A Guide to Oracle®

Including Developer/2000™ and the Oracle WebServer™ and DBA Utilities

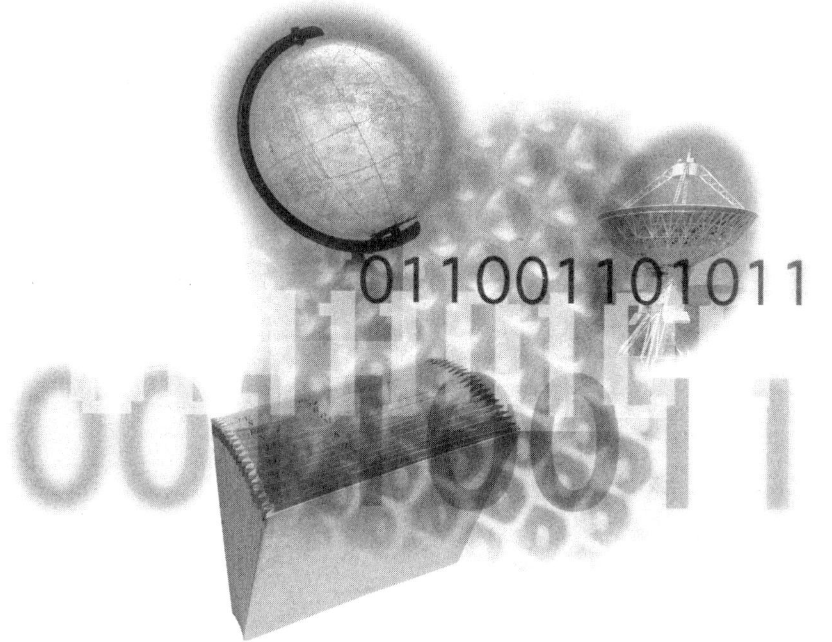

Joline Morrison
University of Wisconsin, Eau Claire

Mike Morrison
University of Wisconsin, Eau Claire

COURSE
TECHNOLOGY

ONE MAIN STREET, CAMBRIDGE, MA 02142

an International Thomson Publishing company I(T)P®

Cambridge • Albany • Bonn • Boston • Cincinnati • London • Madrid • Melbourne • Mexico City
New York • Paris • San Francisco • Singapore • Tokyo • Toronto • Washington

A Guide to Oracle is published by Course Technology.

Managing Editor	Kristen Duerr
Senior Product Manager	Jennifer Normandin
Developmental Editor	Jessica Evans
Production Editor	Melissa Lima
Text Designer	Douglas Goodman
Cover Designer	Cuttriss and Hambleton

For more information contact:

Course Technology, Inc.
One Main Street
Cambridge, MA 02142

ITP Europe
Berkshire House 168-173
High Holborn
London WCIV 7AA
England

Nelson ITP Australia
102 Dodds Street
South Melbourne, 3205
Victoria, Australia

ITP Nelson Canada
1120 Birchmount Road
Scarborough, Ontario
Canada M1K 5G4

International Thomson Editores
Seneca, 53 Colonia Polanco
11560 Mexico D.F. Mexico

ITP GmbH
Konigswinterer Strasse 418
53227 Bonn
Germany

ITP Asia
60 Albert Street, #15-01
Albert Complex
Singapore 189969

ITP Japan
Hirakawacho Kyowa Building, 3F
2-2-1 Hirakawacho
Chiyoda-ku, Tokyo 102
Japan

ISBN 0-7600-4992-0

Printed in the United States of America

10 9 8 7 6 5 4 3 2 1 MZ 02 01 00 99 98

Preface

A Guide to Oracle is designed to provide a comprehensive guide for developing a relational database application using Oracle's database and application development utilities. The goal of this textbook is to support a database development course. It assumes that students already have experience with some other programming language and a basic understanding of relational database concepts.

Organization and Coverage

A Guide to Oracle contains an introductory chapter introducing client/server and relational database concepts. The next two chapters provide hands-on instruction using different Oracle utilities to perform SQL command-line operations as well as create tables, insert data, and perform queries. Chapters 4 through 9 show students how to develop forms, reports, and graphical charts for entering and displaying database data. The final two chapters address developing user interfaces using dynamic Web pages and performing basic database administration tasks. Appendix A provides an overview of PL/SQL, the Oracle procedural programming language.

When students complete this book, they will know how to create and modify database tables and add and modify database data using SQL*Plus, the Oracle command-line SQL environment. Students also will be able to create tables and insert and modify data using the Oracle Navigator, and create queries using Oracle Browser. Students will learn how to create a variety of different user interfaces, reports, and graphical charts for database applications, and develop an integrated database application using the Oracle Developer/2000 application set that includes Oracle Forms, Oracle Reports, and Oracle Graphics. Students also will learn how to program dynamic Web pages to display and manipulate database data. Finally, students will understand basic database administration tasks and how to use the Oracle database administration tools to perform these tasks. This book emphasizes sound database design and development techniques and GUI design skills.

Approach

A Guide to Oracle distinguishes itself from other Oracle books because it is written and designed specifically for students and instructors in educational environments who are participating in the Oracle Academic Alliance Program. The Oracle client/server database software enables educators to illustrate multiuser and client/server database concepts, such as managing concurrent users and sharing database resources; and the problems in this book emphasize the issues that must be considered when developing a client/server database. The book and the Instructor's Manual also address the unique issues that must be considered when installing and using the Oracle software utilities in student laboratory environments and creating and administering student accounts.

Features

A Guide to Oracle is a superior textbook because it also includes the following features:

- **"Read This Before You Begin" Page** This page is consistent with Course Technology's unequaled commitment to helping instructors introduce technology into the classroom. Technical considerations and assumptions about hardware, software, and default settings are listed in one place to help instructors save time and eliminate unnecessary aggravation.

- **Case Approach** Each chapter addresses database-related problems that students could reasonably expect to encounter in business, followed by a demonstration of an application that could be used to solve the problem. Showing students the completed application before they learn how to create it is motivational and instructionally sound. By allowing the students to see the type of application they will create after completing the chapter, students will be more motivated to learn because they can see how the programming concepts that they are about to learn can be used and, therefore, why the concepts are important. The databases referenced in the two ongoing cases represent realistic client/server applications with several database tables, and require supporting multiple users simultaneously at different physical locations. The Clearwater Traders database represents a standard sales order and inventory system, and the Northwoods University database illustrates a student registration system.
- **Step-by-Step Methodology** The unique Course Technology methodology keeps students on track. They click buttons or press keys always within the context of solving the problem posed in the chapter. The text constantly guides students and lets them know where they are in the process of solving the problem. The numerous illustrations include labels that direct students' attention to what they should look at on the screen.
- **HELP?** These paragraphs anticipate the problems students are likely to encounter and help them resolve these problems on their own. This feature facilitates independent learning and frees the instructor to focus on substantive issues rather than on common procedural errors.
- **TIPS** These notes provide additional information about a procedure—for example, an alternative method of performing the procedure.
- **Summaries** Following each chapter is a Summary that recaps the programming concepts and commands covered in the lesson.
- **Review Questions and Problem-Solving Cases** Each chapter concludes with meaningful, conceptual Review Questions that test students' understanding of what they learned in the chapter. Problem-Solving Cases provide students with additional practice of the skills and concepts they learned in the lesson. These exercises increase in difficulty and are designed to allow the student to explore the language and programming environment independently.

The Oracle Server and Client Software

This book was written using Oracle7 Server, Version 7.3, and Oracle WebServer, Version 2.1, installed on a Windows NT database server. The specific client utilities include Personal Oracle7, Version 7.3, Oracle Developer/2000, Version 1.3.2, and Oracle Discoverer/2000 Release 1.3.2, installed on Windows 95 and Windows NT client workstations. Later software versions might have slightly different features, but the core functionality usually is the same. Specific instructions for installation and configuring these applications on a Windows NT server and Windows 95/Windows NT clients are provided in the Instructor's Manual.

The Supplements

All of the supplements for this text are found in the Instructor's Resource Kit, which includes a printed Instructor's Manual and a CD-ROM.

- **Instructor's Manual** The authors wrote the Instructor's Manual and it was quality assurance tested. It is available in printed form and through the Course Technology Faculty Online Companion on the World Wide Web at www.course.com. (Call your customer service representative for the specific URL and your password.) The Instructor's Manual contains the following items:
  - Complete instructions for installing and configuring the server and client software.
  - Answers to all of the review questions and solutions to all of the problem-solving cases.
  - Teaching notes to help introduce and clarify the material presented in the chapters.
  - Technical notes that include troubleshooting tips.
- **Course Test Manager Version 1.1 Engine and Test Bank** Course Test Manager (CTM) is a cutting-edge Windows-based testing software program, developed exclusively for Course Technology, that helps instructors design and administer examinations and practice tests. This full-featured program allows students to generate practice tests randomly that provide immediate on-screen feedback and detailed study guides for incorrectly answered questions. Instructors can also use Course Test Manager to create printed and online tests. You can create, preview, and administer a test on any or all chapters of this textbook entirely over a local area network. Course Test Manager can grade the tests students take automatically at the computer and can generate statistical information on individual as well as group performance. A CTM test bank has been written to accompany your textbook and is included on the CD-ROM. The test bank includes multiple-choice, true/false, short answer, and essay questions.
- **Solutions Files** Solutions Files contain every file students are asked to create or modify in the chapters and cases.
- **Student Files** Student Files, containing all of the data that students will use for the chapters and cases in this textbook, are provided through Course Technology's Online Companion, as well as on the Instructor's Resource Kit CD-ROM. A Readme file includes technical tips for lab management. See the inside covers of this textbook and the "Read This Before You Begin" page before Chapter 1 for more information on Student Files.

Acknowledgments

We would like to thank all of the people who helped to make this book a reality, especially Jessica Evans, our Development Editor, who provided much-needed encouragement and displayed admirable patience and good humor. Thanks also to Kristen Duerr, Managing Editor; Jennifer Normandin, Senior Product Manager; Melissa Lima, Production Editor; and Mike Craig and Tanya Bergner, Quality Assurance testers.

We are grateful to the many reviewers who provided helpful and insightful comments during the development of this book, including George Federman, Santa Barbara Community College; Donovan Young, Georgia Institute of Technology; and Nari Ramarapu, University of Nevada, Reno. Thanks also to Bill Korn and our other colleagues in the MIS department at the University of Wisconsin, Eau Claire who gave us the opportunity to incorporate Oracle into the curriculum and who have supported us during this project. And thanks to all of the students who have taught us about teaching Oracle.

Finally, we would like to dedicate this book to Kyle and Lauren, who can hopefully have their parents back for awhile.

Joline Morrison
Mike Morrison

Contents

chapter 5

CREATING CUSTOM FORMS 165

chapter 6

chapter 7

chapter 9

chapter 10

Read This Before You Begin

To the Student

Student Disks

To complete the chapters and exercises in this book, you need Student Disks. Your instructor will provide you with Student Disks or ask you to make your own.

If you are asked to make your own Student Disks, you will need seven blank, formatted high-density disks. You will need to copy a set of folders from a file server or standalone computer onto your disks. Your instructor will tell you which computer, drive letter, and folders contain the files you need. The following table shows you which folders go on each of your disks, so that you will have enough disk space to complete all the chapters and exercises:

Student Disk	Write this on the disk label	Put these folders on the disk
1	Oracle Chapters 2, 3, 10, Appendix A	Chapter2 Chapter3 Chapter10 AppendA
2	Oracle Chapter 4	Chapter4
3	Oracle Chapter 5	Chapter5
4	Oracle Chapter 6	Chapter6
5	Oracle Chapters 7 and 8	Chapter7 Chapter8
6	Oracle Chapter 9 Clearwater Traders	Chapter9
7	Oracle Chapter 9 Northwoods University	Chapter9

When you begin each chapter, make sure you are using the correct Student Disk. See the inside front or inside back cover of this book for more information on Student Disk files, or ask your instructor or technical support person for assistance.

Using Your Own Computer

You can use your own computer to complete the chapters and exercises in this book, provided you can make a dial-up connection to the server running the Oracle database. To use your own computer, you will need the following:

- **Software** You can download the trial versions of the client software from Oracle's World Wide Web site (http://www.oracle.com). The specific products you will need are Personal Oracle7, Oracle Developer/2000, and Oracle Discoverer. This download is approximately 160 MB of software, so it could take up to 20 hours to complete using a modem with a regular telephone line.

- **Hardware** You must have a computer running Windows 95 or Windows NT workstation, 500 MB of free disk space, a minimum of 32 MB of memory, (64 MB is recommended for Windows NT), and a dial-up networking connection to your database server.

- **Installation and Configuration** To install the downloaded Oracle software, follow the instructions provided in the Installing and Configuring Oracle on the Client and Server Workstations supplement, which you can get from your instructor or electronically through the Internet. See the inside front or back cover of this book for more details. For your home computer, you will use only the following sections:
  1. Installing Developer/2000
  2. Configuring SQL*Net using SQL*Net Easy Configuration—before installing the software, you must get the following information from your instructor or technical support person:
     - Your database server's TCP/IP Host Name (an IP address)
     - Your database instance name (the name given to the database instance when it was created)
  3. Installing Personal Oracle7 and the Oracle Navigator

- **Student Disks** You can get the Student Disk files from your instructor. You will not be able to complete the chapters and exercises in this book using your own computer until you have Student Disks. The student files may also be obtained electronically through the Internet. See the inside front or back cover of this book for more details.

Starting Oracle and Logging on to the Database

When starting an Oracle application, your specific lab configuration might be different from the steps in the book. Your instructor will advise you of the correct method for starting the software and connecting to the database. Your instructor also will advise you of your user name and set up your user account.

Visit Our World Wide Web Site

Additional materials designed especially for you might be available for your course on the World Wide Web. Go to **www.course.com**. Search for this book title periodically on the Course Technology Web site for more details.

To the Instructor

To complete the chapters in this book, your students must use a set of student files. These files are included in the Instructor's Resource Kit. They may also be obtained electronically through the Internet. See the inside front or back cover of this book for more details. Follow the instructions in the Readme file to copy the student files to your server or standalone computer. You can view the Readme file using a text editor such as WordPad or Notepad.

Once the files are copied, you can make Student Disks for the students yourself, or tell students where to find the files so they can make their own Student Disks. Make sure the files get copied correctly onto the Student Disks by following the instructions in the Student Disks section, which will ensure that students have enough disk space to complete all the chapters and exercises in this book.

Because Oracle can be installed with many variations, you or your database administrator should use the instructions provided in the *Installing and Configuring Oracle on the Client and Server Workstations* instructor's supplement for setting up student user names and accounts and for installing and initializing the Oracle DBMS and client utilities. You also should advise students of any differences that they will encounter in the lab, such as how to start the programs.

Course Technology Student Files

You are granted a license to copy the student files to any computer or computer network used by students who have purchased this book.

Chapter 1 objectives

- Identify the differences between client/server databases (such as Oracle) and other popular database environments
- Identify the components of the Oracle database development environment and understand their functions
- Review relational database concepts and terms
- Understand the Clearwater Traders sales order database
- Understand the Northwoods University student registration database

CHAPTER 1

An Introduction to Client/Server Databases

Introduction In this chapter you will learn how a client/server database, such as Oracle, is used to create and maintain data in an organized way. The Oracle development environment includes a client/server database management system (DBMS) and different utilities for developing database systems. In this book you will learn about these utilities and practice using them to build databases for two fictitious organizations—Clearwater Traders and Northwoods University. When you have finished with this chapter, you will have the background you need to begin your exploration of Oracle.

Client/Server Databases

Database management systems (DBMSs), like Microsoft Access and FoxPro, are aimed toward single-user database applications that usually are stored on a single user's desktop computer, or a **client workstation.** When a single-user DBMS is used for a multi-user application, the database application files are stored on a file server and transmitted to the individual users across a network, as shown in Figure 1-1. **Server** is a broad definition for any computer willing to accept requests from other computers and to share some or all of its resources. **Resources** could include printers connected to a server, files stored on hard disks attached to a server, programs running in a server's main memory, and more. A **network** is an infrastructure of telecommunications hardware and software that enables computers to transmit messages to each other.

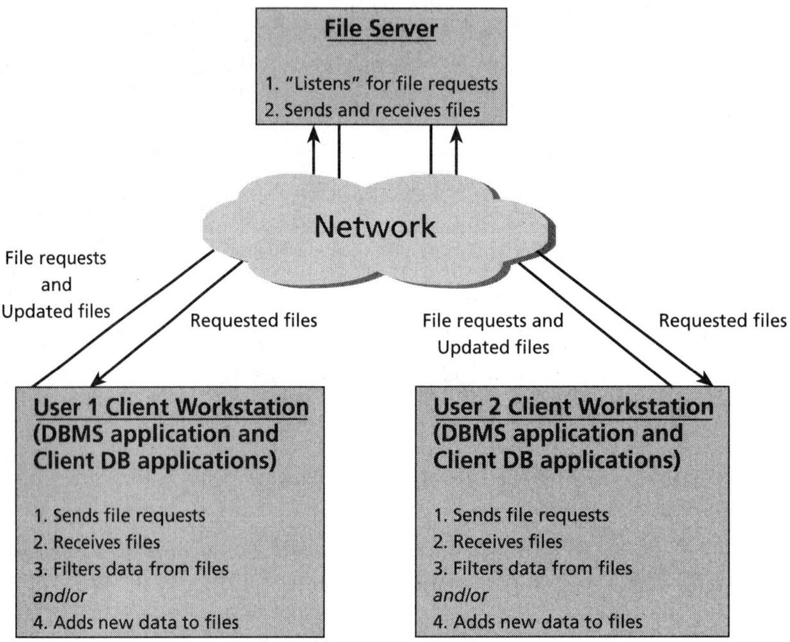

Figure 1-1: Single-user database used for multi-user application

Each client workstation must load the entire database application into main memory along with the client database application to view, insert, update, or print data. A client request for a small amount of data from a large database requires the server to transmit the entire database (that might be hundreds of megabytes in size) to the client's workstation. As a result, non-client/server database management systems put a heavy load on client workstations and on the network. The network must be fast enough to handle the traffic generated when transferring database files to the client workstation and sending them back to the server for database additions and updates. Although system response time depends on the speed of the network, size of the database, and how the database is used, a current typical network might handle 10 users making database transactions at the same time before becoming overloaded.

In contrast, client/server databases like Oracle split the DBMS and applications accessing the DBMS into a "process" running on the server and the applications running on the client, as shown in Figure 1-2. The **client application** sends data requests across the network. When the server receives a request, the server **DBMS**

process retrieves the data from the database, performs the requested functions on the data (sorting, filtering, etc.), and sends *only* the final query result (not the entire database) back via the network to the client. As a result, multi-user client/server databases generate less network traffic than non-client/server databases and are less likely to bog down due to an overloaded network.

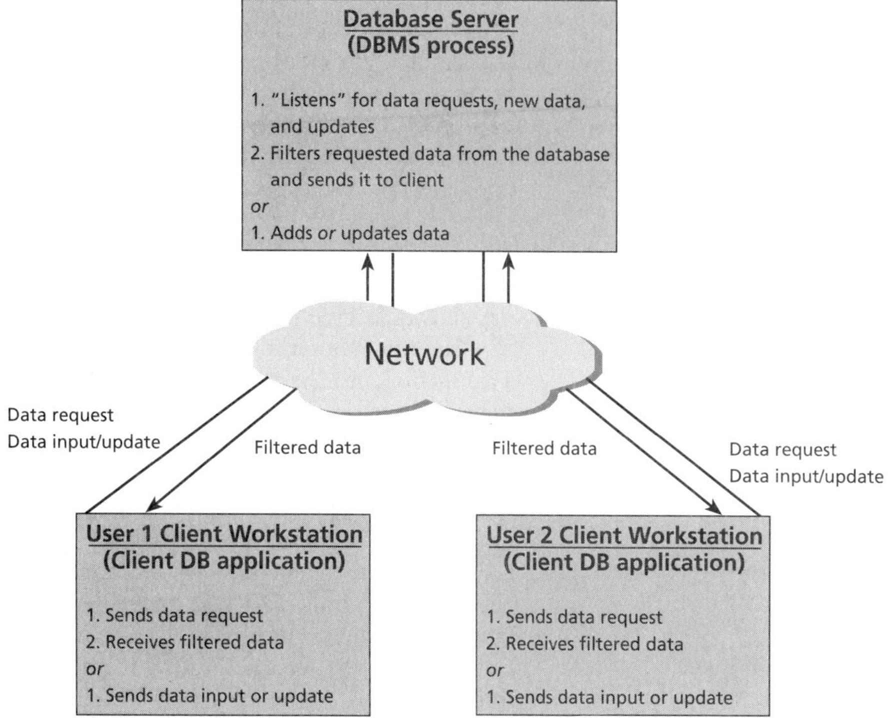

Figure 1-2: Client/server database

Another important difference between client/server and non-client/server databases is how they handle client failures. In a non-client/server system, when a client application fails due to a software malfunction or power failure, the database is likely to become damaged due to interrupted updates, insertions, or deletions. Records in use at the time of the failure are **locked** by the failed client, which means they are unavailable to other users. The database might be repairable, but all users must log off during the repair process, which could take several hours. Updates, deletions, and insertions taking place at the time of the failure often cannot be reconstructed. If repair is not possible, the person responsible for installing, administering, and maintaining the database, called the **database administrator** or **DBA**, can restore the database to the last regular backup, but transactions that occurred since the backup are lost.

On the other hand, a client/server database is not affected when a client workstation fails. The failed client's in-progress transactions are lost, but the failure of a single client does not affect other users. In the case of a server failure, a central synchronized **transaction log** contains a record of all current database changes. The transaction log enables in-progress transactions from all clients to be either fully completed, or to be rolled back. **Rolling back** a database transaction means that the database is made to look like the transaction never took place. Using the transaction log, a DBA can notify users with rolled back transactions to resubmit them. Most client/server DBMS servers have extra features to minimize the chance of failure, and when they do fail, they have fast, powerful recovery mechanisms.

Another important difference is how client/server systems handle competing user transactions. Consider an airline seat ticketing system as an example. In a client/server system such as Oracle, the transaction to sell a ticket causes the database to read the table and simultaneously lock all or part of the table listing available seats prior to updating the table. Then the sold seat is marked as unavailable (or deleted from the table) and the table is unlocked. Without the lock, a second sales agent could read the table after the first agent reads it but before the first agent updates a certain seat as sold. The second agent might see that the given seat still is available and inadvertently sell the same seat to a second customer. By default, a single-user database like Microsoft Access uses **optimistic locking**, or hoping that two competing transactions will not take place at the same time. Optimistic locking, therefore, does not lock the table. Access will notify the second agent the table has been changed since he or she last read it, but then Access offers to proceed and save the update anyway. In this situation, the second agent does not know that the seat already has been sold and sells it again. Access *will* allow developers to write explicit code to lock tables, but it takes a lot more effort than a comparable Oracle application that handles locking automatically.

Another difference is how client/server systems handle transaction processing. **Transaction processing** refers to grouping related database changes into batches that must either all succeed or all fail. For example, assume a customer writes a check from a checking account and deposits it into a money market account. The bank must ensure that the checking account is debited for the amount and the money market account is credited for the same amount. If any part of the transaction fails, then neither account balance should change. Access provides procedures to group related changes, keep a record of these changes in main memory on the client workstation, and roll back the changes if the grouped transactions fail. However, if the client making the changes fails in the middle of a group of transactions, then the transaction log in main memory is lost. There is no file-based transaction log on which to base a rollback, and the partial changes cannot be reversed. Depending on the order of the transactions, a failed client could result in a depleted checking account and unchanged money market account, or an enlarged money market account and unchanged checking account.

Client/server databases are preferred for database applications that retrieve and manipulate small amounts of data from databases containing large numbers of records because they minimize network traffic and improve response times. Client/server systems are essential for mission-critical applications because of their failure handling, recovery mechanisms, and transaction management control. They also have a rich set of database management and administration tools for handling large numbers of users. Some general guidelines are to use a client/server database if your database will have over 10 simultaneous users, if your database is mission critical, or if you need a rich set of administration tools.

The Oracle Environment

The Oracle database development environment includes a client/server DBMS as well as several utilities for developing database systems. In this book, you will learn about the following utilities:

- *SQL*Plus* for creating and testing command-line SQL queries used to create, update, and delete database tables, views, and sequences

- *Oracle Navigator* for creating new tables
- *Oracle Browser* for creating query-by-example (QBE) and SQL queries
- *Oracle Forms* for creating graphical forms and menus for user applications
- *Oracle Reports* for creating reports for displaying and printing data
- *Oracle Graphics* for creating graphics charts based on database data
- *Enterprise Manager* for managing and tuning the database; the enterprise manager uses the following utilities:
  - *Security Manager* for creating and managing user accounts
  - *Storage Manager* for creating and managing tablespaces
  - *Instance Manager* for starting, shutting down, and tuning the database
- *Oracle WebServer* for creating a World Wide Web site that allows users to access Oracle databases and create dynamic Web pages

You also will learn how to use open database connectivity (ODBC) procedures to create a Visual Basic client application for an Oracle database.

Overview of Relational Database Terms

As you learn how to use the Oracle database development utilities, specific terms will be used to describe the different parts of a relational database. A relational database views data in **tables**, or matrixes with columns and rows. **Columns** represent different data categories, and **rows** contain the actual data values. Columns also are called **fields**, and rows also are called **records**. Figure 1-3 shows an example of a relational database that contains two tables.

columns or fields

rows or records

PRODUCT table

PRODUCT_ID	DESCRIPTION	QUANTITY_ON_HAND
1	Plain Cheesecake	8
2	Cherry Cheesecake	10

PURCHASE table

ORDER_ID	PRODUCT_ID	ORDER_QUANTITY
100	1	2
100	2	2
101	2	1
102	1	3

Figure 1-3: A relational database with two tables

Individual records in relational database tables are identified using primary keys. A **primary key** is a field whose value must be unique for each record. Every record must have a primary key, and the primary key cannot be **NULL**, which means its value is indeterminate or undefined. In the PRODUCT table shown in Figure 1-3, the PRODUCT_ID field is a good choice for the primary key because a unique value can be assigned for each product. The DESCRIPTION field might be another choice for the primary key, but there are two drawbacks. First, products always must have unique descriptions, and second, the field is a text field and is therefore prone to typographical, spelling, and punctuation data entry errors. This is a problem because primary key values are used to create relationships with other database tables.

tip

In this textbook, table and field names are identified by typing them in all capital letters.

Relationships among database tables are created by matching key values. For example, suppose order 100 is for two plain cheesecakes and two cherry cheesecakes. Figure 1-4 shows how products 1 and 2 in the PRODUCT table relate to order 100 in the PURCHASE table. A field in a table that is a primary key in another table and thus creates a table relationship is called a **foreign key**. PRODUCT_ID is a foreign key in the PURCHASE table.

PRODUCT table

PRODUCT_ID	DESCRIPTION	QUANTITY_ON_HAND
1	Plain Cheesecake	8
2	Cherry Cheesecake	10

PURCHASE table

ORDER_ID	PRODUCT_ID	ORDER_QUANTITY
100	1	2
100	2	2
101	2	1
102	1	3

foreign key

Figure 1-4: Creating a relationship using a foreign key

A foreign key value must exist in the table where it is a primary key. For example, suppose you have a new record for ORDER_ID 103 that specifies that the customer ordered one unit of product 3. There is no record for PRODUCT_ID 3 in the PRODUCT table, so the purchase record does not make sense. Foreign key values must match the value in the primary key table *exactly*, so that is why it is not a good idea to use text fields, and risk typographical, punctuation, and spelling errors in the primary key.

Sometimes you have to combine multiple fields to create a unique primary key. Figure 1-5 shows an example of this situation. For ORDER_ID 100, the customer purchased two units of product 1, and two units of product 2, so the ORDER_ID value is not unique for each record. However, the combination of the ORDER_ID and PRODUCT_ID values is unique. The combination of fields to create a unique primary key is called a **composite primary key**, or a **composite key**. Note that PRODUCT_ID, which is a foreign key, also can be part of a composite key.

PURCHASE table

composite primary key

ORDER_ID	PRODUCT_ID	ORDER_QUANTITY
100	1	2
100	2	2
101	2	1
102	1	3

Figure 1-5: Example of a composite primary key

Sometimes a database table does not have a field data value that would make a good primary key. Figure 1-6 shows a CUSTOMER table with this problem. The LAST_NAME or FIRST_NAME fields, or even the combination of the two fields, are not good choices for the primary key because many people have the same name. Multiple people can share the same address and phone number, as well. Phone numbers are not a good choice for primary keys because people often get new phone numbers, and if the phone number is updated in the table where it is the primary key, it also must be updated in every table where it is a foreign key. If the phone number is not updated, relationships are lost. A good database development practice is to create a **surrogate key**, which is a numerical value that usually is generated by the database, with the sole purpose of being the primary key identifier for a record. In this case, you probably would call the surrogate key CUSTOMER_ID, and you might start the CUSTOMER_ID numbers at 1 or 100. The CUSTOMER_ID numbers will not change, and every customer gets a unique number.

CUSTOMER table

LAST_NAME	FIRST_NAME	ADDRESS	PHONE
Brown	John	101 Main Street	7155554321
Brown	John	3567 State Street	7155558901
Carlson	Mike	233 Water Street	7155557890
Carlson	Martha	233 Water Street	7155557890
Davis	Carol	1414 South Street	7155555566

Figure 1-6: Table lacking suitable primary key candidates

The Case Study Databases

In this textbook, you will encounter chapter examples and end-of-chapter exercises that illustrate the Oracle utilities using databases developed for Clearwater Traders and Northwoods University, which are two fictional organizations. The focus of this textbook is on database development, and not on database design, so the text does not provide an explanation of the rationale behind the design of these database tables. Instead, the focus of this textbook is on developing applications using the databases.

The described database systems require a client/server database application because they will have many simultaneous users accessing the system from different physical locations. Each database has data examples to illustrate the tasks that are addressed in this textbook, including the development of data entry and maintenance forms, output reports, chart displays, and a Web site application.

The Clearwater Traders Sales Order Database

Clearwater Traders markets a line of clothing and sporting goods via mail-order catalogs and a site on the World Wide Web. Clearwater Traders accepts customer orders via phone, mail, and fax. The company recently experienced substantial growth, and as a result, management decided to offer 24-hour customer order service. The current microcomputer-based database system is not able to handle the current transaction volume that is generated by sales representatives processing incoming orders. Management is concerned that it does not have the failure handling and recovery capabilities needed for an ordering system that cannot withstand any failures or downtime.

When a customer orders an item, the sales representative must check to see if the ordered item is in stock. If the item is in stock, the representative must update the available quantity on hand to reflect that the item has been sold. If the item is not in stock, the representative needs to advise the customer when the item will be available. When new inventory shipments are received, a receiving clerk must update the inventory to show the new quantities on hand. The system must produce invoices that can be included with customer shipments and print reports showing inventory levels, possibly using charts or graphs. Marketing managers would like to be able to track each order's source (particular catalog number or Web site) to help plan future promotions.

The following data items have been identified:

1. Customer name, address, and daytime and evening phone numbers.
2. Order date, payment method (check or credit card), order source (catalog number or Web site), and associated item numbers, sizes, colors, and quantities ordered.
3. Item descriptions, categories (women's clothing, outdoor gear, etc.), price, quantities on hand, and next shipment information for out-of-stock items. Many clothing items are available in multiple sizes and colors. Sometimes the same item has different prices depending on the item size.
4. Information about incoming product shipments and backordered shipments.

Figure 1-7 shows sample data for Clearwater Traders. Five customer records are shown. Customer 107 is Paula Jones, who lives at 1156 Water Street, Apt. #3, Osseo, WI, and her zip code is 54705. Her daytime phone number is 715-555-8943, and her evening phone number is 715-555-9035. CUSTID is the table's primary key.

CUSTOMER

CUSTID	LAST	FIRST	MI	CADD	CITY	STATE	ZIP	DPHONE	EPHONE
107	Jones	Paula	E	1156 Water Street, Apt. #3	Osseo	WI	54705	7155558943	7155559035
232	Edwards	Mitch	M	4204 Garner Street	Washburn	WI	54891	7155558243	7155556975
133	Sorenson	Betty	H	2211 Pine Drive	Radisson	WI	54867	7155558332	7155558332
154	Miller	Lee		699 Pluto St. NW	Silver Lake	WI	53821	7155554978	7155559002
179	White	Alissa	R	987 Durham Rd.	Sister Bay	WI	54234	7155557651	7155550087

CUST_ORDER

ORDERID	DATE	METHPMT	CUSTID	ORDERSOURCE
1057	5/29/99	CC	107	152
1058	5/29/99	CC	232	WEBSITE
1059	5/31/99	CHECK	133	152
1060	5/31/99	CC	154	153
1061	6/01/99	CC	179	WEBSITE
1062	6/01/99	CC	179	WEBSITE

ITEM

ITEMID	ITEMDESC	CATEGORY
894	Women's Hiking Shorts	Women's Clothing
897	Women's Fleece Pullover	Women's Clothing
995	Children's Beachcomber Sandals	Children's Clothing
559	Men's Expedition Parka	Men's Clothing
786	3-Season Tent	Outdoor Gear

INVENTORY

INVID	ITEMID	ITEMSIZE	COLOR	CURR_PRICE	QOH
11668	786		Sienna	259.99	16
11669	786		Forest	259.99	12
11775	894	S	Khaki	29.95	150
11776	894	M	Khaki	29.95	147
11777	894	L	Khaki	29.95	0
11778	894	S	Olive	29.95	139
11779	894	M	Olive	29.95	137
11780	894	L	Olive	29.95	115
11795	897	S	Teal	59.95	135
11796	897	M	Teal	59.95	168
11797	897	L	Teal	59.95	187
11798	897	S	Coral	59.95	0
11799	897	M	Coral	59.95	124
11800	897	L	Coral	59.95	112
11820	995	10	Blue	15.99	121
11821	995	11	Blue	15.99	111
11822	995	12	Blue	15.99	113
11823	995	1	Blue	15.99	121
11824	995	10	Red	15.99	148
11825	995	11	Red	15.99	137
11826	995	12	Red	15.99	134
11827	995	1	Red	15.99	123
11845	559	S	Navy	199.95	114
11846	559	M	Navy	199.95	17
11847	559	L	Navy	209.95	0
11848	559	XL	Navy	209.95	12

Figure 1-7: Sample data for the Clearwater Traders database

SHIPPING

SHIPID	INVID	DATE_EXPECTED	QUANTITY_EXPECTED	DATE_RECEIVED	QUANTITY_RECEIVED
211	11668	09/15/99	25		
211	11669	09/15/99	25		
212	11669	11/15/99	25		
213	11777	06/25/99	200		
214	11778	09/25/99	200		
214	11779	09/25/99	200		
215	11798	08/15/99	100		
215	11799	08/15/99	100		
216	11799	09/25/99	100		
217	11800	08/15/99	100		
218	11845	8/12/99	50	8/15/99	0
218	11846	8/12/99	100	8/15/99	100
218	11847	8/12/99	100	8/15/99	50
218	11848	8/12/99	50	8/15/99	50

BACKORDER

BACKORDERID	SHIPID	INVID	DATE_EXPECTED	QUANTITY_ EXPECTED	DATE_ RECEIVED	QUANTITY_ RECEIVED
1	218	11845	09/15/99	50		
2	218	11847	09/15/99	50		

ORDERLINE

ORDERID	INVID	ORDER_PRICE	QUANTITY
1057	11668	259.99	1
1057	11800	69.96	2
1058	11824	15.99	1
1059	11846	129.95	1
1059	11848	139.95	1
1060	11798	59.95	2
1061	11779	29.95	1
1061	11780	29.95	1
1062	11799	59.95	1
1062	11669	229.99	3

COLOR

COLOR
Sienna
Forest
Khaki
Olive
Teal
Coral
Blue
Red
Navy
Brown

ORDERSOURCE

ORDERSOURCE
99
122
123
145
146
151
152
153
211
WEBSITE

Figure 1-7 (continued): Sample data for the Clearwater Traders database

The CUST_ORDER table shows six customer orders. The first is 1057, dated 5/29/99, method of payment CC (credit card), and ordered by customer 107, Paula Jones. Catalog 152 was the order source. ORDERID is the table's primary key, and CUSTID is a foreign key that creates a relationship to the CUSTOMER table.

The ITEM table contains five different items: Women's Hiking Shorts, Women's Fleece Pullover, Children's Beachcomber Sandals, Men's Expedition Parka, and 3-Season Tent. Item 894, Women's Hiking Shorts, is in the Women's Clothing category. ITEMID is the primary key in this table, and it also is a surrogate key that was created because neither of the other table fields is a good primary key choice—ITEMDESC is a text field, and CATEGORY is also a text field and not unique for every record.

The INVENTORY table contains specific inventory numbers for specific item sizes and colors. It also shows the current price and quantity on hand (QOH) for each item. Items that are not available in different sizes contain NULL, or blank values, in the ITEMSIZE column. Notice that some items have different prices for different sizes. INVID is the primary key of this table, and ITEMID is a foreign key that creates a relationship with the ITEM table.

The SHIPPING table contains a schedule of expected inventory item shipments that includes the inventory item number, the date and quantity of expected items, and the data and quantity of items delivered. Some items will not have expected shipment dates, while other items might have several shipment dates. As you can see in the table, a shipment can consist of one or more inventory items. The primary key of this table is a composite key made of the combination of SHIPID and INVID. Remember that composite keys are required when no single field in the table uniquely identifies each record in the table.

Why is SHIPID needed in this table? First, without SHIPID, the primary key could be composed of both INVID and DATE because it would take both of these entries to identify a record in this table uniquely. But what if there are two separate shipments of the same item arriving on the same day? And what if both shipments have the same quantity? SHIPID provides a useful way to distinguish that there are *two* separate shipments for the same item on the same day.

The BACKORDER table shows backorders corresponding to shipments. Look at the records in the SHIPPING table for shipment 218. When the shipment arrived on 8/15/99, none of the units for items 11845 arrived, and only 50 of the 100 units ordered for item 11847 arrived. Clearwater Traders was notified that the missing units were backordered and would be shipped on 9/15/99. The BACKORDER records show the associated shipment ID, inventory ID, expected date, and expected quantity for these backordered items.

The ORDERLINE table represents the individual inventory items in a customer order. The first line of order 1057 is one Sienna-colored 3-Season Tent, with a price of 259.99. The second line of this order specifies two large coral Women's Fleece Pullovers, with a price of 69.96 each. This information is used to create the printed customer order invoice and to calculate sales revenues. The order prices must be retained to show the actual price paid for an item on a particular order because the price could change in the INVENTORY table since the order was placed. Note that the primary key of this table is not ORDERID because more than one record might have the same ORDERID. The primary key is a composite key made up of the combination of ORDERID and INVID. An order might have several different inventory items, but it will never have the same inventory item listed more than once. Along with being part of the primary key, INVID is also a foreign key in this table because it creates a relationship to the INVENTORY table.

The last two tables, COLOR and ORDERSOURCE, are look-up tables or pick lists. A **pick list** is a list of legal values for a field in another table. Notice the variety of colors shown in the INVENTORY table (Sienna, Forest, Khaki, Olive, Teal, etc.). If users are allowed to type these colors each time an inventory item is added to the table, typing errors might occur. For example, a query looking for sales of items with the Sienna color will not find instances where Sienna is misspelled as Siena, SIENNA, etc. Typically, a user entering a new inventory item will select a color from a pick list so the color is not typed directly, thus reducing errors. Small lists that are unlikely to change over time might be coded directly into an application, but lists with many items that might be added to over time usually are stored in a separate look-up table.

The Northwoods University Student Registration Database

Northwoods University has decided to replace its aging mainframe-based student registration system with a more modern client/server database system. School officials want to provide students with the capability to retrieve course availability information, register for courses, and print unofficial transcripts using personal computers located in the student computer labs. Additionally, administrators must be able to specify course offerings and class sizes, and faculty members must be able to retrieve student course lists, drop and add students to courses, and record course grades. Faculty members must be able to view records for the students they advise. Security is a prime concern, so student and course records must be protected by password access.

Students will log on to the Northwoods system using their name and PIN (personal identification number). They will be given the option of viewing current course listings or viewing information on courses they have completed. They can check what courses are available during the current term by viewing course information such as course names, call IDs, section numbers, days, times, locations, and the availability of open seats in the course. They also could view information about the courses they have taken in the past, and print a transcript report showing past course grades and grade point averages. Faculty members will log on to the system by entering their PINs. Then they can select from a list of the courses they are teaching in the current term, and retrieve a list of students enrolled in the selected course. A faculty member also could retrieve a list of his or her student advisees, select one, and then retrieve that student's past and current course enrollment information. Administrators will enter information about new courses offered for future terms.

The data items for the Northwoods database are:

1. Student name, address, phone number, class (freshman, sophomore, etc.), data of birth, and advisor ID
2. Course call number, name, credit, maximum enrollment, instructor, and term offered
3. Instructor name, office location, phone number, and rank
4. Student/course grades

Figure 1-8 shows sample data for the Northwoods database. Six student records are shown. Student 101 is Sarah Miller, who lives at 144 Windridge Blvd., Eau Claire, WI, and her zip code is 54703. Her phone number is 715-555-9876, she is a senior, her date of birth is 7/14/79, and her faculty advisor is Kim Cox. Note that the SPIN (student PIN) field has been added to store student personal identification numbers to control data access. Only the student or his/her faculty advisor is able to update student record data in this table. SID is the table's primary key. FID is a foreign key that refers to the FID field in the FACULTY table.

STUDENT

SID	SLNAME	SFNAME	SMI	SADD	SCITY	SSTATE	SZIP	SPHONE	SCLASS	SDOB	SPIN	FID
100	Miller	Sarah	M	144 Windridge Blvd.	Eau Claire	WI	54703	7155559876	SR	07/14/79	8891	1
101	Robinson	Brian	D	454 St. John's Place	Eau Claire	WI	54702	7155552345	SR	08/19/79	1230	1
102	Black	Daniel		892 1 Circle Drive	Bloomer	WI	54715	7155553907	JR	10/10/77	1613	1
103	Mobley	Amanda	J	1716 Summit St.	Eau Claire	WI	54703	7155556902	SO	9/24/78	1841	2
104	Sanchez	Ruben	R	1780 Samantha Court	Eau Claire	WI	54701	7155558899	SO	11/20/77	4420	4
105	Connoly	Michael	S	1818 Silver Street	Elk Mound	WI	54712	7155554944	FR	12/4/77	9188	3

FACULTY

FID	FLNAME	FFNAME	FMI	LOCID	FPHONE	FRANK	FPIN
1	Cox	Kim	J	53	7155551234	ASSO	I181
2	Blanchard	John	R	54	7155559087	FULL	1075
3	Williams	Jerry	F	56	7155555412	ASST	8531
4	Perry	Laura	M	55	7155556409	INST	1690
5	Brown	Phillip	E	57	7155556082	ASSO	9899

LOCATION

LOCID	BLDG_CODE	ROOM	CAPACITY
45	CR	101	150
46	CR	202	40
47	CR	103	35
48	CR	105	35
49	BUS	105	42
50	BUS	404	35
51	BUS	421	35
52	BUS	211	55
53	BUS	424	1
54	BUS	402	1
55	BUS	433	1
56	LIB	217	2
57	LIB	222	1

TERM

TERMID	TDESC
1	Fall 1998
2	Spring 1999
3	Summer 1999
4	Fall 1999
5	Spring 2000
6	Summer 2000

COURSE

CID	CALLID	CNAME	CCREDIT
1	MIS 101	Intro. to Info. Systems	3
2	MIS 301	Systems Analysis	3
3	MIS 441	Database Management	3
4	CS 155	Programming in C++	3
5	MIS 451	Client/Server Systems	3

Figure 1-8: Sample data for the Northwoods University database

COURSE_SECTION

CSECID	CID	TERMID	SECNUM	FID	DAY	TIME	LOCID	MAXENRL	CURRENRL
1000	1	5	1	2	MWF	10:00	45	140	135
1001	1	5	2	3	TTH	9:30	51	35	35
1002	1	5	3	3	MWF	8:00	46	35	32
1003	2	5	1	4	TTh	11:00	50	35	35
1004	2	5	2	4	TTh	2:00	50	35	35
1005	3	5	1	1	MWF	9:00	49	30	25
1006	3	5	2	1	MWF	10:00	49	30	28
1007	4	5	1	5	TTh	8:00	47	35	20
1008	5	5	1	2	MWF	2:00	49	35	32
1009	5	5	2	2	MWF	3:00	49	35	35
1010	1	6	1		M-F	8:00	45	50	35
1011	2	6	1		M-F	8:00	50	35	35
1012	3	6	1	3	M-F	9:00	49	35	29

COURSE_UPDATE

CID	FID
1	2
1	5
2	2
3	2
4	3
5	1
5	2

ENROLLMENT

SID	CSECID	GRADE
100	1000	A
100	1003	A
100	1004	B
100	1008	B
101	1003	C
101	1004	B
101	1005	A
101	1008	B
102	1000	C
102	1011	
102	1012	
103	1010	
103	1011	
104	1000	B
104	1004	C
104	1008	C
104	1012	
105	1010	
105	1011	

Figure 1-8 (continued): Sample data for the Northwoods University database

The FACULTY table describes five faculty members. The first record shows faculty member Kim Cox, whose office is located at BUS 424, and her phone number is 715-555-1234. She has the rank of associate professor, and her PIN is 1181. This FPIN (faculty PIN) will be used as a password to determine if a faculty member can update specific student or course records. FID is the primary key, and LOCID is a foreign key that references LOCID in the LOCATION table.

LOCATION is another look-up table. In this case, users will see a sorted list that identifies building codes, room numbers, and room capacities. LOCID is the primary key. After a user makes a selection from the LOCATION table, the LOCID is inserted into the COURSE_SECTION table and FACULTY table. The user never needs to see LOCID.

The TERM table provides a textual description of each term along with an ID number that is used to link the semester to different course offerings. The first record shows a TERMID of 1 for the fall 1998 semester. TERMID is the primary key.

The COURSE table shows five courses. The first, CID 1, has the CALLID MIS 101 and is named "Intro. to Info. Systems." It provides three credits. CID is the primary key, and there are no foreign keys.

The COURSE_SECTION table shows the course offerings for specific semesters in terms of course ID, section number, ID of the instructor teaching the section, and course day, time, location, maximum allowable enrollment, and current enrollment. CSECID is the primary key, and CID, TERMID, FID, and LOCID are all foreign key fields. Notice that the FID field is blank for courses that have not yet been assigned an instructor. The FID field is an example of a foreign key field that can have a NULL value. The first record shows that CSECID 1000 is section 1 of MIS 101. It is offered in the Spring 2000 semester and taught by John Blanchard. The section meets on Mondays, Wednesdays, and Fridays at 10:00 in room CR 101. It has a maximum enrollment of 140 students, and 135 students are enrolled currently.

Only faculty members with administrative privileges for specific courses will be able to update the COURSE and COURSE_SECTION records. The COURSE_UPDATE table shows these record-level security privileges. For example, only faculty members John Blanchard and Phil Brown may update records for CID 1 (MIS 101). Note that the primary key of this table is the combination of CID and FID because one course might have multiple faculty members with update privileges.

The ENROLLMENT table shows students who currently are enrolled in each course section, and their associated grade if it has been assigned. Only the course instructor or faculty members with COURSE_UPDATE privileges can update enrollment records for specific courses. The primary key for this table is a composite key of SID and CSECID.

SUMMARY

- Non-client/server databases download all of the data a user needs to the user's client workstation, manipulate the data, and then upload it back to the server. This process can be slow and cause network congestion.
- Client/server databases send data requests to the server and the results of data requests back to the client workstation. This process minimizes network traffic and congestion.
- Client/server databases have better failure recovery mechanisms than non-client/server databases.
- Client/server databases automatically provide table and record locking.
- Client/server databases maintain a file-based transaction log that is not lost in the event of a client workstation failure.
- Client/server databases have utilities for managing systems with many users.
- The Oracle database development environment has utilities for creating database tables and queries, and developing data forms, reports, and graphics based on database table data.
- The Clearwater Traders sales order database includes the following data entities:
  - customers
  - orders
  - items
  - inventory
  - order lines
  - shipping
  - backorders

- The Northwoods University student registration database includes the following data entities:
  - students
  - courses
  - faculty
  - terms
  - course sections
  - enrollments
- A primary key is a field that uniquely identifies every record in a database table. Primary keys must be unique and cannot be NULL.
- A surrogate key can be created if no single existing data field uniquely identifies each record in a table or if existing primary key candidates are unsuitable because they are text fields or their values might change.
- A composite key is a primary key composed of the combination of two or more fields.
- Foreign keys link related records. A foreign key field in a table must be a primary key in another table.

REVIEW QUESTIONS

Client/Server Database

1. What is the main difference between the way that client/server and non-client/server databases handle and process data?
2. Why can client/server databases handle client failures better than non-client/server systems?
3. Give two examples of database applications that might be appropriate for a client/server system. Give two examples of database applications that might be more appropriate for a non-client/server system. (*Hint:* Non-client/server systems are appropriate for situations where a client/server system is not required.)
4. In a relational database table, what is a field, and what is a record?
5. What is a primary key?
6. What is a foreign key?
7. What is a surrogate key?
8. What is a composite key?
9. What does it mean when a data value is NULL?

Clearwater Traders

Answer the following questions using the database tables shown in Figure 1-7. No computer work is necessary; you will learn how to do these queries using the Oracle database in another chapter.

1. Identify every primary and foreign key field in the Clearwater Traders database.
2. Find the names of every customer who placed orders using the Web site as a source.
3. Find the names of every item that currently is out of stock (QOH = 0).
4. Find the customer name, item description, size, color, quantity, extended total (quantity times order price), and total order amount for every item in order 1057.

5. Find the name and address of every customer who ordered items in the Women's Clothing category.
6. Find the total amount of every order generated from the Web site source.
7. Find the total amount of every order generated from the Catalog 152 source.

Northwoods University

Answer the following questions using the database tables shown in Figure 1-8. No computer work is necessary; you will learn how to do these queries using the Oracle database in another chapter.

1. Identify every primary and foreign key field in the Northwoods University database.
2. Find the name of every course offered during the Summer 2000 semester.
3. List the name of every student that faculty member Kim Cox advises.
4. List the course name and section of every course that is filled to capacity (CURRENRL = MAXENRL) during the Spring 2000 semester.
5. List the course call ID, section number, term description, and grade for every course that student Sarah Miller is taking.
6. Calculate the total credits earned to date by student Brian Robinson.
7. Calculate the total number of students taught by John Blanchard during the Spring 2000 term (use the CURRENRL figures).
8. Calculate the total number of student credits generated during the Spring 2000 term (student credits = CURRENRL times course credits).

Chapter 2

objectives

- Identify the properties of Oracle database tables
- Create and modify database table structures using SQL*Plus
- Create and modify database table structures using the Oracle Navigator
- Use the Oracle online Help system

CHAPTER 2

Creating and Modifying Database Tables

Introduction

Data in relational database tables are inserted, retrieved, and modified using commands called **queries**. Queries are performed using high-level **query languages** that use standard English commands such as INSERT, UPDATE, and DELETE. The standard query language for relational databases is **SQL** (**Structured Query Language**). The structure and syntax of SQL is the same across most database management systems, although different platforms often support slightly different commands.

The first task in developing a database is to create the database tables. You can create tables using SQL*Plus, the Oracle command-line SQL environment, or you can use a table management utility like the Oracle Navigator. In this chapter you will use both approaches to create tables.

Table Names and Properties

A **table** stores user data in a relational database. An Oracle database table specification includes the table name, field names, data types and sizes, and integrity and value constraints. Table and field names can be from 1 to 30 characters long and can consist of only alphanumeric characters and the special characters $ _ #. Table and field names must begin with a letter and cannot contain blank spaces or hyphens. Figure 2-1 shows some invalid SQL table and field names and their descriptions.

Invalid Table or Field Name	Description
STUDENT TABLE	Spaces not permitted
STUDENT-TABLE	Hyphens not permitted
#CUST	Must begin with a letter
US_SOCIAL_SECURITY_NUMBERS_COLUMN	Cannot exceed 30 characters

Figure 2-1: Invalid SQL table and field names

Data Types

When you create a table, you must assign to each column a **data type** to specify what kind of data will be stored in the field. Data types are used for two primary reasons. First, assigning a data type provides a means for error checking. For example, you cannot store the character data "Chicago" in a field declared with a DATE data type. Data types also cause storage space to be used more efficiently by optimizing how specific types of data are stored. The main Oracle character data types are described next.

> Note: A convention used in this book is that all SQL command words, also known as reserved words, appear in all uppercase letters, and all user-supplied variable names appear in lowercase letters. You should use this convention when entering your own queries, as well. While SQL*Plus commands are not case sensitive, this convention makes queries easier to interpret.

VARCHAR2 Character Data Type

The **VARCHAR2** data type stores variable-length character data up to a maximum of 2,000 characters. When you declare a field using VARCHAR2, you must specify a field size. If entered data is smaller than the specified size, only the entered data is stored. Trailing blank spaces are not added to the end of the entry to make it fill the specified column length. If an entered data value is wider than the specified size, an error is returned. Because no trailing blank spaces are added, this data type is recommended for most character data fields. For example, the SLNAME field in the STUDENT table is defined as `slname VARCHAR2(30)`. Examples of data stored in this field include Miller and Robinson.

CHAR Character Data Type

The **CHAR** data type holds fixed-length character data up to a maximum size of 255 characters. If the value stored in a CHAR field is less than the field size you specify, then trailing spaces are added. If no field size is specified, the default size value is one character. An example of a CHAR field definition is the SCLASS field in the STUDENT table in the Northwoods University database. The definition of the SCLASS field is `sclass CHAR(2)`. The data that will be stored in the SCLASS field is SR, JR, SO, FR (senior, junior, sophomore, freshman).

You should use the CHAR data type only for fixed-length character fields that have a restricted set of values, such as in the SCLASS field. Using the CHAR data type on fields that might not fill the column width forces the DBMS to add trailing blank spaces, which causes inconsistent query results in other Oracle applications. The CHAR data type uses data storage space more efficiently than VARCHAR2 and can be processed faster. However, if there is any chance that all column spaces will not be filled, use the VARCHAR2 data type.

NUMBER Data Types

The **NUMBER** data type stores negative, positive, fixed, and floating point numbers between 10^{-130} and 10^{126} with precision up to 38 decimal places. The NUMBER data type is used for all numerical data and must be used for fields that will be used in mathematical operations. When you declare a NUMBER field, you can specify the **precision** (the total number of digits both to the left and to the right of the decimal point), and the **scale** (the number of digits to the right of the decimal point). There are three NUMBER data types: integer, fixed-point, and floating-point.

Integer Numbers An **integer** is a whole number with no digits to the right of the decimal point. For example, the SID field in the STUDENT table stores only integers (student identification numbers), so it is defined as `sid NUMBER(5)`. Example values in this field are 100, 101, 102, etc.

NUMBER(5) specifies that the SID field has a maximum length of five digits and no digits to the right of the decimal point. When you are defining any field, it is important to allow room for growth. Northwoods University begins its SID numbers at 100, but there will be more than 999 students enrolled so the data type is defined to store five digits, or up to 99,999 students.

Fixed-Point Numbers A **fixed-point number** contains a specific number of decimal places. An example is the CURR_PRICE field in the INVENTORY table in the Clearwater Traders database, which is defined as `curr_price NUMBER(5,2)`. Example values are 259.99 and 59.99.

NUMBER(5,2) specifies that all values will have exactly two digits to the right of the decimal point, and that there are a total of five digits. Therefore, no merchandise prices can exceed $999.99. Note that the decimal point itself is *not* included in the precision value.

Floating-Point Numbers A **floating-point value** is a number with a variable number of decimal places. Floating-point values are defined in Oracle by *not* specifying either the precision or scale in the field declaration. While no floating-point values exist in either of the case study databases, a potential floating-point field in Northwoods database could be student grade point average, which might be declared as `s_gpa NUMBER`. A student's GPA might include one or more decimal places, such as 2.7045, 3.25, or 4.0. A floating-point type allows you to store precise numbers.

DATE Data Type The **DATE** data type stores dates from January 1, 4712 BC to December 31, 4712 AD. The DATE data type stores the century, year, month, day, hour, minute, and second. The default date format is DD-MON-YY to indicate the day of the month, a hyphen, the month (abbreviated using three capital letters), another hyphen, and the last two digits of the year. You can use a **format mask** to display the date differently (such as August 15, 1999 instead of 15-AUG-99) in a report. The SDOB field (student date of birth) in the STUDENT table is declared as `sdob DATE`, which stores the values 07-JUL-67 and 12-NOV-73. DATE fields are stored in a standard internal format in the database, so no length specification is required.

tip

"DATE" is a reserved word so it cannot be used as a field name.

Other Data Types

Sometimes you might need to store data that doesn't fit into a character, number, or date field. In these cases, you can use the LONG, RAW, or LONG RAW data types.

LONG Data Type The **LONG** data type is used to store large amounts (up to two gigabytes) of variable-length character data. The LONG data type is appropriate when you need to store an indeterminate amount of unformatted textual data, such as what is found in an invoice, letter, or report. You can include only one LONG field in a table. Suppose you need to store a student's transcript in the STUDENT table. This field would be declared as `s_transcript LONG`. Then the S_TRANSCRIPT field could store each student's transcript in a text format.

RAW and LONG RAW Data Types The RAW and LONG RAW data types store binary data, such as digitized sound and images. These two data types are similar except the RAW data type can be converted to characters and indexed. **Indexing** a data field means that the DBMS creates an internal data structure that enables the data to be retrieved and processed faster. Suppose you need to store a spreadsheet file of an analysis of all orders placed using a given ORDERSOURCE. The data declaration statement in the ORDERSOURCE table would be `order_report LONG RAW`.

Integrity Constraints

An **integrity constraint** allows you to define primary key fields and specify foreign keys and their corresponding table and column references. An example of a primary key definition is the SID field in the STUDENT table. In the CREATE TABLE command for the STUDENT table, the SID field is defined as `sid NUMBER(5) CONSTRAINT student_sid_pk PRIMARY KEY`.

A convention for naming constraints is to use the general format <table-name where the constraint is being created>_<field-name>_<constraint id>, as shown in the example.

This declaration defines a column named SID with a data type of NUMBER and precision 5 as the primary key of the STUDENT table.

The entry `student_sid_pk` is the **constraint variable name** that Oracle uses as the internal name of the primary key constraint for the STUDENT table. If you omit the constraint variable name in a constraint declaration, Oracle will assign a system-generated name to the constraint. It is wise to name the constraint yourself using the naming convention shown so you can interpret the meaning of each given constraint easily. Each constraint variable name must be unique for the entire database; that is, you cannot have two constraints named student_sid_pk. By using the naming convention, you ensure that each constraint variable name is unique.

An example of a foreign key is the LOCID field in the FACULTY table. The CREATE TABLE command for the FACULTY table includes the following definition:

```
locid NUMBER(5) CONSTRAINT faculty_locid_fk
REFERENCES location(locid)
```

Before you can create a foreign key reference, the table where the field is a primary key already must exist, and the field must be defined as a primary key. In this example, before creating the FACULTY table, you must create the LOCATION table and define LOCID as the primary key.

This declaration defines a field named LOCID as an integer field with precision 5. The declaration also specifies that the variable faculty_locid_fk identifies LOCID as a foreign key in the FACULTY table and references the LOCID field in the LOCATION table as well. When a new record is inserted into the FACULTY table, the DBMS checks to make sure that the value to be inserted for LOCID in the FACULTY record already exists in the LOCATION table.

Value Constraints

A **value constraint** restricts what data can be entered into a given field and enables you to specify a default value for that field. For example, you can specify that numeric data must fall between a specific range (entries must be greater than zero but less than 1,000) or that character data must be from a set of specific values (entries must be SR, JR, SO, or FR). Specifying value constraints in table definitions must be done prudently because once the table is populated with data, it is difficult or impossible to modify the constraint—all records must satisfy the constraint. Value constraints should be used only when the number of allowable values is limited and not likely to change. An example of an appropriate use of a value constraint is for a gender field where the values are restricted to "M" or "F." An inappropriate use would be for the COLOR field in the INVENTORY table in the Clearwater Traders database—there are many possible values, and the values change constantly. A better approach is to create a lookup table, such as the one used for the COLOR table.

Each expression in a value constraint must evaluate as true or false, and expressions can be combined using the logical operators AND and OR. When two expressions are joined by the AND operator, both expressions must be true for the expression to be true. When two expressions are joined by an OR operator, only one expression needs to be true for the expression to be true.

An example of a range data check is used in the CCREDIT field when creating the COURSE table to specify that course credits must be greater than 0 and less than 12. The definition is:

The "cc" in course_credit_cc is a commonly used constraint identifier for check condition.

```
ccredit NUMBER(2) CONSTRAINT course_ccredit_cc
CHECK ((ccredit > 0) AND (ccredit < 12))
```

Note that both the expressions (`ccredit > 0`) and (`ccredit < 12`) can be evaluated as either true or false. The AND condition specifies that both conditions must be true for the check condition to be satisfied.

Another check condition in the database checks to ensure that the value entered in the SCLASS field of the STUDENT table is FR, SO, JR, or SR:

```
sclass CHAR(2) CONSTRAINT student_sclass_cc
CHECK ((sclass = 'FR') OR (sclass = 'SO')
OR (sclass = 'JR') OR (sclass = 'SR'))
```

Again, each of the expressions in parentheses can be evaluated as true or false. The OR condition specifies that if any one condition is true, then the check condition is satisfied.

You also can specify whether a field must have a value entered for every record or whether it can be NULL (indeterminate or unknown). When a field is specified as a primary key, it automatically has a NOT NULL constraint. From a business standpoint, some fields, such as a customer's name, should not be NULL. Although foreign keys sometimes can be NULL (meaning there is no link between a given record and another table), sometimes foreign keys should not be NULL. For example, in the Northwoods University database, it doesn't make sense for a COURSE_SECTION record not to have an associated value for a term ID. Foreign key fields that are not allowed to be NULL must have an explicit NOT NULL constraint. The following example declares TERMID as a foreign key in the COURSE_SECTION table, and adds a NOT NULL constraint:

Note that "nn" is commonly used as the constraint identifier for the NOT NULL constraint.

```
termid NUMBER(3) CONSTRAINT course_section_termid_fk
REFERENCES term(termid)
CONSTRAINT course_section_termid_nn NOT NULL
```

You also can specify that a given field value must be unique within a table. For example, although FPIN is not a primary key in the FACULTY table, it must be unique to ensure security. The declaration for the FPIN field is `fpin NUMBER(4) CONSTRAINT faculty_fpin_uk UNIQUE`.

Note that "uk" is commonly used as the constraint identifier for the UNIQUE constraint.

Finally, you can specify that a particular field can have a default value that is inserted automatically for every table record. For example, if all students must live in Wisconsin to attend Northwoods University, the default SSTATE field could be declared with a default value of WI using the declaration `sstate CHAR(2) DEFAULT 'WI'`.

Starting SQL*Plus

Starting an Oracle application such as SQL*Plus is a two-step process. First you start the application on your client workstation, and then you log on to the Oracle database. Your instructor will advise you of the correct logon procedures for your lab. Now you will create some database tables using SQL*Plus, the Oracle command line SQL utility.

Another way to start SQL*Plus is to start Windows Explorer, change to the ORAWIN95\BIN directory, and then double-click the plus33w.exe file. Windows NT users will change to the ORANT folder instead of the ORAWIN95 folder.

To start SQL*Plus:

1. Click the **Start** button on the Windows taskbar, point to **Programs**, point to **Oracle for Windows 95**, and then click **SQL Plus 3.3**. After a few moments, Oracle SQL*Plus starts, opens the Log On dialog box, and requests your user name and password. You must also enter your host string (or connect string) as shown in Figure 2-2.

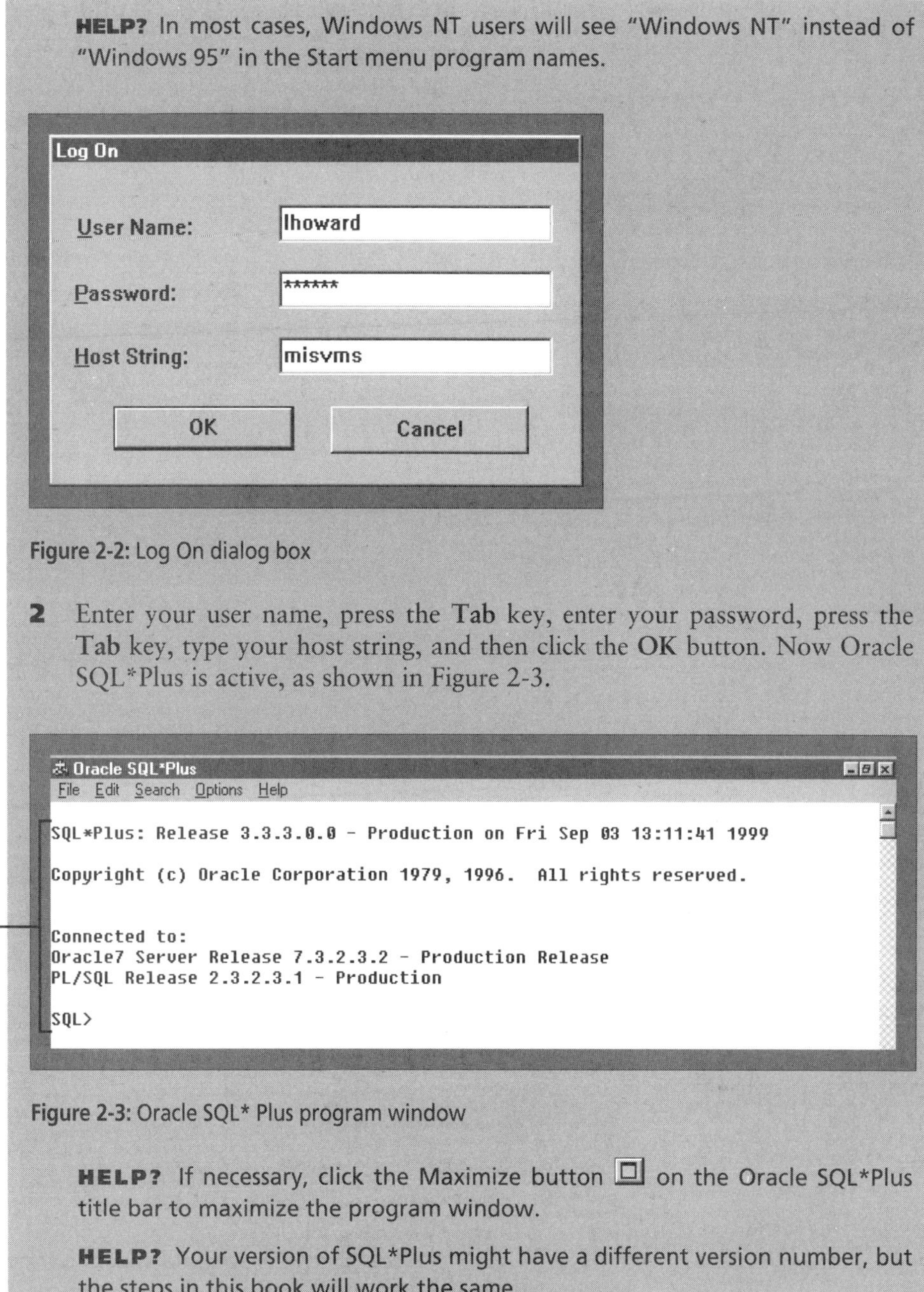

HELP? In most cases, Windows NT users will see "Windows NT" instead of "Windows 95" in the Start menu program names.

Figure 2-2: Log On dialog box

2 Enter your user name, press the **Tab** key, enter your password, press the Tab key, type your host string, and then click the **OK** button. Now Oracle SQL*Plus is active, as shown in Figure 2-3.

tip

Your user name, password, and host string entries are case sensitive.

your SQL*Plus startup information might be different

Figure 2-3: Oracle SQL* Plus program window

HELP? If necessary, click the Maximize button on the Oracle SQL*Plus title bar to maximize the program window.

HELP? Your version of SQL*Plus might have a different version number, but the steps in this book will work the same.

Creating a Database Table Using SQL*Plus

To create the STUDENT table, you will need to create the FACULTY table first because the FID field in the STUDENT table is a foreign key reference to the FID field in the FACULTY table. However, note that the FACULTY table also has a foreign key reference—LOCID in the LOCATION table. The LOCATION table does not have any foreign key references, so you will create it before creating the FACULTY and STUDENT tables.

The SQL command used to create a new table is the CREATE TABLE command.

A convention that is used in this book is that when general code formats are presented, variable names that you will enter are enclosed in angle brackets (< >).

The general format of the CREATE TABLE command appears below.

```
CREATE TABLE <tablename>
(<fieldname1> <data declaration>
CONSTRAINT <integrity constraint declaration>
CONSTRAINT <fieldname1 value constraint declaration>);
```

The constraint declarations are optional. You will create the LOCATION table next.

To create the LOCATION table:

1. Type the query below to create the LOCATION table. Press the Enter key after typing each line to go to the next line, but *do not press* the Enter key after typing the last line of the query. Notice that SQL adds line numbers to your query after you press the Enter key.

   CREATE TABLE LOCATION

   (locid NUMBER(5) CONSTRAINT location_locid_pk PRIMARY KEY,

   bldg_code VARCHAR2(10) CONSTRAINT location_bldg_code_nn NOT NULL,

   room VARCHAR2(6) CONSTRAINT location_room_nn NOT NULL,

   capacity NUMBER(5) CONSTRAINT location_capacity_nn NOT NULL)

2. Type ; after the last line to end the command. SQL commands always end with a semicolon.
3. Press the Enter key to execute the query. See Figure 2-4.

Figure 2-4: SQL query to create the LOCATION table

SQL is not case sensitive, and spaces for formatting are ignored. If your query executes correctly, your screen should display the "Table created" message shown in Figure 2-4. If your query does not execute correctly (and even if it does), proceed to the next section to learn how to edit and debug SQL commands. If necessary, apply these techniques so you can create the LOCATION table.

Editing and Debugging SQL Commands

Many SQL commands are long and complex, and it is easy to make typing errors. There are two editing approaches in SQL*Plus: using the online editing facility or using an alternate text editor. The SQL*Plus environment has some limited online editing capabilities that can be used to make minor changes. For major changes, it is best to use an alternative editing environment in SQL*Plus, such as Notepad or any other Windows text editor.

When you press the Enter key to run a query, the query text is stored in an SQL*Plus memory area called the **edit buffer**. To list the current contents of the edit buffer, type the letter "L" (for list) at the SQL prompt, as shown in Figure 2-5. An asterisk marks the current line, which is the line that is available for editing.

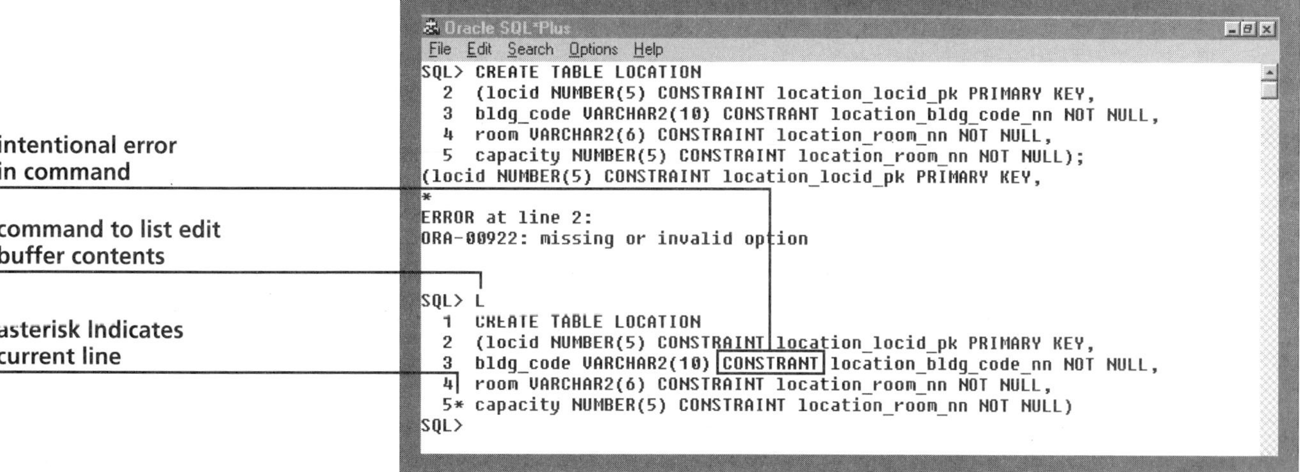

Figure 2-5: Listing the edit buffer contents

You can use the editing commands shown in Figure 2-6 at the SQL prompt to perform the indicated operations. The command is shown in boldface type. The descriptive word that corresponds to the command shown in parentheses and the values you enter for line numbers or text are shown in angle brackets. (You don't type the parentheses or descriptive words—they are listed only to help you understand the meaning of the commands.)

Command	Operation
L (ist)	Shows the complete contents of the edit buffer
<line number>	Changes the current line number to the entered line number and shows the listed line number
A (ppend) **<text>**	Adds the entered text to the end of the current line
C (hange) **/old text/new text/**	Replaces an existing text string in the line (shown here as *old text* and delimited by front slashes) with a new text string (shown here as *new text* and ended with a front slash)
DEL (ete)	Deletes the current line
I (nsert) **<text>**	Creates a new line after the current line that contains the given input text
L (ist) **<line number>**	Shows the indicated line number text
/	Executes the contents of the edit buffer

Figure 2-6: SQL*Plus online editing commands

Figure 2-7 shows examples of how to use these commands. You will learn more about the specific error messages later in the chapter.

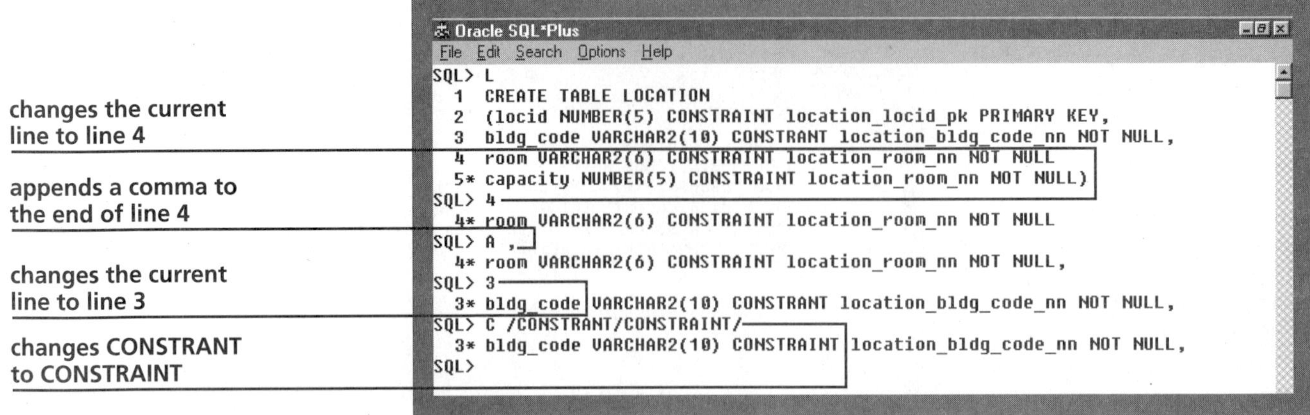

Figure 2-7: Editing in SQL*Plus

You can use an alternate editing environment in SQL*Plus such as Notepad or any other Windows text editor to type your commands. If you run a query and get an error, you can invoke the text editor and SQL*Plus automatically copies the contents of the edit buffer to the text editing environment. From there you can easily edit the query, and then exit the editor and run the query again.

To declare and use the editor:

1. Click **Edit** on the menu bar, point to **Editor**, and then click **Define Editor.** The Define Editor dialog box opens. You use this dialog box to specify the command line to start the program that will be your default editor.
2. If necessary, type **notepad.exe** in the Editor Name dialog box, as shown in Figure 2-8, and then click the **OK** button.

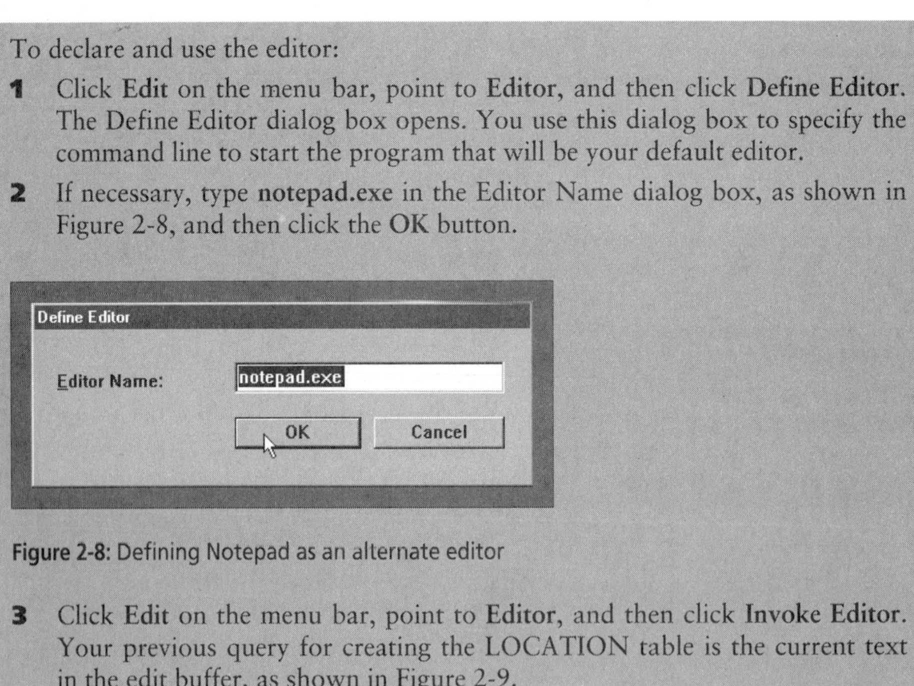

Figure 2-8: Defining Notepad as an alternate editor

3. Click **Edit** on the menu bar, point to **Editor**, and then click **Invoke Editor.** Your previous query for creating the LOCATION table is the current text in the edit buffer, as shown in Figure 2-9.

tip

You also can type EDIT at the SQL prompt to invoke the editor.

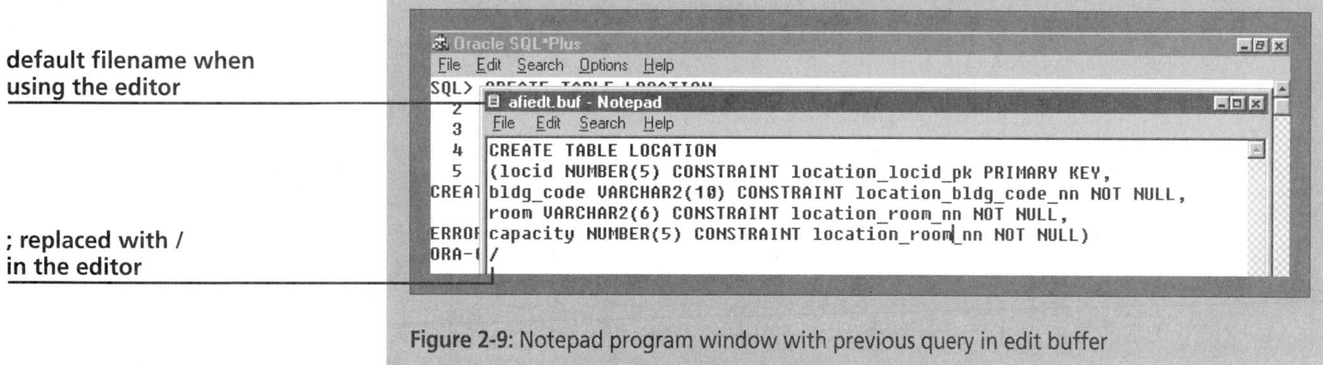

Figure 2-9: Notepad program window with previous query in edit buffer

Now you can edit your query to correct typographical errors. For example, note that in Figure 2-9, the constraint variable for capacity was entered incorrectly as `location_room_nn`. You can change the constraint variable for capacity to `location_capacity_nn` in Notepad (see Figure 2-10), click File on the menu bar, and then click Exit to close Notepad. Click the Yes button to save your changes.

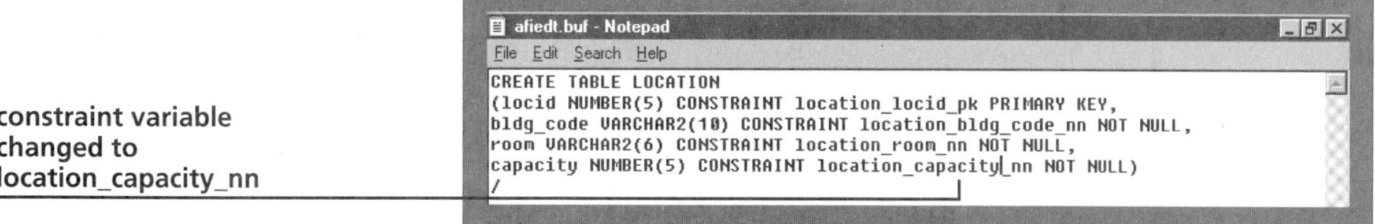

Figure 2-10: Editing a query using Notepad

Your query text will be pasted into SQL*Plus, and then you can execute it by typing a semicolon and then pressing the Enter key. See Figure 2-11 for the query output.

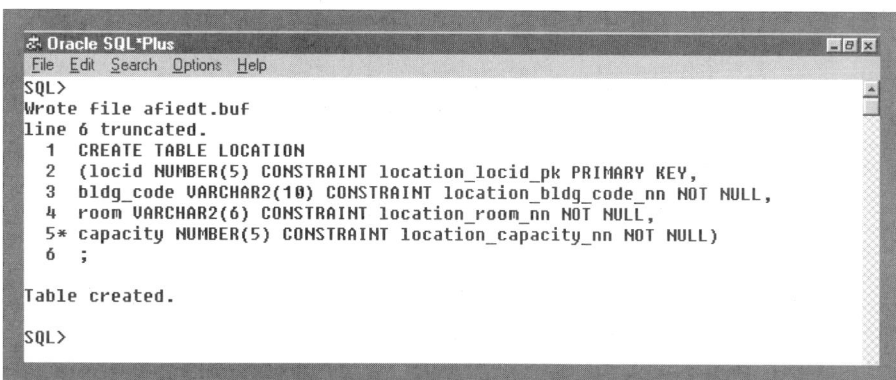

Figure 2-11: Executing the edited query

Another way to use Notepad (or any other Windows-based text editor) to enter commands in conjunction with SQL*Plus is to run both programs concurrently. Type your query text into your text editor, select the desired text by dragging the mouse over it, and then copy the text to the Windows Clipboard by clicking Edit on the menu bar, and then clicking Copy. Switch to SQL*Plus, click Edit on the menu bar, and then click Paste. Your query text will be pasted into the SQL*Plus command line, and then you can execute it by pressing the Enter key.

When you are creating database tables, it is a good idea to save the text of CREATE TABLE queries in a single Notepad text file so you have a record of the original code, and you can easily re-create the tables if changes are required later. To save a text file in Notepad, click File on the menu bar, and then click Save and specify the drive, folder, and filename for the file. You can save more than one CREATE TABLE command in a text file if you want. Just make sure that they are in the proper order so foreign key references are made after their parent tables are created.

Using Online Help

Suppose that when you tried to create the LOCATION table, you got the error message shown in Figure 2-12. The error message shows the line and the position on the line where the error occurred, as well as the error code number and a brief description of the error.

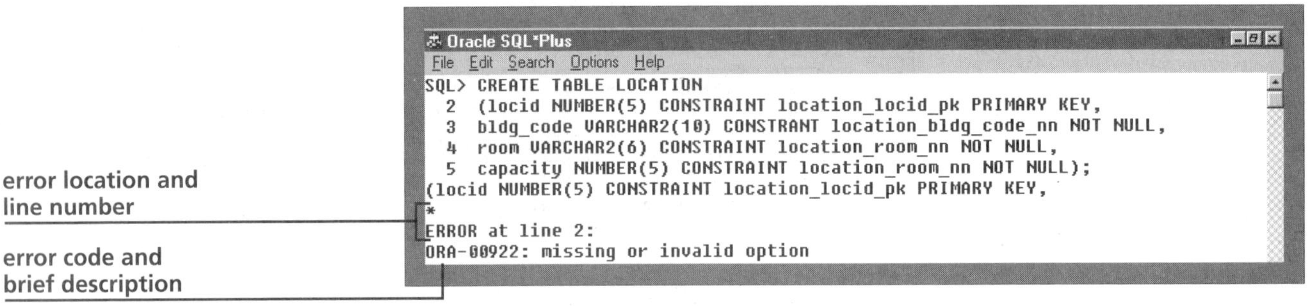

```
Oracle SQL*Plus
File Edit Search Options Help
SQL> CREATE TABLE LOCATION
  2  (locid NUMBER(5) CONSTRAINT location_locid_pk PRIMARY KEY,
  3  bldg_code VARCHAR2(10) CONSTRANT location_bldg_code_nn NOT NULL,
  4  room VARCHAR2(6) CONSTRAINT location_room_nn NOT NULL,
  5  capacity NUMBER(5) CONSTRAINT location_room_nn NOT NULL);
(locid NUMBER(5) CONSTRAINT location_locid_pk PRIMARY KEY,
*
ERROR at line 2:
ORA-00922: missing or invalid option
```

error location and line number

error code and brief description

Figure 2-12: Query error message

The error message indicates that the error occurred on line 2, and the asterisk indicates that it was at the opening parenthesis of the column definitions. Line 2 looks correct. The next step is to use online Help to get a more detailed error description. You will do this next.

To identify the error message:

1. Click the **Start** button, point to **Programs**, point to **Oracle for Windows 95**, and then click **Oracle7 Error Messages**. The Help Topics: Oracle7 Codes and Messages dialog box opens. Oracle does not have a central online Help application for all of its products but has specific online Help applications for each different product. This online Help application provides explanations for DBMS-generated error messages, while other Help applications provide other types of information.
2. Click the **Index** tab, and then type **ORA-00922** in the first text box, as shown in Figure 2-13.

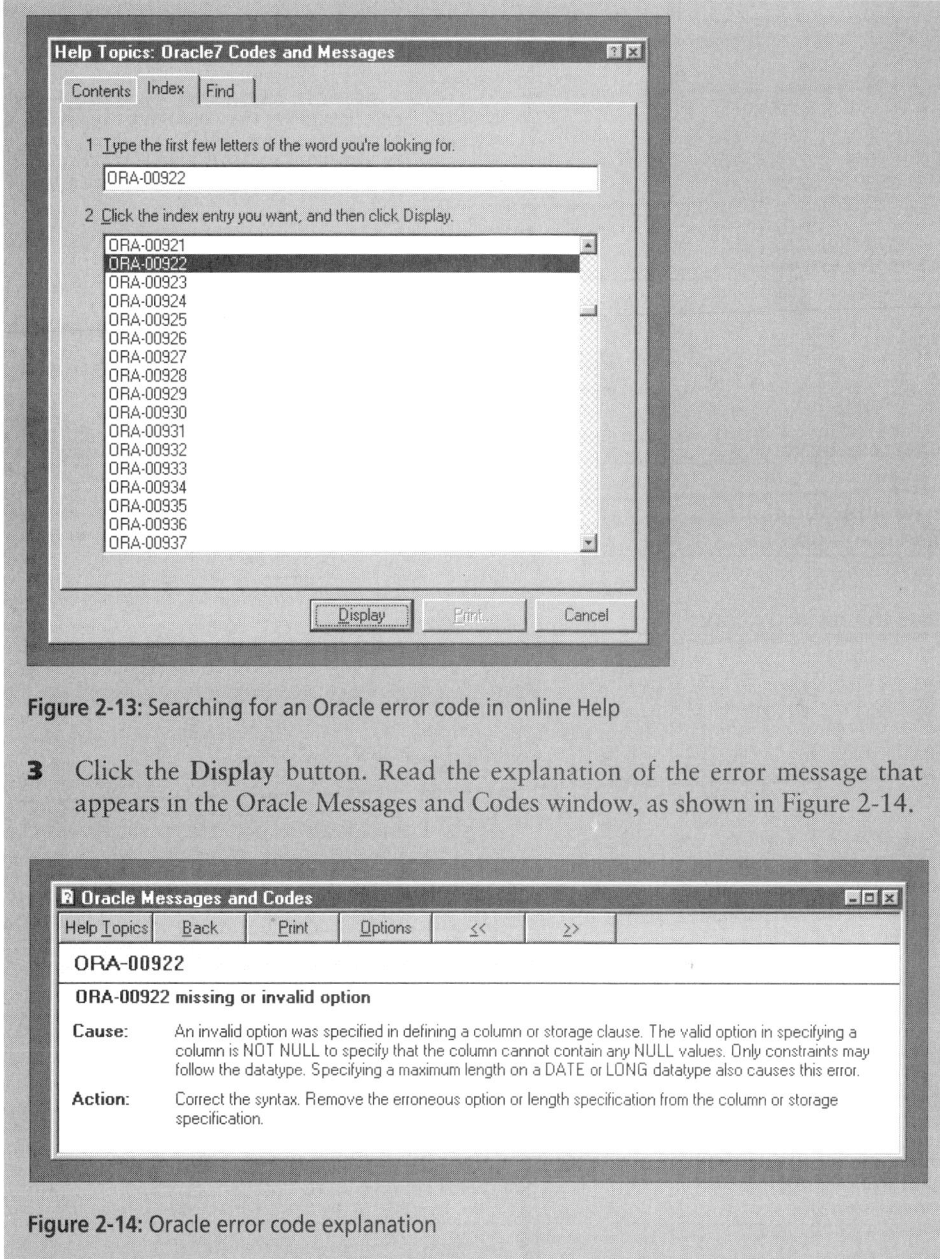

Figure 2-13: Searching for an Oracle error code in online Help

3 Click the **Display** button. Read the explanation of the error message that appears in the Oracle Messages and Codes window, as shown in Figure 2-14.

Figure 2-14: Oracle error code explanation

4 Click the **Close** button ☒ to close Help.

Apparently the error occurred in one of the column definitions. The column definitions begin on line 2, so the error was flagged as occurring on line 2 on the opening parenthesis of the column definitions. However, the problem could be with any one of the column definitions. Look carefully at the query and review each column definition. The problem is that "CONSTRAINT" was spelled as "CONSTRANT" on line 3.

Suppose you fix this typo using the C(hange) online editing command, as shown in Figure 2-15. When you run the query again, you get the new error message shown in the figure.

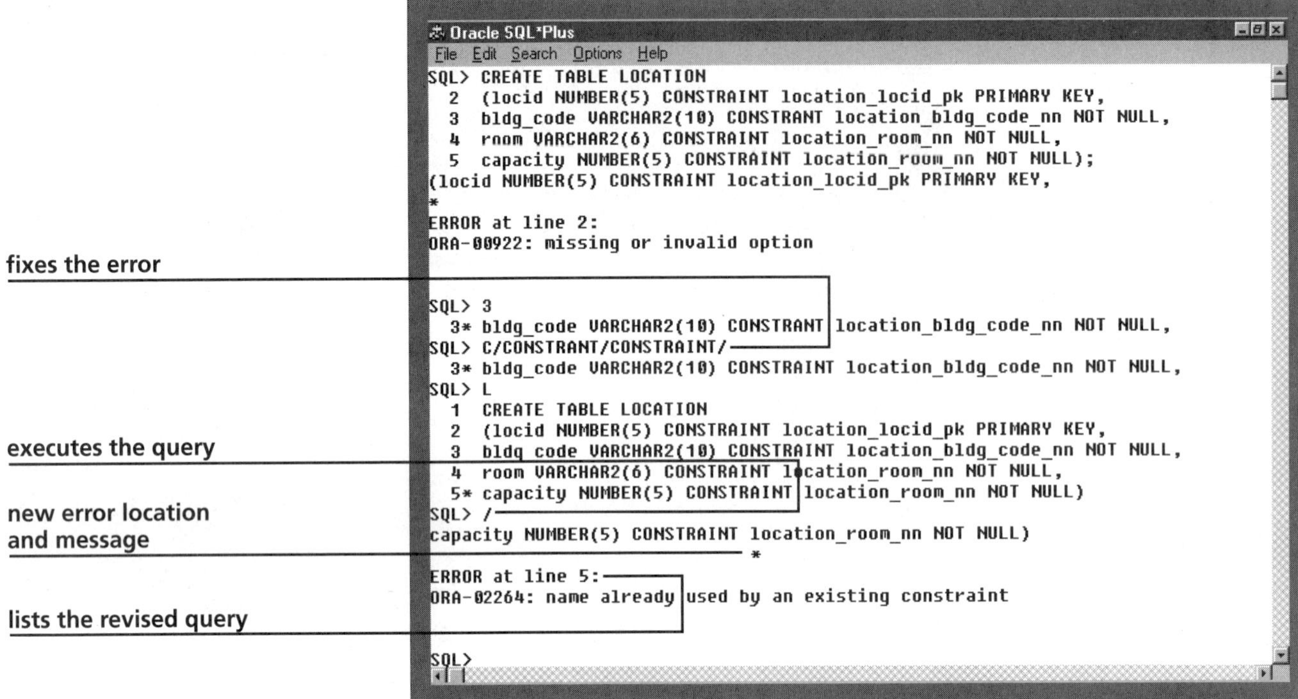

Figure 2-15: Second SQL*Plus error message

This error message and the position of the asterisk suggest that the problem probably has to do with the `location_room_nn NOT NULL` constraint definition. Look at this definition carefully. Note that `location_room_nn` was entered as the constraint variable name for both ROOM and CAPACITY in lines 4 and 5. Remember that every constraint variable in a database must have a unique name. Figure 2-16 shows the process for changing the constraint variable name from `location_room_nn` to `location_capacity_nn`, executing the query again, and then receiving the message that the table was successfully created.

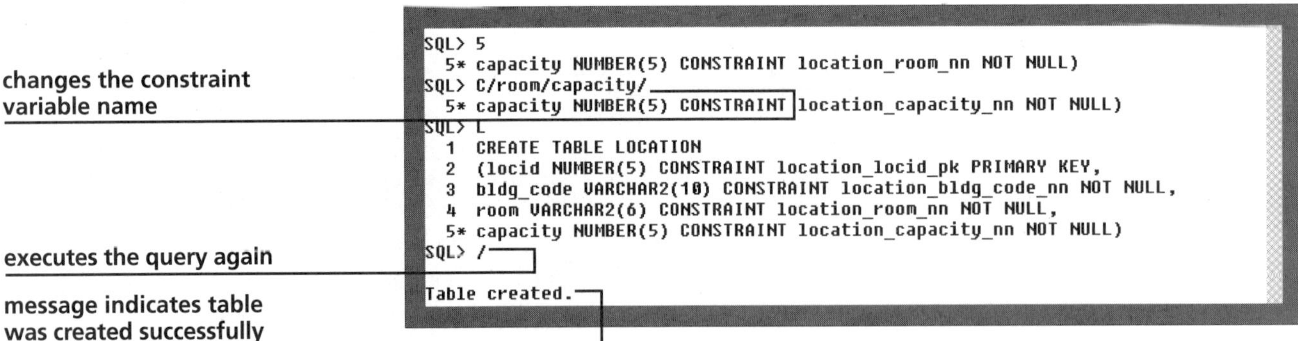

Figure 2-16: Correcting the constraint variable error

Some errors are harder to find than others. For example, the error where CONSTRAINT was misspelled occurred on line 2. Line 2 was fine; the error was actually on line 3. However, the column declarations began on line 2, and the problem was in a subsequent column declaration. To debug SQL queries, always *start* looking for an error at the line referred to in the error message. If the referenced line is correct, examine the error message, and, if necessary, look it up in online Help to identify what type of problem might cause the error. Then examine all the query lines to look for typographical errors, omitted or misplaced commas or parentheses, misspelled words, or repeated constraint variable names.

When you have an error that you cannot locate, a last resort debugging technique is to create the table multiple times and add a new column declaration each time until you find the declaration causing the error, as shown in Figure 2-17.

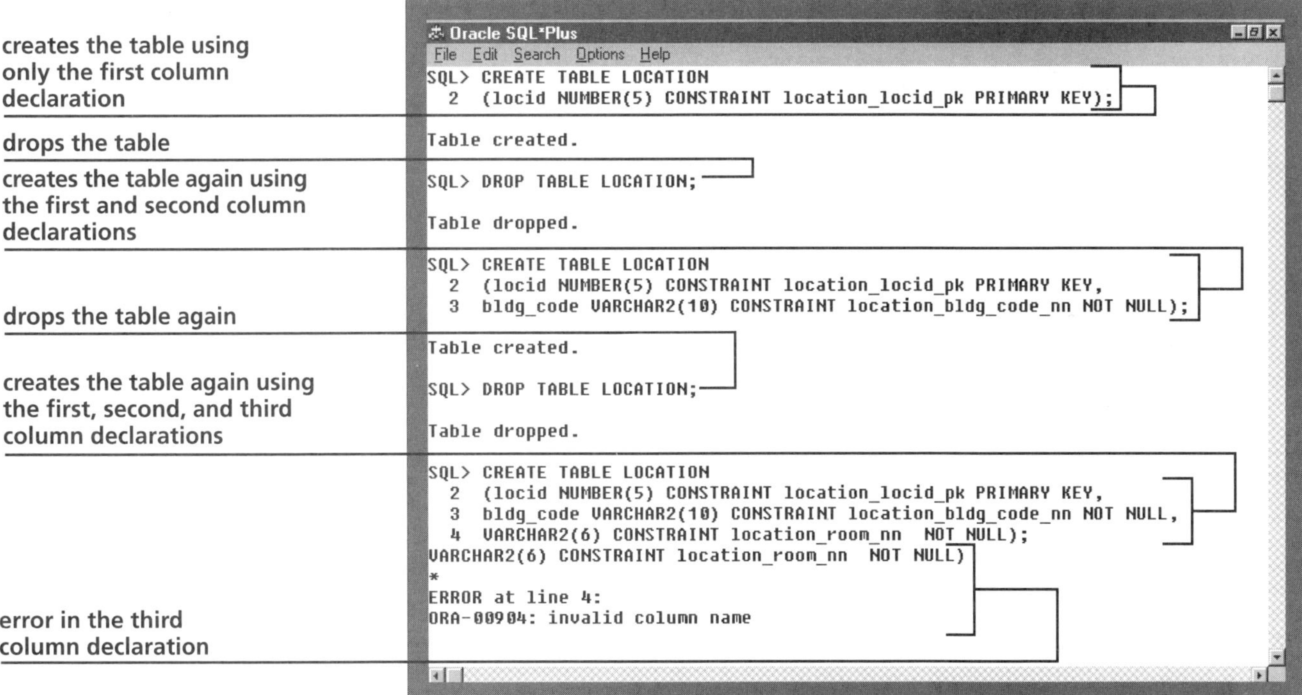

Figure 2-17: Dropping a table to find the location of an error

First paste your non-working query in a Notepad file and modify it so it creates the table with only the first column declared. Copy the modified query, and paste it into SQL*Plus. If the table is created successfully, you now know that the error was not in the first column declaration. Delete the table using the DROP TABLE command, which has the following general format: `DROP TABLE <tablename>;`. Then modify the query in Notepad to create the table using only the first and second column declarations. If this works, you now know that the problem was not in either the first or second column declarations. Drop the table again, and modify the query so the table is created using only the first, second, and third column declarations. Continue this process of adding one more column declaration to the CREATE statement until you locate the column declaration that is causing the error. Figure 2-17 shows how the LOCATION table is created and dropped repeatedly until the error—not specifying a column name—is located on line 4.

Creating the FACULTY and STUDENT Tables

After you successfully create the LOCATION table, you are ready to create some more tables. You will create the FACULTY table next.

You also can click Edit on the menu bar, and then click Select All to select all of the text in the editor.

To create the FACULTY table:

1. Invoke the SQL*Plus text editor.
2. If necessary, use the pointer to select the text currently in the editor, and then press the **Delete** key. Now you can enter the CREATE TABLE command to create the FACULTY table.
3. Type the query shown in Figure 2-18 to create the FACULTY table. Do not include the final semicolon at the end of the query. After typing the last line press the **Enter** key twice so the last line will not get cut off.

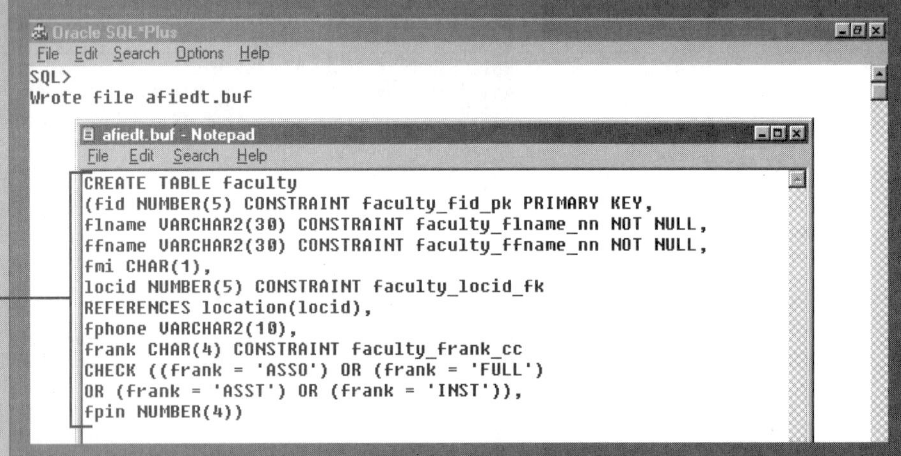

Figure 2-18: Query to create the FACULTY table using Notepad

4. Click **File** on the menu bar, and then click **Exit** to close Notepad. Click the Yes button to save your changes. The text you typed in Notepad is entered in SQL*Plus.
5. Type / and then press the **Enter** key to execute the query. The "Table created" message indicates that your command contained no errors and that Oracle created the table. If you do not get this message, refer back to the section on editing and debugging SQL commands and debug your query until you create the FACULTY table successfully.

Next you will create the STUDENT table.

To create the STUDENT table:

1. Invoke the text editor, type the command shown in Figure 2-19 to create the STUDENT table, and then exit Notepad and save your changes.

type this command

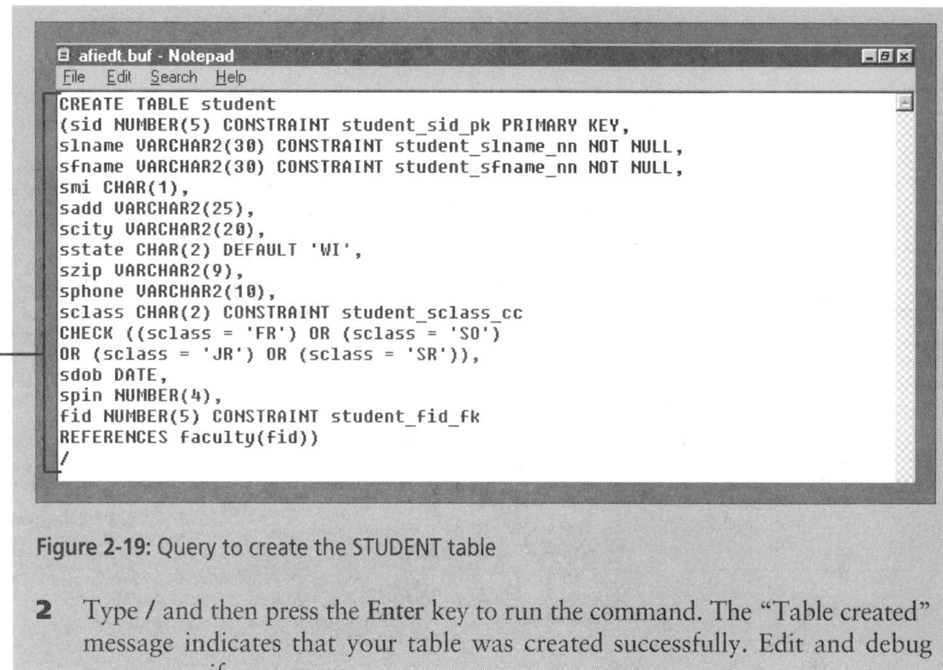

Figure 2-19: Query to create the STUDENT table

2 Type / and then press the **Enter** key to run the command. The "Table created" message indicates that your table was created successfully. Edit and debug your query if necessary.

Viewing Table Structure Information Using SQL*Plus

After you create your database tables and before you begin creating more advanced queries, you often need to review the table names, field and data type values, and constraint types. You can list the names of all of the tables in your user account to see what tables you already have created and which ones still need to be made. To do this, you will execute a query to view data in database tables. (You will learn more about queries in the next chapter.)

To list the tables you own:

1 Type **SELECT table_name,** press the **Enter** key, type **FROM user_tables;**, and then press the **Enter** key to list all of the tables in your account.

The output will show other tables that you own if you have worked in SQL previously.

USER_TABLES is a system database table. **System database tables** are created and maintained by the DBMS for storing information about the database, such as tables and users. This table contains information about all users' data tables, and TABLE_NAME is one of its fields. The query that you just entered shows table names only for the current user. Your output should show the FACULTY, LOCATION, and STUDENT tables.

Viewing Field Definitions

You also might need to view table field names and data types. To do this, you use the DESCRIBE command.

To view the field definitions for the STUDENT table:

1 Type **DESCRIBE student;** and then press the **Enter** key to list the STUDENT table's fields and field data types and sizes. See Figure 2-20.

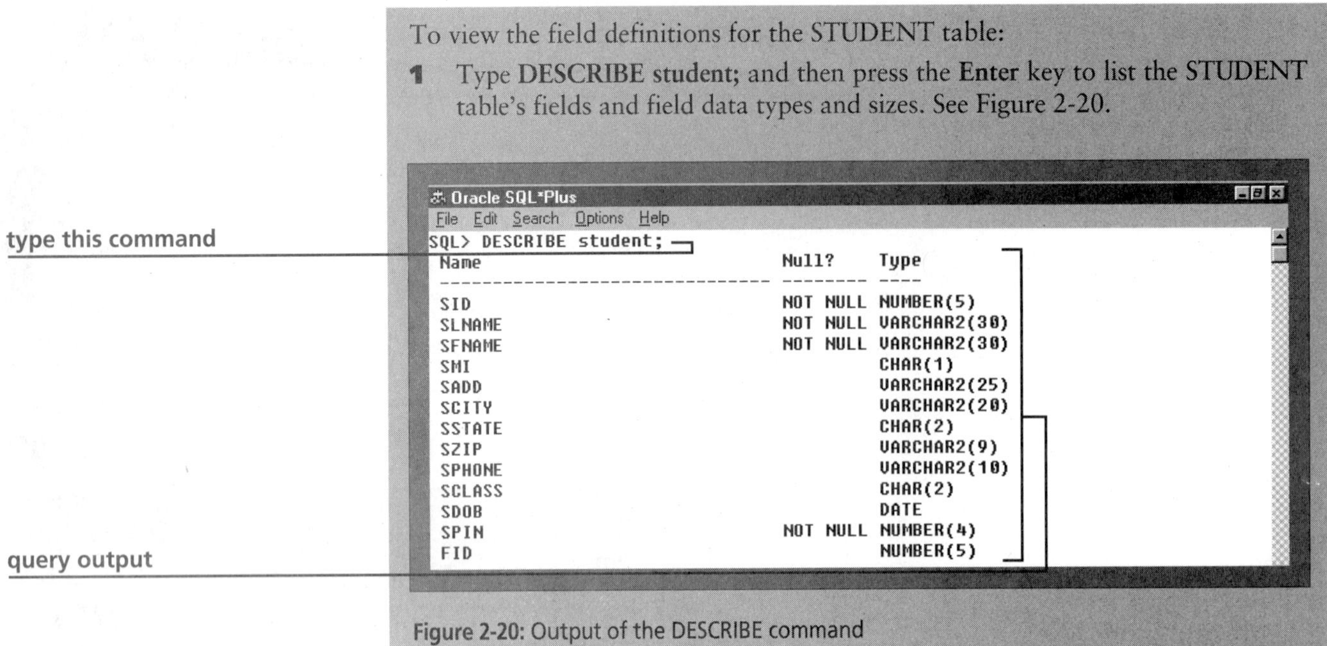

Figure 2-20: Output of the DESCRIBE command

Viewing Constraint Information

You also might need to view information about the constraints that you entered for table fields. To do this, you will query the USER_CONSTRAINTS system database table.

To view the constraint information:

1 Enter and execute the query shown in Figure 2-21. The output shows a listing of all of the constraint variable names assigned to the STUDENT table. Based on the constraint variable naming convention, you can interpret exactly what constraints exist on specific table fields.

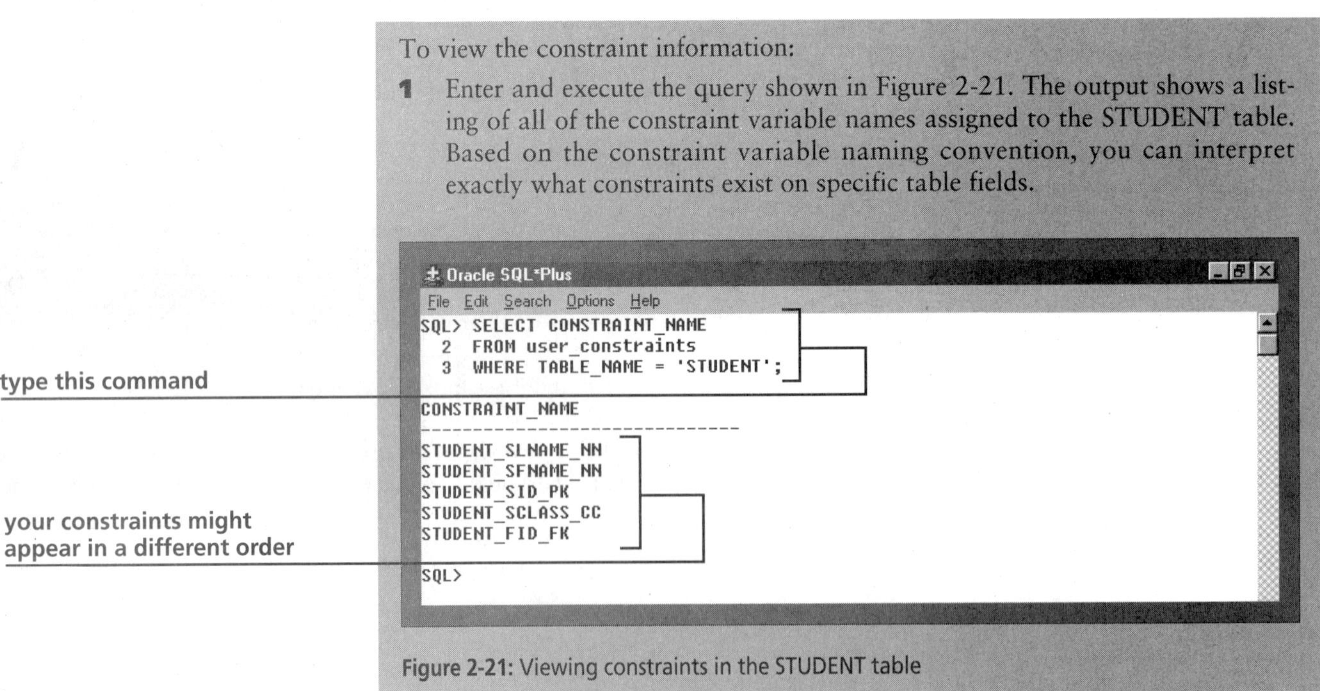

Figure 2-21: Viewing constraints in the STUDENT table

Modifying Tables Using SQL*Plus

After using the DESCRIBE command or selecting the USER_CONSTRAINTS information, you might find that you need to make changes to the column lengths or data types. You should plan your tables carefully to avoid having to make changes to the overall table structure, but inevitably, changes will need to be made. There are some parts of an Oracle database table that you can modify, and others that you cannot. Figure 2-22 shows the restricted and unrestricted actions for a table.

Restricted
Changing a column's data type, size, and default value is allowed only if there is no data in the column being modified
Adding a primary key is allowed only if current field values are unique (no duplicate entries)
Adding UNIQUE and CHECK CONDITION constraints to a column is allowed only if current field values match the added condition
Adding a foreign key is allowed only if current field values are NULL or exist in the referenced table
Changing a column name is not allowed
Deleting a column is not allowed
Unrestricted
Adding a new column to a table
Deleting a primary key constraint (also removes any foreign key references to the field in other tables)
Deleting a foreign key constraint

Figure 2-22: Restricted and unrestricted table changes

Sometimes you might find that you need to make changes that are not allowed in SQL, such as changing the name of a column. One approach is to drop a table so you can re-create it correctly.

Dropping and Renaming Existing Tables

When you drop a table from the database, you delete the table structure and all the data it contains. To delete a table, use `DROP TABLE <tablename>;` command, where *tablename* is the name of that table that you want to drop. To rename a table to a new name, use the `RENAME <oldtablename> TO <newtablename>;` command, and replace the markers *oldtablename* and *newtablename* with the appropriate names.

Adding Fields to Existing Tables

The basic format of the statement to add a new field to a table is:

```
ALTER TABLE <tablename>
ADD <fieldname><data declaration>
CONSTRAINT <integrity constraints>
CONSTRAINT <value constraints>;
```

Suppose that you need to add a field to the FACULTY table that specifies each faculty members' employment start date. The ALTER TABLE command adds a column to an existing table. You will add the STARTDATE field to the FACULTY table next.

To add the STARTDATE field to the FACULTY table:

1 Type **ALTER TABLE faculty ADD (startdate DATE);**, and then press the **Enter** key. The "Table altered" confirmation message appears, as shown in Figure 2-23.

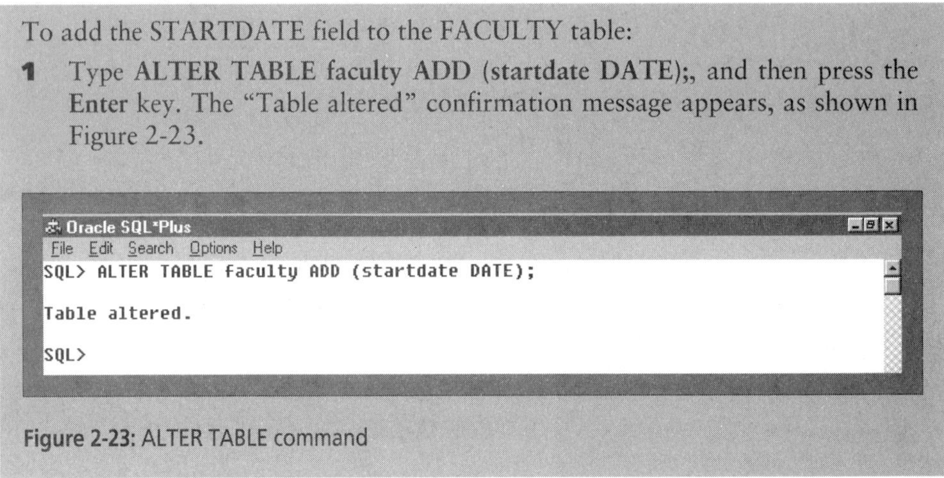

Figure 2-23: ALTER TABLE command

Modifying Existing Fields

The general format of the command to modify an existing field's data declaration is:

```
ALTER <tablename>
MODIFY <fieldname><new data declaration>;
```

However, after you modify an existing field, you must declare the integrity and value constraints again using the ALTER TABLE/ADD command. For example, suppose that you decide to modify the FACULTY table's FRANK field to a data type of VARCHAR2 with a length of six.

To change the data type and size of the FRANK field:

1 Type **ALTER TABLE faculty MODIFY (frank VARCHAR2 (6));**, and then press the **Enter** key to change the data type and size of the FRANK field in the FACULTY table.

This command completely replaces the existing FRANK field definition. Now you must implement again the value constraint check condition that was on the field by using the ALTER TABLE command with the ADD clause.

You can use the ALTER TABLE command to create a composite primary key. For example, to create a composite key of FID and CID in the COURSE_UPDATE table, you would create the table with no primary key constraint, and then modify the table using the command `ALTER TABLE COURSE_UPDATE ADD PRIMARY KEY (cid, fid) ENABLE PRIMARY KEY;`

To add the value constraint check to the FACULTY table:

1 Type the following code exactly as shown:

ALTER TABLE faculty

ADD CONSTRAINT faculty_frank_cc

CHECK ((frank = 'ASSO') OR (frank = 'FULL')

OR (frank = 'ASST') OR (frank = 'INST'));

2 Press the **Enter** key. The "Table altered" message indicates that your changes have been made.

To modify the NOT NULL value constraint, you use the MODIFY command. You want to modify the SPIN field in the STUDENT table so it is UNIQUE and NOT NULL.

To modify the SPIN field in the STUDENT table to NOT NULL:

1 Type **ALTER TABLE student MODIFY (spin NUMBER(4) CONSTRAINT student_spin_nn NOT NULL);**, and then press the Enter key to add a NOT NULL constraint to an existing field.

2 Type **ALTER TABLE student ADD CONSTRAINT student_spin_uk UNIQUE (spin);**, and then press the Enter key to add the UNIQUE constraint.

To change an existing check condition value constraint on a field, you must first drop the existing check condition using the DROP clause, and then add the new check condition. You decide to change the check condition in the SCLASS field in the STUDENT table to allow a GR value for graduate students.

To add the check conditions to the STUDENT table:

1 Type **ALTER TABLE student DROP CONSTRAINT student_sclass_cc;**, and then press the **Enter** key to modify the existing SCLASS field so it no longer has the check constraint.

2 Type the following code to add the new constraint:

ALTER TABLE student

ADD CONSTRAINT student_sclass_cc

CHECK ((sclass = 'FR') OR (sclass = 'SO')

OR (sclass = 'JR') OR (sclass = 'SR')

OR (sclass = 'GR'));

3 Press the **Enter** key to make the change. Next, you would like to make FR (freshman) the default value for the SCLASS field.

4 Type **ALTER TABLE student MODIFY (sclass CHAR(2) DEFAULT 'FR');**, and then press the **Enter** key.

A quirk of the ALTER TABLE command is that the MODIFY clause can be used only to change the data type, size, default values, and the NOT NULL check condition. For all other check condition modifications, you must drop the existing column constraint and then use the ADD clause to define the new constraint.

Figure 2-24 shows when to use the ALTER TABLE/ADD and the ALTER TABLE/MODIFY clauses. Remember that you must drop any existing check condition constraints on the column first before using the ALTER TABLE/ADD clause.

Use ALTER TABLE/ADD when:	Use ALTER TABLE/MODIFY when:
Adding a new column	Modifying a column's data type or size
Adding a new foreign key or check condition constraint	Modifying a column to add a NOT NULL constraint
	Modifying a column to add a default value

Figure 2-24: Summary of using the ALTER TABLE commands

Exiting SQL*Plus

There are three ways to exit SQL*Plus. You can type exit at the SQL prompt, or click File on the menu bar, and then click Exit, or you can click the Close button on the program window title bar. When you connect to a database on a server, your database connection disconnects automatically when you exit SQL*Plus. Use any one of these methods to exit SQL*Plus now.

Creating and Modifying Database Tables Using the Oracle Navigator

The Oracle Navigator is a graphical development tool that enables users to specify table structures visually, instead of from the SQL command prompt. However, both methods of creating tables accomplish the same thing. Most of the database table principles described earlier concerning data types and sizes, field constraints, primary key definitions, and foreign key references are used in the Navigator environment just like they are used in SQL*Plus. However, in this environment you specify the table structure information visually, and the Navigator translates this information to the associated SQL command. You start the Oracle Navigator just like you start any other program. You will start the program next.

To start the Oracle Navigator:

1. Click the **Start** button, point to **Programs**, click **Personal Oracle7 for Windows 95**, and then click **Oracle Navigator**. The Oracle Navigator opens, as shown in Figure 2-25. The Database Connections folder saves past database connection information including your user name, password, and connect string every time that you log on to a database. Next you will connect to the database.

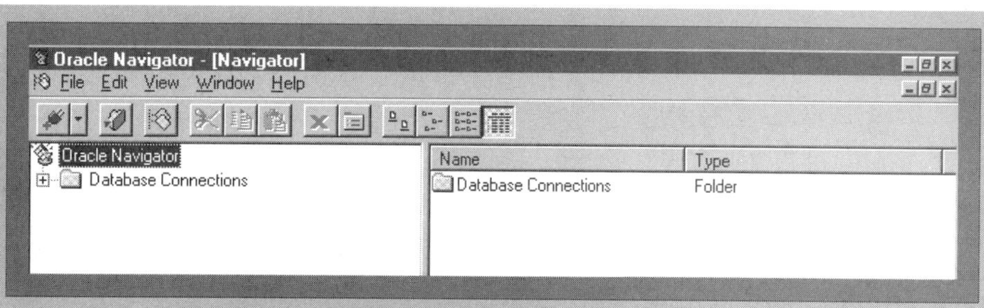

Figure 2-25: Initial Oracle Navigator screen

HELP? If necessary, click the Maximize button on the Oracle Navigator title bar to maximize the program window, and click the Maximize button on the Oracle Navigator title bar to maximize the Oracle Navigator window.

2 Right-click the **Database Connections** folder in the left pane of the Oracle Navigator window, and then click **New**. The New Database Connection Properties dialog box opens, as shown in Figure 2-26. You will enter the name of the connection, your user name, password, and connect string in this dialog box. The connection name can be any descriptive title. Your user name, password, and connect string are the same as the values you entered to log on to SQL*Plus. The Save Password check box gives you the option of having the system save your password so you don't need to retype it the next time you log on.

tip

You also can start the Oracle Navigator by opening Windows Explorer, changing to the \ORAWIN95\BIN\ folder, and then double-clicking the Po7.exe file.

click to clear this check box

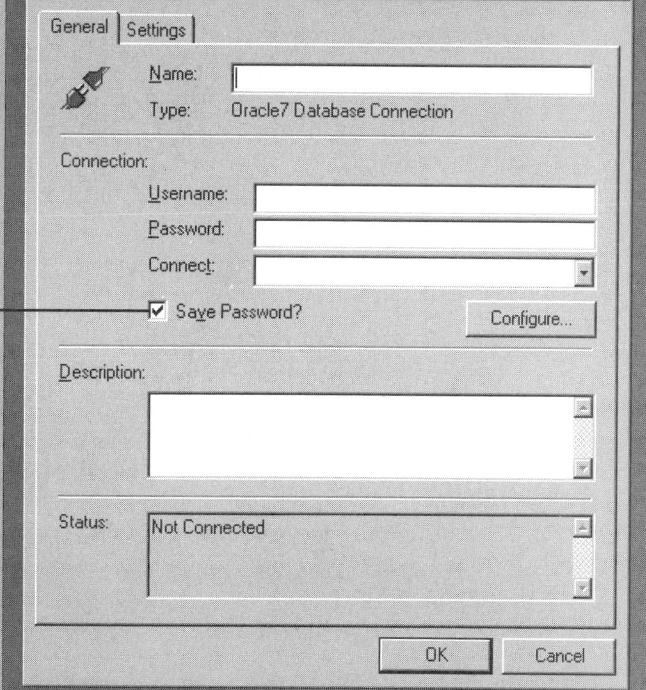

Figure 2-26: New Database Connection Properties dialog box

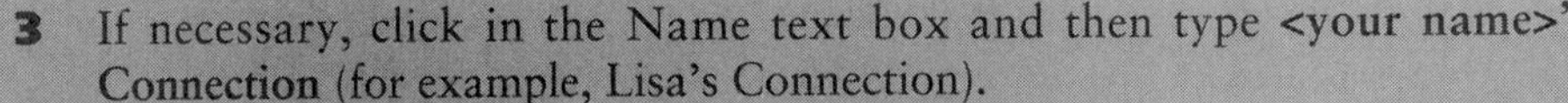

3 If necessary, click in the Name text box and then type <your name>'s **Connection** (for example, Lisa's Connection).

4 Press the **Tab** key and then enter your user name, password, and connect string. Clear the **Save Password?** check box, and then click the **OK** button. The left pane of your screen shows a connected plug-and-socket icon next to your connection name. This icon means that this connection is connected to the database. The right pane shows all of the database objects that you can work with in your connection.

5 Right-click your connection name to see the menu shown in Figure 2-27.

tip

If you are working in a computer laboratory, always make sure that the Save Password? check box is cleared so other users cannot access your database tables if you forget to delete your connection. The steps for deleting a connection are described next.

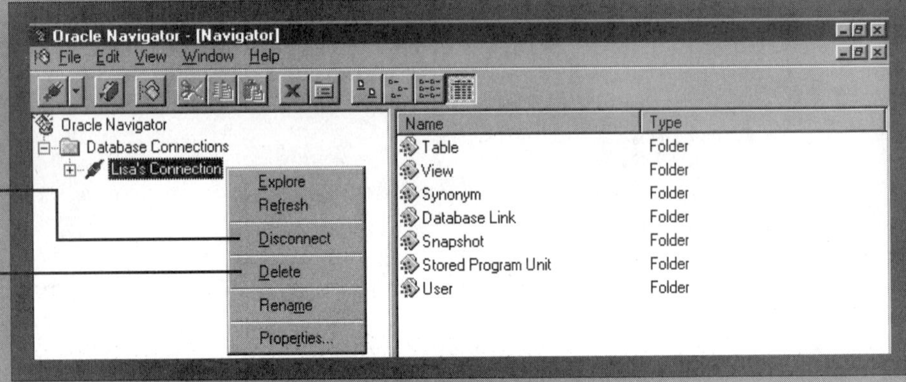

Figure 2-27: Oracle Navigator database connection options

6 Click **Disconnect** on the menu to disconnect from the database.

7 Right-click your connection name again, click **Delete**, and then click the Yes button to delete the connection and all of your user information.

HELP? If you are working in a computer laboratory, you must always delete your connections, or other users will be able to access your database tables.

tip

Disconnecting from the database does not delete your account and password information. The only way to delete your connection information is to use the Delete command.

Creating New Database Tables Using the Oracle Table Wizard

Now you will create some database tables using the Oracle Navigator. You will create the TERM and COURSE tables first because they do not have any foreign keys. There are two methods for creating a new table—using the Table Wizard and creating tables manually. The Table Wizard guides you through a series of steps to create the table; creating the table manually enables you to type the table specifications directly. You will create tables using both methods. You will use the Table Wizard first.

To use the Oracle Table Wizard to create a table:

1 Connect to the database in the Oracle Navigator again.

2 Click the **plus box** ⊞ to the left of your connection to list the available database objects. The Object Navigator lets you manipulate seven types of Oracle objects: tables, views, synonyms, database links, snapshots, stored program units, and users—these objects also display in the right pane of the Navigator window. For now, you will work with tables.

3 Right-click **Table** in the left pane, and then click **New**.

4 Click the **Use table wizard** option button, and then click the **OK** button. The Table Wizard dialog box opens and prompts you to specify the table name.

5 Type **TERM** in the What do you want the name of the new table to be? text box, as shown in Figure 2-28, and then click the **Next** button. In the second dialog box, you enter column definitions.

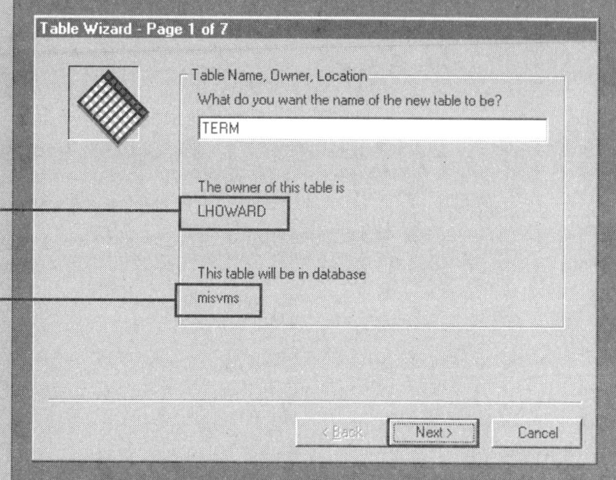

Figure 2-28: Using the Table Wizard to specify the table name

tip

If you want to specify a default value for the field, enter the value in the Does this column have a default value if any? text box. For character data, enter the default value directly without single quotation marks. For date data, the value must be entered in the format DD-MON-YY, for example, 14-JUL-99. You cannot enter a default value for number data because the system always puts single quotation marks around the default values.

6 Type **TERMID** in the Column Name text box, click the **Column Type** list arrow, and then click **NUMBER** from the available data types. Type **5** for Size and **0** for Scale, as shown in Figure 2-29. Click the **New** button to save this column and move to the next column specification screen.

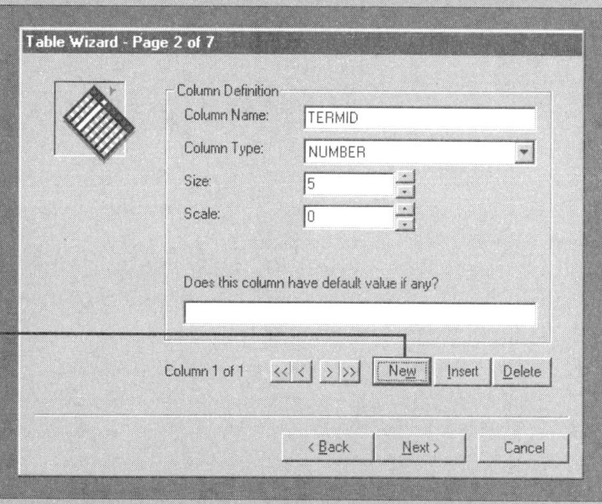

Figure 2-29: Using the Table Wizard to specify the TERMID column

7 Enter the column specifications for TERMDESC, as shown in Figure 2-30, and then click the **New** button.

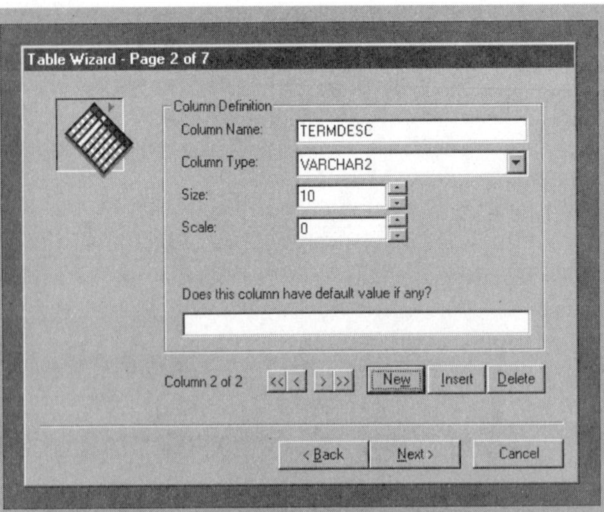

Table Wizard - Page 2 of 7
Column Definition
Column Name: TERMDESC
Column Type: VARCHAR2
Size: 10
Scale: 0
Does this column have default value if any?
Column 2 of 2
<< < > >> New Insert Delete
< Back Next > Cancel

Figure 2-30: Specifying the TERMDESC column

8 Enter the specification for the ENROLLMENT column using a **VARCHAR2** data type with width **20**. Specify a default value of **OPEN**, as shown in Figure 2-31. This is the last column in the table, so click the **Next** button to move to the next page in the Table Wizard.

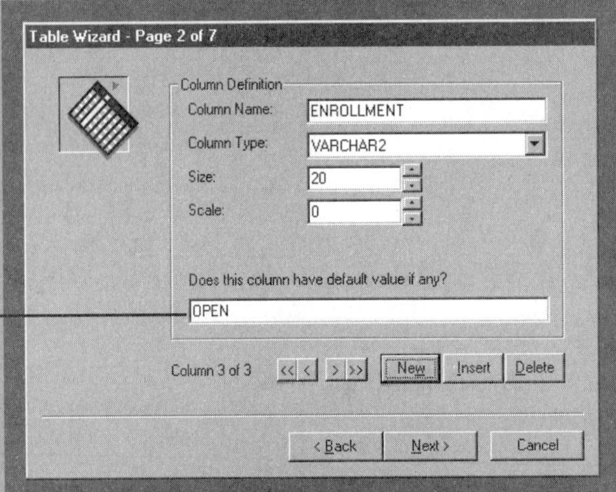

Figure 2-31: Specifying the ENROLLMENT column definition

HELP? If you click the New button after typing a column specification, a blank column is inserted *after* the current column. If you click the Insert button after typing a column specification, a new blank column is inserted *before* the current column. Click the Delete button and then click the Yes button to cancel any unwanted new blank columns.

You can navigate between columns using the navigation arrows on Page 3 of the Table Wizard. Click [<<] to jump to the first column in the table. Click [<] to jump to the column immediately before the selected column, click [>] to jump to the column immediately after the selected column, and click [>>] to jump to the last column in the table. You will use these buttons to navigate through the fields to specify constraints next. First you will specify the unique key and NOT NULL constraints. TERMID is a primary key, so it cannot be NULL and it must be unique.

To specify constraints:

1 If necessary, click [<<] so the TERMID column name displays. Enter the specifications shown in Figure 2-32.

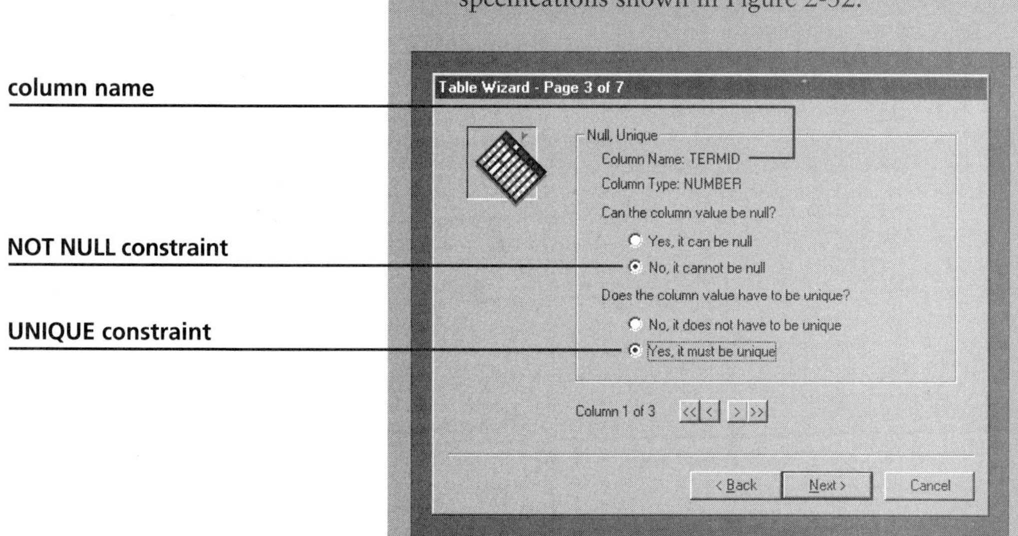

Figure 2-32: Specifying NULL and UNIQUE constraints

2 Click [>] to move to the TERMDESC column specification. This column cannot be NULL either, but it does not have to be unique. Complete this specification.

3 Click [>] to move to the ENROLLMENT column specification. This column cannot be NULL either, and it does not have to be unique. Complete this specification, and then click the **Next** button. The next step is to specify foreign key references and check conditions. The Password dialog box opens first.

4 Enter your password so the DBMS can see what tables are available for foreign key reference, and then click the OK button to go to Page 4 of the Table Wizard, which allows you to specify whether the current column has foreign key references or check conditions. See Figure 2-33. You can move between the columns using the navigational arrows. Neither field in the TERM table has a foreign key or check condition.

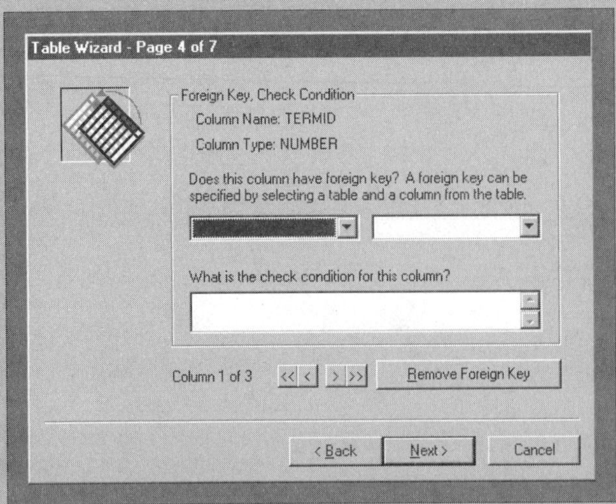

Figure 2-33: Foreign key specification (none specified)

5 Click the **Next** button to go to Page 5 of the Table Wizard, which allows you to specify primary keys. Some tables such as TERM have a single column that serves as the primary key. Other tables require the combination of two columns to be the primary key that uniquely identifies each record.

6 Click in the Primary Key column next to the TERMID column. The number 1 appears, which indicates that TERMID is the first part of the primary key of the table. See Figure 2-34.

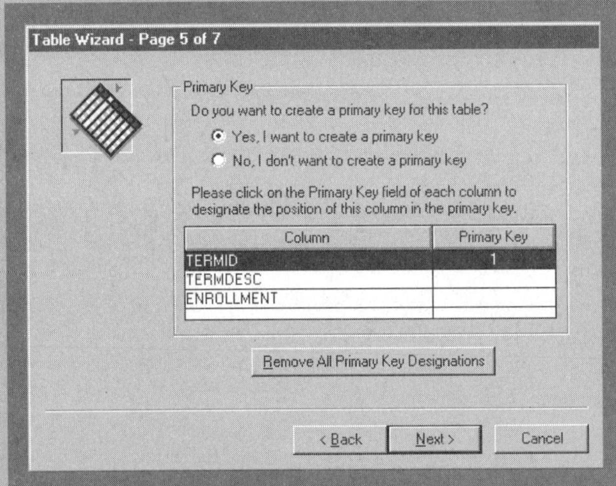

Figure 2-34: Specifying the primary key

7 Click in the Primary Key column for TERMDESC. The number 2 appears, which indicates that TERMDESC is the second part of the table's primary key. You do not want TERMDESC to be part of the primary key, so you need to remove it.

8 Click the **Remove All Primary Key Designations** button to delete the numbers. Now specify TERMID as part 1 of the primary key by clicking the Primary Key column for TERMID.

9 Click the **Next** button to go to Page 6 of the Table Wizard, which allows you to rearrange the order of the columns in the table.

10 Click **termid[NUMBER]** and then click the **Down** button so TERMID is after TERMDESC. See Figure 2-35. The position of the two columns switches. Arrange the columns back so TERMID is first, and then click the **Next** button to go to Page 7 of the Table Wizard, which asks if you want to enter data in the new table. You will not enter any data now, so you will skip this step.

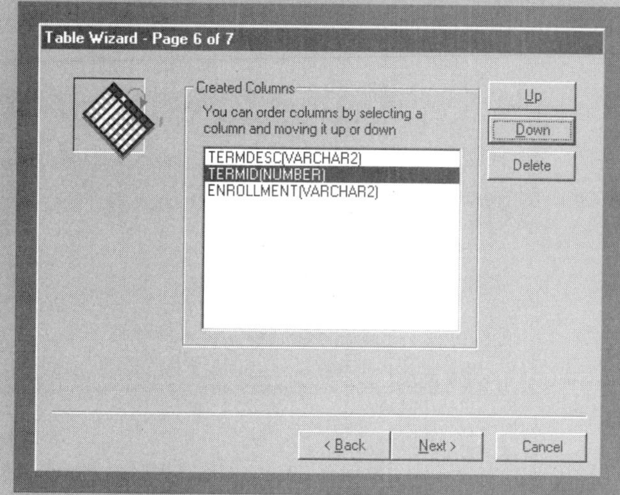

Figure 2-35: Changing the column order

11 Click the **No, I don't want to enter data now** option button, and then click the **Finish** button to return to the Oracle Navigator window.

Next you will create the COURSE table using the Table Wizard.

To create the COURSE table:

1 Create the COURSE table using the Table Wizard. Use the data type and size specifications shown below. When you specify the check condition for CCREDIT, enter ccredit > 0. In general, the check condition in the Oracle Navigator is just the same as the CHECK clause used when you are specifying a check condition when creating a table in SQL*Plus. Do not enter any data in the COURSE table at this time.

Column Name	Data Type and Size	NOT NULL/UNIQUE Specification	Primary Key Specification
CID	NUMBER(6)	NOT NULL, UNIQUE	1
CALLID	VARCHAR2(10)	NOT NULL, NOT UNIQUE	
CNAME	VARCHAR2(25)	NULL OK, NOT UNIQUE	
CCREDIT	NUMBER(2)	NOT NULL, NOT UNIQUE	

Using the Oracle Navigator to Find the Properties of Existing Tables

Now you will create the COURSE_SECTION table, which has four foreign key references: CID, TERMID, FID, and LOCID. Remember that foreign key fields must match their referenced fields' data types and sizes. You know that CID is a NUMBER field with a size of 6 because you just created it. But suppose that you cannot remember the exact field sizes for TERMID, FID, and LOCID. You can use the Oracle Navigator to look up these specifications.

To view the table properties:

1 Double-click the **Table** folder below your connection, and then find your TERM table in the right pane of the Oracle Navigator window. Every table in the database is listed, so make sure you locate the TERM table that lists your user name as the owner. Figure 2-36 shows the TERM table belonging to user LHOWARD.

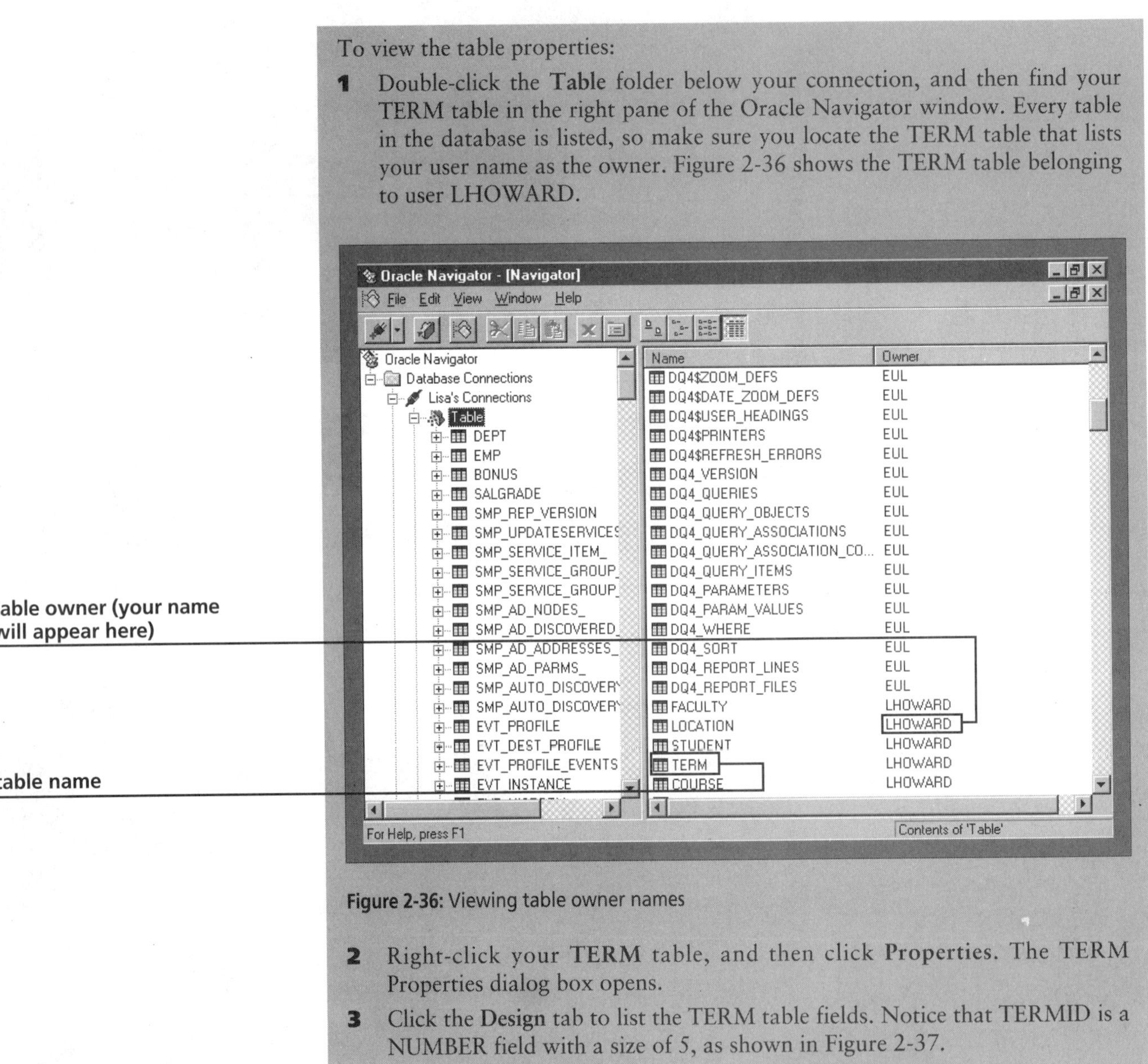

Figure 2-36: Viewing table owner names

2 Right-click your **TERM** table, and then click **Properties**. The TERM Properties dialog box opens.

3 Click the **Design** tab to list the TERM table fields. Notice that TERMID is a NUMBER field with a size of 5, as shown in Figure 2-37.

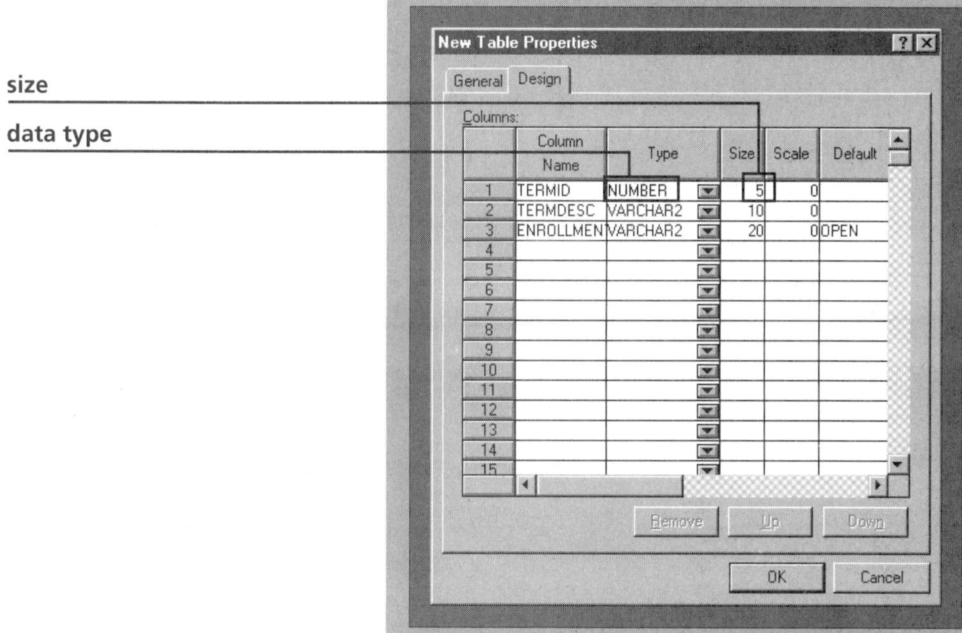

Figure 2-37: Viewing the TERMID column specifications

4 Click the **right scroll arrow** to examine the rest of the table's properties. Notice that the TERMID field's Can be Null? check box is checked. However, if you try to insert a record in this table with TERMID as a NULL value, you will get an error. The primary key designation automatically ensures that this field cannot be NULL.

5 Click the **Cancel** button.

6 Right-click your **COURSE** table in the right pane of the Navigator window, and then click **Properties**. The COURSE Properties dialog box opens. Click the **Design** tab, and then note the CID data type and size (NUMBER, size 6).

7 Click the **Cancel** button.

8 Repeat the previous steps and write down the data types and sizes of the FID and LOCID fields in the FACULTY and LOCATION tables.

You will create the COURSE_SECTION table next.

To create the COURSE_SECTION table:

1 Use the Table Wizard to create a new database table. Name the table **COURSE_SECTION**. Click the **Next** button.

2 On Page 2 of the Table Wizard, specify the table column names, data types, and sizes as shown below. Use the data types and sizes for FID and LOCID that you found in the previous steps. When you are finished specifying all of the columns, click the **Next** button.

Column Name	Data Type and Size	NULL/UNIQUE Specification	Primary Key Specification
CSECID	NUMBER(8)	NOT NULL, UNIQUE	Primary Key 1
CID	NUMBER(6)	NOT NULL, NOT UNIQUE	
TERMID	NUMBER(5)	NULL OK, NOT UNIQUE	
SECNUM	NUMBER(2)	NULL OK, NOT UNIQUE	
FID	Look up in FACULTY table	NOT NULL, NOT UNIQUE	
DAY	VARCHAR2(10)	NULL OK, NOT UNIQUE	
TIME	DATE (no size specification needed)	NULL OK, NOT UNIQUE	
LOCID	Look up in LOCATION table	NULL OK, NOT UNIQUE	
MAXENRL	NUMBER(4)	NOT NULL, NOT UNIQUE	
CURRENRL	NUMBER(4)	NOT NULL, NOT UNIQUE	

3 On Page 3 of the Table Wizard, specify each column's NULL and UNIQUE constraints as shown in Step 2. When you are finished, click the **Next** button.

4 Enter your password to create the foreign key references.

5 On Page 4 of the Table Wizard, use the navigation arrows to move to the CID column.

6 To create the CID foreign key reference, click the left foreign key list arrow, and then scroll down until you see the entry <your user name>.COURSE, and then click it. Figure 2-38 shows what the screen looks like for user LHOWARD.

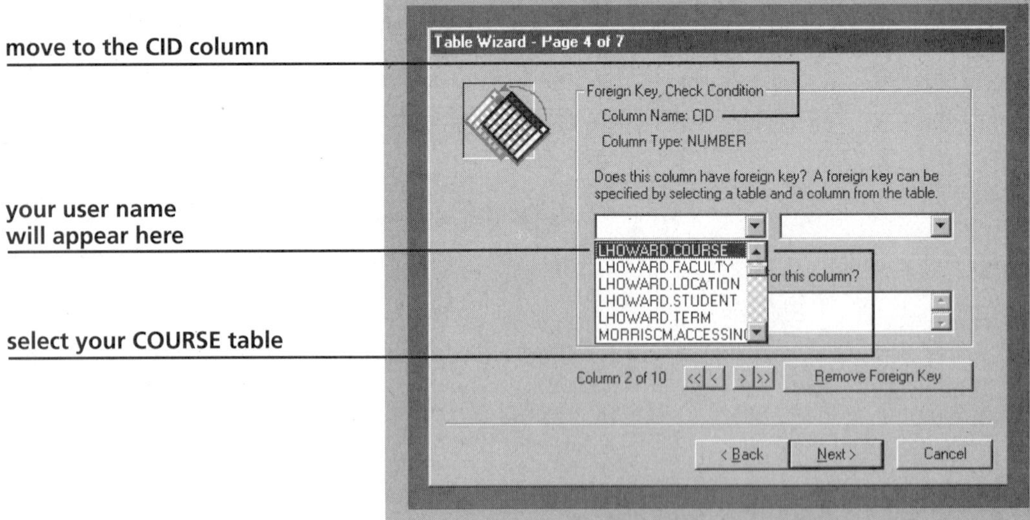

Figure 2-38: Selecting a foreign key table reference

7 Click the right foreign key list arrow, and then click **CID**, as shown in Figure 2-39. This completes the foreign key reference. Click [>] to move to TERMID, FID, and LOCID, and complete their foreign key references to the TERM, FACULTY, and LOCATION tables in a similar manner. When you have completed the foreign key references, click the **Next** button.

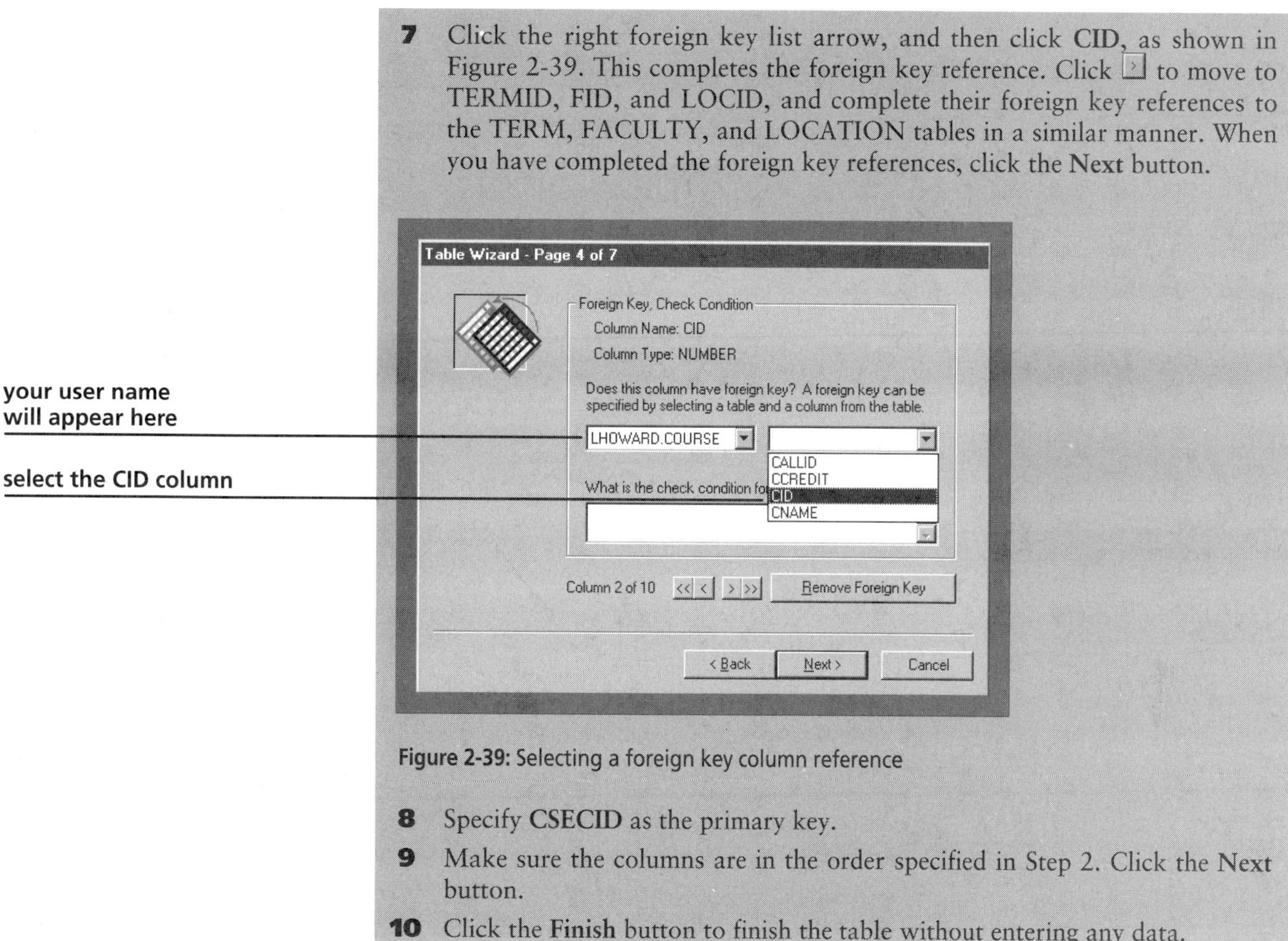

Figure 2-39: Selecting a foreign key column reference

8 Specify **CSECID** as the primary key.

9 Make sure the columns are in the order specified in Step 2. Click the **Next** button.

10 Click the **Finish** button to finish the table without entering any data.

Creating Tables Manually

Next you will create database tables using the Oracle Navigator but without the assistance of the Table Wizard. You will create the COURSE_UPDATE table first.

To create the COURSE_UPDATE table manually:

1 Right-click **Tables,** click **New,** click the **Create table manually** option button, and then click the **OK** button to open the New Table Properties dialog box.

2 Enter **COURSE_UPDATE** as the table name, as shown in Figure 2-40.

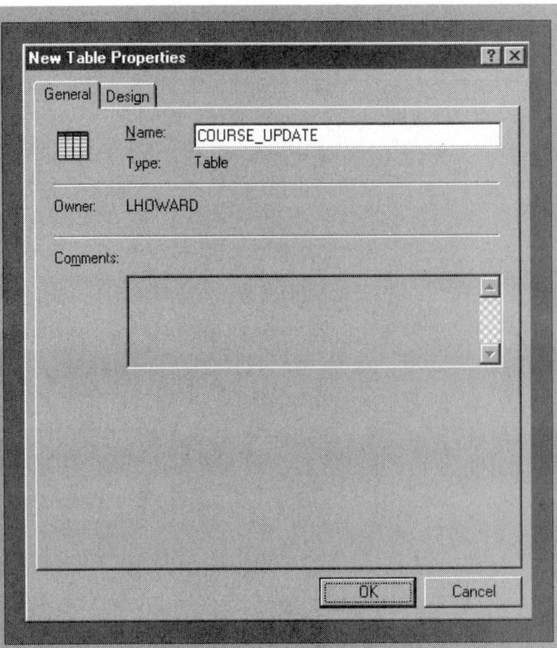

Figure 2-40: Specifying a new table manually

3 Click the **Design** tab, click in the first Column Name box, and then type CID. Press the **Tab** key to go to the Type column, click the **Type** list arrow, and then click **NUMBER.** Press the **Tab** key to go to the Size column, and then type **6**. See Figure 2-41.

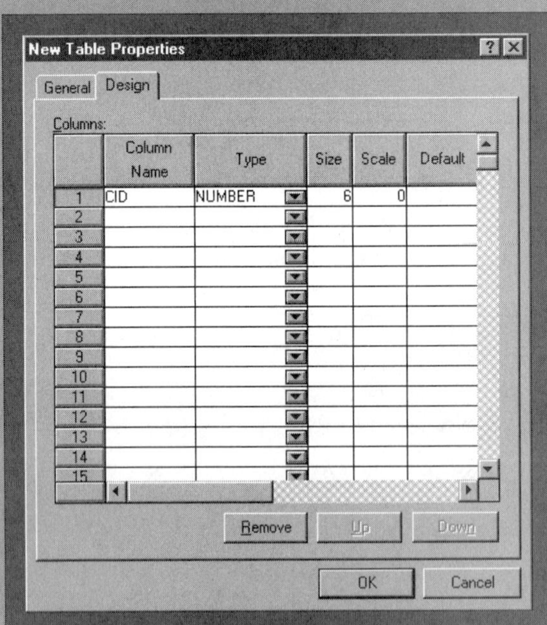

Figure 2-41: Specifying the CID column name, type, and size

4 Press the **Tab** key to move across the columns. Leave Scale = 0, and do not enter a default value.

5 Press the **Tab** key to move across the columns. Leave the Can be Null?, Unique?, and Primary Key columns blank for now.

6 Press the **Tab** key to go the Foreign Key column, and then enter the following foreign key reference for CID: **<your user name>.COURSE(CID)**. This specifies that the foreign key reference is to the CID field in your COURSE table. The foreign key reference for user LHOWARD is shown in Figure 2-42.

your user name will appear here instead of LHOWARD

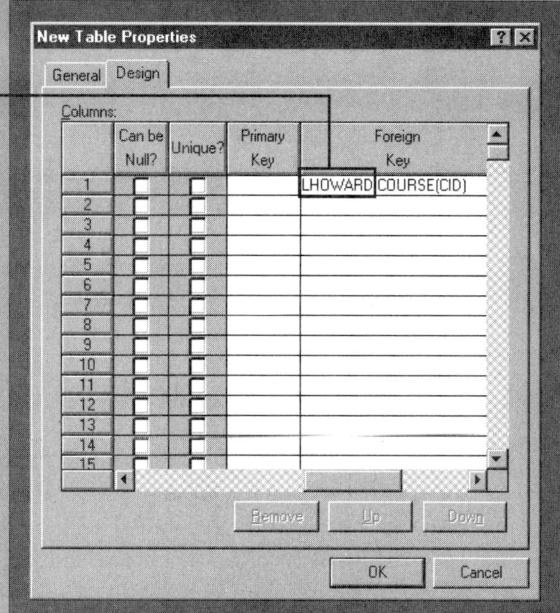

Figure 2-42: Specifying the CID foreign key reference

tip

You can increase the width of the Foreign Key column by placing the pointer on the dividing line between the Foreign Key and Check Condition columns until the pointer changes to , and then dragging the dividing line to the right.

7 Press the **Tab** key until the cursor returns to the Column Name column. Type **FID** as the next column name, with data type **NUMBER**, size 5, and scale 0. The first part of your table design screen should look like Figure 2-43.

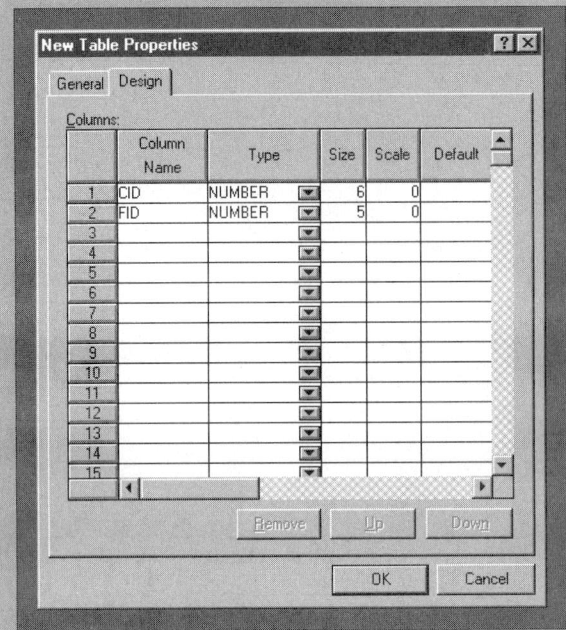

Figure 2-43: Specifying the FID column name, type, and size

8 Specify the FID foreign key reference to the FACULTY table as **<your user name>.faculty(fid)**.

In the COURSE_UPDATE table, each course can have several faculty members who have the privilege of updating course data, so CID alone cannot be the primary key and it will not be unique. Similarly, each faculty member might have the privilege to update the data for several courses, so FID alone cannot be the primary key either and it will not be unique. However, the combination of CID and FID will be the primary key, and it will be unique; therefore, this is a composite primary key. It does not matter which field is the first or second part of the primary key, but you need to specify an order so the database can search for the combination of the two keys faster. In the next set of steps, you will make CID the first part of the primary key, and FID the second part of the primary key.

To declare the composite primary key:

1 Make sure that the check boxes in the Can be Null? columns for CID and FID are cleared. Remember that no part of a primary key can be NULL.

2 Make sure that the Unique Key? check boxes for CID and FID are cleared. Remember that neither field is unique by itself.

3 Click in the Primary Key column of CID so the number 1 appears to specify CID as the first part of the table's primary key.

4 Click in the Primary Key column of FID so the number 2 appears to specify FID as the second part of the table's primary key. Make sure that the second part of your COURSE_UPDATE design screen looks like Figure 2-44.

composite primary key specification

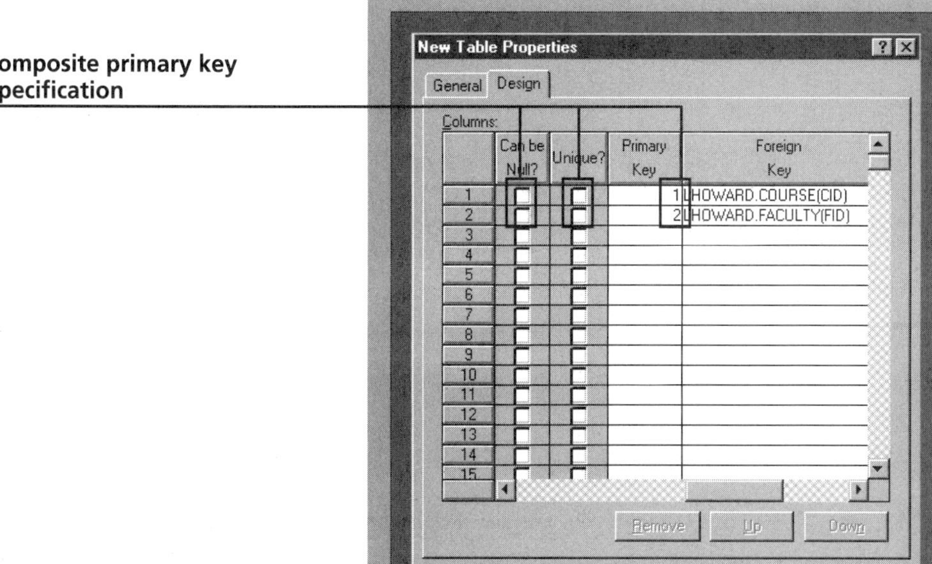

Figure 2-44: Specifying the composite primary key in the COURSE_UPDATE table

5 Click the **OK** button to create the table.

Next, you will create the ENROLLMENT table. It has foreign key references for SID in the STUDENT table and CSECID in the COURSE_SECTION table, so you will open these tables first to determine these fields' data types and sizes.

To create the ENROLLMENT table:

1 Right-click your **STUDENT** table in the right pane, click **Properties**, and then note the data type and size of the SID field.

2 Repeat Step 1 and note the data type and size of the CSECID field in the COURSE_SECTION table.

3 Create a new table using the Create table manually option, and then name the table **ENROLLMENT**. Click the **Design** tab.

4 Enter the following column names, data type and size, UNIQUE/NULL, and primary key specifications. Note that you will specify a composite primary key reference—to find what grade a given student earned in a course, you need to know both the SID and CSECID.

Column Name	Data Type and Size	UNIQUE/NULL Specification	Primary Key Specification
SID	Look up in STUDENT table	NOT UNIQUE NOT NULL	Primary Key 1
CSECID	Look up in COURSE_SECTION table	NOT UNIQUE NOT NULL	Primary Key 2
GRADE	VARCHAR2(1)	NOT UNIQUE NULL OK	

5 Omit the foreign key references at this point. Click the **OK** button to create the table.

Modifying Tables Using the Oracle Navigator

When you modify tables using the Oracle Navigator, you follow the same restrictions as when you modify tables using SQL*Plus. Next you will add the foreign key specifications to the ENROLLMENT table.

To add the foreign keys to the ENROLLMENT table:

1 Right-click your **ENROLLMENT** table in the Oracle Navigator window, and then click **Properties.** Note that you cannot change the table's name. Click the **Design** tab. Note that you cannot change column names, but that you can edit the data type, size, and constraint fields.

2 Add the foreign key reference for SID as **<your user name>.student(sid).**

3 Now add the foreign key reference for CSECID, which will be **<your user name>.course_section(csecid).**

HELP? If you cannot enter the foreign key references, you might be using an older version of the Oracle Navigator that only allows foreign key references up to 20 characters. The same limitation applies to check conditions. If this is the case, you will need to add these constraints using SQL*Plus. Ask your instructor or technical support person for assistance.

4 Click the **OK** button to save your modifications.

The Oracle Navigator provides a more intuitive way to create tables than using SQL*Plus commands, but some operations are not possible using the Navigator so it is important for you to understand both methods.

SUMMARY

- SQL is a high-level language used to query relational databases.
- Reserved words are SQL commands that cannot be used as table or field names.
- Oracle table and field names can be 1 to 30 characters in length and consist of only alphanumeric characters and the special characters $ _ #. Table and field names must begin with a letter and cannot contain spaces.
- Oracle databases contain the following data types: CHAR, VARCHAR2, NUMBER, DATE, LONG, and RAW/LONG RAW.
- In an Oracle database, integrity constraints are enforced through primary key specifications and foreign key references.
- In an Oracle database, value or check constraints on fields specify what values can be entered into those fields, and whether the values can be NULL.
- A convention for naming constraints to ensure that every constraint in the database has a unique name is to use the general format `<tablename where the constraint is being created>_<fieldname>_<constraint identifier>`.
- In an Oracle database, you can specify whether a field has a default value that will be inserted automatically for every record.

- To create a new database table in SQL*Plus, use the CREATE TABLE command followed by the new table name, an opening parenthesis, and then a list of each of the field names, their data type declarations, and constraint declarations, followed by a closing parenthesis.
- You can edit SQL*Plus commands using command-line editing or an alternate text editor. The edit buffer is a memory area in SQL*Plus that stores the text of the last executed query.
- Oracle does not have a central online Help application for all of its products but has specific online Help applications for each different product. Detailed descriptions of Oracle error message codes can be obtained by searching for the code prefix (such as ORA) followed by a hyphen and the error code number (such as -00922) in Oracle Help.
- You can change a column's data type, size, or default value only if there is no data in the column. You can add a primary key constraint to a column only if all of the existing column values are unique. You can add a foreign key constraint to a column only if the existing column values are NULL or if they exist in the referenced table.
- A constraint variable is the internal name used to identify integrity and value constraints. Every constraint variable must have a unique name.
- A system table is a database created and maintained by the DBMS for storing data about database objects such as tables and users.
- You cannot change a column name or table name, or delete a column.
- The Oracle Navigator is a graphical development tool that enables users to specify table structures visually. You can create new tables in the Oracle Navigator manually or by using the Table Wizard.

REVIEW QUESTIONS

1. What is SQL?
2. What are the steps for starting SQL*Plus?
3. Which of the following declarations are legal Oracle table and field names?
   a. SALES-REP-NAME
   b. INVENTORY_TABLE
   c. CLEARWATER_TRADERS_INVENTORY_TABLE
   d. SalesRepID
   e. _ITEM_PRICE
   f. SALESREP TABLE
4. What is the purpose of a data type?
5. List what data type you would recommend for the following data items:
   a. Social Security number
   b. gender (M or F)
   c. telephone number
   d. sales representative last name
   e. sales representative date of birth
6. What are the two types of integrity constraints?
7. What is a value constraint? Give an example using one of the fields from the Clearwater Traders database.
8. Using the general constraint variable naming convention, write valid names for the following constraints:
   a. primary key in the COURSE_SECTION table
   b. SID foreign key reference in the ENROLLMENT table
   c. check condition requiring the enrollment column in the TERM table to have a value of either OPEN or CLOSED
   d. constraint requiring the TDESC column in the TERM table to not be NULL

9. What is a system table?
10. What properties of an Oracle database table can you always change?
11. What properties of an Oracle database table can you never change?
12. What properties of an Oracle database table can you change under certain conditions, and what are the conditions?
13. What is the difference between creating database tables in SQL*Plus and creating them using the Oracle Navigator?
14. What do you need to remember about making a connection to the Oracle Navigator when using a public computer laboratory?
15. What is a composite primary key, and when is it needed?
16. Suppose you have a table with a composite primary key made up of two numerical fields named PKVALUE1 and PKVALUE2. Specify how you would define these fields in the Oracle Navigator's Can Be NULL?, Unique?, and Primary Key columns.

PROBLEM-SOLVING CASES

1. Write the SQL*Plus commands in a Notepad file that make the following modifications on your database tables. Save the file as CH2EX1.txt in the Chapter2 folder on your Student Disk. Test each command by copying and pasting it to the SQL*Plus command line. Make sure each command is modifying the database table as intended. (Depending on the kind of change you are making, you can check by using the DESCRIBE command or querying the USER_CONSTRAINTS table.) When all of the commands are working properly, save the file.
   a. Add a check condition on the GRADE field in the ENROLLMENT table so it allows only values of A, B, C, D, or F.
   b. Modify the STUDENT table so it includes fields for each student's permanent address, city, state, zip code, and telephone number using the following field names, data types, and constraints:

Column Name	Data Type and Size	Constraints
PERMAD	VARCHAR2(30)	NOT NULL
PERMCITY	VARCHAR2(30)	NOT NULL
PERMSTATE	VARHCAR2(2)	NOT NULL
PERMZIP	VARCHAR2(10)	NOT NULL
PERMPHONE	VARCHAR2(10)	NULL OK

   c. Modify the COURSE table so the default value for CCREDIT is 3.
   d. Modify the COURSE_SECTION table so the default value for CURRENRL is 0 (zero).
2. On a piece of paper, write down the column names, data types, sizes, and constraints to use for each of the tables in the Clearwater Traders database shown in Figure 1-7 in Chapter 1. Use the following format:

   TABLE NAME

Column Name	Data Type and Size	NOT NULL/UNIQUE Specification	Primary Key

3. Use Figure 1-7 in Chapter 1 to write the SQL commands to create the CUSTOMER, CUST_ORDER, and ITEM tables in the Clearwater Traders database. Save your commands in a Notepad file as CH2EX4.txt in the Chapter2 folder on your Student Disk. Test your queries in SQL*Plus to make sure they are correct. Do not enter any data into the tables.
4. Use Figure 1-7 in Chapter 1 to create the INVENTORY, SHIPPING, ORDERLINE, COLOR, and ORDERSOURCE tables using the Oracle Navigator. Do not enter any data into the tables.

Chapter 3

objectives

- Learn to automate SQL commands using scripts
- Insert, retrieve, update, and delete data using SQL*Plus
- Retrieve data and create SQL queries using Oracle Browser
- Insert, update, retrieve, and delete data using Oracle Navigator
- Grant table privileges to other users using SQL*Plus and Oracle Navigator

CHAPTER 3

Using Oracle to Add, View, and Update Data

Introduction The next step in developing the Northwoods University database is to insert, view, modify, and delete data records. Ultimately, the database users will perform these operations using data entry and modification forms. To make these forms operational, the database developers often must translate the user input into SQL queries that will be submitted to the database. As a result, the developers must be very proficient with SQL command-line operations. Therefore, it is important that you know how to insert, select, update, and delete data records using SQL*Plus. This chapter will provide the foundation for the SQL commands that you will use in later chapters in this book—it is not intended as a complete SQL reference.

You also will learn how to use Oracle Browser, which is a visual tool that creates queries and generates the corresponding SQL commands and lets users select the query tables from a list of database tables, and then choose the display fields by double-clicking the field names. Then you will learn to use Oracle Navigator to insert, update, delete, and view data sets. Finally, you will learn how to grant the privileges needed to allow other users to manipulate data in your database tables using SQL*Plus and the Oracle Navigator.

Running a SQL Script

A **script** is a text file that contains a sequence of SQL commands that can be executed in SQL*Plus. To run a script, you type the START command at the SQL prompt, followed by a space, and then the full path and filename of the script text file. For example, to start a script saved in the text file A:\Chapter3\myscript.sql, you would enter the following command: `START A:\Chapter3\myscript.sql`. The pathname and text filename and extension can be any legal Windows 95 filename, but they *cannot* contain any blank spaces.

Before you can complete the exercises in this chapter, you need to run a script named emptynu.sql to delete any of the Northwoods University database tables that you already have created and then to re-create the tables.

To run the script file:

1 Start SQL*Plus and log on to the database.

2 Run the emptynu.sql script by typing the following command at the SQL prompt: **START A:\Chapter3\emptynu.sql.**

HELP? Don't worry if you receive an error message on the DROP TABLE command, as shown in Figure 3-1. This error message indicates that the script is trying to drop a table that does not exist. The script is written so it drops all existing Northwoods University database table definitions first before creating the new tables. If a script tries to create a table that already exists, SQL*Plus will generate an error and will not re-create the table.

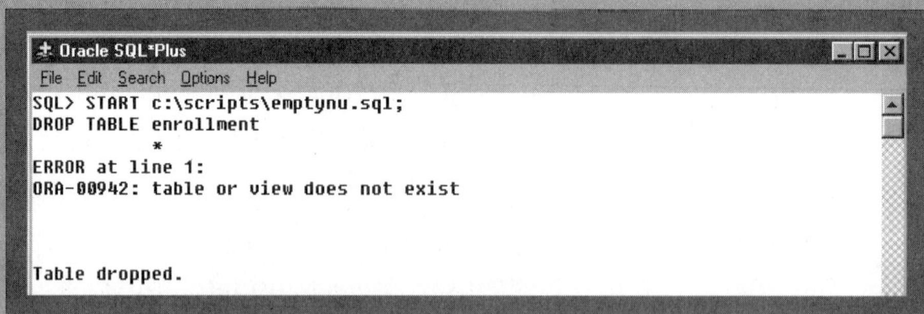

Figure 3-1: Error in the script DROP TABLE command

HELP? If you receive error messages on any script commands other than DROP TABLE, it means that your user account is not set up correctly. Check with your instructor or technical support person to make sure you have the required student account privileges needed to create database tables.

Using SQL*Plus to Insert Data

After running the script to create the tables, you are ready to begin adding data to them. In a business setting, programs called **forms** are used to automate the data entry process. Program developers who create forms usually use the SQL INSERT command in the form program code to insert data into tables.

The INSERT statement can be used two ways: to insert all fields into a record at once or to insert a few selected fields. The basic format of the INSERT statement for inserting all table fields is:

```
INSERT INTO <tablename>
VALUES (column 1 value, column 2 value, …);
```

When you are inserting a value for all record fields, the VALUES clause of the INSERT statement must contain a value for each column in the table. Column values must be listed in the same order as the columns were defined in the CREATE TABLE command.

The basic format of the INSERT statement for inserting selected table fields is:

```
INSERT INTO <tablename> (first column name, second column
name, …)
VALUES (first column value, second column value, …);
```

The column names can be listed in any order. The data values must be listed in the same order as their associated columns, and they must be the correct data type.

Before you can insert a new data record, you must ensure that all the foreign key records that the new record references have been added. For example, in the first STUDENT record, Sarah Miller's FID is 1. This refers to FID 1 (Kim Cox) in the FACULTY table. The FACULTY record must be added before you can add the first STUDENT record, or you will get a foreign key reference error. Look at Kim Cox's FACULTY record, and note that it has a foreign key value of LOCID 53. Similarly, this LOCATION record must be added before you can add the FACULTY record. Thankfully, the LOCID 53 record in the LOCATION table has no foreign key values to reference. Therefore, you can insert LOCID 53 in the LOCATION table, and then insert the associated FACULTY record, and finally add the STUDENT record.

To insert a record:

1 Type the SQL command shown in Figure 3-2, and then press the **Enter** key. The message "1 row created" indicates that the record has been added to the LOCATION table.

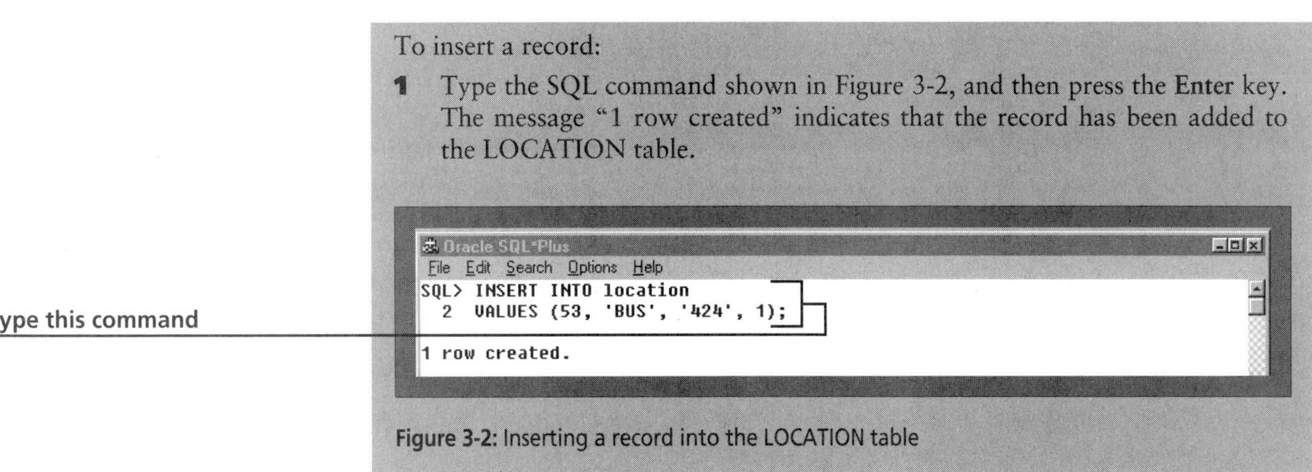

Figure 3-2: Inserting a record into the LOCATION table

Note that the LOCATION table has four columns—LOCID, BLDG_CODE, ROOM, and CAPACITY—and that their associated data types are NUMBER, VARCHAR2, VARCHAR2, and NUMBER. The NUMBER fields are entered as digits, while the VARCHAR2 fields are enclosed within single quotation marks ('). Data stored in CHAR and VARCHAR2 fields must be enclosed in single quotation marks, and the text within the single quotation marks is case sensitive.

The field values in the INSERT statement are entered in the same order as the fields in the table, and a value must be included for every column in the table. When you insert a record into the LOCATION table, the DBMS expects a NUMBER data type, then a VARCHAR2, another VARCHAR2, and then another NUMBER. An error is displayed if you try to insert the values in the wrong order or if you omit a column value. If you cannot remember the order of the columns or their data types, use the DESCRIBE command to verify the table's structure.

The next step is to insert Kim Cox's record into the FACULTY table. Remember that the FACULTY table has been modified to include the STARTDATE field, which has a DATE data type. To insert a date into an Oracle database using SQL*Plus, you will enter the date as a character string, and instruct the DBMS to convert this character string to a DATE using the TO_DATE function. The general format of the TO_DATE function is:

```
TO_DATE('<date that you are inserting>',
'<Oracle date format used for the date you are
inserting>')
```

All dates are stored in the same internal format, but you can select different formats for both entering and displaying date data. The most commonly used Oracle date formats are shown in Figure 3-3.

Format Code	Description
MM	Number of the month
MON	Three-letter abbreviation of month in all uppercase letters
DD	Number of the day of the month
D	Number of the day of the week (Sunday = 1)
DY	Three-letter abbreviation of the day in all uppercase letters (SUN, MON)
YY	Last two digits of the year
YYYY	Full four-digit year
RR	Last two digits of the year, but modified to store dates from different centuries using two digits (If the current year's last two digits are 0 to 49, then years numbered 0 to 49 are assumed to belong to the current century, and years numbered 50 to 99 are assumed to belong to the previous century. If the current year's last two digits are from 50 to 99, then years numbered 0 to 49 are assumed to belong to the next century, and years numbered 50 to 99 are assumed to belong to the current century.)
HH	Hour of the day using a 12-hour clock
HH24	Hour of the day using a 24-hour clock
MI	Minute of the hour
SS	Second of the minute
A.M., P.M.	Displays A.M. or P.M. depending on the time of day

Figure 3-3: Commonly used Oracle date formats

These date formats can be combined using embedded characters such as -/:. For example, the date 08/24/92 is converted to a DATE data type using the following code:

```
TO_DATE('08/24/92', 'MM/DD/YY')
```

To enter the same date as 24-AUG-1992, use the following command:

```
TO_DATE('24-AUG-1992', 'DD-MON-YYYY')
```

Remember that the DATE data type stores times as well. To convert the 10:00 AM start time to a DATE for CSECID 1000 in the COURSE_SECTION table, you would use the following command:

```
TO_DATE('10:00 AM', 'HH:MI AM')
```

Next you will add a record to the FACULTY table. This time you will only enter the specified columns FID, FLNAME, FFNAME, FMI, LOCID, and STARTDATE.

To enter the record for faculty member Kim Cox:

1 Insert the first record into the FACULTY table by typing the SQL command shown in Figure 3-4. The message "1 row created" indicates that the record has been added to the table.

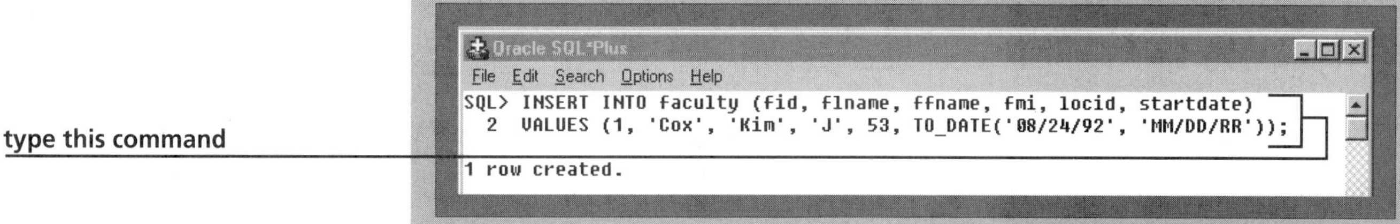

type this command

```
Oracle SQL*Plus
File Edit Search Options Help
SQL> INSERT INTO faculty (fid, flname, ffname, fmi, locid, startdate)
  2  VALUES (1, 'Cox', 'Kim', 'J', 53, TO_DATE('08/24/92', 'MM/DD/RR'));

1 row created.
```

Figure 3-4: Inserting a record with specified columns in the FACULTY table

Next you will add the record for John Blanchard. First you must insert the associated LOCATION record.

To insert the record for John Blanchard:

1 Type the commands shown in Figure 3-5 to insert the records into the LOCATION and FACULTY tables.

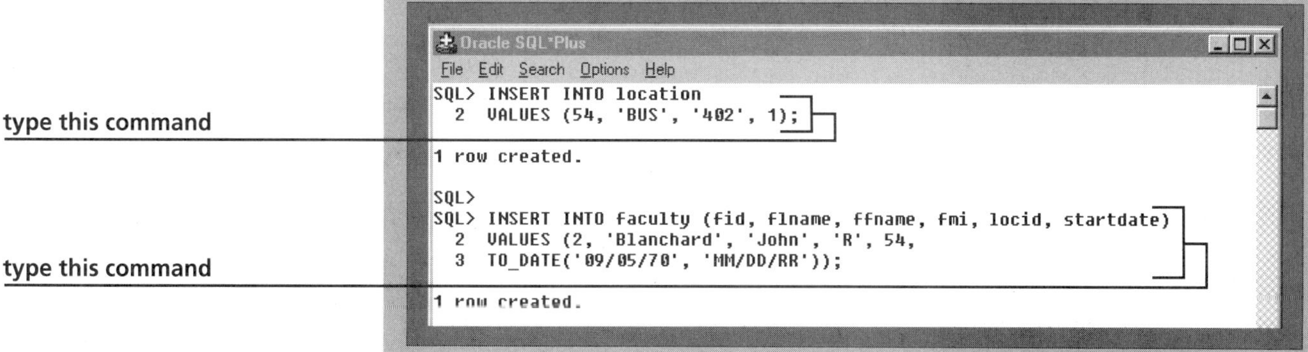

type this command

type this command

```
Oracle SQL*Plus
File Edit Search Options Help
SQL> INSERT INTO location
  2  VALUES (54, 'BUS', '402', 1);

1 row created.

SQL>
SQL> INSERT INTO faculty (fid, flname, ffname, fmi, locid, startdate)
  2  VALUES (2, 'Blanchard', 'John', 'R', 54,
  3  TO_DATE('09/05/70', 'MM/DD/RR'));

1 row created.
```

Figure 3-5: Adding another LOCATION and FACULTY record

Now you can start adding the STUDENT records.

To add the STUDENT records:

1 Enter the first record into the STUDENT table by typing the command shown in Figure 3-6. The message "1 row created" indicates that one record has been added to the table.

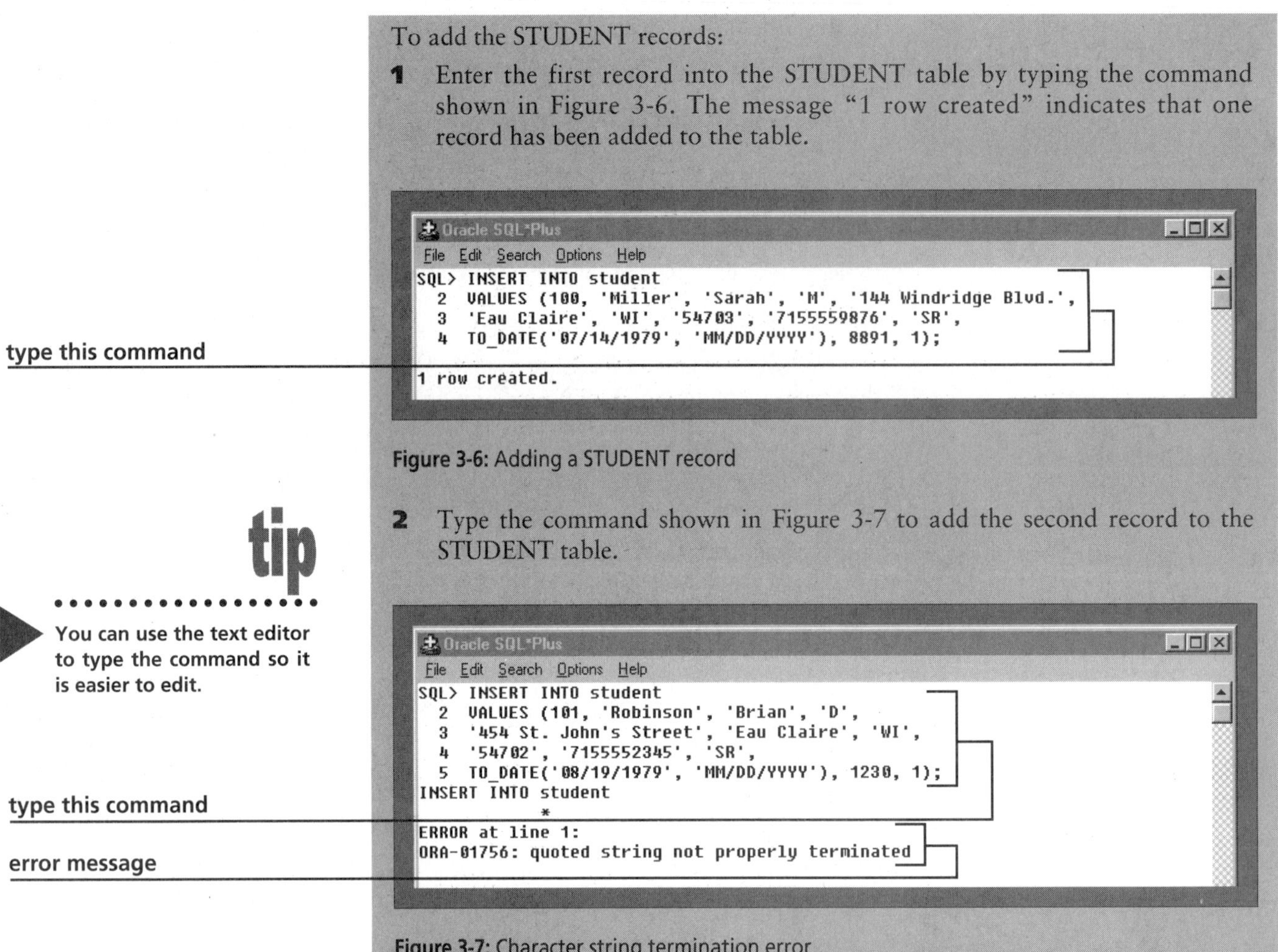

Figure 3-6: Adding a STUDENT record

2 Type the command shown in Figure 3-7 to add the second record to the STUDENT table.

Figure 3-7: Character string termination error

tip

You can use the text editor to type the command so it is easier to edit.

The error message shown in Figure 3-7 appears. What happened? Notice that the SADD value '454 St. John's Street' has a single quotation mark within the text. When the DBMS reached this single quotation mark, it assumed that this was the end of the SADD field, and then it expected a comma. When it found the letter "s" instead, it generated an error. To add text strings with embedded single quotation marks, you need to enter the single quotation mark twice. You will add the correct record next.

To enter text that contains a single quotation mark:

1 Invoke the text editor and change the SADD text to **'454 St. John''s Street'**, and then execute the command again. The message "1 row created" indicates that the record has been added to the table.

2 Enter the record for SID 102 as shown in Figure 3-8. Daniel Black does not have a middle initial, so the word "NULL" is inserted for SMI because a value must be included in the INSERT statement for every column in the table.

type this command

```
SQL> INSERT INTO student
  2  VALUES (102, 'Black', 'Daniel', NULL, '8921 Circle Drive',
  3  'Bloomer', 'WI', '54715', '7155553907', 'JR',
  4  TO_DATE('10/10/1977', 'MM/DD/YYYY'), 1613, 1);

1 row created.
```

Figure 3-8: Adding a STUDENT record with a NULL column value

When inserting a NULL value, do not enclose the word "NULL" in single quotation marks or the character string value "NULL" will be added to the column, instead of a NULL value.

Creating Transactions and Committing New Data

When you create a new table or update the structure of an existing table, the change is effective immediately at the central database on the server. However, when you insert, update, or delete database records, the database on the server is not changed until you explicitly **commit** your changes to make them permanent. To commit changes during your current SQL*Plus session, you use the COMMIT command, as you will see next.

To commit your changes:

1 Type **COMMIT;**. The message "Commit complete" indicates that your changes are made in the central database.

Prior to issuing the commit command, your changes were made to the **database buffer**, which is a memory location that stores the results of changes that add, modify, or delete database records. Other users cannot see the records you added or access the rows you modified because these rows are locked until you commit your changes. When a record is locked, other users cannot change the record until the user who locked the record commits the change and thus releases the lock. SQL*Plus automatically commits your changes when you exit the program. However, it is a good idea to commit your changes often so the records will be available to other users and your changes will be saved if you do not exit normally because of a power failure or workstation malfunction.

A **transaction** is one or more related SQL commands that constitutes a logical unit of work. An example transaction is when a new customer order is taken at Clearwater Traders. The associated CUST_ORDER record must be inserted to record the order ID, date, payment method, customer ID, and order source. Then one or more ORDERLINE records must be inserted to record the inventory ID, order price, and quantity ordered for each item ordered. If all parts of the transaction are not completed, the database will contain inconsistent data. For example, suppose you successfully insert the ORDER record, but before you can insert the ORDERLINE record, your workstation malfunctions. The ORDER record exists but has no associated order line information.

SQL has a process called a **rollback** that enables you to return the database to its original state by undoing the effects of all of the commands since the last COMMIT occurred. An example of a rolled back transaction is shown in Figure 3-9. A new record is inserted into the CUST_ORDER table, and then the ROLLBACK command is issued. The final SELECT statement shows that the record was not inserted into the CUST_ORDER table, and that the INSERT command was effectively rolled back.

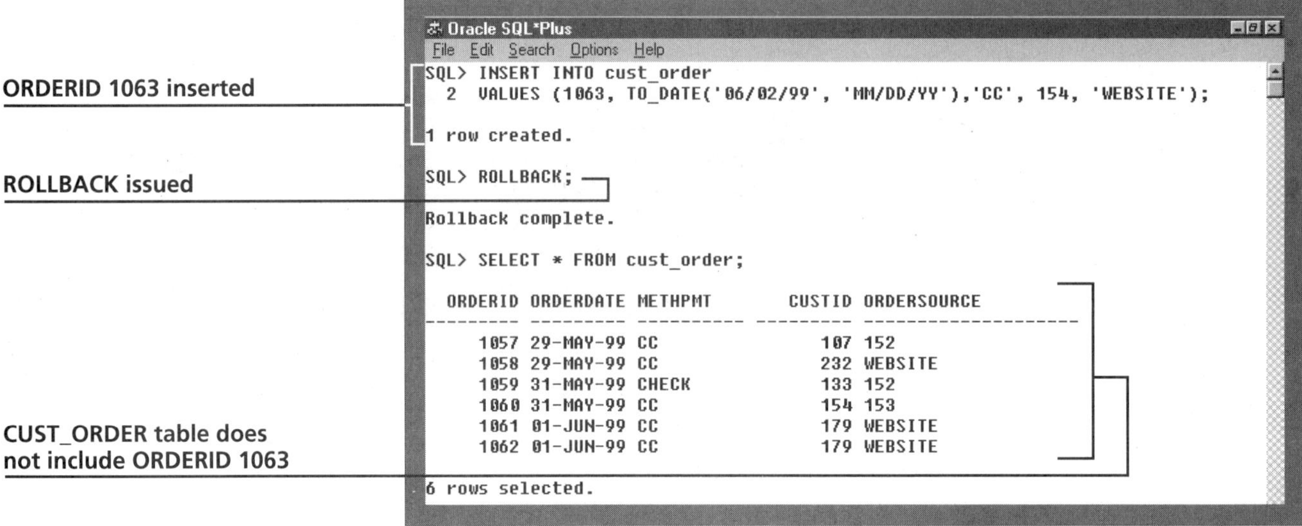

Figure 3-9: Using the ROLLBACK command

Rollbacks can be used with **savepoints** that mark the beginning of individual sections of a transaction. By using savepoints, you can roll back part of a transaction without having to process all of the transaction commands again. Figure 3-10 shows how to create a savepoint and then roll back a SQL*Plus session to that savepoint. A savepoint named ORDER_SAVE is created. A record is inserted for CUST_ORDER 1063, and an associated ORDERLINE record is inserted. Finally a ROLLBACK command to the savepoint is issued, and neither record is saved in the database.

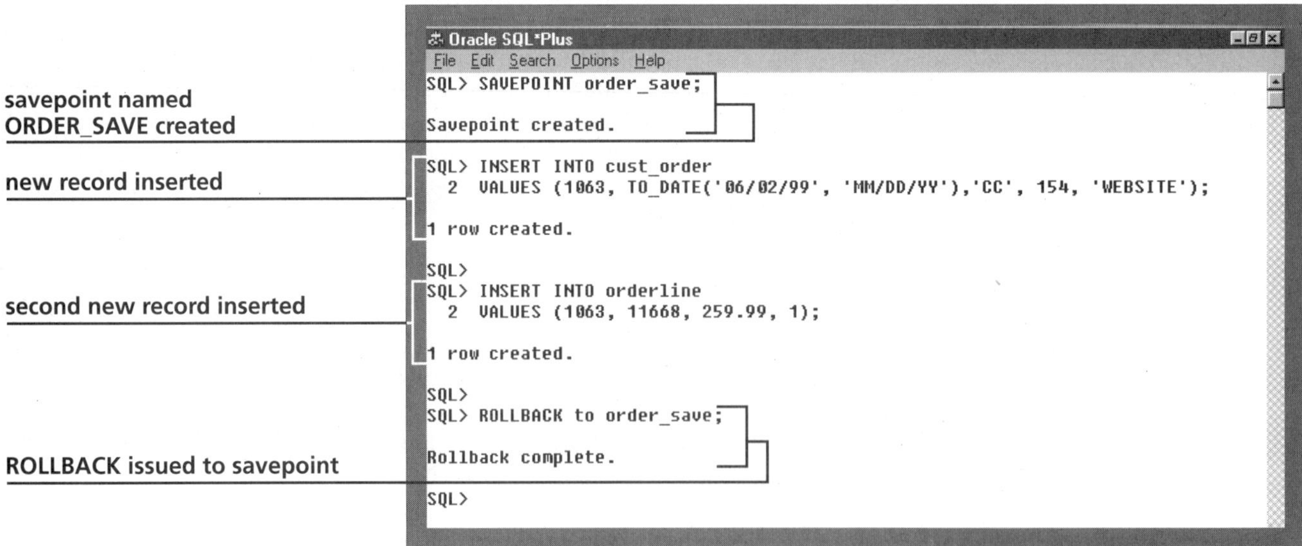

Figure 3-10: Using the ROLLBACK command with a savepoint

Using the SELECT Command to Retrieve Database Data

The SELECT command enables you to view data in relational database tables and join data from multiple tables based on foreign key values. You also can perform calculations on data, such as calculating a person's age from data stored in a date of birth column, or calculating a total for an invoice.

Retrieving Data from a Single Table

The basic format of a SQL query for retrieving data is:

```
SELECT <column1, column2, etc.>
FROM <ownername.table1name, ownername.table2name, …>
WHERE <search condition>;
```

The SELECT clause lists the columns that you want to display in your query. The FROM clause lists the name of each table involved in the query. If you are querying a table that you did not create, then you must preface it with the creator's user name, and the creator must have given you the privilege to SELECT data from that table. To query another user's database tables, you must use the format "ownername.tablename." For example, if you want to query user LHOWARD's LOCATION table, you would write the table name as `LHOWARD.LOCATION`. The WHERE clause is an optional clause that is used to identify which rows to display by applying some search condition.

The SELECT queries in this section will be performed using fully populated Northwoods University database tables that you will create by running the northwoo.sql script on your Student Disk. You will do this next.

To run the script file:

1. Run the northwoo.sql script by typing the following command at the SQL prompt: **START A:\Chapter3\northwoo.sql.**

To retrieve every row in a table, the data does not need to satisfy a search condition, so you omit the WHERE clause. You will retrieve all rows from the STUDENT table next.

To retrieve every row from the STUDENT table:

1. Type the command shown in Figure 3-11 to retrieve every row from the STUDENT table.

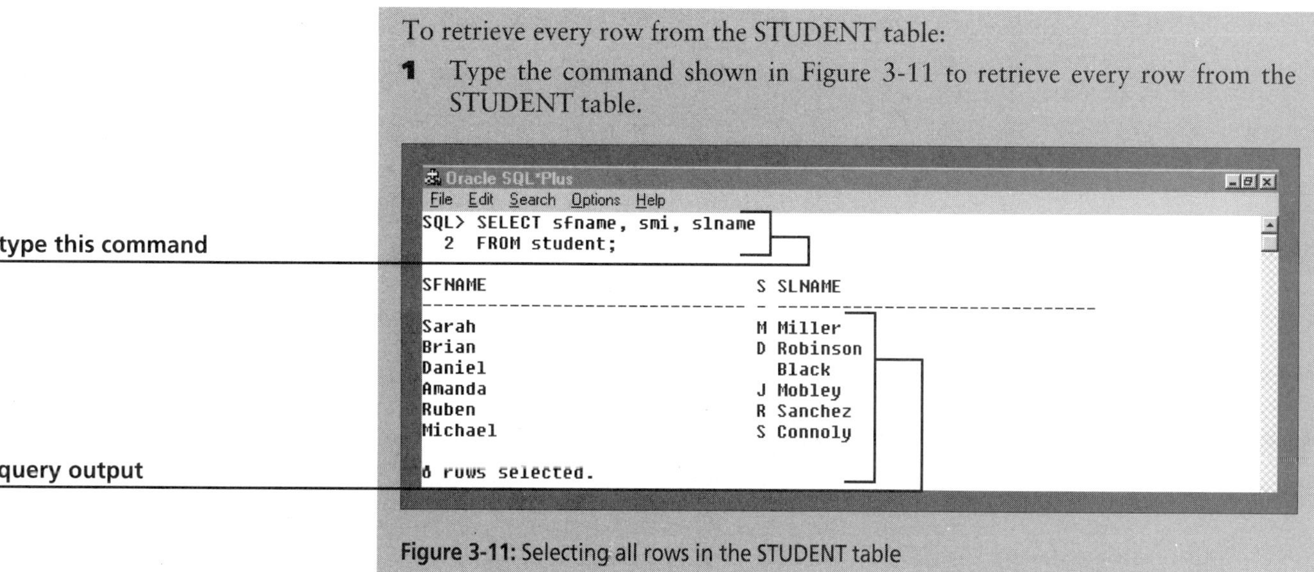

Figure 3-11: Selecting all rows in the STUDENT table

Your output should look like Figure 3-11. Note that the column names appear as column headings. Only the columns included in the SELECT statement are displayed, and the columns appear in the same order as they are listed in the SQL command.

If you want to retrieve all of the columns in a table, you can use an asterisk (*) as a wildcard character in the SELECT statement instead of typing every column name.

To retrieve every row and column from a table:

1 Type the command shown in Figure 3-12 to select all rows and columns from the LOCATION table.

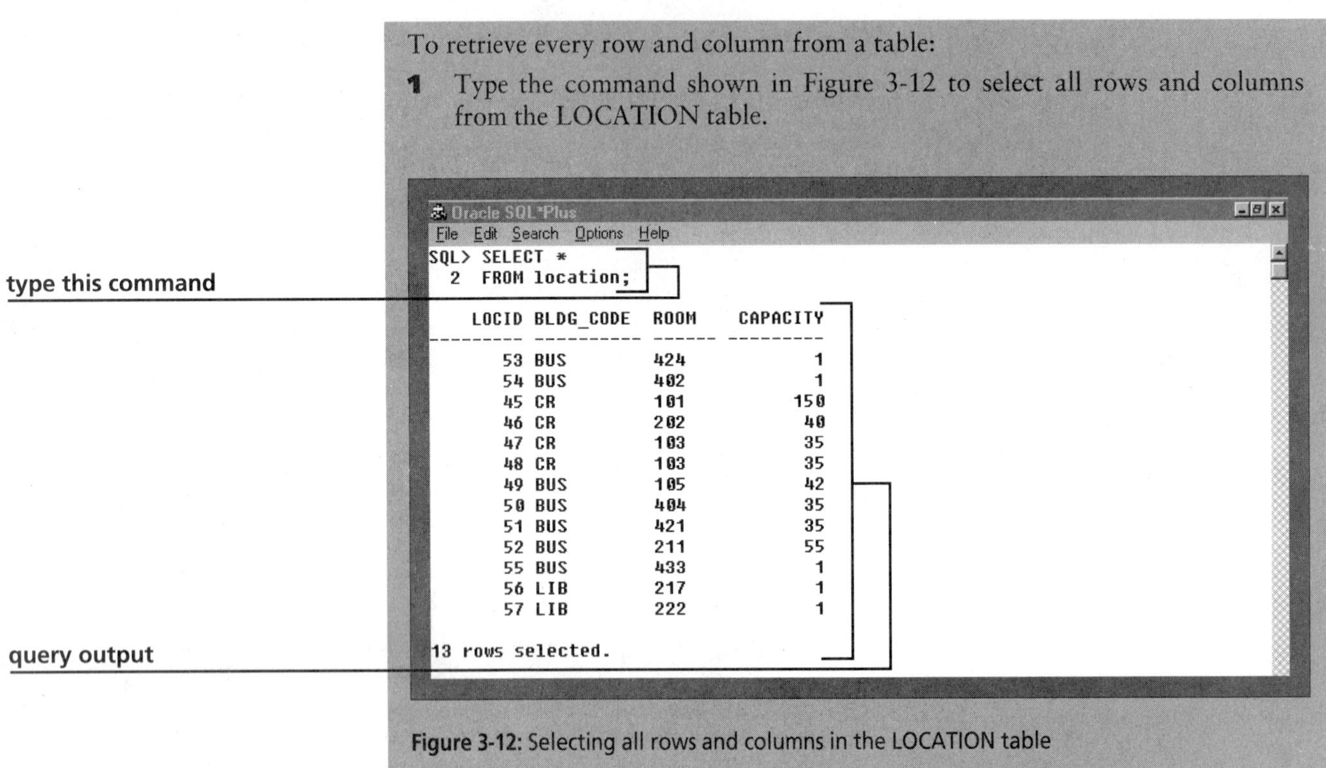

Figure 3-12: Selecting all rows and columns in the LOCATION table

Your output should look like Figure 3-12. Sometimes a query will retrieve duplicate rows. For example, suppose you want to see the different ranks for faculty members.

To retrieve duplicate rows:

1 Type the command shown in Figure 3-13.

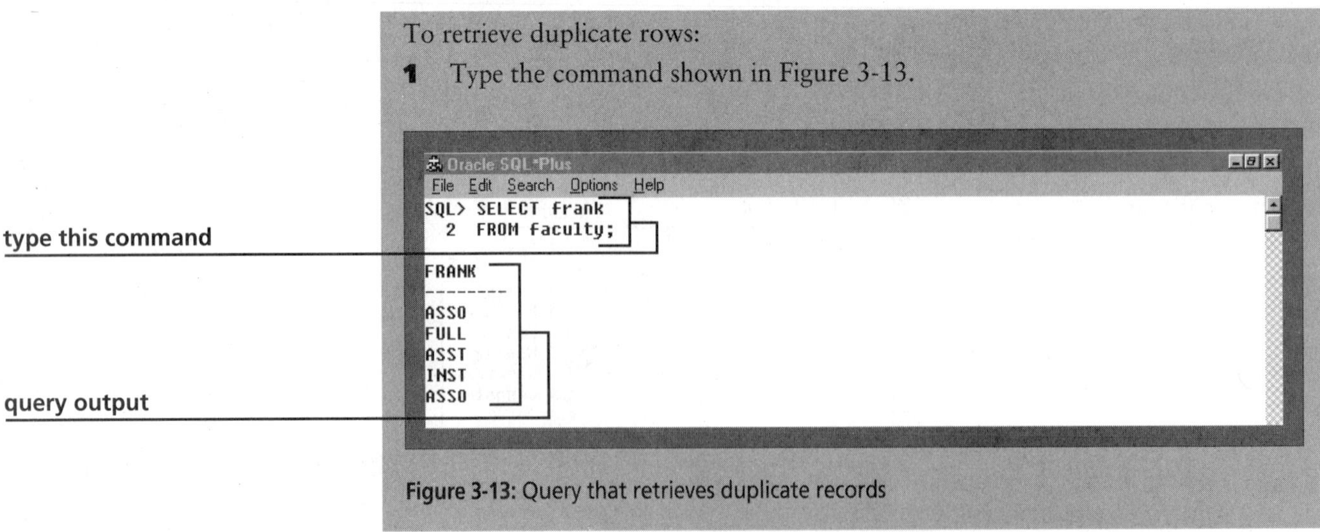

Figure 3-13: Query that retrieves duplicate records

Your output should look like Figure 3-13. The "ASSO" value is listed twice because there are two records in the table with the "ASSO" value in the FRANK field. To suppress duplicate values, use the DISTINCT qualifier immediately after the SELECT command.

To use the DISTINCT qualifier:

1 Type the command shown in Figure 3-14.

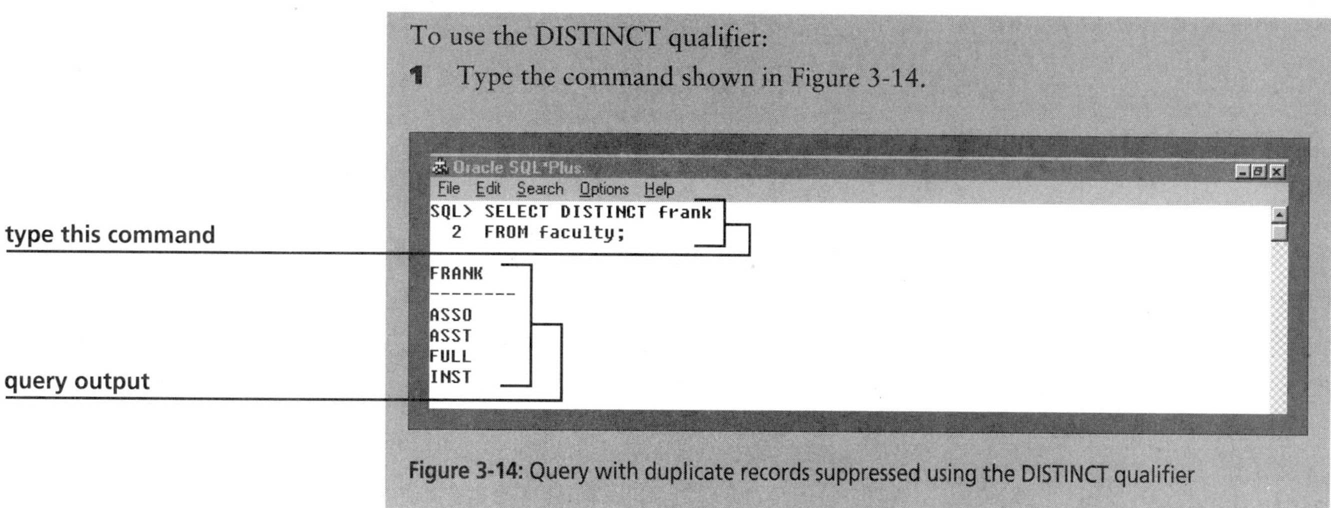

Figure 3-14: Query with duplicate records suppressed using the DISTINCT qualifier

Your output should look like Figure 3-14 with the duplicate rows suppressed.

Writing Queries That Retrieve Specific Records

Search conditions are listed in the WHERE clause to make a query return specific records. The general format of a search condition is:

```
WHERE <expression> <comparison operator> <expression>
```

Expressions usually are field names or constants. Figure 3-15 lists some common comparison operators that are used in SQL expressions.

Operator	Description
=	Equal to
>	Greater than
<	Less than
>=	Greater than or equal to
<=	Less than or equal to
< >	Not equal to

Figure 3-15: Common comparison operators

For example, the condition that finds all locations with a capacity greater than or equal to 50 is `capacity >= 50`. Comparison operators also can compare CHAR and VARCHAR2 values. For example, the expression that finds student records where the SCLASS value is equal to SR is `sclass = 'SR'`.

Next you will use a condition to find values in the FACULTY table.

tip

Don't forget that values enclosed within single quotation marks are case sensitive. If you type `sclass = 'sr'`, you will not retrieve rows in which the sclass value is "SR."

To use a search condition in a SQL command:

1. Type the query shown in Figure 3-16. The query output lists the first name, middle initial, last name, and rank of all faculty members with a rank of "ASSO."

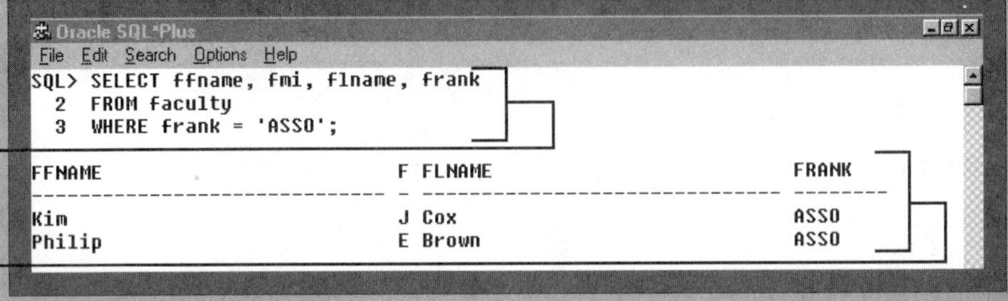

Figure 3-16: Query with a search condition

tip

Oracle pads CHAR values with blank spaces if an entered data value does not fill all of the declared variable's size. For example, suppose you want to declare SCLASS as a CHAR field with size 2 and then enter a data value of 'U' (for unclassified). To search for this value in the WHERE clause, you would have to type SCLASS = 'U ' (with a blank space after the U).

You also can combine multiple search conditions using the AND and OR operators. When you use the **AND operator** to connect two search conditions, both conditions must be true for the row to appear in the query outputs. If no data rows exist that match both conditions, then no data is listed. When you use the **OR operator** to connect two search conditions, only one of the conditions must be true for the row to appear in the query outputs. You will use the AND operator in the next query.

To use the AND operator in a search condition:

1. Type the query shown in Figure 3-17 to find the room numbers of all rooms in the BUS building that have a capacity of greater than or equal to 40. The output displays values that match both conditions in the query.

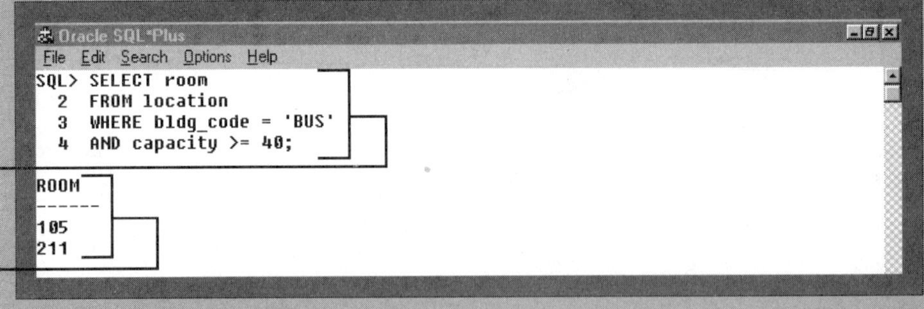

Figure 3-17: Query with multiple search conditions

2 Type the query shown in Figure 3-18 to list the first and last names of all students who are freshmen and were born before January 1, 1977. No STUDENT records match both of the conditions, so no rows are listed in the results, as indicated by the "no rows selected" message.

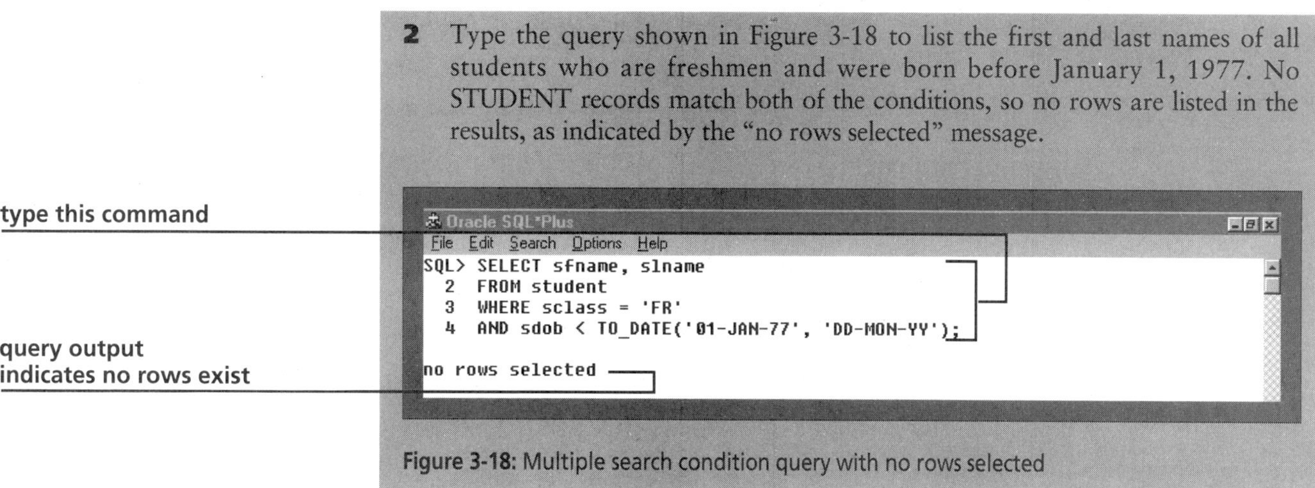

Figure 3-18: Multiple search condition query with no rows selected

When the OR operator is used to connect two conditions, a row is returned if *either* the first or second condition is true. If neither condition is true, no data is returned.

To use the OR operator in a condition:

1 Type the query shown in Figure 3-19 to find the first and last name of every student who was born after January 1, 1978, or whose class standing is FR. The query output lists the students who are freshmen (Sarah Miller, Brian Robinson, and Michael Connoly), along with those students who were born after January 1, 1978, but who are not freshmen (Amanda Mobley).

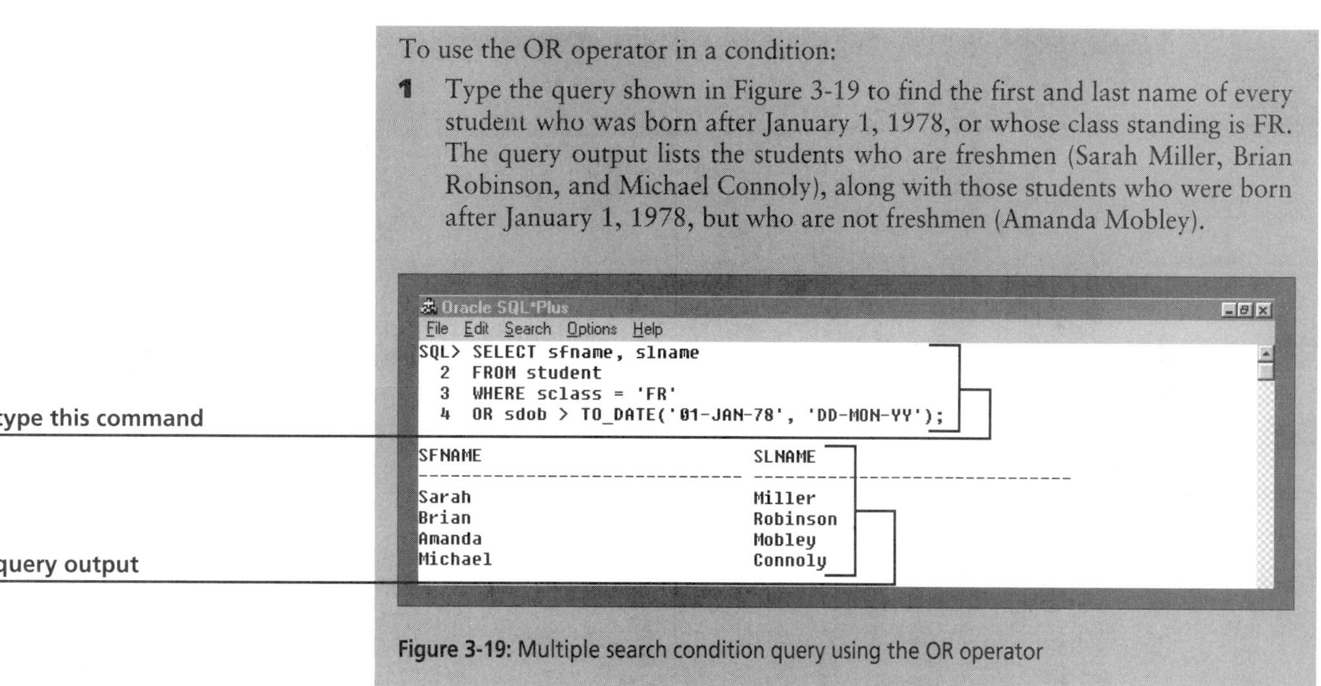

Figure 3-19: Multiple search condition query using the OR operator

You can combine the AND and OR operators in a single query. This is a very powerful operation, but it can be tricky to use. SQL evaluates AND conditions first, and then SQL evaluates the result against the OR condition.

To use the AND and OR operators in a single condition:

1 Type the query shown in Figure 3-20 to find the location ID, building code, room number, and capacity of every room in the BUS or CR building whose capacity is greater than 35.

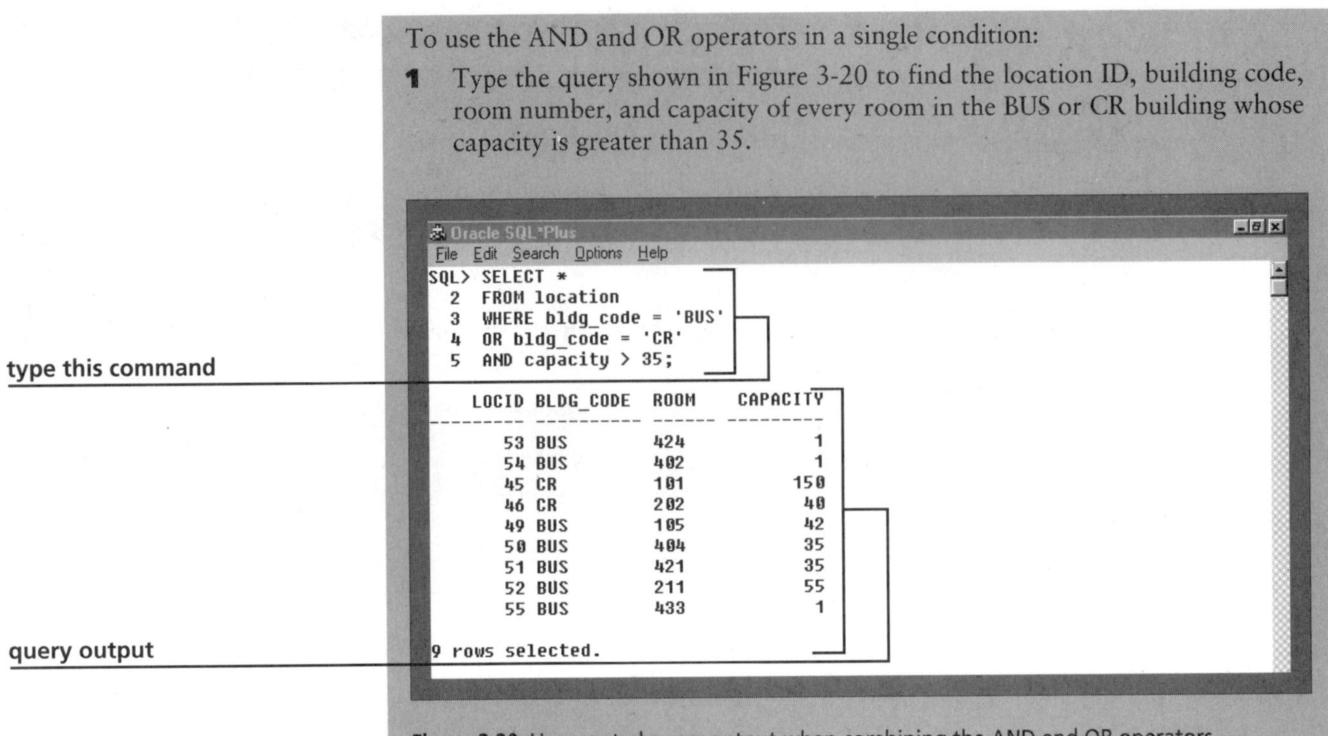

Figure 3-20: Unexpected query output when combining the AND and OR operators

The query output shown in Figure 3-20 is puzzling. Why was every room with a capacity of less than 35 returned? SQL first evaluates the AND condition (`bldg_code = 'CR' AND capacity > 35`), and then returns rows that contain LOCIDs of 45 and 46. Then SQL evaluates the first half of the OR condition (`bldg_code = 'BUS'`), and returns rows that contain LOCIDs of 49, 50, 51, 52, 53, 54, and 55. Finally, SQL combines these results with the result of the AND condition (LOCIDS 45 and 46). Therefore, it returns LOCIDs of 45, 46, and 49 through 55, which is not what you wanted.

The best way to overcome AND/OR ordering problems is to put the operation that should be performed first in parentheses. SQL always evaluates operations in parentheses first—regardless if they contain an AND or OR operator.

To use the AND and OR operators correctly in a single condition:

1 Type the query shown in Figure 3-21. Now the query output is correct. SQL performs the OR operation first (by returning all LOCIDs either in CR or BUS), and then evaluates the AND condition by returning only those locations that have a capacity of greater than 35.

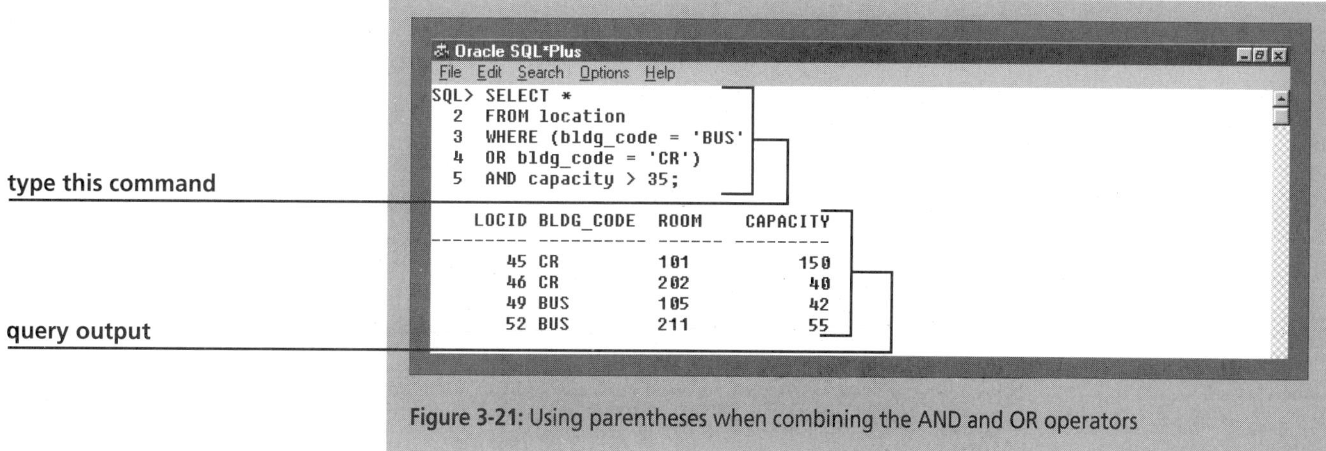

Figure 3-21: Using parentheses when combining the AND and OR operators

You also can use the NOT operator in a condition to express negative conditions, as you will see next.

To use the NOT operator in a condition:

1. Type the query shown in Figure 3-22 to list the first and last name of every student who is not a senior. The query output lists students who are not seniors.

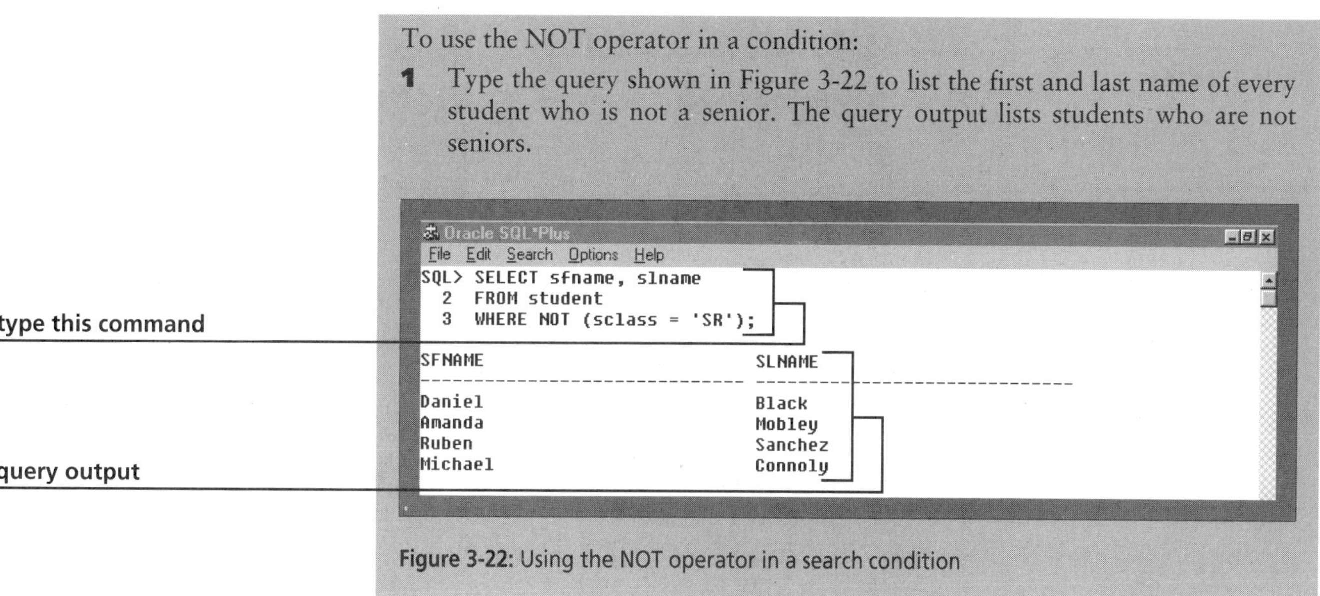

Figure 3-22: Using the NOT operator in a search condition

Sorting the Query Output

The query output you have seen so far has not displayed data in any particular order. You can sort query output by using the ORDER BY clause and specifying the **sort key**, which is the column on which the records will be sorted. The format for the ORDER BY clause is `ORDER BY <column name>`. By default, records are sorted in numerical ascending order if the sort key is a NUMBER column, and in alphabetical ascending order if the sort key is a CHAR or VARCHAR2 column. To sort the records in descending order, insert the DESC command at the end of the ORDER BY clause.

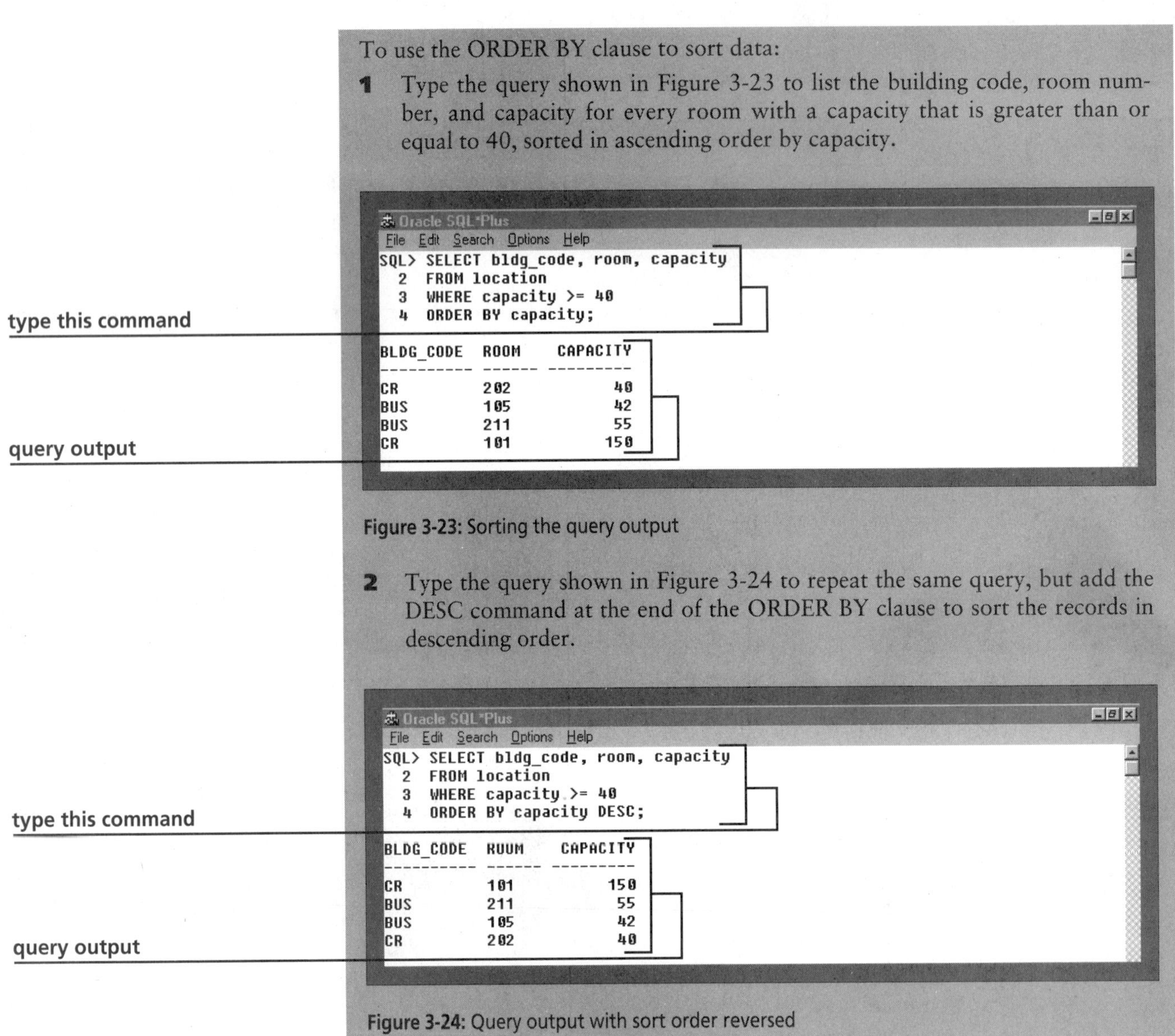

To use the ORDER BY clause to sort data:

1 Type the query shown in Figure 3-23 to list the building code, room number, and capacity for every room with a capacity that is greater than or equal to 40, sorted in ascending order by capacity.


```
SQL> SELECT bldg_code, room, capacity
  2  FROM location
  3  WHERE capacity >= 40
  4  ORDER BY capacity;

BLDG_CODE  ROOM    CAPACITY
---------- ------ ---------
CR         202           40
BUS        105           42
BUS        211           55
CR         101          150
```

Figure 3-23: Sorting the query output

2 Type the query shown in Figure 3-24 to repeat the same query, but add the DESC command at the end of the ORDER BY clause to sort the records in descending order.


```
SQL> SELECT bldg_code, room, capacity
  2  FROM location
  3  WHERE capacity >= 40
  4  ORDER BY capacity DESC;

BLDG_CODE  ROOM    CAPACITY
---------- ------ ---------
CR         101          150
BUS        211           55
BUS        105           42
CR         202           40
```

Figure 3-24: Query output with sort order reversed

You also can specify multiple sort keys to sort query outputs with multiple columns. The next query lists all building codes, rooms, and capacities, sorted first by building code, and then by room number.

To sort data based on multiple columns:

1 Type the query shown in Figure 3-25. The query output lists every row in the LOCATION table, first sorted alphabetically by building code and then sorted within building codes by ascending room numbers.

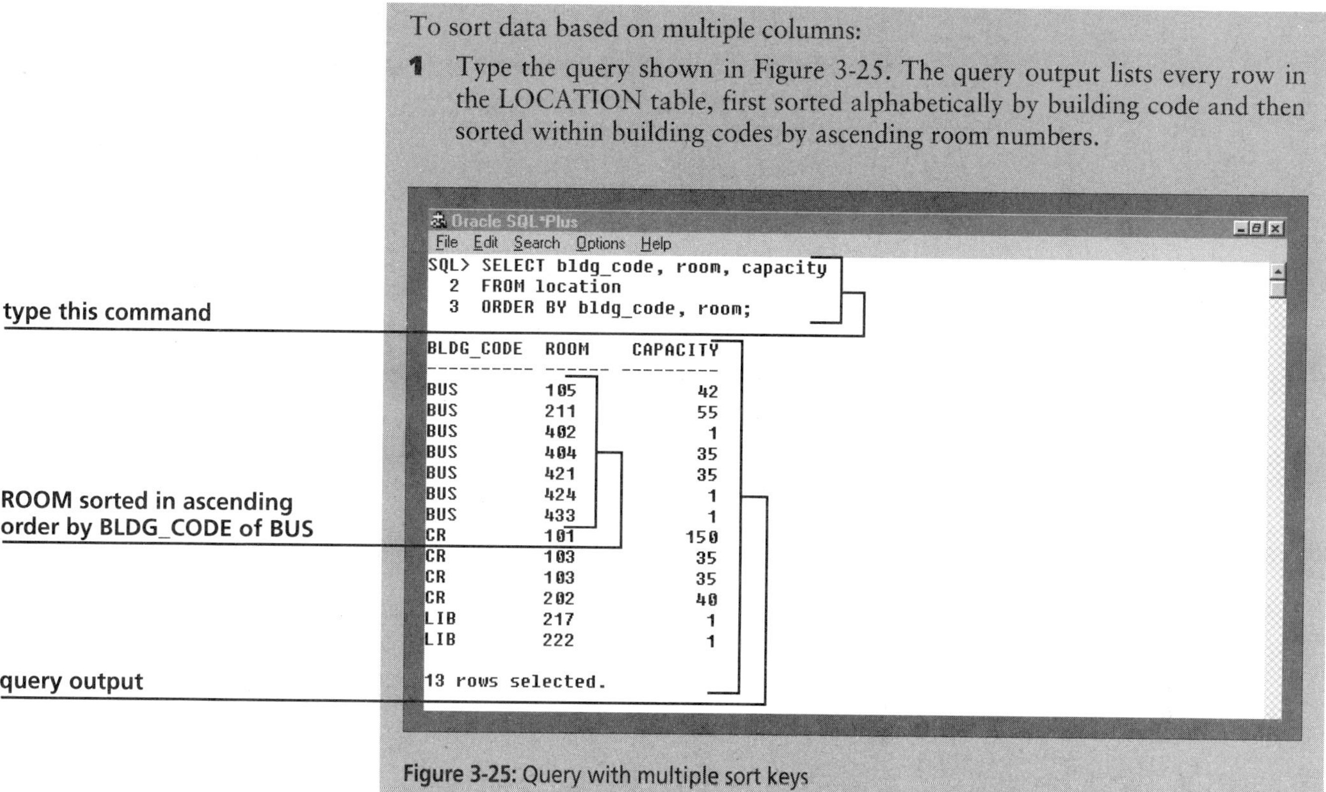

Figure 3-25: Query with multiple sort keys

Using Calculations in a Query

You can perform basic mathematical calculations on retrieved data. Figure 3-26 lists the operations and their associated SQL operators.

SQL Operator	Description
+	Addition
-	Subtraction
*	Multiplication
/	Division

Figure 3-26: SQL operators used in calculations

For example, suppose that you want to display the course section ID, maximum enrollment, current enrollment, and the difference between the maximum enrollment and the current enrollment for each course section.

To calculate data using a SQL query:

1 Type the query shown in Figure 3-27. The query output lists the calculated value by subtracting the CURRENRL value from the MAXENRL value.

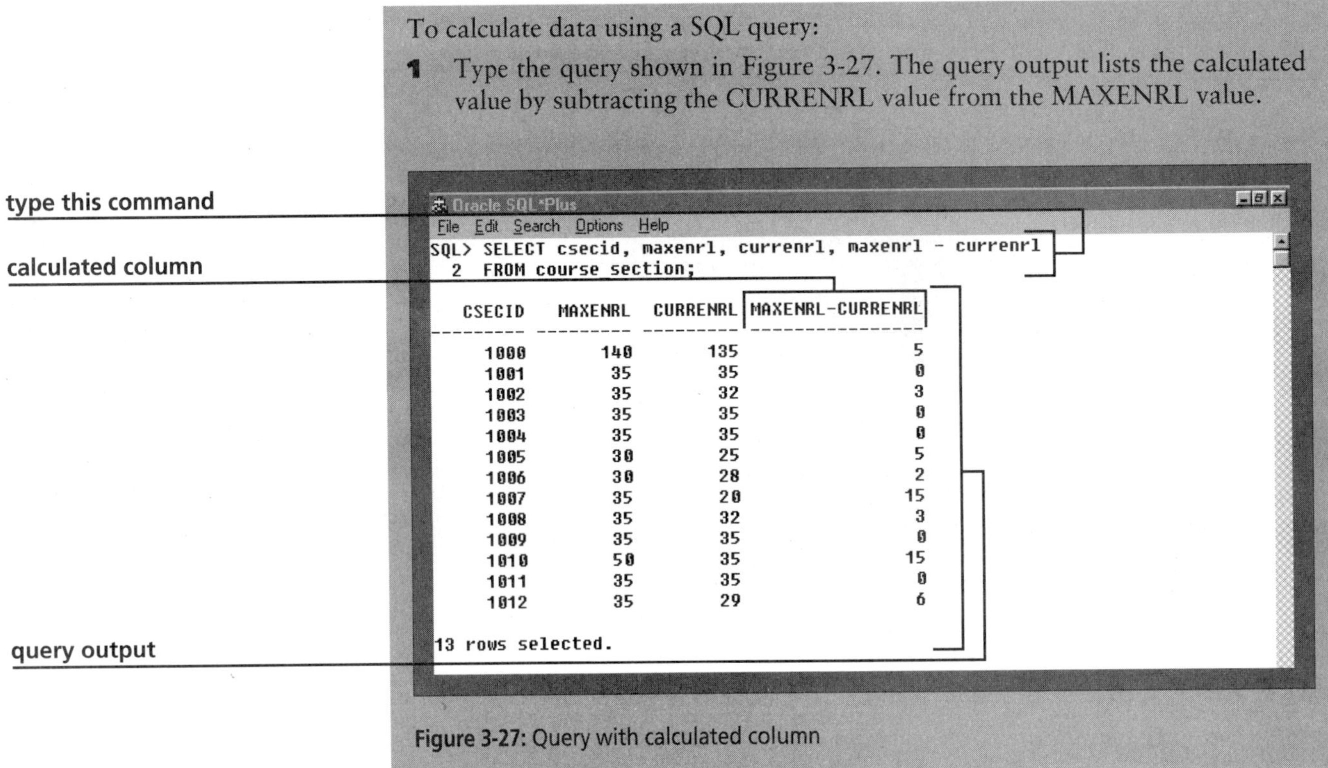

Figure 3-27: Query with calculated column

You also can perform multiple arithmetic operations in a single query.

To perform multiple operations in a single query:

1 Type the query shown in Figure 3-28 to list the student ID, last name, and age for each student. The student age is calculated based on the student's date of birth.

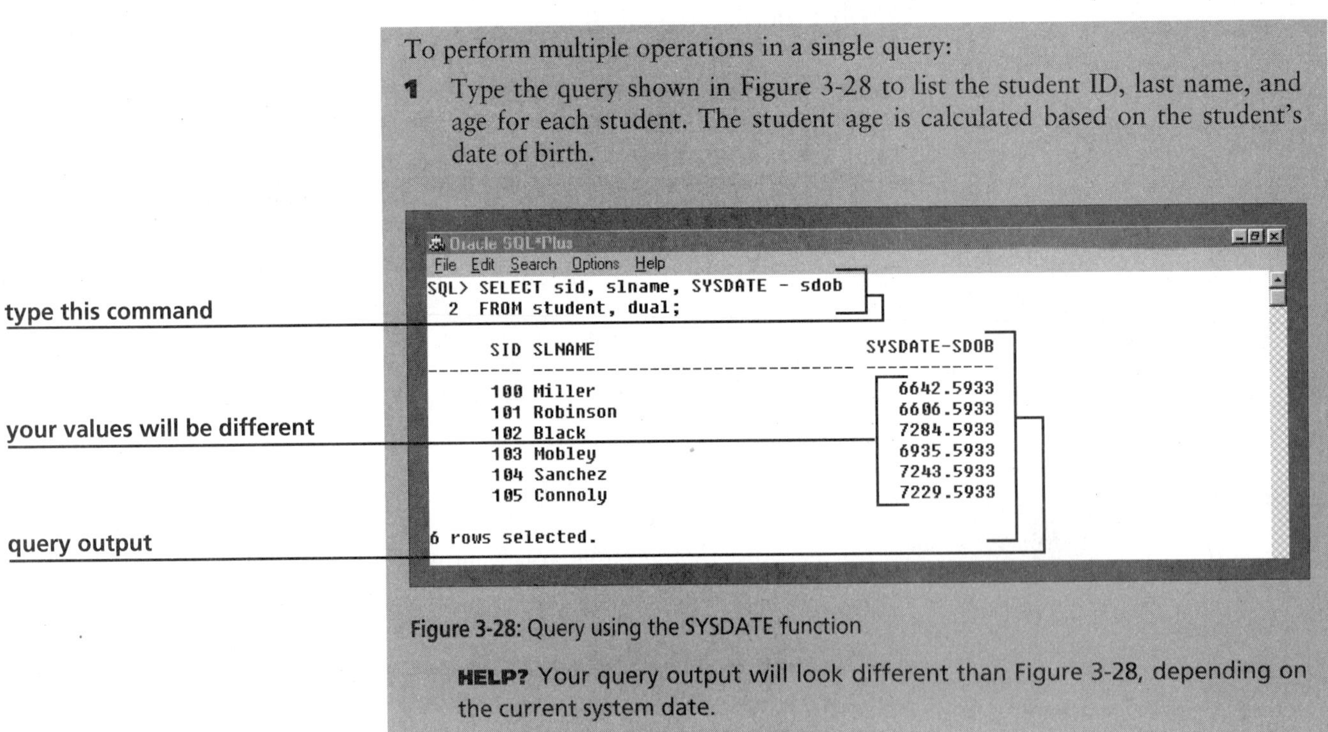

Figure 3-28: Query using the SYSDATE function

HELP? Your query output will look different than Figure 3-28, depending on the current system date.

The SYSDATE function returns the current system (server) date from the system table named DUAL. To retrieve the current system date, use SYSDATE in the SELECT clause, and then specify DUAL in the FROM clause.

The query output lists the calculated ages in days rather than in years. One solution to this problem is to divide this value by the number of days in a year, which is approximately 365.25 days per year including leap years. To display the query output in years, the expression is `SYSDATE – sdob/365.25`.

In mathematics and in other programming languages, expressions that contain more than one operator must be evaluated in a specific order. SQL evaluates division and multiplication operations first, and addition and subtraction operations last. Expressions enclosed within parentheses are evaluated first. Therefore, the previous expression is evaluated as `sysdate - (sdob/365.25)` because the division operation is evaluated before the subtraction operation. However, your intent is to calculate the difference between the current date and the student's date of birth first, and then divide that result by 356.25. You can use parentheses to indicate that the subtraction operation should be evaluated first.

To list students' ages in years:

1 Type the query shown in Figure 3-29. The query output lists the students' ages in years.

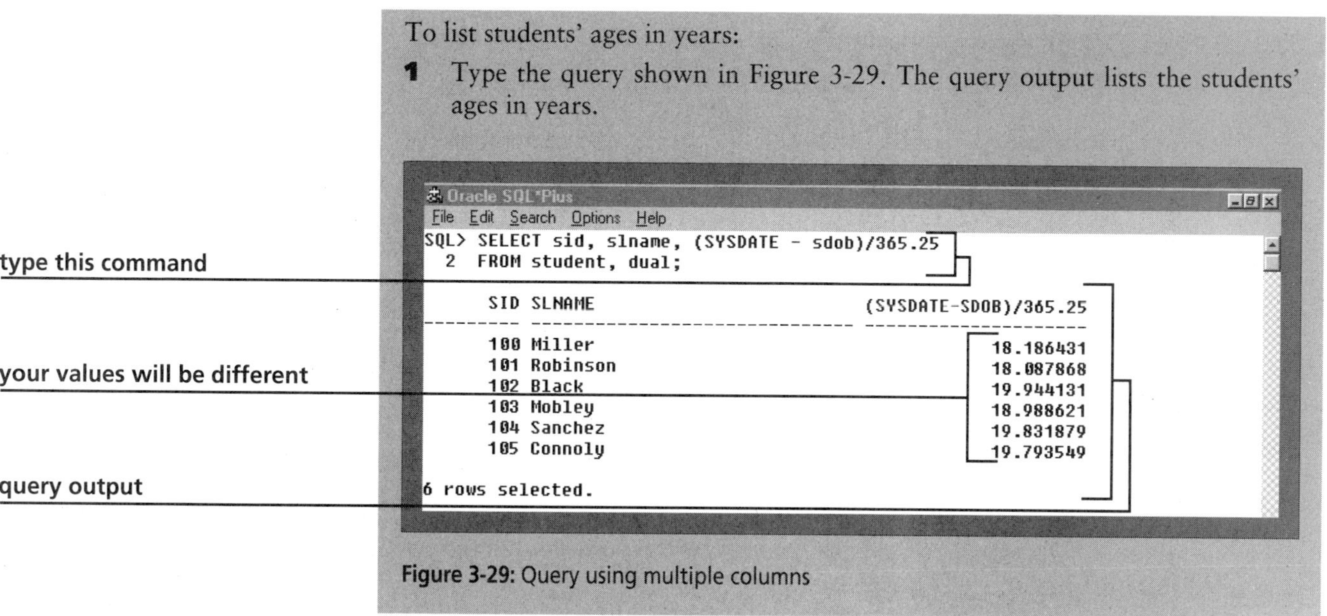

Figure 3-29: Query using multiple columns

Each student's age is shown in years with a fraction that represents the time since the student's last birthday. To remove this fraction, you will need to use a SQL number function. SQL has several **number functions** that manipulate numeric inputs. Figure 3-30 summarizes some of the commonly used SQL number functions.

SQL Function	Description	Example	Result
ABS(*n*)	Returns the absolute value of *n*	SELECT ABS(-1) FROM DUAL;	1
POWER(*n*,power)	Returns *n* raised to the specified power	SELECT POWER(3,2) FROM DUAL;	9
ROUND (*n*, precision)	Returns *n* rounded to the specified precision	SELECT ROUND (123.476, 1) FROM DUAL;	123.5
TRUNC(*n*, precision)	Returns *n* truncated to the specified precision	SELECT TRUNC (123.476, 1) FROM DUAL;	123.4

Figure 3-30: SQL number functions

To use a SQL number function, list the function name followed by the required parameter (or parameters) in parentheses. If parameters are actual numeric values (like rounding the number 123.476), then the general query format is `SELECT <function name (parameter)> FROM DUAL;`. If the parameter is a retrieved or calculated database value, (like truncating the fraction from the retrieved student ages), the general query format is `SELECT <function name>(<field name>) FROM <tablename> WHERE <search condition>;`. The next query demonstrates how to use a number function with a calculated database value. You will use the TRUNC function to truncate the fraction portion of the calculated student ages.

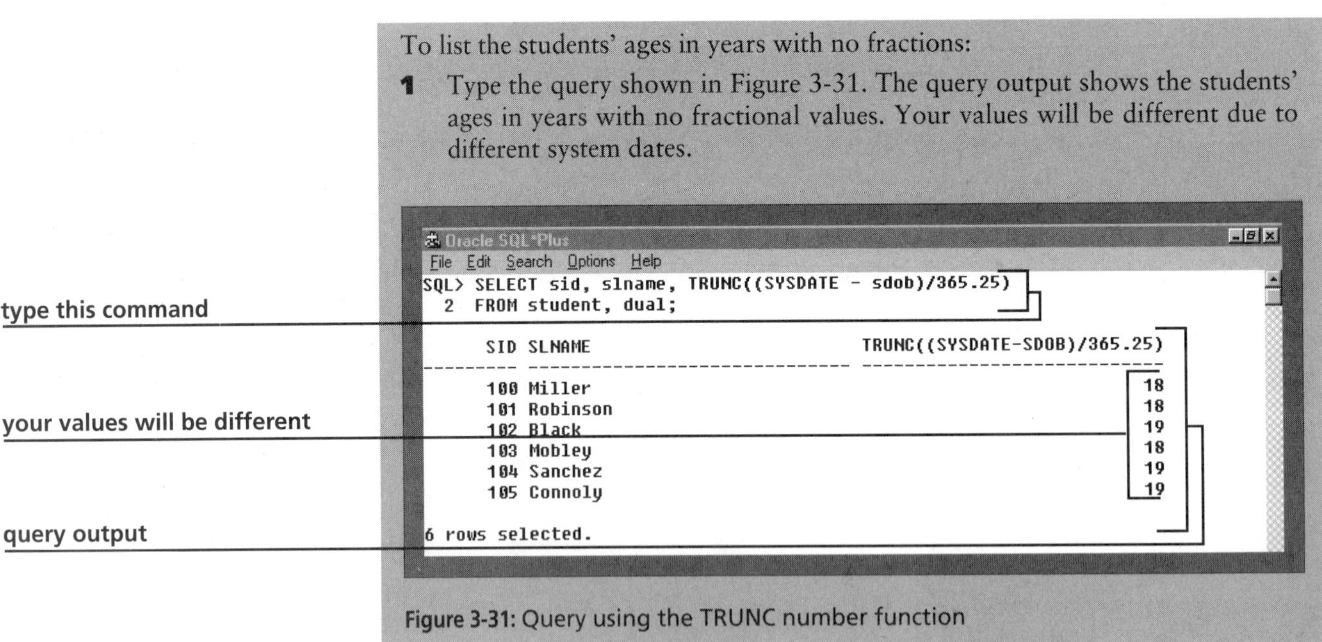

Figure 3-31: Query using the TRUNC number function

Using Group Functions in Queries

A SQL **group function** performs an operation on a group of queried rows and returns a single result such as a column sum. Figure 3-32 describes five commonly used SQL group functions.

Function	Description	Example
AVG	Returns the average value of a numeric column's returned values	AVG(capacity)
COUNT	Returns an integer representing a count of the number of returned rows	COUNT(grade)
MAX	Returns the maximum value of a numeric column's returned values	MAX(currenrl)
MIN	Returns the minimum value of a numeric column's returned values	MIN(currenrl)
SUM	Sums a numeric column's returned values	SUM(ccredit)

Figure 3-32: SQL group functions

To use a group function in a SQL query, list the function name followed by the column name on which to perform the calculation in parentheses. Next, you will enter a query using a group function.

To use a group function in a query:

1 Type the query shown in Figure 3-33 to sum the total current enrollment and calculate the average, maximum, and minimum current enrollment for each course section for the Spring 2000 term (TERMID = 5).

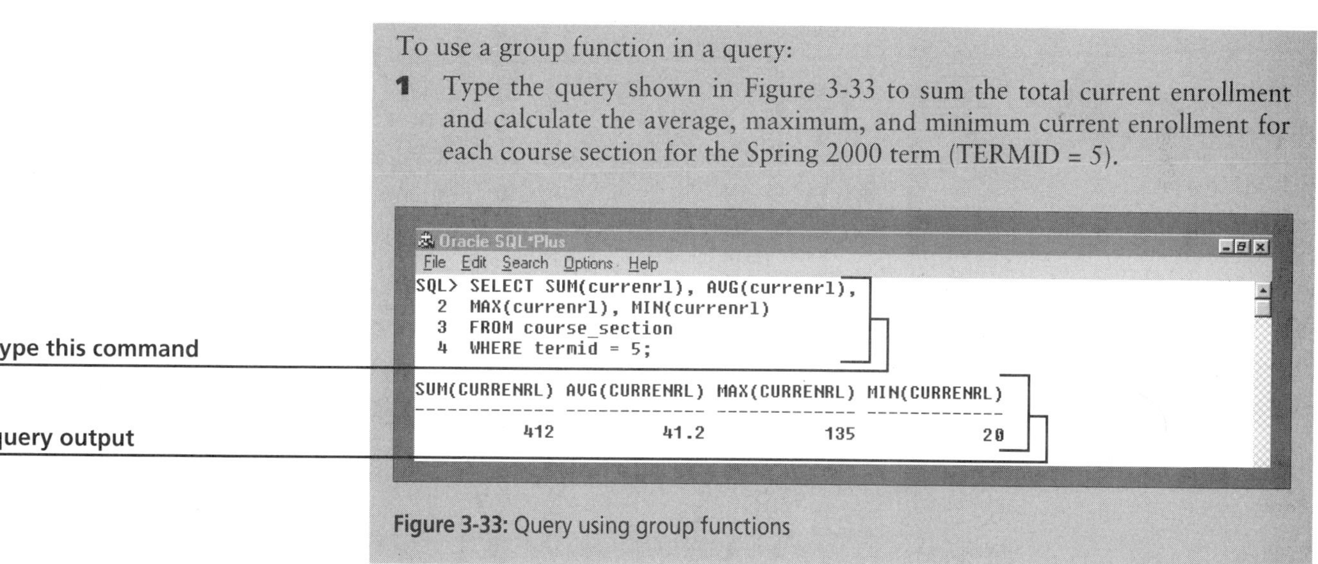

Figure 3-33: Query using group functions

Sometimes you need to divide the query output rows into groups that have matching values and then apply a group function to the grouped data. To do this, use the GROUP BY function.

To use the GROUP BY function to group rows:

1 Type the query shown in Figure 3-34 to list the building code name with the total, average, and maximum room capacities (excluding private offices with a capacity less than 5) of all buildings in the LOCATION table.

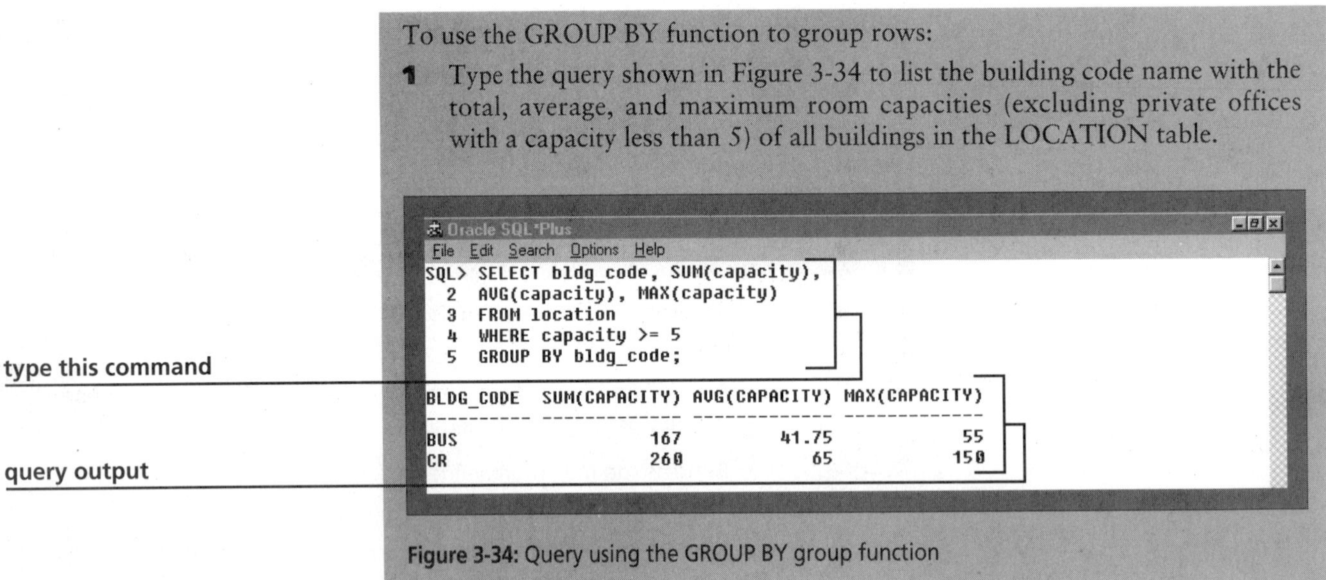

Figure 3-34: Query using the GROUP BY group function

The COUNT group function returns an integer that represents the number of records that are returned by a given query. The COUNT(*) version of this function calculates the total number of rows in a table that satisfy a given search condition. The COUNT(<column-name>) version calculates the number of rows in a table that satisfy a given search condition and also contain a non-null value for the given column. You will use both versions of the COUNT function next.

To use the COUNT group function:

1 Type the query shown in Figure 3-35 to count the total number of students enrolled in CSECID 1010.

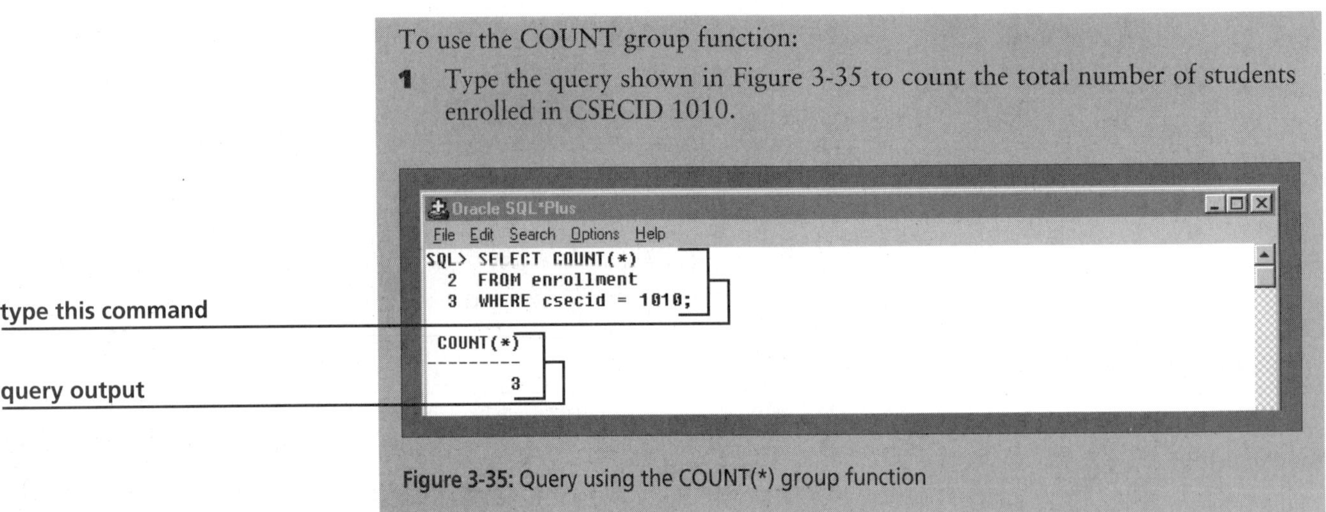

Figure 3-35: Query using the COUNT(*) group function

2 Type the query shown in Figure 3-36 to count the total number of students who have received a value for GRADE in CSECID 1010. Notice the difference between this query output and the query output shown in Figure 3-35. There are three students enrolled in the course, but no student has received a value for GRADE.

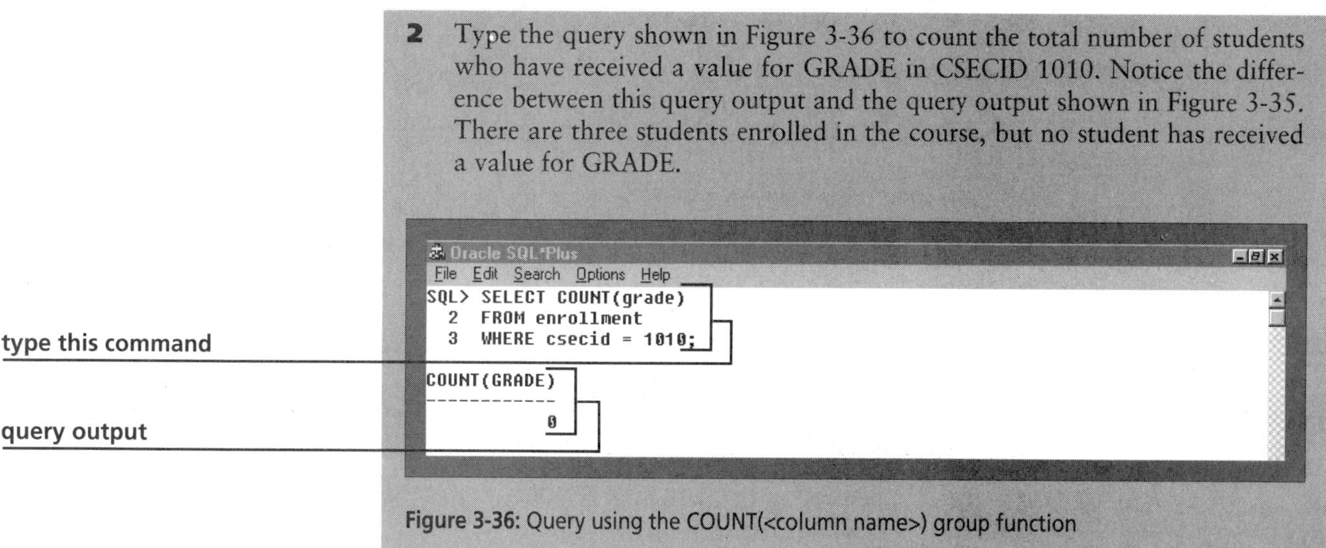

Figure 3-36: Query using the COUNT(<column name>) group function

Using Queries to Join Multiple Tables

All of the queries you have seen so far have retrieved data from a single table. However, one of the strengths of SQL is its ability to **join**, or combine, more than one database table using foreign key references. The general format of a SELECT statement with a join operation is:

```
SELECT <column-name1, column-name 2, …>
FROM tablename1, tablename2
WHERE tablename1.column-name = tablename2.column-name;
```

The SELECT clause contains the names of the columns to display in the query output. If you display a column that exists in more than one of the tables in the FROM clause, you must write the table name, followed by a period, and then write the column name with the name of one of the tables. Otherwise, the DBMS will issue an error. Listing the table name before a column name is known as **qualifying** the column name.

The FROM clause contains the name of each table involved in the join operation. The WHERE clause contains the **join condition**, which specifies the table and column names on which to join the tables. The join condition contains the foreign key reference in one table, and the primary key in the other table. Additional search conditions are listed in the WHERE clause using the AND and OR operators.

To join two tables in a single query:

1 Type the query shown in Figure 3-37 to list the student ID, last name, first name, and advisor last name. You can add additional search conditions in the WHERE clause using the AND operator as demonstrated in the following query.

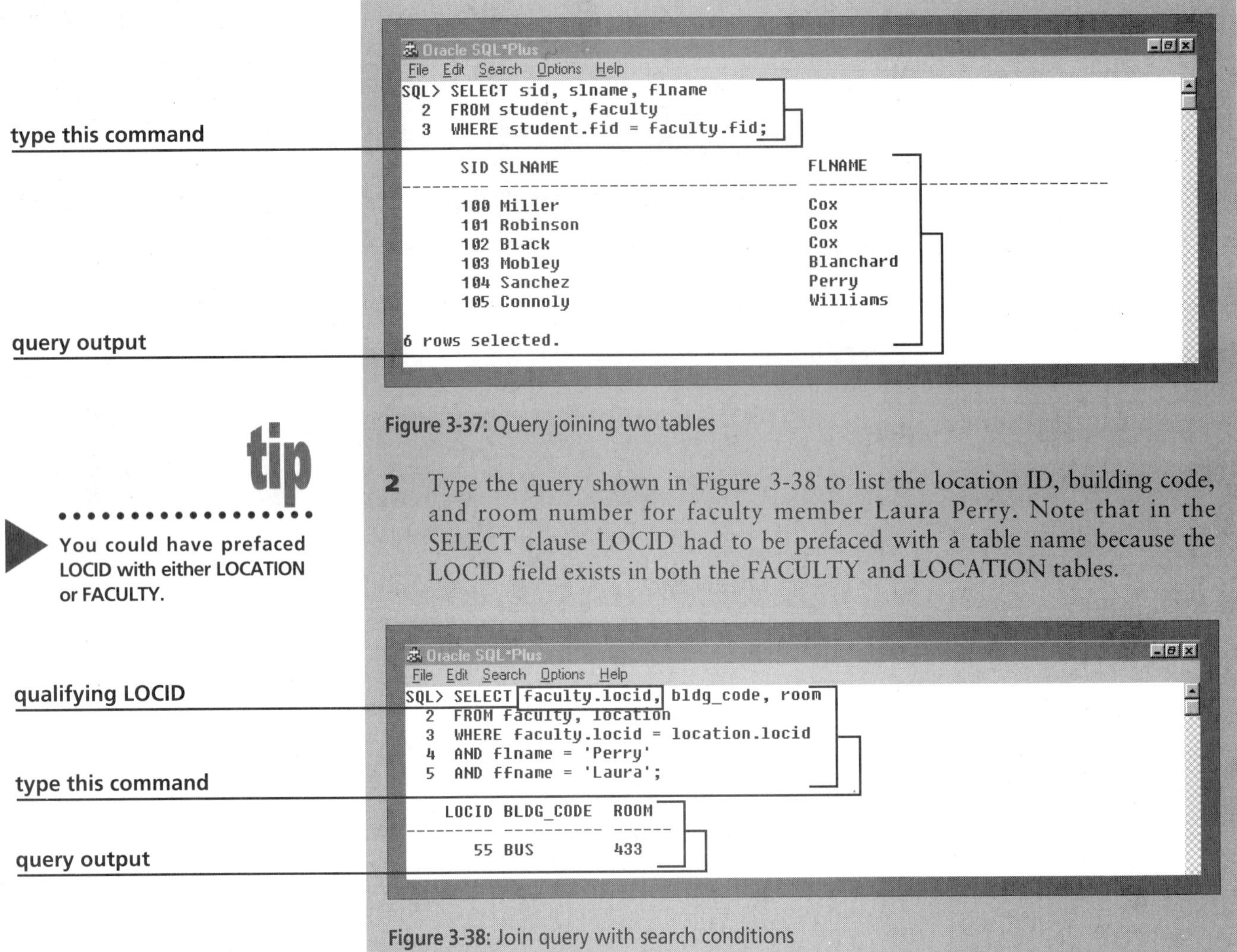

Figure 3-37: Query joining two tables

tip

You could have prefaced LOCID with either LOCATION or FACULTY.

2 Type the query shown in Figure 3-38 to list the location ID, building code, and room number for faculty member Laura Perry. Note that in the SELECT clause LOCID had to be prefaced with a table name because the LOCID field exists in both the FACULTY and LOCATION tables.

Figure 3-38: Join query with search conditions

In the previous examples, you joined two tables, but you can join any number of tables in a SELECT command. When you join more than two tables, each table involved in the query must be listed in the FROM clause, and each table in the FROM clause must be listed in the WHERE clause in a join condition. Suppose that you want to create a query to display the call ID and grade for each of Sarah Miller's courses. This query requires you to join four tables: STUDENT (to search for SFNAME and SLNAME), ENROLLMENT (to display GRADE), COURSE (to display CALLID), and COURSE_SECTION (to join CALLID in COURSE to CSECID in ENROLLMENT). For complex queries like this, it is often helpful to draw a diagram like the one shown in Figure 3-39 to show the columns and associated tables that you need to display and search, as well as the required joining columns and their links.

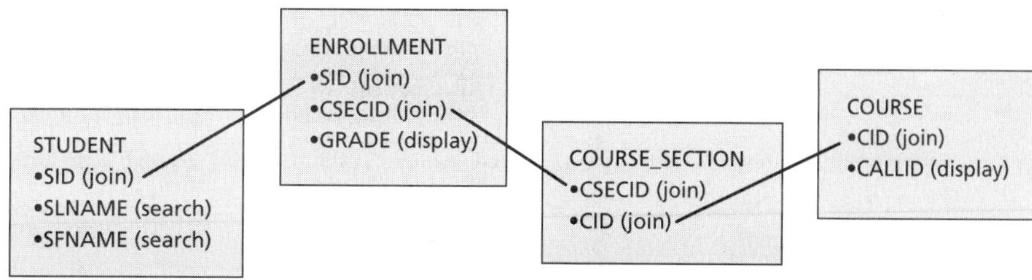

Figure 3-39: Complex join query design diagram

You can derive your query from the diagram by following these steps:

- Place the display fields in the SELECT clause.
- List all of the tables in the FROM clause.
- Include the links in join conditions in the WHERE clause.
- Include all of the search fields in the WHERE clause.

You will create a SQL query to join four tables next.

To join four tables in a single command:

1 Type the query shown in Figure 3-40.

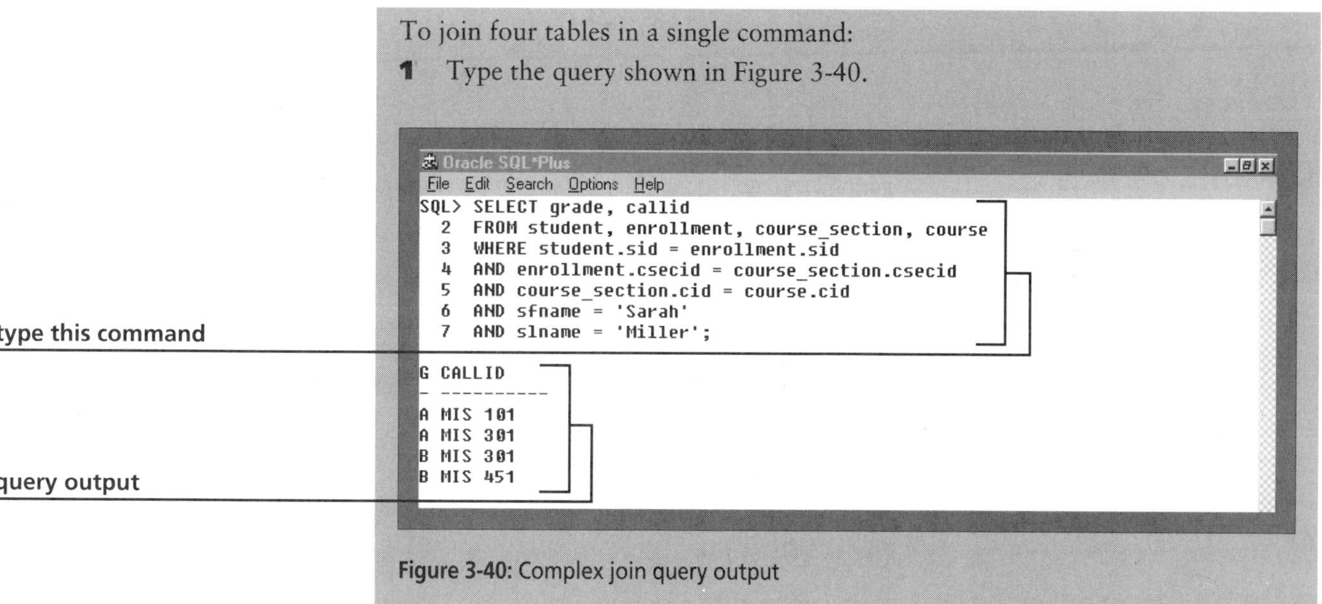

Figure 3-40: Complex join query output

Figure 3-41 shows the output of this query when the join condition between COURSE_SECTION and COURSE is omitted. The actual output doesn't fit on one screen, but a total of 20 records were returned. Here's what happened: Four CSECID records were selected, but then the DBMS joined these records with every record in the COURSE table instead of with the records with matching values for CID. Because there are a total of five records in the COURSE table, the query returned 4 times 5, or 20 records. This is called a **product** of two tables, and was caused by not specifying a join condition between two tables listed in the FROM clause. When a complex join query returns more records than you expect, look for missing join statements.

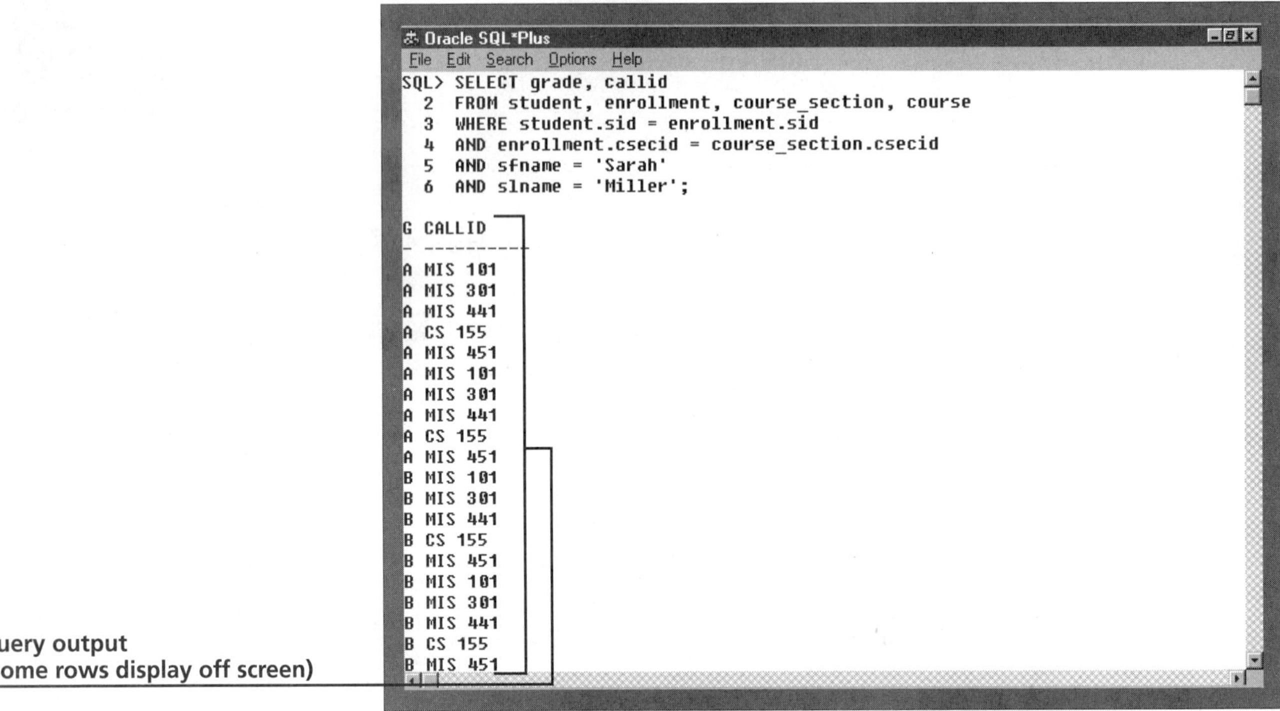

Figure 3-41: Complex join query output with omitted join statement

SQL Unions

You need to create a query to list the last name, first name, and phone number of every student and faculty member in the Northwoods University database. If you enter the SELECT statement shown in Figure 3-42, the output is a product of the FACULTY and STUDENT tables that was caused by omitting a join clause. However, no join clause was included because the relationship between the STUDENT and FACULTY records is not relevant for this query. A list of all student and faculty names and phone numbers has nothing to do with student/advisor relationships. Therefore SQL created a product of the two tables. A SELECT command cannot return data from two unrelated queries as a single output. This query requires a **union**, which combines the outputs of two unrelated queries into a single output result.

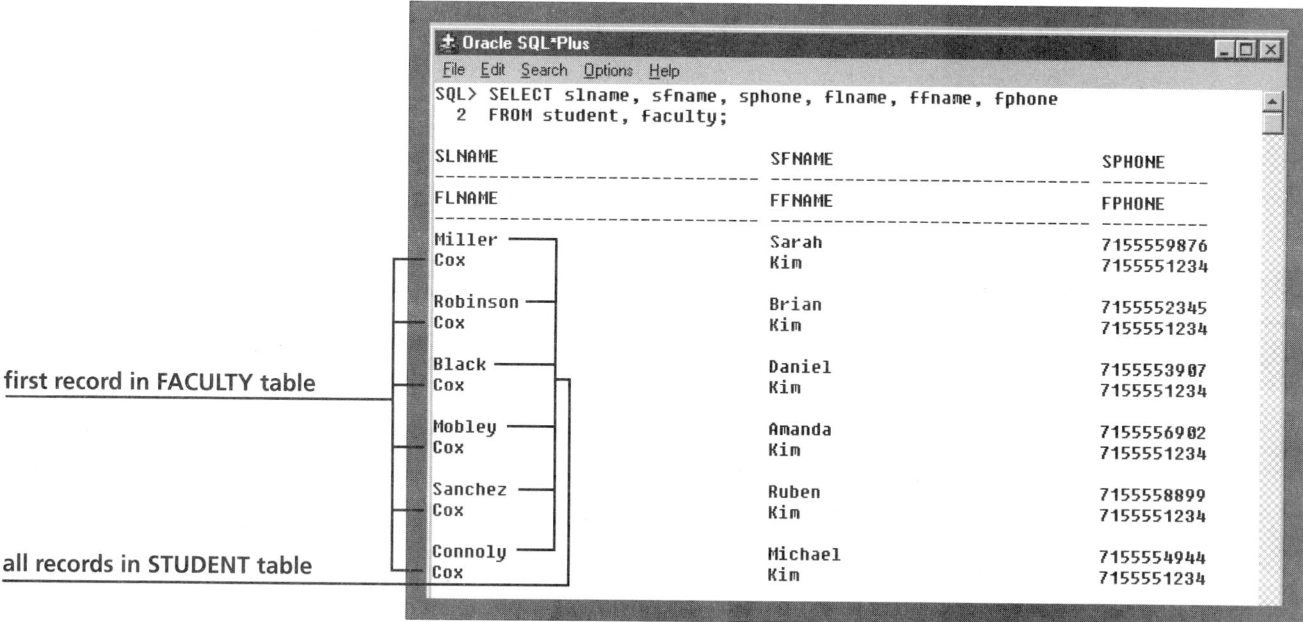

Figure 3-42: Example output that is a product of two tables

A union requires that both queries have the same number of display columns in the SELECT statement, and that each column in the first query must have the same data type as the corresponding column in the second query. The general format of the UNION query is `<query 1> UNION <query 2>`. You will execute a UNION query next.

To execute a UNION query:

1. Type the command shown in Figure 3-43. The query output shows the student and faculty names and phone numbers in a single list. Note that by default the column titles are taken from the column names in the first query's SELECT statement.

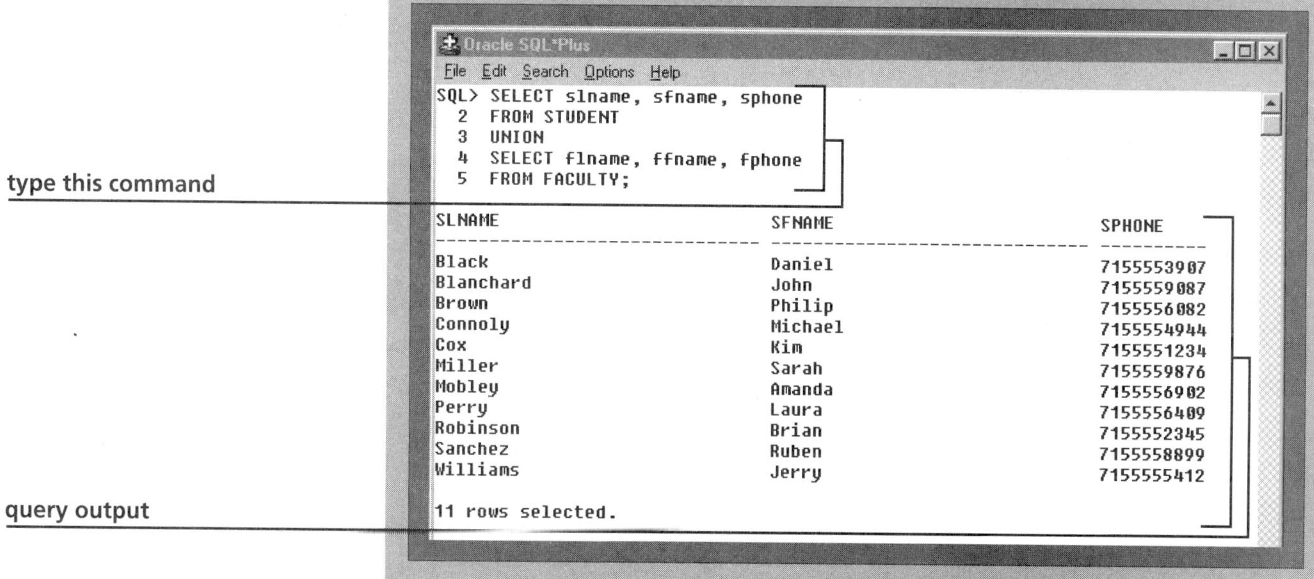

type this command

```
SQL> SELECT slname, sfname, sphone
  2  FROM STUDENT
  3  UNION
  4  SELECT flname, ffname, fphone
  5  FROM FACULTY;

SLNAME                          SFNAME                          SPHONE
------------------------------  ------------------------------  ----------
Black                           Daniel                          7155553907
Blanchard                       John                            7155559087
Brown                           Philip                          7155556082
Connoly                         Michael                         7155554944
Cox                             Kim                             7155551234
Miller                          Sarah                           7155559876
Mobley                          Amanda                          7155556902
Perry                           Laura                           7155556409
Robinson                        Brian                           7155552345
Sanchez                         Ruben                           7155558899
Williams                        Jerry                           7155555412

11 rows selected.
```

query output

Figure 3-43: UNION query

Database Views

A database **view** looks and acts like a database table. A view does not physically exist in the database—it is derived from other database tables. When the data in its source tables is updated, the view reflects the updates as well. Views are useful because you do not have to reenter complex query commands that are used frequently. They also can be used by the DBA to enforce database security and enable certain users to view only selected table fields or records. You can insert and update data, but it is tricky because it is difficult to satisfy the foreign key and NOT NULL constraints of the underlying database tables and probably should be avoided.

The general format for creating a view is `CREATE VIEW <view name> AS <view query specification>`. The following example demonstrates how to create a view named FACULTY_VIEW based on the FACULTY table. This view contains all of the FACULTY columns except the FPIN (faculty PIN). The columns will be sorted by FLNAME.

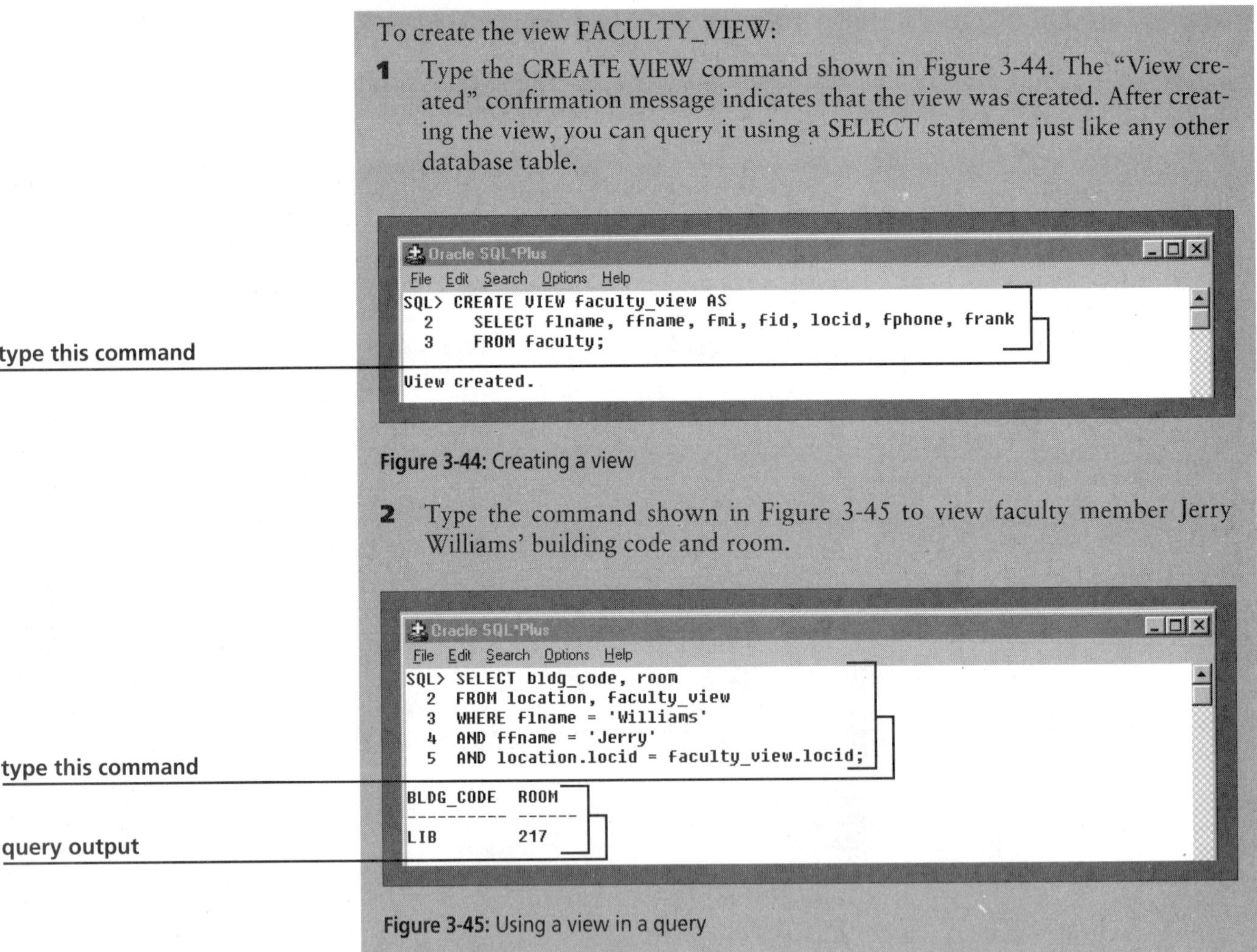

To create the view FACULTY_VIEW:

1 Type the CREATE VIEW command shown in Figure 3-44. The "View created" confirmation message indicates that the view was created. After creating the view, you can query it using a SELECT statement just like any other database table.

Figure 3-44: Creating a view

2 Type the command shown in Figure 3-45 to view faculty member Jerry Williams' building code and room.

Figure 3-45: Using a view in a query

You use the DROP VIEW command to drop a view from the database. Remember that a view is based on a query that executes to display the requested data from the underlying base table. When you drop a view, you do not drop the data that appears in the view—only the view definition is dropped.

To drop the view FACULTY_VIEW:

1. Type **DROP VIEW faculty_view;** to drop FACULTY_VIEW. The "View dropped" confirmation message indicates that the view was dropped.

Updating Existing Records in a Table

An important data maintenance operation is updating existing data records. Student addresses and phone numbers change often, and every year students (hopefully) move up to the next class. The general format of the UPDATE statement is:

```
UPDATE <tablename>
SET <column> = <new data value>
WHERE <search condition>;
```

Search conditions in UPDATE statements work just the same as in SELECT statements.

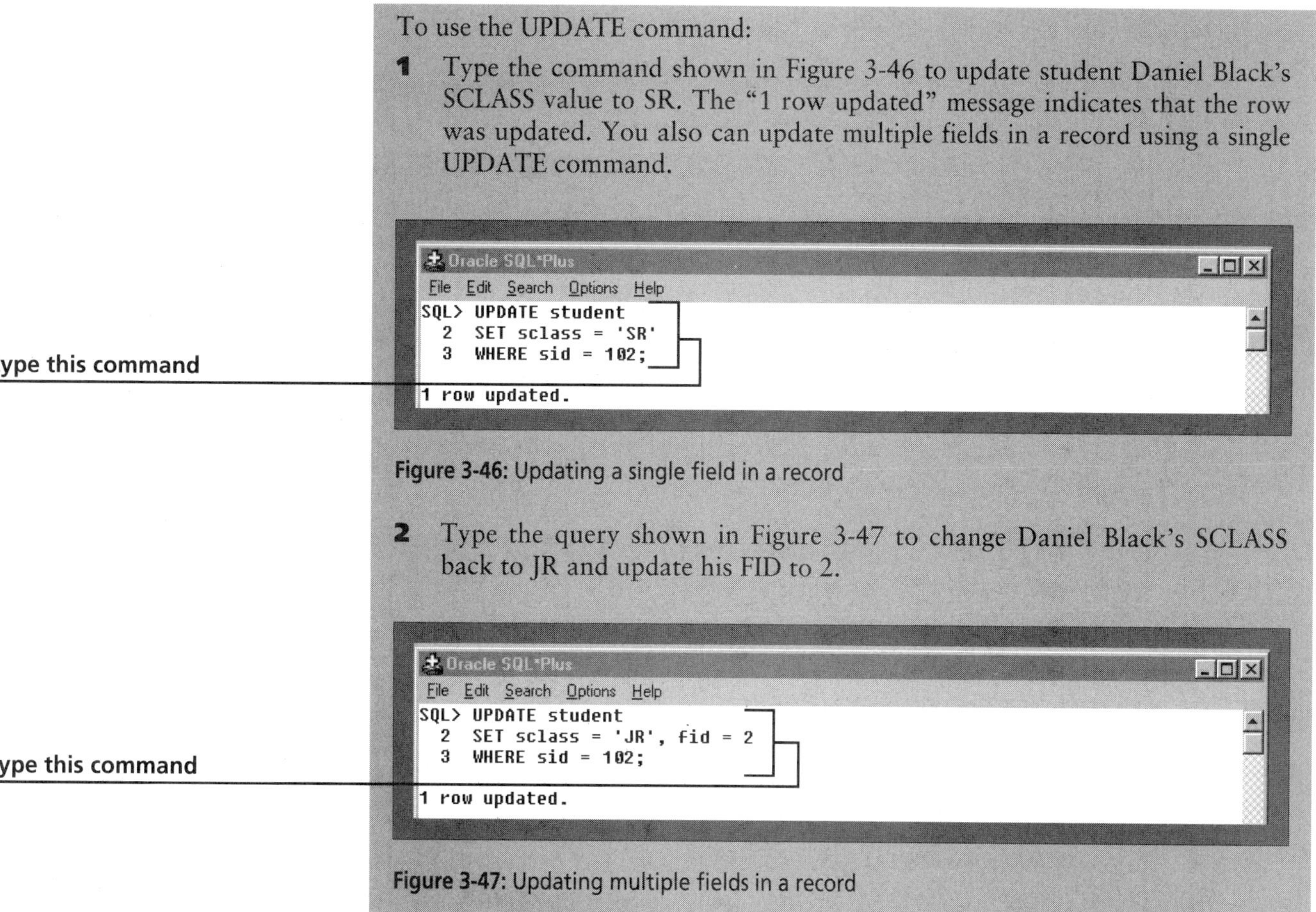

To use the UPDATE command:

1. Type the command shown in Figure 3-46 to update student Daniel Black's SCLASS value to SR. The "1 row updated" message indicates that the row was updated. You also can update multiple fields in a record using a single UPDATE command.

Figure 3-46: Updating a single field in a record

2. Type the query shown in Figure 3-47 to change Daniel Black's SCLASS back to JR and update his FID to 2.

Figure 3-47: Updating multiple fields in a record

You also can update multiple records using a single UPDATE command by specifying a search condition that matches multiple records and uses the greater than (>) or less than (<) mathematical operators, or the AND and OR operators.

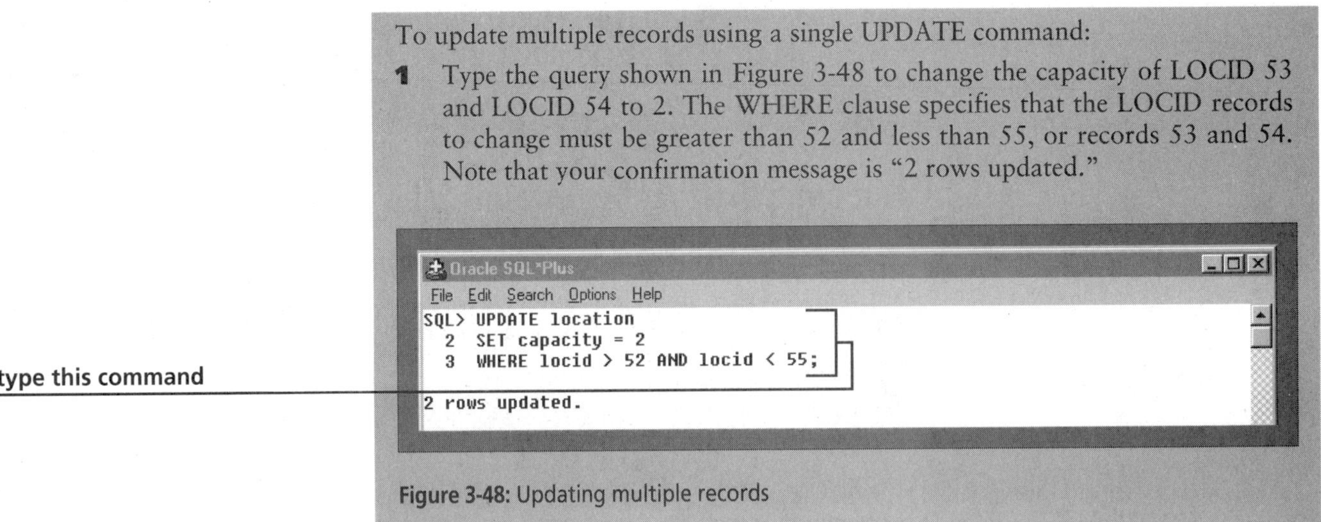

To update multiple records using a single UPDATE command:

1. Type the query shown in Figure 3-48 to change the capacity of LOCID 53 and LOCID 54 to 2. The WHERE clause specifies that the LOCID records to change must be greater than 52 and less than 55, or records 53 and 54. Note that your confirmation message is "2 rows updated."

Figure 3-48: Updating multiple records

Deleting Records

The final table maintenance operation is deleting records. The general format of the DELETE command is:

```
DELETE FROM <tablename>
WHERE <search condition>;
```

Make sure to include a WHERE clause when deleting a record from a table to ensure that the correct record is deleted. Otherwise, all table records will be deleted.

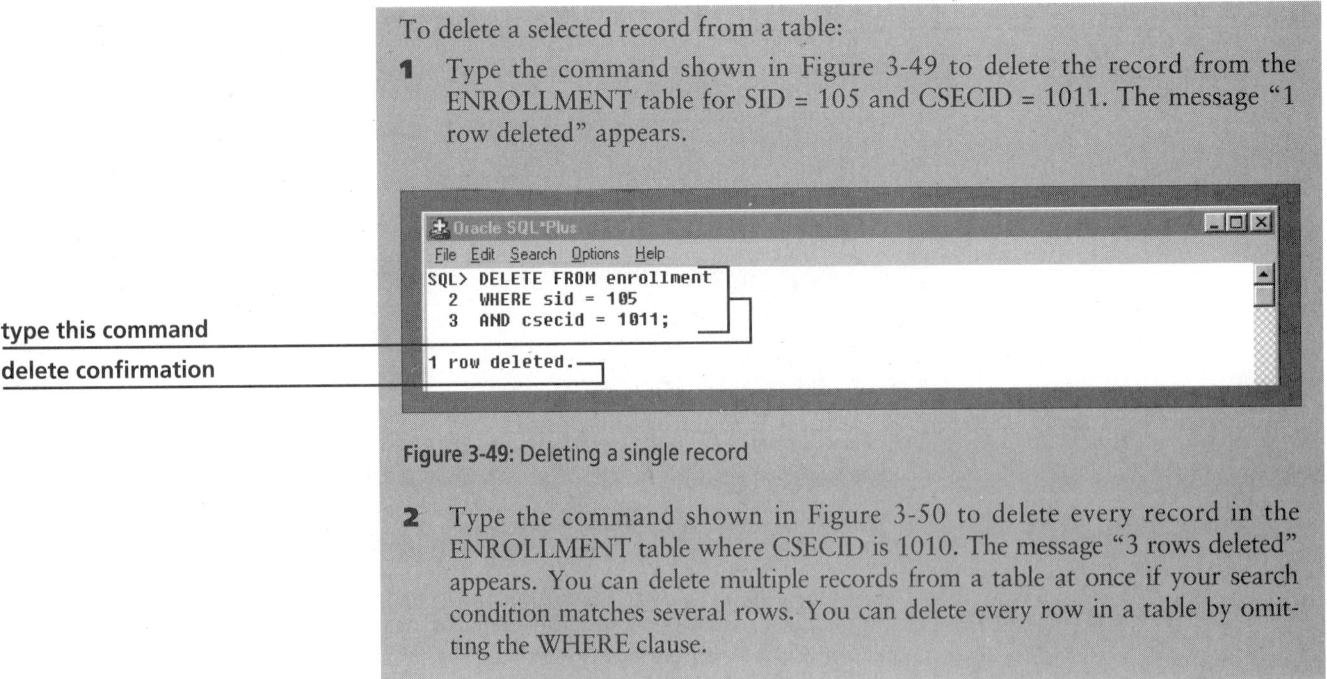

To delete a selected record from a table:

1. Type the command shown in Figure 3-49 to delete the record from the ENROLLMENT table for SID = 105 and CSECID = 1011. The message "1 row deleted" appears.

Figure 3-49: Deleting a single record

2. Type the command shown in Figure 3-50 to delete every record in the ENROLLMENT table where CSECID is 1010. The message "3 rows deleted" appears. You can delete multiple records from a table at once if your search condition matches several rows. You can delete every row in a table by omitting the WHERE clause.

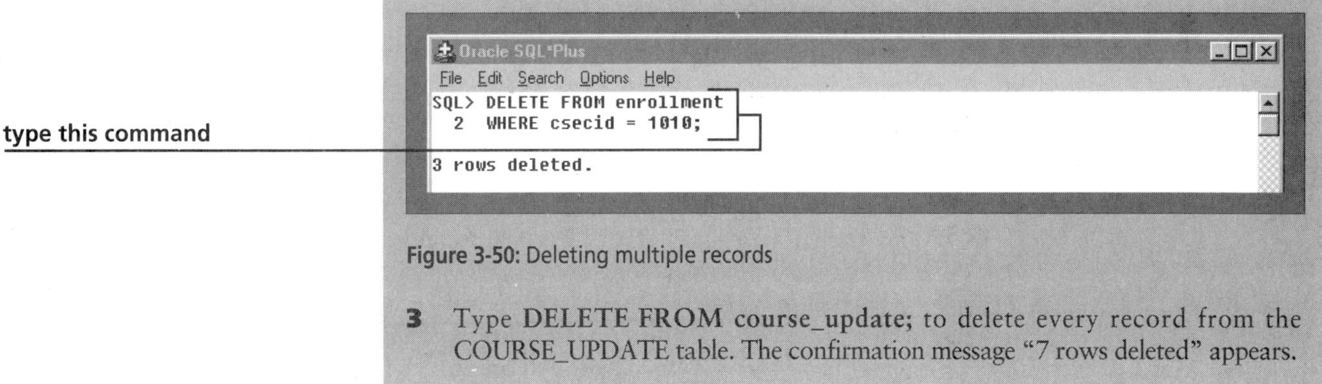

Figure 3-50: Deleting multiple records

3 Type **DELETE FROM course_update;** to delete every record from the COURSE_UPDATE table. The confirmation message "7 rows deleted" appears.

You cannot delete a record if it is a foreign key reference to another record, as you will see next.

To try to delete a record with a foreign key reference:

1 Type the command shown in Figure 3-51 to delete LOCID 53 (Kim Cox's office) from the LOCATION table. The error message shown in Figure 3-54 appears.

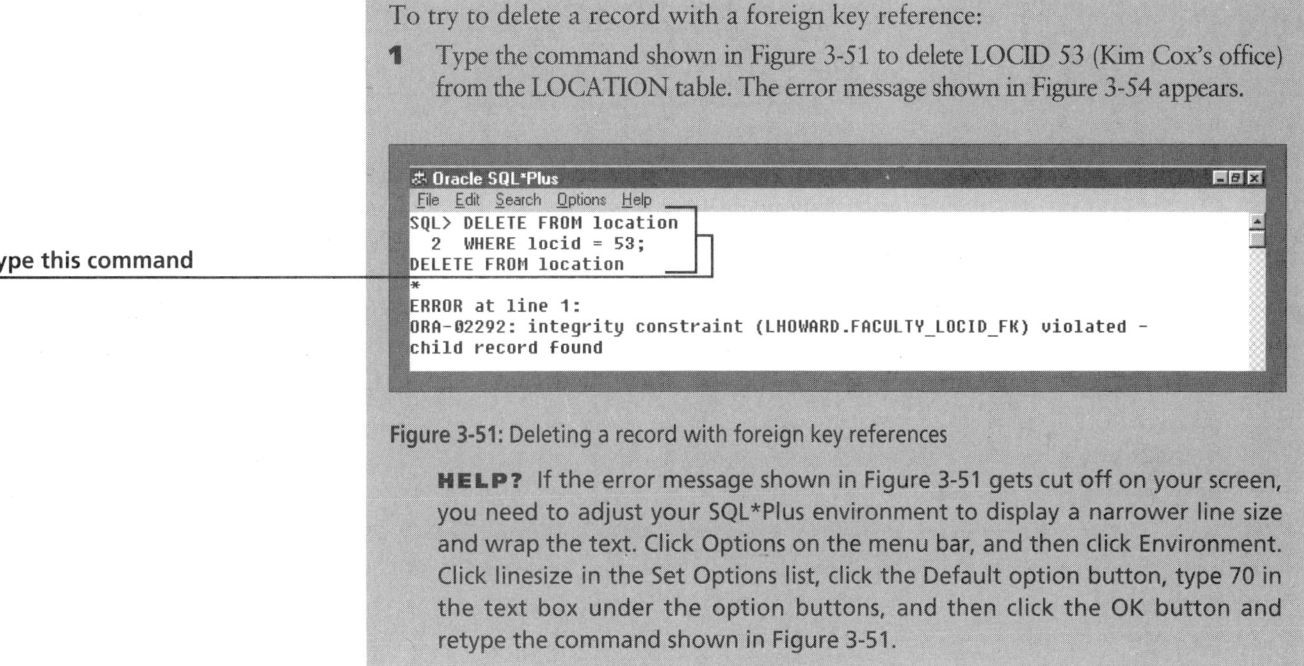

Figure 3-51: Deleting a record with foreign key references

HELP? If the error message shown in Figure 3-51 gets cut off on your screen, you need to adjust your SQL*Plus environment to display a narrower line size and wrap the text. Click Options on the menu bar, and then click Environment. Click linesize in the Set Options list, click the Default option button, type 70 in the text box under the option buttons, and then click the OK button and retype the command shown in Figure 3-51.

The value for LOCID 53 is a foreign key in the FACULTY table for Kim Cox's data record. If you want to delete LOCID 53, you have to delete Kim Cox's FACULTY record first. However, this record (with FID = 1) is referenced in all three of the STUDENT records you previously inserted. To delete LOCID 53, you would have to delete all of the student records that contain FID 1 first, and then delete FID 1.

Selecting Records for Update

When you enter a SELECT command to query database records, no locks are placed on the selected records so other database users can view and update these records simultaneously. This is necessary for databases with many concurrent users because otherwise many or all of the database records would be locked most of the time and work would grind to a halt. However, records that have been changed with an INSERT or UPDATE statement are locked until the user holding the lock releases it by issuing a COMMIT command.

Sometimes you might want to view a record and then update it in the same transaction. For example, when a Clearwater Traders customer wants to order an item, the salesperson first must determine if the item is in stock before placing the order. Suppose that a particular item is in stock and the salesperson verbally confirms this fact to the customer. But, before the salesperson can place the order and commit the update, another salesperson sells the entire inventory on hand.

The general format of the SELECT ... FOR UPDATE command is:

```
SELECT <column names>
FROM <tablenames>
WHERE <search conditions>
FOR UPDATE OF <column names to be updated>
NOWAIT;
```

The column names listed in the FOR UPDATE OF command do not restrict what columns can be updated in the record because the entire record is locked. However, listing these column names helps to document what fields are to be updated. The NOWAIT command causes the system to generate an error message immediately if another user previously locked the selected records. If the NOWAIT command is omitted, the system forces the user to "wait" until the requested records are unlocked, so the user can do no further processing.

Next you will select and update the grades in the ENROLLMENT table for CSECID 1012.

To select, lock, and update the grade records for CSECID 1012:

1 Type the command shown in Figure 3-52 to select and lock the record for CSECID 1012.

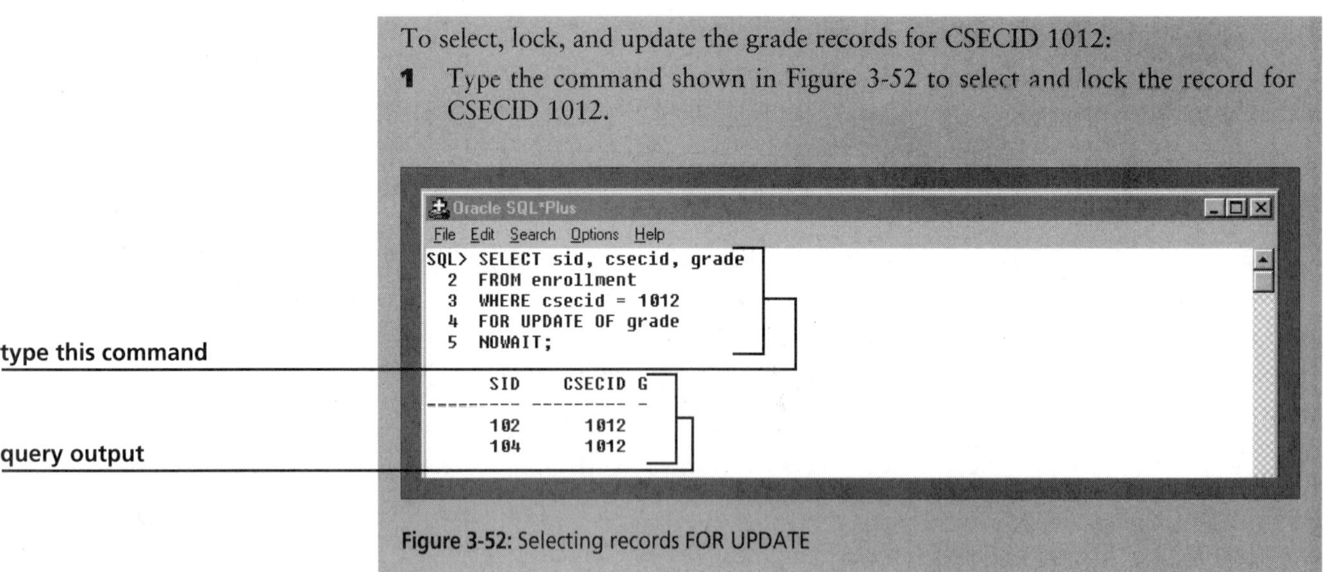

Figure 3-52: Selecting records FOR UPDATE

2 Type the series of UPDATE commands shown in Figure 3-53, and then COMMIT your updates as shown.

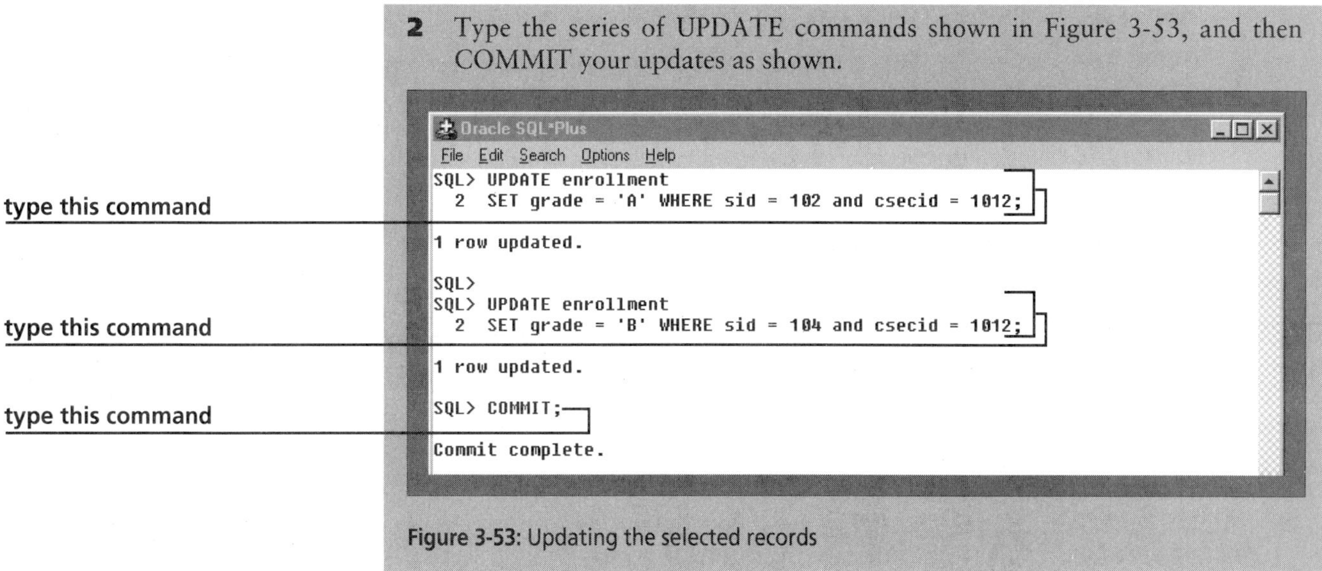

Figure 3-53: Updating the selected records

Figure 3-54 illustrates the effect of using the NOWAIT command. The first command shows the result of a SELECT ... FOR UPDATE command with a NOWAIT clause for records that currently are locked by another user. The second command shows the result of the same command, but without the NOWAIT clause. The "Query is Executing" message will continue to occur until the locked records are released by the other user, or when the current user exits SQL*Plus. Unfortunately, clicking the Cancel button does not cancel the query.

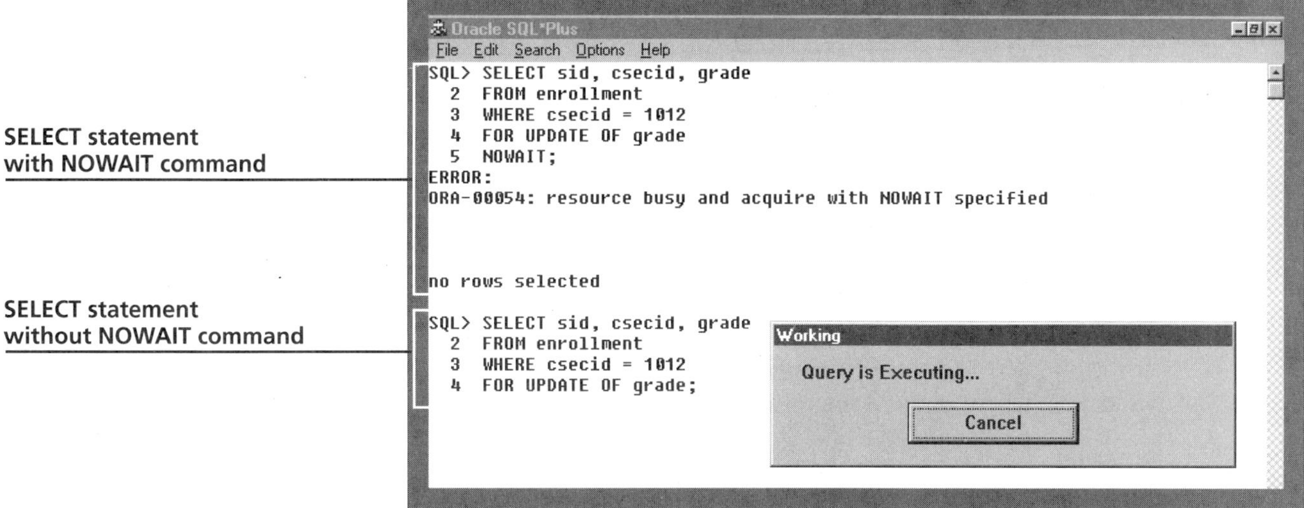

Figure 3-54: Error generated when selecting rows locked by another user

Sometimes you might lock your records inadvertently from yourself if you are multitasking between different Oracle applications. If you get the error message shown in Figure 3-54 while you are working, determine if you have an uncommitted INSERT, UPDATE, or SELECT ... FOR UPDATE command in any application, and then issue a COMMIT.

Using Oracle Browser to Retrieve Data

Oracle Browser is a graphical environment used to create and store SQL SELECT statement queries. To create a Browser query, you select the data tables required in the query, choose the display columns, and then optionally specify search conditions or group functions such as summing, grouping, or ordering. Browser takes care of specifying the join conditions.

First, you need to refresh your Northwoods University database tables by running the northwoo.sql script on your Student Disk.

To run the script file and start Browser:

1. Run the northwoo.sql script by typing the following command: **START A:\Chapter3\northwoo.sql**.
2. Click the **Start** button on the taskbar, point to **Programs**, point to **Discoverer 2000 Win95** (or **Discoverer 2000 NT** for NT users), and then click **Browser 2.0 Extended**.
3. Log on to Browser using your user name, password, and connect string. Leave the Dictionary entry as DEFAULT, as shown in Figure 3-55, and then click the **Connect** button.

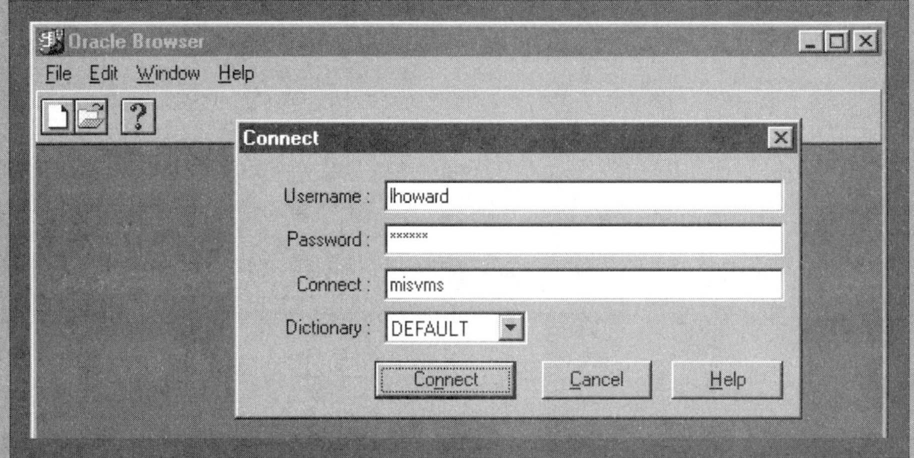

Figure 3-55: Logging on to the Oracle Browser

HELP? If a dialog box opens and displays Browser (BRW-) and Oracle DBMS (ORA-) error messages and codes, it indicates that the person who set up your database did not run some of Browser initialization scripts. Browser still will run correctly, so click the OK button to continue, and then notify your instructor or technical support person.

The Start Oracle Browser dialog box opens, as shown in Figure 3-56. You can use this dialog box to create a new query, open an existing query from the database, or open an existing query from the file system. Browser enables you to create queries, and then save them in the database or in the file system for later retrieval.

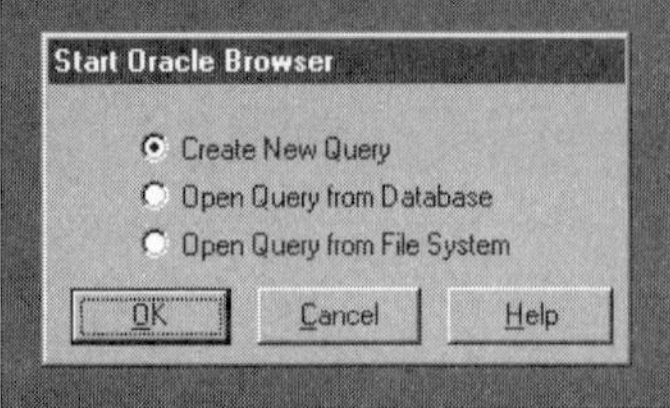

Figure 3-56: Browser query options

4 Make sure that the **Create New Query** option button is selected, and then click the **OK** button. The Oracle Browser program window opens, and then the Select Data Tables dialog box opens, as shown in Figure 3-57. The Show check boxes specify what types of objects are displayed: Tables, Views, Queries, Snapshots, or Synonyms. The center list box allows you to choose whose objects are currently displayed—your user name will display. The bottom list box lists your tables, views, and queries.

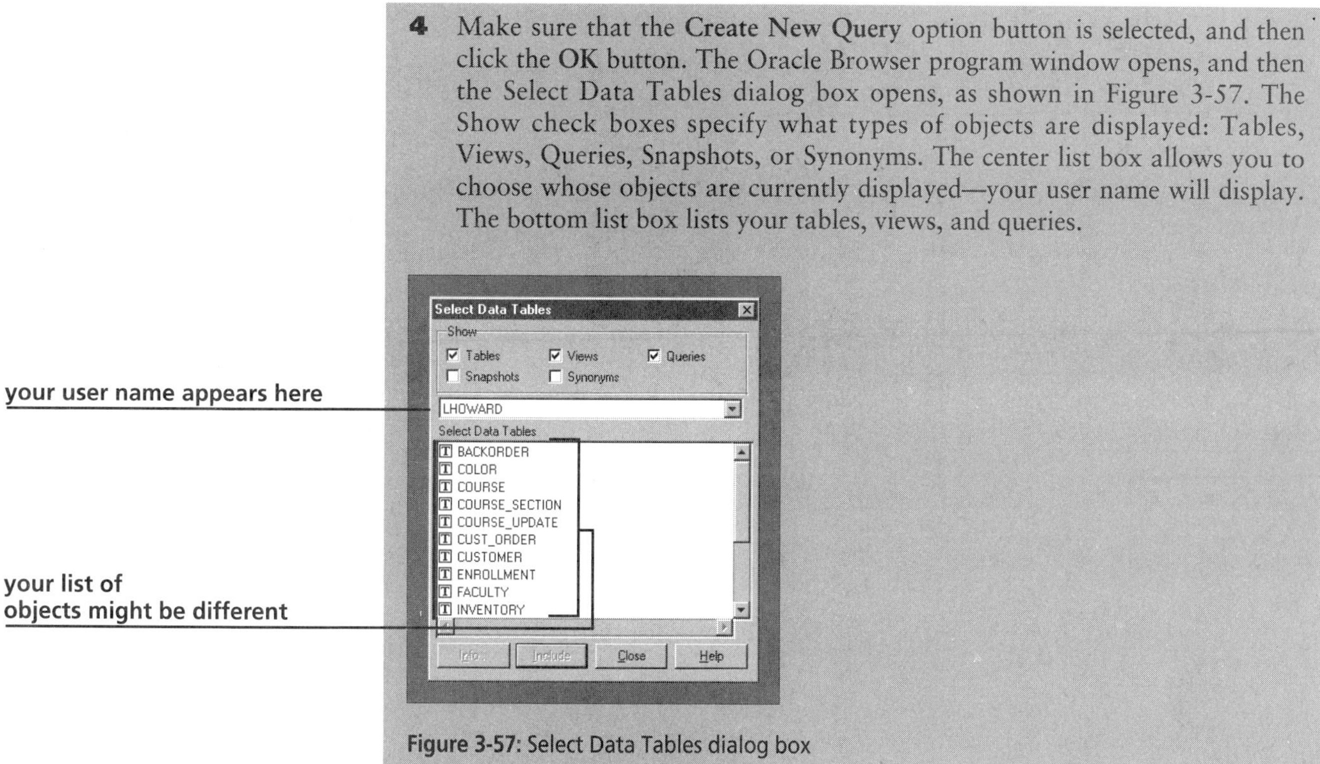

Figure 3-57: Select Data Tables dialog box

Creating a Query Using Browser

Remember the SQL query you created earlier to display the call IDs and grades for all of Sarah Miller's courses? You will re-create that query using Browser next.

To create a query using Browser:

1 Click the **COURSE** table in the Select Data Tables list box, press and hold down the **Ctrl** key, and then click **COURSE_SECTION**, **ENROLLMENT**, and **STUDENT**, as shown in Figure 3-58.

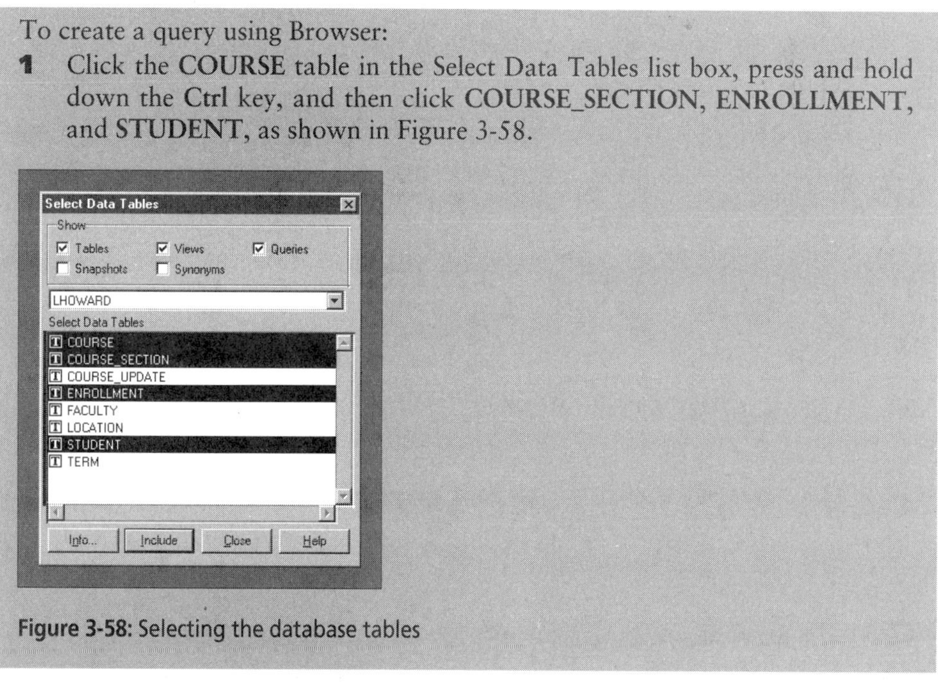

Figure 3-58: Selecting the database tables

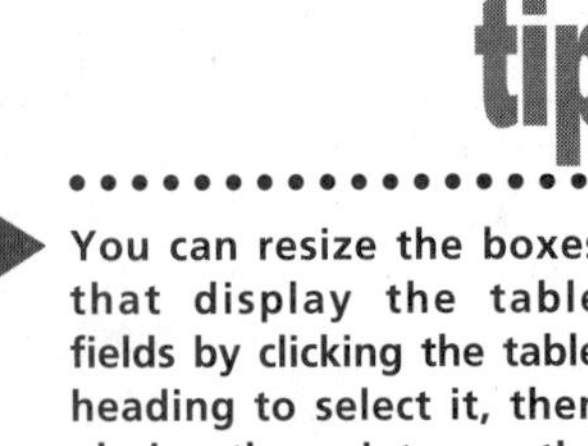

You can resize the boxes that display the table fields by clicking the table heading to select it, then placing the pointer on the lower-right corner until the pointer changes to ↘, and dragging the box to the size you want.

2 Click the **Include** button, wait a moment (the pointer will change from ⌛ to ↖), and then click the **Close** button.

3 Click the **Maximize** button ☐ on the Untitled1: Query window. The Query window shows the tables you selected and the links between the tables created by foreign key relationships.

4 If necessary, drag the tables so they are positioned like the ones shown in Figure 3-59. All tables should display on the screen and all of the foreign key links should be visible.

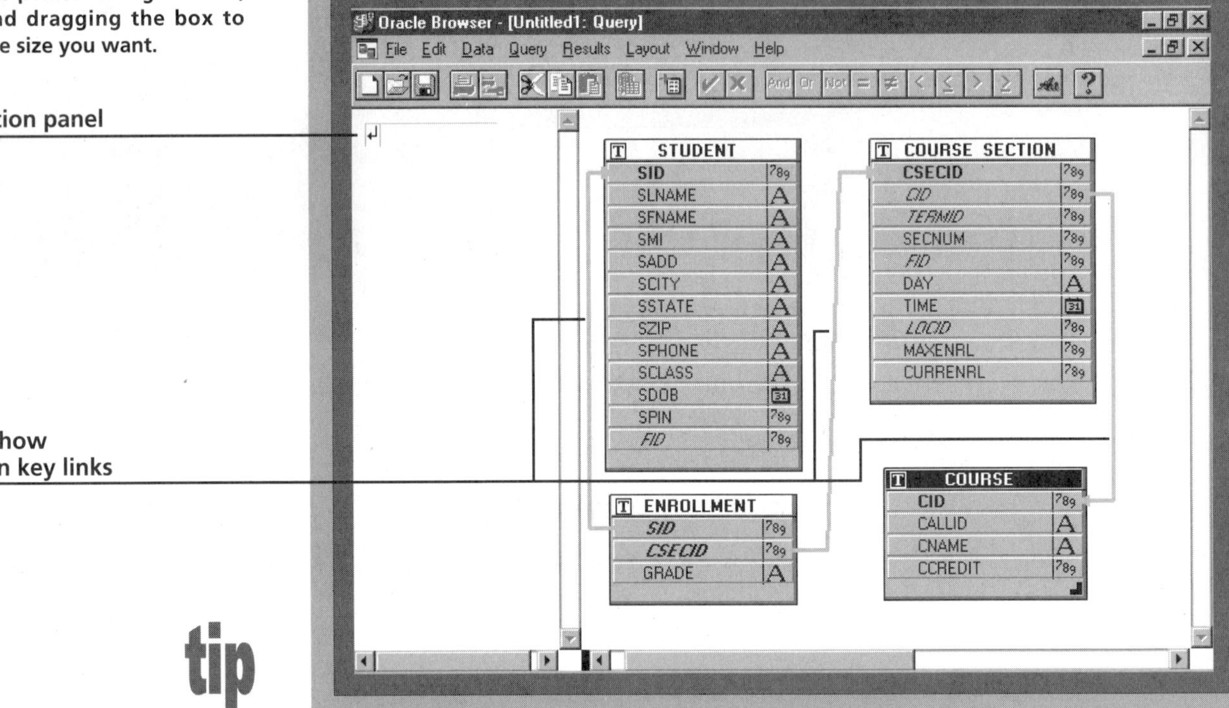

Figure 3-59: Query data tables and foreign key links

The order in which you select the column names will specify the order in which they appear in the query output.

5 Double-click **CALLID** (in the COURSE table) and **GRADE** (in the ENROLLMENT table) to specify them as the display columns. A check mark appears in front of the column names to indicate that they are selected. To deselect a column, double-click it.

Next you will specify the search conditions. Currently the search **Condition panel** is on the left side of the Query window (see Figure 3-59). It is easier to view the search conditions if you configure the Query window so it splits horizontally and the Condition panel appears at the top of the window. Next you will reconfigure the Condition panel and enter the search condition.

To reconfigure the Condition panel and enter the search condition:

1 Click **Edit** on the menu bar, and then click **Preferences.** Click **Query Window** in the Preferences for list box, click the **Vertical** Panel Split Direction option button, and then change the Condition Panel Size value to 20, as shown in Figure 3-60.

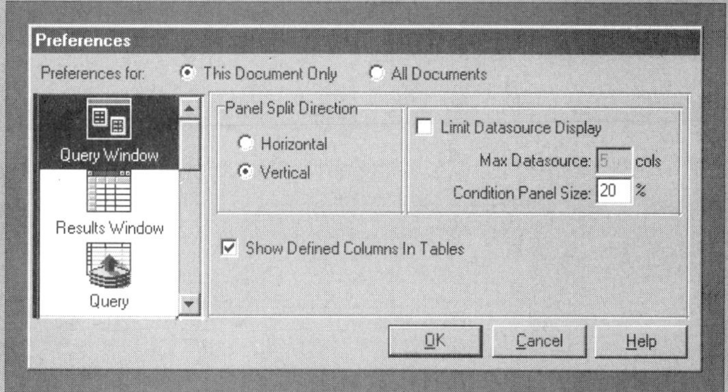

Figure 3-60: Using the Preferences dialog box to change the Query window

2 Click the OK button, click the **Condition Panel** box to activate it, as shown in Figure 3-61, and then click **SLNAME** to add it to the Condition panel.

click here to activate the Condition panel

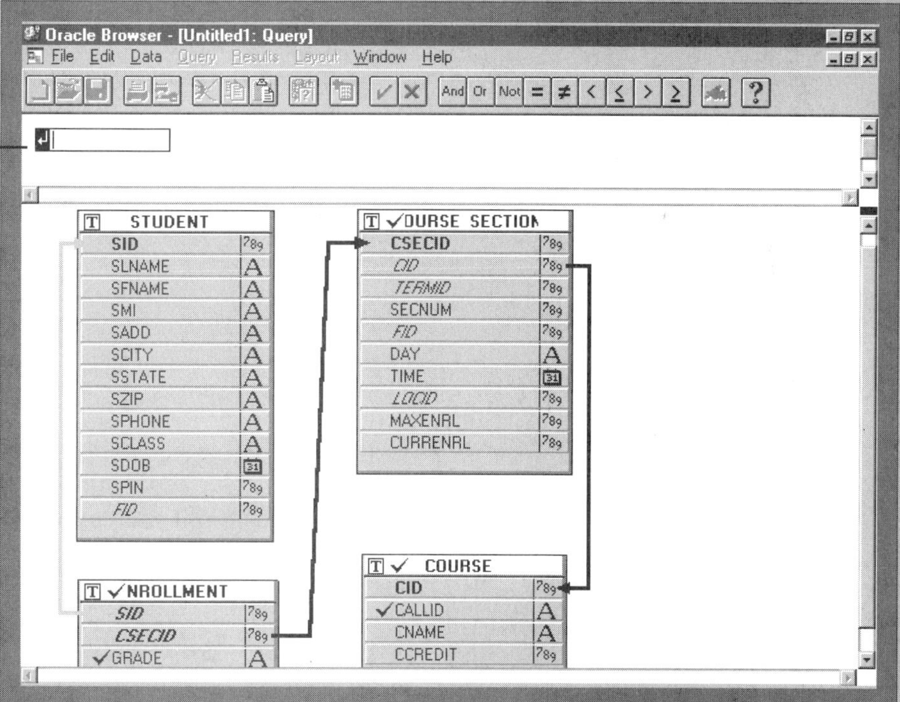

Figure 3-61: Activating the Condition panel

3 Click the **Equal** button [=] on the toolbar to add the equal operator to the Condition panel.

4 Immediately after the =, type **'Miller'** as the first search condition. Make sure that you type the single quotation marks and use the same case as indicated.

5 Click the **And** button [And] on the toolbar to add the AND operator to your expression in the Condition panel.

6 Click **SFNAME** in the STUDENT table to add it to the Condition panel.

7 Click [=] and then type **'Sarah'** as the second search condition, as shown in Figure 3-62.

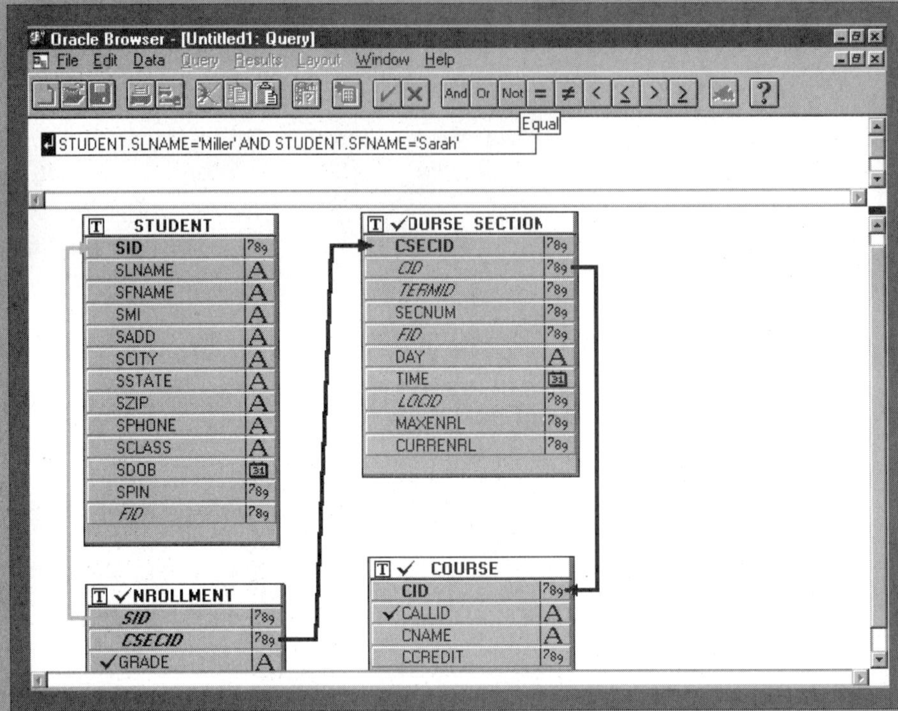

Figure 3-62: Specifying the query search condition

8 Click the **Accept** button on the toolbar to accept the search conditions, and then click the **Execute Query** button on the toolbar to execute the query. The query output is shown in Figure 3-63.

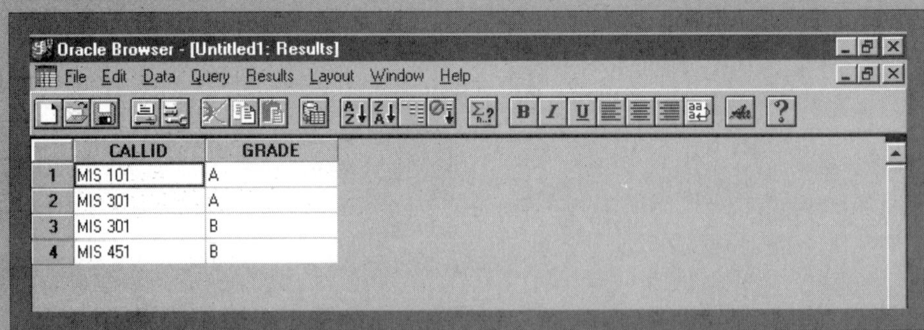

	CALLID	GRADE
1	MIS 101	A
2	MIS 301	A
3	MIS 301	B
4	MIS 451	B

Figure 3-63: Oracle Browser query output

tip

Another way to execute the query is to click Query on the menu bar, and then click Execute Query.

HELP? If the Execute Query button or menu commands are not available to you, you probably forgot to select the display fields. Double-click the fields you want the query to display so a check mark appears in front of their names.

HELP? If your query finds no records, check to make sure that you enclosed the character values within single quotation marks, and that the case of the character strings matches the way the values are entered in the database. If you still have problems, ask your instructor or technical support person for help.

Viewing the SQL Command Code

Browser simplifies the query process, but some knowledge of table relationships and search condition logic still is needed, so Browser probably will not be used by end users as a query tool. However, this utility is useful to create queries like this one that involve several tables because it can generate the SQL syntax that can be copied into other Oracle applications, such as SQL*Plus, Oracle Forms, or Oracle Reports.

To view the SQL command code and copy it to SQL*Plus:

1. Click **Query** on the menu bar, and then click **Show SQL**. The SQL syntax for the query appears, as shown in Figure 3-64.

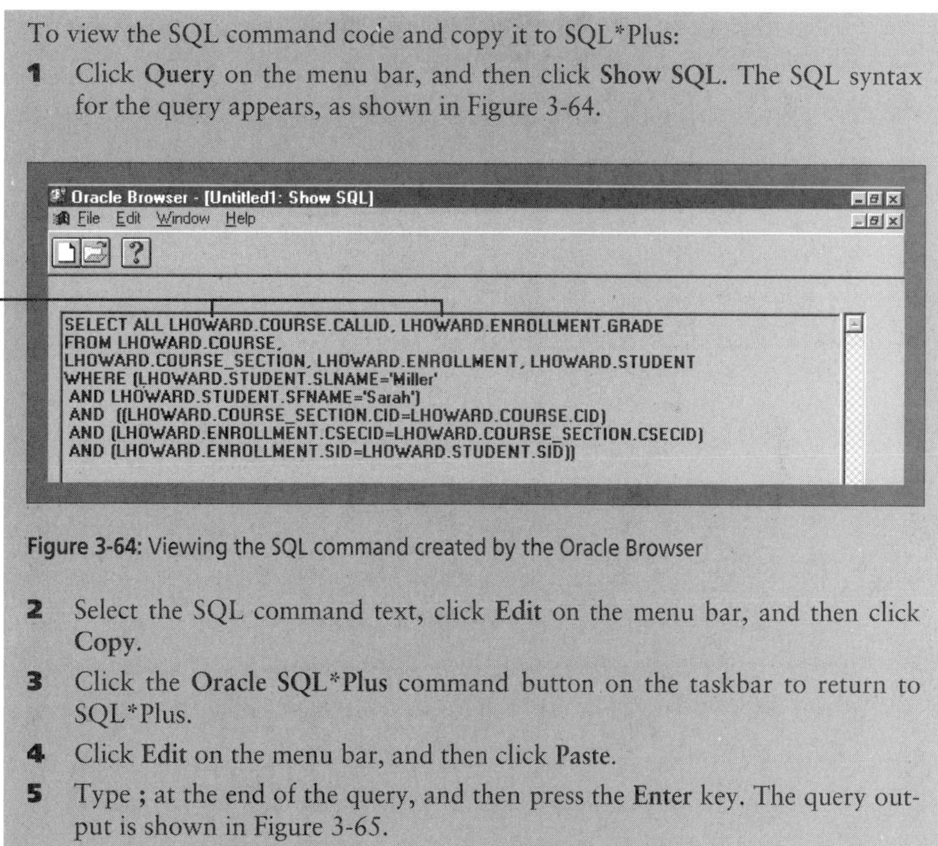

Figure 3-64: Viewing the SQL command created by the Oracle Browser

2. Select the SQL command text, click **Edit** on the menu bar, and then click **Copy**.
3. Click the **Oracle SQL*Plus** command button on the taskbar to return to SQL*Plus.
4. Click **Edit** on the menu bar, and then click **Paste**.
5. Type ; at the end of the query, and then press the **Enter** key. The query output is shown in Figure 3-65.

```
Oracle SQL*Plus
File Edit Search Options Help
SQL> SELECT ALL LHOWARD.COURSE.CALLID, LHOWARD.ENROLLMENT.GRADE
  FROM LHOWARD.COURSE,
  LHOWARD.COURSE_SECTION, LHOWARD.ENROLLMENT, LHOWARD.STUDENT
  WHERE (LHOWARD.STUDENT.SLNAME='Miller'
   AND LHOWARD.STUDENT.SFNAME='Sarah')
   AND  ((LHOWARD.COURSE_SECTION.CID=LHOWARD.COURSE.CID)
   AND (LHOWARD.ENROLLMENT.CSECID=LHOWARD.COURSE_SECTION.CSECID)
   AND (LHOWARD.ENROLLMENT.SID=LHOWARD.STUDENT.SID));

CALLID     G
---------- -
MIS 101    A
MIS 301    A
MIS 301    B
MIS 451    B

SQL>
```

Figure 3-65: Running the Oracle Browser query in SQL*Plus

Saving Your Browser Query

It is useful to be able to save Browser queries so they can be modified later if needed, or so you can run them again and view the results as the data in the database changes. You can save your Browser queries in the database to your file system or as SQL text files. If queries are saved in the database or file system, they can be retrieved only using the Oracle Browser. Queries saved as text files can be copied and then pasted into SQL*Plus or other Oracle applications. The option to save queries in the database might not be available if your database administrator has not run the required Browser initialization scripts.

To save your Browser query:

1. Click the **Oracle Browser** command button on the taskbar to activate Browser.
2. Click **Window** on the menu bar. There are three different windows currently open in your Browser environment: Untitled1: Query (in which you create and edit query specifications), Untitled1: Results (which displays the query output when you run the query), and Untitled1: Show SQL (which shows the SQL command syntax). Click **Untitled1: Query** to activate that window.
3. Click the **Save** button on the toolbar to open the Save As dialog box, as shown in Figure 3-66. You can save the query as a Browser query in the database or in the file system as a file with a .brw extension. The final option is to save to the file system as a .qxf (Oracle Data Query) file. (Oracle Data Query is an end-user query-building tool that is not covered in this book.)

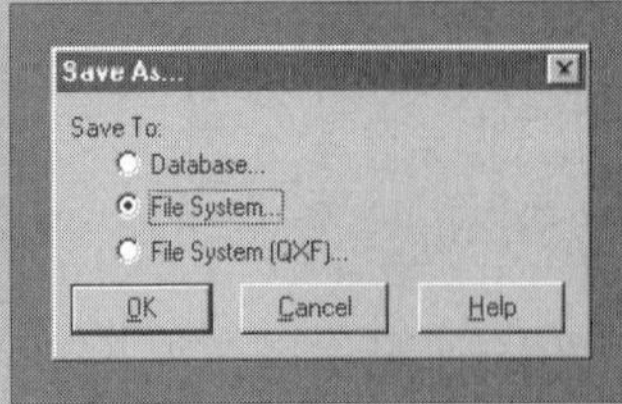

Figure 3-66: Browser query save options

4 Click the **File System** option button, and then click the **OK** button. The Windows Save As dialog box opens.

5 Change the Save in folder to the Chapter3 folder on your Student Disk, and then save the file as **miller.brw**.

6 Click **File** on the menu bar, and then click **Save SQL** to open the Save As dialog box. Save the file as **miller.sql** in the Chapter3 folder on your Student Disk. This saves the query as a text file with a .sql extension that can be opened and modified using any text editor.

7 Click **File** on the menu bar, and then click **Close** to close the Query window.

Other Browser Functions

Browser also has capabilities for creating queries that involve sorting, grouping, or summing data. In the next query, you will list every term, the call IDs for all courses offered during that term, the number of students who were enrolled or currently are enrolled for each course, and the total enrollment for each course and for each term. Figure 3-67 shows the query design diagram that includes the required tables, display fields, search fields, and join fields for this query.

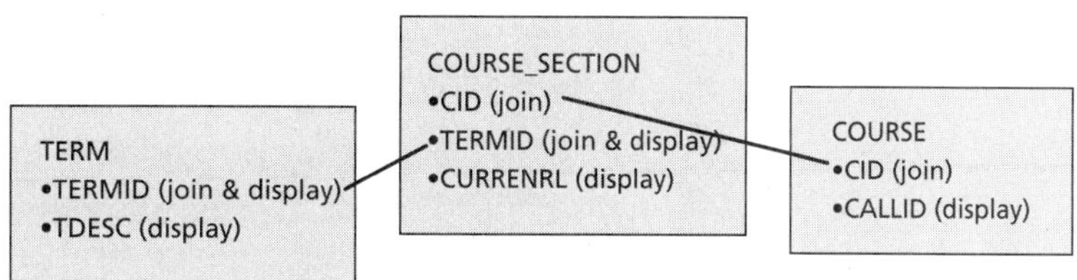

Figure 3-67: Query design diagram for complex Browser query

To create the query:

1 Click the **New** button on the toolbar to create a new Browser query. The Select Data Tables dialog box opens.

2 Click the **COURSE** table, press and hold down the **Ctrl** key, and then click the **COURSE_SECTION** and **TERM** tables. Click the **Include** button, wait a moment, and then click the **Close** button.

3 Click the **Maximize** button on the Query window, and then arrange the tables so you can see the foreign key links.

4 Double-click the display fields in the following order: **TERMID**, **TERMDESC**, **CALLID**, and **CURRENRL**.

tip

Remember that the fields will display in the same order as they are selected.

5 Click **Results** on the menu bar, and then click **Group** to open the Group dialog box. Click **<your user name>.TERM.TERMID** as the first group, and then click the **Copy** button. Note that the field names that appear in more than one table are prefaced by their owner and table names. Click **CALLID** as the second group, and then click the **Copy** button again. See Figure 3-68.

your user name will appear here

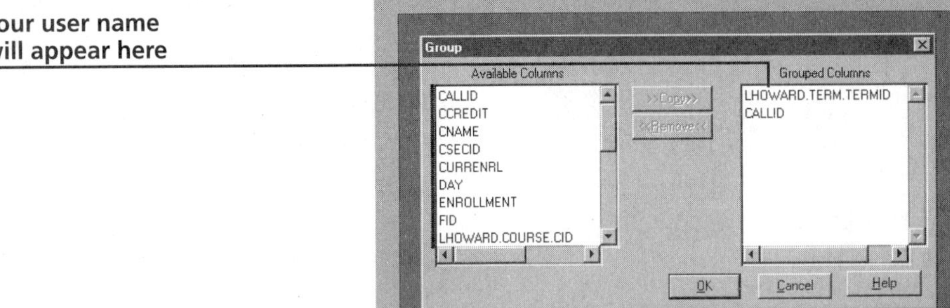

Figure 3-68: Selecting GROUP BY columns in the Browser

6 Click the **OK** button to close the Group dialog box.

7 Click the **Execute Query** button on the toolbar to run the query to check that the grouping is correct, as shown in Figure 3-69. Next, specify the fields to be summed.

data grouped by TERMID

data grouped by CALLID within TERMID

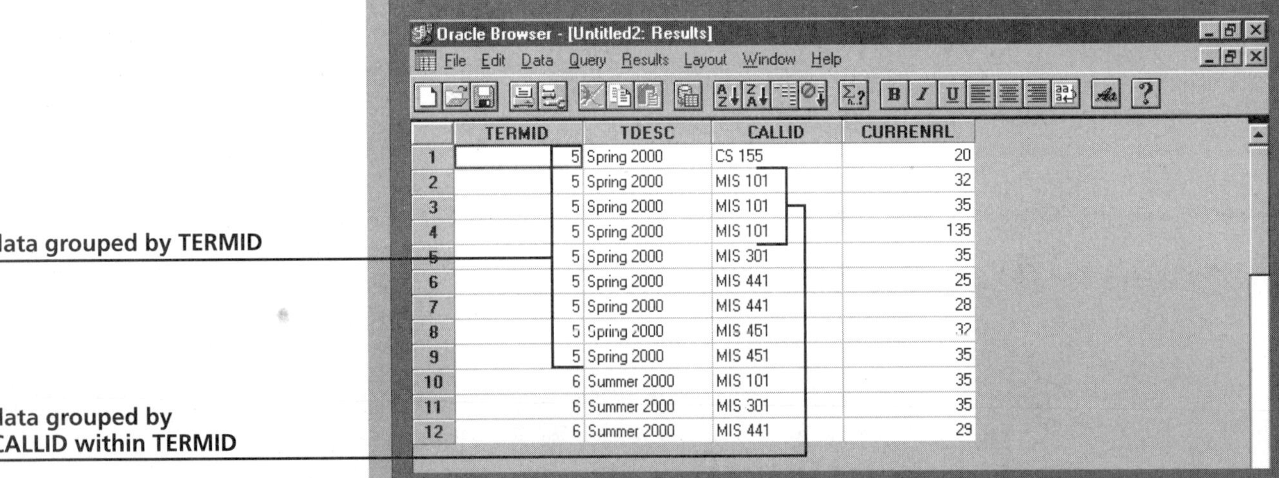

	TERMID	TDESC	CALLID	CURRENRL
1	5	Spring 2000	CS 155	20
2	5	Spring 2000	MIS 101	32
3	5	Spring 2000	MIS 101	35
4	5	Spring 2000	MIS 101	135
5	5	Spring 2000	MIS 301	35
6	5	Spring 2000	MIS 441	25
7	5	Spring 2000	MIS 441	28
8	5	Spring 2000	MIS 451	32
9	5	Spring 2000	MIS 451	35
10	6	Summer 2000	MIS 101	35
11	6	Summer 2000	MIS 301	35
12	6	Summer 2000	MIS 441	29

Figure 3-69: Query output to check grouping

8 Click **Results** on the menu bar, and then click **Totals** to open the Totals dialog box. Click **CURRENRL** as the Select Column, and click the **Total** Summary Operations check box, as shown in Figure 3-70.

your user name will appear here

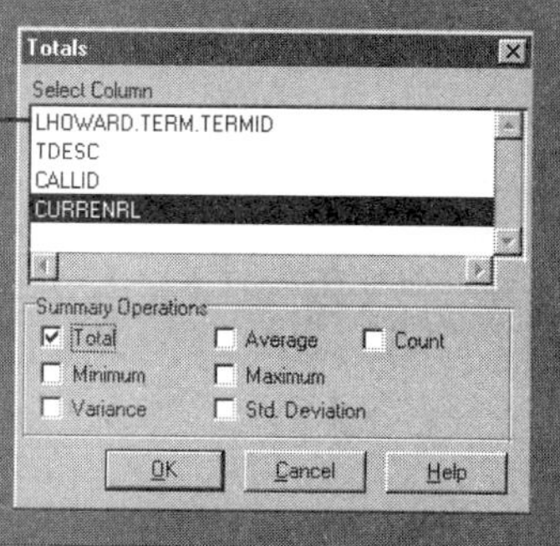

Figure 3-70: Selecting the column to total

9 Click the **OK** button to close the Totals dialog box. The totals for the CURRENRL column should appear, as shown in Figure 3-71.

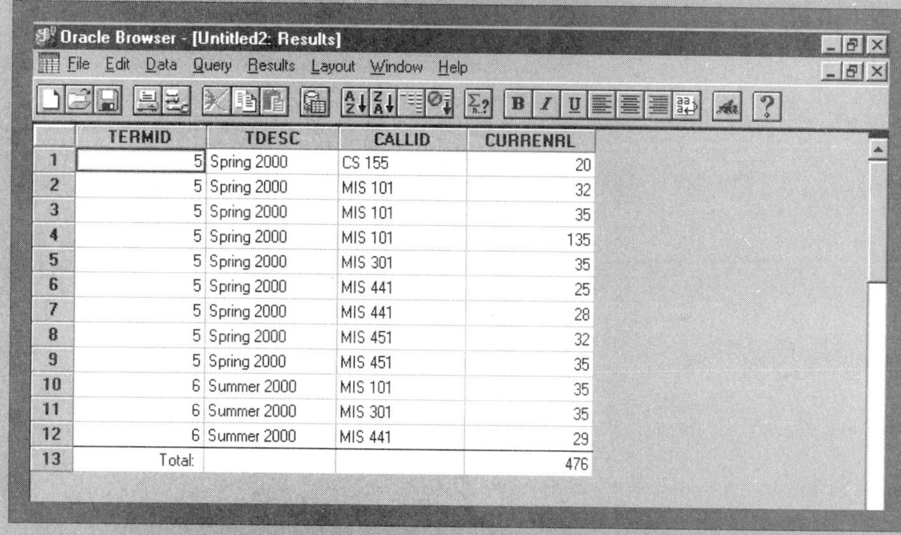

	TERMID	TDESC	CALLID	CURRENRL
1	5	Spring 2000	CS 155	20
2	5	Spring 2000	MIS 101	32
3	5	Spring 2000	MIS 101	35
4	5	Spring 2000	MIS 101	135
5	5	Spring 2000	MIS 301	35
6	5	Spring 2000	MIS 441	25
7	5	Spring 2000	MIS 441	28
8	5	Spring 2000	MIS 451	32
9	5	Spring 2000	MIS 451	35
10	6	Summer 2000	MIS 101	35
11	6	Summer 2000	MIS 301	35
12	6	Summer 2000	MIS 441	29
13	Total:			476

Figure 3-71: Query output showing CURRENRL total

HELP? If the totals do not appear automatically, execute the query again.

The query isn't finished yet—the requirement was to sum the enrollments for each course *and* for each term. To do this, you will have to create a **break** on these fields, which is similar to a SQL GROUP BY statement.

To create a break:

1 Click **Results** on the menu bar, and then click **Break**. Click **<your user name>.TERM.TERMID** as the first break field, click the **Copy** button, click **CALLID** as the second break field, click the **Copy** button, and then click the **OK** button. The query output should look like Figure 3-72.

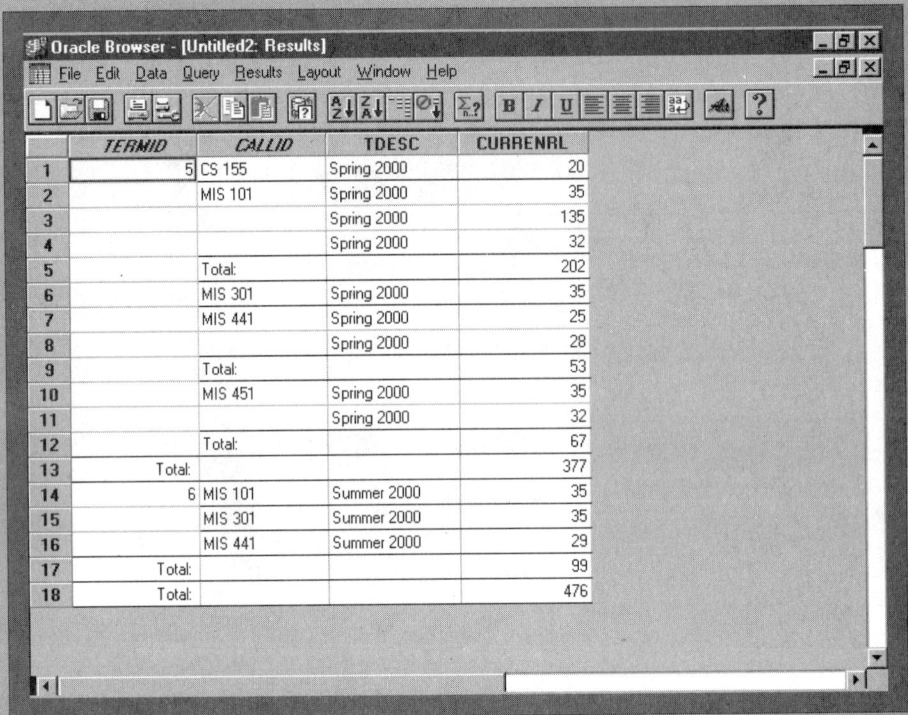

	TERMID	CALLID	TDESC	CURRENRL
1	5	CS 155	Spring 2000	20
2		MIS 101	Spring 2000	35
3			Spring 2000	135
4			Spring 2000	32
5		Total:		202
6		MIS 301	Spring 2000	35
7		MIS 441	Spring 2000	25
8			Spring 2000	28
9		Total:		53
10		MIS 451	Spring 2000	35
11			Spring 2000	32
12		Total:		67
13	Total:			377
14	6	MIS 101	Summer 2000	35
15		MIS 301	Summer 2000	35
16		MIS 441	Summer 2000	29
17	Total:			99
18	Total:			476

Figure 3-72: Final query output

2 Click **Query** on the menu bar, click **Show SQL**, select the SQL text, click **Edit** on the menu bar, and then click **Copy**.

3 Click the **Oracle SQL*Plus** command button on the taskbar, click **Edit** on the menu bar, click **Paste**, and then execute the query. See Figure 3-73.

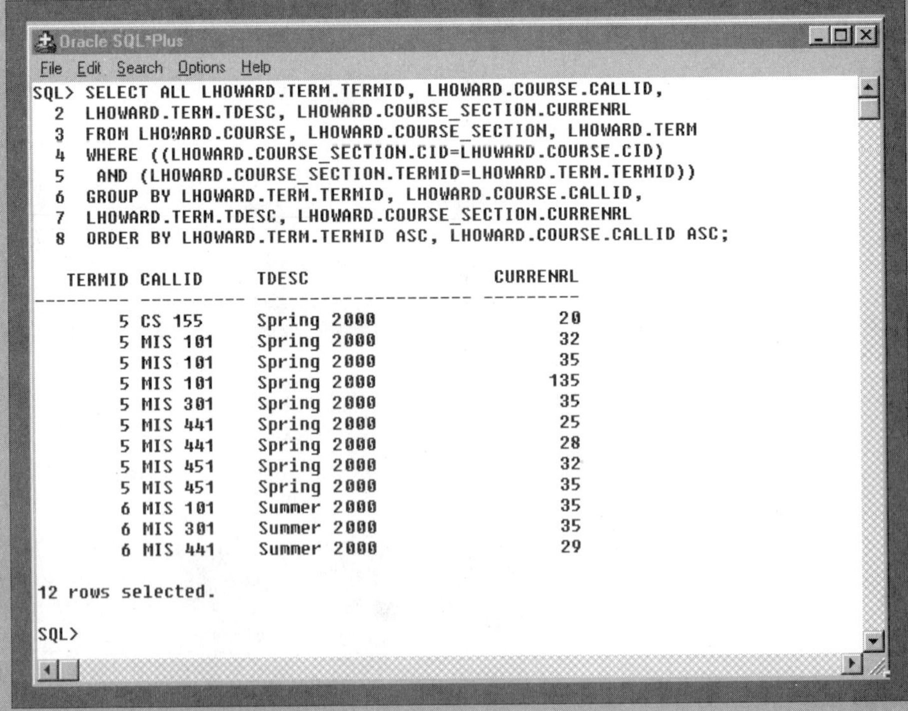


```
SQL> SELECT ALL LHOWARD.TERM.TERMID, LHOWARD.COURSE.CALLID,
  2  LHOWARD.TERM.TDESC, LHOWARD.COURSE_SECTION.CURRENRL
  3  FROM LHOWARD.COURSE, LHOWARD.COURSE_SECTION, LHOWARD.TERM
  4  WHERE ((LHOWARD.COURSE_SECTION.CID=LHOWARD.COURSE.CID)
  5   AND (LHOWARD.COURSE_SECTION.TERMID=LHOWARD.TERM.TERMID))
  6  GROUP BY LHOWARD.TERM.TERMID, LHOWARD.COURSE.CALLID,
  7  LHOWARD.TERM.TDESC, LHOWARD.COURSE_SECTION.CURRENRL
  8  ORDER BY LHOWARD.TERM.TERMID ASC, LHOWARD.COURSE.CALLID ASC;

   TERMID CALLID     TDESC                 CURRENRL
--------- ---------- -------------------- ---------
        5 CS 155     Spring 2000                 20
        5 MIS 101    Spring 2000                 32
        5 MIS 101    Spring 2000                 35
        5 MIS 101    Spring 2000                135
        5 MIS 301    Spring 2000                 35
        5 MIS 441    Spring 2000                 25
        5 MIS 441    Spring 2000                 28
        5 MIS 451    Spring 2000                 32
        5 MIS 451    Spring 2000                 35
        6 MIS 101    Summer 2000                 35
        6 MIS 301    Summer 2000                 35
        6 MIS 441    Summer 2000                 29

12 rows selected.

SQL>
```

Figure 3-73: Final query output in SQL*Plus

The GROUP BY and ORDER BY commands are included in the SQL code, but the SUM command is not. Arithmetic operations in Browser are applied only to the final query output and are not translated into SQL.

Now you will save your query and exit the Oracle Browser.

To save your query and exit Browser:

1. Click the **Oracle Browser** command button on the taskbar, and then click the **Close** button to close the Show SQL window.
2. Click the **Save** button on the toolbar, and then save the query in the Chapter3 folder on your Student Disk as **term.brw**.
3. Click **File** on the menu bar, and then click **Exit** to exit Browser.

Using Oracle Navigator to Insert, Update, and Delete Data

The SQL INSERT, UPDATE, and DELETE statements are the basis for most data operations in Oracle applications. Oracle Navigator provides a visual environment for inserting and modifying small test data sets.

Inserting New Records Using Navigator

You can use Navigator for inserting records, just like you would use a spreadsheet for inserting new data rows. Using Navigator, you can select an existing row and then insert a new empty row either above or below it. You will insert some new data records using Navigator next.

To insert a new record using Navigator:

1. Start the Oracle Navigator, and then connect to the Oracle database.
2. Click the **plus box** to the left of your connection name, and then click to the left of the table icon.
3. Right-click the **LOCATION** table icon, and then click **Open**. All of the data records in the sample database should display.
4. Click the row label for row 13 to select the row, right-click the row, and then click **Insert After**. A blank row appears under row 13.
5. Click in the LOCID box for row 14, type **58**, press the **Tab** key, and then enter the rest of the data shown in Figure 3-74.

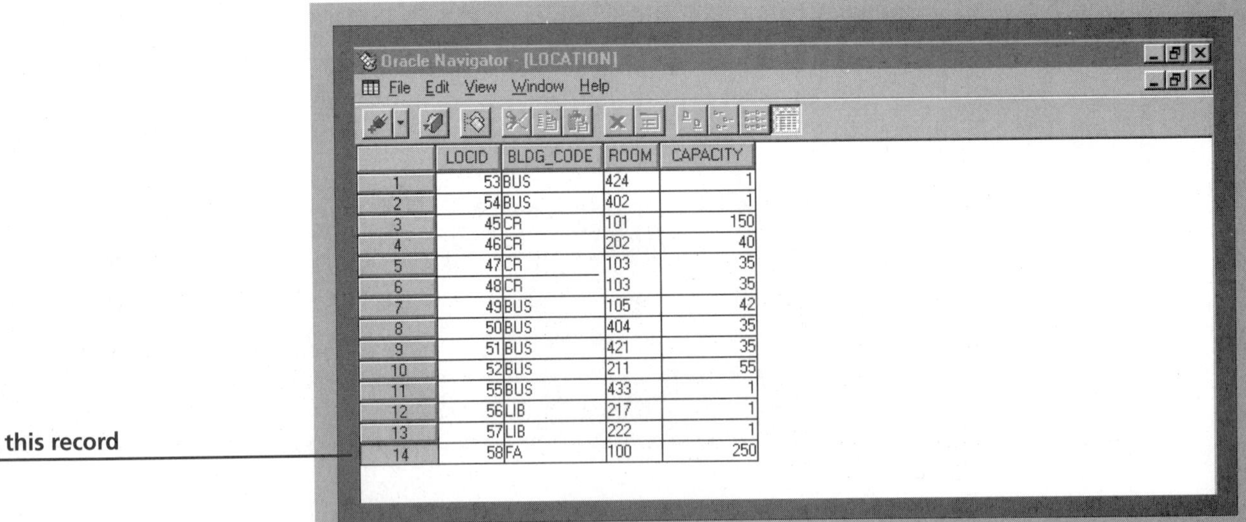

	LOCID	BLDG_CODE	ROOM	CAPACITY
1	53	BUS	424	1
2	54	BUS	402	1
3	45	CR	101	150
4	46	CR	202	40
5	47	CR	103	35
6	48	CR	103	35
7	49	BUS	105	42
8	50	BUS	404	35
9	51	BUS	421	35
10	52	BUS	211	55
11	55	BUS	433	1
12	56	LIB	217	1
13	57	LIB	222	1
14	58	FA	100	250

Figure 3-74: Entering data for LOCID 58

6 Insert a blank row for row 15, and then enter the data for LOCID 59, as shown in Figure 3-75. Then insert another blank row for row 16, and enter the data for LOCID 60 as shown in Figure 3-75.

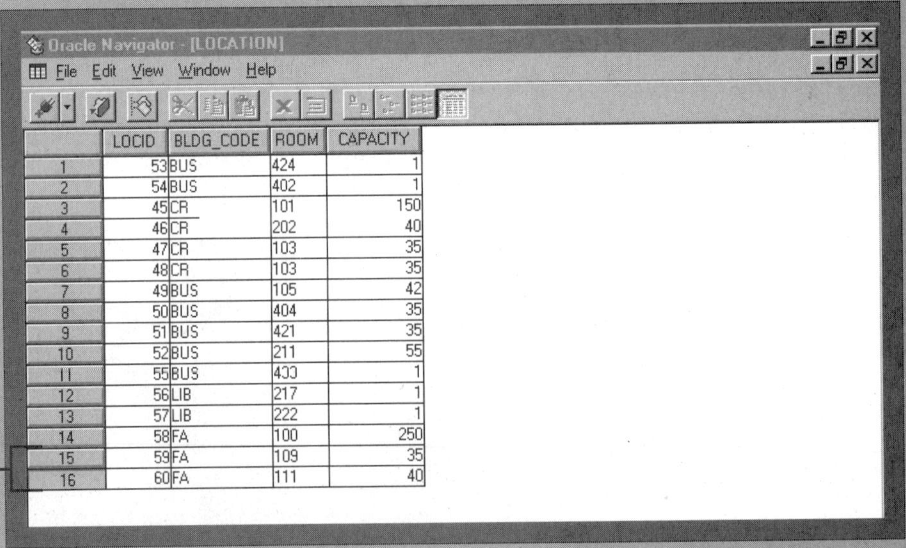

	LOCID	BLDG_CODE	ROOM	CAPACITY
1	53	BUS	424	1
2	54	BUS	402	1
3	45	CR	101	150
4	46	CR	202	40
5	47	CR	103	35
6	48	CR	103	35
7	49	BUS	105	42
8	50	BUS	404	35
9	51	BUS	421	35
10	52	BUS	211	55
11	55	BUS	433	1
12	56	LIB	217	1
13	57	LIB	222	1
14	58	FA	100	250
15	59	FA	109	35
16	60	FA	111	40

Figure 3-75: Entering data for LOCIDs 59 and 60

7 Close the LOCATION table window by clicking the **Close** button ☒, and then click the Yes button to commit the data.

HELP? Some versions of Navigator do not display the message box to confirm committing the data, but your new records still will be saved.

Updating Existing Records Using Navigator

Navigator also enables users to update existing data records. The user can view the given record field, and then select the field and enter a new value or edit the current value. You will update data records using Navigator next.

Selected text is replaced automatically when you start typing.

To update a record using Navigator:

1. Right-click the **STUDENT** table icon, and then click **Open**.
2. Click the **Maximize** button to maximize the STUDENT table window.
3. Click the **SADD** field for row 3, and then change Daniel Black's address by typing **422 State Street.**
4. Press the **Tab** key, and then change SCITY by typing **Eau Claire.**
5. Press the **Tab** key twice, and then change SZIP by typing **54702.**
6. Press the **Tab** key, and then change SPHONE by typing **7155558360.**
7. Click the **Close** button to close the STUDENT table window, and then click the **Yes** button (if necessary) to commit the data.

Deleting Records Using Navigator

To delete a record in Navigator, you select the row to be deleted, right-click, and then select the Delete Row command. You will delete data records using Navigator next.

To delete a record using Navigator:

1. Open the **COURSE_UPDATE** table.
2. Select row 3 (CID = 2, FID = 2) by clicking the row number.
3. Right-click the selected row, and then click **Delete Row.**
4. Click the **Yes** button when you are asked if you are sure that you want to delete the selected row.
5. Click the **Close** button to close the COURSE_UPDATE table window. When you delete a record using the Oracle Navigator, the COMMIT happens immediately rather than when you exit the table window.

Navigator also provides a visual way to insert, modify, and delete data records. However, it is does not allow you to modify or delete multiple records with a single command.

Granting Table Privileges to Other Users

When you create a database table in Oracle, other users cannot modify your tables or view or change your data records unless you give them explicit privileges to do so. Figure 3-76 lists some commonly used table privileges and their descriptions.

Command	Description
ALTER	Allows the user to change a table's structure using the ALTER TABLE command
DELETE	Allows the user to delete records from a table using the DELETE command
INSERT	Allows the user to insert records into a table using the INSERT command
REFERENCES	Allows the user to reference table fields as foreign keys using the REFERENCED BY command
SELECT	Allows the user to view data using the SELECT command
UPDATE	Allows the user to modify data using the UPDATE command
ALL	Grants all privileges to the user

Figure 3-76: Commonly used table privileges

Table privileges are granted to other users using the SQL GRANT command. The general format of the SQL GRANT command is:

```
GRANT <privilege1, privilege2, …>
ON <tablename>
TO <user1, user2, …>;
```

To grant a privilege:

1. Click the **Oracle SQL*Plus** command button on the taskbar to activate SQL*Plus.
2. Type the query shown in Figure 3-77 to grant SELECT and ALTER privileges on your STUDENT table to two other students in your class by substituting the students' user names for MORRISJP and MORRISCM in the query. When your query executes successfully, the confirmation message "Grant succeeded" is displayed. Note that you can grant privileges for only one table at a time, but that you can grant privileges to many users at once. If you want to grant privileges to every database user, you can use the word PUBLIC in the TO clause.

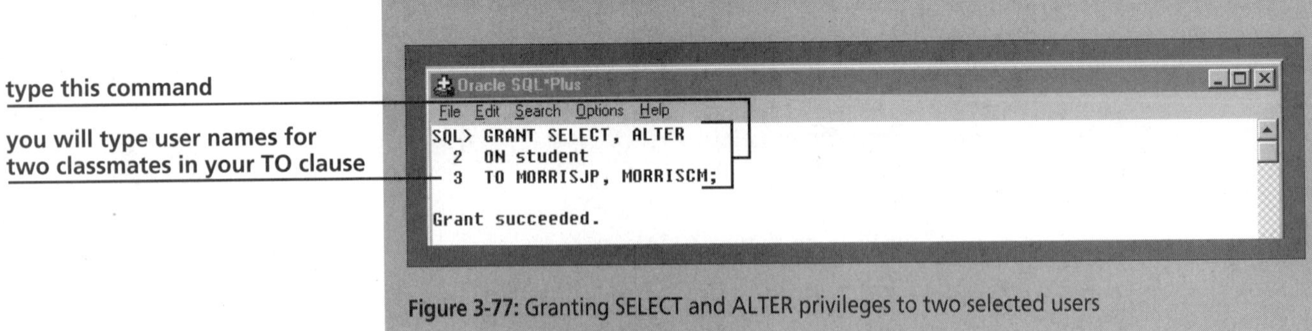

Figure 3-77: Granting SELECT and ALTER privileges to two selected users

3 Type the command shown in Figure 3-78 to grant all privileges on your FACULTY table to all database users.

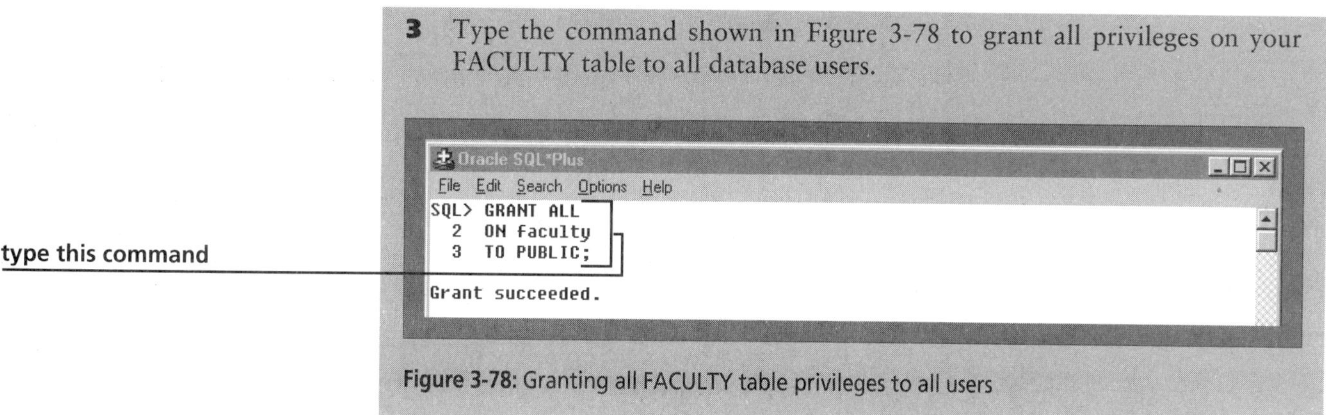

Figure 3-78: Granting all FACULTY table privileges to all users

Revoking Table Privileges

To cancel a privilege to a user, you use the SQL REVOKE command. The general format of the REVOKE command is:

```
REVOKE <privilege1, privilege2, etc.>
ON <tablename>
FROM <user1, user2, etc.>;
```

To revoke a privilege:

1 Type the command shown in Figure 3-79 to revoke the select and alter privileges that you granted to your two fellow classmates on the STUDENT table. Remember that you will have to change the user names from MORRISJP and MORRISCM to the user names you granted these privileges to in Figure 3-77.

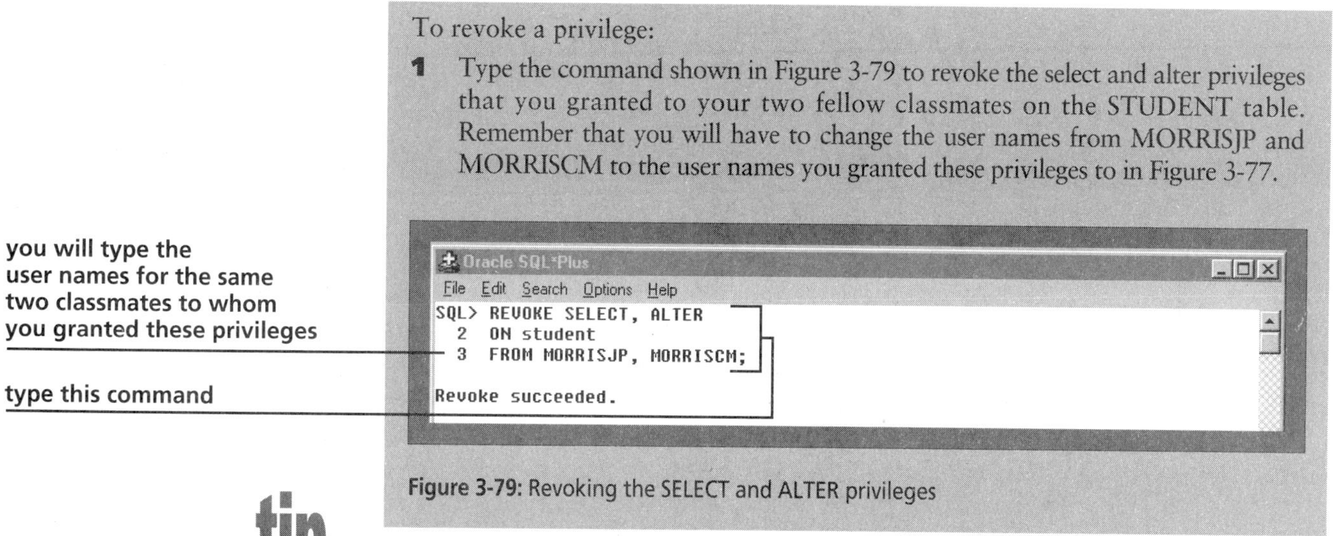

Figure 3-79: Revoking the SELECT and ALTER privileges

If you try to REVOKE a privilege that has not been granted yet, you will receive an error.

Granting and Revoking Table Privileges Using Navigator

You also can use Navigator to grant and revoke table privileges. Next you will grant ALTER and SELECT privileges on your STUDENT table to all database users.

To grant privileges using Navigator:

1 Click the **Oracle Navigator** command button on the taskbar to activate that window.

2 Right-click your **STUDENT** table, and then click **Properties**. Click the **Object Privilege** tab.

3 Click the **Privilege for** list arrow, and then click **PUBLIC**, as shown in Figure 3-80.

your user list will be different

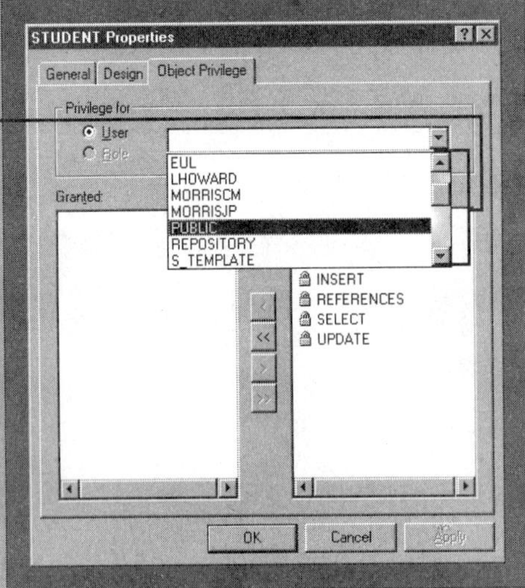

Figure 3-80: Selecting user PUBLIC

4 Click **ALTER** in the Remaining list box, and then click  to move the ALTER privilege into the Granted list box.

5 Double-click **SELECT** in the Remaining list box. Note that this also moves the privilege into the Granted list box, as shown in Figure 3-81.

tip

To select all remaining privileges, click «. To deselect all granted privileges, click ».

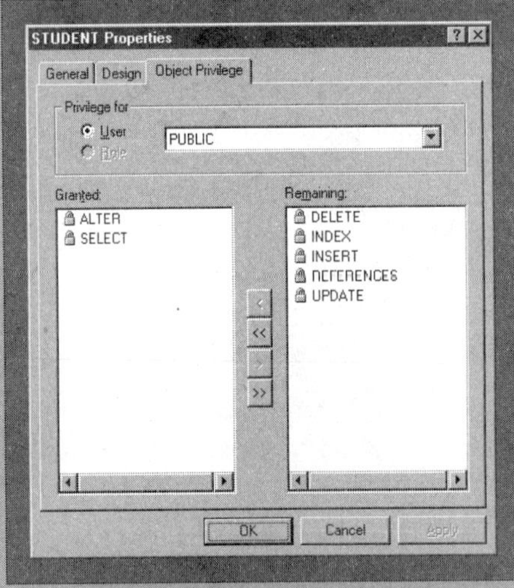

Figure 3-81: Granting ALTER and SELECT privileges to PUBLIC

6 Click the **OK** button to close the STUDENT Properties window.

7 Right-click the **STUDENT** table again, click **Properties**, and then click the **Object Privilege** tab.

8 Click the **Privilege for** list arrow, and then **PUBLIC**. Observe that the privileges granted previously are now displayed in the Granted list box.

9 Revoke these privileges by selecting each one at a time and then clicking .

tip

To revoke all privileges, click ».

10 Click the **OK** button to save your changes and close the STUDENT Properties window.

11 Open the FACULTY Properties window, and revoke all of the privileges you granted to PUBLIC on the FACULTY table.

Now you can delete your Navigator connection and exit the Oracle programs.

To exit the Oracle programs and disconnect from the database:

1 Delete your user connection.

2 Exit the Navigator by clicking the **Close** button ☒.

3 Click the **Oracle SQL*Plus** command button on the taskbar, and then close SQL*Plus by typing **EXIT** at the SQL prompt.

SUMMARY

- Database developers must have a complete understanding of SQL commands for selecting, inserting, updating, and deleting data because these commands are used extensively in Oracle database applications.
- The INSERT command is used to insert new data records into a table. The INSERT command can be used to insert all of the data fields into a record, or to insert only specific fields. Before you can insert a new data record, you must ensure that all of the foreign key records that it references have been previously inserted. Character fields in Oracle are case sensitive, and values must be enclosed within single quotation marks when they are inserted. To add text strings with embedded single quotation marks, type the single quotation mark twice.
- DATE fields are inserted as characters and then converted to dates using the TO_DATE function. DATE fields also store time values.
- A transaction is one or more related SQL commands that constitute a logical unit of work. All parts of the transaction must be completed, or the database will contain inconsistent data.
- When you create a new table or update the structure of an existing table, the change is effective immediately at the central database on the server. When you insert, update, or delete database records, the database on the server is not changed until you explicitly commit your changes using the COMMIT command. Other users cannot see the records you have added or access the rows you have modified because these rows are locked until you commit your changes. It is a good idea to commit your changes often so the records will be available to other users and so your changes will be saved if you do not exit normally because of a power failure or workstation malfunction.
- A rollback enables you to return the database to its original state by undoing the effects of all the commands since the last COMMIT. A savepoint marks the beginnings of individual sections of a transaction. You can roll back transactions to particular savepoints.
- The SELECT statement is used to view database records. Use the SELECT DISTINCT command to suppress duplicate records in query output.
- Query outputs can be sorted using the ORDER BY clause.
- SQL has operations for adding, subtracting, multiplying, and dividing query values and group functions for summing, averaging, finding the maximum or minimum value, or counting the number of records returned by a query.

- To join multiple tables, you must include every involved table in the FROM clause, and include a join condition for every table in the WHERE clause.
- The SYSDATE function returns the current system (server) date.
- A UNION query combines the results of two queries that are not related through foreign key relationships. A union requires that both queries have the same number of display columns in the SELECT clause, and each column in the first query must have the same data type as the corresponding column in the second query.
- A database view looks and acts like a table. It is created from a query and does not physically exist in the database, but it is derived from other database tables.
- Database records are modified using the SQL UPDATE command.
- Database records are deleted using the SQL DELETE command. You cannot delete a record if it exists as a foreign key reference in another record.
- Use the SELECT ... FOR UPDATE command to view a record and then update it in the same transaction. The SELECT ... FOR UPDATE and COMMIT commands must be issued in a transaction that executes without requiring additional user intervention.
- The Oracle Browser provides a visual environment for creating SELECT queries. Browser queries can be saved in the file system or database, and they can be used to generate SQL commands.
- The Oracle Navigator provides a visual environment for inserting, updating, and deleting data records.
- Other users cannot view or modify your database tables unless you give them explicit privileges to do so. Table privileges can be given using the SQL GRANT command, and revoked using the REVOKE command. The Oracle Navigator provides a visual environment for granting and revoking table privileges.

REVIEW QUESTIONS

1. In an INSERT statement, in what order do the column names in the VALUES clause have to be?
2. Write the TO_DATE function that converts the value 09/16/99 to a date using the format DD-MON-YYYY.
3. What is the difference between the YY and RR date format?
4. Write a TO_DATE function to convert the value 10:45:07 P.M. to a date.
5. Why does Oracle require you to issue a COMMIT command?
6. What is the purpose of a savepoint?
7. Write a SELECT statement to retrieve all of the fields and rows from the STUDENT table.
8. Write a SELECT statement to retrieve the SFNAME and SLNAME from the STUDENT table for SID 105.
9. How do you suppress duplicate records in query output?
10. In what order are AND and OR operations evaluated? How can you force a different order?
11. What is the default sort order in the ORDER BY command?
12. What symbols are used to specify addition, subtraction, multiplication, and division operations in SQL?
13. In what order are arithmetic operations evaluated in SQL?
14. What is a group function in SQL?
15. What is the purpose of the GROUP BY clause?
16. What is a join condition?

17. If the result of a query joining multiple tables is many more records than you expected, what probably happened?
18. When do you need to use a union?
19. How do the two queries in a union need to correspond?
20. What is a database view?
21. What is the purpose of the SELECT ... FOR UPDATE command?
22. What is the purpose of the NOWAIT statement in the SELECT ... FOR UPDATE command?
23. What are the three ways to save Oracle Browser queries?
24. Which SQL group functions are translated into SQL code in the Oracle Browser? Which functions are not?
25. How can you specify that a privilege is to be granted to all database users?

PROBLEM-SOLVING CASES

Northwoods University Database

Save all SQL*Plus queries in a text file named CH3NWSQL.TXT in the Chapter3 folder on your Student Disk. Save Browser queries in the Chapter3 folder on your Student Disk using the specified filename with a .brw extension.

1. Create a diagram like the one shown in Figure 3-39 to specify a query that finds the names of all courses offered during the Summer 2000 semester. (*Hint:* Use TERMDESC = 'Summer 2000' as a search condition.) Based on your diagram, write the query in SQL*Plus.
2. Create a diagram like the one shown in Figure 3-39 to write a query that lists the name of every student that faculty member Kim Cox advises. (*Hint:* Use FLNAME and FFNAME in your search conditions.) Based on your diagram, write the query in SQL*Plus.
3. Use SQL*Plus to list the course call ID, section number, term description, and grade for every course taken by student Sarah Miller. (*Hint:* Use SLNAME and SFNAME in your search conditions.)
4. Use SQL*Plus to calculate the total number of students taught by John Blanchard during the Spring 2000 term. Use the CURRENRL figures, and include FLNAME, FFNAME, and TERMDESC in your search condition.
5. Use Browser to create a query that lists the course name and section of all courses that were filled to capacity (CURRENRL = MAXENRL) during the Spring 2000 term. Use TERMDESC in your search condition. Save the query as CH3NW5.brw. Copy your SQL command into a text file named CH3NWSQL.TXT.
6. Use Browser to calculate the total credits earned so far by student Brian Robinson. (*Hint:* Use SLNAME and SFNAME in your search conditions.) Save the query as CH3NW6.brw. Copy your SQL command into a text file named CH3NWSQL.TXT.
7. Use Browser to calculate the total number of student credits generated during the Spring 2000 term (student credits = CURRENRL times course credits). Use TERMDESC in your search condition. Save your query as CH3NW7.brw. Copy your SQL command into a text file named CH3NWSQL.TXT. (*Hint*: You will need to define a new column named STUDENT_CREDITS by clicking Results, and then clicking Define Column on the menu bar.)

8. Write the commands to grant ALTER, DELETE, INSERT, UPDATE, and SELECT privileges to PUBLIC for all of your database tables into a text file named CH3NWSQL.TXT.

Clearwater Traders Database

Save all SQL*Plus queries in a text file named CH3CTSQL.TXT in the Chapter3 folder on your Student Disk. Save Browser queries in the Chapter3 folder on your Student Disk using the specified filename with a .brw extension.

1. Run the script named emptycw.sql to create the Clearwater Traders database tables. Then use SQL*Plus to insert the first record into each of the Clearwater database tables, using Figure 1-7 in Chapter 1. Insert other records required as foreign keys as necessary.

Before doing Exercises 2 through 6, run the script named clearwat.sql to create all of the Clearwater Traders database tables and insert all the sample data records.

2. Use SQL*Plus to find the name of every customer who has placed orders using the Web site as a source. Use ORDERSOURCE in your search condition.
3. Use SQL*Plus to find the name of every item that is currently out of stock (QOH = 0).
4. Use Browser to find the name and address of every customer who ordered items in the Women's Clothing category. Save your query as CH3CW4.brw. Copy your SQL command into a text file named CH3CWSQL.TXT.
5. Use Browser to find the total amount of all orders generated by orders with the Web Site as a source. Save your query as CH3CW5.brw. Copy your SQL command into a text file named CH3CWSQL.TXT.
6. Write the commands to grant ALTER, DELETE, INSERT, UPDATE, and SELECT privileges to PUBLIC for all of your database tables.

Chapter 4 objectives

- View, insert, update, and delete data records using an Oracle form application
- Use the Object Navigator within the Forms Designer
- Create single- and multiple-table data block form applications
- Enhance the appearance of a form using boilerplate text and objects

CHAPTER 4

Creating Oracle Data Block Forms

Introduction The Oracle Developer/2000 applications (Oracle Forms, Oracle Reports, and Oracle Graphics) are used to develop end-user applications that interact with Oracle databases. Oracle Forms is used to create Windows applications for working with data in Oracle database tables. In this chapter, you will learn about **data block forms,** which are forms that are explicitly connected to specific database tables.

Using a Data Block Form Application

Before you learn how to create a data block form, you will run an existing application named CUSTOMER_FORM to become familiar with the appearance and function of a data block form. Before you open the form, you will run a SQL script that drops any existing tables for the Clearwater Traders database and then re-creates the new tables and inserts all of the data values into them.

To run the script:

1. Start SQL*Plus and log on to the database.
2. Type **START A:\Chapter4\clearwat.sql** at the SQL prompt to run the script.

   HELP? If your Student Disk is in another disk drive, substitute the appropriate drive letter in the command to start the script.

   HELP? If you have trouble running the script file, ask your instructor or technical support person for help.

Next you will run the CUSTOMER_FORM application file that is stored on your Student Disk.

When you start an FMX file by double-clicking it, the filename and pathname cannot contain any spaces.

To run the CUSTOMER_FORM application:

1. Start Windows Explorer, double-click the drive that contains your Student Disk, double-click the **Chapter4 folder**, and then double-click the **Custdemo.fmx** file. The Developer/2000 Forms Runtime Logon window opens. Log on to the database, and then click the **Connect** button. The CUSTOMER_FORM application opens, as shown in Figure 4-1.

   HELP? If the Open With dialog box opens instead of the Logon dialog box, your workstation is not configured to open executable Oracle Forms files (which have .fmx extensions) using the Forms Runtime application. Windows 95 users will click the Other button, click the Browse button, click the F45run32.exe file in the ORAWIN95\BIN\ directory, click the Open button, and then click the OK button. Windows NT users will click the Other button, click the \ORANT\BIN\F45run32.exe file, and then click the OK button. Now the Logon dialog box will open automatically when you double-click *.fmx filenames.

   HELP? If the form does not open properly after you create the association, then you probably associated the .fmx file with the wrong program. To delete the association, click View on the Windows Explorer menu bar, and then click Options. Click the File Types tab, and then scroll down in the file list until you find an entry named FMX Files. Click FMX Files, click the Remove button, and then click the Yes button to confirm that you want to remove the association. Click the Close button to close the Options dialog box, and then repeat the steps in the previous HELP? to create the file association.

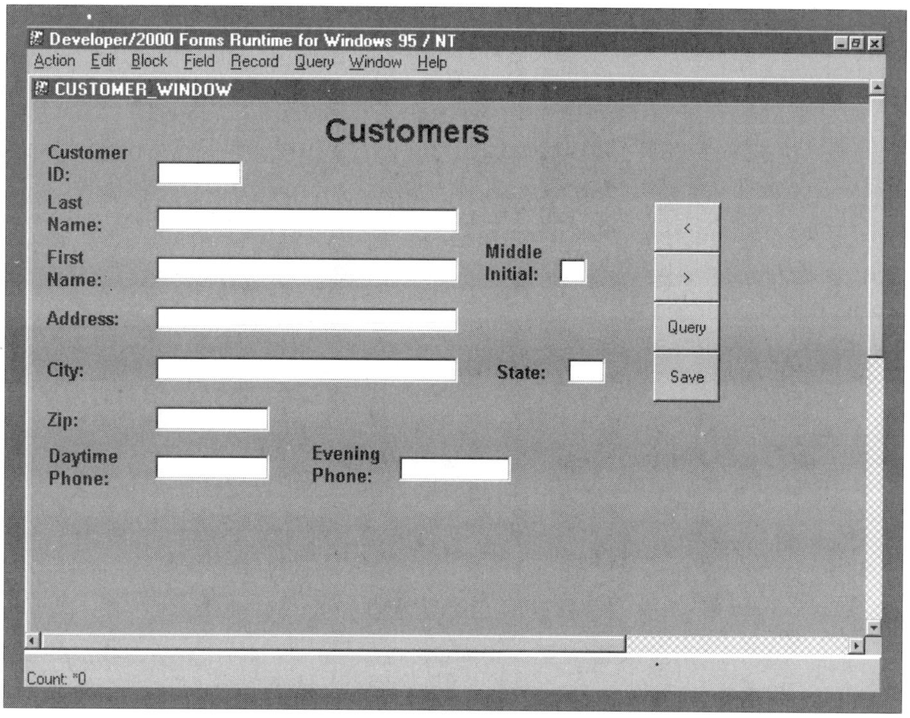

Figure 4-1: CUSTOMER_FORM application

CUSTOMER_FORM is an Oracle Forms application associated with the Clearwater Traders CUSTOMER table. This form can be used to insert new records and modify, delete, or view existing records. First you will insert a new record into the CUSTOMER table. Using a form to add records is the equivalent of adding records in SQL using the INSERT command.

To insert a new record using the CUSTOMER_FORM:

1. Click in the Customer ID field, and then enter **1000**.
2. Press the **Tab** key to move to the Last Name field, and then enter **Chen**.
3. Press the **Tab** key to move to the First Name field, and then enter **Emily**.
4. Press the **Tab** key to move to the Middle Initial field, and then enter **M**.
5. Press the **Tab** key to move to the Address field, and then enter **4340 Pine Drive**.
6. Press the **Tab** key to move to the City field, and then enter **Mondovi**.
7. Press the **Tab** key to move to the State field, and then enter **WI**.

8 Press the **Tab** key to move to the Zip field, and then enter 54705. You will leave the Daytime and Evening Phone fields blank.

9 Click the **Save** button on the Button palette. The confirmation message "FRM-40400: Transaction complete: 1 records applied and saved" appears in the message area in the lower-left corner of the screen, as shown in Figure 4-2.

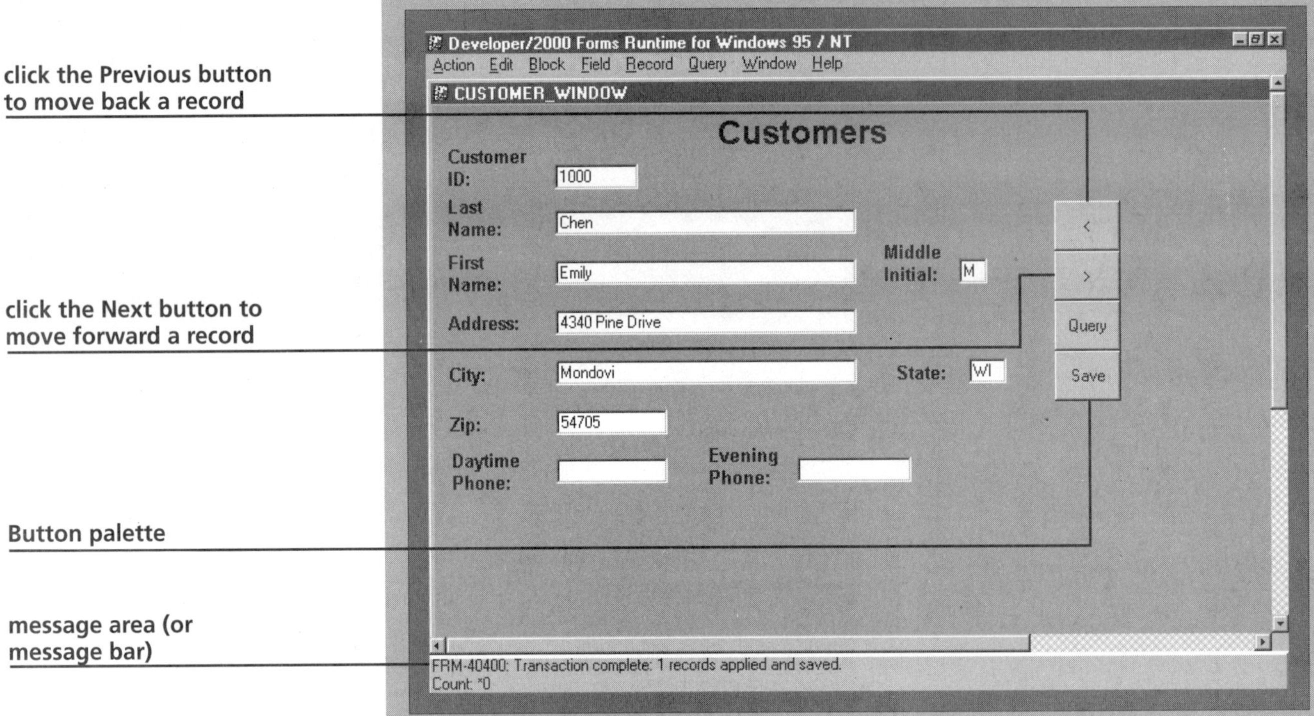

Figure 4-2: Inserting a new record using the CUSTOMER_FORM

Next you will modify an existing record in the CUSTOMER table. Using a form to modify records is the equivalent of modifying records using the SQL UPDATE command. You will change customer Paula Jones's evening phone number next.

To update an existing record:

1 Click the **Query** button on the Button palette. The form fields are cleared, and the form changes to Enter Query mode, as indicated by the mode indicator in Figure 4-3. Forms Runtime has two modes: Normal and Enter Query. The form is in Normal mode until you click the Query button, which changes the form to Enter Query mode. In Enter Query mode, you can enter search parameters in the form fields. To return to Normal mode, you must either execute the query by pressing the F8 key, or cancel the query by pressing Ctrl + Q.

Developer/2000 Forms Runtime for Windows 95 / NT
Action Edit Block Field Record Query Window Help
CUSTOMER_WINDOW
Customers
Customer ID:
Last Name:
First Name:
Middle Initial:
Address:
City:
State:
Zip:
Daytime Phone:
Evening Phone:
<
>
Query
Save
Enter a query; press F8 to execute, Ctrl+q to cancel.
Count: *0 ENTER QUERY

mode indicator

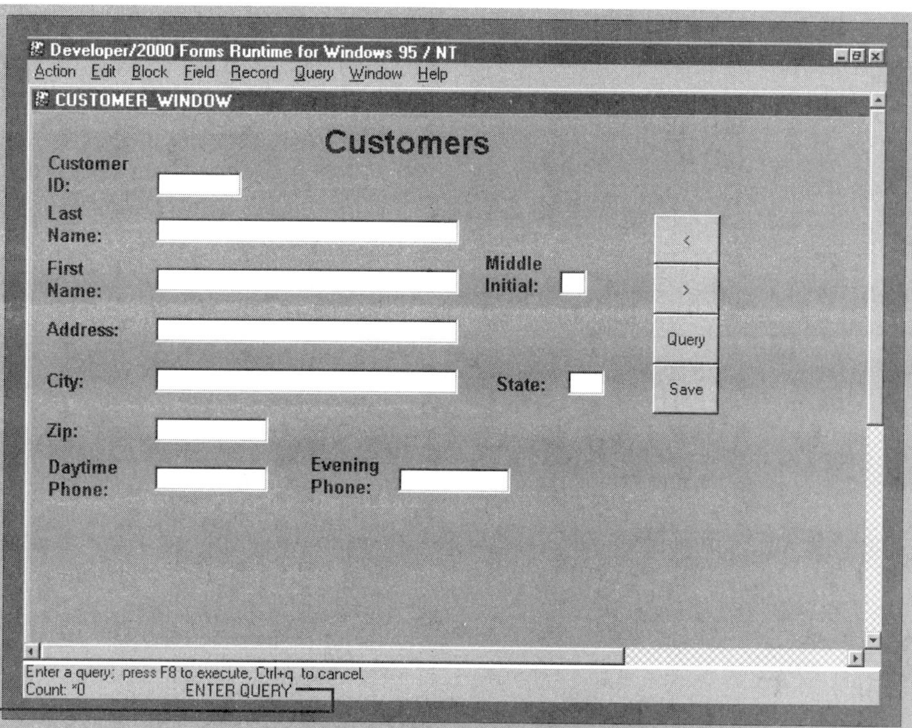

Figure 4-3: CUSTOMER_FORM in Enter Query mode

2 Enter 107 in the Customer ID field.

3 Press the F8 key to execute the query. The complete data record for customer Paula Jones appears in the form. Notice that the messages in the message area and in the mode indicator disappear.

4 Click in the Evening Phone field, and then change the phone number to 7155558975.

5 Click the **Save** button on the Button palette. The confirmation message "FRM-40400: Transaction complete: 1 records applied and saved" appears in the message area, as shown in Figure 4-4.

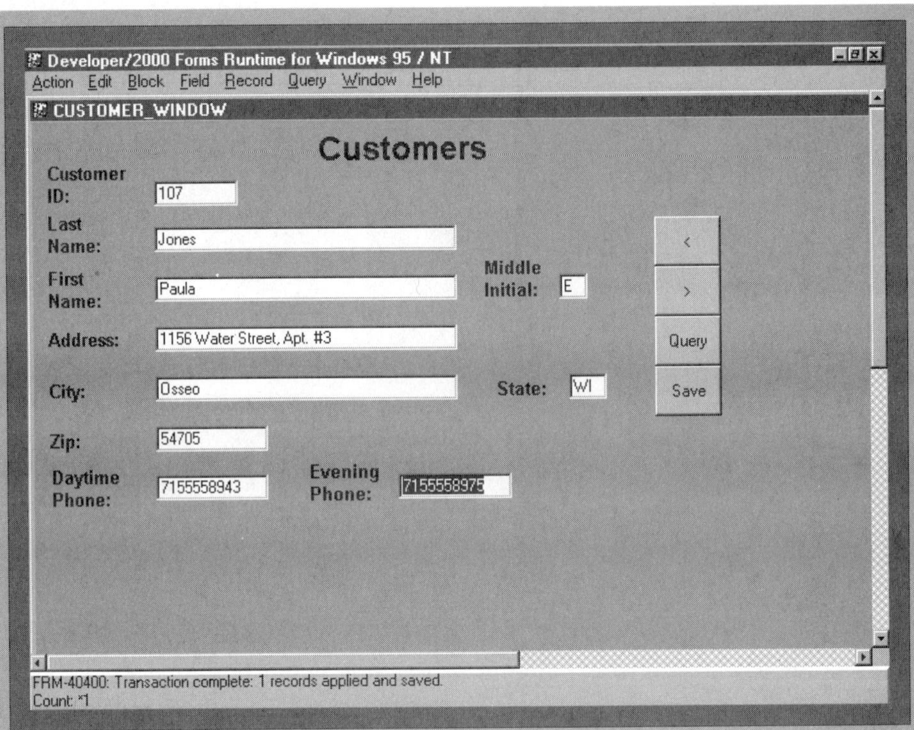

Figure 4-4: Modifying a record

You also can use this form to view data records and step through them sequentially. You will do this next.

To step through the CUSTOMER table records sequentially:

1. Click the **Query** button on the Button palette. The form fields are cleared.
2. Press the **F8** key. Paula Jones's data record (which is the first CUSTOMER record) appears in the form.
3. Click the **Next** button on the Button palette. The next record in the database (customer Mitch Edwards) appears.
4. Click the **Previous** button on the Button palette. Paula Jones's record appears again because it is the record directly in front of Mitch Edwards' record.
5. Click the **Next** button again. Continue clicking the **Next** button until you scroll through all of the CUSTOMER records.

You can use a form to delete data records. You will do this next.

To delete a record from the CUSTOMER table:

1. Click the **Next** button or the **Previous** button on the Button palette until you see customer Emily Chen's record.
2. Click **Record** on the menu bar, and then click **Remove** to delete Emily's record from the form. Alissa White's record now appears in the form because her record was in front of Emily's record in the database.

When you close a form, you are given an option to commit or roll back your changes. You will commit your changes now.

To close the form and commit the changes:

1. Click the **Close** button ☒ on the Forms Runtime title bar. The message window shown in Figure 4-5 appears. You can click the Yes button to commit your changes, the No button to roll back your changes, or the Cancel button to return to the form.

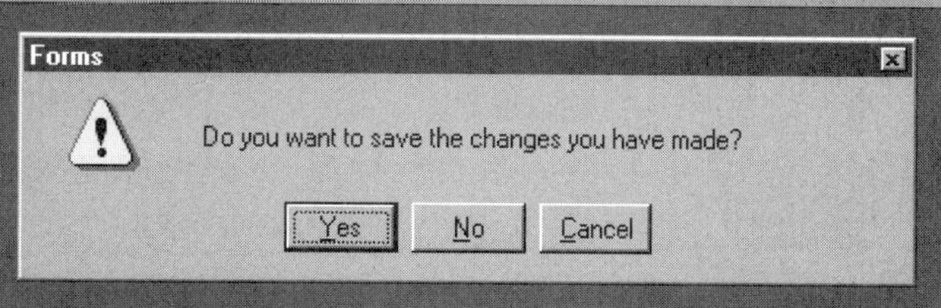

Figure 4-5: Message window asking to save changes

2. Click the Yes button to commit your changes and, if necessary, click the OK button to confirm the commit and close the form.

Form Components and the Object Navigator

Before you start creating an Oracle form, you need to learn about the basic components of a form. Form components are viewed and accessed using an Oracle Forms window called the **Object Navigator**. Figure 4-6 shows the Object Navigator window for the CUSTOMER_FORM. This Object Navigator window shows the form objects in **Ownership View**, where all form object types appear directly below the form module. If an object type has a plus box ⊞ to the left of its name, objects of that type are present in the form.

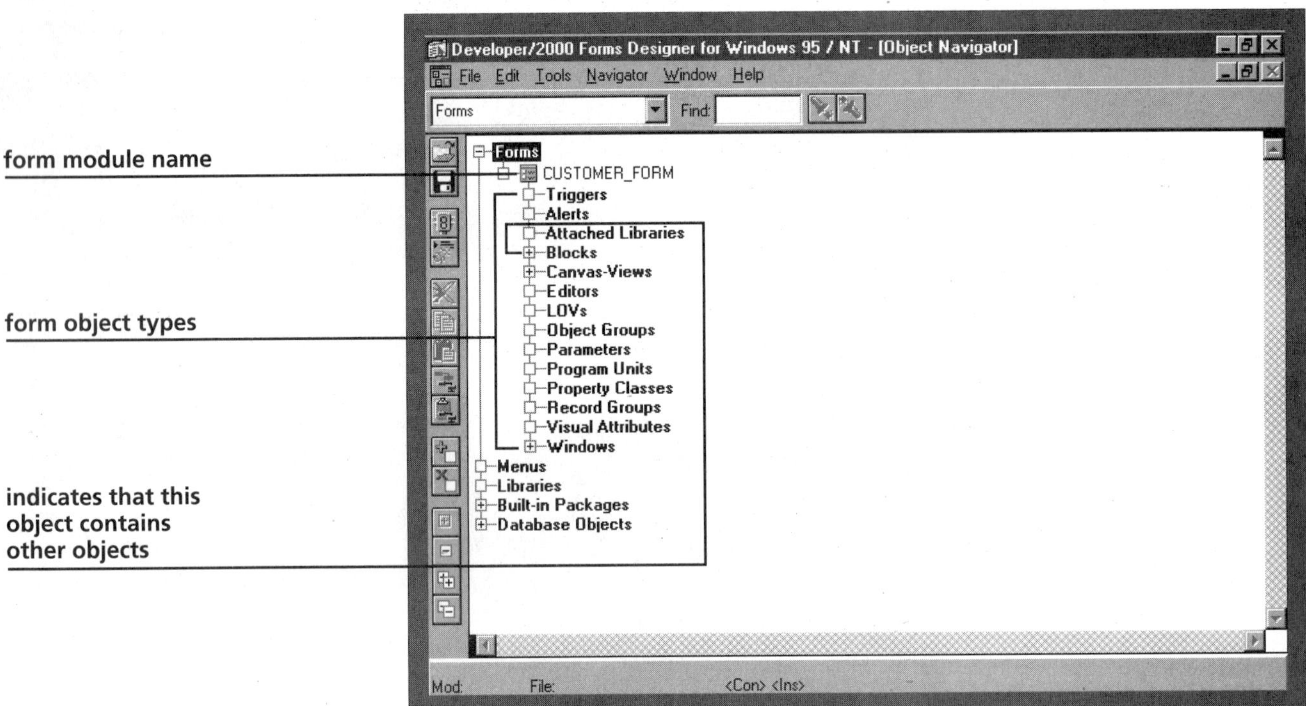

Figure 4-6: CUSTOMER_FORM Object Navigator window in Ownership View

An Oracle Forms application such as the CUSTOMER_FORM application, is called a **form module** or just a form. A form can contain all of the form object types listed. The CUSTOMER_FORM specifically contains blocks, canvas-views, and windows, as indicated by the plus box to the left of the names of these object types. These particular objects are the basic building blocks of a form.

A **window** is the familiar rectangular area on a computer screen that has a title bar at the top. Windows have horizontal and vertical scroll bars, and can be resized, maximized, and minimized. In Oracle Forms applications, you can specify window properties such as title, size, and position on the screen. A form can contain one or more windows. Simple applications usually have only one window, whereas more complex applications might have several windows.

A **canvas-view**, or a **canvas**, is the area in a window where you place **graphical user interface (GUI) objects** such as buttons and text fields. A form window can have multiple canvases. A **block** is a structure that contains a group of GUI objects. A canvas might contain one or more blocks. A **data block** is a block that is related to a database table. When you create a data block, the system automatically generates the text fields and labels for data fields in that table and then creates the code for inserting, modifying, deleting, and viewing data records. In this chapter, you will create form applications using data blocks.

You can expand each object type by clicking the plus box to the left of the object's name. Figure 4-7 shows the expanded view of the CUSTOMER_FORM in the Object Navigator window. The form has two different blocks (CUSTOMER_BLOCK and BUTTON_PALETTE), one canvas (CUSTOMER_CANVAS), and one window (CUSTOMER_WINDOW). The plus boxes to the left of CUSTOMER_BLOCK and BUTTON_PALETTE indicate that these blocks contain more objects that can be viewed by clicking the plus boxes to the left of their names.

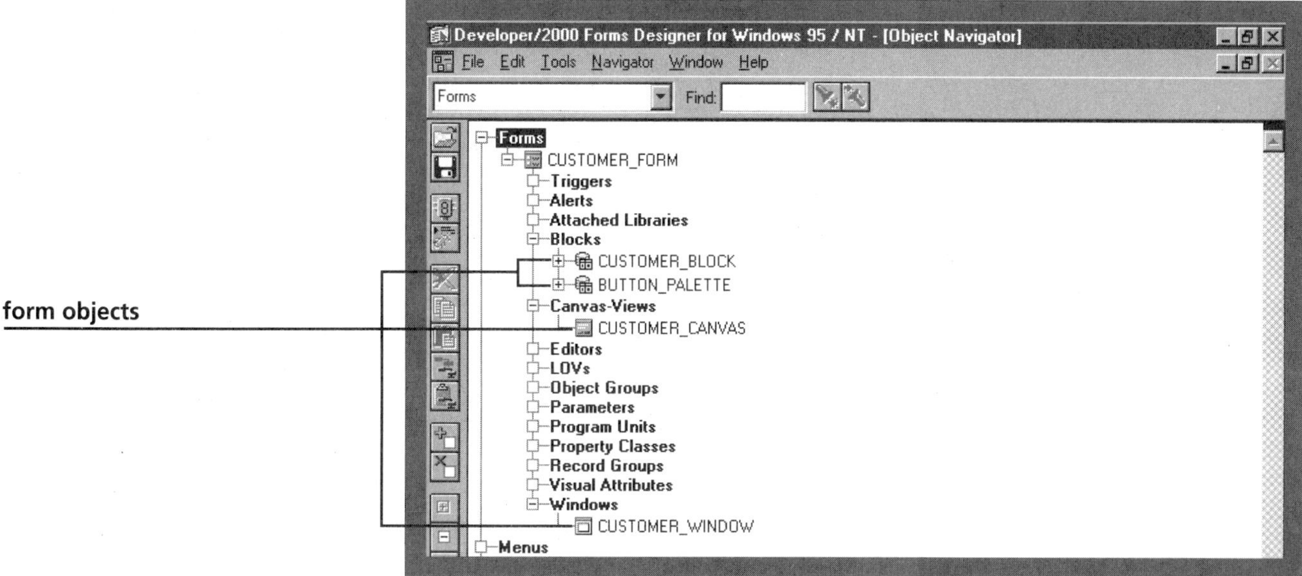

Figure 4-7: Expanding the CUSTOMER_FORM components

Figure 4-8 shows that the CUSTOMER_BLOCK contains triggers and items. Blocks also can contain relations, although the blank box in front of Relations for the CUSTOMER_BLOCK indicates that it contains no relations.

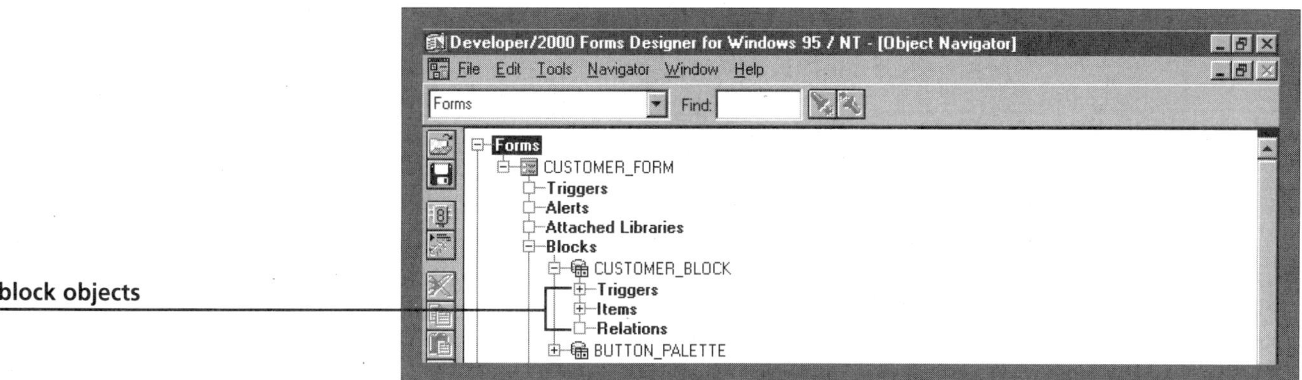

Figure 4-8: CUSTOMER_BLOCK object type

Items are the GUI objects that a user sees and interacts with on the canvas. Figure 4-9 lists some of the common form item types.

Item Type	Description
Check box	Use for selecting options; an option is selected when the box is checked. You can check one or more check boxes in a group.
Button	Use for specifying an action, such as selecting an item from a list or closing an application.
Radio button	Use for selecting options; an option is selected when the center of the button is black. You can select only radio button in a group, and choosing a different button deselects the current one.
Text item	Use for entering or modifying text. Text items often are associated with database fields.

Figure 4-9: Common form item types

Windows applications respond to a user action such as clicking a button or to a system action such as loading a form. These actions are called **events**. In Oracle Forms, events start programs called **triggers**. For example, when you clicked the Save button on the CUSTOMER_FORM, a trigger was executed that inserted or updated the current form record in the database. Triggers are written in **PL/SQL (Programming Language/Structured Query Language)**, which is Oracle's procedural programming language. PL/SQL enables programmers to combine SQL with procedural programming statements and control structures such as if/then statements and loops.

A **relation** is created when you specify a relationship between two data blocks. The CUSTOMER_FORM involves only one database table so it has no relations.

Figure 4-10 shows the CUSTOMER_BLOCK items, which are the text fields that accept input data or display the data in an existing record when you use the CUSTOMER_FORM.

Appendix A contains an overview of PL/SQL.

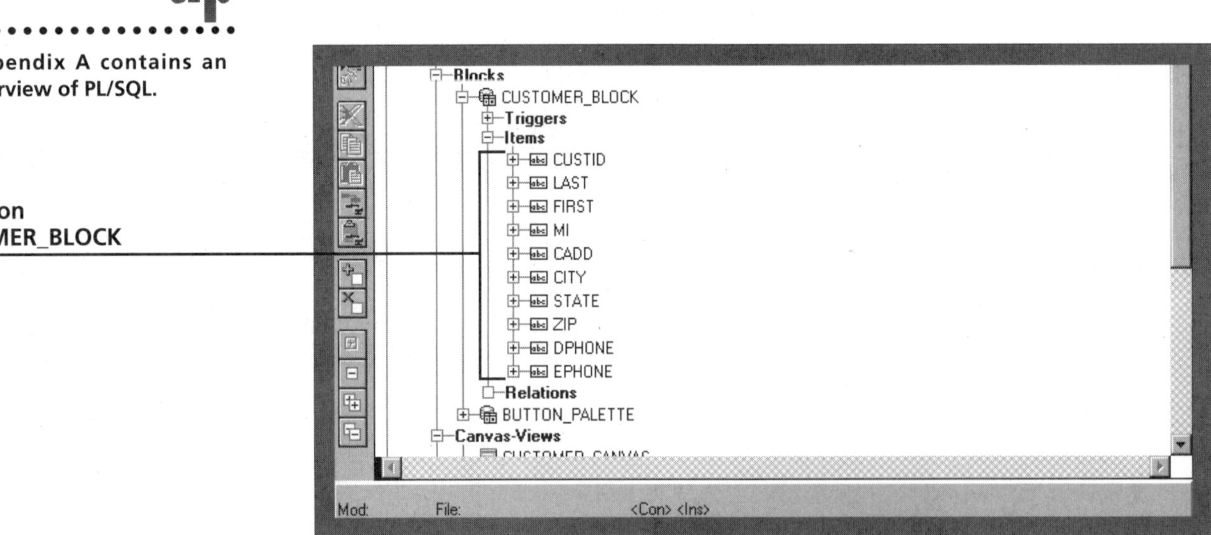

Figure 4-10: CUSTOMER_BLOCK items

The Object Navigator also has a **Visual View** that displays form objects hierarchically. The Visual View shows how objects "contain" other objects. The CUSTOMER_FORM Object Navigator Visual View is shown in Figure 4-11. Visual Attributes and Windows are the highest-level objects in a form module. **Visual Attributes** are form-level settings that specify appearance properties of form objects such as background color and font. The absence of a plus box to the left of an object's name indicates that there are no Visual Attributes objects in the CUSTOMER_FORM.

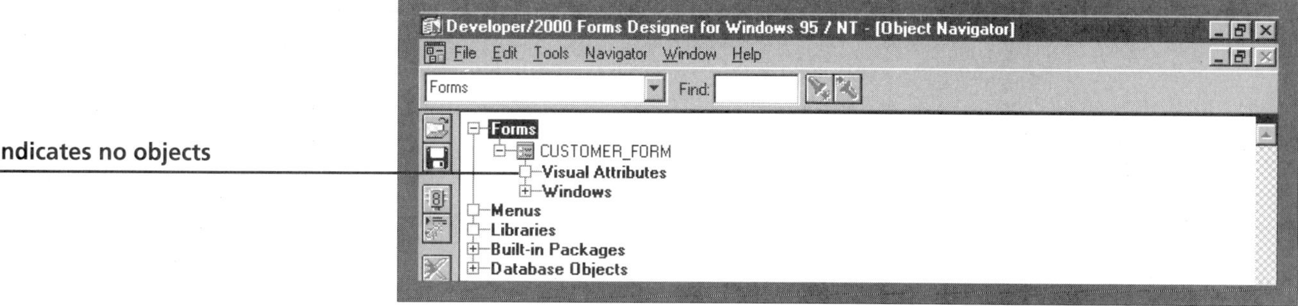

Figure 4-11: CUSTOMER_FORM in Visual View

Several form object types displayed in Ownership View do not display in Visual View.

The plus box to the left of Windows indicates that the form contains Windows objects. The form's Windows objects contain all of the other form objects. Figure 4-12 shows the Visual View expansion of the CUSTOMER_FORM Windows object. Two Windows objects are displayed: the NULL Window, which is created automatically when the form is created but is not displayed on the form, and the CUSTOMER_WINDOW, which contains the rest of the form objects. CUSTOMER_WINDOW contains a canvas named CUSTOMER_CANVAS. The CUSTOMER_CANVAS contains the final level of the Visual View, which contains the form items. Note that blocks are not shown in the Visual View.

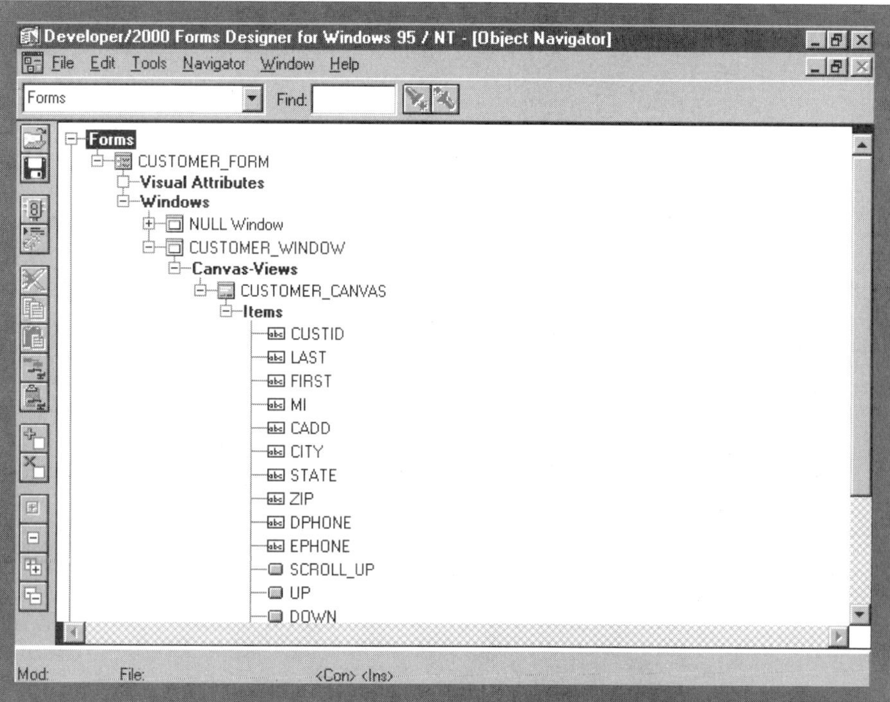

Figure 4-12: Expanding the CUSTOMER_FORM Windows objects

Creating the CUSTOMER_FORM

Now that you understand the basic components of an Oracle form, you are ready to create the CUSTOMER_FORM. First you will start the Oracle Forms Designer application. Like SQL*Plus, starting Oracle Forms is a two-step process—first you start the application on your client workstation, and then you log on to the Oracle database.

tip

Another way to start the Forms Designer is to start Windows Explorer, change to the ORAWIN95\BIN folder, and then double-click the f45des32.exe file (for Windows NT users, click the ORANT\BIN\f45des32.exe file).

To start Oracle Forms:

1. Click the **Start** button on the taskbar, point to **Programs**, point to **Oracle for Windows 95** (or **Oracle for Windows NT**), point to **Developer/2000 for Win95** (or **Developer/2000 for WinNT**), and then click **Forms Designer**.

   HELP? If you cannot find the Forms Designer program, ask your instructor or technical support person for help.

2. Click **File** on the menu bar, and then click **Connect**. Enter your user name, password, and database connect string. See Figure 4-13.

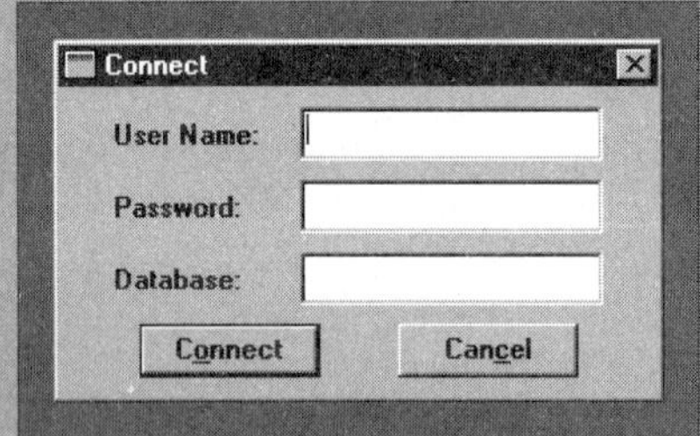

Figure 4-13: Connecting to the database in Oracle Forms

3. Click the **Connect** button. Maximize the Object Navigator program window, if necessary. The Object Navigator window opens in Ownership View.

   HELP? If your window opens in Visual View, click Navigator on the menu bar, and then click Ownership View.

Using the Object Navigator

Figure 4-14 shows the components of the Object Navigator window in Ownership View. The **Current Selection indicator** displays the name of the currently selected object. The **Current Module display line** shows the name of the current form module. The **Object Navigator toolbar** appears on the left side of the window. Now you will change to the Visual View, and then create some form objects.

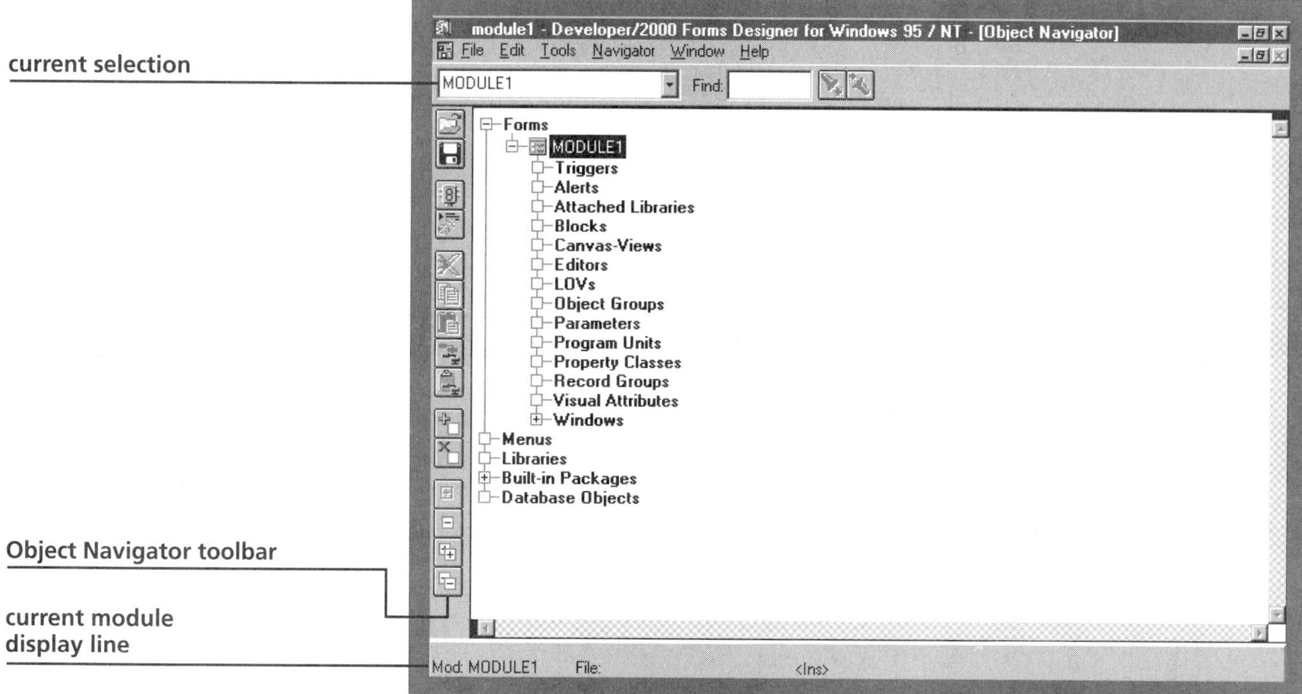

Figure 4-14: Object Navigator in Ownership View

To change to Visual View:

1 Click **Navigator** on the menu bar, and then click **Visual View** to change to Visual View.

The top-level object group is Forms. Remember that each form, or module, is a group of objects (screens, programs, menus, data, etc.) that comprise an Oracle form. MODULE1 is the default module that is created when you first start the Forms Designer. Each module is stored in a separate file on your system, or as a separate object in your database.

Remember that a Navigator object that contains other objects has a plus box to the left of its name. You can see the other objects by clicking the plus box; to hide the other objects, click the minus box ⊟.

A module consists of one or more windows that display when the application is running. For example, a module could have one window that displays information about all customers, and another window that displays order information for a particular customer.

tip

You also can expand or collapse an object by clicking it, and then clicking the Expand ⊞ or Collapse ⊟ button on the Object Navigator toolbar.

To see the module windows:

1 Click the **plus box** ⊞ to the left of the Windows object group under MODULE1. The plus changes to a minus, and the NULL Window and WINDOW0 windows are displayed. These Windows objects are created automatically when you create a new module.

2 Click ⊞ to expand WINDOW0. The Canvas-Views group appears. Remember that a canvas-view, or canvas, has individual screen items such as text fields, labels, and buttons. To create a new object, you select the desired object group, and then click the Create button on the Object Navigator toolbar. To delete an object, select it and then click the Delete button on the Object Navigator toolbar.

3 Click the **canvas-views** object group name to select it. The object name is highlighted to indicate that it is selected.

4 Click the **Create** button on the Object Navigator toolbar to create a new canvas-view object. A new object named CANVAS1 appears.

5 If necessary, click the **CANVAS1** object, and then click the **Delete** button on the Object Navigator toolbar. Click the **Yes** button to delete the selected object.

Creating a Single-Table Form

Now that you are familiar with the basic workings of the Object Navigator, you will create the CUSTOMER_FORM form module that you used earlier. You will change the default name of the form to CUSTOMER, and then save the form on your Student Disk.

To name, save, and create the form:

1 Click **MODULE1** to select it (with a black background), click it again (the background changes to blue), type **CUSTOMER** to change the default form name to CUSTOMER, and then press the **Enter** key.

2 Click the **Save** button on the Object Navigator toolbar to save the form. The Save As dialog box opens. Click the **Save in** list arrow and then change to the drive that contains your Student Disk, double-click the **Chapter4** folder, make sure that **customer.fmb** appears in the File name text box, and then click the **Save** button.

HELP? If you receive the message "FRM_10044: Cannot create file" when you try to save files to your Student Disk, check to make sure that the disk has empty space. If your disk is full, save the file on a new disk.

tip

You also can save a module by clicking File on the menu bar, and then clicking Save, or by pressing Ctrl + S.

3 If necessary, click the **plus box** ⊞ to the left of the Windows object group to expand it, click **WINDOW0** twice so it changes to a blue background, type **CUSTOMER_WINDOW**, and then press the **Enter** key.

4 If necessary, click ⊞ for the **CUSTOMER_WINDOW** group to expand it.

5 Click **Canvas-Views** and then click the **Create** button on the Oracle Navigator toolbar to create a new canvas named CANVAS2.

HELP? Your canvas might have another number, such as CANVAS3. When a new object is created, the object's default name is the name of the object type joined with a number that is one higher than the previous highest object number created. Other form objects use this same naming convention, so you might see different default numbers when you are working in the form. The number does not affect any of your work.

tip

The name of the new module is inserted automatically as the filename. Forms Designer files have an .fmb extension. In this book you will use DOS 8-character filenames to ensure that your forms applications run correctly with the Forms Runtime application.

6 Click the new canvas so its background turns blue, type **CUSTOMER_CANVAS**, and then press the **Enter** key to change the canvas name.

7 Click ⊞ to the left of the CUSTOMER_CANVAS to expand it. A new object group named Items appears. Remember that items are Windows controls such as buttons, text boxes, and check boxes that appear on your form.

The next step is to view your form using the Layout Editor. The **Layout Editor** provides a graphical display of the form canvas that can be used to draw and position form items, and add **boilerplate objects** such as labels, titles, and graphic images. The Layout Editor shows how the form will look when it is running. You will view the form in the Layout Editor next.

You also can change to the Layout Editor by clicking Tools on the menu bar, and then clicking Layout Editor.

To view the form in the Layout Editor:

1 Double-click the **canvas** icon to the left of CUSTOMER_CANVAS to change to the Layout Editor. If necessary, click the **Maximize** button to maximize the Layout Editor program window. Figure 4-15 shows the default form.

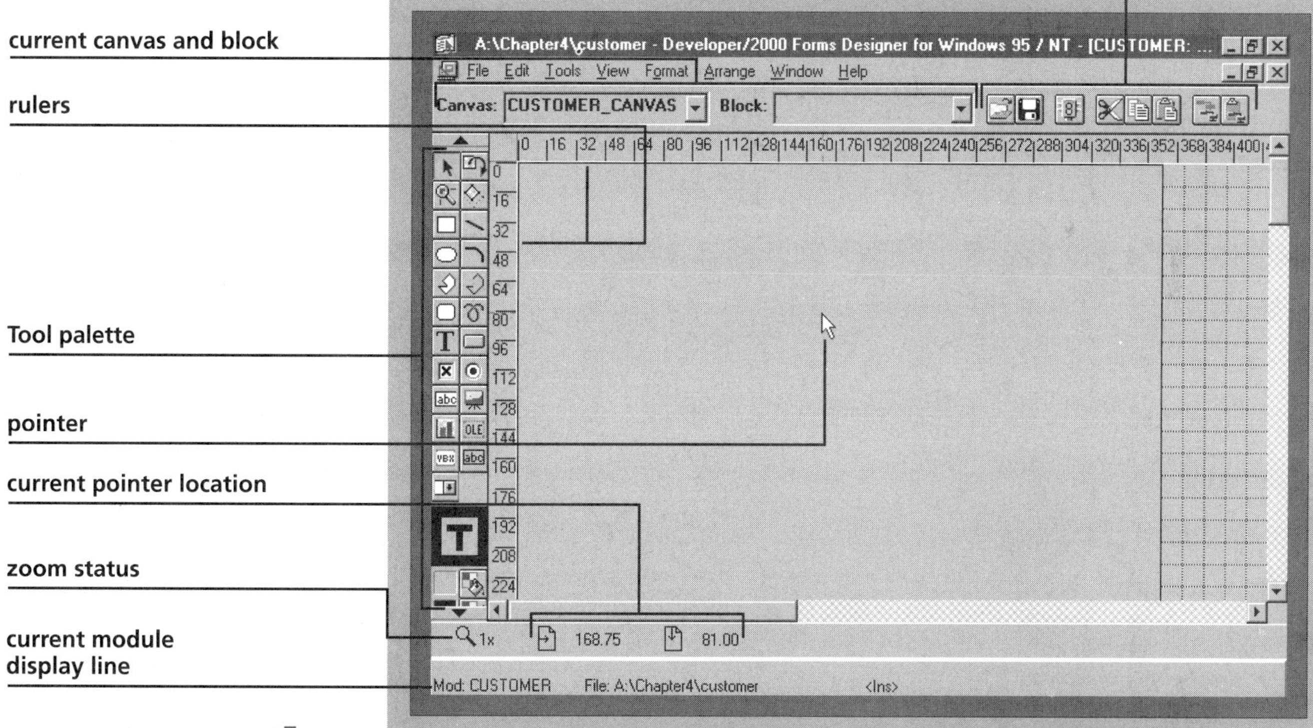

Figure 4-15: Layout Editor window

HELP? If you don't see one of the elements in Figure 4-15 on your screen, click View on the menu bar, and then click the name of the element that you need to turn on.

For zoom status, 1x indicates full size, ½x indicates half full size, and 2x indicates twice full size.

Creating a New Data Block

Currently you have a blank canvas in your Layout Editor window. Remember that a canvas is the area in a window where you place form items such as buttons and text fields. Your new canvas does not have any items on it yet. This is a data block form, so you will create a data block to display the data fields in the CUSTOMER table. Remember that a data block is a block that is related to a database table, and that when you create a data block the system automatically generates the text fields and labels for data fields in that table and creates the code for inserting, modifying, deleting, and viewing data records. You will create a data block related to the CUSTOMER table next.

To create a data block related to the CUSTOMER table:

1 Click **Tools** on the menu bar, and then click **New Block**. The CUSTOMER: New Block Options dialog box opens, as shown in Figure 4-16. You use the General tab to specify the database table that corresponds to the block name and the canvas where you want to display the block.

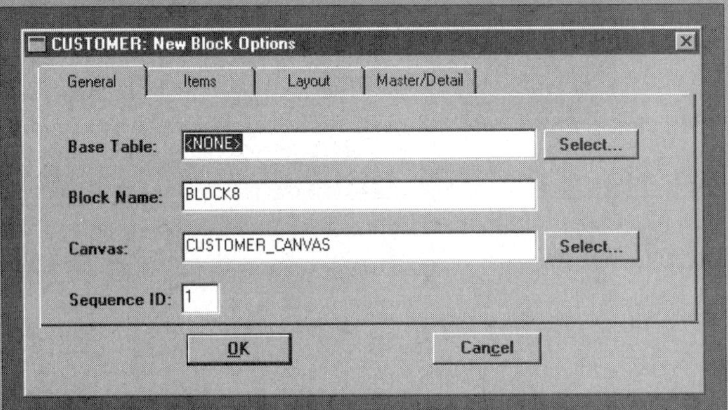

Figure 4-16: Creating a new data block

2 Click the **Select** button for the Base Table text box to open the Tables dialog box, which allows you to select the table to display. The Current User option lists every table that you own, and the Other Users option lists every table in the database. The Other Users option is used if you want to use other users' database tables in your form. You also are given the option of displaying different kinds of database objects: Tables, Views, or Synonyms.

3 Make sure that the **Current User** and **Tables** check boxes are checked, and then click the **OK** button. A list of every table that you own displays.

4 Click the **CUSTOMER** table, and then click the **OK** button to return to the New Block Options window. CUSTOMER appears as the base table and also as the block name. The CUSTOMER_CANVAS is specified automatically because you were viewing the CUSTOMER_CANVAS in the Layout Editor when you created the new block. Note that the default name of the new block is CUSTOMER, which is the same as the database table.

tip

If you select the Other Users check box, all tables in the database will display. This is slow to load and search, so if you are going to choose one of your own tables, check the Current User check box.

If you want other users to be able to use your form with your database table, you must preface the table name with your user name followed by a period.

5 Click in front of the "C" in CUSTOMER in the Base Table text box, and then type your user name followed by a period. See Figure 4-17. *Do not click the OK button.*

HELP? If you click the OK button before you specify all of the block properties, you will have to delete the new block and start over. Click Window on the menu bar, and then click Object Navigator to return to the Object Navigator window and go to Ownership View. Under Blocks, click the new block you just created, click the Delete button on the Object Navigator toolbar, and then click the Yes button to delete the block. Click Tools on the menu bar, and then click Layout Editor to return to the Layout Editor. In the Layout Editor, click Edit on the menu bar, click Select All, click Edit again, and then click Clear to delete all of the labels created by the block. Then repeat the steps to create the block.

enter your user name here

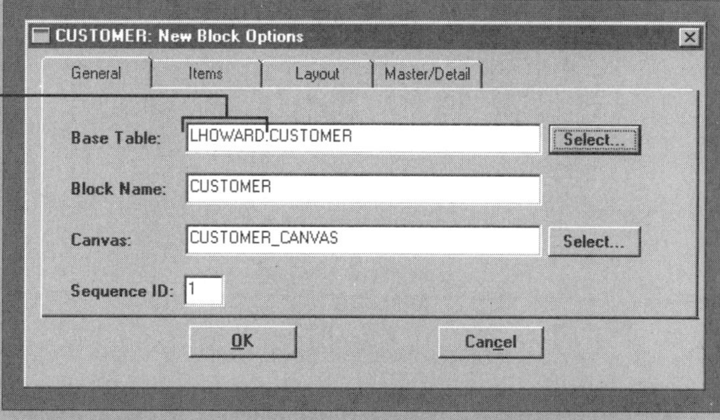

Figure 4-17: Completed General tab

6 Click the **Items** tab.

The Items tab lets you specify what data columns and associated labels and the item types from the CUSTOMER table to display on the canvas. The different types of items that can be linked to database fields are:

- **Text items** For character- or number-based data that can be displayed using either a single or multi-line display. Text items also are called text fields. For example, you entered and modified data in the CUSTOMER_FORM using text fields.
- **Display items** For character- or number-based data that is stored and displayed but not updated. Display items use less memory than text items.
- **Check boxes** For data fields with two possible values, such as true/false or on/off. An example would be to indicate the status of an invoice as paid or not paid.
- **Images** For vector or bitmapped graphic data, for example, saving photographs of inventory items in the Clearwater Traders database.
- **List items** For data fields with a fixed number of data items. Each item can be a text string of up to 30 characters. List items are appropriate for a pick list of the different categories of merchandise items (Women's Clothing, Men's Clothing, etc.) in the ITEM table in the Clearwater database. List items are appropriate only if the list contents do not change.

Use radio button groups when a data field has less than five legal values that do not change. When there are more than five possible values, use a list item.

- **Radio button groups** For displaying a data field with a fixed number of options, of which only one can be selected. An example of a radio button group is the METHPMT field in the ORDER table of the Clearwater database, which has two possible values—CC (for credit card) or CHECK.
- **VBX controls** Standard form controls that are the common form items such as buttons and radio buttons. You might want to add custom controls to your form for specialized tasks, such as printing bar codes or playing sample sounds. You can use the VBX control to associate an external file (called a .vbx file) that provides this function to your form.
- **OLE controls** For associating OLE-enabled applications (such as Microsoft Word or Excel) within Forms applications. An example would be if you wanted to edit an Excel spreadsheet file in a Forms application and then save it in a database table.

Next you will select the individual data columns. You will use this form to insert and update records, so you will display all columns.

To select and display the data columns:

1 Click the **Select Columns** button. The Select Columns list box displays the name of every column in the CUSTOMER table. Columns that will appear on the form have a plus sign (+) in front of their names and a check mark in the Include check box. By default, all columns are displayed. To deselect a column, double-click it to change the plus sign to a minus sign (-). To select a column, double-click it again.

2 Double-click **CUSTID** so a minus sign appears in front of its name. Now the CUSTID column will not display on the form.

3 Double-click **CUSTID** again so the plus sign displays in front of its name. By default, the labels that appear on the form beside the data fields are the same as the table column names. You can change the labels by selecting the field name, clicking the column name in the Select Columns list box, and then entering an appropriate label in the Label text box. You will change the label names next.

4 Click **LAST** in the Select Columns list box. The label "Last" appears in the Label text box, as shown in Figure 4-18.

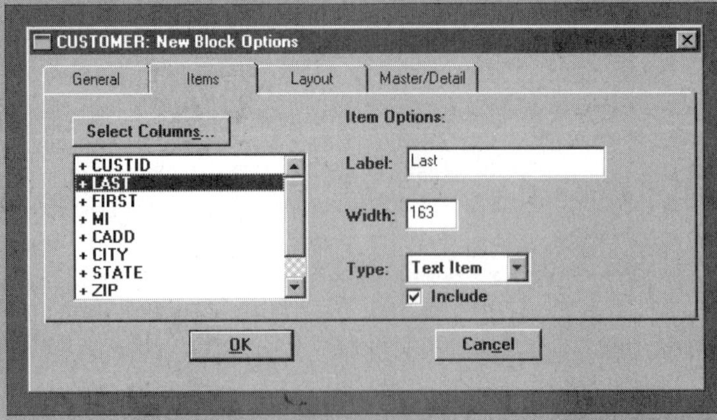

Figure 4-18: Specifying the item settings

5 Click after the last character in the word "Last" in the Label text box, press the **spacebar**, and then type **Name:**.

6 Repeat Steps 4 and 5 to change the default labels to the following new label names. As you select each column name, the value in the Width text box changes to reflect the data widths that were specified when you created the tables. Usually, these values are satisfactory. The default Item Type is Text Item, which is appropriate for your form because you will use this form to add and update records.

Column	**New Label**
FIRST	First Name:
MI	Middle Initial:
CADD	Address:
CITY	City:
STATE	State:
ZIP	Zip:

Note: You will change the labels for the CUSTID, DPHONE, and EPHONE fields later using an alternate approach.

7 *Do not click the OK button.* Click the **Layout** tab.

The layout of a form specifies how the data is displayed. In a **tabular style**, multiple records are displayed on the form. In a **form style**, only one record displays at a time. For the tabular style, the **orientation** of the form determines whether the records are displayed horizontally or vertically on the screen. The records setting specifies how many records display on the form at one time, and the spacing setting defines how many blank spaces appear between successive records.

When you create a form, checking the Integrity Constraints check box signifies that the Forms application will flag violations to the integrity constraints that you established when you created the table (unique primary keys, foreign key references, etc.). This means you will see Oracle Forms-generated error messages rather than ORA-error codes generated by the DBMS. The integrity constraints still will be enforced by the DBMS even if you do not check the Integrity Constraints check box, and users will receive ORA-error codes directly from the DBMS if they violate a table integrity constraint.

You can add a Button palette to the form to provide users with buttons for moving through the records, and for querying and saving records. The Button palette usually is used with the form style. You can add scroll bars to a tabular form to allow the user to navigate through the records using the form.

To change the form layout:

1 Change the settings on your Layout tab to match Figure 4-19. The Master/Detail tab is used to specify a join condition between two tables on a form. You are creating a single-table form so you won't use this tab.

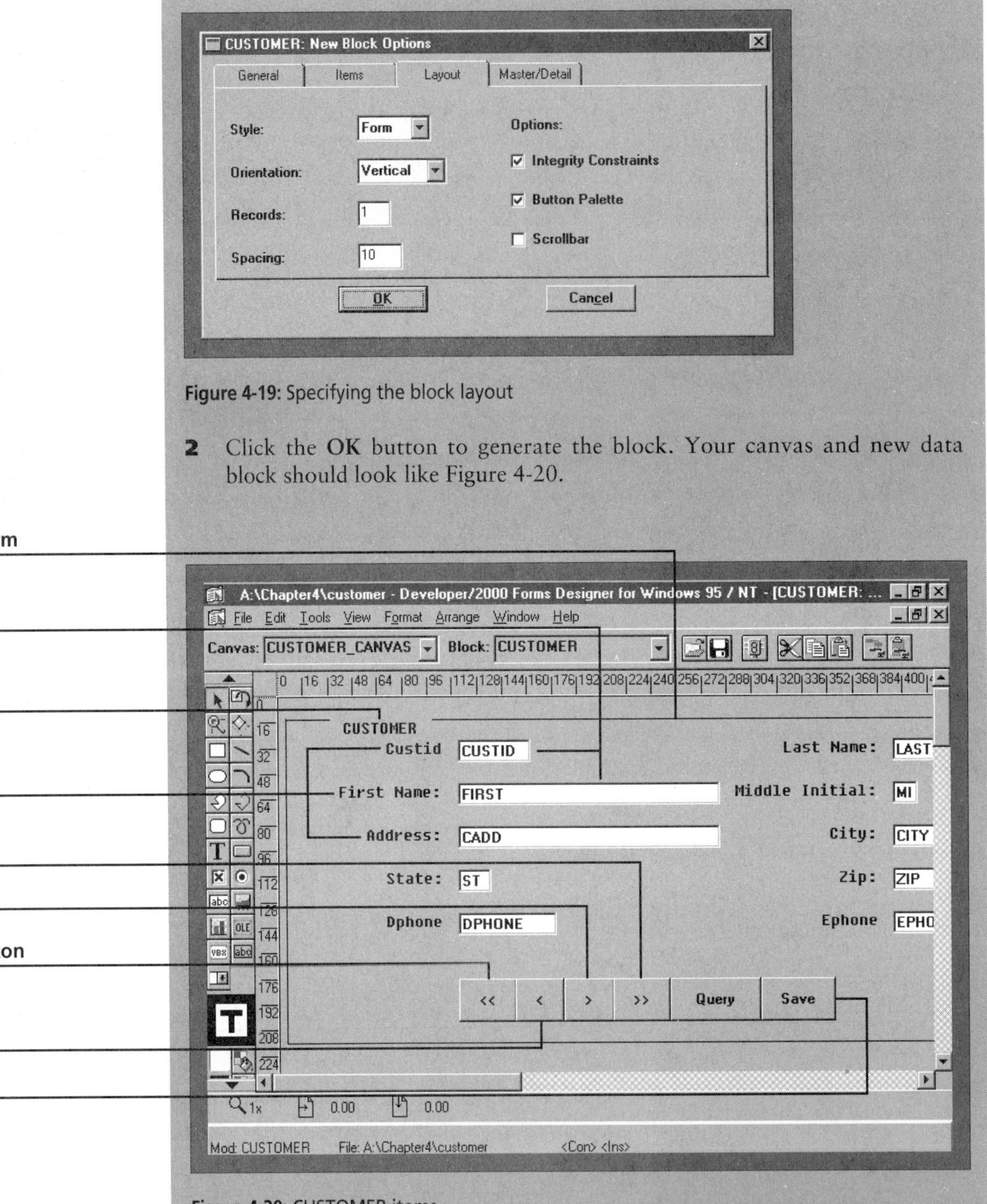

Figure 4-19: Specifying the block layout

2 Click the **OK** button to generate the block. Your canvas and new data block should look like Figure 4-20.

Figure 4-20: CUSTOMER items

3 Click the Save button on the Layout Editor toolbar.

If you want to take a break, you can save your work and begin working again later. Use the following procedure to save your file and close the Forms Designer application.

To save your file and close the Forms Designer application:

1. Click **File** on the menu bar, and then click **Close**.
2. Click the **Yes** button if the message box appears asking if you want to save your changes.

Formatting the Canvas Layout

After creating the block, you can rearrange and format the labels and data fields to improve the form's appearance. If you closed the Forms Designer, you will need to start it again and open your file.

To start the Forms Designer and open your CUSTOMER file:

1. Start the Forms Designer.
2. Click the **Open** button on the Object Navigator toolbar, change to the drive that contains your Student Disk, change to the Chapter4 folder, and then double-click the **customer.fmb** file.
3. Click **Tools** on the menu bar, and then click **Layout Editor**.

The first formatting task is to delete some of the extra form objects.

Deleting Form Objects When you create a data block form, a frame is inserted automatically around the data block fields. You will delete this frame next.

To delete the frame:

1. Click anywhere on the frame. Selection handles appear around the frame to indicate that it is selected.
2. Press the **Delete** key to delete the frame.

   HELP? If you cannot select the entire frame, click the individual lines in the frame and delete them one at a time.

By default, the Button palette includes the six buttons shown in Figure 4-20. The SCROLL_UP and SCROLL_DOWN buttons are used to retrieve "groups" of records when you display several records on the form at one time using a tabular layout. The Next and Previous buttons are used to step through records one at a time. In a form like this one that uses the form layout and displays records one at a time, SCROLL_DOWN and SCROLL_UP have the same function as the Next and Previous buttons. You will delete the SCROLL_UP and SCROLL_DOWN buttons.

To delete the buttons:

1. Click the **SCROLL_UP** button on the Button palette (see Figure 4-20), press and hold down the **Shift** key, click the **SCROLL_DOWN** button on the Button palette, and then release the Shift key. Both buttons should display selection handles.
2. Press the **Delete** key to delete the buttons. Your form should now look like Figure 4-21.

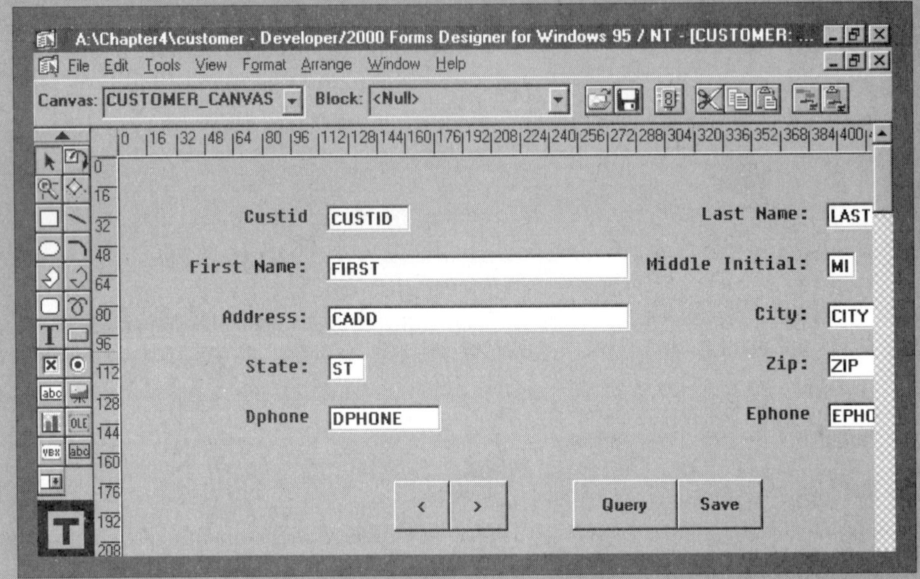

Figure 4-21: Deleting form objects

Editing Text Labels You changed some of the default column labels when you created the form. You also can change column labels in the Layout Editor. Next you will reformat some of the data field labels so they take less screen space and are easier to understand. First format the long labels so they wrap to two lines and take less horizontal space.

To reformat the column labels:

1. Click the **Text** tool on the Tool palette. The pointer changes to ⊞ when you move it over the canvas.
2. Click the **Last Name:** field label, click before the "N" in Name, and then press the **Enter** key. The word "Name:" moves to the next line.
3. Click anywhere on the canvas to deselect the Text tool.
4. Repeat Steps 1 and 2 so the First Name and Middle Initial labels appear on two lines, and then click anywhere on the canvas to deselect the field. See Figure 4-22.

field labels appear on two lines

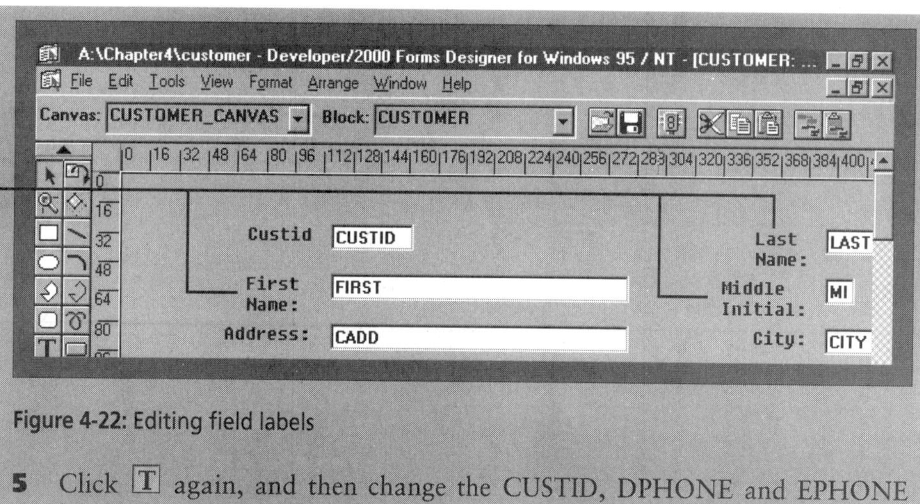

Figure 4-22: Editing field labels

You can change the label text when you create the block, but you must use the Layout Editor to control how lines break.

5 Click T again, and then change the CUSTID, DPHONE and EPHONE labels to **Customer ID:**, **Daytime Phone:**, and **Evening Phone:** so each label appears on two lines.

6 Select all of the labels on the screen by clicking any label, pressing and holding down the **Shift** key, and then clicking the rest of the labels until all labels are selected.

7 Click **Format** on the menu bar, and then click **Font**. Change to 10-point bold Arial font, and then click the **OK** button. See Figure 4-23.

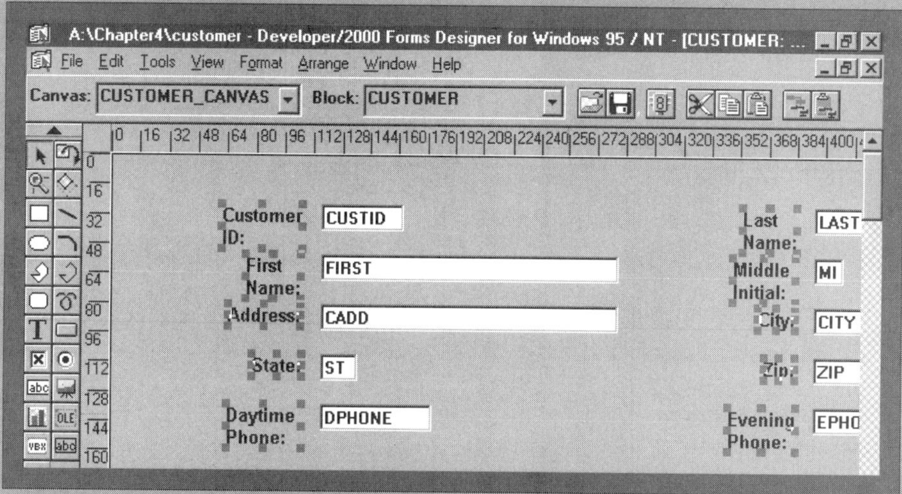

Figure 4-23: Changing the label font

8 Click anywhere on the canvas to deselect the field labels.

Sans serif fonts (such as Arial) usually are more legible on computer screens than serif fonts (such as Times Roman).

Moving and Aligning Groups of Fields and Labels You need to arrange all of your labels and data fields so they are all visible in the window. A good design practice is to arrange the form items on a single screen so users don't have to scroll the form while using it. First you will enable the formatting grid to make aligning items easier.

To enable the formatting grid and rearrange the form items:

1 Click **View** on the menu bar. If Grid Snap does not have a check mark in front of it, click **Grid Snap**. If it is checked, then press the **Esc** key to close the menu. The default grid settings can be adjusted to make a finer or coarser grid.
2 Click **View** on the menu bar, point to **Settings**, and then click **Ruler** to open the Ruler Settings dialog box to change the grid settings.
3 If necessary, click the **Points** option. This specifies that the screen units are being measured in **pixels**, or picture elements. This corresponds to the resolution of your video display. A common video display resolution is 640 pixels wide and 480 pixels long.
4 Change the Number of Snap Points Per Grid Spacing to **4**. The grid gets finer as you increase the grid spacing setting.
5 Click the **OK** button.

When there is a check mark in front of the Grid Snap command, the grid is enabled. To turn off the grid, click View on the menu bar, and then click Grid Snap again.

People read computer screens just like they read a book—top down and left to right. You will arrange the data fields to match this pattern by selecting the different screen objects and dragging them to the new locations. Finally, you will need to fine-tune the alignment and spacing. When designing forms, keep the following formatting tips in mind:

- Place data fields and labels in the basic vicinity where you want them. Align these form objects so they are easy to read and visually appealing. Then adjust the spacing if necessary.
- Move groups of objects whenever possible. To create a group of several objects, select the first object by clicking it, press and hold down the Shift key, and then click to select the next object. Continue to click to select as many objects as you want to include in the group, and then release the Shift key.
- To align a group of items, select all of the items you want to align, click Arrange on the menu bar, and then click Align Objects. You can align groups of objects by their left or right edges, centers, or tops or bottoms. When you select Align Left, all objects in the group are aligned with the object whose edge is currently the farthest to the left; when you select Align Right, all objects are aligned with the right-most object. The same logic works for aligning objects by the top and bottom.
- To space a group of objects evenly, select the object group, click Arrange on the menu bar, click Align Objects, and then click Distribute. This will distribute the objects evenly within their current area.
- To stack a group of objects directly on top of or next to each other, select the object group and use the Stack option.
- You can move, resize, and align the individual buttons on the Button palette just like any other item on the canvas.

You also can create a group by dragging the pointer to draw a box around a group of items.

To rearrange and align the items:

1 Click and drag the items so they are in the same approximate positions as shown in Figure 4-24.

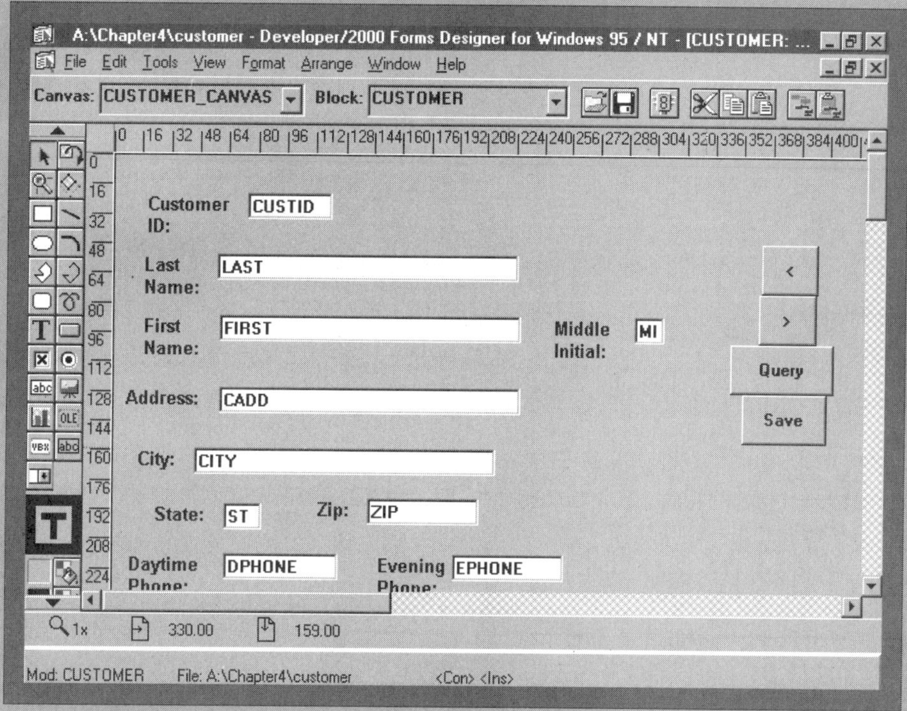

Figure 4-24: Positioning the form items

HELP? If you accidentally double-click an item and open a window titled Properties, close the Properties window, maximize the Layout Editor, and then repeat Step 1.

2 Select the LAST, FIRST, CADD, CITY, ZIP, and DPHONE text fields as a group by clicking **LAST**, pressing and holding down the **Shift** key, clicking the other fields, and then releasing the Shift key. Selection handles appear on each selected object.

3 Drag the group so all of the objects' left edges are to the right of the CUSTID field, as shown in Figure 4-25.

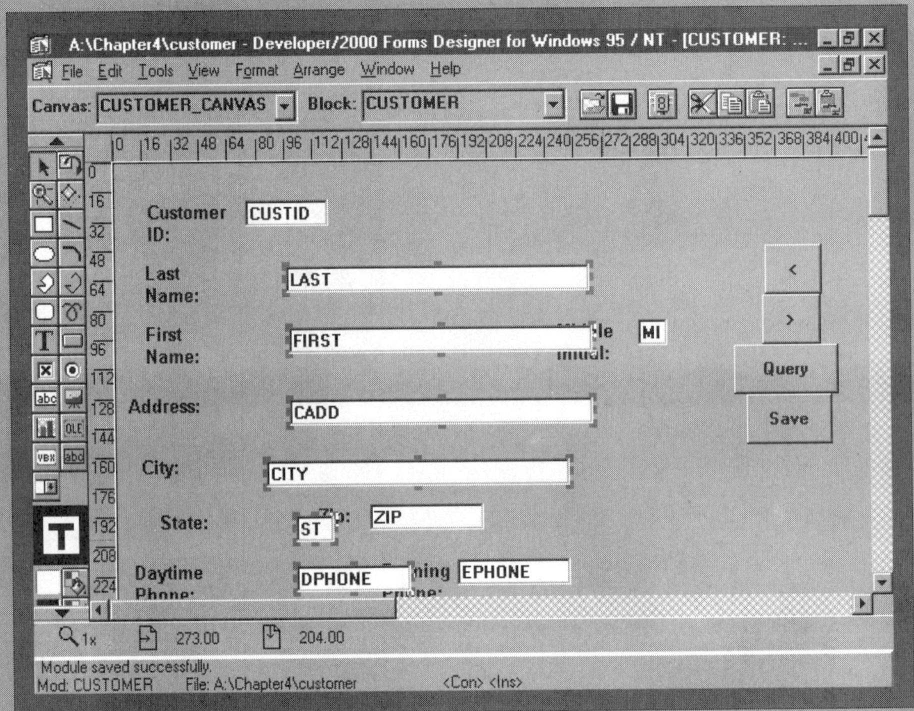

Figure 4-25: Moving the selected text fields to the right of CUSTID

HELP? Don't worry if the text boxes overlap other labels or text fields for now.

4 Press the **Shift** key, click **CUSTID** to add it to your selected group, and then release the Shift key.

5 With the CUSTID, FIRST, LAST, CADD, CITY, STATE, and DPHONE data fields still selected, click **Arrange** on the menu bar, and then click **Align Objects**. The Align Objects dialog box opens.

6 Click the **Align To Each Other, Horizontally Align Left,** and **Vertically Distribute** option buttons, as shown in Figure 4-26.

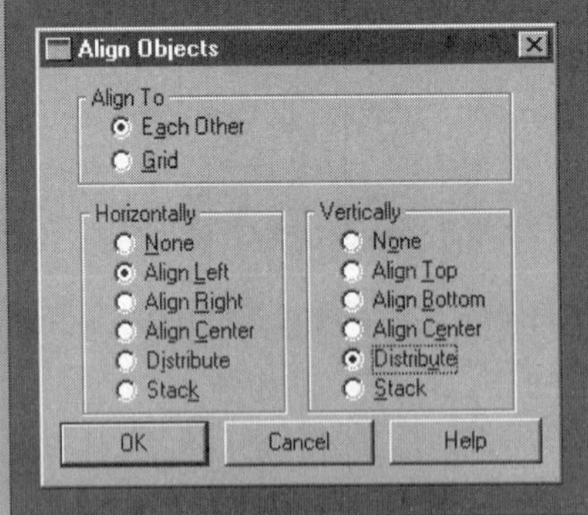

Figure 4-26: Specifying the alignment of the selected text fields

7 Click the **OK** button. Your form should look like Figure 4-27.

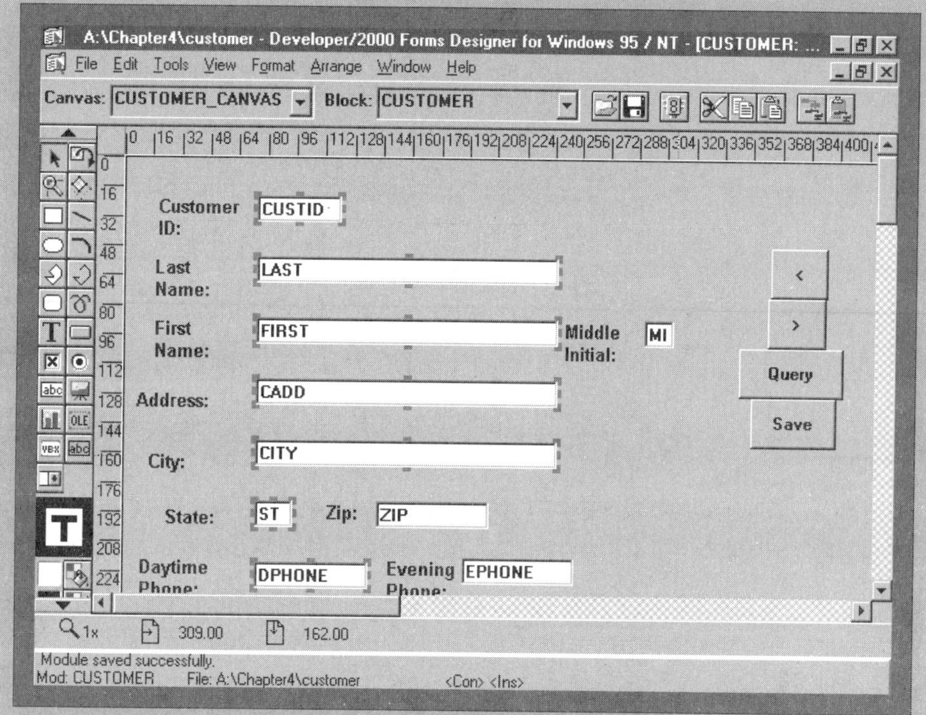

Figure 4-27: Left-aligned text fields

8 Select the **Customer ID**, **Last Name**, **First Name**, **Address**, **City**, **State**, and **Daytime Phone** labels as an object group.

9 Repeat Step 5 to change the alignment to **Align To Each Other**, **Horizontally Align Left**, and **Vertically Distribute**, and then click the **OK** button. Click anywhere on the canvas to deselect the group of labels.

HELP? After clicking the OK button, you might need to reposition the labels manually by selecting and dragging them so they are aligned vertically with their associated data fields.

Now the labels and fields are aligned on the left side of the form. You can continue moving the labels and fields so all items are aligned and visible.

To move the rest of the items:

1 Select the **FIRST** and **MI** text fields as a group.

2 Change the alignment to **Align To Each Other, Horizontally None**, and **Vertically Align Bottom**. The bottoms of the FIRST and MI text boxes are aligned.

3 Align the **STATE** and **ZIP** data field text boxes by their bottom edges.

4 Align the **DPHONE** and **EPHONE** data field text boxes by their bottom edges. Your form should look like Figure 4-28. If necessary, reposition any data labels or text boxes so they match Figure 4-28.

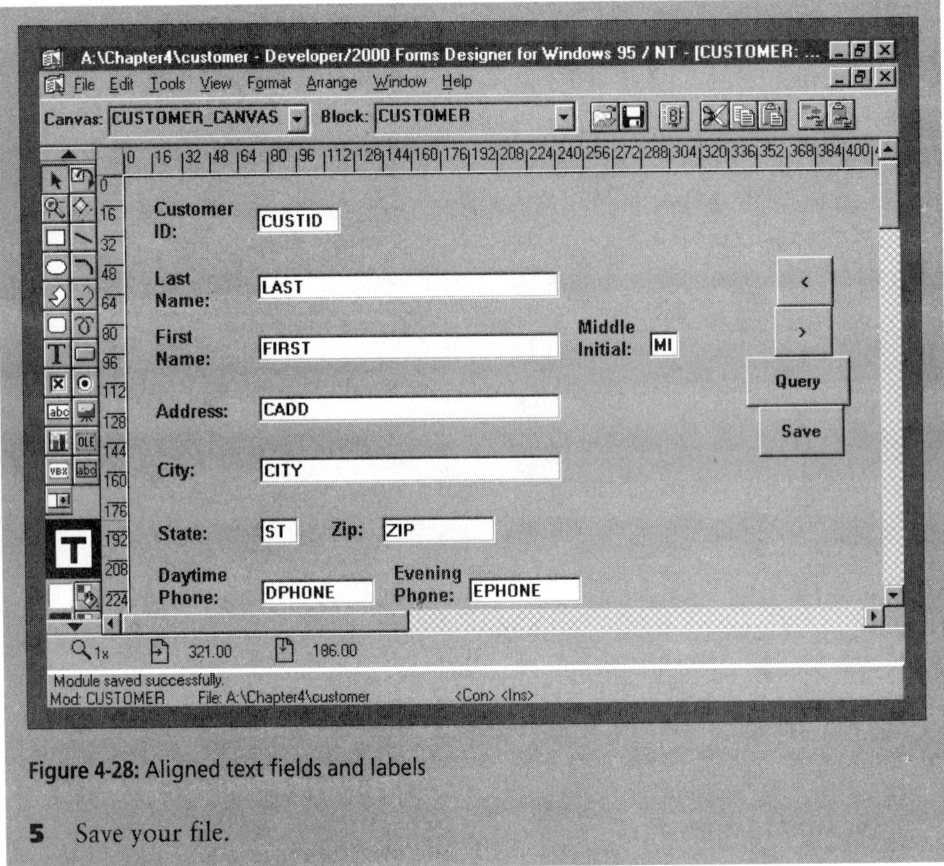

Figure 4-28: Aligned text fields and labels

5 Save your file.

Modifying Item Properties The last formatting task is the Button palette. Currently the buttons have different sizes, and they are not correctly aligned or stacked. First you will resize them. One approach is to select each button and then drag its selection handle to the right size. However, this involves a lot of work and trial and error. An easier approach is to specify the button's Size property. Every canvas object has a **Properties sheet** that specifies a variety of properties specific to the object type. Text fields and buttons have different properties—you use a different Properties sheet to change each object's appearance.

To change the button sizes:

1 Right-click the **Previous** (UP) button on the Button palette, and then click **Properties** to open the Properties sheet, as shown in Figure 4-29. The Properties sheet lists the button name (UP), type, and display properties. The button width is 32, which will be the standard width for each button on the Button palette.

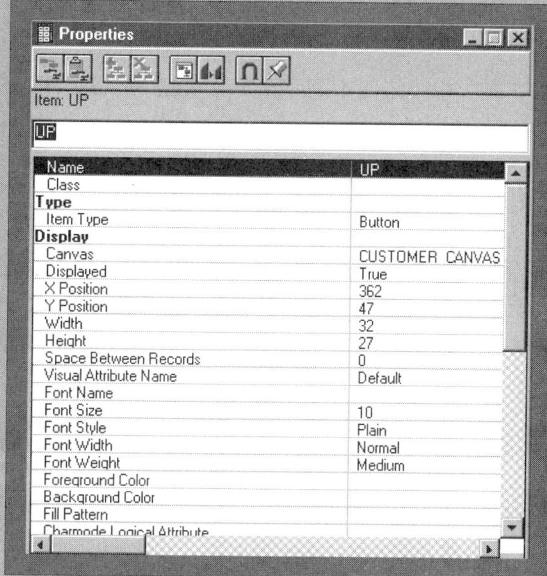

Figure 4-29: Previous button Properties sheet

HELP? If your button width is different, change it to 32 by clicking the Width property, typing 32, and then clicking any other property to save your change.

You also can double-click a button to display its Properties sheet.

2 Close the Previous Properties sheet by clicking the **Close** button.

3 If necessary, maximize your canvas, and then open the Properties sheet for the **Next** button on the Button palette.

4 Confirm that the Width property is 32. If it is not, click the **Width** property to select it, and then type **32**. Click on any other property to save your change, and then click to close the Properties sheet.

HELP? If you do not click another property before closing the Properties sheet, your changes will be lost.

5 If necessary, maximize your canvas again. The widths of the Next and Previous buttons are equal. You can change a property value for a group of items using a group Properties sheet, as you will see next.

6 Press and hold down the **Shift** key and click to select the **Query** and **Save** buttons, and then release the Shift key. Right-click any button in the group, and then click **Properties** to open the Properties sheet for the group, as shown in Figure 4-30. Note that the properties that are the same for all group objects (such as the Item Type and Canvas) are listed, while the properties that are different (such as Name, X Position, and Y Position) are listed as wildcard characters (****).

indicates Properties sheet changes values for multiple items

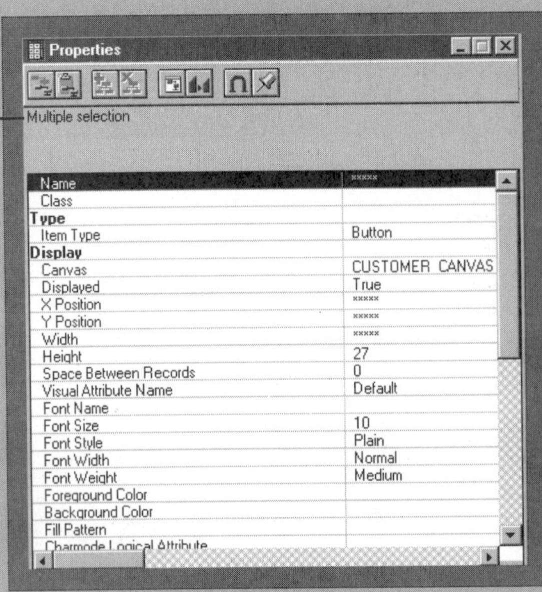

Figure 4-30: Group Properties sheet

7 Change the Width property to **32**, click any other property, and then close the Properties sheet.

8 If necessary, maximize your canvas again. Now all of the buttons on the canvas are the same size.

The buttons are the same size, but they do not align with each other. You will change the button alignment next.

To change the button alignment:

1 Select all of the buttons as an object group by placing the pointer at the top left corner of the button group, and then dragging to draw a box around the entire group. All of the buttons should now have selection handles.

2 Click **Arrange** on the menu bar, click **Align Objects**, and then click the **Align To Each Other, Horizontally Align Left**, and **Vertically Stack** option buttons. Click the **OK** button. The buttons are aligned vertically with each other.

3 If necessary, drag and drop the button group so it is positioned symmetrically beside the data fields. Your canvas should look like Figure 4-31.

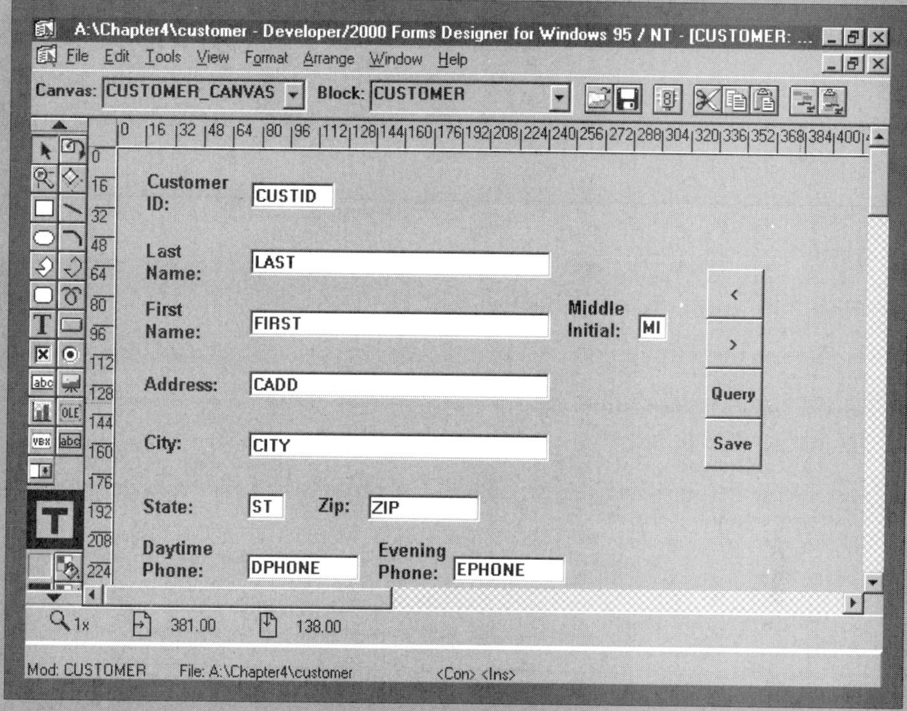

Figure 4-31: CUSTOMER_CANVAS with new placement of Button palette

4 Save your file.

Adding Boilerplate Objects Boilerplate objects, such as a title or a company logo, do not contribute to form functionality, but enhance appearance and ease-of-use. First you will add a title to the form so users can identify the form easily.

To add a title to the form:

1 Click the **Text** tool on the Tool palette. The pointer changes to when you move it over the form.

2 Click at the top center of the canvas under the 160 mark on the horizontal ruler, and then type **Customers**.

3 Drag the pointer over the word "Customers" to select it.

4 Click **Format** on the menu bar, and then click **Font**. Change the font to **18-point bold Arial**, and then click the **OK** button.

5 If necessary, select all of the form text fields and labels, and then drag them down so there is room for the title. Center the **Customers** title text over the data fields and labels.

Next add a colored frame around the data block. First change the default fill and line colors.

To add the frame and change the colors:

1 Click the **Fill Color** button on the Tool palette.

HELP? If necessary, click the Down button on the Tool palette to display the rest of the toolbar buttons. You might have to scroll to the bottom of the canvas to see the Fill Color button.

2 Click any **light gray** color.

3 Click the **Rectangle** tool on the Tool palette. The pointer changes to when you move it over the form.

4 Click **View** on the menu bar, and then click **Zoom Out** so you can see all of your form on the screen. Next use the Rectangle tool to draw a rectangle around the data fields and labels.

5 Click in the top left corner of the canvas, and then drag the pointer down and to the left until a rectangle encloses all of the canvas elements. See Figure 4-32. After you release the mouse button, the rectangle covers the Customers title and the labels. You need to send the colored rectangle to the back of the form so the labels are on top.

tip

Use subtle colors like you see in popular Windows applications in your forms. Intense, saturated colors look less professional and can cause eyestrain. Ensure that there is sufficient contrast between the background and text colors so titles and labels are highly visible.

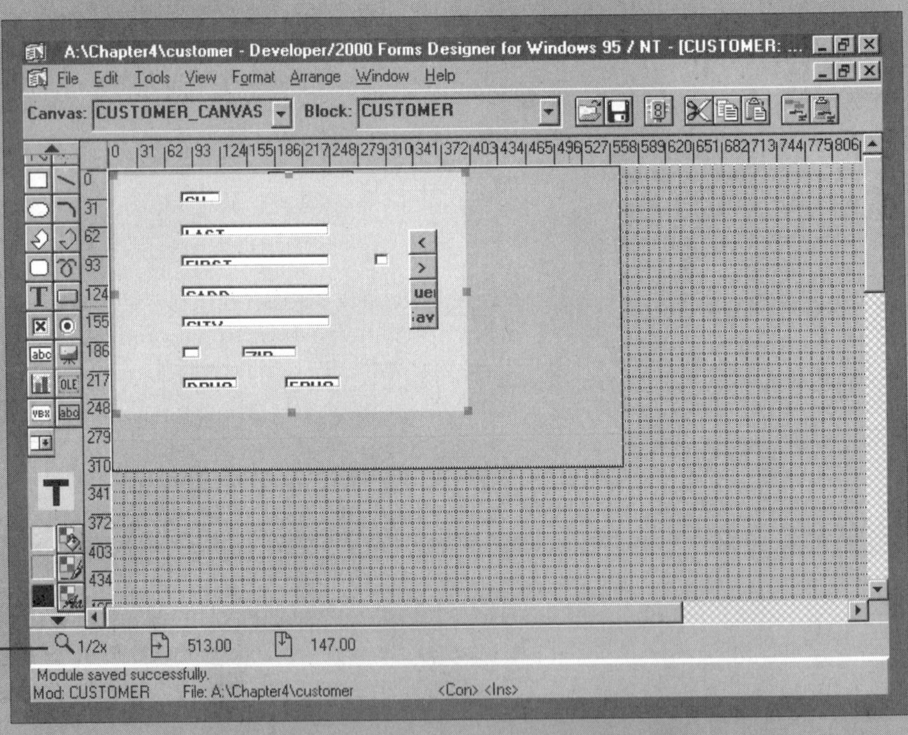

Figure 4-32: Rectangle covering labels

HELP? If necessary, resize the rectangle by clicking a corner selection handle and dragging it to make the object larger or smaller to match Figure 4-32.

6 Click the rectangle to select it. When it is selected, selection handles appear around the rectangle.

7 Click **Arrange** on the menu bar, and then click **Send to Back**. The labels should now be visible and the rectangle appears in the background.

8 With the rectangle still selected, click the **Line Color** tool on the Tool palette, and then click a **dark gray** color.

9 Select all of the canvas objects, and move them so the rectangle is flush with the top and left edge of the canvas. Your completed form should look like Figure 4-33.

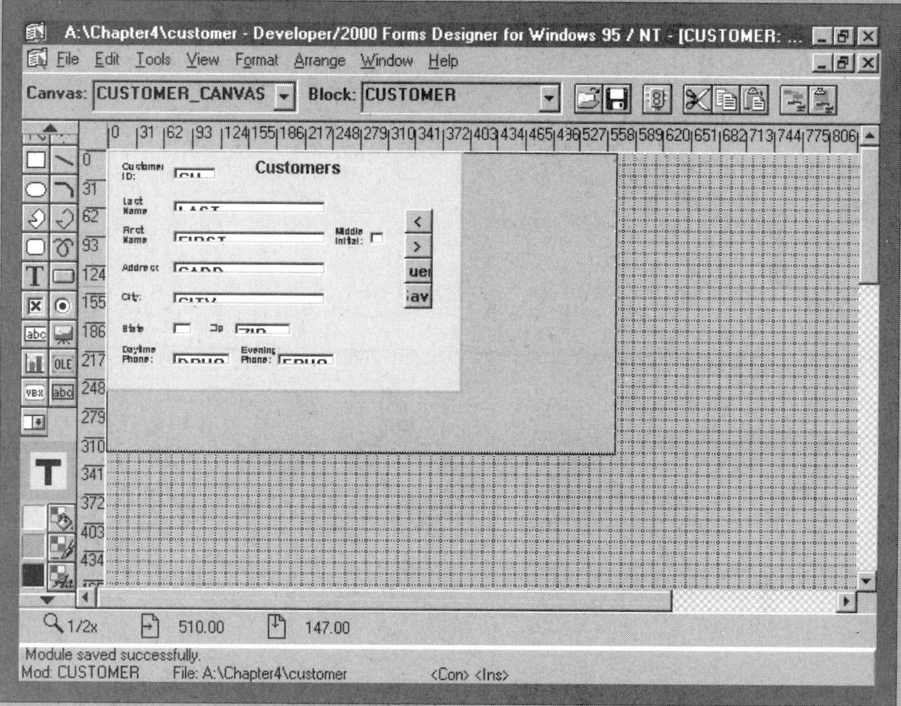

Figure 4-33: Completed CUSTOMER_CANVAS

HELP? If necessary, adjust the positioning of the data fields, labels, or query buttons to match Figure 4-33.

HELP? If your Customers title has a black outline and a different background color than the form, click the title to select it, click the Line Color tool on the Tool palette and then click No Line. Then click the Fill Color button on the Tool palette and then click No Fill.

10 Click **View** on the menu bar, and then click **Normal Size** to return to the normal Layout Editor view. Drag the scroll bars to view the upper-left corner of the Layout Editor window.

11 Save your file.

Running the Form

The next step is to run your form and confirm that it correctly displays, and that you can use it to insert, update, and delete records from the CUSTOMER table. Currently, your application is saved in a file named customer.fmb. Before you can run your form and display data in the data fields, the Forms Designer must generate an executable file that will be named customer.fmx. After generating this executable file, the Forms Designer can run the form using the Forms Runtime application. Remember that Forms Designer files have an .fmb extension, while Forms Runtime files have an .fmx extension. Before you generate and run your form, you will change some of the setup options to automate the process.

To change the setup options and run the form:

1 Click **Tools** on the menu bar, and then click **Options**. The Options dialog box opens, as shown in Figure 4-34. The Save Before Generate check box instructs the system to save your design (.fmb) file automatically each time you run your form. The Generate Before Run check box instructs the system to generate your .fmx file again automatically before running it. It is advisable to check both of these boxes so your design file will be saved automatically and generated each time you run your form.

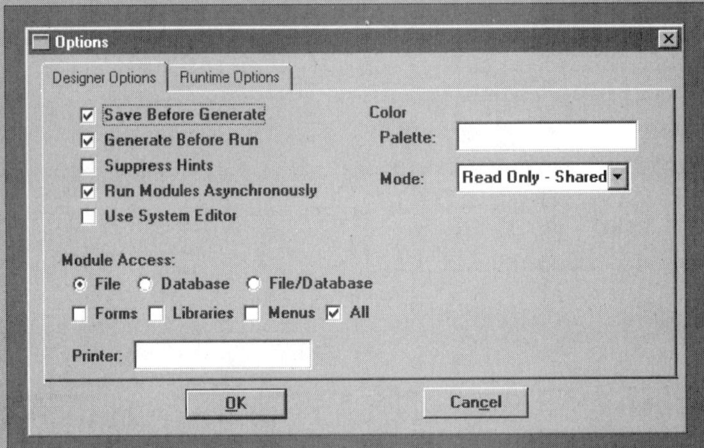

Figure 4-34: Forms Designer setup options

2 Make sure that the **Save Before Generate** and **Generate Before Run** check boxes are checked, and then click the OK button. Do not check or clear any other check boxes or change any other options.

3 Click the **Run** button on the Layout Editor toolbar to run your form. After a few moments, your form should appear in the Developer/2000 Forms Runtime Window. Maximize the Forms Runtime window if necessary.

You can run a form by clicking on the Object Navigator toolbar, or by clicking File on the menu bar, and then clicking Run, or by pressing Ctrl + R.

Viewing Table Records Sequentially First you will test to see that you can scroll through the CUSTOMER records sequentially.

To scroll through the records:

1. Click **Query** button on the Button palette, and then press the **F8** key to execute the query. The first record from the CUSTOMER table appears in your form, as shown in Figure 4-35.

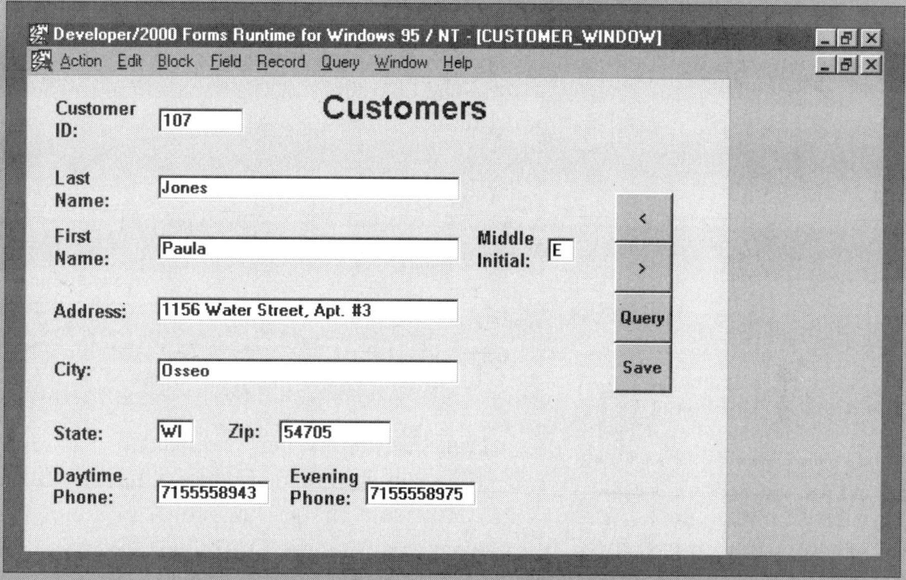

Figure 4-35: CUSTOMER_FORM in Forms Runtime

2. Click the **Next** button on the Button palette to display the record for Mitch Edwards. Click the **Next** button until you have viewed all of the records.
3. Click the **Previous** button and view the records until you return to the first record.

Viewing Specific Records Using Search Conditions Sequentially viewing all records works well for the small sample databases you are using with this book, but it won't work when you are looking for a specific record in a database that contains thousands of records. When you are working with large databases, you can use another approach. You can enter search conditions in a form to retrieve specific records, just like when you use the WHERE clause in a SQL command.

tip

You also can click Query on the menu bar, and then click Enter to go to Enter Query mode.

To use a query to find a specific record:

1. Click the **Query** button on the Button palette. The message in the message area prompts you to enter a query.
2. Click in the Zip field, enter **53821**, and then press the **F8** key to execute the query. Lee Miller's customer record appears. Queries can retrieve multiple records, as you will see next.

3 Click the **Query** button again, and note that the fields are cleared. Enter **WI** in the State field, and then press the **F8** key to execute the query.

4 Click the **Next** button on the Button palette to confirm that all five CUSTOMER records are retrieved.

So far you have done exact searches. You can do approximate searches by using the percent sign (%) to indicate that there are any number of wildcard characters either before or after a search string. For example, if you want to retrieve the records for all customers whose zip code begins with 54, you would enter the search condition as `54%`. If you want to retrieve the records of all customers who have the characters "Apt" anywhere in their address, you would enter the search condition `%Apt%`.

To search using a wildcard character:

1 Click the **Query** button on the Button palette, enter **54%** as the Zip search condition, and then press the **F8** key. Four records are retrieved.

2 Click the **Query** button again, enter **%Apt%** as the Address search condition, and then press the **F8** key. The query finds the record for Paula Jones.

When you are in Enter Query mode, you must execute the query by pressing the F8 key, or cancel the query by pressing Ctrl + Q.

Counting Query Hits When you execute a query, it is useful to know how many total records will be returned without having to execute the query and download all of the data from the server. You can count the number of records that would be retrieved by using the Count hits command prior to executing the query.

To use the Count hits command:

1 Enter a query with the search condition **%Street%** in the Street field to determine which customers have the word "Street" in their address, but *do not press the F8 key.*

HELP? If you press the F8 key by mistake, just repeat Step 1.

2 Click **Query** on the menu bar, and then click **Count hits**. The message "Query will retrieve 2 records" appears in the message area.

3 Press the **F8** key to execute the query and view the two records.

Inserting New Records At the beginning of the chapter, you used a form to enter CUSTOMER records. Now you will test to confirm that the form you created inserts new CUSTOMER records correctly.

To use your form to add a new record to the CUSTOMER table:

1 Click **Record** on the menu bar, and then click **Insert**. A blank row appears, and the insertion point moves to the Customer ID field.

2 Enter the following data: Customer ID: **1001**; Last Name: **Brian**; First Name: **Sarah**; Middle Initial: **M**; Address: **1444 Spring Street**; City: **Elk Mound**; State: **WI**; and Zip: **54705**. You will not enter the daytime and evening phone numbers.

HELP? If you press the Tab key to navigate between the text fields, the entry order might not flow from left to right and down the screen. You will learn to specify the navigation order of form text fields in a later chapter. Click in the field to enter values into it.

3 Click the **Save** button on the Button palette. The confirmation message "FRM-40400: Transaction complete: 1 records applied and saved" appears in the message area.

Updating Records To update an existing database record, you first need to display the record. Then you can enter the field you want to update, delete the existing value, and enter the new value.

To update a record:

1 Execute a new query to retrieve Alissa White's record by entering a query using **White** as the search condition in the Last Name field.
2 Select the value in the Evening Phone field, type **7155557644**.
3 Click the **Save** button on the Button palette. The message "1 records applied and saved" appears in the message area.
4 Change Alissa's evening phone number back to the original value (7155550087), and then save your changes.

Deleting Records Remember that to delete a record you must execute a query to display the record, and then click Record on the menu bar, and click Remove.

To delete a record:

1 Execute a query to retrieve Sarah Brian's record.
2 Click **Record** on the menu bar, and then click **Remove**.
3 Click the **Save** button on the Button palette. When you save a form you commit the delete to the database.
4 Execute another query to retrieve Sarah Brian's record to confirm that it has been deleted. The message "Query caused no records to be retrieved. Re-enter." indicates that the record doesn't exist in the database.
5 Press the F8 key to return to Normal mode.

Clearing the Form Fields and Exiting from Forms Runtime Suppose you begin to enter a data record, and then decide you don't want to save it. There is an easy way to clear all of the form fields.

To clear the form fields:

1 Enter **1002** in the Customer ID field.
2 Enter **Potter** in the Last Name field.
3 Clear the fields by clicking **Action** on the menu bar, and then clicking **Clear All**. Click the **Yes** button to confirm that you want to clear the form fields.

To exit from the Forms Runtime application, close the window by clicking the Close button on the title bar. If you have made any changes (insertions, updates, or deletions) since the last time you clicked the Save button, you will be asked if you want to save your changes. If you click the Yes button, your changes will be committed to the database. If you click the No button, your changes will not be saved. Always exit the Forms Runtime application when you return to the Forms Designer, or you will have multiple Forms Runtime processes running on your computer and you will eventually run out of memory.

tip

You also can click Action on the menu bar, and then click Exit to close Forms Runtime.

To exit Forms Runtime:

1 Click the **Close** button on the Forms Runtime title bar to close the application.

HELP? If you cannot exit the program, press the F8 key to return to Normal mode, and then repeat Step 1.

2 If a message box appears and asks if you want to save your changes, click the **Yes** button to commit your changes.

Creating a Multiple-Table Form

Now that you have learned how to create a single-table data block form, the next task is to create a form using multiple tables with master/detail relationships. You will create a form that allows users to select a customer record, and then display and edit customer order and order line information. You will create the master block first, which will be the list of customers. When the user selects a specific customer, the details about this customer's orders will be shown in the detail block.

To create the new form:

1 Return to the Object Navigator and change to Visual View.
2 Click the **minus sign** for CUSTOMER_FORM to close all CUSTOMER_FORM objects.
3 Create a new form by clicking the **Forms** object, and then clicking the **Create** button on the Object Navigator toolbar. A new form module (named MODULE2) appears. Rename it **CUST_ORDERS**, and then press the **Enter** key.
4 Click the **plus box** to the left of Windows under CUST_ORDERS, and rename WINDOW0 to **CUST_ORDERS_WINDOW**.

5 Create a new canvas in CUST_ORDERS_WINDOW, and name it **CUST_ORDERS_CANVAS.**

6 Double-click the **CUST_ORDERS_CANVAS** icon to go to the Layout Editor, and maximize the window if necessary.

Creating the CUSTOMER Master Data Block

First you will create the master block. This block will be like the CUSTOMER block you created in the previous form, except that it will show several customer records on the form at the same time.

To create the CUSTOMER master block:

1 Click **Tools** on the menu bar, and then click **New Block** to create a new data block linked to the CUSTOMER table. Name the block **CUSTOMER.** On the General tab, make sure that you preface the base table name with your user name (followed by a period).

2 Click the **Items** tab, and change the settings to display all data fields by clicking the **Select Columns** button. Do not change the field labels.

3 Click the **Layout** tab, and then specify a **tabular** format, vertical orientation, 3 records, and check the **Integrity Constraints, Button Palette,** and **Scrollbar** check boxes.

HELP? You do not specify the master/detail relationship in the master block. You will specify it when you create the detail block.

4 Click the **OK** button to create the new data block.

5 Save the file as **cust_orders** in the Chapter4 folder on your Student Disk.

HELP? If you have trouble using the scroll bars to scroll to areas on the right side or bottom of your canvas, click and drag the mouse pointer to the area of the canvas that you want displayed to scroll the screen.

Next you need to format the data fields so they look like Figure 4-36.

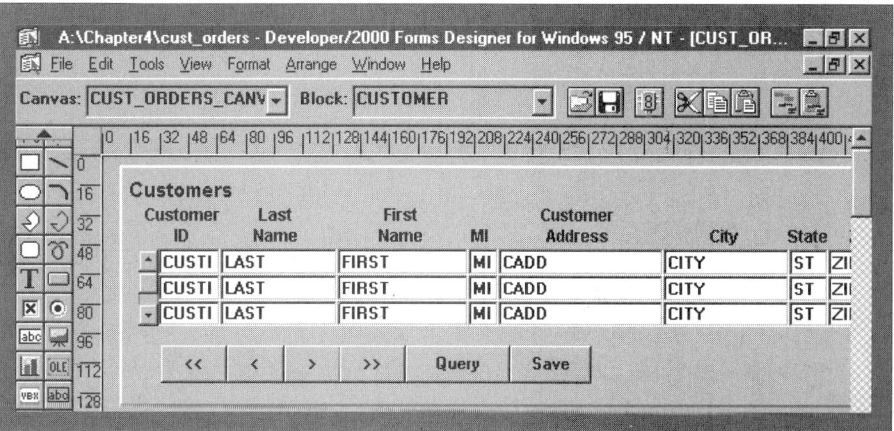

Figure 4-36: Formatting the CUSTOMER_BLOCK

To format the data fields:

1. Delete the frame around the data fields.
2. Select all of the buttons as an object group, and change their group Height property to 20.
3. Click one of the **LAST** text fields, position the pointer on the bottom right handle, and then drag it to the left to decrease the field width.
4. Repeat Step 3 and reduce the widths of the other text fields to match Figure 4-36.
5. Select all the text fields as a group, and then change the Height property to 14 in the group Properties sheet.
6. With all of the fields still selected, move them all as far to the left as possible.
7. With all of the fields still selected, click **Arrange** on the menu bar, click **Align Objects**, and then click the **Horizontally Stack** and **Vertically Align Bottom** option buttons.
8. Reposition the scroll bar if necessary so it is stacked horizontally on the left edge of the CUSTID field.
9. Save the file.

Next you will format the field labels. You also will create a form title.

To complete these formatting tasks:

1. Change the labels as follows. Labels that have two words should display on two lines. (The City, State, and Zip labels don't need to be changed.)

Old Label	**New Label**
Custid	Customer ID
Last	Last Name
First	First Name
Mi	MI
Caddress	Address
Dphone	Daytime Phone
Ephone	Evening Phone

2. Select all of the labels as a group, click **Format** on the menu bar, click **Font**, and then change the label fonts to **9-point bold Arial**.
3. Select the words in the two-line labels as a group, click **Format** on the menu bar, point to **Alignment**, and then click **Center** to center the labels with respect to their top and bottom lines.
4. Reposition the labels so they are centered over their associated text fields.
5. Select all of the labels, click **Arrange**, point to **Align Objects**, and then click the **Horizontally None**, **Vertically Align Bottom** option buttons. Click the OK button.
6. Use the **Text** tool [T] on the Tool palette to add the title **Customers** at the top of the form, and then change its font to **11-point bold Arial**.
7. Save the form.

The final formatting task is to create the raised rectangle that encloses the text fields and title. This rectangle groups the Button palette with this data block.

To create the raised rectangle:

1. Use the **Rectangle** tool on the Tool palette to draw a rectangle around the data fields, labels, and Button palette. Change the fill color to **light gray**, and then change the line color to **dark gray**.
2. Click the rectangle to select it, click **Format** on the menu bar, point to **Bevel**, and then click **Raised** to change it to a three-dimensional image.
3. Click **Arrange** on the menu bar, and then click **Send to back** to send the color to the background.
4. Reposition the Button palette so it is aligned with the left edge of the text fields.
5. Select all of the form objects, and move them to the upper-left edge of the canvas.
6. Save the form.

Creating the CUST_ORDER Detail Data Block

When the user selects a customer in the CUSTOMER block, the form will show the selected customer's order information. Next you will create a detail block called CUST_ORDER that is associated with the Clearwater Traders CUST_ORDER table to show the related order information.

To create the CUST_ORDER data block:

1. Create a new block named **CUST_ORDER** that is associated with your CUST_ORDER database table. Make sure that you preface the base table name with your user name.
2. Click the **Items** tab, and display all data fields.
3. Click the **Layout** tab, and then specify a **tabular** style, vertical orientation, 2 records, and check the **Integrity Constraints** and **Scrollbar** check boxes. *Do not check the Button Palette check box.* You do not need the Button palette because the user will not navigate through the records in this block directly, but will scroll through the CUSTOMER records, and the records in this block will be updated depending on the selected customer record. The next step is to specify the master/detail relationship.
4. Click the **Master/Detail** tab. The text boxes for entering the master block and join condition appear, as shown in Figure 4-37. The next step is to specify the master/detail relationship between the CUSTOMER block and the CUST_ORDER block. The CUSTOMER block will be the master block because it will hold the records that the user will select. Then the CUST_ORDER detail block will show detailed order information about the selected master record.

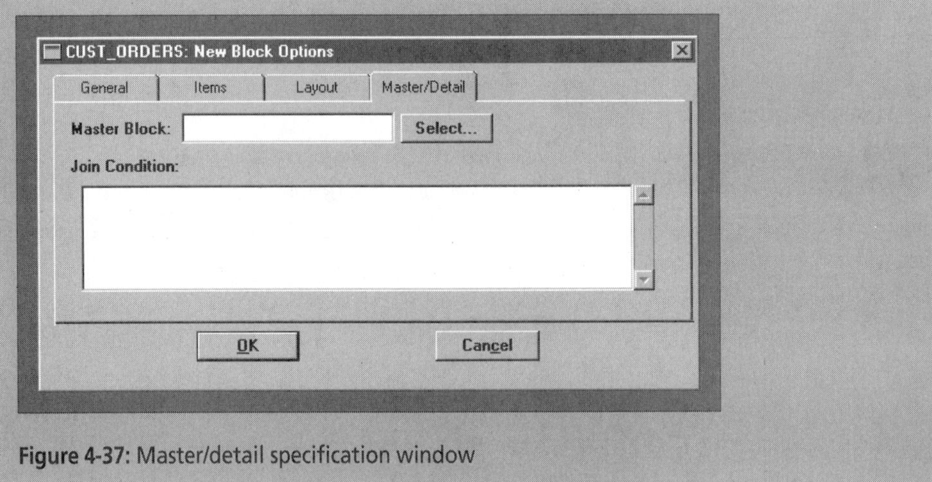

Figure 4-37: Master/detail specification window

The join condition specifies the block and item names that you are joining the two blocks on using the general format `<master block name>.<join item name> = <detail block name>.<join item name>`. When you create a detail block, the block name always defaults to its associated table name, even if you specified a different block name on the General tab. The associated database tables must have foreign key constraints on the specified join fields.

The name in the Master Block text box is the block name—not the table name. You must create the master block before you can specify a master/block relationship in a detail block.

To specify the master/detail relationship:

1. Enter **CUSTOMER** as the master block name.
2. Press the **Tab** key to move to the Join Condition text box, and then enter the join condition shown in Figure 4-38.

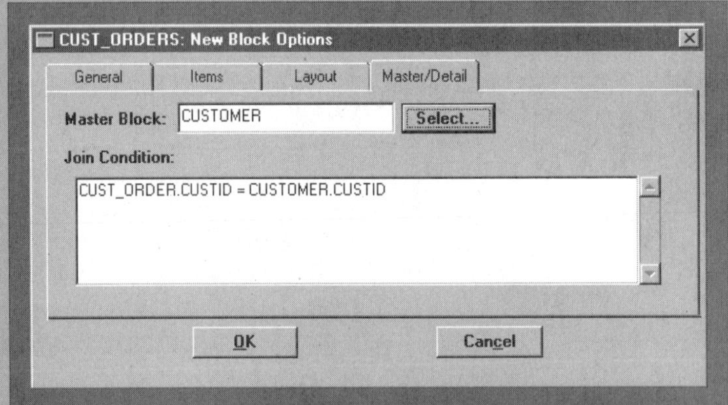

Figure 4-38: Specifying the CUSTOMER/CUST_ORDER master/detail relationship

3. Click the **OK** button to create the block.

HELP? Sometimes when you click the Select button to the right of the Master Block text box, a selection list of available master blocks displays. When you select a master block from the list, the join condition is entered automatically in the Join Condition text box. However, if you receive a message stating that no master blocks are available, even though some do indeed exist, you can enter the master block name and the join condition as shown in Figure 4-38.

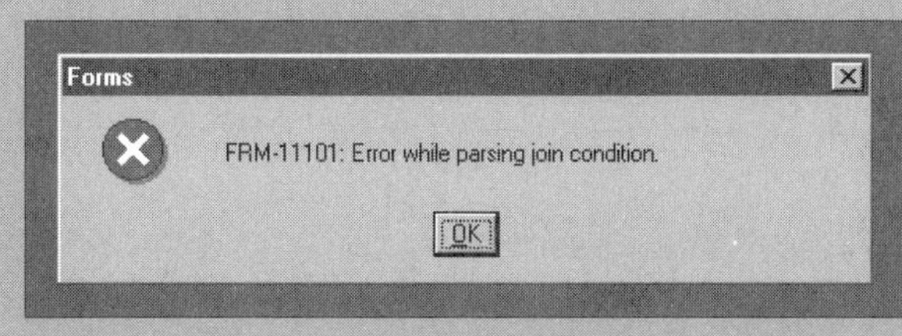

Figure 4-39: Master/detail block error

HELP? If you received the error message shown in Figure 4-39, it means that you did not specify the join condition correctly. Click the OK button to close the message box, and then click the Cancel button to close the New Block Options window. Open the Object Navigator window in Ownership View, and then check that the name of the block that you specified as the master block is correct. Also, be sure that the join item is listed as an item in the master block. Then, re-create the detail block using the correct master block and join item name.

Finally, you need to format the CUST_ORDER block. You will do this next.

To format the CUST_ORDER block:

1 Format the CUST_ORDER block as shown in Figure 4-40 using the same steps you used to format the CUSTOMER block.

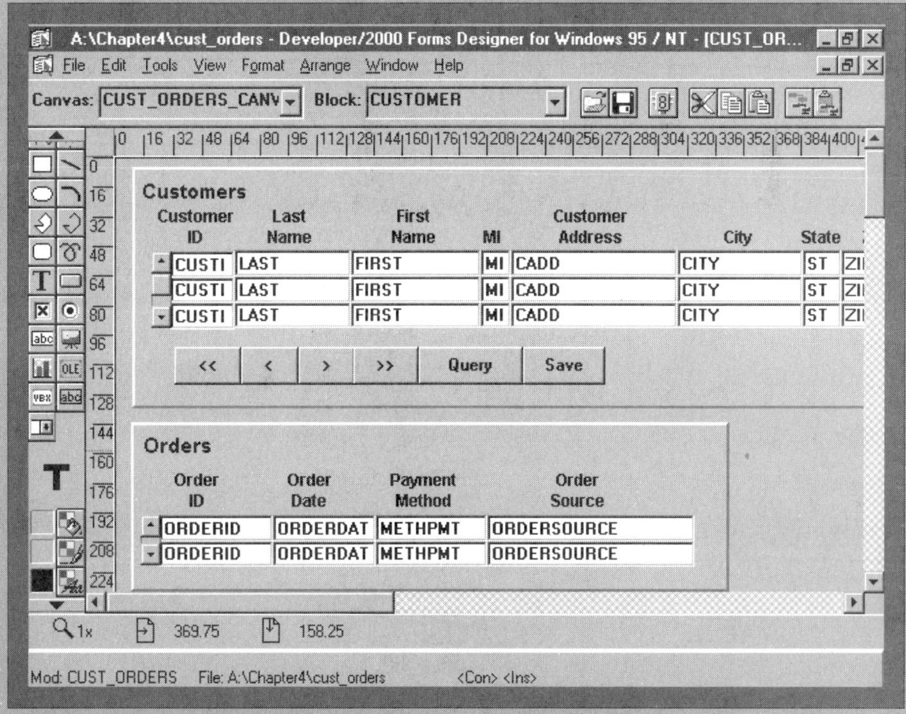

Figure 4-40: Formatting the CUST_ORDER block

2 Save the file.

When you run your form, Oracle creates a text file named <form name>.err that records compilation messages and errors. These messages also are displayed on the screen, so you probably will not use this file. However, you can open it in any text editor to review its contents.

Running the Master/Detail Form and Modifying the Window Properties

Now run the form to test its runtime appearance.

To run the form:

1. Click the **Run** button on the Layout Editor toolbar. Your form in the Forms Runtime application should look like Figure 4-41. Notice that part of the CUSTOMER block data fields are cut off, and that there are no scroll bars to allow users to scroll to the right to see the rest of the fields. Also note the window title CUST_ORDERS_WINDOW is descriptive for programming but isn't right for the finished application. You will need to change some properties of the CUST_ORDER_WINDOW to solve these problems.

inappropriate window title

data fields display off the screen

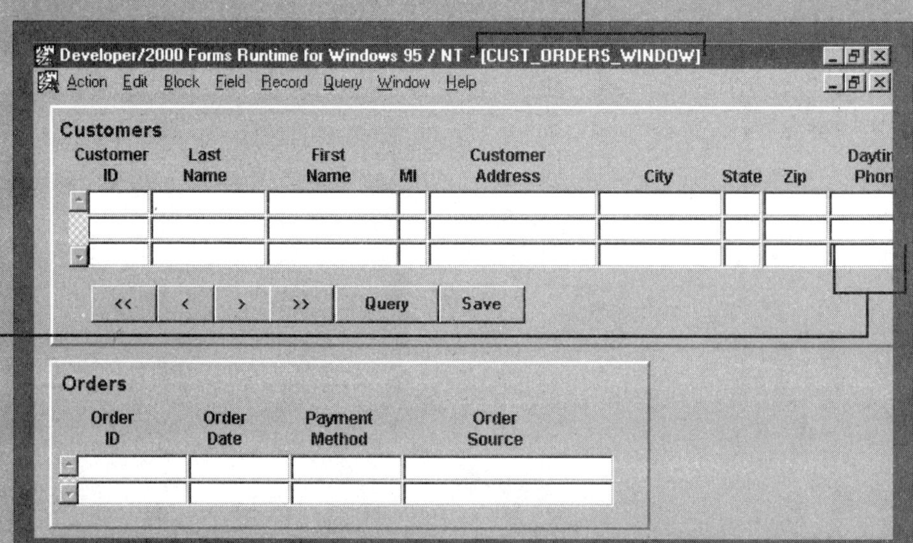

Figure 4-41: Running the CUST_ORDERS form

2. Close the Forms Runtime application.
3. Open the Object Navigator window.
4. Right-click **CUST_ORDERS_WINDOW**, and then click Properties to open its Properties sheet. Scroll down and note the Width and Height properties. The maximum width and height that can be displayed on a monitor screen depends on the type of monitor and how it is configured. Some common screen resolutions are 640 x 480 or 800 x 600 to indicate the number of pixels that display on the screen. You will change the width and height to 640 x 480 next.
5. Click the Width property, and then type **640**, and then click the Height property to save the new width value.
6. With the Height property selected, type **480**, and then click any other property to save the new height value.

7 Change the Title property to **Customer Orders**, click any other property to save your change. See Figure 4-42.

change these values

change the title

A:\Chapter4\cust_orders - Developer/2000 Forms Designer for Windows 95 / NT
File Edit Tools Window Help
Properties
Window: CUST_ORDERS_WINDOW
CUST_ORDERS_WINDOW
Name CUST_ORDERS_WINDOW
Class
Display
X Position 0
Y Position 0
Width 640
Height 480
Bevel Lowered
Title Customer Orders
Visual Attribute Name Default
Font Name
Font Size 10

Figure 4-42: Modified CUST_ORDERS_WINDOW

8 Scroll down the Properties sheet, and then change the Horizontal Scroll Bar and Vertical Scroll Bar properties to **True** by double-clicking them.

9 Close the Properties sheet, and then save the form.

10 Run the form. You should now be able to see your new title as well as all of the canvas objects using the scroll bars. See Figure 4-43.

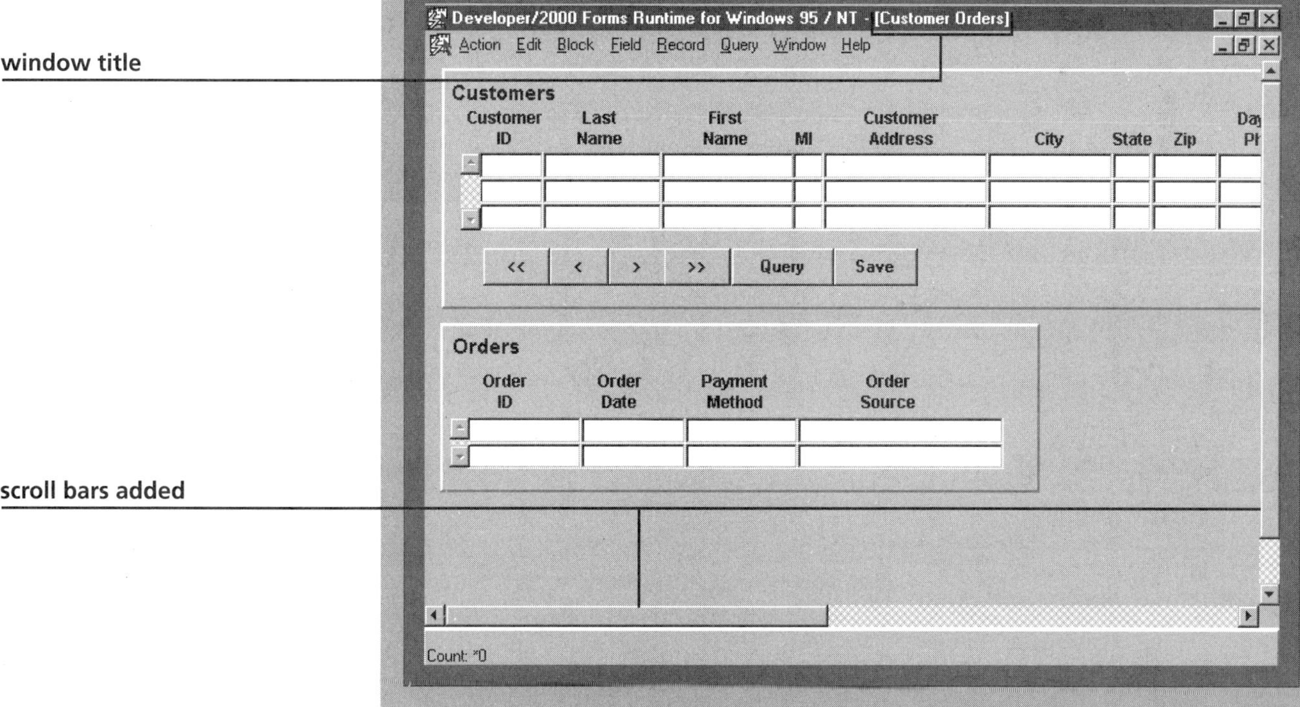

Figure 4-43: CUST_ORDERS form with modified window properties

Using Master/Detail Forms

You can add, update, delete, and query database records in a form that is based on multiple tables, just as you did in the single-table form. The only difference is that you need to activate the data block first where the record is that you want to add, modify, or query.

To query the form:

1. Click **Query** on the menu bar, and then click **Execute**. The insertion point moves to the first record in the CUSTOMER data block (Paula Jones). Note that Order ID 1057 (the order for Paula Jones) displays in the CUST_ORDER block.
2. Use the pointer to click other customer records, or use the scroll bars or navigation buttons to select other customer records. As you select other records, the customer order information changes in the form. The location of the pointer determines which block and record are active.
3. Click the insertion point in any data field in the CUSTOMER data block.
4. Click the **Query** button, type **White** in the Last Name field, and then press the **F8** key to execute the query. The query retrieves the customer and order information for Alissa White.
5. Change Alissa's daytime phone number to **7158300920**, press the **Enter** key, and then click the **Save** button. Note the confirmation message in the message bar.
6. Change Alissa's daytime phone number back to **7155558943**, and then click the **Save** button.
7. Click in the Order ID 1062 field in the CUST_ORDER data block, click **Record** on the menu bar, and then click **Insert**. A blank row appears.
8. Enter the following new order information in the new record: Order ID: 1063; Date: **17-JUN-99**; Payment Method: **CHECK**; and Order Source: 153.
9. Click the Save button on the Button palette. Note the save confirmation message.
10. Click anywhere in the CUSTOMER block, click **Record** on the menu bar, and then click **Clear** to clear the contents of the CUSTOMER data fields.
11. Click **Query** on the menu bar, click **Execute** to refresh the customer records, and then select Alissa White's record. Scroll through her orders to confirm that order 1063 was added.
12. Click **Order ID 1063**, click **Record** on the menu bar, and then click **Remove** to delete the record. Order 1063 disappears. Click the **Save** button to commit the changes.
13. Close the Forms Runtime application.

Adding Another Detail Data Block to the CUST_ORDERS Form A form can have multiple master/detail data block relationships. Next you will create an ORDERLINE data block to show the order lines that correspond to a particular customer order. CUST_ORDERS will be the master block in this relationship, and ORDERLINE will be the detail block. CUST_ORDERS is the master block because when the user selects a particular CUST_ORDER record, the detail information about the individual order lines for that order appears automatically.

To create the second master/detail data block relationship:

1 Open **CUST_ORDERS_CANVAS** in the Layout Editor, and then create a new data block named **ORDERLINE** linked to your ORDERLINE database table.

2 Click the **Items** tab, and then display all data fields.

3 Click the **Layout** tab, and then specify the **tabular** style, vertical orientation, 5 records, and check the **Integrity Constraints** and **Scrollbar** check boxes. *Do not check the Button Palette option button.*

4 Click the **Master/Detail** tab, type **CUST_ORDER** as the master block name, and then type the following join condition: **CUST_ORDER.ORDERID = ORDERLINE.ORDERID.**

5 Click the **OK** button to create the data block.

6 Format the ORDERLINE block as shown in Figure 4-44.

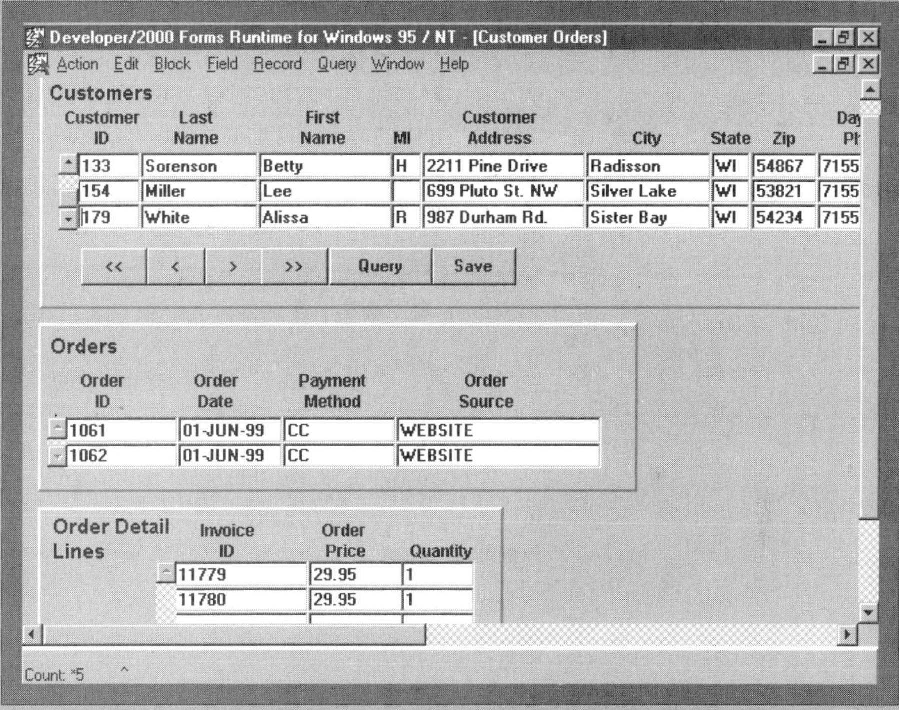

Figure 4-44: Formatting the ORDERLINE block

7 Run the form.

8 In the Forms Runtime application, click **Query** on the menu bar, and then click **Execute**. Now, as you scroll down through the customer records, the associated inventory IDs, order prices, and quantities are displayed for each customer order.

9 Scroll down through the customer records until you get to Alissa White's record, as shown in Figure 4-45. Notice that this data relationship shows that Alissa White has two orders in the CUST_ORDER block. Although there is no way to tell visually, the order detail lines correspond to the first order record.

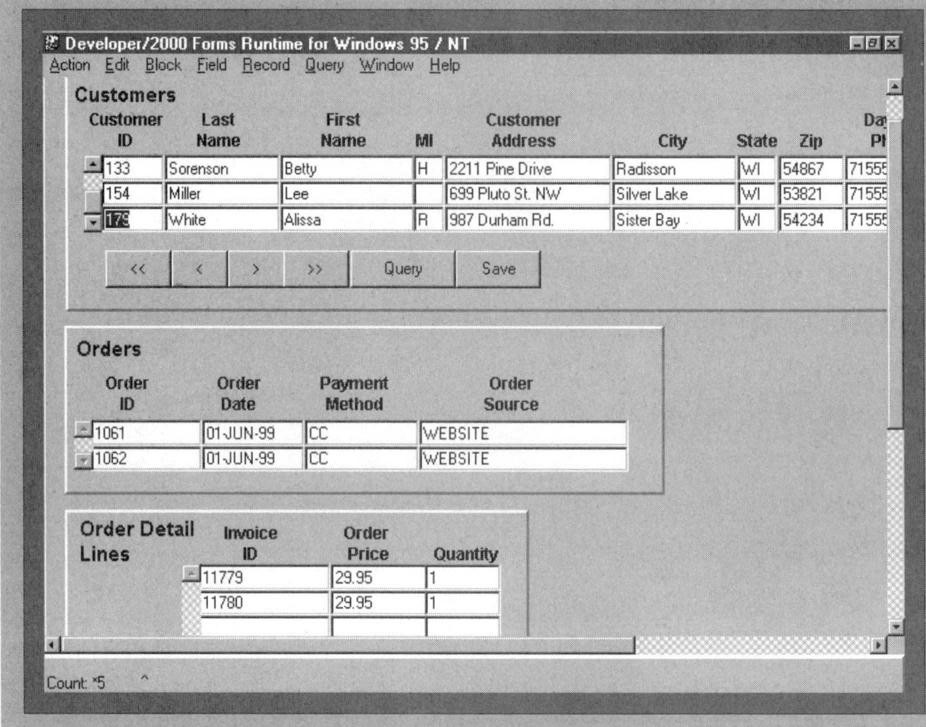

Figure 4-45: Viewing a submaster block

10 Click **Order ID 1062** in the CUST_ORDER block and note that the order detail lines are updated.

You can insert, update, and delete data records just as before. For example, next you will add another item to Order ID 1061.

To add another item to an order:

1 Click **Order ID 1061** in the CUST_ORDER block.

2 Click **Invoice ID 11780** in the ORDERLINE data block, click **Record** on the menu bar, and then click **Insert** to insert a new record.

3 Enter the following data in the form: Invoice ID: **11846**; Order Price: **199.95**; and Quantity: **1**.

4 Click the **Save** button on the Button palette. Note the confirmation message at the bottom left of the screen.

5 Delete the record you just entered by clicking **Record** on the menu bar, and then clicking **Remove**. Click the **Save** button on the Button palette to commit the record deletion.

6 Close the Forms Runtime application. Do not save your changes.

7 Close the Forms Designer application. Click the **Yes** button to save the changes to your CUST_ORDERS and CUSTOMER forms.

Now you are familiar with creating and using Oracle data block forms. In Chapter 5, you will learn advanced techniques for creating customized forms.

SUMMARY

- Oracle Forms is used to create applications for inserting, updating, deleting, and querying database data, and for integrating Oracle Forms applications with Oracle Reports and Graphics applications.
- Data block forms are explicitly associated with database tables.
- Using a form to add records is the equivalent of adding records in SQL using the INSERT command. Using a form to modify records is the equivalent of updating records in SQL using the UPDATE command.
- The Object Navigator in Oracle Forms enables you to access all form objects either by object type (Ownership View) or hierarchically by opening objects that contain other objects (Visual View).
- Form modules contain windows. Windows contain canvases; and canvases contain items such as data fields and labels. The Layout Editor shows a visual view of the actual layout of your canvas items.
- Data blocks are created to display database table fields.
- If you want other users to be able to use your form application to access your database tables, you must preface the table name in the Base Table text box on the General tab with your user name.
- On the Items tab, Text Items are used to display database fields that can be updated, while Display Items are used to display database fields for viewing only. List Items are used to display pick lists of items that do not change frequently. Radio Groups are used to display database fields with a fixed number of options (usually no more than about five). Item labels can be edited on the Items tab when creating a data block or in the Layout Editor.
- On the Layout tab, the form style displays one record per form, whereas the tabular style displays as many records at a time as you specify in the Records text box. Checking the Integrity Constraints check box enforces integrity constraints in the Forms environment. Checking the Button Palette check box generates buttons for navigating through the data records, querying the database, and saving new records. Checking the Scrollbar check box generates a scroll bar for moving through data records that are displayed in the tabular style.
- When you are formatting a canvas, a good strategy is to get all of the data fields and labels in the correct general vicinity before doing the final alignment.
- Almost every canvas item has a Properties sheet that you can use to specify an item's size, position, and a variety of other properties. You can change a property for a group of selected items using a group Properties sheet where values that are different for each group item are shown as wildcard characters (****).
- Boilerplate objects are text, graphics, and other objects that do not contribute to the functionality of a form but enhance its appearance and ease-of-use.
- Use subtle colors on forms and ensure that there is adequate contrast between background colors and foreground text.
- Forms Designer files are saved with an .fmb extension, whereas executable Forms Runtime files are saved with an .fmx extension. Whenever you make a change to your .fmb file, you must regenerate it to create an updated .fmx file before you can run it.
- The Next and Previous buttons on the Button palette navigate among database records one at a time. The SCROLL_UP and SCROLL_DOWN buttons retrieve groups of records when they are displayed in the tabular style.
- Forms Runtime has two modes: Normal and Enter Query. You are in the Normal mode until you click the Query button, which switches you to Enter Query mode. When you are in Enter Query mode, you must execute the query (by pressing the F8 key) or cancel the query (by pressing Ctrl + Q) to return to Normal mode.

- You can do exact searches in forms by entering the exact data you would like to match, or approximate searches where you surround a search string with a % to indicate a variable number of wildcard characters on either side of the search string.
- When creating master/detail data blocks, create the master block first, and then specify the master/detail information on the Master/Detail tab of the detail block. On the Master/Detail tab, the Master Block text box contains the name of the master *block* name (not the database table name), and the Join Condition text box contains the *block* and *item* names (not the table and field names).
- You can change a window's size and add horizontal and vertical scroll bars using the window's Properties sheet.
- You can add, update, delete, and query database records in master/detail blocks just like in single-table data blocks except that you need to activate the data block first before performing the insert, update, or query.
- A single form can have multiple master/detail block relationships.

REVIEW QUESTIONS

1. What views are available in the Object Navigator, and how are they different?
2. How do you create new objects in the Object Navigator?
3. How do you rename objects in the Object Navigator?
4. Describe two ways to go to the Layout Editor from the Object Navigator.
5. Why is it important to preface your table name with your user name when you create a new data block?
6. What is the difference between the form and tabular styles in a data block?
7. What is the difference between a text item and a display item?
8. When should you use a radio group, and when should you use a list item?
9. Why should you check the Integrity Constraints check box on the Layout tab when you create a new data block?
10. When should you check the Scrollbar check box on the Layout tab?
11. How do you group canvas items? Name two tasks that are completed more easily if you select items as a group.
12. How do you access an item's Properties sheet from the Layout Editor?
13. What is a boilerplate object?
14. What is the difference between the files named customer.fmb and customer.fmx?
15. What is the difference between the Next and SCROLL_UP buttons?
16. What are the two modes that exist in the Forms Runtime application? How do you move between these modes?
17. Specify an approximate search condition that would return the records for all items with the word "Children" in the description. (Specify the search condition so there could be text either before or after the word "Children.")
18. When creating a master/detail relationship, how do you decide which block is the master block and which block is the detail block? Which block do you create first?
19. When specifying a master/detail relationship, what do the items in the Join Condition text box refer to, and how can you ensure that they are correct?

PROBLEM-SOLVING CASES

Northwoods University Database

For each form that you create in the Exercises below, save the .fmb and .fmx files in the Chapter4 folder on your Student Disk.

1. Run the northwoo.sql script to create the Northwoods University database and populate the tables. The script file is stored in the Chapter4 folder on your Student Disk.
2. Create a single-table form named LOCATION for inserting, updating, and viewing records in the LOCATION database table. Name the window LOCATION_WINDOW and the canvas LOCATION_CANVAS. Use a tabular layout style, and vertical orientation with five records displayed, and include a Button palette. Format the layout attractively using the design and formatting concepts discussed in this chapter.
3. Create a master/detail form named LOC_FAC showing faculty members and their associated LOCATION information. Use a tabular layout style and vertical orientation for all blocks and display five records in each block. The user should be able to scroll through the FACULTY records, and the associated LOCATION information should be displayed. Use the same naming conventions for forms, windows, and other form objects as specified in Exercise 2, and follow good formatting and design practices.
4. Create a multiple-table form named CRS_ENR showing course sections, their associated enrollments, and their associated students. When the user selects a specific COURSE_SECTION, the associated ENROLLMENT information will be displayed. When the user selects an ENROLLMENT record, the associated STUDENT information will be displayed. Use a tabular layout style and vertical orientation for all blocks and display five records in each block. Use the same naming conventions for forms, windows, and other form objects as specified in Exercise 2, and follow good formatting and design practices.
5. Create a multiple table form named TERM that shows TERM information. When the user selects a given TERM record, the associated COURSE_SECTION records are displayed. When the user selects a given COURSE_SECTION record, the associated FACULTY and COURSE records are displayed. Use a tabular layout style and vertical orientation for all blocks and display five records in each block. Use the same naming conventions for forms, windows, and other form objects as specified in Exercise 2, and follow good formatting and design practices.

Clearwater Traders Database

For each form that you create in the Exercises below, save the .fmb and .fmx files in the Chapter4 folder on your Student Disk.

1. Run the clearwat.sql script to create the Clearwater Traders database and populate the tables. The script file is stored in the Chapter4 folder on your Student Disk.

2. Create a single-table form named ITEM for inserting, updating, and viewing records in the ITEM database table. Call the window ITEM_WINDOW, and the canvas ITEM_CANVAS. Use a tabular layout style, and vertical orientation with five records displayed, and include a Button palette. Format the layout attractively using the design and formatting concepts discussed in this chapter.
3. Create a multiple-table form named ITM_INV that displays items and their associated inventory, shipping, and back order information. When a user selects an ITEM record, the associated INVENTORY information should appear. When the user selects an INVENTORY record, the associated SHIPPING and BACKORDER records should appear. Use a tabular layout style and vertical orientation for all blocks and display five records in each block. Use the same naming conventions for forms, windows, and other objects as specified in Exercise 2, and follow good formatting and design practices.

Chapter 5

objectives

- Use sequences to generate surrogate keys automatically
- Create custom Oracle forms using SQL statements for inserting, updating, deleting, and viewing data
- Create single-table and multiple-table lists of values (LOVs) to provide pick lists of data values
- Create triggers, which are the programs that run when a user performs an action such as clicking a button
- Reuse form objects
- Interpret form error messages
- Use Oracle format masks

CHAPTER 5

Creating Custom Forms

Introduction The data block forms you created in Chapter 4 were easy to create and useful for performing basic database operations. However, sometimes data block forms are not flexible enough to support certain operations. For example, a data block form requires the user to press the F8 key to go into Enter Query mode, and then type a search command to retrieve records. However, you might want to create a form that allows the user to select a search condition from a list without having to press the F8 key or type a search condition.

Another more serious limitation of data block forms is how they display master/detail data relationships. Each data block displays data from only one table. You cannot create a data block display to show information from multiple tables that is formatted to look like a single record. For example, suppose you want to display a line on a customer invoice. This requires data from three different tables: INVENTORY (for inventory ID, size, color, and price), ITEM (for item description), and ORDERLINE (for quantity). This kind of display requires a custom form. **Custom forms** require the form developer to write programs to control how the form works. Custom forms allow more flexibility in the way data is displayed on the form and how the user interacts with the form.

In this chapter you will see how a custom form works by running a custom form to insert, update, view, and delete database records. You also will learn how to use Oracle sequences to generate surrogate key values for primary key fields automatically. System-generated primary keys are preferable to user-entered primary keys for busy database systems with many users because it might be difficult for users to ensure that entered primary key values are unique. Finally, you will learn how to create custom forms that use sequences to generate primary key values automatically and how to write programs that control how the form looks and works.

Sequences

Oracle **sequences** are sequential lists of numbers that are generated automatically by the database. Sequences are useful for creating unique surrogate key values for primary key fields when no field exists to use as the primary key. For example, you might assign a sequence for a customer ID field so each record is unique. Fields using sequences must have a NUMBER data type. In the following exercises, you will become familiar with creating and manipulating sequences using SQL*Plus.

Creating New Sequences

You must create sequences in SQL*Plus, but you can access and increment a sequence within a form using SQL statements. The general format that you will use for creating a new sequence is shown below, with optional commands enclosed in square brackets:

```
CREATE SEQUENCE <sequence name>
[INCREMENT BY <number>]
[START WITH <start value number>]
[MAXVALUE <maximum value number>]
[NOMAXVALUE]
[MINVALUE <minimum value number>]
[CYCLE]
[NOCYCLE]
[CACHE <number of sequence values to cache>]
[NOCACHE]
[ORDER]
[NOORDER];
```

Every sequence must have a unique name, and the naming rules are the same as for Oracle data tables and fields. The CREATE SEQUENCE command is the only command required to create a sequence; the rest of the commands are optional. The following list describes these optional commands and their default value if the command is omitted:

- INCREMENT BY specifies the value by which the sequence is incremented. The default value is 1.
- START WITH specifies the sequence start value. The default value is 1. It is necessary to specify a start value if you already have data in the fields where the sequence will be used to generate primary key values. For example, in the ITEM table, the highest existing ITEMID is 995, so you would start the sequence with 996.
- MAXVALUE specifies the maximum value to which the sequence can be incremented. If you don't specify a maximum value, the maximum allowable value for a sequence variable is 1.000 + E27. The default is NOMAXVALUE, which specifies that the sequence will keep incrementing until the maximum allowable value is reached.
- MINVALUE specifies the minimum value of the sequence.
- CYCLE specifies that, when the sequence reaches its MAXVALUE, it cycles back and starts again at the MINVALUE. For example, if you specify a sequence with a maximum value of 10 and a minimum value of 5, the sequence would increment up to 10 and then start again at 5. The default value is NOCYCLE, which specifies that the sequence will continue to generate values until MAXVALUE and will not cycle.
- CACHE specifies that, whenever you request a sequence value, the Oracle database server automatically generates several sequence numbers and stores them in a server memory area called a **cache** to improve system performance. The default number of sequence values stored in the cache is 20. To specify a different number of sequence values to be cached, use the CACHE command along with the number of sequence values you want to generate and store.
- NOCACHE directs the server not to cache any sequence values.
- ORDER guarantees that the sequence numbers are granted in the exact chronological order in which they are requested. For example, the first user that requests a number from the sequence would be granted sequence number 1, the second user that requests a number from the sequence would be granted sequence number 2, and so forth. This is useful for tracking the order in which specific transactions occur. The default value is NOORDER.
- NOORDER specifies that the sequence values are not necessarily granted in chronological order, which means that although users are guaranteed to get unique sequence numbers, the order of the values might not correspond with the order in which the sequence numbers were requested.

Next you will create a sequence for the ITEMID field in the ITEM table in the Clearwater Traders database. Before you create a new sequence, you need to run the script that deletes all Clearwater Traders database tables, re-creates them, and then inserts all of the data records. You will do this next.

To run the script:

1. Start SQL*Plus and log on to the database.
2. Place your Student Disk in the disk drive, and then type **START A:\Chapter5\clearwat.sql** at the SQL prompt to run the script.

Now you will create a sequence named ITEMID_SEQUENCE that starts with 996 and has no maximum value. The sequence will increment by 1, so you will accept the default value and not use the INCREMENT BY command. You do not want the sequence to CYCLE, so you omit the CYCLE command and accept the NOCYCLE default. You will not have the server to cache sequence values, which means that you will not include the NOCACHE command.

To create the ITEMID_SEQUENCE:

1. Type the SQL command shown in Figure 5-1. The sequence will start at 996, and it has no maximum value. The confirmation message "Sequence created" indicates that the ITEMID_SEQUENCE sequence was created.

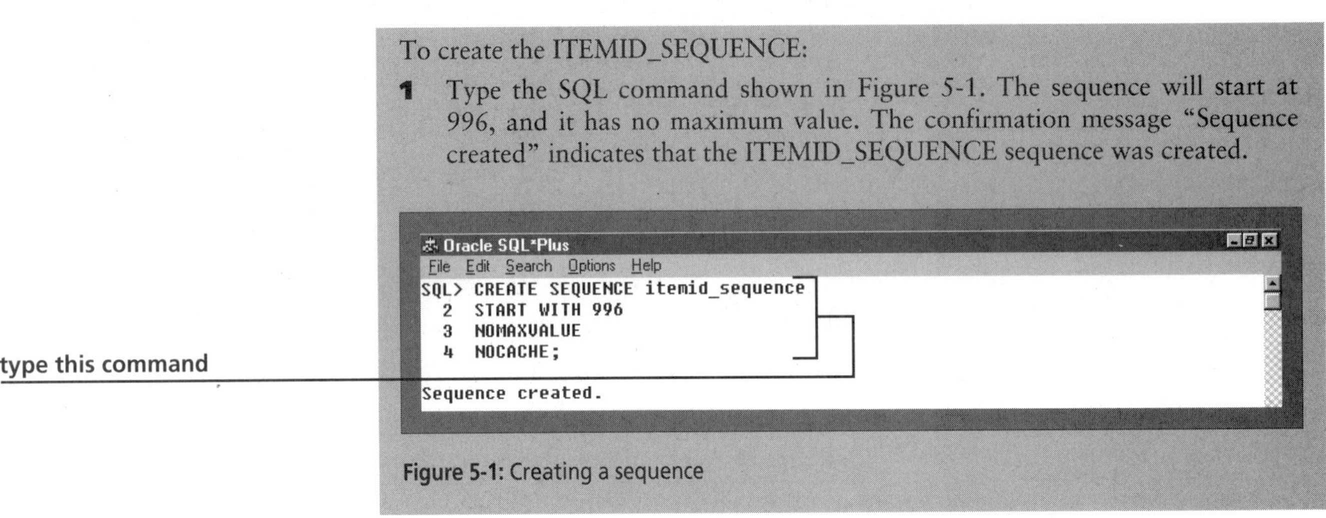

Figure 5-1: Creating a sequence

Accessing the Next Sequence Value

To access the next value in a sequence and use that value when you insert a new data record, use the following general command:

```
INSERT INTO <tablename>
VALUES (<owner user name>.<sequence name>.NEXTVAL, <field
2 data value>, <field 3 data value>, …);
```

tip

This command assumes that the primary key associated with the sequence is the first table field.

You don't have to preface the sequence name with your user name when you are using your own sequences. However, it is a good practice to use your user name because other users might use your sequences to insert data records.

Next you will insert a new item record in the Clearwater Traders database for an item with description "Heavy Duty Day Pack" in the Outdoor Gear category.

To insert a new ITEM record using the sequence:

1 Type the SQL command shown in Figure 5-2, and substitute your user name for lhoward. The confirmation message "1 row created" indicates that you inserted one record. Next you will see what was inserted for ITEMID.

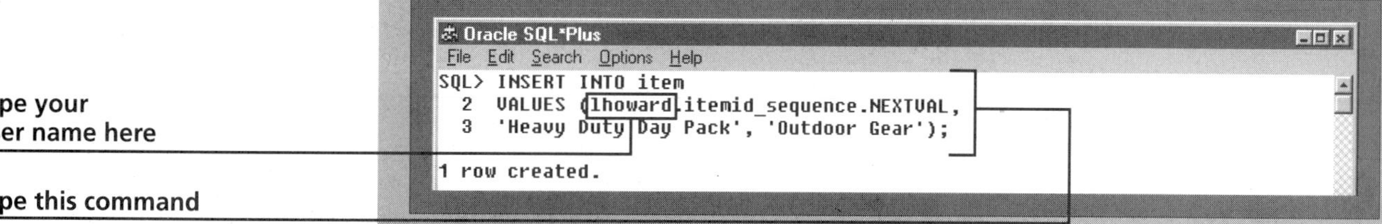

Figure 5-2: Inserting a new record using a sequence

2 Type the command shown in Figure 5-3. The new item has ITEMID 996. Now insert another customer record to confirm that the sequence increments correctly using the SELECT command.

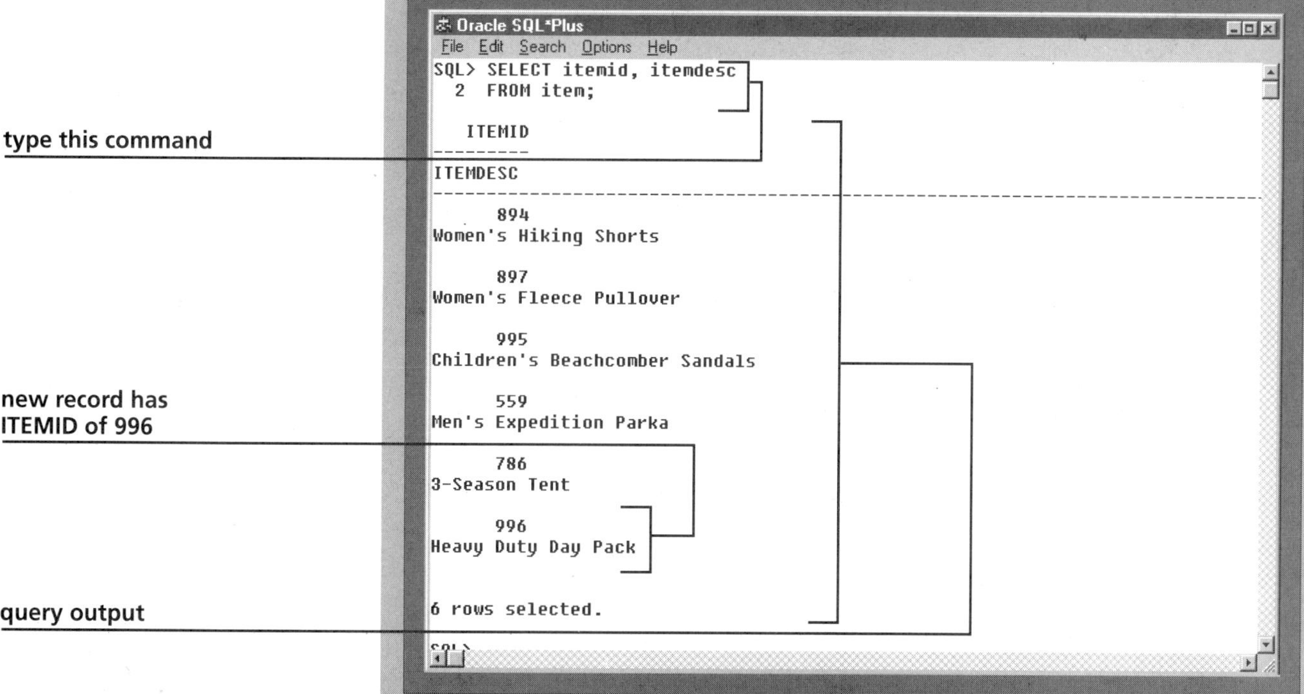

Figure 5-3: Viewing the new record inserted using the sequence

3 Type the SQL command shown in Figure 5-4, and substitute your user name for lhoward. You should receive the "1 row created" message again.

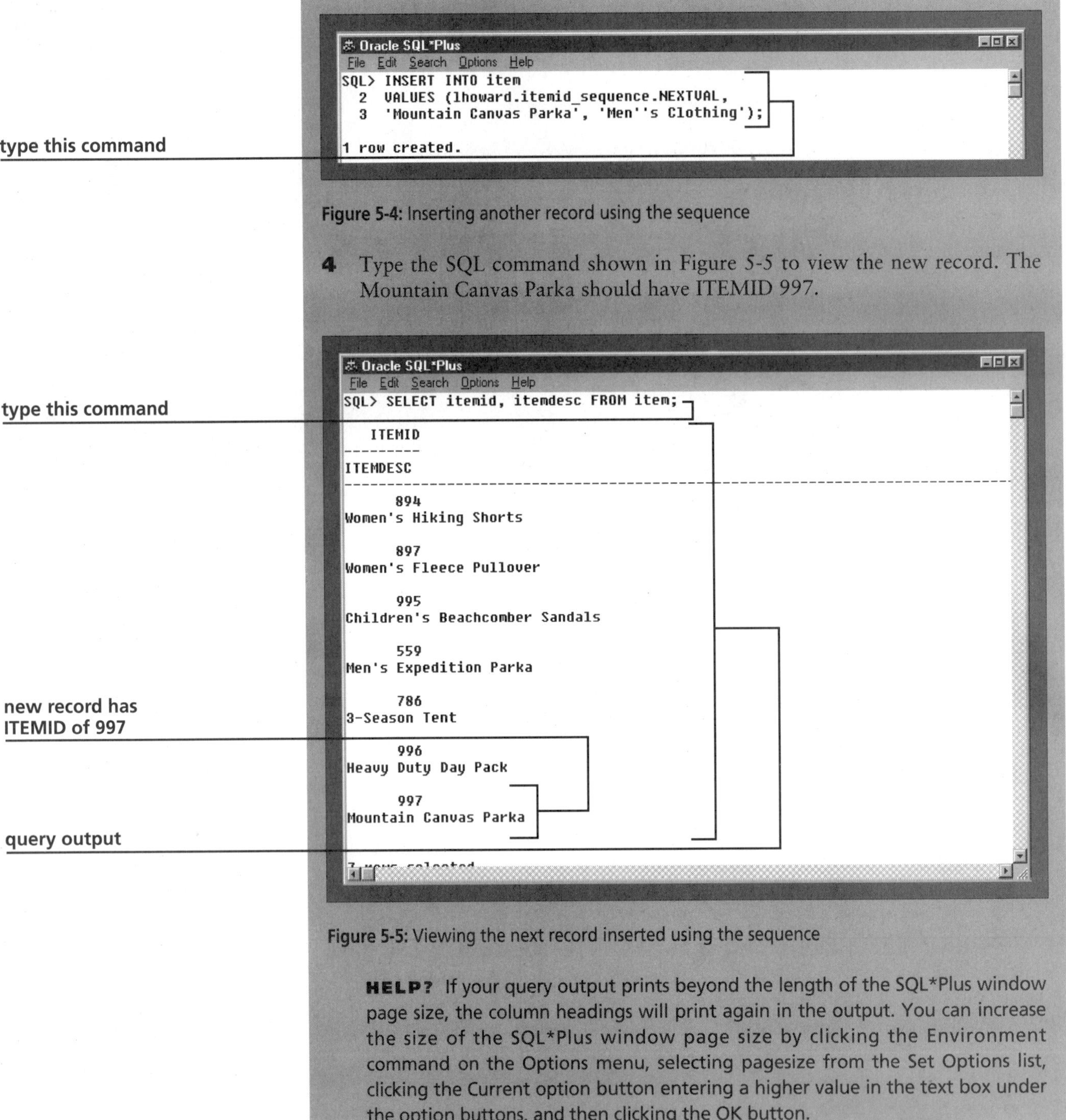

Figure 5-4: Inserting another record using the sequence

4 Type the SQL command shown in Figure 5-5 to view the new record. The Mountain Canvas Parka should have ITEMID 997.

Figure 5-5: Viewing the next record inserted using the sequence

HELP? If your query output prints beyond the length of the SQL*Plus window page size, the column headings will print again in the output. You can increase the size of the SQL*Plus window page size by clicking the Environment command on the Options menu, selecting pagesize from the Set Options list, clicking the Current option button entering a higher value in the text box under the option buttons, and then clicking the OK button.

Sometimes you need to access the next value of a sequence, but you don't want to insert a new record. For example, suppose you want to create a new customer order and display the ORDERID on the order form, but you need to have the user enter more information before you actually insert the new record. To do this, you use the SELECT command with the Oracle system database table DUAL. **DUAL** is a system database table that is used with a variety of SQL commands.

To use the SELECT command to access the next value in a sequence:

1. Type the SQL command shown in Figure 5-6, and substitute your user name for lhoward. Your query result should show 998 as the NEXTVAL in the ITEMID_SEQUENCE. Now that it has been accessed, it is the current value of the sequence, and the next value will be 999.

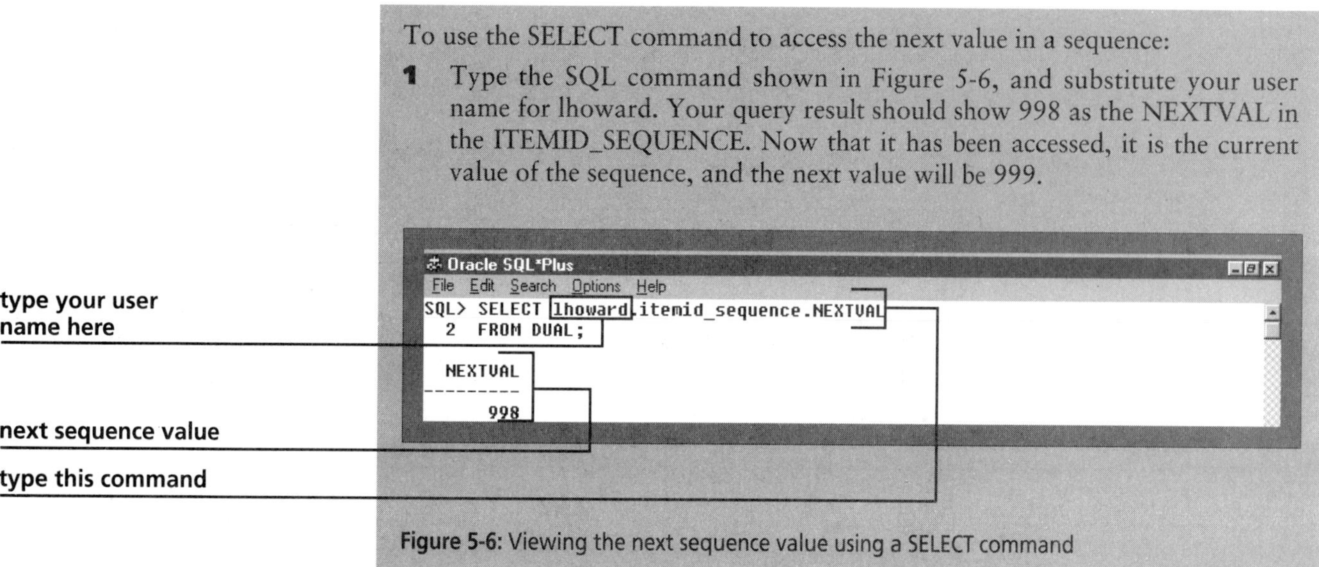

Figure 5-6: Viewing the next sequence value using a SELECT command

You can confirm that 999 is the next value by accessing it, as you will see next.

To make sure that the sequence increments correctly:

1. Confirm that 999 is the next value by typing L and pressing the **Enter** key at the SQL prompt to list your previous SQL command. Then type / and press the **Enter** key to execute the command. Your query output should look like Figure 5-7.

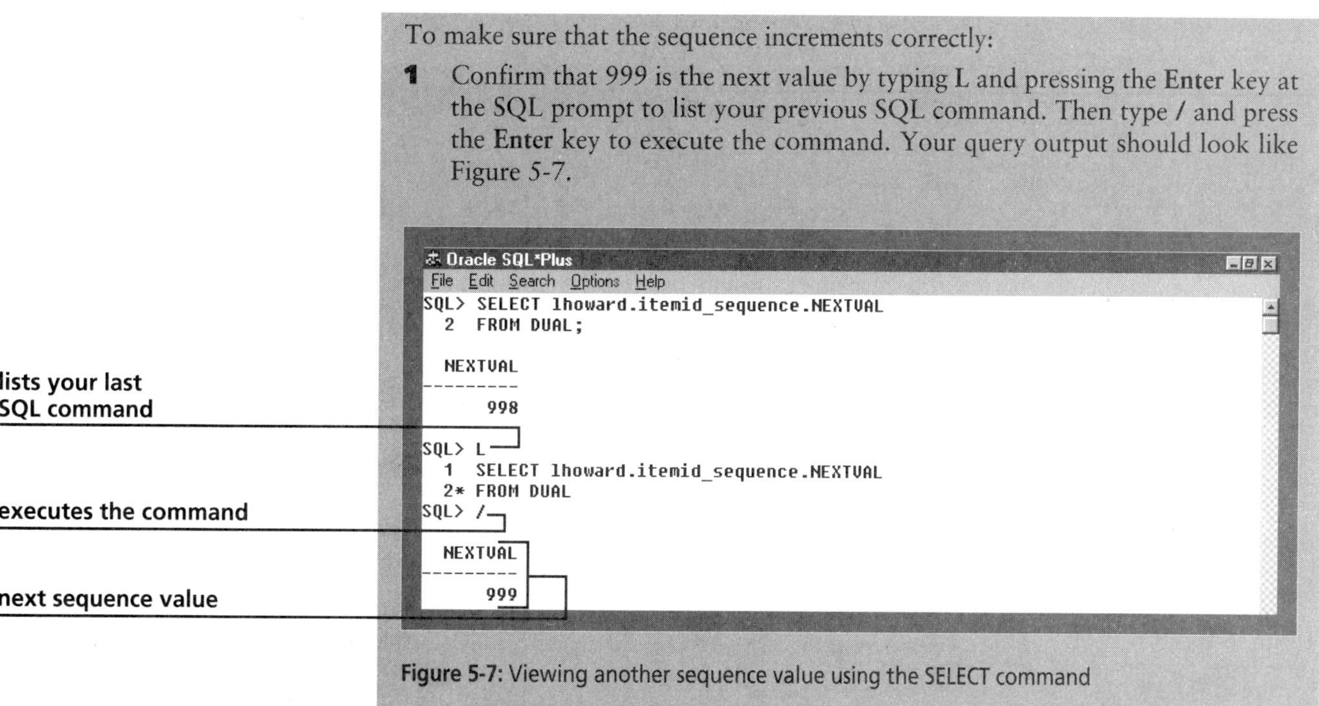

Figure 5-7: Viewing another sequence value using the SELECT command

Once you move on to the next value, the previous sequence value cannot be accessed using the sequence commands to prevent you (or anyone else) from accidentally using the same sequence value as the primary key for two different records. In the previous example, 998 is "lost" as a sequence value. But that's okay—it is better to lose a sequence value than to use the same value as the primary key for two different records.

Accessing the Current Sequence Value

While you cannot access past sequence values, you can access the current value using the CURRVAL command.

To use the CURRVAL command:

1. Confirm that 999 is the current sequence value by typing the SQL command shown in Figure 5-8, and substitute your user name for lhoward.

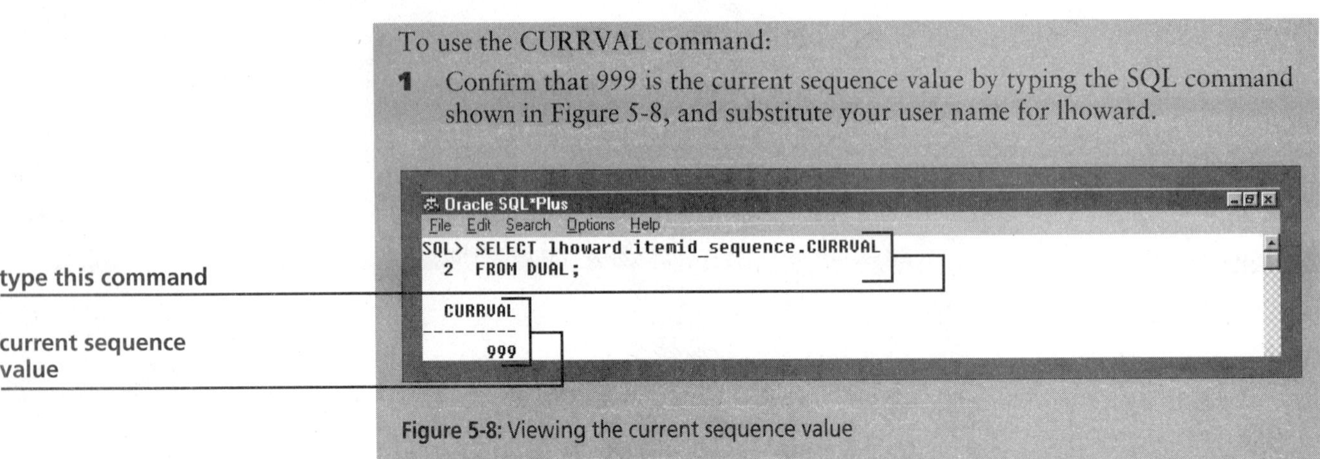

Figure 5-8: Viewing the current sequence value

The tricky thing about using the CURRVAL command is that it can be used only in the same database session and immediately after using the NEXTVAL command. This prevents two different database users or processes from assigning the same sequence value to two different records. Next you will prove this by exiting SQL*Plus, starting it again, and then trying to use the CURRVAL command.

To make sure that the CURRVAL command works properly:

1. Exit SQL*Plus.
2. Start SQL*Plus again and log on to the database.
3. Type the SQL command shown in Figure 5-9. The error message indicates that the CURRVAL command will not select a value because you exited SQL*Plus and then started a new SQL*Plus session.

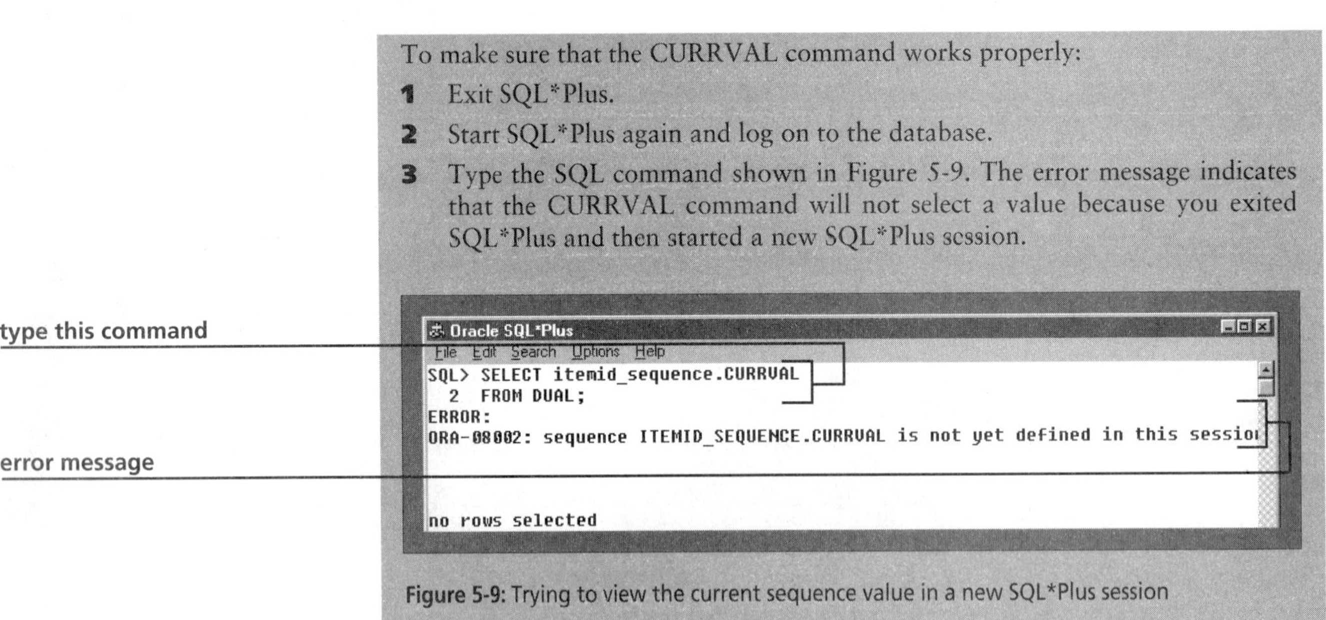

Figure 5-9: Trying to view the current sequence value in a new SQL*Plus session

Granting Sequence Privileges to Other Users

You must grant other users explicit privileges to use your sequences. You grant sequence privileges using the following general command format: `GRANT SELECT ON <sequence name> TO <user name 1, user name 2, …>`. Next you will grant privileges on your ITEMID_SEQUENCE to user PUBLIC.

To grant sequence privileges using the GRANT command:

1. Type the SQL command shown in Figure 5-10. The confirmation message "Grant succeeded" enables all database users to use the NEXTVAL, CURRVAL, and SELECT commands with your ITEMID_SEQUENCE. If you want to grant this privilege to only a small group of users, you would enter individual user names (separated by commas) instead of PUBLIC.

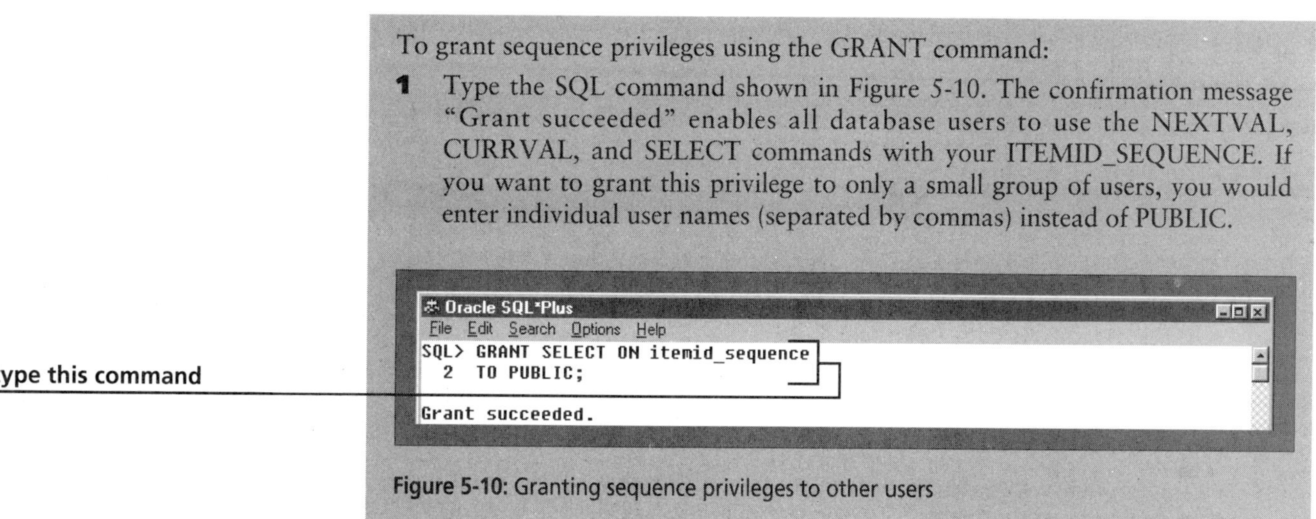

Figure 5-10: Granting sequence privileges to other users

Viewing and Deleting Sequences

Sometimes you might need to review the names and properties of your sequences after you create them. You can do this by querying the USER_SEQUENCES system table using a SELECT command.

To review the properties of your sequences:

1. Type the SQL command shown in Figure 5-11. The query output lists your current sequence names and properties, including the minimum and maximum allowable values that were established when you created the sequence and the value by which the sequence increments. The CYCLE and ORDER parameter values of "N" indicate that cycling and ordering are not used. The cache size is shown as 0 because you specified not to cache sequence values using the NOCACHE command. The next value of the sequence is 1000.

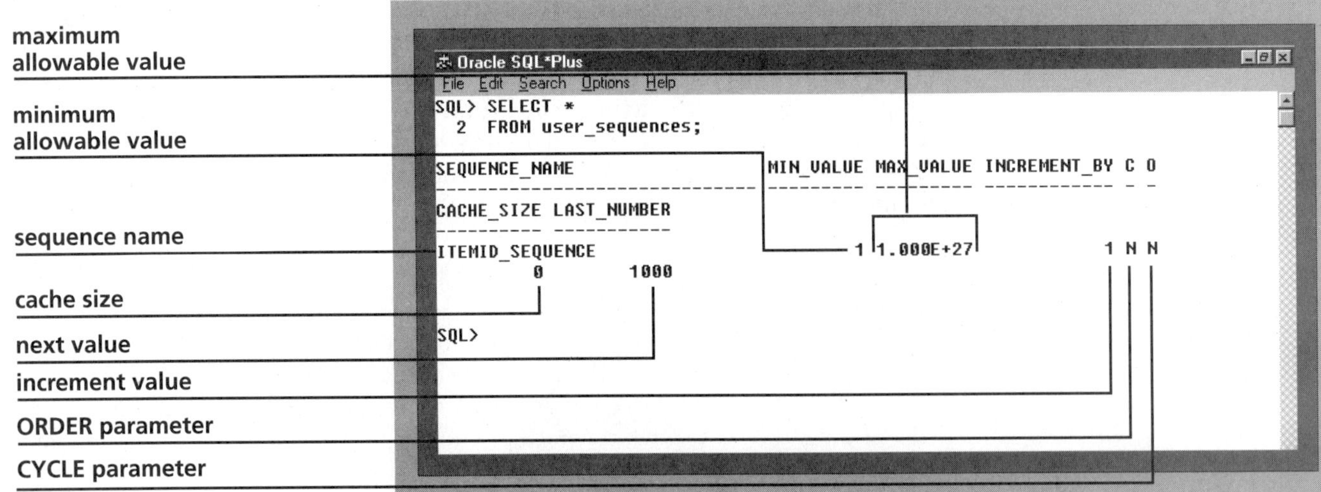

Figure 5-11: Current sequence names and properties

HELP? If the query output scrolls off the screen, you need to adjust the SQL*Plus linesize property. Click Environment on the Options menu, and then select linesize from the Set Options list. Click the Current option button, enter 75 in the Value text box, and then click the OK button. (You might need to enter a larger or smaller value depending on your video display properties.)

You might need to delete a sequence if you want to change its name or one of its other properties. When you need to delete a sequence, use the `DROP SEQUENCE <sequence name>;` command.

Using a Custom Form

Next you will run a custom form named CUSTITEM_FORM that inserts, views, updates, and deletes records in the Clearwater Traders ITEM table and allows users to select records from a list. You will run this form from a file on your Student Disk so you can see how a custom form works.

To run the file and insert a new record using the CUSTITEM_FORM:

1. Start Windows Explorer, change to the drive that contains your Student Disk, and then double-click the **custdemo.fmx** file in the Chapter5 folder. The Developer/2000 Forms Runtime Logon window opens. Log on to the database in the usual way, and then click the **Connect** button. The CUSTITEM_FORM window opens, as shown in Figure 5-12. (Maximize the window, if necessary.)

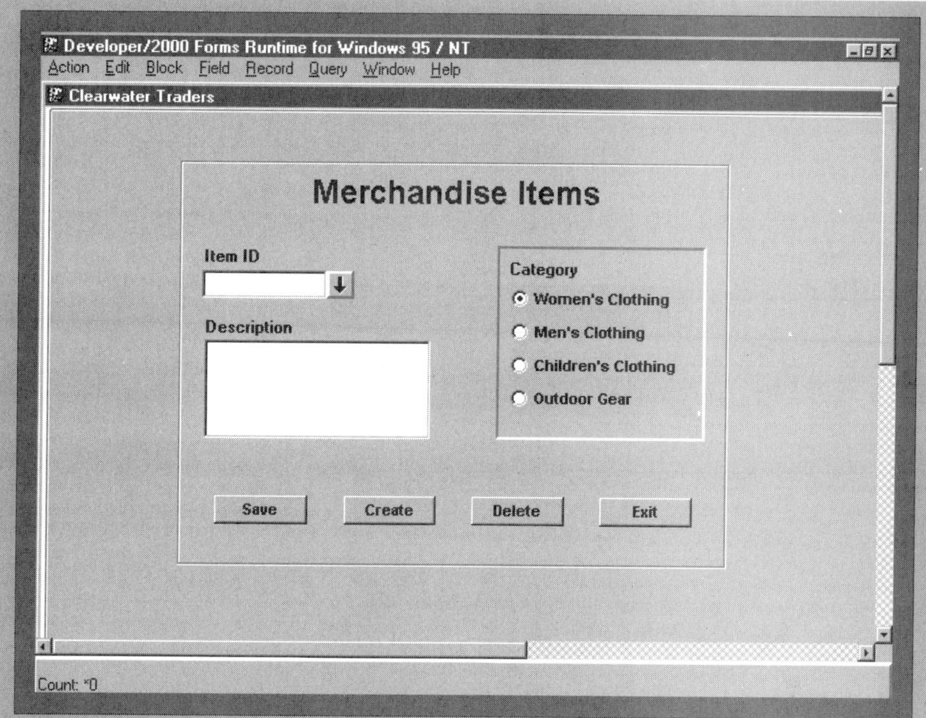

Figure 5-12: CUSTITEM custom form

HELP? If the Open With dialog box opens instead of the Logon dialog box, it means that the workstation you are using does not have an association between executable Oracle Forms Designer files (which have .fmx extensions) and the Oracle Forms Runtime application. Refer to the instructions in Chapter 4 to learn how to create the association.

HELP? If you try to start custdemo.fmx from another folder, the application will generate an error message if any of the folder names in the path contain blank spaces.

2 Click the **Create** button. The value 1000 appears in the Item ID text field.

HELP? Your value might be different depending on the current value of your ITEMID_SEQUENCE.

3 The insertion point is now in the Description text box. Type **Children's Raincoat.**

4 Click the **Children's Clothing** option button. Your screen should look like Figure 5-13.

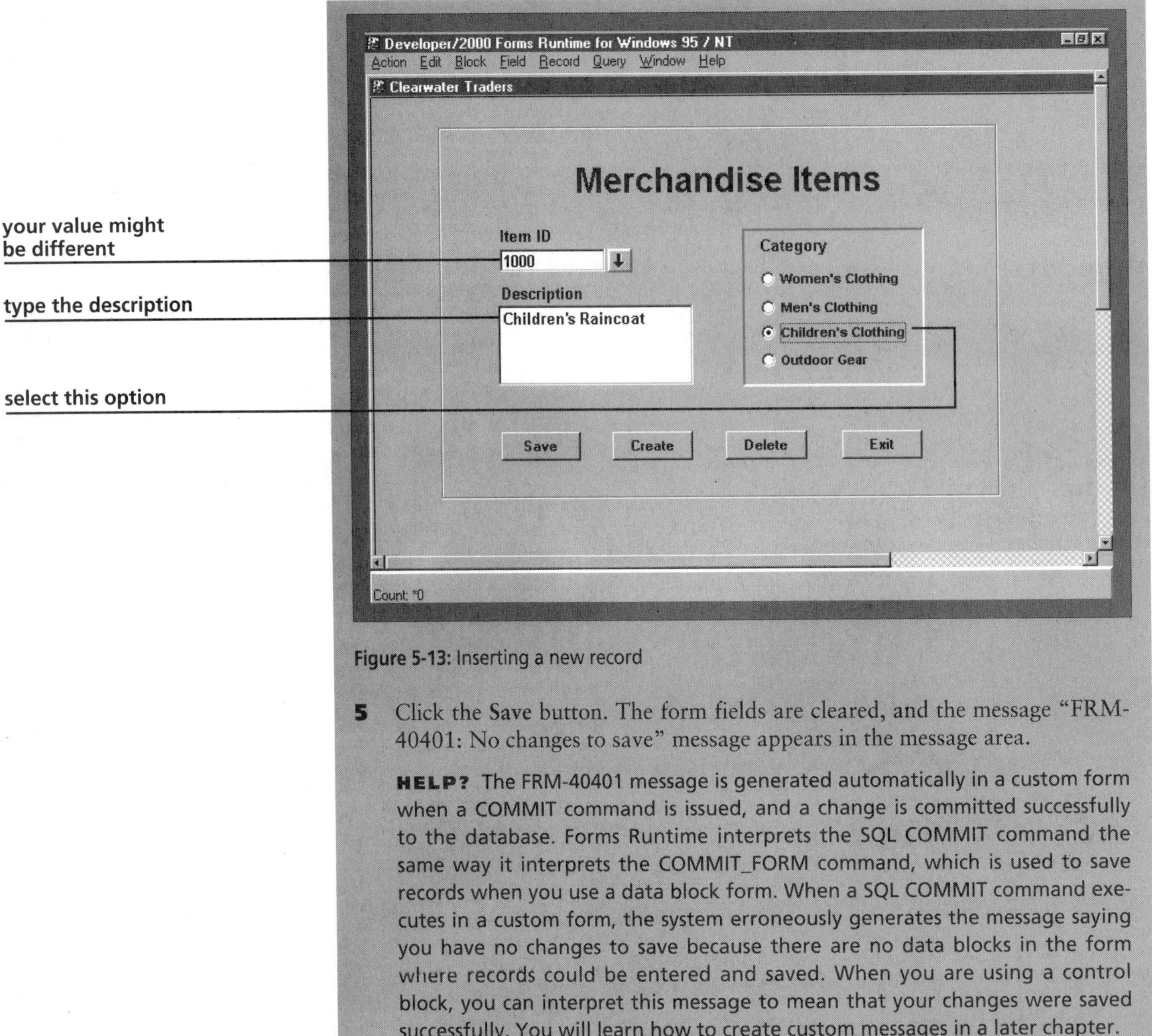

Figure 5-13: Inserting a new record

5 Click the **Save** button. The form fields are cleared, and the message "FRM-40401: No changes to save" message appears in the message area.

HELP? The FRM-40401 message is generated automatically in a custom form when a COMMIT command is issued, and a change is committed successfully to the database. Forms Runtime interprets the SQL COMMIT command the same way it interprets the COMMIT_FORM command, which is used to save records when you use a data block form. When a SQL COMMIT command executes in a custom form, the system erroneously generates the message saying you have no changes to save because there are no data blocks in the form where records could be entered and saved. When you are using a control block, you can interpret this message to mean that your changes were saved successfully. You will learn how to create custom messages in a later chapter.

Next you will use the CUSTITEM_FORM to update the record you just inserted. You will select the record using a **list of values** (**LOV**), which displays a list of the current item description records in the ITEM table.

To select and update the Children's Raincoat record:

1 Click the **Item ID LOV** button on the form. The LOV shows all of the item description records that are currently in the ITEM table, as shown in Figure 5-14.

LOV

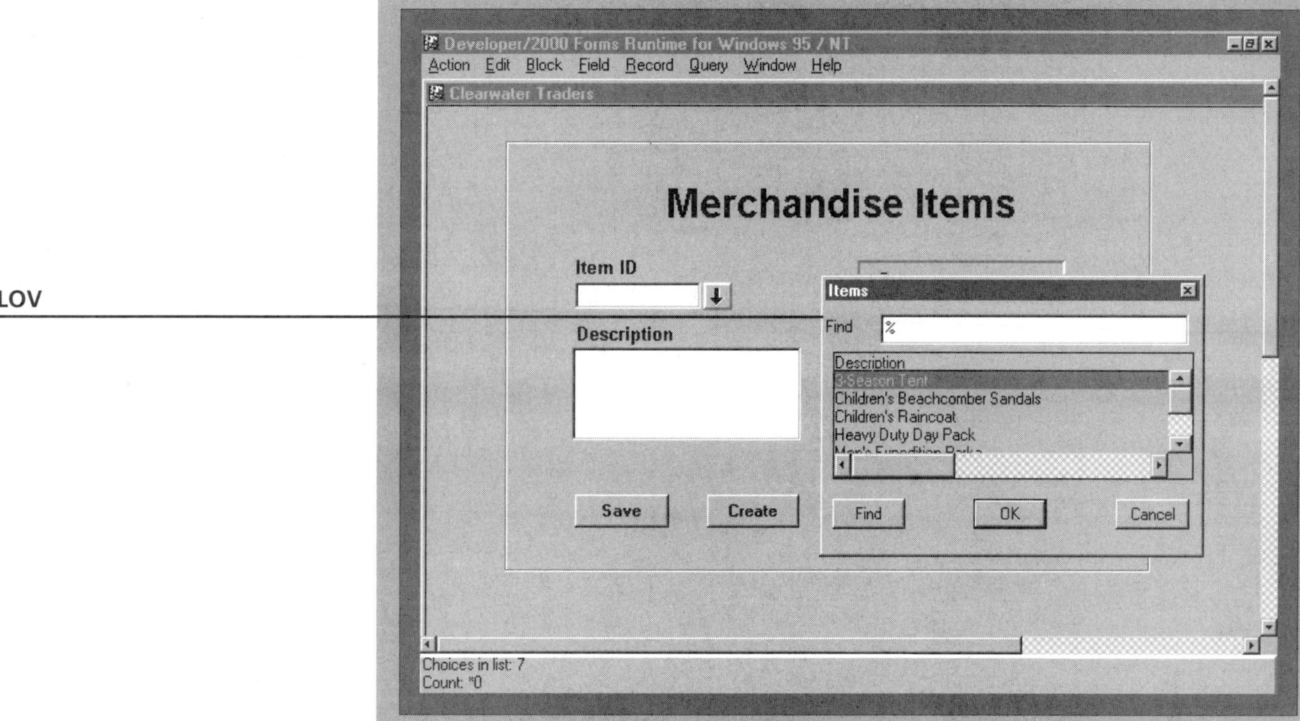

Figure 5-14: CUSTITEM_FORM Item ID LOV

2 Click **Children's Raincoat** in the Description text field, and then click the OK button. The record's data values appear in the form text fields.

3 Click in the Description text field, and then edit the description so it reads **Children's Rain Gear**, as shown in Figure 5-15.

new description

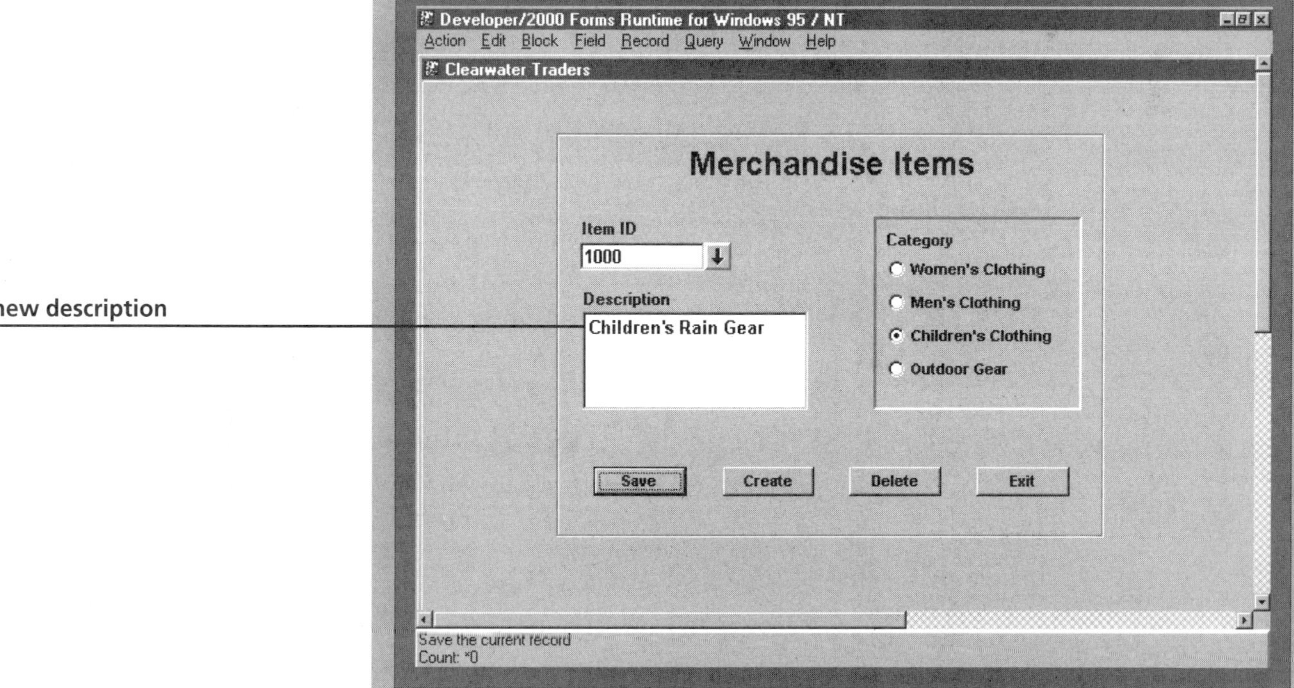

Figure 5-15: Updating the record

4 Click the **Save** button. The form fields clear, and the message "FRM-40401: No changes to save" message appears in the message area, indicating that the record was updated.

Finally, you will delete this record.

To delete the record:

1 Click the **Item ID LOV** button [↓] again. Click **Children's Rain Gear** in the Description text field, and then click the **OK** button.

2 Click the **Delete** button. The confirmation message indicates that the record was deleted successfully.

3 Click [↓] again and confirm that Children's Rain Gear is no longer in the list of items.

4 Click the **Exit** button to exit the form.

Creating a Custom Form

Custom forms do not contain data blocks that are associated with specific database tables. Instead, they use SQL statements to manipulate data. These SQL statements are embedded in special programs called **triggers** that run when a user performs an action such as clicking a button. For example, when you clicked the Save button in the CUSTITEM_FORM, a program containing a SQL INSERT command was executed. In a data block form, the triggers were generated automatically when you created the data block. In a custom form, the person who develops the form must write the triggers for each button. The trigger for the Create button on the CUSTITEM_FORM retrieves the next value in the ITEMID_SEQUENCE and displays it in the Item ID field on the form. The Delete button's trigger contains a SQL DELETE command, and the Exit button's trigger closes the form.

To create a custom form, you will create a control block rather than a data block. **Control blocks** are not connected to a particular database table. Instead, they have text items that correspond with database table columns. The control block for the CUSTITEM_FORM will contain an item for each field in the ITEM table. It will also contain the Create, Save, Delete, and Exit buttons, and the Item LOV button.

To create the control block:

1 Start the Forms Designer and log onto the database.

2 If necessary, maximize the Object Navigator window and change to Visual View. Click **MODULE1** so its background color changes to blue, change the form name to **CUSTITEM_FORM**, and then press the **Enter** key.

3 Open the Windows object, click **WINDOW0** twice, change the window name to **CUSTITEM_WINDOW**, and then press the **Enter** key.

4 Open **CUSTITEM_WINDOW**, select **Canvas-Views**, and then click the **Create** button on the Oracle Navigator toolbar to create a new canvas. Change the new canvas-view's name to **CUSTITEM_CANVAS**.

5 Save the form as **custitem.fmb** in the Chapter5 folder on your Student Disk.

HELP? Oracle might rename your form name from CUSTITEM_FORM to custitem.fmb to match the filename that you gave the file in Step 5. If this happens, change the form name back to CUSTITEM_FORM in the Oracle Navigator.

6 Click **Tools** on the menu bar, and then click **Layout Editor** to go to the Layout Editor.

7 Click **Tools** on the menu bar, and then click **New Block** to create a new control block.

8 Complete the General tab as shown in Figure 5-16 by changing the block name to **ITEM_CONTROL_BLOCK.** You will not select a base table for the block, so you will not specify information on the Items or Layout tabs.

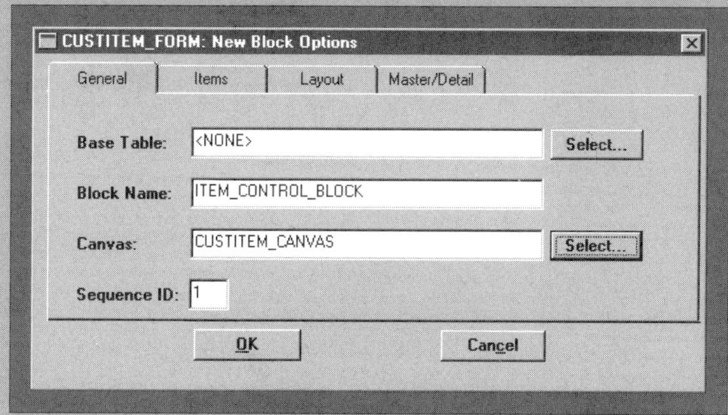

Figure 5-16: Specifying the ITEM_CONTROL_BLOCK

9 Click the **OK** button to create the block.

Creating the Text Items

The Layout Editor displays a blank canvas and shows the current canvas and block. First you will create the text items to correspond to the ITEMID and ITEMDESC database table fields as shown in Figure 5-17. You will not create a text item to correspond to the CATEGORY field because its values will be displayed as selections in a radio button group.

NOTE: If you are not working in ITEM_CONTROL_BLOCK, or if it is a data block rather than a control block, your form will not work correctly.

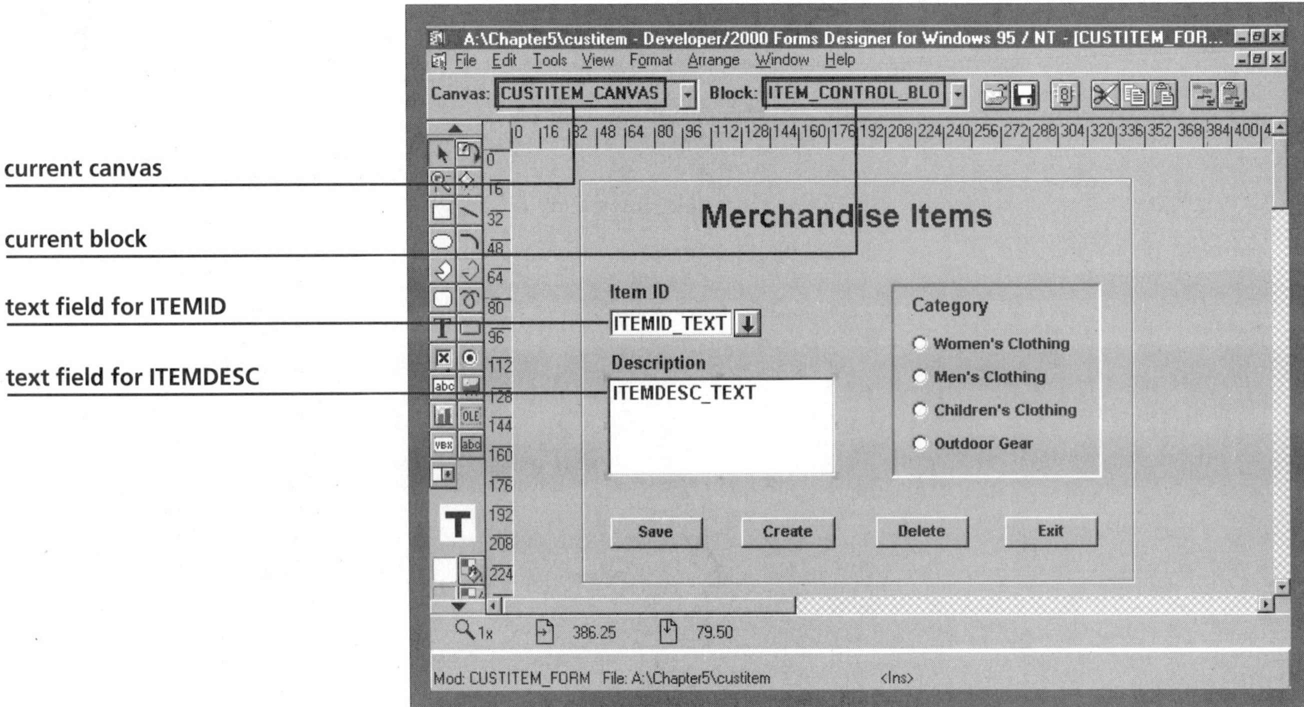

Figure 5-17: CUSTITEM_FORM text items

To create the text items:

1 Confirm that you are working in the ITEM_CONTROL_BLOCK. Click the **Text Item** tool on the Tool palette, and then draw a rectangular box for the ITEMID field in the ITEM table, as shown in Figure 5-18.

HELP? The default name on your text field might be different. This is a system-generated name that you will change.

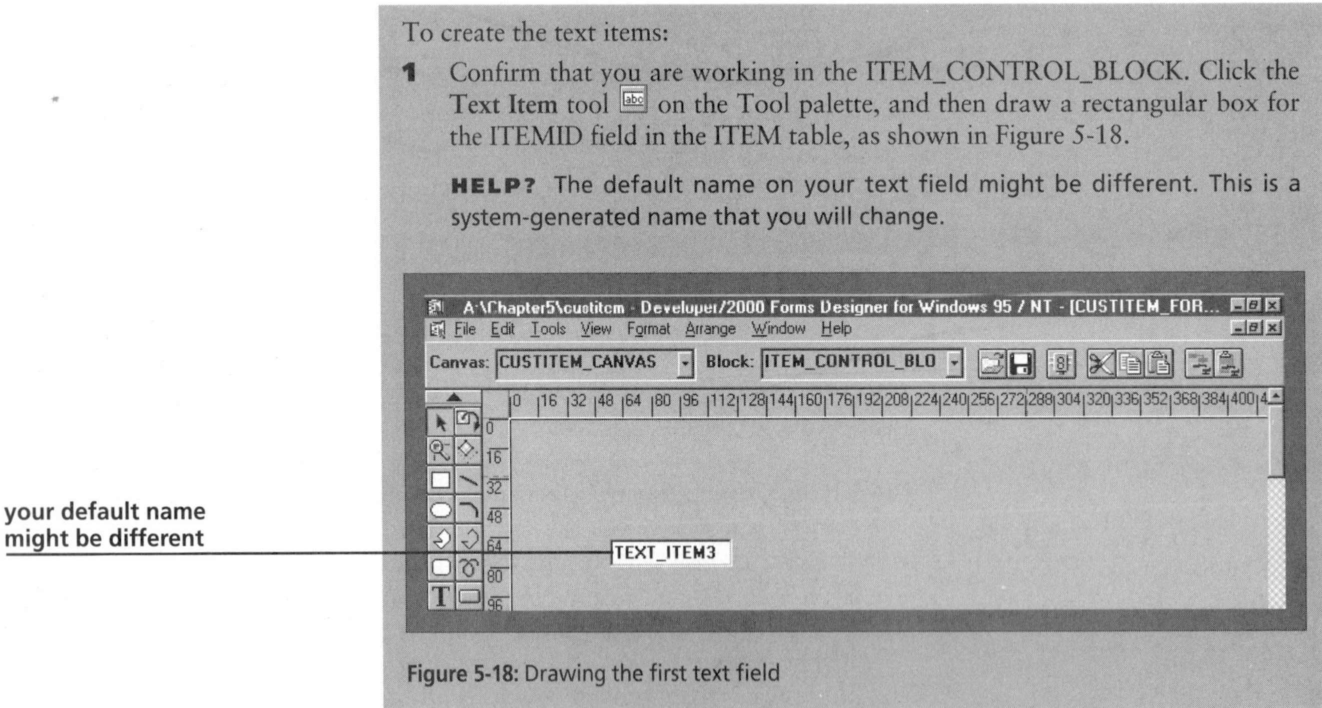

Figure 5-18: Drawing the first text field

The next step is to specify the properties of the new text item. One of the most important properties is the Name property, which is used whenever you refer to the item in a trigger. You will specify the text item's Name property next.

To specify the text item's Name property:

1 Right-click your new text item, and then click **Properties** to open its Properties sheet.

HELP? If no menu appears when you right-click your new text item, make sure that you draw the text field using the Text Item tool and not one of the other tools on the Tool palette. If you drew the text field using a different tool, delete it and then redraw it using the Text tool.

2 Change the Name property to **ITEMID_TEXT** by clicking the Name property and typing the new name at the top of the sheet, and then click any other property to save your changes.

When the ITEM table was created, ITEMID was specified as a NUMBER field of size 8. Text items that display database records must have the same data type and maximum length as the corresponding data field in the database.

To change the data type and size:

1 Scroll down the Properties sheet, and then double-click the **Data Type** property to change it from Char to **Number**.

2 Scroll down to the Maximum Length property, click it, type **8**, and then click any other property to save the change.

3 Close the Properties sheet, and then maximize the Layout Editor window if necessary. The new name appears in the text item.

Next you will create the text item for the ITEMDESC data field.

To create the ITEMDESC text item:

1 Draw a text item under ITEMID_TEXT for the ITEMDESC field, as shown in Figure 5-19.

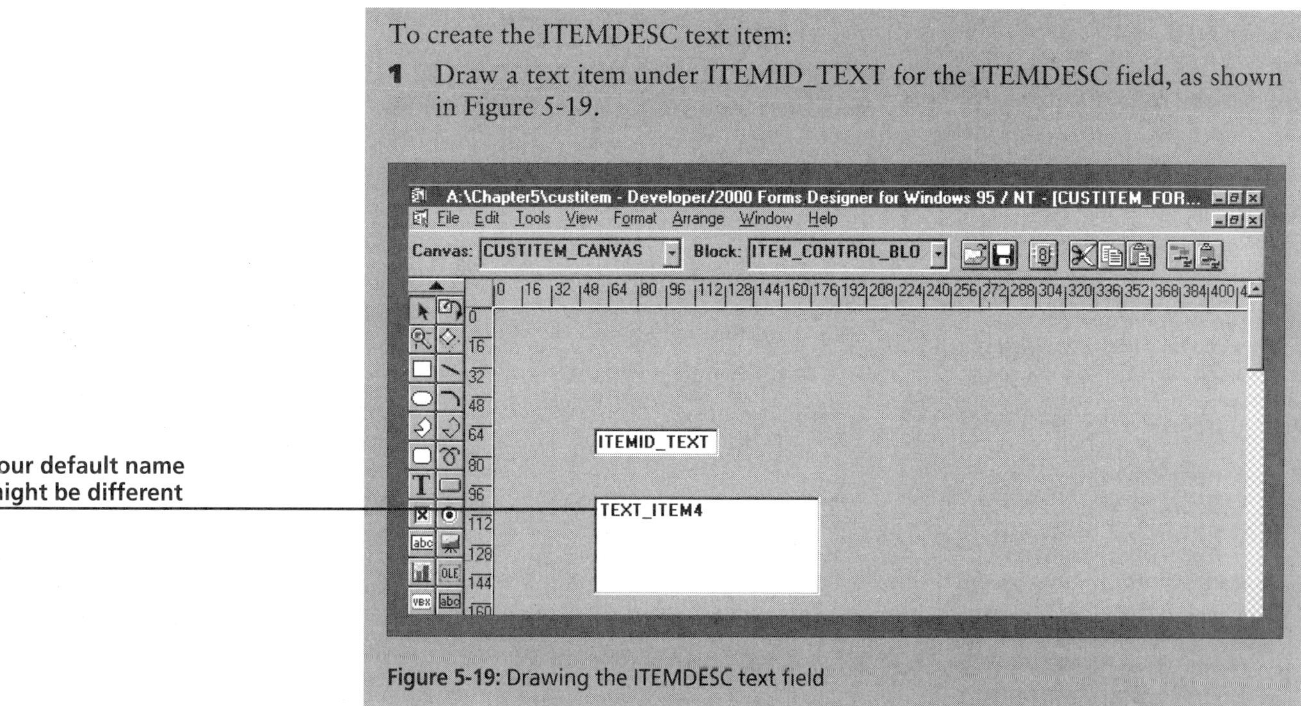

Figure 5-19: Drawing the ITEMDESC text field

2 Open the new text item's Properties sheet, and then change its Name property to **ITEMDESC_TEXT**.

3 Scroll down the Properties sheet, and confirm that the Data Type property is **Char**. If it is not, double-click the Data Type value until Char appears.

4 Change the Maximum Length property to **100**.

5 Close the Properties sheet and then maximize the Layout Editor.

6 Save the form.

Creating a Radio Button Group

The CATEGORY field currently is limited to four different values: Women's Clothing, Men's Clothing, Children's Clothing, and Outdoor Gear. When you have a limited number of values, you can use a radio button group to make it easier for users to enter data. First you will create the individual radio buttons.

To create the individual radio buttons:

1 Click the **Radio Button** tool on the Tool palette, and then draw a rectangle on the canvas to correspond with the radio button for the Women's Clothing category, as shown in Figure 5-20. After you release the mouse button, you will see the radio button and its corresponding label.

your default name might be different

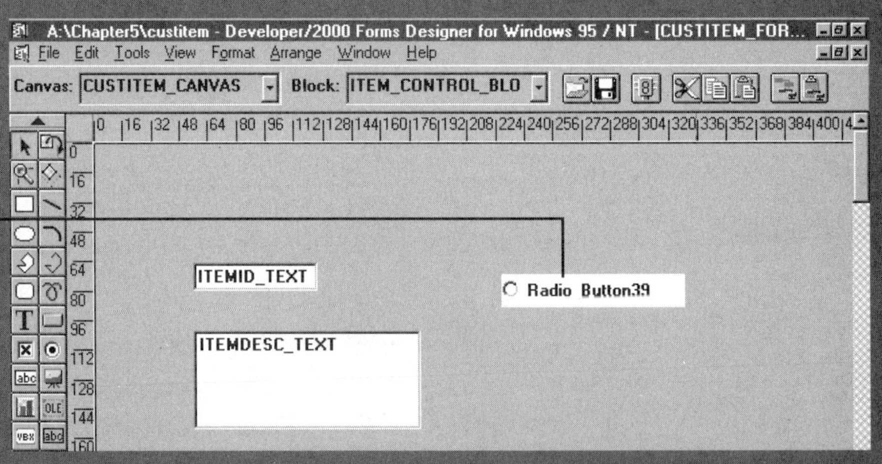

Figure 5-20: Drawing the first radio button

The Value property is the actual database data value that is associated with the radio button—in this case it happens to be the same as the label, but this is not always the case. For example, if you create a radio group to display the METHPMT values in the CUST_ORDER table, the actual data values stored in the database are CC (for credit card) and CHECK. The corresponding radio button labels are "Credit Card" and "Check."

2 Double-click the new radio button to open its Properties sheet, and then change the following properties. When you are finished, close the Properties sheet and maximize the Layout Editor.

Property	New Value
Name	WC_RADIO_BUTTON
Label	Women's Clothing
Value	Women's Clothing

You also can press Ctrl + C to copy and Ctrl + V to paste, or click Copy or Paste on the Edit menu.

3 Click the WC_RADIO_BUTTON to select it. If necessary, make the label larger by dragging the bottom right selection handle toward the right edge of the canvas so the entire label is visible.

4 With the WC_RADIO_BUTTON still selected, click the **Copy** button on the Layout Editor toolbar to make a copy of the radio button.

5 Click the **Paste** button on the Layout Editor toolbar to paste the copied radio button to the canvas.

6 Click two more times to create two more radio buttons.

7 Select all of the radio buttons into an object group by clicking the first radio button, pressing and holding down the **Shift** key, clicking the remaining radio buttons, and then releasing the Shift key.

8 Click **Arrange** on the menu bar, click **Align Objects**, and then click the **Horizontally Align Left** and **Vertically Stack** option buttons. Click the **OK** button. The four radio buttons should now appear with their left edges aligned and stacked on top of each other.

9 Click anywhere on the canvas to deselect the object group.

10 Change the properties of the second, third, and fourth buttons in the group as follows:

Property	Button 2	Button 3	Button 4
Name	MC_RADIO _BUTTON	CC_RADIO _BUTTON	OG_RADIO _BUTTON
Label	Men's Clothing	Children's Clothing	Outdoor Gear
Value	Men's Clothing	Children's Clothing	Outdoor Gear

11 When you are finished changing the radio button properties, close the Properties sheet and maximize the Layout Editor. Your canvas should look like Figure 5-21.

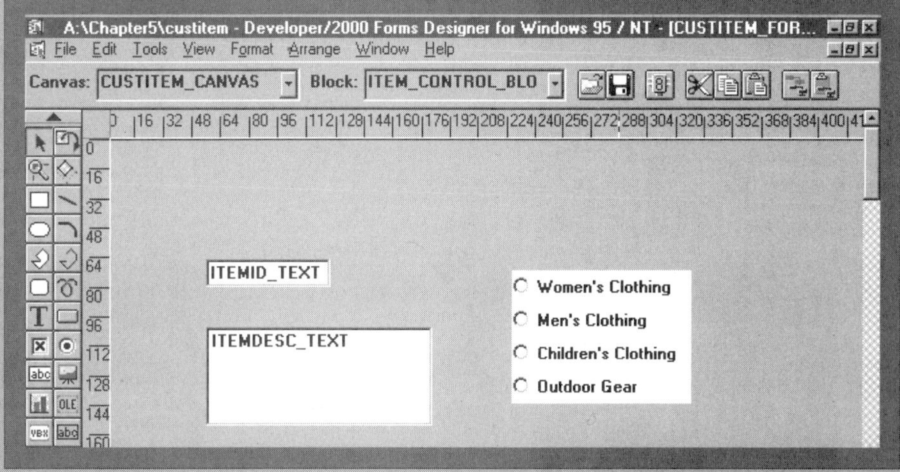

Figure 5-21: Finished radio buttons

12 Save the form.

In a collection of related radio buttons, only one button can be selected at a time. Therefore, radio buttons always exist within a form object called a **radio group**. Whenever you draw radio buttons in the Layout Editor, Oracle automatically creates a radio group. Next you will view the radio group you just created in the Object Navigator, and change some of the radio group's properties.

To view the radio group:

1 Click **Window** on the menu bar, and then click **Object Navigator** and change to Ownership View if necesary. A new radio group appears, as shown in Figure 5-22.

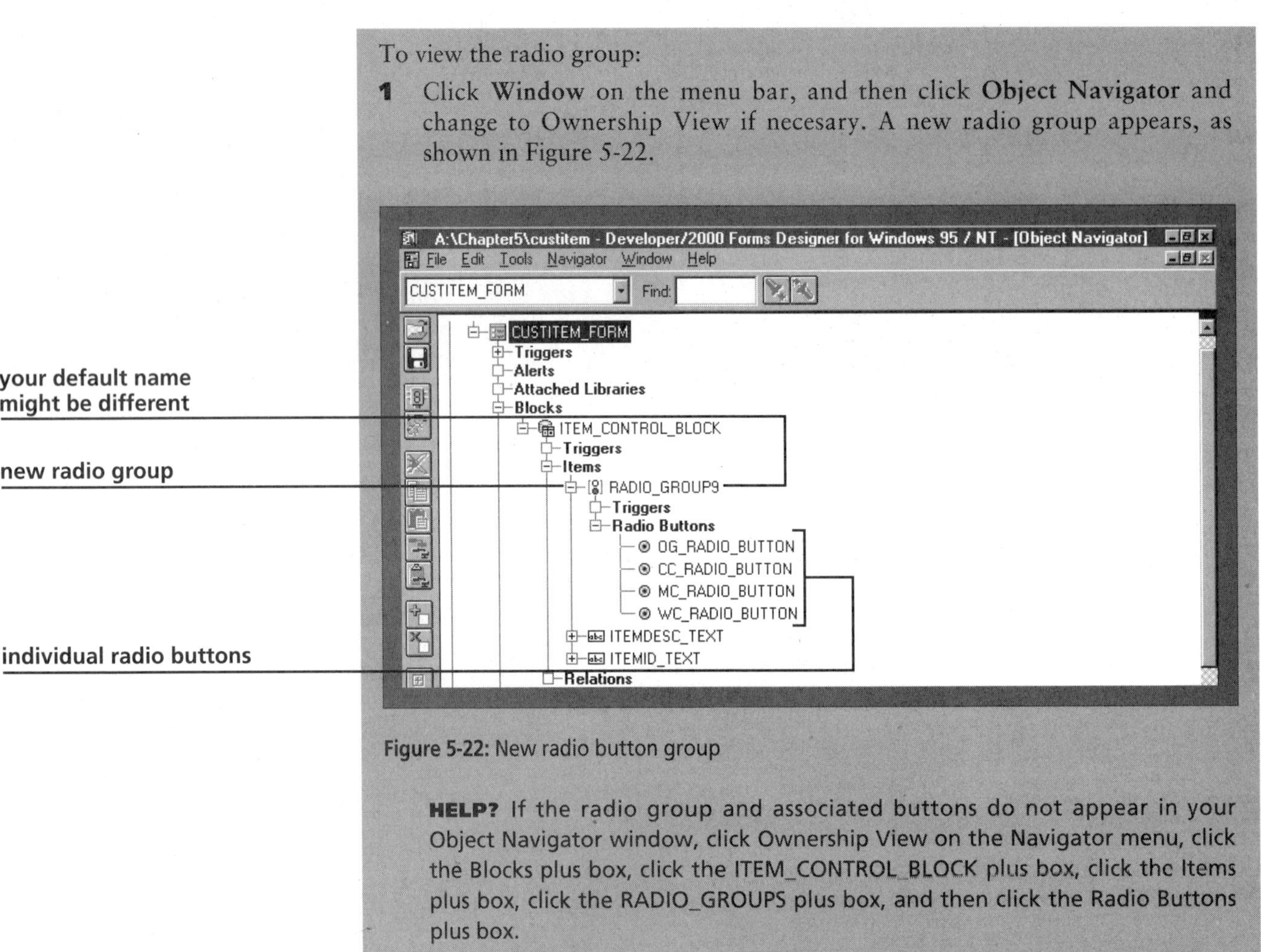

Figure 5-22: New radio button group

HELP? If the radio group and associated buttons do not appear in your Object Navigator window, click Ownership View on the Navigator menu, click the Blocks plus box, click the ITEM_CONTROL_BLOCK plus box, click the Items plus box, click the RADIO_GROUPS plus box, and then click the Radio Buttons plus box.

Figure 5-22 shows the radio buttons under the new RADIO__GROUP9. (Your radio group default name might be different.) The Value property in each radio button's Properties sheet represents the radio group's value when that particular button is selected. For example, when WC_RADIO_BUTTON is selected, this radio group has the value "Women's Clothing."

Next you will change the radio group's name and default value. The **default value** is the value that the radio group has when the form is first displayed.

To change the radio group's name and default value:

1 Right-click **RADIO_GROUP9** (or the default name of your radio group) in the Object Navigator window, and then click **Properties**.

2 Change the name of the radio group to **CATEGORY_RADIO_GROUP**.

The radio group's default value is the radio button value that is selected when the form is first displayed. Usually the default value is the most common choice or the first choice in the radio button group.

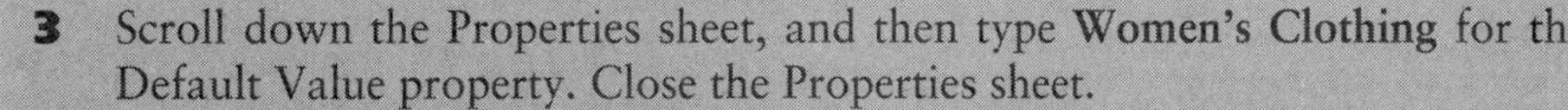

3 Scroll down the Properties sheet, and then type **Women's Clothing** for the Default Value property. Close the Properties sheet.

4 If necessary, click **Window** on the menu bar, and then click **CUSTITEM_CANVAS** to return to the Layout Editor.

5 Save the form.

Next you will create the form boilerplate objects. These objects include labels for the text fields and radio button group, a rectangle box to highlight the radio button group, and the form title. First you will create and format the form labels.

To modify the Fill Color property, select the label and then click the Fill Color button on the Tool palette. To modify the Line Color property, select the label and then click the Line Color button on the Tool palette.

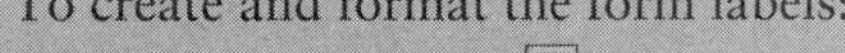

To create and format the form labels:

1 Use the **Text** tool on the Tool palette to create labels titled **Item ID** and **Item Description** for the text items, and **Category** for the radio group, as shown in Figure 5-23. If necessary, modify the text Fill Color property to No Fill, and the text Line Color property to No Line.

new form labels

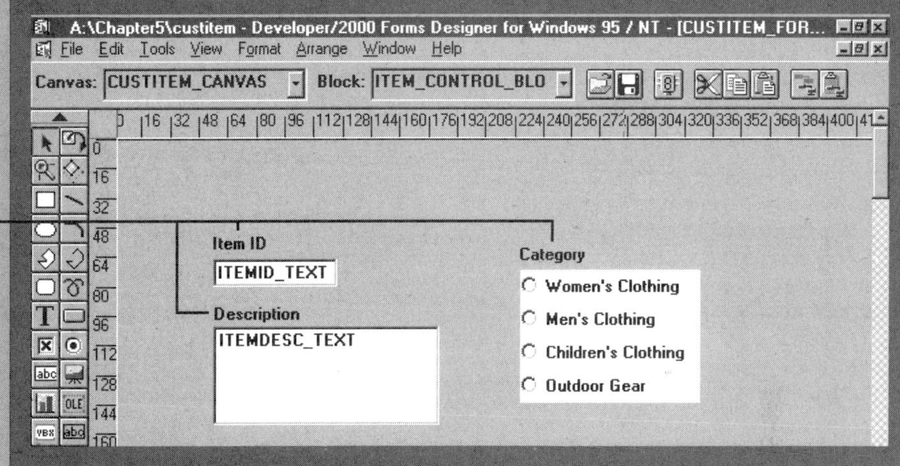

Figure 5-23: Form field labels

To select objects as a group, select one of the labels, press and hold the Shift key, and then select the rest of the labels.

2 Select all of the field item labels as a group, and then change the font to **10-point bold Arial.**

Next you will create the rectangle around the radio group and format the radio button labels.

To draw a rectangle around the radio button group and format the radio button labels:

1 Click the **Rectangle** tool on the Tool palette, and then draw a rectangle around the radio button group and Category label, as shown in Figure 5-24.

draw rectangle here

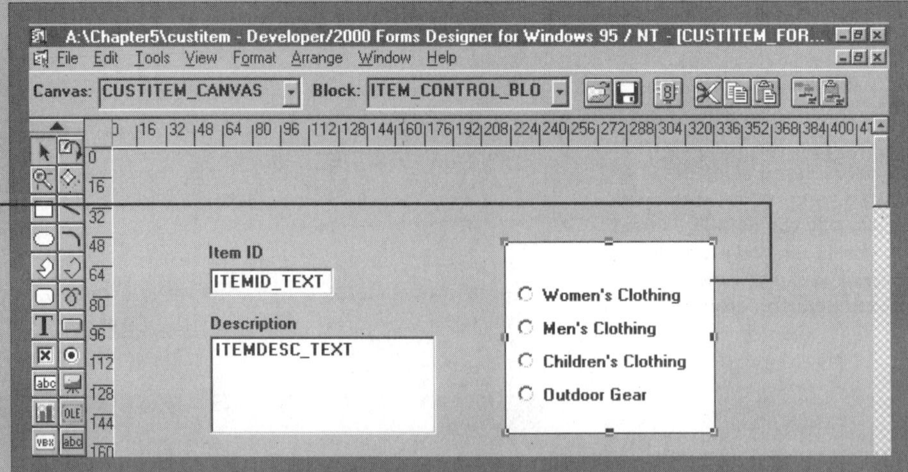

Figure 5-24: Drawing the rectangle around the radio button group

2 If necessary, change the rectangle Fill Color property to **No Fill.**

3 If necessary, change the rectangle Line Color property to **black.**

4 Click **Format** on the menu bar, point to **Bevel**, and then click Lowered to format the rectangle with a lowered bevel edge.

5 Click **Arrange** on the menu bar, and then click **Send to Back** to send the rectangle to the back of the canvas.

6 Select all of the radio buttons as a group, and then change the font to **8-point bold Arial.**

7 Change the Fill Color property of the radio buttons to the same color as the canvas background.

HELP? You cannot change the Fill Color property of the radio buttons to No Fill. Instead, you will need to match their fill color to the background color of the canvas.

If a rectangle does not have a line color, changing the Bevel property will not change the rectangle's appearance.

The final step is to create and format the form title.

To create and format the form title:

1 Use the **Text** tool [T] on the Tool palette to add a title at the top of the form with the text **Merchandise Items.**

2 Select the title, click **Format** on the menu bar, click **Font**, and then change the title's font to **18-point bold Arial.**

3 If necessary, change the title label Fill Color property to **No Fill** and the text Line Color property to **No Line.**

4 Align and reposition your form objects on the canvas as necessary to match Figure 5-25.

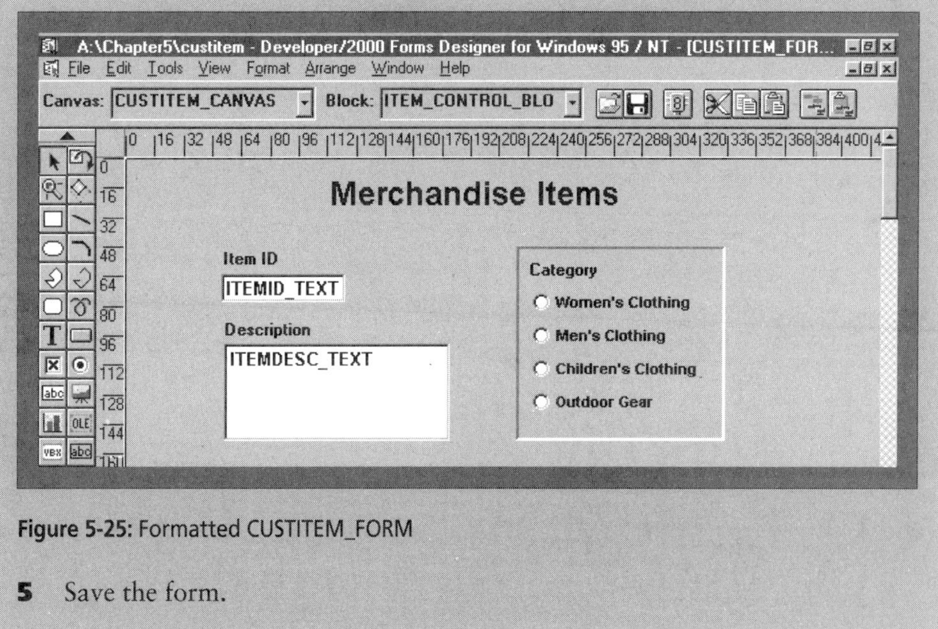

Figure 5-25: Formatted CUSTITEM_FORM

5 Save the form.

Creating the Form Buttons

In your CUSTITEM_FORM, when the user clicks the Create button, the form fields clear and a new ITEMID is retrieved from the ITEMID_SEQUENCE. Then the user can enter the new item information. When the user clicks the Save button, a new record is inserted into the ITEM table or an existing record is updated. When the user clicks the Delete button, the displayed record is deleted. When the user clicks the Exit button, the form closes. For your form to function properly, you need to draw the buttons on the canvas, and then write the triggers, which are the program procedures that provide the underlying functionality.

Recall that a trigger is program code written by the program developer that contains explicit instructions about what the form is supposed to do when the user clicks a particular button or right-clicks a particular area on the form. Triggers also can be associated with specific things that are done by the system, such as loading the form or exiting the form. To write a trigger, you must specify the event that it is associated with, such as clicking a button. Now you will draw the form buttons and create the associated triggers.

To create the form buttons:

1 Click the **Push Button** tool on the Tool palette, and then draw a rectangular button below your text items and on the left side of the canvas, as shown in Figure 5-26.

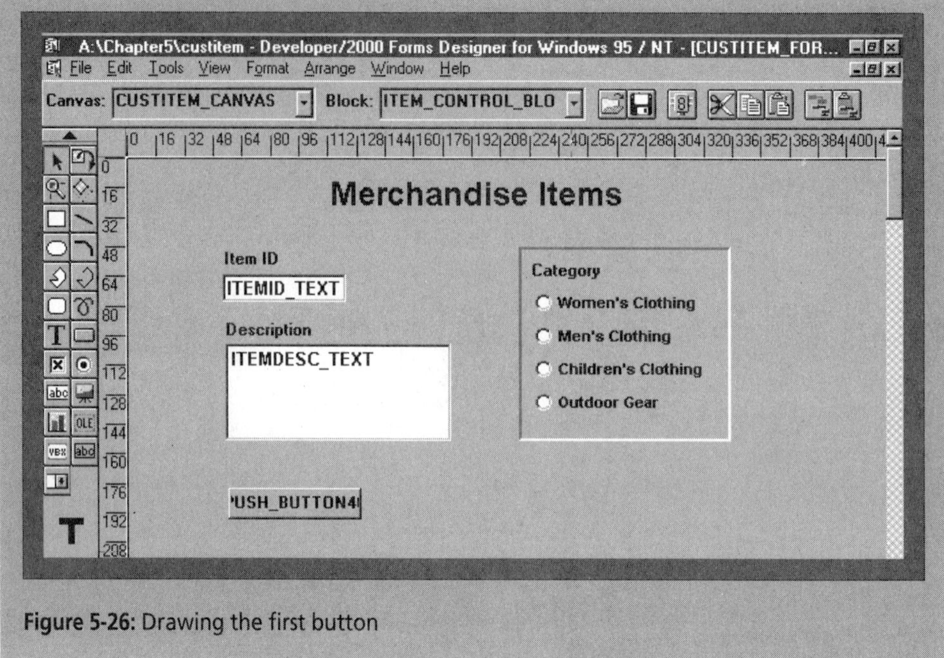

Figure 5-26: Drawing the first button

This button will be part of a button group consisting of the Save, Create, Delete, and Exit buttons. Before creating the button group, you will configure the size and font properties of the Save button.

As a general guideline, buttons should be about 18 pixels high with an 8-point font used for the label. Buttons in a group should be the same size and should be wide enough to accommodate the longest label.

To change the Auto hint property to True, double-click the current Auto hint property value.

To configure the size and font for the Save button:

1. Open the Properties sheet for the button you just drew.
2. Change the properties as follows:

Name	SAVE_BUTTON
Width	55
Height	18
Label	Save
Hint	Save the current record
Auto hint	True

3. Close the SAVE_BUTTON Properties sheet, and then maximize the Layout Editor.
4. Click the **SAVE_BUTTON** to select it, and then change its label font to **8-point bold Arial.**
5. Close the Properties sheet and then save the form.

When the Auto hint property is True, the text in the Hint property is displayed when the item is selected on the form. Text items can be selected by clicking the mouse pointer in them; buttons are selected when the user moves the insertion point from a text field to a button by pressing the Tab key. Windows applications should be self-documenting, so you should always add on-screen hints to canvas items. Hints should be short and to the point.

Next you need to copy the SAVE_BUTTON and paste it three times to create the Create, Delete, and Exit buttons. Then you will change the individual properties of the new buttons.

To create the Create, Delete, and Exit buttons:

1 Copy the SAVE_BUTTON, and then paste it three times to create all four buttons.

Depending on the screen layout, button groups can be oriented horizontally and centered at the bottom of the screen, or oriented vertically at the right edge of the screen. You will position the new buttons in a horizontal arrangement.

To rearrange the button group:

1 Rearrange the buttons, align the button group vertically, and distribute the buttons horizontally. Your canvas should look like Figure 5-27.

Buttons should be aligned and evenly spaced, and you shouldn't put more than five buttons in a group.

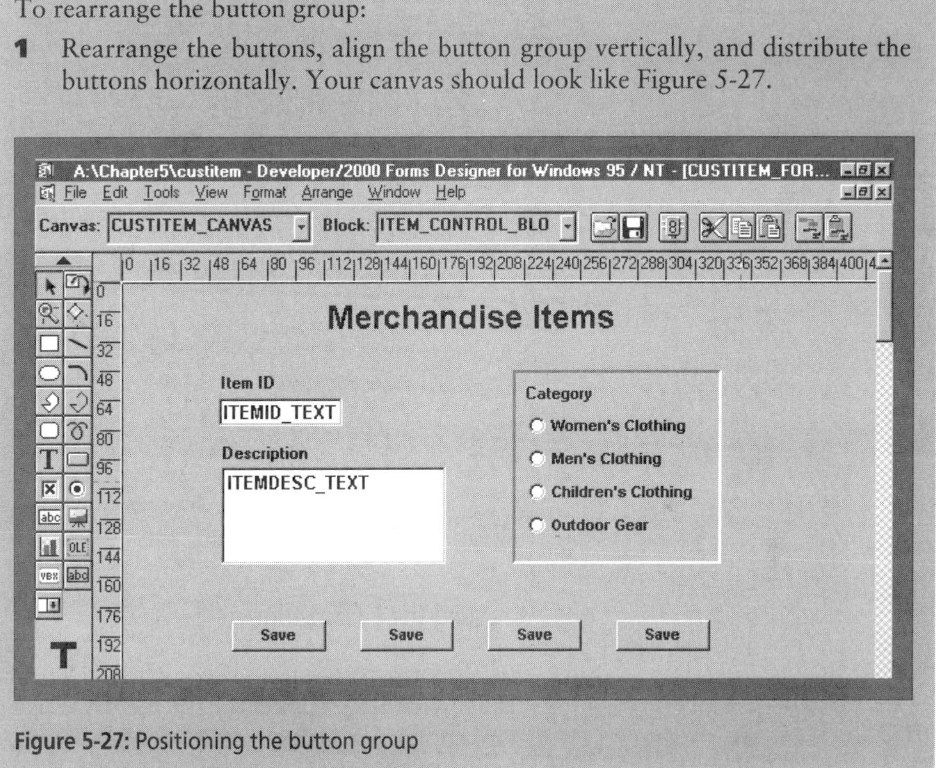

Figure 5-27: Positioning the button group

Finally you need to specify the individual button properties. You should put the **default button**, which is the button most likely to be used, in the button group first, either at the left side in a horizontal button group or at the top in a vertical group. If you have a Help button, it should always be placed last. The Save button probably will be used most, so it will be placed first, followed by the Create, Delete, and Exit buttons.

To change the button properties:

1 Change the button properties of the new buttons as shown. Your formatted button group should look like Figure 5-28.

Button Name	Label	Hint
CREATE_BUTTON	Create	Create a new record
DELETE_BUTTON	Delete	Delete the current record
EXIT_BUTTON	Exit	Exit the form

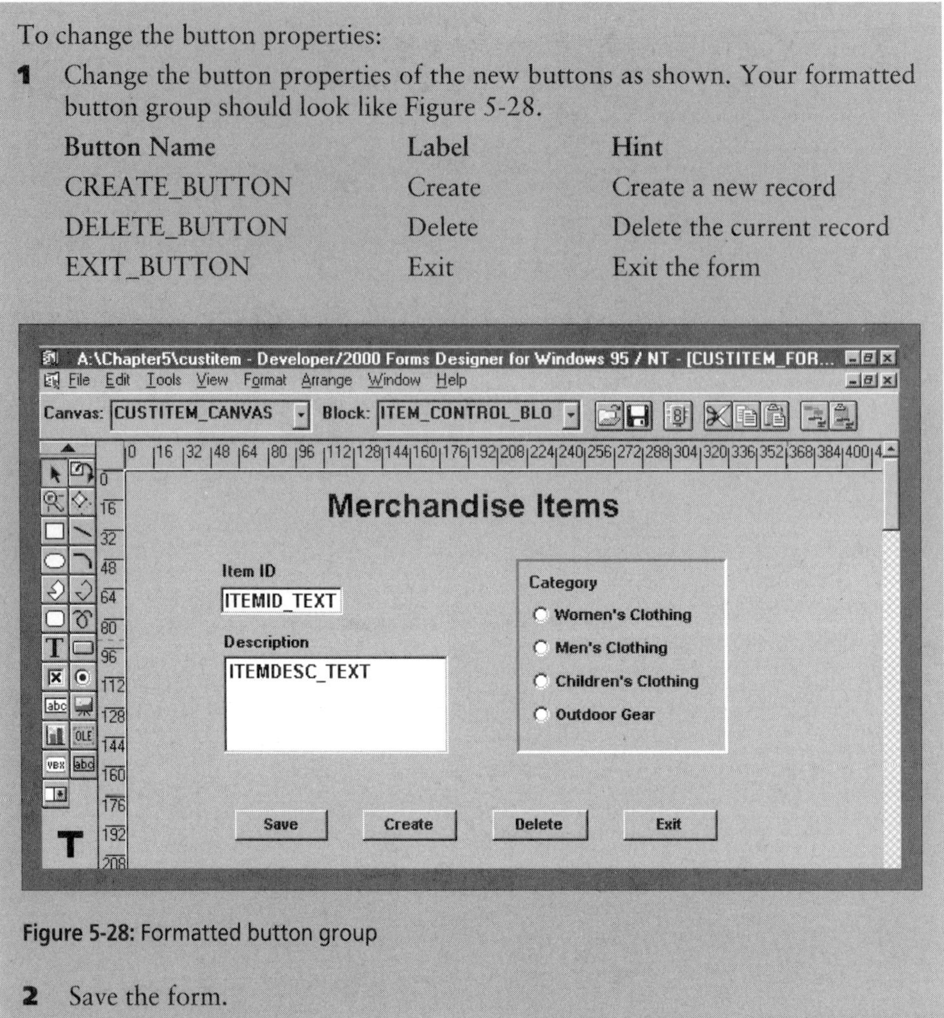

Figure 5-28: Formatted button group

2 Save the form.

Creating the Button Triggers

Recall that when a user clicks the Save button, a procedure called a trigger is run that inserts a new record in the database using a SQL INSERT statement. Oracle Forms triggers are written in PL/SQL, Oracle's programming language. PL/SQL is a lot like other procedural programming languages such as Basic, COBOL, and Pascal. It allows users to declare variables, assign values to variables, and manipulate variable values. It has basic control structures such as if/then statements and loops. What makes it different is that programmers can combine PL/SQL procedural programming statements with SQL commands to insert, update, view, and delete data records. An overview of PL/SQL commands is provided in Appendix A.

The triggers in this form will be kind of tricky because the Save button is used for inserting new records as well as for updating existing records. The approach you will use is that the form will have two states—INSERT and UPDATE. It will be in the UPDATE state all of the time except when the user clicks the Create button. This will move it to the INSERT state and signal the Save button to insert a new record. As soon as the new record is inserted, the form will return to the UPDATE state. The form will remain in the UPDATE state when an existing record is updated or deleted. Figure 5-29 shows the form's state diagram.

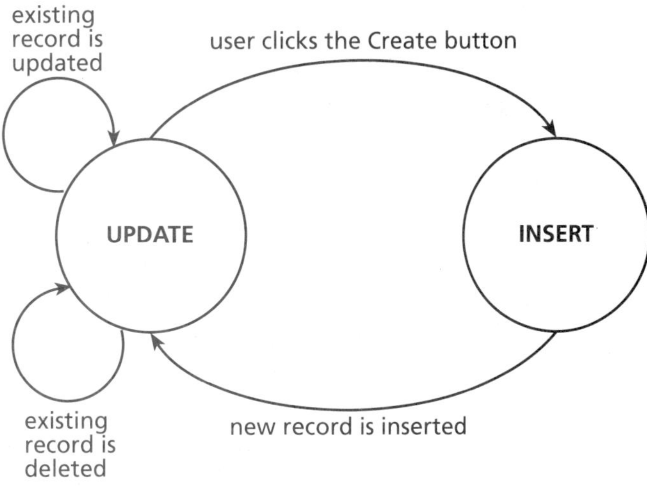

Figure 5-29: CUSTITEM_FORM state diagram

Writing the CREATE_BUTTON Trigger The first trigger you will write is for the Create button. This trigger needs to put the form in the INSERT state. It also needs to get the next value in the ITEMID_SEQUENCE and display it in the Item ID text field on the form. First you will create the trigger by associating the form object (the CREATE_BUTTON) with the associated trigger event (the user clicking the button).

To make the CREATE_BUTTON trigger:

1. Right-click the **CREATE_BUTTON** in the Layout Editor, and then click **PL/SQL Editor**. You have not created any triggers for the CREATE_BUTTON yet, so you are prompted to create a new trigger with the **CUSTITEM_FORM: Triggers** dialog box, which shows all of the button events that can have associated triggers. You want to attach this trigger to the WHEN-BUTTON-PRESSED event.
2. Drag the mouse pointer over the % in the Find text box, type **w**, and then press the **Enter** key. This automatically scrolls the list box down to the beginning of the events that start with the letter *w*, as shown in Figure 5-30.

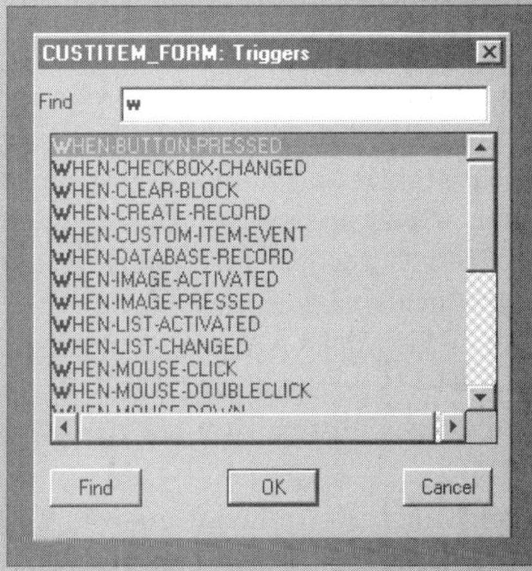

Figure 5-30: Selecting the trigger event

3 Click the **WHEN-BUTTON-PRESSED** event, and then click the **OK** button. The PL/SQL Editor opens, as shown in Figure 5-31.

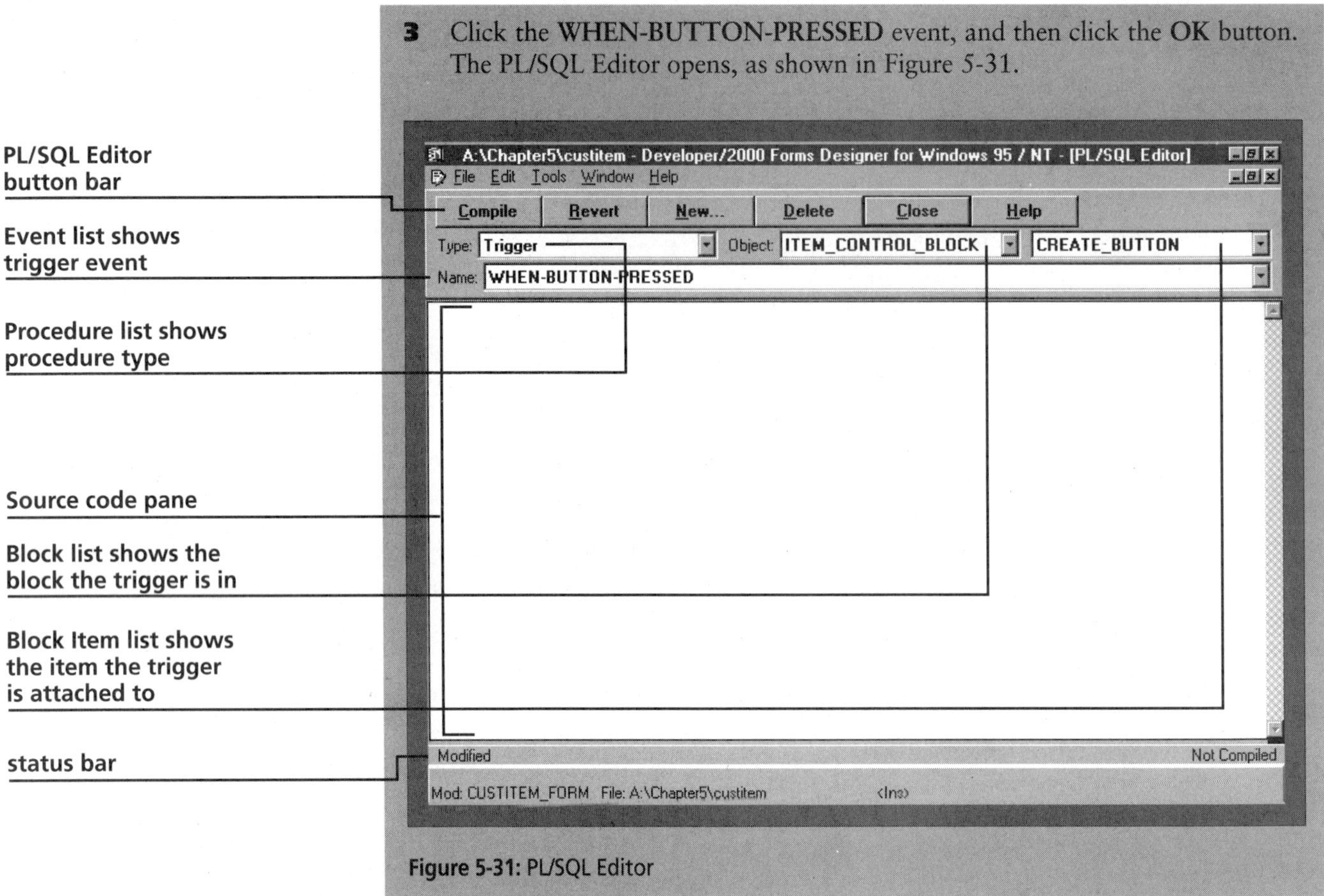

Figure 5-31: PL/SQL Editor

In the PL/SQL Editor, the **Procedure list** shows the procedure type, which is a trigger. (Procedures also can be **program units**, which are sub-programs that are called by triggers.) The **Block list** displays the name of the block that the trigger is in, and the **Block Item list** shows the name of the item the trigger is attached to. The **Event list** shows the event associated with the trigger. The **Source code pane** is where you type the PL/SQL program statements. The **status bar** shows the trigger's current modification status (Modified or Not Modified) and compile status (Not Compiled, Successfully Compiled, or Compiled with Errors).

The PL/SQL button bar has the following buttons:

- **Compile**, which compiles the program statements in the Source code pane. The compiler detects syntax errors and references to incorrectly specified database tables and fields and form objects.
- **Revert**, which reverts the source code to how it was since it was last compiled or since the last time the Revert button was clicked.
- **New**, which creates a new procedure.
- **Delete**, which deletes the current procedure.
- **Close**, which closes the PL/SQL Editor.
- **Help**, which allows the user to get help while working in the PL/SQL Editor.

Now you will enter the code for the CREATE_BUTTON trigger. To specify that the form is in the INSERT state, you will create a global variable named mode that stores the form's state (INSERT or UPDATE). Global variables provide a way to share information among different form triggers. They are referenced using the following general format: `:GLOBAL.<variable name>`. For example, the global variable mode will be referred to as :GLOBAL.mode.

When working in PL/SQL, keep the following conventions in mind:

- PL/SQL comment lines are inserted by starting the line with two hyphens (--).
- PL/SQL commands are not case sensitive except for text strings enclosed within single quotation marks. In this book, PL/SQL reserved words appear in uppercase letters.
- The general format for referencing the contents of a form text item is:`:<block name>.<item name>`.
- Always precede the block name with a colon (:).

Now you will enter the PL/SQL code for the CREATE_BUTTON trigger.

To enter the CREATE_BUTTON trigger code:

1 Click anywhere in the Source code pane in the PL/SQL Editor, and then type the code shown in Figure 5-32.

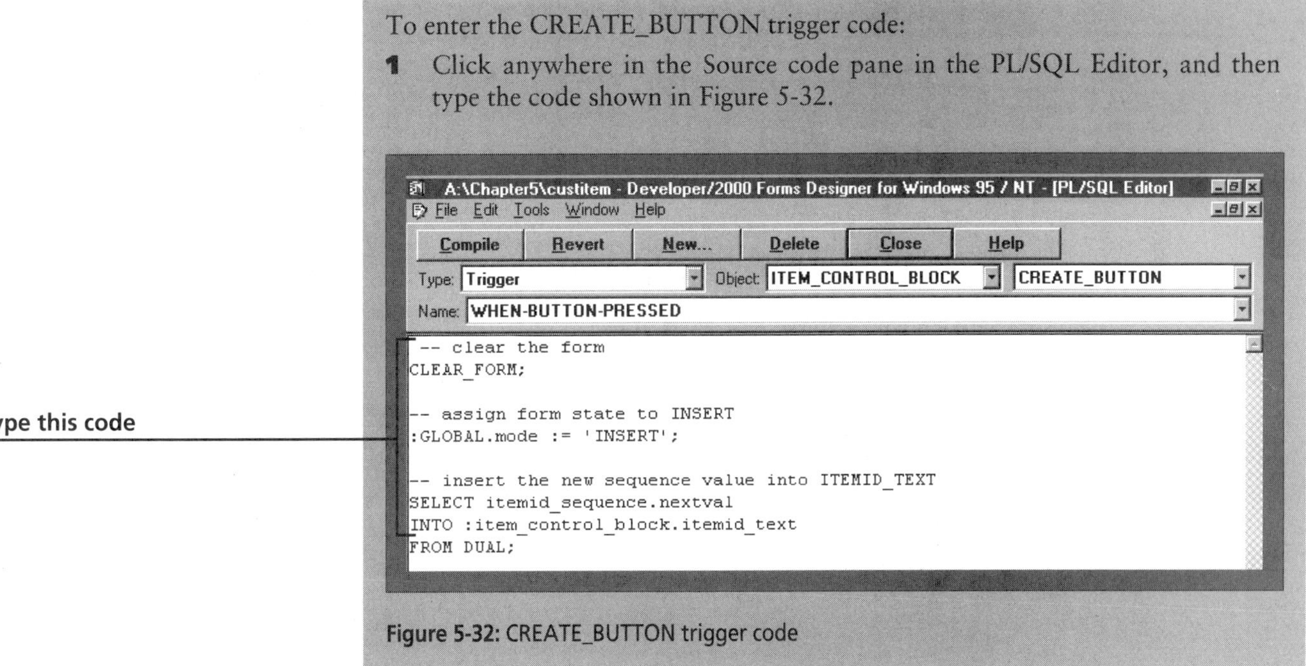

Figure 5-32: CREATE_BUTTON trigger code

Triggers must be **compiled**, or converted to executable code. When a trigger is compiled, it is checked for syntax errors and for references to database tables or fields or form objects that are not specified correctly or do not exist. Oracle Forms automatically compiles all triggers when you generate a form to create the executable (.fmx) file, but it is better to compile each procedure just after you enter the source code so you can find and correct errors immediately. When an error is detected, the program displays the line number of the statement causing the error with an error description. Next you will compile the CREATE_BUTTON trigger.

To compile the trigger:

1. Click the **Compile** button on the PL/SQL Editor button bar. If the trigger compiles successfully, the "Successfully Compiled" message appears on the status bar.
2. If your trigger compiled successfully, click the **Close** button on the PL/SQL button bar to close the PL/SQL Editor. If it did not compile successfully, don't worry—you will now learn about debugging triggers.
3. Save the form.

Debugging Triggers Figure 5-33 shows an example of a compile error generated when compiling the CREATE_BUTTON trigger. The **Compilation messages pane** displays the line numbers and error messages, as well as a correction suggestion. The selected error is the error message that is selected in the Compilation messages pane. The insertion point shows the location for the selected error in the Source code pane. You can select a different error message by clicking the message.

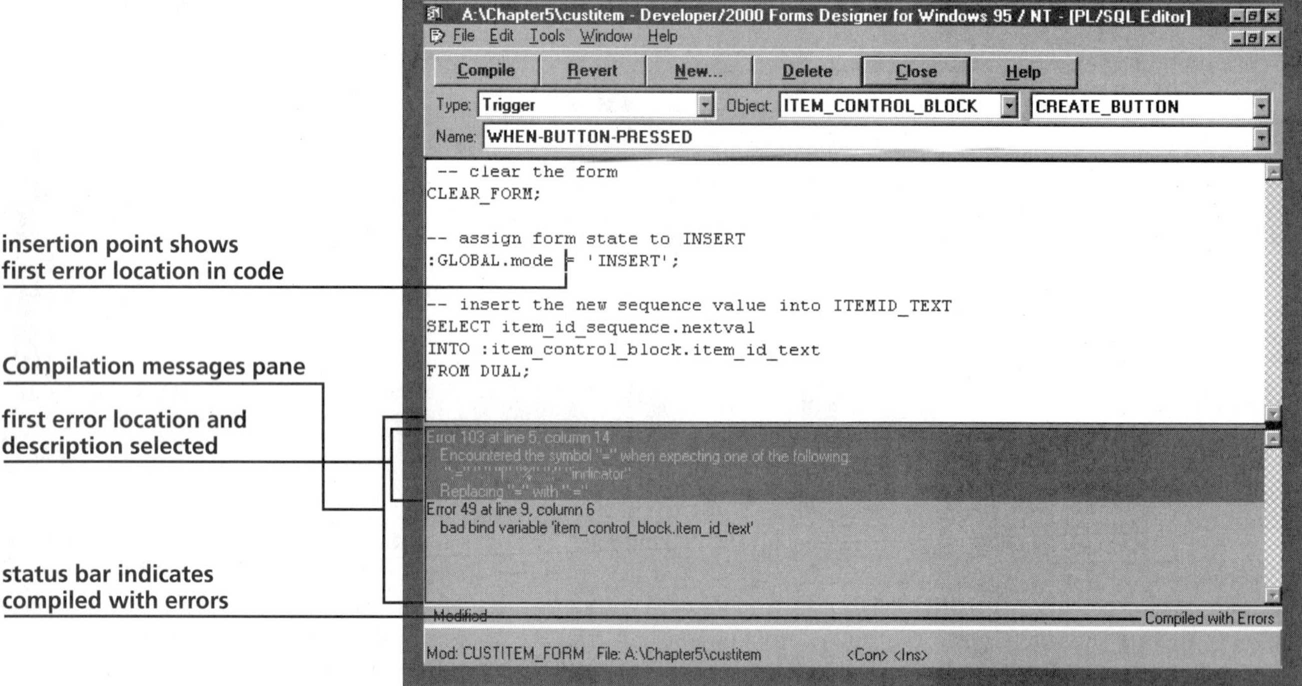

Figure 5-33: Trigger with compilation errors

The error shown in Figure 5-33 is a PL/SQL syntax error. The compiler expects the assignment operator (:=) when the variable :GLOBAL.mode is assigned the value 'INSERT'. (The **assignment operator** is used to assign a value to a variable.) Instead, the developer erroneously entered the **comparison operator** (=), which is used to compare two values to see if they are equal. This error can be corrected by changing = to := and then clicking the Compile button to recompile the trigger.

Figure 5-34 illustrates another common compile error. The error message "bad bind variable 'item_control_block.item_id_text'" indicates that the indicated form item does not exist. The probable cause is that the block name or text item name was entered incorrectly. If you closed the PL/SQL Editor and checked in the Object Navigator, you would see that the name of the text field is ITEMID_TEXT, instead of ITEM_ID_TEXT. To correct the error, you would enter the correct text field name, and then recompile the trigger.

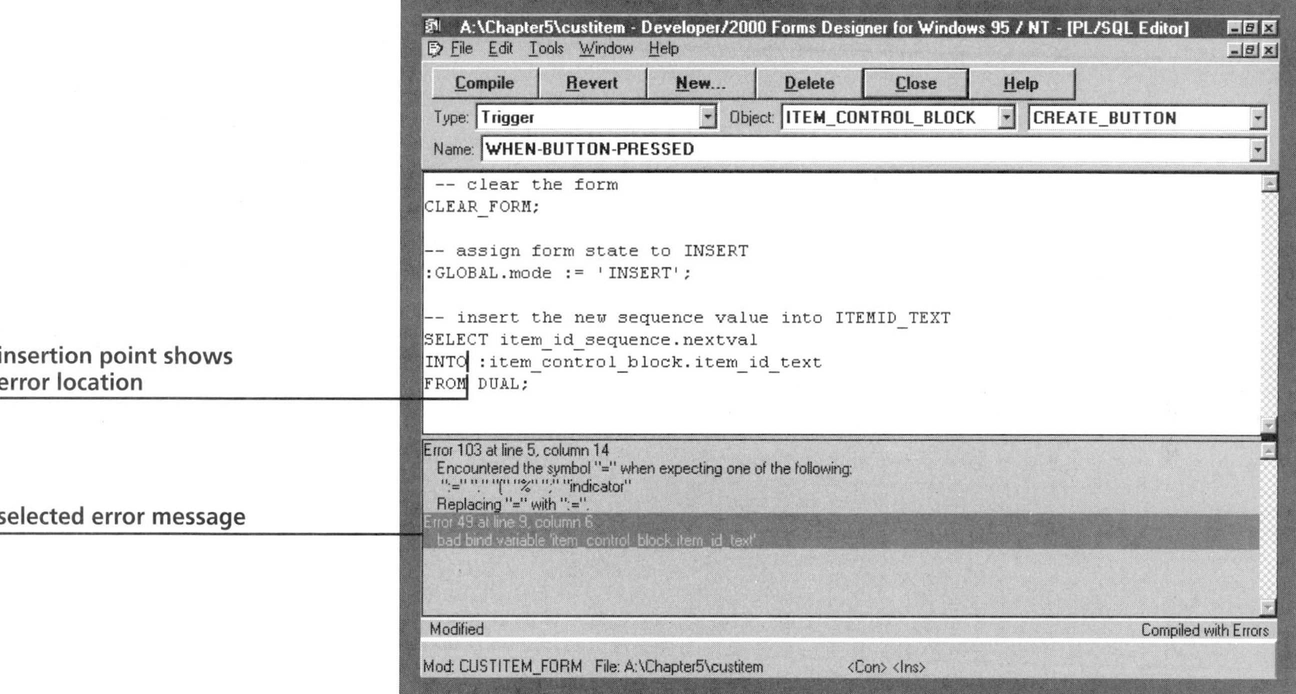

Figure 5-34: Compilation error generated by referring to a nonexistent form item

The "user must have access" error message will be generated if you are not connected to the database when you compile a trigger with a SELECT command for *any* database table, not just DUAL.

Another common compile error message, shown in Figure 5-35, is "'DUAL' (or some other table name used in the trigger) must name a table to which the user has access." This error (or one naming a database table other than DUAL) is generated when you are not connected to the database at the time you compile the trigger. The solution is to click Connect on the File menu, connect to the database in the usual way, and then recompile the trigger.

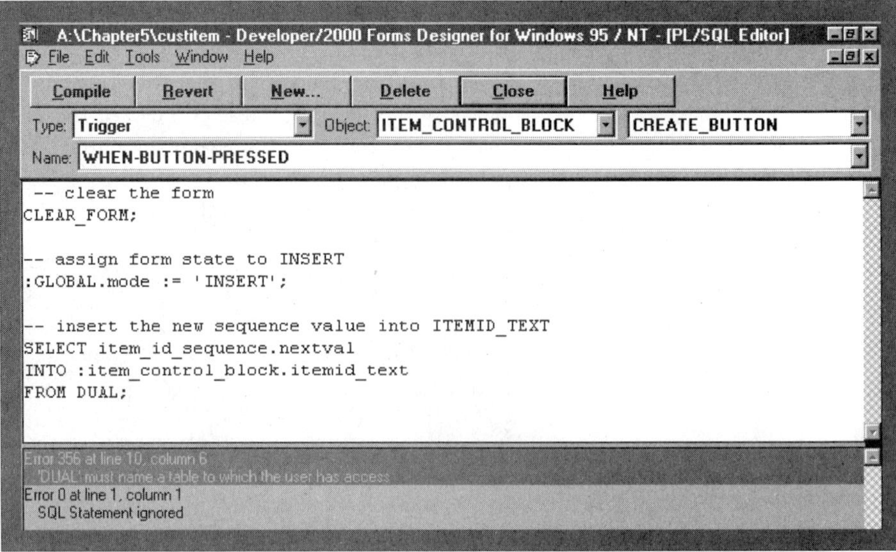

Figure 5-35: Compilation error generated when the user is not connected to the database

Figure 5-36 shows another common error message. The error message "qualifier 'ITEM_ID_SEQUENCE' must be declared" indicates that the compiler cannot identify the given variable name, in this case, ITEM_ID_SEQUENCE. Because the variable is a database object, the compiler cannot find it in any of your database objects, which include your tables, fields, and sequences. If you check the names of your sequences using SQL*Plus, you would find that the name of the sequence is ITEMID_SEQUENCE, not ITEM_ID_SEQUENCE. Entering the sequence name correctly and then recompiling the trigger corrects this error.

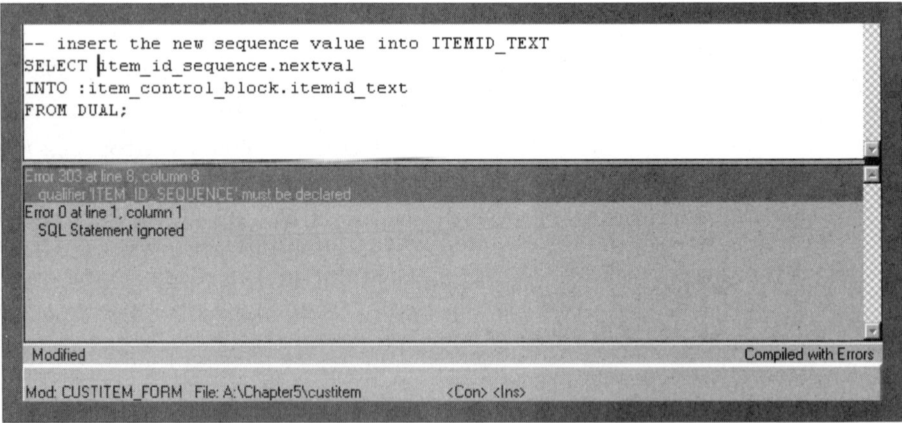

Figure 5-36: Compilation error generated by referring to a nonexistent database object

Often compile errors result when a SQL command is not correct. If you suspect that this is the case, copy the SQL command into a text editor, and then remove the INTO command used in the trigger SQL statement to place the query output into the form fields. Paste the edited SQL query into SQL*Plus and see if the query output is correct. Figure 5-37 shows how the SELECT command from Figure 5-36 was run in SQL*Plus without its INTO command. The SQL*Plus error message immediately identifies that the error occurred because the sequence name does not exist.

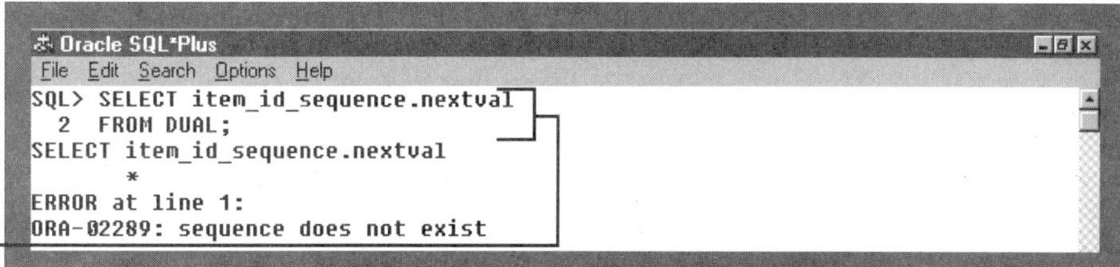

Figure 5-37: Testing a trigger SQL command in SQL*Plus

There are many more possible compile errors, but these are some of the most common ones. The best way to locate errors is to carefully examine the source code line that contains the error and make sure that the form objects and database objects are specified correctly and that the PL/SQL syntax is correct. If you cannot spot the error visually, test the SQL commands in SQL*Plus to make sure that they are correct.

Testing the CREATE_BUTTON Trigger After you successfully compile the trigger, the next step is to test it to be sure that it is working correctly. It is a good idea to run the form each time you create a new trigger or add new code to an existing trigger so if there are errors, you know exactly what code caused them.

To test the trigger:

1. If necessary, correct any syntax errors in your trigger, and then recompile the code until it successfully compiles.
2. Click the **Close** button on the PL/SQL Editor button bar to close the PL/SQL Editor.
3. Click the **Run** button on the Layout Editor toolbar to run the form in the Forms Runtime application and then maximize the window.
4. Click in the Item ID text field, and then press the **Tab** key to navigate to your buttons. Verify that the hints appear in the message area for each button.

   HELP? Don't worry if the buttons are accessed out of order when you press the Tab key. You will fix this later.
5. Click the **Create** button to confirm that a new ITEMID value is retrieved into the ITEMID_TEXT text field.
6. Close the Forms Runtime application by clicking the **Close** button on the Forms Runtime title bar.

Writing the SAVE_BUTTON Trigger When the Save button is clicked, the trigger determines if the form state is INSERT. If it is, a new record that has the values that are displayed in the form text fields is inserted, and the form state is set back to UPDATE. If the form state is UPDATE, the record displayed in the form text fields is updated. The last program line in the trigger clears the form fields so the current record is not displayed and the form is ready for the next operation.

To write the SAVE_BUTTON trigger:

1. Right-click the **SAVE_BUTTON**, and then click **PL/SQL Editor**.
2. Select the **WHEN-BUTTON-PRESSED** event, and then click the **OK** button.
3. Type the code shown in Figure 5-38 in the Source code pane.

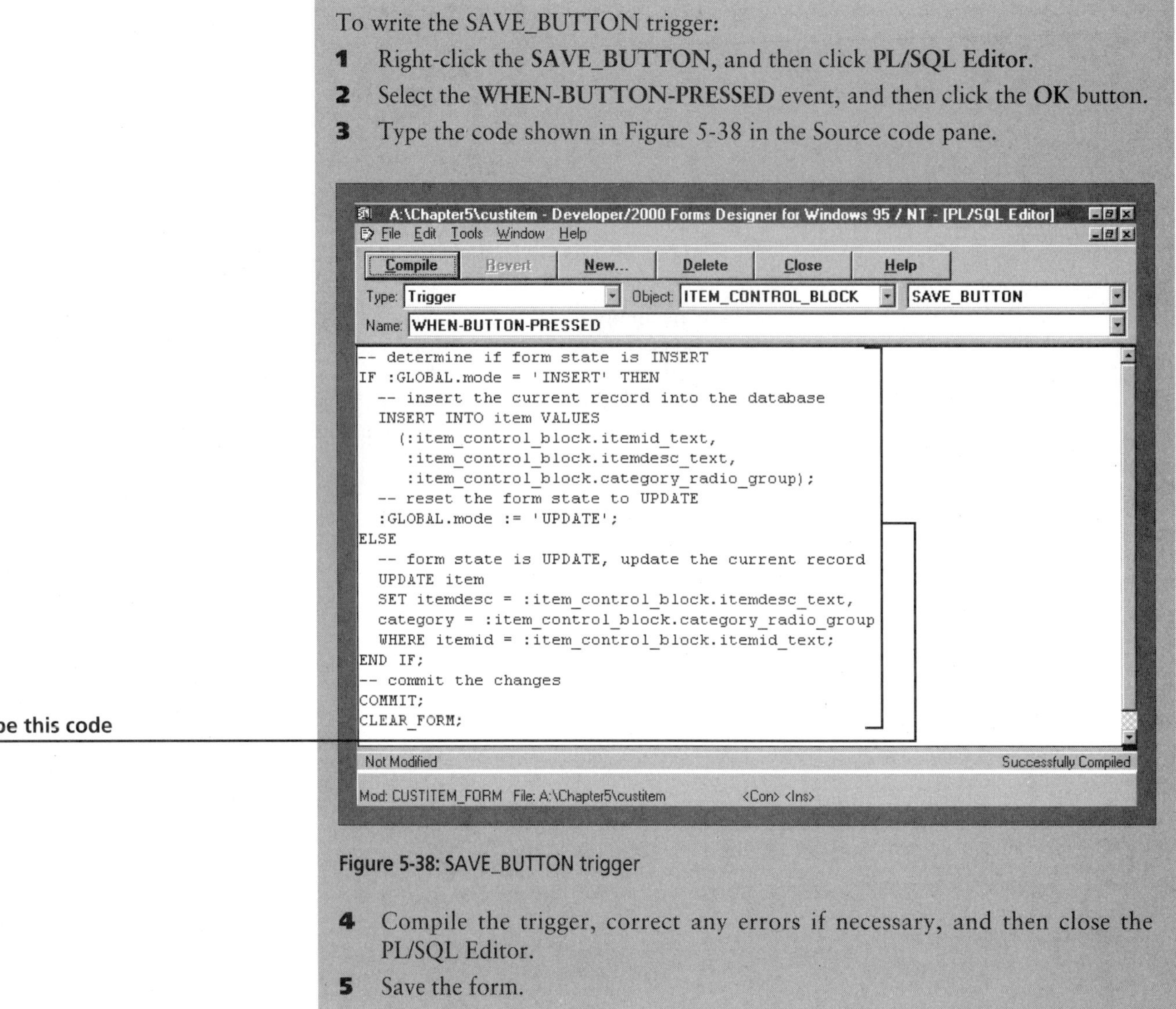

Figure 5-38: SAVE_BUTTON trigger

4. Compile the trigger, correct any errors if necessary, and then close the PL/SQL Editor.
5. Save the form.

Testing the SAVE_BUTTON Trigger Next you will test the SAVE_BUTTON trigger to be sure that it is working correctly to insert new records and update existing records. You will try to insert a new record first.

To test to see if the trigger works for inserting a new record:

1. Run the form.
2. Click the **Create** button to generate a new Item ID.
3. Type the new item description and select the category as shown in Figure 5-39.

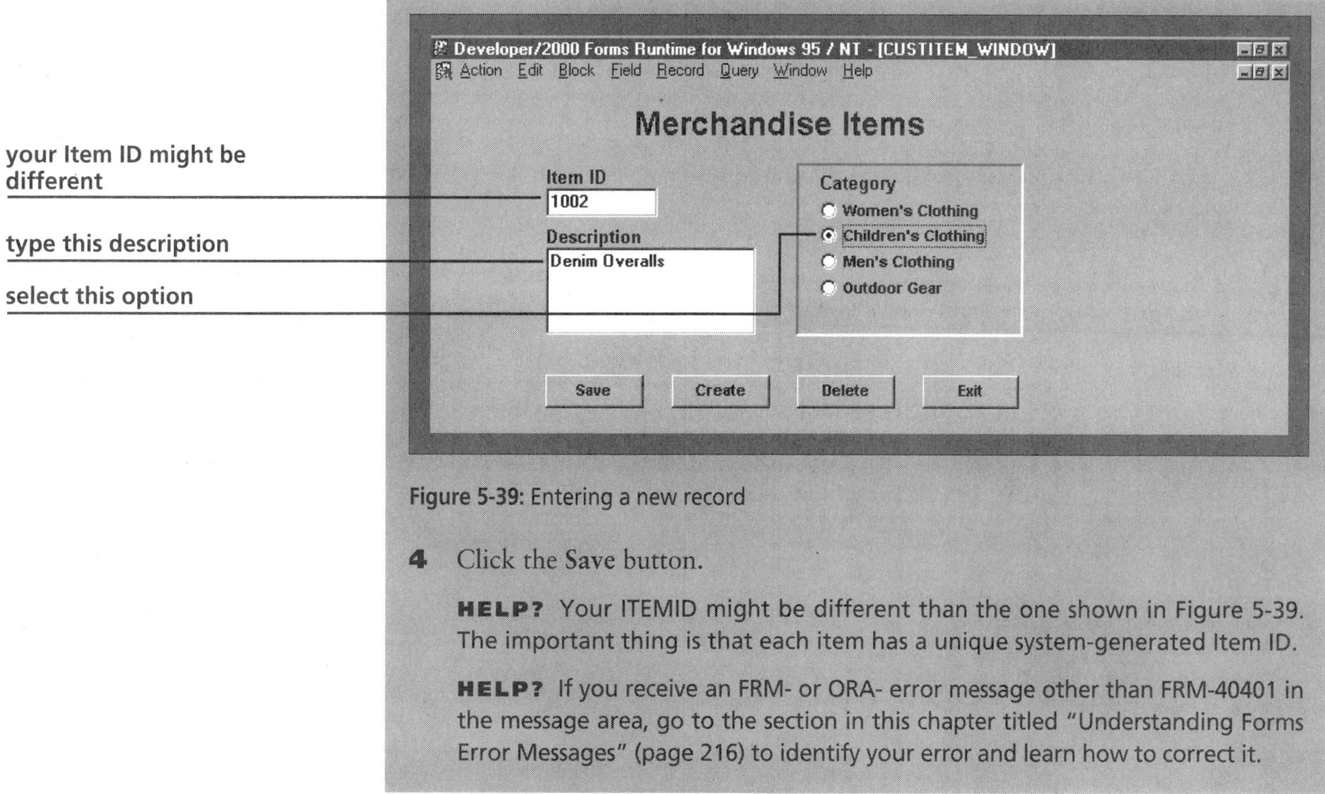

Figure 5-39: Entering a new record

4 Click the **Save** button.

HELP? Your ITEMID might be different than the one shown in Figure 5-39. The important thing is that each item has a unique system-generated Item ID.

HELP? If you receive an FRM- or ORA- error message other than FRM-40401 in the message area, go to the section in this chapter titled "Understanding Forms Error Messages" (page 216) to identify your error and learn how to correct it.

If the record was inserted successfully, the "FRM-40401: No changes to save" message should appear in the message area. This message is generated automatically when a COMMIT is issued following a SQL INSERT or UPDATE statement. You will learn how to substitute a more informative message for this message in Chapter 6. Now you can close the Forms Runtime application.

To close the Forms Runtime application:

1 Click the **Close** button [X] on the Forms Runtime title bar to close the application.

Creating the List of Values (LOV)

Before you can use this form to update or delete existing records, you must retrieve an existing record into the form text fields. When you ran the CUSTITEM_FORM earlier, you clicked a LOV (list of values) button that displayed a list of the descriptions of the items in the ITEM table. A LOV displays a **record group**, which is a list of data records that is based on a SQL query. When you create a new LOV, you can create a new record group or link the LOV to an existing record group.

To create the LOV:

1 Click **Window** on the menu bar, and then click **Object Navigator**.

2 In the Object Navigator window, click **Navigator** on the menu bar, and then click **Ownership View**.

3 Select **Forms** at the top of the Ownership View object tree, and then click the **Collapse All** button on the Object Navigator toolbar to close all open objects. When you create a LOV, it is useful to display all of your canvas item names so you can see all of the item names and therefore reference them correctly.

4 Click the **Forms plus box** ⊞, click the **CUSTITEM_FORM plus box** ⊞, click the **Blocks plus box** ⊞, click the **ITEM_CONTROL_BLOCK plus box** ⊞, and then click the **Items plus box** ⊞. Your screen should look like Figure 5-40.

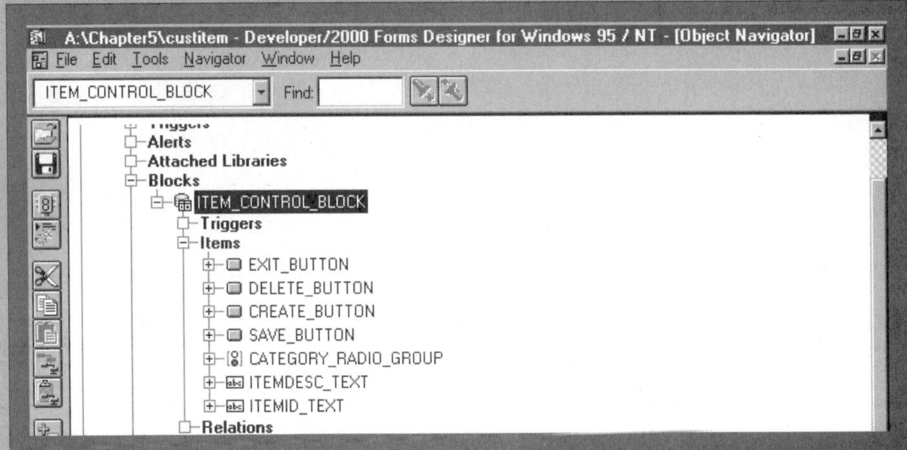

Figure 5-40: Viewing the form items

5 Click **LOVs** and then click the **Create** button on the Object Navigator toolbar to open the CUSTITEM_FORM: New LOV dialog box.

6 Make sure that the **New Record Group Based on the Query below** option button is selected, and then type the query shown in Figure 5-41. This query retrieves the ITEMID, ITEMDESC, and CATEGORY records from the ITEM table. When the user selects a record in the LOV and clicks the OK button, it places the selected record values into the ITEMID_TEXT, ITEMDESC_TEXT, and CATEGORY_RADIO_GROUP items on the form. Note that the item records in the LOV will be ordered by ITEMDESC.

7 Click the **OK** button. The new LOV appears in the Object Navigator window.

HELP? If you received the error message "FRM-11905: Item referenced in select statement does not exist," it means you did not enter the query correctly. Here are some debugging tips:

- Immediately copy the query text into a text editor so you can edit it by dragging the query text to select it, and then pressing Ctrl + C.
- Errors usually are caused by not specifying the table, field, block, or item names correctly. Move the New LOV dialog box on the screen so you can see the exact names of all of your text items behind it in the Object Navigator.
- If you cannot spot the error, try to isolate it systematically. In the text editor, remove the INTO clause, and then copy and run the query in SQL*Plus. If it runs, you know the problem is in the block and item names listed in the INTO clause.

tip

In a LOV command, the block names do not have to be preceded with a colon. No error is generated if you place a colon before the block names, however.

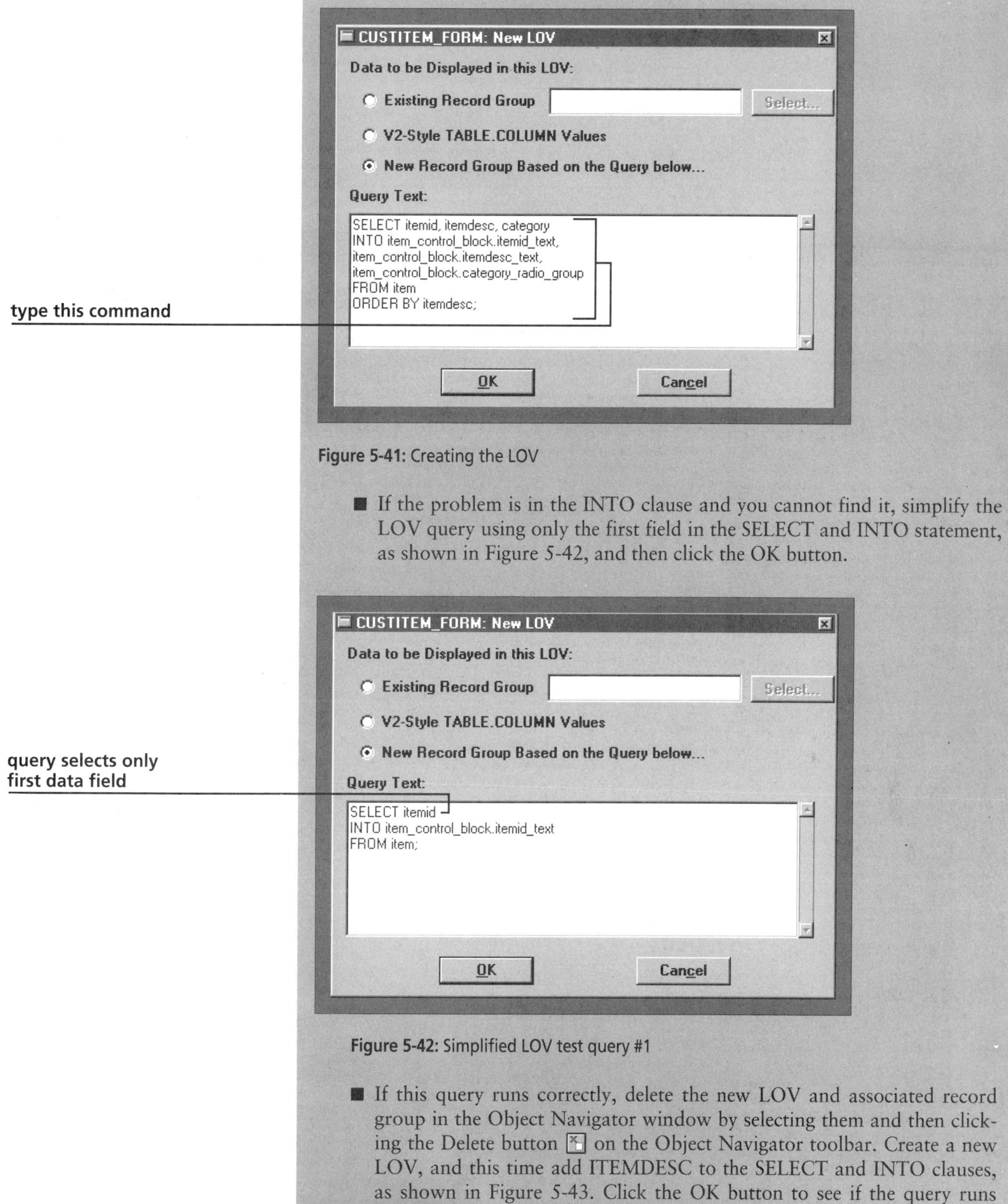

Figure 5-41: Creating the LOV

- If the problem is in the INTO clause and you cannot find it, simplify the LOV query using only the first field in the SELECT and INTO statement, as shown in Figure 5-42, and then click the OK button.

Figure 5-42: Simplified LOV test query #1

- If this query runs correctly, delete the new LOV and associated record group in the Object Navigator window by selecting them and then clicking the Delete button on the Object Navigator toolbar. Create a new LOV, and this time add ITEMDESC to the SELECT and INTO clauses, as shown in Figure 5-43. Click the OK button to see if the query runs correctly. Continue this process until you isolate the error.

query selects only the first two data fields

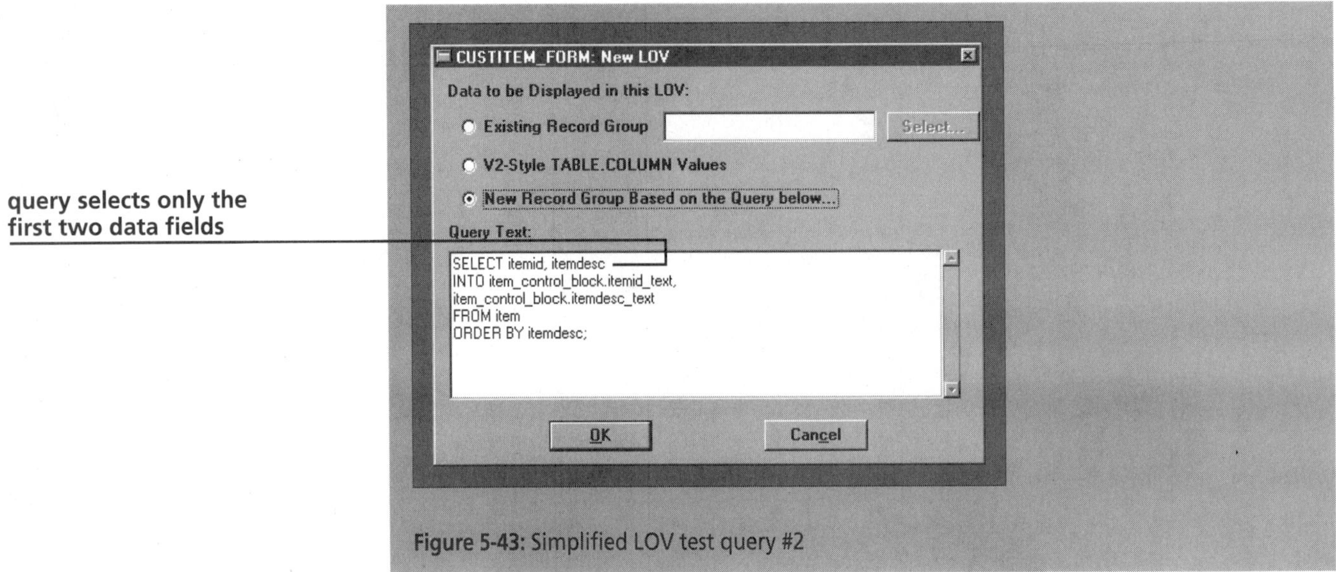

Figure 5-43: Simplified LOV test query #2

After you successfully create the LOV, new items appear in the Object Navigator screen under LOVs and Record Groups. You need to give these new items descriptive names.

To change the names of the LOV and record group:

1 Rename both the LOV and record group to **ITEM_LOV**, as shown in Figure 5-44.

rename these items

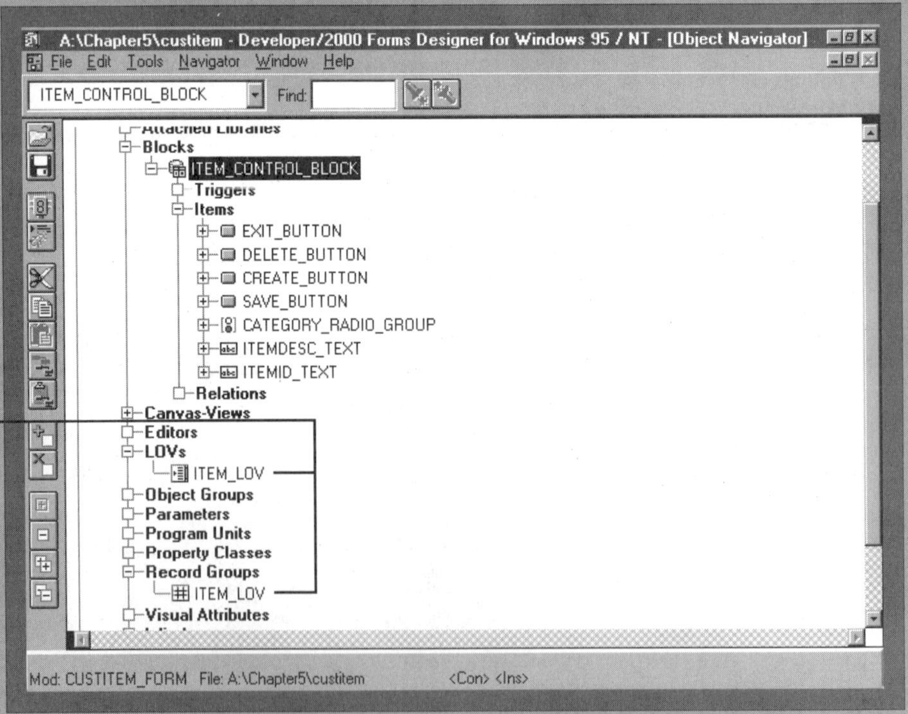

Figure 5-44: Renaming the new LOV and record group

2 Save the form.

Formatting the LOV Display The **LOV display** is the list that displays the record group data. By default, the display fields have the same column widths and titles as the corresponding database fields, which might result in column titles that are hard to understand and column widths that are too wide for the display screen. To modify the LOV display, you will use the Column Mapping dialog box shown in Figure 5-45.

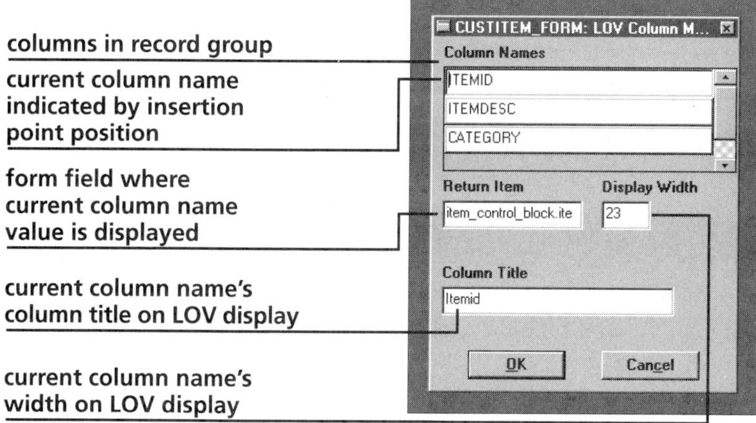

Figure 5-45: LOV Column Mapping dialog box

The Column Mapping dialog box is accessed through the ITEM_LOV Properties sheet. It lists the column names that are selected by the LOV's record group. The **current column name** is determined by the position of the insertion pointer. The **return item** specifies the form field that corresponds to the current Column Names selection where the user's LOV selection will be transferred. For example, the current column name is ITEMID, and its return item is ITEM_CONTROL_BLOCK .ITEMID_TEXT. If the user selects Women's Hiking Shorts in the LOV display and then clicks the OK button, the Item ID for Women's Hiking Shorts (894) is displayed in the ITEMID_TEXT field on the form. The **display width** specifies the current column name's width on the LOV display. The **column title** specifies the column title for the current Column Names selection on the LOV display.

By default, the LOV display shows all of the record group columns. However, a column containing a surrogate key, such as ITEMID, might not help the user identify a specific record, so you might want to omit it from the LOV display. (Surrogate keys must be included in the LOV record group because they contain the primary key value used to retrieve the record.) In this LOV, you will display only the item description. To omit a column from a LOV display, you set its display width to 0.

Next you will format the LOV display and hide all of the display fields except DESCRIPTION.

tip

When you create a new LOV, try to display the minimum number of fields that will enable the user to identify a specific item. Otherwise, the LOV display might not fit on a single screen.

To format the LOV display:

1 Open the Properties sheet for the LOV named ITEM_LOV (not the record group).

2 Change the Title property to **Items**. This is the title that will appear in the LOV window title bar.

3 Click the **Column Mapping** property, and then click the **More** button at the top of the Properties sheet. The CUSTITEM_FORM: LOV Column Mapping dialog box opens (see Figure 5-45).

4 Click the **ITEMID** field in the Column Names list box to select ITEMID as the current column name, and then change its Display Width to **0**, to indicate that you don't want to display it on the LOV display. The column will not be displayed, so you do not need to change the column title.

5 Click the **ITEMDESC** field in the Column Names list box to select ITEMDESC as the current column. Leave the Display Width at its current value, and then change the Column Title to **Description**.

6 Click the **CATEGORY** field in the Column Names list box, and then change the Display Width to **0**. It will not be displayed in the LOV display, so you do not need to change the title. Do not click the blank field below CATEGORY.

HELP? If you accidentally click the blank field below CATEGORY, click the Cancel button and then repeat the steps to format the LOV display.

7 Click the **OK** button to close the CUSTITEM_FORM: Column Mapping dialog box.

8 Close the LOV Properties sheet.

9 Save the form.

Creating the LOV Button

The next step is to create a button that the user can click to open the LOV display. You will add a button with a down arrow symbol (like a Windows list arrow) on the right edge of the ITEMID_TEXT text field. This type of button is called an **iconic button** because an **icon**, or picture, of a list arrow will appear on it. To create an iconic button, you create a regular button, change its Iconic property to True, and then change the Icon Name property to the name of the file that contains the icon that you want to display on the button. Filenames entered in the Icon Name property must be in the ORAWIN\ICONS (or ORANT\ICONS) folder on your client workstation. You do not include the path or extension on the filename in the Icon Name property.

To create the LOV button:

1 Go to the Layout Editor.

2 Use the **Push Button** tool on the Tool palette to draw a small square button positioned just to the right of ITEMID_TEXT, as shown in Figure 5-46.

draw the LOV button here

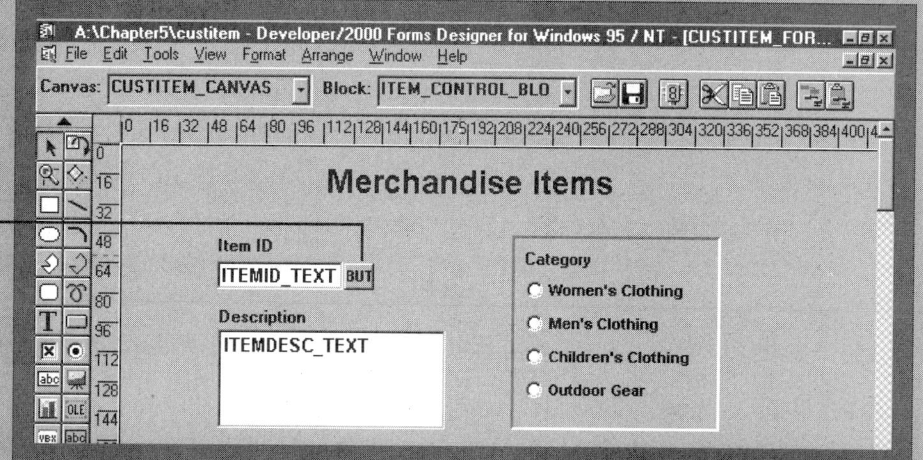

Figure 5-46: Drawing the LOV button

HELP? Sometimes when you try to draw a small button, the Forms Designer will automatically transform it to a default-sized larger button. If this happens, resize the button to match Figure 5-46.

The down.ico file is stored on your Student Disk in the Chapter5 Folder.

3 Change the button's properties as follows:

Name	ITEM_LOV_BUTTON
Height	15
Width	15
Mouse Navigate	False
Label	(Delete any default label—it will have an icon instead)
Iconic	True
Icon Name	Down

4 Close the ITEM_LOV_BUTTON Properties sheet. The icon should appear on your button.

HELP? If the icon does not appear, verify that you have changed the button's Iconic property to True, and entered Down for the Icon Name property. Verify that the down.ico file is in the ORAWIN\ICONS (or ORANT\ICONS) folder on your workstation. If the icon still does not appear, contact your instructor or technical support person regarding installation of the icon files.

5 Select the **ITEMID_TEXT** text field and the **ITEM_LOV_BUTTON** as a group, and set their alignment to **Horizontally Stack** and **Vertically Align Top**. Your screen should look like Figure 5-47.

LOV button with Down icon

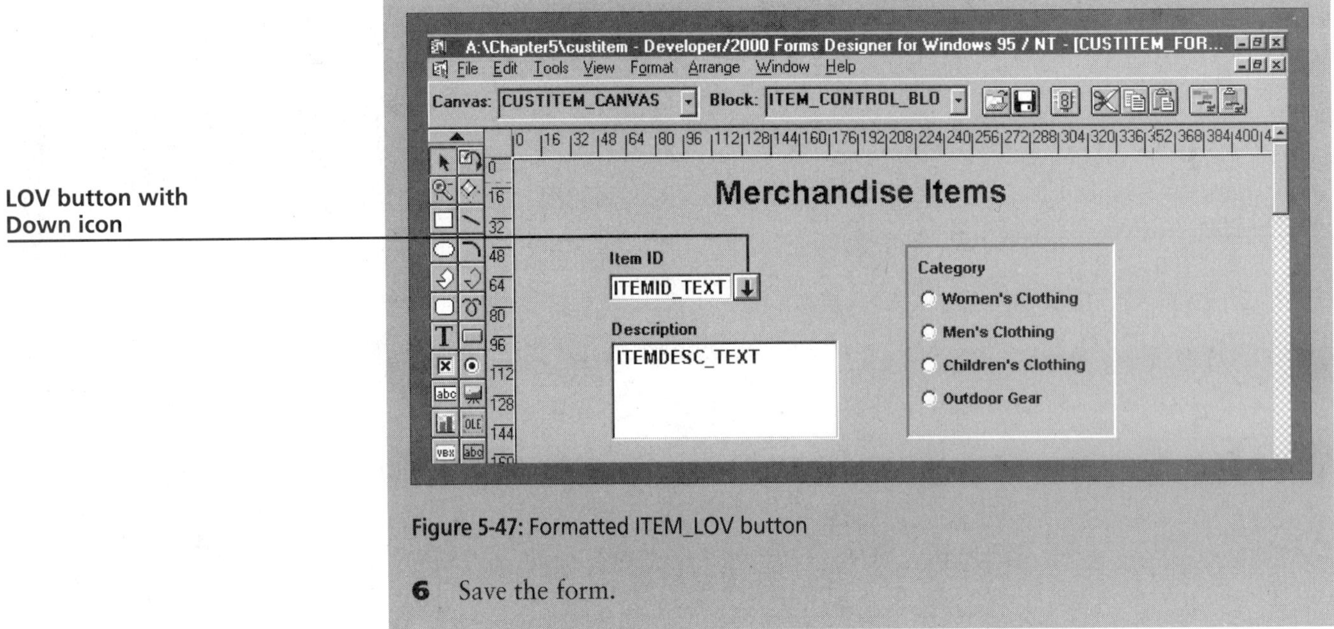

Figure 5-47: Formatted ITEM_LOV button

6 Save the form.

You must associate the LOV with a text field on the form. Usually, you associate the LOV with the text field that is the primary key of the record that you are displaying in the LOV. To associate a LOV with a text field, you set the text field's LOV property to the name of the LOV. To display the LOV, you must put the insertion point in the associated text field, and then issue the LIST_VALUES command. First you will associate the ITEM_LOV with the ITEMID_TEXT text field.

To associated the ITEM_LOV with the ITEMID_TEXT text field:

1 Open the ITEMID_TEXT Properties sheet.

2 Scroll down to the LOV property, and then double-click the LOV property so **ITEM_LOV** appears, as shown in Figure 5-48.

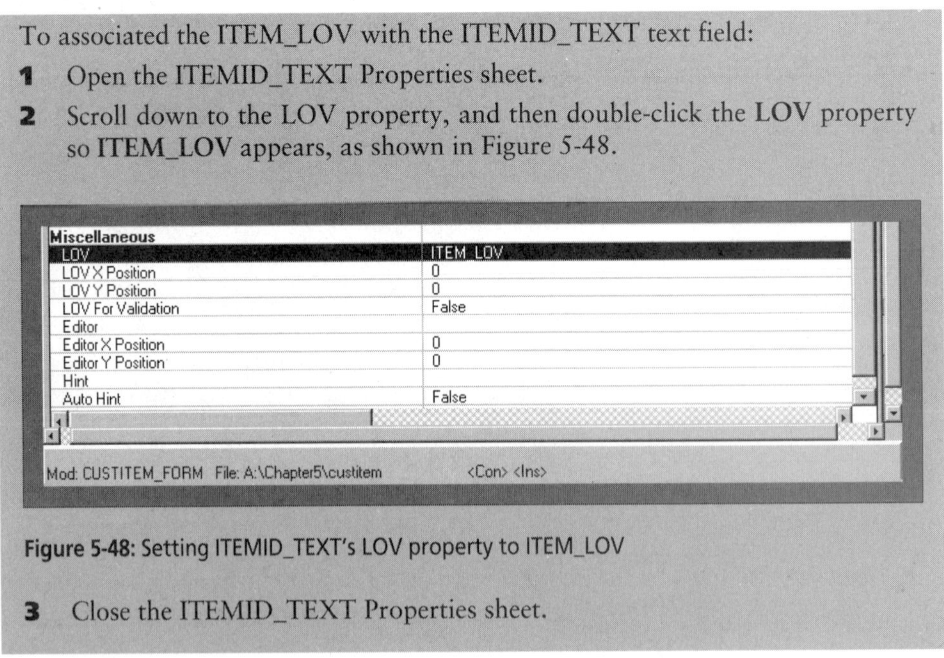

Figure 5-48: Setting ITEMID_TEXT's LOV property to ITEM_LOV

3 Close the ITEMID_TEXT Properties sheet.

Next you will create the ITEM_LOV_BUTTON trigger that will put the insertion point into ITEMID_TEXT and then display the LOV.

To create the ITEM_LOV_BUTTON trigger:

1 Right-click the **ITEM_LOV_BUTTON**, click **PL/SQL Editor**, and then create a new trigger using the **WHEN-BUTTON-PRESSED** event.

2 Type the code shown in Figure 5-49.

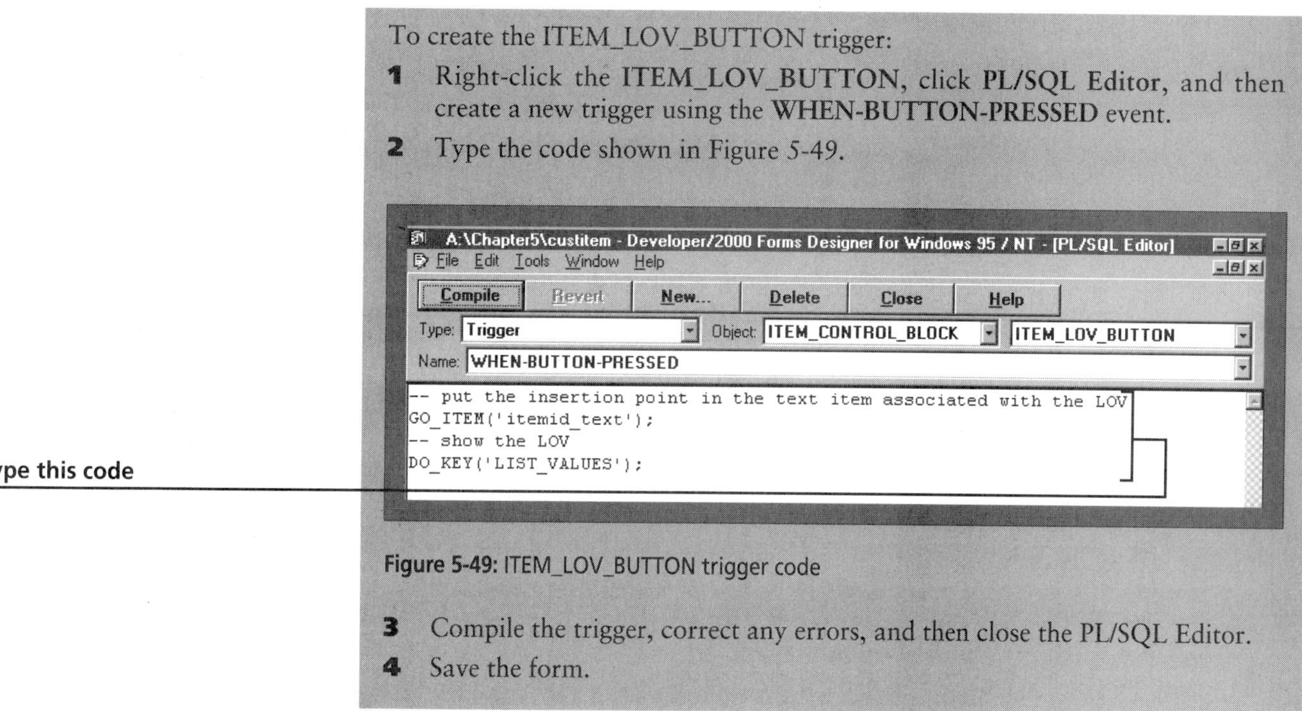

Figure 5-49: ITEM_LOV_BUTTON trigger code

3 Compile the trigger, correct any errors, and then close the PL/SQL Editor.

4 Save the form.

Next you will test the form to verify that the LOV display appears and that the selected record values are placed in the form text fields.

To test the LOV:

1 Run the form.

2 Click the **ITEM_LOV_BUTTON** to display the LOV. See Figure 5-50.

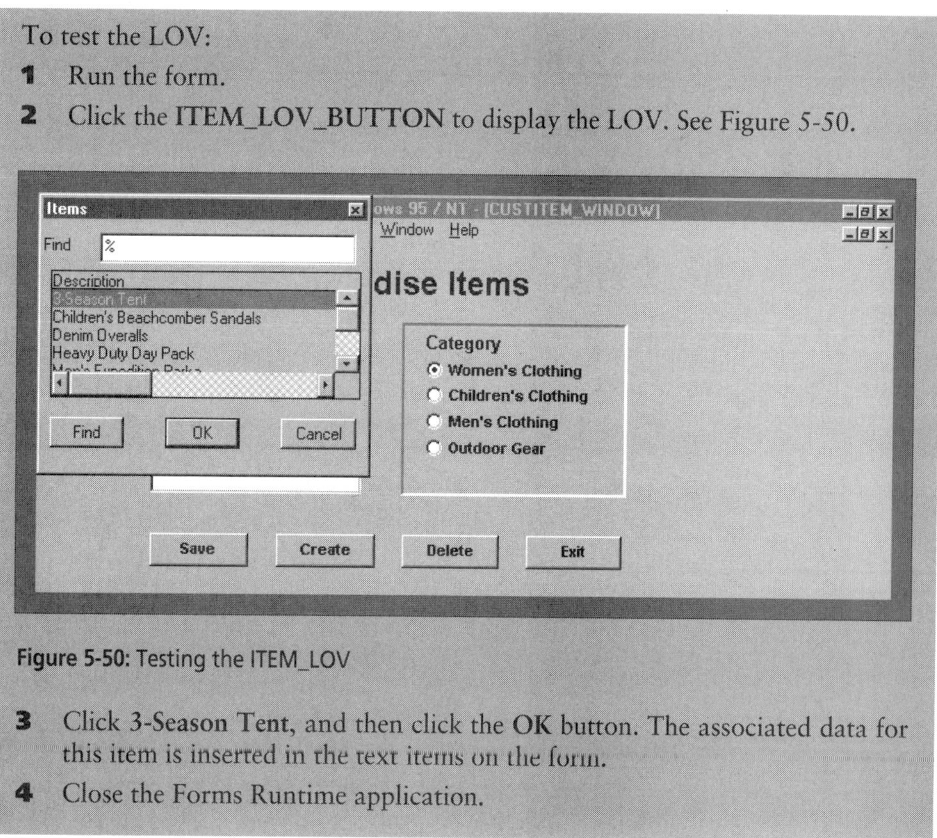

Figure 5-50: Testing the ITEM_LOV

3 Click **3-Season Tent**, and then click the **OK** button. The associated data for this item is inserted in the text items on the form.

4 Close the Forms Runtime application.

Creating a PRE-FORM Trigger

Review the state diagram for the form shown in Figure 5-29. The form is in the UPDATE state all of the time except when the user clicks the Create button. You will need to initialize the :GLOBAL.mode variable so that it is equal to UPDATE when the form first is displayed.

Currently, when the form first is displayed, the global variable does not exist. It is first initialized when the user clicks the Create button. But what if the user opens the form, retrieves a record using the LOV, modifies the record, and then clicks the Save button? The Save button trigger won't recognize the :GLOBAL.mode variable and will issue an error message. Therefore, you need to create a PRE-FORM trigger to initialize :GLOBAL.mode to UPDATE. A **PRE-FORM trigger** is attached to a form and executes when the form first displays. A form can have only one PRE-FORM trigger, which usually is used to initialize global variable values or to set up display parameters such as automatically maximizing the form window. You will create the PRE-FORM trigger next.

To create the PRE-FORM trigger:

1. Open the Object Navigator window, right-click the **CUSTITEM_FORM** module, and then click **PL/SQL Editor.**
2. Click the **New** button on the PL/SQL Editor button bar to open the CUSTITEM_FORM: Triggers dialog box.
3. Click the **PRE-FORM** event, and then click the **OK** button.
4. Type the following code in the Source code pane: **:GLOBAL.mode := 'UPDATE';**.
5. Compile the trigger, correct any typing errors, and then close the PL/SQL Editor.
6. Save the form.

Next you will test the form to see if the PRE-FORM trigger sets the form state to UPDATE when the form is first displayed. To do this, you will test to see if you can start the form and immediately update a record.

To test the PRE-FORM trigger:

1. Run the form.
2. Click the **ITEM_LOV** button, and then click **Denim Overalls.**
3. Change the item description to **Children's Denim Overalls,** as shown in Figure 5-51, and then click the **Save** button. The "FRM-40401: No changes to save" confirmation message indicates that the record was updated successfully. Therefore, the form was initialized to the UPDATE state correctly.

change this value

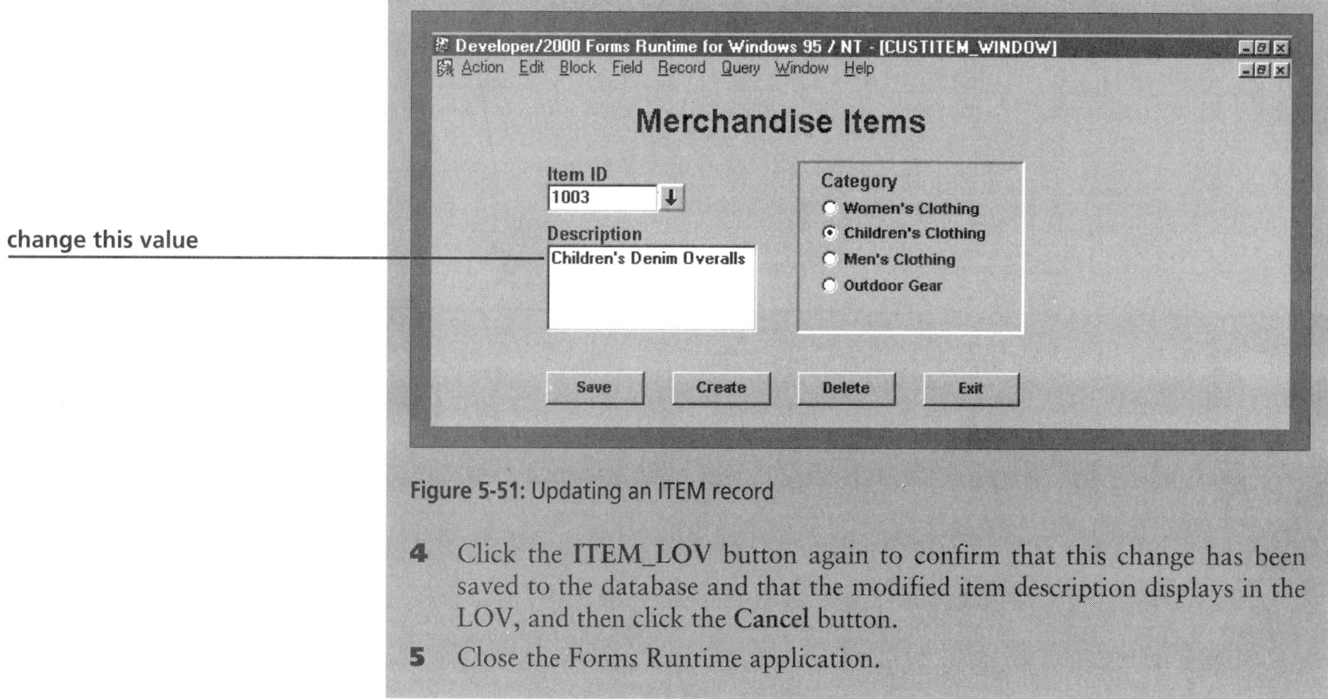

Figure 5-51: Updating an ITEM record

4 Click the **ITEM_LOV** button again to confirm that this change has been saved to the database and that the modified item description displays in the LOV, and then click the **Cancel** button.

5 Close the Forms Runtime application.

Creating the DELETE_BUTTON and EXIT_BUTTON Triggers The final step for completing the form is to create the triggers for the Delete and Exit buttons. First you will write the DELETE_BUTTON trigger, which will have a SQL command to delete the current record from the database, and then the trigger will use the CLEAR_FORM command to clear the form fields and set them for the next task.

To create the DELETE_BUTTON trigger:

1 Create a WHEN-BUTTON-PRESSED trigger for the DELETE_BUTTON.

2 Type the code shown in Figure 5-52 in the Source code pane.

type this code

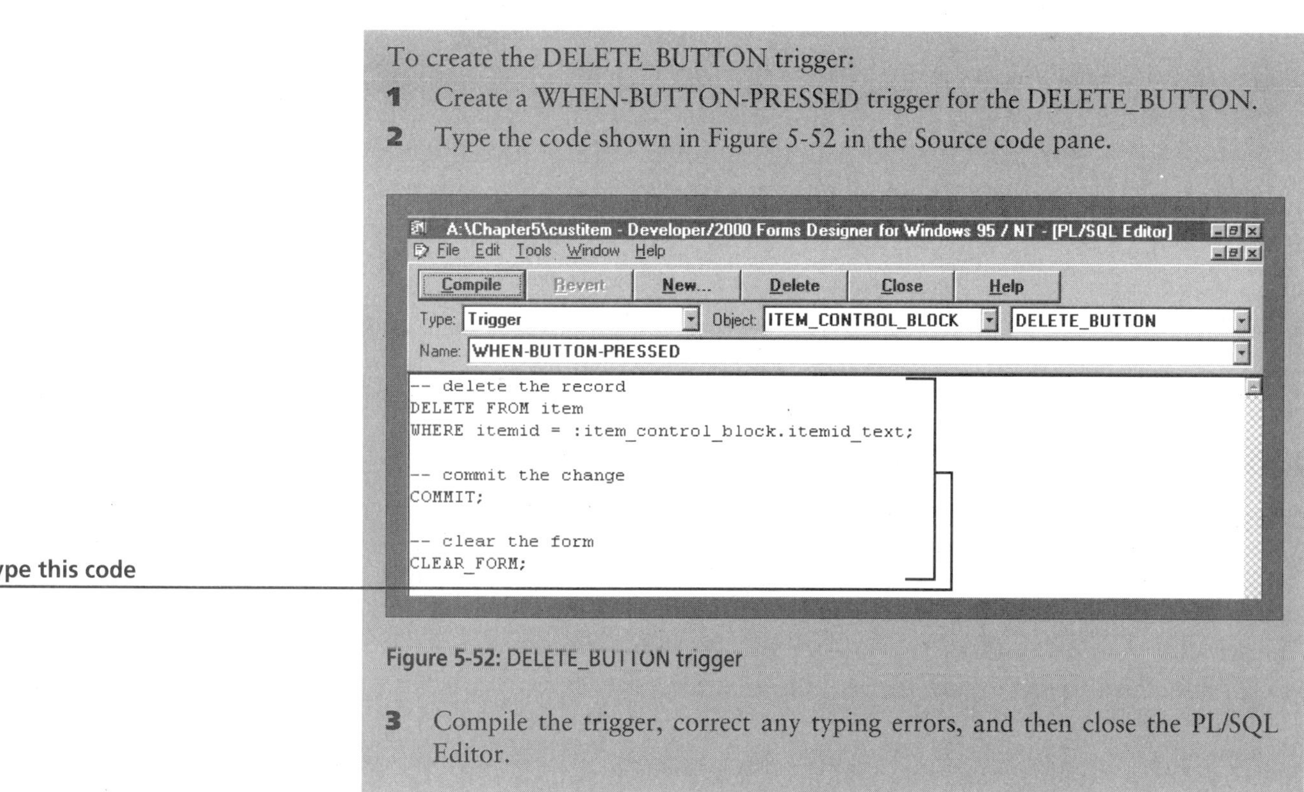


```
-- delete the record
DELETE FROM item
WHERE itemid = :item_control_block.itemid_text;

-- commit the change
COMMIT;

-- clear the form
CLEAR_FORM;
```

Figure 5-52: DELETE_BUTTON trigger

3 Compile the trigger, correct any typing errors, and then close the PL/SQL Editor.

Next you will create the trigger for the EXIT_BUTTON, which will close the form using the CLOSE_FORM command.

To create the EXIT_BUTTON trigger:

1 Create a WHEN-BUTTON-PRESSED trigger for the EXIT_BUTTON.

2 Type the following code in the PL/SQL Editor Source code pane: **EXIT_FORM;**.

3 Compile the trigger, correct any typing errors, and then close the PL/SQL Editor.

4 Save the form.

Now you need to test the form to verify that the Delete and Exit buttons work correctly.

To test the Delete and Exit buttons:

1 Run the form.

2 Click the **LOV** button, click **Children's Denim Overalls**, and then click the **OK** button. Click the **Delete** button. The "FRM-40401: No changes to save" confirmation message indicates that the record was deleted successfully.

3 Click the **LOV** button again to confirm that the record was deleted, and then click the **Cancel** button.

4 Click the **Exit** button to verify that it closes the form.

Finalizing the Format of the Form

To make the CUSTITEM_FORM form attractive and professional looking, you will add some final formatting touches. The first thing you will do is change the canvas size so it covers the entire screen, and then draw a background rectangle on the canvas so you can change the form's background color.

tip

The solid-colored area in the Layout Editor is the canvas, and the patterned area is the background behind the canvas.

To change the canvas size and draw a rectangle so you can change the background color:

1 Go to the Object Navigator window, select **CUSTITEM_CANVAS** under Canvas-Views, and then right-click to open its Properties sheet.

2 Change the canvas Width to 640 and the Height to 480.

3 Close the CUSTITEM_CANVAS Properties sheet.

4 Open the Layout Editor, click **View** on the menu bar, and then click **Zoom Out** as many times as necessary so you can see your entire canvas.

5 Click the **Rectangle** tool  on the Tool palette, and then draw a rectangle that is nearly the same size as the canvas. See Figure 5-53.

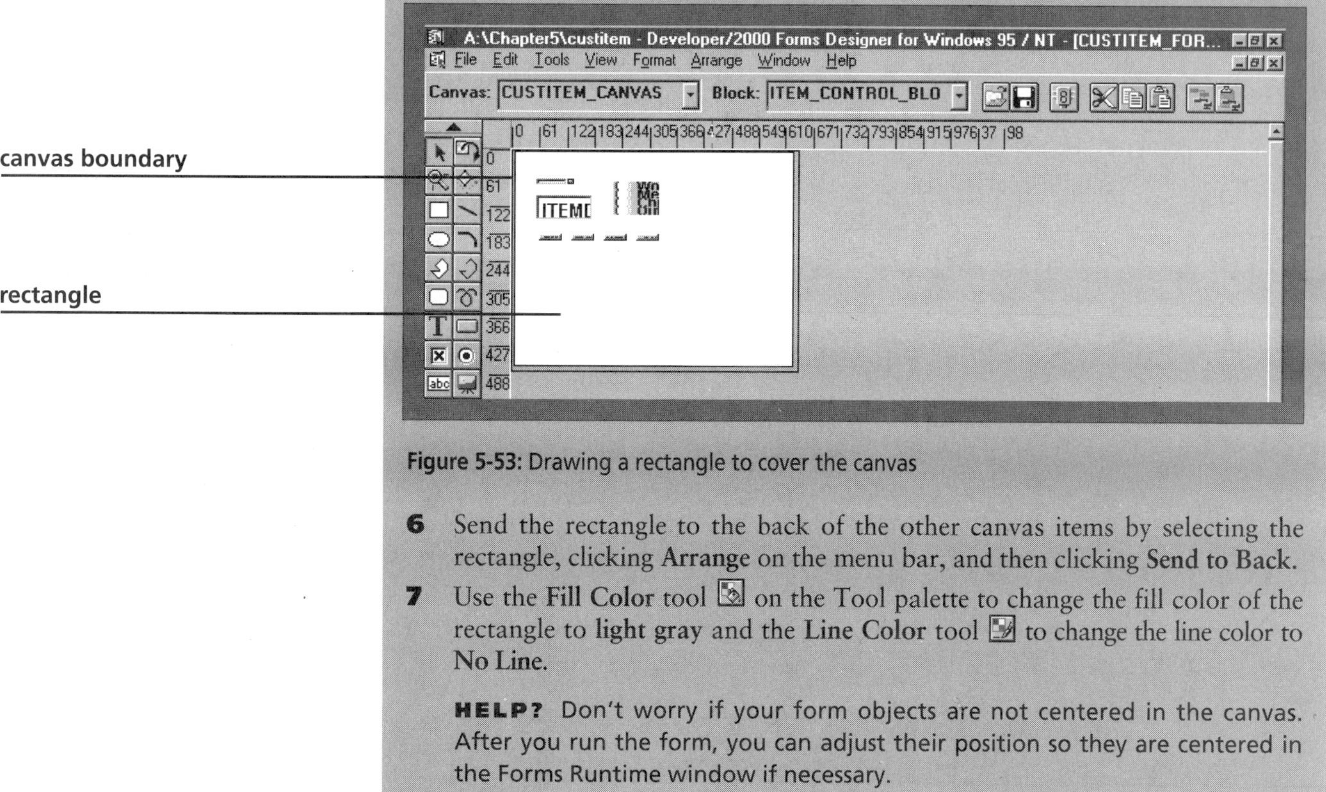

Figure 5-53: Drawing a rectangle to cover the canvas

6 Send the rectangle to the back of the other canvas items by selecting the rectangle, clicking **Arrange** on the menu bar, and then clicking **Send to Back.**

7 Use the **Fill Color** tool on the Tool palette to change the fill color of the rectangle to **light gray** and the **Line Color** tool to change the line color to **No Line.**

HELP? Don't worry if your form objects are not centered in the canvas. After you run the form, you can adjust their position so they are centered in the Forms Runtime window if necessary.

Next you will draw a smaller rectangle to enclose the form items.

To draw the smaller rectangle:

1 If necessary, click **View** on the menu bar, and then click **Zoom In** so you can see all of your form objects.

2 Click the **Rectangle** tool on the Tool palette, and then draw a smaller rectangle to enclose the form items. See Figure 5-54.

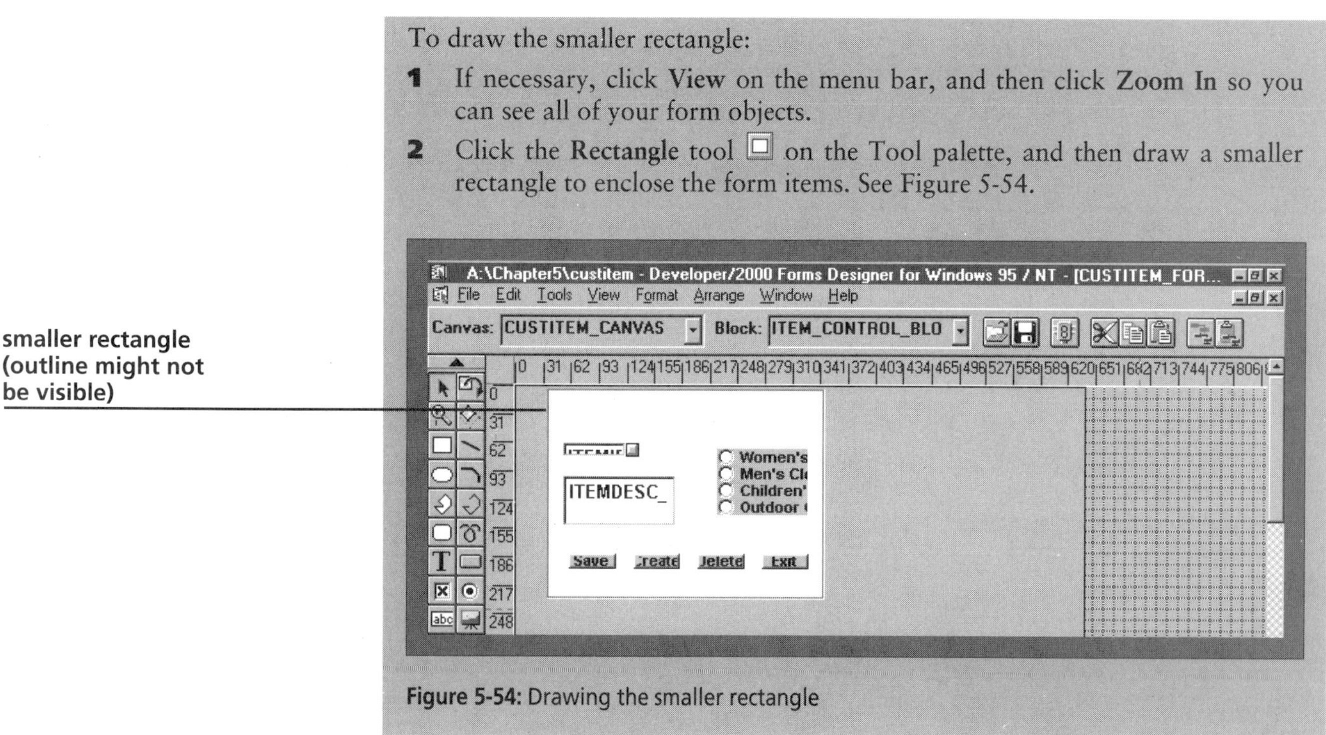

Figure 5-54: Drawing the smaller rectangle

3 Change the smaller rectangle's Fill Color property to **No Fill**, and the Line Color property to **black**.

HELP? The outline of the smaller rectangle might not be visible if its line color is the same as the background color.

4 Click **Format** on the menu bar, point to **Bevel**, and then click **Inset**.

5 Select the smaller rectangle, click **Arrange** on the menu bar, and then click **Send to Back**. The smaller rectangle is now under the larger one.

6 Select the larger rectangle, click **Arrange** on the menu bar, and then click **Send to Back**. The smaller rectangle is now visible on top of the larger one.

7 Click **View** on the menu bar, and then click **Normal Size**.

8 If necessary, scroll to the top left corner of the Layout Editor.

9 If necessary, select all of the radio buttons as a group, and then change the radio group Fill Color property so it is the same as the background rectangle.

HELP? Sometimes it is difficult to get the radio button fill color to exactly match the background fill color. If this happens, select a different background color until you find one that can match a radio button fill color.

10 Change the position of the form objects if necessary to make your form look like Figure 5-55.

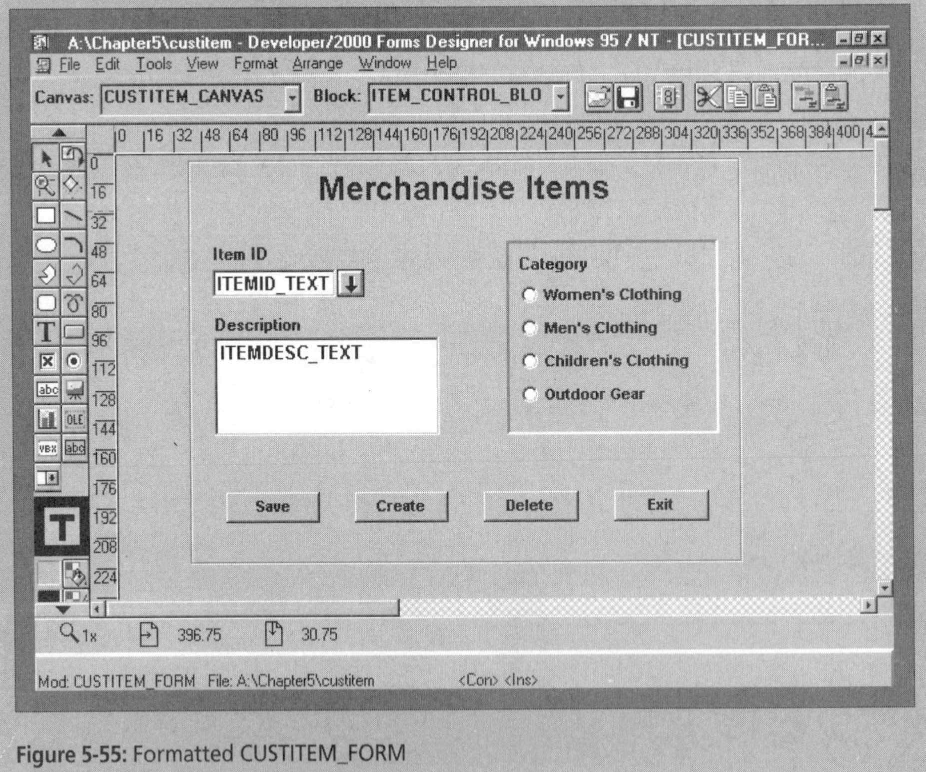

Figure 5-55: Formatted CUSTITEM_FORM

Always remember to change the window title and the window size so it is the same size as the screen. You will do this next.

To change the window title and size:

1. Open the CUSTITEM_WINDOW Properties sheet.
2. Change the Title property to **Clearwater Traders.**
3. If necessary, change the Width to **640** and the Height to **480**, and then close the Properties sheet.
4. Save the form.

Modifying the LOV Display Position The next formatting task is to change the position of the LOV display. Currently, it appears in the upper-left corner of the form. It will look better if it is positioned to the right of the ITEMID_TEXT field. You should position a LOV display close to its associated LOV button so users do not have to move the pointer very far to make a selection.

To change the position of the ITEM_LOV display:

1. If necessary, maximize the Layout Editor. Place the pointer at the top right corner of the ITEMID_TEXT field, and then note the X- and Y-positions at the bottom of the screen, as shown in Figure 5-56.

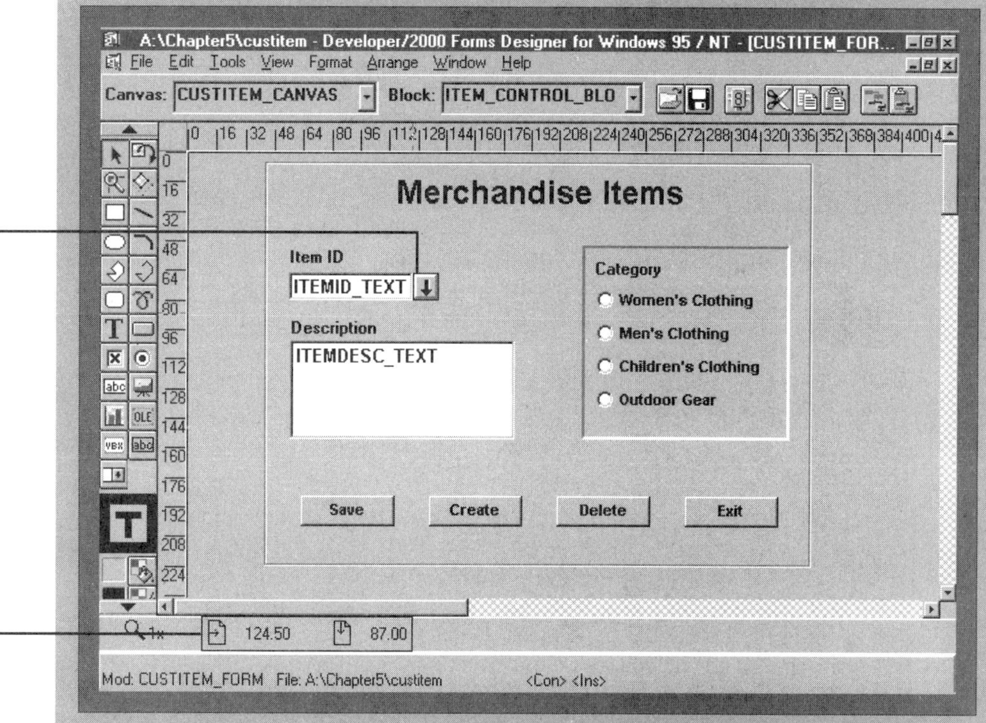

Figure 5-56: Finding the X- and Y-positions for the LOV display

HELP? Your X- and Y-positions might be different from those shown in the figure, so be sure to note them.

2. Go to the Object Navigator window, and then select the **ITEM_LOV**.

tip

The X Position and Y Position values of a LOV display must be entered in whole numbers.

3 Open the ITEM_LOV Properties sheet, and then change the X Position and Y Position to the values noted in Step 1. Round the values to the nearest whole number. The entered values for the pointer coordinates in Figure 5-56 are shown in the ITEM_LOV Properties sheet in Figure 5-57.

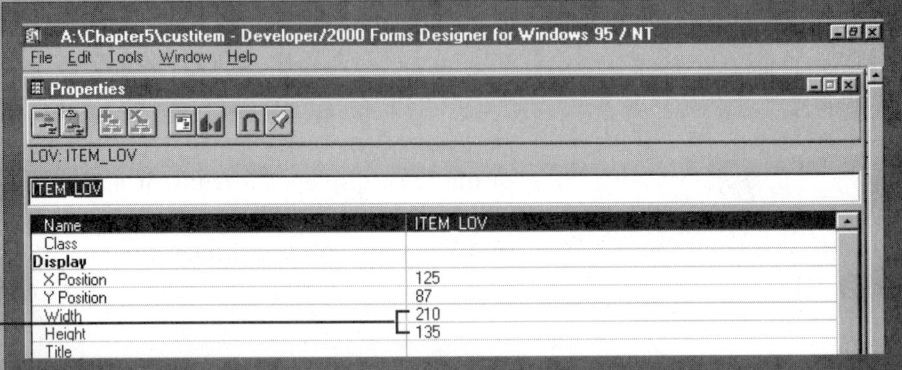

Figure 5-57: Entering the X- and Y-position coordinates in the ITEM_LOV Properties sheet

4 Close the ITEM_LOV Properties sheet.

5 Save the form.

6 Run the form and click the **LOV** button. Your form should look like Figure 5-58. If necessary, return to the Layout Editor, and adjust the size and position of your items to match the figure.

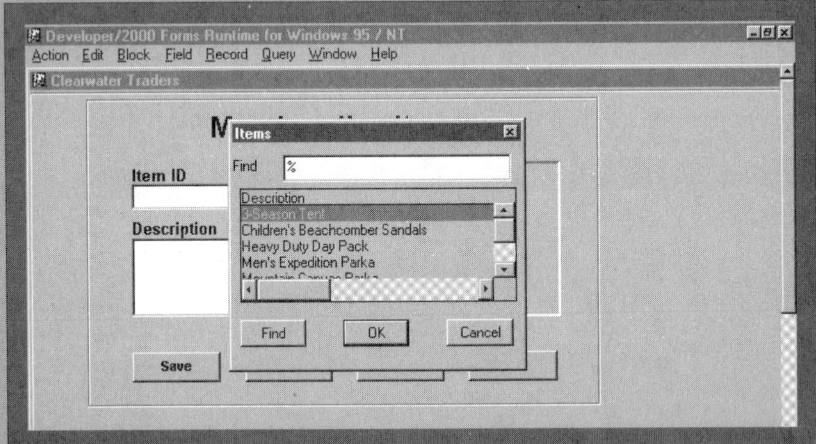

Figure 5-58: New ITEM_LOV display position

HELP? To adjust the position of the form objects so they are centered in the Forms Runtime window, zoom out so you can see the entire canvas. Select all of the form objects, except the large background rectangle, as a group by clicking and dragging the pointer to draw a box around the objects. Then drag all of the form objects (except the large background rectangle) to the desired position.

7 Click the **OK** button to close the LOV.

Changing the Item Navigation Sequence When you are running a form, you can move between canvas items by pressing the Tab key. Users read and enter data from top to bottom and left to right. The order that the insertion point moves through the canvas items when the user presses the Tab key is called the **navigation sequence.** Next you will examine the current navigation sequence for the CUSTITEM_FORM form to make sure that the movements are logical; then you will change the order of the sequence if necessary.

To examine the current navigation sequence for the CUSTITEM_FORM form and make necessary changes:

1. Click the **ITEMID_TEXT** field so the insertion point appears.
2. Press the **Tab** key to move from item to item. Notice that the item focus moves among the buttons and text items in no apparent order. Actually, there is an order—it is the order in which the items are listed in the Object Navigator.
3. Close the Forms Runtime application.
4. Open the Object Navigator window in Ownership View.
5. Select the **CUSTITEM_FORM** and then click the **Collapse All** button on the Object Navigator toolbar to close all open objects.
6. Open the **CUSTITEM_FORM Blocks, ITEM_CONROL_BLOCK,** and **Items** objects. The canvas items are listed in the reverse order in which they were created.

Next you will modify the navigation sequence so the items are accessed left to right and top to bottom in the following order: ITEMID_TEXT, ITEMDESC_TEXT, ITEM_LOV_BUTTON, CATEGORY_RADIO_GROUP, SAVE_BUTTON, CREATE_BUTTON, DELETE_BUTTON, and EXIT_BUTTON.

To correct the navigation sequence for the CUSTITEM_FORM form items:

1. Click **ITEMID_TEXT** and then drag it so it is the first item listed under Items. You will have to drag it so the "line" that appears is above the current first item.
2. Click **ITEMDESC_TEXT** and then drag it so the "line" is directly under ITEMID_TEXT.
3. Continue this process until the canvas items are in the desired order. Your Object Navigator screen should look like Figure 5-59.
4. Save the form.
5. Run the form to confirm that the navigation sequence is correct.
6. Exit the Forms Runtime application.
7. Click **File** on the menu bar, and then click **Close** to close CUSTITEM_FORM in the Forms Designer application. If necessary click the **Yes** button to confirm your changes.

put the block items in this order

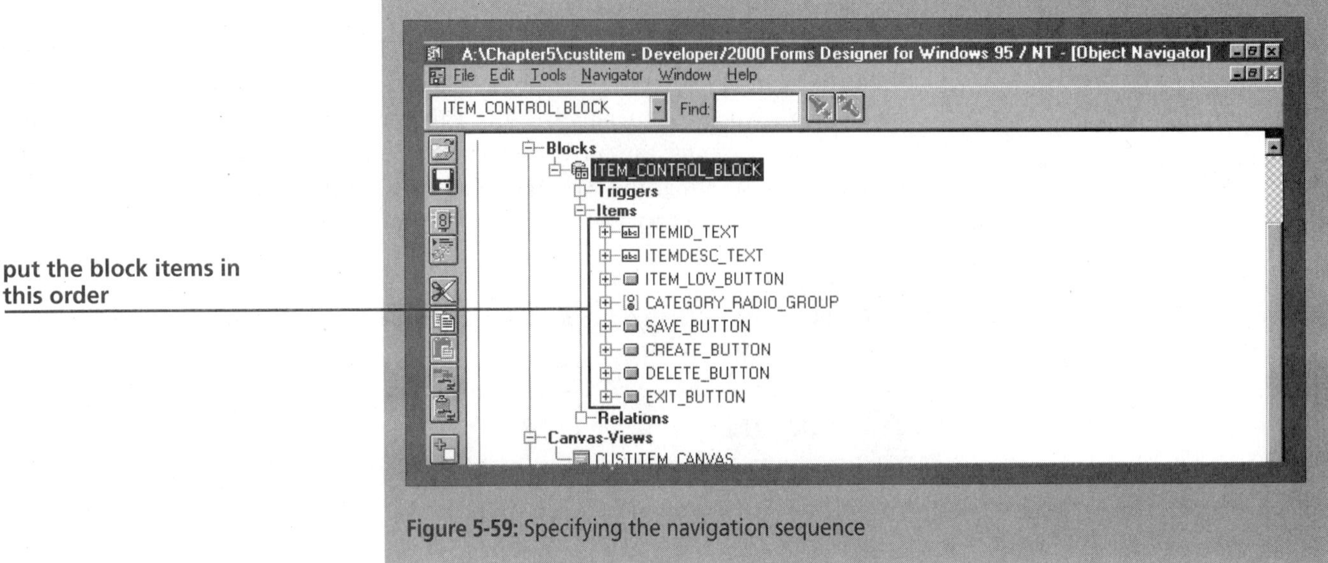

Figure 5-59: Specifying the navigation sequence

Now you are finished with the CUSTITEM_FORM. You can use the techniques you just learned to develop a form to insert, update, and delete data in any database table that does not have a foreign key field. Before you learn how to handle tables with foreign keys, you will learn how to understand and interpret Oracle Forms error messages. You can take a break now if you want.

Understanding Forms Error Messages

System messages appear in the message area of the Forms Runtime window. It is important to know how to use online Help to find what these messages mean, especially when you are trying to debug a form that is not running correctly. There are two likely kinds of messages you will see: ORA- messages are issued by the Oracle database, and FRM- messages are issued by the Forms Runtime application.

Finding ORA- Message Explanations

The ORA- message codes are generated by the database when errors occur that violate database constraints, such as inserting a primary key value that is not unique or a foreign key value that does not exist in the foreign key table. These are the same message codes that you saw in SQL*Plus in Chapter 2. To decode a message, click the Start button on the taskbar, point to Programs, point to Oracle for Windows 95 (or Windows NT), click Oracle7 Error Messages, and then search for the given message, as you learned in Chapter 2.

Finding FRM- Message Explanations

FRM- message explanations can be found in online Help in the Forms Designer application.

To use Help in the Forms Designer application:

1 If necessary, start the Oracle Forms Designer.

2 Click **Help** on the menu bar, and then click **Contents.**

3 Click the **Index** tab, and then type **FRM** in the first text box. Oracle Forms doesn't have a search engine to find explanations for individual messages, so you have to choose a block of error messages and then manually search to find a particular error code. Most system-generated messages that you will encounter are in the block labeled 10200-91119, as shown in Figure 5-60.

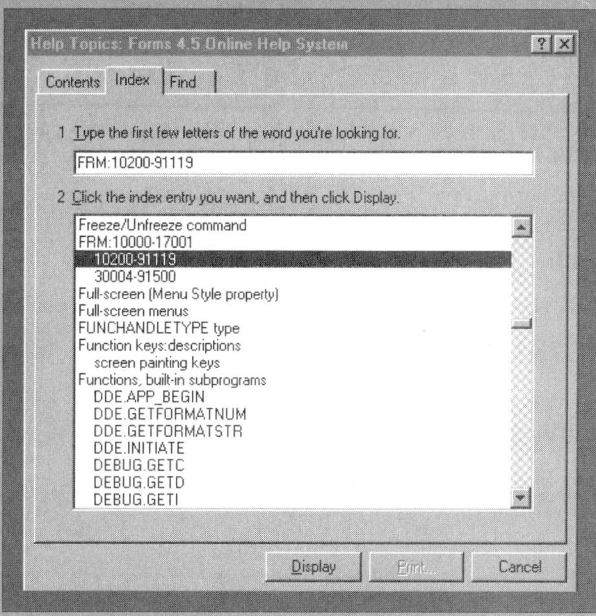

Figure 5-60: Finding FRM- error message explanations

4 Click the **10200-91119** block, click the **Display** button, and then maximize the Help screen if necessary, as shown in Figure 5-61. The FRM- error messages are listed sequentially, beginning with error message 10200.

5 Scroll down until you find FRM-40401, as shown in Figure 5-62. Note the cause, action, and level for FRM-40401. This message occurs because the system thought you tried to do a COMMIT to a data block, but there are no data blocks on your form, so the system assumed that no new records have been added or modified. No action is required, so the severity level of this message is low (5).

6 Scroll up until you see FRM-40361. Now note the cause, action, and level for FRM-40361. This message occurs if you try to do an inexact search using the % wildcard in a TIME data type field. The action requires you to restate your query, and the severity level is higher (>25). All error messages that require user actions have higher severity levels. In Chapter 6, you will learn how to substitute your own error message for the system error message. Your error message will tell users what to do to correct the problem rather than requiring the users to look up the cause and action in online Help.

7 Close the Help window.

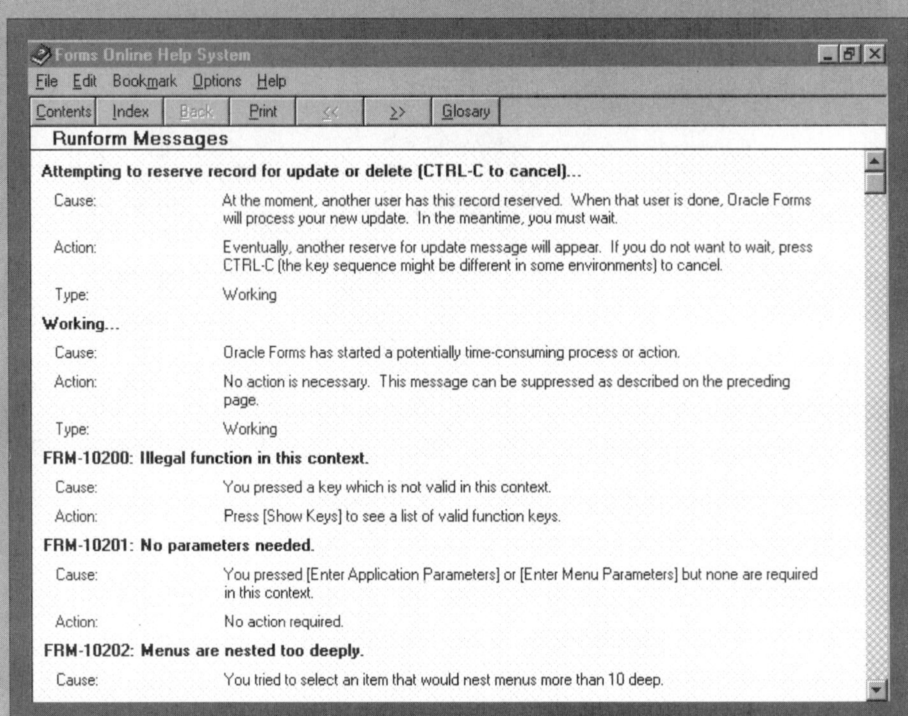

Forms Online Help System

File Edit Bookmark Options Help

Contents | Index | Back | Print | << | >> | Glosary

Runform Messages

Attempting to reserve record for update or delete (CTRL-C to cancel)...

Cause: At the moment, another user has this record reserved. When that user is done, Oracle Forms will process your new update. In the meantime, you must wait.

Action: Eventually, another reserve for update message will appear. If you do not want to wait, press CTRL-C (the key sequence might be different in some environments) to cancel.

Type: Working

Working...

Cause: Oracle Forms has started a potentially time-consuming process or action.

Action: No action is necessary. This message can be suppressed as described on the preceding page.

Type: Working

FRM-10200: Illegal function in this context.

Cause: You pressed a key which is not valid in this context.

Action: Press [Show Keys] to see a list of valid function keys.

FRM-10201: No parameters needed.

Cause: You pressed [Enter Application Parameters] or [Enter Menu Parameters] but none are required in this context.

Action: No action required.

FRM-10202: Menus are nested too deeply.

Cause: You tried to select an item that would nest menus more than 10 deep.

Figure 5-61: FRM help screen

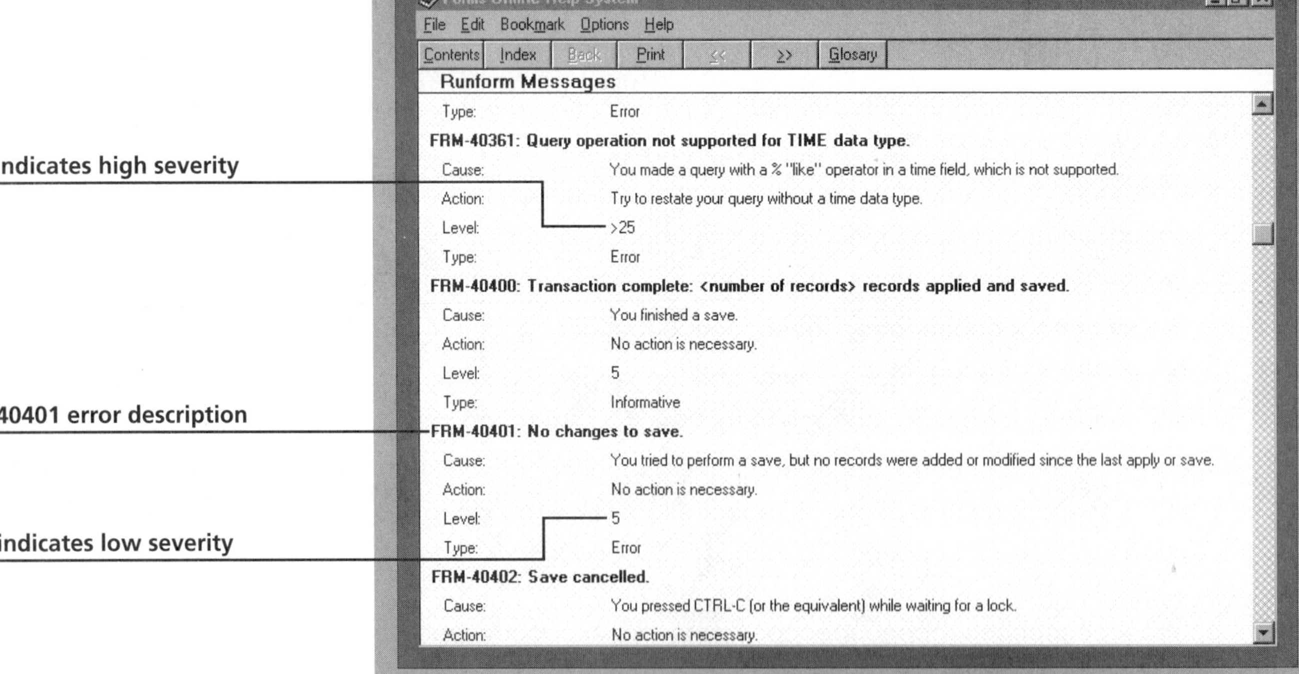

Forms Online Help System

File Edit Bookmark Options Help

Contents | Index | Back | Print | << | >> | Glosary

Runform Messages

Type: Error

FRM-40361: Query operation not supported for TIME data type.

Cause: You made a query with a % "like" operator in a time field, which is not supported.

Action: Try to restate your query without a time data type.

Level: >25

Type: Error

FRM-40400: Transaction complete: <number of records> records applied and saved.

Cause: You finished a save.

Action: No action is necessary.

Level: 5

Type: Informative

FRM-40401: No changes to save.

Cause: You tried to perform a save, but no records were added or modified since the last apply or save.

Action: No action is necessary.

Level: 5

Type: Error

FRM-40402: Save cancelled.

Cause: You pressed CTRL-C (or the equivalent) while waiting for a lock.

Action: No action is necessary.

Figure 5-62: FRM error explanations and severity levels

Creating a Form with Complex LOVs

In the CUSTITEM_FORM, a single LOV was used to list the existing records in the ITEM table. In the next set of steps, you will create a custom form for the INVENTORY table that has a LOV to allow the user to select existing inventory entries based on data from the INVENTORY and ITEM tables. INVENTORY has two foreign key fields (ITEMID and COLOR), so the form also will have LOVS to provide existing ITEMID and COLOR values for creating new inventory records. Also, you will learn how to use objects (such as buttons and triggers) that you created before in the CUSTITEM_FORM in your new form.

To create the window, canvas, text items, and labels for the new form:

1. Go to the Object Navigator window in Visual View. Create a new form module by clicking **Forms**, and then clicking the **Create** button on the Object Navigator toolbar.
2. Name the new form module **CUSTINV_FORM.**
3. Click **Windows** and then rename the window **CUSTINV_WINDOW.**
4. Create a new canvas, and then name it **CUSTINV_CANVAS.**
5. Create a new control block named **INVENTORY_BLOCK.**
6. Go to the Layout Editor, and then draw text items to correspond to the data fields in the INVENTORY table and for the ITEMDESC field in the ITEM table. Position the fields as shown in Figure 5-63, and use the following names, data types, and sizes:

Database Field	Form Field Name	Data Type	Maximum Length
INVID	INVID_TEXT	Number	10
ITEMID	ITEMID_TEXT	Number	8
ITEMSIZE	ITEMSIZE_TEXT	Char	10
COLOR	COLOR_TEXT	Char	20
CURR_PRICE	CURR_PRICE_TEXT	Number	8
QOH	QOH_TEXT	Number	4
ITEMDESC	ITEMDESC_TEXT	Char	100

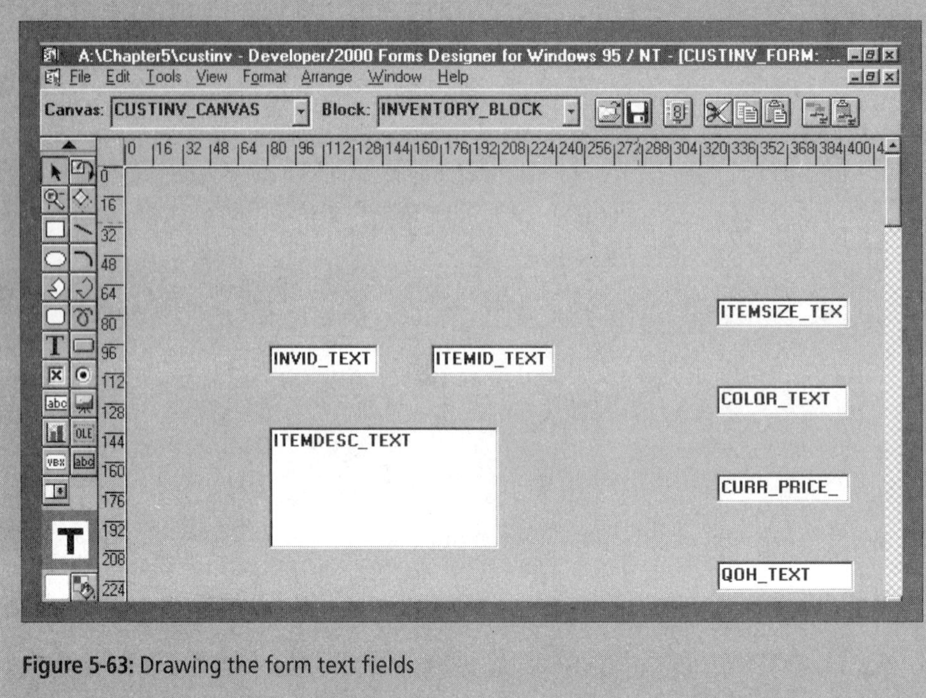

Figure 5-63: Drawing the form text fields

7 Save the form as custinv.fmb in the Chapter5 folder on your Student Disk.

8 If necessary, rename the form CUSTINV_FORM in the Object Navigator.

In this form, you will display the ITEMDESC rather than the ITEMID because item descriptions provide more meaningful information to the user than ID numbers. You still need to keep track of the current record's ITEMID, however, because that value is needed if you want to insert or modify a record. To store but not display the ITEMID value, you will set the Displayed property for ITEMID_TEXT to False. You will do this next.

To set the Displayed property of ITEMID_TEXT to False:

1 Open the ITEMID_TEXT Properties sheet.

2 Double-click the **Displayed** property so it changes to **False**.

3 Close the ITEMID_TEXT Properties sheet, and then maximize the Layout Editor window.

Next you need to create labels for each of the text items on the form.

To create the text item labels:

1 Create labels for each of the text items using a 9-point bold Arial font, as shown in Figure 5-64.

create these labels

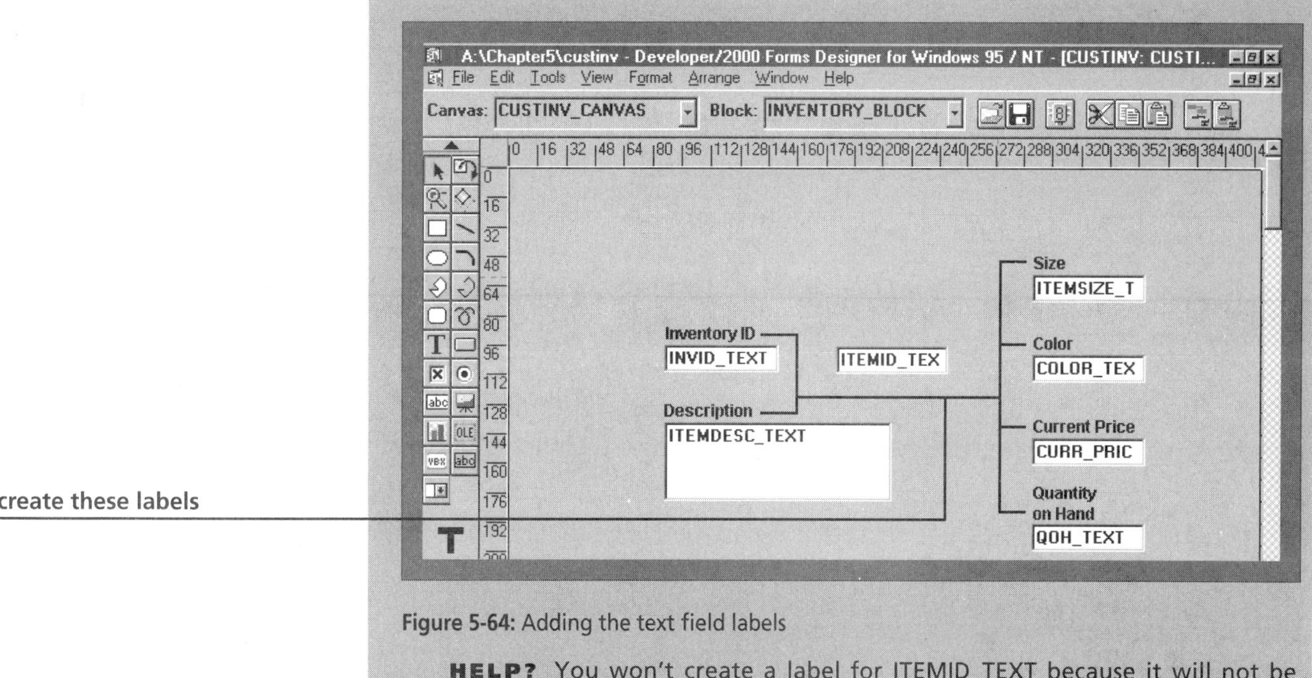

Figure 5-64: Adding the text field labels

HELP? You won't create a label for ITEMID_TEXT because it will not be displayed when you run the form.

Copying the Buttons and PRE-FORM Trigger from CUSTITEM_FORM

Next you need to create the form's Save, Create, Delete, and Exit buttons. You could draw the buttons, format them, and then enter the trigger code like you did when you made the CUSTITEM_FORM. However, the buttons in this form are almost identical to the buttons you created before, so it will save a lot of time if you copy the buttons from CUSTITEM_FORM, paste them into CUSTINV_FORM, and then modify their triggers as necessary. First you will copy the buttons from the CUSTITEM_FORM.

To copy and paste the buttons:

1. Go to the Object Navigator window in Ownership View.
2. Click **CUSTINV_FORM** and then click the **Collapse All** button on the Object Navigator toolbar to close all of the open items in CUSTINV_FORM.
3. Click **File** on the menu bar, click **Open**, and then double-click **custitem.fmb**. CUSTITEM_FORM appears in the Object Navigator window along with CUSTINV_FORM.
4. If necessary, click the **CUSTITEM_FORM plus box** ⊞, and then open the following objects: **Blocks**, **ITEM_CONTROL_BLOCK**, and **Items**.
5. Select the SAVE_BUTTON, CREATE_BUTTON, DELETE_BUTTON, and EXIT_BUTTON as an object group by clicking the **SAVE_BUTTON**, pressing and holding down the **Shift** key, and then clicking the other three objects. Your screen should look like Figure 5-65, with CUSTITEM_FORM as your current form, and the ITEM_CONTROL_BLOCK items selected.

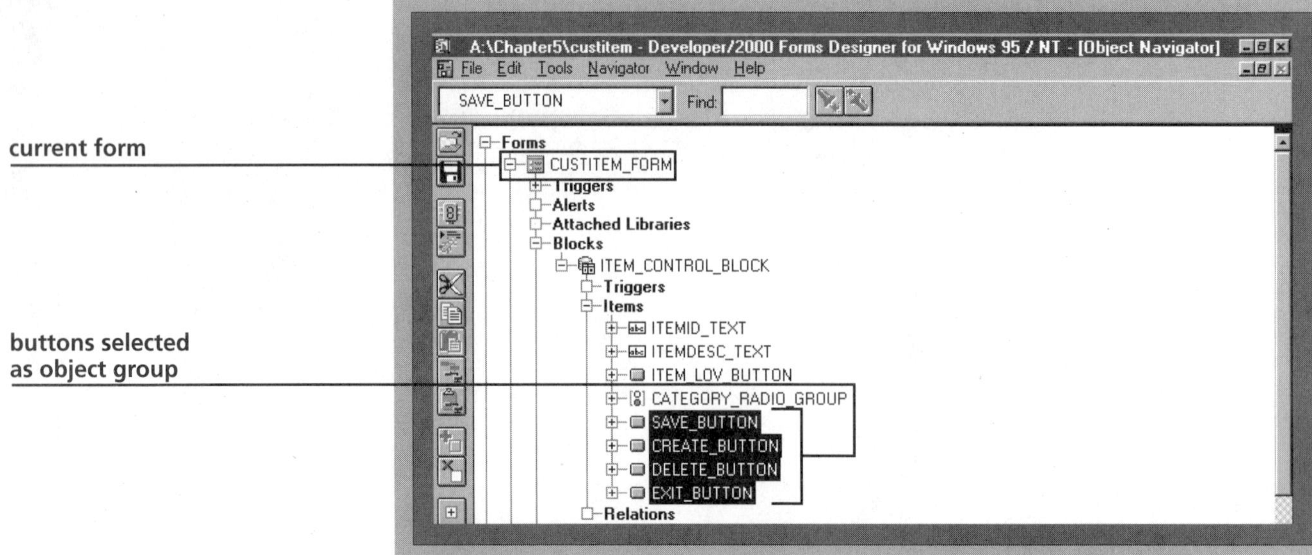

Figure 5-65: Selecting the SAVE, CREATE, DELETE, AND EXIT buttons in CUSTITEM_FORM

6 Click the **Copy** button on the Object Navigator toolbar to copy the buttons.

7 Click **CUSTITEM_FORM** and then click to close all of the open items in CUSTITEM_FORM.

Next you will paste the copied buttons into CUSTINV_FORM.

To paste the buttons into CUSTINV_FORM:

1 Click the **CUSTINV_FORM plus box**, and then open the following objects: **Blocks**, **INVENTORY_BLOCK**, and **Items**.

2 Click the **Paste** button on the Object Navigator toolbar. The four buttons appear under Items in the CUSTINV_FORM, as shown in Figure 5-66.

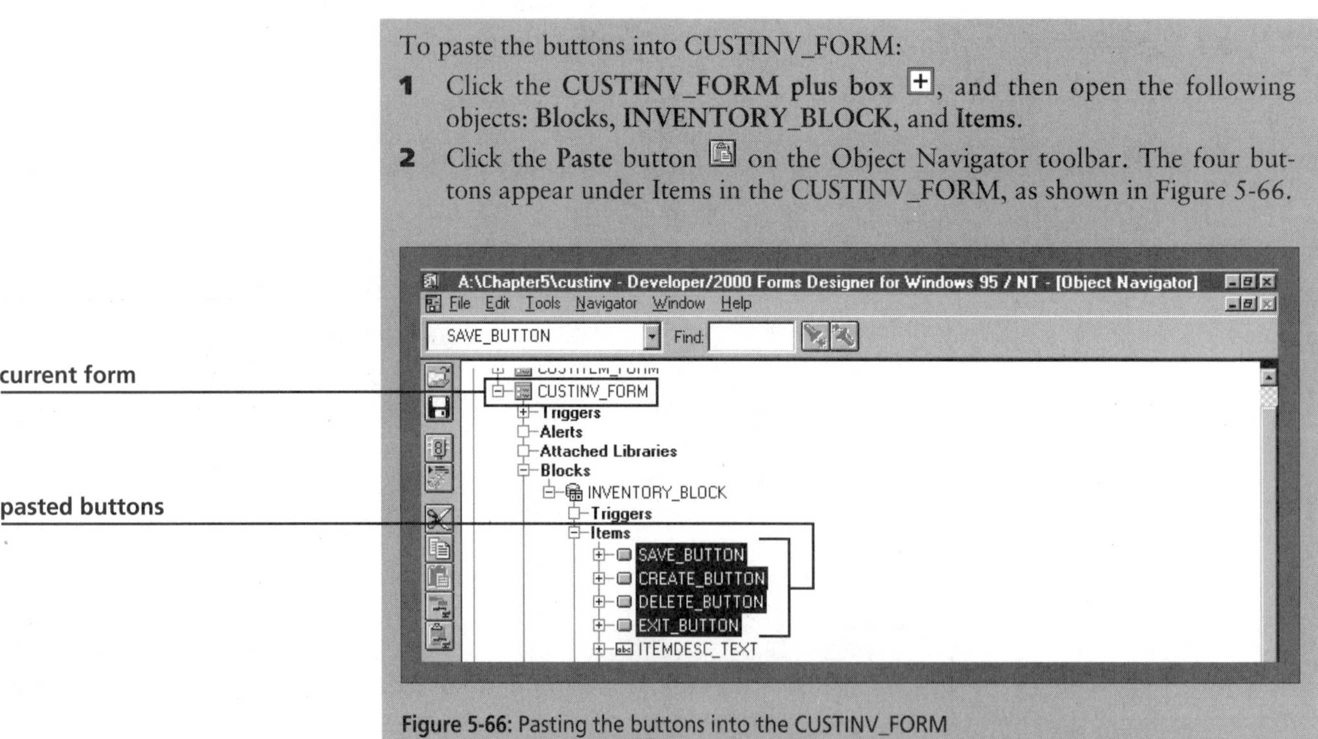

Figure 5-66: Pasting the buttons into the CUSTINV_FORM

When you copy items from one form into another in the Object Navigator window, you must change the Canvas property of the pasted items. Currently, the Canvas property of the buttons is CUSTITEM_CANVAS, which is the name of the canvas in the CUSTITEM_FORM. It needs to be changed to CUSTINV_CANVAS so the buttons will display on the canvas in the CUSTINV_FORM. You will do this next.

Make sure that you select the SAVE_BUTTON in CUSTINV_FORM and not in CUSTITEM_FORM. Otherwise, you wil modify the wrong button.

When two or more forms are open, you must select the form you want to view in the Object Navigator before you open the Layout Editor.

To change the Canvas property of the pasted buttons:

1. Right-click the **SAVE_BUTTON** in the CUSTINV_FORM, and then open its Properties sheet.
2. Double-click the SAVE_BUTTON's **Canvas** property. The property value becomes blank.
3. Double-click the **Canvas** property again. CUSTINV_CANVAS appears.
4. Close the SAVE_BUTTON Properties sheet, and then maximize the Object Navigator window if necessary.
5. Repeat the steps to change the Canvas property for the CREATE_BUTTON, DELETE_BUTTON, and EXIT_BUTTON to **CUSTINV_CANVAS.**
6. Click **CUSTINV_FORM** in the Object Navigator window.
7. Click **Tools** on the menu bar, and then click **Layout Editor.** The pasted buttons appear on the CUSTINV_CANVAS.
8. If necessary, reposition the buttons on the canvas to match Figure 5-67.

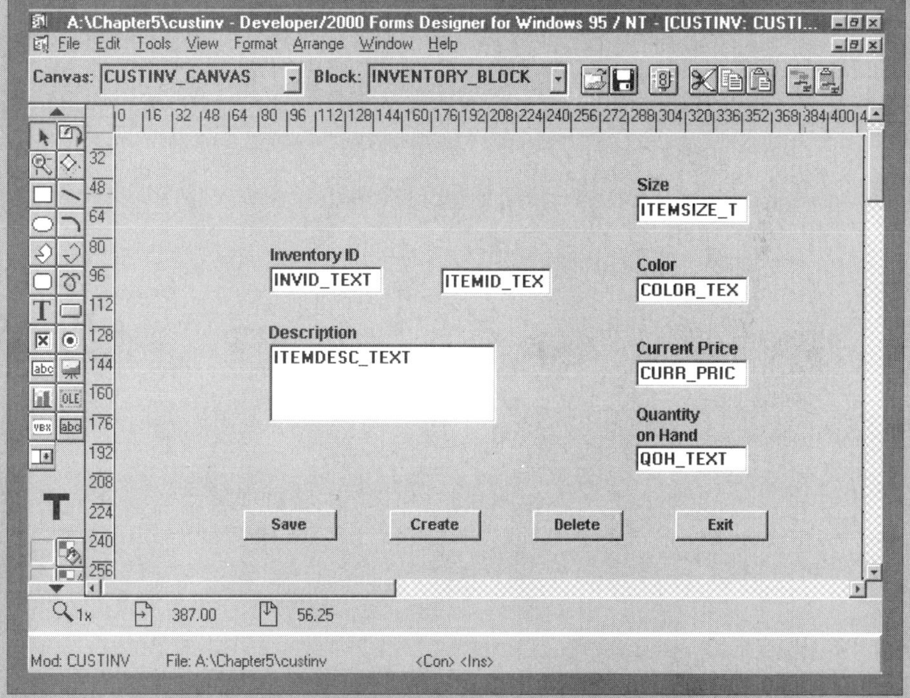

Figure 5-67: Pasted buttons on CUSTINV_CANVAS

9. Save the form.

Next you need to modify the triggers of the pasted buttons. Currently, the triggers contain the same code that you used in the CUSTITEM_FORM to insert, update, and delete records from the ITEM table. You will need to modify the triggers to do the same operations, but for the INVENTORY table instead of the ITEM table. First you will modify the CREATE_BUTTON trigger. Currently, the trigger inserts the NEXTVAL of the ITEMID_SEQUENCE into ITEMID_TEXT. You will need to create a new sequence to generate sequence numbers for INVID. You will do this next.

To create the new sequence:

1. Start SQL*Plus and log on to the database.
2. Type the commands shown in Figure 5-68 to create a new sequence named **INVID_SEQUENCE** that starts at 11849, has no maximum value, and instructs the DBMS to not cache values and to grant SELECT privileges to PUBLIC for INVID_SEQUENCE.

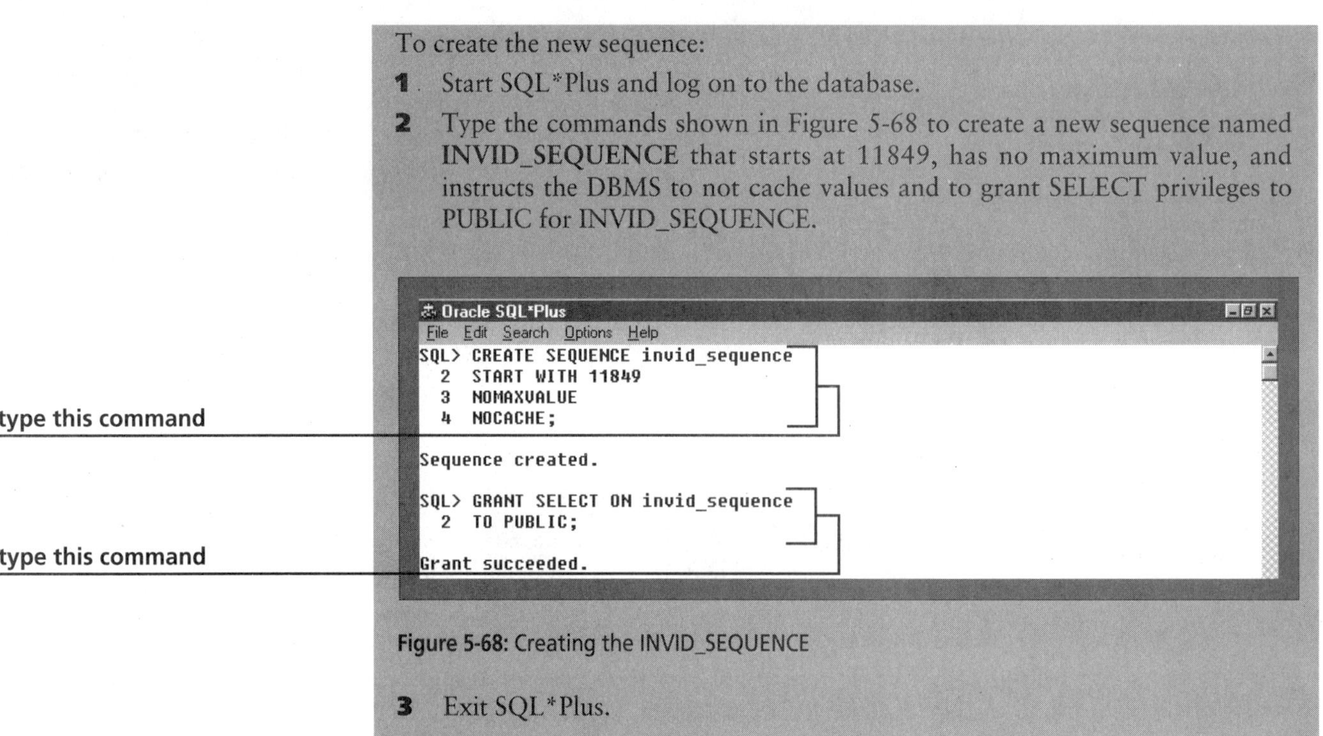

Figure 5-68: Creating the INVID_SEQUENCE

3. Exit SQL*Plus.

Next you will modify the CREATE_BUTTON trigger code so it retrieves the NEXTVAL of the INVID_SEQUENCE and then inserts the retrieved value into the INVID_TEXT field on the form. You need to change the sequence name, block name, and text field name to match the ones for CUSTINV_FORM.

To modify the CREATE_BUTTON trigger:

1. Right-click the **CREATE_BUTTON**, and then click **PL/SQL Editor**.
2. Modify the code as shown in Figure 5-69.

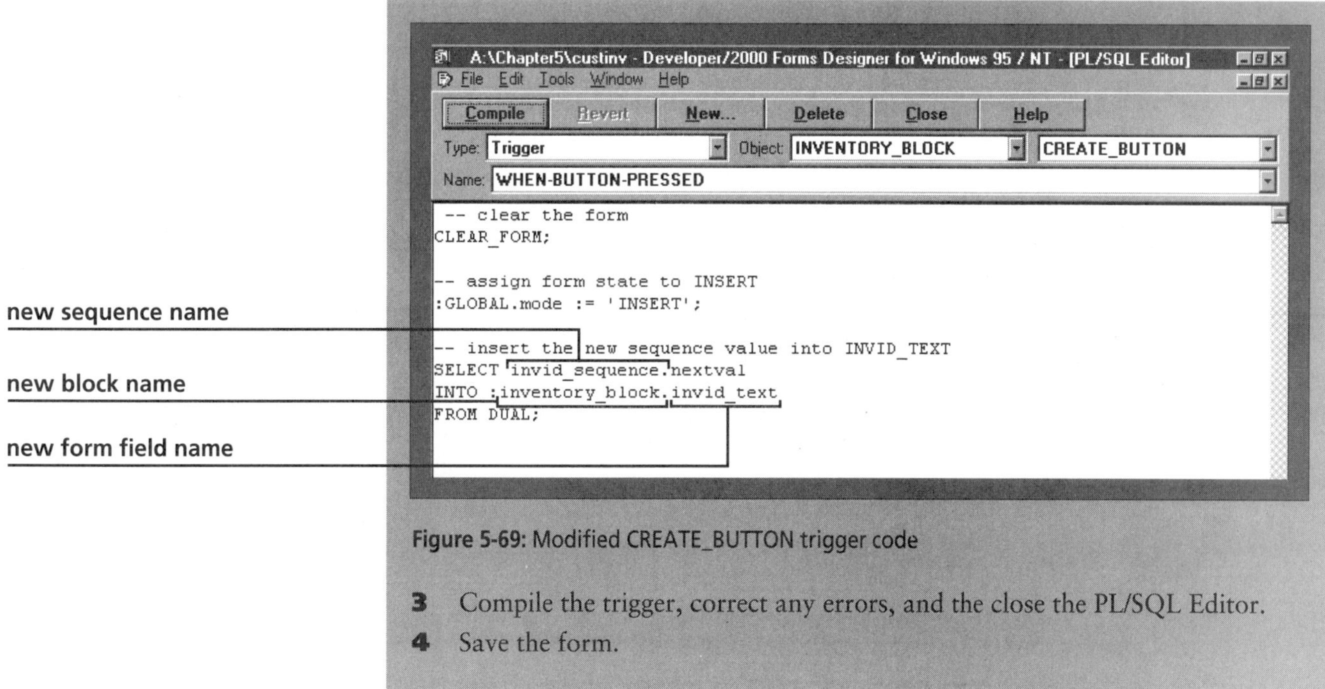

Figure 5-69: Modified CREATE_BUTTON trigger code

3 Compile the trigger, correct any errors, and the close the PL/SQL Editor.

4 Save the form.

Next you will modify the DELETE_BUTTON trigger by modifying the SQL DELETE command so it deletes the record currently displayed on the form. You will need to change the table name from ITEM to INVENTORY and change the search condition in the DELETE so that the INVID of the record that is deleted matches the current value in the INVID_TEXT field. You will do this next.

To modify the DELETE_BUTTON trigger:

1 Open the DELETE_BUTTON trigger in the PL/SQL Editor.

2 Modify the code as shown in Figure 5-70.

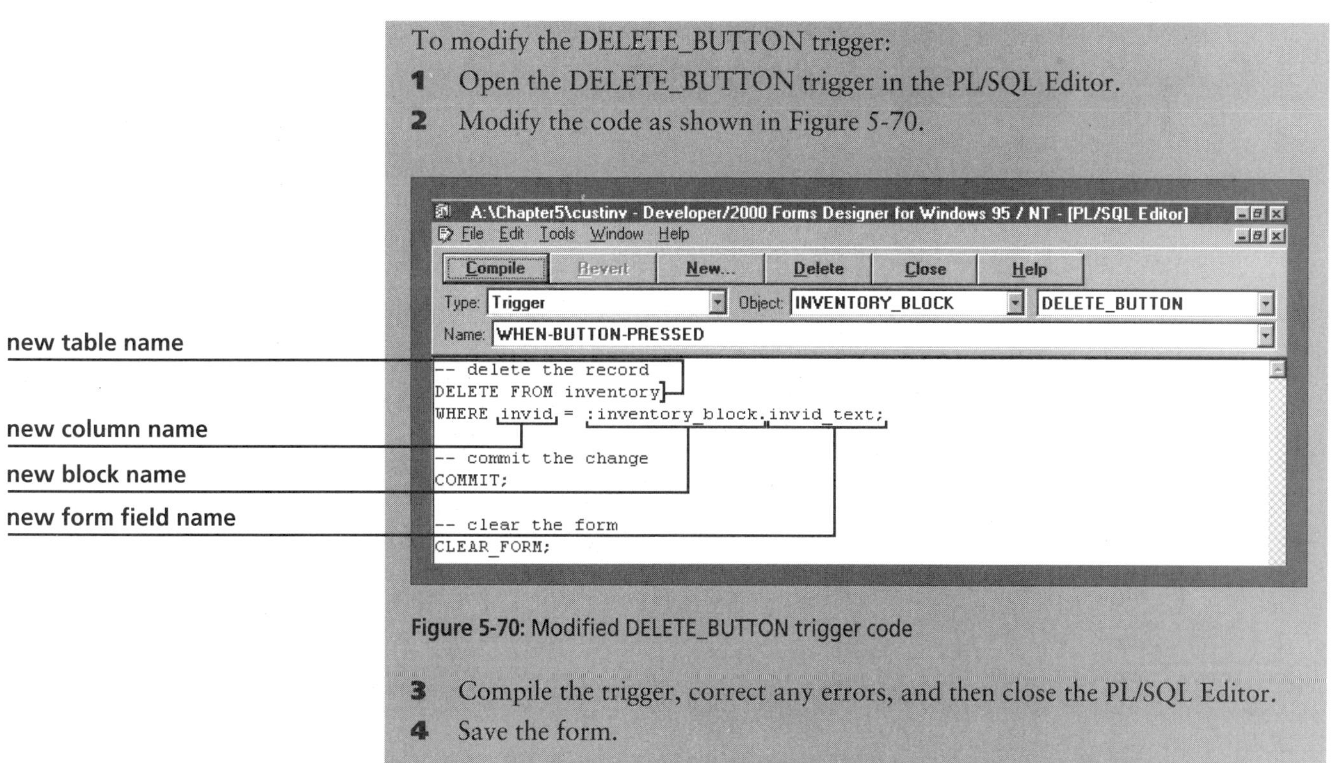

Figure 5-70: Modified DELETE_BUTTON trigger code

3 Compile the trigger, correct any errors, and then close the PL/SQL Editor.

4 Save the form.

Next you will modify the SAVE_BUTTON trigger. The INSERT and UPDATE statements will reference the INVENTORY table instead of the ITEM table, and the block and field names will need to be the ones on the CUSTINV_FORM instead of the ones on the CUSTITEM_FORM. You will need to change every reference to ITEM_BLOCK to INVENTORY_BLOCK and change every reference to the ITEM table to INVENTORY. You also will need to change all of the field name references from the field names in the CUSTITEM_FORM to the field names in the CUSTINV_FORM.

To modify the SAVE_BUTTON trigger:

1 Modify the WHEN-BUTTON-PRESSED trigger for the Save button in the PL/SQL Editor, as shown in Figure 5-71.

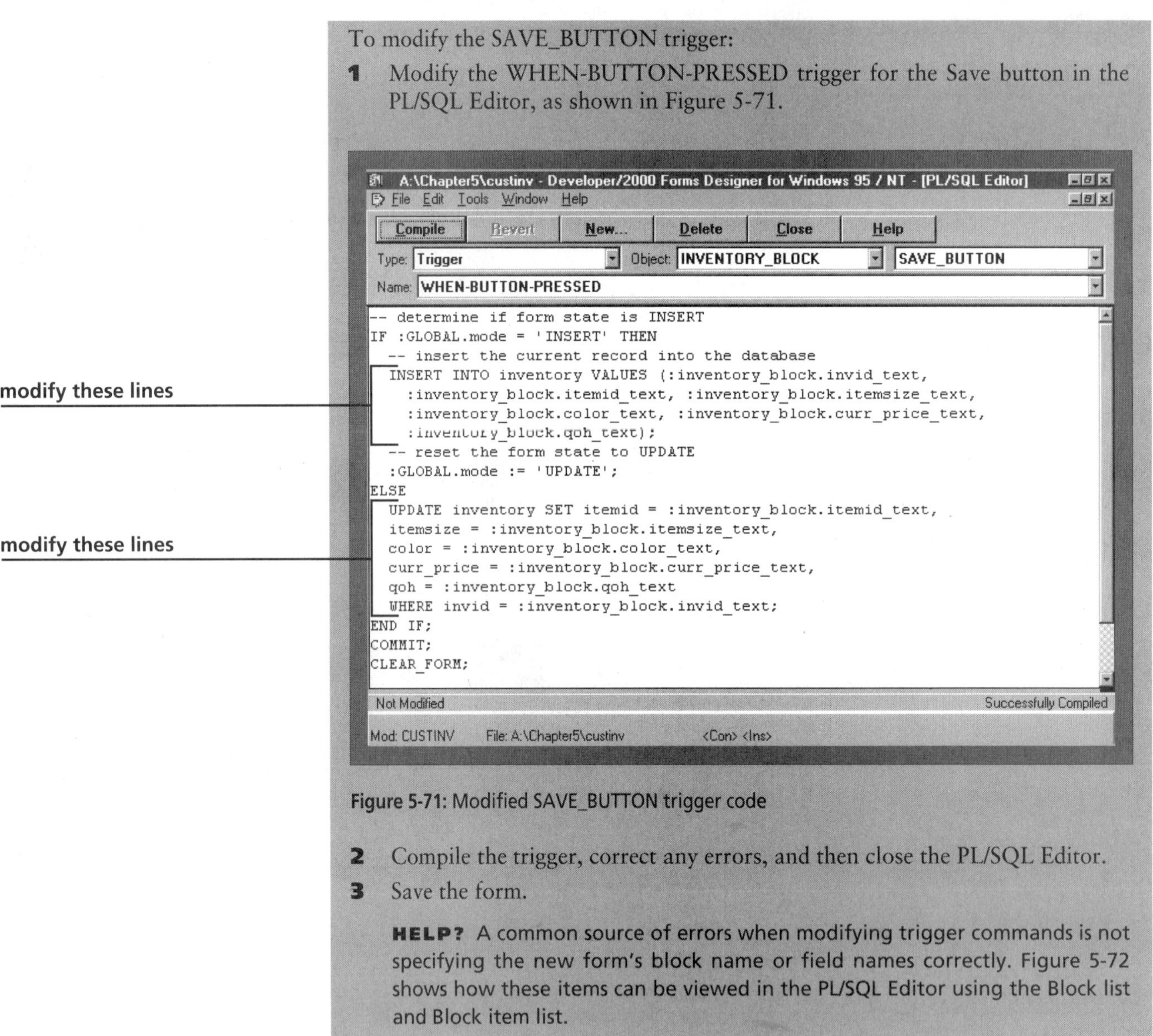

Figure 5-71: Modified SAVE_BUTTON trigger code

2 Compile the trigger, correct any errors, and then close the PL/SQL Editor.

3 Save the form.

HELP? A common source of errors when modifying trigger commands is not specifying the new form's block name or field names correctly. Figure 5-72 shows how these items can be viewed in the PL/SQL Editor using the Block list and Block item list.

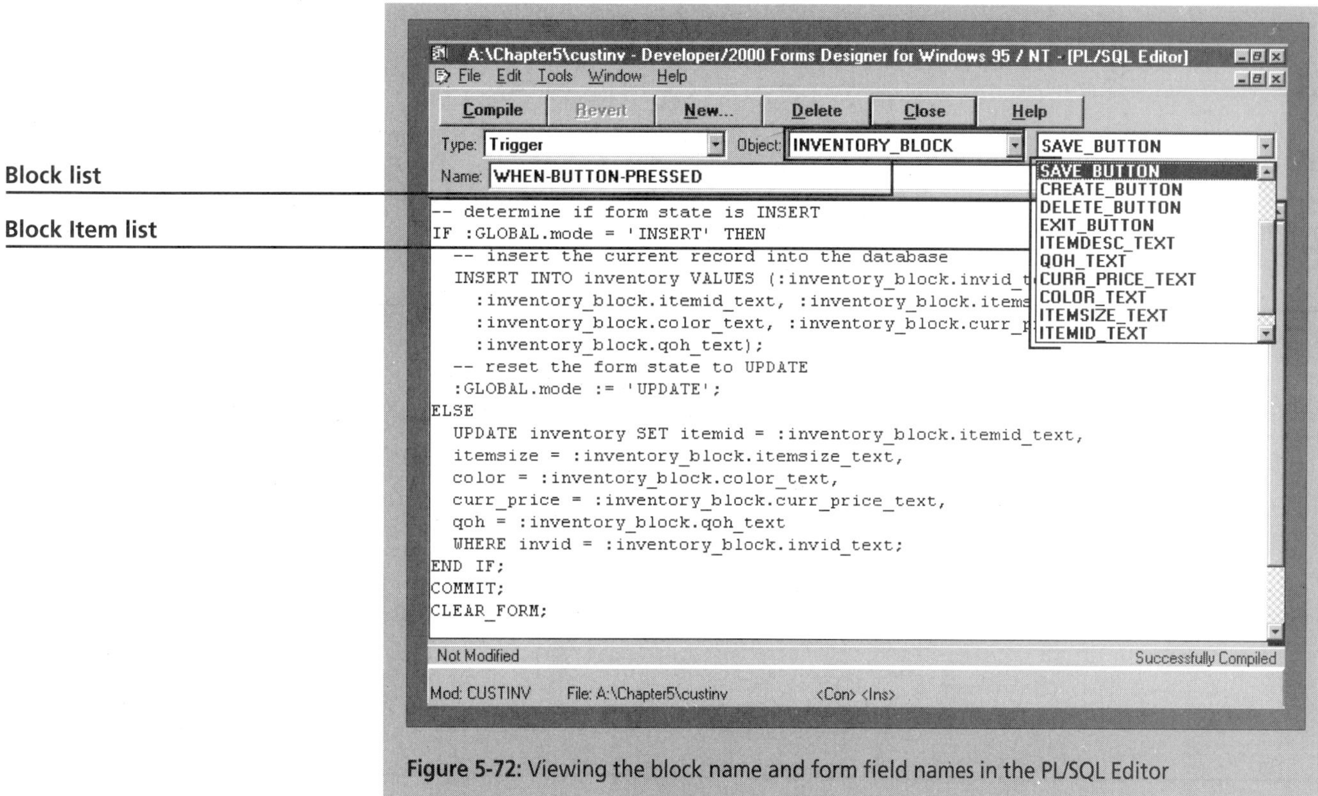

Figure 5-72: Viewing the block name and form field names in the PL/SQL Editor

Finally, you need to copy the PRE-FORM trigger from the CUSTITEM_FORM to the CUSTINV_FORM. The PRE-FORM trigger performs the same exact function in both forms (initializing the :GLOBAL.mode variable to UPDATE), so it will not require any modification.

To copy the PRE-FORM trigger:

1. Go to the Object Navigator window in Ownership View.
2. Click **Forms** and then click the **Collapse All** button on the Object Navigator toolbar.
3. Click the **Forms plus box** ⊞, and then open the **CUSTITEM_FORM** and **Triggers** objects.
4. Click the **PRE-FORM** trigger. Your screen should look like Figure 5-73.

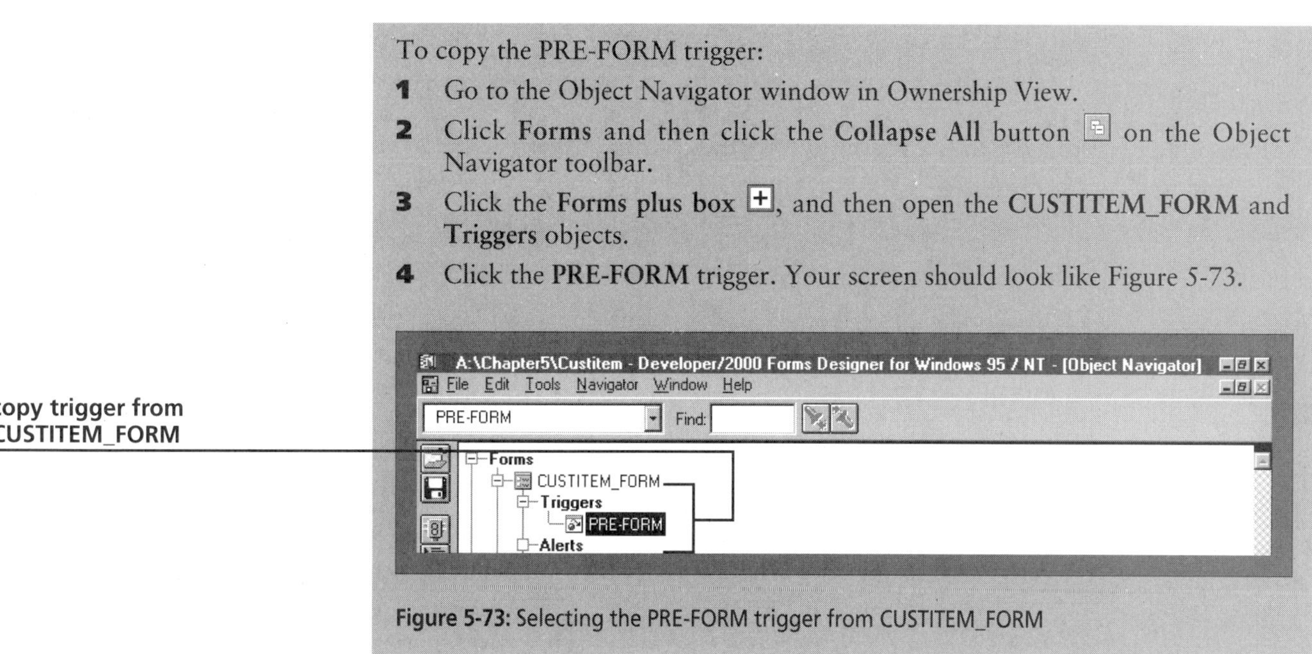

Figure 5-73: Selecting the PRE-FORM trigger from CUSTITEM_FORM

5 Click the **Copy** button on the Object Navigator toolbar to copy the PRE-FORM trigger.

6 Click the **CUSTITEM_FORM minus box** to close the form objects.

7 Click the **CUSTINV_FORM plus box** to open the form objects.

8 Click **Triggers** and then click the **Paste** button on the Object Navigator toolbar to paste the trigger into CUSTINV_FORM. Your screen should look like Figure 5-74.

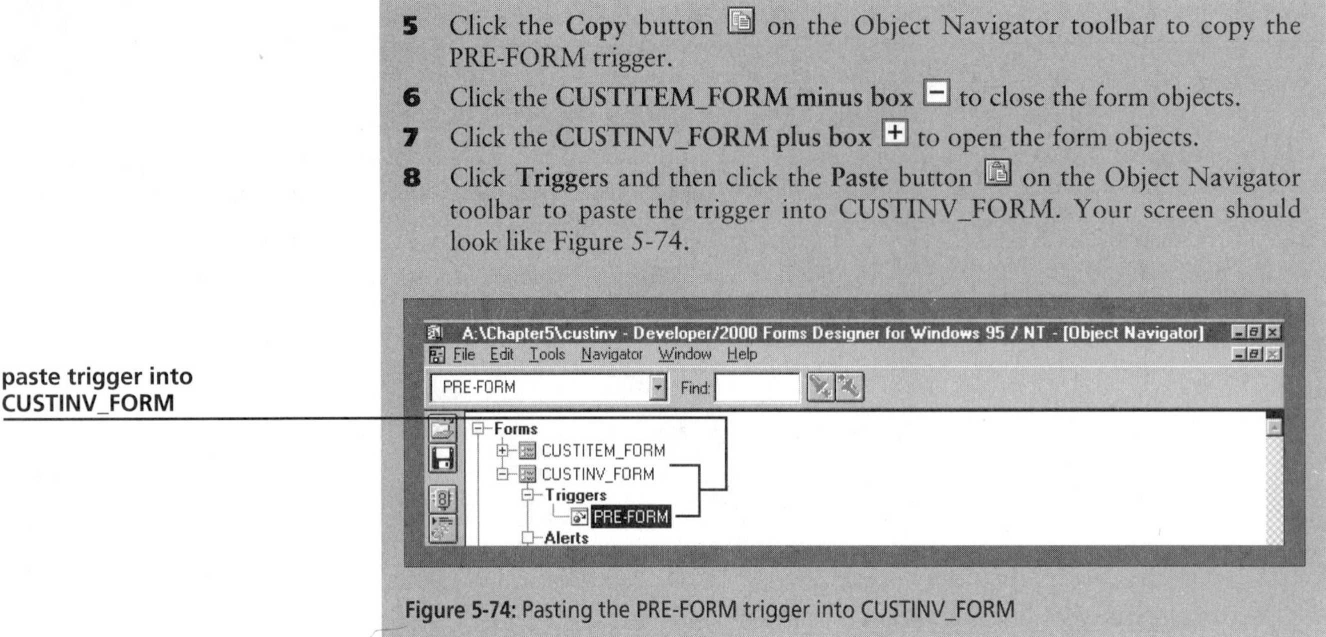

Figure 5-74: Pasting the PRE-FORM trigger into CUSTINV_FORM

Remember that foreign key values must already exist in the tables where they are primary keys. ITEMID values that are used in INVENTORY records already must exist in the ITEM table, and the COLOR values already must exist in the COLOR table.

Creating the LOVs and LOV Buttons

The INVENTORY table has two foreign key fields—ITEMID and COLOR. If you want to create a new INVENTORY record or modify an existing one, the form will have LOVs to provide lists of existing item IDs in the ITEM table and colors in the COLOR table. If you want to update an existing INVENTORY record, the form also will have a LOV to allow you to select a specific record based on the inventory ID, item description, color, and size.

The form's LOV buttons will be placed beside the INVID_TEXT, ITEMDESC_TEXT and COLOR_TEXT fields, as shown in Figure 5-75. When you click the INVID_TEXT LOV button, a list of the existing inventory item descriptions, sizes, colors, current prices, quantities on hand, and inventory IDs appears. When you click the ITEMDESC_TEXT LOV button, a list of the existing item descriptions in the ITEM table appears. When you click the COLOR_TEXT LOV button, a list of existing colors in the COLOR table appears.

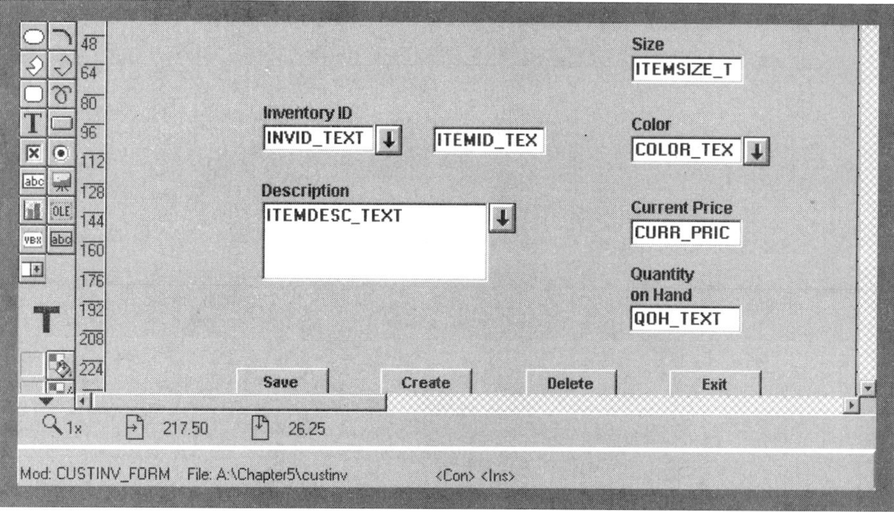

Figure 5-75: Position of the LOV buttons

First you will create the LOV associated with the button beside the Description field to display the item ID and description. This LOV will return its values to the ITEMID_TEXT and ITEMDESC_TEXT form fields. The first step is to create the LOV in the Object Navigator window.

To create the new LOV for the ITEM table fields:

1. Go to the Object Navigator window in Ownership View.
2. Click **Forms** and then click the **Collapse All** button on the Object Navigator toolbar to close all of the form objects.
3. Click the **Forms plus box** to display the two form modules. Open **CUSTINV_FORM** and then click **LOVs**.
4. Click the **Create** button on the Object Navigator toolbar to create a new LOV using the following SQL command:

```
SELECT itemid, itemdesc
INTO :inventory_block.itemid_text,
:inventory_block.itemdesc_text
FROM item
ORDER BY itemdesc;
```

5. Rename the new LOV and record group **ITEM_LOV**.

The next step is to format the LOV display on the ITEM_LOV Properties sheet. You will change the LOV display title, the column width of the ITEMID field so ITEMID is not displayed, and the ITEMDESC column title.

To change the ITEM_LOV properties:

1 Open the Properties sheet for the LOV named ITEM_LOV.

2 Change the Title to Items.

3 Click **Column Mapping** then click the **More** button at the top of the Properties sheet.

4 Click **ITEMID** in the Column Names list box, and change the Display Width to 0 so the ITEMID is not displayed in the LOV.

5 Click **ITEMDESC** in the Column Names list box, and then change the Column Title to **Description**.

6 Click the **OK** button to close the Column Mapping dialog box.

7 Close the ITEM_LOV Properties sheet, and then maximize the Layout Editor.

Next you need to associate the ITEM_LOV with the ITEMDESC_TEXT field on the form so when the insertion point is in the ITEMDESC_TEXT form field and the user clicks the LOV button, the ITEM_LOV display appears. You will do this by changing the LOV property in ITEMDESC_TEXT Properties sheet to ITEM_LOV.

To associate the ITEM_LOV with ITEMDESC_TEXT:

1 Open the ITEMDESC_TEXT Properties sheet.

2 Double-click the **LOV** property so **ITEM_LOV** appears.

3 Close the ITEM_DESC_TEXT Properties sheet, and then maximize the Layout Editor.

The final step is to create the LOV button. Instead of creating a new button, you will copy the ITEM_LOV_BUTTON from the CUSTITEM_FORM, paste it into the CUSTINV_FORM, and then modify its properties and trigger. First you will copy the button from the CUSTITEM_FORM.

To copy the LOV button from the CUSTITEM_FORM:

1 Go to the Object Navigator window in Ownership View.

2 Click **Forms** and then click the **Collapse All** button on the Object Navigator toolbar to close all of the form objects.

3 Open the following objects: **Forms**, **CUSTITEM_FORM**, **Blocks**, **ITEM_CONTROL_BLOCK**, and **Items**.

4 Select the **ITEM_LOV_BUTTON**, and click the **Copy** button on the Object Navigator toolbar.

5 Click **Forms**, and then click .

6 Open the following objects: **Forms**, **CUSTINV_FORM**, **Blocks**, **INVENTORY_BLOCK**, and **Items**.

7 Click the **Paste** button on the Object Navigator toolbar. The ITEM_LOV_BUTTON appears in the INVENTORY_BLOCK items.

You are finished copying items from CUSTITEM_FORM, so you can close it.

To close the CUSTITEM_FORM:

1 Select the **CUSTITEM_FORM** in the Object Navigator window.

2 Click **File** on the menu bar, and then click **Close**. The CUSTITEM_FORM disappears from the Object Navigator window.

Next you will modify the ITEM_LOV_BUTTON Canvas property so the button displays on the CUSTINV_CANVAS.

To modify the ITEM_LOV_BUTTON:

1 In the Object Navigator window, select the **ITEM_LOV_BUTTON** in the CUSTINV_FORM, and open its Properties sheet.

2 Modify the ITEM_LOV_BUTTON's Canvas property by double-clicking the current value twice so **CUSTINV_CANVAS** appears.

3 Close the ITEM_LOV_BUTTON Properties sheet, and maximize the Layout Editor if necessary.

4 Reposition the ITEM_LOV_BUTTON if necessary so it is aligned with the top right edge of ITEMDESC_TEXT. See Figure 5-76.

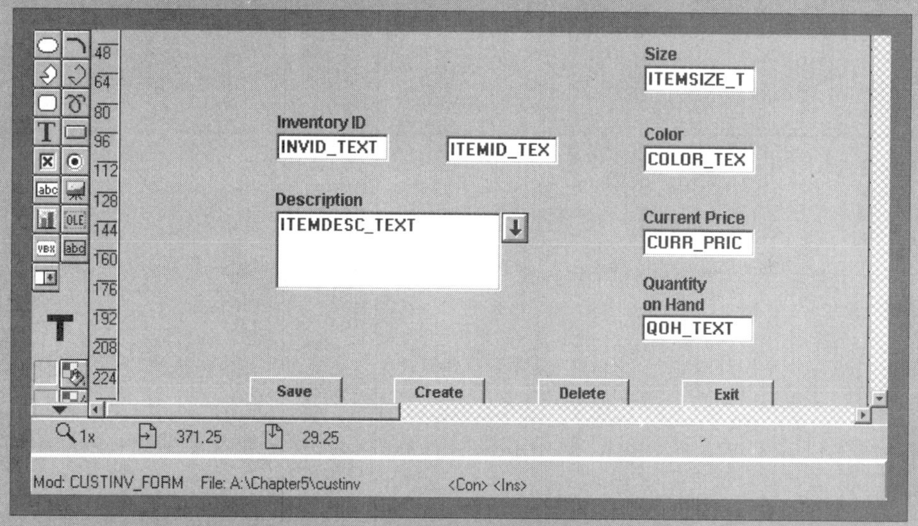

Figure 5-76: Positioning the ITEM_LOV_BUTTON

Finally, you will modify the ITEM_LOV_BUTTON's trigger so it places the insertion point in the ITEMDESC_TEXT form field and then displays the LOV.

To modify the ITEM_LOV_BUTTON trigger:

1 Select the **ITEM_LOV_BUTTON**, right-click, and then click **PL/SQL Editor**.

2 Modify the trigger code as shown in Figure 5-77.

change the insertion point location to the form field associated with the LOV

```
A:\Chapter5\custinv - Developer/2000 Forms Designer for Windows 95 / NT - [PL/SQL Editor]
File Edit Tools Window Help
Compile  Revert  New...  Delete  Close  Help
Type: Trigger   Object: INVENTORY_BLOCK   ITEM_LOV_BUTTON
Name: WHEN-BUTTON-PRESSED
-- put the cursor in the text item associated with the LOV
GO_ITEM ('itemdesc_text');
-- show the LOV
DO_KEY ('LIST_VALUES');
```

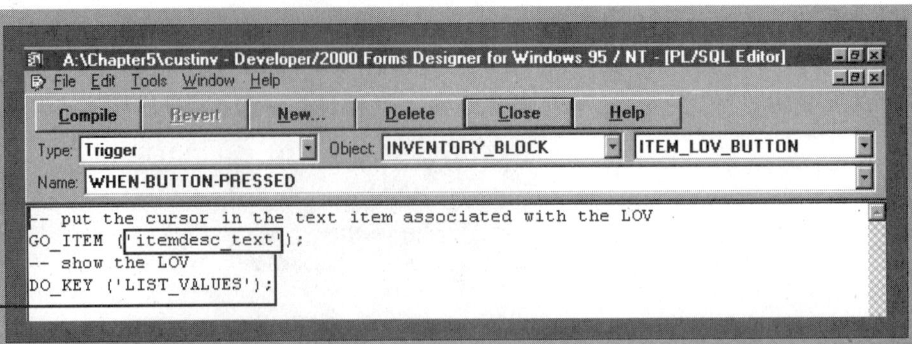

Figure 5-77: Modifying the ITEM_LOV_BUTTON trigger code

3 Compile the trigger, correct any errors, and then close the PL/SQL Editor.

4 Save the form.

Next you will create the LOV that will appear beside COLOR_TEXT and display the COLOR table records.

To create the COLOR_LOV:

1 Create a new LOV that displays the colors in the COLOR table using the following SQL command:

SELECT *
INTO :inventory_block.color_text
FROM color;

2 Rename the new LOV and associated record group **COLOR_LOV.**

3 Open the COLOR_TEXT Properties sheet, and then change the LOV property to **COLOR_LOV.**

4 In the Layout Editor, click the **ITEM_LOV_BUTTON**, copy it, and then paste it on the canvas.

5 Position the button that you copied in Step 3 so it is aligned with the top right edge of COLOR_TEXT.

6 Change the new button's name to **COLOR_LOV_BUTTON.**

7 Modify the WHEN-BUTTON-PRESSED trigger for COLOR_LOV_BUTTON so it places the insertion point in the COLOR_TEXT field before issuing the LIST_VALUES command using the following code:

--put the cursor in the text item
associated with the LOV
GO_ITEM ('color_text');
-- show the LOV
DO_KEY ('LIST_VALUES');

8 Compile the code, correct any errors, and then close the PL
9 Save the form.

Next you will make the LOV that will retrieve the existing inventory records. It should display what is needed to identify a specific inventory item: item description, size, and color. This will require performing a join on the ITEM and INVENTORY tables in the LOV. Users can search on the first field in a LOV display. You will assume that Clearwater Traders users are likely to search on the ITEMDESC field, so you will put it first.

To create the LOV to display inventory information:

1 Create a new LOV using the command shown in Figure 5-78.

type this command

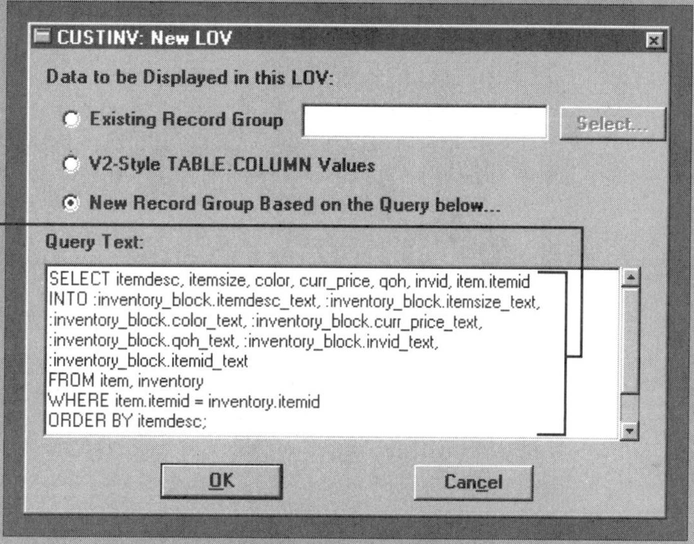

CUSTINV: New LOV

Data to be Displayed in this LOV:

- Existing Record Group [Select...]
- V2-Style TABLE.COLUMN Values
- New Record Group Based on the Query below...

Query Text:

```
SELECT itemdesc, itemsize, color, curr_price, qoh, invid, item.itemid
INTO :inventory_block.itemdesc_text, :inventory_block.itemsize_text,
:inventory_block.color_text, :inventory_block.curr_price_text,
:inventory_block.qoh_text, :inventory_block.invid_text,
:inventory_block.itemid_text
FROM item, inventory
WHERE item.itemid = inventory.itemid
ORDER BY itemdesc;
```

OK Cancel

Figure 5-78: Command to create the LOV to display inventory information

tip

The ITEMID field is prefaced by a table name because ITEMID exists in both the ITEM and INVENTORY tables. You could use either table name.

2 Rename the LOV and associated record group to **INV_LOV**.

3 Open the Properties sheet for the LOV named INV_LOV, and then change the Title to **Inventory Items**, the Width to **400**, and the Height to **200**.

4 Change the Column Mapping for INV_LOV as follows:

Column Name	Title	Display Width
ITEMDESC	Description	150
ITEMSIZE	Size	25
COLOR	Color	60
CURR_PRICE	Price	25
QOH	QOH	25
INVID	ID	25
ITEMID	Column is not displayed, so no title is needed	0

HELP? The LOV Display Width, Height, and Column Width properties are determined by initially accepting the default values, running the form and viewing the LOV display, and then adjusting the properties as necessary. This is generally an iterative process and requires a lot of trial and error to make the display look attractive.

5 Copy and paste the COLOR_LOV button, and then position the copy on the right edge of INVID_TEXT.

6 Change the new button's name to **INV_LOV_BUTTON**.

7 Change the LOV property of INVID_TEXT to **INV_LOV**.

8 Modify the WHEN-BUTTON-PRESSED trigger for INV_LOV_BUTTON so it places the insertion point in INVID_TEXT.

9 Save the form.

Testing the Form

Now you have completed the form, and you need to test it to make sure everything is working correctly. You will need to test the following operations: creating a new record and saving it to the database; retrieving a record using the INV_LOV, modifying the record, and then saving it to the database; and, retrieving a record and then deleting it. First you will test the Create/Save combination by inserting a new inventory record.

To test the Create/Save combination:

1 Run the form.

2 Click the **Create** button and verify that a new INVID displays.

3 Click the **LOV** button beside the Description field, click **Women's Fleece Pullover**, and then click the **OK** button.

4 Click the **Size** field and then type **XS**.

5 Click the **LOV** button beside the Color field, and then click **Coral**.

HELP? If you click a LOV button and see the message "FRM 41800: List of Values not available for this field," it means that the form field that currently holds the insertion point does not have a value for LOV in its Properties sheet. Close the Forms Runtime application, open the LOV Properties sheet, change the LOV value, and then run the form again.

6 Enter **59.95** for Current Price and **50** for Quantity on Hand.

7 Click the **Save** button. The "No changes to save" confirmation message indicates the record was committed to the database successfully.

Next you will test the INV_LOV button, and perform a search on the ITEM records.

To test the INV_LOV button:

1. Click the **LOV** button beside the Inventory ID field. The LOV display appears, as shown in Figure 5-79. Next you will perform a search on the Description column.

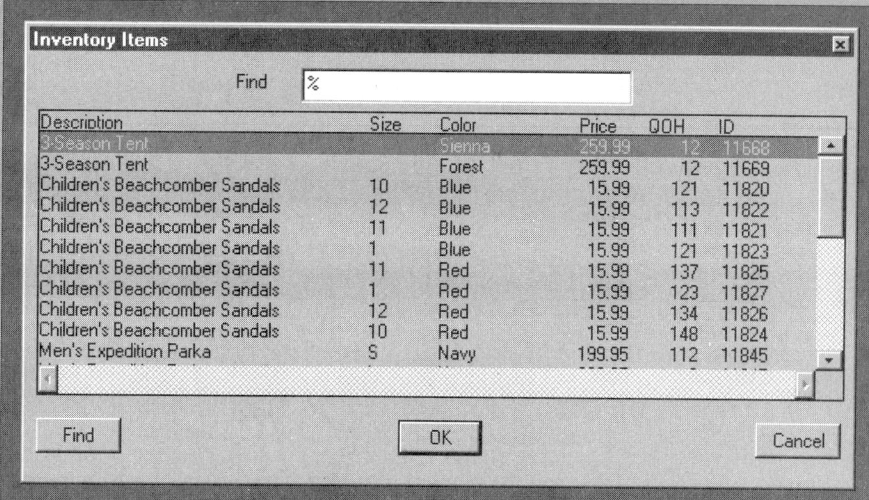

Figure 5-79: INV_LOV display

2. Select **%** in the Find box, type **Women's,** and then press the **Enter** key. See Figure 5-80. All item descriptions beginning with the string "Women's" are listed. You also can perform exact and inexact searches in a LOV, as you learned in Chapter 4.

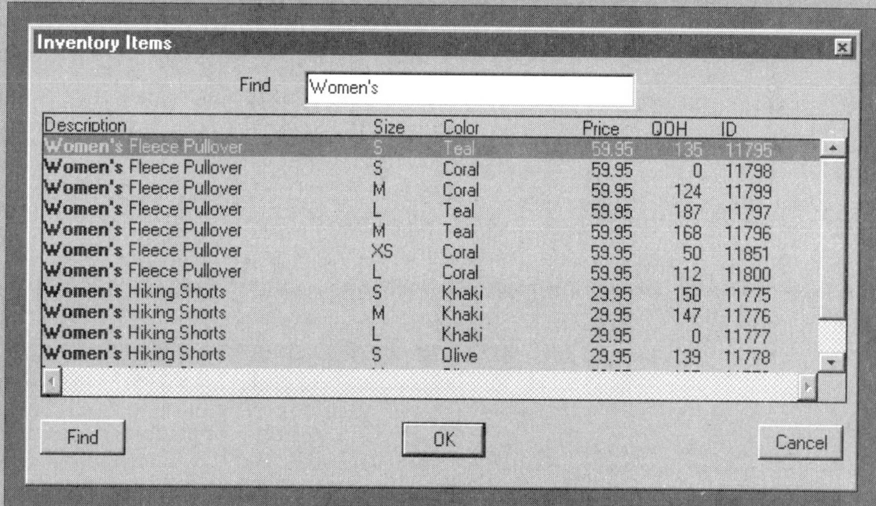

Figure 5-80: Performing a search in a LOV display

Now you will use the INV_LOV to retrieve an inventory record and then update it.

To retrieve and update an inventory record:

1. In the Find text box, replace "Women's" by typing 3, and then press the **Enter** key.
2. Click **3-Season Tent,** color **Sienna,** and then click the **OK** button.
3. Click the **Color LOV** button, and then click **Khaki.**
4. Click the **Save** button. The "No changes to save" confirmation message indicates that the updated record was committed to the database successfully.
5. Retrieve the 3-Season Tent inventory record by clicking the **LOV** button next to the Inventory ID field again to confirm that the color has been updated to Khaki and then click the **Cancel** button.

Finally, you will test the DELETE and EXIT buttons by deleting a record and exiting the form.

To test the DELETE and EXIT buttons:

1. Click the **LOV** button beside the Inventory ID field, click **Women's Fleece Pullover,** size **XS,** and then click the **OK** button.
2. Click the **Delete** button. The "No changes to save" confirmation message indicates that the record was deleted successfully.
3. Click the **LOV** button beside the Inventory ID field again, confirm that the Women's Fleece Pullover size XS has been deleted, and then click the **Cancel** button.
4. Click the **Exit** button to exit the Forms Runtime application.

Using Format Masks

To complete the CUSTINV_FORM, you will need to specify format masks. A **format mask** is a text item property that specifies how data will display in a form. For example, the default date display format in Oracle is DD-MON-YY, which displays a date as 22-JUL-99. To change the date's format to 07/22/99, you would enter MM/DD/YY in the Format Mask property for the date's text item. Format masks only impact how the data displays or prints; the full data value is stored in the database. Figure 5-81 lists how the numeric data value stored as 059783 displays using some common numerical data format masks.

Format Mask	Explanation	Sample Data
99999	Number of 9s determines display width	59783
099999	Displays leading zeros	059783
$99999	Prefaces the value with dollar sign	$59783
99999MI	Displays "-" before negative values	-59783
99999PR	Displays negative values in angle brackets	<59783>
99,999	Displays a comma in the indicated position	59,783
99999.99	Displays a decimal point in the indicated position	59783.00

Figure 5-81: Common numerical format masks

Figure 5-82 shows some common date format masks using the example date of 5:45:35 PM, Friday, January 15, 1999.

Format Mask	Explanation	Sample Data
YYYY	Displays four-digit year	1999
YYY or YY or Y	Displays last 3, 2, or 1 digits of year	999, 99, 9
MM	Month displays as digit (01-12)	01
MONTH	Displays name of month, spelled out (for months with less than 9 characters in their name, trailing blank spaces are added to pad the name to 9 characters)	JANUARY
DD	Displays day of month (01-31)	15
DDD	Displays day of year (01-366)	15
DAY	Displays day of week, spelled out	FRIDAY
DY	Displays name of day as a 3-letter abbreviation	FRI
AM, PM, A.M., P.M.	Meridian indicator (without or with periods)	PM
HH	Displays hour of day using 12-hour clock	05
HH24	Displays hour of day using 24-hour clock	17
MI	Displays minutes (0-59)	45
SS	Displays seconds (0-59)	35

Figure 5-82: Common date format masks

Front slashes, hyphens, and colons can be used as separators between different date elements. For example, the format mask MM/DD/YY would appear as 01/15/99, and the mask HH:MI:SS would appear as 05:45:35. Additional characters such as commas, periods, and blank spaces must be included within double quotation marks. For example, the format mask "DAY", "MONTH" "DD", "YYYY" would appear as FRIDAY, JANUARY 15, 1999.

You can embed characters within character data by preceding the format mask with the characters "FM" to specify that the user will not have to enter the embedded format characters and the double quotation marks. Figure 5-83 lists some commonly used character data format masks.

Data Item	Format Mask	Stored Value	Displayed Value
Phone number	FM"("999") "999"-"9999	7155551234	(715) 555-1234
Social Security number	FM099"-"999"-"9999; omits leading 0 if one exists	123456789 012345678	123-45-789 12-34-5678

Figure 5-83: Common character format masks

It is a good idea to make the Maximum Length property of form fields that will include format masks wider than the longest possible formatted data value. If the Maximum Length property is not wide enough to display the formatted data, the data will appear as pound signs (###).

To specify a format mask for a form text field, you set the field's Format Mask property to the desired format mask specification. It is important that you remember to update the Maximum Length property of the text field so it can accommodate the formatted data value as well. For example, a DATE data item that will be formatted as DD-MONTH-YYYY (such as 15-SEPTEMBER-1999) must have a maximum length of 17. This includes 9 spaces for the month name, 2 spaces for the hyphens, 2 spaces for the day of the month, and 4 spaces for the year. Similarly, a NUMBER value with a format mask $9,999.99 must have a format mask of 9, although the size and scale of the NUMBER data field in the database might only be (6,2).

Next you will add a format mask to the CUSTOM_INVENTORY form.

To add a format mask to the CUSTINV_FORM:

1 Open the Properties sheet for CURR_PRICE_TEXT, and then change the Format Mask property to **$999,999.99**, and change the Maximum Length property to **11** to allow room for the dollar sign, commas, and decimal point. See Figure 5-84.

modify these values

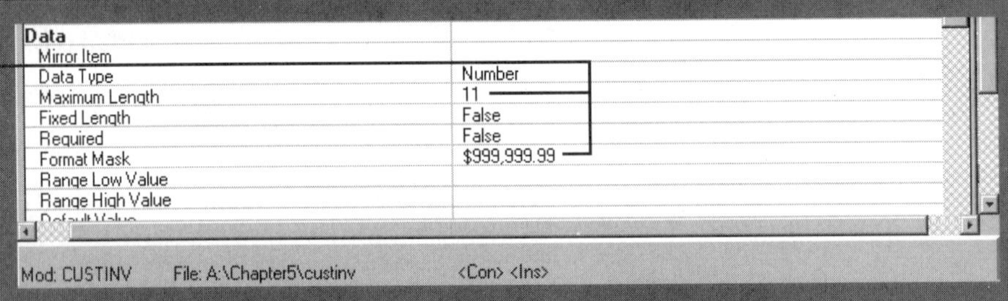

Figure 5-84: Adding a fomat mask to CURR_PRICE_TEXT

2 Close the Properties sheet, run the form, click the **INV_LOV** button, and then select the **3-Season Tent** and color **Forest**. Note how the current price is formatted.

3 Close the Forms Runtime application.

Final Formatting Checklist

A checklist of final formatting tasks you should perform every time you complete a form appears below:

- Change the window title.
- Change the canvas background color by drawing a background rectangle.
- Change the text fill colors for maximum contrast between text and backgrounds.
- Change the font types and sizes to ensure legibility, and use larger fonts for emphasis.
- Modify text field widths if necessary so they are wide enough to accommodate most of the data records that they will display.
- Add the form title (such as "Inventory").
- Update the item navigation sequence.
- Increase the window size so the form can be maximized when it runs.
- Center the canvas items in the maximized window.

- Add other formatting items such as rectangles so the form's appearance is consistent with other forms in the database.
- For a LOV display with one or two columns, reposition the LOV display on the right edge of the text field associated with the LOV so the top edge of the display is even with the top edge of the text field. For LOVs with several columns, center the LOV display in the middle of the screen.
- Realign canvas items if necessary.
- Add format masks if necessary.

You will finish formatting the CUSTINV_FORM as an end-of-chapter exercise. Now you will save your form and close the applications.

1. Save your changes.
2. Close all open Oracle applications.

SUMMARY

- Custom forms created using SQL queries provide more flexibility in how forms look and work.
- Sequences are sequential lists of numbers that are generated automatically by the database for creating unique surrogate key values for primary key fields. Sequences are created using SQL*Plus, but can be accessed and manipulated in other Oracle applications such as the Forms Designer. Once you move on to the next sequence value, the previous value cannot be accessed using the sequence commands to prevent two users from accidentally using the same sequence value for a primary key. You have to grant explicit privileges to other users to use your sequences.
- Custom forms have all of their items in a control block that is not connected to any database table. A control block text item's data type and maximum size must match the data type and maximum size of the corresponding database field that it will display.
- The Value property of a radio button represents the corresponding value of the data field that is stored in the database.
- The Default Value of a radio group is the value that is selected when the form first displays, which is usually the most common choice or the first choice in the radio button group.
- Buttons should have a height of 18 pixels with an 8-point font used for labels. Buttons in a button group should be the same size and should be wide enough to accommodate the longest label. Button groups can be oriented horizontally and centered at the bottom of the screen, or oriented vertically at the right edge of the screen.
- A trigger is a procedure or function that is attached to an event, such as loading a form or clicking a button. Triggers are written in the PL/SQL Editor, which combines SQL commands with procedural programming statements and control structures, such as if/then statement and loops.
- Global variables provide a way to pass data values among different triggers and PL/SQL programs.
- A LOV displays a list of data records, called a record group, based on a SQL query that a user can use to select a particular record and have the corresponding values inserted into text items on a form. The LIST VALUES command in a LOV button trigger displays the LOV associated with the text item at the current location of the insertion point.
- A PRE-FORM trigger is a procedure that runs just before a form first appears.

- The order that the insertion point moves through the canvas items when the user presses the Tab key is called the navigation sequence.
- Oracle Forms displays ORA- messages that are issued by the Oracle database, and FRM- messages that are issued by the Forms Runtime application.
- When you paste an item from one form to another in the Object Navigator window, you must modify the pasted item's Canvas property so it displays on your current canvas.
- LOV record groups can contain fields from multiple tables created using a SQL join.
- Format masks specify how data will be displayed, but do not affect how the data is stored in the database.

REVIEW QUESTIONS

1. What is a sequence, and what is it used for?
2. Write the SQL command to create a sequence named PRACTICE_SEQUENCE that begins with 1 and has no maximum value.
3. Write the SQL command to access the next value in PRACTICE_SEQUENCE.
4. What is the difference between a custom form and a data block form?
5. What is the difference between a data block and a control block?
6. How do you create a control block?
7. What does the Value property for a radio button specify?
8. What is a radio group? What is the Default Value property of a radio group?
9. What is a trigger? How does a trigger relate to an event?
10. When do you need to use a global variable?
11. What is the general format for referencing the value of a canvas item?
12. What is a LOV, and when do you use it?
13. What two things do you specify in the LOV Column Mapping property?
14. What is the relationship between the insertion point position on the screen and the LIST_VALUES command?
15. What is the item navigation sequence? How is it modified?
16. What are the two types of error messages that can be displayed in forms? Where do you find explanations for both types of errors?
17. How do you perform searches in a LOV?
18. What is a format mask? List the correct format masks for the following values:

Stored Data Value	Displayed Value	Format Mask
0123456789	123,456,789	________
0123456789	01234567.89	________
888888888	888-88-8888	________
8888888888	(888)-888-8888	________
15-JUL-2000	15/07/00	________
6:33 PM 15-JUL-2000	18:33:00 PM	________
6:33 PM 15-JUL-2000	6 PM	________

PROBLEM-SOLVING CASES

Northwoods University Database

Before you begin these exercises, run the SQL script A:\Chapter5\northwoo.sql from your Student Disk to rebuild your Northwoods University database tables. Save all forms created in the exercises to the Chapter5 folder on your Student Disk.

1. Create a custom form named LOCATION_FORM that contains all of the fields in the LOCATION table and has buttons for creating, updating, and deleting records, and for exiting the form. Save your form as location.fmb in the Chapter5 folder on your Student Disk.
   a. Create a sequence named LOCID_SEQUENCE to use for inserting new locations that starts with 58, has no maximum value, and does not cache sequence values. Grant SELECT privileges to PUBLIC.
   b. Format your form using the formatting checklist at the end of the chapter.
2. Create a custom form named FACULTY_FORM that contains all of the fields in the FACULTY table, and has buttons for creating, updating, and deleting records, and for exiting the form. Save your form as faculty.fmb in the Chapter5 folder on your Student Disk.
   a. Create a sequence named FID_SEQUENCE to use for inserting new faculty members that starts with 6, has no maximum value, and caches 5 sequence values at a time. Grant SELECT privileges to PUBLIC.
   b. Use radio buttons for the FRANK field with choices (and corresponding values) for full (FULL), associate (ASSO), assistant (ASST), and instructor (INST).
   c. Create a LOV with a LOV button beside the form field for LOCID to show LOCATION information including building codes and rooms.
   d. Use an appropriate format mask for the FPHONE field.
   e. Format your form using the formatting checklist at the end of the chapter.
3. Create a custom form named STUDENT_FORM that contains all of the fields from the STUDENT table, and has buttons for creating, updating, and deleting records, and for exiting the form. Save your form student.fmb in the Chapter5 folder on your Student Disk.
   a. Create a sequence named SID_SEQUENCE to use for inserting new students that starts with 106, has a maximum value of 10,000, caches 10 values at a time, and guarantees that the sequence values will be granted in the order they are requested. Grant SELECT privileges to PUBLIC.
   b. Use radio buttons for the SCLASS field with choices (and corresponding data values) for freshman (FR), sophomore (SO), junior (JR), senior (SR), and graduate student (GR).
   c. Create a LOV with a LOV button beside the form field associated with the FID field that displays faculty last name, first name, building code, and room number.
   d. Use format masks for the SPHONE field so phone numbers are formatted as (715) 555-5555, and so SDOB fields are formatted as MM/DD/YYYY.
   e. Format your form using the formatting checklist at the end of the chapter.

Clearwater Traders Database

1. Complete all of the formatting checklist items so your finished CUSTINV_FORM looks like Figure 5-85. Make sure to move the LOV displays so the user does not have to move the pointer very far to make a selection. Change the navigation order so the cursor moves top to down, left to right as follows: INVID_TEXT, INV_LOV_BUTTON, ITEMDESC_TEXT, ITEM_LOV_BUTTON, ITEMSIZE_TEXT, COLOR_TEXT, COLOR_LOV_BUTTON, CURR_PRICE_TEXT, QOH_TEXT, SAVE_BUTTON, CREATE_BUTTON, DELETE_BUTTON, EXIT_BUTTON.

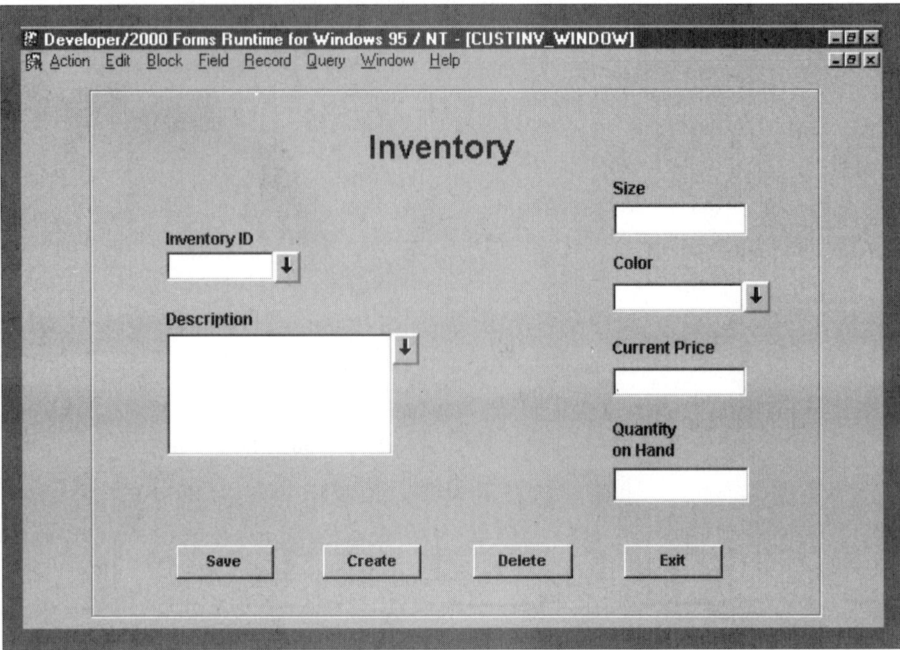

Figure 5-85

2. Create a custom form named CUSTOMER_FORM that contains all of the fields in the CUSTOMER table, and has buttons for creating, updating, and deleting records, and for exiting the form. Save your form as customer.fmb in the Chapter5 folder on your Student Disk.
   a. Create a sequence named CUSTID_SEQUENCE to use for inserting new customers that starts with 233, has no maximum value, and does not cache sequence values. Grant SELECT privileges to PUBLIC.
   b. Use appropriate format masks for DPHONE and EPHONE so phone numbers are formatted as (715) 555-5555.
   c. Format your form using the formatting checklist at the end of the chapter.
3. Create a custom form named CUST_ORDER_FORM that contains all of the fields in the CUST_ORDER table, and has buttons for creating, updating, and deleting records, and for exiting the form. Save your form as cust_ord.fmb in the Chapter5 folder on your Student Disk.
   a. Create a sequence named ORDERID_SEQUENCE to use for inserting new orders that starts with 1063, and has a maximum value of 100,000. The sequence should CYCLE, and begin again with a minimum value of 1000. The sequence should cache 20 sequence values. Grant SELECT privileges to PUBLIC.
   b. Create radio buttons for the payment method field with choices (and corresponding data values) for Credit Card (CC) or Check (CHECK).
   c. Create a LOV for the customer ID field that displays customer first and last name, middle initial, address, city, state, and zip code.
   d. Create a LOV for the order source field.
   e. Use a format mask for DATE so the date appears in the format 15-OCTOBER-1999.
   f. Format your form using the formatting checklist at the end of the chapter.

Chapter 6

objectives

- Design and create custom forms to support business processes
- Create a form that has multiple windows
- Use the Oracle Debugger
- Anticipate system errors and create customized error messages

CHAPTER 6

Creating Forms to Support Business Applications

Introduction The forms that you have created so far were based on a single database table. Some of your forms retrieved data from other tables to use as foreign key values, but the basic INSERT, UPDATE, and DELETE operations involved a single table. However, normal business operations usually do not rely on a single relational database table. Users are required to insert, update, and delete records from many related tables. In this chapter you will learn how to create forms that integrate several database tables and support realistic business processes. You will create two custom business forms: one for supporting the Clearwater Traders merchandise receiving process and one for handling the customer order process. While developing these forms, you will learn how to use the Oracle Debugger and explore how to intercept system-level messages and replace them with custom messages.

The Clearwater Traders Merchandise Receiving Process

To create a custom database application, first you must identify the processes and corresponding database tables. The best way to start is to describe the process. The first form you will develop supports the merchandise receiving function at Clearwater Traders, which is described next.

When Clearwater Traders purchases new merchandise from its suppliers, it records information about anticipated shipments in the SHIPPING table. This information includes the inventory ID of the purchased item, the quantity expected, and the date the shipment is expected. When a new shipment arrives, the receiving clerk first has to determine if the incoming shipment is a pending or backordered shipment. Pending shipment data is stored in the SHIPPING table, and backordered shipment data is stored in the BACKORDER table. After finding the record, the clerk enters the following information from the incoming shipment's packing list: the shipment quantity received, quantity backordered (if any), and expected date that the backordered items will arrive. If the record came from the SHIPPING table (i.e., it was not a backorder), then the system updates the DATE_RECEIVED field in the SHIPPING table to the current date and updates the QUANTITY_RECEIVED field to the quantity received. If the record came from the BACKORDER table, then these same updates are made in the BACKORDER table. If the incoming shipment reports a backorder, then a new record must be created in the BACKORDER table, and values are inserted for the date the backorder will arrive and the expected quantity. Finally, the system updates the QOH field in the INVENTORY table to include the quantity of goods actually received.

Figure 6-1 illustrates these processing steps using a flowchart to show more detailed design information. The clerk retrieves all information about pending new and backordered shipments from the SHIPPING and BACKORDER tables using a Shipment LOV. Then the clerk enters the quantity received, quantity backordered, and expected backorder receipt date. The system determines if the selected shipment came from the SHIPPING or BACKORDER table by executing a SELECT query on the SHIPPING table first. If no record is found in the SHIPPING table, the system executes a SELECT query on the BACKORDER table. The appropriate SHIPPING or BACKORDER record is updated with the date and quantity received. If there is a backorder, the system creates new backorder record. Regardless of whether there is a backorder, the system finds the current QOH of the inventory item using a SELECT ... FOR UPDATE query, and then updates the current QOH in the INVENTORY table by adding the quantity received to the current QOH.

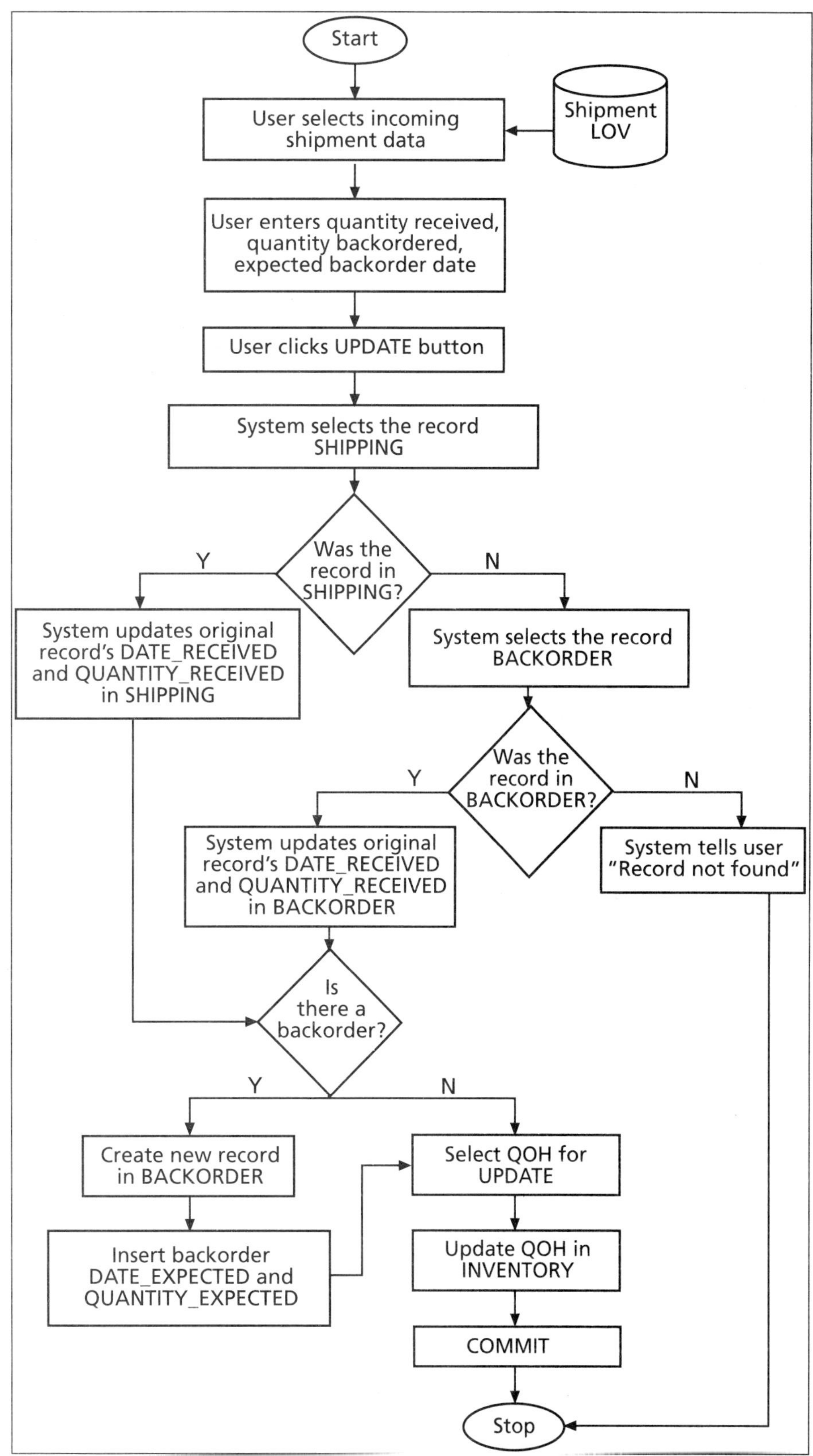

Figure 6-1: Clearwater Traders' receiving process flowchart

It is necessary to do a SELECT ... FOR UPDATE to lock the QOH record for update for the following reason: suppose two inventory clerks are entering shipment information at the same time and both are processing a shipment of the same inventory item that was received. Both processes read the current QOH to be 100. The first shipment contains 50 units of the inventory item, so the process calculates the current QOH to be 100 + 50, or 150, and then updates the QOH record and commits the change. The second shipment contains 100 units of the inventory item, so the process calculates QOH to be 100 + 100, or 200, and then updates the QOH and commits the change just after the first process committed its update. The current QOH in the database is now 200, but it should be 250, and the first update is lost.

Creating the Interface Design

The next step is to visualize how the user interface will look. Figure 6-2 shows a design sketch of the interface design. The form will display the shipment ID, inventory ID, and inventory description information, and the expected date for receipt and quantity expected for each item. The form will have fields for inserting the quantity received, quantity backordered, and the expected backorder arrival date. Buttons will be included to display the SHIPPING LOV, to update the SHIPMENT and INVENTORY tables, to cancel the current information and clear the screen, and to exit the form.

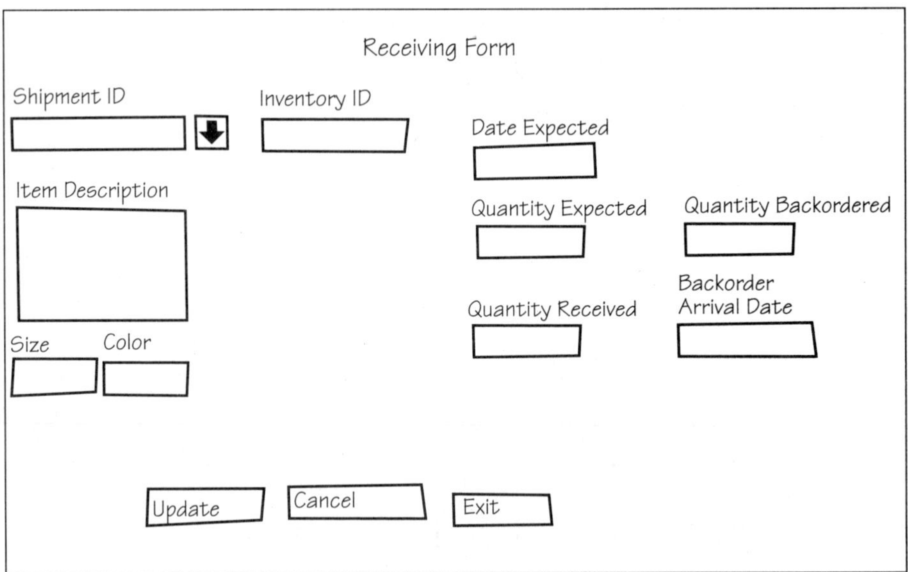

Figure 6-2: Design of the receiving form

Before working on the form, you will refresh your Clearwater Traders database tables by running the script that re-creates the tables and inserts all of the sample data records. You also will run a script that drops your sequences and then re-creates them and adds new sequences that you will use in this chapter. Then you will start the Forms Designer and create the new form.

To refresh the Clearwater Traders database, and create the new form:

1 Start SQL*Plus, log on to the database, and then type **START A:\Chapter6\clearwat.sql** at the SQL prompt to refresh your database.

2 Type **START A:\Chapter6\clearseq.sql** at the SQL prompt to create the new sequences. Now you are ready to create the form using the Forms Designer.

HELP? If the program displays an error message that says "ORA-02289: sequence does not exist," the script tried to drop a sequence that does not exist. You can ignore this error, as the script will create all of the sequences that you need.

3 Start the Forms Designer and then go to the Object Navigator in Visual View.

4 Create a new form named **RECEIVING_FORM.**

5 Create a new window named **RECEIVING_FORM_WINDOW**, and then create a new canvas named **RECEIVING_FORM_CANVAS.**

6 Create a new control block named **RECEIVING_BLOCK.**

Next you will create the text fields and labels for the fields in the SHIPPING table that will appear on the form. You will copy the INVENTORY table fields from the form you created in Chapter 5 later.

To create the SHIPPING table fields and labels:

1 Create text fields with the following properties. Position the text fields on the canvas as shown in Figure 6-3. By default, the quantity backordered will be zero unless the user changes it.

Name	Data Type	Maximum Length
SHIPID_TEXT	Number	10
EXP_DATE_TEXT	Date	20
QUANT_EXP_TEXT	Number	4
QUANT_REC_TEXT	Number	4
QUANT_BO_TEXT	Number	4
BO_DATE_TEXT	Date	20

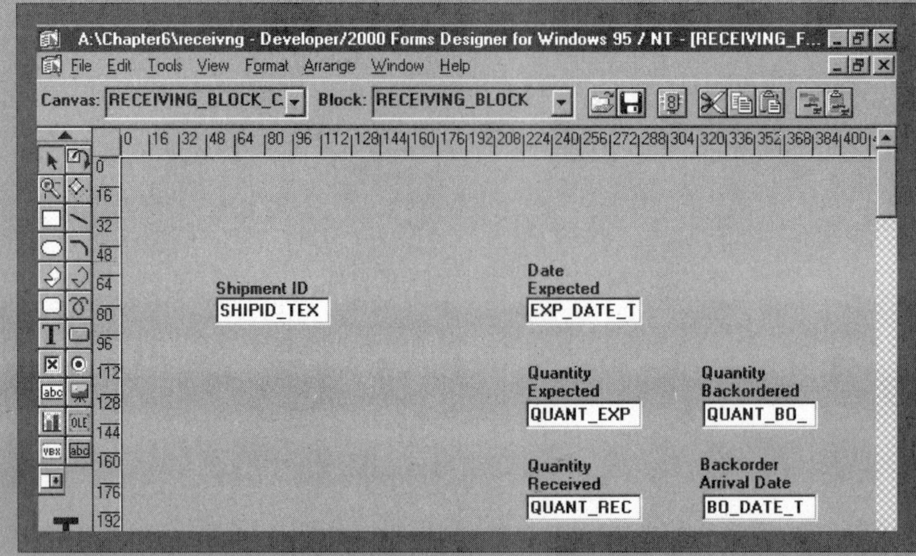

Figure 6-3: Creating the SHIPPING table fields and labels

2 Open the QUANT_BO_TEXT Properties sheet, and then change the Default Value property to **0**.

3 Create the labels shown in Figure 6-3 for each of the text fields you just created.

4 Save the form as **receivng.fmb** in the Chapter6 folder on your Student Disk and then change the form name back to RECEIVING_FORM in the Object Navigator.

You created the INVENTORY fields and labels that will display on this form in the CUSTINV_FORM that you created in Chapter 5. You can open that form and copy the fields and labels into the new form.

To open the form and copy the fields:

1 Click the **Open** button on the Layout Editor toolbar, change to the Chapter5 folder on your Student Disk, and then double-click the **custinv.fmb** file to open it. The Object Navigator window opens.

2 Change to Ownership View, and then open **Blocks, INVENTORY_BLOCK,** and **Items** in the CUSTINV_FORM.

3 Press and hold down the **Ctrl** key, and then select the **INVID_TEXT, ITEMDESC_TEXT, ITEMSIZE_TEXT,** and **COLOR_TEXT** items, as shown in Figure 6-4.

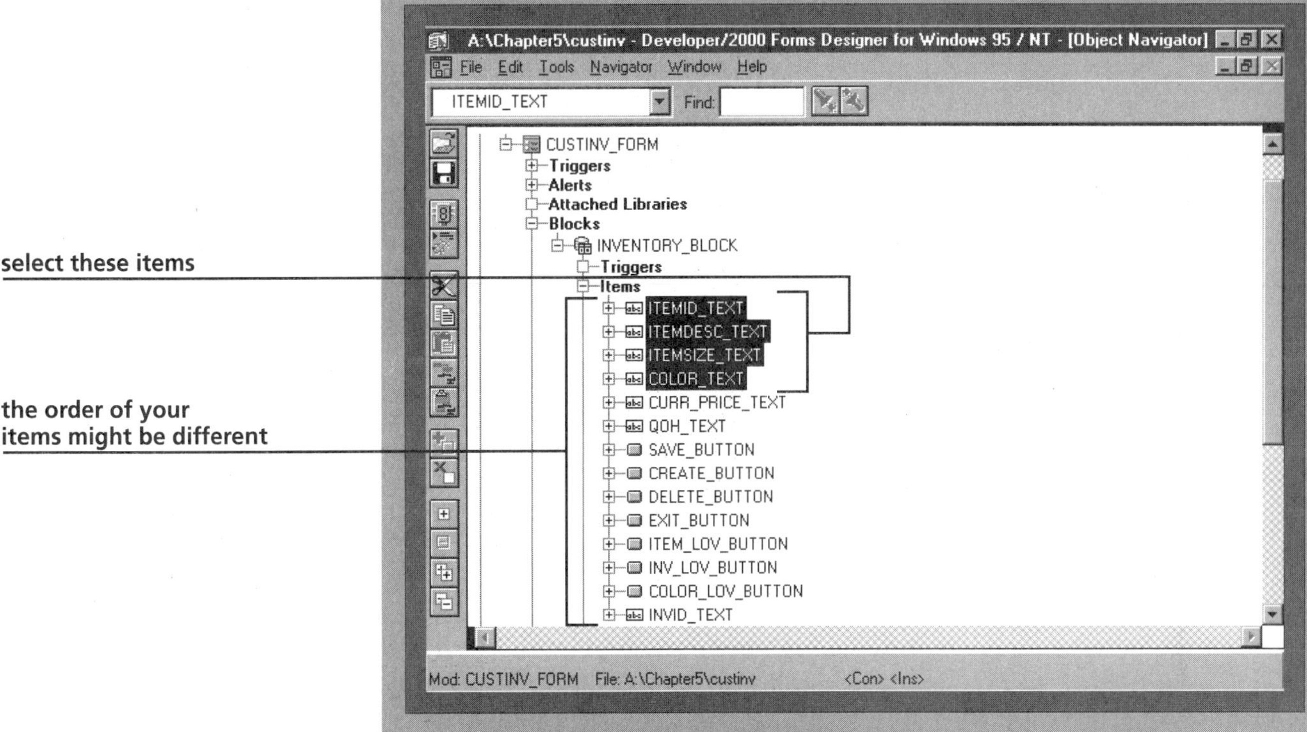

Figure 6-4: Selecting fields to copy from CUSTINV_FORM

4 Click the **Copy** button on the Object Navigator toolbar to copy the text fields.
5 Click **Forms** and then click the **Collapse All** button on the Object Navigator toolbar to close all of the Object Navigator objects.
6 Open **Forms, RECEIVING_FORM, Blocks, RECEIVING_BLOCK,** and **Items.**
7 Click the **Paste** button on the Object Navigator toolbar. The copied text fields appear in the RECEIVING_BLOCK items, as shown in Figure 6-5.

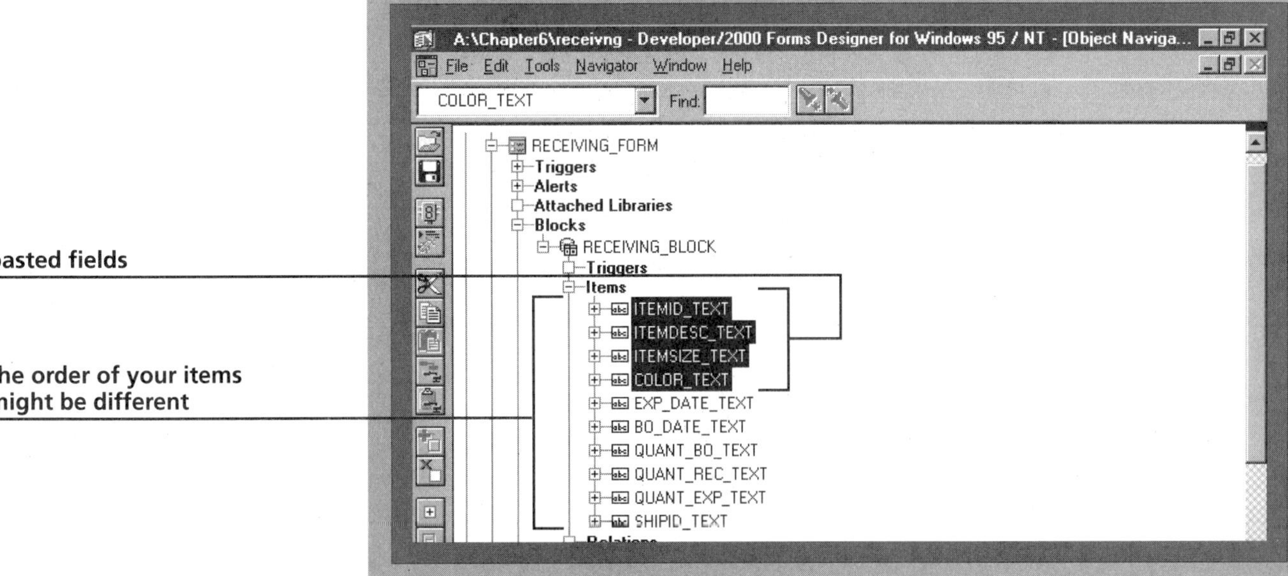

Figure 6-5: Pasting the copied fields into RECEIVING _FORM

Next you will modify some of the properties of the pasted text fields. You will need to change every field's Canvas property to RECEIVING_FORM_CANVAS so the fields will display on the current form, and then you will need to delete the LOV property in the fields that had LOVs in the previous form. You will do this next using the group Properties sheet.

To modify the pasted field properties:

1 In the Object Navigator window, press and hold down the **Shift** key, and then select **COLOR_TEXT, ITEMSIZE_TEXT, ITEMDESC_TEXT,** and **INVID_TEXT**. With the Shift key still pressed, right-click the selected items, and then click **Properties** to open the group Properties sheet.

2 Change the Canvas property to **RECEIVING_FORM_CANVAS**, and then close the group Properties sheet.

3 In the Object Navigator window, press and hold down the **Ctrl** key, and then select **COLOR_TEXT, ITEMDESC_TEXT,** and **INVID_TEXT**.

4 Press and hold down the **Shift** key, right-click the selected objects, and then click **Properties**. Double-click the **LOV** property to delete it, and then close the Properties sheet.

5 Maximize the Layout Editor window, and then position the pasted fields and create labels so your form looks like Figure 6-6.

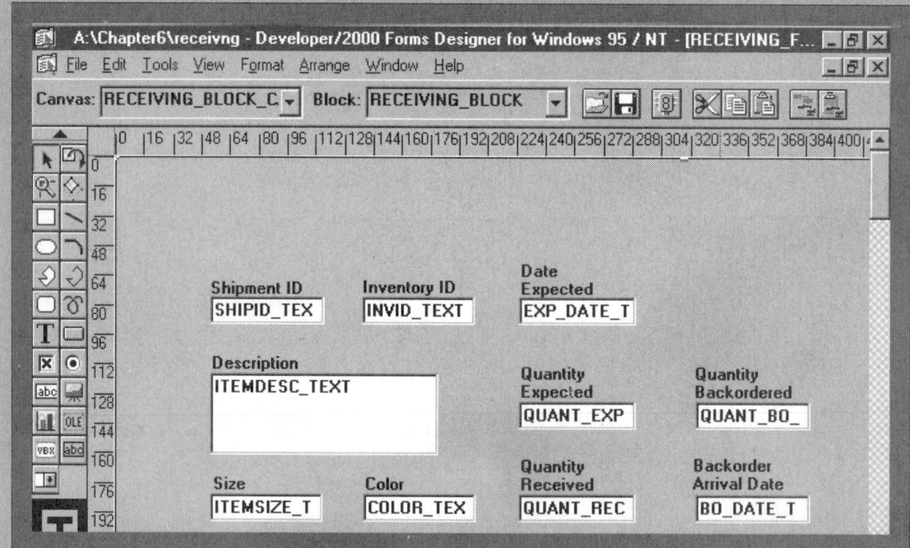

Figure 6-6: Positioning the INVENTORY fields and labels

6 Save the form.

Creating the LOV

Next you will create the LOV to retrieve data from the SHIPPING and BACKORDER records that have not arrived. This LOV will display the SHIPID, INVID, and QUANTITY_EXPECTED fields and the corresponding ITEMDESC, ITEMSIZE, and COLOR data for each inventory item. This query requires a UNION because it needs to return all records from both the SHIPPING and BACKORDER tables where the DATE_RECEIVED field is NULL. However, a LOV in a form cannot be derived from a UNION—it can be derived only from a conventional SELECT query. To get around this limitation, you will create a database view that contains all SHIPPING records and their associated inventory information where the date received is NULL, and then uses a UNION to join these records with a second query that retrieves all BACKORDER records and their associated inventory information where the date received is NULL.

To create the database view:

1 Click the **Oracle SQL*Plus** command button on the taskbar to switch to SQL*Plus.

2 Type the command shown in Figure 6-7 to create the view named SHIPVIEW.

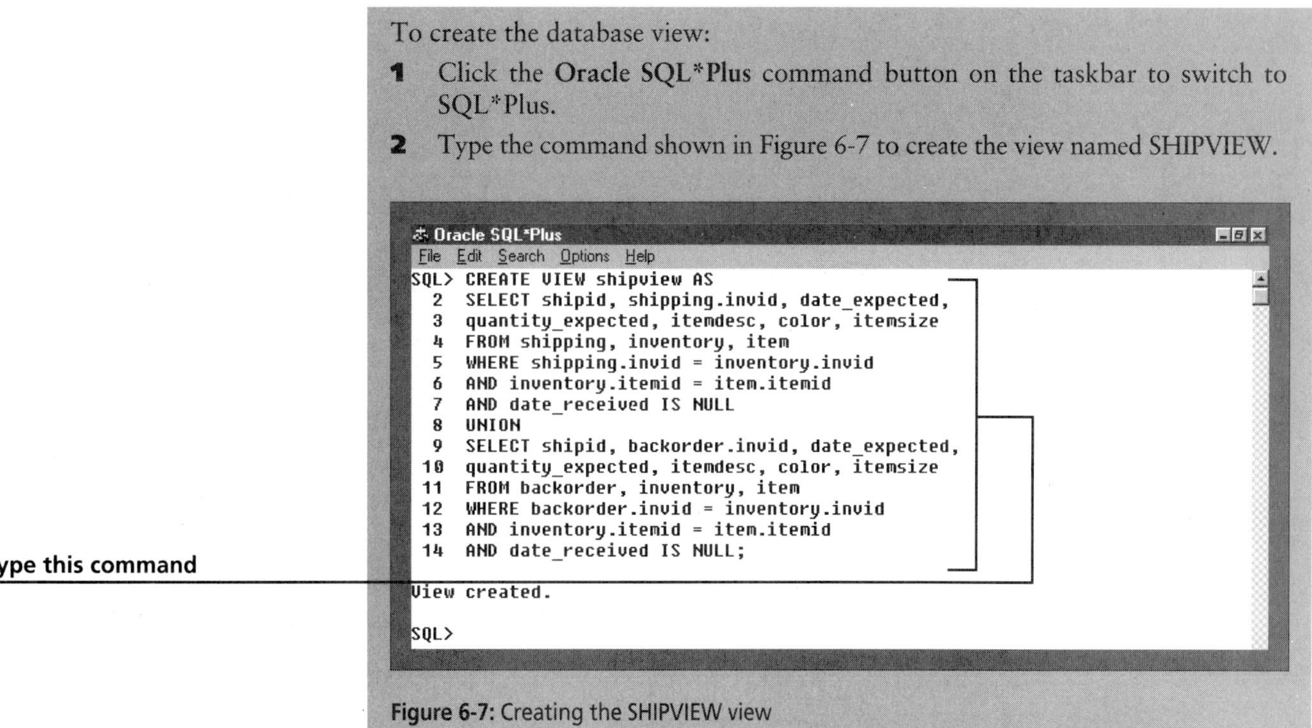

Figure 6-7: Creating the SHIPVIEW view

Next you will create the LOV to display the SHIPVIEW data.

To create the LOV:

1 Click the **Forms Designer** command button on the taskbar, and then change to the Object Navigator window if necessary.

2 Click **LOVs** under RECEIVING_FORM and then click the **Create** button on the Object Navigator toolbar to create a new LOV.

3 Type the query text shown in Figure 6-8, and then click the **OK** button.

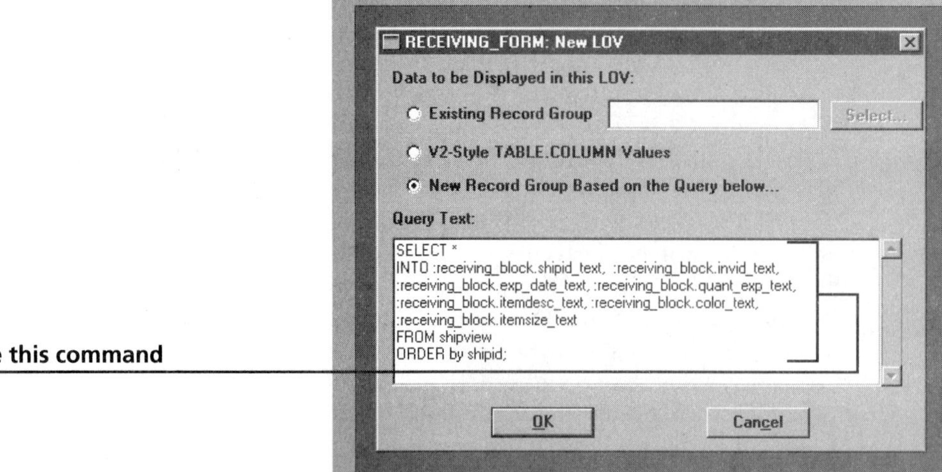

Figure 6-8: LOV query text

4 Rename the new LOV and associated record group to **SHIPPING_LOV**.

5 Open the SHIPPING_LOV (LOV) Properties sheet, and then change the Title property to **Expected Shipments**, which will be the title of the LOV display, and then close the Properties sheet.

6 Copy any LOV button from your CUSTINV_FORM (it doesn't matter which one) and then paste it into the RECEIVING_FORM.

7 Rename the pasted button to **SHIPPING_LOV_BUTTON**, and then modify its Canvas property to **RECEIVING_FORM_CANVAS**.

8 Maximize the Layout Editor window, and then place the SHIPPING_LOV _BUTTON on the right edge of the SHIPID_TEXT field.

9 Modify the trigger for SHIPPING_LOV_BUTTON so it places the insertion point into the SHIPID_TEXT field by changing the GO_ITEM command to **GO_ITEM('shipid_text');**.

10 Update the LOV property of SHIPID_TEXT to **SHIPPING_LOV**.

11 Run the form, click the **Shipment ID LOV** button to confirm that the SHIPPING _LOV is displayed and that the values of the selected shipment are displayed correctly in the form fields, and then close the Forms Runtime application.

HELP? If the SHIPPING_LOV does not display, switch to SQL*Plus and verify that the view exists in your account and that its fields correspond to the text fields specified in the INTO clause in Figure 6-8. If the SHIPPING_LOV does not display correctly, or the returned values do not display correctly, close the Forms Runtime application, open the SHIPPING_LOV (LOV) Properties sheet, and then examine the column mapping to confirm that the column names are listed correctly and that each column is mapped to the correct return item.

12 Open the Object Navigator window, open the SHIPPING_LOV Properties sheet, and then modify the SHIPPING_LOV Column Mapping, Height, and Width properties so the LOV display looks like Figure 6-9. Modify the X- and Y-Position properties so the LOV is centered on the screen.

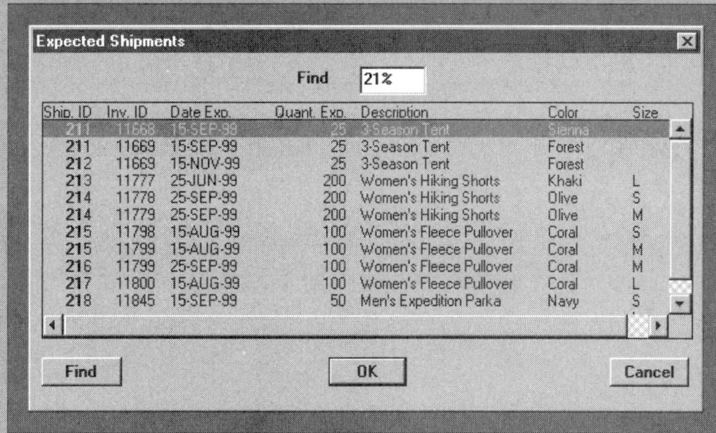

Figure 6-9: Shipping LOV

13 Save the form.

The next step is to create the Update, Cancel, and Exit buttons.

To create the Update, Cancel, and Exit buttons:

1 In the Layout Editor, draw a button and then change its Name property to **UPDATE_BUTTON**; Width to 60, Height to 18; and Label to **Update**, and then close the Properties sheet.

2 Copy this button and paste it two times to create the Cancel and Exit buttons. Change the Name property of the buttons to **CANCEL_BUTTON** and **EXIT_BUTTON**, and then change the Label property to **Cancel** and **Exit**, respectively.

3 Move the buttons so they appear aligned and evenly distributed at the bottom of the canvas, as shown in Figure 6-10.

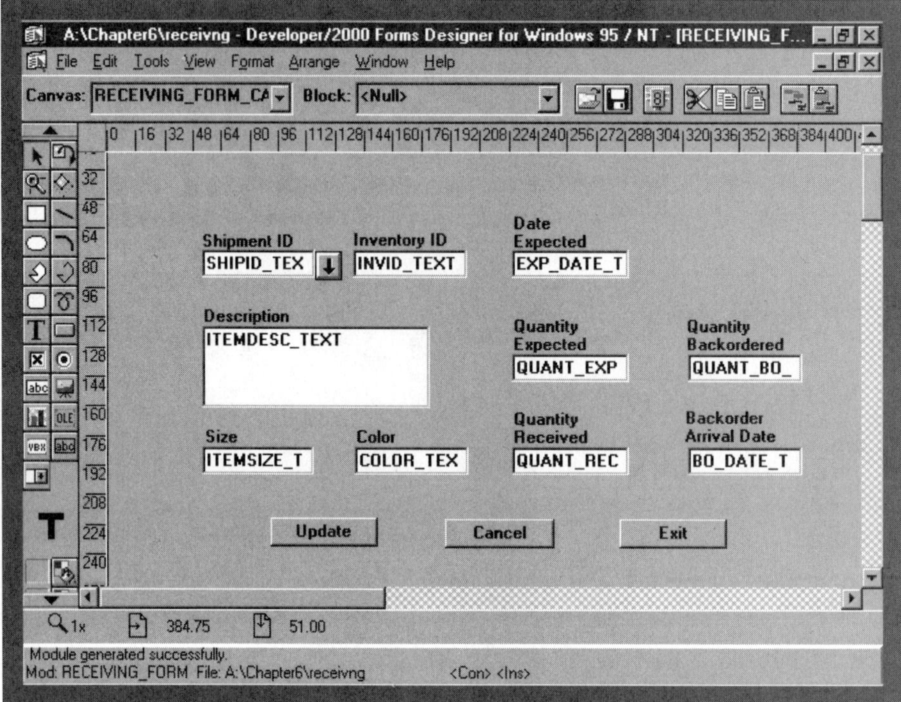

Figure 6-10: Positioning the form buttons

Now you need to write the trigger for the Update button. Review the process design in Figure 6-1. The user first retrieves the shipment information, enters the quantity received, quantity backordered, and expected backorder date, and then clicks the Update button. The UPDATE_BUTTON trigger first must determine if the selected record came from the SHIPPING table by trying to select the record for update. If the record is not found in the SHIPPING table, then the trigger must try to select the record from the BACKORDER table. To create these queries, you will have to create a cursor.

A **cursor** is a variable corresponding to a memory location that holds a compiled SQL query. Cursors can be implicit or explicit. **Implicit cursors** are created using the general format `SELECT <table fields> INTO <form fields>`. An implicit cursor is not declared in the DECLARE section of a PL/SQL procedure or trigger, but it is declared implicitly in the SELECT command. If an implicit cursor does not retrieve any records, a system error is generated. In a LOV, this error is handled internally by the system.

Explicit cursors are declared formally in the DECLARE section of a PL/SQL procedure or trigger. Explicit cursors must be used in PL/SQL SELECT commands that might retrieve variable numbers of records or no records at all. To determine if the shipment record selected through the LOV came from the SHIPPING or BACKORDER table, the trigger first will query the SHIPPING table, and there is a possibility that no records will be returned. If no records are returned from the SHIPPING table, then the trigger will query the BACKORDER table, and again there is a possibility that no records will be returned. Therefore this operation requires explicit cursors for the SELECT commands for both the SHIPPING and BACKORDER tables. You will type the DECLARE section for the Update button trigger that declares the explicit cursors next.

To create the DECLARE section of the UPDATE_BUTTON trigger:

1. Create a WHEN-BUTTON-PRESSED trigger for the UPDATE_BUTTON.
2. Type the code shown in Figure 6-11 in the PL/SQL Editor Source code pane. *Do not* compile the trigger yet. You entered only the DECLARE section, so you will receive compile errors.

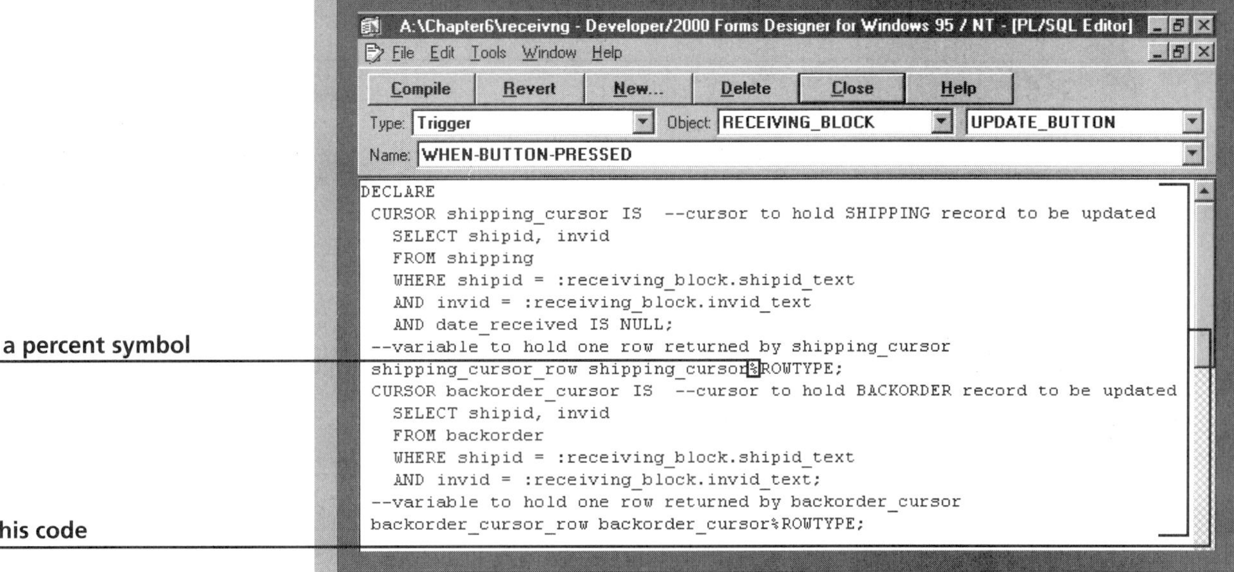

Figure 6-11: DECLARE section of UPDATE_BUTTON trigger

3. Click the **Close** button on the PL/SQL Editor button bar to save your code and close the editor.
4. Save the form.

A good coding practice when creating triggers is to make each trigger as short as possible so it is easier to understand and debug. One way to simplify a trigger is to create subprograms called **program units** that contain a series of executable statements to single out a procedure that corresponds to a single process, such as what is shown in a single flowchart step. A program unit can be a **procedure**, which is simply a series of statements that change variable values, or a **function**, which returns a value. You can pass variables to and from program units.

Figure 6-12 shows the program units you will create for the UPDATE_BUTTON trigger. UPDATE_SHIPPING will update the selected record in the SHIPPING table, and UPDATE_BACKORDER will update the selected record in the BACKORDER table. PROCESS_BO will determine if the user has entered a quantity backordered, and if so, it will create a new BACKORDER record. UPDATE_QOH will select the current QOH for update, update the quantity received, and commit the queries. You will create these four program units next.

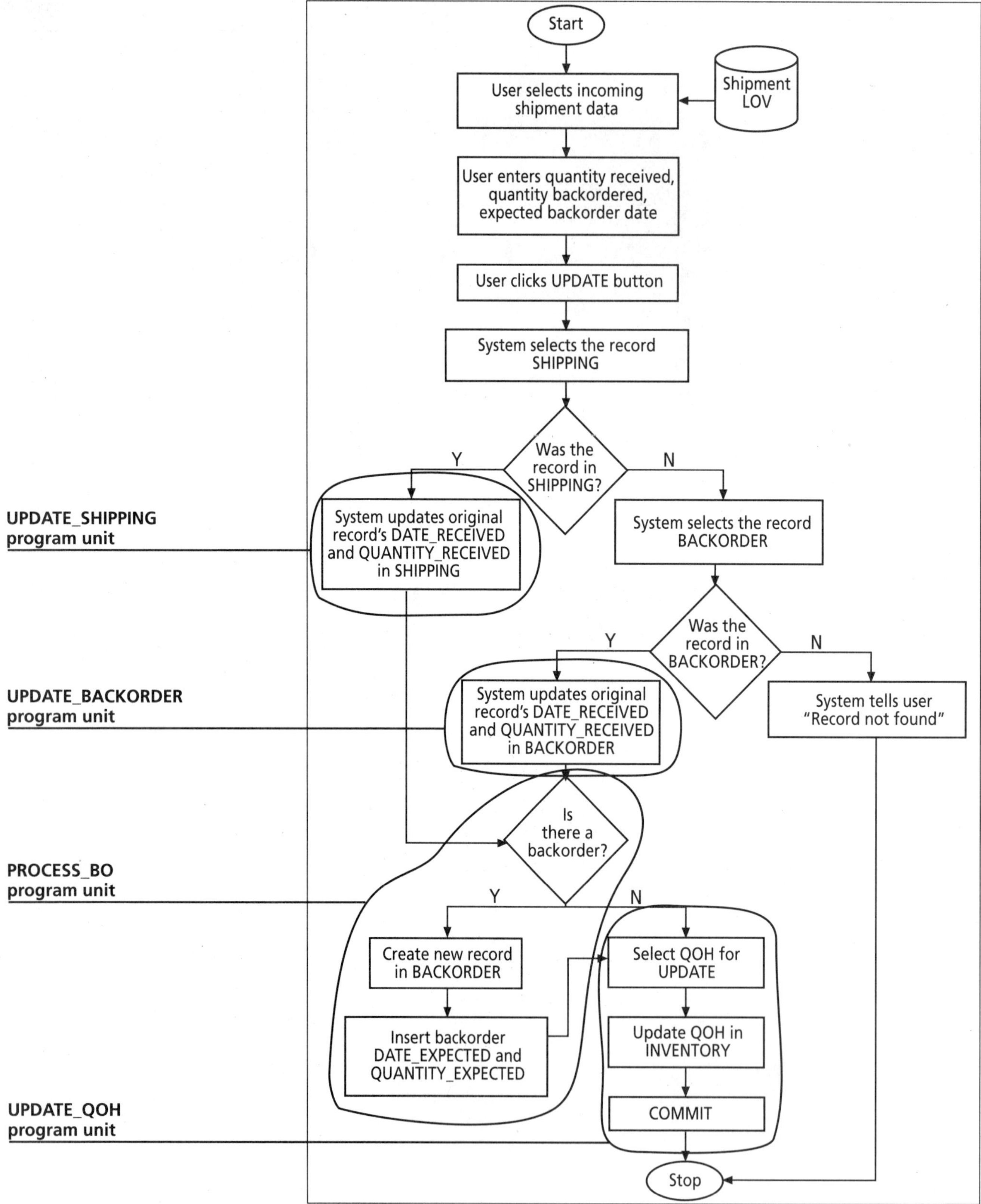

Figure 6-12: UPDATE_BUTTON program units

To create the program units:

1 Open the Object Navigator window in Ownership View, click **Program Units**, and then click the **Create** button on the Object Navigator toolbar. The New Program Unit dialog box opens, as shown in Figure 6-13.

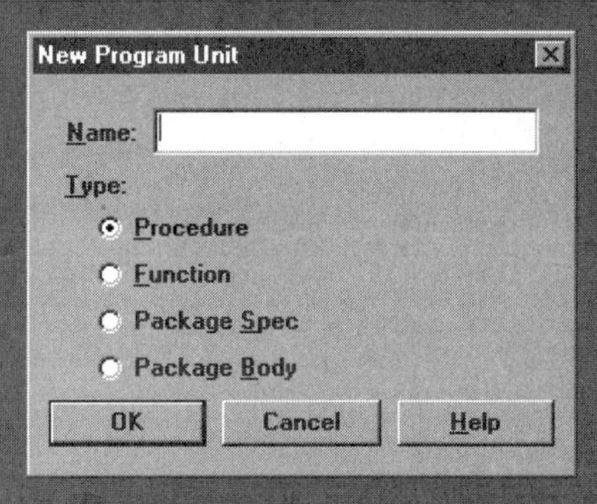

Figure 6-13: New Program Unit dialog box

2 Type **UPDATE_SHIPPING** in the Name text box, make sure that the **Procedure** option button is selected, and then click the **OK** button. The PL/SQL Editor opens.

3 Type the code shown in Figure 6-14, and then compile your code and correct any syntax errors.

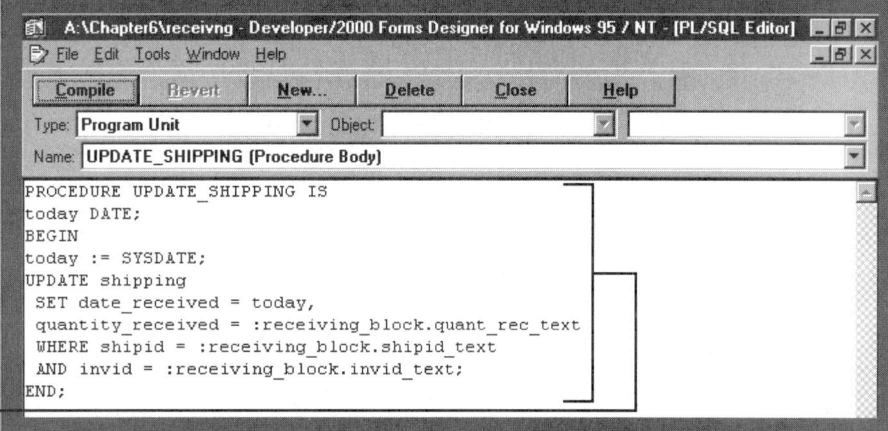


```
PROCEDURE UPDATE_SHIPPING IS
today DATE;
BEGIN
today := SYSDATE;
UPDATE shipping
 SET date_received = today,
 quantity_received = :receiving_block.quant_rec_text
 WHERE shipid = :receiving_block.shipid_text
 AND invid = :receiving_block.invid_text;
END;
```

Figure 6-14: UPDATE_SHIPPING program unit

4 Click the New button on the PL/SQL Editor button bar, type **UPDATE_BACKORDER** in the Name text box, make sure that the **Procedure** option button is selected, and then click the **OK** button.

5 Type the code shown in Figure 6-15, and then compile your code and correct any syntax errors.

A:\Chapter6\receivng - Developer/2000 Forms Designer for Windows 95 / NT - [PL/SQL Editor]

File Edit Tools Window Help

Compile | Revert | New... | Delete | Close | Help

Type: Program Unit Object:

Name: UPDATE_BACKORDER (Procedure Body)

```
PROCEDURE UPDATE_BACKORDER IS
today DATE;
BEGIN
today := SYSDATE;
UPDATE backorder
  SET date_received = today,
  quantity_received = :receiving_block.quant_rec_text
  WHERE shipid = :receiving_block.shipid_text
  AND invid = :receiving_block.invid_text;
END;
```

type this code

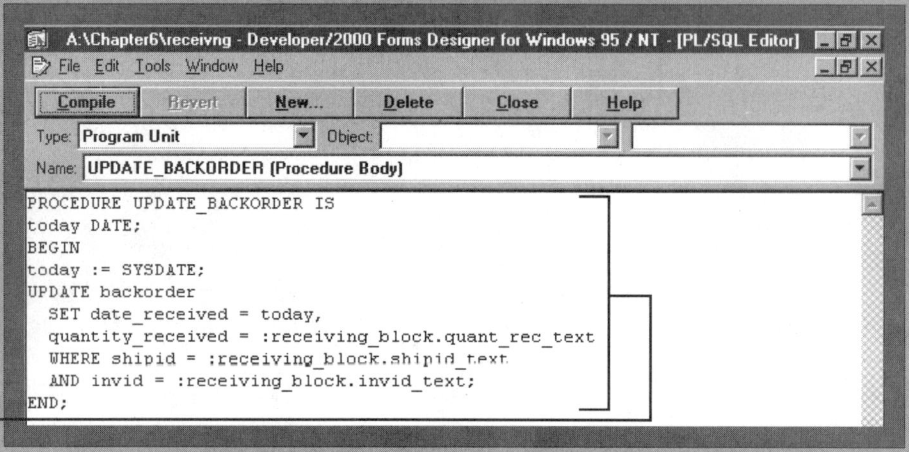

Figure 6-15: UPDATE_BACKORDER program unit

6 Create the PROCESS_BO program unit shown in Figure 6 16.

A:\Chapter6\receivng - Developer/2000 Forms Designer for Windows 95 / NT - [PL/SQL Editor]

File Edit Tools Window Help

Compile | Revert | New... | Delete | Close | Help

Type: Program Unit Object:

Name: PROCESS_BO (Procedure Body)

```
PROCEDURE PROCESS_BO IS
BEGIN
  IF :receiving_block.quant_bo_text = 0 THEN
    INSERT INTO backorder VALUES
      (backorderid_sequence.nextval, :receiving_block.shipid_text,
      :receiving_block.invid_text, :receiving_block.bo_date_text,
      :receiving_block.quant_bo_text, NULL, NULL);
  END IF;
END;
```

this sequence was created when you ran the clearseq.sql script

type this code

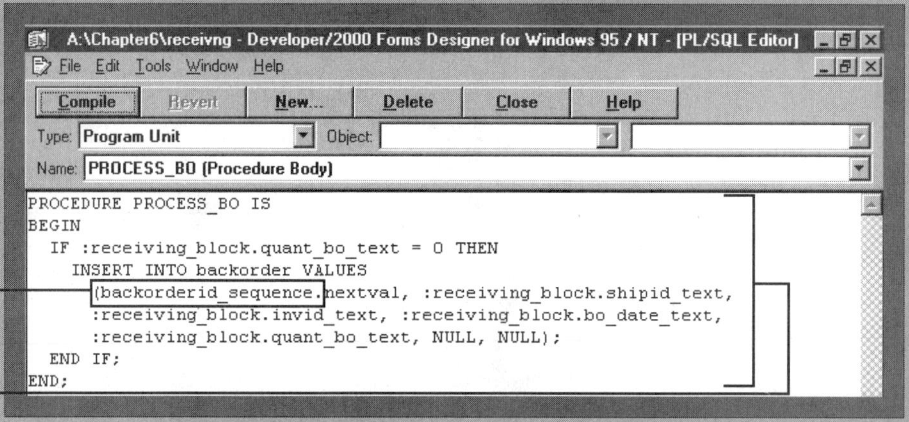

Figure 6-16: PROCESS_BO program unit

7 Create the UPDATE_QOH program unit shown in Figure 6-17.

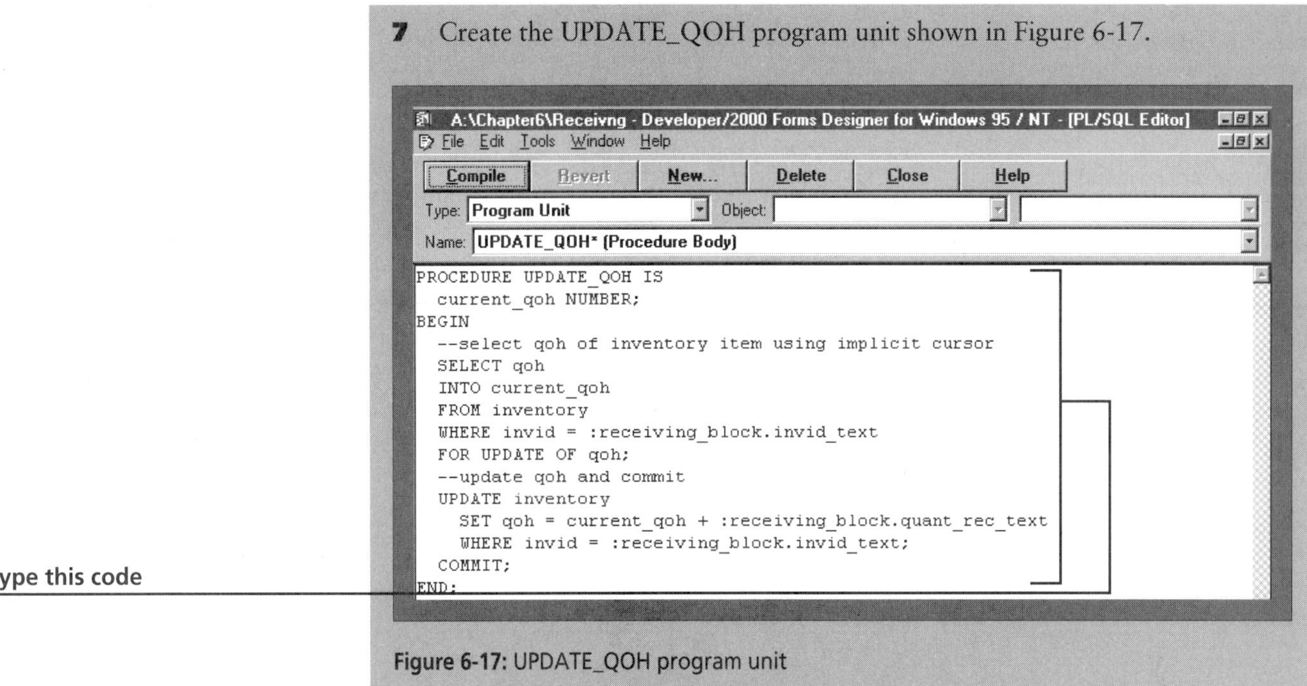


```
PROCEDURE UPDATE_QOH IS
  current_qoh NUMBER;
BEGIN
  --select qoh of inventory item using implicit cursor
  SELECT qoh
  INTO current_qoh
  FROM inventory
  WHERE invid = :receiving_block.invid_text
  FOR UPDATE OF qoh;
  --update qoh and commit
  UPDATE inventory
    SET qoh = current_qoh + :receiving_block.quant_rec_text
    WHERE invid = :receiving_block.invid_text;
  COMMIT;
END;
```

Figure 6-17: UPDATE_QOH program unit

Now you will enter the body of the trigger for the Update button. The following steps show how you can move to the UPDATE_BUTTON trigger easily without closing the PL/SQL Editor.

To move to the UPDATE_BUTTON trigger:

1 In the PL/SQL Editor, click the **Type** list arrow, and then click **Trigger**.

2 Select the object the code is attached to, which can be either a form (for PRE-FORM triggers) or a specific block in a form. Click the first **Object** list arrow, and then click **RECEIVING_BLOCK.**

3 To select the specific item (button, text field, etc.) associated with the trigger, click the second **Object** list arrow, and then click **UPDATE_BUTTON**, as shown in Figure 6-18, to return to the code for the UPDATE_BUTTON trigger.

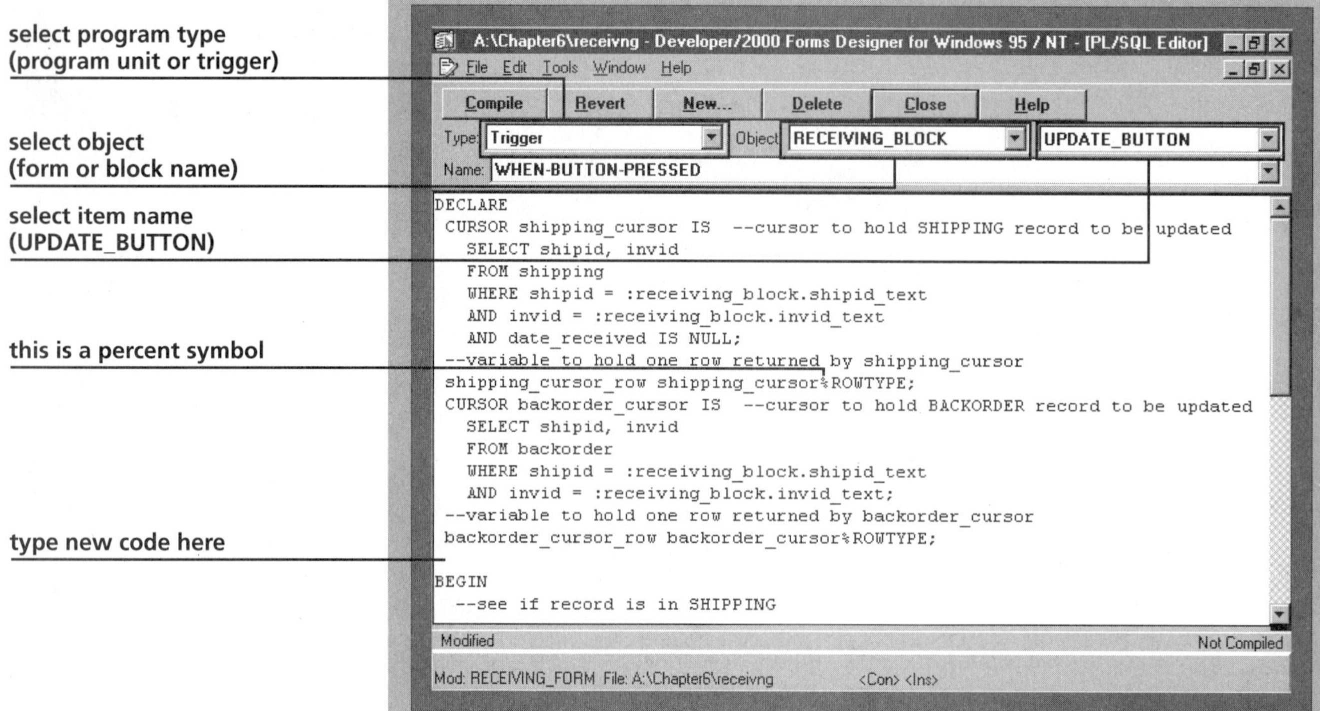

Figure 6-18: Moving to the UPDATE_BUTTON trigger

4 Type the following code at the end of the DECLARE section (see Figure 6-18) to complete the UPDATE_BUTTON trigger:

```
BEGIN
--see if record is in SHIPPING
   OPEN shipping_cursor;
   FETCH shipping_cursor INTO shipping_cursor_row;
   IF shipping_cursor%FOUND THEN -- record is in SHIPPING
     Update_Shipping;
     Process_BO;
     Update_QOH;
     CLOSE shipping_cursor;
   ELSE --confirm record is in BACKORDER
     OPEN backorder_cursor;
     FETCH backorder_cursor INTO backorder_cursor_row;
     IF backorder_cursor%FOUND THEN -- record is in BACKORDER
        Update_Backorder;
        Process_BO;
        Update_QOH;
        CLOSE backorder_cursor;
     ELSE --display message showing record not found
        MESSAGE('Record not found');
     END IF; --backorder cursor found
   END IF; --shipping found
   CLEAR_FORM;
END;
```

5 Compile the trigger, correct any syntax errors, and then click the **Close** button on the PL/SQL Editor button bar.

HELP? If you get the error message that one of your program units is "not declared in this scope" (such as "PROCESS_BO not declared in this scope"), it means that the program unit either has not been created or has not been successfully compiled. Confirm that the specified program unit exists and has been successfully compiled.

Finally, you will create the triggers for the Cancel and Exit buttons.

To create the Cancel and Exit buttons:

1 Create a WHEN-BUTTON-PRESSED trigger for the Cancel button with the following code: **CLEAR_FORM;**.

2 Create a WHEN-BUTTON-PRESSED trigger for the Exit button with the following code: **EXIT_FORM;**.

3 Save the form.

Testing the RECEIVING_FORM

To test the RECEIVING_FORM and confirm that it works correctly, you need to examine all possible cases:

1. The selected shipment is from the SHIPPING table, and there is no backorder.
2. The selected shipment is from the BACKORDER table, and there is no new backorder.
3. The selected shipment is from the SHIPPING table, and there is a new backorder.
4. The selected shipment is from the BACKORDER table, and there is another backorder.

You will test the first case next. You will record receipt of Shipment ID 212 (3-Season Tent, Color Forest, and Quantity 25) from the SHIPPING table, and assume that all 25 tents were received.

To test the first case in the RECEIVING_FORM:

1 Run the form.

2 Click the **Shipment ID LOV** button, click **212**, and then click the **OK** button.

3 Type 25 in the Quantity Received field.

4 Click the **Update** button. An error message appears at the bottom of the screen, as shown in Figure 6-19.

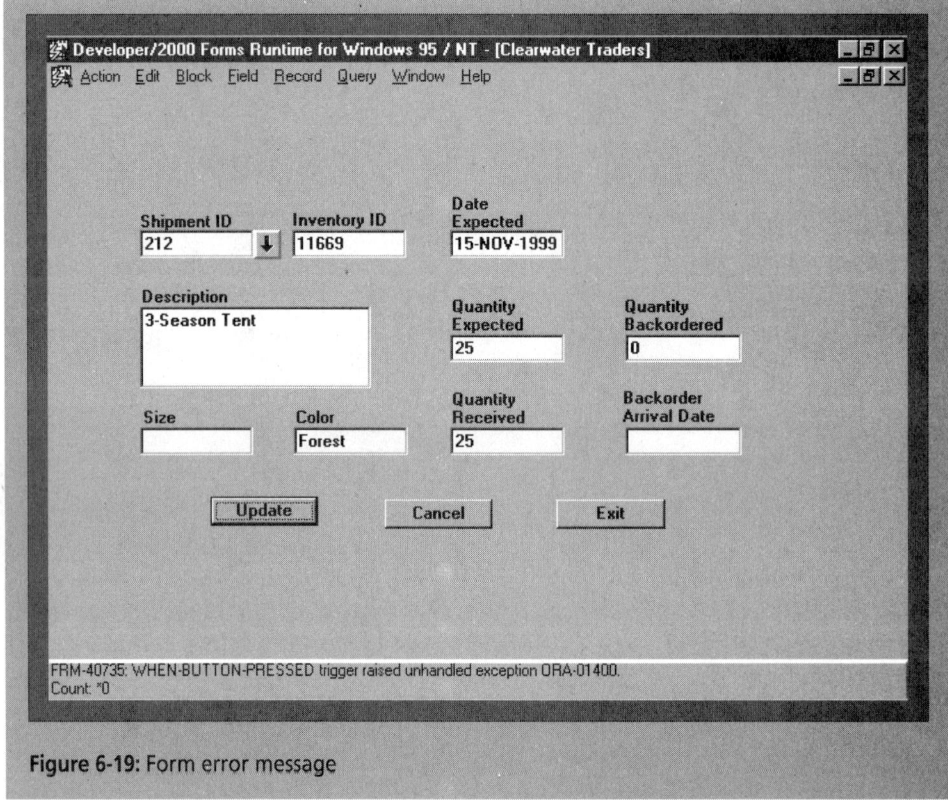

Figure 6-19: Form error message

This is a good time to review how to interpret error codes and learn how to use the Oracle Debugger.

Using the Oracle Debugger to Find Errors

The first step in correcting an error is to find out what the FRM- and ORA- error codes mean.

To find the description of the error message:

1. Close the Forms Runtime application.
2. Click the **Start** button on the taskbar, click **Programs,** point to **Oracle for Windows 95** (or **Windows NT**), and then click **Oracle7 Error Messages.**

3 Click the **Index** tab, type **ORA-01400** in the first text box, and then click the **Display** button to see the error explanation shown in Figure 6-20. The ORA-01400 message indicates that you did not specify a value for a column that cannot be NULL. Close the Oracle Messages and Codes window. Now you will use the Oracle Debugger to locate where the error is occurring.

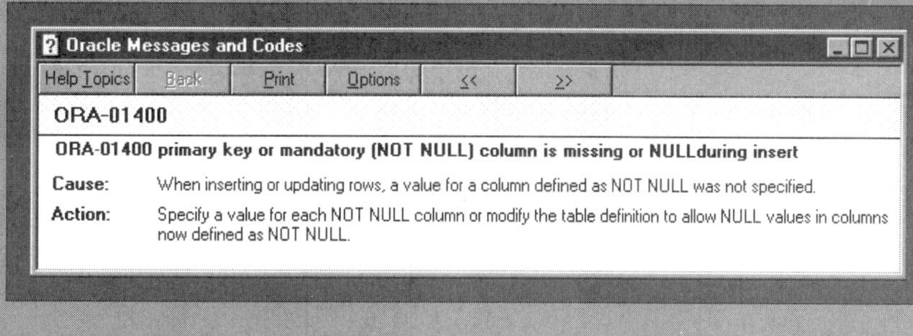

Figure 6-20: Error explanation

The Oracle Debugger allows you to step through triggers and other PL/SQL programs one line at a time to examine the values of variables during execution. To use the Oracle Debugger, you must change to Debug mode and then run your form and specify **breakpoints** that temporarily halt execution so you can single-step through specific program lines to examine program flow and variable values.

To use the Oracle Debugger:

1 Open the Object Navigator window, and then click the **Debug Mode** button on the Object Navigator toolbar. The button changes to indicate that you are in Debug mode.

HELP? You also can click Tools on the menu bar, and then click Debug Mode to turn Debug mode on and off.

2 Run the form.

3 Maximize the Debugger window so it looks like Figure 6-21. The Debugger window has a toolbar with buttons that perform debugger commands, a Source code pane to show the code you are debugging, a Navigator pane similar to the Object Navigator that allows you to navigate among form and database objects, and a command line interpreter for entering command-line debugger commands.

You can maximize the Debugger window by double-clicking the title bar.

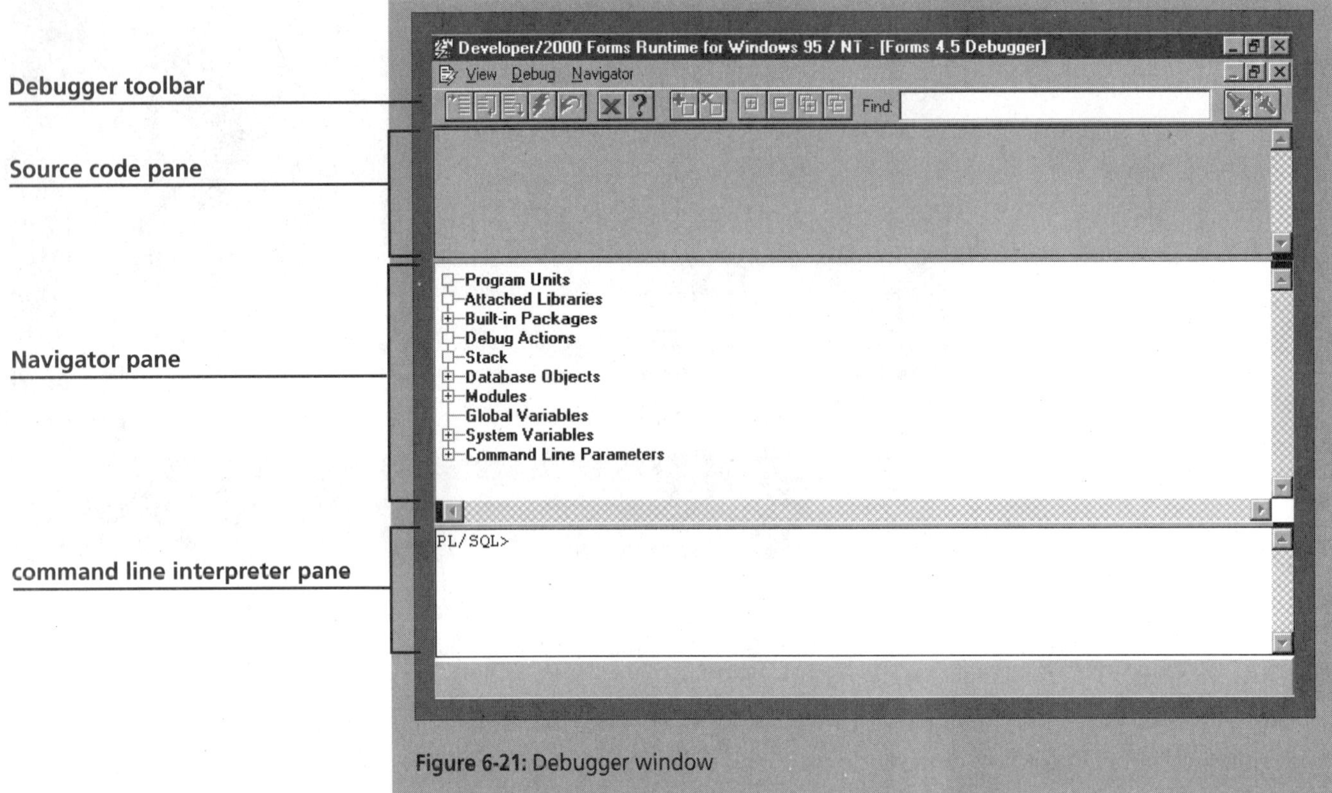

Figure 6-21: Debugger window

Setting Breakpoints

The first step in using the Oracle Debugger is to set breakpoints to halt program execution. The Navigator pane lists the system objects that you might want to access while you are debugging. An object with a plus box to the left of its name indicates that the specific object might exist in the code you currently are running. You will first open the Modules object, which lists the forms and form objects in your current application.

To open the Modules object:

1 Click the **Modules plus box** ⊞ in the Navigator pane, and then open the following objects: **RECEIVING_FORM**, **Blocks**, **RECEIVING_BLOCK**, **Items**, **UPDATE_BUTTON**, **Triggers**, and **WHEN-BUTTON-PRESSED**. The source code for the UPDATE_BUTTON trigger appears in the Source code pane. Next you need to enlarge your Source code and Navigator panes. You will control the Oracle Debugger by clicking buttons rather than typing commands so you can close the command line interpreter pane.

2 Move the pointer over the line between the Navigator and command line interpreter panes so the pointer changes to ↕. Click and drag down so the command line interpreter pane is no longer visible.

3 Move the pointer over the line between the Source code and Navigator panes so the pointer changes to ↕. Click and drag down so each pane occupies about one-half of the screen, as shown in Figure 6-22. Next you will set a breakpoint at the beginning of this trigger so you can single-step through it and examine how the program (and the Oracle Debugger) works.

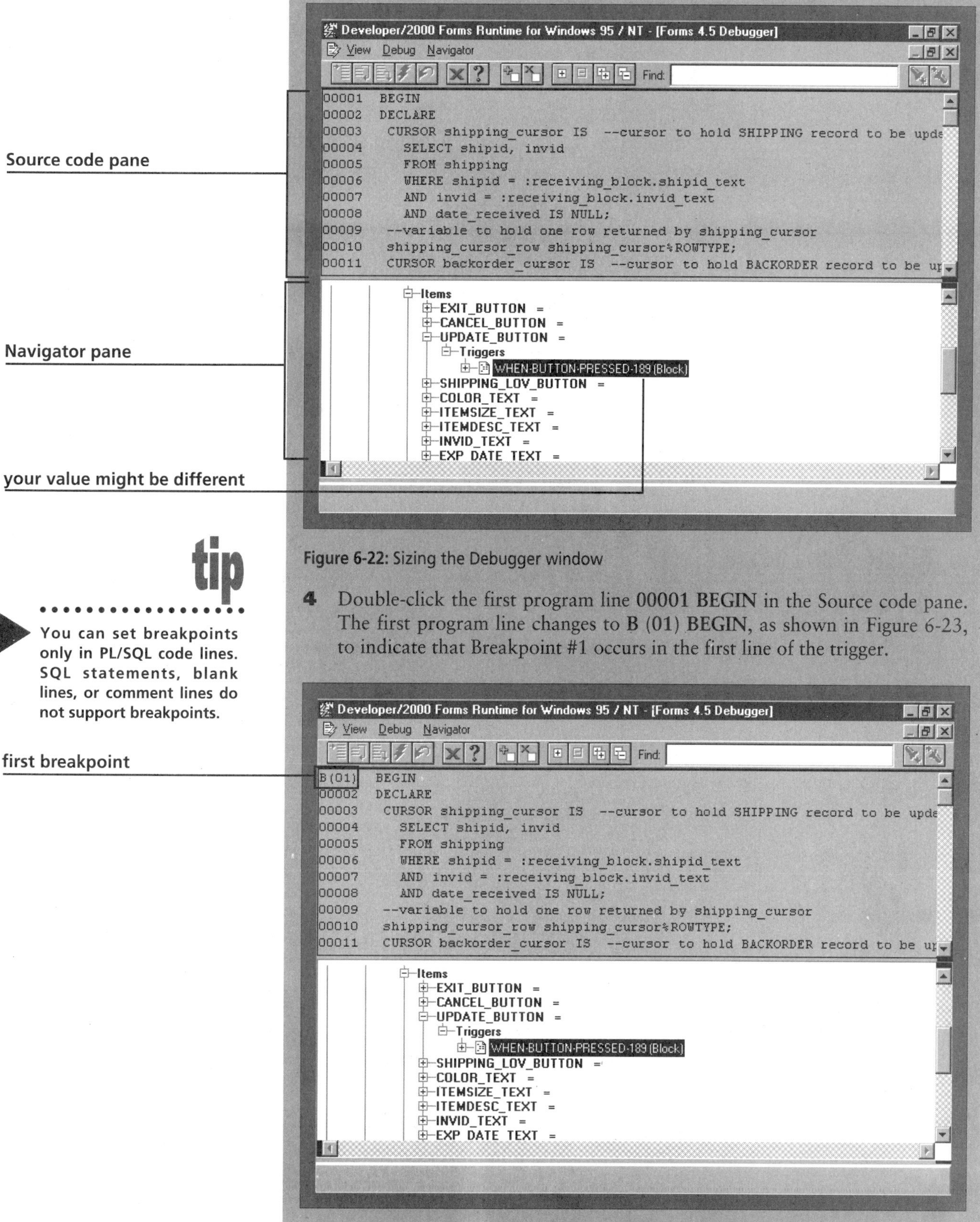

Figure 6-22: Sizing the Debugger window

tip

You can set breakpoints only in PL/SQL code lines. SQL statements, blank lines, or comment lines do not support breakpoints.

4 Double-click the first program line 00001 BEGIN in the Source code pane. The first program line changes to B (01) BEGIN, as shown in Figure 6-23, to indicate that Breakpoint #1 occurs in the first line of the trigger.

Figure 6-23: Creating a breakpoint

5 Close the Debugger window by clicking the **Close** button [X] on the Debugger toolbar. The Debugger window closes, and your form appears in Forms Runtime.

Monitoring Program Execution and Variable Values

Now you will select the shipment ID, enter the quantity received, and click the Update button. As the trigger runs, you will be able to single-step through each source code line to see how the program executes, and you will be able to examine the values of form variables at specific times during execution.

To monitor the program execution:

1 Click the **Shipment ID LOV** button, click **212**, and then click the **OK** button.

2 Type **25** in the Quantity Received field, and then click the **Update** button. The Debugger window opens, as shown in Figure 6-24.

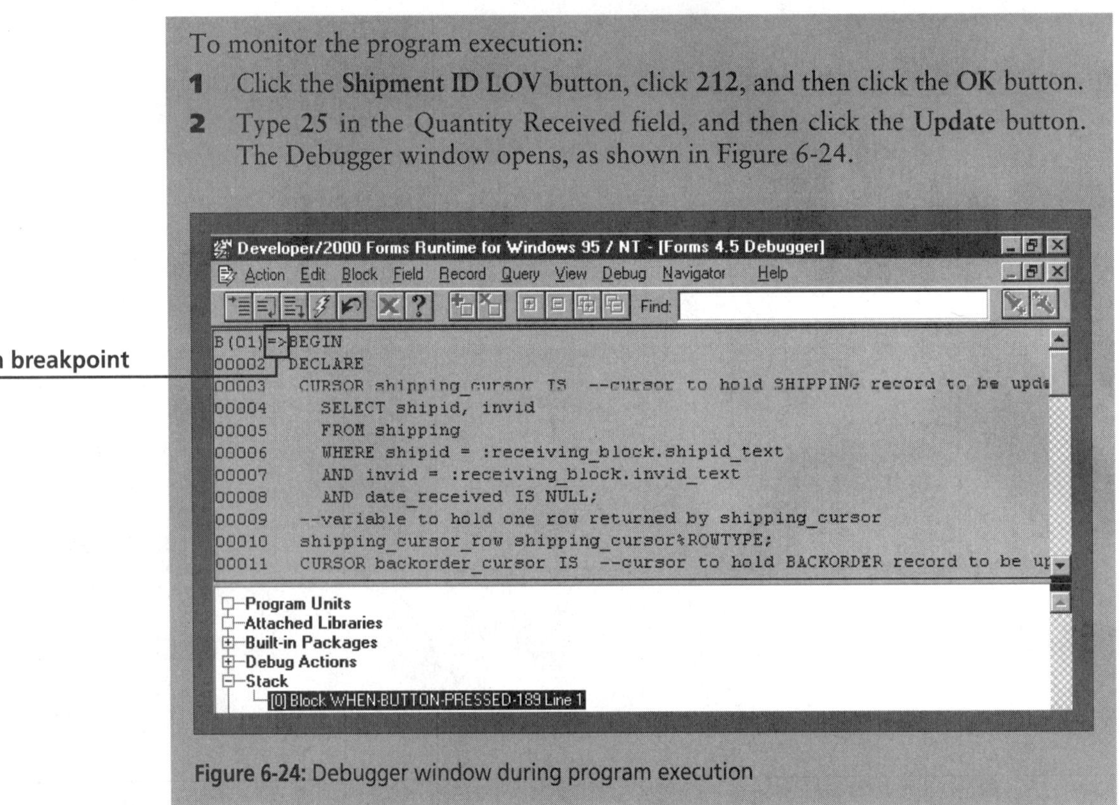

Figure 6-24: Debugger window during program execution

Notice the debugger command buttons that are active on the toolbar. The **Step Into** button allows you to step through the program one line at a time. The **Step Over** button allows you to bypass a call to a program unit. The **Step Out** button executes all program lines to the end of the current trigger. The **Go** button allows you to pass over the current breakpoint and run the program until the next breakpoint is called or the program is terminated. The **Reset** button terminates execution and returns the form to the point before you clicked the Update button and started the current trigger.

Also notice the position of the execution arrow on the first line of the trigger. The **execution arrow** shows what line of the procedure the Oracle Debugger will execute next. As you step through the program, the execution arrow stops on PL/SQL statements and skips comment lines and SQL statements.

Finally, notice the objects displayed in the Navigator pane. You can open these objects during program execution to examine the current values of program variables. The three most common object types that you will examine are Stack, Modules, and Global Variables. The **Stack** object contains **stack variables**, which are the variables that are initialized in the DECLARE statements of individual triggers and procedures. Stack variables sometimes are called **local variables** because only the procedure or trigger where they are declared uses them. **Modules** allow you to select a specific block and then examine the current values of block items in the form (such as SHIPID_TEXT and INVID_TEXT). **Global Variables** display current values for global variable values.

To single-step through the trigger:

1. Click the **Step Into** button on the Debugger toolbar again. The execution arrow stops on the first variable declaration (CURSOR shipping_cursor IS).
2. Click again. The execution arrow stops on the next variable declaration (shipping_cursor_row).
3. Click again, and then scroll down in the Source code pane if necessary so you can see the line on which the execution stopped.
4. Continue clicking until you have stepped through the DECLARE section and the execution arrow is in the BEGIN section and on line 00021, as shown in Figure 6-25.

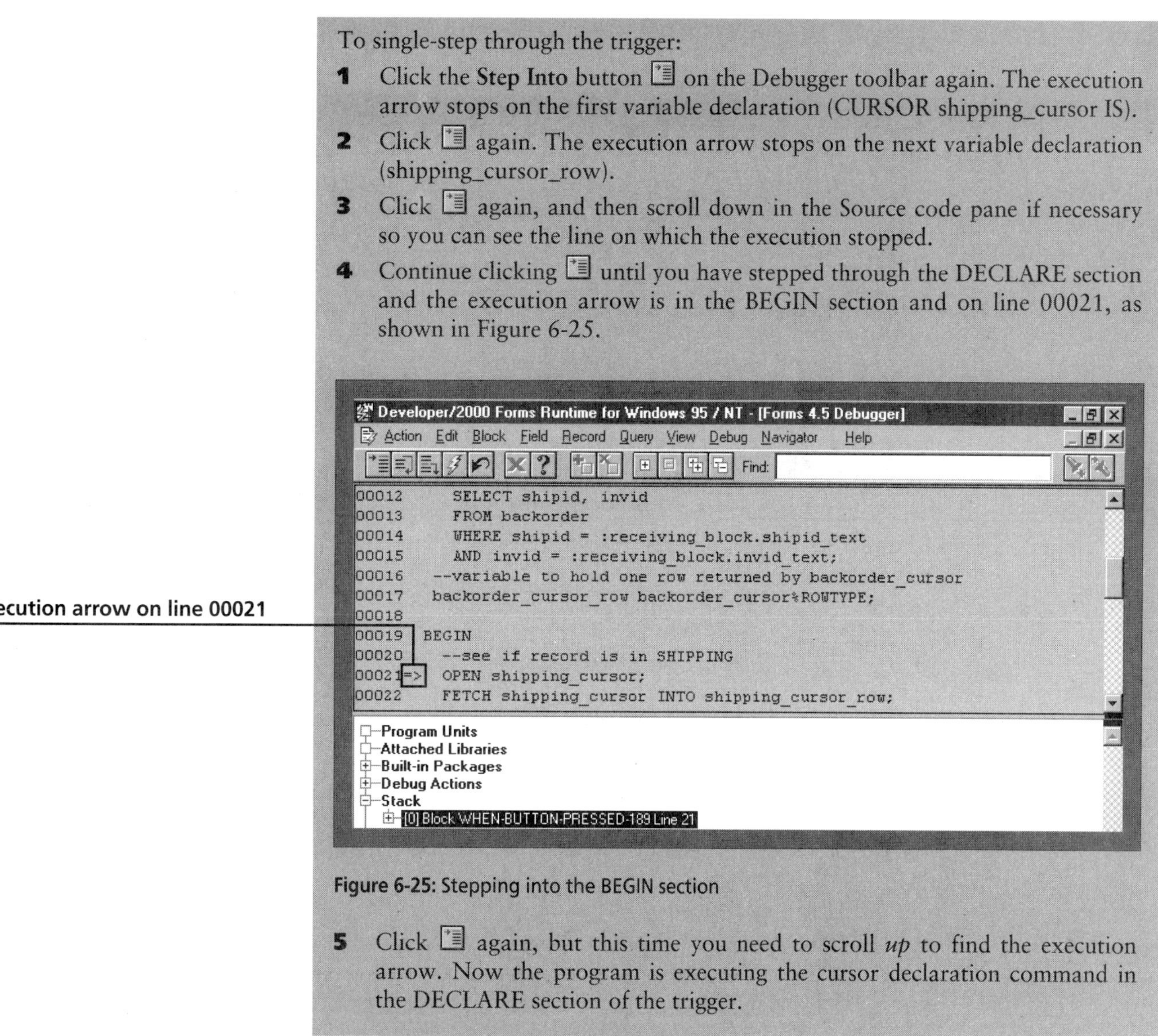

Figure 6-25: Stepping into the BEGIN section

5. Click again, but this time you need to scroll *up* to find the execution arrow. Now the program is executing the cursor declaration command in the DECLARE section of the trigger.

Note that in the cursor declaration, the search field for SHIPID is `:receiving_block.shipid_text`, and the search field for INVID is `:receiving_block.invid_text`. Before you open and fetch the data values, you need to check the values of these block variables so you will know if the cursor retrieves the record correctly.

To examine the values of the block variables:

1 Click the **plus boxes** [+] for **Modules**, **RECEIVING_FORM**, **Blocks**, **RECEIVING_BLOCK**, and **Items** in the Navigator pane.

2 Enlarge the Navigator pane by dragging the border between the source code and Navigator panes so you can see all of the block text items, as shown in Figure 6-26. Notice that SHIPID_TEXT is 212, and INVID_TEXT is 11669. These are the values that you selected when you ran the form and the values that will be used in the search statements of the cursor query. Notice that QUANT_REC_TEXT is 25, which is the value you entered before you clicked the Update button.

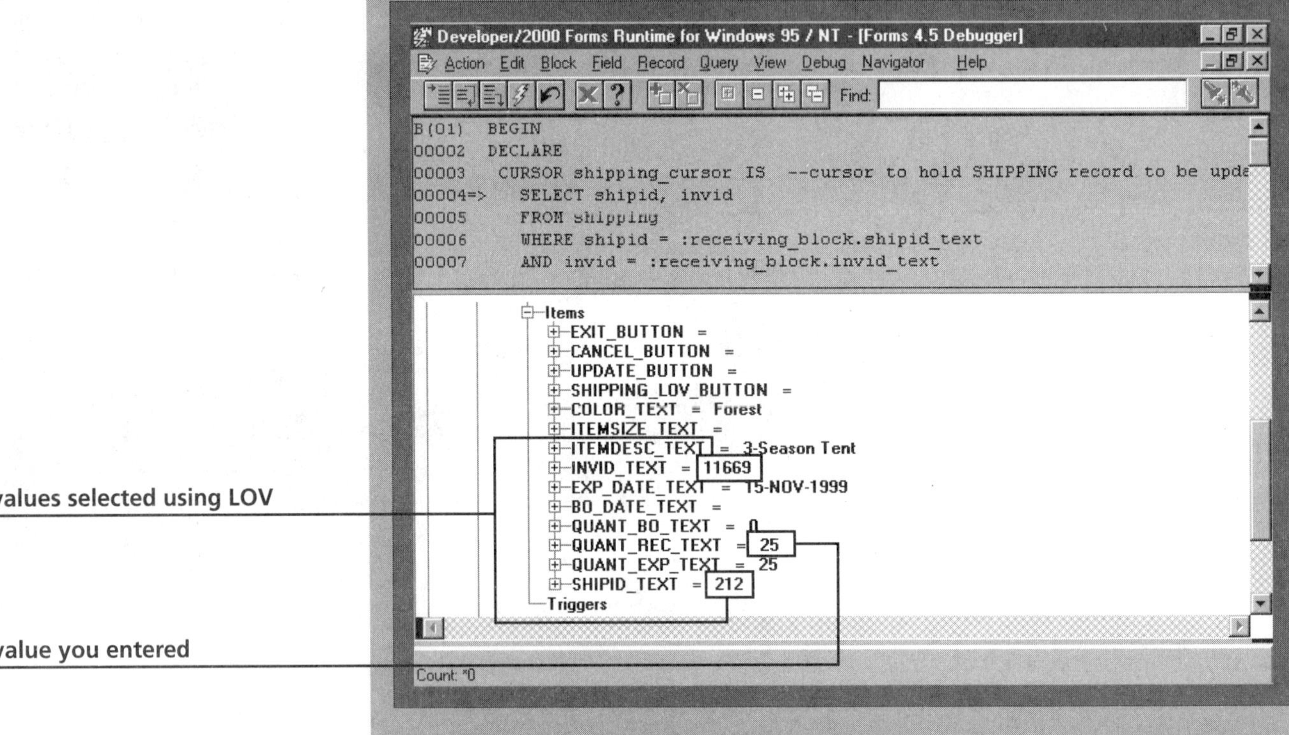

Figure 6-26: Displaying block variable values

Next you will continue to step through the trigger, fetch the row values into the cursor row variable, and then see exactly which values have been fetched by the cursor SELECT statement. Cursors are declared in the DECLARE section of the trigger, so cursor row values are local variables, and their values are found under the Stack object.

To examine the data values returned by the cursor:

1 Click the **Step Into** button on the Debugger toolbar, and then scroll down if necessary. The execution arrow appears on the FETCH shipping_cursor INTO shipping_cursor_row command (line 00022).

2 Click again, and then scroll down if necessary. The execution arrow appears on line 00023 (IF shipping_cursor%FOUND THEN).

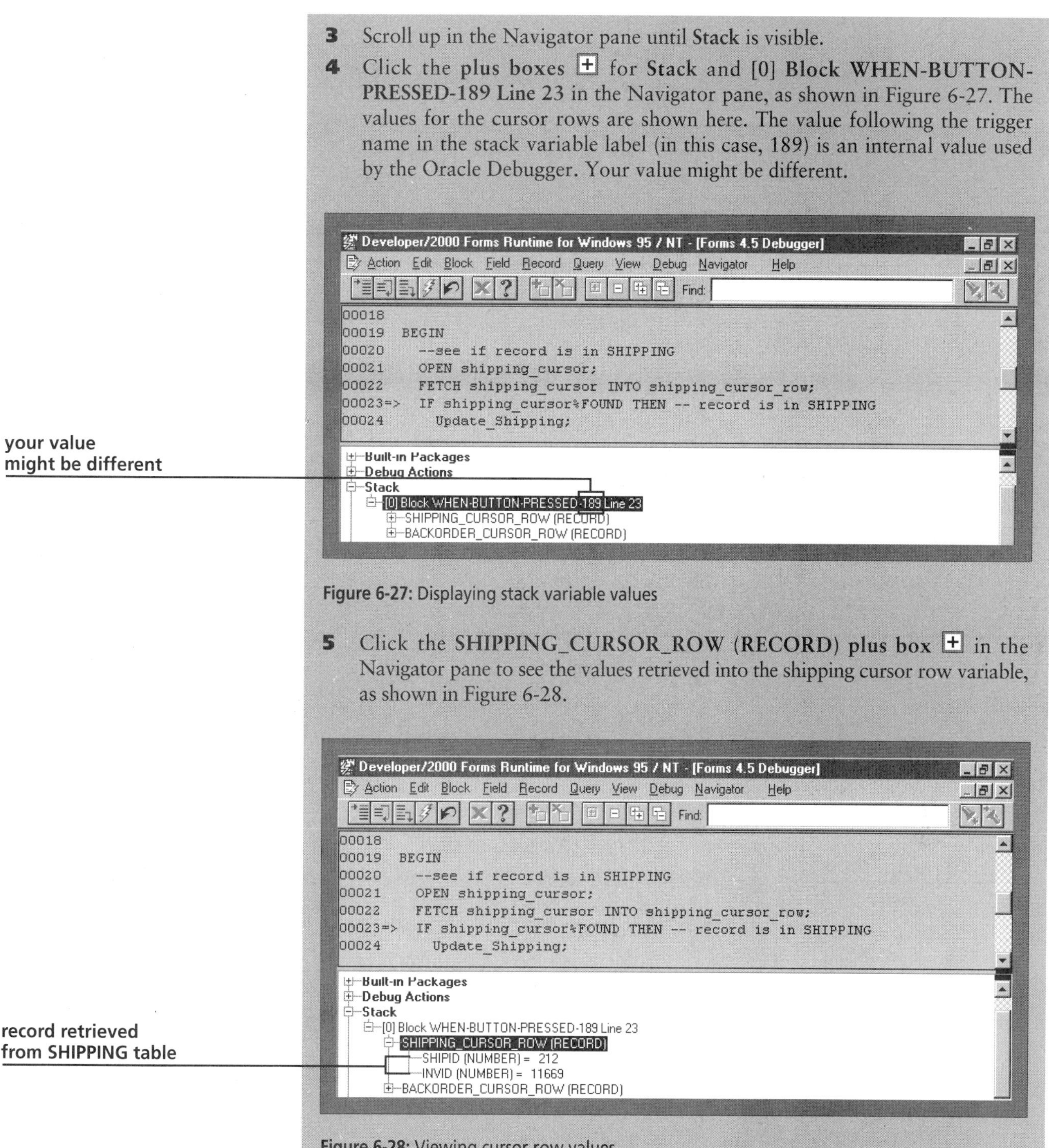

3 Scroll up in the Navigator pane until **Stack** is visible.

4 Click the **plus boxes** ⊞ for **Stack** and **[0] Block WHEN-BUTTON-PRESSED-189 Line 23** in the Navigator pane, as shown in Figure 6-27. The values for the cursor rows are shown here. The value following the trigger name in the stack variable label (in this case, 189) is an internal value used by the Oracle Debugger. Your value might be different.

Figure 6-27: Displaying stack variable values

5 Click the **SHIPPING_CURSOR_ROW (RECORD) plus box** ⊞ in the Navigator pane to see the values retrieved into the shipping cursor row variable, as shown in Figure 6-28.

Figure 6-28: Viewing cursor row values

This confirms that the cursor selected the record from the SHIPPING table successfully, so the next step is to update the record and step through the program to see if the update works correctly.

To check if the SHIPPING record is updated correctly:

1. Click the **Step Into** button on the Debugger toolbar, and then scroll down if necessary to see the execution arrow, which is on the program line that calls the UPDATE_SHIPPING program unit.
2. Click again. The execution arrow is now on the first line of the UPDATE_SHIPPING program unit.
3. Click again. The execution arrow is on line 00004, where the variable today will be set to SYSDATE.
4. Click again. The execution arrow cannot stop on SQL commands, so it skips over the UPDATE command and goes back to the BEGIN statement. At this point, you should check the values of the block and stack variables that are used in the UPDATE command.
5. Click the **Procedure Body UPDATE_SHIPPING plus box** in the Navigator pane. The value for the TODAY variable should be the current date, as shown in Figure 6-29.

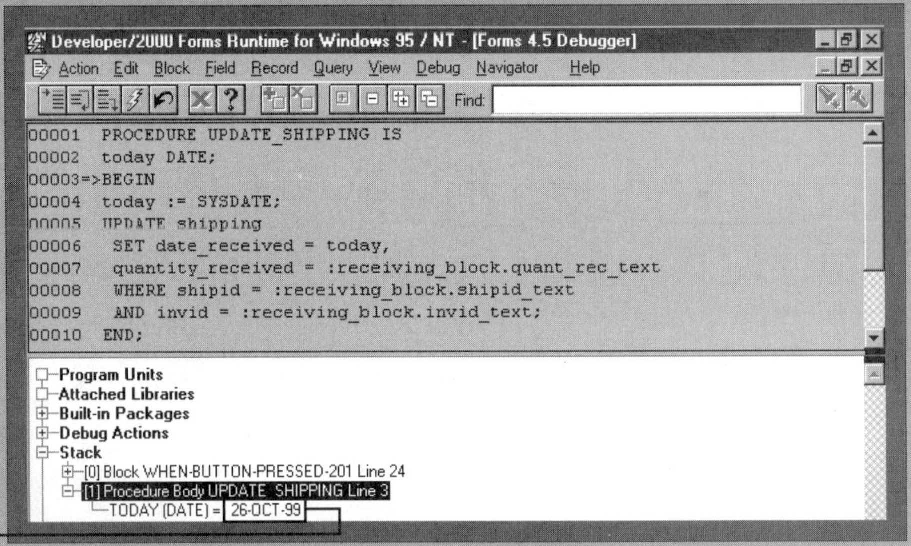

Developer/2000 Forms Runtime for Windows 95 / NT - [Forms 4.5 Debugger]

Action Edit Block Field Record Query View Debug Navigator Help

```
00001  PROCEDURE UPDATE_SHIPPING IS
00002  today DATE;
00003=>BEGIN
00004  today := SYSDATE;
00005  UPDATE shipping
00006   SET date_received = today,
00007   quantity_received = :receiving_block.quant_rec_text
00008   WHERE shipid = :receiving_block.shipid_text
00009   AND invid = :receiving_block.invid_text;
00010  END;
```

- Program Units
- Attached Libraries
- Built-in Packages
- Debug Actions
- Stack
  - [0] Block WHEN-BUTTON-PRESSED-201 Line 24
  - [1] Procedure Body UPDATE_SHIPPING Line 3
    - TODAY (DATE) = 26-OCT-99

today's date appears here

Figure 6-29: Viewing the value of the stack variable for TODAY

6. Click the **Stack minus box** to close it.
7. If necessary open **Modules**, **RECEIVING_FORM**, Blocks, **RECEIVING_BLOCK**, and **Items**. Note the values of the block variables that will be used in the UPDATE command, as shown in Figure 6-30. These variables all look okay, so the UPDATE command should run correctly.

variables to be used in the UPDATE command

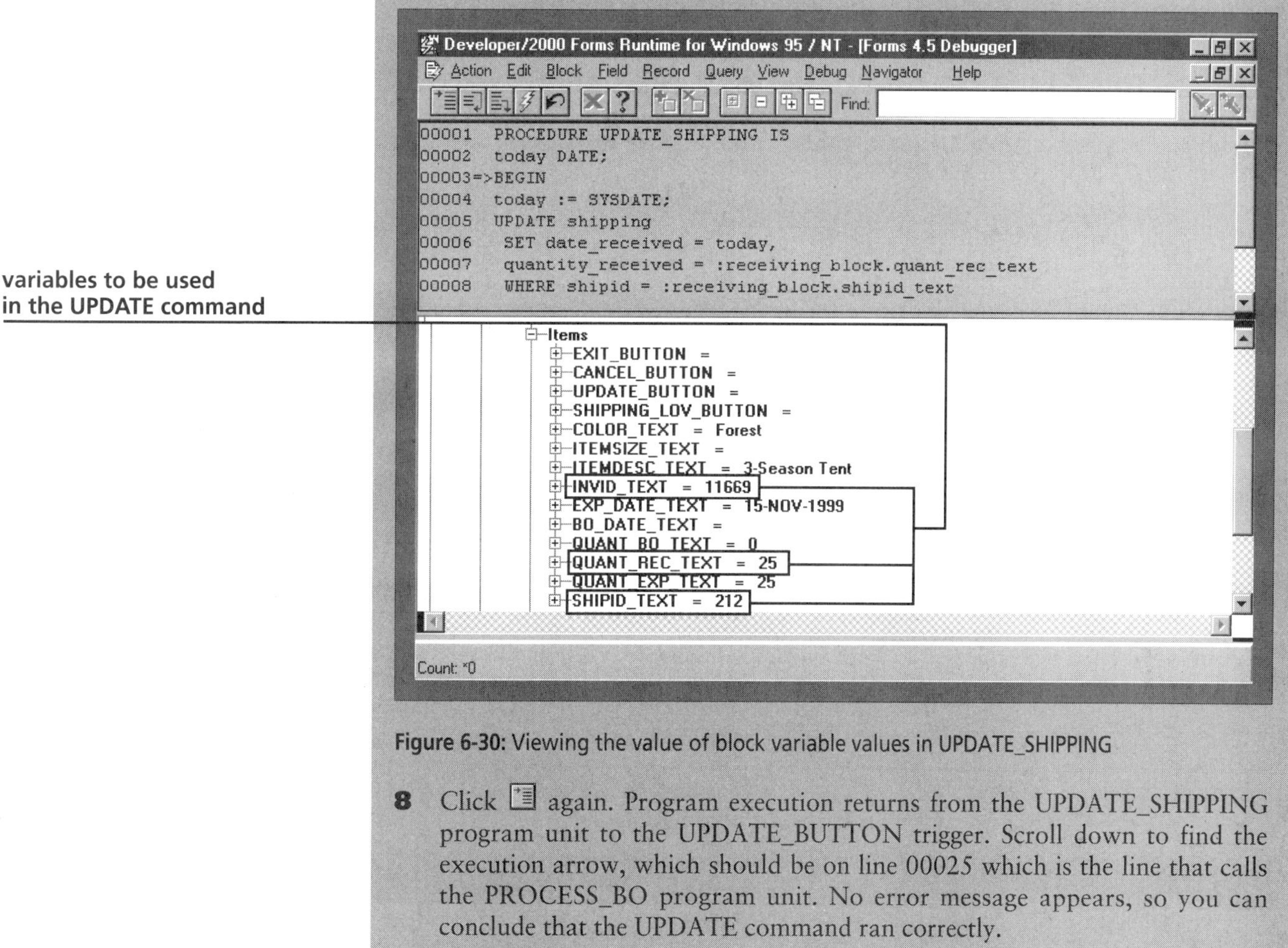

Figure 6-30: Viewing the value of block variable values in UPDATE_SHIPPING

8 Click [icon] again. Program execution returns from the UPDATE_SHIPPING program unit to the UPDATE_BUTTON trigger. Scroll down to find the execution arrow, which should be on line 00025 which is the line that calls the PROCESS_BO program unit. No error message appears, so you can conclude that the UPDATE command ran correctly.

No error occurred in the UPDATE_SHIPPING program unit, so you know that the error is in one of the other parts of the code. Next you will step through the PROCESS_BO program unit that processes potential backorders. Your test case does not involve a backorder, so no new backorder record should be inserted.

To step through the PROCESS_BO program unit:

1 Click the **Step Into** button [icon] on the Debugger toolbar. The execution arrow appears on the first line of the PROCESS_BO program unit.

2 Click [icon] again. The execution arrow is on line 00003, which determines if there is a backorder or not. Before you step into the INSERT command, you need to examine all of the block variable values included in the INSERT command.

3 In the Navigator pane, view **Modules**, **RECEIVING_FORM**, **Blocks**, **RECEIVING_BLOCK**, and **Items**. Scroll and resize the pane so it looks like Figure 6-31, and note the value of QUANT_BO_TEXT is 0, which it should be. But the source code says that if QUANT_BO_TEXT equals zero, then a new backorder record should be created. That doesn't make sense—you should create a new backorder record only if QUANT_BO_TEXT is greater than zero. Note the values that will be used in the INSERT command; the value for BO_DATE_TEXT is NULL. This could be the error.

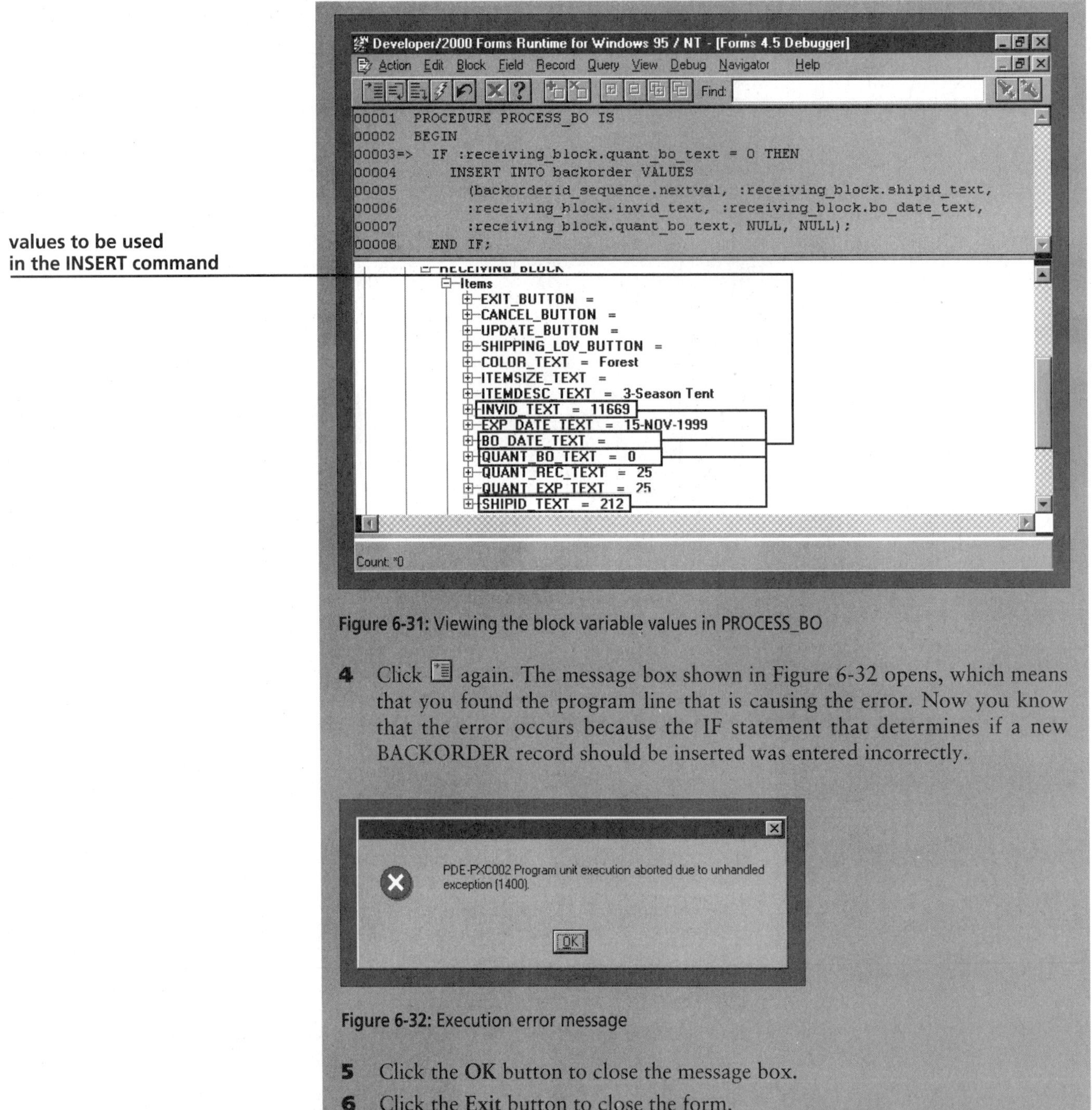

Figure 6-31: Viewing the block variable values in PROCESS_BO

4 Click [icon] again. The message box shown in Figure 6-32 opens, which means that you found the program line that is causing the error. Now you know that the error occurs because the IF statement that determines if a new BACKORDER record should be inserted was entered incorrectly.

Figure 6-32: Execution error message

5 Click the **OK** button to close the message box.

6 Click the **Exit** button to close the form.

Now that you have used the Oracle Debugger to locate the program line that is causing the error, you need to fix it. Next you will return to the Forms Designer and correct the PROCESS_BO program unit code.

To correct the program unit code:

1 If necessary, click the **Developer/2000 Forms Designer** command button on the taskbar to activate the program window.

2 If necessary, open the Object Navigator window in Ownership View, open **Program Units**, and then double click the **program unit** icon beside the PROCESS_BO program unit. A new backorder record should be inserted only if the user enters a value for QUANT_BO_TEXT.

3 Change the program line IF :receiving_block.quant_bo_text = 0 THEN to **IF :receiving_block.quant_bo_text > 0 THEN.**

4 Compile the program unit, correct any syntax errors, and then close the PL/SQL Editor.

5 Save the form.

Now you need to test the form again to see if this change corrects the error.

To test the form again:

1 Click the **Debug Mode** button on the Object Navigator toolbar to turn off Debug mode.

2 Run the form.

3 Click the **Shipping ID LOV** button, select Shipment ID **212** and Inventory ID **11669**, and then click the OK button.

4 Type 25 in the Quantity Received field, and then click the **Update** button. The "No changes to save" confirmation message appears, which seems to confirm that an update to the SHIPPING table with no backorder works correctly. Before you can be totally confident that this operation worked correctly, you should double-check the values in the SHIPPING and INVENTORY tables. You will do that next in SQL*Plus.

HELP? If an error message appears instead of the confirmation message, repeat the debugging exercise until you find the location of the next error. Then analyze the values of the stack and block variables at the time of the error so you can determine the cause of the error.

5 Click the **Oracle SQL*Plus** command button on the taskbar.

6 Type the query shown in Figure 6-33 to confirm that the DATE_EXPECTED and QUANTITY_EXPECTED fields were updated correctly.

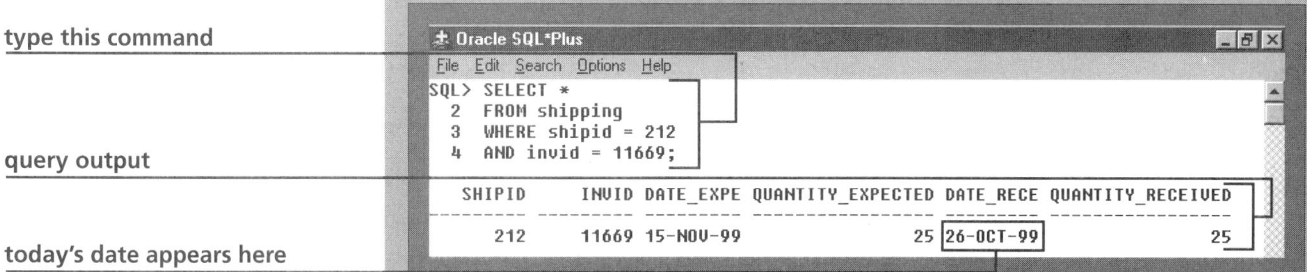

Figure 6-33: Confirming that the SHIPPING table was updated correctly

The query output confirms that DATE_RECEIVED is the current date and the QUANTITY_RECEIVED is 25. Next you need to determine if QOH was updated properly in the INVENTORY table. The original QOH for item 11669 in the INVENTORY table was 12. You just received 25 additional items, so the new QOH should be 37.

To verify that the INVENTORY table was updated correctly:

1 Type the query shown in Figure 6-34. The query output indicates that QOH was updated correctly.

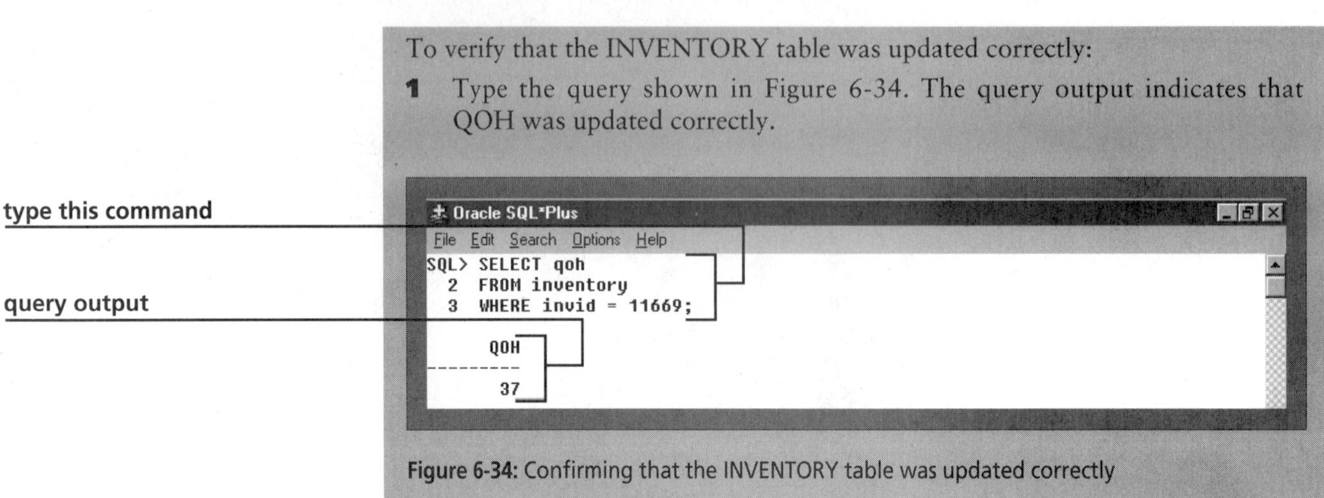

Figure 6-34: Confirming that the INVENTORY table was updated correctly

Next you need to test whether the form works correctly when a shipment with a backorder is recorded. Assume that shipment 215 was received today, and all 100 of the Women's Fleece Pullovers, color Coral, size S were received, but none of the size M were received. One hundred items with size M are backordered and expected to arrive on December 1, 1999.

To test the form when a shipment with a backorder is recorded:

1 Click the **Developer/2000 Forms Runtime** command button on the taskbar.

2 Select the size S items for shipment **215**, and then click the **OK** button. Enter that **100** items were received, and then click the **Update** button.

3 Select the size **M** items for shipment **215**. Enter that **0** items were received, and that **100** items are backordered and expected on **01-DEC-1999**, as shown in Figure 6-35.

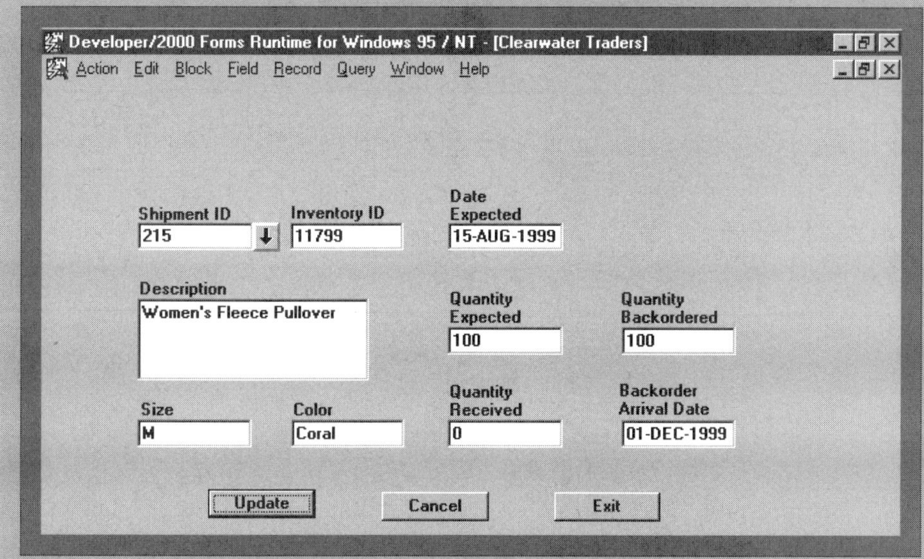

Figure 6-35: Entering a shipment with a backorder

4 Click the **Update** button. The "No changes to save" confirmation message indicates that the update works correctly. You also need to confirm that the information was stored correctly in the database.

5 Click the **Oracle SQL*Plus** program button on the taskbar.

6 Type the command shown in Figure 6-36 to check the status of the SHIPPING table. The query output confirms that the DATE_RECEIVED was updated to today's date and that QUANTITY_RECEIVED is 0.

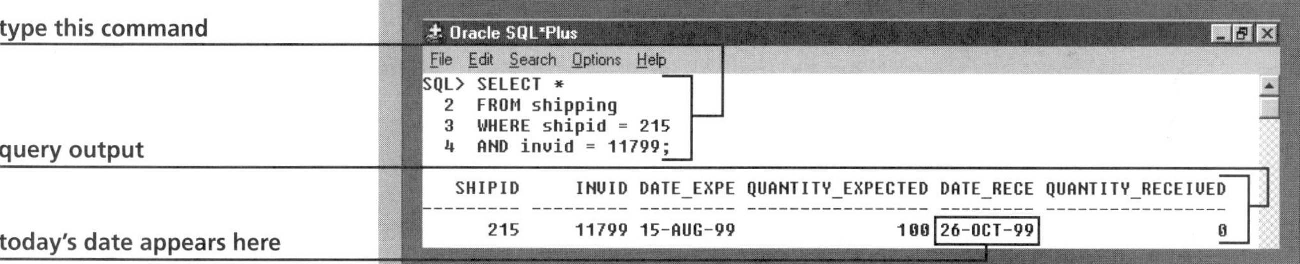

Figure 6-36: Confirming that the SHIPPING table was updated correctly

7 Type the command shown in Figure 6-37 to confirm that a new BACKORDER record was added. The query output confirms that a new BACKORDER record was created with the DATE_EXPECTED field as 01-OCT-1999 and the QUANTITY_EXPECTED equal to 100. (Your BACKORDERID value might be different depending on the current value of your sequence.)

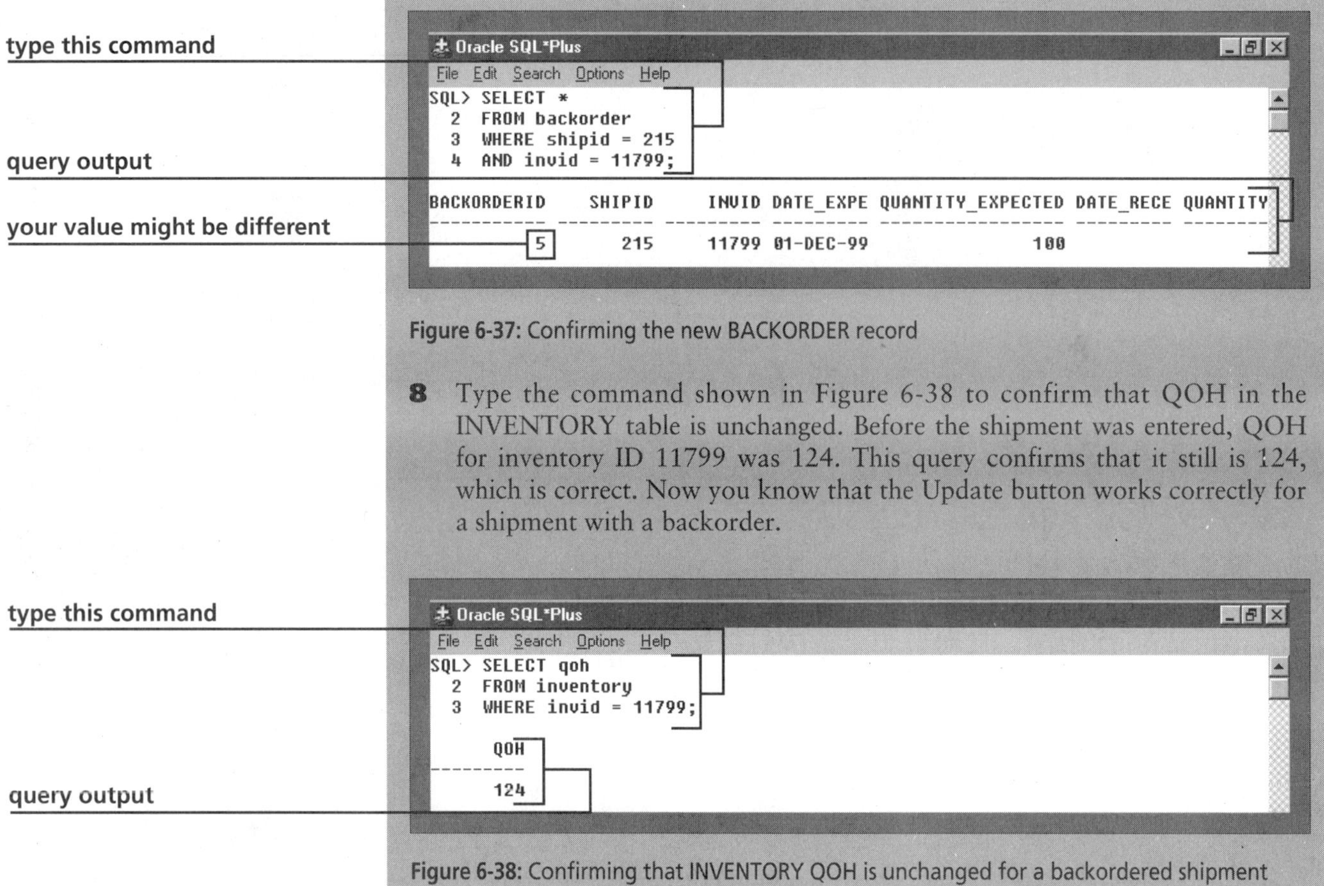

Figure 6-37: Confirming the new BACKORDER record

8 Type the command shown in Figure 6-38 to confirm that QOH in the INVENTORY table is unchanged. Before the shipment was entered, QOH for inventory ID 11799 was 124. This query confirms that it still is 124, which is correct. Now you know that the Update button works correctly for a shipment with a backorder.

Figure 6-38: Confirming that INVENTORY QOH is unchanged for a backordered shipment

Your next task is to ensure that the database is updated correctly when Clearwater Traders receives a backordered shipment that does not require another backorder. You will need to enter the receiving information using the receiving form and then confirm the updates made on the BACKORDER and INVENTORY tables.

To check the updates when Clearwater Traders receives a backordered shipment with no additional backorder:

1 Click the **Developer/2000 Forms Runtime** command button on the taskbar.

2 Click the **Shipping ID LOV** button, and then select Shipment ID **215** and Inventory ID **11799**. This shipment is the one that you backordered in the previous set of steps. Click the **OK** button.

3 Type **100** in the Quantity Received field.

4 Click the **Update** button. The "No changes to save" confirmation message indicates that the change was made. Now you need to check the BACKORDER and INVENTORY tables to confirm that they were updated correctly.

5 Click the **Oracle SQL*Plus** program button on the taskbar.

6 Type the command shown in Figure 6-39. The query output shows that the DATE_RECEIVED is today's date and the QUANTITY_RECEIVED is 100 items.

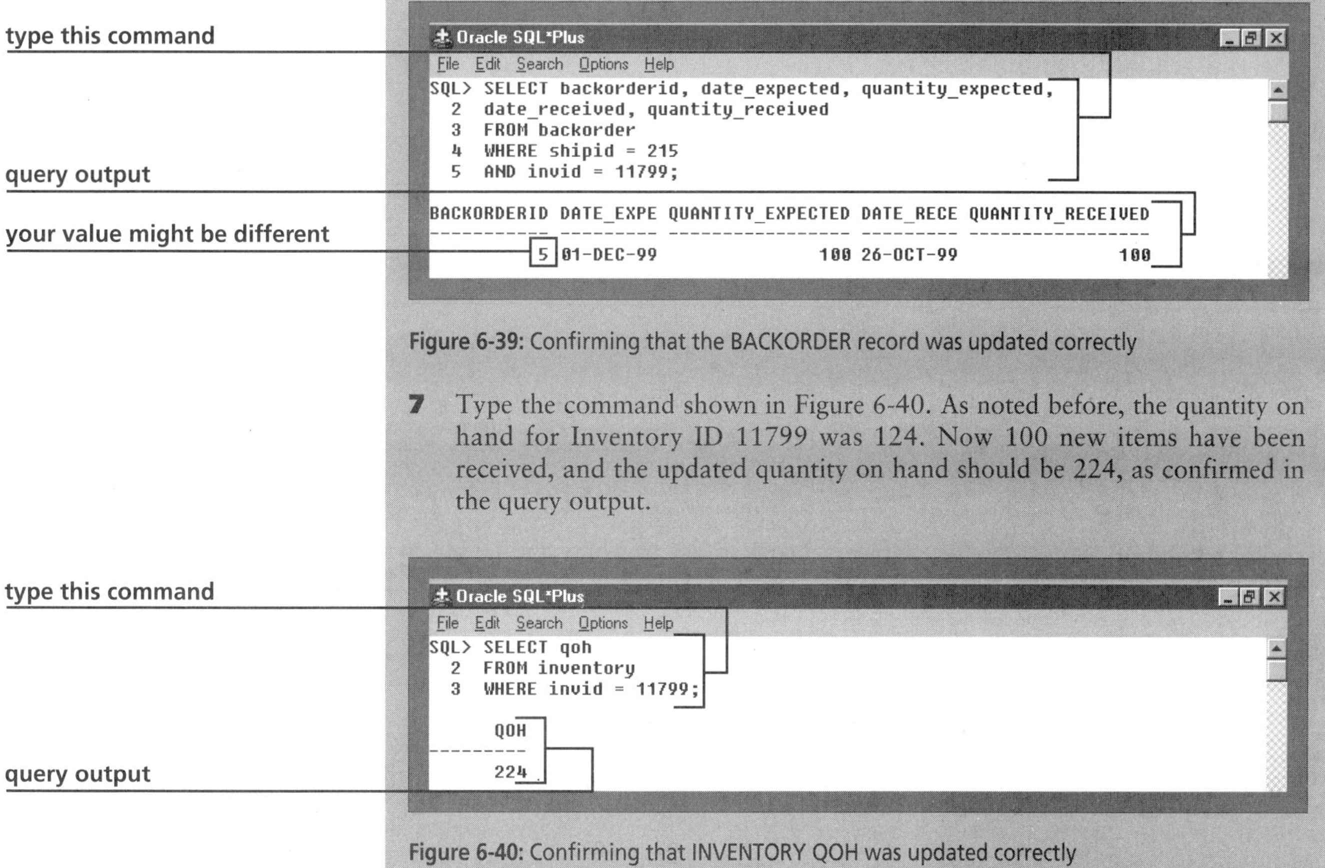

Figure 6-39: Confirming that the BACKORDER record was updated correctly

7 Type the command shown in Figure 6-40. As noted before, the quantity on hand for Inventory ID 11799 was 124. Now 100 new items have been received, and the updated quantity on hand should be 224, as confirmed in the query output.

Figure 6-40: Confirming that INVENTORY QOH was updated correctly

The last test case is when Clearwater Traders receives a backordered shipment that is backordered again. A notification for shipment 213 for 200 pairs of Women's Hiking Shorts, color Khaki, size L is received stating that all 200 pairs are backordered with an expected shipment date of 15-NOV-1999. Then, a few days later, you receive another notification about the shipment stating the expected shipment date will be 15-DEC-1999. You will create the first backorder record, and then you will update it with the second backorder notification.

To check whether the update is correct for a backordered record that is backordered again:

1 Click the **Developer/2000 Forms Runtime** command button on the taskbar.

2 Click the **Shipment ID LOV** button, and then select Shipment ID **213** and Inventory ID **11777**. Click the **OK** button.

3 Enter 0 for Quantity Received, **200** for Quantity Backordered, and **15-NOV-1999** for Backorder Arrival Date, and then click the **Update** button. Now enter the record for the second backorder notification with the later shipment date.

4 Click the **Shipment ID LOV** button, select the same shipment record again (Shipment ID **213** and Inventory ID **11777**), and then click the **OK** button.

5 Enter 0 for Quantity Received, **200** for Quantity Backordered, and **15-DEC-1999** for Backorder Arrival Date, and then click the **Update** button.

Next you need to use SQL*Plus to check how the records were updated in the BACKORDER table, and confirm that QOH was not updated.

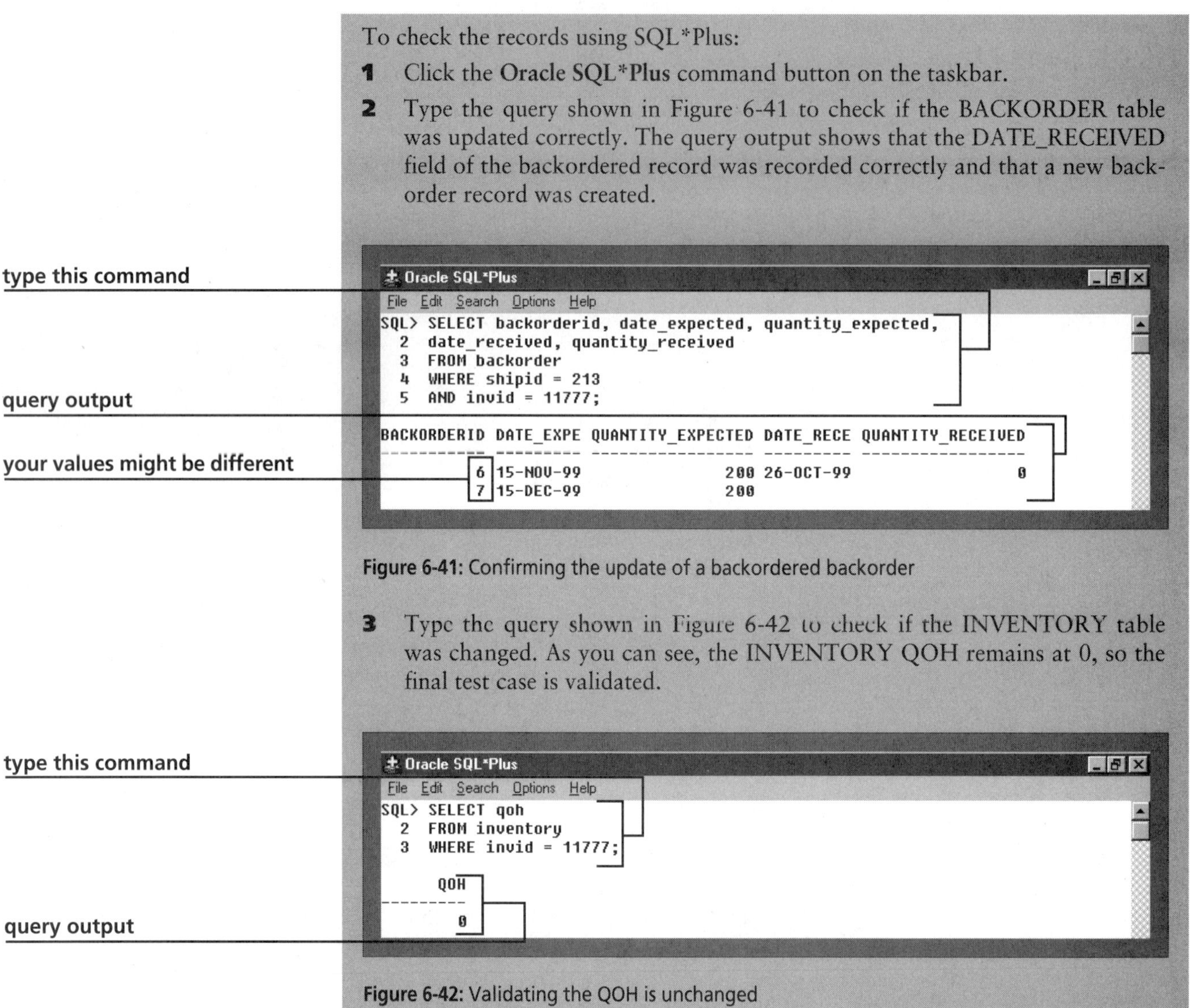

To check the records using SQL*Plus:

1. Click the **Oracle SQL*Plus** command button on the taskbar.
2. Type the query shown in Figure 6-41 to check if the BACKORDER table was updated correctly. The query output shows that the DATE_RECEIVED field of the backordered record was recorded correctly and that a new back-order record was created.

Figure 6-41: Confirming the update of a backordered backorder

3. Type the query shown in Figure 6-42 to check if the INVENTORY table was changed. As you can see, the INVENTORY QOH remains at 0, so the final test case is validated.

Figure 6-42: Validating the QOH is unchanged

Finally, you need to test the Cancel and Exit buttons.

To test the Cancel and Exit buttons:

1. Click the **Developer/2000 Forms Runtime** command button on the taskbar.
2. Click the **Shipment ID LOV** button, select any Shipment ID, and then click the **OK** button.
3. Click the **Cancel** button. The form fields should clear.
4. Click the **Exit** button to close the Forms Runtime application.

Finalizing the RECEIVING_FORM

The first step in finalizing the RECEIVING_FORM is to format it so it looks like a finished application. To do this, you need to complete the following tasks.

To format the form:

1. Change the window title to **Clearwater Traders.**
2. Create a text title label **Receiving Form,** and then change the font to **18-point bold Arial.**
3. Change the canvas background color to **light gray** by drawing a background rectangle.
4. Draw a smaller rectangle to outline the form objects, and set its bevel to **Inset.**
5. Change the field labels to **8-point bold Arial** font.
6. Update the item navigation sequence so it progresses from left to right and from top to bottom.
7. Increase the RECEIVING_CANVAS size by changing Width to **640** and Height to **480.**
8. Increase the window size by changing Width to **640** and Height to **480,** so the user can maximize the form when it runs.

You learned in Chapter 5 that a successful form is one that is easy to understand and use. You probably have noticed that every time you run your form, you have to maximize the Forms Runtime window and the form window. You can create a PRE-FORM trigger with commands that automatically maximize these windows.

MDI (Multiple Document Interface) is the Microsoft Windows window management system that allows programs to display an outer "parent" window (called the application window) and an inner document or dialog window.

To create the PRE-FORM trigger for maximizing the form:

1. Open the Object Navigator window in Ownership View, click **Triggers** (directly under the RECEIVING_FORM module), and then click the **Create** button on the Object Navigator toolbar.
2. Click the **PRE-FORM** event.
3. Type the folllowing code in the PL/SQL Editor to maximize the application window (which is named FORMS_MDI_WINDOW) at runtime:

```
-- maximize the runtime and forms windows
SET_WINDOW_PROPERTY (FORMS_MDI_WINDOW,
WINDOW_STATE, MAXIMIZE);
SET_WINDOW_PROPERTY ('RECEIVING_FORM_WINDOW',
WINDOW_STATE MAXIMIZE);
```

4. Compile the code, correct any syntax errors, and then close the PL/SQL Editor.
5. Run the form to confirm that both windows maximize automatically.
6. Close the Forms Runtime application.

Suppressing System Messages

By now you are familiar with the FRM- and ORA- messages that display in the message area when you execute your forms. These error messages are useful for determining what error occurred while you are running your forms. However, you need to suppress these messages and provide more explicit message descriptions for your forms' users. Next you will learn how to suppress the system-generated messages, how to generate customized messages, and how implement triggers for avoiding common user errors.

Oracle system messages are categorized by severity level and message type. Figure 6-43 (which you saw in an earlier chapter) illustrates the different types of messages. **Informative messages** provide information about what is happening and usually do not require any user action. Informative messages have low severity levels (usually 5). **Error messages** require some user action and their severity levels are higher, ranging from 15, 20, or >25. Oracle Forms determines what message severity level to display in the message area using a system variable named **:SYSTEM.MESSAGE_LEVEL**. You can set the level of this variable in a PRE-FORM trigger to control which messages display when the form is used. You will now modify a PRE FORM trigger to set the level so only the most severe messages (severity level >25) display.

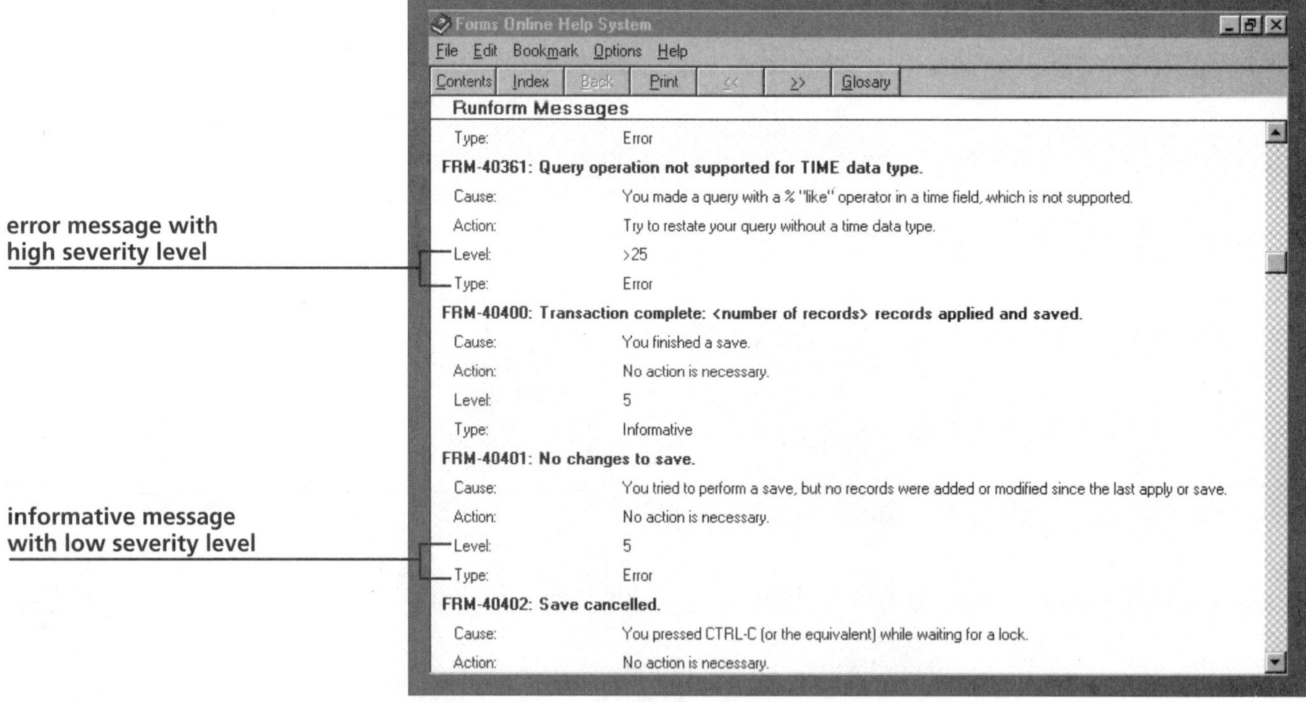

Figure 6-43: System message levels and types

To display only severe messages:

1. If necessary, open the Object Navigator window in Ownership View, and double-click the **trigger** icon next to the PRE-FORM trigger. The PL/SQL Editor opens.
2. Type the code shown in Figure 6-44 to modify the PRE-FORM trigger.

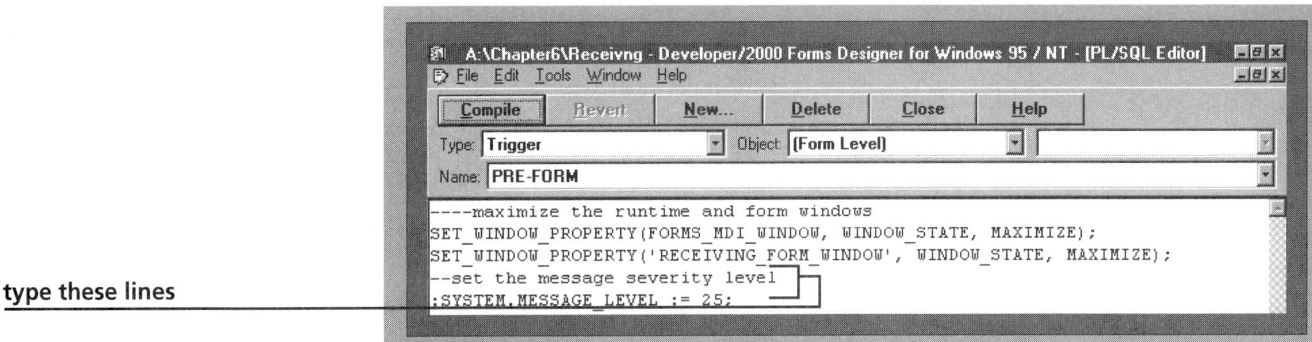

type these lines

```
----maximize the runtime and form windows
SET_WINDOW_PROPERTY(FORMS_MDI_WINDOW, WINDOW_STATE, MAXIMIZE);
SET_WINDOW_PROPERTY('RECEIVING_FORM_WINDOW', WINDOW_STATE, MAXIMIZE);
--set the message severity level
:SYSTEM.MESSAGE_LEVEL := 25;
```

Figure 6-44: Modifying the PRE-FORM trigger

3 Compile the trigger, correct any syntax errors, and then close the PL/SQL Editor. Now run a test to see the effect of this action. Assume that the shipment of 50 Men's Expedition Parkas, color Navy, size S, has arrived.

4 Run the form.

5 Select Shipment ID 218 and Inventory ID **11845**.

6 Enter 50 for Quantity Received, and then click the **Update** button. Notice that the usual confirmation message does not appear.

7 Close the Forms Runtime application.

Your form fields were cleared when you clicked the Update button, and you did not receive any confirmation message in the message area. Now you are confident that the trigger executed correctly and the new PRE-FORM trigger suppressed the confirmation message. However, you need to provide users with explicit system feedback using form messages called ALERTS.

Creating Alerts to Provide System Feedback

An important principle of graphic user interface design is to give users feedback as to what is happening and to make applications "forgiving" so users can undo unintended operations. Right now, this application does not provide any confirmation that the SHIPPING and INVENTORY update operations were successful or any opportunity for canceling the updates. An **alert** is a message box that provides information to users and allows them to choose from different options. You will create an UPDATE_ALERT to inform the user that the SHIPPING and INVENTORY tables were updated and to give the option of continuing, canceling the operation, or clicking Help to get more information. If the user chooses to continue, the user will see the CONFIRM_ALERT to confirm that the records were updated successfully. If the user chooses to cancel, the user will see the ROLLBACK_ALERT confirming that the change has been cancelled. If the user chooses Help, the user will see the HELP_ALERT, which provides suggestions for using the form. Finally, you will create an ERROR_ALERT for when the user enters a backorder quantity but forgets to enter the expected backorder receipt date.

To create the alerts:

1 Open the Object Navigator window in Ownership View.

2 Click the **Alerts** object.

3 Click the Create button on the Object Navigator toolbar to create a new alert.
4 Rename the alert to **UPDATE_ALERT**.
5 Create the following alerts: **CONFIRM_ALERT**, **ROLLBACK_ALERT**, **HELP_ALERT**, and **ERROR_ALERT**.

Setting Alert Properties

The alert properties you will use are Title, Style, Button, and Message. The Title property determines the title that appears in the alert window title bar. Style determines the icon that appears on the alert—possible styles are note, caution, and stop. Note alerts contain an "i" for information, caution alerts contain an exclamation point (!), and stop alerts contain a red "X." The Button property determines what labels will appear on the alert buttons. If you completely delete the label for a given button, the button will not display. The Message property is the text that is displayed in the alert. Figure 6-45 shows an example of an information alert with one alert button.

Figure 6-45: Example of an information alert with one button

Double-click the Alert Style property to change its style.

To change the properties of the new alerts:

1 Double-click the beside each alert to open its Properties sheet, and then change each alert's properties as follows:

Name	UPDATE_ALERT	CONFIRM_ALERT	ROLLBACK_ALERT
Title	Update Alert	Records Updated	Rollback Alert
Alert Style	Caution	Note	Note
Button 1	OK	OK	OK
Button 2	Cancel	<deleted>	<deleted>
Button 3	Help	<deleted>	<deleted>
Message	You are about to update the database records.	Records successfully updated.	Database successfully rolled back, no records updated.

Name	HELP_ALERT	ERROR_ALERT
Title	Help Alert	Error
Alert Style	Note	Stop
Button 1	OK	OK
Button 2	<deleted>	<deleted>
Button 3	<deleted>	<deleted>
Message	Be sure that you have chosen the correct inventory item and entered the correct quantity received, quantity backordered, and expected backorder receipt date.	If there is a backorder, you, MUST enter a value for expected backorder receipt date.

2 Save the form.

Showing Alerts

To display an alert on the screen, you use the SHOW_ALERT function. In programming, a function always returns a value. The SHOW_ALERT function returns a numeric value. To display an alert during the execution of a trigger, you need to declare a numeric variable and then assign this variable to the value returned by the SHOW_ALERT function. This value corresponds to the alert button that the user clicks, so you can specify different actions depending on what value is returned. The following example shows the commands used within a trigger to call and manipulate an alert:

```
DECLARE
 -- declare the variable that will be assigned to
 -- SHOW_ALERT
 alert_button number;
BEGIN
 -- show the alert
 alert_button := SHOW_ALERT ('UPDATE_ALERT');
 IF alert_button = ALERT_BUTTON1 THEN
 -- do what you need to for first button
ELSE
 IF alert_button = ALERT_BUTTON2 THEN
 -- do what you need to for second button
 ELSE
 -- do what you need to for third button
 END IF;
END IF;
END;
```

Next you will create a new program unit named DISPLAY_ALERTS that will call the SHOW_ALERT function and display the UPDATE_ALERT, which has three buttons—OK, Cancel, and Help. If the user clicks the OK button, the transaction is committed and the CONFIRM_ALERT is displayed. If the user clicks the Cancel button, the transaction is rolled back and the ROLLBACK_ALERT is displayed. If the user clicks the HELP button, the transaction is rolled back and the HELP_ALERT is displayed.

To create the program unit:

1 In the Object Navigator window, click **Program Units**, and then click the **Create** button on the Object Navigator toolbar.

2 Type **DISPLAY_ALERTS** for the new program unit name.

3 Type the code shown in Figure 6-46 in the PL/SQL Editor.

variable to hold value returned by SHOW_ALERT function
user clicked first button (OK)
user clicked second button (Cancel)
user clicked third button (Help)
type this code
A:\Chapter6\receivng - Developer/2000 Forms Designer for Windows 95 / NT - [PL/SQL Editor]
File Edit Tools Window Help
Compile Revert New... Delete Close Help
Type: Program Unit Object:
Name: DISPLAY_ALERTS (Procedure Body)
PROCEDURE DISPLAY_ALERTS IS
alert_button NUMBER;
BEGIN
alert_button := SHOW_ALERT('UPDATE_ALERT');
IF alert_button = ALERT_BUTTON1 THEN --user clicked OK, go ahead and commit
COMMIT;
alert_button := SHOW_ALERT('CONFIRM_ALERT');
CLEAR_FORM;
ELSE
IF alert_button = ALERT_BUTTON2 THEN -- user clicked Cancel, do rollback
ROLLBACK;
alert_button := SHOW_ALERT('ROLLBACK_ALERT');
GO_ITEM('quant_rec_text');
ELSE --user clicked Help, do rollback and show help alert
ROLLBACK;
alert_button := SHOW_ALERT ('HELP_ALERT');
END IF;
END IF;
END;
Not Modified
Successfully Compiled
Mod: RECEIVING_FORM File: A:\Chapter6\receivng
<Con> <Ins>

Figure 6-46: DISPLAY_ALERTS program unit code

4 Compile the DISPLAY_ALERTS program unit code, and correct any syntax errors if necessary.

Next you need to modify the UPDATE_QOH program unit so it calls the DISPLAY_ALERTS program unit instead of committing the transaction to the database.

To modify the UPDATE_QOH program unit:

1 In the PL/SQL Editor, click the **Name** list arrow to display the list of program units, and then click **UPDATE_QOH**, as shown in Figure 6-47. The UPDATE_QOH program unit code appears.

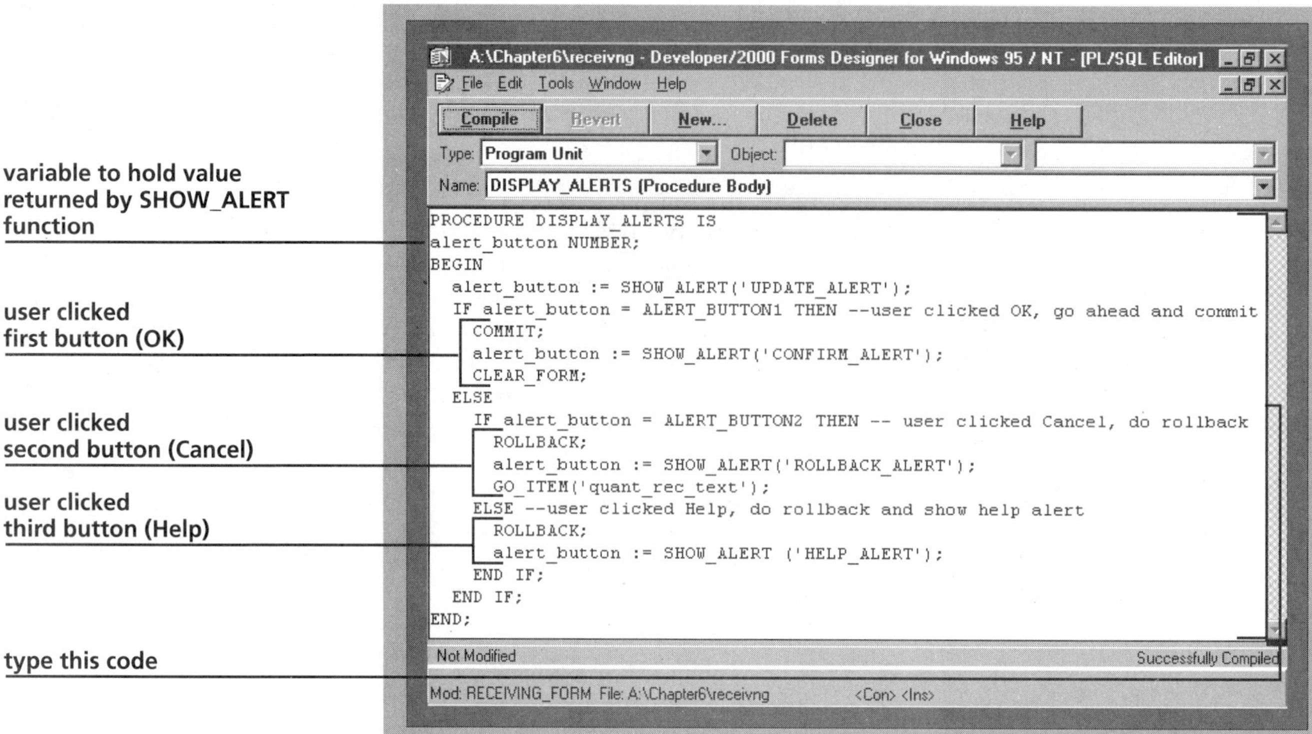

A:\Chapter6\receivng - Developer/2000 Forms Designer for Windows 95 / NT - [PL/SQL Editor]
File Edit Tools Window Help
Compile Revert New... Delete Close Help
Type: Program Unit Object:
Name: DISPLAY_ALERTS (Procedure Body)
DISPLAY_ALERTS (Procedure Body)
PROCESS_BO (Procedure Body)
UPDATE_BACKORDER (Procedure Body)
UPDATE_QOH (Procedure Body)
UPDATE_SHIPPING (Procedure Body)
IF alert_button = ALERT_BUTTON1 THEN --user clicked OK, go ahead and commit
COMMIT;

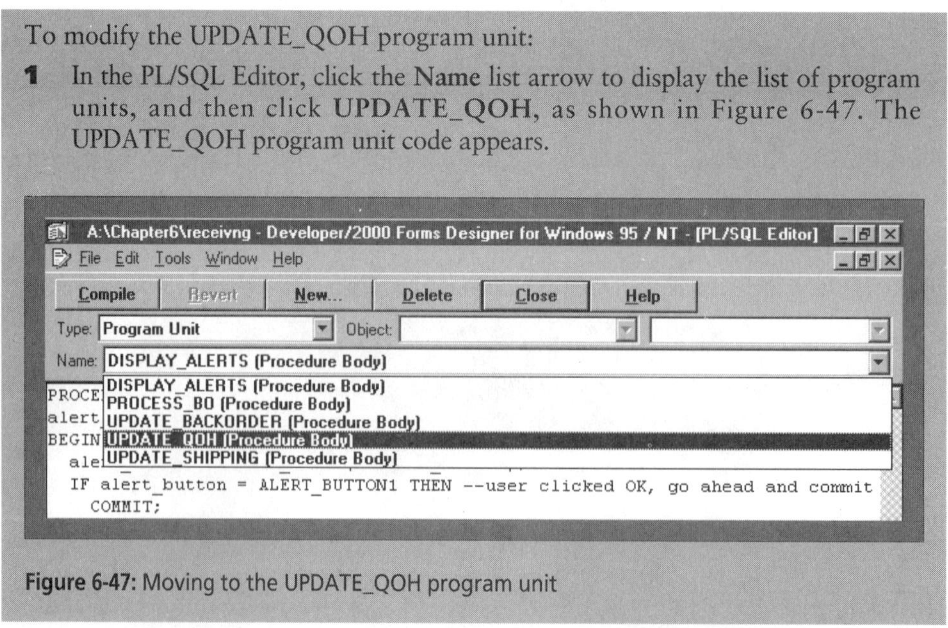

Figure 6-47: Moving to the UPDATE_QOH program unit

2 Replace the COMMIT command with **DISPLAY_ALERTS**. Your modified UPDATE_QOH program unit should look like Figure 6-48.

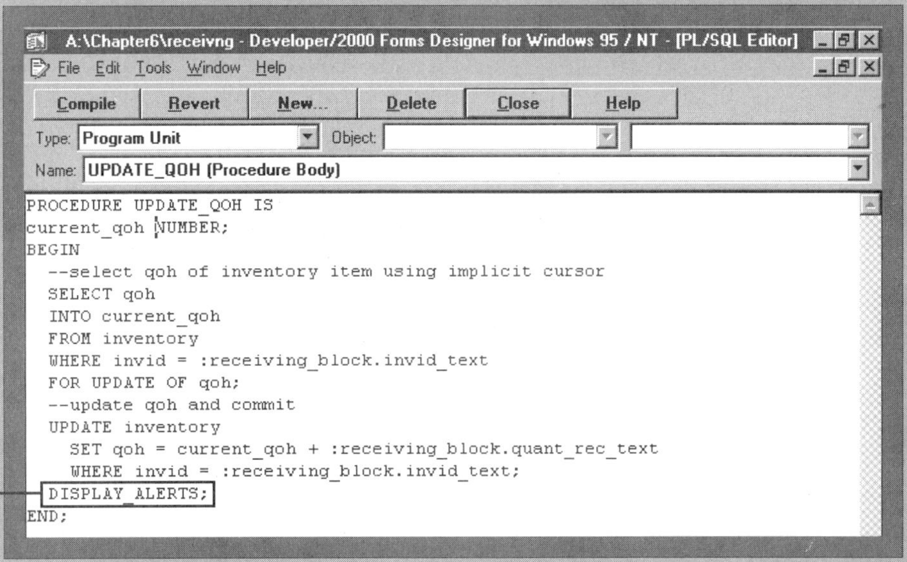

replace COMMIT;
with DISPLAY_ALERTS;

```
PROCEDURE UPDATE_QOH IS
current_qoh NUMBER;
BEGIN
  --select qoh of inventory item using implicit cursor
  SELECT qoh
  INTO current_qoh
  FROM inventory
  WHERE invid = :receiving_block.invid_text
  FOR UPDATE OF qoh;
  --update qoh and commit
  UPDATE inventory
    SET qoh = current_qoh + :receiving_block.quant_rec_text
    WHERE invid = :receiving_block.invid_text;
  DISPLAY_ALERTS;
END;
```

Figure 6-48: Modifying the UPDATE_QOH program unit

3 Compile the program unit, correct any syntax errors, and then close the PL/SQL Editor.

4 Save the form.

Next you need to test the UPDATE_ALERT to see if it correctly informs the user that the database is about to be updated and then gives the user the option to save or cancel the changes or see the Help instructions.

To test the UPDATE_ALERT:

1 Run the form, click the **Shipment ID LOV** button, click **218**, (Men's Expedition Parka, Navy, L), and then click the **OK** button. All 50 parkas in the order were received, so enter 50 for Quantity Received, and then click the **Update** button. The UPDATE_ALERT opens the Update Alert dialog box, as shown in Figure 6-49.

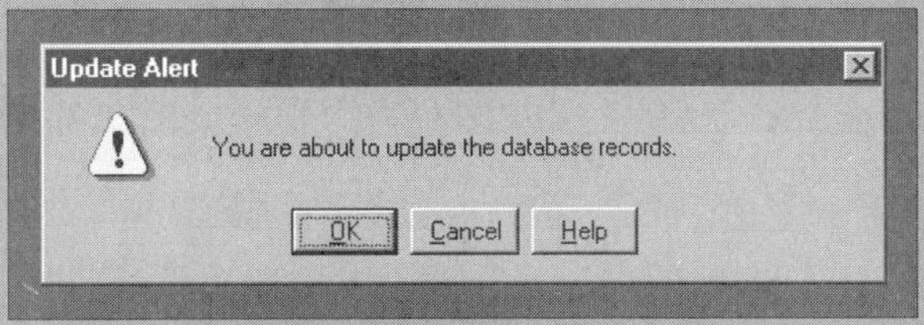

Update Alert

You are about to update the database records.

OK | Cancel | Help

Figure 6-49: Update Alert

2 Click the **OK** button. The CONFIRM_ALERT opens the Records Updated dialog box, as shown in Figure 6-50.

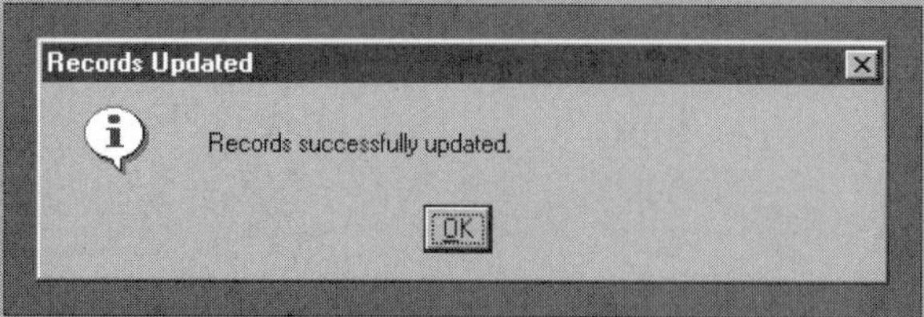

Figure 6-50: Confirm alert

3 Click the **OK** button again to clear your form fields.

4 Select Shipment ID **214** and Inventory ID **11778**, (Women's Hiking Shorts, Olive, S). Enter **200** for Quantity Received, and then click the **Update** button. You decide not to update the record, so you will cancel your changes.

5 Click the **Cancel** button. The ROLLBACK_ALERT opens the Rollback Alert dialog box, as shown in Figure 6-51.

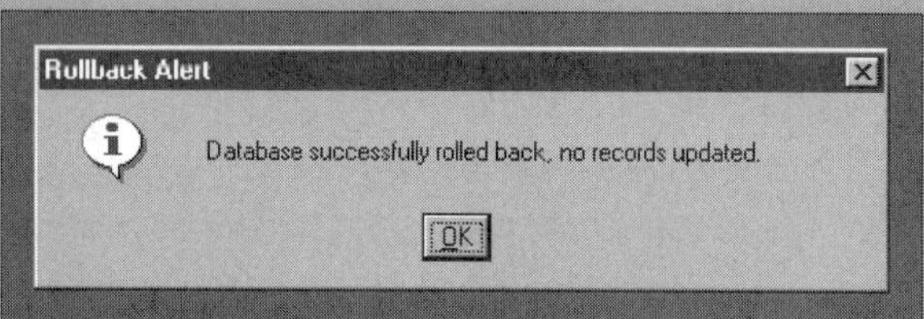

Figure 6-51: Rollback Alert

6 Click the **OK** button.

7 Select Shipment ID **214** and Inventory ID **11778**, (Women's Hiking Shorts, Olive, S), and then enter **200** for Quantity Received. Click the **Update** button, and then click the **Help** button. The HELP_ALERT opens the Help Alert dialog box, as shown in Figure 6-52.

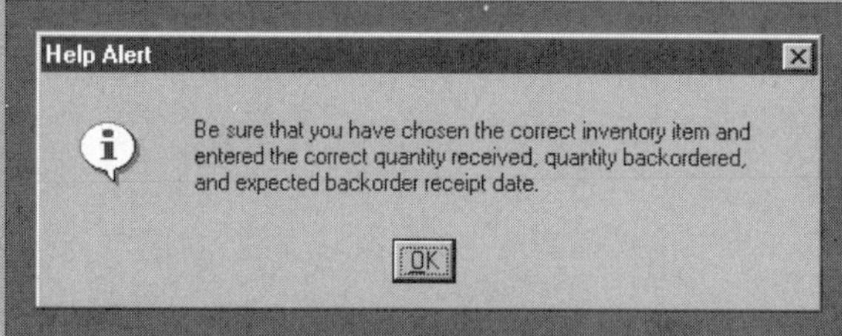

Figure 6-52: Help Alert

8 Click the **OK** button.

Adding Error Traps

Your forms should include ways to keep users from making mistakes and ways to help them correct their mistakes. To do this, you will create error traps. An **error trap** is program code that either does not allow a user to perform an illegal action, or that detects an illegal action after it is performed and then provides suggestions to the user for correction.

Next you will purposely perform an illegal action in the RECEIVING_FORM by updating a primary key value to see what happens.

To update a primary key value:

1. Select Shipment ID **214** and Inventory ID **11778**, and then click the OK button.
2. Select the current shipment ID number, and then change it to **220**, for which a value does not exist in either the SHIPPING or BACKORDER table.
3. Click the **Update** button. The "Record not found" message appears in the message area. See Figure 6-53. This is the error message you put in the UPDATE_BUTTON trigger that displays if no record is found in either the SHIPPING or BACKORDER table that matches the user's LOV selection.

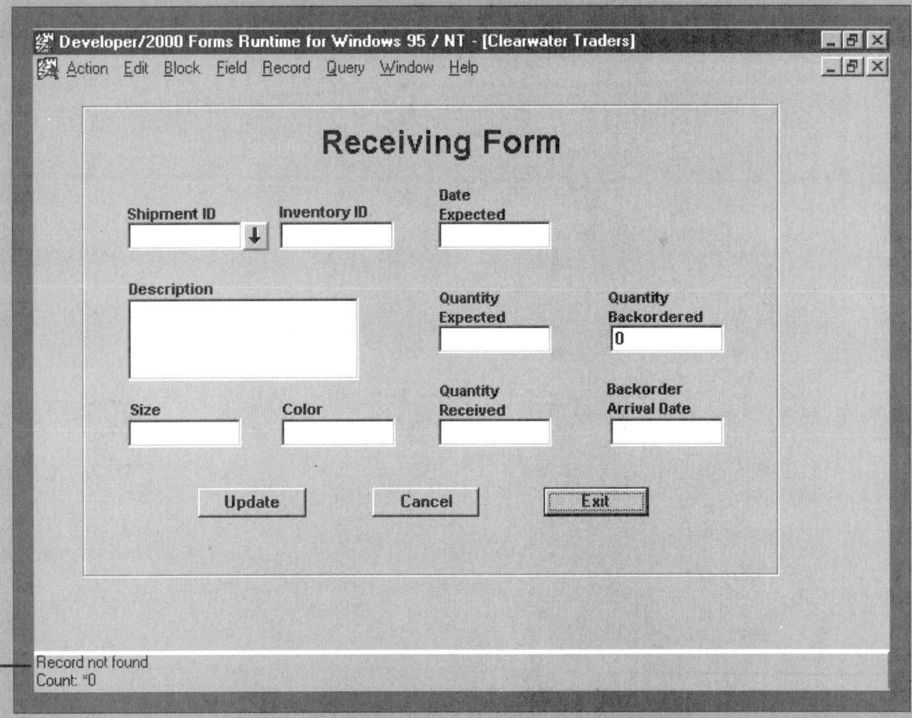

Figure 6-53: Error message generated when user changes shipment ID to a value that does not exist in SHIPPING or BACKORDER table

The code in the UPDATE_BUTTON trigger that generated this message is shown in Figure 6-54.

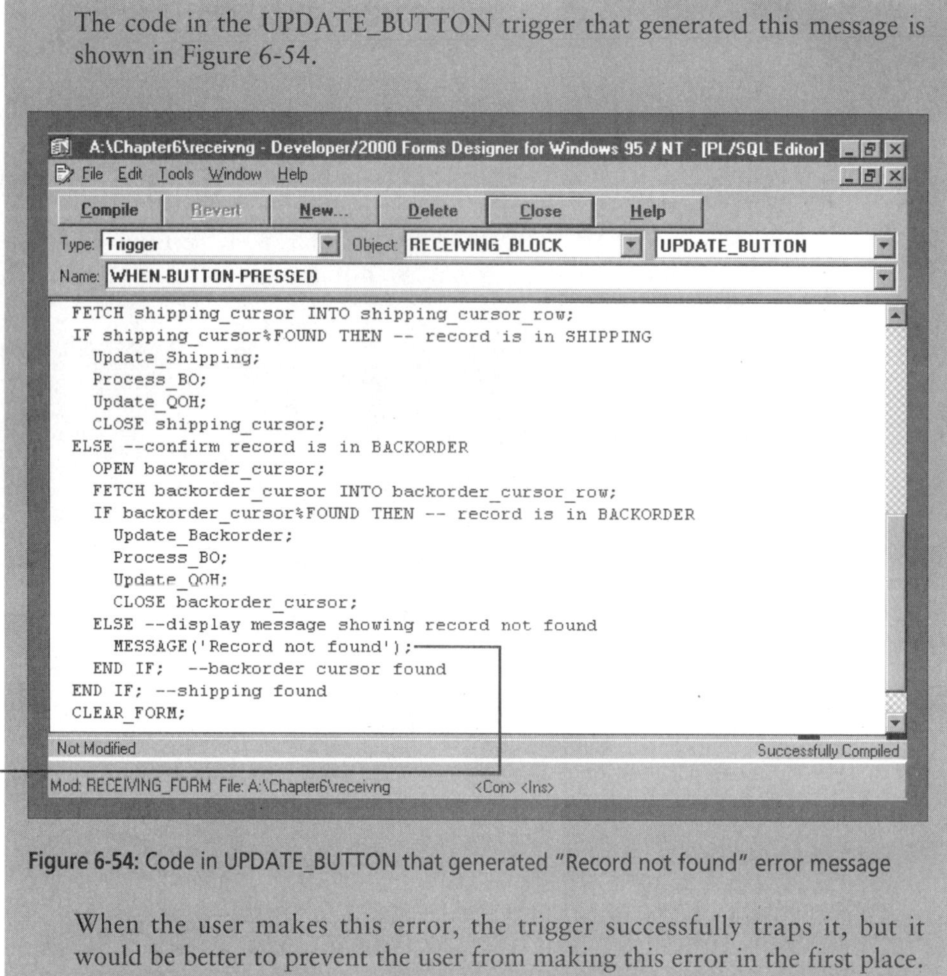

Figure 6-54: Code in UPDATE_BUTTON that generated "Record not found" error message

When the user makes this error, the trigger successfully traps it, but it would be better to prevent the user from making this error in the first place. You will learn how to do this next.

4 Click the **Exit** button to exit the form.

Obviously you do not want to give users the opportunity to update or delete primary and foreign key fields, or to delete NOT NULL fields. One strategy is to make these fields **non-navigable**, which means the user cannot select the field using the insertion point. To do this, you need to set the field's Navigable property to False, so the only way a user can get to the field is by using the pointer. Then you need to create a trigger that moves the insertion point to somewhere else on the form whenever a user clicks the field.

To make the Shipment ID field non-navigable:

1 Click the **Developer/2000 Forms Designer** command button on the taskbar.

2 Go to the Layout Editor, right-click **SHIPID_TEXT**, click **Properties**, and then change its Navigable property to False. Close the Properties sheet, and then maximize the Layout Editor if necessary.

3 In the Layout Editor, right-click **SHIPID_TEXT**, and then click **PL/SQL Editor**. You will search for triggers that include mouse-related events.

4 Type **%mouse%** in the Find box of the RECEIVING_FORM: Triggers dialog box, and then press the **Enter** key. The mouse-related triggers appear in the list, as shown in Figure 6-55.

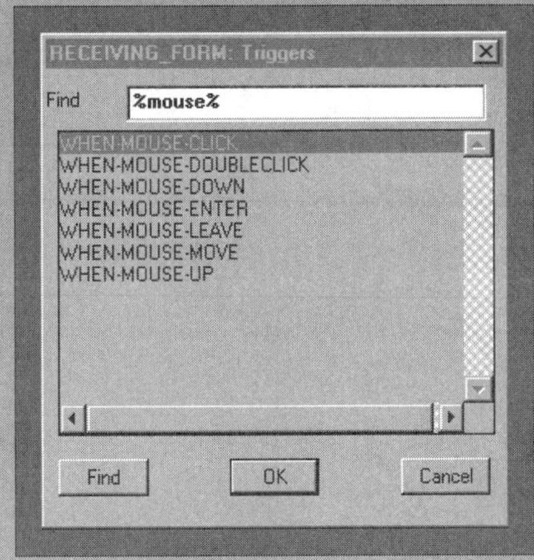

Figure 6-55: Mouse-related trigger events

You could use the WHEN-MOUSE-CLICK event because users usually click the mouse button to enter a text item. However, you would have to create an identical trigger for the WHEN-MOUSE-DOUBLECLICK event because some users might double-click the field to enter a text item. If you use the WHEN-MOUSE-DOWN event, the trigger will be called whenever any mouse button is clicked in the item. Next you will create a WHEN-MOUSE-DOWN trigger that places the insertion point in a different form field whenever the user clicks in the SHIPID_TEXT field. Because this is a RECEIVING_FORM, the Quantity Received field seems like a good place to move the insertion point.

To create the MOUSE-DOWN trigger to move the insertion point:

1 Click **WHEN-MOUSE-DOWN** in the list, and then click the **OK** button.

2 Type **GO_ITEM('quant_rec_text');** in the PL/SQL Editor to switch the form focus to the QUANT_REC_TEXT field.

3 Compile the trigger, correct any syntax errors, and then close the PL/SQL Editor.

4 Save the form and then run it.

5 Click the **Shipment ID LOV** button, and then select any shipment ID.

6 Try to select SHIPID_TEXT using the mouse pointer. The focus moves the insertion point to QUANT_REC_TEXT.

7 Click the **Exit** button to close the form.

Next you will change the other read-only text fields on the form (Inventory ID, Item Description, Size, Color, Date Expected, and Quantity Expected) to non-navigable by changing their Navigable properties to False and creating WHEN-MOUSE-DOWN triggers that change the form focus to QUANT_REC_TEXT.

To change the other read-only text fields to non-navigable:

1. Open the Layout Editor, click **INVID_TEXT**, press and hold down the Shift key, and then click **ITEMDESC_TEXT**, **ITEMSIZE_TEXT**, **COLOR_TEXT**, **EXP_DATE_TEXT**, and **QUANT_EXP_TEXT** to select all of the read-only fields as a group.
2. Right-click while keeping the Shift key pressed, and then click **Properties** to open the group Properties sheet.
3. Change the Navigable property to **False**, and then close the group Properties sheet.
4. Open the Object Navigator window, click the **WHEN-MOUSE-DOWN** trigger below the SHIP_ID_TEXT object, and then click the **Copy** button on the Object Navigator toolbar.
5. Click the **INVID_TEXT** item, and then click the **Paste** button on the Object Navigator toolbar.
6. Paste the trigger into ITEMDESC_TEXT, ITEMSIZE_TEXT, COLOR_TEXT, EXP_DATE_TEXT, and QUANT_EXP_TEXT.
7. Save the form.
8. Run the form and confirm that the triggers work correctly. You should not be able to move the insertion point into the fields, and the trigger should move the insertion point to the QUANT_REC_TEXT.
9. Click the **Exit** button to close the form.
10. Close the RECEIVING_FORM in the Forms Designer application.

General Error Handling

There are common errors that apply to a variety of forms, such as trying to delete a record that is referenced as a foreign key by other records or trying to insert a new record when NOT NULL fields are left blank. To investigate how to handle these errors, you will use the CUSTINV_FORM form you created in Chapter 5. First you will experiment with trying to delete a record that you know is referenced by another record.

To try to delete the record:

1. Open the **custinv.fmb** form file from the Chapter5 folder on your Student Disk.
2. Click **File** on the menu bar, and then click **Save As** and save the file as **cinv_mod.fmb** in the Chapter6 folder on your Student Disk.
3. Run the form.
4. Select Inventory ID **11668** (3-Season Tent, Sienna).
5. Click the **Delete** button. The error message, shown in Figure 6-56, appears in the message area.

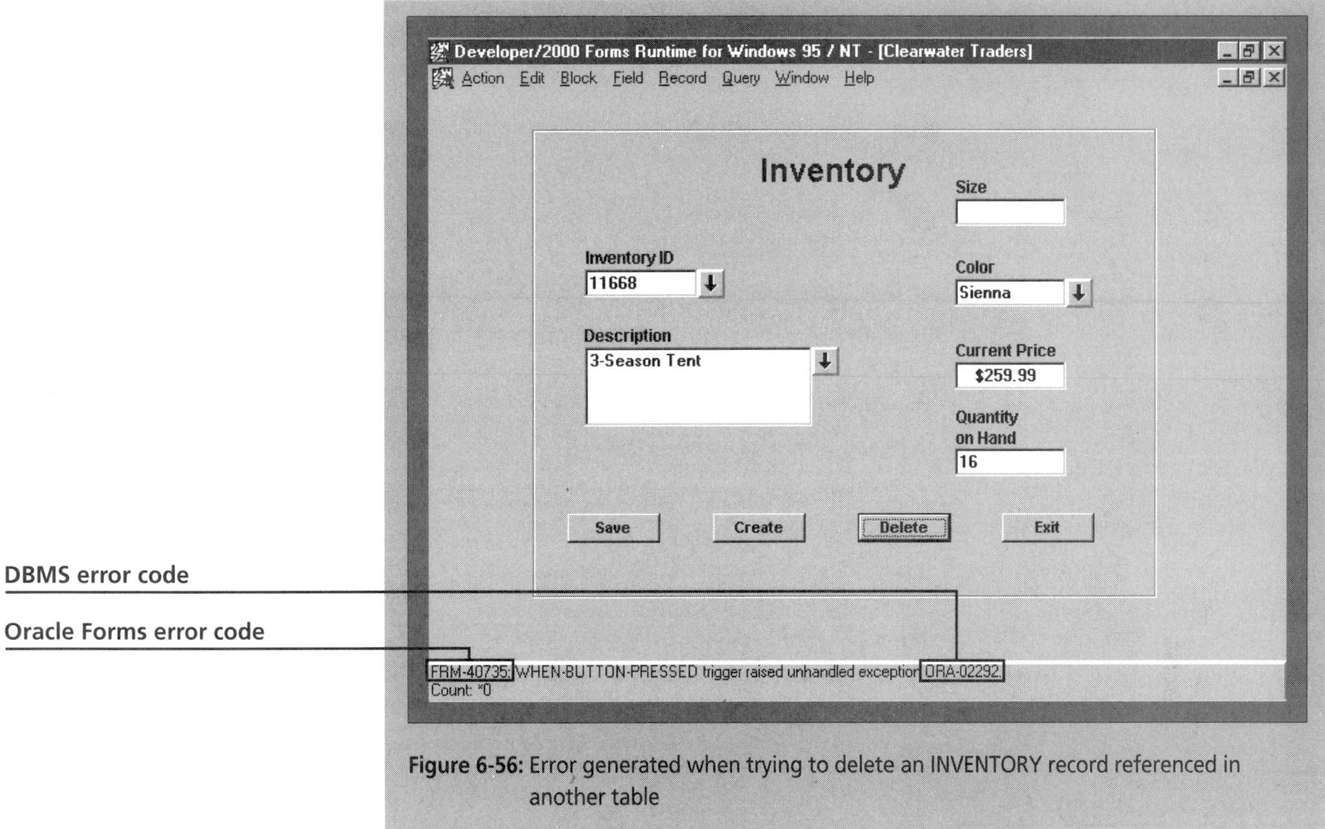

Figure 6-56: Error generated when trying to delete an INVENTORY record referenced in another table

Forms Runtime has error handling routines that intercept DBMS (ORA-) error messages and then generate the associated Forms (FRM-) error messages. If you look up FRM-40735, the explanation states that the trigger raised an "unhandled exception," which means that there is no associated FRM- error message for this error. Therefore you need to use the ORA- error message code to determine the cause of the error. If you look up the ORA-02292 error code in the Help system, it warns that this record is referenced in other tables and should not be deleted, as shown in Figure 6-57.

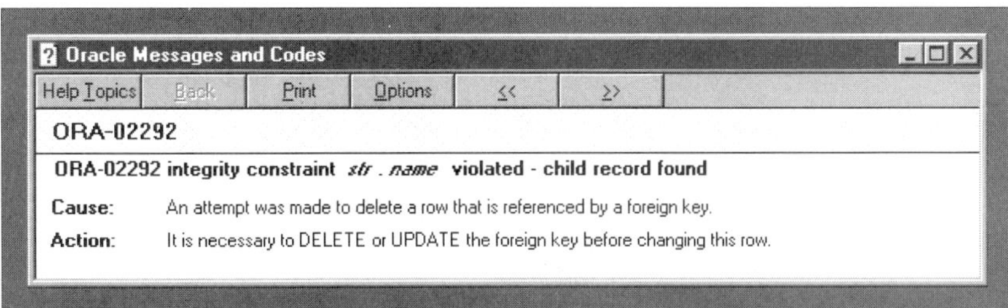
Oracle Messages and Codes

Help Topics | Back | Print | Options | << | >>

ORA-02292

ORA-02292 integrity constraint *str . name* violated - child record found

Cause: An attempt was made to delete a row that is referenced by a foreign key.

Action: It is necessary to DELETE or UPDATE the foreign key before changing this row.

Figure 6-57: ORA-02292 error message text

This record is referenced in the SHIPPING and ORDERLINE tables—the user should not be able to delete it. But it probably is not reasonable to expect users to look up ORA- error code messages to find out why they cannot complete a task, so you need to intercept the DBMS error message and handle the error in your form.

You can intercept DBMS error messages by creating a form-level trigger that corresponds to the ON-ERROR event. Whenever a DBMS error is generated while a form is running, this trigger will execute. It can trap specific ORA- messages and display custom-made alerts to provide informative messages and alternatives.

If a DBMS error is generated that is not anticipated in the trigger, it displays the ORA- error message explanation in the message area.

To create the ON-ERROR trigger:

1 Click the Exit button to close the Forms Runtime application, return to the Object Navigator window in Ownership View, and then click **Triggers** directly below CUSTOM_INVENTORY.

2 Click the **Create** button on the Object Navigator toolbar to create a new trigger that corresponds to the ON-ERROR event.

3 Type the code shown in Figure 6-58 in the PL/SQL Editor.

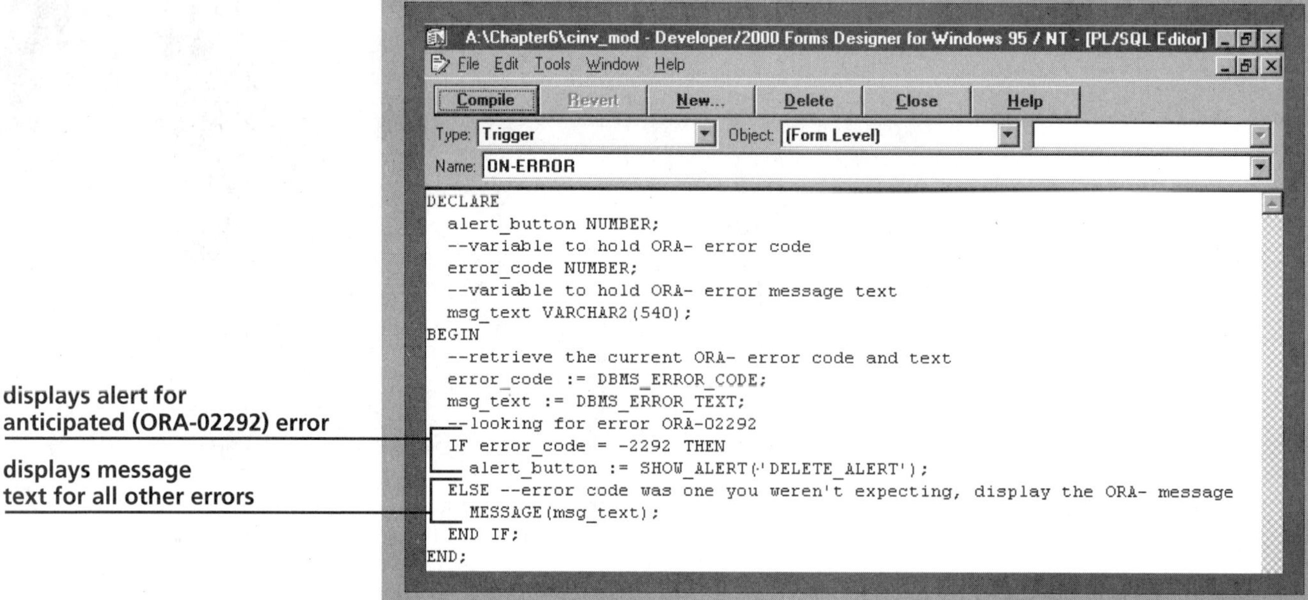

A:\Chapter6\cinv_mod - Developer/2000 Forms Designer for Windows 95 / NT - [PL/SQL Editor]

File Edit Tools Window Help

Compile | Revert | New... | Delete | Close | Help

Type: Trigger Object: (Form Level)

Name: ON-ERROR

```
DECLARE
  alert_button NUMBER;
  --variable to hold ORA- error code
  error_code NUMBER;
  --variable to hold ORA- error message text
  msg_text VARCHAR2(540);
BEGIN
  --retrieve the current ORA- error code and text
  error_code := DBMS_ERROR_CODE;
  msg_text := DBMS_ERROR_TEXT;
  --looking for error ORA-02292
  IF error_code = -2292 THEN
    alert_button := SHOW_ALERT('DELETE_ALERT');
  ELSE --error code was one you weren't expecting, display the ORA- message
    MESSAGE(msg_text);
  END IF;
END;
```

displays alert for anticipated (ORA-02292) error

displays message text for all other errors

Figure 6-58: ON-ERROR trigger code

4 Compile the code, correct any syntax errors, and then close the PL/SQL Editor.

Next you need to create a new alert named DELETE_ALERT that will appear instead of the ORA-02292 error code.

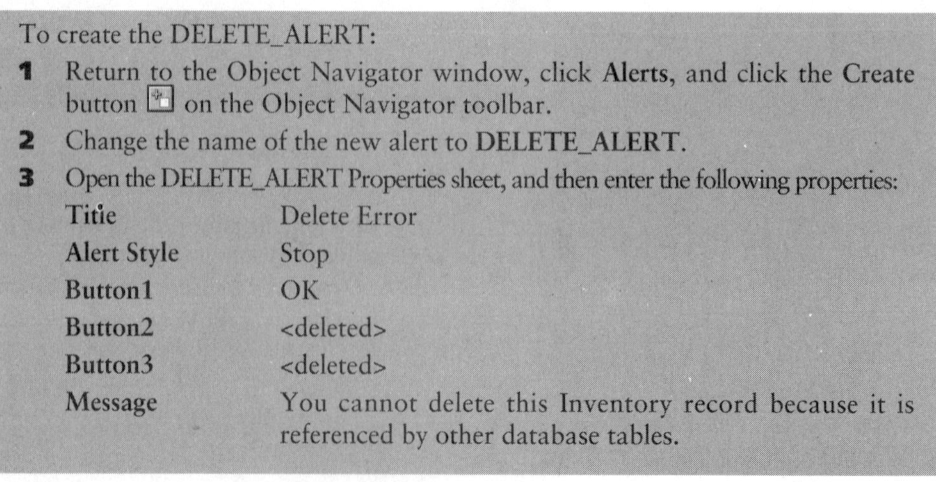

To create the DELETE_ALERT:

1 Return to the Object Navigator window, click **Alerts**, and click the **Create** button on the Object Navigator toolbar.

2 Change the name of the new alert to **DELETE_ALERT**.

3 Open the DELETE_ALERT Properties sheet, and then enter the following properties:

Title	Delete Error
Alert Style	Stop
Button1	OK
Button2	<deleted>
Button3	<deleted>
Message	You cannot delete this Inventory record because it is referenced by other database tables.

4 Close the Properties sheet, and then save the form. Now you need to test your ON-ERROR trigger and DELETE_ALERT.

5 Run the form, select Inventory ID **11668** (3-Season Tent, Sienna), and then click the **Delete** button. The DELETE_ALERT opens the Delete Alert dialog box, as shown in Figure 6-59. Click the **OK** button to close the alert message box. Now you will test to see what happens when an unexpected error occurs that is not listed in the ON-ERROR trigger.

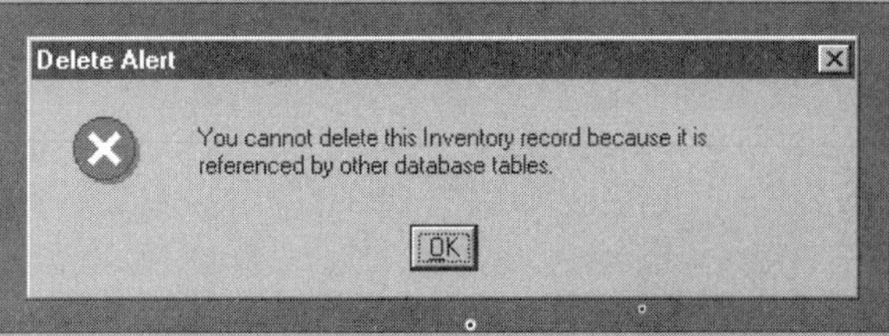

Figure 6-59: Delete Alert

6 Click the **Create** button. The form fields are cleared and a new inventory ID appears.

7 Click the **Save** button to generate an error by not entering data in the NOT NULL fields. The error message shown in Figure 6-60 is an ORA- error, and not an error that you anticipated in the ON-ERROR trigger.

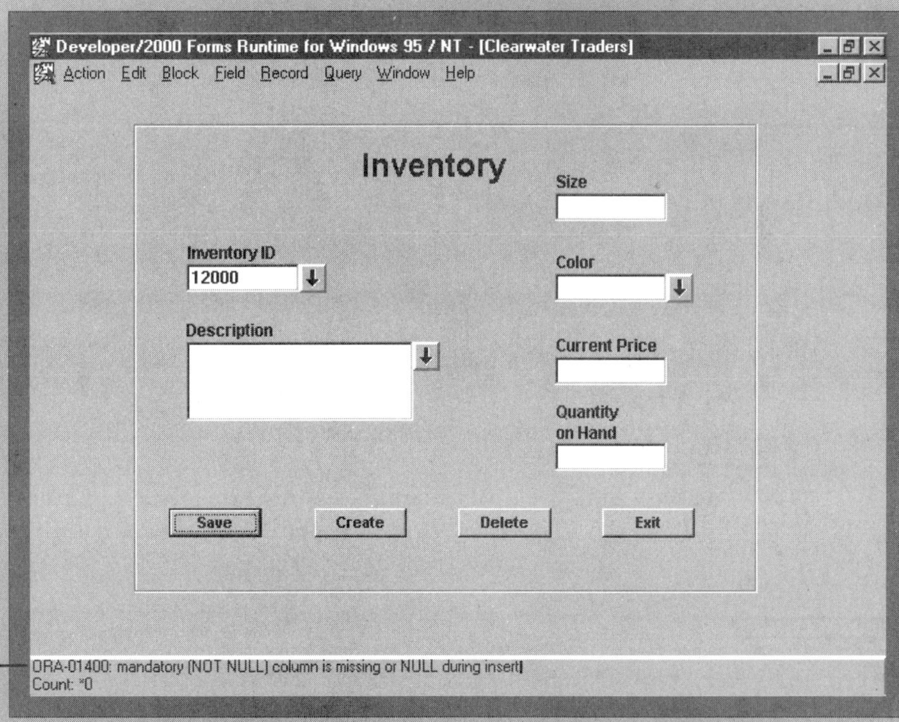

Figure 6-60: Untrapped error message

8 Click the **Exit** button to close the form.

You will need to trap this error in the ON-ERROR trigger, and then create a customized alert to display a message to the user. You will do this next.

To trap the error in the ON-ERROR trigger:

1. Double-click the trigger icon beside the ON-ERROR trigger to open the PL/SQL Editor.
2. Modify the BEGIN section of the ON-ERROR trigger by adding the code shown in Figure 6-61.

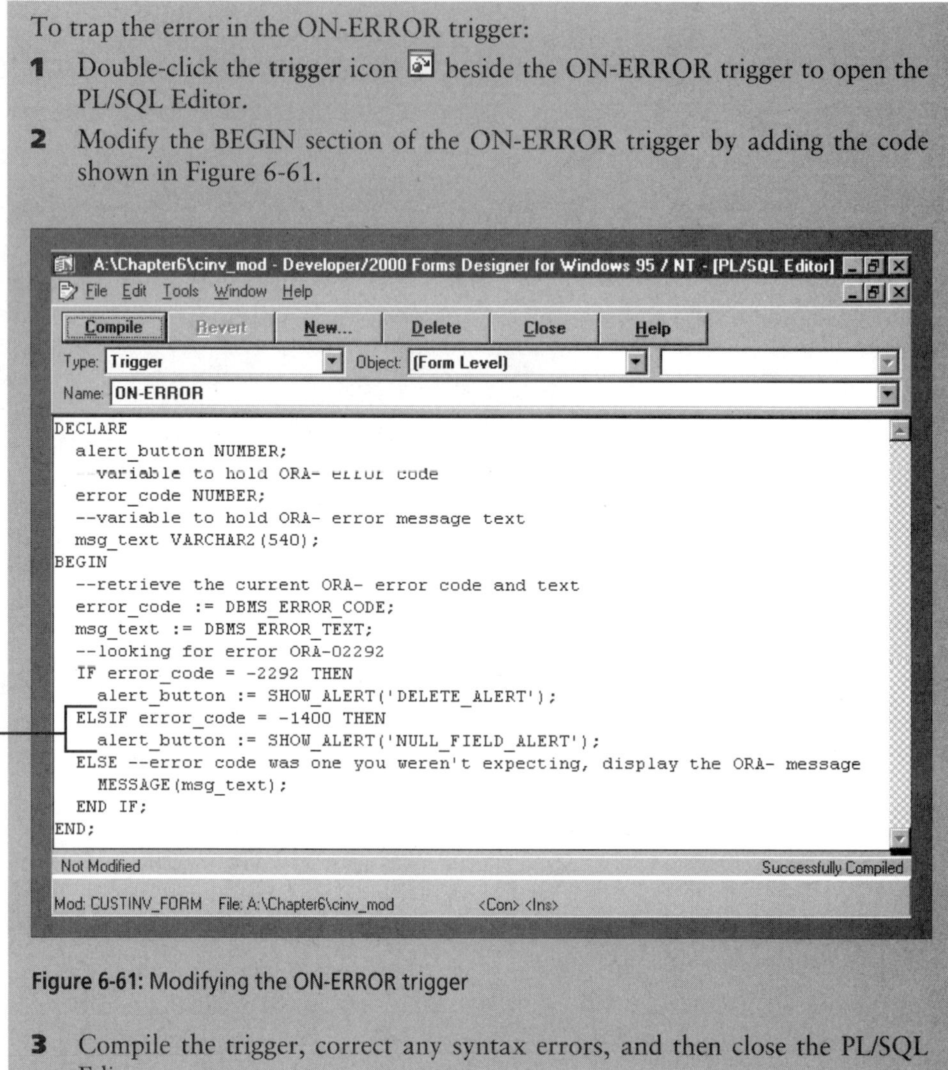

Figure 6-61: Modifying the ON-ERROR trigger

3. Compile the trigger, correct any syntax errors, and then close the PL/SQL Editor.

tip

Note that the PL/SQL syntax for the ELSE IF command in an IF/THEN/ELSE IF program structure is "ELSIF."

Next you need to create an alert that notifies the user that some required field values were not entered. You will do this by copying the DELETE_ALERT and modifying its properties.

To create the new alert:

1. Switch to the Object Navigator window, click **DELETE_ALERT**, and click the **Copy** button on the Object Navigator toolbar.
2. Click the **Paste** button on the Object Navigator toolbar to create a new alert that is a copy of DELETE_ALERT.
3. Rename the new alert **NULL_FIELD_ALERT**.

4 Modify its properties as follows: Title: **Missing Field Values**; and Mess **You MUST select an Item ID and enter values for Current Price and Quantity on Hand.**
5 Close the Properties sheet.
6 Save the form.
7 Verify that this error trap is working by running the form, clicking the **Create** button, and then clicking the **Save** button without entering any data. Your new alert should display as shown in Figure 6-62.

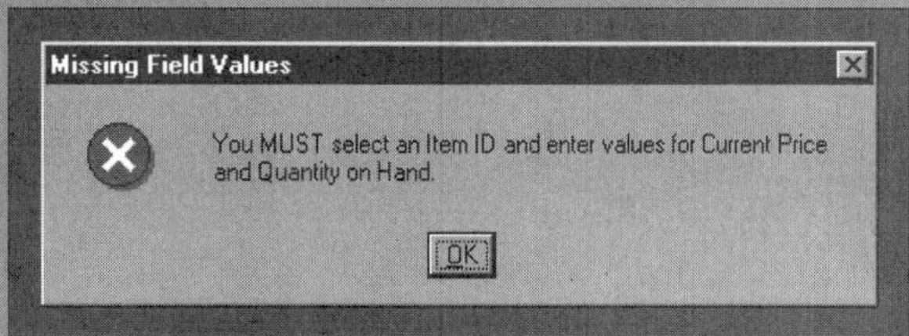

Figure 6-62: NULL fields alert

HELP? If your alert does not display, go to the Object Navigator window and verify that its name is NULL_FIELD_ALERT and that you have changed its title and message properties. Then open the ON-ERROR trigger and verify that your code looks exactly like Figure 6-61. If you still have problems, ask your instructor for help.

8 Click the **OK** button to close the alert message box.
9 Exit the form, and then close the cinv_mod.fmb file.

The Clearwater Customer Order Process

Next you will create a form that calls another form and switches between different form windows. At Clearwater Traders, new customer orders are entered using an on-screen form that an order processor completes when the customer calls the company. The first window in this form displays customer information, calls a second form that allows the order processor to enter a new customer record if necessary, and then switches to a second window that displays information about the order. This process is described in detail next.

The person processing a new customer order first must create a new CUSTOMER record for new customers or retrieve the existing CUSTID for existing customers. Then the order processor must enter the payment method and order source (catalog number or Web site) and create a new CUST_ORDER record. Next the order processor must enter the first item number and quantity desired and check the item availability in the INVENTORY table. If the item is available, a record is inserted in the ORDERLINE table. This process is repeated for all items in the order. When there are no more items, the order processor reports the total order cost (including sales tax and shipping and handling) to the customer.

Figure 6-63 illustrates the customer order process in a flowchart. If the customer is a new customer, the application activates a different form for adding new customer information, and then returns the new CUSTID to the current application. If the customer is an existing customer, a LOV is used to retrieve the CUSTID. Then the method of payment and order source is entered, and the CUST_ORDER record is inserted.

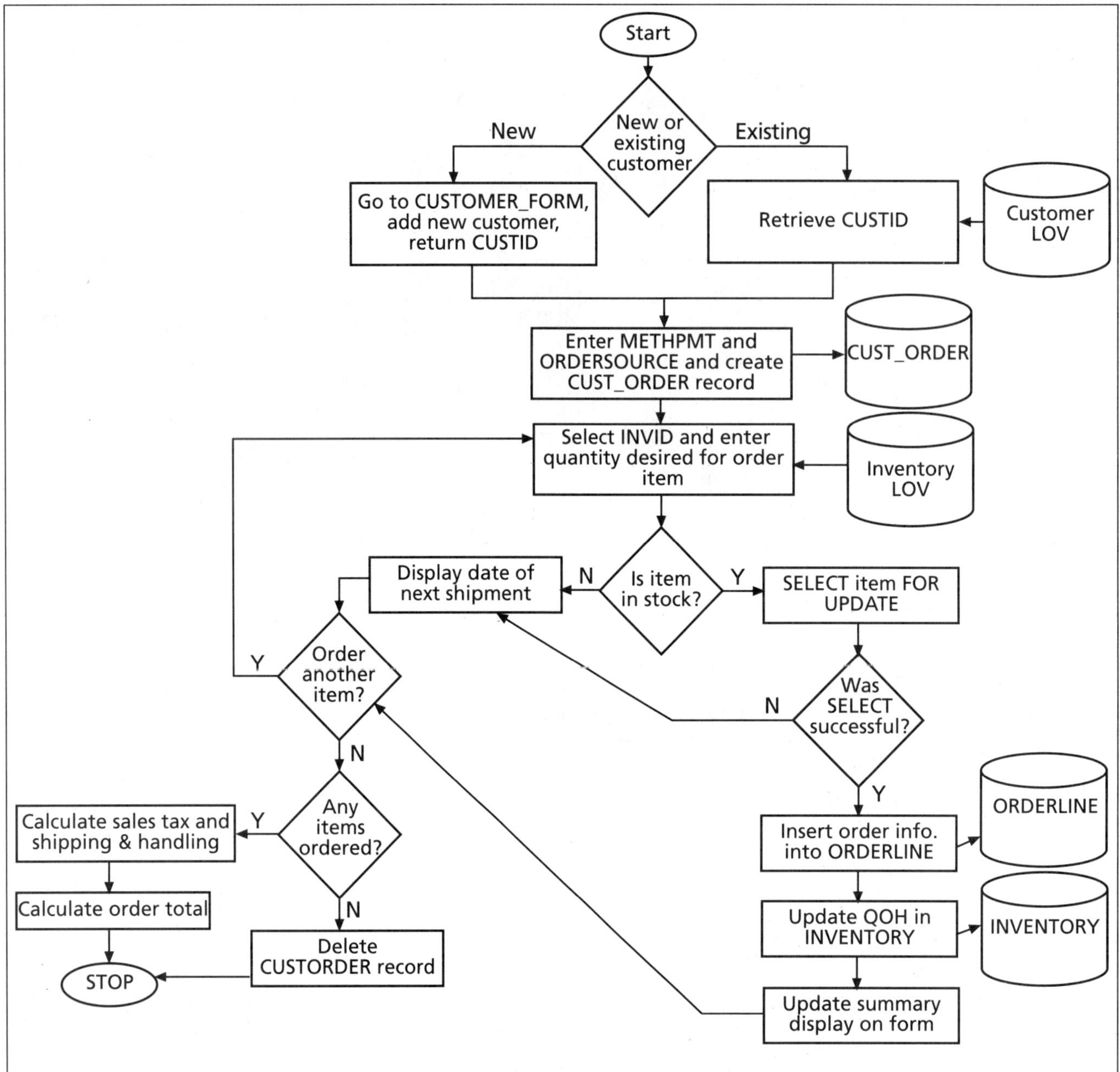

Figure 6-63: Clearwater Traders customer sales process flowchart

The first item's inventory ID is retrieved using a LOV. The INVENTORY table is queried to determine if the item is in stock. If the inventory item is in stock, it is selected using a SELECT ... FOR UPDATE query to lock the record. If the item still is available, the item order specification is inserted into the ORDERLINE table, the quantity on hand is updated in the INVENTORY table, and a summary of the ordered items appears on the form. If the item is not in stock or not available for the SELECT ... FOR UPDATE, the order processor tells the customer the date of the next expected shipment and asks the customer if he or she wants to order another item. When the customer is finished ordering, if no items were ordered because the desired item(s) were not in stock, the CUSTORDER record is deleted. Otherwise, the form calculates the sales tax, and shipping and handling charges, and the order total.

Creating the Interface Design

The interface for this form will involve two separate windows—the first window (named CUST_ORDER) will hold the customer and order information, and the second window (named ORDERLINE) will contain the information about the specific order items. The design sketch for the CUST_ORDER window (see Figure 6-64) has a text field and associated LOV button for selecting the customer ID, and a New Customer button that activates a form to allow the user to enter new customer information, if necessary. The user can select the payment method (check or credit card type) and enter the customer's credit card information as needed. The user also can select the order source using a LOV that will show valid order sources from the ORDERSOURCE table. The Order ID field will contain the ORDERID of the new order record that is inserted into the CUST_ORDER table. After entering this information, the user can click the Enter Items button to insert the new order record into the CUST_ORDER table and move to the next window to enter the order items, the Cancel Order button to clear the form fields, or the Exit button to exit the form.

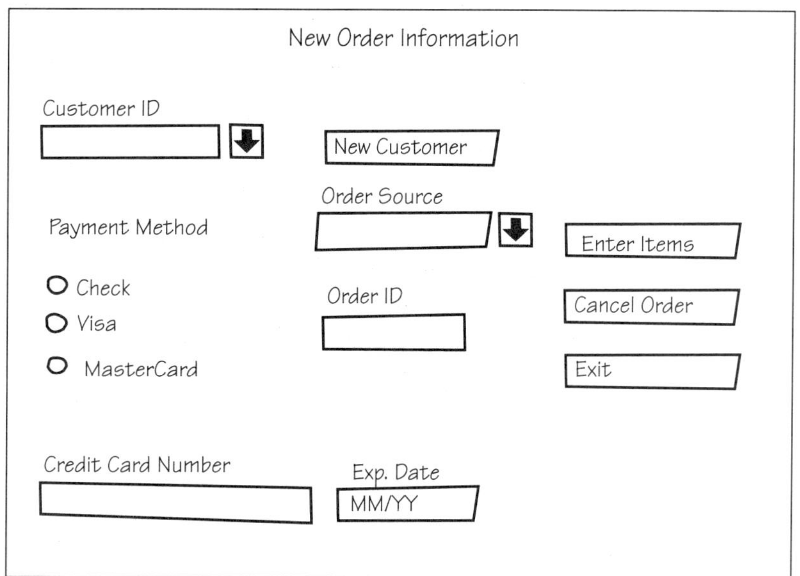

Figure 6-64: Design of the CUST_ORDER window

The ORDERLINE window (see Figure 6-65) has fields to display inventory item information (ID, description, size, color, and price) and the desired quantity. As items are added to the order using the Add Item to Order button, an Order Summary display field dynamically shows each order line's item ID, quantity, description, size, color, and price. When all order items are entered, the user clicks the Finish Order button to calculate the subtotal, sales tax, shipping and handling, and final total. The user can click the New Order button to switch back to the CUST_ORDER window and begin taking a new customer's order information, or click the Cancel Order button to cancel the order.

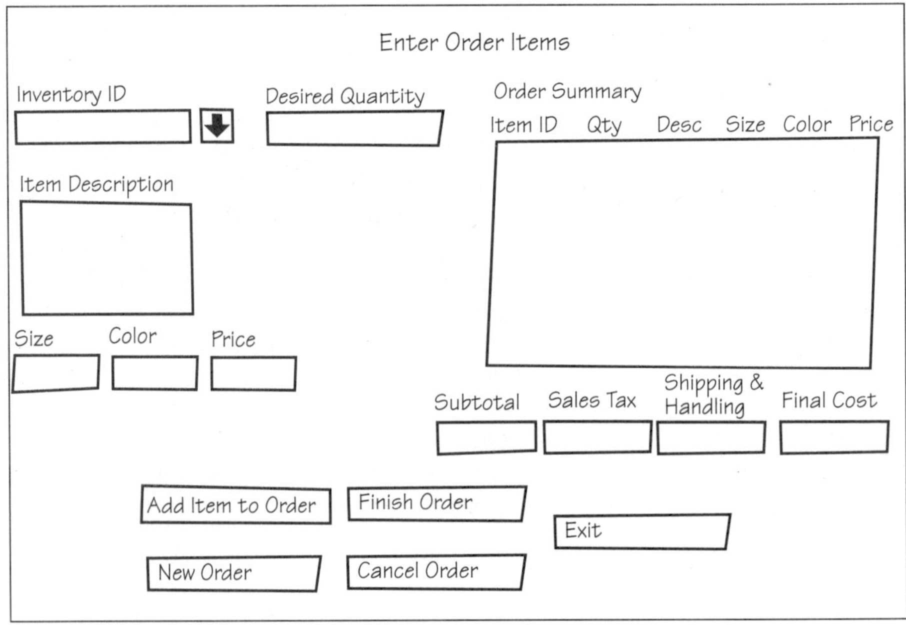

Figure 6-65: Design of the ORDERLINE_WINDOW

Now that the design work is completed, you can create the form.

To create the form:

1. Go to the Object Navigator window in Visual View, and then create a new form named **SALES_FORM**.
2. Rename the default window to **CUST_ORDER_WINDOW**.
3. Create a new window named **ORDERLINE_WINDOW**.
4. Create a new canvas in the CUST_ORDER_WINDOW named **CUST_ORDER_CANVAS**.
5. Create a new canvas in the ORDERLINE_WINDOW named **ORDERLINE _CANVAS**.
6. Change the CUST_ORDER_WINDOW and ORDERLINE_WINDOW Width property to **640**, and Height property to **480**.
7. Change the CUST_ORDER_CANVAS and ORDERLINE_CANVAS Width property to **640**, and Height property to **480**.
8. Save the form as **sales.fmb** in the Chapter6 folder on your Student Disk, and then change the form name back to SALES_FORM, if necessary.

Next you will create a PRE-FORM trigger to maximize the windows automatically at runtime and set the SYSTEM.MESSAGE_LEVEL to 25.

To create the PRE-FORM trigger to maximize the windows and set the message level:

1. Switch to the Object Navigator window in Ownership View.

2 Click **Triggers** below SALES_FORM, and then click the **Create** button on the Object Navigator toolbar to create a new trigger.

3 Select the **PRE-FORM** event for the new trigger, and then click the **OK** button.

4 Type the code shown in Figure 6-66 in the PL/SQL Editor to create the trigger.

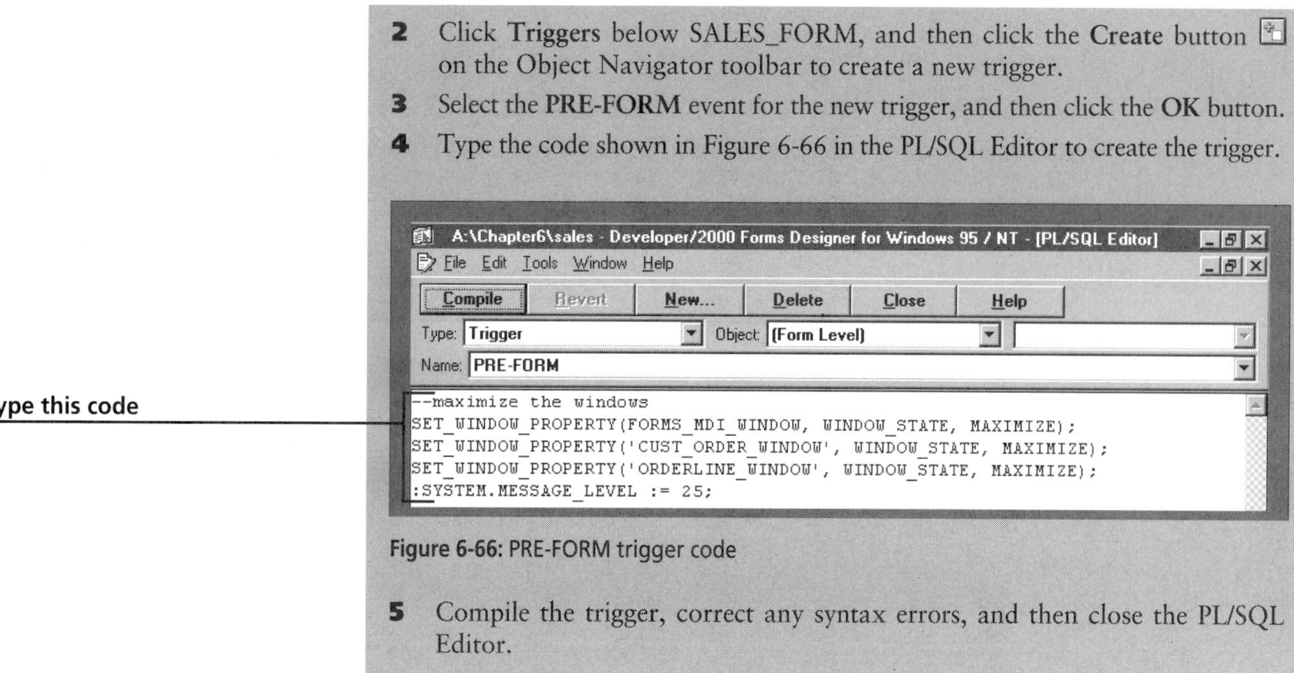

Figure 6-66: PRE-FORM trigger code

5 Compile the trigger, correct any syntax errors, and then close the PL/SQL Editor.

Creating the CUST_ORDER_WINDOW Items

First you will create the text fields, labels, and radio button group shown in Figure 6-64 on the CUST_ORDER_CANVAS in the CUST_ORDER_WINDOW. To do this, you must open the canvas and then create a new control block on the canvas.

To create the CUST_ORDER_WINDOW block items:

1 Open the Object Navigator window in Ownership View, and then double-click the **canvas** icon beside CUST_ORDER_CANVAS to open the canvas in the Layout Editor.

2 Click **Tools** on the menu bar, and then click **New Block** to create a new control block on the CUST_ORDER_CANVAS. Name the new block **CUST_ORDER_BLOCK**, and then click the **OK** button.

3 If necessary, select the **CUST_ORDER_BLOCK** from the Block list on the CUST_ORDER_CANVAS, as shown in Figure 6-67.

tip

When a form has multiple canvases and multiple blocks, you must make sure that the correct block is selected for a canvas in the Layout Editor.

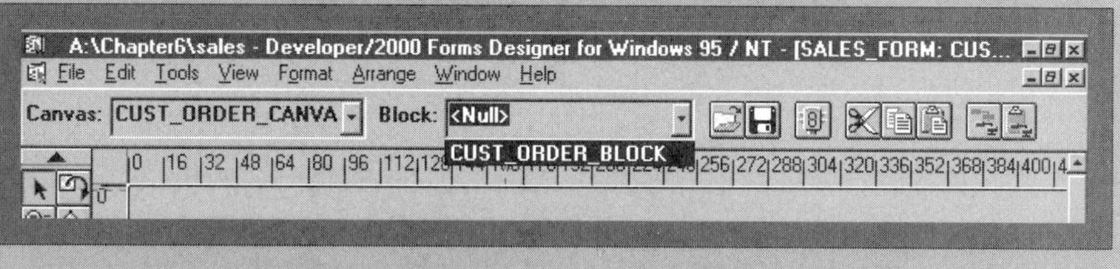

Figure 6-67: Selecting the CUST_ORDER_BLOCK on the CUST_ORDER_CANVAS

4 Create the following text fields on the CUST_ORDER_CANVAS in the CUST_ORDER_BLOCK:

Name	Data Type	Maximum Length	Height	Width	Format Mask
CUSTID_TEXT	Number	5	15	70	
CCNUMBER_TEXT	Char	30	15	115	
CCEXP_TEXT	Date	5	15	35	MM/YY
ORDERSOURCE_TEXT	Char	20	15	60	
ORDERID_TEXT	Number	10	15	60	

5 Position the text fields and add the labels as shown in Figure 6-68 using a 9-point bold Arial font.

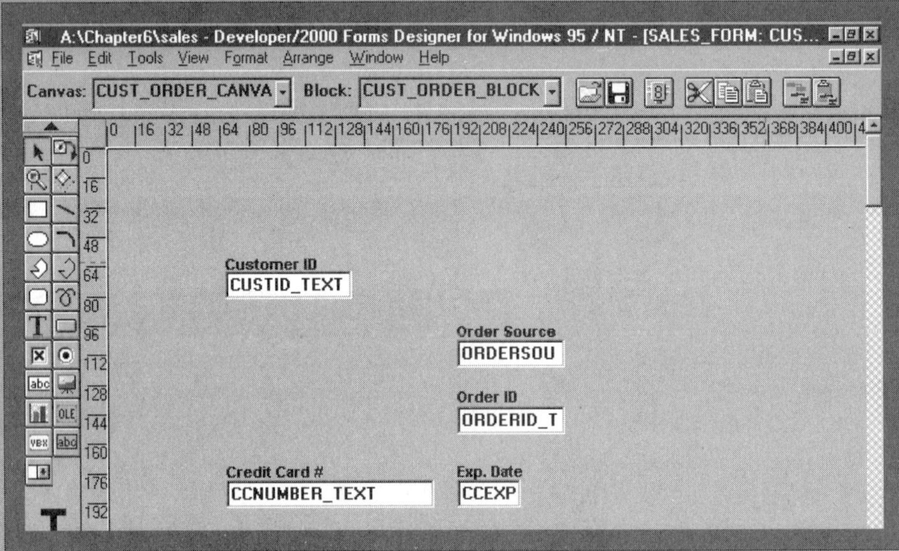

Figure 6-68: Positioning the CUST_ORDER_CANVAS text fields and labels

Next you will create the radio button group to display the payment method choices and the form buttons.

To create the radio button group and form buttons:

1 Create the following radio buttons:

Name	Label	Value
CHECK_RADIO_BUTTON	Check	CHECK
VISA_RADIO_BUTTON	Visa	CC
MC_RADIO_BUTTON	MasterCard	CC

2 Open the Object Navigator window, and then rename the new radio button group to **PMT_RADIO_GROUP**.

3 Open the PMT_RADIO_GROUP Properties sheet, and then change the Default Value to **CHECK**.

4 Align the radio buttons, and then create a label for the radio group with the text **Payment Method**.

5 Draw a rectangle around the radio button group, and then set its Bevel to **Lowered**.

Finally, you will create the form buttons and format the form.

To create the buttons and format the form:

1 Create the following new buttons:

Name	Label	Height	Width
NEW_CUST_BUTTON	New Customer	15	75
ENTER_ITEM_BUTTON	Enter Items	15	75
CANCEL_BUTTON	Cancel Order	15	75
EXIT_BUTTON	Exit	15	75

2 Create a form title with the text **New Order Information** using a 16-point bold Arial font.

3 Format your form so it looks like Figure 6-69.

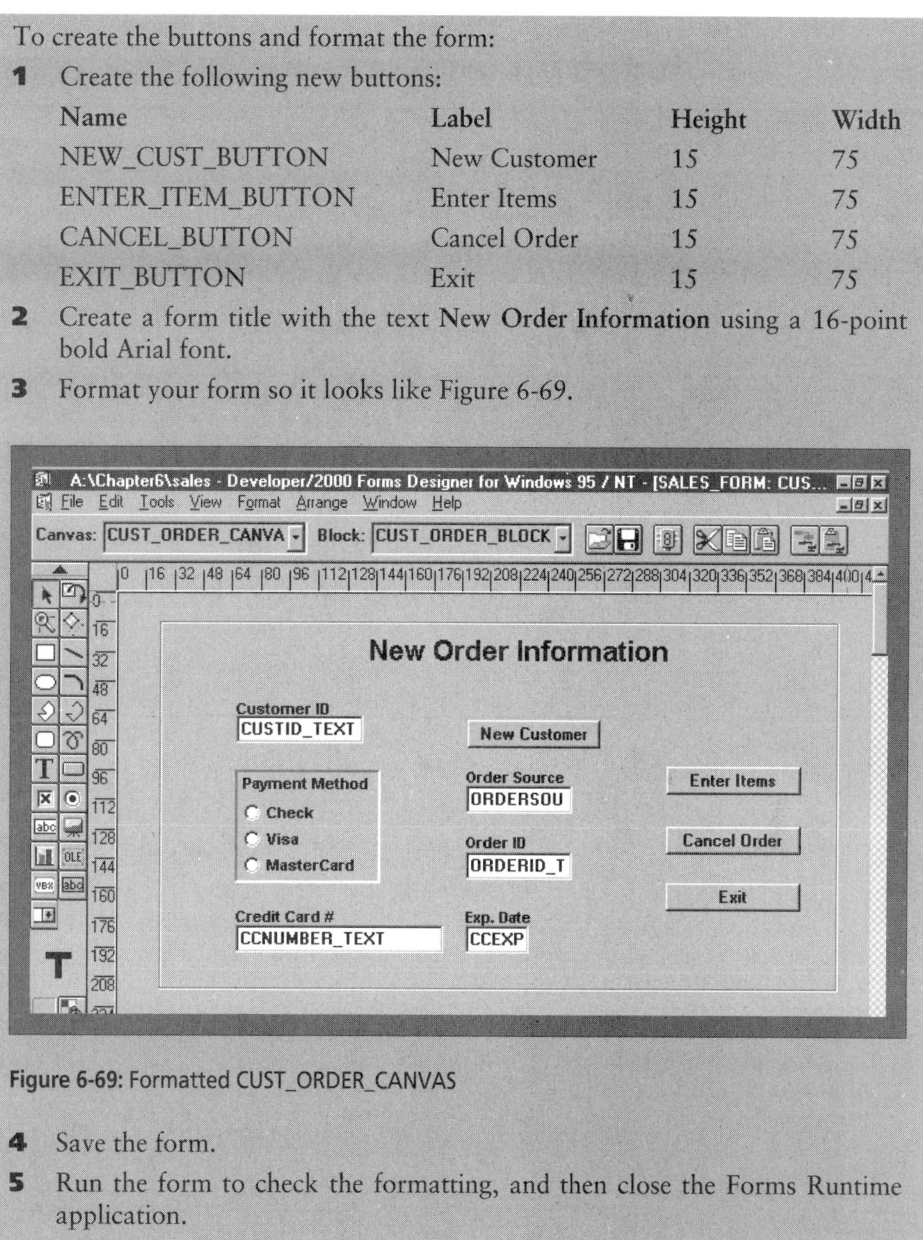

Figure 6-69: Formatted CUST_ORDER_CANVAS

4 Save the form.

5 Run the form to check the formatting, and then close the Forms Runtime application.

Next you will create the LOVs to show customer and order source information. The customer LOV lets the user search using customer evening phone numbers, and displays the customer ID, last and first name, address, city, state, and zip code. The LOV should enter only the selected customer's ID into CUSTID_TEXT on the form. To do this, you will omit the INTO clause that normally maps the LOV display fields into the form fields, and then map the CUSTID field into CUSTID_TEXT manually using the LOV Column Mapping property.

To create the LOV:

1 Open the Object Navigator window, and then create a new LOV.

2 Enter the query text shown in Figure 6-70 to create the LOV to display customer information, and then click the **OK** button. Note that the INTO clause that normally maps the LOV display fields into the form fields is omitted.

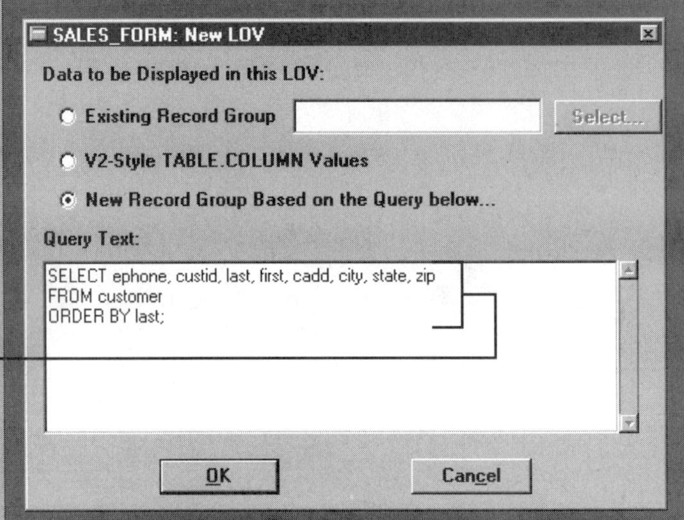

Figure 6-70: Query to create the CUST_LOV

3 Name the new LOV and record group **CUST_LOV**.

4 Open the LOV Properties sheet for CUST_LOV and change the Title to **Customers**, the Width to **400**, and the Height to **200**.

5 Click the **Column Mapping** property, and then click the More button. Update the fields as follows:

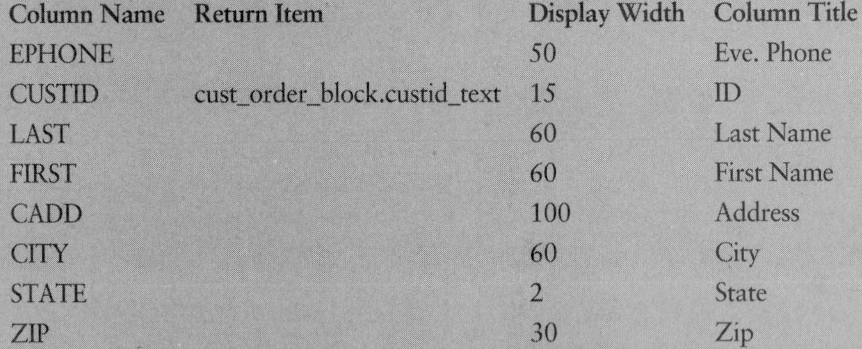

Column Name	Return Item	Display Width	Column Title
EPHONE		50	Eve. Phone
CUSTID	cust_order_block.custid_text	15	ID
LAST		60	Last Name
FIRST		60	First Name
CADD		100	Address
CITY		60	City
STATE		2	State
ZIP		30	Zip

6 Click the **OK** button to close the Column Mapping dialog box, and then close the CUST_LOV Properties sheet.

7 Save the form.

tip

When you want to return only one column from a LOV to a form field, omit the INTO clause in the LOV query and create the column mapping manually in the LOV Properties sheet by entering the form field name into the item's Return Item property.

To finish the LOV, you need to copy a LOV button from another form and paste it onto your canvas. Instead of copying the button in the Object Navigator and then changing its canvas property so it will display on the current canvas, you will copy the button directly onto the canvas.

To copy the LOV button onto the canvas:

1 Open the Object Navigator window in Ownership View, click **Forms**, and then click the **Collapse All** button on the Object Navigator toolbar to close all of the open items in SALES_FORM.

2 Click **File** on the menu bar, and then click **Open** and open the **receivng.fmb** file in the Chapter6 folder on your Student Disk.

3 Click **Tools** on the menu bar, and then click **Layout Editor**. The RECEIVING _FORM opens.

4 Click the **LOV button** next to SHIPID_TEXT.

5 Click the **Copy** button on the Layout Editor toolbar to copy the LOV button.

6 Click **File** on the menu bar, and then click **Close** to close the RECEIVING _FORM. You did not make any changes to the form, so you can click the **No** button when you are asked if you want to save your changes to RECEIVING_FORM.

7 Click **Tools** on the menu bar, and then click **Layout Editor**. There are two canvases in this form, so you must select which one you want to view. Select **CUST_ORDER_CANVAS**, as shown in Figure 6-71, and then click the **OK** button. The CUST_ORDER_CANVAS appears.

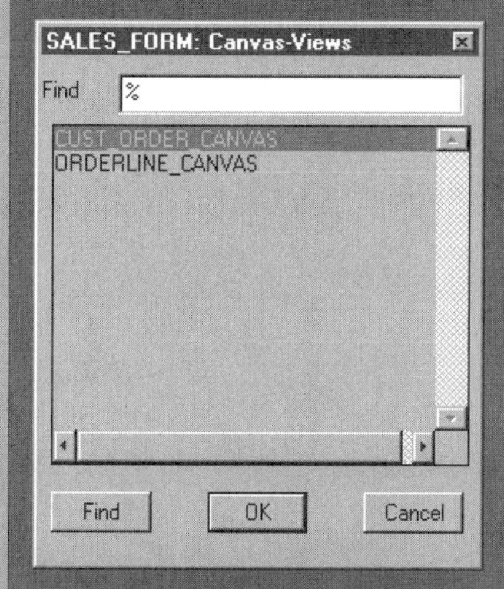

Figure 6-71: Selecting the canvas to display in the Layout Editor

8 Click the **Paste** button on the Layout Editor toolbar. The LOV button appears on the CUST_ORDER_CANVAS.

9 Drag the LOV button so it is positioned on the right edge of CUSTID_TEXT.

To finish the LOV, you will modify the properties of the LOV button and CUSTID_TEXT field so they work correctly with the CUST_LOV.

To finish the LOV:

1. Right-click the new **LOV button**, click **Properties**, change the name of the new button to **CUST_LOV_BUTTON**, and then close the Properties sheet.
2. Right-click the **CUST_LOV_BUTTON**, click **PL/SQL Editor**, and then modify the trigger as shown in Figure 6-72.

modify this line

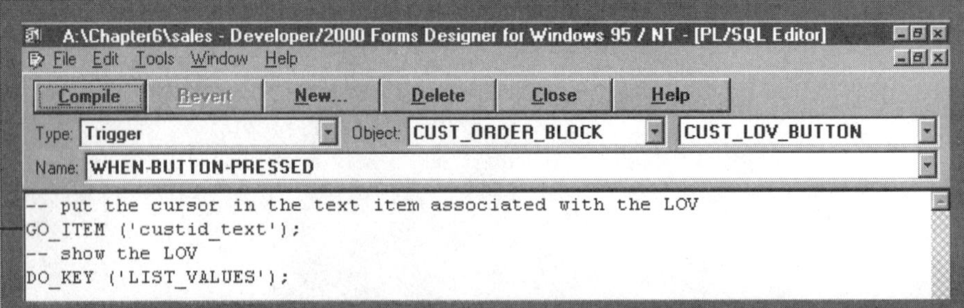

Figure 6-72: Modifying the CUST_LOV_BUTTON trigger

3. Compile the trigger, correct any syntax errors, and then close the PL/SQL Editor.
4. Open the CUSTID_TEXT Properties sheet, and then change the LOV property to **CUST_LOV**.
5. Save the form.
6. Run the form and click the LOV button to test the LOV. Your LOV display should look like Figure 6-73.

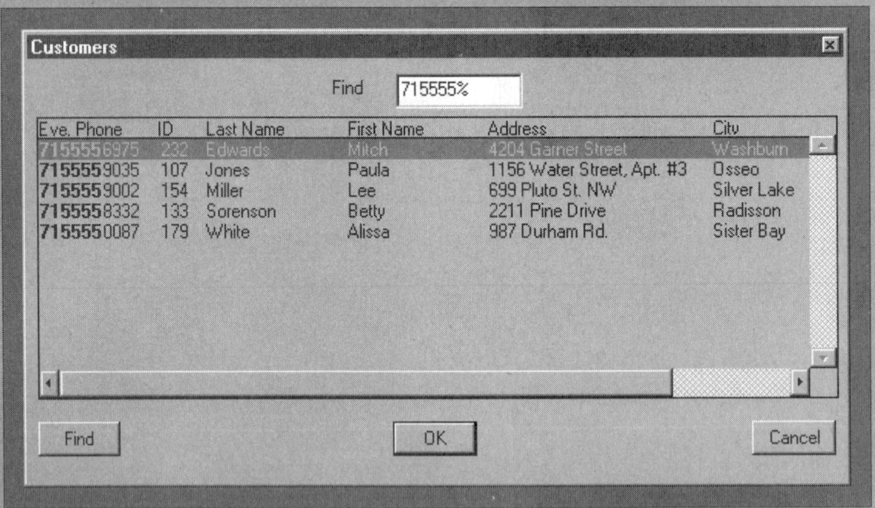

Figure 6-73: CUST_LOV display

7. Click the Cancel button to close the LOV display, and then close the Forms Runtime application.

Now you need to create the LOV to display the records in the ORDERSOURCE table so the user can select a value to insert into the ORDERSOURCE_TEXT field on the form.

To create a LOV to display the records in the ORDERSOURCE table:

1 Create a new LOV that selects the ORDERSOURCE field from the ORDERSOURCE table and maps it into the ORDERSOURCE_TEXT field.
2 Rename the LOV and record group to **ORDERSOURCE_LOV**.
3 Open the LOV PROPERTIES sheet for ORDERSOURCE_LOV and change the Title property to **Order Source**, the Width to **75**, and the Height to **200**. Open the Column Mapping window, and then change the ORDERSOURCE column's title to **Order Source** and the Column Width to **75**. Change the X- and Y-Position properties so the LOV display is directly under ORDERSOURCE_TEXT on the canvas.
4 Make a copy of the CUST_LOV_BUTTON, and position the copy next to ORDERSOURCE_TEXT. Change the Name property of the copy to **ORDERSOURCE_LOV_BUTTON.**
5 Change the trigger for the ORDERSOURCE_LOV_BUTTON GO_ITEM command so it places the insertion point in ORDERSOURCE_TEXT.
6 Change the LOV property of ORDERSOURCE_TEXT to **ORDERSOURCE _LOV**.
7 Save the form.
8 Run the form and test the LOV. Your display should look like Figure 6-74.

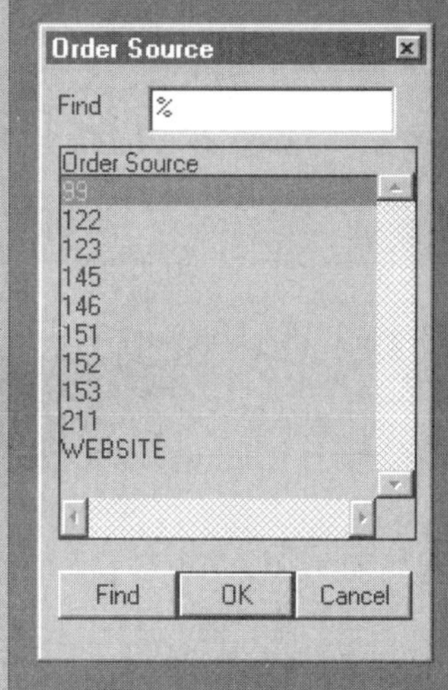

Figure 6-74: ORDERSOURCE _LOV display

HELP? If the selected Order Source does not appear in ORDERSOURCE_TEXT on the form when you test the LOV, you probably forgot the INTO statement on your LOV query. To correct this error, map the ORDERSOURCE field into the ORDERSOURCE_TEXT field on the LOV Properties sheet.

Creating the Form Triggers

The first trigger you need to create is for the NEW_CUST_BUTTON. This trigger needs to call a form named CUSTOMER_FORM that allows the user to create a new customer record. Then this form needs to pass the new CUSTID for the customer record back to the SALES_FORM. You will use the CALL_FORM command to call

If your file is stored on a different drive or in a different folder, you can use it as long as you specify the full pathname. However, the pathname cannot contain any blank spaces.

CUSTOMER_FORM, which has the following general format: `CALL_FORM('<full path to form's .fmx file>')`. Note that you must use the executable (.fmx) file in the CALL_FORM statement. Figure 6-75 illustrates how the NEW_CUST_BUTTON trigger will work with the SAVE_BUTTON trigger on the CUSTOMER_FORM. When the user clicks NEW_CUST_BUTTON, the trigger immediately calls CUSTOMER_FORM. The user enters the new customer information and then clicks the SAVE_BUTTON. The SAVE_BUTTON trigger inserts the new customer record into the database, and then sets the new CUSTID value equal to a global variable named :GLOBAL.newcustid. The user exits the CUSTOMER_FORM. Program control returns to the next line in the NEW_CUST_BUTTON trigger, which then displays the new customer ID in the CUSTID_TEXT field.

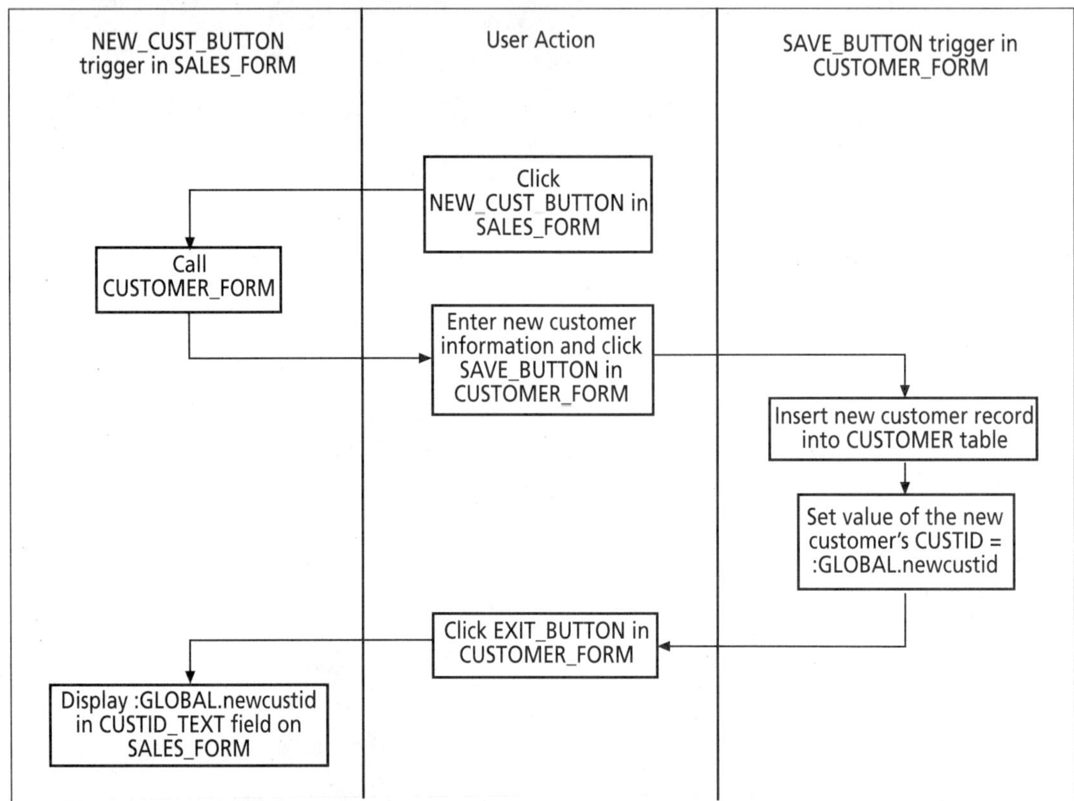

Figure 6-75: Calling CUSTOMER_FORM and passing the new CUSTID as a global variable

To create the NEW_CUST_BUTTON trigger:

1 Create a new WHEN-BUTTON-PRESSED trigger for NEW_CUST_BUTTON, and then type the code shown in Figure 6-76 in the PL/SQL Editor. The executable file for CUSTOMER_FORM will be stored in the Chapter6 folder on your Student Disk and will be named cust_mod.fmx.

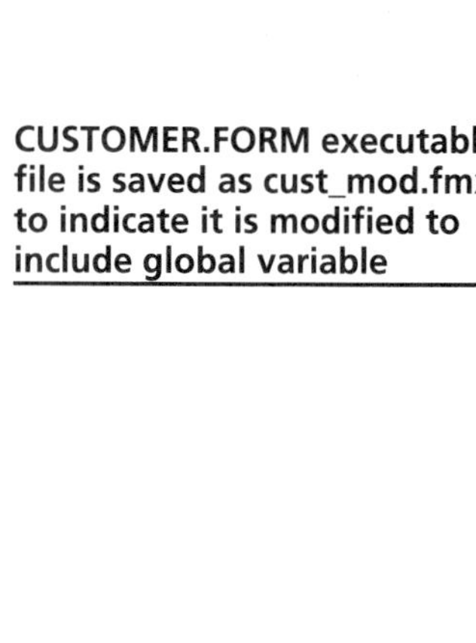

CUSTOMER.FORM executable file is saved as cust_mod.fmx to indicate it is modified to include global variable

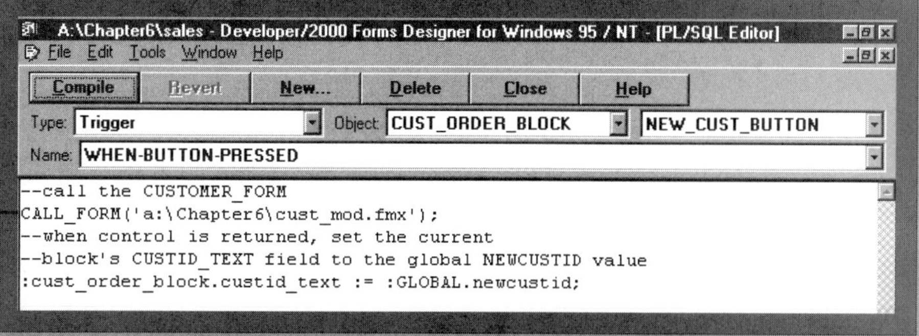

Figure 6-76: NEW_CUST_BUTTON trigger

2 Compile the trigger, correct any syntax errors, and then close the PL/SQL Editor. Next you need to modify the CUSTOMER_FORM so it sets the global variable when the user clicks the Save button.

3 Open the Object Navigator window, click **Forms**, then click the **Collapse All** button on the Object Navigator toolbar to close all of the open items in SALES_FORM.

4 Open the **customer.fmb** file from the Chapter6 folder on your Student Disk, and then save it as **cust_mod.fmb** in the same folder.

5 Click **CUSTOMER_FORM** in the Object Navigator, click **Tools** on the menu bar, and then click **Layout Editor**. The CUSTOMER_FORM appears in the Layout Editor.

6 Right-click the **Save button**, and click **PL/SQL Editor** to open the button's trigger.

7 Modify the Save button trigger so it saves the value of the new customer ID by adding the code lines shown in Figure 6-77.

add these lines

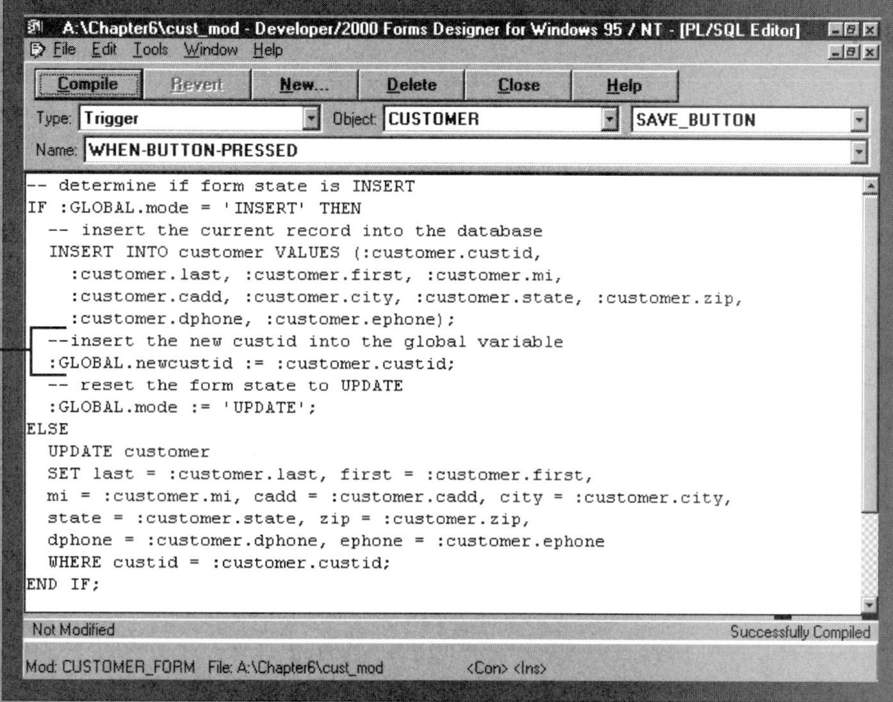

Figure 6-77: Modifying SAVE_BUTTON trigger in CUSTOMER_FORM

When you call a form from another form, remember that the .fmx file (and not the .fmb file) is called. Whenever you make changes to the .fmb file of a form that is being called, don't forget to generate a new .fmx file.

You also can run the form to generate a new .fmx file.

8 Compile the modified trigger, correct any syntax errors, and then close the PL/SQL Editor.

9 Save the file.

Before you can test to see if you can successfully call the CUSTOMER_FORM from the SALES_FORM, you need to generate your modified customer_mod.fmb file to create a new customer_mod.fmx (executable) file.

To create the new customer.fmx file:

1 Click **File** on the menu bar, point to **Administration**, and then click **Generate**.

2 Close the CUSTOMER_FORM by clicking **File** on the menu bar, and then clicking **Close**.

Now you need to test to make sure that calling the CUSTOMER_FORM from the SALES_FORM is working correctly. You will run the Sales form, click the New Customer button to call the CUSTOMER_FORM, insert a new customer record, and then see if the value for the customer ID appears on the SALES_FORM.

To test if calling the CUSTOMER_FORM from the SALES_FORM is working:

1 Run the Sales form.

2 Click the **New Customer** button. The CUSTOMER_FORM should appear.

3 Click the **Create** button. Enter a new customer record for **Terry L. Harris**, **3879 Edgewater Drive**, **Superior**, **WI**, **54880**, daytime phone **7155552008**, and evening phone **7155552388**.

4 Click the **Save** button. The "No changes to save" message appears to confirm that the new record was inserted.

5 Click the **Exit** button. The new customer's CUSTID should appear in the CUSTID_TEXT field in the SALES_FORM.

6 Close the Forms Runtime application.

HELP? If the CUSTOMER_FORM does not appear, check the NEW_CUST_BUTTON trigger and make sure you entered the path to A:\Chapter6\cust_mod.fmx correctly, and verify that the cust_mod.fmx file exists in the Chapter6 folder on your Student Disk.

Creating a Trigger to Dynamically Set Form Properties Sometimes you need to change a property of a form item during form execution. For example, the current default choice for the PMT_RADIO_GROUP is CHECK. If CHECK is the selected payment method, then the user will not need to enter values for credit card number or expiration date, so these fields should be disabled when check is selected, and enabled when either Visa or MasterCard are selected. You can dynamically change the properties of these text fields during form execution using the SET_ITEM_PROPERTY command, which has the following general format: `SET_ITEM_PROPERTY('<form item name>', <property name>, <property value>)`.

Next you will create a trigger for the radio group's WHEN-RADIO-CHANGED event so the credit card number and expiration date text fields are not enabled or navigable unless the selected payment method is credit card.

For more information about the SET_ITEM_PROPERTY command and how to use it for other properties, search for SET_ITEM_PROPERTY in Oracle Forms online Help.

To make the WHEN-RADIO-CHANGED trigger to dynamically change the credit card text field properties:

1 Open the Layout Editor for the CUST_ORDER_CANVAS, select the **CC_NUMBER_TEXT** and **CC_EXP_TEXT** items as a group, change their Enabled and Navigable properties to **False**, and then close the Properties sheet.

2 In the Object Navigator window, right-click **PMT_RADIO_GROUP**, and then click **PL/SQL Editor**. The PL/SQL Editor opens.

3 Click the New button on the PL/SQL button bar, scroll down and select the **WHEN-RADIO-CHANGED** event, and then click the **OK** button.

4 Type the code shown in Figure 6-78 in the PL/SQL Editor to disable the credit card text fields if the radio group value is CHECK, and enable the credit card text fields if the radio group value is CC.

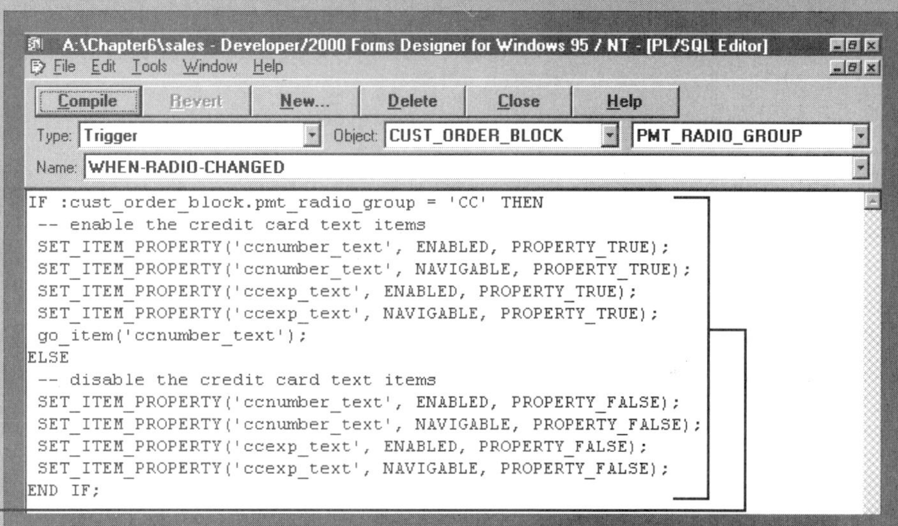

Figure 6-78: PMT_RADIO_GROUP trigger

5 Compile the trigger, correct any syntax errors, and then close the PL/SQL Editor.

6 Run the form.

7 Leave the **Check** option button selected, and then confirm that you cannot enter data in the credit card number or expiration date fields.

8 Click the **Visa** option button, and then confirm that you can enter data in the credit card number and expiration date fields.

9 Close the Forms Runtime application.

Creating the ENTER_ITEMS Trigger When the user clicks the Enter Items button, the system needs to insert a new order record into CUST_ORDER and then display the ORDERLINE_WINDOW. You will create the ENTER_ITEMS trigger next.

To create the ENTER_ITEMS trigger:

1 Open the Layout Editor for the CUST_ORDER_CANVAS, and then create a WHEN-BUTTON-PRESSED trigger for the Enter Items button by typing the code shown in Figure 6-79 in the PL/SQL Editor.

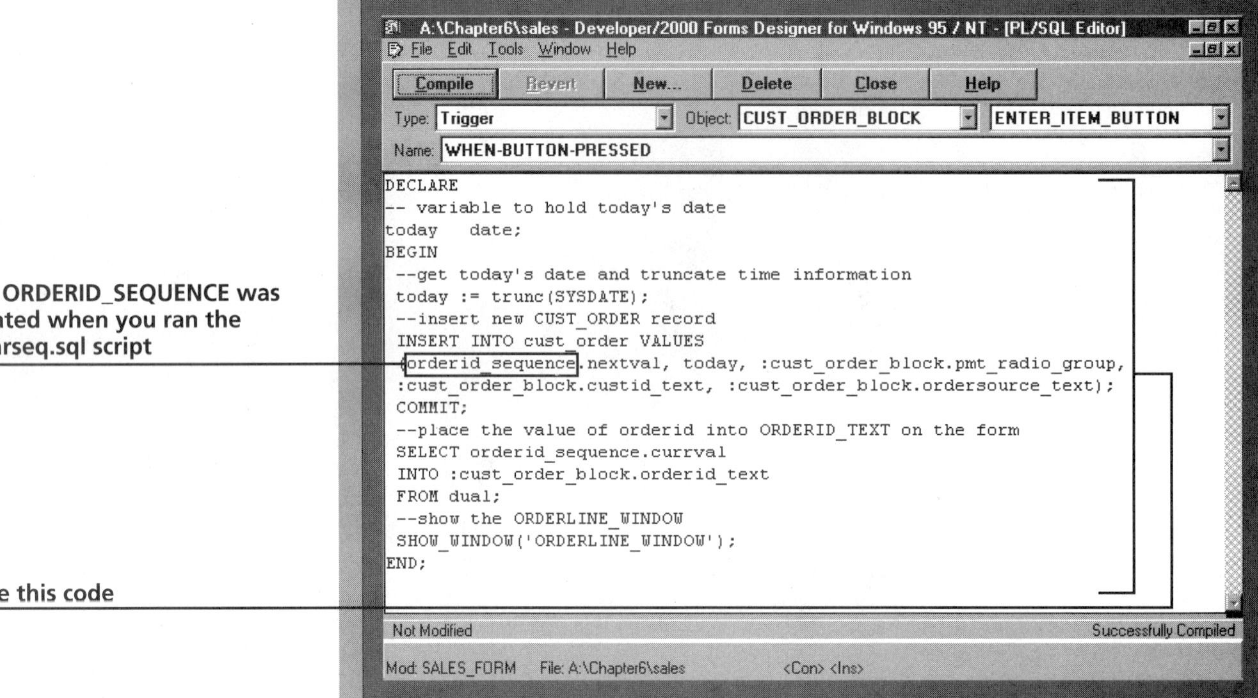

Figure 6-79: ENTER_ITEM_BUTTON trigger

2 Save the form and then run it. To test the trigger, suppose that customer Mitch Edwards is making an order. He wants to pay by check, and he has indicated that the order source is Catalog 151.

3 Use the LOVs to enter Mitch's customer and order source data, and then click the **Enter Items** button. The new order ID number appears in the Order ID field, but the CUST_ORDER_WINDOW still appears. What happened to the ORDERLINE_WINDOW?

4 Click **Window** on the menu bar. You should see that both windows now are present in the application, as shown in Figure 6-80. However, CUST_ORDER_WINDOW is the *active window* because it contains the item that currently has the application's focus, which is the Enter Items button. You will set the focus to an item on the ORDERLINE_WINDOW later after changing some items.

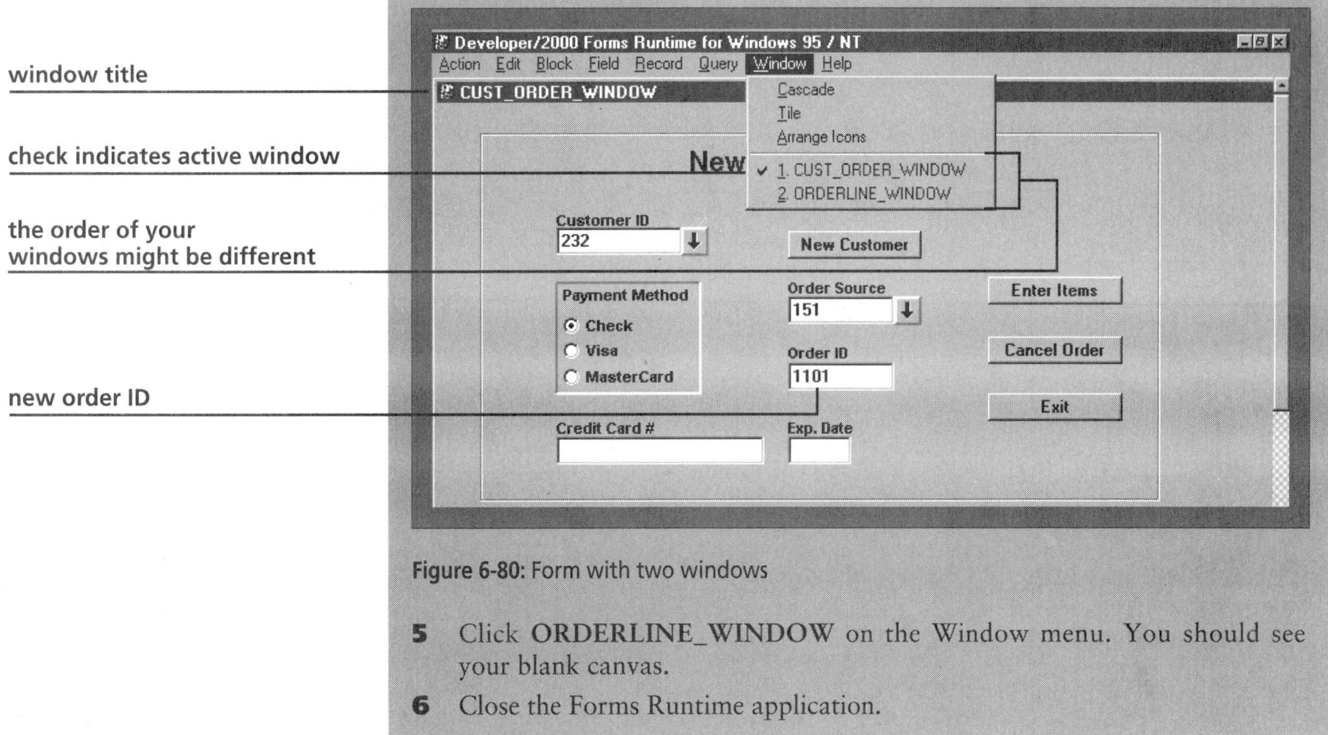

Figure 6-80: Form with two windows

5 Click **ORDERLINE_WINDOW** on the Window menu. You should see your blank canvas.

6 Close the Forms Runtime application.

As you can see, the window Title property is more than just cosmetic—it is what users see in the Windows menu in a multi-window application. Next you will change your window titles so they are more descriptive.

To change the window titles:

1 Open the Object Navigator window, and then change the Title property of CUST_ORDER_WINDOW to **Customer Order Information.**

2 Change the Title property of ORDERLINE_WINDOW to **Order Item Information.**

Creating Triggers for the Cancel Order and Exit Buttons Before you begin working on the ORDERLINE_WINDOW, you need to finish the CUST_ORDER_WINDOW by creating triggers for the Cancel Order and Exit buttons. The Cancel Order button will clear the form fields, and the Exit button will exit the form.

To create the Cancel Order and Exit triggers:

1 Create a WHEN-BUTTON-PRESSED trigger for the Cancel Order button with the following trigger code: **CLEAR_FORM;**.

2 Create a WHEN-BUTTON-PRESSED trigger for the Exit button with the following trigger code: **EXIT_FORM;**.

3 Save the form.

4 Test your form to make sure that these triggers work correctly.

Creating the ORDERLINE_WINDOW Items

Now you need to create the ORDERLINE_WINDOW items as proposed in the design shown in Figure 6-65. First you will create a control block called ORDERLINE_BLOCK, and then you will create the form text fields. You also will create fields for ITEMID and QOH because these values are needed to update the database, but they are not displayed. The INVENTORY fields that will be retrieved using the LOV (Inventory ID, Description, Size, Color, and Current Price) will be set as non-navigable so the user will not be able to update or delete their values.

To create the ORDERLINE_WINDOW block and text fields:

1 Open the Object Navigator window in Ownership View, and then double-click the **canvas** icon beside ORDERLINE_CANVAS to open the Layout Editor.

2 Create a new control block named **ORDERLINE_BLOCK.**

3 Make sure that **ORDERLINE_BLOCK** is selected in the Block list box in the Layout Editor.

HELP? If the ORDERLINE_BLOCK is not selected, click the list arrow, and then click ORDERLINE_BLOCK.

4 Create the following text fields, and then position the text fields as shown in Figure 6-81 and add the associated labels using a 9-point bold Arial font:

Name	Data Type	Maximum Length	Display	Navigable	Format Mask
ITEMID_TEXT	Number	8	False	False	
INVID_TEXT	Number	10	True	False	
ITEMDESC_TEXT	Char	100	True	False	
ITEMSIZE_TEXT	Char	10	True	False	
COLOR_TEXT	Char	20	True	False	
CURR_PRICE _TEXT	Number	9	True	False	$9,999.99
QOH_TEXT	Number	4	False	False	
ORDER_QUANT _TEXT	Number	4	True	True	
SUBTOTAL _TEXT	Number	9	True	True	$9,999.99
SH_TEXT	Number	9	True	True	$9,999.99
TAX_TEXT	Number	9	True	True	$9,999.99
FTOTAL_TEXT	Number	9	True	True	$9,999.99

HELP? If you get a message that the item names CUSTID_TEXT and ORDERID_TEXT are not unique, then you probably are creating your text items in the CUST_ORDER_BLOCK. Make sure ORDERLINE_BLOCK is the block that appears in the Block list box at the top of the Layout Editor. If you accidentally created some text items in the CUST_ORDER_BLOCK, you can cut and paste them into the ORDERLINE_BLOCK in the Object Navigator.

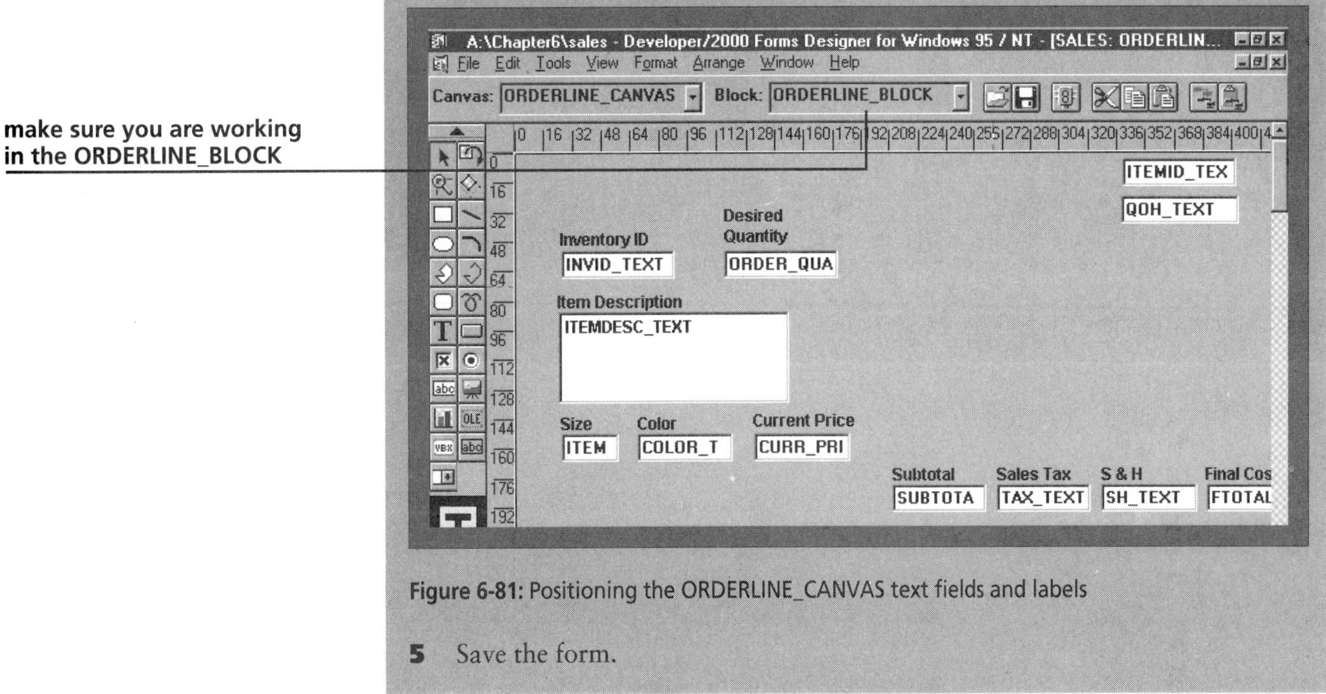

Figure 6-81: Positioning the ORDERLINE_CANVAS text fields and labels

5 Save the form.

Next you will create a display item to show the information about each ordered item, including the item ID, quantity, description, size, color, and price. Recall that a display item is used to display text that is cannot be changed directly by the user, or by a user selecting values into it using a LOV.

To create the display item:

1 Click the **Display Item** tool on the Tool palette, and then draw a box to hold the Order Summary as shown in Figure 6-82.

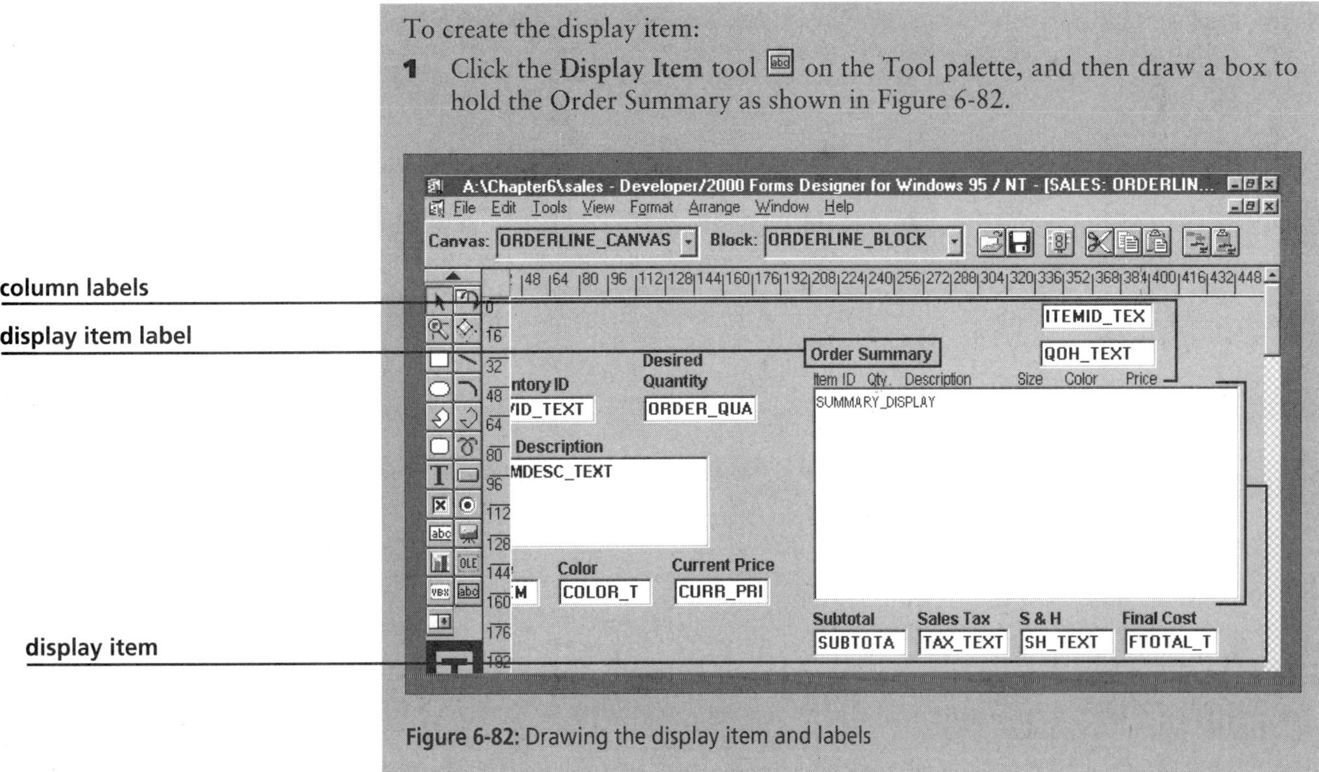

Figure 6-82: Drawing the display item and labels

2 Right-click the new display item, click **Properties**, and then change the display item name to **SUMMARY_DISPLAY**, the Font Name to **Arial Narrow**, the Font Size to 8, the Font Weight to **Light**, and the Maximum Length property to **32000**.

3 Create labels for the display item and for the individual summary columns as shown in Figure 6-82. Use a 9-point bold Arial font for the display item label, and a 10-point Arial Narrow font for the column labels.

4 Save the form.

To finish the canvas layout, you need to create the buttons and format the canvas. You will do this next.

To finish the canvas layout:

1 Create buttons with the following properties, and then position the buttons as shown in Figure 6-83.

Name	Label
ADD_BUTTON	Add Item to Order
FINISH_BUTTON	Finish Order
NEW_ORDER_BUTTON	New Order
OL_CANCEL_BUTTON	Cancel Order
OL_EXIT_BUTTON	Exit

Figure 6-83: Positioning the ORDERLINE_CANVAS buttons

2 Add a title with the text **Enter Order Items.** Format the title as 18-point **bold Arial** font.

3 Save the form.

tip

Rather than calling the buttons on this canvas CANCEL_BUTTON and EXIT_BUTTON, name them OL_CANCEL_BUTTON and OL_EXIT_BUTTON to indicate that they are on the ORDERLINE_BLOCK. You should use unique item names even when items are in different blocks to avoid confusion.

When you run the form, you want the CUST_ORDER_WINDOW to appear first. The way to ensure this is to create a WHEN-NEW-FORM-INSTANCE trigger that fires just after the form is loaded. In this trigger, you will put a command to set the form focus on the CUSTID_TEXT field, which is in the CUST_ORDER_WINDOW. As a result, the CUST_ORDER_WINDOW always will appear first when the form starts.

To create a new WHEN-NEW-FORM-INSTANCE trigger:

1 Open the Object Navigator window, and then click **Triggers** directly under SALES_FORM.

2 Click the **Create** button on the Object Navigator toolbar, and then select the **WHEN-NEW-FORM-INSTANCE** event.

3 Type the following code in the PL/SQL Editor: **GO_ITEM('custid_text');**.

4 Compile the trigger, correct any syntax errors, and then close the PL/SQL Editor.

5 Save the form, and then run the form to confirm that the CUST_ORDER_WINDOW appears first.

HELP? If the ORDERLINE_WINDOW appears instead of the CUST_ORDER_WINDOW, close the Forms Runtime application, open the Object Navigator in Visual View, and confirm that CUSTID_TEXT is on the CUST_ORDER_CANVAS, and that the CUST_ORDER_CANVAS is in the CUST_ORDER_WINDOW. If it is not, drag and drop the items as necessary so they are on the correct canvas and in the right window.

6 Close the Forms Runtime application.

Now you need to modify the Enter Items button trigger in CUST _ORDER_BLOCK so the ORDERLINE_WINDOW will be displayed when the user clicks the Enter Items button. To do this, you will use the GO_ITEM command to move the insertion point to an item in the ORDERLINE_BLOCK. The first action the user will make in the ORDERLINE_WINDOW is to select an inventory item, so you will set the form's focus to the INVID_TEXT field.

To modify the Enter Items button trigger so it changes the focus to the INVID_TEXT field:

1 Open the Layout Editor, and then select the **CUST_ORDER_CANVAS** from the canvas list.

2 Modify the Enter Items button trigger in the PL/SQL Editor so the last line is: **GO_ITEM('invid_text');**.

3 Compile the trigger, correct any syntax errors, and then close the PL/SQL Editor.

4 Save the form and then run the form.

5 Click the **Customer LOV** button, and select customer **Mitch Edwards**.

6 Click the **Order Source** LOV button, and select Order Source **151**.

7 Click the **Enter Items** button. The Order Item Information window opens.

8 Close the Forms Runtime application.

Creating the Inventory LOV

Next you need to create the Inventory LOV on the ORDERLINE_CANVAS to allow the user to search for inventory items, and display and return inventory IDs, item descriptions, colors, sizes, and current prices. The LOV also must return (but not display) the item ID and quantity on hand.

To create the Inventory LOV:

1. Open the Object Navigator window, click **LOVs**, and then click the **Create** button on the Object Navigator toolbar.
2. Type the query text shown in Figure 6-84.

type this command

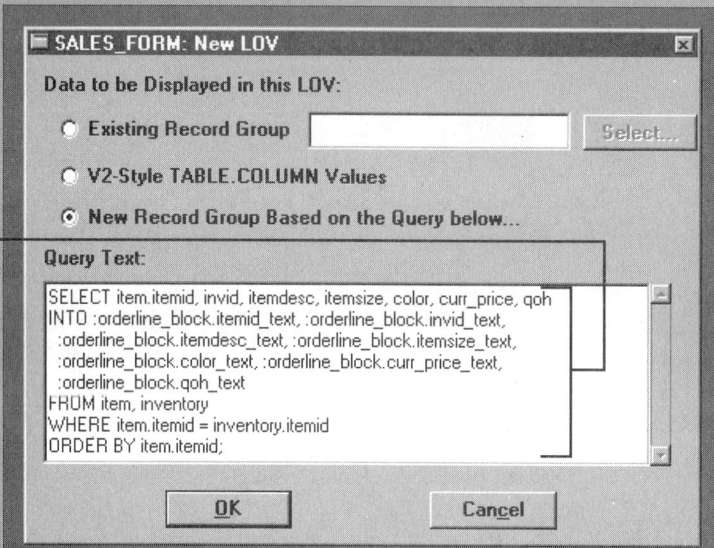

Figure 6-84: Query to create the INV_LOV

tip

If you have trouble creating the LOV, copy the SELECT statement into a text editor by selecting the text and then pressing Ctrl + C, and then click the Cancel button. Then look in the Object Navigator window (Visual View) and verify that all of the text fields referenced in the INTO clause are in ORDERLINE_BLOCK.

3. Rename the LOV and record group to **INV_LOV**.
4. Change the Title property for the INV_LOV display to **Inventory**.
5. Modify the Column Mapping for INV_LOV as follows:

Column	Title	Width
ITEMID	Item ID	30
INVID	<not displayed>	0
ITEMDESC	Description	140
ITEMSIZE	Size	25
COLOR	Color	40
CURR_PRICE	Price	30
QOH	<not displayed>	0

6. Open the Layout Editor, select **CUST_ORDER_CANVAS** from the canvas list, and then copy the **CUST_LOV_BUTTON**.
7. Select **ORDERLINE_CANVAS** from the canvas list, and then paste the LOV button onto the ORDERLINE_CANVAS. Drag the new button so it is positioned on the right edge of INVID_TEXT.
8. Select the new button and open its Properties sheet. Change the button's name to **INV_LOV_BUTTON**, and then close the Properties sheet.
9. Right-click the new LOV button, and then click **PL/SQL Editor** to open the PL/SQL Editor. Modify the GO_ITEM command in the trigger as follows: **GO_ITEM('invid_text');**.
10. Compile the trigger, correct any syntax errors, and then close the PL/SQL Editor.

11 Open the Layout Editor, and open the INVID_TEXT Properties sheet. Set the LOV property to **INV_LOV**.

12 Save the form.

Now you can run the form to confirm that the INV_LOV works correctly.

To confirm that the INV_LOV works correctly:

1 Run the form, and then click the **Enter Items** button on the CUST_ORDER_CANVAS. (Normally you would enter the customer order information, but you will skip this step for testing the INV_LOV.)

2 Click the **Inventory ID LOV** button, and then select the first item (Men's Expedition Parka, S, Navy). The selected fields display as shown in Figure 6-85.

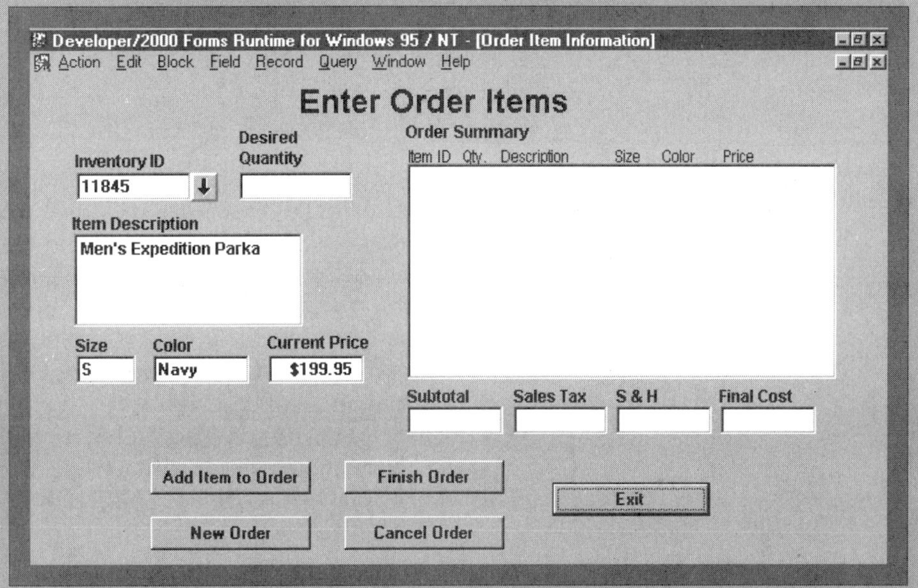

Figure 6-85: Retrieving an inventory item

3 Close the Forms Runtime application, and then resize the LOV display if necessary so all of the fields are visible.

Creating the ORDERLINE_WINDOW Triggers

You will create the triggers for the EXIT_BUTTON and NEW_ORDER buttons first. The EXIT_BUTTON trigger exits the form, and the NEW_ORDER trigger clears the form fields and sets the form focus to the CUSTID_TEXT field in the CUST_ORDER_CANVAS.

To create the EXIT_BUTTON and NEW_ORDER buttons:

1. Create a WHEN-BUTTON-PRESSED trigger for the EXIT_BUTTON. Type the following code in the PL/SQL Editor: **EXIT_FORM;**.
2. Compile the trigger, correct any syntax errors, and then exit the PL/SQL Editor.
3. Create a WHEN-BUTTON-PRESSED trigger for the NEW_ORDER_BUTTON with the following code:

   CLEAR_FORM;

   GO_ITEM('custid_text');.
4. Compile the trigger, correct any syntax errors, and then exit the PL/SQL Editor.
5. Save the form, and then run the form and verify that the EXIT_BUTTON and NEW_ORDER buttons work correctly.

The ADD_BUTTON trigger will need to determine if the desired quantity of the selected inventory item is in stock, and then either process the order or display the date the next shipment is expected. Figure 6-86 shows how this process will be divided into program units. If the item is in stock, the system needs to insert a new record in the ORDERLINE table and subtract the quantity from the INVENTORY table. This will be done by the UPDATE_OL_AND_QOH program unit. The system then needs to update the summary display, which will be done by the UPDATE_SUMMARY_DISPLAY program unit. If the desired item quantity is not in stock, then the user needs to be notified of the date the next shipment is due. This will be done by the SHOW_SHIPMENT_ALERT program unit.

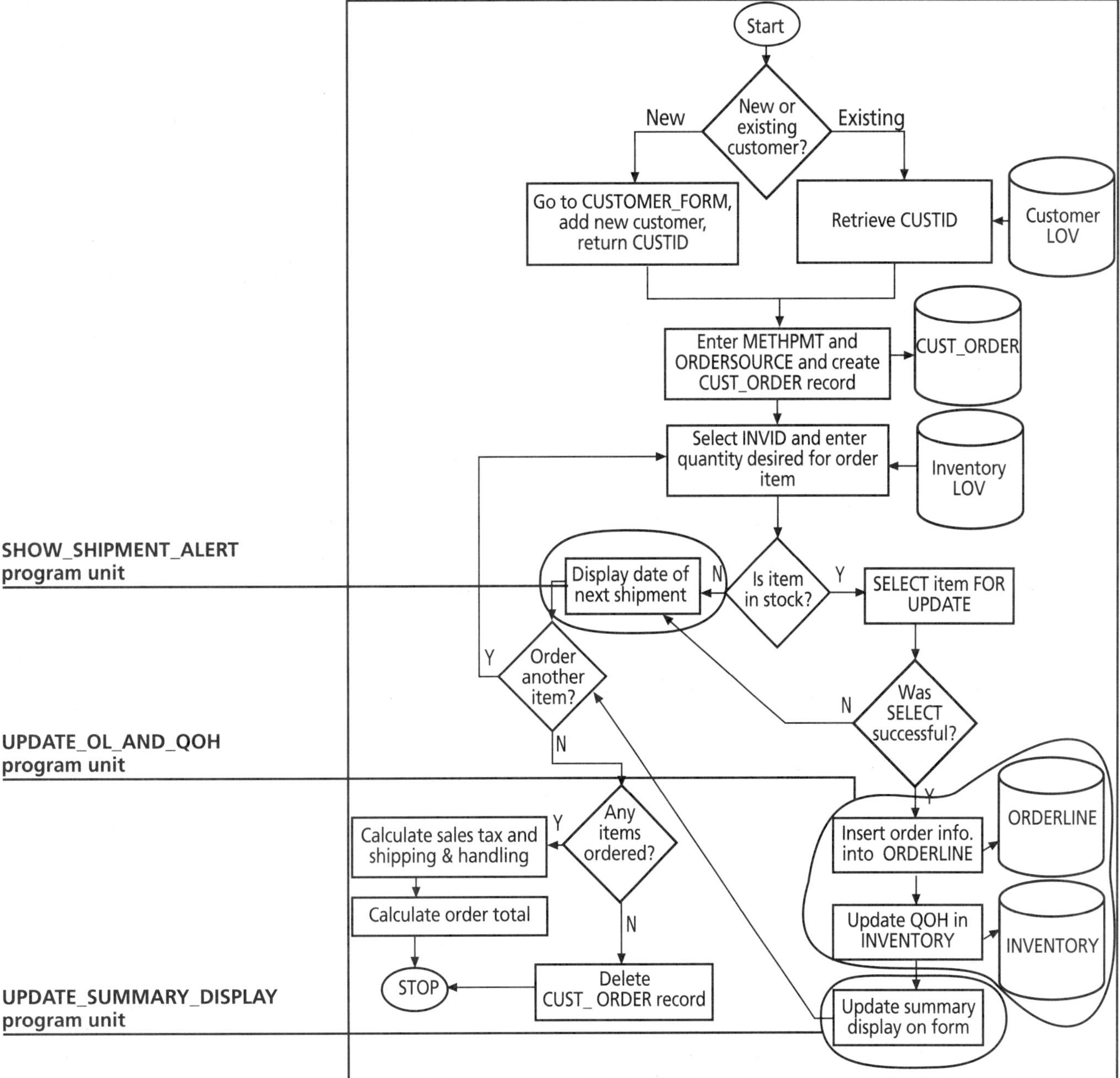

Figure 6-86: ADD_BUTTON program units

First you will create the ADD_BUTTON trigger. If the item is in stock, the trigger will call the UPDATE_OL_AND_QOH program unit, call a program unit to clear the fields on the ORDERLINE_CANVAS, and then call the UPDATE_SUMMARY_DISPLAY program unit. If the item is not in stock, the trigger will call the SHOW_SHIPMENT_ALERT program unit.

To create the ADD_BUTTON trigger:

1 Create a new WHEN_BUTTON_PRESSED trigger for the ADD_BUTTON by typing the code shown in Figure 6-87 in the PL/SQL Editor. Do not compile the trigger yet, because you have to make the program units first.

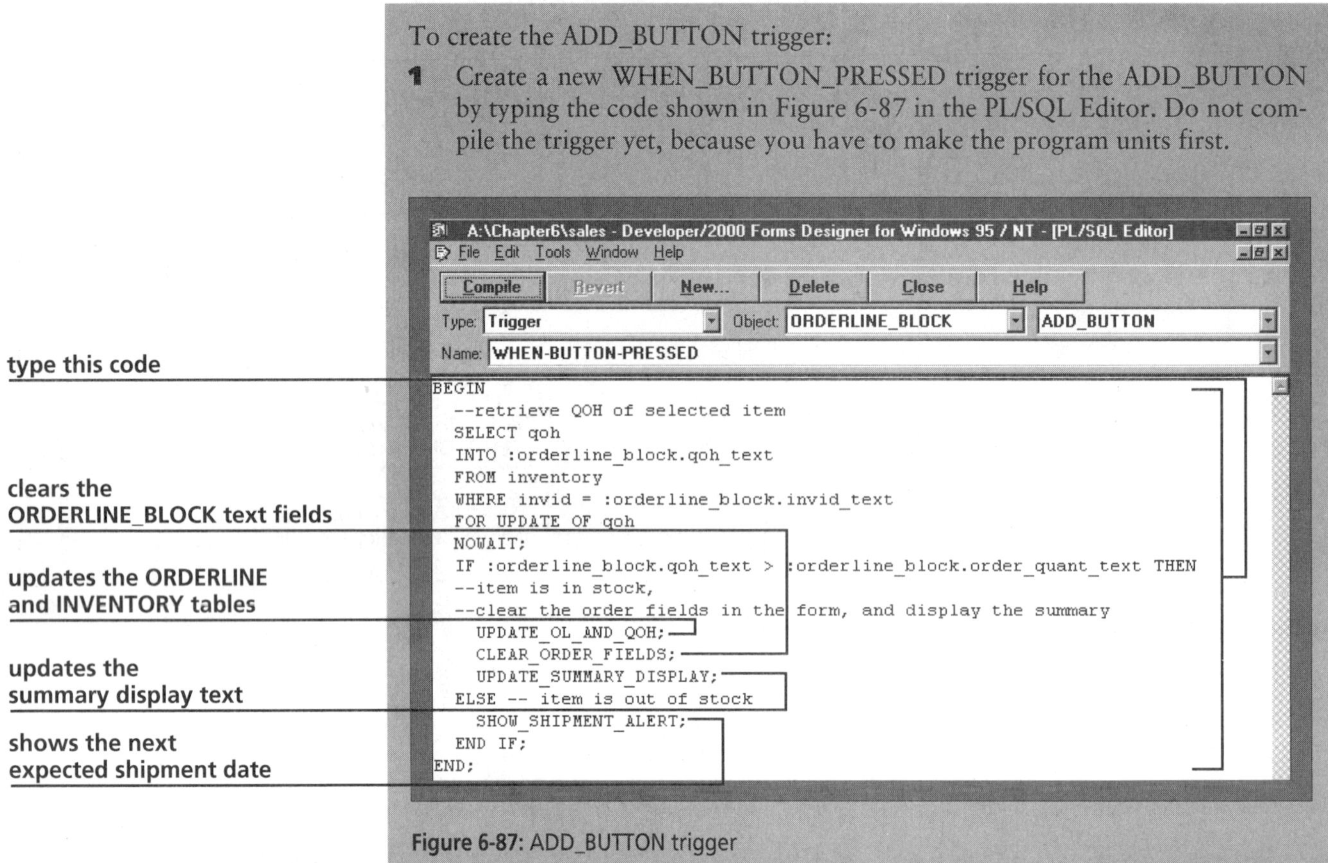

Figure 6-87: ADD_BUTTON trigger

First you will make the UPDATE_OL_AND_QOH program unit to insert the new order line information into ORDERLINE and to update QOH in INVENTORY.

To create the new program unit:

1 In the PL/SQL Editor, click the **Type** list arrow, click **Program Units**, and then click the **New** button on the PL/SQL Editor button bar.

2 Name the new program unit **UPDATE_OL_AND_QOH**, make sure that the **Procedure** option button is selected, and then click the **OK** button.

3 Type the code shown in Figure 6-88.

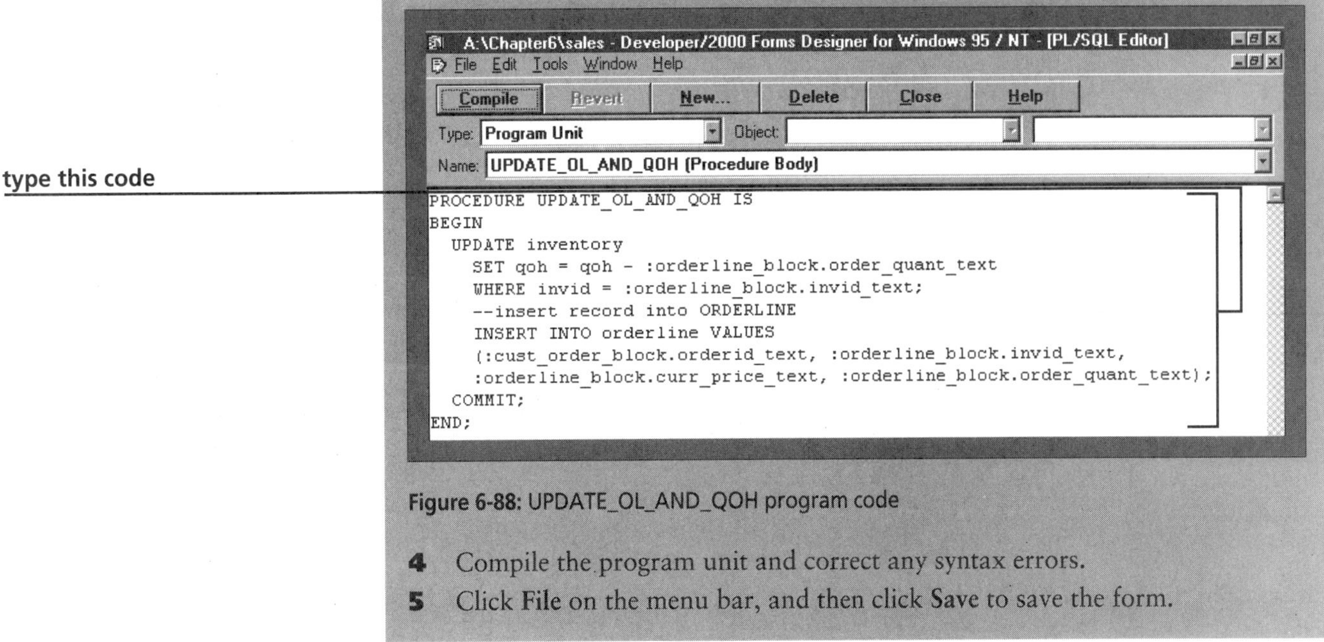

Figure 6-88: UPDATE_OL_AND_QOH program code

4 Compile the program unit and correct any syntax errors.

5 Click **File** on the menu bar, and then click **Save** to save the form.

Next you need to create a program unit named CLEAR_ORDER_FIELDS that clears the ORDERLINE_BLOCK text fields that contain the information about the inventory item that was just processed. You cannot use the CLEAR_FORM function because it clears all of the fields in the form, and you want to retain the customer order information on the CUST_ORDER_CANVAS.

To create the CLEAR_ORDER_FIELDS program unit:

1 In the PL/SQL Editor, confirm that **Program Units** is selected in the Type list, and then click the **New** button on the PL/SQL Editor button bar.

2 Name the new program unit **CLEAR_ORDER_FIELDS**. Make sure that the **Procedure** option button is selected, and then click the **OK** button.

3 Type the code shown in Figure 6-89 in the PL/SQL Editor for the CLEAR_ORDER_FIELDS program unit.

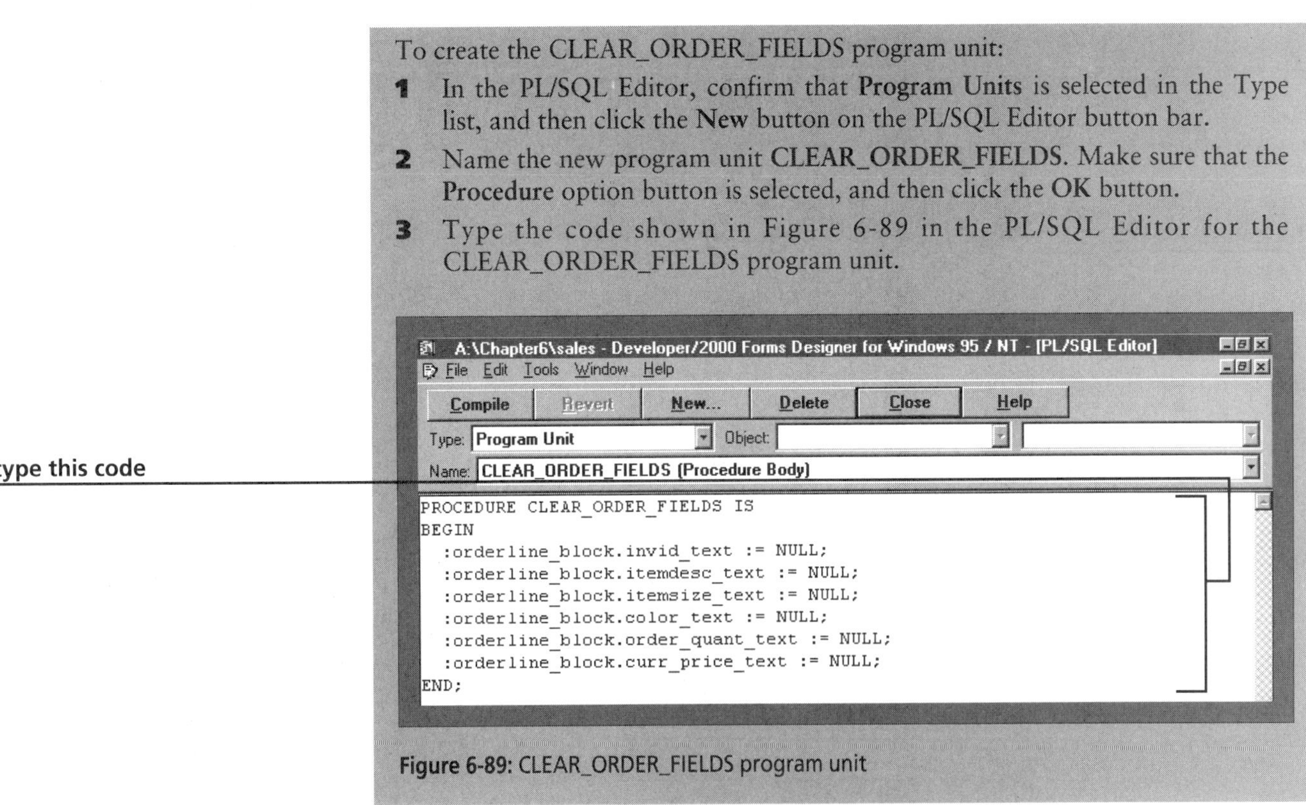

Figure 6-89: CLEAR_ORDER_FIELDS program unit

4 Compile the code and correct any syntax errors.

The next step is to create the UPDATE_SUMMARY_DISPLAY that summarizes all of the order lines in the display item. This program unit requires an explicit cursor because there will be a variable number of ORDERLINE entries to display. The program unit will fetch each ORDERLINE record for the current order, and then place the information in a variable named SUMMARY_TEXT. As each new data record is fetched, the results are **concatenated**, or joined, to the current value of SUMMARY_TEXT using the double-bar (||) symbol, which is used to concatenate text strings in PL/SQL.

To format the display, you will need to trim all of the trailing blank spaces from each returned data value using the RTRIM function, and then pad each data value with blank spaces using the RPAD function so each column is the same width. You will convert the numerical values (ITEMID and QUANTITY) to characters using the TO_CHAR function. You must put a fixed number of blank spaces between each data field so the data values will be displayed in a columnar fashion with blank space in between values.

To create the UPDATE_SUMMARY_DISPLAY program unit:

1 In the PL/SQL Editor, click the **New** button on the PL/SQL Editor button bar.

2 Name the new program unit **UPDATE_SUMMARY_DISPLAY**. Make sure that the **Procedure** option button is selected, and then click the **OK** button.

3 Type the code shown in Figure 6-90 for the DECLARE section of the program unit.

type this code

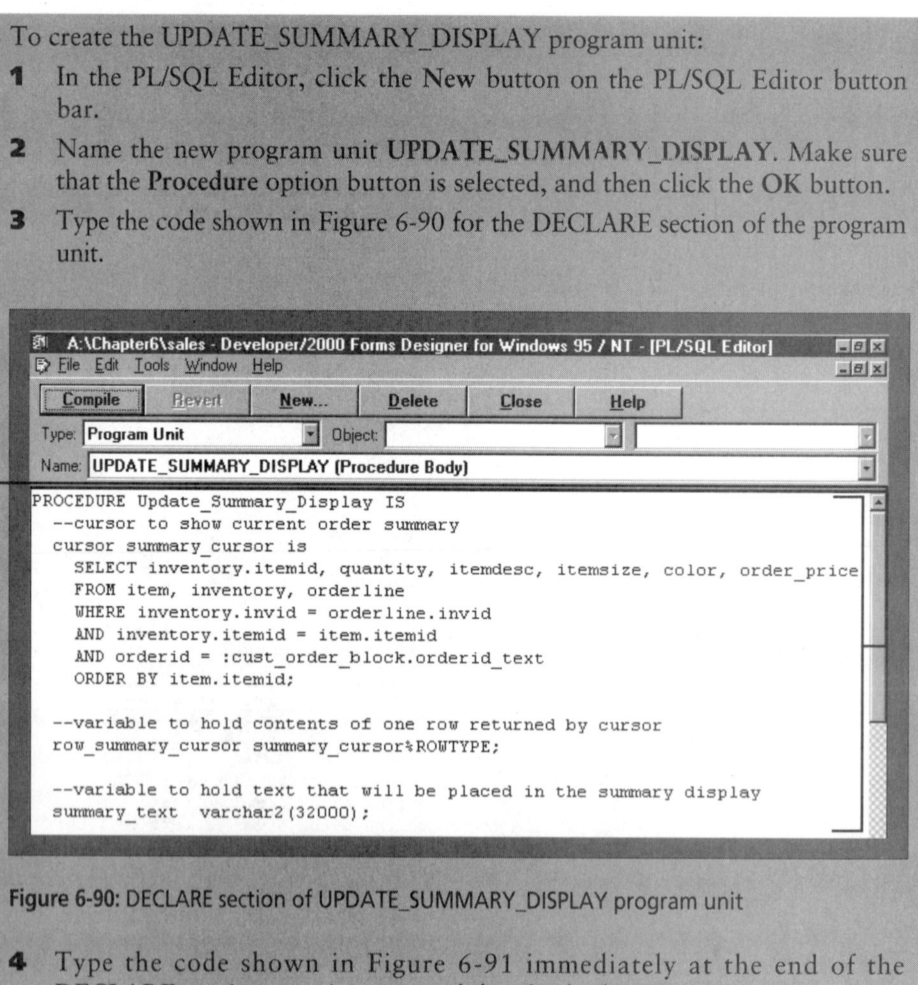


```
PROCEDURE Update_Summary_Display IS
  --cursor to show current order summary
  cursor summary_cursor is
    SELECT inventory.itemid, quantity, itemdesc, itemsize, color, order_price
    FROM item, inventory, orderline
    WHERE inventory.invid = orderline.invid
    AND inventory.itemid = item.itemid
    AND orderid = :cust_order_block.orderid_text
    ORDER BY item.itemid;

  --variable to hold contents of one row returned by cursor
  row_summary_cursor summary_cursor%ROWTYPE;

  --variable to hold text that will be placed in the summary display
  summary_text  varchar2(32000);
```

Figure 6-90: DECLARE section of UPDATE_SUMMARY_DISPLAY program unit

4 Type the code shown in Figure 6-91 immediately at the end of the DECLARE section you just entered for the body (BEGIN section) of the program unit.

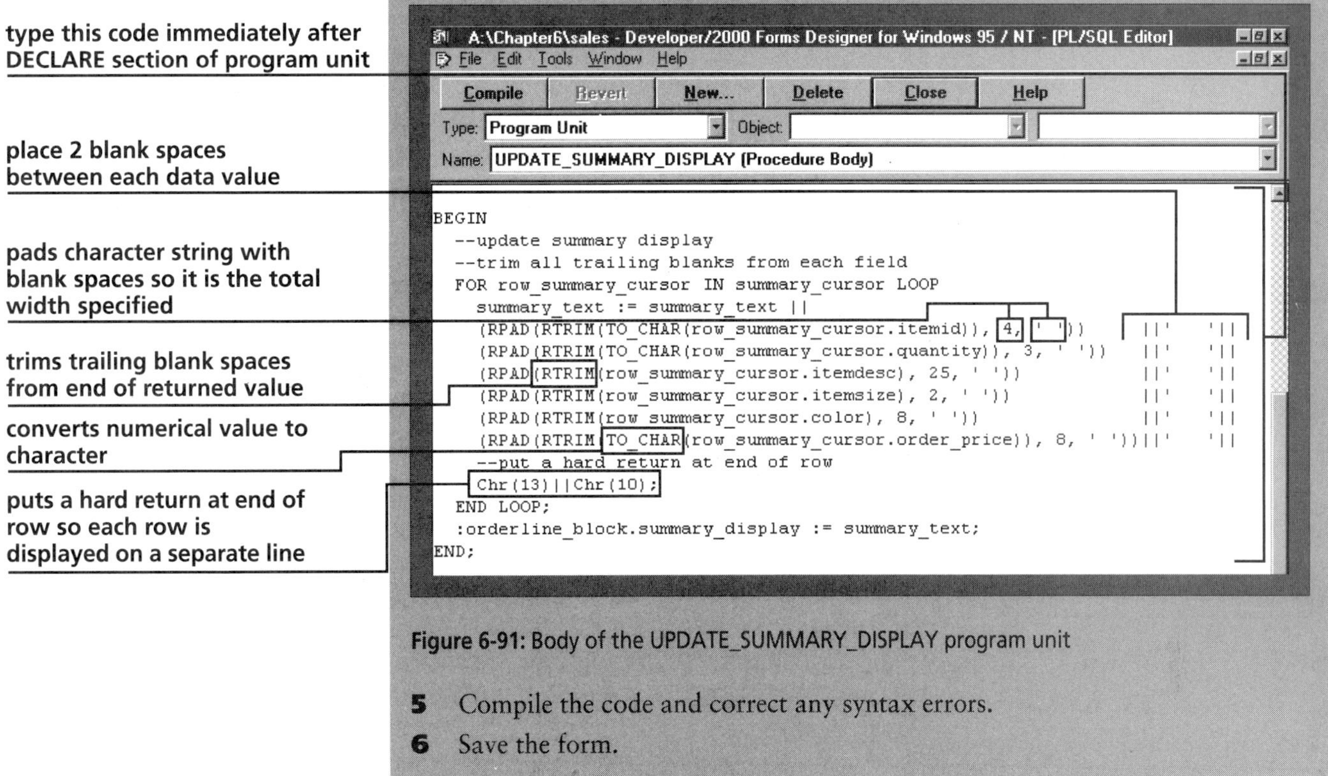

Figure 6-91: Body of the UPDATE_SUMMARY_DISPLAY program unit

5 Compile the code and correct any syntax errors.

6 Save the form.

The final program unit, SHOW_SHIPMENT_ALERT, involves the case where a "stockout" has occurred. Normally when you create an alert, the alert message is a fixed property set in the alert Properties sheet at design time. In this alert, the message will be configured while the program is running to show the dates that the next shipment of the out-of-stock item is expected. First you will create the STOCKOUT_ALERT.

To create the STOCKOUT_ALERT:

1 Return to the Object Navigator window in Ownership View, and then create a new alert named **STOCKOUT_ALERT**.

2 Change the Title property to **Item Out of Stock**, the Alert Style property to **Stop**, and the Button1 property to **OK**. Delete the Button2 property.

3 Leave the Message property blank because you will set it while the form is running and just before the alert is displayed.

4 Close the STOCKOUT_ALERT Properties sheet.

5 Save the form.

Now you will create the SHOW_SHIPMENT_ALERT program unit that configures the alert message. To configure the message, the program unit queries the database to retrieve new shipment records for the given inventory item using an explicit cursor. It places the retrieved records in a character variable named SHIPMENT_TEXT. The LENGTH function is used to determine if the length of SUMMARY_TEXT field is greater than one. If it is greater than one, it means some SHIPPING or BACKORDER records were found, and new shipments are expected.

The program unit then sets the Message property of the STOCKOUT_ALERT equal to a message stating the dates the new shipments are expected using the SET_ALERT_PROPERTY command. The expected shipment dates are displayed as a list of dates separated by blank spaces. If no new shipments exist, then the message states that no new shipments are expected. After the alert is displayed, the form fields are cleared and the user can select a new inventory item.

To create the SHOW_SHIPMENT_ALERT program unit:

1 In the Object Navigator, click **Program Units**, and then click the **Create** button on the Object Navigator toolbar.

2 Name the new program unit **SHOW_SHIPMENT_ALERT**. Make sure that the **Procedure** option button is selected, and then click the **OK** button.

3 Type the code shown in Figure 6-92 for the DECLARE section of the SHOW_SHIPMENT_ALERT program unit.

type this code

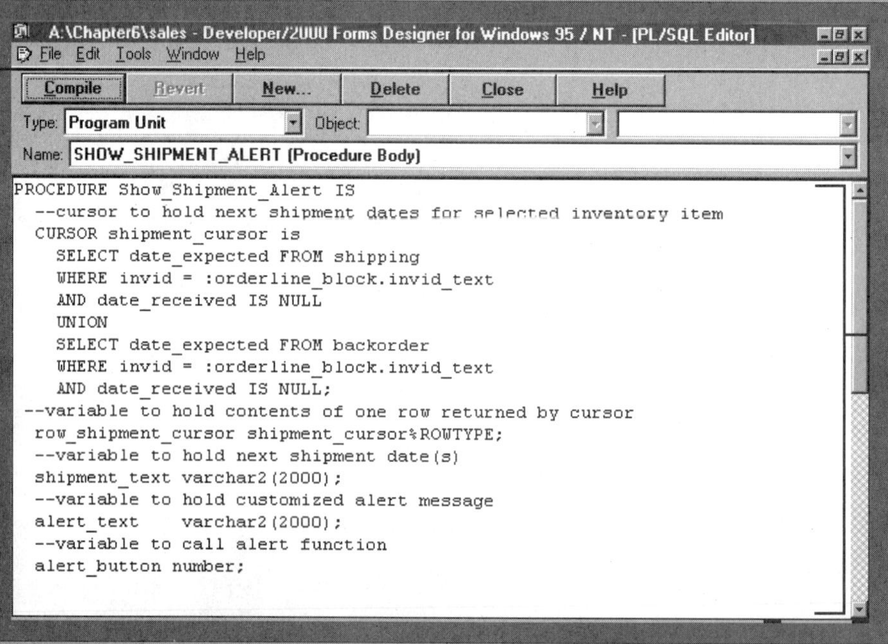


```
PROCEDURE Show_Shipment_Alert IS
  --cursor to hold next shipment dates for selected inventory item
  CURSOR shipment_cursor is
    SELECT date_expected FROM shipping
    WHERE invid = :orderline_block.invid_text
    AND date_received IS NULL
    UNION
    SELECT date_expected FROM backorder
    WHERE invid = :orderline_block.invid_text
    AND date_received IS NULL;
 --variable to hold contents of one row returned by cursor
  row_shipment_cursor shipment_cursor%ROWTYPE;
  --variable to hold next shipment date(s)
  shipment_text varchar2(2000);
  --variable to hold customized alert message
  alert_text    varchar2(2000);
  --variable to call alert function
  alert_button number;
```

Figure 6-92: DECLARE section of SHOW_SHIPMENT_ALERT program unit

4 Type the code shown in Figure 6-93 for the body of the program unit. Type this code immediately after the DECLARE section.

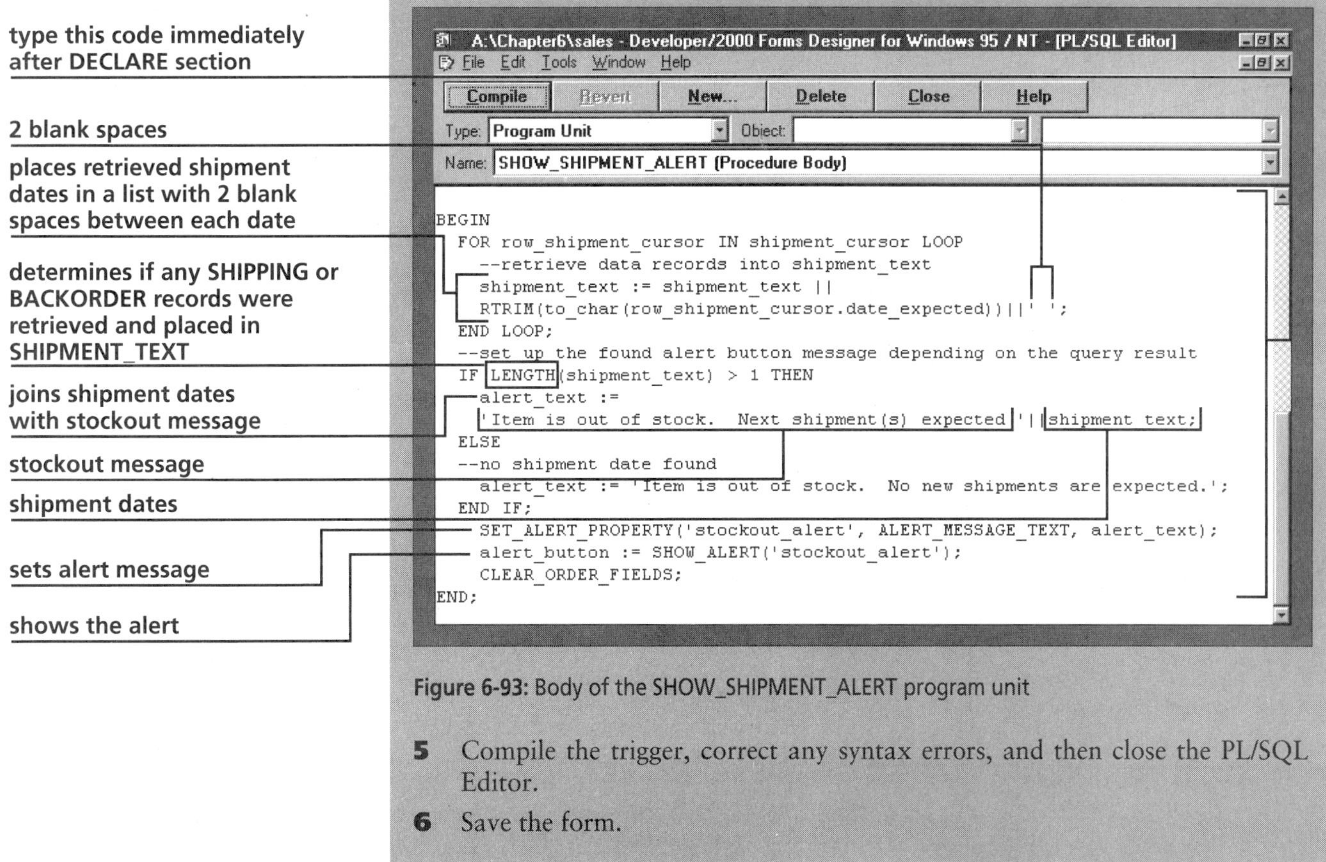

Figure 6-93: Body of the SHOW_SHIPMENT_ALERT program unit

5 Compile the trigger, correct any syntax errors, and then close the PL/SQL Editor.

6 Save the form.

Now that you have completed the alerts, you will test the form to see if the ADD_BUTTON trigger correctly handles the case where an ordered item is in stock.

To test the form when an item in stock:

1 Run the form.

2 Select customer **Mitch Edwards** and Order Source **122**, and then click the **Enter Items** button.

3 Select Item ID **559** (Men's Expedition Parka, S, and Navy).

4 Enter **1** for Desired Quantity.

5 Click the **Add Item to Order** button. If your trigger works correctly, your screen should look like Figure 6-94.

you might need to adjust the positions of your column headings or the number of blank spaces between your columns to align the headings and columns

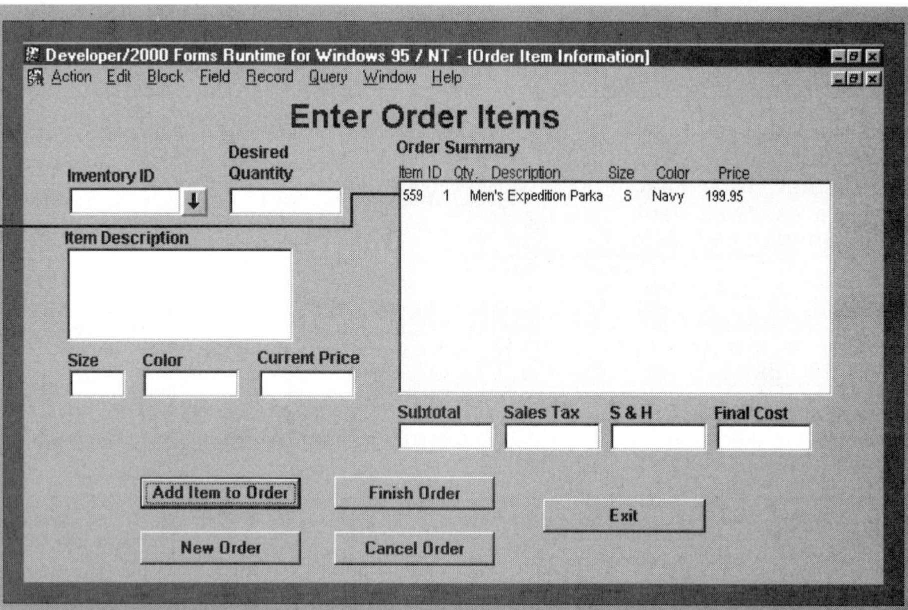

Figure 6-94: Ordered item in the Order Summary display

HELP? If your trigger does not work correctly, look up the explanations for any ORA- or FRM- error codes that occur, and then click the Exit button to exit the form. Run the form using the Oracle Debugger, place a breakpoint on the first line of the ADD_BUTTON trigger, and single-step through the trigger to determine what part of the code is causing the error.

Next you will test to see if the STOCKOUT_ALERT is displayed when you try to order an item that is out of stock. To ensure that the item you select is out of stock, first you will update the INVENTORY record in SQL*Plus and set quantity on hand to zero.

To update the record in SQL*Plus and then test the form when an item is out of stock:

1 Click the **Oracle SQL*Plus** command button on the taskbar.

2 Type the UPDATE and COMMIT commands shown in Figure 6-95 to set the quantity on hand for Inventory ID **11777** (Women's Hiking Shorts, L, Khaki) to zero.

type this command

type this command

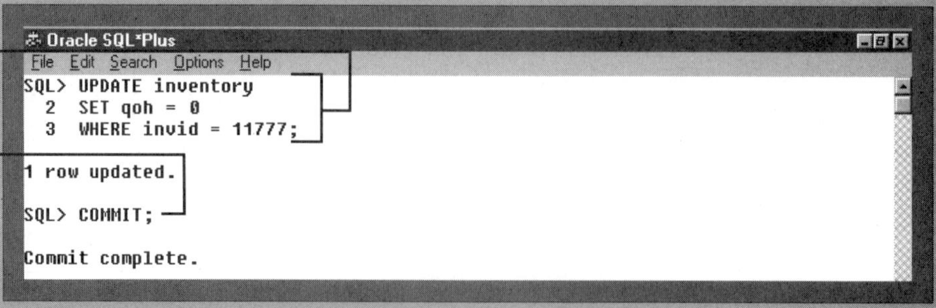

```
SQL> UPDATE inventory
  2  SET qoh = 0
  3  WHERE invid = 11777;

1 row updated.

SQL> COMMIT;

Commit complete.
```

Figure 6-95: Setting Inventory ID 11777's quantity on hand to zero

3 Click the **Developer/2000 Forms Runtime** command button on the taskbar.

4 Click the **Inventory ID LOV** button, and then select Item ID 894 (Women's Hiking Shorts, L, Khaki). Enter **1** for Desired Quantity, and then click the **Add Item to Order** button. The STOCKOUT_ALERT opens the Item Out of Stock dialog box and displays the date of the next shipment, as shown in Figure 6-96.

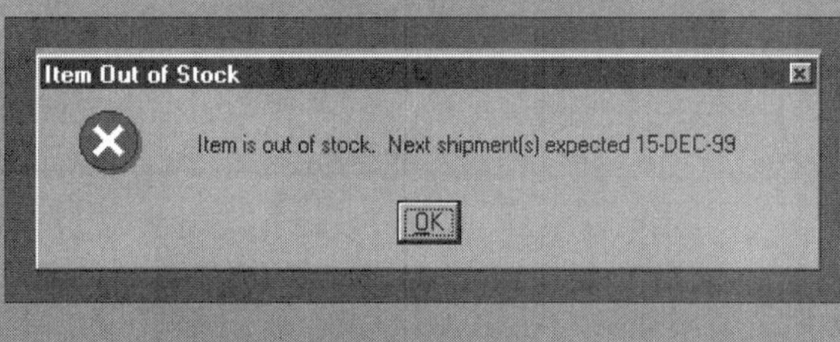

Figure 6-96: Stockout alert

5 Click the **OK** button.

6 Exit the form.

The FINISH_ORDER button calculates the order subtotal, which is the sum of each order line's quantity ordered times the price of each item. The FINISH_ORDER button also needs to determine the sales tax amount (which will be 6% for Wisconsin residents and zero for all others), and the shipping and handling. The final order cost is the total of the subtotal, tax, and shipping and handling fields. You will create program units to calculate the sales tax and the shipping and handling. You will create the program unit to calculate the sales tax first.

To create the program unit to calculate the sales tax:

1 Open the Object Navigator window in Ownership View, click **Program Units**, and then click the **Create** button on the Object Navigator toolbar.

2 Name the new program unit **CALC_TAX**, and then click the **OK** button.

3 Type the code shown in Figure 6-97.

type this code

```
PROCEDURE CALC_TAX IS
  --variable to hold customer's state
  cust_state    VARCHAR2(2);
BEGIN
  -- determine if customer is a WI resident and has to pay sales tax
  SELECT state
  INTO cust_state
  FROM customer
  WHERE custid = :cust_order_block.custid_text;
  IF cust_state = 'WI' THEN
    --calculate sales_tax
    :orderline_block.tax_text := .06*:orderline_block.subtotal_text;
  ELSE
    :orderline_block.tax_text := 0;
  END IF;
END;
```

Figure 6-97: CALC_TAX program unit

4 Compile the program unit and correct any syntax errors.
5 Save the form.

Next you need to create a program unit to calculate shipping and handling. Shipping and handling is calculated as a flat rate depending on the amount of the order subtotal. The shipping and handling rate for orders for less than or equal to $25 is $3.50; for orders between $25 and $75 is $5; and for orders over $75 the rate is $7.50.

To create the program unit to calculate shipping and handling:

1 In the PL/SQL Editor, click the **New** button on the PL/SQL Editor button bar, enter **CALC_SHIPPING** for the program unit name, and then click the **OK** button.
2 Type the code shown in Figure 6-98.

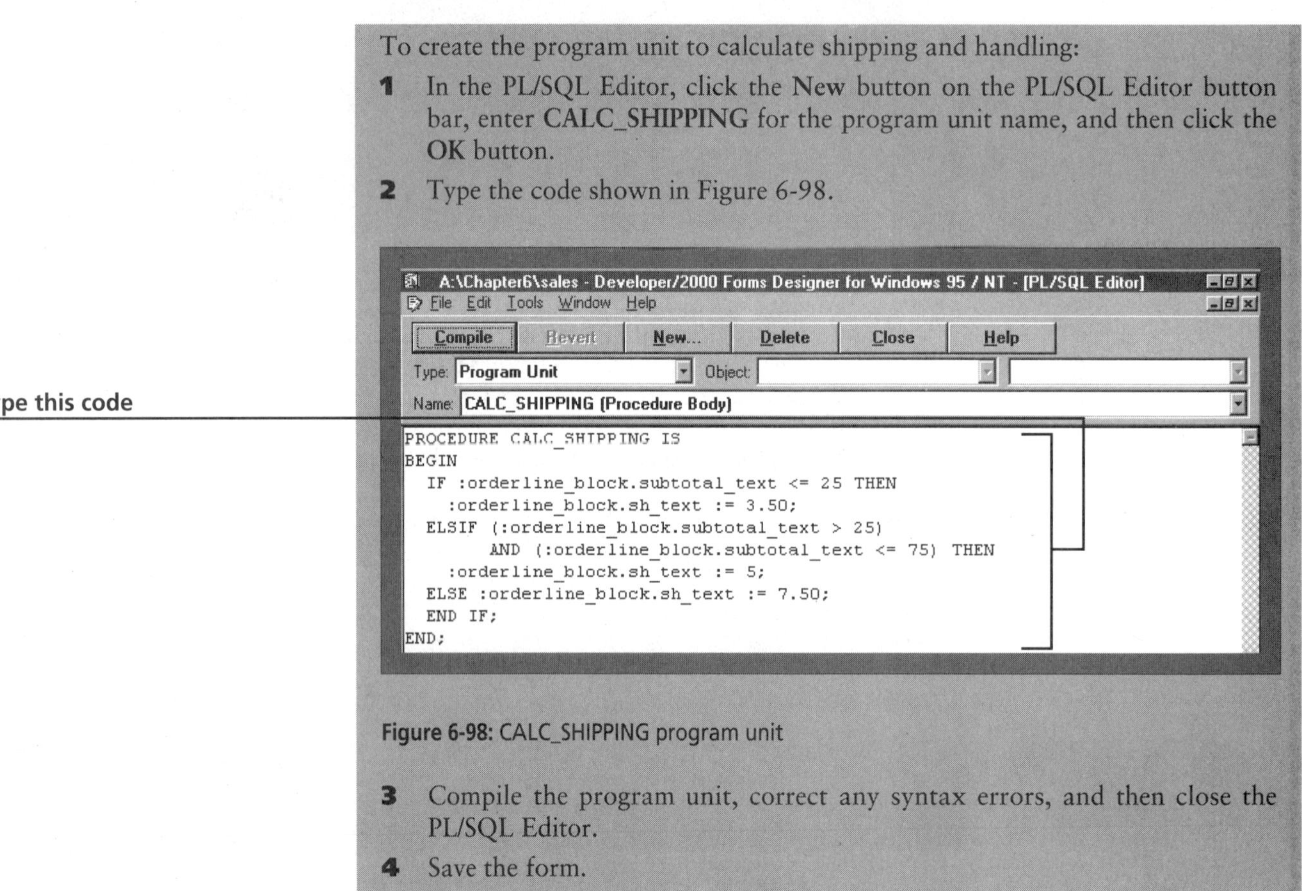


```
PROCEDURE CALC_SHIPPING IS
BEGIN
  IF :orderline_block.subtotal_text <= 25 THEN
    :orderline_block.sh_text := 3.50;
  ELSIF (:orderline_block.subtotal_text > 25)
        AND (:orderline_block.subtotal_text <= 75) THEN
    :orderline_block.sh_text := 5;
  ELSE :orderline_block.sh_text := 7.50;
  END IF;
END;
```

Figure 6-98: CALC_SHIPPING program unit

3 Compile the program unit, correct any syntax errors, and then close the PL/SQL Editor.
4 Save the form.

Now you will create the trigger for the FINISH_BUTTON, which will calculate the order subtotal, call the program units to calculate tax and shipping and handling, and then calculate the order total.

To create the FINISH_BUTTON trigger:

1 Open the Layout Editor to the ORDERLINE_CANVAS, right-click the **Finish Order** button, and then click **PL/SQL Editor**. Select the **WHEN-BUTTON-PRESSED** event.
2 Type the code shown in Figure 6-99 in the PL/SQL Editor.

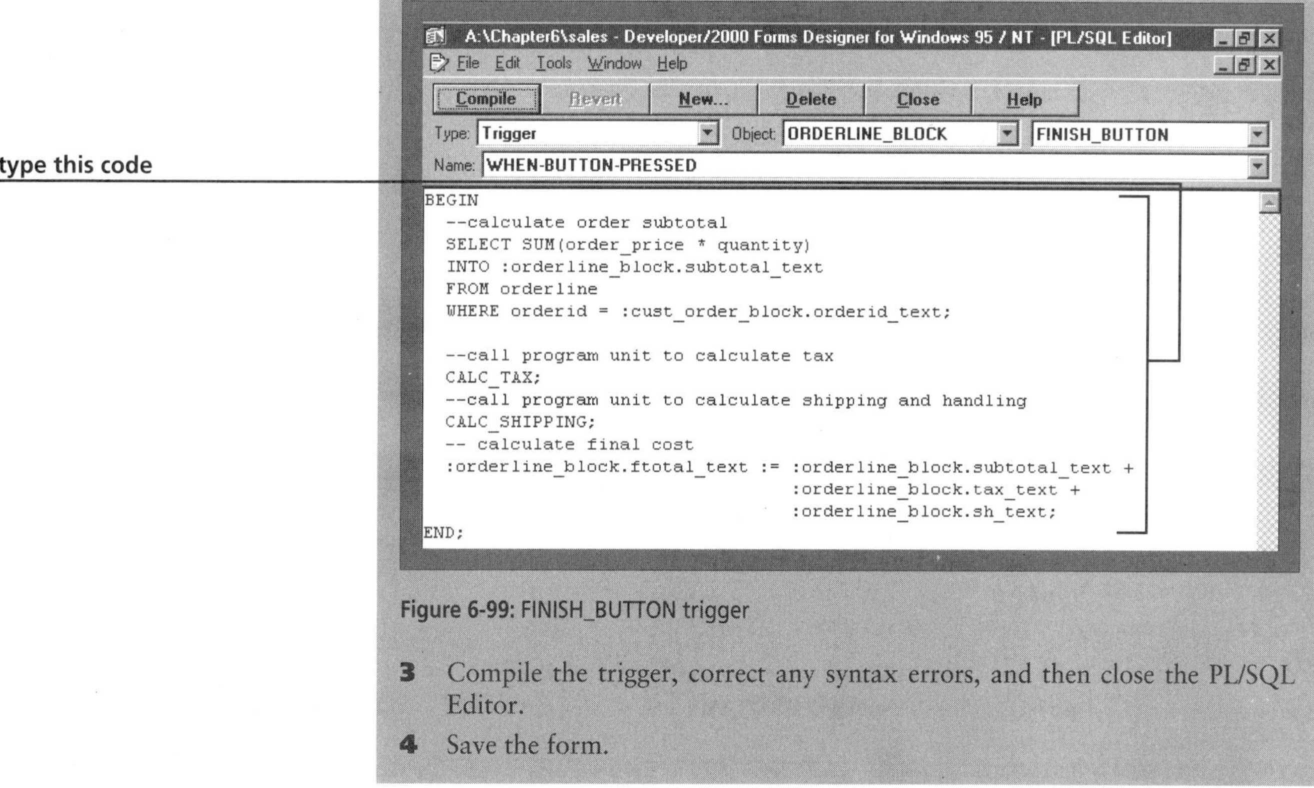

Figure 6-99: FINISH_BUTTON trigger

3 Compile the trigger, correct any syntax errors, and then close the PL/SQL Editor.

4 Save the form.

Now you will run the form to test if the Finish Button calculates the order totals correctly.

To test the Finish button:

1 Run the form.

2 Create a new order for customer **Mitch Edwards**, payment type **Check**, order source **122**, and then click the **Enter Items** button.

3 Select Item ID **559** (Men's Expedition Parka, S, Navy). Enter **1** for Desired Quantity, and then click the **Add Item to Order** button.

4 Select Item ID **894** (Women's Hiking Shorts, Khaki, S). Enter **2** for Desired Quantity, and then click the **Add Item to Order** button.

5 Click the **Finish Order** button. The subtotal, sales tax, shipping and handling, and final cost displays in the form, as shown in Figure 6-100.

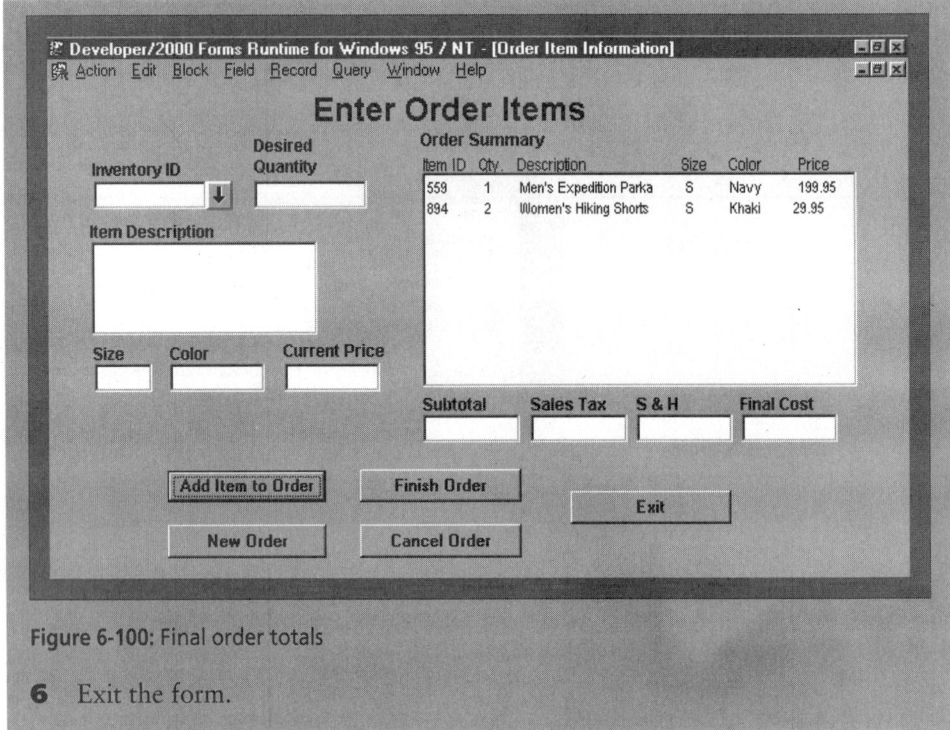

Figure 6-100: Final order totals

6 Exit the form.

tip

The columns in the summary display might not be aligned perfectly because the font used in the display item was a proportional font and some of the characters were wider than others. You can adjust the columns by using a non-proportional font such as Courier.

The Cancel button will need to delete each ORDERLINE cntry and add back the quantity ordered to the INVENTORY table. Returning the items to stock requires a cursor that retrieves the ORDERLINE records, and then processes each record sequentially in a FOR loop by deleting the ORDERLINE record and updating the associated INVENTORY QOH field. After executing the FOR loop, the trigger will delete the CUST_ORDER record and return to the CUST_ORDER_WINDOW.

To create the trigger for the Cancel button:

1 Open the Layout Editor, right-click the **CANCEL_BUTTON**, and click **PL/SQL Editor.**

2 Create a new WHEN-BUTTON-PRESSED trigger by typing the DECLARE section of the trigger as shown in Figure 6-101.

type this code

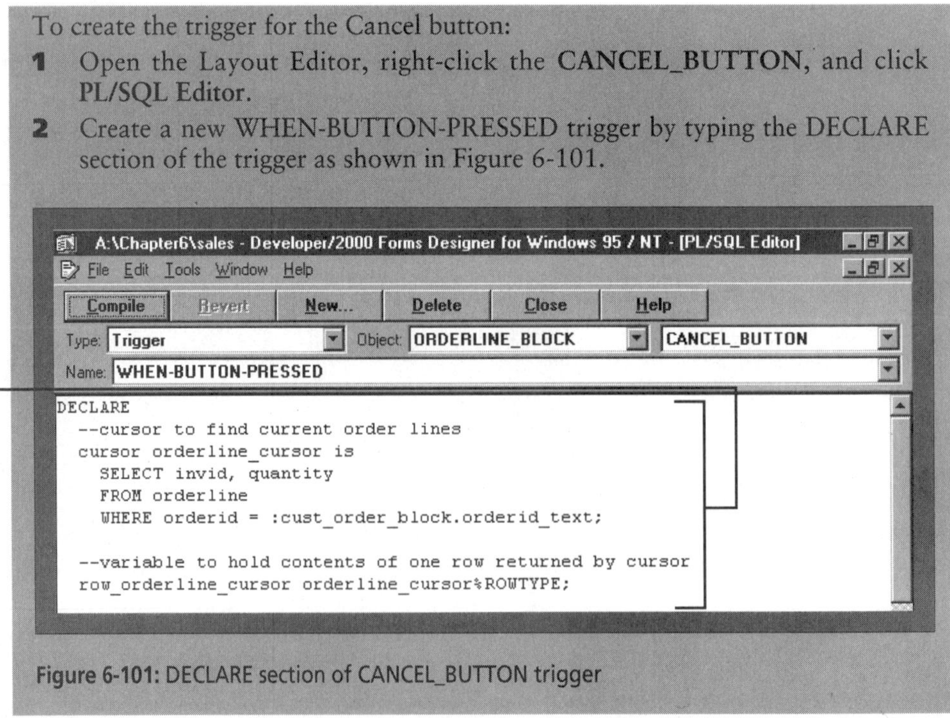


```
DECLARE
  --cursor to find current order lines
  cursor orderline_cursor is
    SELECT invid, quantity
    FROM orderline
    WHERE orderid = :cust_order_block.orderid_text;

  --variable to hold contents of one row returned by cursor
  row_orderline_cursor orderline_cursor%ROWTYPE;
```

Figure 6-101: DECLARE section of CANCEL_BUTTON trigger

3 Enter the body of the trigger as shown in Figure 6-102.

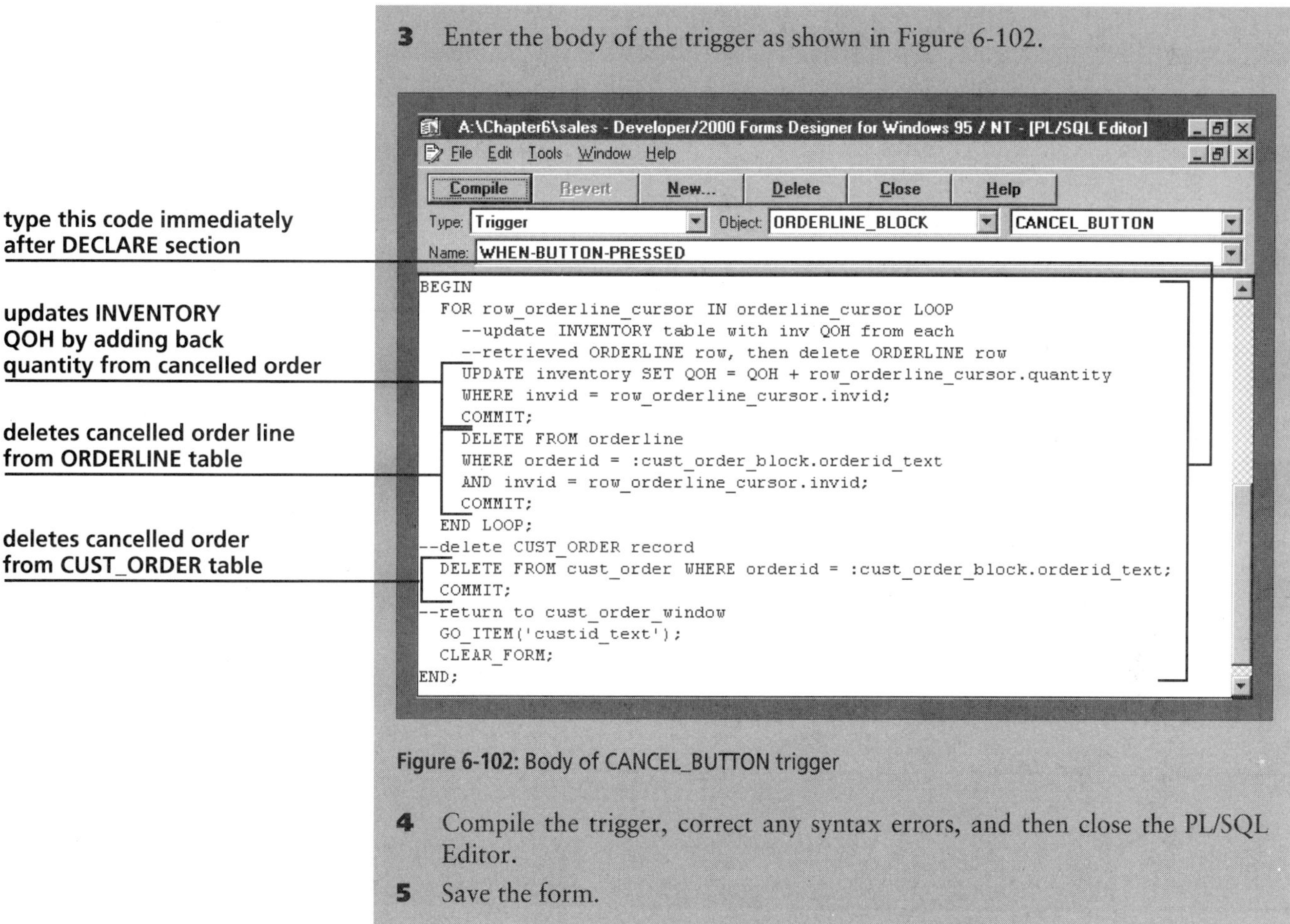


```
BEGIN
  FOR row_orderline_cursor IN orderline_cursor LOOP
    --update INVENTORY table with inv QOH from each
    --retrieved ORDERLINE row, then delete ORDERLINE row
    UPDATE inventory SET QOH = QOH + row_orderline_cursor.quantity
    WHERE invid = row_orderline_cursor.invid;
    COMMIT;
    DELETE FROM orderline
    WHERE orderid = :cust_order_block.orderid_text
    AND invid = row_orderline_cursor.invid;
    COMMIT;
  END LOOP;
--delete CUST_ORDER record
  DELETE FROM cust_order WHERE orderid = :cust_order_block.orderid_text;
  COMMIT;
--return to cust_order_window
  GO_ITEM('custid_text');
  CLEAR_FORM;
END;
```

Figure 6-102: Body of CANCEL_BUTTON trigger

4 Compile the trigger, correct any syntax errors, and then close the PL/SQL Editor.

5 Save the form.

Now you will test the SALES_FORM to verify that it creates the required records in CUST_ORDER and ORDERLINE correctly, and changes the inventory quantity on hand when an item is selected. First you will return your CUST_ORDER and ORDERLINE tables back to the point they were when you started the chapter by running the clearwat.sql script.

To run the script and test the SALES_FORM:

1 Click the **Oracle SQL*Plus** command button on the taskbar, and then type **START A:\Chapter6\clearwat.sql** at the SQL command prompt.

2 Click the **Developer/2000 Forms Designer** command button on the taskbar, and then run the form.

3 Create a new order for customer **107** (Paula Jones), payment method **Check**, and order source **122**, and then click the **Enter Items** button.

4 Switch to SQL*Plus, and then type the query shown in Figure 6-103 to verify that the new record was added to the CUST_ORDER table. Make a note of the ORDERID value.

5 Switch back to your form, select Item ID 559 (Inventory ID 11845, Men's Expedition Parka, S, Navy), enter **1** for Desired Quantity, and then click the **Add Item to Order** button.

6 Select Item ID 786 (Inventory ID 11668, 3-Season Tent, Sienna), enter **1** in Desired Quantity, and then click the **Add Item to Order** button.

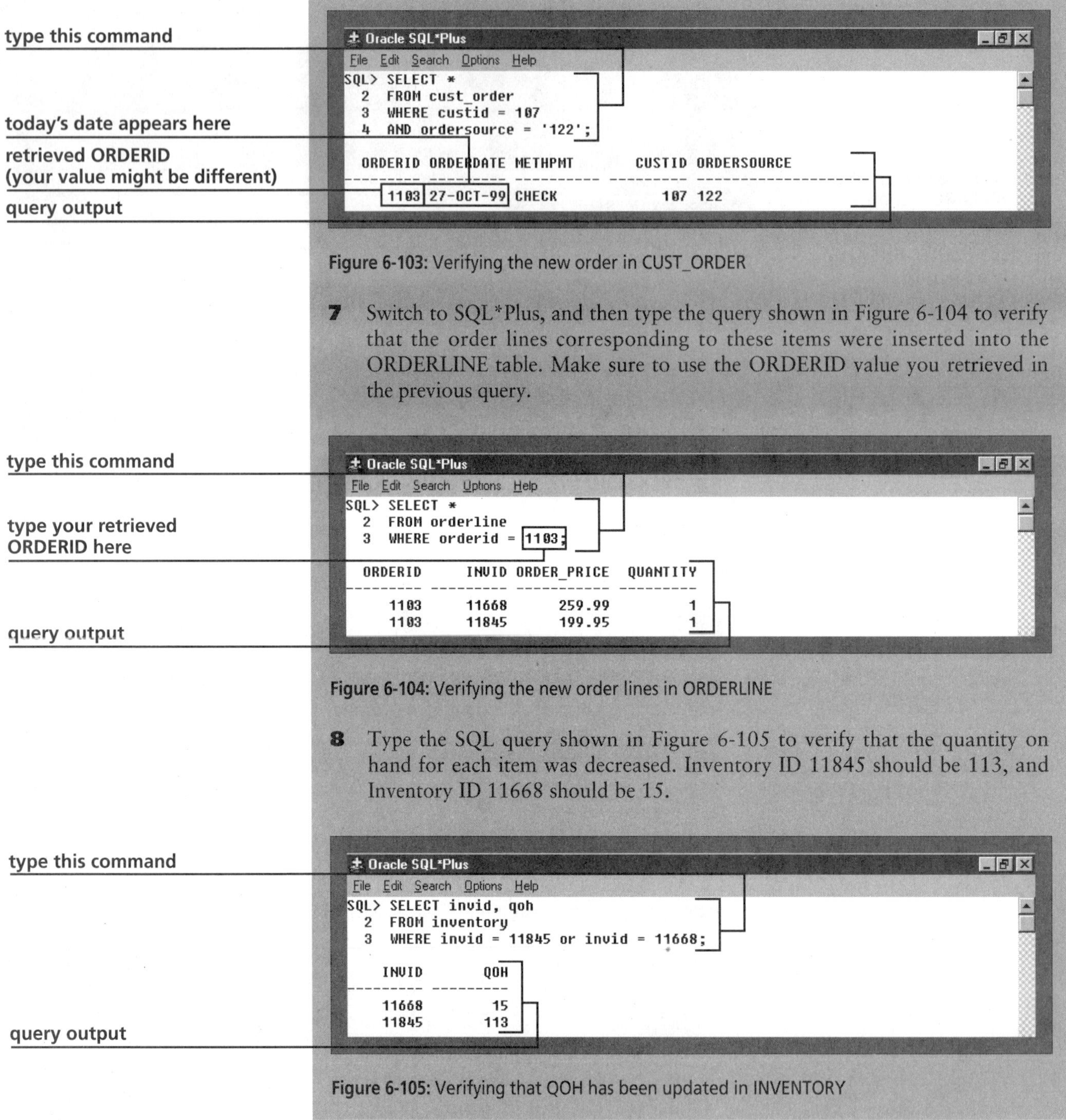

Figure 6-103: Verifying the new order in CUST_ORDER

7 Switch to SQL*Plus, and then type the query shown in Figure 6-104 to verify that the order lines corresponding to these items were inserted into the ORDERLINE table. Make sure to use the ORDERID value you retrieved in the previous query.

Figure 6-104: Verifying the new order lines in ORDERLINE

8 Type the SQL query shown in Figure 6-105 to verify that the quantity on hand for each item was decreased. Inventory ID 11845 should be 113, and Inventory ID 11668 should be 15.

Figure 6-105: Verifying that QOH has been updated in INVENTORY

Now you will test the CANCEL_BUTTON trigger to verify that it removes the order records and updates the inventory correctly.

To test the CANCEL_BUTTON:

1 Return to your form, and then click the **Cancel Order** button to clear the fields.

2 Switch to SQL*Plus, type **L** to list the contents of the buffer, and then type **/** to run the previous SQL command and verify that the inventory was restored. Inventory ID 11845 should be 114, and Inventory ID 11668 should be 16.

3 Type the SQL command shown in Figure 6-104 again to verify that the order records were deleted from the ORDERLINE table. You should receive the message "no rows selected."

4 Type the SQL command shown in Figure 6-106 to verify that the CUST_ORDER record was deleted.

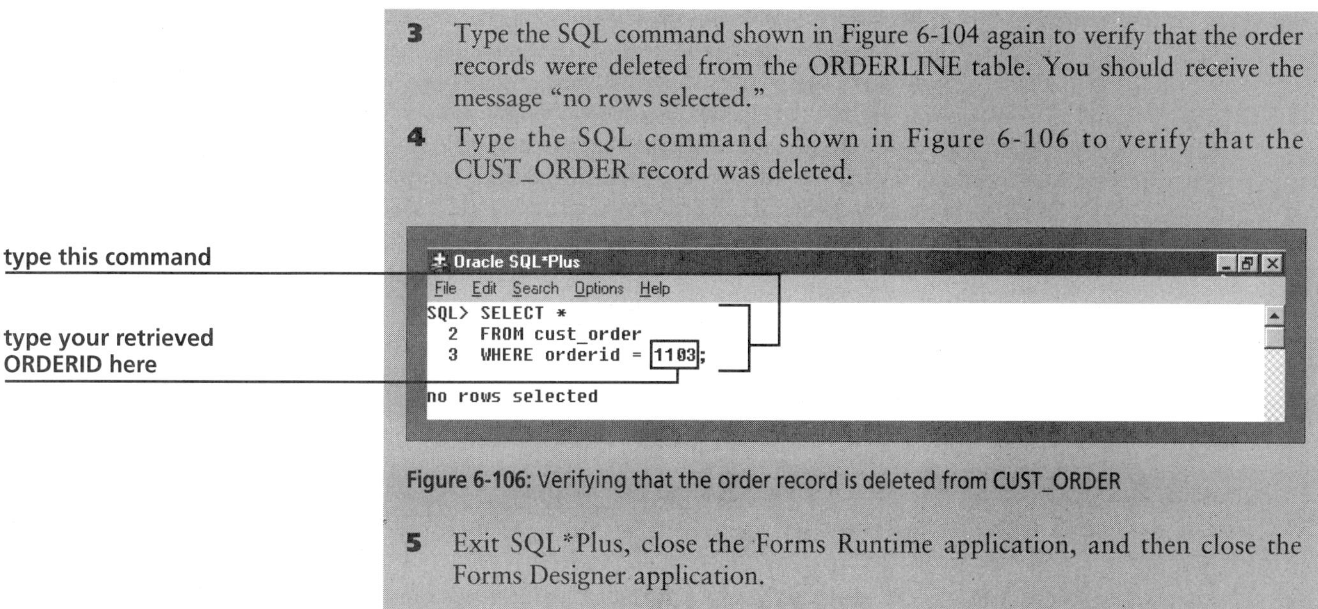

Figure 6-106: Verifying that the order record is deleted from CUST_ORDER

5 Exit SQL*Plus, close the Forms Runtime application, and then close the Forms Designer application.

SUMMARY

- Process text descriptions, flowcharts, and sketches of the user interface for a form are important tools to use when designing complex Oracle Forms applications.
- The Oracle Debugger allows you to step through PL/SQL programs one line at a time to examine values of variables during execution. The Oracle Debugger has a Source code pane that shows program code lines, a Navigator pane that is similar to the Object Navigator for viewing variable values, and a command line interpreter for entering command-line debugger commands.
- Breakpoints are places in PL/SQL programs where you can pause program execution so you can single-step through the code that follows and/or examine current variable values. You can put breakpoints only on PL/SQL code lines. SQL statements, blank lines, and comment lines cannot contain breakpoints. The Oracle Debugger execution arrow stops on PL/SQL statements and skips over comment lines and SQL statements.
- The Stack object in the Oracle Debugger allows you to examine the values of local variable values. The Modules object in the Oracle Debugger allows you to examine the values of form items, such as text fields. The Global Variables object in the Oracle Debugger allows you to examine the values for global variables.
- MDI (Multiple Document Interface) is the Microsoft Windows window management system where applications display an outer "parent" window (called the application window) and an inner document or dialog window. You can maximize the MDI runtime window and the form window in a Forms application using a PRE-FORM trigger.
- You can suppress lower-level Oracle Forms messages by setting the :SYSTEM.MESSAGE_LEVEL variable to a higher value in a PRE-FORM trigger.
- An important principle of graphic user interface design is to provide feedback to users about form operations while they are working and to make applications "forgiving" so users can cancel unintended operations.
- Alerts are form messages that provide information to users and allow them to choose from different options. The alert Style property determines what icon is displayed on the alert. Note alerts include an "i" for information, caution alerts include an exclamation point, and stop alerts include a red "X."

- System-level errors correspond to the form-level ON-ERROR event, so you can use a trigger to catch system error messages and substitute your own messages.
- To run another form from your current Forms application you use the CALL_FORM command in your current form to call the next form's executable (.fmx) file.
- You can show multiple windows in a single Forms application by using the SHOW_WINDOW command and then setting the form's focus to the new window using the GO_ITEM command.
- You can set an alert's message at runtime using the SET_ALERT_PROPERTY command.
- A cursor is a variable corresponding to a memory location that holds a compiled SQL query. Cursors are useful in Oracle Forms applications for processing multiple records that are retrieved by a SQL query.
- When you are testing an Oracle Forms application and monitoring changing data values in SQL*Plus, always enter a COMMIT after updating or deleting values in SQL*Plus or your tables will be locked and inaccessible to your Forms application.

REVIEW QUESTIONS

1. What three tools can be used to design a forms application to support a complex business process?
2. How does the Oracle Debugger help you to find programming errors?
3. How do you use the source code and Navigator panes in the Debugger window?
4. What is a breakpoint?
5. On what kinds of program lines can you set breakpoints? On what kinds of lines can you not set breakpoints?
6. How do you set a breakpoint?
7. What is the purpose of the Step Into button in the Debugger window?
8. What is the execution arrow?
9. What kinds of program lines does the execution arrow stop on? What kinds of lines does it skip?
10. What are stack variables in the Oracle Debugger?
11. What are block item values in the Oracle Debugger?
12. Where would you go in the Oracle Debugger Navigation pane to find the value of a variable named :custom_block.cust_name_text?
13. What is the MDI window? How can you maximize it at runtime?
14. What is message severity level? Are high-severity level messages more or less serious than low-severity messages?
15. How can you suppress some system-level messages? What messages cannot be suppressed?
16. What is an alert? Why should you make alerts in forms applications?
17. What are the three alert styles, and how are they different?
18. What is the purpose of the TRUNC command?
19. How can you prevent a user from entering and changing a primary or foreign key field value?
20. How can you intercept FRM- and ORA- error messages and replace them with your own alerts?
21. What is a database cursor?
22. What is the difference between an implicit cursor and an explicit cursor?
23. When must you use an explicit cursor?

PROBLEM-SOLVING CASES

Clearwater Traders Database

1. Modify the SALES_FORM ORDERLINE_WINDOW that you created in the chapter as follows:
   a. Create an error trap so the user cannot enter or modify the Inventory ID, Item Description, Size, and Color fields.
   b. Modify the ADD_BUTTON trigger so that if the user fails to enter a value for the Desired Quantity field, an alert is displayed stating that no value was entered for the quantity ordered. When the user clicks the OK button on the alert, the insertion point is placed in the Desired Quantity field. (*Hint:* Check to see if the ORDER_QUANT_TEXT field is greater than zero.)
2. Copy the CANCEL_BUTTON trigger into a text editor or word processor, and then print the code. Run the SALES_FORM with the Oracle Debugger enabled, and set a breakpoint on the BEGIN statement of the CANCEL_ORDER trigger. Then create a new customer order for customer Betty Sorenson, with Check as the payment method, and the WEBSITE as the order source. Enter the following order items:
   1 pair Red Children's Beachcomber Sandals, size 10
   1 pair Blue Children's Beachcomber Sandals, size 1
   Then click the Cancel_Order button.
   a. What are the values of the variables in the CUST_ORDER_BLOCK and ORDERLINE_BLOCK when the execution arrow is on the break point?
   b. Show on your trigger printout each place that the execution arrow stops. Number the first stop as 1, the second stop as 2, etc.
   c. What are the values of the stack variables during each execution of the FOR loop?

Northwoods University Database

1. Create a flowchart and user interface design for a university registration system application that allows faculty members to log on by selecting their name and entering their SPIN as a password. (You can keep a text item from showing on the screen and have asterisks show in its place by setting its Security property to True.) Faculty members should be able to choose a term, and then select items from a list of courses that they taught (or currently are teaching) during that term. After selecting a course, faculty members should be able to view the names of all students who are (or were) enrolled in the course and each student's grade.
2. Implement your design for Exercise 1 and save your file as facreg.fmb in the Chapter6 folder on your Student Disk.
3. Create a flowchart and user interface design for an application that allows students to log on to the university registration system by selecting their name and entering their SPIN as a password. After logging in, students should be able to select a given semester and view their past course and grade information for semesters with CLOSED enrollment, or enroll in courses that have remaining seats (CURRENRL <= MAXENRL) for semesters with OPEN enrollment. Students also should be able to drop courses. When a student enrolls or drops a course, the CURRENRL field needs to be updated.
4. Implement your design for Exercise 3, and save your file as studreg.fmb in the Chapter6 folder on your Student Disk.

Chapter 7

objectives

- Create and format a single-table Oracle Reports application
- Create a report that shows master/detail relationships
- Calculate retrieved data in a report
- Customize report output with user input parameters

CHAPTER 7

Using Oracle Reports

Introduction Oracle Reports is the Oracle Developer/2000 application used for creating data reports that can viewed on the screen, printed to a file, or printed on paper. Reports applications retrieve database data using SQL queries, perform mathematical or summary calculations on the retrieved data, and format the output to look like invoices, form letters, or other business documents. In this chapter, you will learn about the Oracle Reports environment and create a simple report based on data from a single table. Then you will explore how to create master/detail reports, reports that calculate retrieved data fields, and reports that allow users to specify input parameters.

Creating a Single-Table Report

The best way to become familiar with the Reports environment is to create a simple report that involves a single database table. You will create a student report for Northwoods University that shows the current date and each student's last name, first name, middle initial, address, city, state, zip code, and phone number. The report page number will appear at the bottom of each page. Figure 7-1 shows a sketch of the report. The **data fields** are the fields that will be retrieved from the database, and each row will repeat the data fields for every retrieved student record. The **parameter fields** are report elements, such as page numbers, that will display on every report page.

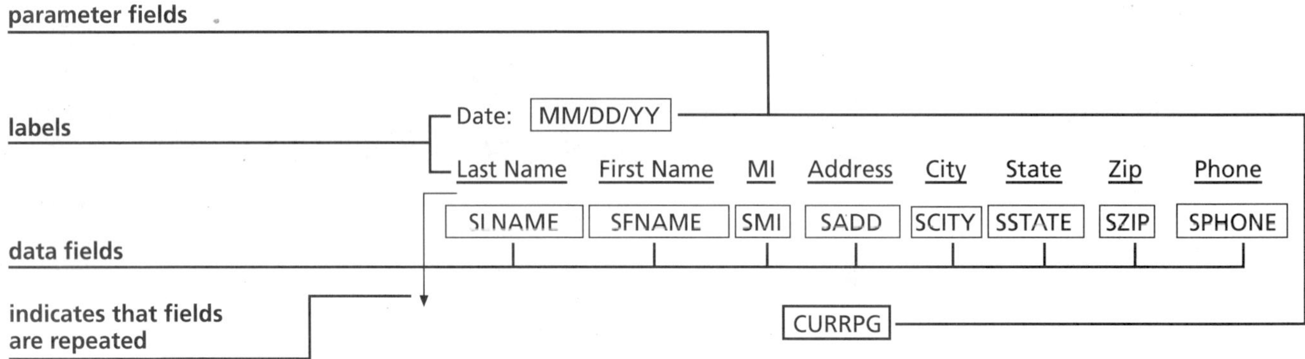

Figure 7-1: Student report design

To be sure that you are starting with a complete database, you will run the northwoo.sql script file on your Student Disk.

To run the script file and start the Reports Designer:

1. Start SQL*Plus and log on to the database.
2. Type **START A:\Chapter7\northwoo.sql** at the SQL prompt to drop your old tables and re-create and add values to the new tables.
3. Exit SQL*Plus.
4. Click the **Start** button on the taskbar, point to **Programs**, click **Oracle for Windows95** (or **Oracle for Windows NT**), click **Developer/2000 for Win95** (or **Developer/2000 for Windows NT**), and then click **Reports Designer.** Like the other Oracle applications you have been using, after you start the Reports Designer you must connect to the database.

   HELP? Your system configuration might be different; the Reports Designer should be in the same place as the Forms Designer.

5. Click **File** on the menu bar, click **Connect**, and then connect to the database. After connecting to the database, maximize the Reports Designer program window, if necessary. The Oracle Reports Object Navigator window appears, as shown in Figure 7-2.

tip

You also can start Windows Explorer, change to the ORAWIN\BIN directory, and then double-click the r25des.exe file to start the Reports Designer. (Windows NT users can change to the ORANT\BIN directory, and then double-click the r25des.exe file.)

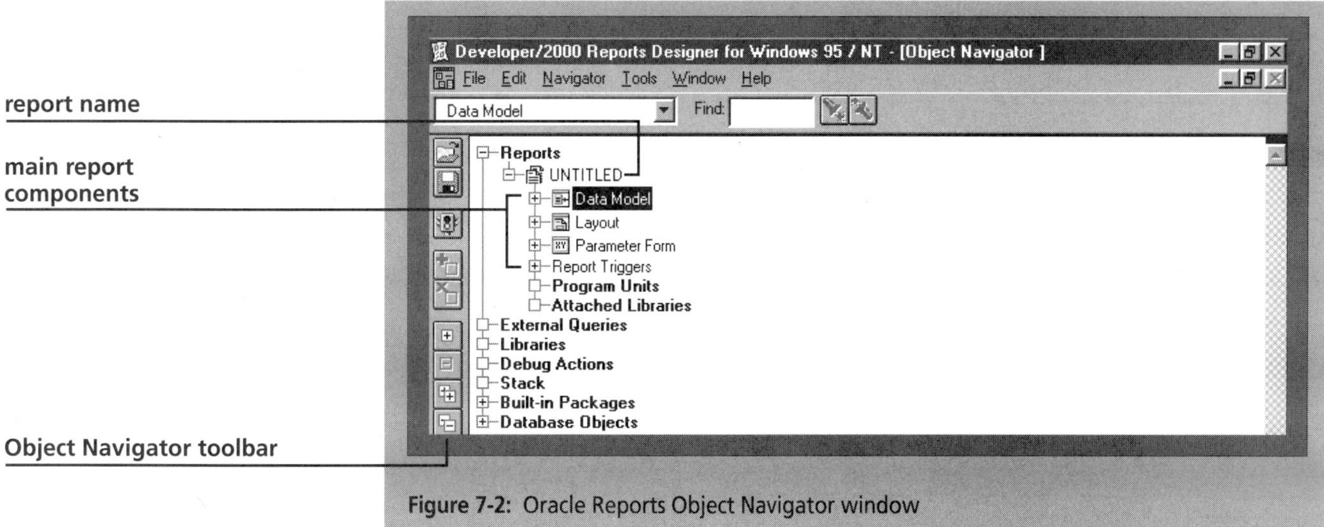

Figure 7-2: Oracle Reports Object Navigator window

The Oracle Reports Object Navigator is used to access the components of a report. The top-level object is **Reports**, and the default report name shown in Figure 7-2 is UNTITLED. The main report components are the data model, layout, parameter form, and report triggers. The **data model** contains one or more related SQL queries that specify the database data that is shown in the report. The data model also can contain specifications for calculated fields. The **layout** specifies the position and format of the text fields that display the retrieved and calculated data, and also contains boilerplate objects such as labels and titles. A **parameter form** is a form with fields where users can enter input values to define the data that is displayed in the report. **Report triggers** are programs that are associated with report events running the report or accessing the next report page. A report also can contain program units, which are the PL/SQL programs you created when you worked in Oracle Forms, and **attached libraries**, which are libraries of PL/SQL programs that can be used by many different Oracle applications.

Naming the Report

The first step in creating a new report is to name the report by saving it either in the file system or the database. In this book you will save your reports in the file system.

You also can click File on the menu bar, and then click Save to save a file.

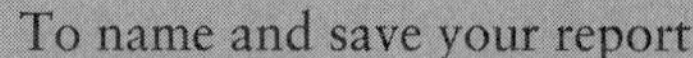

To name and save your report:

1. Click the **Save** button on the Object Navigator toolbar. The Save dialog box opens, as shown in Figure 7-3. The Save To option determines where the report will be saved. The Display options let you specify what types of files or objects will be displayed when you open a report: all files, report files (which have an .rdf extension), query files (which have a .sql extension), or PL/SQL library files (which have a .pll extension).

Figure 7-3: Save dialog box

2. Make sure that the **File** option button and the **Reports** check box are selected, and then click the **OK** button. A new Save dialog box opens with the default filename "Untitled" selected in the File name text box.
3. Type **student.rdf** in the File name text box, change to the Chapter7 folder on your Student Disk, and then click the **Save** button. You return to the Object Navigator and your report is named STUDENT.

To change the name of the report in the Object Navigator, click File on the menu bar, click Save As, and then type the new name in the File name text box. The report name in the Object Navigator is always the same as the report filename.

Building the Data Model

A report is really just another way of formatting the output of a SQL query. Reports are created by specifying the data to be displayed using a SQL query, and then arranging how the output will look on a printed page or on the screen. You specify your report data fields using the Data Model Editor. The Data Model Editor window, as shown in Figure 7-4, has a Tool palette for creating queries and a toolbar for specifying program operations such as opening and saving files and running and printing reports. The **painting region** is an area of the window that displays queries and their associated record group fields. The **status line**, located at the bottom of the window, shows the current **zoom factor**, where 1x means normal size, 1/2x means half of normal size, etc. The status line also shows the current pointer position in inches.

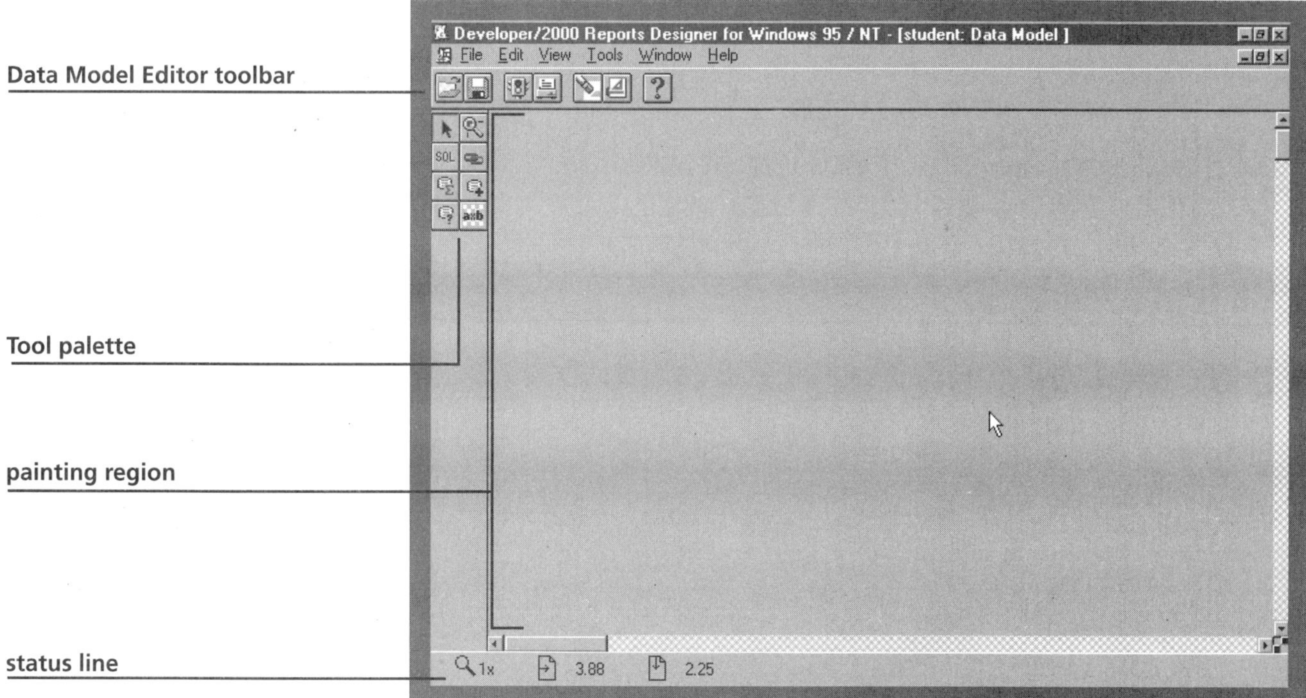

Figure 7-4: Data Model Editor window

To create a query in the Data Model Editor, you click the Query button on the Tool palette and then draw a rounded rectangle in the painting region to represent the query. The rounded rectangle is called the query. Then you specify the data records that the query will display in its record group by defining a SQL command using the Query Editor, which is opened by double-clicking the query. Each query defines a record group, which is a list of data records. After you specify the SQL command, the record group fields are displayed automatically directly under the query. The order of the fields in the record group represents the order that the fields will display in the default report layout. You will build the data model for your report next.

You also can right-click the Data Model icon and then click Editor, or click Tools on the menu bar, and then click Data Model Editor to open the Data Model Editor.

To build the report data model:

1 Double-click the **Data Model** icon under STUDENT in the Object Navigator to open the Data Model Editor. First you will specify the SQL command that defines this report.

2 Click the **Query** button on the Tool palette. The pointer changes to + when you move it into the painting region.

3 Draw the rounded rectangle shown in Figure 7-5 to represent your query. The query is labeled Q_1, to indicate that it is the first query in this data model. Next you need to open the Query Editor to define the SQL query.

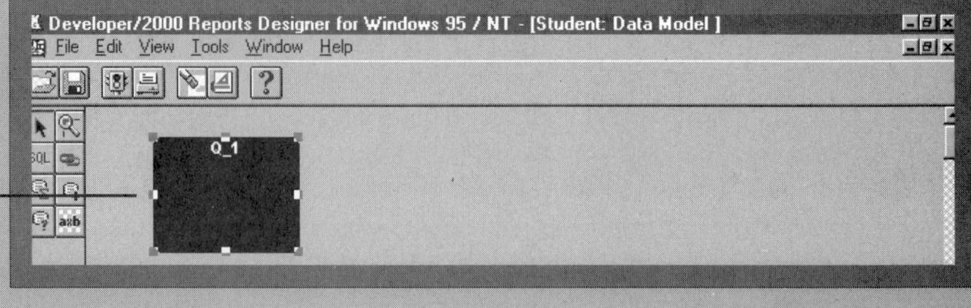

Figure 7-5: Creating a query

You also can right-click the Q_1 query, and then click Properties on the menu to open the Query Editor.

4 Double-click the Q_1 query to open the Query Editor, as shown in Figure 7-6. You use the Query Editor to change the query name, specify the maximum number of data rows the query will retrieve, specify a query that is in a text file with a .sql extension, or enter a SQL command. First you will change the query name.

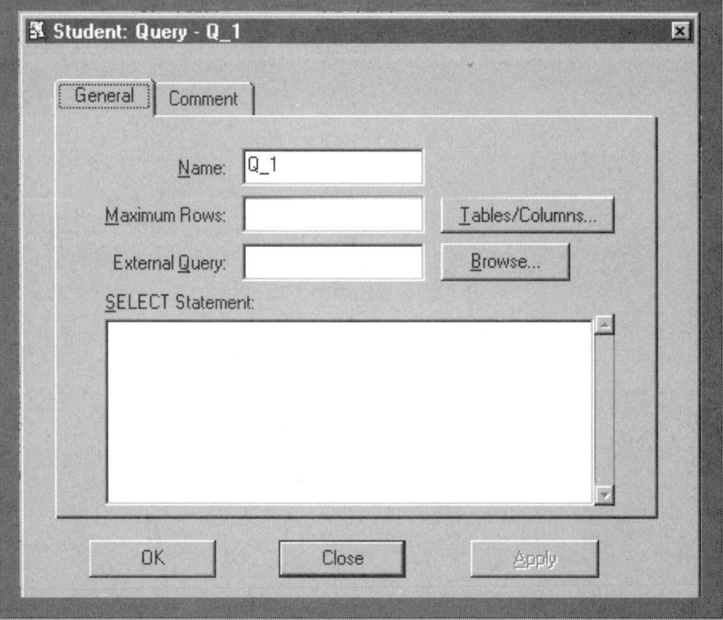

Figure 7-6: Query Editor

5 Select the default name in the Name text box, and then type **Q_student.**

You can limit the maximum number of data rows a query returns by entering a value in the Maximum Rows text box. You might do this while you are developing and testing a new report because loading and processing a large number of data rows might take a long time.

The next step is to specify the SQL command for the query that defines the data to use in your report. There are three ways of defining the SQL command: You can enter the query using the Tables/Columns button if your data is stored in a single table. You can select an External Query file, which is a text file with a .sql extension. Or you can type a SQL command in the SELECT Statement text box. Your report data is stored in only one table—the STUDENT table—so you will use the Tables/Columns button.

To define the SQL query for the report:

1 Click the **Tables/Columns** button in the Query Editor. The Table and Column Names dialog box opens. You use this dialog box to select the database object (in this case, the STUDENT table) and columns that contain the data for your report.

2 Scroll down the Database Objects list, and then click **STUDENT**. The Columns list box now displays the columns in the STUDENT table.

3 Press and hold down the **Ctrl** key, and then click the report display fields, which are **SID, SLNAME, SFNAME, SMI, SADD, SCITY, SSTATE, SZIP,** and **SPHONE**, as shown in Figure 7-7. You will include SID in the record group but you will not display it in the report.

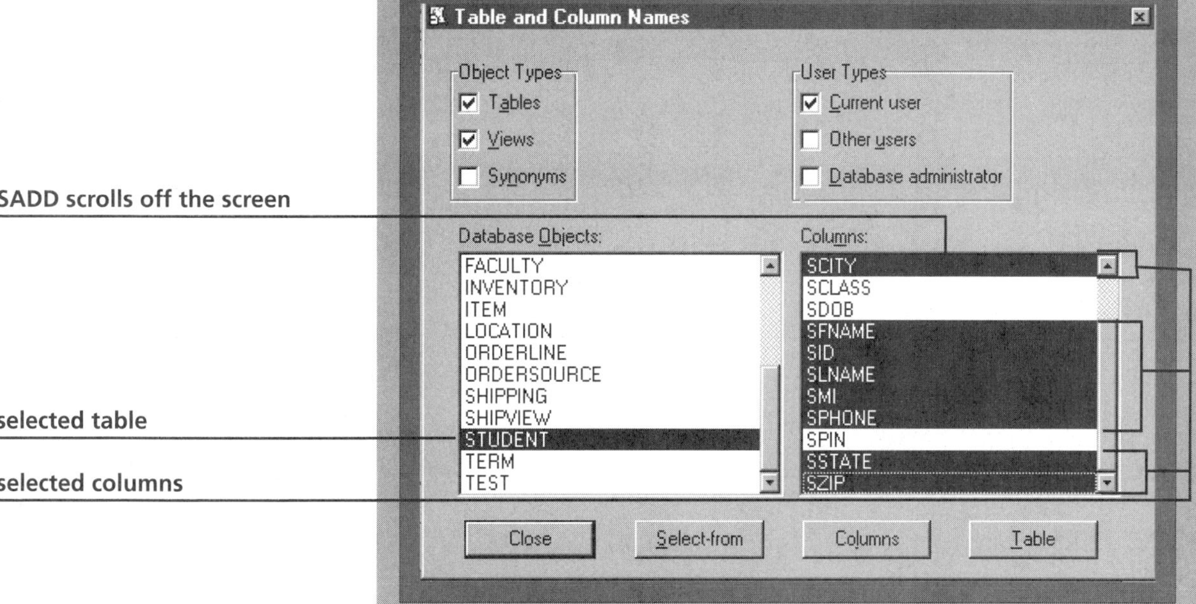

Figure 7-7: Specifying the query using the Tables/Columns button

4 Click the **Select-from** button, and then click the **Close** button. The Table and Column Names dialog box closes, and your SELECT statement appears in the SELECT Statement text box in the Query Editor, as shown in Figure 7-8.

tip

The order in which you select the fields in the Columns text box does not matter—the column names will appear alphabetically in the SELECT statement.

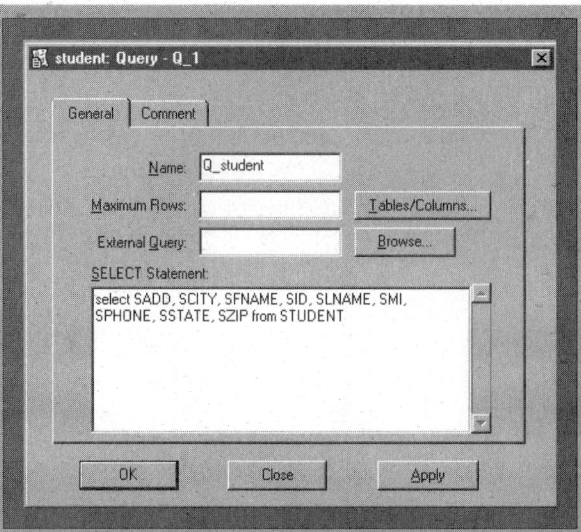

student: Query - Q_1

General | Comment

Name: Q_student

Maximum Rows:

External Query:

Tables/Columns...

Browse...

SELECT Statement:

select SADD, SCITY, SFNAME, SID, SLNAME, SMI, SPHONE, SSTATE, SZIP from STUDENT

OK | Close | Apply

Figure 7-8: Q_student SELECT statement

HELP? If your SELECT statement does not look like the one shown in Figure 7-8, delete the current command and then repeat Steps 1 through 4 to redefine the query.

5 Click the OK button, and then maximize the Data Model Editor window, if necessary. The Q_student query appears with its associated record group, which is titled G_student, as shown in Figure 7-9. Next you will enlarge the record group so all fields display, and rearrange the fields so they are in the correct order for your report output.

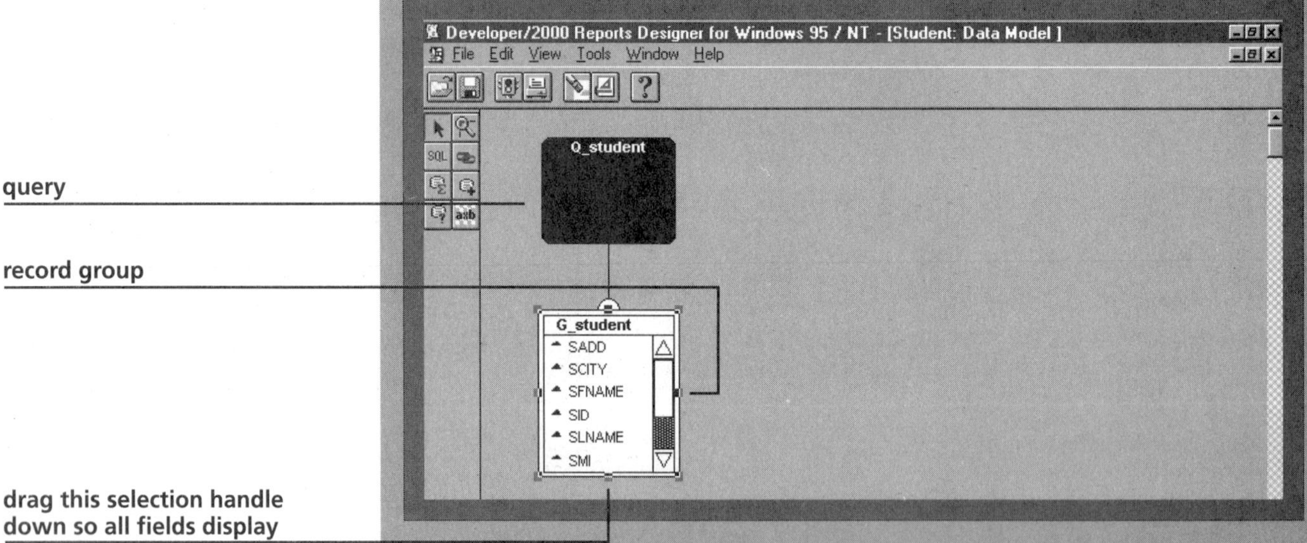

Figure 7-9: Q_student query and G_student record group

6 If necessary select the **G_student** record group by clicking it, and then drag the bottom center handle down so all fields are displayed and the scroll bar disappears.

7 Click **SID** in the record group, and then drag it up so it is on top of the first field in the record group.

HELP? If you drag the field up and it displays as the last field in the list, then you dragged it up too far. Click the SID field again, and then drag it up so it is on top of the first field in the list. If you dragged the field and it displays outside of the record group box, click Edit on the menu bar, click Undo, and then repeat Step 7.

8 Click **SLNAME** and then drag it up so it is the second field in the record group.

9 Rearrange the rest of the fields in the record group so they look like Figure 7-10.

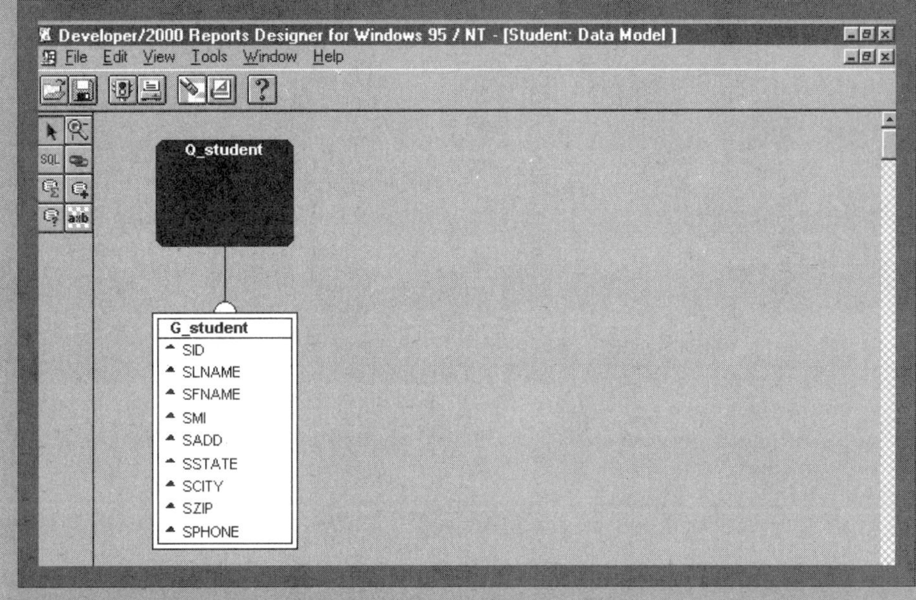

Figure 7-10: Ordered G_student record group

10 Save your report by clicking the Save button on the Data Model Editor toolbar.

Developing the Report Layout

The next step is to specify how the data fields will display on the report. You use the Reports Layout Editor to change the position of objects in the report, just like you used the Forms Layout Editor to change objects in a form. The Layout Editor window (see Figure 7-11), like the Data Model Editor, has a Tool palette, toolbar, painting region, and status line. The painting region also has rulers and gridlines to help you position report components.

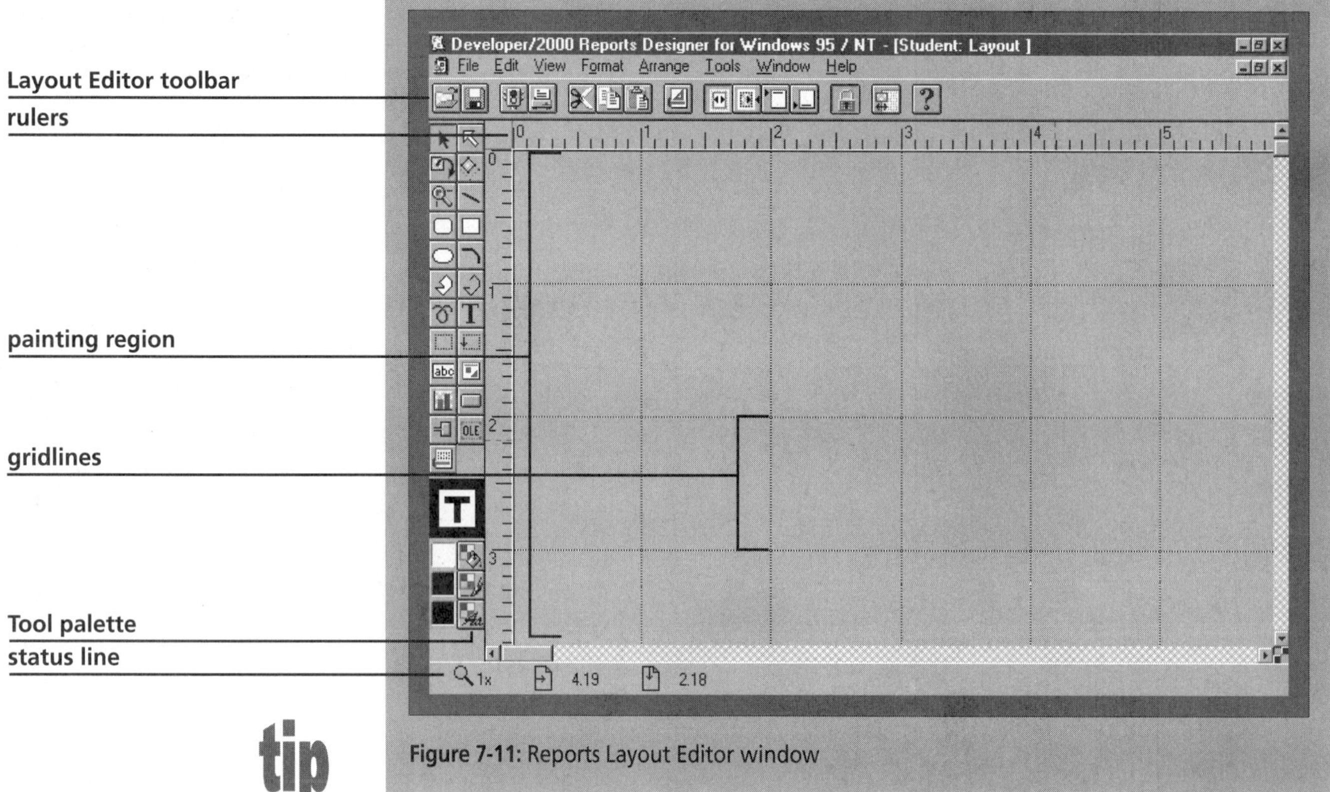

Figure 7-11: Reports Layout Editor window

tip

You can change the measurement units on the rulers and gridlines by clicking View on the menu bar, pointing to View Options, and then clicking Rulers.

Next you will open the Layout Editor and develop the report layout.

To open the Layout Editor:

1 Click **Tools** on the menu bar, and then click **Layout Editor**. The Reports Layout Editor window opens.

The Reports Layout Editor is similar to the Forms Layout Editor, but the Reports Layout Editor includes specific tools for creating reports. You can create your own report by drawing fields and connecting them to record group fields, but most of the time it is easier to use one of the default layouts that the program generates. A **default layout** automatically positions the data fields for standard report layouts, such as columns, mailing labels, or form letters. You select and generate a default layout using the Default Layout dialog box.

Before you open the Default Layout dialog box and generate your layout, you need to choose the default values for your page layout and font. If you do not choose default values, your layout will have the program default values, which are a portrait orientation and a 10-point Courier font. This report will display multiple columns across the page, and some of the fields are long, so you will use a landscape layout and a smaller font size.

To change the Layout Editor default page setup and font and open the Default Layout dialog box:

1 Click **File** on the menu bar, click **Page Setup**, click the **Landscape** option button, and then click the **OK** button to change the page to landscape orientation.

2 Click **Format** on the menu bar, click **Font**, change the settings to **8-point regular Arial Narrow** font, and then click the **OK** button to change the default font. This is a small but legible font that works well when you display multiple data rows on the same page.

3 Click the **Fill Color** tool on the Tool palette and select **No Fill** as the line color.

4 Click the **Line Color** tool on the Tool palette and select **No Line** as the line color.

5 Click the **Default Layout** button on the Layout Editor toolbar to open the Student: Default Layout dialog box, as shown in Figure 7-12.

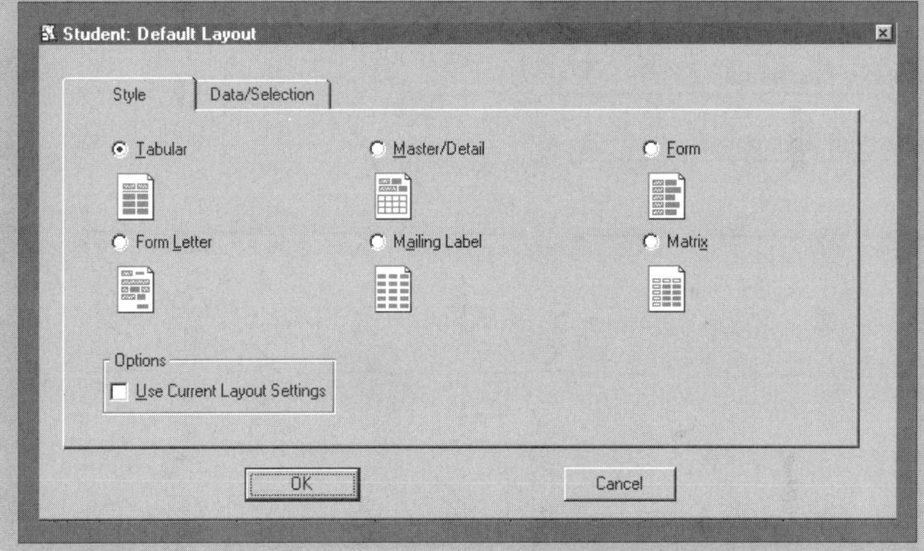

Figure 7-12: Default layout style options

The Default Layout dialog box allows you to specify the layout style, which data model fields will display on the report, and how the fields will display. The Style tab shows the default style options that are available. The tabular style displays multiple data records on a page, with a column heading at the top of each field. The master/detail style displays one-to-many data relationships in a tabular style. For example, a master/detail report in the Northwoods University database could show the data for a faculty member, and then list the data for each course section that the faculty member teaches below the faculty member data. The form style is similar to the tabular style, except field headings appear to the left of the fields instead of above them. The form letter layout allows you to create a form letter by mixing text with data fields. The mailing label layout prints multiple records in multiple columns on the page so you can create mailing labels.

Matrix layouts contain records both across the top and down the left side of the page. A matrix layout is used to display data that relate to the combination of two records at the intersection point. For example, a matrix report could show student names down the left side of the page, course names across to the top of the page, and the grade the student earned in the course at the intersection point of the student name and the course name. For your report, you will use a tabular style.

To change to the tabular style and view the Data/Selection options:

1 Make sure that the **Tabular** option button is selected, and then click the **Data/Selection** tab. The Data/Selection options appear, as shown in Figure 7-13.

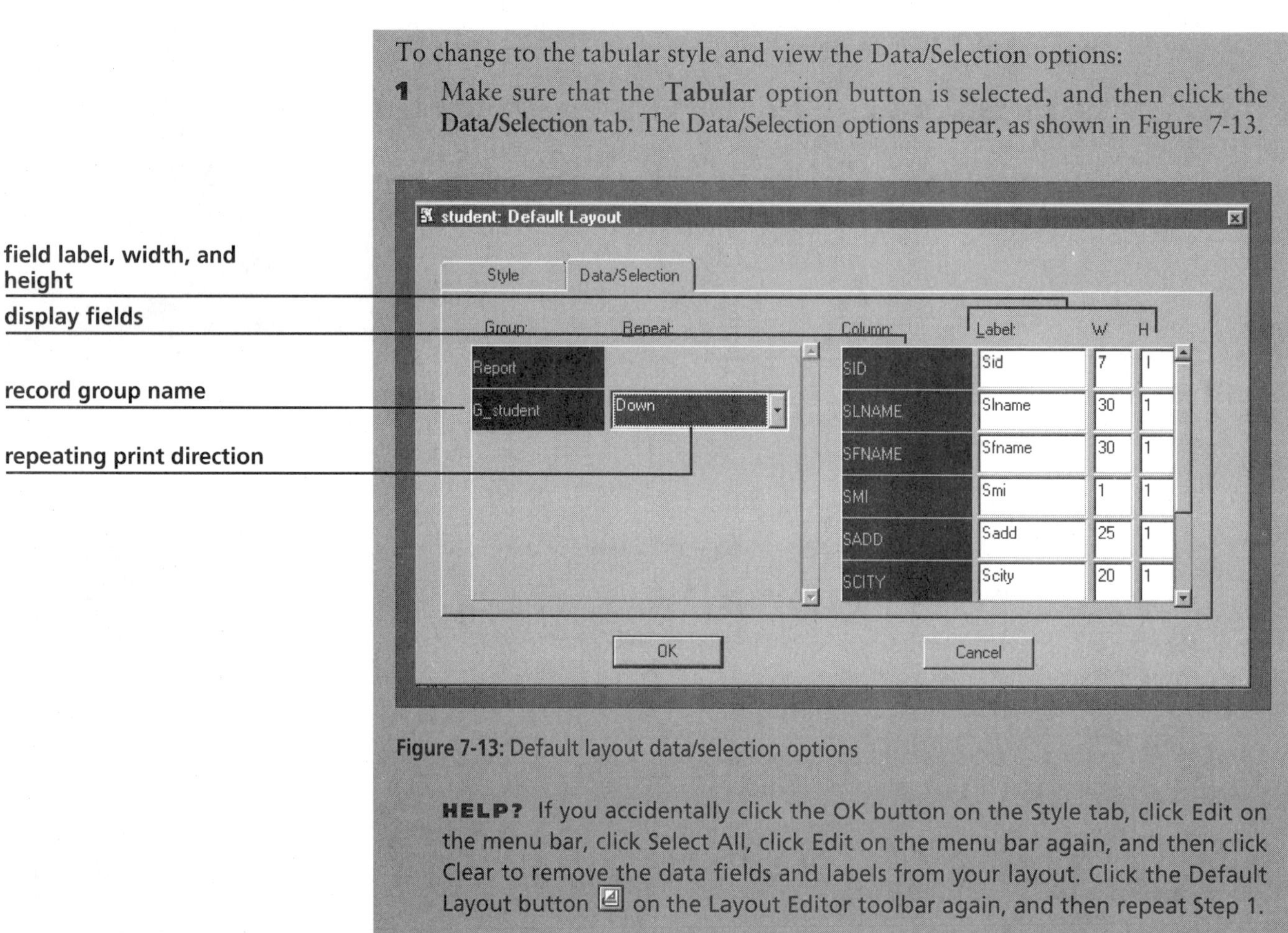

Figure 7-13: Default layout data/selection options

HELP? If you accidentally click the OK button on the Style tab, click Edit on the menu bar, click Select All, click Edit on the menu bar again, and then click Clear to remove the data fields and labels from your layout. Click the Default Layout button on the Layout Editor toolbar again, and then repeat Step 1.

The left side of the Data/Selection tab allows you to specify how you want data records to repeat for each report record group. Figure 7-14 illustrates the different repeating print options for how a record group, which is also called a frame, is printed on a report. The Across repeating option specifies to print the frames across the page until the page is filled horizontally. Only one row of frames is printed per page. The Across/Down repeating option specifies to print as many frames as will fit horizontally across a page, and then to print the next row of frames directly beneath the first row. When the page is filled, printing moves to the next page. The Down repeating option specifies to print each frame directly below its predecessor in a single column. When the page is filled, printing moves to the next page. The Down/Across repeating option specifies to print one column of frames on the page, and then print a second column to the right of the first column. This continues until no more frame columns will fit horizontally on the page and then printing continues on the next page. The Matrix repeating option, which is valid only with the matrix layout style, specifies that frames will be printed at the intersections of rows and columns.

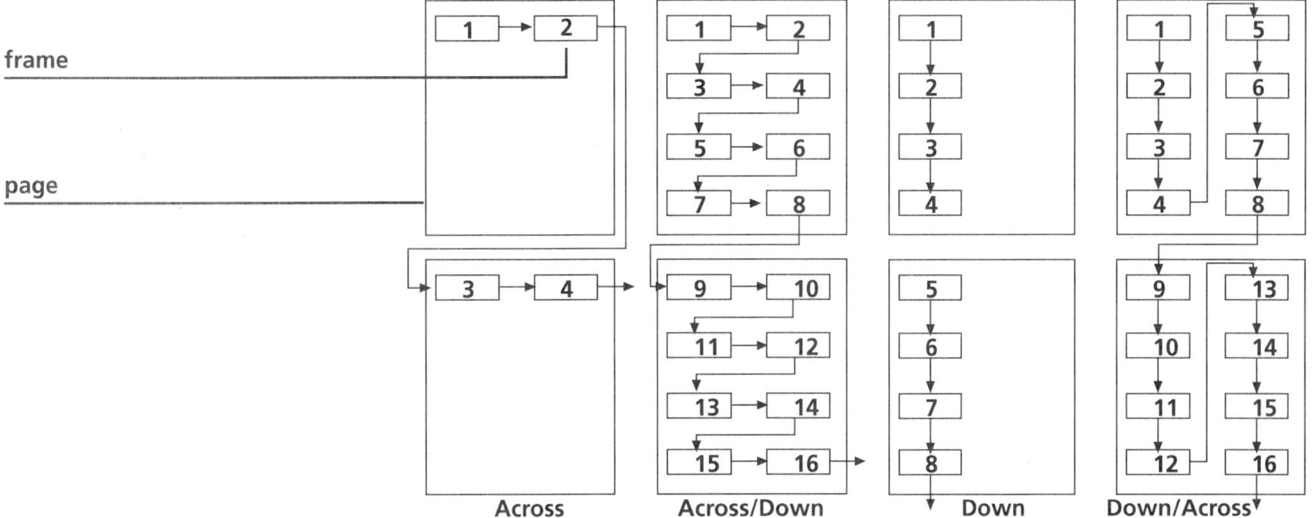

Figure 7-14: Repeating print directions

The right side of the Data/Selection tab allows you to specify which fields to display in the report and their label texts and widths. By default, all fields display in the report. Your report will print student frames using a down repeating print direction, and will display all fields except SID.

To set the repeating print direction and specify the display fields:

1. Make sure that the Repeat style for G_student is **Down**. Click **SID** in the Column column. Note that the box changes color to indicate that the field will not display in the report.
2. Change the field labels and widths as follows using the Data/Selection tab. You will need to scroll down the columns to change all of the values. Your completed Data/Selection tab should look like Figure 7-15.

Field	**Label**	**W(idth)**
SLNAME	Last Name	25
SFNAME	First Name	15
SMI	MI	1
SADD	Address	25
SCITY	City	15
SSTATE	State	2
SZIP	Zip	5
SPHONE	Phone	15

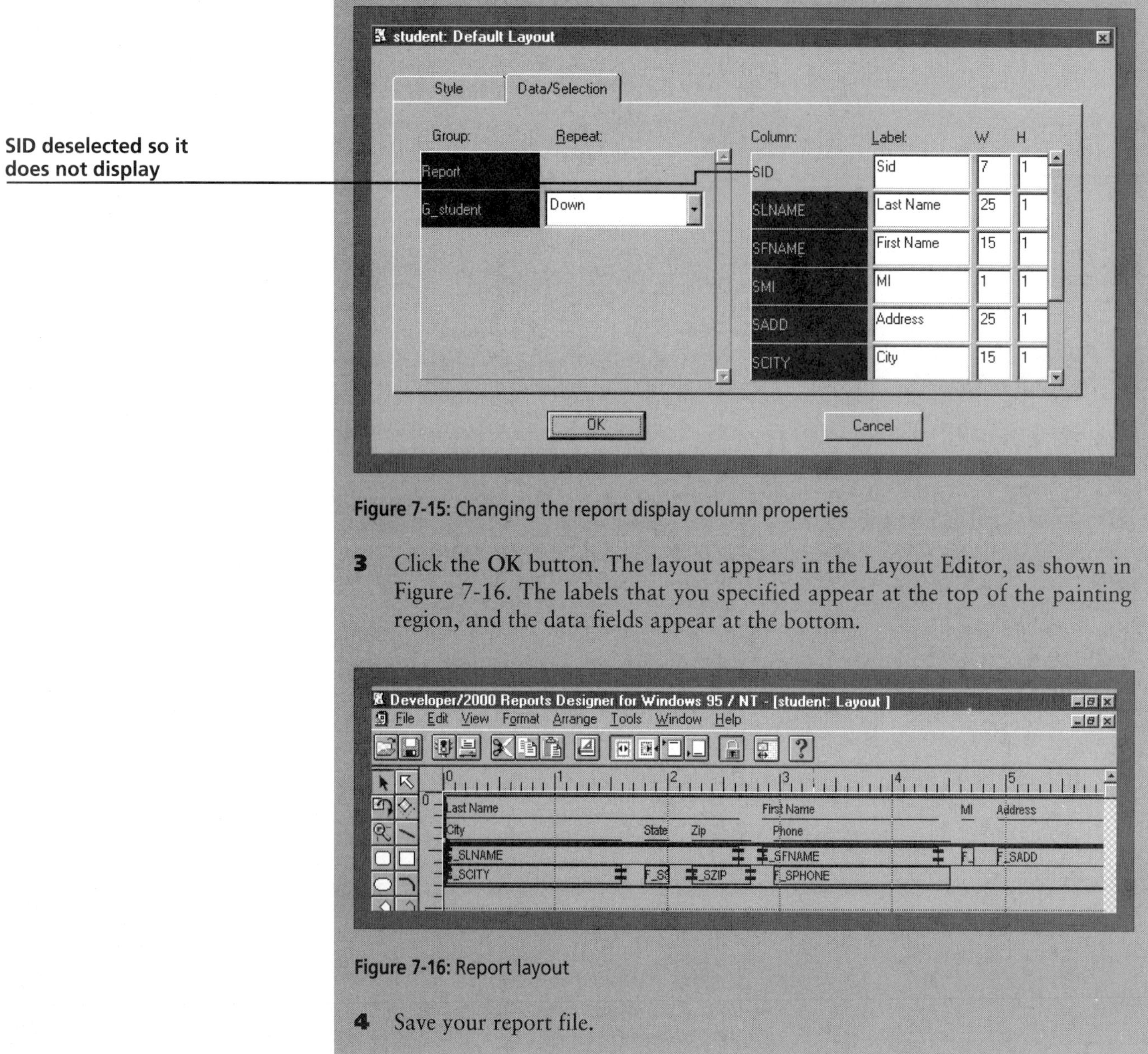

Figure 7-15: Changing the report display column properties

3 Click the **OK** button. The layout appears in the Layout Editor, as shown in Figure 7-16. The labels that you specified appear at the top of the painting region, and the data fields appear at the bottom.

Figure 7-16: Report layout

4 Save your report file.

Next you will run the report to see how it looks. When you click the Run button on the Layout Editor toolbar, the Reports Runtime window opens first. When you click the list arrow, the screen looks like Figure 7-17. You use this window to specify the report's output destination—to the screen, printed to a file, or to the printer. You also can send the report via electronic mail to e-mail addresses specified in the Destination Name text box if your e-mail system supports Microsoft Mail API (application programming interface) protocol. Preview sends the report to the screen using PostScript formatting, which will show how the report will look if it is printed using a PostScript printer. You will run the report to the screen.

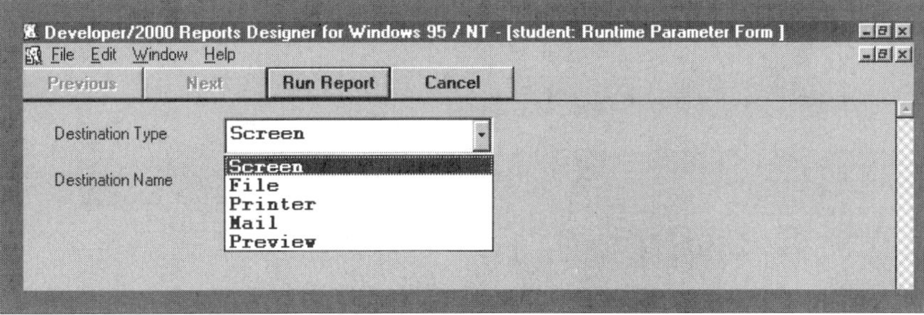

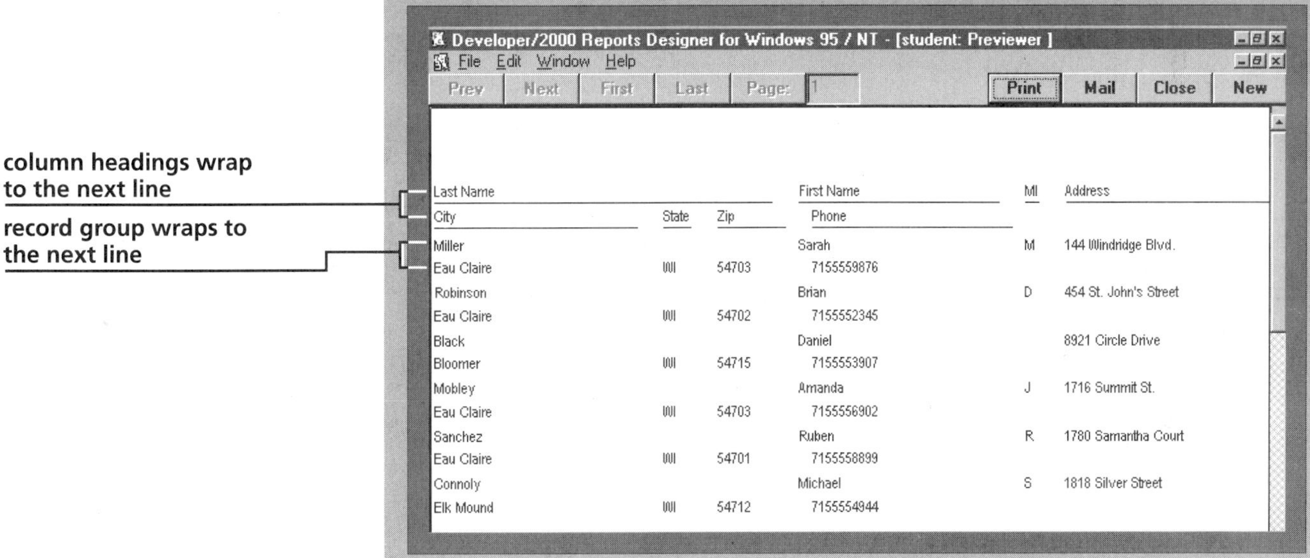

Developer/2000 Reports Designer for Windows 95 / NT - [student: Runtime Parameter Form]
File Edit Window Help
Previous
Next
Run Report
Cancel
Destination Type
Screen
Destination Name
Screen
File
Printer
Mail
Preview

Figure 7-17: Reports Runtime destinations

To run the report:

1. Click the **Run** button on the Layout Editor toolbar.
2. Click the **Destination Type** list arrow, and then click **Screen**.
3. Click the **Run Report** button. After a few moments, the report appears in the Previewer window, as shown in Figure 7-18.

column headings wrap to the next line
record group wraps to the next line
Developer/2000 Reports Designer for Windows 95 / NT - [student: Previewer]
File Edit Window Help
Prev
Next
First
Last
Page:
Print
Mail
Close
New
Last Name
First Name
MI
Address
City
State
Zip
Phone
Miller
Sarah
M
144 Windridge Blvd.
Eau Claire
WI
54703
7155559876
Robinson
Brian
D
454 St. John's Street
Eau Claire
WI
54702
7155552345
Black
Daniel
8921 Circle Drive
Bloomer
WI
54715
7155553907
Mobley
Amanda
J
1716 Summit St.
Eau Claire
WI
54703
7155556902
Sanchez
Ruben
R
1780 Samantha Court
Eau Claire
WI
54701
7155558899
Connoly
Michael
S
1818 Silver Street
Elk Mound
WI
54712
7155554944

Figure 7-18: Report output in Previewer window

HELP? When you run a report using this set of steps, the system does not create an executable file. When you finish the application, you will create an executable .rep file that can be run independently of the Oracle Reports Designer application using the Administration/Generate commands on the File menu.

Some of the data fields in your report are too wide, which forces each record to wrap to the next line and makes the report difficult to read. You will adjust the data field widths next.

To adjust the data field widths:

1. Click the **Close** button to return to the Layout Editor.
2. Click the **Default Layout** button on the Layout Editor toolbar.
3. On the Style tab, click the **Use Current Layout Settings** check box to select it so the program will apply any changes you make to the current layout instead of generating a new layout on top of the existing layout.
4. Click the **Data/Selection** tab, and then change the following field widths:

Field	**W(idth)**
SLNAME	10
SFNAME	10
SADD	15
SCITY	10
SPHONE	7

5. Click the **OK** button, and then click the **Yes** button to replace your existing layout body.
6. Run the report again to the screen to see the revised layout. Your screen output should look like Figure 7 19.

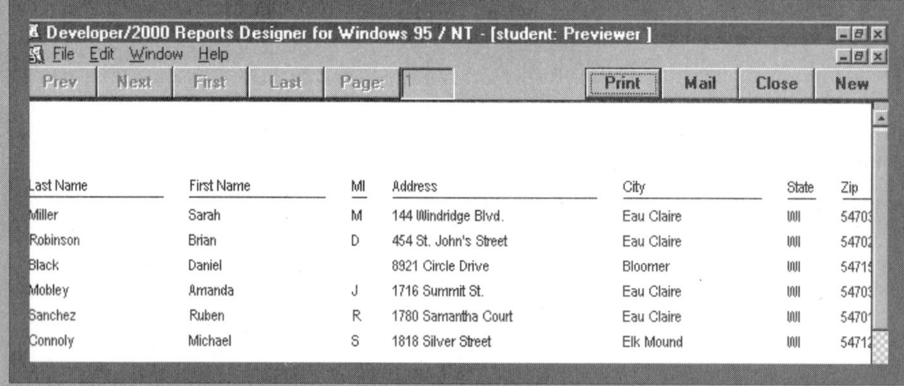

Figure 7-19: Revised report output

7. Click the **Close** button to return to the Layout Editor.
8. Save your report file.

Understanding Layout Frames

Next you will take a closer look at the report layout you just created so you can understand how the Reports Designer works.

To examine the Reports Designer:

1. In the Layout Editor, click **View** on the menu bar, click **Zoom In**, click **View** on the menu bar again, and then click **Zoom In** again. Scroll to the upper-left corner of your layout so your screen looks like Figure 7-20.

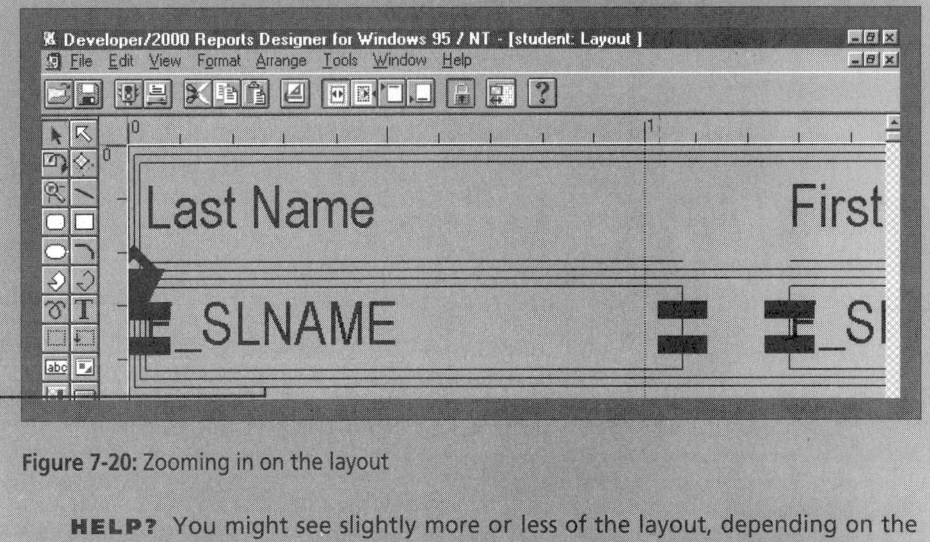

Figure 7-20: Zooming in on the layout

HELP? You might see slightly more or less of the layout, depending on the video resolution of your computer.

You can see that there is a large box around each report item, and other boxes around the labels and data fields. These boxes are called frames. **Frames** are containers for grouping related objects. There are two different types of frames. **Group frames** enclose and keep related groups of objects together, and **repeating frames** enclose objects that are repeated multiple times in a report that displays multiple records. For example, in your report the column headings display only once at the top of the page, so they will display in a group frame. There is more than one student record, so the student data fields will display in a repeating frame. You can identify a particular frame's type by selecting it and then opening its Properties sheet and viewing its name.

To examine the frame properties:

1 Right-click the outer rectangle (see Figure 7-20) so handles appear around its edges, and then click **Properties** on the menu. The student: Frame - M_student_GRPFR dialog box opens, as shown in Figure 7-21. The frame name (M_student_GRPFR) and the selected object type (Enclosing Object) indicate that this is the main frame, or the enclosing group frame, of the report. You can use the General Layout tab to specify layout property values for pagination, print condition, and sizing. The Printer Codes tab specifies numeric printer codes that control print properties such as margins, fonts, and other page elements. Normally you will accept the default values on these tabs. The Comment tab provides a text box for the developer to enter product documentation.

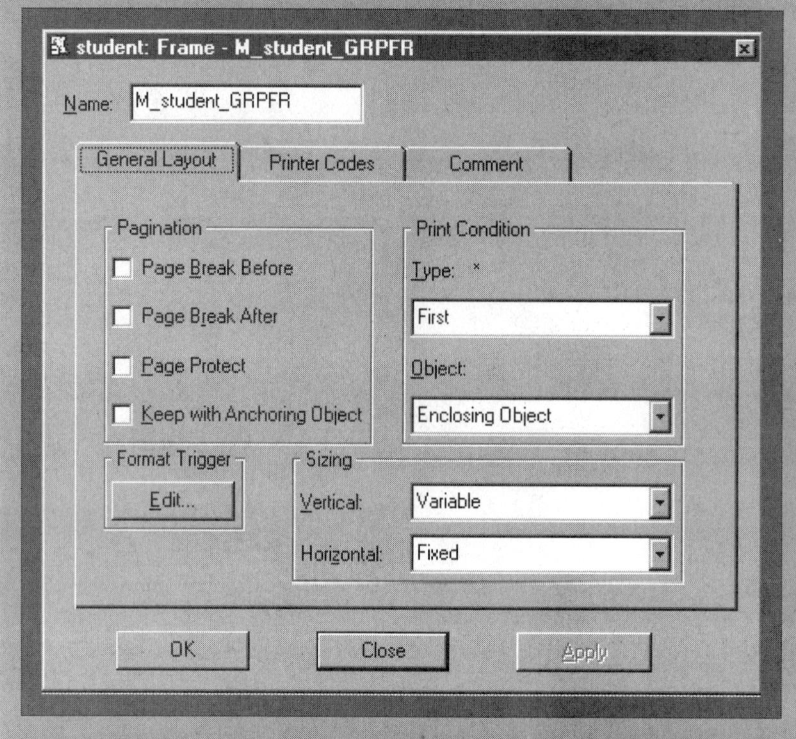

Figure 7-21: M_student_GRPFR frame Properties sheet

2 Click the **Close** button to accept the default settings and close the dialog box.

Sometimes when you move objects around in the layout, you might find that you cannot move or drag an object such as a text field or label outside its enclosing frame. This is because your report layout is in **confine mode**, which ensures that enclosing objects (such as M_student_GRPFR) must completely enclose the objects they contain (which are called child objects). You can turn confine mode off by clicking the Confine button on the Layout Editor toolbar, and turn it back on by clicking the Confine Off button. It usually is best to leave confine mode on because, if a group frame does not enclose all of the objects inside it, you will get an error message when you run the form. Next you will examine what happens when you try to move objects outside their enclosing frame with confine mode on, and see the error message that is generated when an object is moved outside its enclosing frame.

To examine the behavior of enclosing frames with confine mode on and off:

1 Drag the bottom left handle of the M_student_GRPFR frame down so it is at least two-tenths of an inch below the next frame inside, as shown in Figure 7-22.

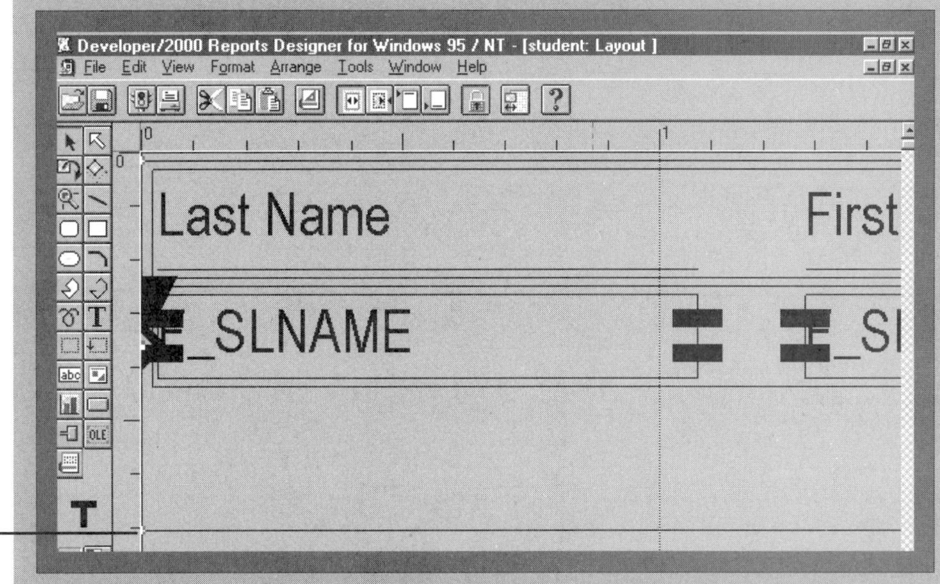

Figure 7-22: Enlarging the M_student_GRPFR frame

2 Try to drag the bottom left handle of the M_student_GRPFR frame to the right about one-tenth of an inch so it overlaps some of the frames it encloses. Note that you cannot make the group frame smaller than the objects inside because the Layout Editor currently is in confine mode.

3 Click the **Confine** button on the Layout Editor toolbar. The Confine button changes to the Confine Off button.

4 Drag the bottom left handle of the M_student_GRPFR frame to the right one-tenth of an inch again. This time you should succeed, and your screen should look like Figure 7-23.

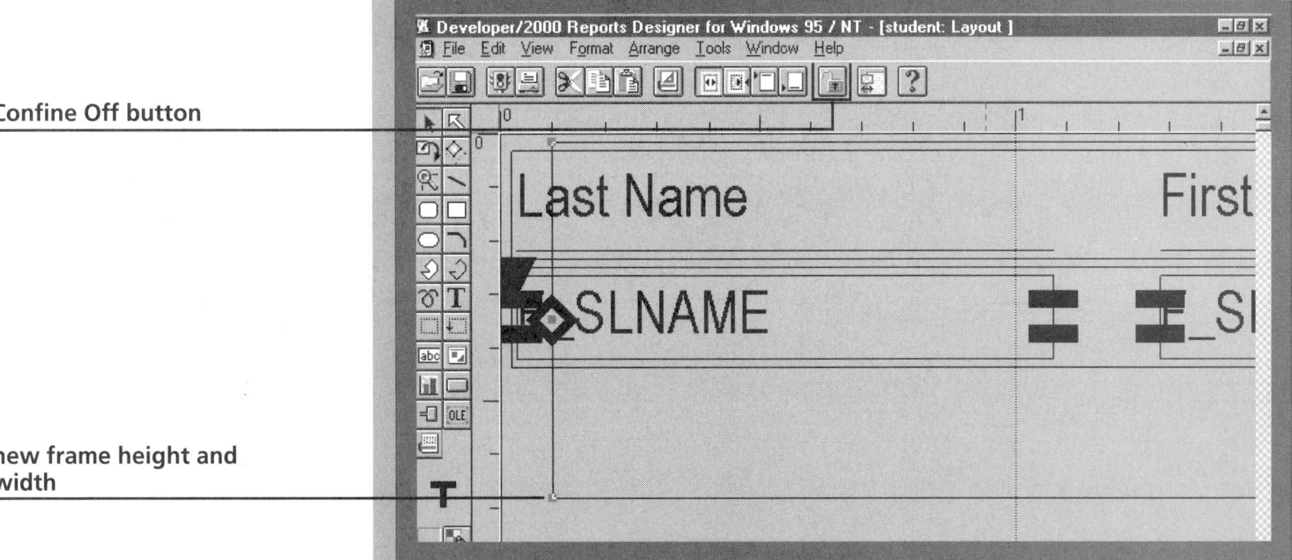

Figure 7-23: Resizing the M_student_GRPFR frame

5 Run the report to the screen. A warning dialog box opens with the message "REP-1035: Warning: Frame M_student_GRPFR intersects but does not enclose object 'R_student'." The warning occurs because you turned off confine mode and decreased the size of the group frame so it did not completely enclose the repeating frame.

6 Click the **Continue** button. A second message indicates that M_student_GRPFR did not enclose object M_student_HDR.

7 Click the **Continue** button again. Your report appears in the Previewer window. As you can see, changing the group frame size so it does not enclose all of its objects causes error messages, but does not keep the report from running. It is best to keep confine mode on. If you find you need to turn confide mode off when you are positioning objects in the report layout, find the enclosing frame named in the warning message and make sure that it completely encloses its child objects.

8 Click the **Close** button to return to the Layout Editor, resize the M_student_GRPFR frame so it encloses all of the child objects, and then click to turn confide mode back on.

9 Right-click the **R_student** frame just inside the bottom edge of M_student_GRPFRM, and then click **Properties** on the menu. The student: Repeating Frame - R_student dialog box opens, as shown in Figure 7-24.

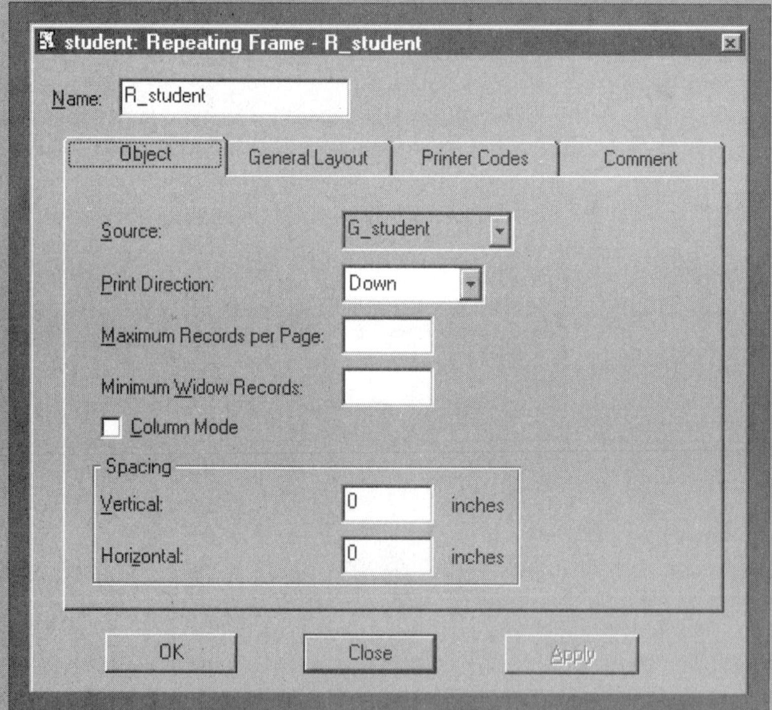

Figure 7-24: R_student Properties sheet

HELP? If the name of your dialog box is different, click the Close button and then repeat Step 8.

You should now see the R_student Properties sheet. The R_ prefix in its name indicates that R_student is a repeating frame, which means that the objects inside this frame will repeat as many times as necessary to show all of the records retrieved in the student record group. On the Properties sheet, you can specify the print direction, maximum records per page, and spacing to control how records repeat in the frame. Next you will experiment with the spacing.

The horizontal spacing is affected only when you are displaying frames across the page using the across/down or down/across print direction.

To change the spacing in the repeating frame:

1. Change the value in the Vertical text box to .5 inches, and then click the OK button.
2. Run the report to the screen. Notice that there is more space between the student records now.
3. Click the **Close** button.
4. Open the **R_student** Properties sheet again, and change the Vertical Spacing property back to **0** inches, and then click the **General Layout** tab. Notice that R_student also is an enclosing object—it encloses the individual data fields in the record. You rarely change the default values on the General Layout or Printer Codes tabs for a repeating frame.
5. Click the **OK** button to save your spacing change and to close the R_student Properties sheet.

Next you will examine the column label frame and the individual data fields, as shown in Figure 7-25. The frame around the column labels is a group frame rather than a repeating frame because the labels print only once per page. Data fields display the retrieved or calculated data values. Each data field has a default name of F (for field), an underscore, and then the name of the associated field in the G_student record group. Data fields can be generated automatically using one of the default layouts, or drawn manually using the Field tool [abc] on the Tool palette. If you draw a data field manually, you must associate it with record group field. In this report, all data fields are enclosed in a repeating frame because a row of data fields will display for each student record retrieved from the database.

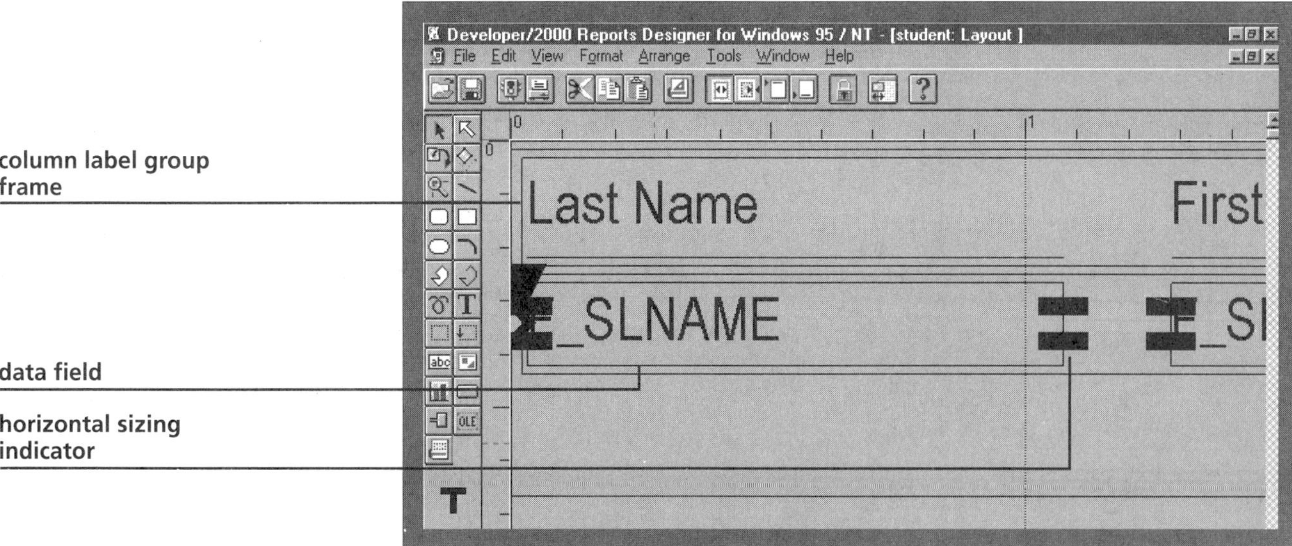

Figure 7-25: Column label group frame and data field

The horizontal marks on the sides of the data field reflect the data field's sizing properties. **Sizing** determines whether a field's size is fixed on the printed report, or whether it can expand or contract automatically depending on the size of the retrieved data value. Figure 7-26 illustrates the different sizing options and associated markings on the field's horizontal and vertical borders. The markings on the left and right edges specify the horizontal sizing property, and the markings on the top and bottom specify the vertical sizing. Fixed sizing means the field will have the size shown in the layout, and extra text will be truncated. Contract sizing means that the field will contract if the data value is smaller than the layout size, but wider data will be truncated. Expand sizing means that the data field will expand automatically to accommodate wider data values, but narrower data values will still occupy the entire space shown in the layout. Variable sizing means that the data field will contract or expand as needed to fit the data value.

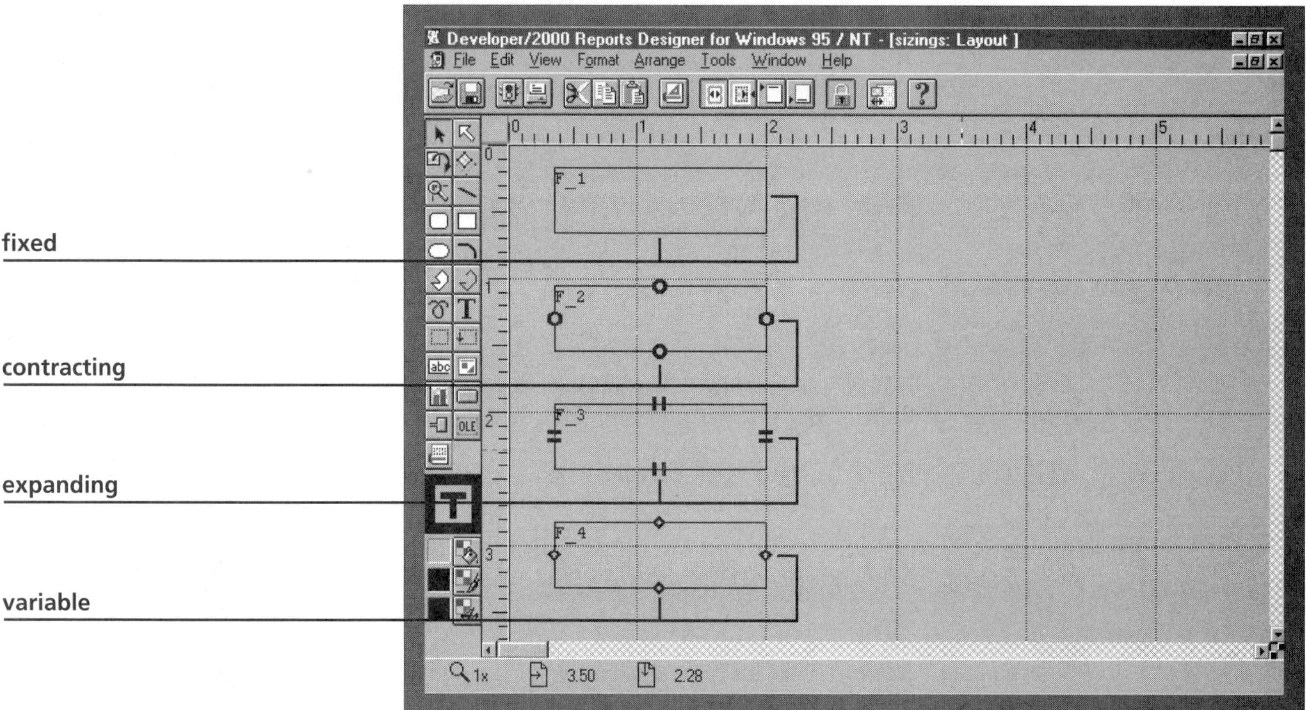

Figure 7-26: Data field sizing indicators

To examine the properties of the column label frame and data fields:

1. Right-click the column label group frame just inside the top edge of M_student_GRPFR (see Figure 7-25), and then click **Properties** on the menu. The student: Frame - M_student_HDR dialog box opens. The M_student_HDR frame contains the column heading objects. Just like the other frames, you rarely change the properties of the frame.
2. Click the **Close** button to close the M_student_GRPFR Properties sheet.
3. Right-click the **F_SLNAME** data field, and then click **Properties**.

You might not be able to see the "F" in F_SLNAME because of the elements that display on top of it. You will not need to scroll the form.

4. Click the **Source From** list arrow to display a list of all of the fields in the G_student record group. You could select a different record group field such as SPHONE, and then the student phone numbers would display in this data field when you run the report. Make sure that **SLNAME** is selected.
5. Click the **Format Mask** list arrow. Note that nothing happens. You can specify format masks only for NUMBER and DATE fields in a report, and the Source From data type indicates that SLNAME is a VARCHAR2 field.
6. Click the **General Layout** tab. Options are provided for changing the data field pagination, print condition, and sizing. Again, you usually accept the default values on the General Layout or Printer Codes tabs for a default layout data field. Click the **OK** button to close the F_SLNAME Properties sheet.

Now see what happens when you move a data field outside of its repeating frame.

To move a data field outside of its repeating frame:

1. Click the **Confine** button on the Layout Editor toolbar to turn confine mode off.
2. In the Layout Editor, click and drag **F_SLNAME** so it is completely outside of R_student.
3. Run the report to the screen. The error message "REP-1213: Field 'F_SLNAME' references column 'SLNAME' at a frequency below its group" indicates that the data column (SLNAME) potentially could retrieve multiple records, but the layout field (F_SLNAME) is not in a repeating frame. To fix this problem, you need to move the field back into its repeating frame.
4. Click the **OK** button. This is a fatal error that keeps your form from running.
5. Move **F_SLNAME** back into R_student.
6. Click the **Confine Off** button on the Layout Editor toolbar to turn confine mode on again.

Now that you are acquainted with frames, what they are for, and some of the problems that they can cause, you will regenerate the default layout.

To regenerate the default layout:

1. Click **View** on the menu bar, and then click **Normal Size**.
2. Click the **Default Layout** button on the Layout Editor toolbar, click the **OK** button to regenerate the default layout, and then click the **Yes** button to replace your existing layout.
3. Save the report.

Formatting the Report

There are three report regions that you can access in the Layout Editor—the header, body, and trailer. The **header** is an optional page (or multiple pages) that appears at the beginning of the report and can contain text, graphics, data, and computations. The report **body** is not optional—it contains the majority of the report's data and computations. So far, you have been working in the report body. A top and bottom margin appears on each body page where you can put text such as page numbers. The default margin size is one-half inch each for the top and bottom margins and zero for the left and right margins. The report **trailer**, like the header, is an optional page (or multiple pages) that appears at the end of the report. The trailer can include summary data, or for a report with hundreds of pages, it could contain text that indicates the end of the report.

Adding Parameter Fields and Labels to the Body Margins

The Layout Editor toolbar contains a navigation button group that enables you to switch to different report layout regions. The first button in this group is the Body button, which currently is pressed because you are viewing the body portion of the layout. Next you will move to the margin region and add the parameter fields and labels to show the current date and the report page number. You will add the date to the top margin first.

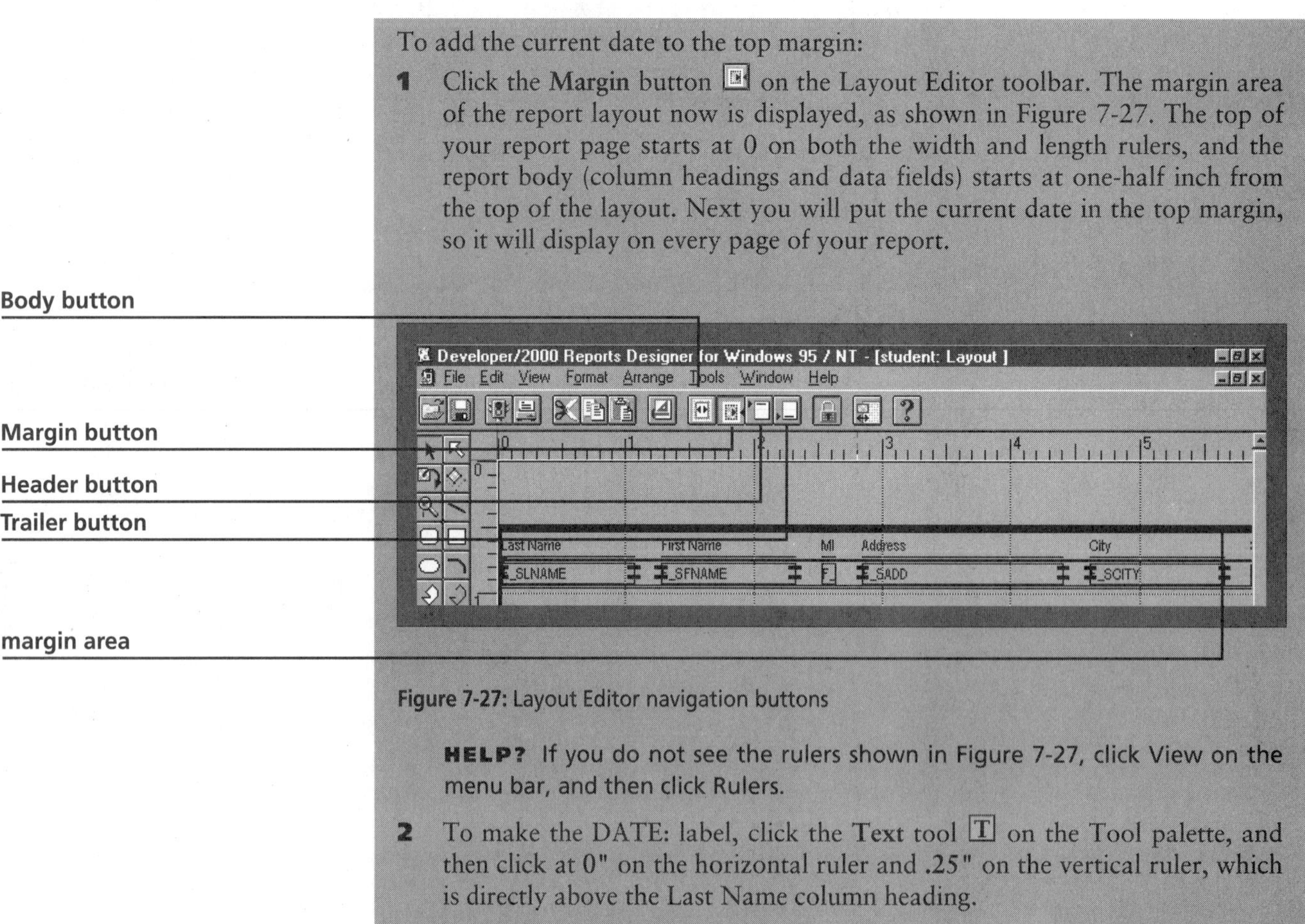

To add the current date to the top margin:

1 Click the **Margin** button on the Layout Editor toolbar. The margin area of the report layout now is displayed, as shown in Figure 7-27. The top of your report page starts at 0 on both the width and length rulers, and the report body (column headings and data fields) starts at one-half inch from the top of the layout. Next you will put the current date in the top margin, so it will display on every page of your report.

Figure 7-27: Layout Editor navigation buttons

HELP? If you do not see the rulers shown in Figure 7-27, click View on the menu bar, and then click Rulers.

2 To make the DATE: label, click the Text tool on the Tool palette, and then click at 0" on the horizontal ruler and .25" on the vertical ruler, which is directly above the Last Name column heading.

To reposition an object exactly, click the object, press and hold down the Shift key, and then use the arrow keys on the keyboard to move the object.

3 Type DATE: and then click anywhere else on the painting region.

4 Click the **Field** tool on the Tool palette, and then draw a field to the right of your DATE: label, as shown in Figure 7-28. The new field is labeled F_1. If necessary, drag the label and data field so they are positioned correctly.

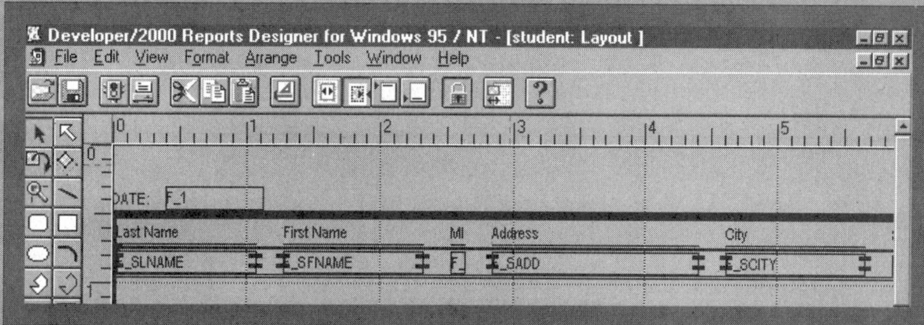

Figure 7-28: Creating the field to display the date

5 Right-click the new field, and then click **Properties** on the menu. The student: Layout Field - F_1 dialog box opens with the default field name selected in the Name text box.

6 Type F_**date** to rename the field.

7 Click the **Source From** list arrow, and then click **&Current Date** to display the current date in the field.

8 Click the **Format Mask** list arrow, and then scroll down and click **MM/DD/YY**. Your F_date Properties sheet should look like Figure 7-29. Click the **OK** button.

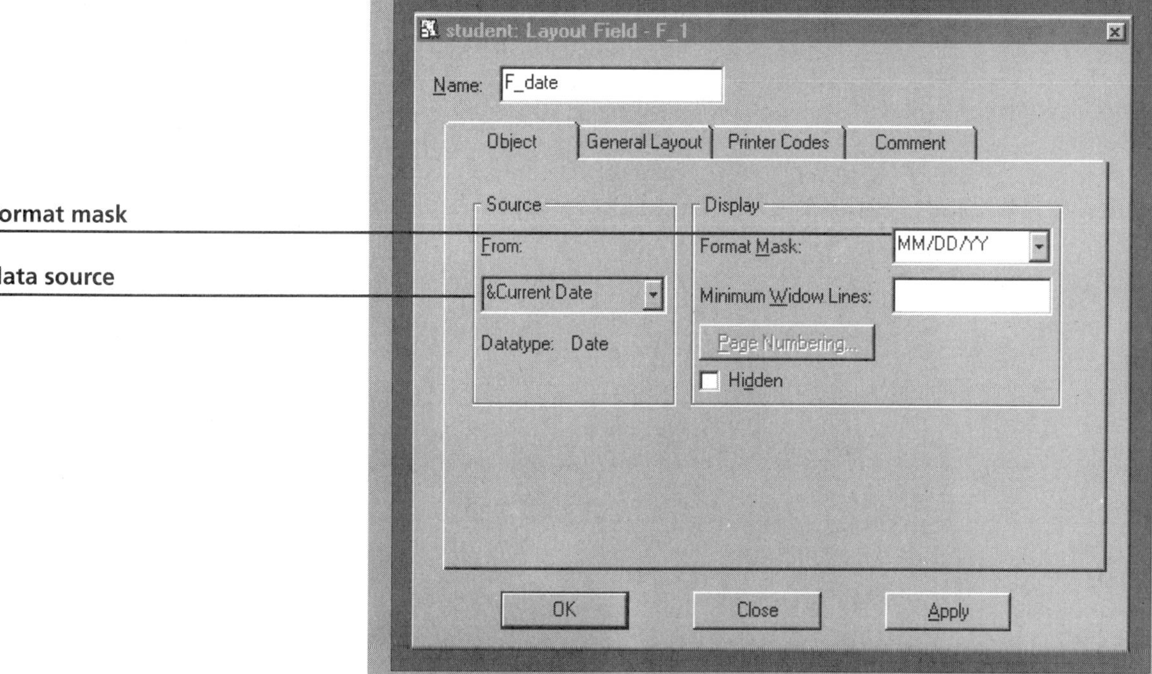

Figure 7-29: F_date Properties sheet

Next you will add the parameter field to display the report page number on the bottom margin.

To add the report page number:

1. Click **View** on the menu bar, and then click **Zoom Out**. Scroll to the bottom of the Layout Editor. Note that there is a heavy black line at 10½" from the top of the page to show where the bottom margin area begins. You will put the page number below this line in the bottom margin area.
2. Click the **Field** tool on the Tool palette, and then draw a field in the center of the page below the bottom margin line at **4.25"** on the horizontal ruler and below **10.5"** on the vertical ruler. Right-click the field, click **Properties**, and then change the Name property to **F_page#** and change its Source From property to **&Physical Page Number**, and then click the **OK** button to close the F_page# Properties sheet.
3. Run the report to the screen, and make sure that the date and page numbers display correctly, and then click the **Close** button to return to the Layout Editor.
4. Save the report.

tip

A logical page can be any size the designer wants it to be. The physical page size is determined by how the logical page contents are printed by a particular printer.

Creating a Header with Text and a Graphic Image

Next you will create a header page with the Northwoods University logo and some header text. This page will be the cover page for your report.

To create the header page:

1. In the Layout Editor, click the **Header** button on the Layout Editor toolbar to display the header page.

   HELP? The right side of the page should be at 8 1/2" on the horizontal ruler so you can see the entire page width. If you cannot see the entire page width, click View on the menu bar, and then click Zoom Out.
2. Click **Edit** on the menu bar, point to **Import**, and then click **Image**. The Import Image dialog box opens.
3. Click the **File** option button, and then click the **Browse** button.
4. Change to the Chapter7 folder on your Student Disk, click the **nwlogo.jpg** file, click the **Open** button, accept the default values for the Format and Quality options, and then click the **OK** button in the Import Image dialog box to close it and add the Northwoods University logo to the header.
5. Drag the image so its upper-left corner is at 3" on the horizontal ruler and 3" on the vertical ruler to center it.
6. Click View on the menu bar, and then click **Zoom In**. Zoom In again if necessary so you can see the image, and then scroll so the area directly under the image is visible.
7. Click the Text tool on the Tool palette, click below the image, and then type **Student Report** to add the title to the report. Click outside the text box to select the field and to deselect the Text tool.
8. Click **Format** on the menu bar, click **Font**, and then change the font to **20-point bold Arial** font. Drag the bottom right handle down and to the right to increase the size of the text box so all of the label will be visible.

tip

To delete a header or trailer page, open the Object Navigator window, select the items under the Header or Trailer items, and then press the Delete key.

9 Click **Format** on the menu bar, point to **Alignment**, and then click **Center** to center the text within the text box. If necessary, position the text box under the logo so it looks like Figure 7-30.

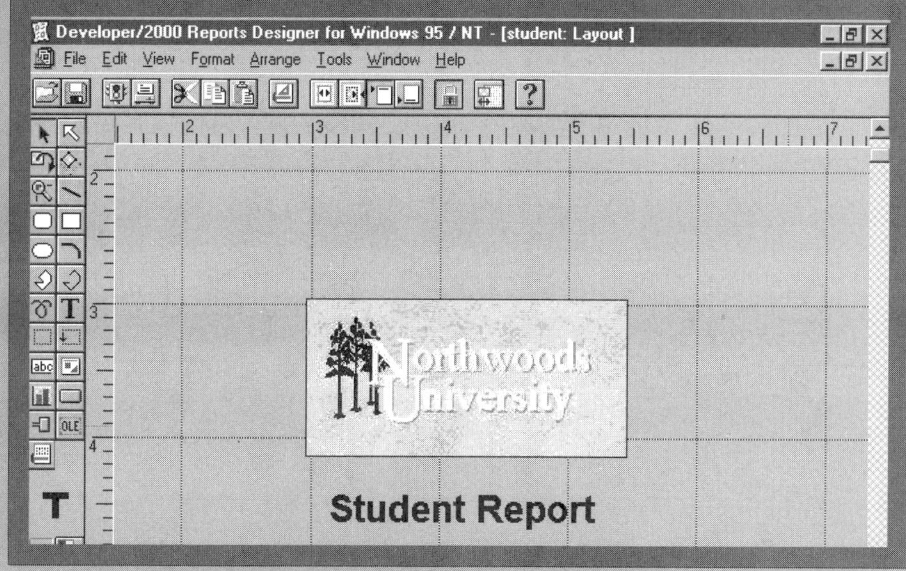

Figure 7-30: Report header

There are additional report pages when the Next button is active in the Previewer window.

10 Save your changes, and then run the report to the screen. After you view the header screen, click the **Next** button to view the report body.

11 Click the **Close** button to close the report and return to the Layout Editor.

Creating a Report Trailer

Finally you will create a trailer to identify the end of the report. In a short report like this one, a trailer page usually is unnecessary, but a trailer page is helpful when the report includes hundreds of pages.

To create the report trailer:

1 In the Layout Editor, click the **Trailer** button on the Layout Editor toolbar. The trailer page looks just like the header page.

2 Click **View** on the menu bar, and then click **Zoom Out**. Continue zooming out until you can see the full page width.

3 Click the **Text** tool on the Tool palette, click at 2" on the horizontal ruler and 5" on the vertical ruler, and then type *** * * END OF REPORT * * ***.

4 If necessary, change the font to **20-point bold Arial**, and then center the text on the trailer page.

5 Save your changes, run the report to the screen, and then view your trailer page by clicking the **Next** button twice.

HELP? There is no zoom feature in the Previewer, so you might have to scroll down to see your trailer text.

6 Click the **Close** button to close the report and return to the Layout Editor.

7 Save the report.

Generating the Report Executable File

After you finish a report, you need to create an executable (.rep) file, which can be run independently of the Reports Designer application. You might develop a report for non-programmers and not want them to run it through the Reports Designer, where they might change design elements accidentally.

To generate and run the report executable file:

1 Click **File** on the menu bar, point to **Administration**, and then click **Generate.** The Generate dialog box opens. The default filename is the same as the report filename, so you will accept the default filename.

2 Change to the drive that contains your Student Disk, open the Chapter7 folder, and then click the **Save** button to accept the default filename and generate the student.rep executable file. To run a .rep file, double-click the filename in Windows Explorer. Before the file will run, an association must exist on your workstation between files with an .rep extension and the Oracle Reports Runtime application. In Windows95/NT, this is called a registered file type.

3 Start Windows Explorer.

4 Go to the Chapter7 folder on your Student Disk, and then double-click **student.rep**. If you see the Oracle Database Connect dialog box, then .rep files are already a registered file type, so you can go to Step 5. If not, follow the steps in the HELP paragraphs that follow.

HELP? If the Open With dialog box opens instead of the Logon dialog box, your workstation is not configured to open executable Oracle Reports files (which have .rep extensions) using the Oracle Reports Runtime application. For Windows 95 users, click the Other button, click the Browse button, click the R25run32.exe file in the ORAWIN95\BIN\ directory, click the Open button, and then click the OK button. For Windows NT users, click the Other button, click the R25run32.exe file in the \ORANT\BIN\ folder, and then click the OK button. Now the Logon dialog box will open automatically when you double-click .rep filenames.

HELP? If the report does not run properly, then you probably associated the .rep file with the wrong executable filename. To delete an association, click View on the Windows Explorer menu bar, and then click Options. Click the File Types tab, and then scroll down in the file list until you find an entry called REP Files. Click REP Files, click the Remove button, and then click the Yes button to confirm that you want to remove the association. Click the Close button to close the Options dialog box, and then repeat the steps to create the file association.

5 Close the report in the Reports Runtime application.

6 Close Windows Explorer.

7 Close the report file in the Reports Designer application by clicking **File** on the menu bar, and then clicking **Close**. If you are asked to save changes, click the **Yes** button. You return to the Object Navigator.

Creating a Master/Detail Report

The student report data fields came from a single database table. You also can create reports that retrieve data from multiple tables and format these reports to show master/detail relationships. Recall that a master/detail relationship exists when one record can have many associated records. Next you will create a master/detail report to show faculty last and first names, and the last and first names, address, and phone numbers of each faculty members' advisees, as shown in Figure 7-31. The report will have a title and show the current date, page number, and total number of pages in the top margin. The FACULTY data fields will be the master records, and the STUDENT data fields will be the detail records. A faculty record will display, followed by the group of student detail records for that faculty member. Then the next faculty record will display, followed by the associated group of student detail records.

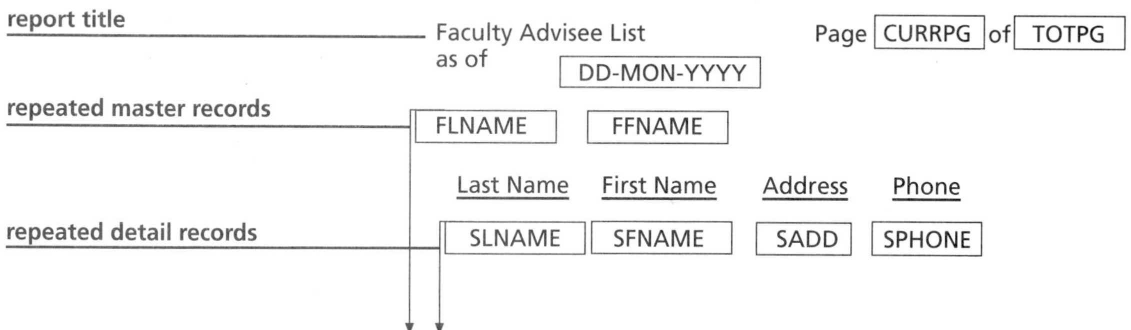

Figure 7-31: FACULTY master/detail report design

To create the master/detail report:

1. Click the **Reports** object in the Object Navigator window, and then click the **Create** button on the Object Navigator toolbar.
2. Click the **Save** button on the Object Navigator toolbar, and save your report as **faculty.rdf** in the Chapter7 folder on your Student Disk. Notice that the name of the form changes automatically to FACULTY after you save it.

tip

You also can click Navigator on the menu bar, and then click Create to create a new report.

Creating the Data Model

When you create a master/detail report, you must create the data model to define the data to retrieve and display in the report. The data model in a master/detail report is slightly different than the report you created previously because it must include a break that separates the master and detail fields. A master/detail relationship is also known as a **one-to-many relationship**, which means that one record in one table could have many related records in another table. Figure 7-32 shows how one faculty member advises many students. The master record group is the *one* side of the relationship, or in this case, the FACULTY fields. The detail record group is the *many* side of the relationship, or in this case, the STUDENT fields.

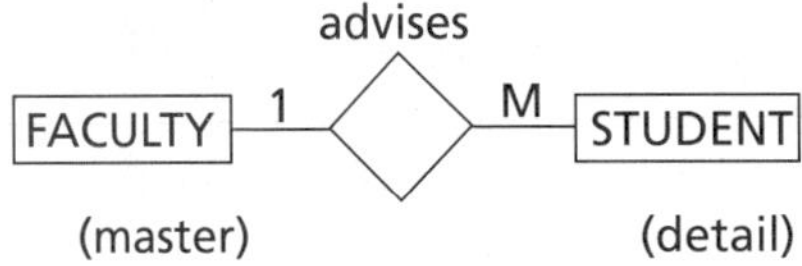

Figure 7-32: FACULTY/STUDENT master/detail relationship

In a master/detail report, the first query you create contains all of the report data fields. Then you move the master (FACULTY) records into a separate record group to create the master/detail relationship.

To create the query to show both the FACULTY and STUDENT records:

1. Double-click the **Data Model** icon, click the **Query** button on the Tool palette, and then draw a query.
2. Right-click the query, click **Properties** on the menu to open the faculty: Query - Q_1 box, and then change the default query name to **Q_student**.
3. Type the SQL query shown in Figure 7-33 to show the faculty last and first names, the student last and first names, student address, and student phone number.

type this command

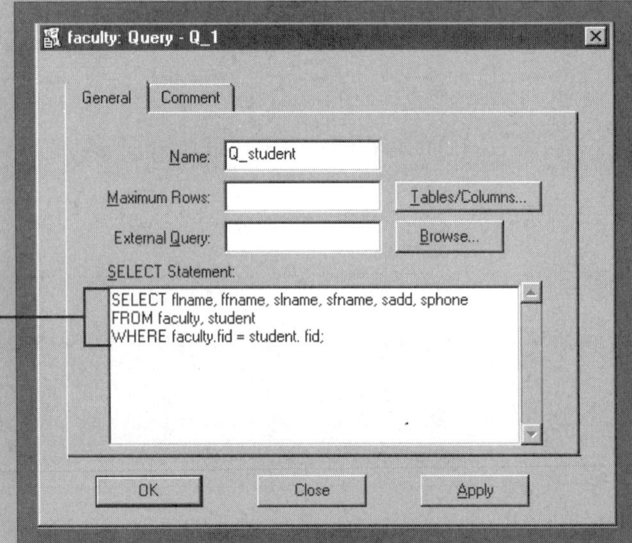

Figure 7-33: Q_student SELECT statement

4. Click the **OK** button. Your Q_student data model should look like Figure 7-34.

tip

You cannot use the Tables/Columns button in the Query Editor if your query involves more than one database table.

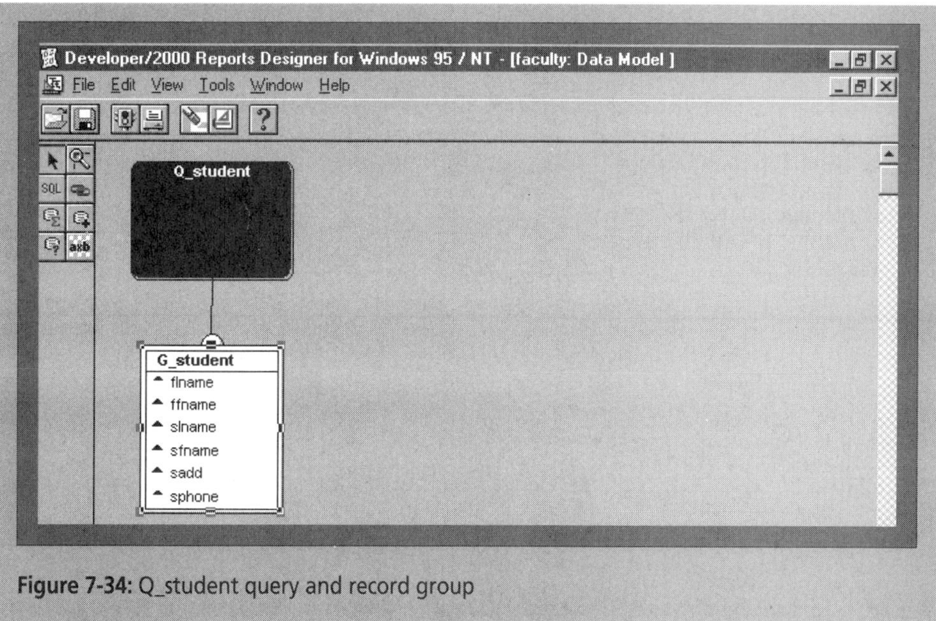

Figure 7-34: Q_student query and record group

The next step is to move the FACULTY records into a separate record group. To do this, you "break out" the master fields by selecting them and then drag them outside the original record group to create a new record group.

To break out the FACULTY records:

1. Click **flname** and then drag it outside the G_student record group, as shown in Figure 7-35. A new record group named G_1 appears, with lines connecting it to both Q_student and G_student. The connecting lines show that the new record group is the master record group because it appears above the G_student group in the data model hierarchy. You might need to reposition your record groups to look like Figure 7-35.

master record group

detail record group

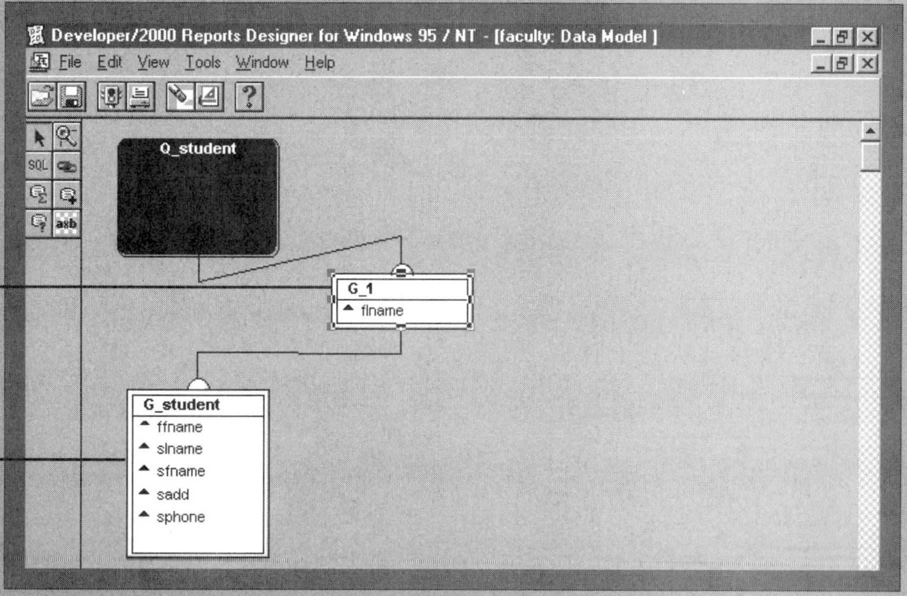

Developer/2000 Reports Designer for Windows 95 / NT - [faculty: Data Model]
File Edit View Tools Window Help
Q_student
G_1
flname
G_student
ffname
slname
sfname
sadd
sphone

Figure 7-35: Data model with break

When creating a master/detail relationship, always create a record group with all of the required records, and then break out the master records.

2 Right-click G_1 and then click **Properties** on the menu. Change the name to **G_faculty**, and then click the **OK** button.

HELP? If you open the flname column Properties sheet by mistake, you will not be able to change the record group name. Click the Close button, and then repeat Step 2.

3 Drag the bottom center handle for **G_faculty** down about one-half inch on the screen to make it larger.

4 Click **ffname** and then drag it from G_student into G_faculty. It should now be listed below flname. Your finished data model should look like Figure 7-36.

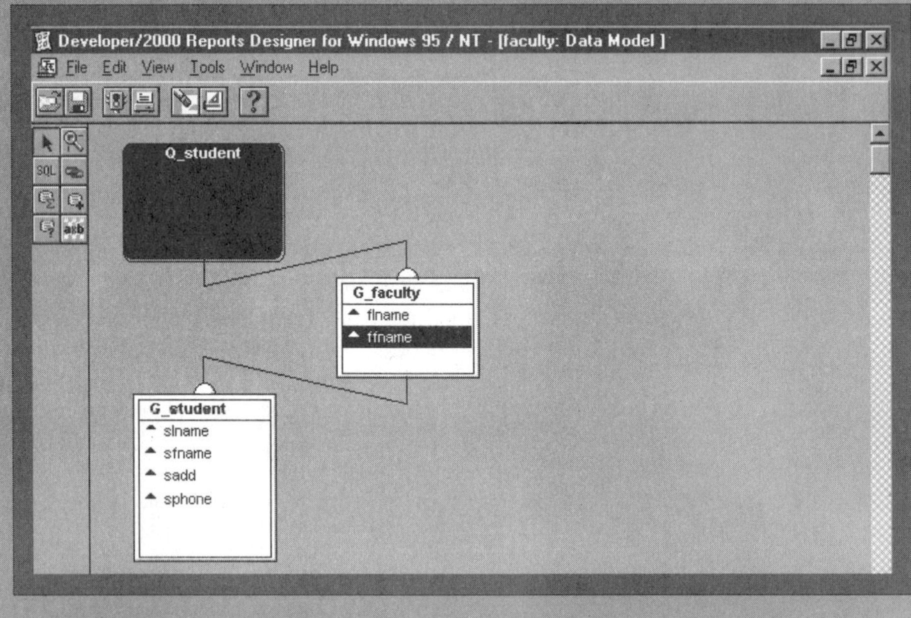

Figure 7-36: Finished data model

5 Save the report file.

Formatting the Layout

Next you need to format the layout. First you will select the default layout style and then specify the display labels and field sizes. Then you will preview the report, and adjust the layout as necessary.

To format the layout:

1 Click **Tools** on the menu bar, and then click **Layout Editor** to go to the Layout Editor.

2 Click **Format** on the menu bar, click **Font**, and then change the default font to **8-point Arial Narrow**, and then click **File** on the menu bar, click **Page Setup**, and then click the **Portrait** option button to change the page orientation.

3 Click the **Fill Color** tool on the Tool palette and confirm that the Fill Color is **No Fill**.

4 Click the **Line Color** tool on the Tool palette and confirm that the Line Color is **No Line.**

5 Click the **Default Layout** button on the Layout Editor toolbar, and then click the **Master/Detail** option button. This layout automatically formats your master/detail records correctly.

6 Click the **Data/Selection** tab, and then change the field labels and widths as follows:

Field Name	Label	W(idth)
FLNAME	<no label>	20
FFNAME	<no label>	15
SLNAME	Last Name	20
SFNAME	First Name	15
SADD	Address	20
SPHONE	Phone	10

7 Click the **OK** button to generate the layout.

8 Save the report.

9 Run the report to the screen. Your initial report preview display should look like Figure 7-37. If the report default properties (such as font, fill color, or line color) are not correct, change the default properties in the Layout Edition and then click the Default Layout button and regenerate the report.

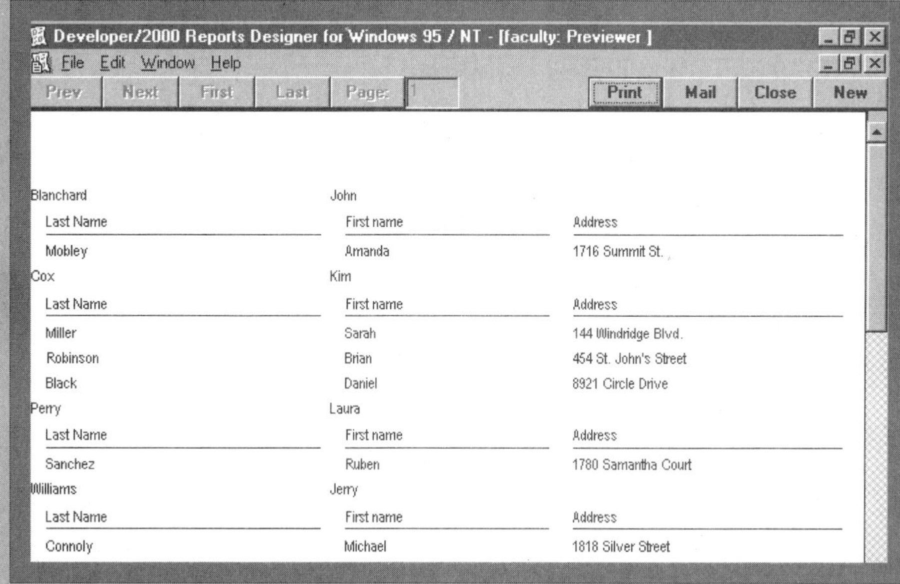

Figure 7-37: Initial report in Previewer window

The report spacing needs to be adjusted so the master records stand out from the detail records. You will increase the vertical spacing at the end of each set of detail lines so there is some white space between each master/detail group.

To increase the vertical spacing at the end of each detail record group:

1 Click the **Close** button to close the Previewer window, then click **View** on the menu bar, and then click **Zoom In** and scroll to the top left corner so you can see the individual frames.

If you have trouble selecting a specific frame, zoom in again to increase the space between the frames. If two frames appear to be on top of one another, select the inside frame and make it slightly smaller or select the outside frame and make it slightly larger.

2 Select the outer frame, and open its Properties sheet to make sure the frame name is M_faculty_GRPFR. You only can change vertical spacing on repeating frames, so this frame won't help. Click the **Close** button to close the M_faculty_GRPFR Properties sheet.

3 Select the next frame in, and open its Properties sheet to make sure the frame name is R_faculty (if the name is *not* R_faculty, click the Close button, and select another frame until you see R_faculty). Do you want to increase the spacing between each repeating faculty name? The answer is yes—that will leave more space between the last student name in a list and the next faculty name.

4 Change the Vertical Spacing property on R_faculty to **.25** inches, and then click the **OK** button.

5 Save your changes, run the report to the screen. and then evaluate the effect of the change. Your revised report should look like Figure 7-38.

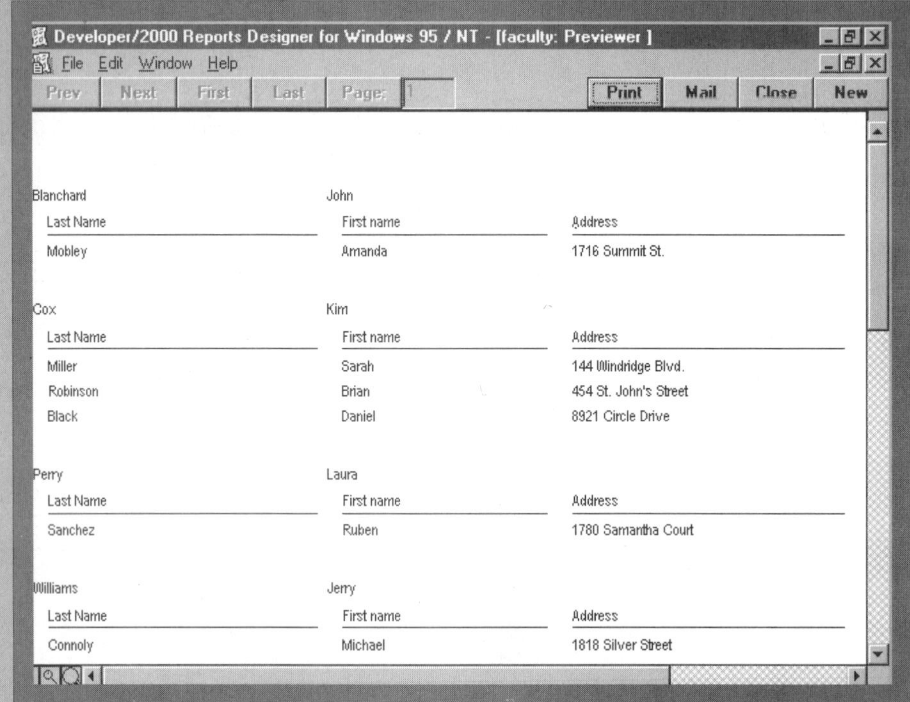

Figure 7-38: Report with increased vertical spacing between FACULTY records

6 Click the **Close** button to close the Previewer window and return to the Layout Editor.

The report looks better, but it still doesn't look like the design sketch shown in Figure 7-31. You need to emphasize the FACULTY fields by formatting them with a larger font.

To format the FACULTY fields:

1 Select the f_flname and f_ffname fields in the Layout Editor by clicking **f_flname**, pressing and holding down the **Shift** key, and then clicking **f_ffname.**

2 Click **Format** on the menu bar, and then click **Font** and change the font to **10-point bold Arial Narrow.**

3 Save the report, run the report to the screen, and then close it.

The report looks pretty good. The last formatting task is to add the title, date, and page numbers in the top margin.

To add the title, date, and page numbers:

1 Click the **Margin** button on the Layout Editor toolbar so the top report margin is visible.

2 Click the **Text** tool on the Tool palette, click .2" down from the top margin space one inch from the top edge and directly on the left edge, type **Faculty Advisee List**, and then click anywhere on the painting region to deselect the Text tool.

3 Click again, click the top margin space .4" from the top margin and directly below the "Faculty Advisee" label, type **as of**, and then click anywhere on the painting region to deselect the Text tool.

4 Click the **Field** tool on the Tool palette, and draw a data field just to the right of the **as of** label. A new field named F_1 appears.

5 Open the F_1 Properties sheet, and change the Name to **F_date**, the Source From to **&Current Date**, and the Format Mask to **DD MON YYYY**. Click the **OK** button to close the Properties sheet. The F_date field appears in the report, as shown in Figure 7-39.

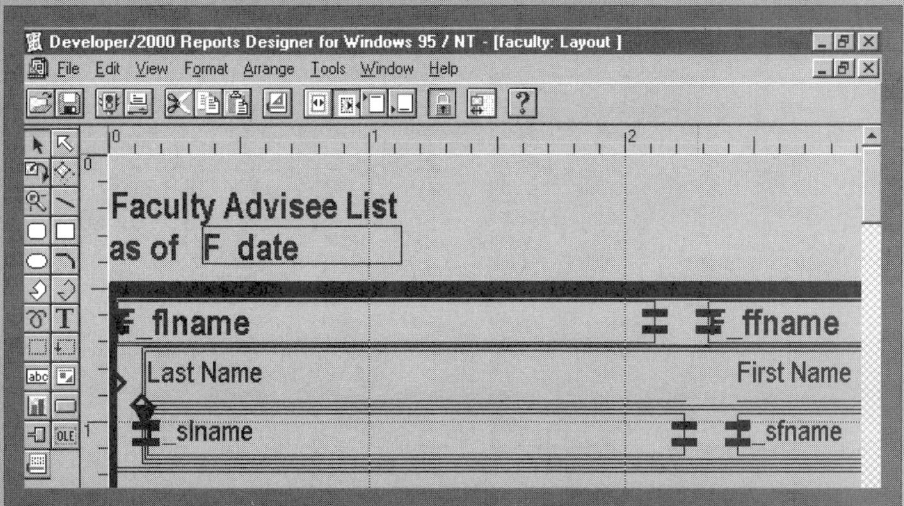

Figure 7-39: Drawing the date field

6 Click the **as of** label, press the **Shift** key, and then click **F_date** so both are selected. Click **Arrange** on the menu bar, click **Align Objects**, and then specify no horizontal alignment and an **Align Top** vertical alignment.

7 Add the page number labels and fields so their left edge is about 4.5" from the left edge of the report, as shown in Figure 7-40. Name the current page number data field **F_currpage**, and set its Source From property as

&Physical Page Number; name the total page number data field F_totpage, and set its Source From as &Total Physical Pages. Align the page number fields with each other and with the "as of" and F_date fields.

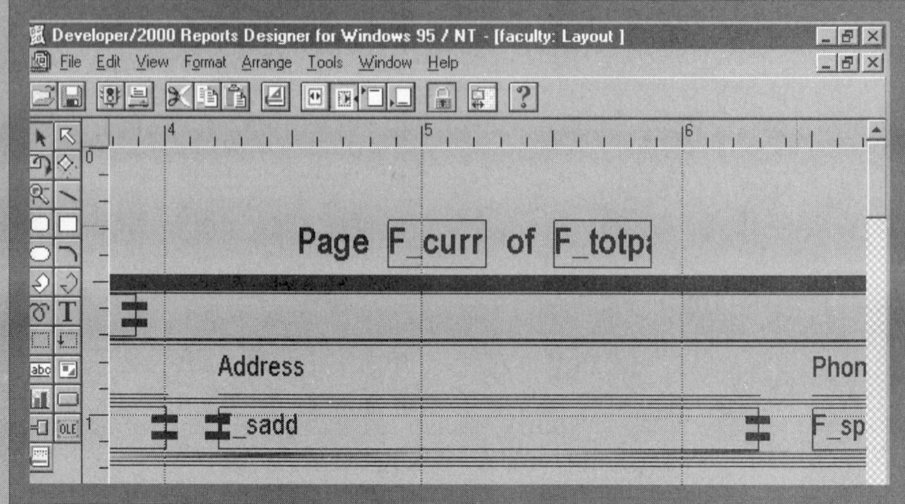

Figure 7-40: Creating the page number labels and fields

8 Save the report file, and then run it to the screen to check your changes. Your finished report should look like Figure 7-41.

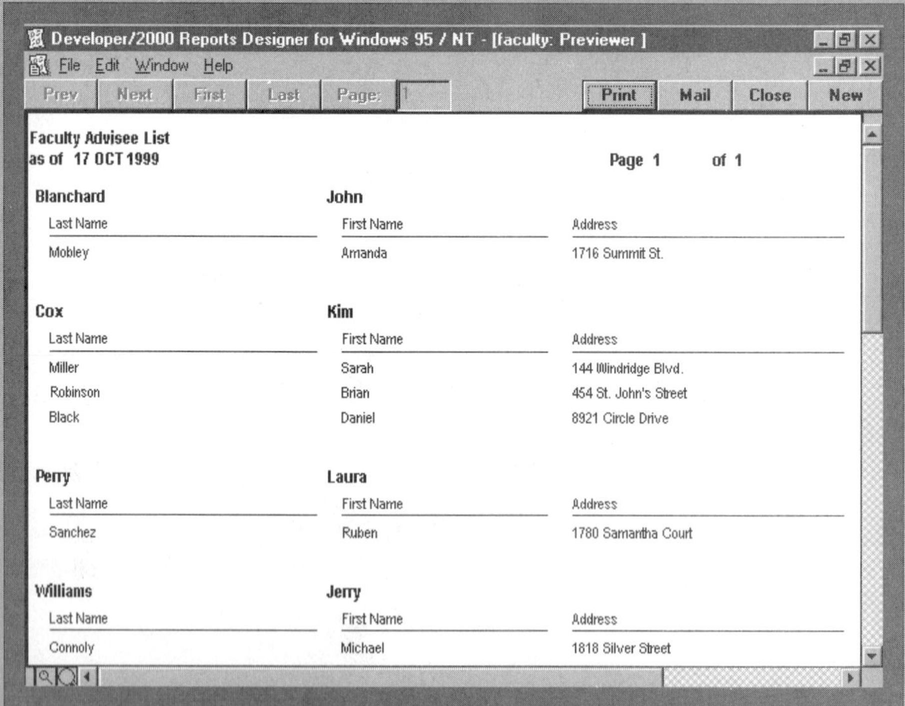

Figure 7-41: Final report display

9 Close the Previewer window.

10 Generate an executable file named **faculty.rep**, and save it in the Chapter7 folder on your Student Disk.

11 Close the report file.

Creating a Report with Calculated Values and Input Parameters

Next you will learn how to create calculated fields and parameters to let users specify report inputs. Your report will allow the user to select a specific student and then print that student's transcript. The transcript information will include the student name and mailing address, the names of every course taken each term, the associated grades, and the student's total term credits and term grade point average. Figure 7-42 shows the design sketch for this report.

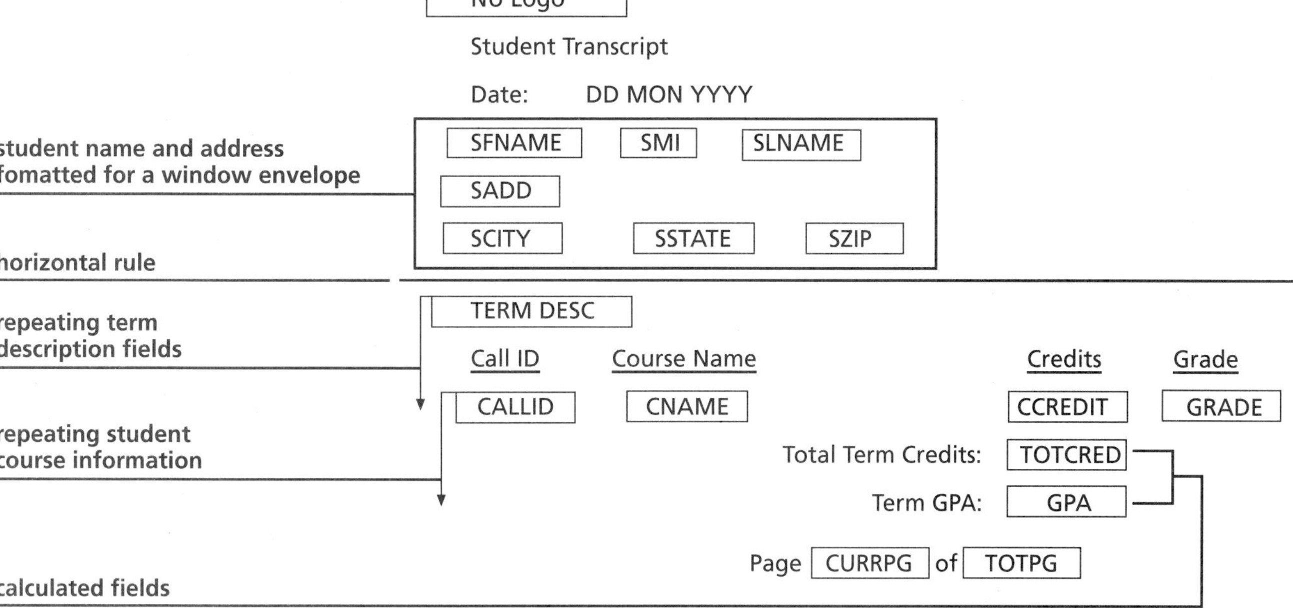

Figure 7-42: Student transcript report design

The Northwoods University logo will appear at the top of the report body, followed by the report title and current date. Then the student name and address will appear in a format appropriate for displaying through a window envelope. This will be followed by a horizontal rule to separate the heading information from the report data. The first term description is followed by its detail records that include the course call ID, name, credits, and grade. After all course records are printed, calculated fields appear to show the total term credits and term grade point average. The bottom margin displays the current page number and number of total pages.

The first step is to create the report and save it on your Student Disk.

To create and save the report:

1 Create and save a report named **tscript.rdf** in the Chapter7 folder on your Student Disk.

Next you will create the query to retrieve all of the report data.

To create the report data model:

1. Open the Data Model Editor, and then create a new query named **Q_courses.**
2. Enter the query shown in Figure 7-43 to retrieve the report data.

type this command

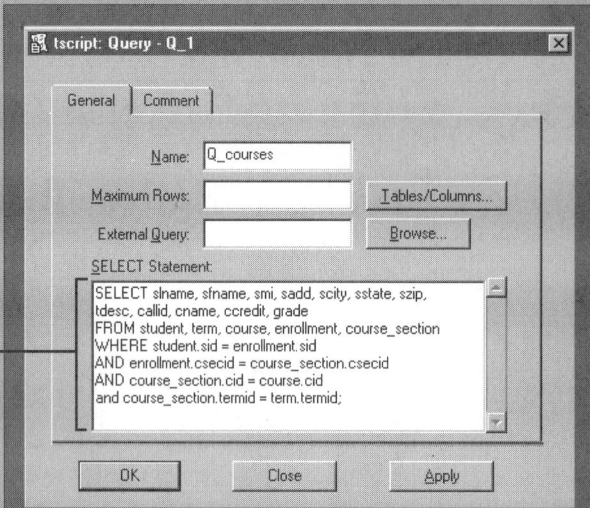

Figure 7-43: Q_courses SQL command

tip

When you create a complex SQL query for a report, it is a good idea to generate the SQL command using Oracle Browser or to preview the query output using SQL*Plus so you are sure that your query retrieves the correct records.

3. Enlarge the G_courses record group, if necessary, so all data fields are displayed and your record group looks like Figure 7-44.

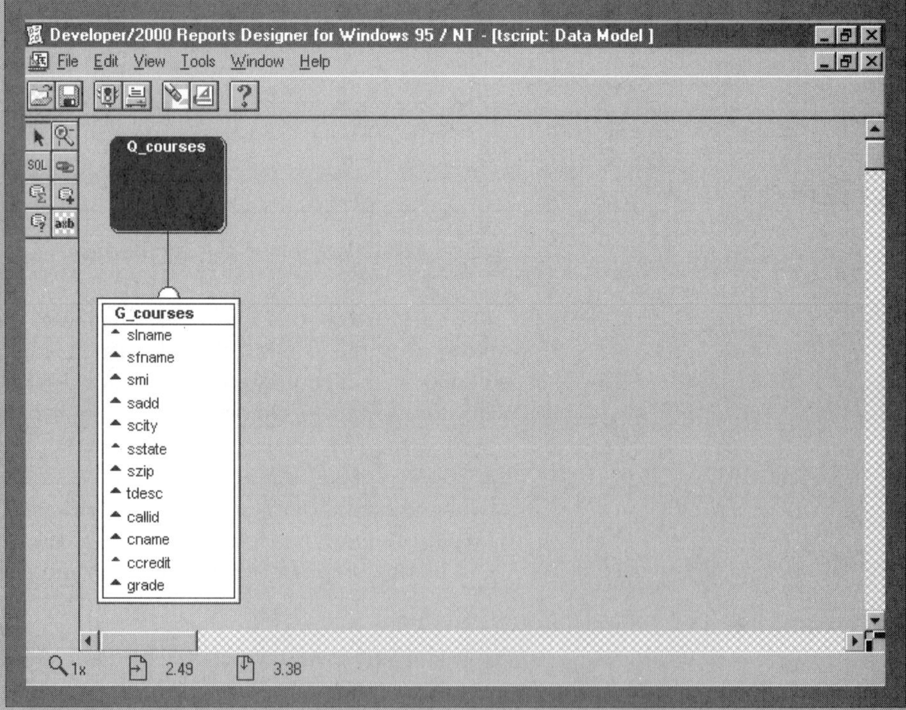

Figure 7-44: Initial data model

Remember that when you are creating master/detail relationships, you always "break out" the master lines. In this data model, there are two master/detail relationships—a student could be enrolled during many terms, and during a single term a student could be enrolled in many courses. Figure 7-45 shows the relationship for this description.

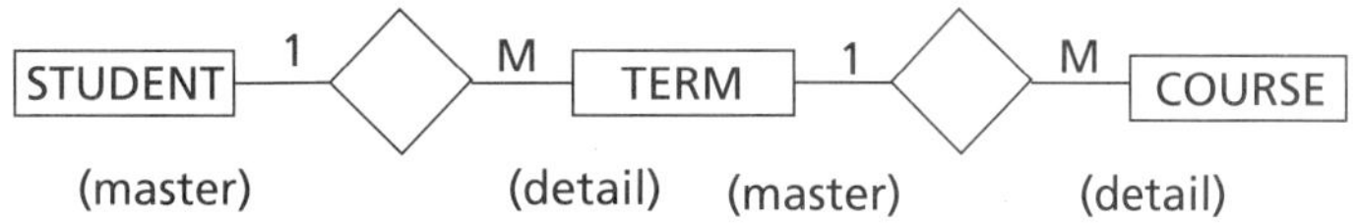

Figure 7-45: STUDENT/TERM/COURSE master/detail relationships

To create the first data model break, you need to break out all of the STUDENT and TERM fields and leave only the final set of detail fields—the COURSE fields. (You named the first query Q_courses because the COURSE fields will stay in the initial record group.)

tip

You can select and drag the fields as a group by clicking s/name, pressing the Shift key, and then clicking the rest of the STUDENT fields. While keeping the Shift key pressed, drag the group into G_terms.

To create the first data model break:

1. Drag the **tdesc** field outside of the G_courses record group.
2. Rename the new record group **G_terms**, and then enlarge the record group so it will hold eight additional fields.
3. Drag the following fields into the G_terms record group: **sfname, smi, slname, sadd, scity, sstate,** and **szip.**
4. Resize and reposition your record groups so your data model looks like Figure 7-46.

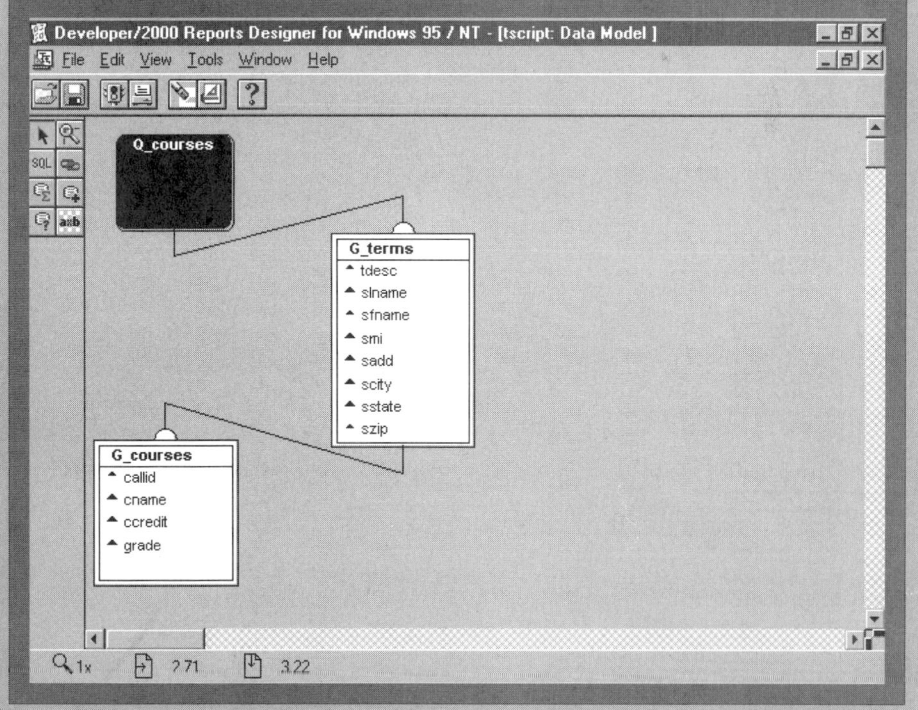

Figure 7-46: Data model after first break

Now you need to break out the first set of master fields—the STUDENT fields.

To break out the STUDENT fields:

1. Drag **s/name** out of the G_terms record group.
2. Rename the new record group **G_students**, and then enlarge the record group so it will hold six more fields.
3. Drag the rest of the STUDENT fields into **G_students**.
4. Resize and reposition the record groups so your completed data model looks like Figure 7-47.

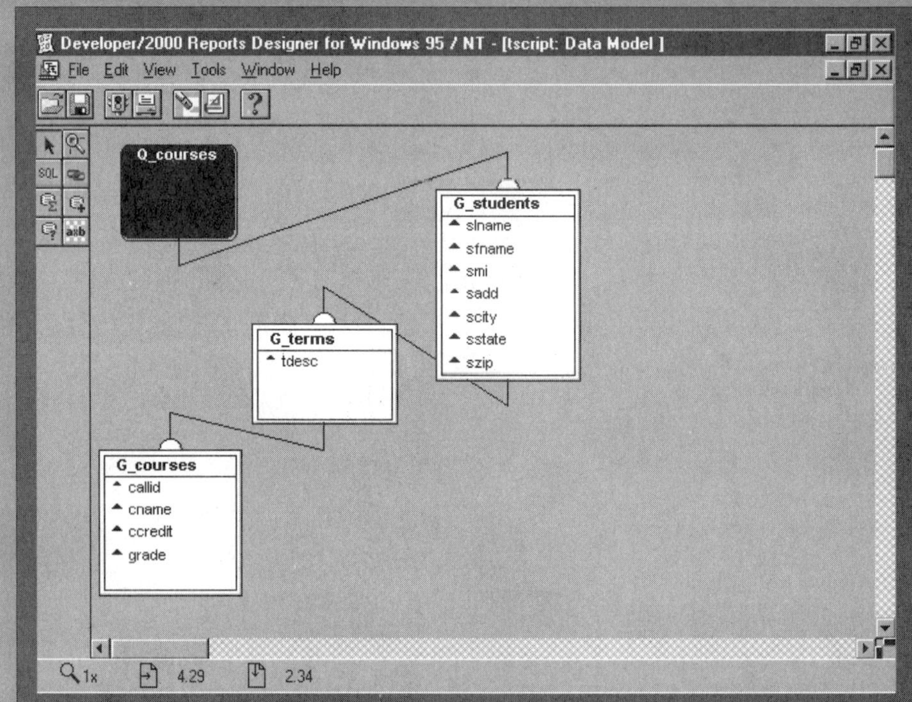

Figure 7-47: Completed data model

HELP? Your record group boxes might appear in different positions and be different sizes than what is shown in Figure 7-40, in which case the breaks might look different. Just make sure that you have the correct fields in each record group, and that the fields are in the correct order.

5. Save the report file.

Next you will create the report layout. You will use a master/detail default layout and then rearrange the fields so the display looks like Figure 7-42. Note that the only field labels in the design sketch are for the student course records, so you will delete the other field labels. After you create the default layout, you will preview the report to make sure that the data displays correctly and to see what additional formatting is needed. Before you select the layout, you will change the page and font defaults.

tip

Whenever you create a report with a master/detail relationship, always use the master/detail default layout because it is difficult to lay out a master/default report manually.

To create the layout and preview the report:

1. Click **Tools** on the menu bar, click **Layout Editor**, and then use the Page Setup command to change the page orientation to **Portrait** and the Format Font command to change the default font to **10-point regular Arial.**
2. Click the **Default Layout** button on the Layout Editor toolbar, and then click the **Master/Detail** option button.
3. Click the **Fill Color** tool on the Tool palette and confirm that the Fill Color is **No Fill.**
4. Click the **Line Color** tool on the Tool palette and confirm that the Line Color is **No Line.**
5. Click the **Data/Selection** tab, and then delete the labels for **SLNAME, SFNAME, SMI, SADD, SCITY, SSTATE, SZIP,** and **TDESC.**
6. Change the CALLID, CNAME, CCREDIT, and GRADE field labels as follows:

Field	**Label**
CALLID	Call ID
CNAME	Course Name
CCREDIT	Credits
GRADE	Grade

7. Click the **OK** button, and then save the report.
8. Run the report to the screen. Your initial report output should look like Figure 7-48. Note that student Daniel Black has taken courses during two different terms, so you can see if the multiple master/detail relationship is working correctly, with the STUDENT information appearing first, followed by the term descriptions and associated course information.
9. Scroll down through the report, and then click the **Next** button to view the next page. There should be one master/detail display for each student, for a total of six student records.

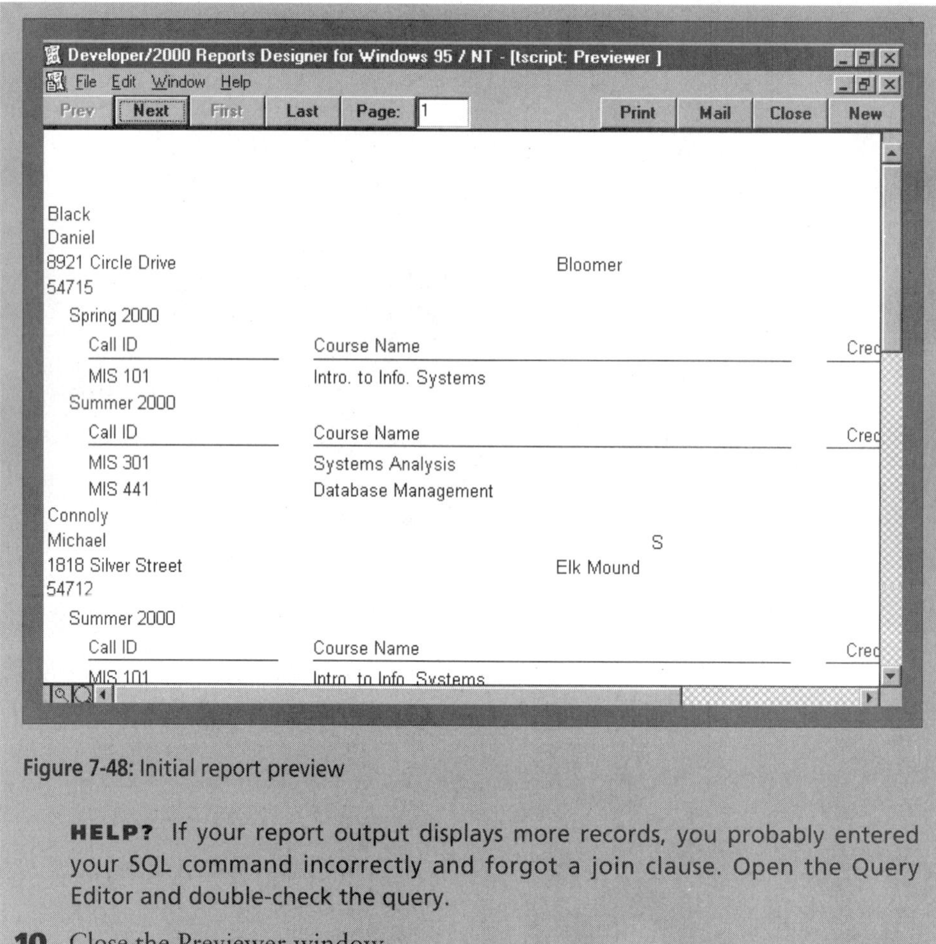

Figure 7-48: Initial report preview

HELP? If your report output displays more records, you probably entered your SQL command incorrectly and forgot a join clause. Open the Query Editor and double-check the query.

10 Close the Previewer window.

Now you need to format the report so each student transcript appears on a separate page.

To format the records to display on separate pages:

1 Zoom in and scroll up and left so you can see the individual frames.

2 Click the **R_students** frame, and then open its Properties sheet. (It will be the second frame from the outside.)

3 On the Object tab, change the Maximum Records per Page setting to 1, and then click the **OK** button.

4 Run the report to the screen to test the effect of the change. You should now see each student's transcript on a separate report page. Click the Next button to scroll through all of the records.

5 Close the Previewer window, and then save your changes.

Next reposition the fields on the page so it looks more like a real transcript. First you need to enlarge the frames so you can distinguish between them in a full-page view.

To enlarge the frames and reposition the data fields:

1. With the Layout Editor view still zoomed in so you can see the individual frames, click the outermost frame (**M_students_GRPFR**).
2. Drag the bottom left handle for M_student_GRPFR down to 3" on the vertical ruler. The report canvas will scroll down when you drag the frame down.
3. Drag down the frames for **R_students**, **M_terms_GRPFR**, **R_terms**, **M_courses_GRPFR**, and **R_courses**, as shown in Figure 7-49.

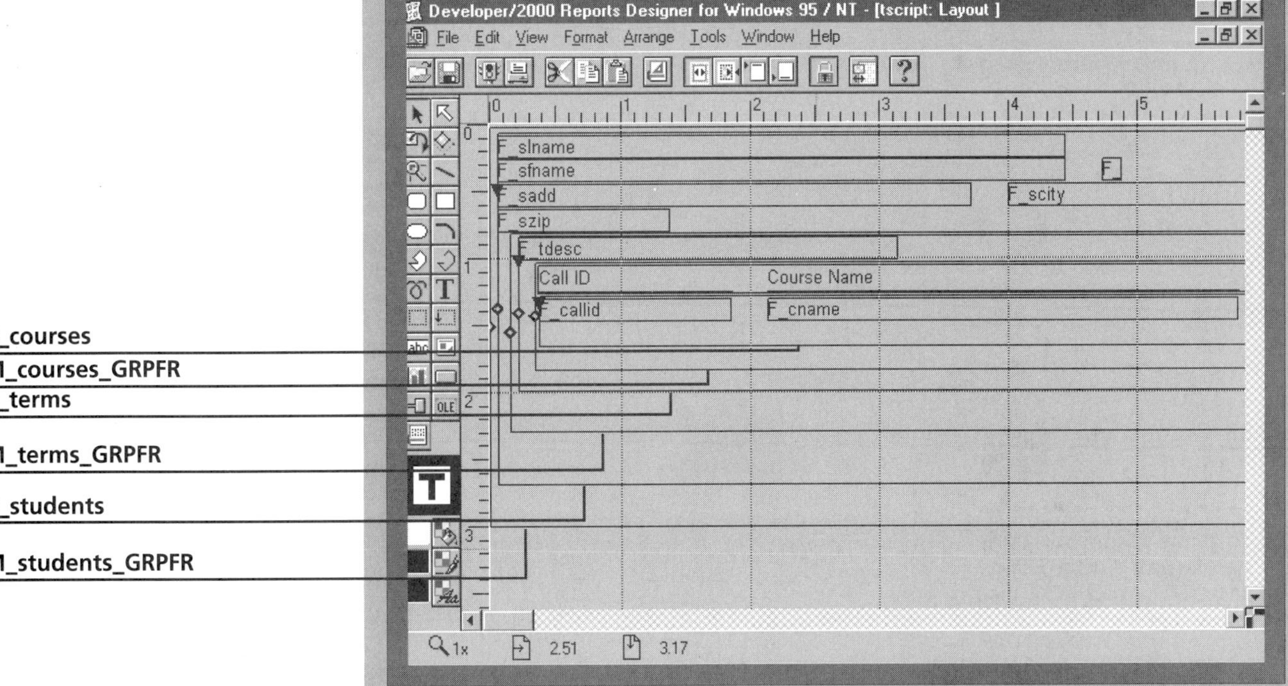

Figure 7-49: Enlarging the frames

4. Click **View** on the menu bar, and then click **Zoom Out** until you can see the entire report page area (8.5" wide and 11" long).
5. Resize **M_students_GRPFR** until it is 8" wide and 10" long.
6. Resize **R_students** until it also covers almost the entire page but is still inside M_students_GRPFR, as shown in Figure 7-50.

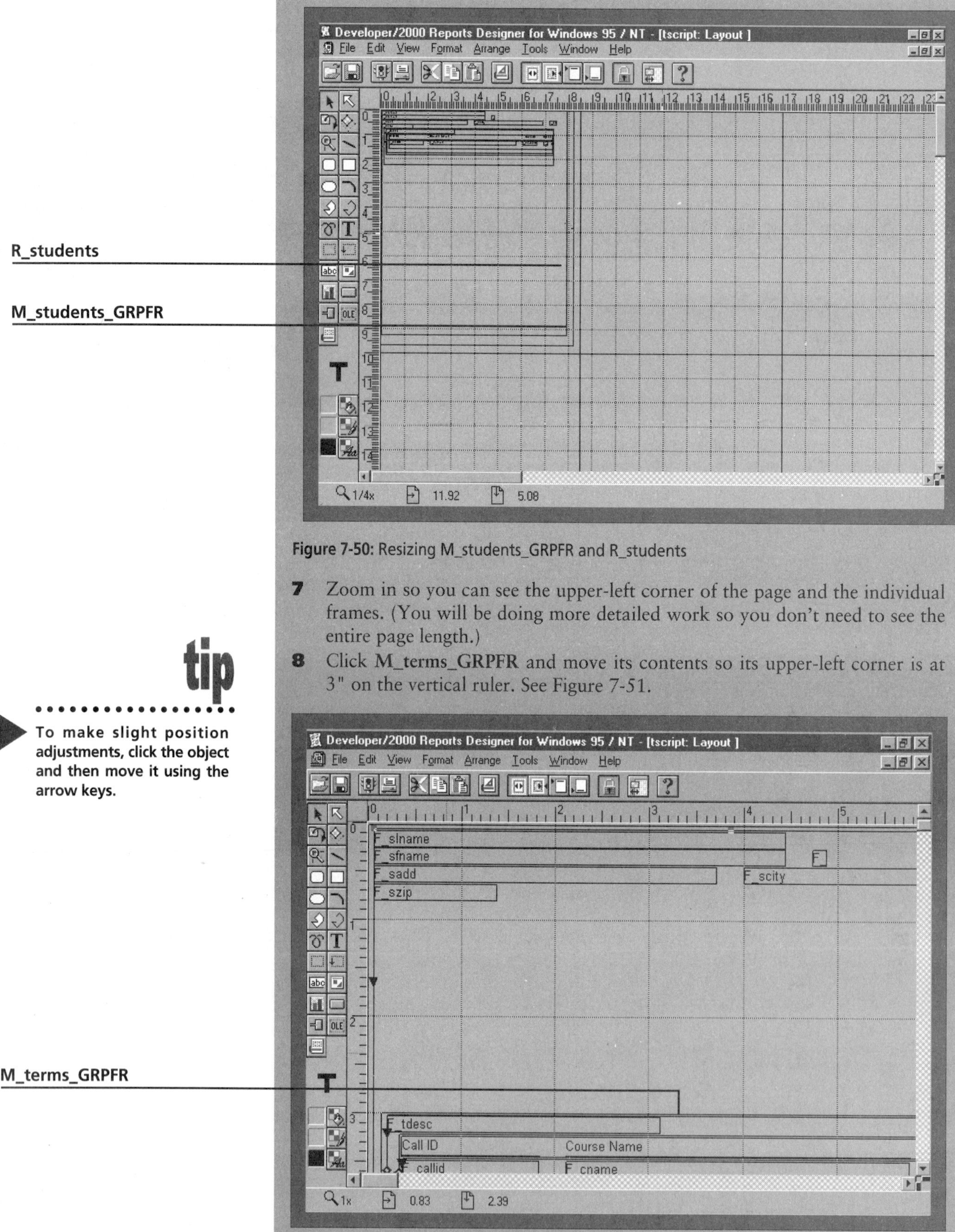

Figure 7-50: Resizing M_students_GRPFR and R_students

7 Zoom in so you can see the upper-left corner of the page and the individual frames. (You will be doing more detailed work so you don't need to see the entire page length.)

8 Click **M_terms_GRPFR** and move its contents so its upper-left corner is at 3" on the vertical ruler. See Figure 7-51.

tip

To make slight position adjustments, click the object and then move it using the arrow keys.

Figure 7-51: Repositioning M_terms_GRPFR

9 Resize and reposition the STUDENT data fields so your screen looks like Figure 7-52. Use the Align Objects command on the Arrange menu to align the fields horizontally and vertically.

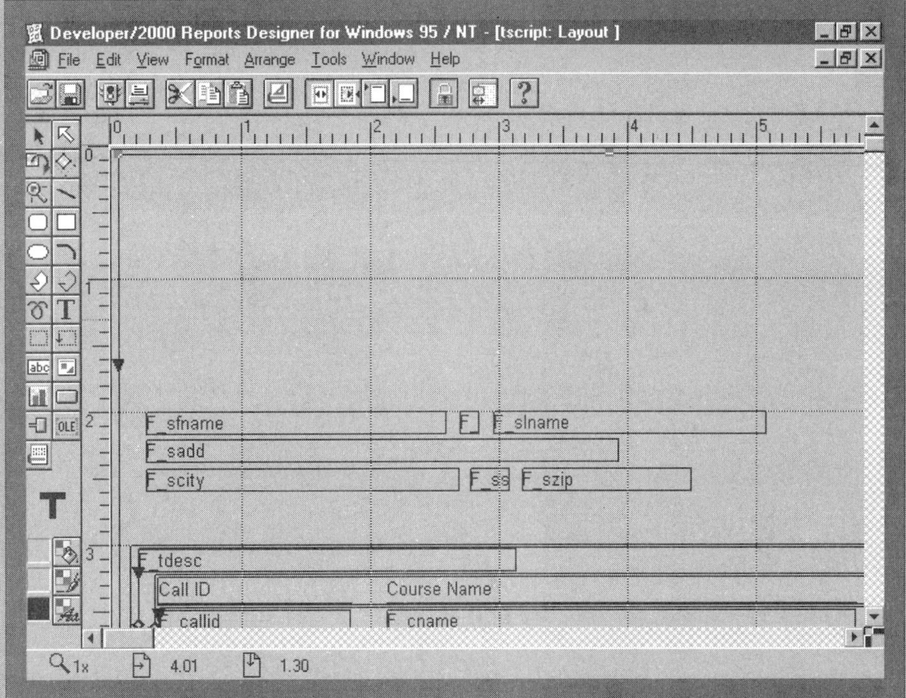

Figure 7-52: Sizing and positioning the STUDENT data fields

HELP? If you accidentally change the height of the data fields, you can make all of the fields the same height by selecting all of the fields as a group and clicking Arrange on the menu bar, and then clicking Size Objects. Click the No Change option button for Width, the Largest option button for Size, and then click the OK button.

10 Save the report file.

11 Run the report to the screen. Your Previewer window should look like Figure 7-53.

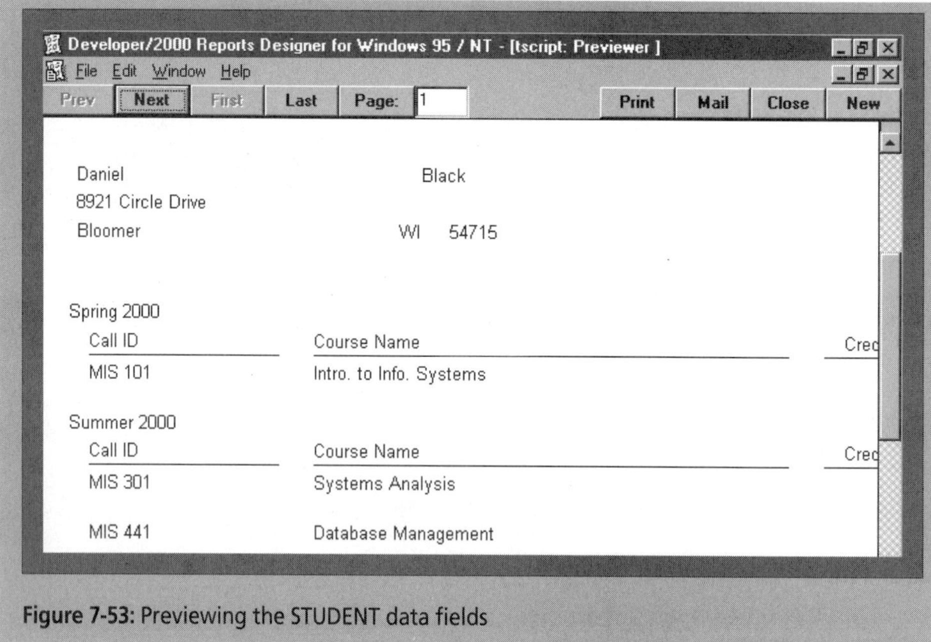

Figure 7-53: Previewing the STUDENT data fields

Notice that in the Previewer window there is a wide gap between the student's first and last name and between the city and state names. You can adjust the sizing property of the data fields so they expand or contract automatically depending on the width of the current data value. Then you can create **anchors** to pull the data fields together so they display directly beside one another. Anchors have child objects and parent objects. The child object is attached to the parent and moves with the parent as the parent's size increases or decreases. To create an anchor, first you select the child object with the Anchor tool, and then double-click the parent object.

To adjust the data field sizing and create anchors:

1. Close the Previewer window.
2. Open the F_sfname Properties sheet, click the **General Layout** tab, change the Horizontal Sizing property to **Variable**, and then click the **OK** button. Note that a diamond symbol appears on the top and bottom borders of F_sfname to indicate that the horizontal sizing is now variable.
3. Change the Horizontal Sizing property of F_smi and F_slname to **Variable**.
4. Zoom in so you can see the lower-left corner of F_slname clearly, and click the **Anchor** tool on the Tool palette. The pointer changes to + as you move it across the painting region.
5. Create an anchor with the student's last name as the child object, and the student's middle initial as the parent object. Click the lower-left corner of F_slname, move the pointer towards F_smi, and then double-click the lower-right corner of F_smi. The anchor appears, as shown in Figure 7-54.

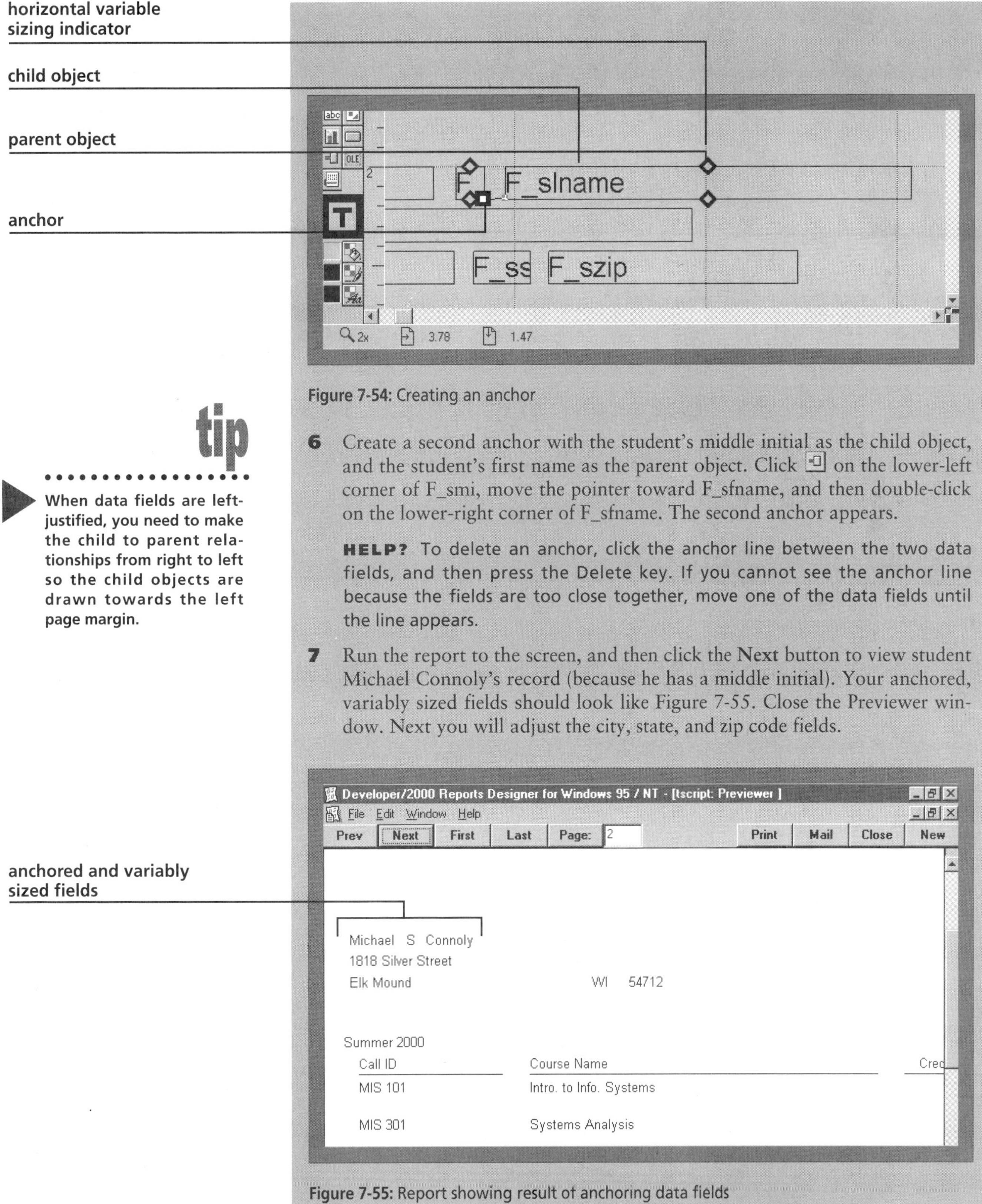

Figure 7-54: Creating an anchor

tip

When data fields are left-justified, you need to make the child to parent relationships from right to left so the child objects are drawn towards the left page margin.

6 Create a second anchor with the student's middle initial as the child object, and the student's first name as the parent object. Click the anchor tool on the lower-left corner of F_smi, move the pointer toward F_sfname, and then double-click on the lower-right corner of F_sfname. The second anchor appears.

HELP? To delete an anchor, click the anchor line between the two data fields, and then press the Delete key. If you cannot see the anchor line because the fields are too close together, move one of the data fields until the line appears.

7 Run the report to the screen, and then click the **Next** button to view student Michael Connoly's record (because he has a middle initial). Your anchored, variably sized fields should look like Figure 7-55. Close the Previewer window. Next you will adjust the city, state, and zip code fields.

Figure 7-55: Report showing result of anchoring data fields

8 Change the horizontal sizing property of the F_scity, F_sstate, and F_szip data fields to **Variable**.

9 Create an anchor with F_szip as the child object and F_sstate as the parent object.

10 Create another anchor with F_sstate as the child object and F_scity as the parent object.

11 Save the report, and then run the report to the screen to view your variably sized and anchored data fields.

12 Close the Previewer window.

To increase the blank space between anchored data fields, move the fields farther apart in the painting region.

Next you need to add boilerplate objects to format the transcript so it looks like Figure 7-56. First you will import the Northwoods University logo and add a report title.

To add the boilerplate objects:

1 Import the **nwlogo.jpg** file from the Chapter7 folder on your Student Disk and move it to the upper-left corner of the report, if necessary. Make sure that the image is inside of all of the frames or you will receive warning messages when you run the form.

2 Create a **Student Transcript** text label using a **16-point regular Arial** font. Position it under the logo.

3 Create a **Date:** label using **12-point regular Arial** font under the Student Transcript label.

4 Create a parameter field named **F_date** to display the current date next to the **Date:** label. Format the date as DD MON YYYY.

5 Click the **Rounded Rectangle** tool on the Tool palette, and then draw a rectangle around the student name and address fields. If necessary, change the Line Color to **black**, and the Fill Color to **No Fill.**

6 Select the **F_tdesc** field, and change it to **10-point bold Arial** font.

7 Create the horizontal rule between the student and term records by clicking the **Line** tool on the Tool palette, and then draw a 7.5" horizontal line just below the rounded rectangle enclosing the student address information.

8 Increase the Vertical Spacing property of R_terms to **1** inch. (You will need the extra space to include the term summary information.)

9 Move to the bottom margin region of the report, and create a parameter data field named **F_currpg** to show the current page number.

10 Create a parameter data field named **F_totpg** to show the total number of pages in the report.

11 Create labels so you can format the page numbers as **Page F_currpg of F_totpg**. Change the font of both the parameter fields and labels to an **8-point italic Arial** font. Save your changes, and then run the report to the screen. Click the **Next** button until you view the transcript report for student Ruben Sanchez on page 6 of the report. The formatted report should look like Figure 7-56.

Student Transcript
Date: 17 OCT 1999

Ruben R Sanchez
1780 Samantha Court
Eau Claire WI 54701

Spring 2000

Call ID	Course Name	Credits	Grade
MIS 101	Intro. to Info. Systems	3	B
MIS 301	Systems Analysis	3	C
MIS 451	Client/Server Systems	3	C

Summer 2000

Call ID	Course Name	Credits	Grade
MIS 441	Database Management	3	
MIS 101	Intro. to Info. Systems	3	

Figure 7-56: Formatted transcript record

12 Close the Previewer window.

Creating a Summary Column

A **summary column** is used to total another data column. Next you will create a column to sum the total credits for each term. This is a two-step process—first you modify the data model, and then you update the layout.

To modify the data model:

1 Click **Tools** on the menu bar, and then click **Data Model Editor** to return to the Data Model Editor.

2 Click the **Summary Column** tool on the Tool palette. The pointer changes to + when you move it into the painting region. The summary column will appear once for every term record, so you will place it in the **G_terms** record group.

3 Click the **G_terms** record group. A new column named *CS_1* appears, as shown in Figure 7-57.

new summary column

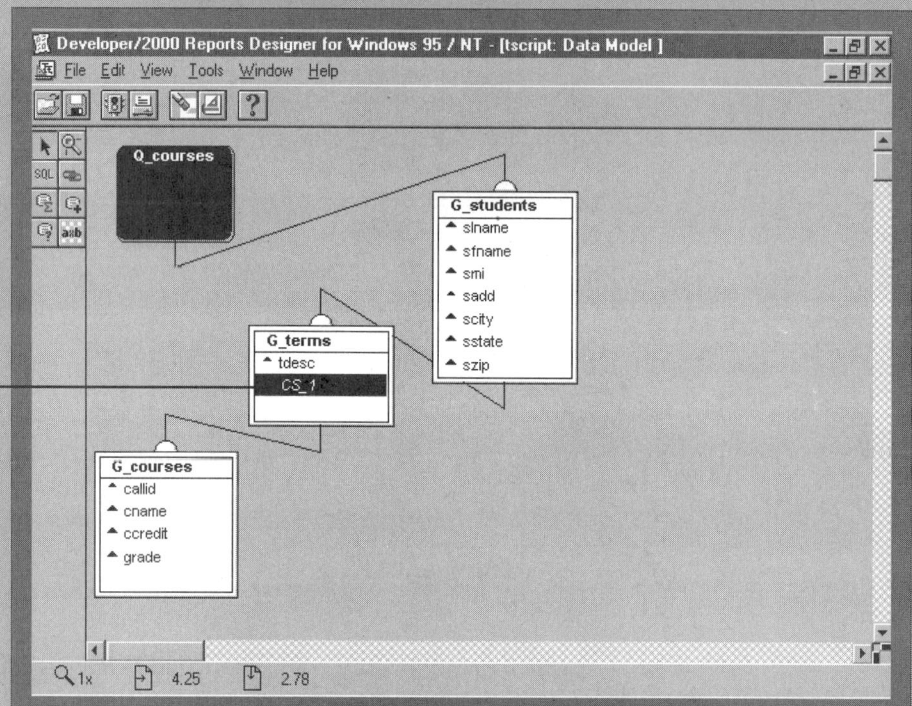

Figure 7-57: Creating a new summary column

4 Right-click *CS_1*, and then click **Properties** on the menu. Rename the column to **CS_term_credits**. *Do not click the OK button.*

5 Click the **Source From** list arrow, scroll down, and then click **ccredit** so the summary column will sum the CCREDIT column.

6 Click the **Reset At** list arrow, scroll down, and then click **G_terms** so the summary column value will be reset for every new term group.

7 Make sure that the Width is **2**. (No student will take a total of more than 99 credits during a single term.) Your completed CS_term_credits Properties sheet should look like Figure 7-58.

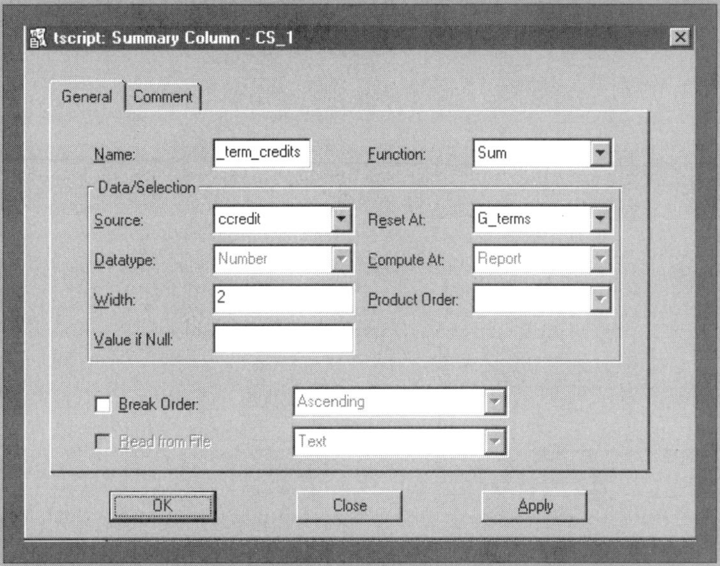

Figure 7-58: CS_term_credits Properties sheet

8 Click the **OK** button.

Now you need to draw a field in the report layout to display the summary column under the course credit data fields. This field must be *inside* the R_terms repeating frame so it will display once for every term. However, it cannot be in the R_courses repeating frame or M_courses_GRPFR because it is summing the value for all of the courses. Summary columns must be outside the group frame of the fields they are summing.

To create the field to display the credits summary:

1 Go to the Layout Editor, and then scroll so you can see the credit (**F_CCREDIT**) column and the space under it.

2 If necessary, enlarge the **M_terms_GRPFR** and **R_terms** frames so you can create a field under F_CCREDIT that is inside R_terms but not inside M_courses_GRPFR.

3 Click the **Field** tool on the Tool palette, and then draw a field under the F_CCREDIT field and within the R_terms frame, as shown in Figure 7-59.

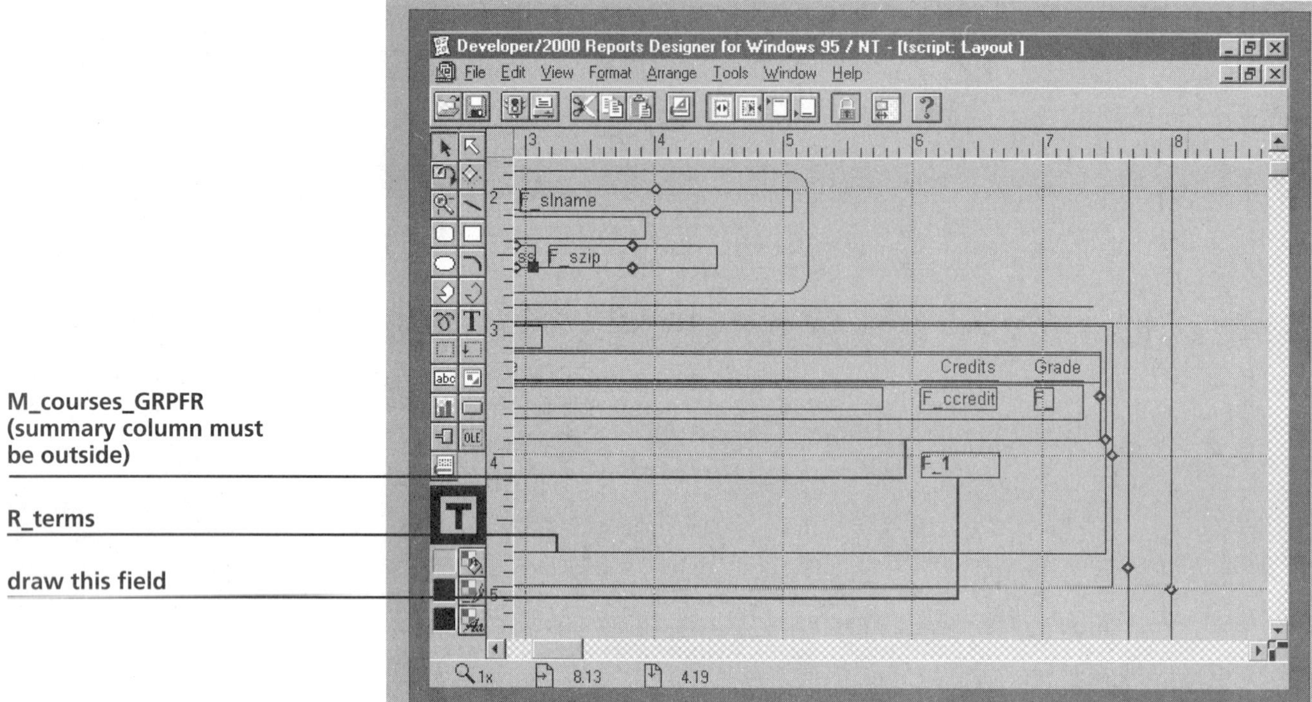

Figure 7-59: Drawing the summary column field

4 Open the new field's Properties sheet, and then rename it to **F_total_term_credits.**

5 Click the **Source From** list arrow, scroll down, and then click **CS_term_credits.** Your F_total_term_credits Properties sheet should look like Figure 7-60.

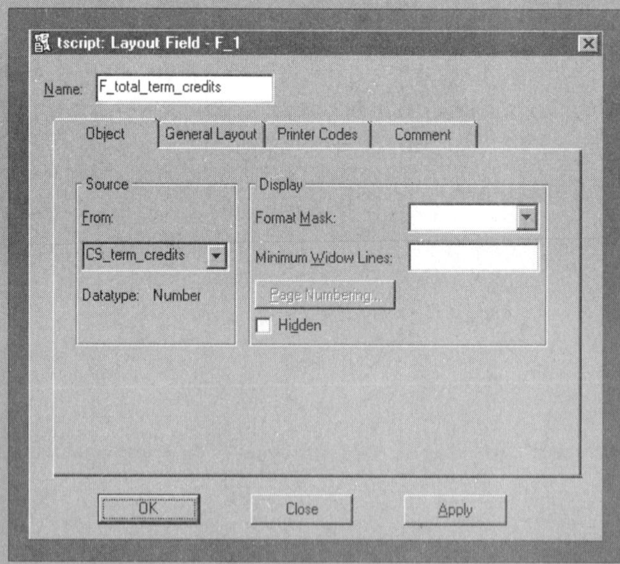

Figure 7-60: Summary column field Properties sheet

6 Click the **OK** button.

7 Click the **F_total_term_credits** field, and change the font to **10-point regular Arial**. You will need to right-justify the summary column text.

8 Click **F_total_term_credits**, click **Format** on the menu bar, point to **Alignment**, and then click **Right**.

9 Save the report and then run the report to the screen to make sure that the summary column works correctly. Your report for the first student record should look like Figure 7-61.

summary columns

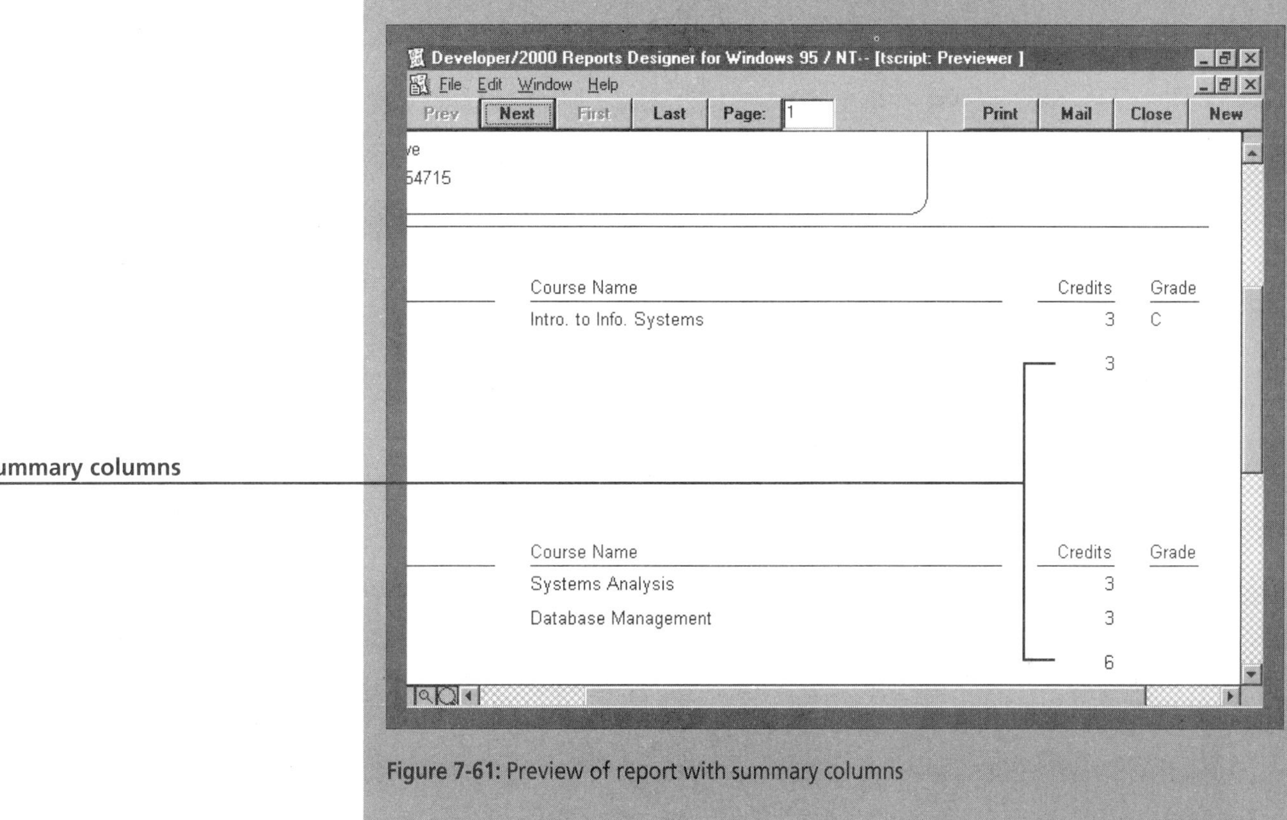

Figure 7-61: Preview of report with summary columns

10 Close the Previewer window.

Now you need to create a label and a line above the summary total as shown in Figure 7-62.

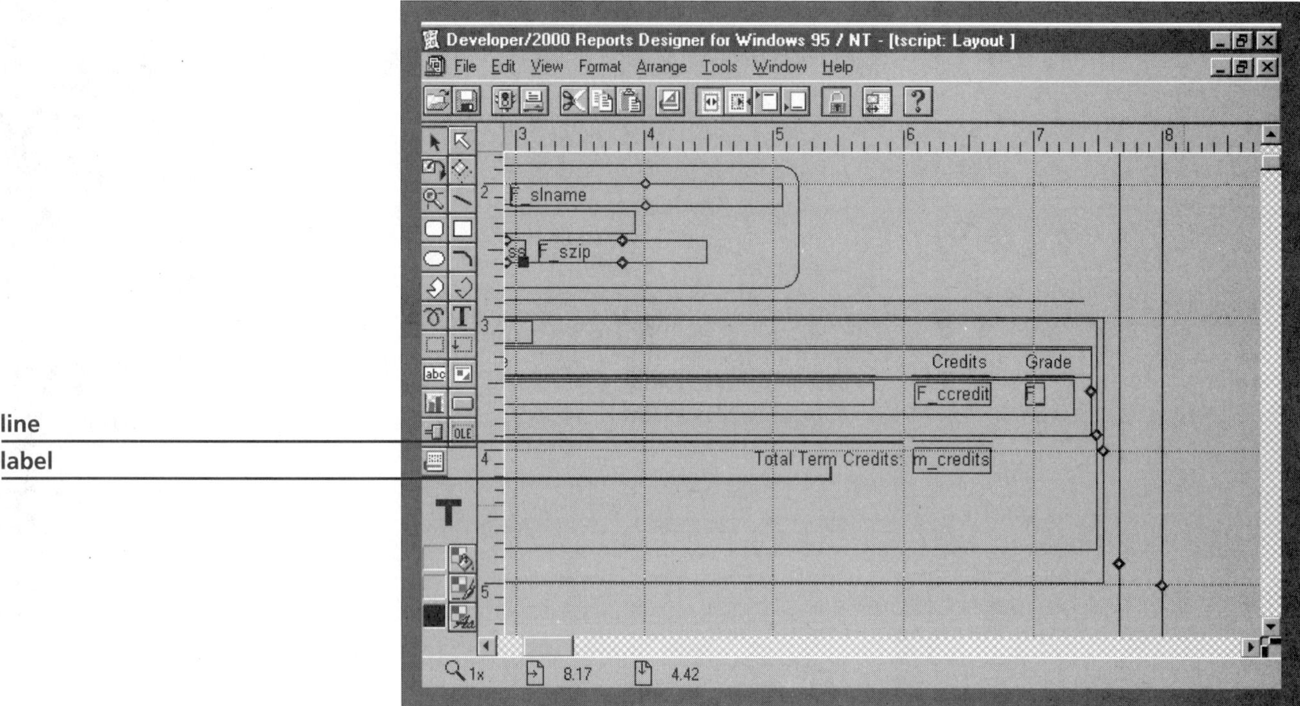

Figure 7-62: Summary column label and line

To create the summary column label and line:

1. Create a **Total Term Credits** label, and place it just to the left of the summary column field.
2. Click the **Line** tool on the Tool palette, and then draw a line that is about the same length as the Credits column width. Place it directly above the summary column field.
3. Save your changes and then run the report to the screen to check the label and line appearance.
4. Close the Previewer window.

Creating Formula Columns

Formula columns return the value of a function that performs mathematical computations on retrieved data values. You will need to use formula columns to calculate the student's grade point average for each term. Grade point average is calculated as follows:

$$\frac{\Sigma(\text{Course Credits} * \text{Course Grade Points})}{\Sigma(\text{Course Credits})}$$

Course grade points are awarded as follows:

Grade	Grade Points
A	4
B	3
C	2
D	1
F	0

First you will create a formula column to calculate the credit points, which is Course Credits * (multiplied by) Course Grade Points. For example, if a student got an A in a 3-credit course, the credit points would be 3 (the course credits) times 4 (the grade points for an A), or 12.

To create a column to calculate course credit points:

1. Go to the Data Model Editor. You will calculate this column value for each course record, so the formula column will go in the G_courses record group.
2. Click the **Formula Column** tool on the Tool palette. The pointer changes to + when you move it into the window.
3. Click the **G_courses** record group. A new formula column named *CF_1* appears in the record group, as shown in Figure 7-63.

new formula column

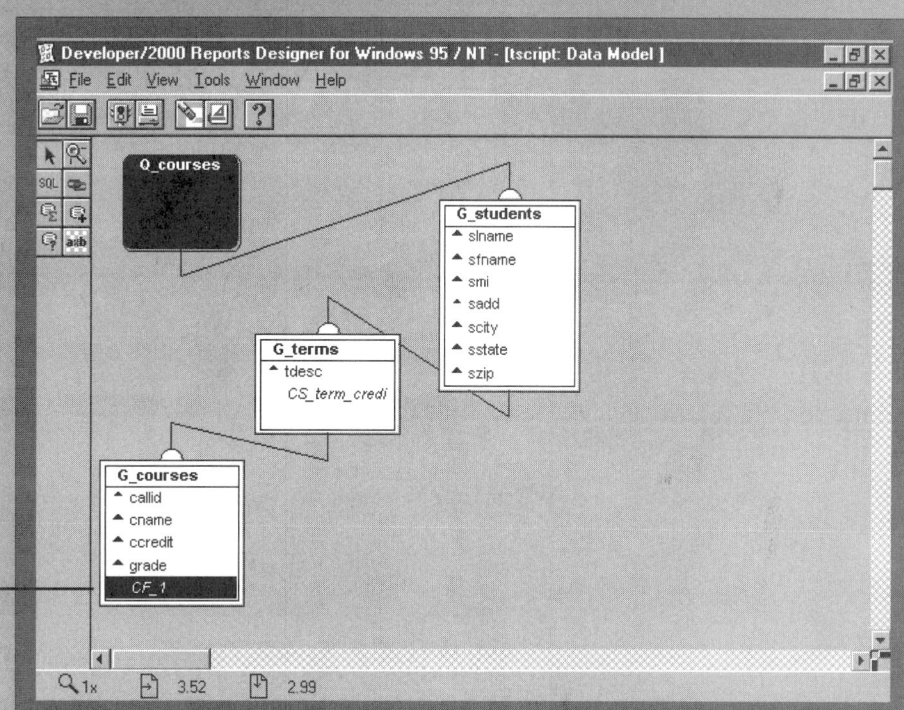

Figure 7-63: Creating a new formula column

4. Open the *CF_1* Properties sheet and change the Name to **CF_credit_points.** *Do not click the OK button.*
5. Click the **Edit** button on the Properties sheet to open the PL/SQL Editor. This is where you will enter the program code to calculate the course credit points.
6. Click the **OK** button to save the new column name and close the Properties sheet. The PL/SQL Editor still should be open.

Every formula column has an associated function written in PL/SQL. The function can perform computations on the values in the report's database columns, summary columns, and other formula columns. Usually you declare a local variable in the function, and then perform calculations so this variable is the value you want displayed in the formula column. To reference a report field in the PL/SQL formula column function, preface its name with a colon.

To write the PL/SQL code for the calculated column:

1 Type the code shown in Figure 7-64 in the PL/SQL Editor to return the credit points value for a specific course/grade combination.

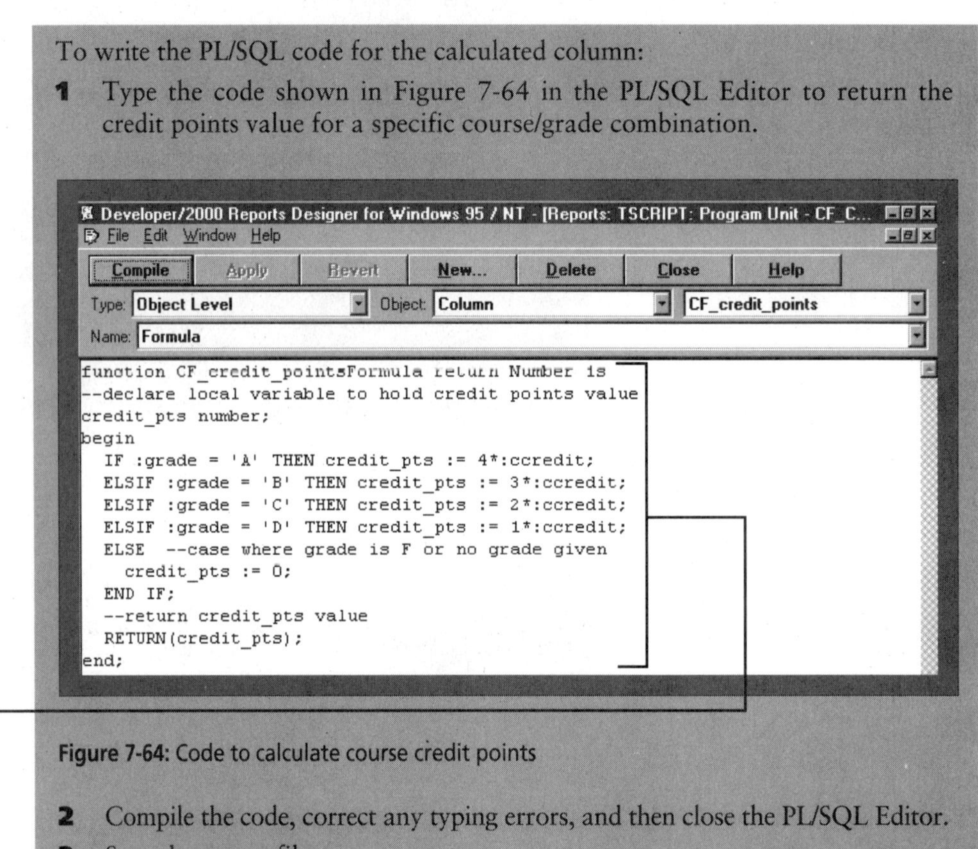

Figure 7-64: Code to calculate course credit points

2 Compile the code, correct any typing errors, and then close the PL/SQL Editor.

3 Save the report file.

Next you need to create a holding field to "hold" the value of CF_credit_points for each course record. A **holding field** is not displayed on the final report but serves to hold the value of a calculated or summed column that will be used in another computation so you can check its value and confirm that it is calculated correctly. Fields that display formula column values must be in the same frame as the most detailed value in the formula. For example, because this field will display a value for each course record, it must be in the R_courses frame that contains the individual course records.

To create the holding field for each course record:

1 Go to the Layout Editor.

2 Enlarge the **R_courses** frame by dragging it to the right edge of the painting region, and then draw a new field inside the R_courses frame, as shown in Figure 7-65. You probably will need to enlarge R_courses and its surrounding frames.

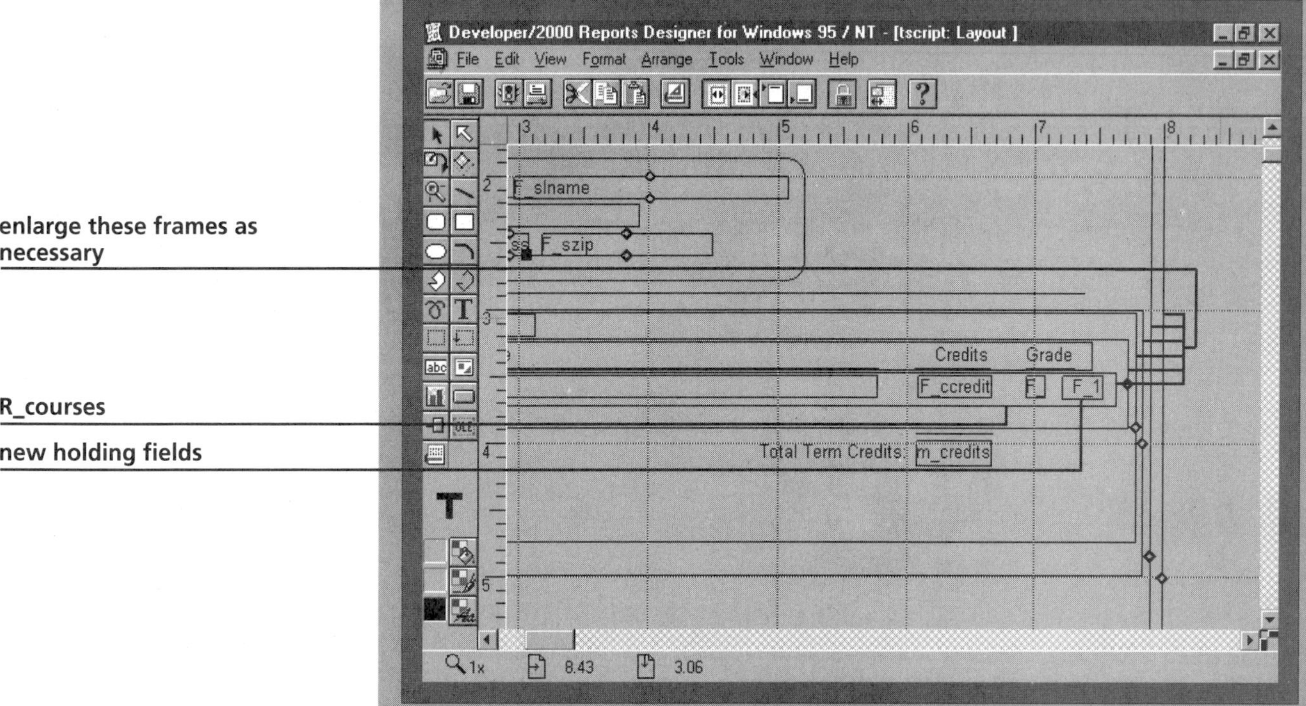

Figure 7-65: Holding field for value of CF_credit_points

3 Open the new field's Properties sheet, change the Name to **F_credit_points**, and then change the Source From to **CF_credit_points**. Note that there is a Hidden check box on the Properties sheet. Don't check it yet—you should view the credit points value first to make sure it is calculated correctly.

4 Click the **OK** button.

5 Save the file and then run the form to the screen. Ruben Sanchez's transcript (page 6 of the report) looks like Figure 7-66. The credit points column appears to work correctly.

tip

Don't check the Hidden check box on any holding fields until the entire report is finished, so you can make sure all fields work correctly.

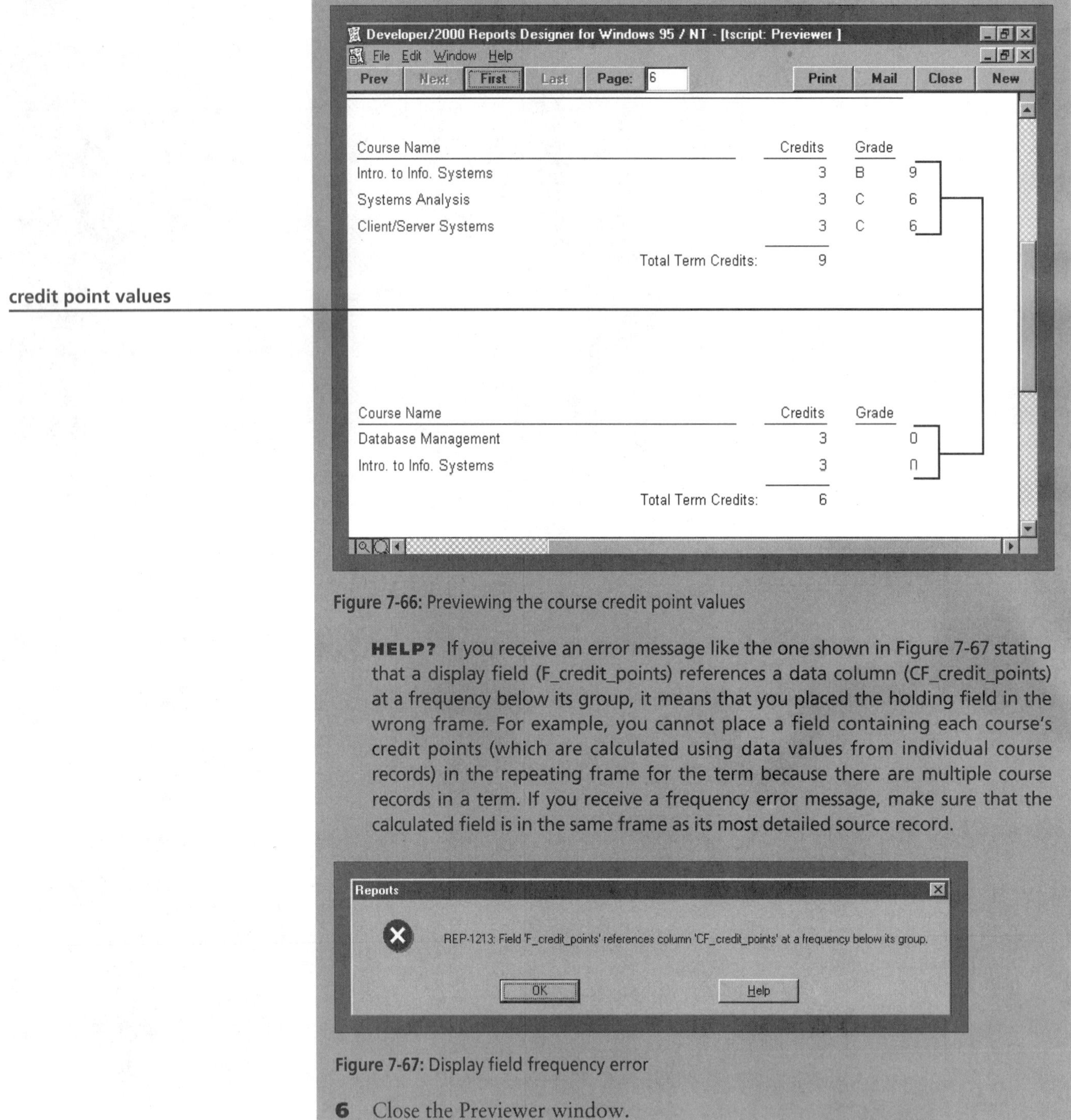

Figure 7-66: Previewing the course credit point values

HELP? If you receive an error message like the one shown in Figure 7-67 stating that a display field (F_credit_points) references a data column (CF_credit_points) at a frequency below its group, it means that you placed the holding field in the wrong frame. For example, you cannot place a field containing each course's credit points (which are calculated using data values from individual course records) in the repeating frame for the term because there are multiple course records in a term. If you receive a frequency error message, make sure that the calculated field is in the same frame as its most detailed source record.

Figure 7-67: Display field frequency error

6 Close the Previewer window.

You can sum a formula column just like a database column. Next you will sum the course credit points for each term.

To create the credit points summary column:

1 In the Data Model Editor, create a new summary column in the G_terms record group.

2 Open the new summary column's Properties sheet, rename the new summary column to **CS_credit_points**, and set its Source property as **CF_credit_points.**

3 You want the summary column to calculate the total credit points for every term, so set the Reset At property to **G_terms.**

4 Go the Layout Editor and then create a holding field named **F_total_term_credit_points** at the bottom of the credit points column to hold the value of CS_credit_points. Set the Source From property to **CS_credit_points.**

5 Save the file and then run the form to the screen to confirm that your F_total_term_credit_points column works correctly. The printout of Ruben Sanchez's record should look like Figure 7-68.

term credit points summary values

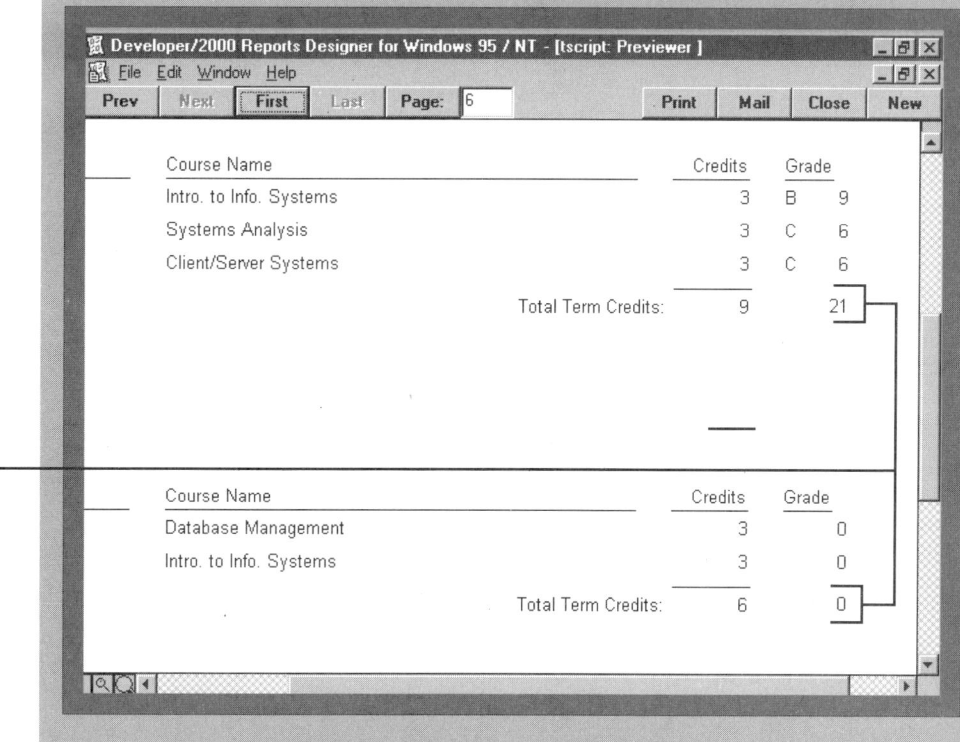

Figure 7-68: Previewing the term credit points summary values

6 Close the Previewer window.

Finally you need to create a formula column to calculate the student grade point average for each term. Remember that GPA = Σ(Course Credits * Course Grade Points)/Σ(Course Credits). In the report, this requires dividing the course credit points summary field (CS_credit_points) by the term credits summary field (CS_term_credits). Remember that to reference columns in a formula function, you preface the column name with a colon.

To create the term GPA formula column:

1 In the Data Model Editor, create a new formula column in the G_term record group.

2 Open the new formula column's Properties sheet, and then name the column **CF_term_gpa**. Click the **Edit** button to open the PL/SQL Editor, and then click the **OK** button to close the Properties sheet. The PL/SQL Edition should be open.

3 Type the code shown in Figure 7-69 to calculate the student GPA. Compile the code, correct any syntax errors, and then close the PL/SQL Editor.

type this code

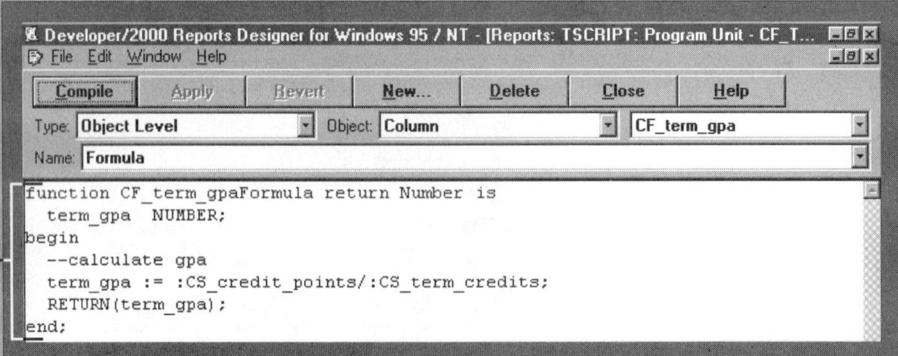

Figure 7-69: Code to calculate term GPA

4 In the Layout Editor, draw a new layout field to hold **CF_term_gpa**. Place the field directly below the total term credits summary field.

5 Open the new field's Properties sheet, and then change the Name to **F_term_gpa**. Set the Source From property to **CF_term_gpa**, and enter **N.00** as the format mask to make the field display to a precision of two decimal places even if the value is a whole number. The completed F_term_gpa Properties sheet should look like Figure 7-70.

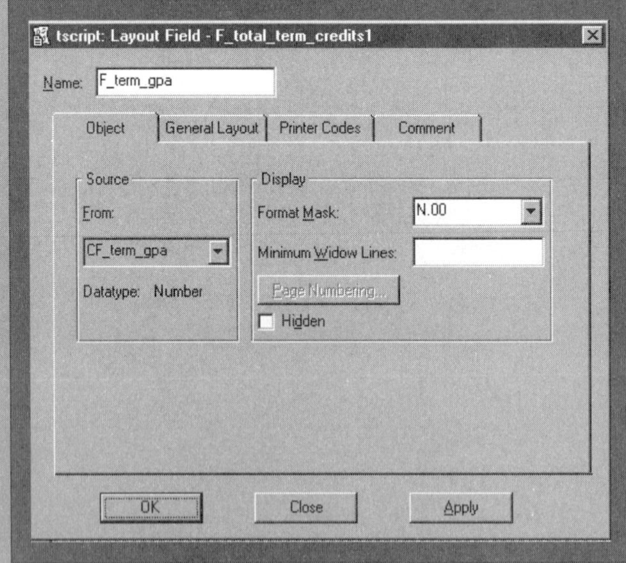

Figure 7-70: F_term_gpa Properties sheet

6 Click the **OK** button to close the Properties sheet.

7 Create a new label with the text **Term GPA:** and place it to the left of the term GPA field. Your completed term GPA field and label should look like Figure 7-71.

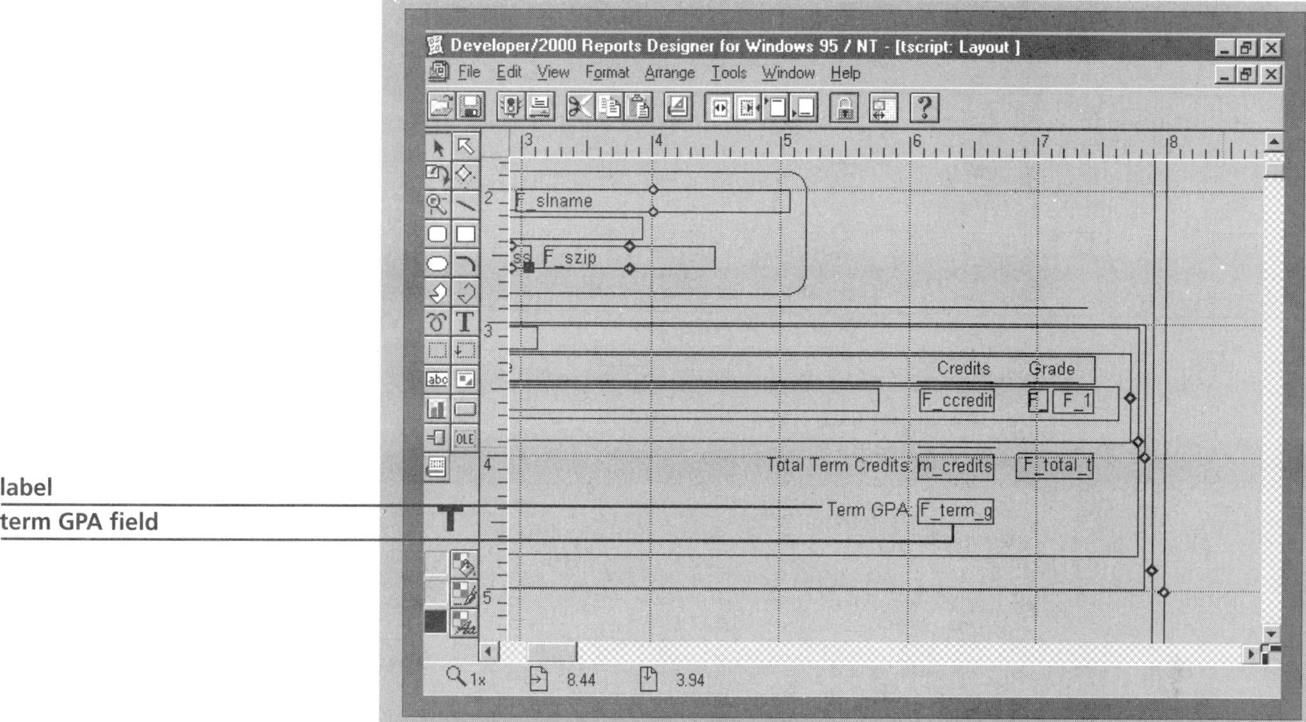

Figure 7-71: Creating the term GPA field and label

8 Save the file and then run the report to the screen to confirm that the GPA is calculated correctly. Your display of Ruben Sanchez's record (page 6) should look like Figure 7-72.

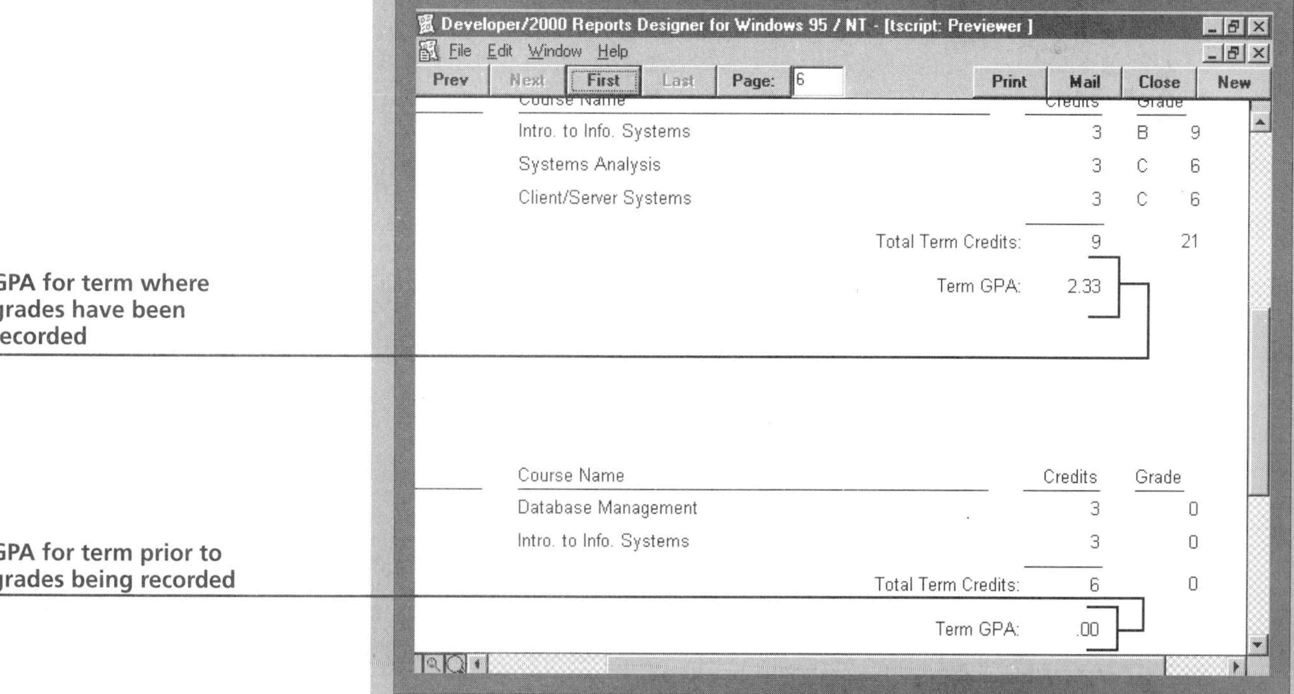

Figure 7-72: Calculated GPA values

9 Close the Previewer window.

Now that all of the calculated fields are complete, you can hide the fields that you don't want to display in your report, and then print the report.

To hide the fields in the report display:

1 In the Layout Editor, click the **Hidden** check box on the Properties sheets for F_credits_points and F_total_term_credit_points.

2 Save the file and then run the report to the screen to confirm that the holding columns do not display. Close the Previewer window.

3 Run the report again, but this time click **Printer** in the Destination Type list. Confirm that your printer name and location is specified in the Destination Name list, as shown in Figure 7-73.

Developer/2000 Reports Designer for Windows 95 / NT - [tscript: Runtime Parameter Form]
File Edit Window Help
Previous | Next | Run Report | Cancel
Destination Type: Printer
Destination Name: Epson Stylus COLOR ESC/P 2, LPT1:

your printer name and location will appear here

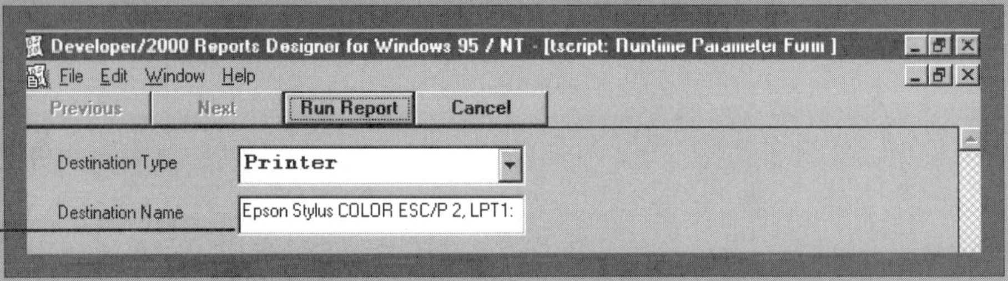

Figure 7-73: Running the report to the pointer

4 Click the **Run Report** button. The Print dialog box shown in Figure 7-74 opens.

Print
Printer
Name: Epson Stylus COLOR ESC/P 2 | Properties
Status: Ready
Type: Epson Stylus COLOR ESC/P 2
Where: LPT1:
Comment:
Print to file
Print range
All
Pages from: 6 to: 6
Copies
Number of copies: 1
OK | Cancel

specify to print page 6 only

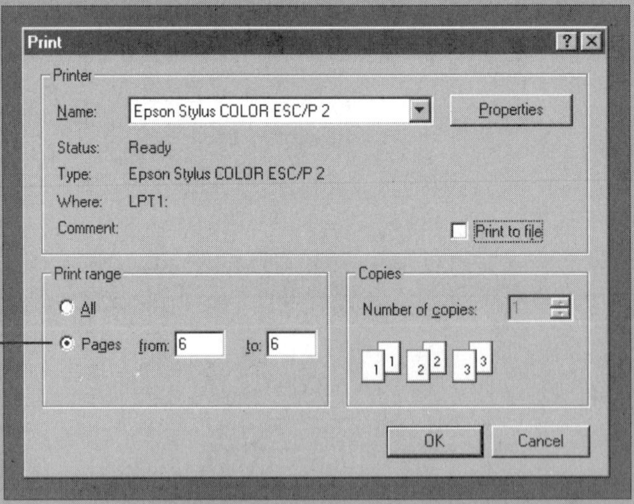

Figure 7-74: Print dialog box

5 Click the **Pages** option button, enter **6** in the From and To text boxes so you only print page 6 of the report, and then click the **OK** button. Your printed report page should look like Figure 7-75.

Student Transcript
Date: 17 OCT 1999

Ruben R Sanchez
1780 Samantha Court
Eau Claire WI 54701

Spring 2000

Call ID	Course Name	Credits	Grade
MIS 101	Intro. to Info. Systems	3	B
MIS 301	Systems Analysis	3	C
MIS 451	Client/Server Systems	3	C
	Total Term Credits:	9	
	Term GPA:	2.33	

Summer 2000

Call ID	Course Name	Credits	Grade
MIS 441	Database Management	3	
MIS 101	Intro. to Info. Systems	3	
	Total Term Credits:	9	
	Term GPA:	.00	

Figure 7-75: Printed report

HELP? If your report does not print correctly, ask your instructor or technical support person for help.

Creating a User Input Parameter

Someone using this report probably would want to print a particular student's transcript rather than printing all student transcripts. You can create a **user input parameter** that allows the user to choose which student's transcript to display or print in the report. You will create a user parameter that displays a list of possible report input values, which will be the student names. Then you will modify the SQL query in your data model to use the selected student's SID as a search condition. As a result, the report will be generated only for the selected student.

To create the user input parameter:

1. Go to the Object Navigator.
2. Click **User Parameters** under the Data Model object, and then click the **Create** button on the Object Navigator toolbar to create a new user parameter.
3. Change the name of the new user parameter to **P_STUDENT**.
4. Open the P_STUDENT Properties sheet by double-clicking the to the left of its name. The P_STUDENT Properties sheet displays, as shown in Figure 7-76.

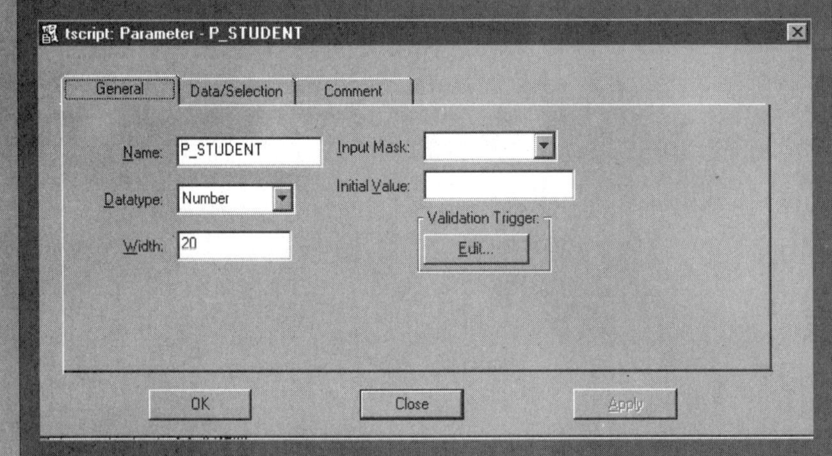

Figure 7-76: P_STUDENT Properties sheet

tip

You also can right-click P_STUDENT and then click Properties on the menu to open the Properties sheet.

The General tab of the user parameter Properties sheet lets you specify the user parameter name and the properties of the data field that will be used to specify the data query—data type, maximum width, and input format mask. Although the user will select from a list of student names, the user parameter that will be passed to the data model will be the associated student ID, so you will change the properties to match those of the SID field in the STUDENT table.

The Data/Selection tab lets you specify the list of values that the user can choose from for the report input. You can enter a static list of predetermined input values or a list based on a database query. You will use a SQL query that retrieves student IDs and last names, first names, and middle initials. The query must return the primary key (SID) so it can be used as a search condition in the report's data model query. However, you will not display the SID in the user parameter list.

To specify the P_STUDENT properties:

1. If necessary, change the Datatype to **Number** and the Width to 5, and then click the **Data/Selection** tab.
2. Click the **SELECT Statement** option button.

3 Type the query shown in Figure 7-77 in the Enter Query text box.

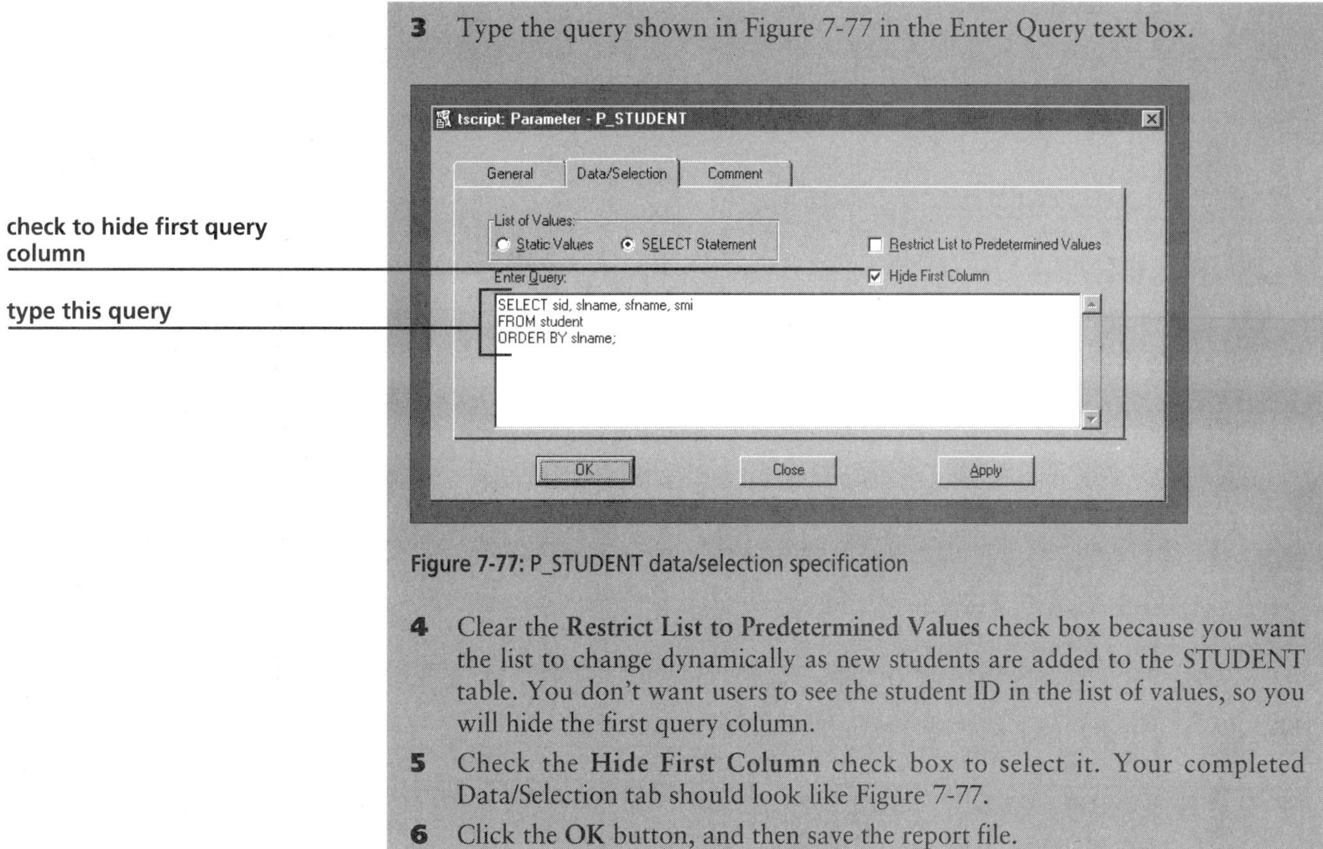

Figure 7-77: P_STUDENT data/selection specification

4 Clear the **Restrict List to Predetermined Values** check box because you want the list to change dynamically as new students are added to the STUDENT table. You don't want users to see the student ID in the list of values, so you will hide the first query column.

5 Check the **Hide First Column** check box to select it. Your completed Data/Selection tab should look like Figure 7-77.

6 Click the **OK** button, and then save the report file.

Now you need to modify the data model query to return only the record for the student selected by the user input parameter. You will modify the SQL command by adding a search condition that SID equals the value of the input parameter, which is expressed as :P_STUDENT.

To modify the data model query:

1 Go to the Data Model Editor, and then double-click the **Q_courses** query to view the original data model SELECT statement.

2 Modify the SELECT statement as shown in Figure 7-78 to return only the SID value specified by the P_STUDENT input parameter.

add this line

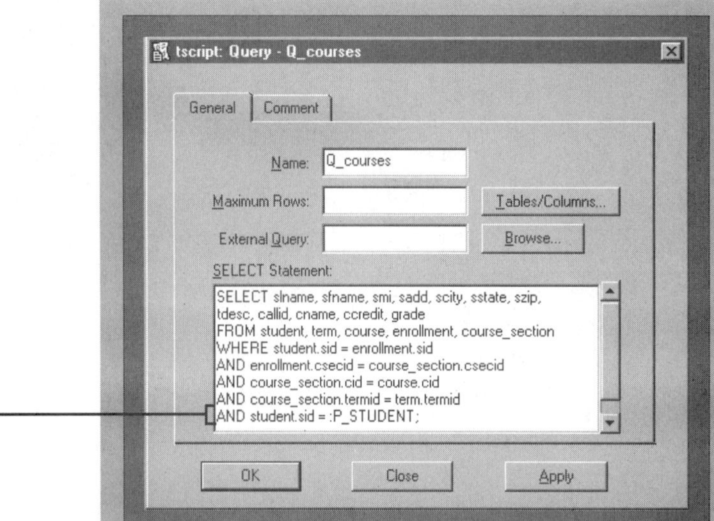

Figure 7-78: Modifying the data model query

3 Click the OK button.

4 Save the report file and then run the report. The initial Reports Runtime window displays the user parameter input screen with a list arrow for selecting student names, as shown in Figure 7-79.

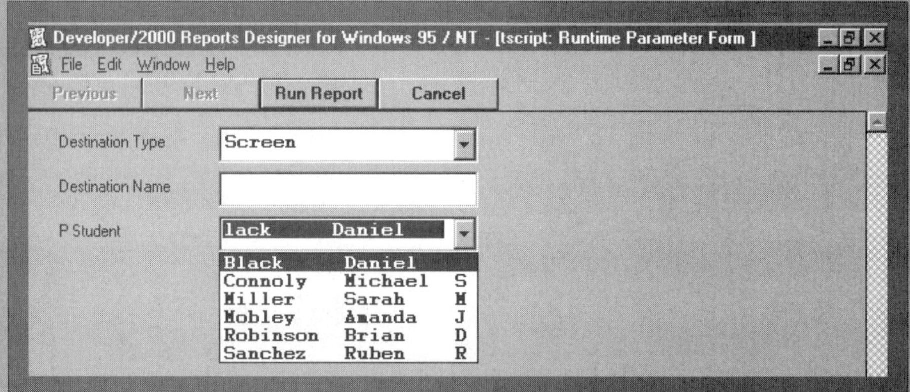

Figure 7-79: User parameter input screen

HELP? The "B" in Daniel Black's name might not display in the list box, which is normal.

5 Select a student name and then run the report to the screen to confirm that that the correct student's transcript is generated.

6 Close the Previewer window.

7 Generate an executable file named **tscript.rep**, and save it in the Chapter7 folder on your Student Disk.

8 Close the Reports Designer application.

SUMMARY

- In a report, data fields are retrieved from the database, and rows will repeat for every retrieved record. Parameter fields are report parameters such as page numbers that are displayed on every report page.
- To name a report, you must save the report to the database or file system. The report has the same name as the saved report.
- The Data Model Editor is used to specify the SQL query (or queries) that define your report data. Each query has one or more associated record groups.
- The default layout automatically generates layouts for common report styles.
- The tabular layout style displays multiple data records on a page with a column heading at the top of each field.
- The master/detail layout style displays one-to-many data relationships in a tabular style.
- You can specify how repeated records are printed down and/or across pages.
- When you run a Reports .rdf file, no executable file is generated, so the file must be generated each time you run it in the Reports Designer application. After you finish developing the report, you can create an executable .rep file.
- The report output destinations are the screen, a file, your printer, an electronic mail address, or preview.
- Frames are containers for grouping related objects. Group frames enclose and keep related groups of objects together. Repeating frames enclose objects that are repeated multiple times for a data column that displays multiple record values. To avoid Reports Runtime warning messages, make sure that frames completely enclose the objects inside them.
- You can adjust the spacing between repeating records and the number of records that will appear on a page on the repeating frame's Properties sheet. Data fields that could potentially retrieve multiple records must be in repeating frames or you will receive a system error message.
- When a report is in confine mode, you cannot move an object out of its containing object.
- Sizing determines whether a field's size is fixed on the printed report, or whether it can expand or contract automatically depending on the size of the retrieved data value. You can combine variably sized fields with anchors so data records with different widths are always displayed or printed beside each other. Anchors have child and parent objects. You always select the child object first, and then anchor it to the parent.
- The report header is an optional page (or multiple pages) that appears at the beginning of the report and can contain text, graphics, data, and computations.
- The report body contains the majority of the report's data and computations. The report body has a top and bottom margin where you can place text, such as page numbers or the current date. The default report margin size is one-half inch each for the top and bottom margins and zero for the left and right margins.
- The report trailer is an optional page (or multiple pages) that appears at the end of the report that can contain text, graphics, data, or computations.
- You can import a variety of graphic image types into a report using the Import, Image command on the Edit menu.
- A master/detail report is created when a record can have many associated records.
- The data model in a master/detail report must include a "break" that separates the master and detail fields. In a master/detail relationship, you always "break out" the master fields.

- A summary column sums the data values in a repeating data column. To create a summary column, you first define it in the data model, and then you create a display field in the layout editor to display it on the report. Summary columns must be outside the group frame of the fields they are summing.
- A formula column returns the value of a function that makes mathematical computations on other columns. Formula columns must be displayed in the same frame as the most detailed data column in their formula.
- A holding field is a report layout field that does not display in the final report, but serves to hold the value of a calculated or summed column that is not displayed but will be used in another computation so you can confirm that its value is correct.
- User input parameters allow users to specify inputs to generate specific reports. A user input parameter list of values can be a static list of predetermined values or a list based on a database query.

REVIEW QUESTIONS

1. How do you change a new report's name in the Object Navigator?
2. What is the purpose of the Data Model Editor?
3. What is the difference between. rdf and .rep files?
4. How do you create .rep files?
5. List and define three Reports Runtime destinations.
6. What is a frame? How can you tell the difference between a group frame and a repeating frame? What is the difference between a group frame and a repeating frame?
7. What does it mean when the Layout Editor is in confine mode? What should you do if you get a Reports Runtime warning message stating that a group frame does not enclose an object?
8. What should you do if you get a Reports Runtime error message stating that a field references a column at a frequency below its group?
9. What are the three report regions, and what kind of data do they contain?
10. When should you create a report trailer?
11. What data types can you add format masks to in a report?
12. What is a master/detail data relationship?
13. How do you determine which records are the master records and which records are the detail records?
14. What is a break in a data model?
15. In a master/detail data relationship, do you "break out" the master or detail data fields?
16. What is an anchor, and when do you use one?
17. What is a summary column? In what frame do you place the display field for a summary column?
18. What is a formula column? In what frame do you place the display field for a formula column?
19. What is a holding field?
20. What is a user input parameter? How do you create one?

PROBLEM-SOLVING CASES

Northwoods University Database

Save the files that you create in the Exercises below in the Chapter7 folder on your Student Disk.

1. Create a report named FAC_LIST that lists the last name, first name, middle initial, phone number, rank, building code, and room for every faculty member. Create a header page with the title FACULTY LIST as of <current date>. Add page numbers to the center of the bottom page margin. Format the report so each faculty record is on a single line with the column headings at the top of the page.
2. Update the following records in the ENROLLMENT table: SID = 102, CSECID = 1011, GRADE = B; SID = 102, CSECID = 1012, GRADE = A; SID = 104, CSECID = 1012, GRADE = B. Then modify the TSCRIPT report so it displays only information for courses where the student has been assigned a grade, and so it displays total student credits earned for all terms and overall student grade point averages in addition to total term credits and term grade point averages. (*Hint*: You will not need to modify the data model using the search condition "AND grade IS NOT NULL." You can check your report for students Daniel Black and Ruben Sanchez.)
3. Create a master/detail report named ST_SCHED. Allow the user to select from a list of student last names, first names, and middle initials, but use SID as the actual input parameter. The report should list the selected student's current (where TERM.Enrollment = 'OPEN') course call IDs, course names, section number, day, time, building code, and room number. Format the report so each course section record is on a single line, with the column headings at the top of the page. Put the Northwoods logo at the top of the report, and add the title STUDENT SCHEDULE under the logo. Include the student's mailing address in the top part of the report.
4. Create a master/detail report named F_CR_SEC. Allow the user to select from a list of faculty last names, first names, and middle initials, but use FID as the actual input parameter. The report should show the faculty member's current (where TERM.Enrollment = 'OPEN') course call IDs and section numbers, as well as a list of every student (last name, first name, middle initial) enrolled in the course section. Print each student record on a single line with column headings at the top of the page. Make each course section start on a new page. Add the title FACULTY CLASS LIST FOR at the top of each page, and include the faculty member's name on the right edge of the title. Add the current date in the top margin of each page.

Clearwater Traders Database

Save the files that you create in the Exercises below in the Chapter7 folder on your Student Disk.

1. Create a report named CUST_REP that lists each current customer's last and first name, middle initial, address, city, state, zip code, daytime phone, and evening phone. Print each customer record on a single line, with the column headings at the top of the page. Create a header page with the title CLEARWATER TRADERS CUSTOMER LIST. Add the current date under the title. Include page numbers on the center of the bottom margin of the report body.
2. Modify the CUST_REP you created in Exercise 1 so it also includes the dates of each customer's orders. (*Hint:* Change the report type to a master/detail report). Name the modified report CUST_ORD.
3. Create a report named INV_REP that lists every item number and item description along with its corresponding inventory ID, size, color, current price, quantity on hand, and expected date(s) of next shipment(s). Print each inventory record on a single line,

with column headings at the top of the page. Create a header page with the title CLEARWATER TRADERS INVENTORY REPORT. Add the current date under the title. Add page numbers to the center of the bottom margin of the report body.

4. Create a report named CUST_INV that allows the user to select from a list of customer last and first names, middle initials, and order IDs. The report should look like the customer invoice shown in Figure 7-80. Use anchors to format the customer name and address information. The extended total is a formula column calculated by multiplying the order line price times quantity. The subtotal is the sum of all of the extended total fields. Calculate the sales tax based on five percent of the subtotal for Wisconsin residents, and zero percent for all other states. Shipping and handling is calculated based on the order subtotal, and $3.50 for orders less than $25, $5.00 for orders between $25 and $75, and $7.50 for orders over $75. The final order total is the sum of the subtotal, tax, and shipping and handling fields.

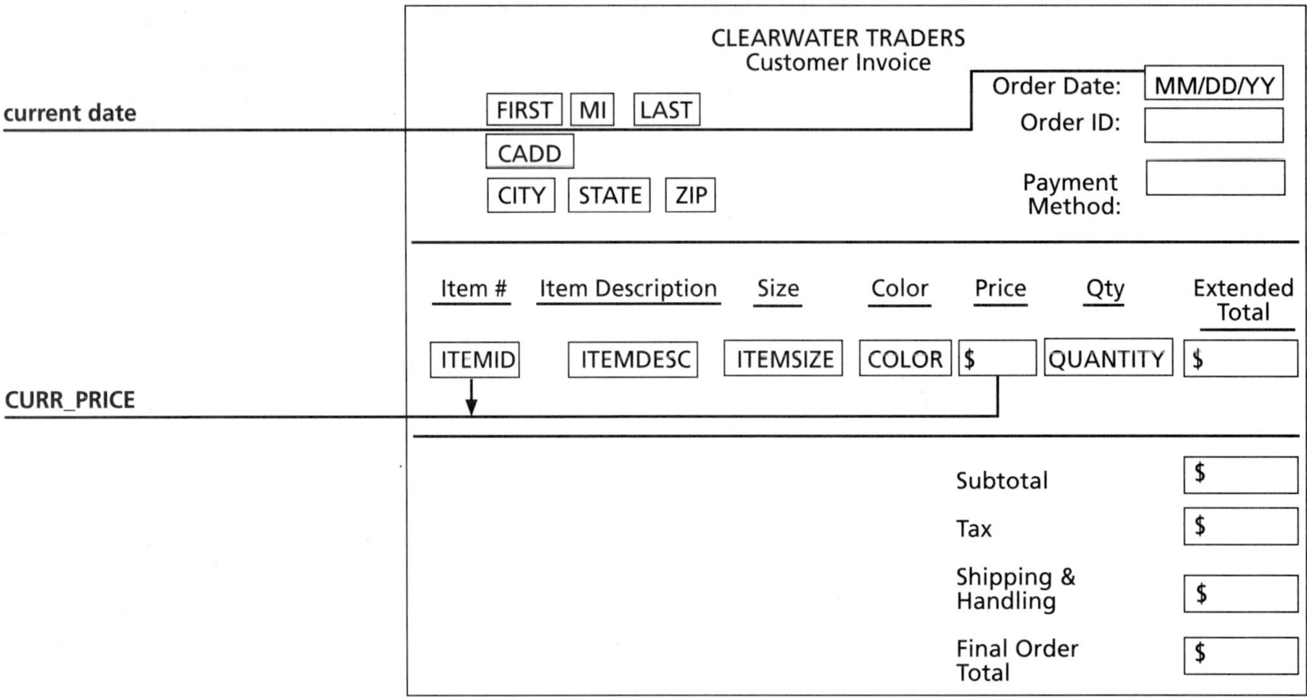

Figure 7-80: Design for the Clearwater Traders customer invoice

Chapter 8

objectives

- Use Oracle Graphics to create pie and bar charts based on database data
- Link two charts using a drill-down relationship
- Create an Oracle Forms application that dynamically passes user inputs to an Oracle Graphics chart
- Create an Oracle Reports application that displays an Oracle Graphics chart that corresponds to report data records

CHAPTER 8

Using Oracle Graphics

Introduction Oracle Graphics is the Oracle Developer/2000 application used for creating graphical displays of database data. Graphics applications can run as stand-alone applications, or they can be embedded within Forms or Reports applications. In this chapter, you will learn how to create simple pie and bar charts and how to embed charts in Forms and Reports applications. You also will learn how to create an interactive drill-down relationship between two related charts that allows you to select a value in one chart and to view related data in a second chart.

Creating a Chart

Before you create a chart, it is important to consider the type of data you want to chart and the purpose of what you want to illustrate in your chart. Figure 8-1 lists the chart types you can create using Oracle Graphics, describes what each chart is designed to illustrate, and provides an example application.

Chart Type	Description	Example
Column	Shows discrete values using vertical columns	Display current quantities on hand for different inventory items
Bar	Shows discrete values using horizontal bars	Same as column
Gantt	Shows task or project scheduling or progress information	Display work schedule information by showing hours of the day on the X-axis and names of employees on the Y-axis, with horizontal bars showing each employee's scheduled start and stop times
High-Low	Shows multiple Y-axis values for a single X-axis point	Display a student's highest, lowest, and average GPA
Line	Shows data values as points connected by lines to show trends	Display total order revenues for each item category for each month of the past year
Mixed	Combines a column and line chart	Display total order revenues for each month of the past year as columns, with a line connecting the top of the columns to show sales trends
Pie	Shows how individual data values make up a total amount	Illustrate what each item category (Women's Clothing, Men's Clothing, etc.) contributes to total sales
Scatter	Presents two sets of potentially unrelated data for identifying trends	Plotting student age versus GPA
Table	Shows text data in columns	Show a listing of all Northwoods University course call IDs, descriptions, days, times, and locations
Double Y-charts	Shows a line chart with two different sets of Y-axis data for the same X-axis values	Illustrate how revenue dollars and units sold have varied over the same time period

Figure 8-1: Oracle Graphics chart types and uses

The management at Clearwater Traders wants to create a chart to display what portion of its total order revenue comes from specific catalogs and from the Web site. A pie chart is appropriate because it is used to compare individual components (such as revenue from each order source) to an overall total (such as total order revenue). Figure 8-2 shows a design sketch for how the order source pie chart will look. If Clearwater Traders had $1000 in total revenue and one-third came from Catalog 152, one-third came from Catalog 153, and one-third came from the Web site, each of these three sources would contribute one-third to the total revenue, so each represents one-third of the pie. The chart labels show the source name as well as the value that it contributes to the total revenue. Now you will start Oracle Graphics Designer and then create the order revenue sources pie chart.

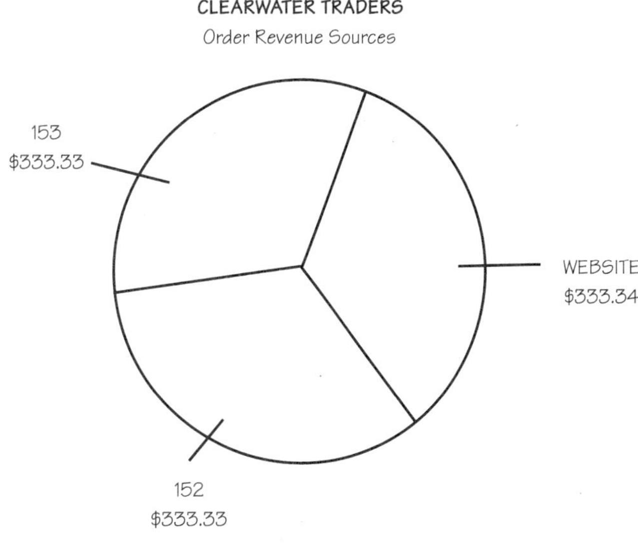

Figure 8-2: Design sketch for pie chart

Starting the Oracle Graphics Designer

Just like any other Oracle application, you must start the Graphics Designer and then log on to the database. You will start the Graphics Designer and then run the SQL script to refresh your Clearwater Traders database.

tip

Another way to start the Graphics Designer is to open Windows Explorer, change to the ORAWIN\BIN (or ORANT\BIN) folder, and then double-click the file g25des32.exe.

To start the Graphics Designer and run the SQL script:

1 Click the **Start** button on the taskbar, point to **Programs**, point to **Developer/2000 for Win95** (or **Developer/2000 for WinNT**), and then click **Graphics Designer.**

2 Click **File** on the menu bar, click **Connect**, and then connect to the database in the usual way. Graphics Designer opens the Object Navigator window, as shown in Figure 8-3.

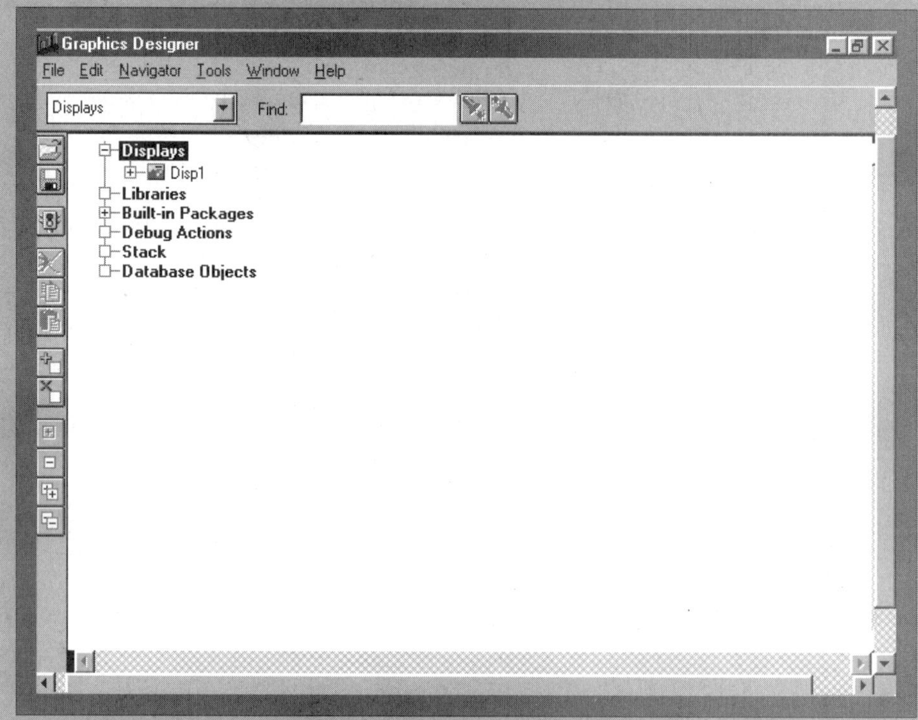

Figure 8-3: Oracle Graphics Designer Object Navigator window

HELP? The Graphics: Disp1: Layout Editor window might open when you start the Graphics Designer. If this happens, click Window on the menu bar, click Object Navigator, and then maximize the Object Navigator window.

3 Start SQL*Plus, log on to the database, and then type the following to refresh your database tables: **START A:\Chapter8\clearwat.sql**.

4 Exit SQL*Plus.

An Oracle Graphics chart object is called a **display**. When you start the Graphics Designer, a new display object named Disp1 is created automatically. To change the display name, you need to save it with a different filename in the database or file system.

To change the display name:

1 In the Object Navigator window, click **Disp1**.

2 Click the **Save** button on the Object Navigator toolbar. The Save dialog box opens.

3 If necessary, click the **File System** option button, and then click the OK button. The Save As dialog box opens.

4 Change to the Chapter8 folder on your Student Disk, type ord_srce in the File Name text box, and then click the **Save** button.

For the first chart, you will use the Chart Genie in the Layout Editor to automate the chart creation process.

To start the Chart Genie:

1 In the Object Navigator, click **Window** on the menu bar, click **Graphics: ord_srce.ogd: Layout Editor** to go to the Layout Editor, and then maximize the Layout Editor window if necessary. The Graphics Layout Editor is similar to the Forms and Reports Layout Editors.

2 Click **Chart** on the menu bar, and then click **Create Chart** to open the Chart Genie - New Query dialog box.

Creating the Query

Creating a new chart is a two-step process—first you create the query to define the data that you want to display in the chart, and then you define the chart properties. Depending on the chart type, the query will define the data that is displayed in the pie slices of a pie chart or on the X- and Y-axes of a column, bar, or line chart. When writing the query to retrieve the chart data, visualize what the chart will look like. In this case, you want to display data that show the total revenue amount for each order source, which is a catalog or the Web site. For a pie chart, the different pie slice labels will be values in one column, and their corresponding numerical contribution to the whole pie will be a label on the chart and a value in another query column. Therefore you need to create a query where the first column shows the names of the different order sources and where the second column shows the total revenue (ORDER_PRICE multiplied by (*) QUANTITY from the ORDERLINE table) from each source.

To define the query:

1 Change the query name to **ordersource_query**. To define your chart, you can enter a SQL statement or import the data from Microsoft Excel SYLK files, Lotus WKS files, or ASCII PRN files. You also can import a custom query created in PL/SQL. The File text box is used to specify the external filename if an external file is used.

2 If necessary, click the **Type** list arrow, and then click **SQL Statement**. You will create a SQL query to retrieve the data for the pie chart, so you will not enter anything in the File text box.

3 Click in the SQL Statement text box, and then type the query shown in Figure 8-4.

command to create an alias for a calculated column

type this command

Chart Genie - New Query

Define a new query for the chart.

Query | Data

Name: ordersource_query

Type: SQL Statement

File:

SQL Statement

```
SELECT ordersource,
SUM(order_price * quantity) AS revenue
FROM cust_order, orderline
WHERE cust_order.orderid = orderline.orderid
GROUP BY ordersource;
```

Browse... | Connect... | Import SQL... | Export SQL...

Execute | OK | Cancel | Help

Figure 8-4: SQL command for ordersource_query

HELP? Notice that the SQL SELECT command is written as `SELECT ordersource, SUM (order_price * quantity) AS revenue`. The "AS revenue" command creates an **alias**, which is an alternate name for a column retrieved in a **SELECT** command. The general format for creating an alias is `SELECT <field name> AS <alias name>`. An alias often is used to give descriptive names to columns with calculated values. When you use a calculated value in a query for a Graphics chart, you must create an alias for the calculated values column or some advanced Graphics functions will not work correctly.

4 Click the **Execute** button to execute the SQL statement and to go to the Data tab of the Chart Genie - New Query dialog box, which shows different order sources and their respective revenues, as shown in Figure 8-5.

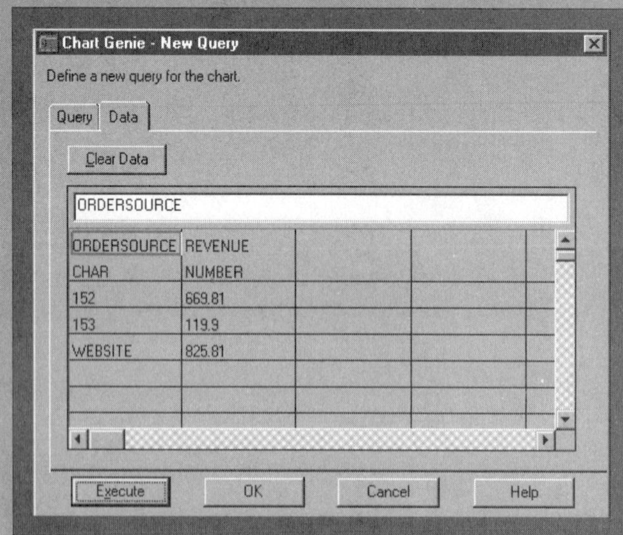

Figure 8-5: Data tab for ordersource_query

HELP? If you receive a DBMS (ORA-) error message when you try to execute a query, or if your query does not return the data you expect, then you probably made a SQL error, such as forgetting a join clause. Use Oracle Browser to generate the query, or create the query in a text editor and then test it using SQL*Plus. When the command is correct, copy the tested SQL code into the SQL Statement text box on the Query tab and execute the query again.

5 Click the **OK** button to accept the data and open to the Chart Properties dialog box, as shown in Figure 8-6.

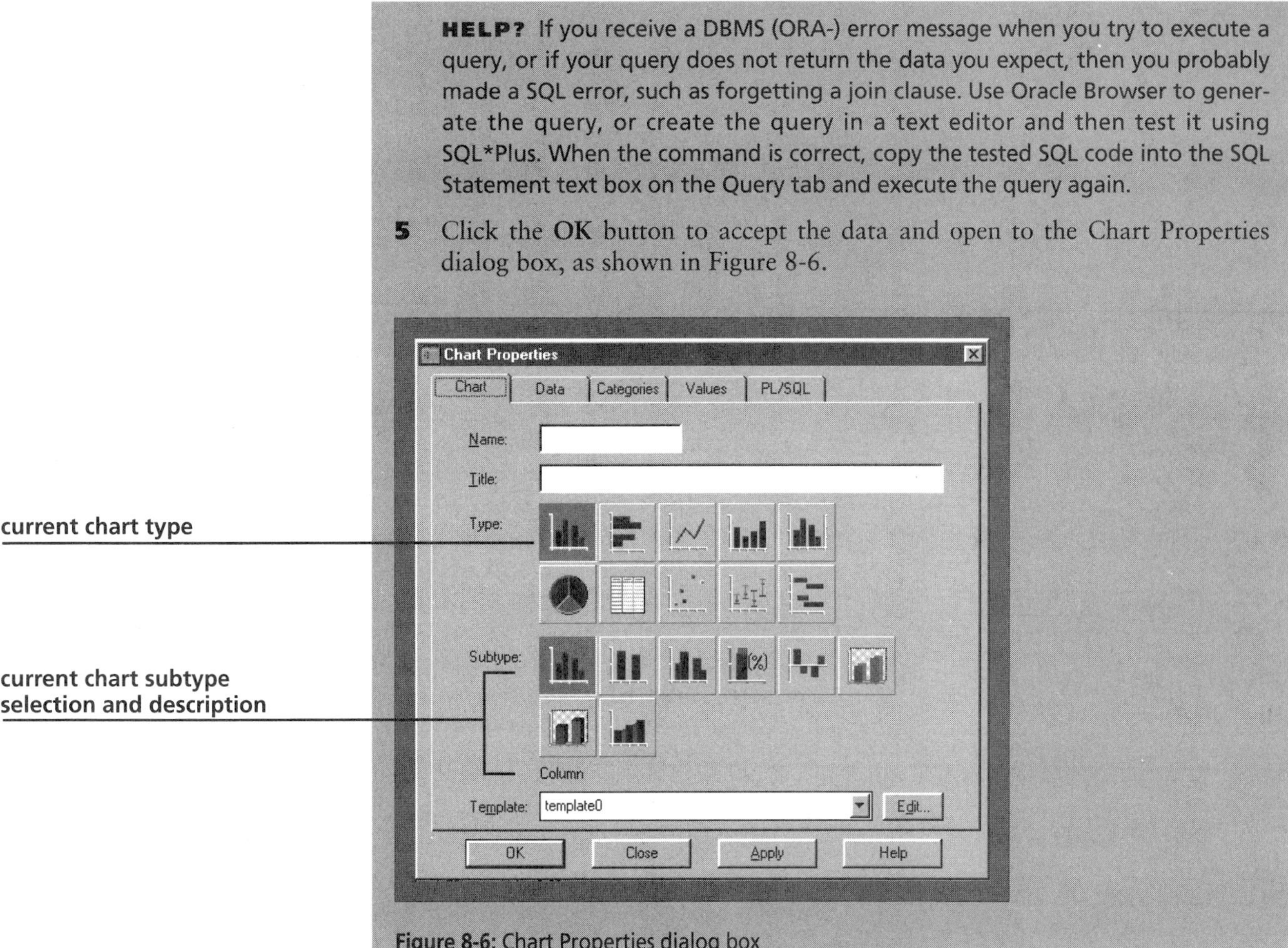

Figure 8-6: Chart Properties dialog box

Defining the Chart Properties

The Chart Properties dialog box lets you configure how the chart will look. You use the Chart tab of the Chart Properties dialog box to specify the chart name, title, type, subtype, and a template on which to base the chart. The chart name should be different from the query name because you might have several charts that use the same query to define the data that they illustrate. The chart title is what is displayed at the top of the chart. The **chart type** defines the type of chart you want to create—pie, bar, column, etc. The **subtype** defines the different display and shading options for the selected chart type. The default chart type is column, which is currently selected. The default chart subtype is also column; the name of the current subtype appears above the Template list box.

To name the chart and change its properties:

1. Click in the Name text box, and then type **ordersource_chart**.
2. Click in the Title text box, and then type **Clearwater Traders Order Revenue Sources.**
3. Click the **Pie** chart type (the first chart type in the second row). Note that the Subtype options change to show different variations of the pie chart.
4. Click the **Pie with depth** subtype (the third subtype from the left). Your Chart tab should look like Figure 8-7.

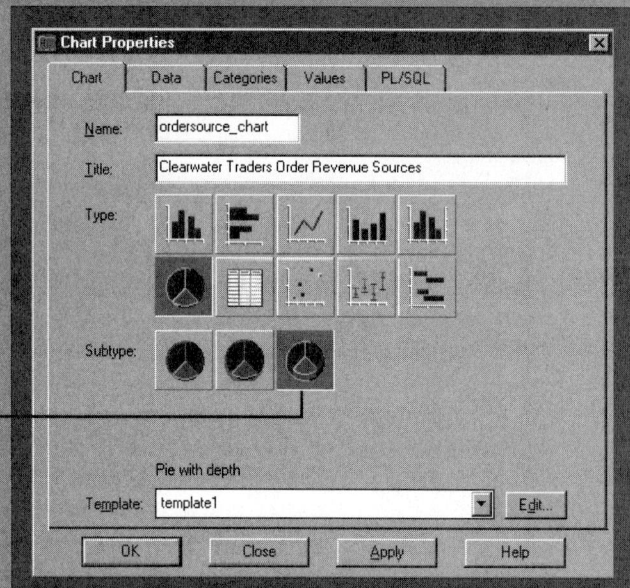

Figure 8-7: Completed Chart tab

5. Click the OK button to close the Chart Properties dialog box and create the chart in the Layout Editor window, as shown in Figure 8-8. Each slice of the pie chart shows the approximate proportion of revenue for each of the different sources, but it would be more informative if it listed the actual dollar figures along with the source names.

selection handles indicate entire chart (not individual components) is selected

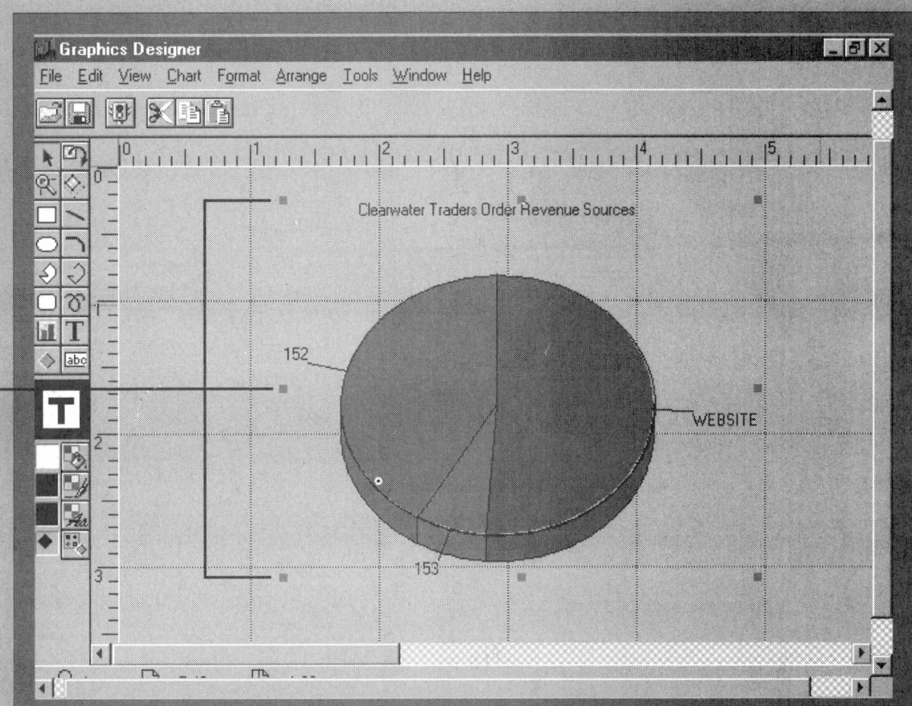

Figure 8-8: Chart in the Layout Editor window

6 If necessary click anywhere in the pie chart to select it. Selection handles appear around a square perimeter of the chart, as shown in Figure 8-8, to indicate that the chart is selected.

HELP? If selection handles appear around the chart and the individual pie slices, you selected the chart's individual components rather than the entire chart. Click anywhere outside the chart, and then single-click the chart to select it.

7 Right-click anywhere on the gray background within the selected area, and then click **Properties** on the menu to open the Chart Properties dialog box.

8 Click the **Categories** tab. This tab allows you to specify what data values are displayed. Currently ORDERSOURCE is the only query column that is displayed in the Chart Categories list. You want to display the revenue amounts for each slice of the pie.

9 Click **REVENUE** in the Query Columns list box, click the **Insert** button to copy REVENUE into the Chart Categories list, and then click the **OK** button. The chart now includes revenue amounts, as shown in Figure 8-9.

tip

You also can double-click anywhere on the background area around the chart to open the Chart **Properties** dialog box.

revenue values

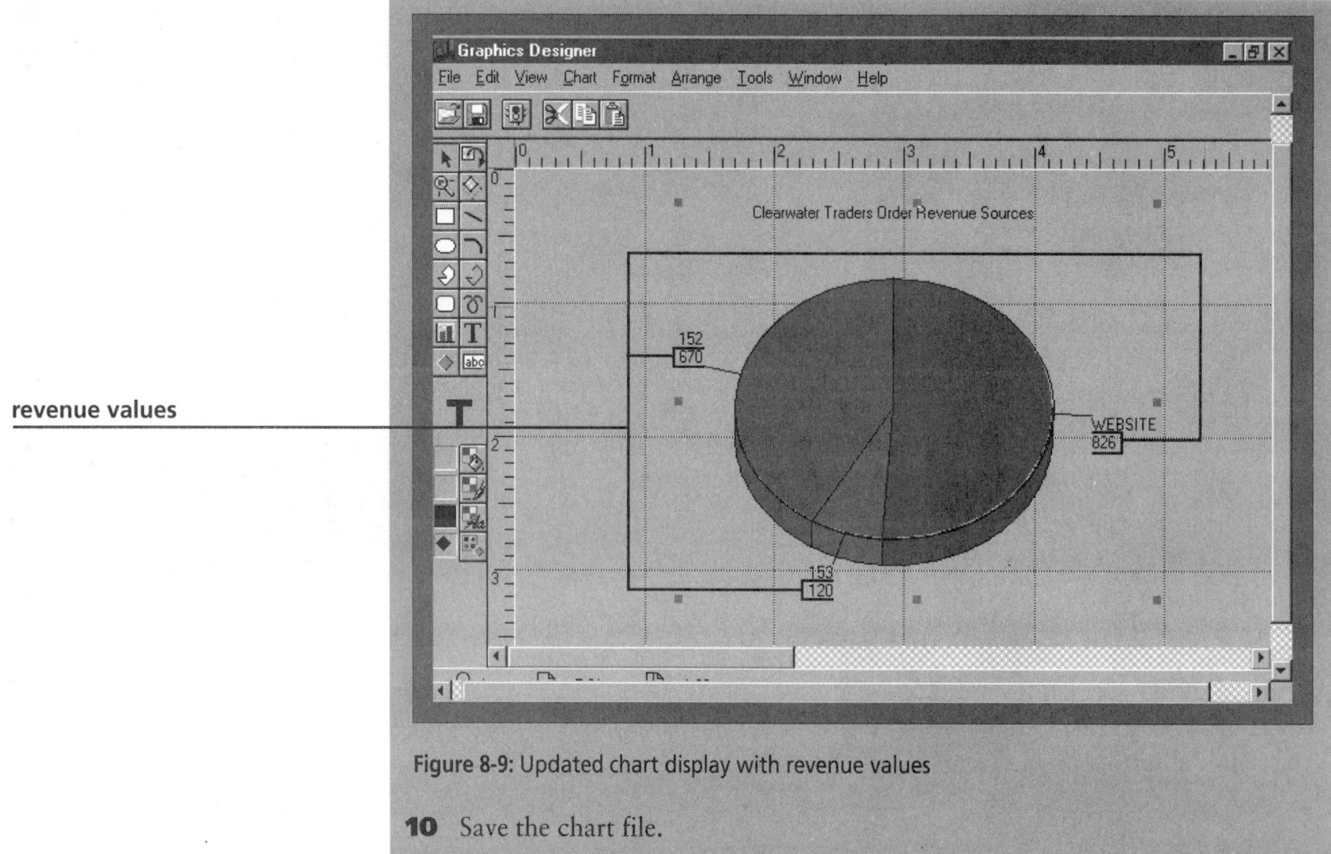

Figure 8-9: Updated chart display with revenue values

10 Save the chart file.

Formatting the Chart Display

Now the chart includes the revenue amounts, but they display as numbers instead of as currency, which makes it hard to differentiate the catalog numbers from the revenue amounts. You can apply a format mask to the revenue amounts so they will display with dollar signs and two decimal places. Then you will reposition the chart and change the chart labels to make them more prominent and enhance the chart's appearance.

To format the revenue amounts as currency:

1 Click the chart to select it, and then click any of the revenue values to select them as a group. Selection handles should appear around each revenue value, as shown in Figure 8-10.

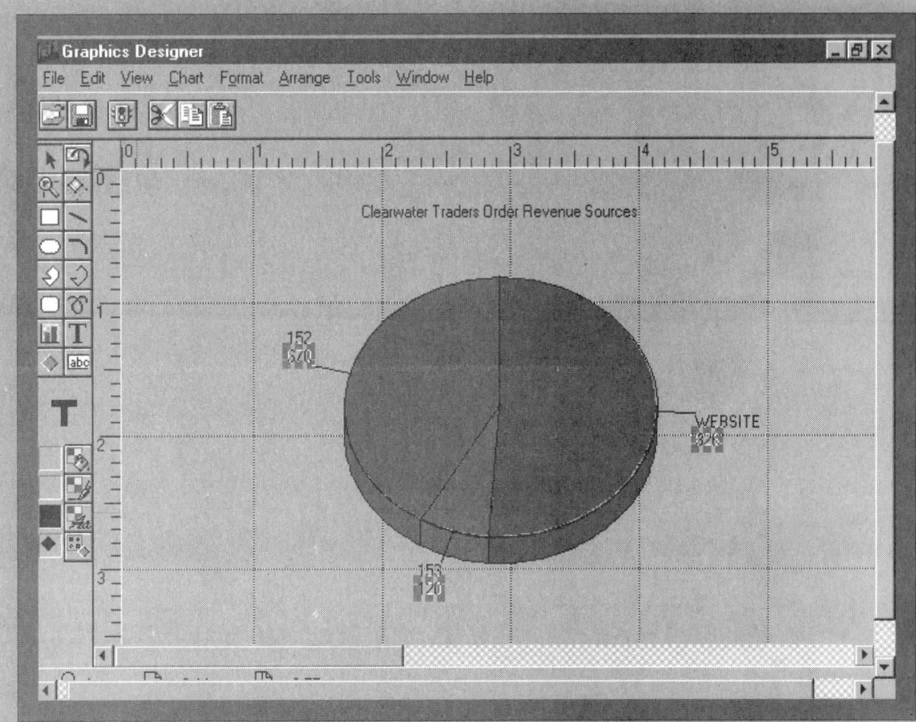

Figure 8-10: Chart revenue values selected

You can apply format masks only to NUMBER and DATE data types.

2 With the revenue values selected, click **Format** on the menu bar, click **Number** to open the Number Format dialog box, click **$999,990.99**, and then click the **OK** button to apply the selected format mask to the selected objects. The currency values now should be formatted correctly in the Layout Editor window.

HELP? If the format mask you want to use does not appear in the list of available format masks, click Format on the menu bar, and then click Number. Type the format mask you want to use in the Format text box, click the Add button, and then click the OK button.

Now the revenues display as currency with two decimal places. Next you will reposition and resize the chart, and then format the chart labels.

To reposition and resize the chart, and format the labels:

1 Drag the chart to the top left corner of the Layout Editor, and then use the rulers to resize the chart so it is about 3.9" wide and 3.2" long.

2 Select the entire chart, and then click the middle of the chart and drag it up to the upper-left corner of the Layout Editor window so the upper-left corner of the chart is .2" from the top and .2" from the left edge of the window.

HELP? If the rulers do not display at the top and left edges of the Layout Editor window, click View on the menu bar, and then click Rulers to turn them on.

3 Click **Chart** on the menu bar, and then click **Update Chart** to refresh the chart display. You should update the chart when you change the size of the chart so you are sure the new size is presented in the Layout Editor. Next you will format the chart text.

4 Click the chart title so selection handles appear around the title, click Format on the menu bar, click **Font**, and then change the font to **10-point Arial bold.**

HELP? You might need to move the chart title text box so it appears at the top of the chart display, or increase the size of the chart title text box so the entire chart title text is visible.

5 Click any one of the order source labels to select them as a group, and then change the font to **8-point bold Arial** font.

6 Click any one of the revenue figures to select them as a group, and then change the font to **8-point regular Arial** font.

7 Save the file.

Running and Generating the Chart

Now that the chart looks the way you want it in the Layout Editor, you need to run it in the Graphics Runtime application to see how it looks when run. Like the other Oracle Developer/2000 applications, Oracle Graphics allows you to save Graphics charts both as design files (with an .ogd extension) and as finished executable files (with an .ogr extension).

To run the chart and create an executable file:

1 Click the **Run** button  on the Layout Editor toolbar to run your chart in the Graphics Runtime window, as shown in Figure 8-11.

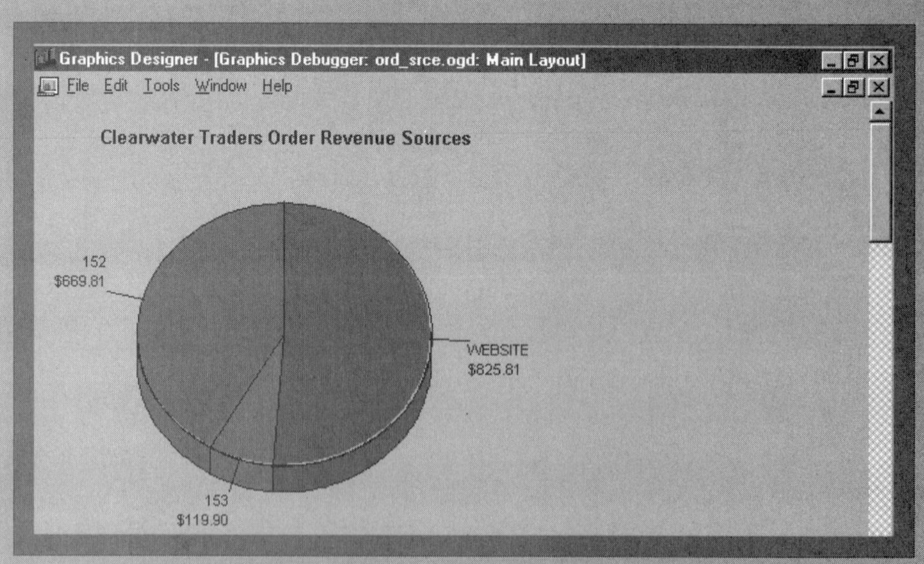

Figure 8-11: Chart displayed in the Graphics Runtime window

tip

The Graphics Runtime window has the title "Graphics Debugger" because you only use this window while you are developing and debugging your chart.

2 Close the Graphics Runtime window by clicking **File** on the menu bar, and then clicking **Close**. *Do not click the Close* ☒ *button because you will exit the Graphics Designer as well.* You will create an executable file next.

3 Click **File** on the menu bar, point to **Administration**, point to **Generate**, and then click **File System**. The Save As dialog box opens.

4 Make sure that the Chapter8 folder on your Student Disk is selected in the Save in text box and that the filename is **ord_srce.ogr**, and then click the **Save** button. The executable file is saved on your Student Disk. You can run the executable file by double-clicking the filename in Windows Explorer or by calling the chart within a form or report, as you will learn later in this chapter.

Creating a Column Chart

Next you will create a column chart to display a detailed analysis of the revenue generated by each individual item sold through the Web site order source. Figure 8-12 shows the design sketch for the revenue detail column chart. Each individual item is shown as a separate column on the X-axis, and total revenue determines each column's height on the Y-axis. You will add this chart to the ord_srce.ogd file that you just created. For this chart, you will create the query and layout components manually instead of using the Chart Genie.

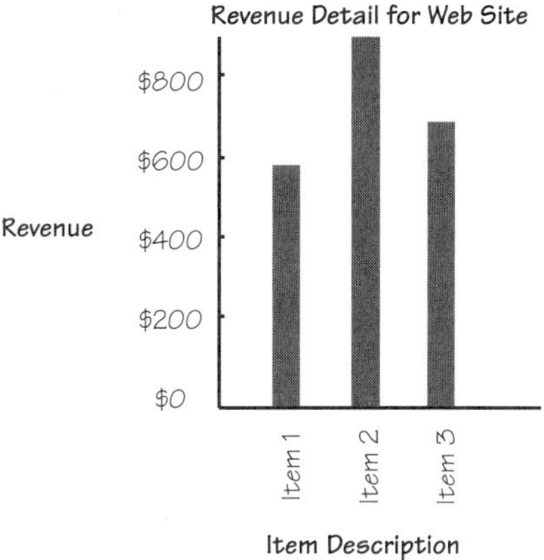

Figure 8-12: Design sketch for the revenue detail column chart

Creating a Query Manually

When you created the pie chart, you used the Chart Genie to specify the query and format of your chart. You also can create the query manually, as you will see next. However, first you will save the file with a new filename, so your original ord_srce.ogd file remains intact.

To create a query manually:

1 If necessary, start the Graphics Designer and open the **ord_srce.ogd** file from the Chapter8 folder on your Student Disk that you created in the previous exercise.

2 Click **File** on the menu bar, click **Save As**, and then click **File System**. If necessary change to the Chapter8 folder on your Student Disk. Type **rev_detl.ogd** in the File Name text box, and then click the **Save** button.

3 If necessary, click **Window** on the menu bar, and then click **Object Navigator** to go to the Object Navigator.

4 Click **Queries** and then click the **Create** button on the Object Navigator toolbar. The Query Properties dialog box opens.

5 Name the new query **revdetail_query**. For this chart, you want to display the item descriptions on the X-axis and show the total revenue generated by each item as a column value on the Y-axis. Therefore, the query will need to return item descriptions in one column and associated total revenue for all orders placed using the Web site as the source in the other column.

6 If necessary, click the **Type** list arrow, and then click **SQL Statement**, and then click in the SQL Statement text box and type the query shown in Figure 8-13.

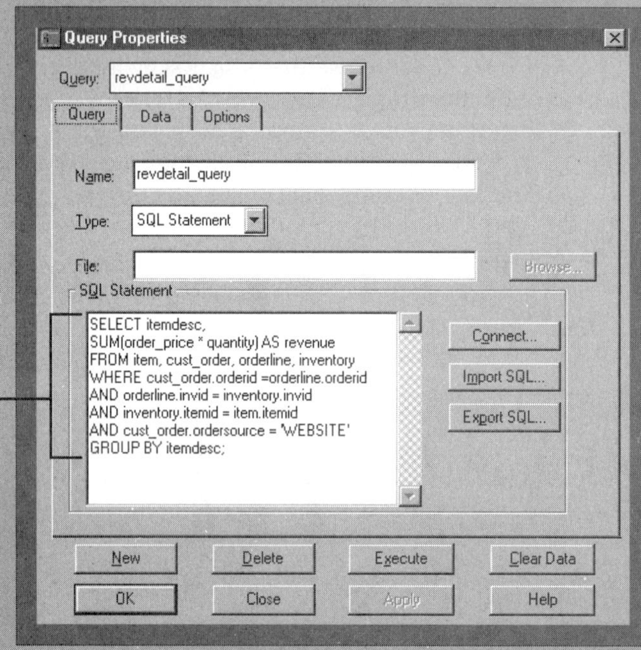

Figure 8-13: SQL command for revdetail_query

7 Click the **Execute** button to execute the SQL statement and to go to the Data tab, as shown in Figure 8-14. If your data is different, double-check to make sure you typed the SQL command correctly.

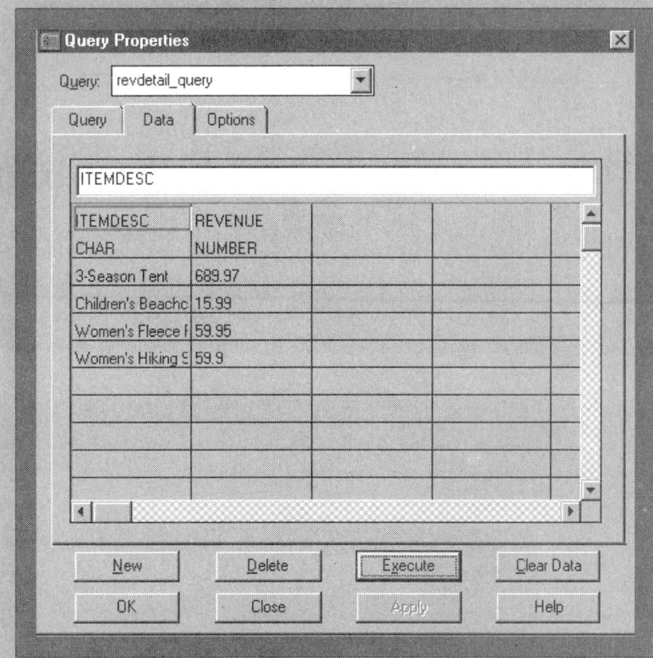

Figure 8-14: Data for revdetail_query

8 Click the **OK** button to accept the data and to close the Query Properties dialog box.

Creating a Manual Layout

Next you will go to the Layout Editor where the pie chart is displayed. You will create the layout for the column chart in the area to the right of the pie chart.

To create the layout for the column chart:

1 Click **Window** on the menu bar, and then click **Graphics: rev_detl.ogd: Layout Editor** to go to the Layout Editor.

2 Click **View** on the menu bar, and then click **Zoom Out**. Zoom out again if necessary until you can see at least five inches of blank space to the right of the pie chart.

3 Click the **Chart** tool on the Tool palette, and then click anywhere in the layout area and to the right of the pie chart. The Chart Genie dialog box opens and prompts you for a query source.

4 Make sure that the **Existing Query** option button is selected and that **revdetail_query** is displayed in the query list, and then click the **OK** button. The Chart Properties dialog box opens.

5 Type **revdetail_chart** as the chart name and **Revenue Detail for Web Site** as the chart title.

6 Click the **Column** chart type, click the **Column with depth** chart subtype (the first box in the second subtype row), and then click the **OK** button to close the dialog box and create the column chart. Move the column chart if necessary so it is on the page next to the pie chart layout.

7 Click **View** on the menu bar, and then click **Zoom In** so you can see the chart in detail. Move the column chart so its top edge is .2" from the top edge of the layout screen and so it does not overlap the pie chart.

Formatting the Layout

Now you need to format the chart layout. The current chart layout is shown in Figure 8-15. First you will format the X- and Y-axis labels. Currently the axis labels are the same as the query column titles—ITEMDESC and REVENUE. You will create custom labels so the labels match the design sketch shown in Figure 8-12. You also will format the **tick labels**, which are the labels on the individual tick mark items on the axes. You also will add a currency format mask for the Y-axis revenue values, and then change the font size and style for the chart title and axis labels.

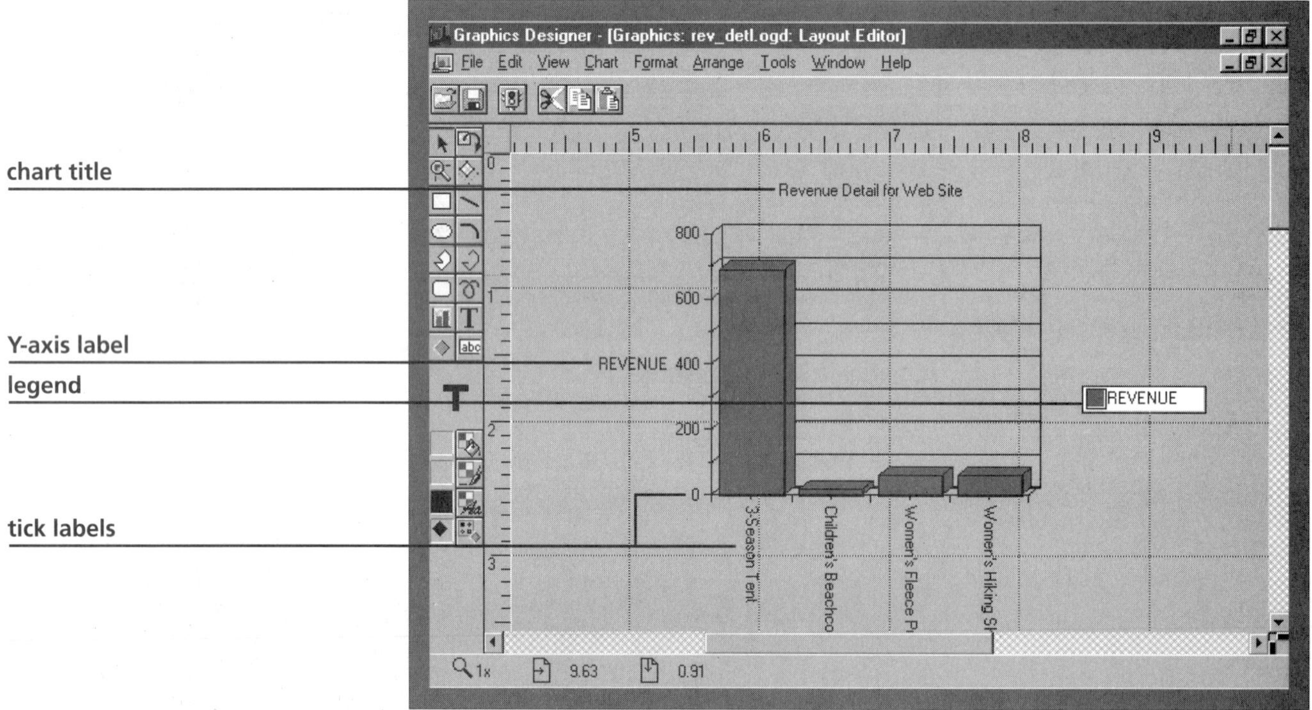

Figure 8-15: Chart layout elements

To format the chart axes:

1 Select the column chart, right-click it, and then click **Axes** on the menu. The Axis Properties dialog box opens, as shown in Figure 8-16. You use this dialog box to select either the X- or Y-axis and then specify the axis display properties such as the label, direction, tick mark style, tick label rotation, and number of tick marks per interval. You will change the Y-axis first.

click to select axis

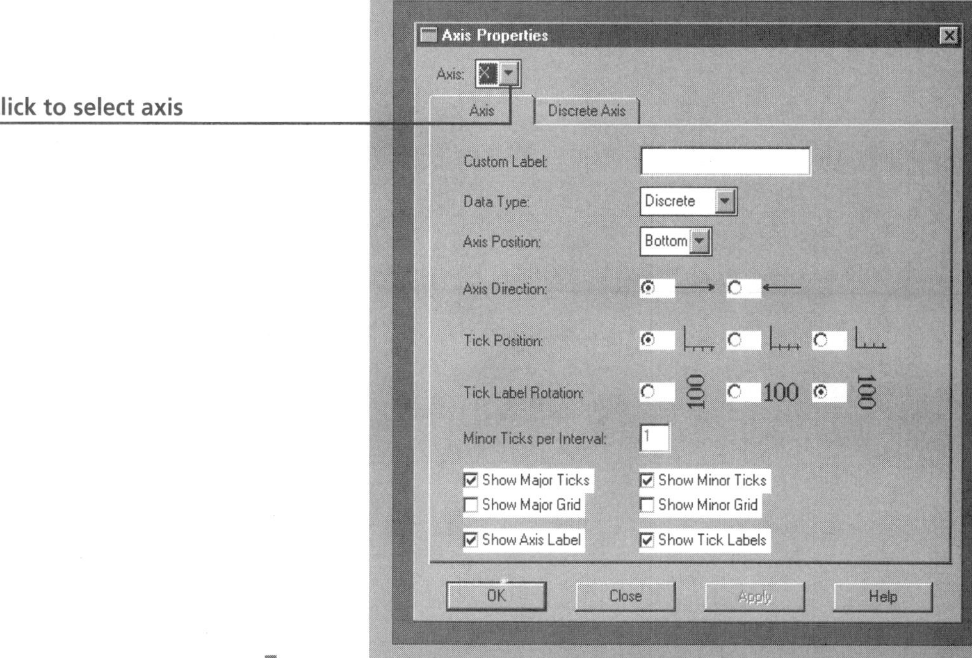

Figure 8-16: Axis Properties dialog box

tip

The Y-axis is labeled Y1 because you could have two Y-axes in a double-Y chart.

2 Click the **Axis** list arrow, and then click **Y1**.
3 Click in the Custom Label text box, and then type **Revenue**.
4 Click the **Apply** button to save your change.
5 Click the **Axis** list arrow, and then click **X**.
6 Click in the Custom Label text box, and then type **Item Description**.
7 Click the first **Tick Label Rotation** option button so the tick labels are displayed right-side up and parallel to the right edge of the page or screen, and then click the **OK** button. The Axis Properties dialog box closes. The X-axis labels change to display vertically.
8 To change the revenue values to display as currency, click any one of the revenue value labels on the Y-axis to select the group, click **Format** on the menu bar, click **Number**, click **$999,990** in the Number Format dialog box, and then click the **OK** button.
9 Select the column chart title, and then change it to **10-point bold Arial** font.
10 Change the X- and Y-axis labels (Item Revenue and Description) to **8-point bold Arial** font, change the X- and Y-axis tick labels (currency values and item descriptions) to an **8-point Arial regular** font, and then save the file.

By default, the chart displays a legend that shows the current columns that display the REVENUE data values. There is only one data series in the chart, so you will delete the legend. Also, the columns currently are the same color on their front, side, and top surfaces. Two-dimensional objects achieve a three-dimensional appearance as a result of the illusion of light shining on one surface with the other surfaces in shadow. You can enhance the appearance of the three-dimensional columns if you choose a light shade for the front surface and a slightly darker shade of the same color for the side and top surfaces.

To hide the legend and change the appearance of the column bars:

1 To hide the legend, select the column chart, right-click it, and then click **Frame** on the menu to open the Frame Properties dialog box. Click the **Show Legend** check box to clear it (and hide the legend), and then click the **OK** button.

2 Click the front bar surface on one of the column bars in the column chart, click the **Fill Color** button on the Tool palette, and then change the fill color to **light blue**.

3 Click the side surface of any column bar to select it, click , and then change the fill color to the same slightly **darker blue** shade as used on the side surface of the bars.

HELP? You cannot select the front, side, and top surfaces of a column bar as a group because they do not belong to the same group.

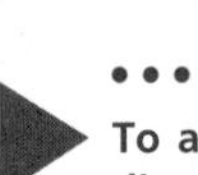

To achieve the best three-dimensional effect, choose colors that are directly beside each other on the Fill Color palette.

4 Click the top surface of any column bar to select it, click , and then change the fill color to a slightly **darker blue**.

5 Resize the pie and column charts so you can see both the pie and column charts in the Layout Editor window at normal size (1×), as shown in Figure 8-17. If necessary, move the Item Description label below the item descriptions.

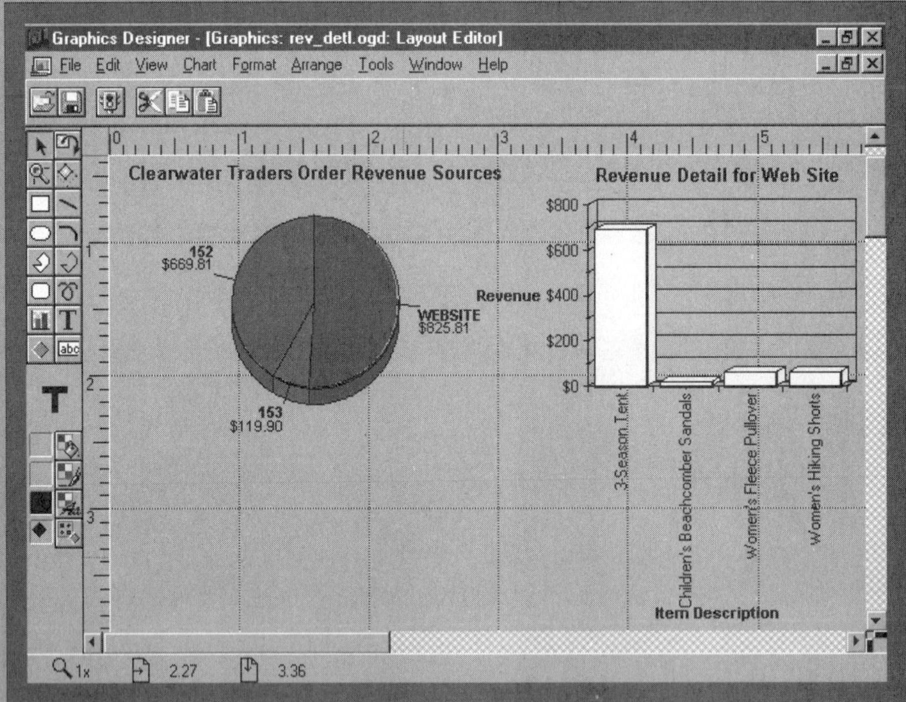

Figure 8-17: Resizing and repositioning the pie and column charts

HELP? After you move the axis label, you might need to update the chart layout by clicking Chart on the menu bar and then clicking Update Chart.

6 Save the file and then run the file to view your charts in the Graphics Runtime application.

7 Click **File** on the menu bar, and then click **Close** to exit the Graphics Runtime application.

Creating a Chart Drill-Down Relationship

Next you will see how to create a drill-down relationship between the two charts that you just created. An example of a **drill-down relationship** is when the user selects the catalog 152 pie slice in the pie chart, and then the detail information about catalog 152 orders is displayed in the column chart automatically. You can create a drill-down relationship with any two charts that have a master/detail relationship where the first (master) chart specifies values that the user can select as search conditions for the second (detail) chart's query.

The first step in creating a drill-down relationship between the pie chart and bar chart you created is to modify the chart layout as shown in Figure 8-18. You will modify the column chart title to be more general because data for different order sources will be displayed. You also will need to add instructions to direct the user to click a pie slice to view the associated revenue detail information.

modify column chart title to "Revenue Detail for Selected Order Source"

add user instructions here

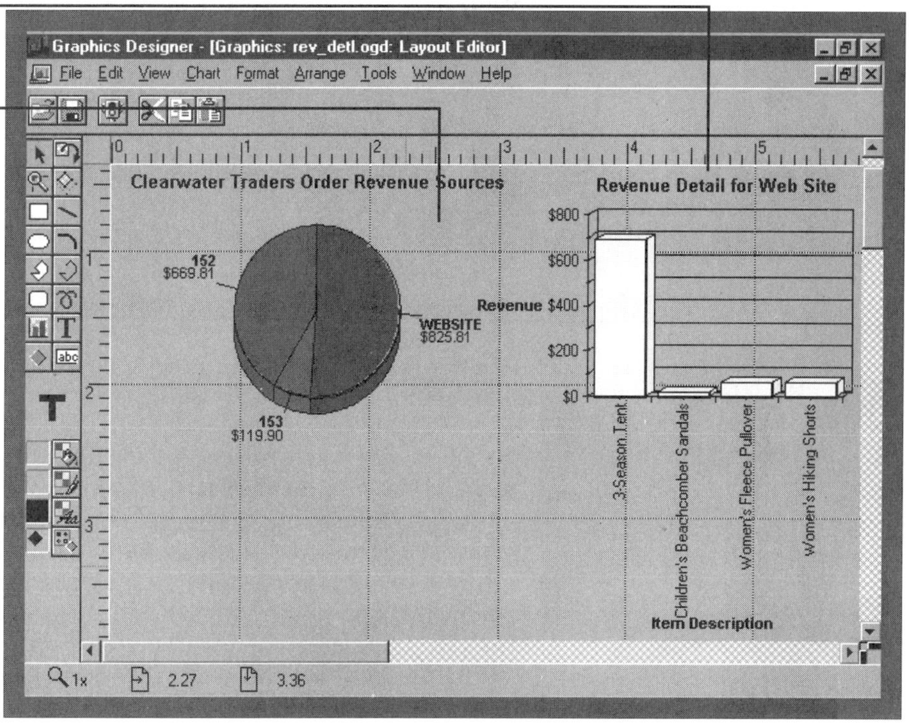

Figure 8-18: Modifying the chart layout for the drill-down relationship

To modify the chart layout for the drill-down relationship:

1. Select the column chart, right-click it, and then click **Properties** on the menu and change the chart title to **Revenue Detail for Selected Order Source.** Click the **OK** button to close the Properties sheet.
2. Click the **Text** tool [T] on the Tool palette, click in the location shown in Figure 8-18, and then create a text label with the following text: **Select a pie slice to update Revenue Detail.** Divide the text into three lines as shown in Figure 8-18 by pressing the **Enter** key at the end of each line.

3 Format the text as a **10-point regular Arial** font with no background color, and then change the text alignment to **Center**.

4 Click the **Ellipse** tool  on the Tool palette, and then draw an ellipse to hold the user instructions as shown in Figure 8-18. Set the fill color to **No Fill**, and select **black** for the line color. Your modified chart layout should look like Figure 8-19.

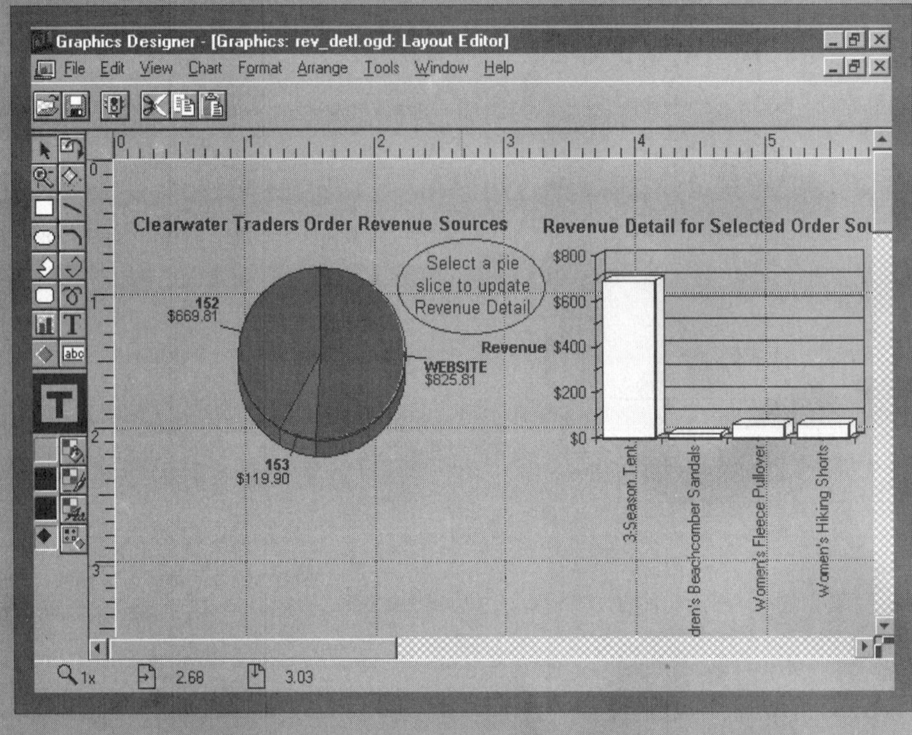

Figure 8-19: Modified chart layout

Next you need to modify the chart properties to create the drill-down relationship. You must create a **parameter** first, which is a variable whose value is set when the user clicks one of the pie chart slices and selects a specific order source. Then this parameter value is passed to the column chart query, and the values displayed on the column chart change to display the data for the selected parameter. You also must change the column chart query so the retrieved data is for the parameter value rather than its current search condition, which is WEBSITE. First you will create the parameter for the slices in the pie chart.

tip

If you already created a parameter, the New button to the right of the Set Parameter text box will be named Edit. Clicking the Edit button will allow you to create a new parameter just like when you click the New button.

To create the drill-down parameter:

1 In the Layout Editor, click the pie chart, and then click any one of the pie slices so all the slices are selected as individual objects.

2 Right-click anywhere in the selected objects, and then click **Properties** on the menu. The Object Properties dialog box opens for the REVENUE_slices object.

3 Click the **Drill-down** tab, and then click the **New** button to the right of the Set Parameter text box. The Parameters dialog box opens.

4 Type **selected_source** for the parameter name, and make sure that Char is the data type.

5 Type **WEBSITE** in the Initial Value text box. (This value will change when the chart runs, but an initial value must be entered.) This text is a query search condition so it is case-sensitive. Your completed Parameters dialog box should look like Figure 8-20.

your default parameter name might be different

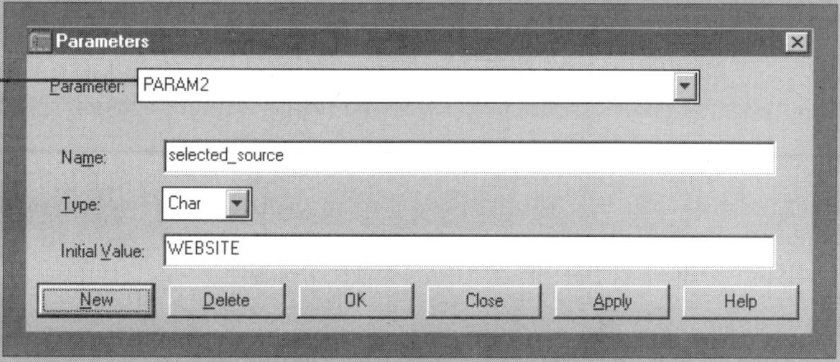

Parameters
Parameter: PARAM2
Name: selected_source
Type: Char
Initial Value: WEBSITE
New | Delete | OK | Close | Apply | Help

Figure 8-20: Creating the parameter

HELP? The initial parameter name in your Parameter text box might be different than the one shown in Figure 8-20. By default, the first parameter you create is labeled PARAM0, the second is PARAM1, etc.

6 Click the **OK** button.

Next you need to specify that the new parameter will be the value for the ORDERSOURCE field in the column chart query, which is the revdetail_query.

To specify the new parameter value:

1 In the Object Properties dialog box, click the **To Value of** list arrow, and then click **ORDERSOURCE**. This specifies that the parameter will take the ORDERSOURCE value of the pie slice that is selected by the user in the pie chart.

2 To specify that the parameter will be used in the column chart revdetail_query, click the **Execute Query** list arrow, and then click **revdetail_query**. Your Object Properties dialog box should look like Figure 8-21. Do not click the OK button yet.

parameter name

parameter value comes from current ORDERSOURCE selection in pie chart

parameter is used in column chart's revdetail_query

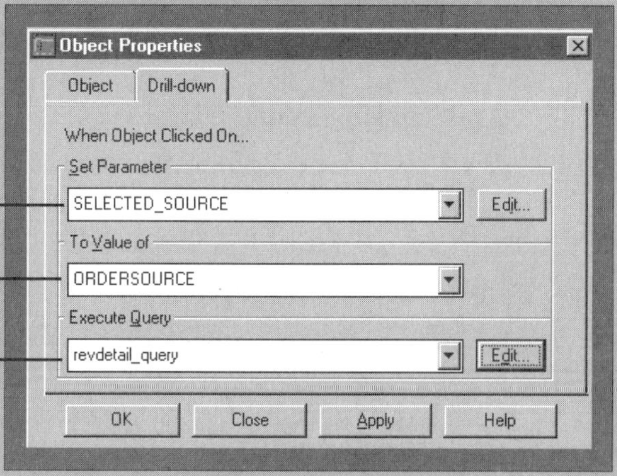

Object Properties
Object | Drill-down
When Object Clicked On...
Set Parameter
SELECTED_SOURCE | Edit...
To Value of
ORDERSOURCE
Execute Query
revdetail_query | Edit...
OK | Close | Apply | Help

Figure 8-21: Specifying the drill-down properties

Finally you need to edit the orderdetail_query so the parameter name is used for the search condition instead of the WEBSITE value that you entered when you originally created the query.

To edit the revdetail_query:

1 In the Object Properties dialog box, click the **Edit** button to the right of the Execute Query text box. The Query Properties dialog box opens. If necessary, click the **Query** tab so you can view the SQL query.

2 Modify the query as shown in Figure 8-22. You will substitute the parameter name (:selected_source) for the initial search condition (WEBSITE).

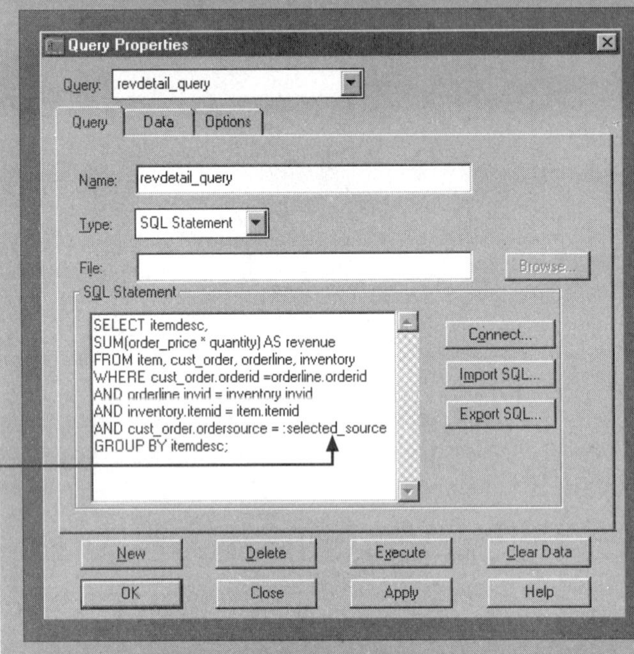

Figure 8-22: Modifying revdetail_query

3 Click the **Apply** button to accept the changes, and then click the **OK** button to close the Query Properties dialog box.

4 Click the **OK** button to close the Object Properties dialog box.

5 Save the file.

Now you can run the chart to confirm that the drill-down relationship works correctly.

To test the drill-down relationship:

1 Run the chart. As you select different pie slices, the values displayed in the column chart are dynamically updated.

HELP? If your drill-down relationship does not work correctly, close the Debugger window, go to the Object Navigator, find the parameter you just created, and then delete it. Repeat the steps to create the parameter. If you still have problems, ask your instructor or technical support person for help.

2 Close the Graphics Runtime application.

3 Close the rev_detl.ogd file.

Creating a Form with an Embedded Graphics Chart

Oracle Graphics charts usually are embedded within forms or reports. In this section, you will learn how to embed charts in these applications and dynamically pass parameters to the chart to change its display.

First you will create a combined Forms/Graphics application where the user selects an item from the Clearwater Traders' ITEM table using a LOV, and the corresponding inventory colors, sizes, and quantities on hand are displayed in an Oracle Graphics column chart. The design sketch for this application is shown in Figure 8-23. The user clicks the LOV button, selects a particular item ID, and the item description displays in the Item Description text box. The associated inventory sizes and colors display as columns on the column chart, and the column height represents the quantity on hand for each inventory item.

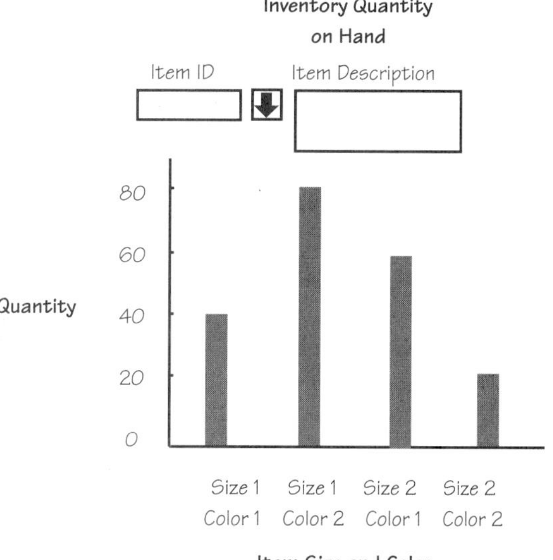

Figure 8-23: Design sketch for form displaying INVENTORY QOH chart

Creating the Graphics Application

First you will create the Graphics column chart to show the size and color information for a particular item ID on the X-axis and the corresponding quantity on hand amount on the Y-axis. The first step is to name and save the Graphics chart.

To name and save the Graphics chart:

1 If necessary, start the Oracle Graphics Designer.

2 In the Object Navigator, create a new display named **inventry.ogd**, and save it to the file system in the Chapter8 folder on your Student Disk.

You need to create a query that shows all item sizes, colors, and quantities on hand for a given item ID. Ultimately, you will pass the item ID as a parameter from the Forms application. For now, you will use item ID 995 as your search condition to make sure that the query works correctly.

To create the query:

1 Go to the Object Navigator window, expand **inventry.ogd**, click **Queries**, and then click the **Create** button on the Object Navigator toolbar.

2 If necessary click the **Query** tab, name the query **inventory_query**, and then type the SQL statement shown in Figure 8-24.

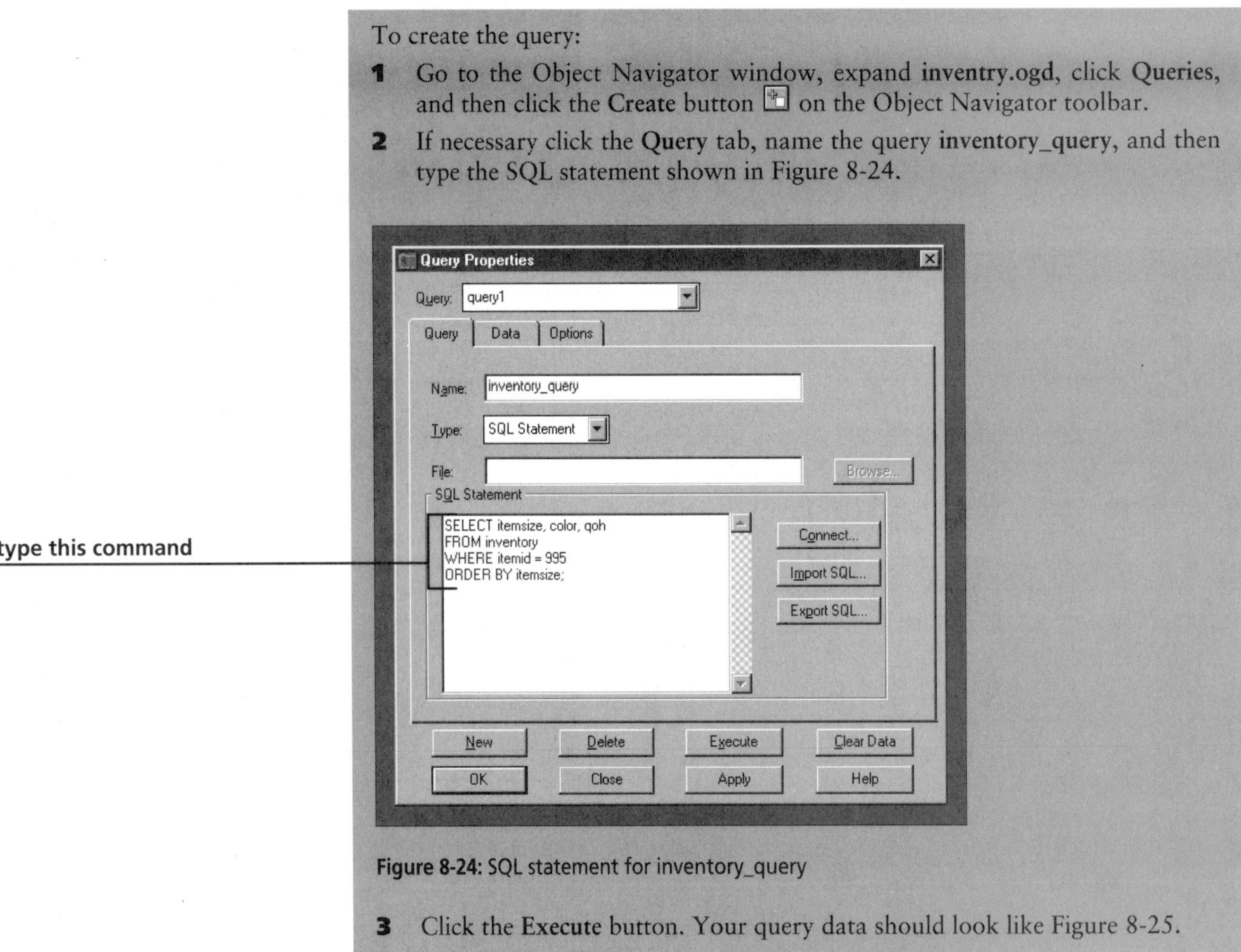

Figure 8-24: SQL statement for inventory_query

3 Click the **Execute** button. Your query data should look like Figure 8-25.

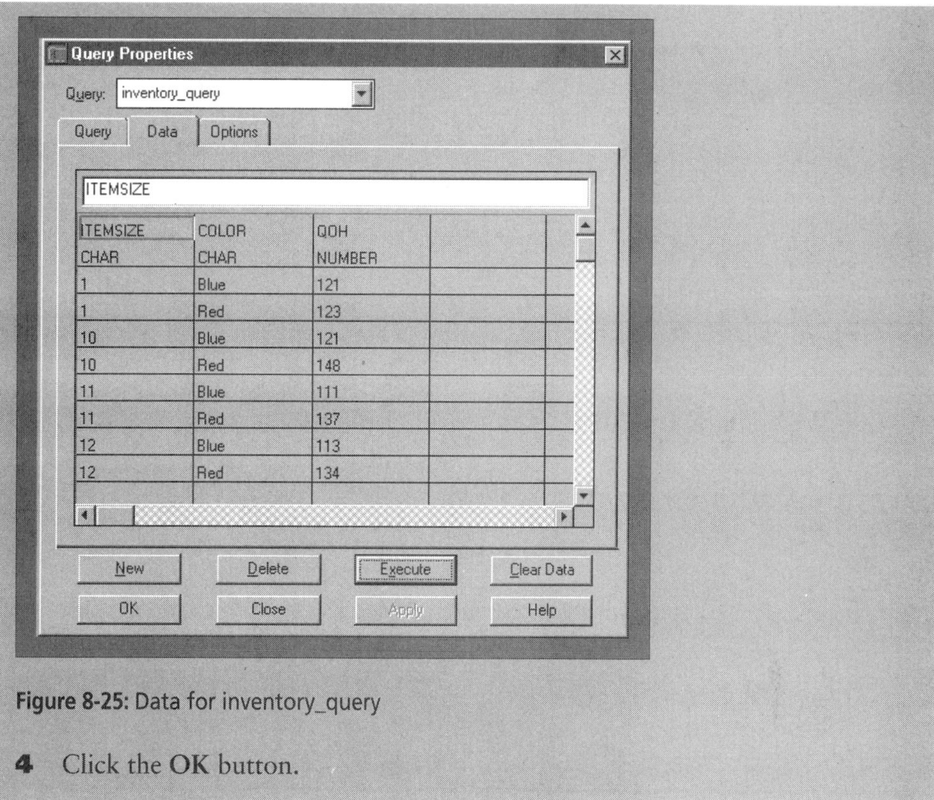

Figure 8-25: Data for inventory_query

4 Click the **OK** button.

Now that you have created the query, the next step is to create the chart layout.

To create the chart layout:

1 Open the Layout Editor, click the **Chart** tool on the Tool palette, and then click anywhere in the blank layout area. Make sure that the **Existing Query** option button is selected and that **inventory_query** is displayed in the query list, and then click the OK button.

2 Name the chart **inventory_chart**, and then type **Inventory Quantity on Hand** as the title.

3 Select a **Column** chart and the **Column with shadows** chart subtype (the last chart in the first subtype row).

4 Click the **Categories** tab. Currently, only the ITEMSIZE will display on the X-axis. Click **COLOR**, and then click the **Insert** button to specify to display both ITEMSIZE and COLOR on the X-axis.

5 Click the **OK** button to create the chart. Your current chart layout should look like Figure 8-26. If necessary, reposition the chart in the Layout Editor window.

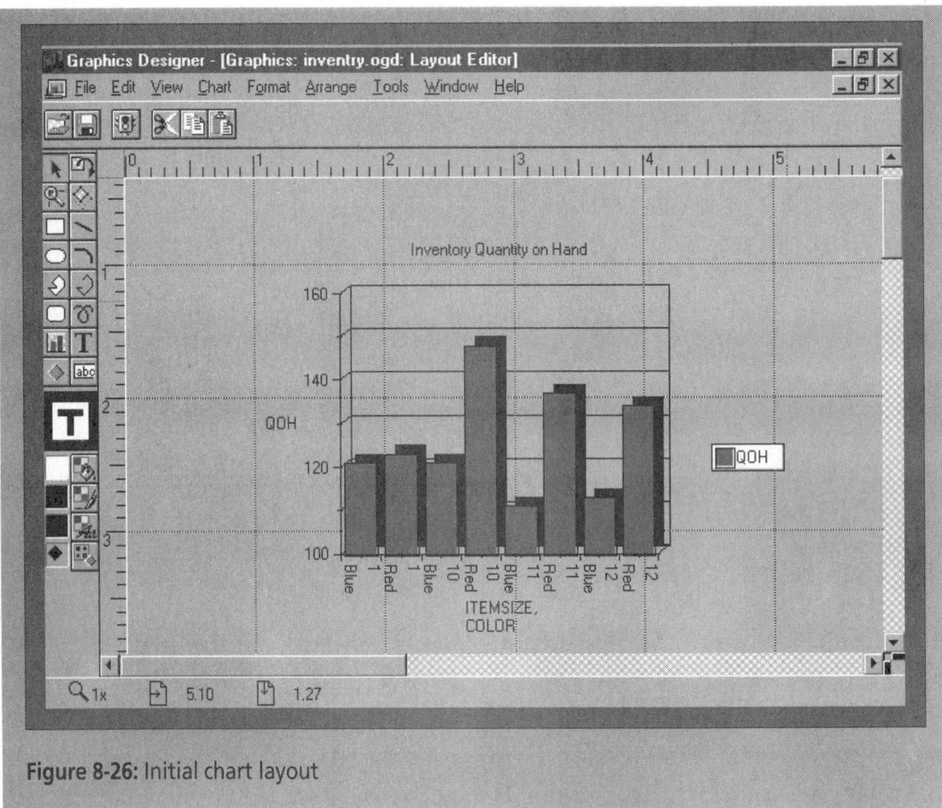

Figure 8-26: Initial chart layout

Next you will need to format the axis labels so they look like Figure 8-23. You will create custom labels for the X- and Y-axis, and then change the orientation of the X-axis tick labels. You also will hide the chart legend and format the label fonts.

To format the axis labels:

1 Select the chart, right-click it, and then click **Axes** on the menu.
2 Select the X-axis, and then change the label to **Item Size and Color**.
3 Click the second **Tick Label Rotation** option button so the labels are displayed horizontally.
4 Clear the **Show Minor Ticks** check box so the minor tick marks are not displayed on the X-axis. Click the **Apply** button to save your changes.
5 Select the Y1-axis, and then change the label to **Quantity**. Click the **Apply** button, and then click the **OK** button.
6 Right-click the chart, and then click **Frame** on the menu. Clear the **Show Legend** check box to hide the legend, and then click the **OK** button.
7 Change the chart title to **10-point bold Arial** font, change the axis titles to **8-point bold Arial** font, and then change the tick mark labels to **8-point regular Arial** font.
8 Save the file and then run the chart. Your formatted chart display should look like Figure 8-27 in the Graphics Runtime application.

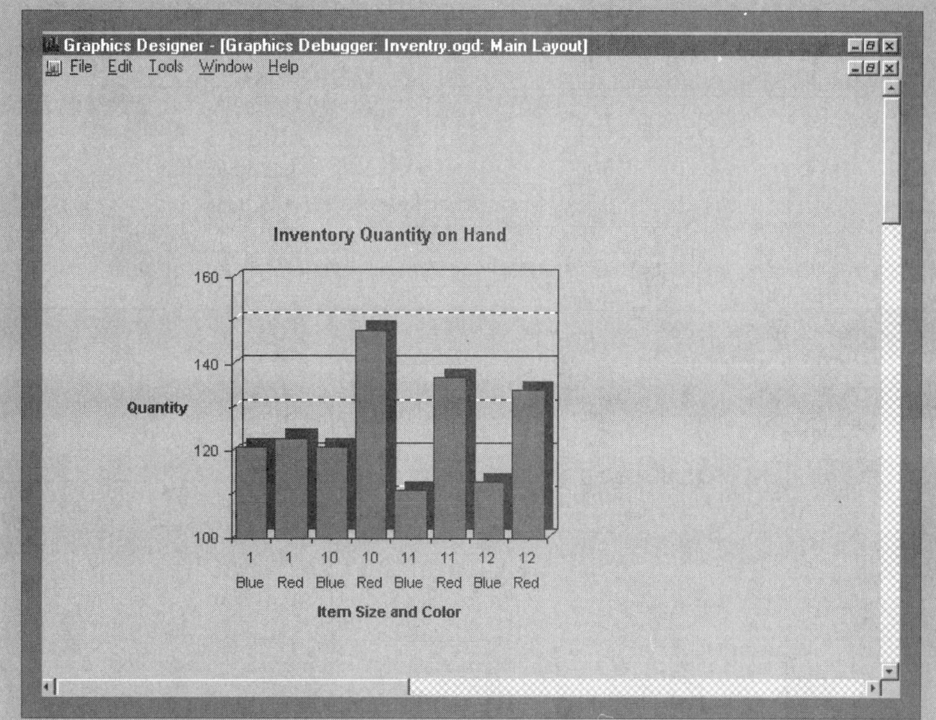

Figure 8-27: Formatted chart in Graphics Runtime application

HELP? Sometimes when you run a chart, you will receive an error message that says "No SQL statement specified." However, your chart still displays successfully and has a working query with a SQL statement. This error is caused by having an additional query that does not contain a SQL statement as a chart object. If you see this error, open the Object Navigator, look under Queries, determine if an extra query exists, and then delete it.

9 Close the Graphics Runtime window.

The final step in creating the chart is to create the input parameter that will be passed to the chart from the Oracle Forms application.

To create the input parameter:

1 Go to the Object Navigator, click **Parameters**, and then click the **Create** button on the Object Navigator toolbar to create a new parameter. The Parameters dialog box opens.

2 Type **item_id** in the Name text box, select **Number** as the data type, and then change the value in the Initial Value text box to **995**, as shown in Figure 8-28.

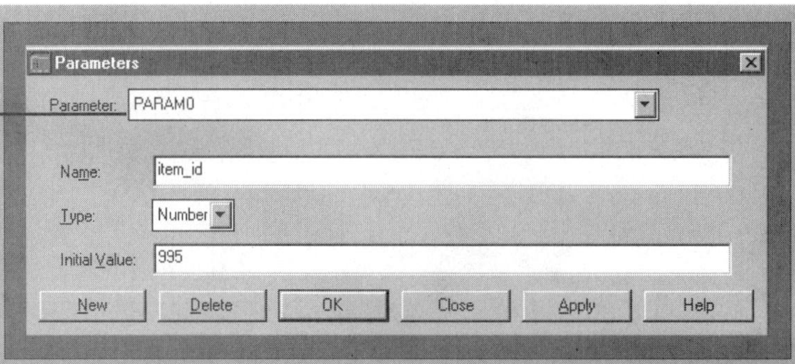

your default parameter name might be different

Figure 8-28: Specifying the query parameter

3 Click the OK button to create the parameter. Now you need to reference the parameter name in the query.

4 In the Object Navigator, double-click the **Query** icon next to inventory_query to open the Query Properties dialog box. Modify the SQL Statement on the Query tab as shown in Figure 8-29 so the query will use the value of the item_id parameter to determine what data the chart displays.

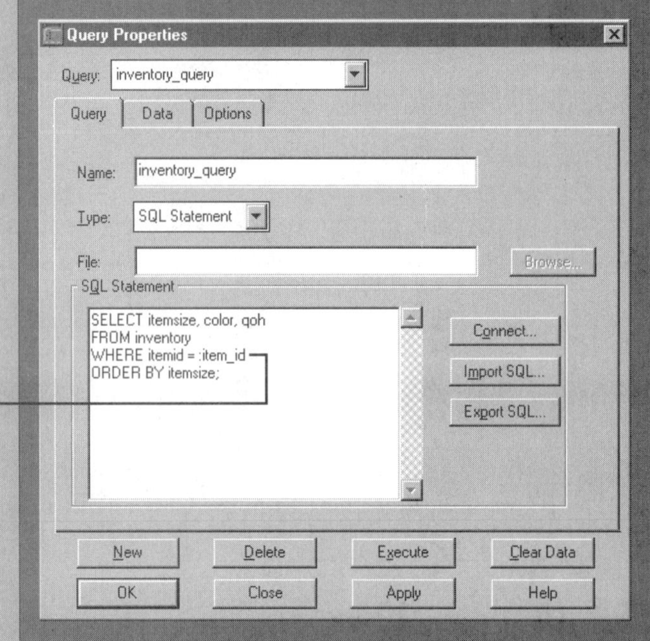

Figure 8-29: Modifying the inventory_query to use the :item_id input parameter

5 Click the **OK** button to save the query change, and then save the file.

6 Run the chart to confirm that the parameter works correctly in the Graphics Runtime application. The chart should still look like Figure 8-27.

HELP? If your chart does not run correctly, close the Graphics Runtime application. Open the item_id Parameters Properties sheet, and make sure that it looks like Figure 8-28. Then open the inventory_query Query Properties sheet, and confirm that the modified query looks like Figure 8-29. If you still have problems, ask your instructor or technical support person for help.

7 Generate the **inventry.ogr** file, and save it in the Chapter8 folder on your Student Disk.

HELP? If the Generate command is dimmed on your menu, open the Layout Editor and then repeat Step 7.

8 Close the Graphics Designer application.

Creating the Forms Application

The Forms application will allow the user to select an item ID and description using a LOV. As soon as the user selects the item, the associated inventory sizes, colors, and associated quantities on hand will appear in a column chart on the form.

To create the form items and LOV:

1 Start the Forms Designer, and then connect to the database.

2 Open the Object Navigator in Visual View, and then create a new form named **CHART_INV**.

3 Create a new window named **CHART_INV_WINDOW**. Resize the window by changing its Width to **640** and Height to **480**, and then change the window title to **Clearwater Traders Inventory QOH**.

4 Create a new canvas named **CHART_INV_CANVAS**. Resize the canvas by changing its Width to **640** and Height to **480**.

5 Go to the Layout Editor, and then create a new control block named **CHART_INV_BLOCK**.

6 Create a text item named **ITEMID_TEXT** to hold the ITEMID field. It should be a **Number** data type, with Maximum Length equal to **8**. Position ITEMID_TEXT as shown in Figure 8-23.

7 Create a text item named **ITEMDESC_TEXT** to hold the ITEMDESC field. It should be a **Char** data type, with Maximum Length equal to **100**, and Multi-Line set as **TRUE** so the item description can wrap to multiple lines if necessary.

8 Create item text labels with the text **Item ID** and **Item Description** and place them above the ITEMID_TEXT and ITEMDESC_TEXT field boxes, as shown in Figure 8-23. Change the labels to **10-point bold Arial** font.

9 Create a form title with the text **Item Quantity on Hand**. Change the label to **12-point bold Arial** font.

10 Save your file as **chart_inv.fmb** in the Chapter8 folder on your Student Disk.

Next you need to create the LOV that will display the item IDs and descriptions and then return the selected values into the ITEMID_TEXT and ITEMDESC_TEXT text fields.

To create the LOV:

1 Open the Object Navigator window in Ownership View, and then create a new LOV. Type the SQL command shown in Figure 8-30 into the Query Text text box, and then click the **OK** button.

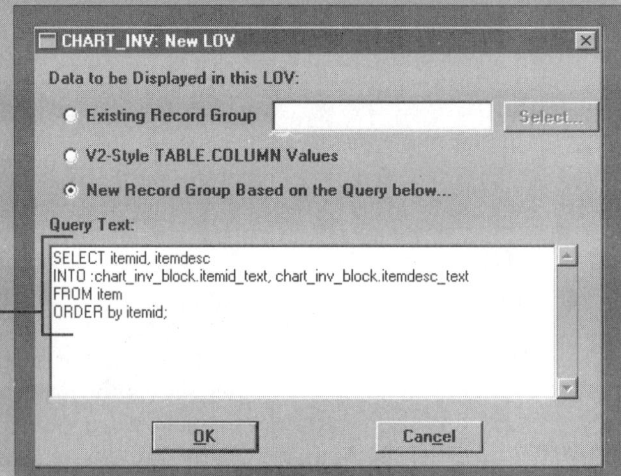

Figure 8-30: Creating the LOV to display item IDs and descriptions

2 Rename the new LOV and record group to **CHART_INV_LOV**.

3 Open the CHART_INV_LOV Properties sheet, and then change the title to **Inventory Items**, the X Position to **125**, and the Y Position to **75**.

4 In the CHART_INV_LOV **(LOV)** Properties sheet, select **Column Mapping**, and then click the **More** button and change the column mapping properties as follows:

Column	**Title**	**Display Width**
ITEMID	Item ID	25
ITEMDESC	Description	150

5 Click the **OK** button to close the Column Mapping dialog box, and then close the CHART_INV_LOV Properties sheet.

6 Click the **Push Button** tool on the Tool palette, draw the LOV button, and then position it on the right edge of the ITEMID_TEXT field. Change its properties as follows:

Name	CHART_INV_LOV_BUTTON
Width and Height	15
Label	<deleted>
Iconic	True
Icon Name	Down

7 Create a WHEN-BUTTON-PRESSED trigger for CHART_INV_LOV_BUTTON with the following code:

```
GO_ITEM('itemid_text');
LIST_VALUES;
```

8 Open the ITEMID_TEXT Properties sheet, and then change the LOV property to **CHART_INV_LOV**.

9 Save the file and then run the form and test the LOV. It should look like Figure 8-31.

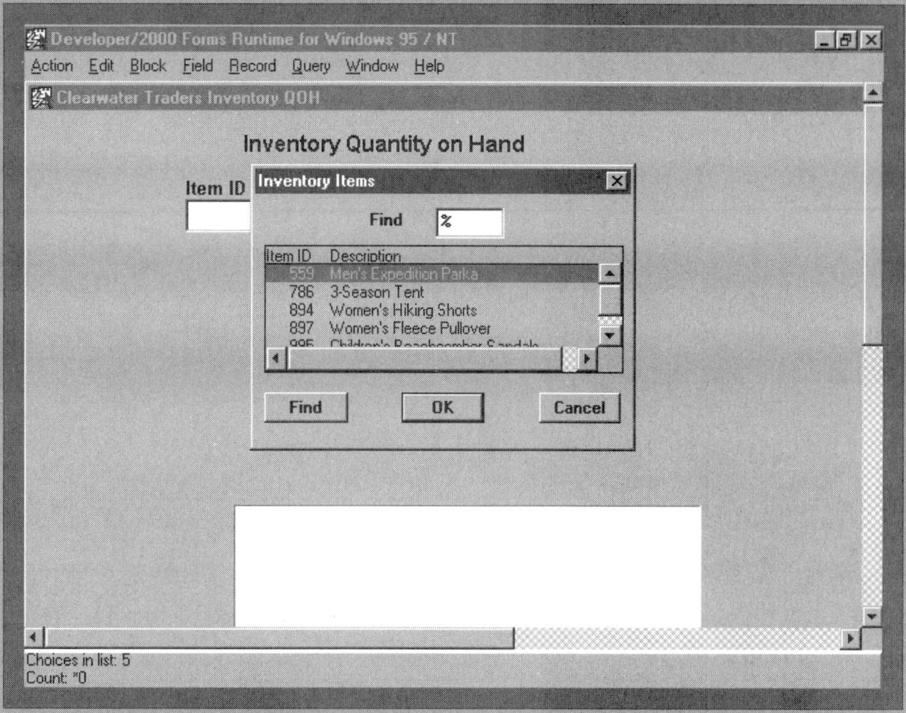

Figure 8-31: CHART_INV_LOV display

10 Close the Forms Runtime application.

Next you will create the chart object on the form to hold the Graphics display that you created previously.

To create the chart object to hold the chart:

1 Open the Layout Editor, click the **Chart** tool on the Tool palette, and then draw a chart object under your text items. Your zoomed-out canvas should look like Figure 8-32.

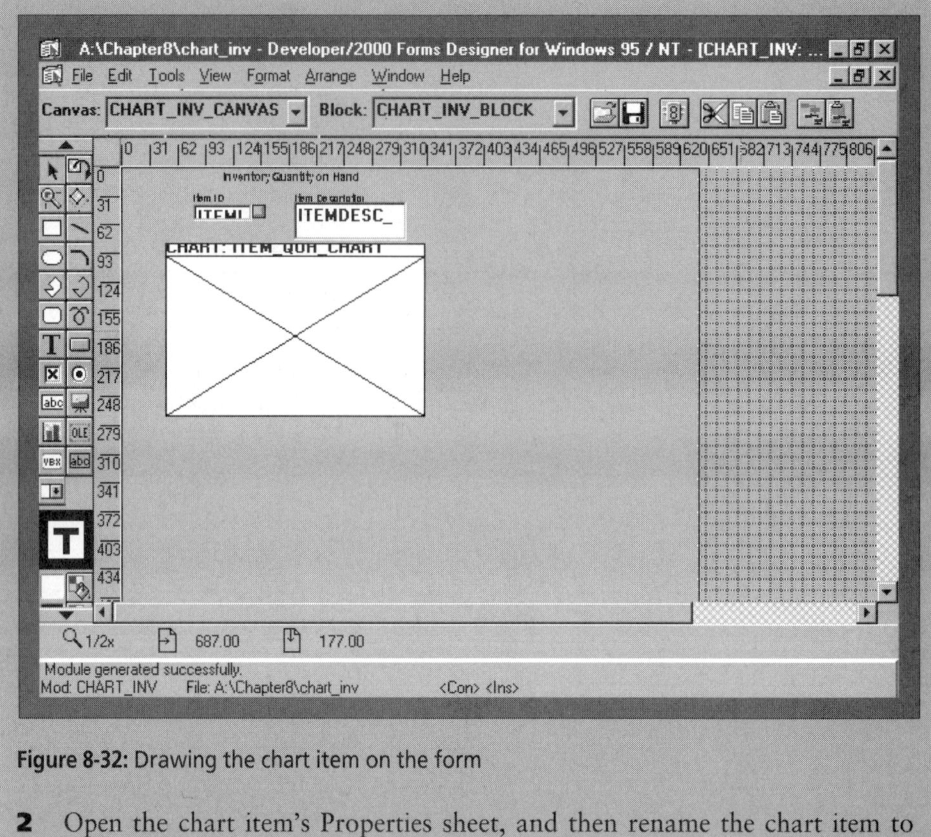

Figure 8-32: Drawing the chart item on the form

2 Open the chart item's Properties sheet, and then rename the chart item to ITEM_QOH_CHART, and then close the Properties sheet.

3 Save the file.

Calling the Graphics File

Now you need to modify the LOV push button trigger so that after the user selects an item the Graphics application is called and the selected item ID is passed as a parameter. You will do this using the Oracle RUN_PRODUCT procedure, which can be used in Oracle Forms to call a Graphics application and pass it the selected item ID using a parameter list.

Creating a Parameter List A **parameter list** is a list of variables that is used to pass data values from one Developer/2000 application to another. Parameter lists are created in triggers or program units using PL/SQL. To create a parameter list, you first have to declare a variable with the data type PARAMLIST to hold the list's internal identifier. You also need to declare a VARCHAR2 variable to hold the list name. These declarations are done in the DECLARE section of the PL/SQL code using the following general code:

```
DECLARE
 --variable to hold internal parameter list id
 param_list_id PARAMLIST;
 --variable to hold parameter list name
 param_list_name VARCHAR2(20);
```

The next step in creating a parameter list is to name the list and then create the list, which is done in the body of the PL/SQL procedure using the following general code:

```
BEGIN
--initialize the parameter list name to any name
param_list_name := 'param_list';
--create the list using this name
param_list_id := CREATE_PARAMETER_LIST(param_list_name);
```

After creating the parameter list, the ADD_PARAMETER procedure is used to add the parameter values to the parameter list using the following general format: `ADD_PARAMETER(LIST, KEY, PARAMTYPE, VALUE);`. This command requires the following items:

- **LIST** is the list ID of the parameter list that you defined when you created the parameter list. In the general code example, this was `param_list_id`.
- **KEY** is the name of the parameter as it was defined in the application it is being passed to. KEY is passed as a character string, so it must be enclosed in single quotation marks. For your inventory_chart, the key is `item_id` because this is the name of the parameter that is expected in the inventory_query (see Figure 8-29).
- **PARAMTYPE** can have a value of either TEXT_PARAMETER or DATA_PARAMETER. The only types of data that can be passed in a parameter list are character strings or record groups. Use TEXT_PARAMETER if the parameter is a character string, or use DATA_PARAMETER if it is a record group name.
- **VALUE** is the actual parameter character string or record group name. In the form you created, you want to pass the value currently stored in ITEMID_TEXT. This would be included in the ADD_PARAMETER command as `chart_inventory_block.textid_text`.

The following code illustrates how to add the current value of ITEMID_TEXT, which is a NUMBER data type, to the parameter list created using the general code example, and how to pass it to the item_id input parameter created in the Graphics chart. Note that because the value you are passing (:`chart_inventory_block.textid_text`) is a NUMBER data type, it must be converted to a CHAR data type first before it can be passed in the parameter list, using the following code:

```
--convert itemid_text to a character variable type
textid_char := to_char(:chart_inv_block.itemid_text);
--add the value of itemid_text to the parameter list
ADD_PARAMETER(param_list_id, 'item_id', TEXT_PARAMETER,
textid_char);
```

Destroying a Parameter List After you finish using a parameter list, you must destroy it or it will remain in the database's memory. The general format of the DESTROY command is `DESTROY_PARAMETER_LIST(param_list_id);`.

Using the RUN_PRODUCT Procedure The RUN_PRODUCT procedure is used to start the Graphics Runtime application and pass it the parameter list. The general format of the RUN_PRODUCT command is:

```
RUN_PRODUCT(PRODUCT, DOCUMENT, COMMUNICATION MODE,
EXECUTION MODE, LOCATION, PARAMETER LIST, DISPLAY);
```

This code requires the following items:

- **PRODUCT** specifies which product you want to run. RUN_PRODUCT can be used to run either Reports or Graphics applications, so its value could be either REPORTS or GRAPHICS.
- **DOCUMENT** specifies the complete path and filename of the Graphics .ogr file, which is specified as a character string enclosed in single quotation marks. If your file is named inventry.ogr and it is stored on drive A in the Chapter8 folder, the DOCUMENT value would be `'A:\Chapter8\inventry.ogr'`.
- **COMMUNICATION MODE** can be either SYNCHRONOUS or ASYNCHRONOUS. **SYNCHRONOUS** specifies that control returns to Oracle Forms only after the called product (Reports or Graphics) has closed. **ASYNCHRONOUS** specifies that control returns to the calling application immediately. For most applications, the SYNCHRONOUS mode is used.
- **EXECUTION MODE** can be either BATCH or RUNTIME. Use **BATCH** when running a Graphics application so the chart is displayed directly in the form chart object and the Graphics Runtime environment is not displayed. Use **RUNTIME** when running a Reports application so control is transferred to the Reports Runtime environment and the user can specify where the display is to be routed (screen, printer, etc.).
- **LOCATION** can be either FILESYSTEM or DB (database), and specifies where the document to be run is stored. Oracle Corporation has not yet implemented the DB option, so all documents used in the RUN_PRODUCT command must be stored in the file system at this time.
- **PARAMETER LIST** is the ID of the parameter list to be passed, if there is one. If there is no parameter list, this value must be passed as NULL.
- **DISPLAY** is needed only when you are running a Graphics chart. DISPLAY specifies the name of the Oracle Forms chart item that will contain the Oracle Graphics display. The name of the chart item must be specified in the format `block_name.item_name`. For the CHART_INV form, this value will be `chart_inv_block.item_qoh_chart`.

The command to run the Oracle Graphics inventory_chart you created (assuming it is stored on drive A in the Chapter8 folder) is:

```
RUN_PRODUCT (GRAPHICS, 'a:\chapter8\inventry.ogr',
SYNCHRONOUS, BATCH, FILESYSTEM, param_list_id,
'chart_inv_block.item_qoh_chart');
```

Modifying the LOV Trigger

Now you will put these commands into the LOV button's WHEN-BUTTON-PRESSED trigger so that when the user clicks the button, the LOV will be displayed, and then the selected value will appear in a parameter list and pass to the Oracle Graphics application.

To modify the LOV button trigger and test the form:

1 Right-click the **CHART_INV_LOV** button, and then click **PL/SQL Editor** on the menu. Add the DECLARE section above the existing trigger code as shown in Figure 8-33.

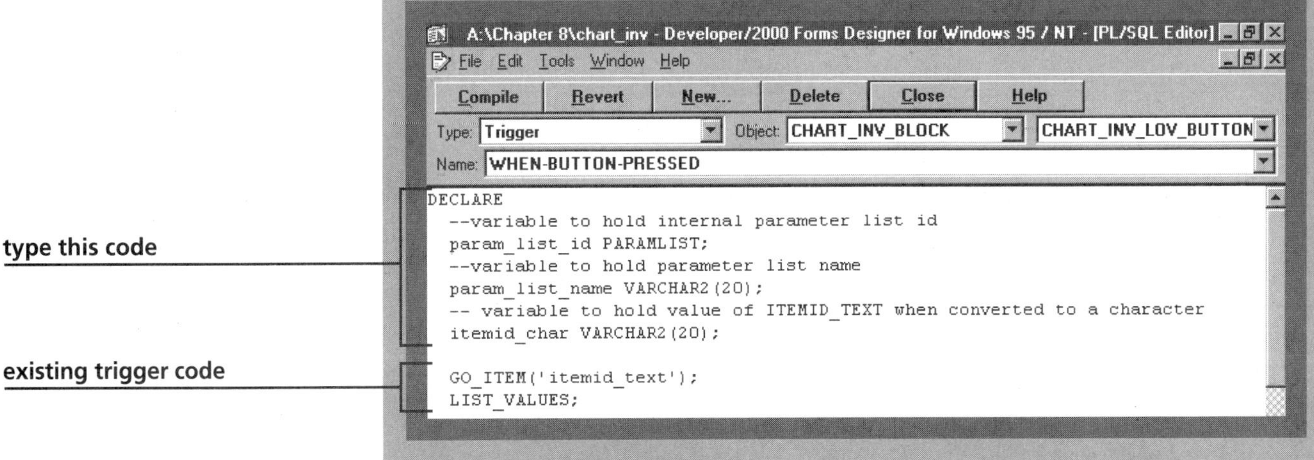

Figure 8-33: Adding the DECLARE section to the LOV button trigger

2 Modify the body of the trigger as shown in Figure 8-34.

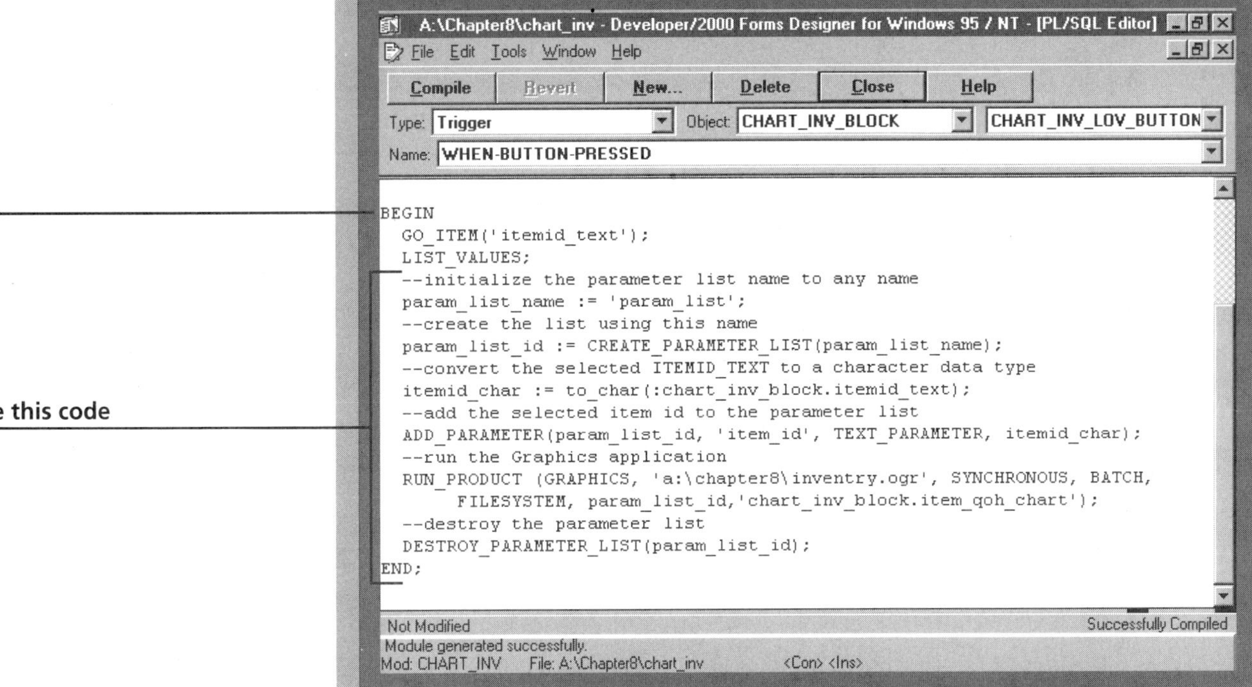

Figure 8-34: Modifying the body of the LOV button trigger

3 Compile the trigger, correct any syntax errors, and then close the PL/SQL Editor.

4 Save the file and then run the form.

5 Select Item ID 995 (Children's Beachcomber Sandals). Your form display should look like Figure 8-35.

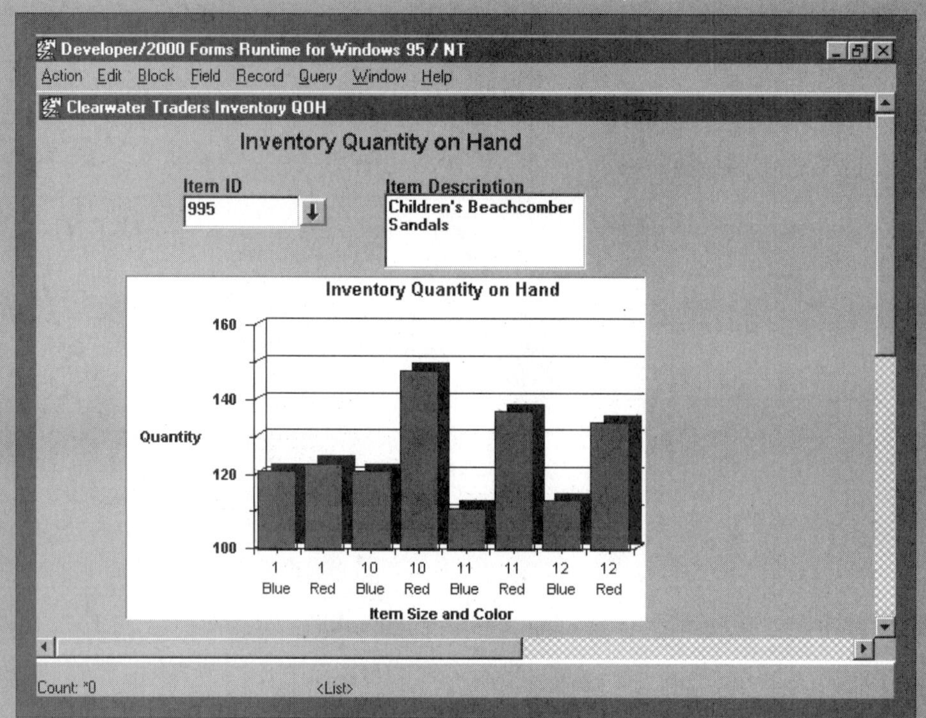

Figure 8-35: Completed Forms/Graphics application

6 Click the **LOV** button to select some of the other items to confirm that the Graphics chart updates correctly.

HELP? If your chart does not display, exit the Forms Runtime application and examine the LOV button trigger in the PL/SQL Editor to confirm that you modified your trigger exactly as shown in Figures 8-33 and Figure 8-34. Also make sure that your Graphics application is on your Student Disk as A:\Chapter8\inventry.ogr. If you still have problems, ask your instructor or technical support person for help.

7 Close the Forms Runtime application.

8 Close the Forms Designer application.

9 Click the **Oracle Graphics Batch** application command button on the taskbar, and then close the application. This application starts whenever you call a Graphics application using the RUN_PRODUCT command using the BATCH execution mode.

Creating a Report with an Embedded Graphics Chart

Next you will create a report that contains a graphics chart to display some of the report data visually. Clearwater Traders needs an inventory report that shows each item ID and description; lists all of the associated inventory numbers, sizes, colors, current prices, and quantities on hand; and provides a chart that shows the associated quantity on hand for each inventory item size/color combination. The design sketch for this report is shown in Figure 8-36. The report data appears in a master/detail layout on the left side of the page, with the item information as the master record and the inventory information as repeating the detail records. The chart shows the size, color, and quantity on hand information visually. To create this inventory report, you will embed the inventory_chart that you created into a report that displays the data textually. The first step is to create the report.

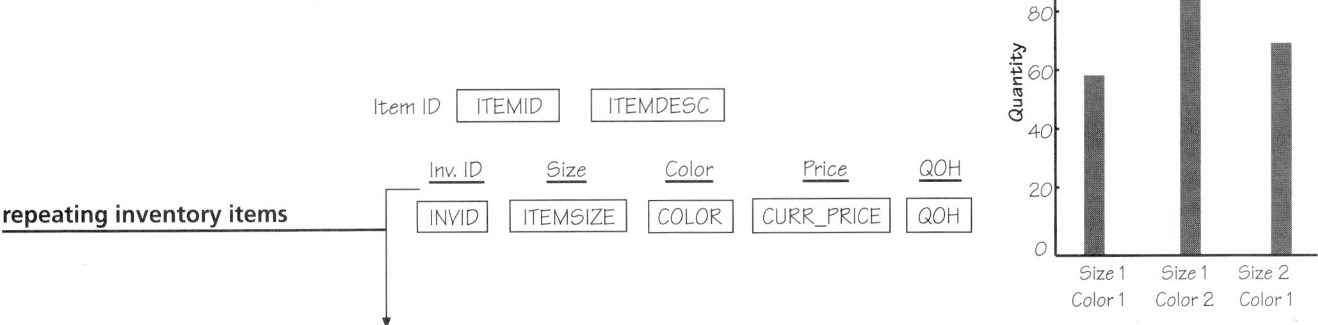

Figure 8-36: Design sketch for report with chart display

To create the report:

1. Start the Reports Designer, and then connect to the database.
2. Create a new report named **chart_rep.rdf**, and save it in the Chapter8 folder on your Student Disk.

Now you need to create a query to show item IDs and descriptions and their associated inventory numbers, sizes, colors, current prices, and quantities on hand.

To create the query:

1. Go to the Data Model Editor.
2. Create a new query named **Q_inventory**, and then type the SELECT statement shown in Figure 8-37 to retrieve the report data.

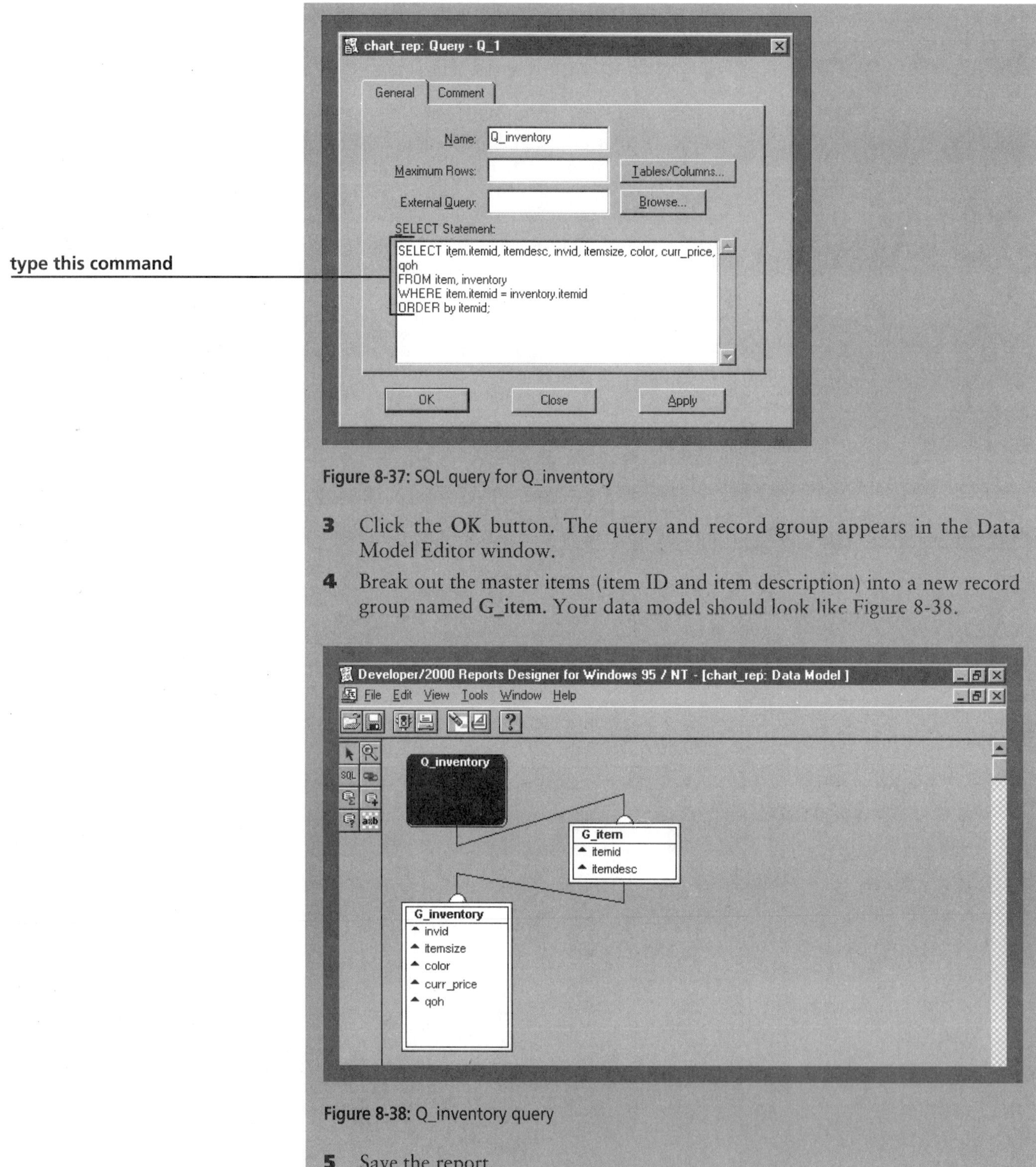

Figure 8-37: SQL query for Q_inventory

3 Click the OK button. The query and record group appears in the Data Model Editor window.

4 Break out the master items (item ID and item description) into a new record group named **G_item**. Your data model should look like Figure 8-38.

Figure 8-38: Q_inventory query

5 Save the report.

Next you will specify the report layout using a master/detail default layout. From the design sketch (see Figure 8-23), you see that you need to delete the label for the ITEMDESC, and change the labels for the other columns.

To specify the report layout:

1. Go to the Layout Editor, and change the default font to **8-point regular Arial Narrow** and the page layout to portrait. Change the fill color to **No Fill** and the line color to **No Line.**
2. Click the **Default Layout** button on the Layout Editor toolbar, and then specify a **Master/Detail** style.
3. Click the **Data/Selection** tab, and then change the column titles and widths as follows:

Column	Title	W(idth)
ITEMID	Item ID	10
ITEMDESC	<deleted>	20
INVID	Inv. ID	6
ITEMSIZE	Size	6
COLOR	Color	10
CURR_PRICE	Price	8
QOH	QOH	6

4. Click the **OK** button to generate the layout.
5. Run the report to the screen to confirm that the fields are displayed correctly. Your layout should look like Figure 8-39.

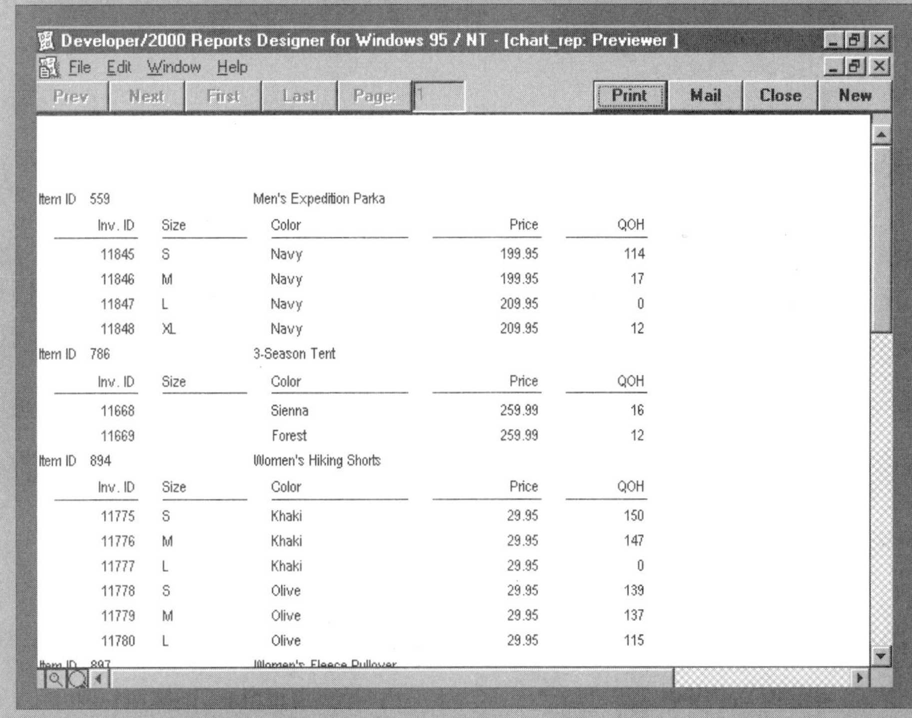

Figure 8-39: Initial report layout

6. Close the Previewer window, and then save the report.

Next you will format the ITEM field and label fonts so they are emphasized, and enlarge the report frames so they are large enough to hold the chart item.

To format the report:

1 Format the item ID field and label and the item description field in an **8-point bold Arial Narrow** font.

2 Zoom in on your layout, and then enlarge the outermost frame (**M_item_GRPFR**) and next frame inside (**R_item**) so you can distinguish between them in a zoomed-out view.

3 Zoom out so you can see the entire page width.

4 Enlarge **M_item_GRPFR** so it is about 3" long and 8" wide.

5 Enlarge **R_item** so it is almost as large as M_item_GRPFR.

6 Open the **R_item** Properties sheet, and then type **2** in the Maximum Records per Page text box so only two records will display per page, so the inventory chart will print next to its text display. Change the vertical spacing to **1** inch, and then click the **OK** button to close the Properties sheet.

Next you need to create a graphics display item on the report layout to hold the chart.

To create the graphics display item:

1 Click the **Graphics Display** tool on the Tool palette, and then draw a graphics display item to the right of the data fields inside the R_item frame (because the graphics display will repeat for each item record group). Your layout should look like Figure 8-40.

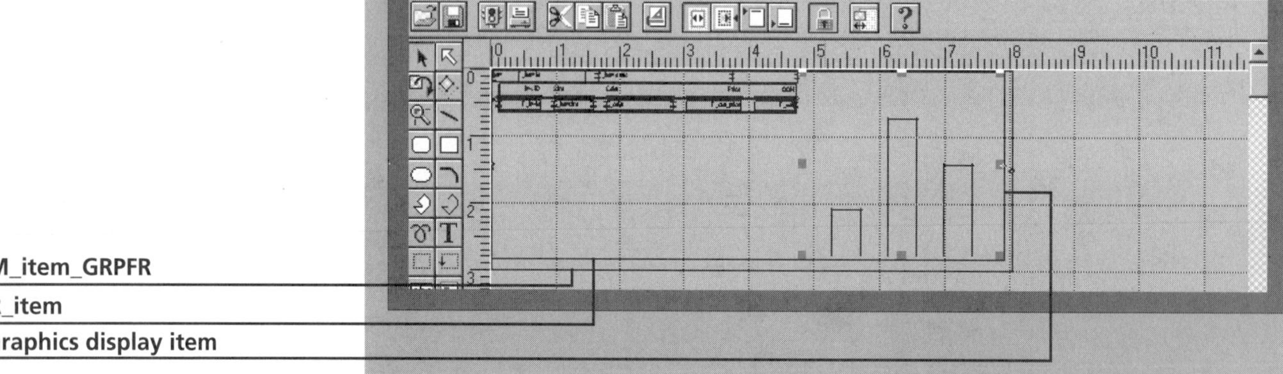

Figure 8-40: Creating the graphics display item

2 Right-click the new graphics display item, and then click **Properties** on the menu.

3 Rename the item to **D_inventory_chart**, *but do not click the OK button.*

Now you need to connect the D_inventory_chart graphics display item to the inventry.ogd Graphics file you created earlier. First you will specify the filename in the Display Name text box.

When you are linking a report to a form chart display item, use the design (.ogd) file rather than the executable (.ogr) file.

To create the report/graphic link:

1 Click the **Browse** button in the D_inventory_chart Properties dialog box, click the **inventry.ogd** file in the Chapter8 folder on your Student Disk, and then click the **Open** button. The filename appears in the Display Name text box, as shown in Figure 8-41. *Do not click the OK button.*

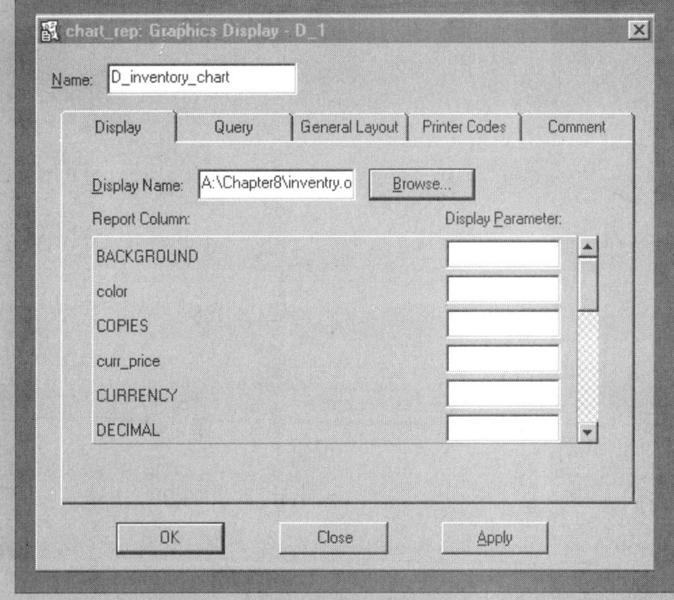

Figure 8-41: Specifying the Graphics .ogd file

Next you need to create a link between the data fields in the current report record and the data that is displayed in the chart adjacent to the records. There are two approaches to doing this—using the data that already has been retrieved by the report, or using one of the report values as an input parameter, and then re-querying the database to generate the chart display. First you will learn how to use the data that already have been retrieved by the report.

To instruct the chart to use the retrieved data values that are displayed in the report record, you first specify the name of record group in the report, which will be the data source, and the associated chart query, which will be the data recipient. Then you link the appropriate report record group fields to their associated chart display columns.

To use the report's data to generate the chart display:

1 Click the **Query** tab. First you will enter the name of the query that is displayed by the chart. This is the query name that you specified in the Graphics file.

2 Type **inventory_query** in the Display Query text box. Next you will specify the record group in the report that will be the data source for the query.

3 Click the **Source** list arrow, and then click **G_inventory**. The G-inventory record group provides the data (item size, color, quantity on hand) that will be displayed in the chart. Now you will select the specific report record group source data columns.

4 Click **color** in the Report Column list to select it, scroll down, and then click the **itemsize** and **qoh** columns to specify the report data values that will be displayed in the chart. The next step generally is to specify the associated display column names. However, you don't need to change the display column names because the column names in both the Graphics and Report queries have the same names as the database fields. If you renamed one of the columns in either the report or the chart using the SQL AS clause, you would link the different names using the Display Column text box. Your completed Query tab should look like Figure 8-42.

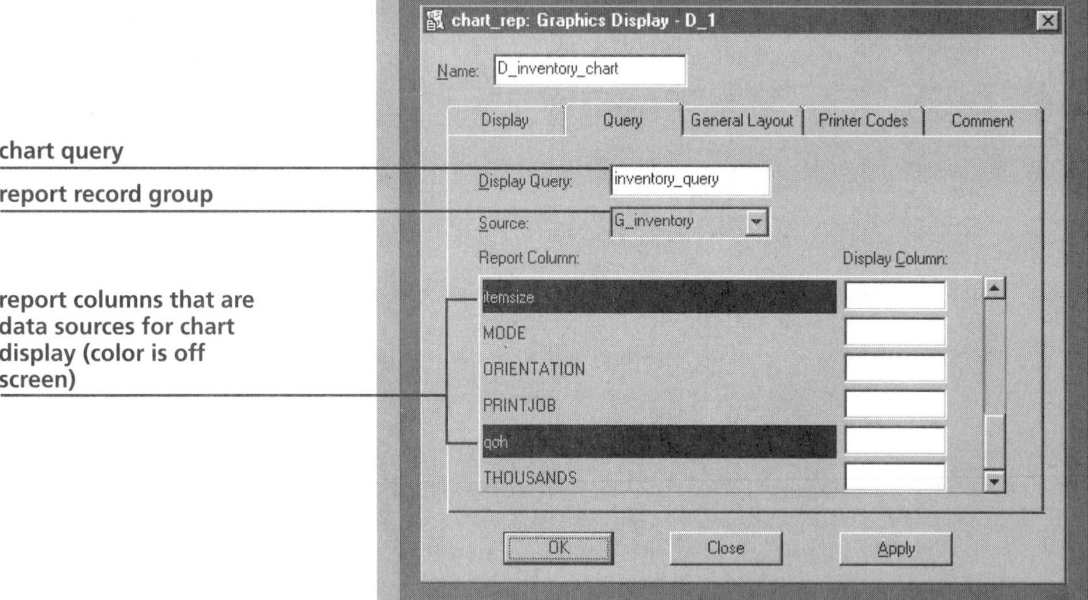

Figure 8-42: Specifying the chart data using the report data

5 Click the **OK** button.

6 Save the report and then run the report to the screen. The first page of your output should look like Figure 8-43.

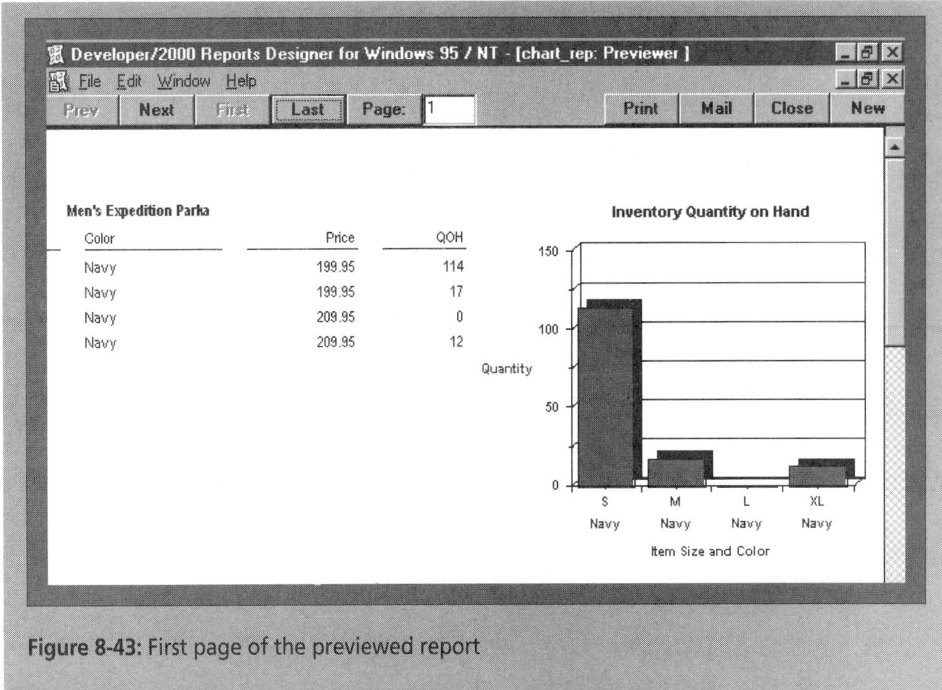

Figure 8-43: First page of the previewed report

7 Close the Previewer window.

The advantage to using the report data to generate the chart display is that the same data is used in both the report and the chart, so the data is retrieved from the database and sent over the network only once. However, this approach won't work when you want to display data in the chart that isn't shown in the report. In that case, you will have to create a link between the current report record to the chart's input parameter by passing the current value of ITEMID to the item_id input parameter in the chart. To do this, you will delete the current graphics display item on the report and create a new one because it is difficult to modify the existing chart object so it will run correctly. Then you will specify the input parameter on the new graphics display item's Properties sheet.

To generate the chart display using the input parameter:

1 Save your report as **chart_ip.rdf** in the Chapter8 folder on your Student Disk.

2 In the Layout Editor, delete the **D_inventory_chart** item.

3 Create another graphics display item in the same place as the D_inventory_chart was on the report, open the Properties sheet for the new graphics display, and then name it **D_inventory_chart.**

4 Click the **Browse** button, click the **inventry.ogd** file in the Chapter8 folder on your Student Disk, and then click the **Open** button.

5 Scroll down in the Report Column list until you find **itemid**, and then click it.

6 Type **item_id** (the parameter name from the Graphics chart, as shown in Figure 8-29) in the Display Parameter text box. Your Properties sheet should look like Figure 8-44.

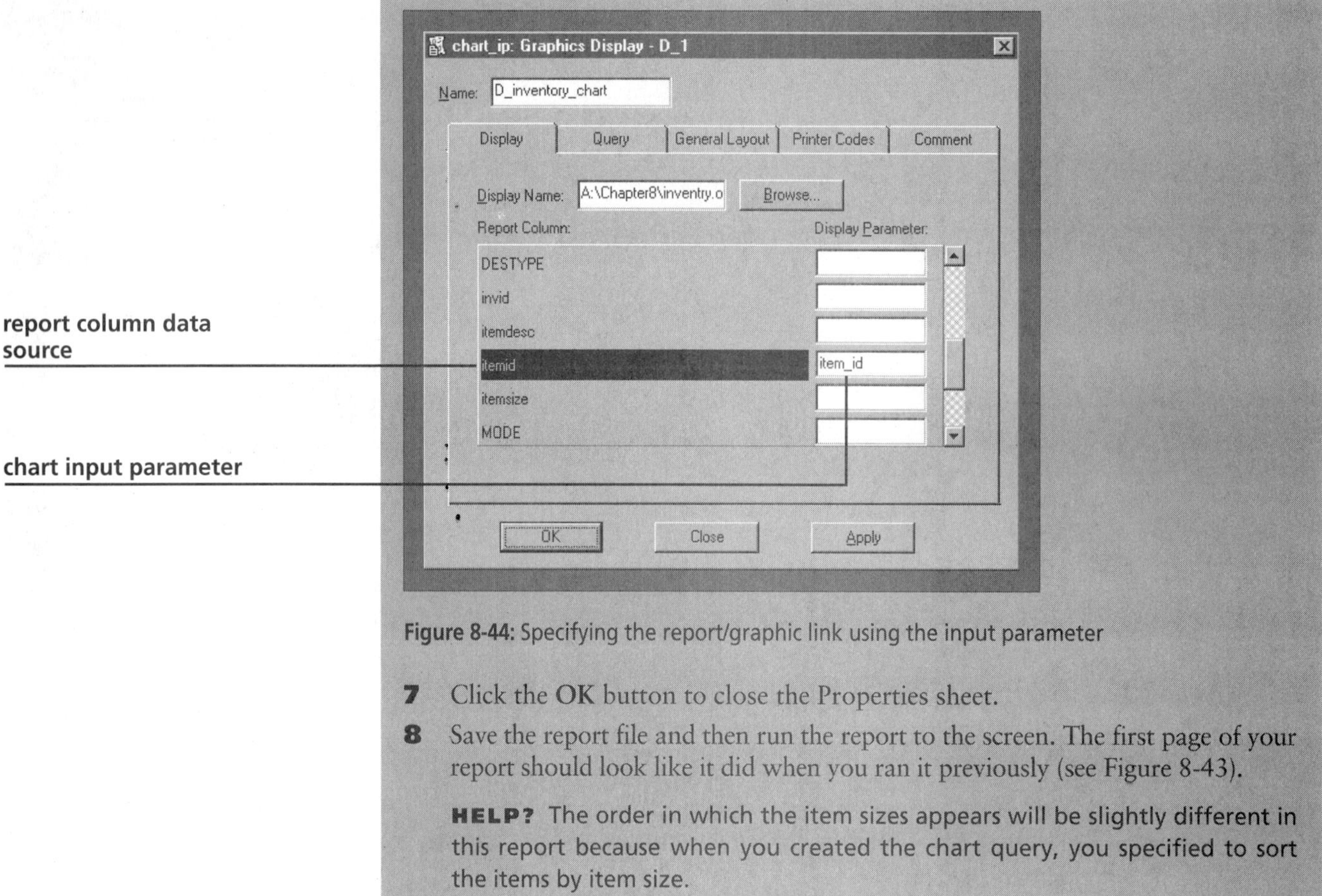

Figure 8-44: Specifying the report/graphic link using the input parameter

7 Click the **OK** button to close the Properties sheet.

8 Save the report file and then run the report to the screen. The first page of your report should look like it did when you ran it previously (see Figure 8-43).

HELP? The order in which the item sizes appears will be slightly different in this report because when you created the chart query, you specified to sort the items by item size.

The disadvantage to using input parameters to generate chart data is that when you generate the report, the database must send the same information to the client workstation twice—once for the report and once for the chart. For a report with thousands of records, the required time and network traffic generated by transmitting all of the data twice mandates that you use this approach only if the report doesn't contain all of the data required in the chart display.

Now you can close the applications.

To close Oracle Reports:

1 Close the screen display.

2 Exit the Reports Designer.

3 Click the Oracle Graphics Batch button on the taskbar, and then close the application.

SUMMARY

- To change the name of an Oracle Graphics chart display, save the chart to the database or file system using the desired name.
- To create a new chart, create the query to define the chart, and then define the chart display properties.
- For pie charts, the different pie slices will be the values of one query data column, and their corresponding numerical contribution to the whole pie will be the values in the second query column.
- For column charts, the X-axis item labels will be the values of one query data column, and their Y-axis values will be the values in the second query column.
- When creating calculated column values using SQL arithmetic or aggregate functions in Oracle Graphics, you should assign the calculated column an alias using the SQL AS clause.
- Oracle Graphics allows you to save Graphics charts both as design files (with an .ogd extension) and as finished executable files (with an .ogr extension).
- A drill-down relationship can be created for any two charts that have a master/detail relationship where one chart specifies different values that the user can select from to be a search condition for the second chart's query.
- Use the Oracle RUN_PRODUCT procedure to run Reports or Graphics applications from Oracle Forms. A parameter list is used to pass parameters in the RUN_PRODUCT procedure. Parameter lists can pass values only as character data types. After you are finished using a parameter list, you must destroy it or it will remain in the database's memory.
- In the RUN_PRODUCT procedure, use the BATCH execution mode when running an Oracle Graphics application.
- You can link the current report record to an embedded Graphics display using either the Graphics display input parameters or the current report data. The disadvantage to using input parameters is that when you generate the report, the database must send the same information to the client station twice—once for the report, and once for the chart.
- The only time you cannot use current report data in a Graphics display is when the chart requires data that is not in the report.

REVIEW QUESTIONS

1. What are the ten different types of charts you can create using Oracle Graphics, and how would you use each one?
2. How can you change the name of a chart display?
3. What columns does a pie chart query need to return?
4. What columns does a column chart query need to return?
5. What data types does Oracle Graphics allow you to apply format masks to?
6. What is the difference between an .ogd and an .ogr file?
7. What is a drill-down relationship?
8. What procedure do you use to call an Oracle Reports or Graphics application from Oracle Forms?
9. What is a parameter list?

10. Why do you need to destroy parameter lists?
11. What data type(s) can be passed in a parameter list?
12. What are the two methods for linking the current report data to an embedded Graphic display, and when should you use each approach?

PROBLEM-SOLVING CASES

Save the files that you create in the cases in the Chapter8 folder on your Student Disk.

Northwoods University

1. Create a pie chart named location.ogd that shows each building code as a pie slice, with the total capacity of the building's rooms as the proportion of the pie. List the total capacity of each building as a label on the pie chart. Change the chart title to "Building Capacities."
2. Create a column chart named faculty.ogd that shows the faculty ranks (ASSO, FULL, INST, ASST) on the X-axis, and shows how many faculty members there are in each rank as column values on the Y-axis. (*Hint*: Use the SQL COUNT(*) function, and modify the Y-axis so it is specified as a continuous axis on the Axes Properties sheet.) Give the chart a descriptive title and custom axis labels, and delete the legend.
3. Open the location.ogd file you created in Exercise 1, and save it as loc_detl.ogd. Then create a bar chart on the layout that shows building room numbers on the X axis and room capacities on the Y axis. Create a drill-down relationship so that when you select a given building's pie slice you see the selected building's room numbers and capacities. Provide a descriptive title for the chart, add custom axis labels, and delete the legend.
4. Modify your faculty.ogd chart from Exercise 2 to include a table chart showing faculty member last and first names and middle initials. Create a drill-down relationship so that when you select a given faculty rank on the column chart the data for faculty members with the selected rank is displayed. Save the modified chart as faculty2.ogd.
5. Create a Forms file named crs_enrl.fmb that allows a user to select a given course call ID and name using a LOV. Depending on the selected course, create an embedded Oracle Graphics column chart that shows the term description on the X-axis and the current enrollment figure for the course for the term on the Y-axis. Provide a descriptive title for the chart, add custom axis labels, and delete the legend. Format your form using the form formatting checklist at the end of Chapter 5.
6. Modify Exercise 5 so that the enrollment figures are shown in a line chart rather than in a column chart. Save the modified file as l_enrl.fmb.
7. Create a report named location.rdf that lists all building codes, room numbers, and their capacities. Create an embedded Graphics column chart on the report that shows each building's room numbers on the X-axis and capacities on the Y-axis. Provide a descriptive title for the chart, add custom axis labels, and delete the legend.
8. Create a report named cur_enrl.rdf that lists each term and for each term lists each offered course call ID and name. For each course, the report then should list all of the offered section numbers, maximum enrollments, and current enrollments. Create an embedded column chart that shows the section numbers on the X-axis and the associated maximum and current enrollments as grouped columns on the Y-axis. (*Hint:* Specify the displayed columns on the Values tab of the chart Properties sheet.) Provide a descriptive title for the chart, add custom axis labels, and delete the legend.

Chapter 9

objectives

- Design a database user interface
- Use timers in an Oracle Forms application to create a splash screen
- Create custom picture buttons
- Use the CALL_FORM procedure to call one Oracle Forms application from another
- Create an Oracle Forms application that starts and passes data values to a report
- Create pull-down menus
- Specify different pull-down menu modules in called forms

CHAPTER 9

Creating an Integrated Database Application

Introduction Now that you have created a variety of individual forms and reports, you can integrate them into a database application that allows users to access all of the individual forms and reports from a single entry point. The user interface will be a separate Oracle Forms application that will serve as the starting point for the individual Forms, Reports, and Graphics applications.

Organizing the Forms and Reports

tip

When you create your own integrated database applications, make sure that your application files are in the same folder. You must modify all applications that reference other applications so they find the referenced files in the correct drive and folder.

When you create an integrated database application, all of the called forms and reports must be on the same disk and in the same folder. All of the executable files required for this chapter are saved in the Chapter9 folder on your Student Disk. Also, all applications that call other applications must have been modified so they access the called applications from this folder. CHART_INV has been modified so it calls the inventry.ogr Graphics file from the Chapter9 folder instead of the Chapter8 folder, and CHART_REP has been modified in the same way so it calls the inventry.ogd Graphics application from the Chapter9 folder instead of the Chapter8 folder.

Your integrated database application will be for the Clearwater Traders database. Figure 9-1 summarizes the forms, reports, and graphics that you created for Clearwater Traders that will be used in the integrated application.

Name	Location	Description
CUSTOMER_FORM	A:\Chapter6\custmod.fmx	Displays and edits CUSTOMER data records using a custom form
CUSTITEM_FORM	A:\Chapter5\custitem.fmx	Displays and edits ITEM data records using a custom form
CUSTINV_FORM	A:\Chapter5\custinv.fmx	Displays and edits INVENTORY data records using a custom form and displays associated ITEM foreign key records
RECEIVING_FORM	A:\Chapter6\receivng.fmx	Records information about new inventory item shipments in the INVENTORY, SHIPPING, and BACKORDER tables
SALES_FORM	A:\Chapter6\sales.fmx	Records information about new customer sales orders in the CUST_ORDER, ORDERLINE, and INVENTORY tables
CHART_INV	A:\Chapter8\chart_inv.fmx and A:\Chapter8\inventry.ogr	Form that displays a column chart showing quantities on hand of different inventory items for a selected product
ORD_SRCE	A:\Chapter8\ord_srce.ogr and A:\Chapter8\rev_detl.ogr	Drill-down graphics application that shows total revenue from different order sources in a pie chart and related inventory detail information in a column chart
CHART_REP	A:\Chapter8\chart_rep.rdf and A:\Chapter8\inventry.ogd	Report that displays ITEM and INVENTORY information with an embedded chart that shows the size, color, and quantity on hand information

Figure 9-1: Summary of items to be used in the integrated database application

Designing the Main Application Screen

The first step is to design the main application screen that lets users access the different forms and reports. A database application should have a front-end entry screen, or splash screen, to introduce the application. The main application screen also needs a **switchboard** that enables fast and easy access to commonly used features that can be implemented using picture buttons with descriptive icons and labels. All application functions should also be accessible through pull-down menus for users who prefer to use the keyboard rather than the mouse pointer. Pull-down menus provide access to less-used features and to features that have multiple levels of choices. For example, you could have a pull-down menu titled Reports, and then the next level menu would list the different report titles that the system could generate.

Figure 9-2 shows a design sketch for the main application screen for the Clearwater Traders order processing system. The two main business processes—processing new orders and receiving incoming shipments—have switchboard access using picture buttons. The associated .fmx files that each picture button will call are shown beside the picture button labels to help speed up the implementation process later.

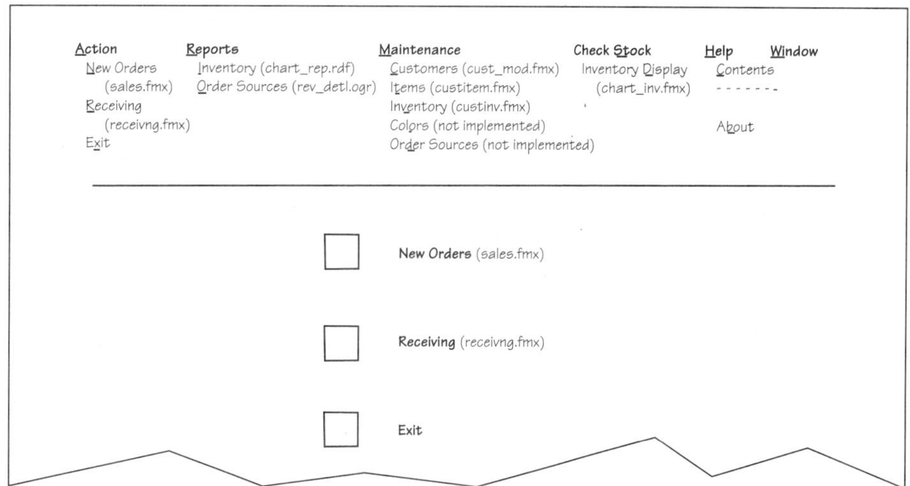

Figure 9-2: Main application screen design

The first pull-down menu selection is Action. This menu contains selections for processing new orders and incoming shipments, and an Exit command. Note that every pull-down menu choice contains an underlined letter. These letters are the access keys that users can press to access the main menu choice through the keyboard by pressing the Alt key and the specified key (for example, Alt + A + X exits the system). Every main menu selection will have a unique access key.

The Reports pull-down menu provides access to the Inventory and Order Sources reports. The Maintenance pull-down menu provides access to the basic forms that let users insert, update, and delete records from each database table. Note that forms for two of the selections (Colors and Order Sources) have not been implemented yet. You will learn how to develop **stubs**, or programs that handle undeveloped system features, later in this chapter.

The Check Stock pull-down menu provides access to the combined Forms/Graphics inventory display application that allows users to select a given item number, and then see the stock levels of the associated inventory items graphically. The Check Stock menu command is included as a pull-down selection

tip

Most GUI applications have Help as the last menu choice, but Oracle Forms automatically places Window as the last selection in the Forms Runtime window.

because a sales order clerk might want to access the form while processing a new order. The final two commands in the Clearwater Traders database application are Help and Window. The Help selection has two second-level selections—Contents, which provides access to the help search engine, and About, which gives details about the current application. The Window pull-down menu allows users to move between windows in a multiple-window application.

Creating a Splash Screen

A **splash screen** is the first image that appears when you run an application. It introduces the application and usually identifies the system author(s) and copyright information. To implement the splash screen, you will create a form with two windows. (Recall that a form can have multiple windows. For example, the SALES_FORM you created in Chapter 6 had one window for entering CUST_ORDER information and another window for entering ORDERLINE information.) When the user starts the program, the first window will display the splash screen shown in Figure 9-3 for a few seconds. Then the application will switch to the second window and display the main application screen shown in Figure 9-2. To implement this, you will create a PRE-FORM trigger that loads the splash screen image and then sets a timer. The splash screen window will appear first, and when the timer expires, a form-level trigger named WHEN-TIMER-EXPIRES executes. This trigger sets the application's focus to an item on the main application window, causing the main application window to appear.

Figure 9-3: Splash screen

The first step in developing the splash screen is to create the form, and the splash screen and main application screen windows. You will do this next.

To create the form and windows:

1. Start the Oracle Forms Designer and open the Object Navigator window in Visual View.
2. Create a new form module named **MAIN**.
3. Create two new windows in MAIN and name the first window **SPLASH_WINDOW** and the second window **MAIN_WINDOW**.
4. Create a new canvas in SPLASH_WINDOW named **SPLASH_CANVAS**, and then create a new control block on SPLASH_CANVAS named **SPLASH_BLOCK**.
5. Create a new canvas in MAIN_WINDOW named **MAIN_CANVAS**, and then create a new control block named **MAIN_BLOCK**.
6. Save your file as **main.fmb** in the Chapter9 folder on your Chapter 9 Clearwater Traders Student Disk.

Configuring the Splash Screen Window

Windows applications are displayed in a main application window. This window can run in its normal state, where multiple application windows are visible on the screen display, or in a maximized state, where the application window fills the screen display. For a form, the main application window is the Forms Runtime window. Windows within a form can be **document windows**, which are displayed within the main application window frame. If the user resizes the main application window so that it is smaller than the document window inside it, the document window is clipped and scrollbars appear. So far, all of the windows in your forms have been document windows. Windows within a form can also be **dialog windows**, which are displayed in their own window frame. You will configure the splash screen window as a dialog window so it displays only the window title bar and no pull-down menu selections from the Forms Runtime application. You also will modify the Remove on Exit property so the window disappears from the screen as soon as the application focus switches to the main application window.

To configure the splash screen window:

1. Open the SPLASH_WINDOW Properties sheet, and then scroll to the Window Style property. Double-click the **Window Style** property so it changes from Document to **Dialog**. Double-click the **Remove on Exit** property to change it to **True**. You also will need to change the width and height of the splash screen window and canvas so they fill the entire screen.
2. Change the Width and Height properties of the SPLASH_WINDOW and SPLASH_CANVAS to Width **470** and Height **335**.

   HELP? The dimensions in Step 2 assume that your monitor has a screen resolution of 640 by 480. If you are using a different resolution monitor, your instructor might provide you with different width and height settings.
3. Change the title of SPLASH_WINDOW to **Clearwater Traders**.
4. Save your file.

Creating an Image Item in the Splash Window

The splash screen image is a graphics file that will appear on the SPLASH_CANVAS. There are two approaches to displaying graphics files on a form. The first approach is to create the image as a boilerplate image like you did when you imported the Northwoods University logo into the report that you created in Chapter 7. This approach stores the image inside the .fmb file at design time. However, this approach will not work for a splash screen because the image is the only item on the canvas, and a canvas with only boilerplate objects and no items under the Item category in the Object Navigator will not be displayed by the Forms Runtime application.

You will use the second approach, which is to create an image item on the SPLASH_CANVAS. The image item is an empty item container in the .fmb design file, and the actual image is loaded into it at runtime. This method must be used when you display a canvas with no items other than a graphic image.

To create an image item for the SPLASH_CANVAS:

1 Go to the SPLASH_CANVAS in the Layout Editor.

2 Zoom out so you can see the entire canvas.

3 Click the **Image Item** tool on the Tool palette, and then draw a box that is about the same size as the canvas and just inside the canvas borders, as shown in Figure 9-4.

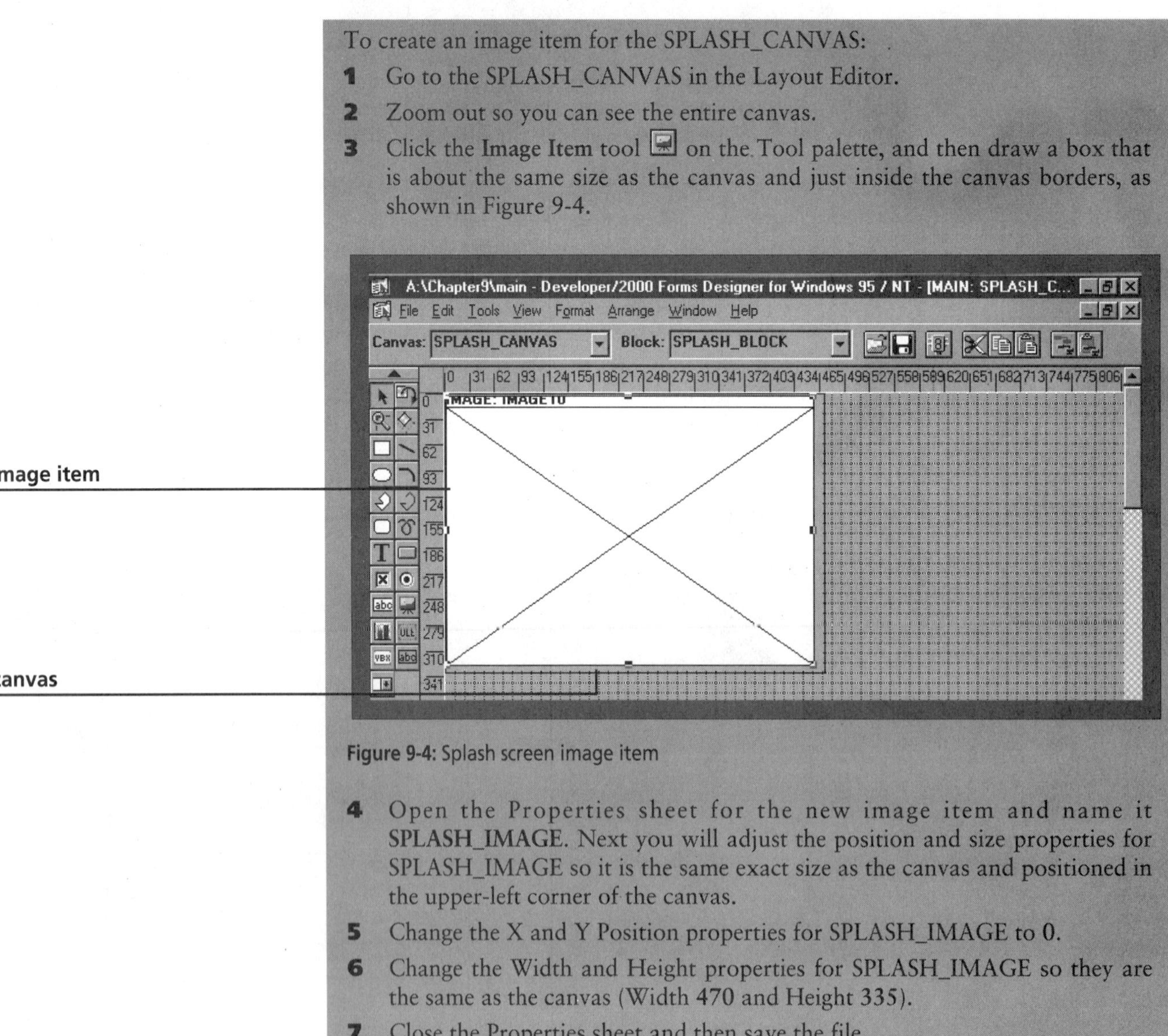

Figure 9-4: Splash screen image item

4 Open the Properties sheet for the new image item and name it **SPLASH_IMAGE**. Next you will adjust the position and size properties for SPLASH_IMAGE so it is the same exact size as the canvas and positioned in the upper-left corner of the canvas.

5 Change the X and Y Position properties for SPLASH_IMAGE to **0**.

6 Change the Width and Height properties for SPLASH_IMAGE so they are the same as the canvas (Width **470** and Height **335**).

7 Close the Properties sheet and then save the file.

Creating the PRE-FORM Trigger

Next you will create the PRE-FORM trigger to load the graphic file into the image item before the form appears and create a timer that determines how long the splash screen appears on the screen.

tip

The different image file types depend on what graphics application is used to create the file, and how the image is compressed to make it take less file space. Bitmap (BMP) files are usually uncompressed, while PCX, GIF, and TIFF files use different compression methods. PICT and PCD files are made by specific graphics applications, and CALS files are used to compress black and white images for FAX transmissions. Most popular graphics applications support one of these types of files.

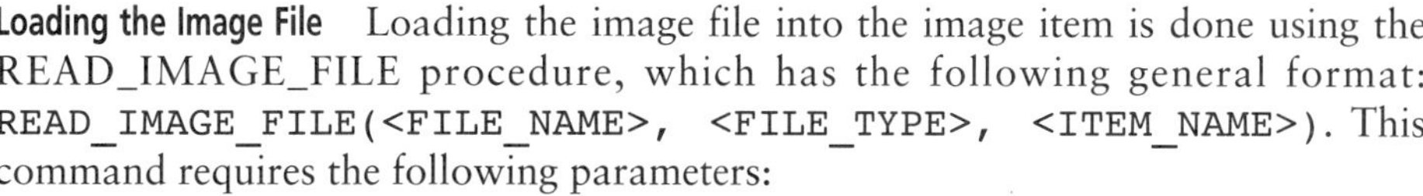

Loading the Image File Loading the image file into the image item is done using the READ_IMAGE_FILE procedure, which has the following general format: `READ_IMAGE_FILE(<FILE_NAME>, <FILE_TYPE>, <ITEM_NAME>)`. This command requires the following parameters:

- **FILE_NAME** is the complete path and filename, passed as a character string in single quotation marks. If the image file is named cwsplash.tif and stored in the Chapter9 folder on your Student Disk, the parameter would be `'A:\Chapter9\cwsplash.tif'`.
- **FILE_TYPE** is the type of image file being used, which is passed as a character string in single quotation marks. Legal values are the following file types (extensions): BMP, PCX, PICT, GIF, CALS, PCD, and TIFF. For the TIFF file used in the previous example, the parameter would be passed as `'TIFF'`.
- **ITEM_NAME** is the name of the image item where the file will be displayed, which is passed as a character string in single quotation marks in the format `block name.item name`. For the image item you just created, the parameter would be `'splash_block.splash_image'`.

Creating the Timer To create a timer, use the CREATE_TIMER function, which has the following general format: `TIMER_ID := CREATE_TIMER(<TIMER_NAME>, <MILLISECONDS>, <ITERATE>);`. This command requires the following parameters:

- **TIMER_ID** is a previously declared variable of data type TIMER.
- **TIMER_NAME** can be any character string up to 30 characters long. TIMER_NAME is entered as a character string in single quotation marks. An example timer name is `'splash_timer'`.
- **MILLISECONDS** is a numeric value that specifies the time duration until the timer expires in milliseconds. (When the timer expires, it calls a form-level trigger named WHEN-TIMER-EXPIRED, which you will create later in this chapter.)
- **ITERATE** specifies whether the timer should be reset immediately after it expires. Valid values are **REPEAT** (meaning it should be reset) and **NO_REPEAT** (meaning it should stay expired). The splash screen will be displayed only once so you will use the NO_REPEAT option.

Now you will create the PRE-FORM trigger to maximize the main application window, load the image into the SPLASH_WINDOW, and create the timer.

To create the PRE-FORM trigger:

1 Create a PRE-FORM trigger using the PL/SQL code shown in Figure 9-5.

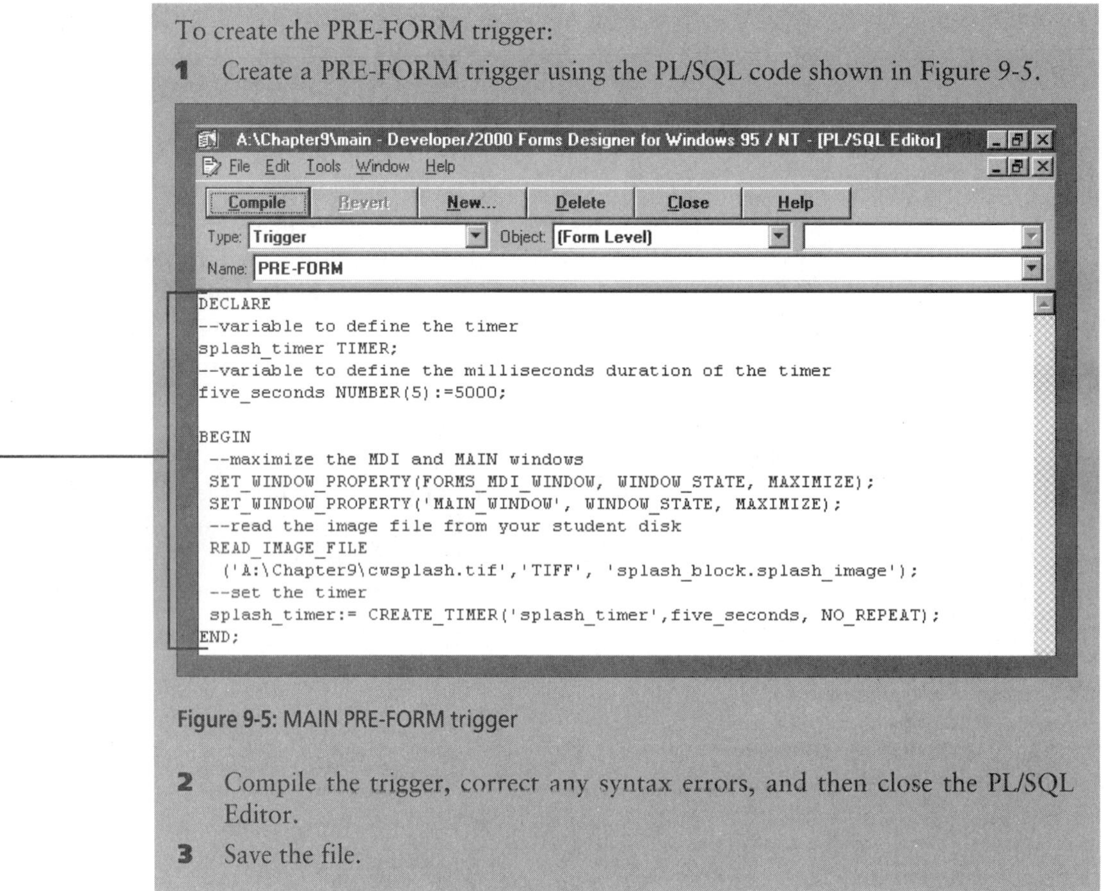

Figure 9-5: MAIN PRE-FORM trigger

2 Compile the trigger, correct any syntax errors, and then close the PL/SQL Editor.

3 Save the file.

Creating the WHEN-TIMER-EXPIRED Trigger

When a form timer expires, the form-level WHEN-TIMER-EXPIRED trigger is called. If no WHEN-TIMER-EXPIRED trigger exists, nothing happens. If such a trigger does exist, then the code in the trigger is executed. The next step is to create a WHEN-TIMER-EXPIRED trigger that displays the main application window. Remember that to show a window in a multiple-window application, you first show the window using the SHOW_WINDOW command, and then set the application's focus to an item on that window using the GO_ITEM command. Therefore, you first need to create an item in the main application window so you can switch the application's focus to that item.

To create an item in the MAIN_WINDOW:

1 Go to the **MAIN_CANVAS** in the Layout Editor.

2 If necessary, select **MAIN_BLOCK** from the Block list box in the Layout Editor. You will create a button that will become the picture button that will call the sales.fmx file. You will adjust the button size and position later.

3 Create a button named **NEW_ORDERS_BUTTON**. This will be the picture button beside the New Orders label.

4 Save the file.

Next you will create the WHEN-TIMER-EXPIRED trigger to show the MAIN_WINDOW and switch the application's focus to the NEW_ORDERS_BUTTON.

To create the WHEN-TIMER-EXPIRED trigger:

1. Go to the Object Navigator window in Ownership View.
2. Under the MAIN module, select **Triggers** to make a form-level trigger.
3. Create a WHEN-TIMER-EXPIRED trigger with the following code:

```
--show the main window
SHOW_WINDOW('main_window');
--set the application focus to an item in main_window
GO_ITEM('new_orders_button');
```

4. Compile the trigger, correct any syntax errors, and then close the PL/SQL Editor.
5. Save the file.

When an Oracle Forms application runs, the Forms Runtime application displays the window that contains the item that is first in the form's navigation sequence. Remember that the navigation sequence is determined by the order that the blocks and items are listed in the Object Navigator. Therefore SPLASH_BLOCK must be the first block listed and SPLASH_ITEM must be the first item in the block. Next you will double-check the navigation sequence to make sure that the window with the splash screen will be the first window displayed.

To check the navigation sequence:

1. Go to the Object Navigator window in Ownership View.
2. Double-check that the navigation sequence looks like the one shown in Figure 9-6. If it does not look like Figure 9-6, drag the blocks and items into the correct position, and verify that SPLASH_IMAGE is in SPLASH_BLOCK, and NEW_ORDERS_BUTTON is in MAIN_BLOCK.

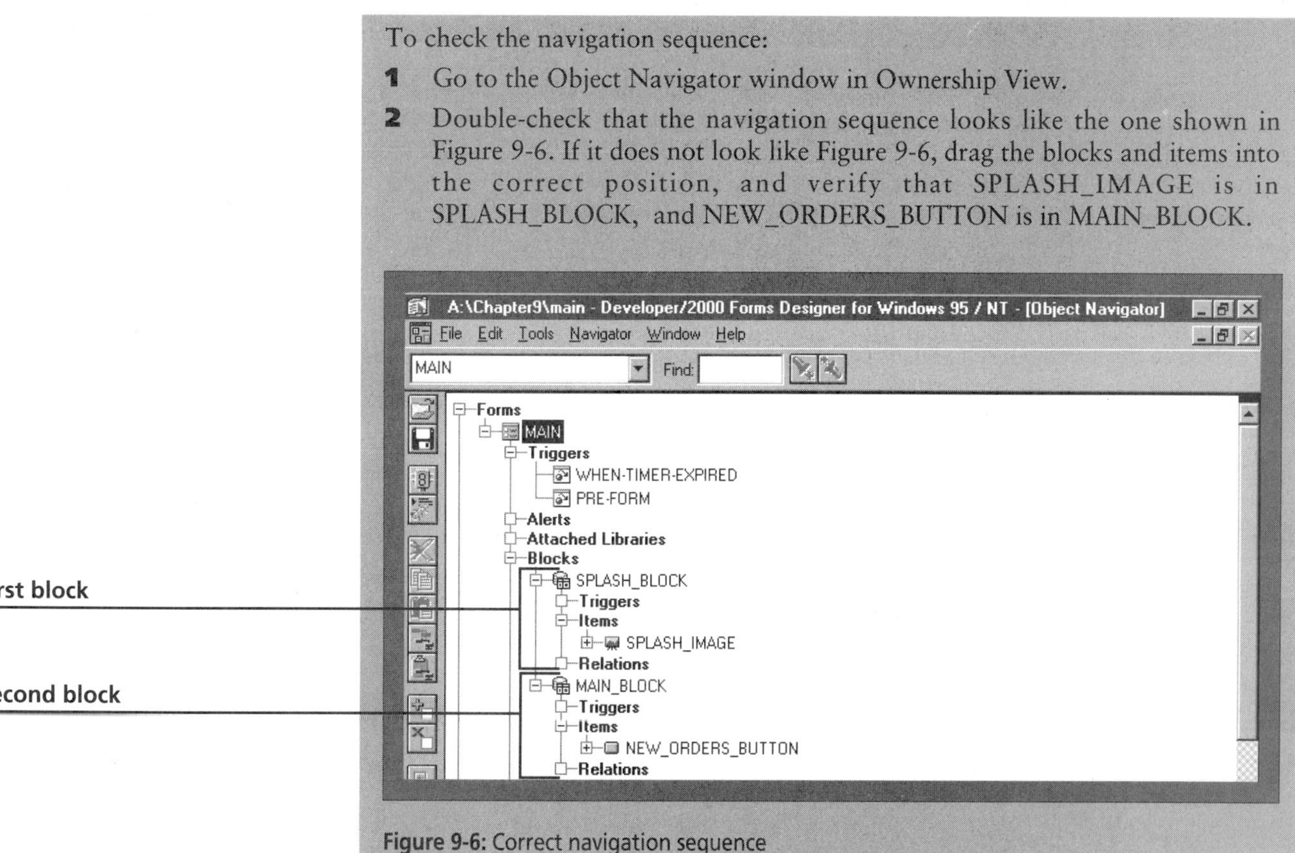

Figure 9-6: Correct navigation sequence

Now you can test the splash screen.

To test the splash screen:

1 Run the application. The splash screen should display for five seconds, and then switch to the main window.

HELP? You might need to adjust the window and canvas size in the Layout Editor or the TIFF image size using a program for editing graphic images to make the splash screen appear as a full-screen image on your monitor. Ask your instructor or technical support person for help.

2 Close the Forms Runtime application.

The icon files used in the steps are stored in the Chapter9 folder on your Clearwater Traders Student Disk.

To make icons appear on buttons in the Forms Designer environment, the icons must be stored in the ORAWIN\ICONS (or ORANT\ICONS) folder on your client workstation. When you run the application by double-clicking the .fmx file, the icons can be stored either in the ICONS folder or in the same folder as the .fmx file.

Creating the Picture Buttons

Next you will format the MAIN_WINDOW and create the picture buttons and labels shown in Figure 9-7. These picture buttons are similar to the LOV push buttons you first created in Chapter 5 where the picture comes from an icon (.ico) file specified in the button's Properties sheet. From a design standpoint, it is important to use an icon image that relates to the button's function and to provide a hint when the user positions the mouse pointer on the button.

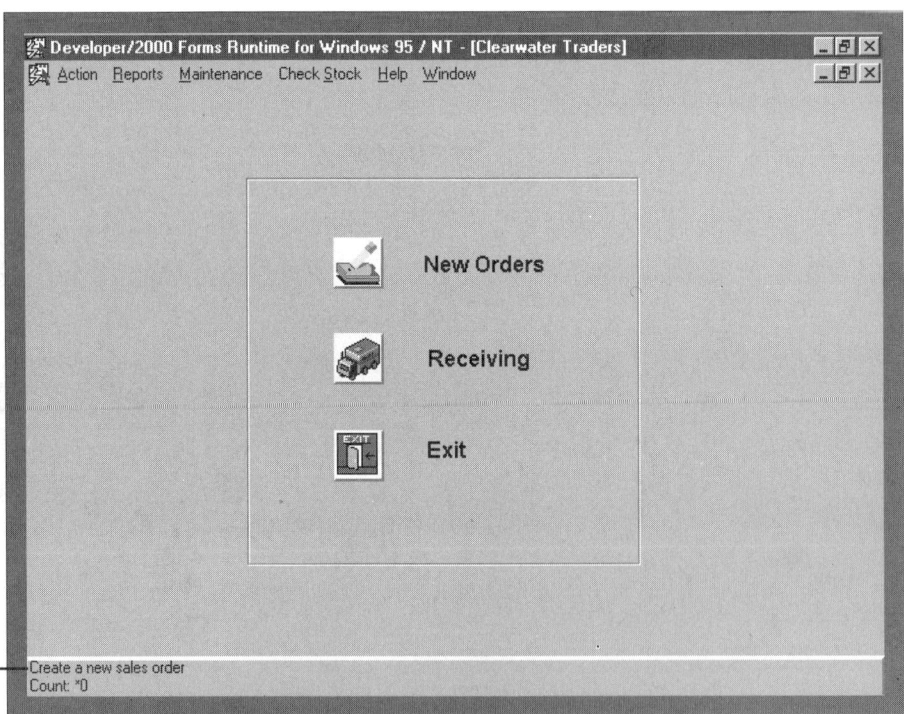

Figure 9-7: Picture button layout

To format the MAIN_WINDOW and create the picture buttons:

1 Change the Width and Height properties of the MAIN_CANVAS and MAIN_WINDOW to Width 470 and Height 335 so they will display full screen.

HELP? These values assume that your screen resolution is set to 640 by 480. You might need to adjust these values if your actual monitor resolution is different.

2 Change the title of MAIN_WINDOW to **Clearwater Traders.**

3 Go to the MAIN_CANVAS in the Layout Editor.

4 Open the NEW_ORDERS_BUTTON Properties sheet, and then change the following properties. The "Notepadg" icon (green notepad) should appear on the NEW_ORDERS_BUTTON after you close the button's Properties sheet.

Property	Value
Width	28
Height	28
Label	<deleted>
Iconic	True
Icon Name	Notepadg
Hint	Create a new sales order
AutoHint	True

HELP? This button size assumes you are using a 640 by 480 screen resolution. If your screen resolution is different, you might need to change the size of the buttons to make the icons appear correctly.

HELP? If the icon does not appear on the button, it is probably because the icon file is not in the \ORAWIN\ICONS (or ORANT\ICONS) folder on your client workstation, and you need to copy it from the Chapter9 folder on your Student Disk. If the icon file is there, then it probably means that the default icon directory for your database has not been set to ORAWIN\ICONS, and you need to contact your instructor or technical support person for help.

5 Copy the button and paste it two times to make the next two picture buttons.

6 Modify the properties of the new buttons as follows:

Name	Icon Name	Hint
RECEIVING_BUTTON	Movingva	Receive a new shipment
EXIT_BUTTON	Exit	Exit the application

7 Position the buttons and create the associated labels and boilerplate rectangles as shown in Figure 9-7. Format the labels using a **12-point bold Arial** font.

8 Save the file.

9 Run the form and then adjust the item positions and sizes if necessary.

Creating the Button Triggers

Now you need to create the WHEN-BUTTON-PRESSED triggers for the three picture buttons. To call one form from another, you use the CALL_FORM procedure, which has the following general format: `CALL_FORM(<FORM MODULE NAME>, <DISPLAY>, <SWITCH_MENU>);`. This command requires the following parameters:

- FORM MODULE NAME is the full path and filename, including the drive letter, to the called form's .fmx file. FORM MODULE NAME is passed as a character string in single quotation marks, for example, `'A:\Chapter9\sales.fmx'`.

- **DISPLAY** specifies whether the calling form is hidden or not hidden by the called form. Valid values are HIDE and NO_HIDE.
- **SWITCH_MENU** specifies whether the called form's pull-down menus are inherited from the calling form or if custom menus will replace the called form's pull-down menus specified by the programmer. Valid values are **NO_REPLACE** (pull-down menus are inherited from the calling form) and **DO_REPLACE** (pull-down menus are specified by the programmer).

To create the button triggers:

1. For the NEW_ORDERS_BUTTON, create a WHEN-BUTTON-PRESSED trigger by typing the following code in the PL/SQL Editor: **CALL_FORM('A:\Chapter9\sales.fmx', HIDE, DO_REPLACE);**.
2. Compile the trigger, correct any syntax errors, and then close the PL/SQL Editor.
3. Save the file and then run the form to confirm that the SALES_FORM is called correctly.

HELP? If the SALES_FORM does not appear when you click the NEW_ORDERS_BUTTON, check to be sure that you entered the path to the .fmx file correctly in the CALL_FORM command, and then confirm that the sales.fmx file is in the Chapter9 folder on your Student Disk.

4. Exit the Forms Runtime application.
5. For the RECEIVING_BUTTON, create a similar WHEN-BUTTON-PRESSED trigger so it calls **A:\Chapter9\receivng.fmx.**
6. Create a trigger for the EXIT_BUTTON with the code **EXIT_FORM;**.
7. Save the file and then run the form to confirm that the new button triggers work correctly.
8. Exit the Forms Runtime application.

tip

By using the DO_REPLACE parameter, the SALES_FORM will have the default Oracle Forms pull-down menus. If you used the NO_REPLACE parameter, the SALES_FORM would inherit the pull-down menus from the MAIN_FORM.

Adding the Pull-Down Menus

Currently, whenever you run a form, the default pull-down menu choices of Action, Edit, Block, Field, Record, Query, Window, and Help are displayed. To replace these default menu choices with custom menu choices like the ones shown in Figure 9-2, you will need to create a menu module. A **menu module** is a separate Oracle application that can contain individual menus as well as other objects such as program units and parameters. A menu module is saved in the file system as a design file with an .mmb extension and as an executable file with an .mmx extension. The executable (.mmx) menu file can be attached to any form module. After you create a menu module, you create one or more **menus** that contain a customized set of pull-down menu choices. The top-level menu choices on the menu bar are called **parent menu items** and the lowest-level selections are called **child menu items**. When the user selects a child menu item, a program called an **action trigger** runs that issues commands to perform actions such as calling another form, calling a report, or clearing the form. For example, when a user clicks Action and then clicks New Orders, an action trigger executes that calls the SALES_FORM. Next you will create a new menu module and a menu for your integrated database application.

To create the menu module and menu:

1 Go to the Object Navigator window, click **Menus**, and then click the **Create** button on the Object Navigator toolbar to create a new menu module.

2 Rename the new menu module **CW_MENU**.

3 Click the **Menus** module under CW_MENU, and then click. A new menu item with the default name MAIN_MENU is created. By default, the first menu in a menu module is always named MAIN_MENU.

4 Double-click the Menu icon to open the Menu Editor.

5 Click **File** on the menu bar, and then click **Save** and save the menu module as **cw_menu.mmb** in the Chapter9 folder on your Student Disk.

You also can click MAIN_MENU and then click the Menu Editor command on the Tools menu to open the Menu Editor.

Using the Menu Editor

The Menu Editor window (see Figure 9-8) enables you to build a pull-down menu structure and define the underlying action triggers to carry out the user selections. Like other Oracle applications, it has a toolbar and status line at the bottom of the screen. By default, a new menu item contains a default menu selection named New_Item. Before you create any menus, it is important to configure the Menu Editor environment so the menu design file is saved automatically when you generate an executable file. You will do this next.

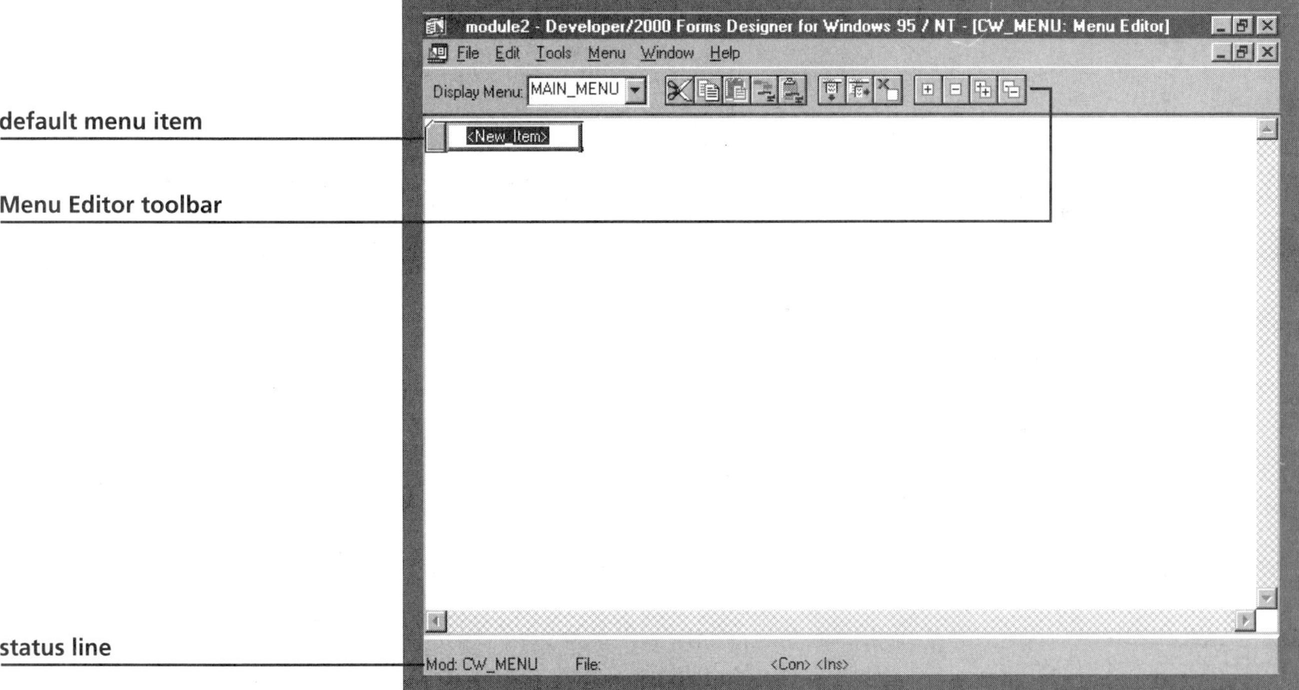

Figure 9-8: Menu Editor window

To configure the Menu Editor:

1. Click **Tools** on the menu bar, and then click **Options** to open the Options dialog box.
2. Make sure that the **Save Before Generate** check box is selected, and then click the **OK** button to save the changes.

Now you can create the menu items. You can use the Menu Editor to create the menu items visually by creating the parent menu items across the screen and the child menu items below their associated parent selections.

To create the menu items:

1. Double-click the <New Item> box directly on the label text so the label is selected, and then type **Action** to rename the first parent menu item.
2. Click the **Create Down** button on the Menu Editor toolbar to create a child menu item under the Action menu item.
3. Type **New Orders** to change the <New Item> menu item name to New Orders.
4. Click again to create another child menu item, and change the new menu item name to **Receiving.**
5. Click again to create another child menu item, and change the new menu name to **Exit**.
6. Press the key three times to select the Action menu item.
7. Click the **Create Right** button on the Menu Editor toolbar to create a new parent menu item to the right of the Action menu item.
8. Type **Reports** to rename the new menu item.
9. Repeat the previous steps to create the menu items shown in Figure 9-9. Use the **Create Down** button and the **Create Right** button on the Menu Editor toolbar until you have created the entire menu structure.

You also can select the Action menu item by clicking it with the mouse.

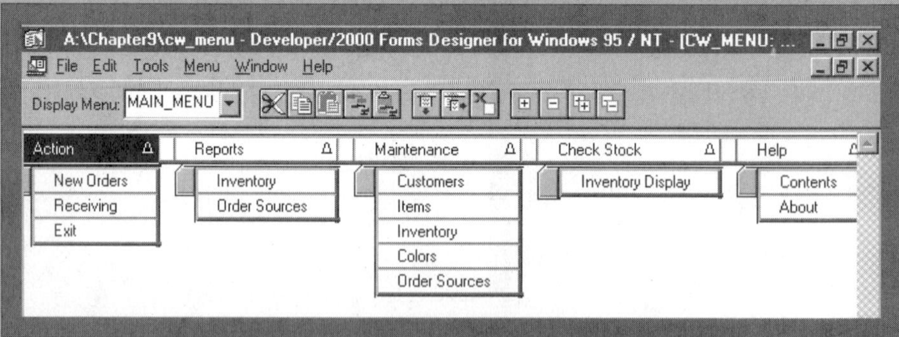

Figure 9-9: Menu structure

HELP? If you accidentally create a menu item that you don't need, click on the menu item you want to delete, click the Delete button on the Menu Editor toolbar, and then click the Yes button to confirm the deletion.

HELP? You do not create the Window menu selection shown in Figure 9-2 because it will be added automatically in the Forms Runtime window.

Your menu structure almost is finished—you are missing the Window menu selection, which the system automatically adds at runtime, so you don't need to create it on your menu structure. Now you will create the separator bar in the Help submenu that separates Contents and About.

To create the separator bar:

1. Select the **Contents** child-level item, and then click the **Create Down** button on the Menu Editor toolbar to create a new child menu item under Contents.
2. Right-click the new menu item (to the right of the <New Item> text), and then click **Properties** to open the Properties sheet for the new menu item.
3. Change the name of the menu item to **SEPARATOR_BAR**.
4. Double-click the **Menu Item Type** property selection several times until **Separator** appears, and then close the Properties sheet. If necessary, click **Window** on the menu bar, and then click **CW_MENU: Menu Editor** to return to the Menu Editor window.

Accessing Menu Module Files

Menu modules are stored separately from Forms applications. Therefore, to access a menu module file, you need to retrieve it from the file system independently of the Forms application. To illustrate how to do this, suppose you decide to take a break and close your application and work on it later.

To close and then reopen the menu module file:

1. Close the Menu Editor by clicking the **Close** button on the Menu Editor title bar.
2. Close the Forms Designer, and then start the Forms Designer again.
3. Click the **Open** button on the Object Navigator toolbar, and then open the **main.fmb** file from the Chapter9 folder on your Student Disk. In the Object Navigator, note that there are no items in the Menus node. The CW_MENU module is not retrieved with the Form file. You will need to retrieve the menu file.
4. In the Object Navigator window, click **Menus**.
5. Click again, click the **Files of type** list arrow, click **Menus (*.mmb)**, and then click **cw_menu.mmb** to open the file.
6. To return to the **Menu** Editor, click the **Menu** icon beside CW_MENU. Notice that each parent menu item with underlying selections choices has a down-pointing tab beside the label name. To open a parent item, click the tab.
7. Click the **Action** tab to display the child menu items. Note that the Action tab now points upward, indicating that its child items now are displayed. Also, note that the child items do not have tabs beside them.
8. Click the **Action** tab to close the Action menu.

If you want an ampersand to display in a menu choice, type the ampersand twice. For example, a menu selection of Research & Development would be entered as Research && Development.

Creating the Access Key Selections

By default, the first letter of each menu item name is the access key that the user can press to access the menu from the keyboard by pressing the Alt key and the first menu letter key. Sometimes it is necessary to change the default access key because it already has been used or because another key seems more intuitive. For example, the access key for Exit is *x* rather than *E* because *x* sounds more like Exit. To override the default access key choice, type an ampersand (&) before the desired access key menu letter. The ampersand will not appear at runtime.

To change the access keys:

1. Open the **Action** menu item so **Exit** is displayed.
2. Select the **Exit** child item by clicking it, and then click it again to go into text editing mode.
3. Type & before the x so the label now reads E&xit.
4. Modify all other menu items whose access key is not the first letter of the label to the underlined access keys in Figure 9-2.
5. Save the file.

Creating the Menu Item Action Triggers

Every child menu item must have an associated action trigger that is executed when the user selects the item. You will create the action trigger for the New Orders menu selection next. It will have exactly the same code as the NEW_ORDERS_BUTTON, so you will copy that code and then paste it into the menu item's action trigger.

To create the New Orders menu item action trigger:

1. Open the Layout Editor for the MAIN_CANVAS, right-click the **NEW_ORDERS_BUTTON**, and then click **PL/SQL Editor** to view the trigger code. Select all of the code, click **Edit** on the menu bar, click **Copy**, and then close the PL/SQL Editor.
2. To reopen the Menu Editor window, click **Window** on the menu bar, and then click **CW_MENU: Menu Editor**.
3. Right-click the **New Orders** menu selection, and then click **PL/SQL Editor** on the menu. An action trigger for the menu choice is created automatically, and you can enter the code that will execute when the menu item is selected.
4. Click **Edit** on the menu bar, and then click **Paste** to paste the copied trigger code into the Source code pane.
5. Compile the trigger, correct any syntax errors, and then close the PL/SQL Editor.

Next you will create the triggers for the Receiving and Exit menu items. For the Receiving item, you will copy the code from the RECEIVING_BUTTON trigger, and then paste it into the action trigger for the Receiving menu item.

To create the action triggers for the Receiving and Exit menu items:

1. Open the Layout Editor for the MAIN_CANVAS, right-click the **RECEIVING_BUTTON**, and then click **PL/SQL Editor** to view the trigger code. Copy the code and then close the PL/SQL Editor.
2. Click **Window** on the menu bar, and then click **CW_MENU: Menu Editor** to open the Menu Editor window.
3. Right-click the **Receiving** menu selection, and then click **PL/SQL Editor** on the menu. Paste the copied trigger code into the Source code pane, compile the trigger, and close the PL/SQL Editor.
4. Right-click the **Exit** menu selection, and then click **PL/SQL Editor** to open the Editor again.
5. Type **EXIT_FORM;** in the PL/SQL Editor.
6. Compile the trigger, correct any syntax errors, and then close the PL/SQL Editor.
7. Save the menu file.

The next child menu item that needs an action trigger is Inventory (under the Reports menu) for calling the inventory chart report. Running a report from a Forms application is similar to running a Graphics file because it requires using the RUN_PRODUCT procedure like you used in Chapter 8. Recall that the general format of the RUN_PRODUCT procedure is:

```
RUN_PRODUCT(PRODUCT, DOCUMENT, COMMUNICATION MODE,
EXECUTION MODE, LOCATION, PARAMETER LIST, DISPLAY);
```

The RUN_PRODUCT procedure requires the following parameters:

- **PRODUCT** specifies which product you want to run. This is a report so the product will be REPORTS. GRAPHICS indicates a Graphics chart.
- **DOCUMENT** specifies the complete path and filename to the Report .rdf file or the Graphics.ogr file, specified as a character string in single quotation marks. You will be calling the chart.rep file stored in the Chapter9 folder on your Student Disk, so this will be specified as 'A:\Chapter9\chart_rep.rdf'.
- **COMMUNICATION MODE** can be either SYNCHRONOUS or ASYNCHRONOUS. **SYNCHRONOUS** specifies that control returns to Oracle Forms only after the called product (Reports or Graphics) has closed. **ASYNCHRONOUS** specifies that control returns to the calling application immediately. For most applications, the SYNCHRONOUS mode is used.
- **EXECUTION MODE** can be either BATCH or RUNTIME. Use RUNTIME when running a Reports application when control is transferred to the Reports or Graphics Runtime application. Use BATCH when running a Graphics application so the chart appears directly in the form chart object.
- **LOCATION** will be FILESYSTEM.
- **PARAMETER LIST** is the ID of the parameter list to be passed, if there is one. If there is no parameter list, this value must be passed as NULL.
- **DISPLAY** is only needed when you are running a Graphics chart that is displayed in a chart item on a form. DISPLAY specifies the name of the Oracle Forms chart item that will contain the Oracle Graphics display. The name of the chart item must be specified in the format `block_name.item_name`.

Next you will create the Inventory menu item's action trigger to run the report.

tip You cannot test your trigger until you complete every child item trigger. If any child menu item doesn't have an action trigger, you will get a menu generation error.

To create the Inventory menu item's action trigger:

1 Select the **Inventory** child item selection under Reports, and then open the PL/SQL Editor and type the following code:

RUN_PRODUCT(REPORTS, 'A:\Chapter9\chart_rep.rdf ', SYNCHRONOUS, RUNTIME, FILESYSTEM, NULL, NULL);

2 Compile the trigger, correct any syntax errors, and then close the PL/SQL Editor.

3 Save the menu file.

The next menu selection under Reports is Order Sources, which will display the ord_srce.ogr Graphics application. This action trigger will use the RUN_PRODUCT procedure just like the previous action trigger, except you will substitute GRAPHICS for REPORTS as the product name, and change the filename.

To create the Order Sources action trigger:

1 Right-click the **Order Sources** child menu item under Reports, click **PL/SQL Editor** on the menu, and then create an action trigger for the Order Source selection using the code: **RUN PRODUCT(GRAPHICS, 'A:\Chapter9\rev_detl.ogr', SYNCHRONOUS, FILESYSTEM, RUNTIME, NULL, NULL);**.

2 Compile the trigger, correct any syntax errors, and then close the PL/SQL Editor.

The first three Maintenance menu selections (Customers, Items, and Inventory) and the Inventory Display selection under Check Stock all require action triggers to call .fmx files. These triggers will use the CALL_FORM command just like you used when you created the picture button triggers. You will create these action triggers next.

To create the action triggers to call the .fmx files:

1 Right-click the **Customers** child menu item, and then click **PL/SQL Editor** on the menu.

2 Type the following trigger code **CALL_FORM('A:\Chapter9\cust_mod.fmx', HIDE, DO_REPLACE);**. Compile the code and correct any syntax errors, and then close the PL/SQL Editor.

3 Create and compile similar triggers for the Items, Inventory, and Inventory Display menu child items using the following trigger code:

Child Menu Item	Trigger Code
Items	CALL_FORM('A:\Chapter9\custitem.fmx', HIDE, DO_REPLACE);
Inventory	CALL_FORM('A:\Chapter9\custinv.fmx', HIDE, DO_REPLACE);
Inventory Display	CALL_FORM('A:\Chapter9\chart_inv.fmx', HIDE, DO_REPLACE);

4 Save the menu file.

Next you need to create the stubs for the menu selections (Color and Order Sources under Maintenance and About under Help) that are not implemented yet. To do this, you will create an alert to inform the user that the feature has not been implemented, and then create the action triggers to display the alert.

To create the alert and action triggers for the unimplemented menu items:

1. Go to the Object Navigator window in Ownership View, and then create an alert named **NOT_DONE_ALERT**.
2. Open the NOT_DONE_ALERT Properties sheet, and then change the following properties:

Title	Not Implemented
Alert Style	Stop
Button1	OK
Button2	Deleted
Message	Feature Not Yet Implemented

3. Create action triggers for the Colors and Order Sources menu selections (under Maintenance) and the About selection (under Help) to display the NOT_DONE_ALERT using the trigger code shown in Figure 9-10.

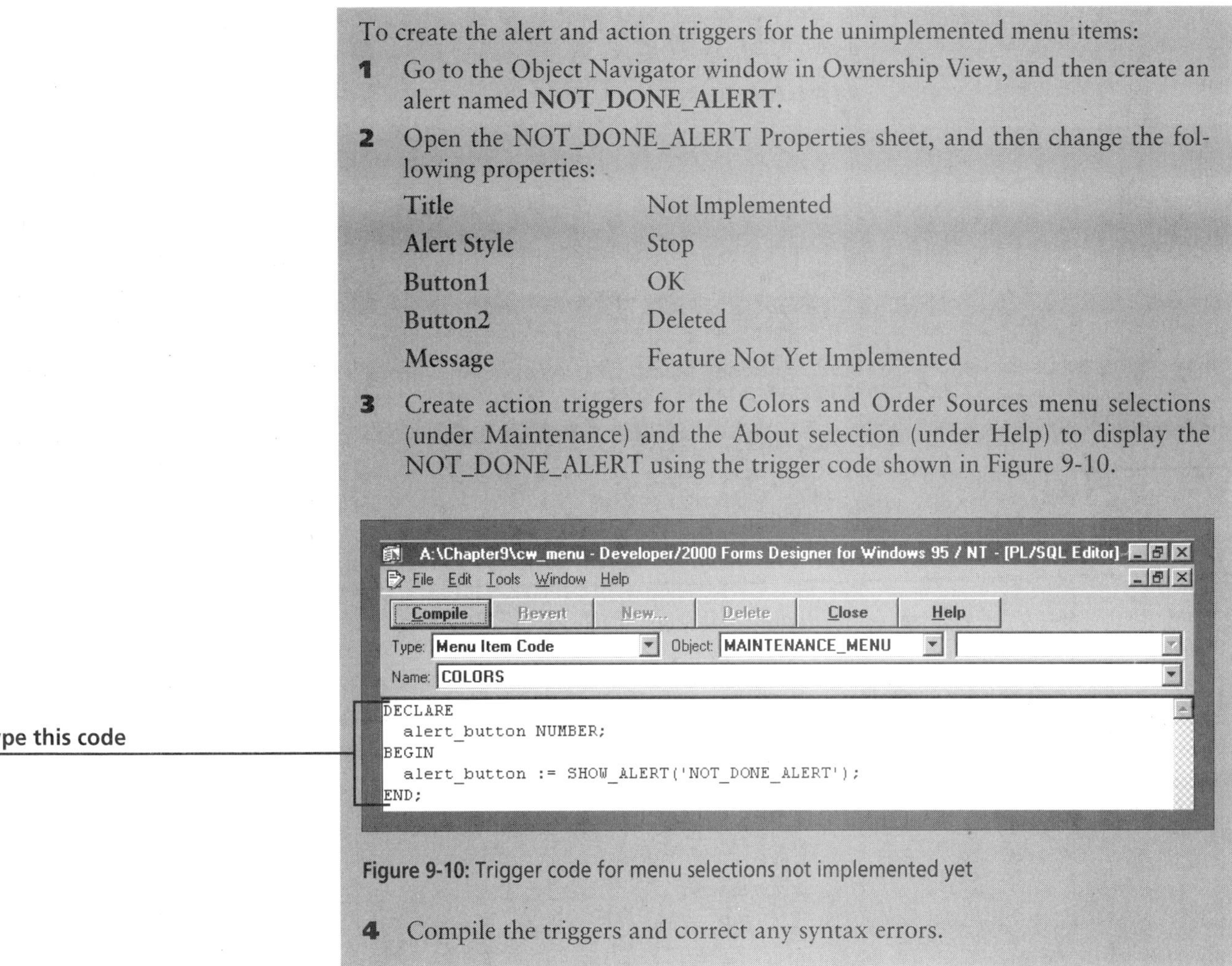

Figure 9-10: Trigger code for menu selections not implemented yet

4. Compile the triggers and correct any syntax errors.

Finally, you will create an action trigger for Contents (under Help) to activate the Forms Designer Help screen.

To create the action trigger for Contents:

1. Create and compile an action trigger for the Contents menu selection (under Help) with the code **DO_KEY('help');**.
2. Save the menu file.

Generating the Executable Menu File

Before you attach a menu to a form, you must generate the executable (.mmx) menu file. Every time you modify your menu module, you must regenerate the .mmx file. Otherwise, your form will use your old .mmx file and not show your recent changes.

To generate the executable menu file:

1. Open the Menu Editor window (if necessary), click **File** on the menu bar, point to **Administration**, and then click **Generate**. If you have not logged onto the database yet, you will be prompted to do so. The message "Module generated successfully" on the status line indicates that the executable file was created successfully.

   HELP? If your menu module did not successfully compile, read the next section on menu module debugging.

2. Close the Menu Editor window by clicking its **Close** button ☒ on its title bar.

Menu Module Debugging Receiving the menu generation error message shown in Figure 9-11 is very common. The "No PL/SQL source code" error indicates that there is a child menu item with no associated action trigger. The "Compilation error on CONTENTS menu item" message indicates that the Contents menu item is missing its trigger. If you encounter a similar error, add the necessary trigger code under the menu selection indicated in the error message and then regenerate the menu file.

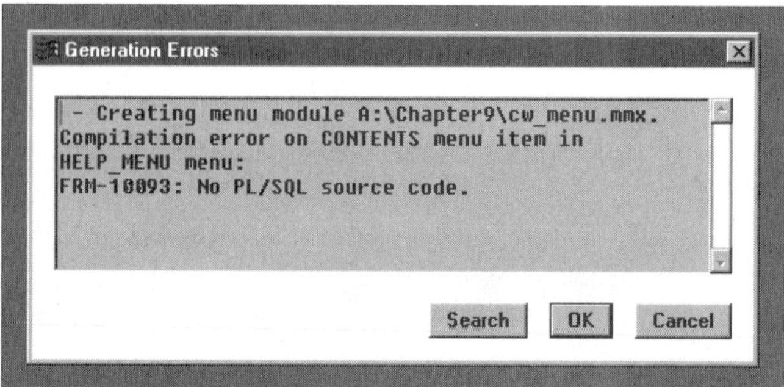

Figure 9-11: Menu generation error #1

Figure 9-12 shows another common menu generation error. If you look up this error code in online Help, you will find the explanation, "You are generating a module that has a menu which contains no items." However, you can visually see that your Help menu item has two child items, Contents and About. What's going on?

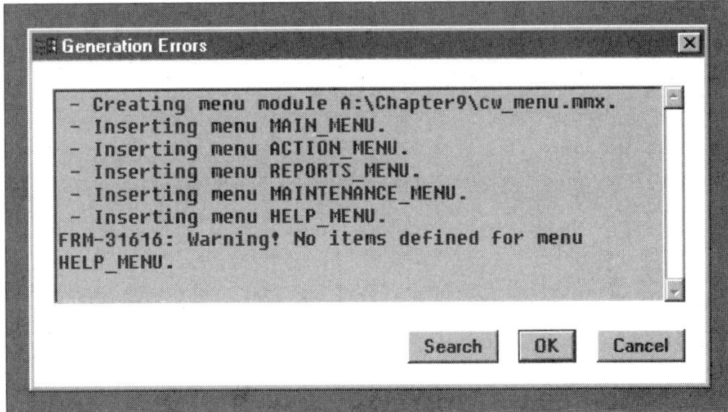

Figure 9-12: Menu generation error #2

The key is to go to the Object Navigator and examine how menu items are structured. Figure 9-13 shows the first part of the CW_MENU objects. The first menu object is MAIN_MENU, with items corresponding to each of the parent menu items (ACTION, REPORTS, MAINTENANCE, CHECK_STOCK, and HELP). The next menu is ACTION_MENU, with items corresponding to each of its child menu items (NEW_ORDERS, RECEIVING, and EXIT). Each parent menu should have items for each of its child selections.

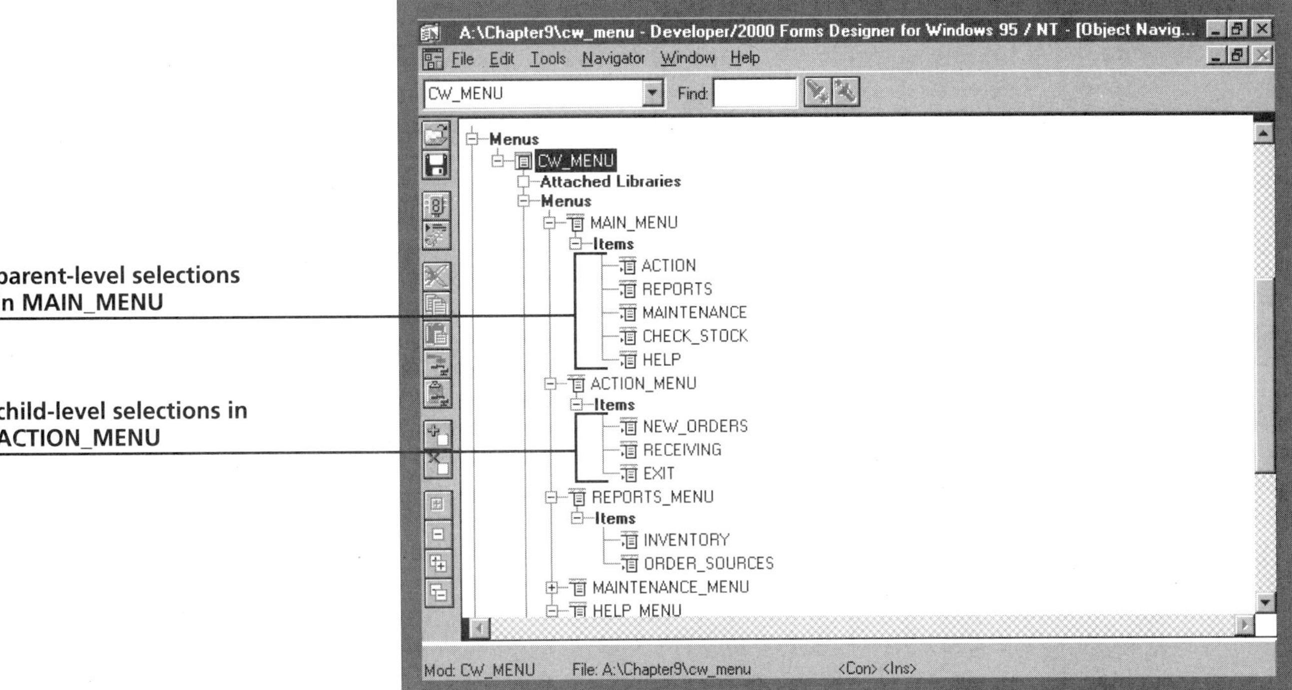

Figure 9-13: Menu structure in the Object Navigator (screen #1)

You can generate a menu module in the Object Navigator by clicking File, pointing to Administration, and then clicking Generate as long as one of the menu items is selected. If a form item is selected, this will generate the current form rather than the menu module.

As you examine the rest of the parent-level menu objects and their child-level items shown in Figure 9-14, you should notice something strange—there is a parent menu named HELP_MENU and another parent menu named HELP_MENU23. What happened is that the programmer created a menu selection with the label Help, and the system named the corresponding menu object HELP_MENU. Then the programmer created a second item with the label Help. No two objects can have the same name, so the system gave the second object the default name HELP_MENU23. The programmer deleted the first Help item from the Menu Editor, but it was not deleted from the Object Navigator. To delete the unused HELP_MENU and remove the error message, select HELP_MENU, press the Delete key, and then click the Yes button. Then you would need to regenerate the menu module.

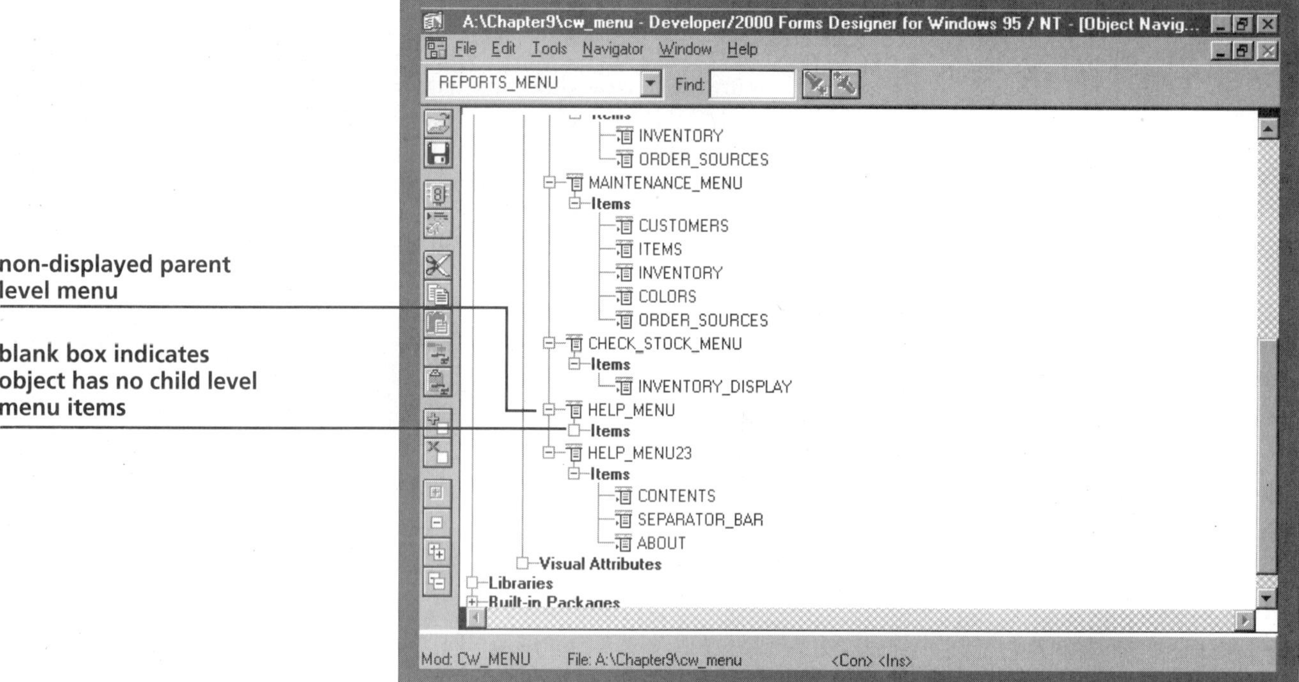

Figure 9-14: Menu structure in the Object Navigator (screen #2)

Attaching the Menu Module to the Form and Testing the Menus

The final step is to attach the menu module to the form in the MAIN module's Properties sheet and then to test the menus.

To attach the menu module to the form and test the menus:

1. In the Object Navigator window, open the MAIN module Properties sheet by double-clicking the **Forms** icon, and scroll down to the Menu Module property. The current value should be DEFAULT.
2. Change the value to the full path and filename of your newly generated menu module, which is **A:\Chapter9\cw_menu.mmx**, as shown in Figure 9-15.

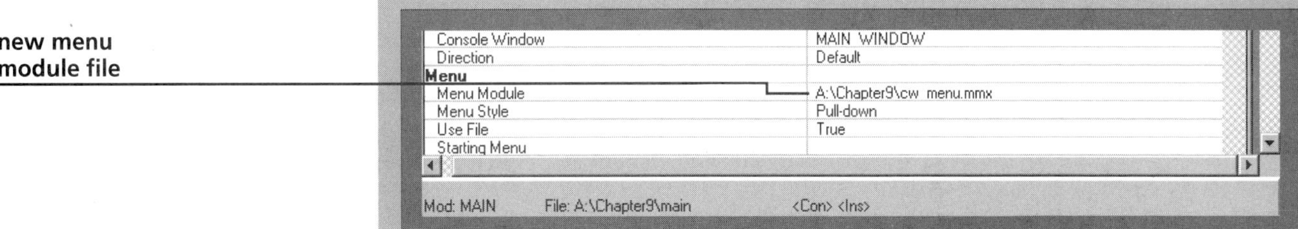

Figure 9-15: Specifying the menu module file

3 Close the form's Properties sheet.

4 Save the form file and then run the form. Your pull-down menus should look like Figure 9-16.

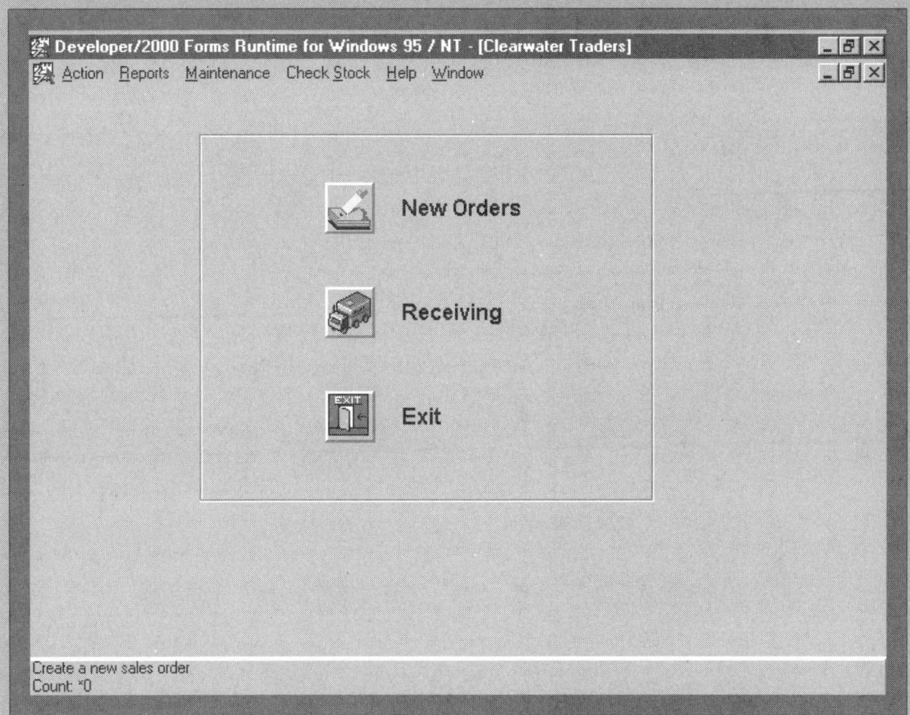

Figure 9-16: Pull-down menus

5 Test all of your pull-down menu choices to confirm that they call the correct form, report, or graphic, and that the NOT_DONE_ALERT displays for unimplemented selections.

HELP? If your menus do not work correctly, it is usually because the name or path of the executable file (.fmx, .rdf, or .ogr) is not specified correctly or that the correct file is not in the specified folder. For example, you might have mistakenly typed the path to the Order Sources graphic under the Reports menu selection as A:\Chapter8\rev_detl.ogr. There is no Chapter8 folder on your Chapter9 Student Disk, so you will receive an error message that the file could not be found. After making any changes in the menu action triggers, always remember to regenerate your menu file before you run it again.

6 Test all of the pull-down menu choices using the access keys to confirm that they work correctly as well.

HELP? If the access key selection does not work, confirm that you are pressing the correct access key. If you are, then confirm that the selection works when you use the mouse pointer.

7 Exit the Forms Runtime application.

Replacing Called Form Pull-Down Menus

Every time you called a form in this application, you used the DO_REPLACE option in the CALL_FORM procedure. As a result, each time a new form was called, the pull-down menu in the MAIN_FORM was replaced by the default menu that was previously attached to the called form. When you want a called form to have the same pull-down menu as the calling form, use the NO_REPLACE parameter in the CALL_FORM procedure.

When you are creating an integrated database application, you do not want called forms to inherit the main form's pull-down menus because every time a user calls a form from a pull-down menu, the calling form remains in memory on the client workstation. If the user calls several forms in succession from the pull-down menus without exiting any of the forms, the application eventually will run out of memory. Generally, it is best to force the user to exit each form and return to the main application screen before calling another form. If you want a called form to have a different pull-down menu than the default menu module, create and generate a new custom menu module, and then specify the custom menu module's path and filename as the Menu Module property on the called form's Properties sheet. When you call a form with a custom menu module, be sure to use the DO_REPLACE option in the CALL_FORM command.

SUMMARY

- When you create an integrated Oracle database application, put all of the files in the same folder, and modify all of the applications that call other applications so the paths point to this common folder.
- A splash screen is the first image that appears when you run an application. It introduces the application and usually identifies the system author(s) and copyright information.
- All application features should be available through pull-down menus, and the most commonly used features should have easy switchboard access.
- A user interface should support both mouse and keyboard access for all choices. Access keys are the underlined letters in pull-down menus that allow users to access the main menu choice using the keyboard by pressing the Alt key and the underlined key. Every main menu selection must have a unique access key. Users can select submenu access keys by pressing the indicated key when the parent menu selection is open.
- Stubs are programs that handle how an application accesses other programs that have not been implemented yet.
- When you use picture buttons in a user interface, it is important to use an icon image that relates to the button's function and to provide a hint when the user positions the mouse on the button.

- Oracle Forms automatically places Window as the last pull-down menu selection. In a menu module, the Window menu selection is added automatically at runtime, so you don't need to create it.
- Document windows are always displayed within the main application window frame and are clipped if the user resizes the main application window so that it is smaller than an embedded document window. Dialog windows are displayed in their own window frame.
- Different image file types depend on what graphics application was used to create the file and how the image information is compressed to make it take less file space.
- If an imported graphics image is the only image on a canvas, you must create an Image item to store the graphic, or the canvas will not be displayed at runtime.
- Boilerplate graphic image items are loaded at design time, while Image item graphic images are loaded at runtime using the READ_IMAGE_FILE procedure.
- When a timer expires, the WHEN-TIMER-EXPIRED trigger is called. If no WHEN-TIMER-EXPIRED trigger exists, nothing happens. If the trigger does exist, then the code in the trigger is executed.
- To show a different window in a form, use the SHOW_WINDOW command, and then navigate to an item in the window using the GO_ITEM command.
- When an Oracle Forms application runs, the Forms Runtime application displays the window that contains the item that is first in the form's navigation sequence.
- To replace the Forms Runtime default menu with a custom menu, you must create a new menu module. Menu modules are saved in the file system as design files with an .mmb extension and as executable files with an .mmx extension. The executable (.mmx) menu file can be attached to any form module.
- Main menu items with underlying selections are called parent menu items. Menu choices without submenu choices under them are called child menu items.
- An action trigger is the procedure that is executed when a user selects a pull-down menu item. Every child menu item must have an associated action trigger that is executed when the user selects the item.
- The default access key for menu selections is the first letter of the selection label. To override the default, type an ampersand (&) before the desired new access key.
- Every time you modify your menu module, you must regenerate the .mmx file.
- To display a different menu module in a called form, specify the new menu module filename in the form's Menu Module property, and then call the form using the DO_REPLACE option in the CALL_FORM command.

REVIEW QUESTIONS

1. When should you use pull-down menus in a user interface, and when should you use picture buttons?
2. What is an access key?
3. What is a splash screen, and when do you use it?
4. What is the difference between the dialog and document window styles?
5. What are the two methods for displaying an imported graphics image file in a form?
6. Why must you use an image item to display a graphic on a splash screen rather than creating a boilerplate object?
7. How do timers work in Oracle Forms?
8. How do you display a different window in a multiple-window form?
9. Which window is displayed first when you start a Forms application?
10. What is the purpose of the SWITCH_MENU parameter in the CALL_FORM command?

11. What is the difference between an .mmb and an .mmx file?
12. What is a parent menu item? What is a child menu item?
13. What is the default access key for pull-down menu selections? How do you override the default access key?
14. What is an action trigger? Why do you have to wait to test an individual action trigger until all of the child menu items have action triggers?
15. Why must you regenerate your menu module every time you modify it?
16. How do you replace the menu module in a called form?

PROBLEM-SOLVING CASES

Save the files that you create in the cases in the Chapter9 folder on your Clearwater Traders or Northwoods University Student Disk.

Clearwater Traders Database

1. Create a new form named about.fmb to serve as the About window for the Clearwater Traders Order Processing System. Look at other Windows-based applications to help design the form. Modify the CW_MENU module so the new form is called from the pull-down menu.
2. Create a custom menu module named about.mmb for the About form in Exercise 1 that has a File parent menu item, with an Exit child menu item. Make x the access key for Exit. Attach the new menu module to the About form, and make sure to call the form so the new menu is displayed.

Northwoods University Database

1. Create a menu design based on the one shown in Figure 9-2 for the Northwoods University student registration system.
2. Create a splash screen for the Northwoods University system. Use the graphics file nwsplash.tif, which is saved in the Chapter9 folder on your Northwoods University Student Disk, or use your own graphics file.
3. Implement the Northwoods University menu design in an integrated application named nw_main.fmb. Call the actual forms and reports that you have implemented from past chapter exercises whenever possible, and create an alert stating that a feature is not yet finished for non-implemented selections.

Chapter 10

objectives

- Learn about Web addressing
- Identify the differences between static and dynamic Web pages
- Learn how dynamic Web pages are generated
- Use PL/SQL in Oracle WebServer applications
- Create a dynamic Web page generated from a PL/SQL procedure
- Learn how to send user inputs from a Web form to a PL/SQL program
- Generate a Web page response to form inputs
- Learn how to debug a PL/SQL Web program
- Learn how the POST method improves Web form security

CHAPTER 10

Creating Web Applications with the Oracle WebServer

Introduction

The **World Wide Web** (**WWW**) has become synonymous with the Internet. Commercial Web sites are becoming profitable, and Web-generated sales are projected to climb into the billions of dollars in the next few years. Selling products from WWW sites requires more than advertising, however. Customers need the ability to submit information to a server and a way to receive a response about their inquiries.

The Oracle WebServer provides several methods for dynamically creating Web pages that respond to user requests. The focus of this chapter is on using PL/SQL and Oracle WRB (Web Request Broker) commands to generate dynamic Web pages containing database information.

Building a complex Web page requires a significant knowledge of Hypertext Markup Language (HTML) for creating Web pages, along with in-depth knowledge of PL/SQL. Creating a dynamic Web application takes longer and is harder to debug than a comparable Developer/2000 Forms or Reports application. The motivation for using this approach, however, is that Internet access is available to a large percentage of users, and once you create a Web interface to your database, the entire world becomes your customer. This approach also is valuable for organizations using Intranets, which are Internet-based applications including Web pages that are private to the organization. Almost any computer can run a Web browser, but only newer and faster personal computers can run Developer/2000 applications. Developer/2000 also is focused primarily on computers running a Microsoft Windows operating system. Although most organizations have a diverse mix of old and new computers running a variety of operating systems, nearly everyone in the organization can use a Web browser regardless of his or her operating system or type of computer.

HTML and dynamic Web development is a large topic. This chapter will cover only the HTML commands needed to complete the Web exercises included here. The whole area of dynamic Web development is undergoing the quickest and most profound changes ever seen in the computer industry. The goal of this chapter is to provide you with an understanding of how Web browsers interact with Web servers and how programs running on Web servers respond to requests from browsers. Although this chapter uses Oracle's PL/SQL Agent to illustrate these interactions, many of the concepts presented carry over to other Web development environments.

Web Fundamentals

The Internet is built upon on protocols called the **Transmission Control Protocol** and the **Internet Protocol**. Both protocols are required, so they usually are abbreviated and referred to as **TCP/IP**. Any computer connected to a network using TCP/IP protocols loads software into its memory for processing TCP/IP network traffic. The computer might be used to browse the Web, or it might be used as a Web server. In either situation TCP/IP processing software will be loaded.

Internet messages are broken into **packets**, or small chunks of data that can be routed independently through the Internet. TCP is responsible for reassembling network packets into complete messages. IP specifies how messages are addressed, and for Web users and programmers, is the more important aspect of the TCP/IP protocol. Next you will learn about IP addresses and see how they are used to build Web addresses. Then you will see how more than one server can run on the same computer and at the same IP address. Finally, you will learn about static and dynamic Web pages.

Internet Protocol Addresses

IP addresses are 32-bit numbers that are generally expressed in base 10 as four numbers (ranging in value from 0 to 255) separated by periods (or decimals). For example, an IP address often used in this text is `137.28.224.5`.

Numbers of this type are difficult to remember, so IP addresses usually are represented by **domain names**. Domain name servers maintain tables with pairs of domain names matched with their corresponding IP address. Anytime you enter a domain name, such as www.uwec.edu, as part of a Web address, your browser sends a message to a domain name server requesting the IP numeric address corresponding to the domain name. After receiving the IP address, your browser will try to contact the server listening on that address. If you know the desired IP address, a domain name is not necessary; using a domain name slows response time by the amount of time required to learn the IP address from a domain name server. Domain names generally are recommended if they exist, however. An administrator might decide to change a server's IP address while retaining the same domain name. If you are accessing www.uwec.edu, for example, you will not be aware that the IP address changed. If you have been typing `137.28.1.25` in your address, your address will quit working if www.uwec.edu is moved to a different IP address.

Web Addresses

Web addresses are called **Uniform Resource Locators** (**URLs**). When a URL refers to a remote computer, it includes a domain name or IP address. The **Hypertext Transfer Protocol** (**HTTP**) is the most common Web protocol. HTTP addresses always begin with "http://<domain name or IP address>/". For example, the University of Wisconsin-Eau Claire's Web URL is `http://www.uwec.edu/`. Older Internet protocols such as the File Transfer Protocol (FTP) and Gopher also are supported. FTP still is the primary technology used for transferring files on the Web. Gopher sites are menu driven and primarily store text documents. Although Gopher sites still exist, they are being phased out rapidly in favor of Web sites. If a URL refers to an FTP site, the address will take the form of "ftp://<domain name or IP address>/". A Gopher URL begins with "gopher://". If the protocol is not specified, Web browsers by default assume an http:// address. Web servers also reference files located on the Web server with URLs. For example, a file URL could be `file:///c:/orant/ows21/new/index.htm`.

A shorthand notation is also available that assumes the starting directory is the Web server's root document directory. For example, an HTML document named example1.htm located in the c:\orant\ows21\new\examples\ folder on a server with the IP address 137.28.224.5 can be addressed as `http://137.28.224.5/examples/example1.htm` if c:\orant\ows21\new is the server's root document folder.

Multiple Servers at the Same Address (Running on the Same Computer)

Most Web sites run an FTP server as well as a Web server to allow Web developers to send new Web pages to their Web sites. Some Web sites run a second Web server listener to respond to and process administrator requests. This is managed through the concept of **ports**. The TCP/IP standard specifies that server processes will be assigned to numeric "ports." A message addressed to a specific IP address also will specify the port assigned to the listening server process. Web servers are by default assigned to port 80; however, an administrator can change this to any other port if desired. Web browsers assume a Web server is assigned to port 80 unless you tell them otherwise. To access a Web server listening on port 81, you would modify your URL to: `http://137.28.224.5:81/examples/example1.htm`.

Some port numbers are reserved for other common TCP/IP server processes. An FTP server usually listens on port 21. An Internet e-mail server usually runs two listening processes—one on port 25 for receiving and sending messages and one on port 110 for users reading their mail. The default port for Oracle's WebServer administrator listener process is port 9999. Assuming this port assignment isn't changed, a WebServer administrator can access a WebServer site remotely and modify the Web server's configuration, as well as perform a limited number of administrative tasks for Oracle databases by accessing a URL similar to `http://137.28.224.5:9999/`.

When you access a Web server and do not specify a file, such as example1.htm, you get the default home page. Default Web home pages often are named index.htm or home.htm.

Static Web Pages

A **Web page** is a file containing HTML tags and text. HTML is a document-layout language with additional hypertext-specification capabilities. HTML is not a programming language although it can contain embedded programming commands. HTML's primary task is to define the structure and appearance of documents and to allow documents to embed hypertext links to other documents. HTML tags usually take the form of <tag>...</tag>. Tags are not displayed in a Web page—they just define how the text or hyperlinks will appear when displayed in a Web browser. A basic HTML document skeleton is as follows:

```
<html>
<head>
<title>text</title>
</head>
<body>
<h2>text</h2>
...... Add the rest of your document here ......
</body>
</html>
```

Notice the beginning <html> and ending </html> paired tags. These tags tell a Web browser that the enclosed text is to be treated as an HTML document. The <head>...</head> tags enclose the document's header section. The <title>...</title> tags delimit text that will be displayed in the title bar of the browser window. The <body>...</body> tags enclose the text (and other tags) that compose the actual Web page. In a **static Web page**, tags and text are fixed at the time the page is created. Each time a static page is accessed, it will display the same information.

Dynamic Web Pages

Static Web pages are useful for displaying and navigating between HTML pages, much like flipping through pages in a book. Of course, a hyperlink to Chapter 7 will get you there much faster than flipping through pages. Perhaps more useful, however, are **dynamic Web pages** that can respond to user inputs, such as "I want to purchase 10 widgets and 6 wodgets at $100 for each widget and $225 for each wodget" and "What is my current checking account balance?" The ability to respond to these requests is creating a new system of commerce. So how can a Web server interactively read and respond to user requests?

Currently, the technologies supporting interactive Web pages can be grouped into three categories. The first uses forms to collect and send user inputs to a Web server. A program running on the Web server processes the form inputs and composes a Web page reply. When the program finishes, the Web server sends the Web page response back to the user's Web browser. Programs processing form inputs originally used the **Common Gateway Interface (CGI)** specification. The CGI specification still might be the most common method used at interactive Web sites. Its biggest limitation, however, is that each form submitted to a Web server starts its own copy of the CGI program. A busy Web server can run out of memory easily when it starts and services all of the CGI requests. As interactive Web sites have gained popularity, Web server vendors have developed proprietary technologies to process form inputs without starting a new copy of the servicing program for every form. Oracle's Web Request Broker (WRB), Netscape's Netscape Service Application Programming Interface (NSAPI), and the Microsoft Internet Server Application Programming Interface (ISAPI) are designed to address this issue.

The second technology stores binary code on a Web server, downloads it to a Web browser when requested, and runs it from the user's Web browser. The browser or user operating system must have the ability to run the downloaded binary file. This downloaded program interacts with the user and as needed sends and retrieves data from other servers. Examples falling into this category are Java, Java Beans, and ActiveX. More natural user interfaces can be created because user inputs can be validated and responded to from a local Java or ActiveX program rather than from a remote Web server.

The third technology writes uncompiled code directly into an HTML document. Special tags indicate to a browser that the following text is to be interpreted as code. The browser must have the capability of recognizing and interpreting the embedded code. Examples of this technology include JavaScript and VBScript. As with Java or ActiveX, more natural user interfaces are possible with this approach.

It isn't clear if any one of these technologies will dominate the others. The first technology (forms with Web server processing) is the most widely used. The extra network traffic and server processing required to send a response back to a user who forgot to enter his phone number is making all Web developers take a long look at the second and third technologies. For now, most Web browsers support forms. Only the latest browsers support the second and third technologies. To reach the widest audience today, forms seem to be the best choice.

Oracle's WebServer

The Oracle WebServer maintains a listener process on a Web server that listens for user HTTP requests. Requests that reference stored database procedures are forwarded to the **Web Request Broker (WRB)**. The WRB retrieves the stored procedure from an Oracle database. The database can be on the same server as the WebServer application or on a database server located somewhere else on the network. The WRB runs the stored procedure and sends the resulting HTML-encoded Web page response back to the browser. Figure 10-1 shows how the WRB works.

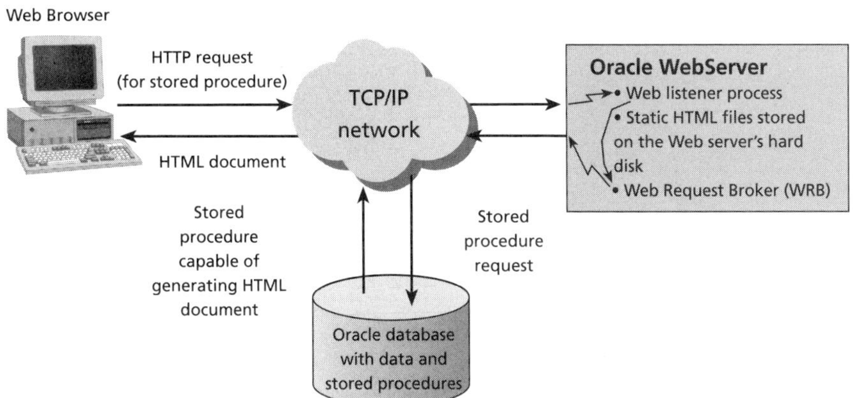

Figure 10-1: Oracle WebServer architecture

For example, a customer enters her customer ID and payment information into a form. After submitting this information to an Oracle Web server, the Web listener receives this information and determines it should be forwarded to the WRB by reading and interpreting its address. (The /owa_default_service/owa/ part of the address is what tells the Web listener the message is intended for the WRB.) A stored PL/SQL procedure named startorder is then called by the WRB to process the information and prepare a response.

Oracle's WRB enables one copy of a Web program in main memory to service many simultaneous requests. The WRB uses **cartridges**, or programs that interpret inputs from Web browsers, to generate dynamic Web pages. Some examples of current cartridges are:

- **PL/SQL Agent** Processes PL/SQL, which you will use in this chapter. The PL/SQL Agent is optimized better for database access than Oracle's Javacartridge, but lacks some of Java's functionality.
- **Javacartridge** Allows Java execution on the server and enables Java server applications to use PL/SQL.
- **LiveHTML** Allows the output of any executable program supported by your operating system to be included in Web pages.

You will use Web forms with Oracle's PL/SQL Agent, although the PL/SQL Agent might not see a lot of use in industry. Newer technologies like Java or JavaScript allow more natural user interfaces and might make forms obsolete. On top of this, PL/SQL Agent development is slow, and debugging is difficult. Oracle has added Java generation to the latest suite of Developer/2000 tools, which allows a much more interactive and "friendly" interface than what is possible with HTML forms. Web interface development using the Forms Designer and the Reports Designer should be faster and easier than developing interfaces by entering HTML codes in a PL/SQL program. Unfortunately, the Java generated by Forms Designer or Reports Designer is not yet supported by current Web browsers. Most Web sites still are using forms, however, and this is likely to remain the case for a few more years. For this reason, there is value in using the PL/SQL Agent to explore the strengths and weaknesses of Web forms. At the same time, you will gain experience in writing server processes (as Oracle stored procedures) and creating client interfaces (as HTML documents).

Creating Dynamic Web Pages

Dynamic Web pages are generated by running stored PL/SQL procedures. These procedures are created and coded using Oracle's Procedure Builder. In this section you will create your first "Helloworld" Web page using a PL/SQL stored procedure. Although most of this coding can be done using a static Web page, you will use the PL/SQL SYSDATE function to return to the current day of the week. The returned page displays different output depending on the day of the week, so it is a dynamic Web page. It isn't interactive, however, because it doesn't vary its results based on user inputs. You will see how to create interactive inputs in the next section.

The Oracle Procedure Builder

You used the Procedure Builder's PL/SQL Editor in Chapter 6 when you created program units using Oracle Forms. The Procedure Builder is integrated into Forms Designer, Reports Designer, and other Developer/2000 tools. For example, in Forms Designer, when you use the Object Navigator in Forms, Reports, and Graphics to create a program unit, the Procedure Builder's PL/SQL Editor opens. You also can use the Object Navigator in Forms, Reports, and Graphics to open database objects, open your user account, and create stored program units using the Procedure Builder.

Although the Procedure Builder provides a debugging environment for program units, it does not provide debugging support for *stored* program units. For that reason, this chapter will not explore the Procedure Builder's debugging capabilities. The following section on stored program units will explain how a stored program unit differs from a program unit.

Stored Program Units and Packages

Database triggers are programs that are invoked by a database action, such as inserting or updating a record. They are similar to the action triggers you created in Oracle Forms, which invoked a program as a result of a user or program action.

The www_user account is a special user account that the Oracle WebServer uses to interact with the database. Web developers must have privileges to execute the www_user's stored program units, and www_user must have privileges to manipulate user database tables.

In Chapter 6 the Form Designer program units were stored in form files that run on the user's PC. Program units also can be stored in separate library files and accessed by many different forms or reports. Program units stored in library files still are executed on the local user's PC. **Stored program units** are PL/SQL procedures or functions that are stored and run on the database server. When used in non-Web Oracle programs, they usually are used as database triggers. Database triggers are stored program units invoked by actions such as inserting, deleting, or updating a database table. A database trigger might add a record to an audit table each time a user modifies a table, or automatically add a primary key to a new record. When used with Oracle's WebServer, stored procedure units do much more. They create the entire user Web interface, process and respond to user inputs, and update the Oracle database as needed. In this chapter, you will use the www_user.htp.p procedure in the HTP package. (Note that www_user is the user account that owns [created] the stored procedure, and htp is the name of the package storing the procedure.) For other users to access procedures in the HTP package, www_user must grant execute privileges on HTP to these users. P is the name of a stored procedure in HTP. P sends text strings to a Web page that your stored procedure composes to respond to a user's input.

Packages are groups of related procedures, functions, variables, cursors, and other PL/SQL program items that provide a way to manage large numbers of related programs and variables. The package specification declares the public interface to the package, or the programs and variables other program units can call. The package body contains the code of the procedures declared in the specification. A specification doesn't have to have a body if the specification is used only to declare public variables and data types. Calling a program stored in a package requires prefacing the program with the package name, a period, and the program name. For example, calling the function lookup_customer stored in the package named billing and passing it to a parameter named custid would be written as `cust_name := billing.lookup_customer(custid);`. Accessing a variable named current_num declared in the billing package specification would be written as `temp_var := billing.current_num;`. Variables declared in a package specification are global variables. Now you will start the Oracle Procedure Builder and verify that it is configured for PL/SQL Web applications.

To verify Oracle is configured for PL/SQL Web applications:

1. Click the **Start** button on the taskbar, point to **Programs**, point to **Developer 2000 for Win95** (or **Developer 2000 for WinNT**), and then click **Procedure Builder**.
2. Click **File** on the menu bar, and then click **Connect** and connect to the database in the usual way.
3. Maximize the Object Navigator window. This is the vertical window on the left side of Figure 10-2.

maximizes the Object Navigator window

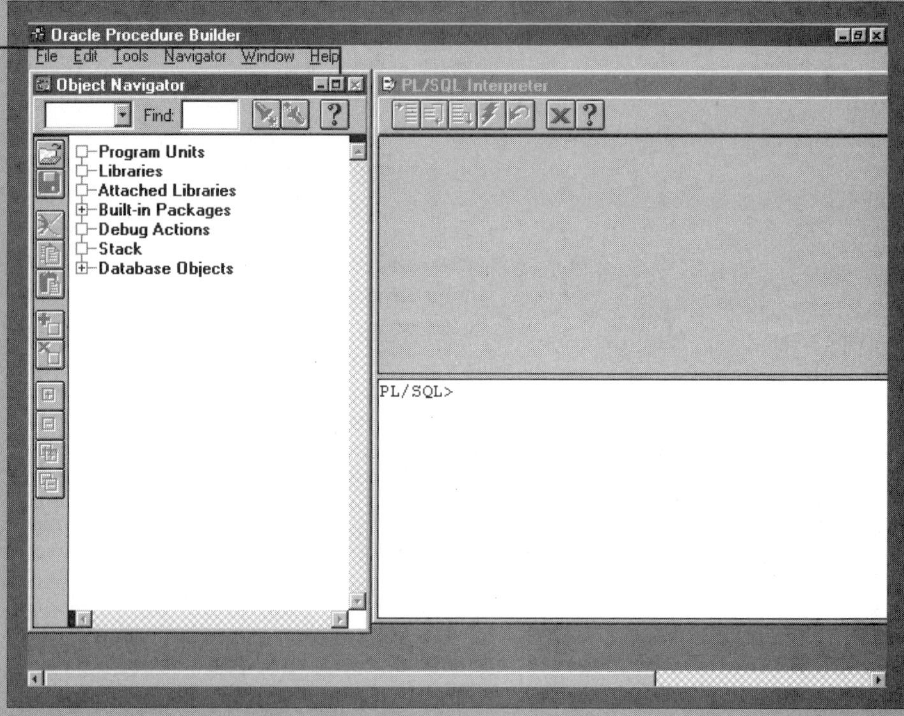

Figure 10-2: Procedure Builder window

4. Click the **Database Objects plus box** ⊞ to open it.
5. Scroll down and click ⊞ for **WWW_USER** and **Stored Program Units**, and make sure that you see the same entries as shown in Figure 10-3.

make sure you have these objects

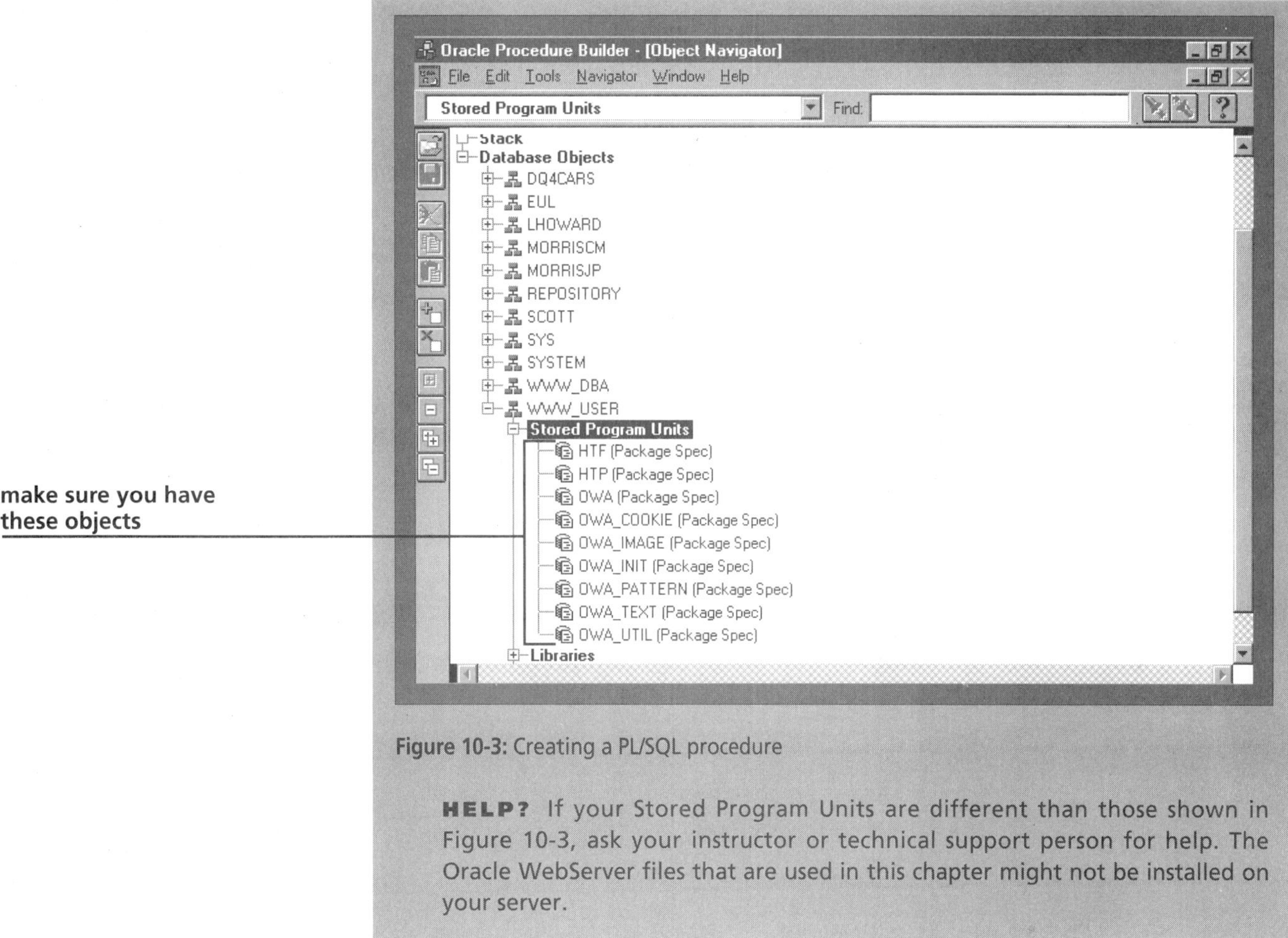

Figure 10-3: Creating a PL/SQL procedure

HELP? If your Stored Program Units are different than those shown in Figure 10-3, ask your instructor or technical support person for help. The Oracle WebServer files that are used in this chapter might not be installed on your server.

Next you will create the helloworld stored program unit.

Note: The HTML code used in this book will work with Microsoft Internet Explorer 3.01 or higher and Netscape Navigator 3 or higher.

To create the helloworld stored program unit:

1. Click the **plus box** ⊞ for your user name.
2. Click **Stored Program Units**, and then click the **Create** button on the Object Navigator toolbar to create a new program unit. The New Program Unit dialog box opens. You use this dialog box to create a new program unit.
3. Type **helloworld** in the Name text box, make sure that the **Procedure** option button is selected, and click the **OK** button. The Procedure Builder opens.

4 Type the code shown in Figure 10-4 in the Procedure Builder. Substitute your name and e-mail address where indicated without the parentheses around them. (If you don't have an e-mail address, make one up.)

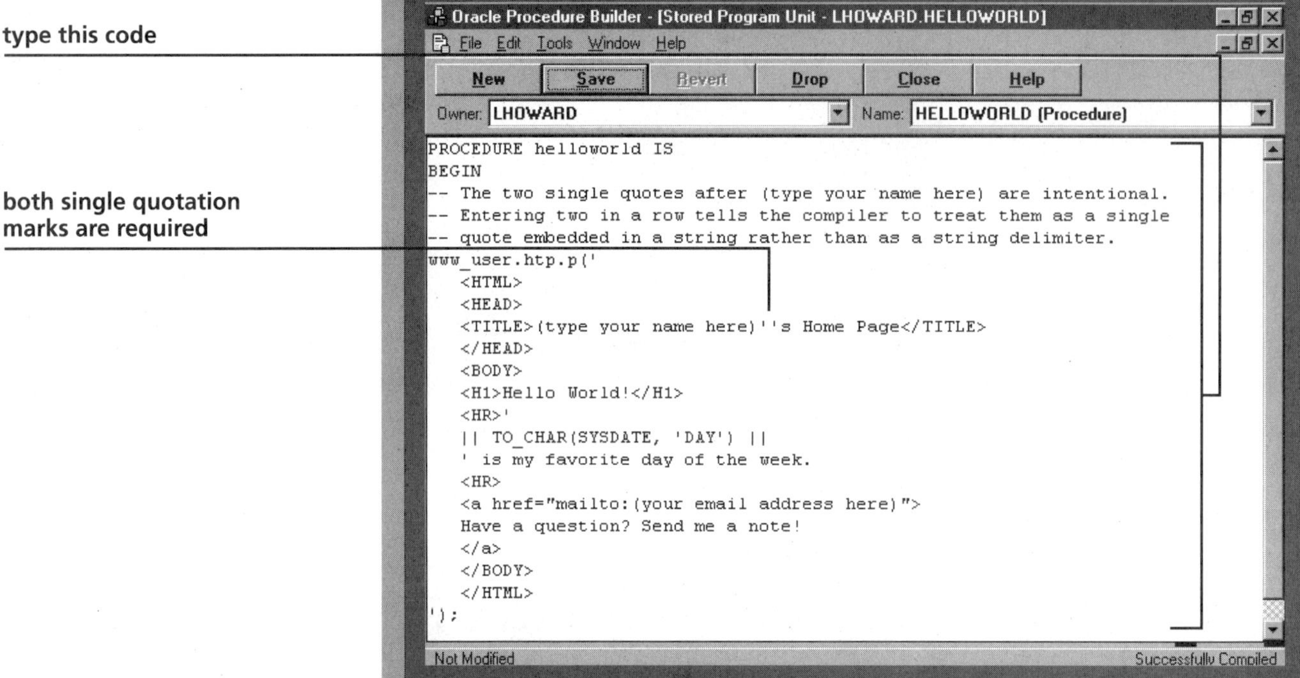

Figure 10-4: Stored program unit for helloworld

5 Click the **Save** button to compile and save this procedure. Next you will confirm your new stored procedure works.

HELP? If you get an error message stating "The source of the stored program unit is incomplete," then you omitted a single quotation mark or added an extra single quotation mark. Check your code carefully and then compile it again.

HELP? If you receive other errors, make sure that your code matches the code shown in Figure 10-4, and then save the procedure again. If you still have problems, ask your instructor or technical support person for help.

6 Now you must grant execute privileges on your program unit to WWW_USER. Start SQL*Plus, log on to the database, type **GRANT EXECUTE ON helloworld TO WWW_USER;** at the SQL prompt, and then press the **Enter** key.

7 Start Internet Explorer or your default Web browser, type the following address in the Address text box: **http://<your Web server's domain name or IP address>/owa_default_service/owa/<your user name>.helloworld**, and then press the **Enter** key. Your home page appears in the Web browser, as shown in Figure 10-5.

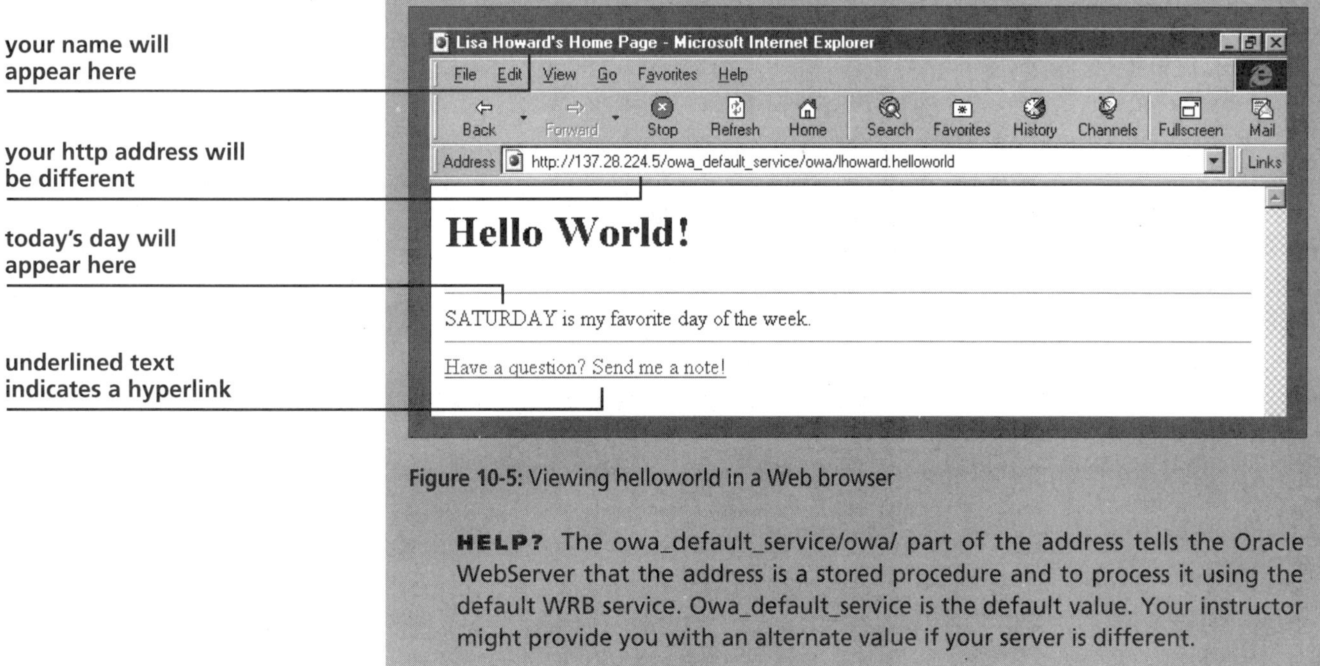

Figure 10-5: Viewing helloworld in a Web browser

> **HELP?** The owa_default_service/owa/ part of the address tells the Oracle WebServer that the address is a stored procedure and to process it using the default WRB service. Owa_default_service is the default value. Your instructor might provide you with an alternate value if your server is different.

The SYSDATE function makes this Web page dynamic because the page displays the current day each time the page appears.

Creating a Web Form

Next you will create a Web front end for the Northwoods University database. This Web front end allows students and faculty members to access information using Web browsers, such as Microsoft Internet Explorer or Netscape Navigator. Before creating the Web form, you will refresh your database tables to their original settings.

To refresh your Northwoods University database:

1. Switch to SQL*Plus.
2. Type **START A:\Chapter10\northwoo.sql** at the SQL prompt to refresh your database tables.

When you have finished the following steps, you will be able to access a Web page that allows you to enter a student ID, PIN, and a desired report, and then submit your entries to a Web program for processing. First you will create a package specification named SRecords that contains the names of the different package procedures, and then you will create the package body that contains the actual program code for the package procedures.

To create the Web page:

1. Click the Procedure Builder program button on the taskbar.
2. If necessary, open **Database Objects**, **your account**, and **Stored Program Units**. Select **Stored Program Units**, and then click the **Create** button on the Object Navigator toolbar.
3. Enter **SRecords** as the new program unit name, and then click the **Package Spec** option button, as shown in Figure 10-6 to create the package specification.

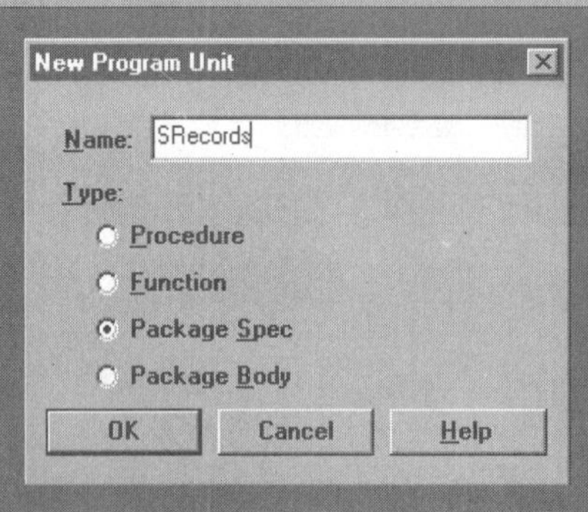

Figure 10-6: Creating a package specification

4. Click the OK button to close the dialog box. This automatically opens the Procedure Builder's Code Editor (which is called the PL/SQL Editor in the Forms Designer).
5. Type the code shown in Figure 10-7 to specify the names of the procedures in the package.

your user name will appear here

type this code

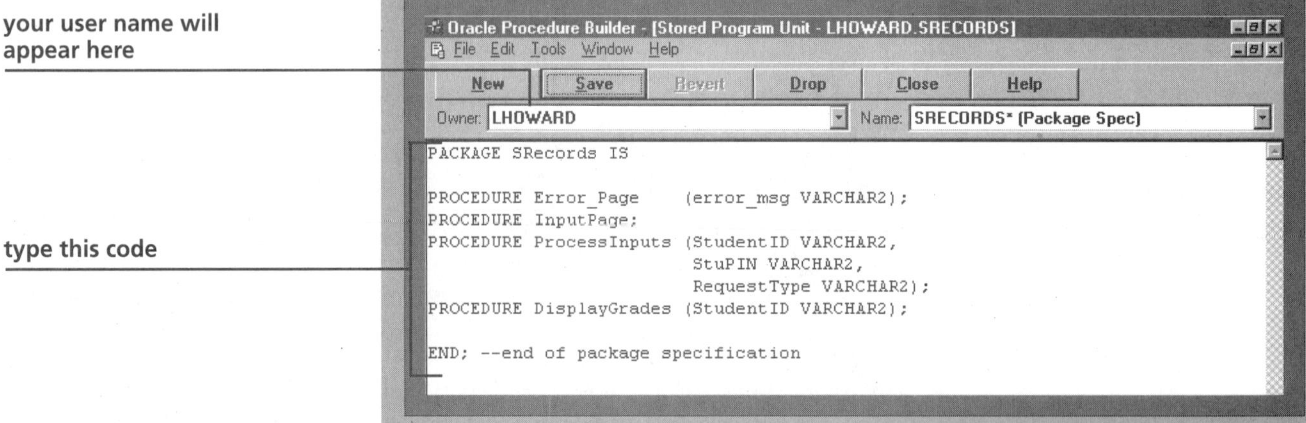


```
PACKAGE SRecords IS

PROCEDURE Error_Page     (error_msg VARCHAR2);
PROCEDURE InputPage;
PROCEDURE ProcessInputs (StudentID VARCHAR2,
                         StuPIN VARCHAR2,
                         RequestType VARCHAR2);
PROCEDURE DisplayGrades (StudentID VARCHAR2);

END; --end of package specification
```

Figure 10-7: Adding procedures to a package specification

6. Save the code, correct any syntax errors, and close the Procedure Builder.
7. Create a new package body named **SRecords**.
8. Save your empty package body. Compile errors will occur because you haven't entered any code. Ignore them for now.

9 Open the SRecords package specification, and then use the mouse pointer to select the declarations you previously entered, and copy them by pressing Ctrl + C.

10 Close the package specification, open the **SRecords** package body, and then paste the declarations into the package body by pressing **Ctrl + V**.

11 Modify your declarations using the code shown in Figure 10-8.

Oracle Procedure Builder - [Stored Program Unit - LHOWARD.SRECORDS]

File Edit Tools Window Help

New Save Revert Drop Close Help

Owner: LHOWARD Name: SRECORDS* (Package Body)

type this code

```
PACKAGE BODY SRecords IS
PROCEDURE Error_Page (error_msg VARCHAR2) IS
BEGIN
END;

PROCEDURE InputPage IS
BEGIN
END;

Procedure ProcessInputs (StudentID VARCHAR2,
                         StuPIN VARCHAR2,
                         RequestType VARCHAR2) IS
BEGIN
END;

PROCEDURE DisplayGrades (StudentID VARCHAR2) IS
BEGIN
END;

END; --end of package body
```

Figure 10-8: Coding the package body

12 Save the code. Although a compile error is generated, you succeeded in saving your work in the Oracle database. PL/SQL does not compile procedures without code in them.

Now you are ready to add the code to generate the Web page shown in Figure 10-9.

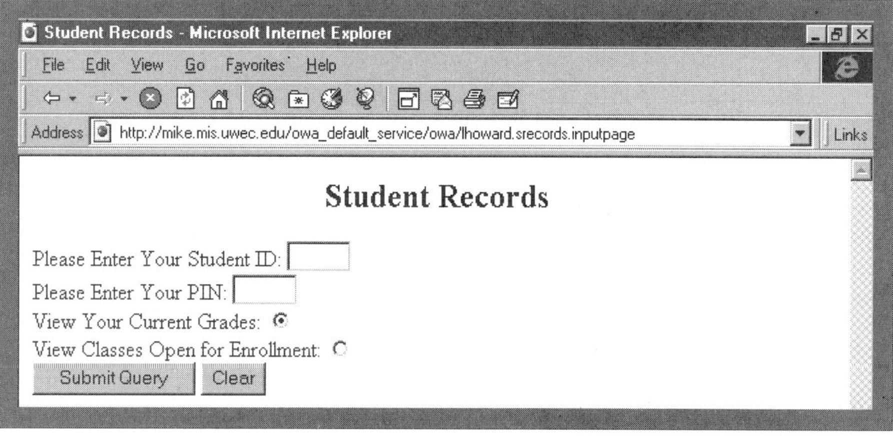

Figure 10-9: Viewing the input page in a Web browser

To add code to generate the Web page:

1 Modify your SRecords package body to the following:

```
PACKAGE BODY SRecords IS

PROCEDURE Error_page(error_msg VARCHAR2) IS
BEGIN
www_user.htp.p('
  <html><head>
  <title>Error Page</title>
  </head>
  <body>
  <center>'
  || error_msg ||
  '</center>
  </body></html>
');
END;

PROCEDURE InputPage IS
BEGIN
www_user.htp.p('
  <HTML>
  <HEAD>
  <TITLE>Student Records</TITLE>
  </HEAD>
  <BODY>
  <center>
  <H2>Student Records</H2>
  </center>
  <form action=<your user name>.srecords.processinputs>
  Please Enter Your Student ID:
   <input type=text name=StudentID size=5 maxlength=5><br>
  Please Enter Your PIN:
   <input type=text name=StuPIN size=5 maxlength=4><br>
  View Your Current Grades:
   <input type=radio checked name=requesttype value="GRADES"><br>
  View Classes Open for Enrollment:
   <input type=radio name=requesttype value="OPENCLASSES"><br>
   <input type=submit> <input type=reset value="Clear">
```

calls procedure named ProcessInputs

```
   </form>
   </BODY>
   </HTML>
');
END;

PROCEDURE ProcessInputs (StudentID   VARCHAR2,
                  StuPIN      VARCHAR2,
                  RequestType VARCHAR2) IS
BEGIN
 <your user name>.srecords.error_page('ProcessInputs'  ||
         '<br>StudentID:'   || StudentID ||
         '<br>StuPIN:'      || StuPIN    ||
         '<br>RequestType:' || RequestType);
END;

PROCEDURE DisplayGrades (StudentID VARCHAR2) IS
BEGIN
 <your user name>.srecords.error_page('DisplayGrades');
END;
END; -- end of package body
```

2 Save your package body and correct any syntax errors. If you can't resolve the compile errors, see the section entitled "Debugging Tips" near the end of this chapter for advice on debugging.

3 Switch to SQL*Plus and then type **GRANT EXECUTE ON srecords TO WWW_USER** at the SQL prompt.

4 Confirm your stored procedures work by starting your Web browser, entering the following address in the Address text box: **http://<your Web server's domain name or IP address>/owa_default_service/owa/<your user name>.srecords.inputpage**, and then pressing the **Enter** key. Your Web page should look like Figure 10-9. You cannot test your form yet because you have not written the procedures to process the form inputs.

The parameters passed to ProcessInputs are form inputs in the Web page generated by the procedure InputPage. The name attribute of each input must be identical to the parameter name passed into ProcessInputs, and the order of the <input…> variables in InputPage must be the same as the order in which they are declared in ProcessInputs. For example, the InputPage procedure creates the following user inputs:

```
<input type=text name=StudentID size=5 maxlength=5>
<input type=text name=StuPIN size=5 maxlength=4>
<input type=radio checked name=requesttype value="GRADES">
<input type=radio name=requesttype value="OPENCLASSES">
<input type=submit>
<input type=reset value="Clear">
```

The name attributes of these inputs are StudentID, StuPIN, and requesttype. Although two of the <input> tags include requesttype, this is treated as a single input parameter that must take the value of the selected radio button.

Second, what is that www_user.htp.p('...'); function doing and where *is* this function? If in the Procedure Builder, you open WWW_USER, Stored Program Units, and the HTP package specification; then you can scroll down to find the following entries:

```
-- Output Procedures
procedure print (cbuf in VARCHAR2 DEFAULT NULL);
procedure print (dbuf in DATE);
procedure print (nbuf in NUMBER);

-- Abbrev call to print()
procedure p (cbuf in VARCHAR2 DEFAULT NULL);
procedure p (dbuf in DATE);
procedure p (nbuf in NUMBER);
```

PRINT is defined three times, and each definition is slightly different. P is offered as a shorter way to call PRINT. In the HTP package body, the first P procedure is:

```
procedure p (cbuf in VARCHAR2 DEFAULT NULL) is
begin print(cbuf); end;
```

Similarly, the other P procedures reference the PRINT procedure. Inside a package, procedures and functions can be **overloaded**, which means that if there is more than one procedure or function with the same name but with different parameters, each procedure is treated separately and can have different code and actions. In this chapter's exercises, the first procedure is named "print" and "p" because a VARCHAR2 type variable is passed. The P and PRINT procedures add the contents of the parameter passed to them to a Web page that will be returned to the user.

Aligning Text and Form Inputs Using HTML Tables

When you look at your Web page, you should notice the text boxes and the radio buttons are not aligned. HTML tables are used to align text and form inputs in a Web page. HTML tables are enclosed between the <table> ... </table> tags. Table rows are indicated with the <tr> ... </tr> tags. You can add as many rows as you like to a table. Within a table row, the <td> ... </td> tags delimit the contents of a table cell (and also define a table column). Additional attributes can be specified within these tags. Modifying a table tag to `<table width="%95">` ... `</table>` tells the browser to size the table to span 95% of the available screen width. Modifying cell/column tags to `<td width="20%">` ... `</td>` tells the browser to size the cell (and column) to span 20% of the total table width. These column widths should total 100% even when the <table> tag width is less than 100%. The column width is in relation to the table, not the screen; you should include the width attribute in the <td> .... </td> tags only in a table's first row. The first row controls column/cell width and width = ".." attributes will be ignored in later rows. Similarly, the first row determines the number of columns in a table. You should include the same number of <td>..</td> tags in every row of the table.

If a row <tr> tag doesn't have a corresponding </tr> tag, or a column <td> doesn't have a matching </td> tag, the resulting page in the browser will be affected in strange ways. For example, review the following HTML table and how it is displayed in a browser:

```
<table width="95%" border=1>
<tr>                 -- the first row in the table
<td width="20%">One</td>
<td width="20%">Two</td>
<td width="20%">Three</td>
<td width="20%">Four</td>
<td width="20%">Five</td>
</tr>
<tr>                 -- the second row in the table
<tr>Six</td>         -- Error: <tr> doesn't match the </td>
<td>Seven</td>
<td>Eight</td>
<td>Nine</td>
<td>Ten</td>
</tr>
</table>
```

Here is what is displayed in Netscape 4 and Internet Explorer 4:

Six

One	Two	Three	Four	Five
Seven	Eight	Nine	Ten	

The next exercise will use a table to align the contents of your Web page.

To align the text and form inputs:

1 Modify your InputPage procedure so it is the same as the code that appears below and on the next page. Don't miss any of the new table entries, and also notice that the <center> tags are rearranged slightly.

```
PROCEDURE InputPage IS
BEGIN
www_user.htp.p('
  <HTML>
  <HEAD>
  <TITLE>Student Records</TITLE>
  </HEAD>
  <BODY>
  <center>
  <H2>Student Records</H2>
  <form action=<your user name>.srecords.processinputs>
  <table width="95%">
  <tr>
   <td width="60%">Please Enter Your Student ID:</td>
   <td width="40%"><input type=text name=StudentID size=5
     maxlength=5></td>
  </tr><tr>
```

```
    <td>Please Enter Your PIN:</td>
    <td><input type=text name=StuPIN size=5 maxlength=4></td>
   </tr><tr>
    <td>View Your Current Grades:</td>
    <td><input type=radio checked name=requesttype value ="GRADES"></td>
   </tr><tr>
    <td>View Classes Open for Enrollment:</td>
    <td><input type=radio name=requesttype value="OPENCLASSES"></td>
   </tr><tr>
    <td><input type=submit></td>
    <td><input type=reset value="Clear"></td>
   </tr>
   </table>
   </center>
   </form>
   </BODY>
   </HTML>
  ');
  END;
```

2 Save your revised code (which also compiles it). If you have compile errors, see the "Debugging Tips" section later in this chapter for advice on debugging. Test your revised Web page either by refreshing the page if it still appears in Internet Explorer, or by starting your Web browser, entering the following address in the Address text box: **http://<your Web server's domain name or numeric address>/owa_default_service/owa/<your user name>.srecords.inputpage**, and pressing the Enter key. The Web page should look like Figure 10-10.

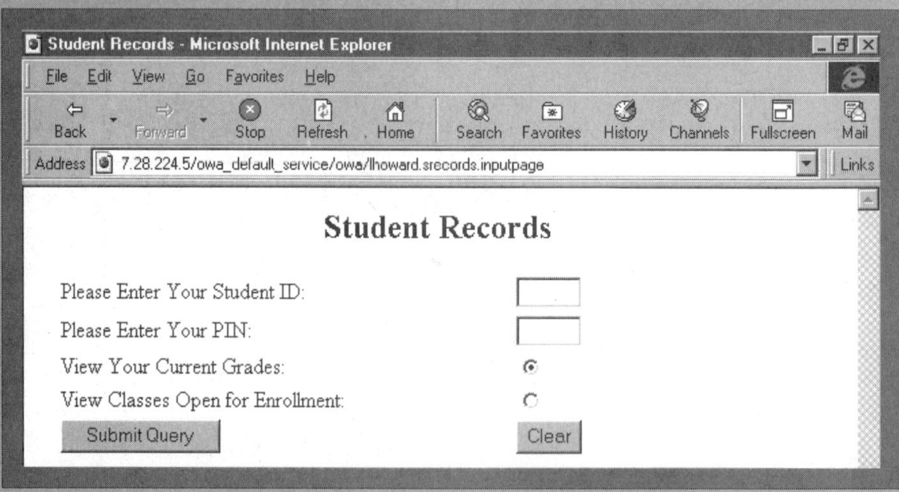

Figure 10-10: Aligning input page entries with an HTML table

Processing Form Inputs

There are four steps necessary to process form inputs. Steps 1 through 3 on the next page demonstrate how to query the database, validate a student's entries, and return a Web page informing the student of an error if the student ID or PIN is entered incorrectly. Step 4 adds the code to return a Web page with a student's grades.

Step 1's SELECT statement uses an implicit cursor. As explained in Chapter 6, an implicit cursor might be used if you are sure a SELECT statement will return a single record. If no records are returned or more than one record is returned, an error occurs. The variable(s) receiving the data from the query in the INTO clause must be of the same data types as the returned fields.

A user might enter a student ID that does not exist in the database, so an exception handler is added to the end of the ProcessInputs procedure. In the PL/SQL language, system or application errors of any kind are treated as exceptions. Many of these exceptions have been assigned names. Named exceptions usually are raised by a PL/SQL error (for example, dividing by zero) or a database processing error. ProcessInputs takes advantage of the NO_DATA_FOUND named exception to notify the user that the student ID was not in the database table. The OTHER named exception is a handy way to catch and respond to any errors, named or unnamed, that might occur. The SQLCODE function returns the status code of the last executed line of code (which caused the error). SQLERRM is a function that returns the text of the error message.

To handle exceptions:

1 Modify the ProcessInputs procedure to the following:

```
PROCEDURE ProcessInputs (StudentID   VARCHAR2,
                         StuPIN      VARCHAR2,
                         RequestType VARCHAR2) IS
  stu_pin <your user name>.student.spin%TYPE;
BEGIN
  -- the following SELECT is an example of an implicit cursor
  SELECT spin INTO stu_pin FROM <your user name>.student WHERE
  sid = StudentID;
  IF stu_pin = StuPIN THEN
    -- personal identification number was entered correctly
    IF RequestType = 'GRADES' THEN
      <your user name>.srecords.displaygrades (StudentID);
    ELSE
      error_page ('OpenClasses isn''t implemented...');
      <your user name>.srecords.inputpage;
    END IF;
  ELSE
    <your user name>.srecords.error_page ('Unable to find your StudentID
     or PIN' ||
    '<br>Please try again...');
    <your user name>.srecords.inputpage;
  END IF;
```

```
EXCEPTION
  WHEN NO_DATA_FOUND THEN -- happened on the SELECT spin
    <your user name>.srecords.error_page ('Unable to find your StudentID
    or PIN' ||
    '<br>Please try again...');
    <your user name>.srecords.inputpage;
  WHEN OTHERS THEN        --check for unanticipated system errors
    <your user name>.srecords.error_page ('SQLCODE: ' || SQLCODE ||
    '<br>ErrorText: ' || SUBSTR(SQLERRM, 1, 200));
END;
```

2 Save your code and use the "Debugging Tips" section to correct any syntax errors until the code compiles successfully.

3 Refresh your Web page if your browser is still running; or start your Web browser and then enter the address for your InputPage procedure. Test your changes by entering **Student ID 100** and **Student PIN 8891**, and then clicking the **Submit Query** button. When your application runs correctly, you will see the Display Grades form, which will be blank because you have not written the code to display the grades yet. Try an invalid Student ID/PIN combination to confirm that you see the "Unable to find your Student ID or PIN" message.

HELP? If your code does not compile successfully, or if it compiles but you receive the message "Request Failed. We were unable to process your request at this time. Please try again later.", go to the section on Debugging Tips at the end of this chapter to locate and correct your error.

Next you will create an explicit cursor in the DisplayGrades procedure. As you recall from Chapter 6, explicit cursors are used when you anticipate returning more than one record in your SELECT statement. They are written in the DECLARE section and processed in the procedure body. In the DisplayGrades procedure, you will create an explicit cursor named STU_CUR.

You also will modify DisplayGrades to call a new procedure named AddPoints. AddPoints is not declared in the package specification because it is a private procedure used only in this package. To enable DisplayGrades to access AddPoints, you will put the code for AddPoints before the DisplayGrades procedure. If you wanted to place AddPoints procedure *after* DisplayGrades, a forward declaration of AddPoints would have to be placed in the package body before DisplayGrades. A **forward declaration** involves declaring a function or procedure before you actually write the code for the function or procedure. The purpose of a forward declaration is to allow other functions and procedures to call the declared program without getting compile errors. A forward declaration is coded identically to a declaration in a package specification. For example, you would use the following code to write a forward declaration for the AddPoints function: `FUNCTION AddPoints (hours NUMBER, grade CHAR);`.

Note: When you enter the following code for DisplayGrades, you will crash the Web server if you forget to FETCH the next record or forget to EXIT the LOOP when the last record has been processed (these lines are italicized). Some (not all) infinite loops on a Web server consume all the Web server's main memory which results in a crash (making you unpopular with your system administrator and fellow students—Web and database access logs will identify who is responsible for doing this). Other infinite loops will not crash the Web server, but will consume most of the available CPU time and make the server unusable until an administrator stops the runaway process.

To create the explicit cursor:

1 Type the following code *before* DisplayGrades in the Srecords package body, and then click the **Save** button to compile and save the function.

```
FUNCTION AddPoints(hours NUMBER, grade CHAR) RETURN
NUMBER IS
BEGIN
 IF UPPER(grade) = 'A' THEN
   RETURN hours * 4;
 ELSIF UPPER(grade) = 'B' THEN
   RETURN hours * 3;
 ELSIF UPPER(grade) = 'C' THEN
   RETURN hours * 2;
 ELSIF UPPER(grade) = 'D' THEN
   RETURN hours * 1;
 ELSIF UPPER(grade) = 'F' THEN
   RETURN 0;
 ELSE
   RETURN 0;
 END IF;
END;
```

2 Modify the DisplayGrades procedure as follows. (The text for the modified DisplayGrades procedure is saved in the dgrades.txt file in the Chapter10 folder on your Student Disk, or you can type it directly.)

```
PROCEDURE DisplayGrades (StudentID VARCHAR2) IS
  -- the following CURSOR is an example of an explicit cursor
  CURSOR stu_cur IS SELECT slname, sfname, smi, tdesc, callid,
                    secnum, ccredit, grade
              FROM  <your user name>.enrollment, <your user name>.student,
                   <your user name>.course_section, <your user name>.course,
                    <your user name>.term
              WHERE  student.sid=StudentID
                    AND enrollment.sid=student.sid
                    AND enrollment.csecid=course_section.csecid
```

```
                     AND course_section.cid=course.cid
                     AND course_section.termid=term.termid
                 ORDER BY term.termid DESC, callid;
  stu_row stu_cur%ROWTYPE;
  CompHours   NUMBER := 0;
  GradePoints NUMBER := 0;
  CurrentTerm testuser.term.tdesc%TYPE := 'type a space here ';
BEGIN
  OPEN stu_cur;
  FETCH stu_cur INTO stu_row;
  IF stu_cur%NOTFOUND THEN -- make sure the query returned something!
    CLOSE stu_cur; -- Close your cursor when you are finished!
    teststudent.srecords.error_page
    ('The system found your StudentID and ' ||
    'PIN.<br>But didn't find '  ||
    'any other information.<br>'  ||
    'Please notify the Student '  ||
    'Records Office.');
    <your user name>.srecords.inputpage;
  ELSE
  www_user.htp.p('
  <HTML>
  <HEAD>
  <TITLE>Student Grade Report</TITLE>
  </HEAD>
  <BODY>
  <center>
  <H2>Student Grade Report</H2>' || TO_CHAR(SYSDATE) || '<br>For: '
  || stu_row.sfname || ' ' || stu_row.smi      || ' ' || stu_row.slname ||
  '<br>
  <form action=<your user name>.srecords.inputpage>
  <br><input type=submit value= "Return to Start"><br>
  <table width=95%>
  <tr>
   <td width="20%">
    <strong><u>Term</u></strong></td>
   <td width="20%">
    <strong><u>ClassID</u></strong></td>
   <td width="20%">
    <strong><u>Credit</u></strong></td>
   <td width="20%">
```

```
      <strong><u>Section</u></strong></td>
    <td width="20%">
      <strong><u>Grade</td></u></strong></tr>
’);
    -- Now display the grades
    LOOP
      www_user.htp.p(‘<tr>’);
      IF CurrentTerm <> stu_row.tdesc THEN
        www_user.htp.p(‘<td>’ || stu_row.tdesc  || ‘</td>’);
        CurrentTerm := stu_row.tdesc;
      ELSE
        www_user.htp.p(‘<td> </td>’);
      END IF;
        www_user.htp.p(‘<td>’ || stu_row.callid ||
                ‘</td><td>’ || stu_row.ccredit ||
                ‘</td><td>’ || stu_row.secnum  || ‘</td>’);
        IF stu_row.grade IS NULL THEN
          www_user.htp.p(‘<td>Incomplete</td></tr>’);
        ELSE
          www_user.htp.p(‘<td>’ || stu_row.grade || ‘</td></tr>’);
        END IF;
      IF NOT stu_row.grade IS NULL AND LENGTH(stu_row.grade) > 0
      THEN
         CompHours := CompHours + stu_row.ccredit;
         GradePoints := GradePoints +
                  AddPoints(stu_row.ccredit, stu_row.grade);
      END IF;
        -- get the next record
      FETCH stu_cur INTO stu_row;
        -- exit if there are no more records to retrieve
      IF stu_cur%NOTFOUND THEN EXIT; END IF;
    END LOOP;
    www_user.htp.p(
    ‘<tr>
      <td> </td>
      <td> </td>
      <td><strong>_____</strong></td>
      <td> </td>
      <td><strong>_____</strong></td></tr>
     <tr>
      <td> 
      </td><td>Completed Hours:
```

Type five underscores (_) here

Type five underscores (_) here

```
      </td><td>' || TO_CHAR(CompHours) ||
      '</td><td>GPA:</td>
      <td>' || TO_CHAR(GradePoints/CompHours, '9D99') || '</td></tr>
     </table>
');
    CLOSE stu_cur; -- Close your cursor when you are finished!
  END IF;

EXCEPTION
  WHEN OTHERS THEN         -- check for unanticipated system errors
    <your user name>.srecords.error_page ('SQLCODE: ' || SQLCODE ||
                        '<br>ErrorText: ' ||
                        SUBSTR(SQLERRM, 1, 200));
END;
```

2 Save your code and correct any syntax errors. See the "Debugging Tips" section if necessary.

3 Test the program using your Web browser. Your Web browser should look like Figure 10-11 after entering a valid student ID and PIN.

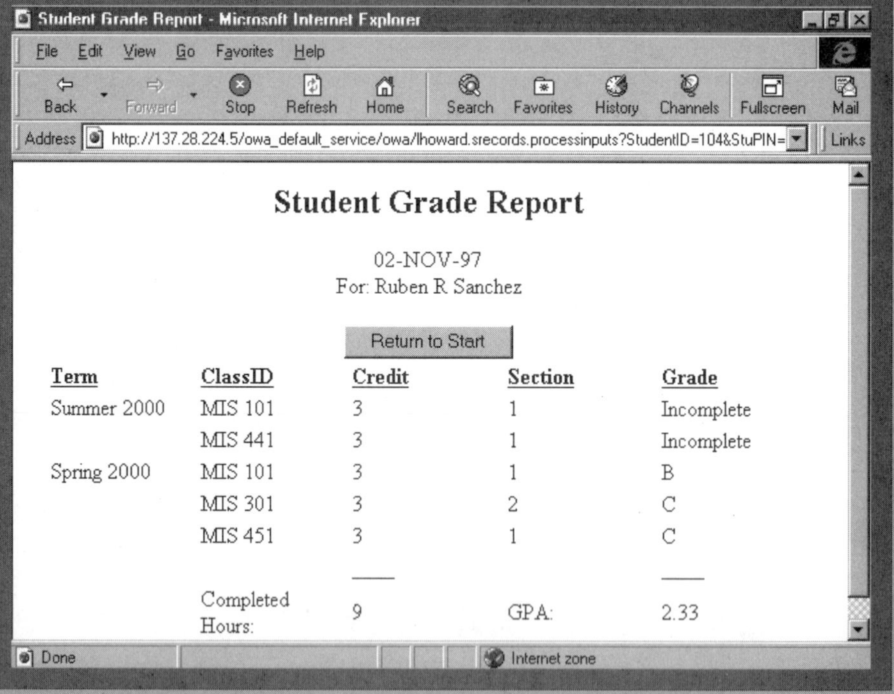

Figure 10-11: Viewing student grades in a Web browser

Procedures declared in the package specification are **public procedures**. Any PL/SQL procedure in any package can access these procedures. If needed, variables can be declared in a package specification. These variables become global variables that are accessible from any other procedure or function.

Debugging Tips

When you are compiling PL/SQL procedures, even a simple typing error can result in multiple compile errors. This section introduces you to some common errors and shows you how to interpret and correct them.

After you save (compile) your code, the "PDE-USWOO2 The source of the stored program unit source is incomplete" error message indicates that you omitted a single quotation mark in one of your character strings. This error often is difficult to find. You can use the /* */ block comment delimiters to remove a block of code from the compile process temporarily. For example, place /* */ around the following block of code prior to saving it:

```
/* www_user.htp.p('<H2>Student Grade Report</H2>' ||
                  TO_CHAR(SYSDATE) || '<br>For:'  ||
                  stu_row.sfname   || ' '         ||
                  stu_row.smi      || ' ||stu_row.slname
                  || '<br>' ||
                  <form action=<your user name>.srecords
                  .inputpage>'); */
```

After adding the block comment markers, save the program. If it compiles without the error, you know to look for the missing single quotation mark in the block you commented out. (Incidentally, the above block of code is missing a single quotation mark in the fourth line.)

The "PLS-00103 Encountered the symbol 'this varies based on your code' when expecting" message indicates that you omitted a semicolon at the end of a line of code. This error is easier to spot and rarely requires block commenting to find it, but you can use the comment markers if necessary to find the error.

Finally, remember that double-clicking an error message often moves the insertion point to the approximate area in the code where the error occurred. This process works well for omitted semicolons, but it usually does not find missing single quotation marks.

HTML Errors

After saving your program, you still might find errors in the HTML code generated by your program. If you skipped the "Aligning Text and Form Inputs Using HTML Tables" section, return to this section and read the part about table errors.

A form's "action" attribute determines the Web program that will process the form's inputs. In the InputPage procedure, the form action attribute refers to your ProcessInputs procedure (`<form action=<your user name>.srecords .processinputs>`.

The <input type =... name=...> tags create and name parameters that will be passed to the program listed in the form's action attribute. The processing program expects to be passed these parameters. If it doesn't receive them, it quits and the Web server returns a Web page that says "Request Failed. We were unable to process your request at this time. Please try again later."

The InputPage procedure creates the following form inputs:

```
<input type=text name=StudentID size=5 maxlength=5>
<input type=text name=StuPIN size=5 maxlength=4>
<input type=radio checked name=requesttype value="GRADES">
<input type=radio name=requesttype value="OPENCLASSES">
```

The ProcessInputs procedure expects StudentID, StuPIN, and RequestType to be passed to it in this order and with these names. Any of the following uses will cause the "Request Failed" error:

- Misspelling name as nmae: `<input type=text nmae=StudentID size=5 maxlength=5>`
- Misspelling StudentID as StudntID: `<input type=text name=StudntID size=5 maxlength=5>`
- Omitting an input:

```
<input type=text name=StudentID size=5 maxlength=5>
<input type=radio checked name=requesttype value="GRADES">
<input type=radio name=requesttype value="OPENCLASSES">
```

- Wrong order:

```
<input type=text name=StuPIN size=5 maxlength=4>
<input type=text name=StudentID size=5 maxlength=5>
<input type=radio checked name=requesttype value="GRADES">
<input type=radio name=requesttype value="OPENCLASSES">
```

Security Issues for Web Browsers

You might notice that the student's ID and PIN appear in the address shown in Figure 10-11. It is tempting to think that because the output is displayed for the student after he or she enters these numbers, it shouldn't matter if this information appears. However, Internet Explorer and other Web browsers maintain a history of visited Web sites that includes addresses like the one shown in Figure 10-11. Any student can view a history list, enter the student ID and PIN found in the history list, and then display student name and grades, which are supposed to be confidential.

For customers accessing a commercial site from home, this probably is not an issue. The customer knows the information required to log in, and seeing the information in a Web address isn't going to be a problem unless other people use their home PCs and are security risks. In a business environment, an employee's personal PC might be locked in the employee's office, which also could reduce the security risk. In a university PC lab, anyone might sit down at any time in front of any of the lab PCs. As you can see, keeping a history of visited Web sites becomes a major problem.

One solution is to disable the histories kept by the browser if more than one person will use the same PC or if security is an issue. For Internet Explorer this is done by clicking View on the menu bar, clicking Options, and then clicking the Navigation tab. Then you clear the current history and set the number of days to keep pages in the history to 0. In Netscape Navigator 3.x, click Options on the menu bar, click General Preferences, click the Appearance tab, click the Expire Now button, and then set the Expire After value to 0 days. The history is cleared when the user exits the system, so the user still can use the history during a single Web session. When you clear the history, you need to tell users to close their Web browsers before physically leaving the PC, so they can ensure that the PC is secure. You also should alert users to the fact that while they are working, other users can see confidential user parameters passed to the Web program by simply looking at the address.

A better solution is to prevent form inputs from appearing in a URL. Web forms have two primary methods for sending their inputs to a Web server. The default method, which was used in these exercises, is the GET method. With the GET method, inputs are passed as command line parameters in the URL to the Web server. After receiving form inputs, a GET request is passed to the program processing the request as an environment variable. Environment variables typically are limited to 255 characters in length. Due to length restrictions and security concerns, the POST method is more commonly used. Form inputs are not displayed in a URL when using POST and there are no restrictions on the length of these inputs. After receiving form inputs using the POST method, a Web server passes the inputs to the processing program as though they were directly typed into the program from the keyboard (using STDIN, or standard input). To correct this problem in your Web program, do the following:

1. Modify `<form action=<your user name>.srecords.inputpage>` in InputPage and DisplayGrades to `<form action=<your user name>.srecords.inputpage method="POST">`.
2. Test your program again in your Web browser and confirm that the form inputs are no longer displayed in the URLs.

The Oracle WebServer supports a variety of encryption standards to ensure security. If transmitting unencrypted passwords and sensitive information across a network is unacceptable, you will need to investigate these capabilities and implement them. This topic is beyond the scope of this book.

The Future of Oracle on the Web

The latest version of Developer/2000 allows Developer/2000 applications to be converted into Java code and run from Oracle's WebServer. Without a doubt, this is the future for Oracle's dynamic Web pages, but at the time this book is published Oracle does not support these capabilities because current Web browsers do not support this standard. However as Web technologies gain popularity and become simpler and more refined, many organizations will use the Oracle WebServer to allow users to access databases.

SUMMARY

- A Web listener reads all IP addresses embedded in all network messages passing through the network it is on and forwards messages with the server's address to higher level server processes.
- IP addresses are 32-bit numbers but usually are expressed as domain names that are easier to remember.
- Web addresses are called Uniform Resource Locators (URLs). URLs referring to a Web server start with "http://". URLs also might refer to FTP servers (ftp://), files (file:///), and more.
- More than one server process can run on the same computer. A Web server usually is assigned to the TCP/IP port 80. An FTP server running on the same computer usually would be assigned to port 21. An e-mail server running on the same computer usually would be assigned to port 25. Any number of server processes can run on the same computer with the same IP address so long as they are assigned different port numbers.

- Oracle's Web Request Broker (WRB) supports the PL/SQL Agent, Javacartridge, and LiveHTML. Additional cartridges are used to expand the capabilities of the WRB.
- Static Web pages are files that contain HTML codes and text. They always display the same information.
- Dynamic Web pages are generated by a server program when they are accessed by a Web browser. The generated page will vary depending on the inputs to the program. These inputs can come from the user, the operating system, files stored on the server, or from database tables accessed by the program.
- Oracle's PL/SQL Web page programs are saved and accessed as stored program units in an Oracle database. This database might run on the same computer the Oracle WebServer runs on, or it might run from a different location.
- Oracle's HTP package contains procedures for generating HTML documents (Web pages). Web pages are generated by sending their contents and HTML tags as a parameter to the htp.p procedure. The htp.p procedure is really three different procedures, depending on the data type of the parameter passed to it. Assigning the same name but different numbers or types of parameters to PL/SQL procedures is called overloading.
- Block comment delimiters /*...*/ are useful for finding compiler errors. Block out sections of code until the code compiles, and then add it back until you find the compile error. Double-clicking an error message often moves the insertion point to the approximate location of the error.
- Dynamically generated form input parameters are usually visible as part of the Web address, which means that users can view them in their Web browser's address window and history list. User IDs and passwords often appear in the Web browser in this manner, so PCs used by more than one user present a security risk. Turning off a Web browser's history is one way of minimizing this risk.
- Procedures, functions, and variables declared in a package specification are public, which means that any procedure or function in any package can access them.
- Procedures or functions declared in a package body (and not declared in the package specification) are private procedures or functions, which means that only procedures or functions in the same package body can call them. In addition, they must be declared in the package body before any other procedure or function can call them.

REVIEW QUESTIONS

1. Give two reasons for creating a Web database application rather than a Developer 2000 database application.
2. How is an IP address determined from a domain name?
3. What server process is normally assigned to TCP/IP port 80?
4. What is the function of the Web Request Broker?
5. Why might you choose the PL/SQL Agent rather than Java for building your Oracle Web application?
6. How does the Oracle WebServer know a Web address refers to a PL/SQL program?
7. Assume you have a form with three input items named LNAME, FNAME, and ADDRESS and that these inputs are displayed in that order. Will a stored procedure with the parameters LASTNAME, FIRSTNAME, and ADDRESS (in that order) successfully receive this form's inputs?
8. What is procedure (or function) overloading in PL/SQL?
9. When should you use an explicit cursor?
10. How would you create a global variable?

PROBLEM-SOLVING CASES

Northwoods University

1. Review the partial Northwoods University database structure shown in Figure 10-12. Modify the explicit cursor in DisplayGrades to include the last name of the faculty member teaching a particular section of a course. Modify DisplayGrades to include the faculty member's last name as a new column after Section and before Grade.

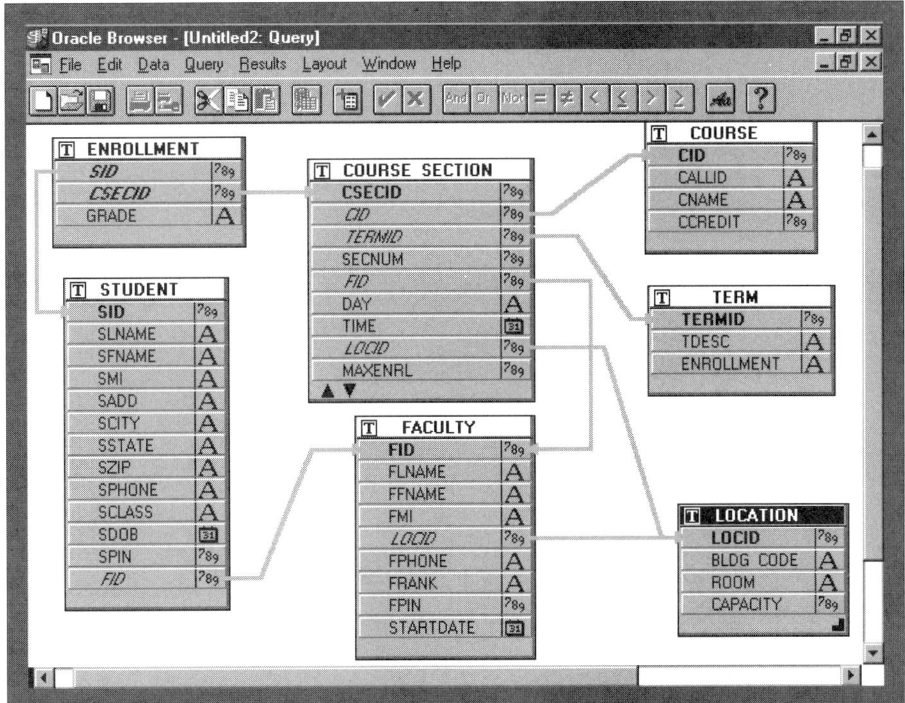

Figure 10-12

2. Modify DisplayGrades to add a new row at the end of each term with the completed hours and GPA for the displayed term. Modify the text to differentiate the overall GPA and completed hours from each term's completed hours and GPA.

Chapter 11 objectives

- Learn the duties of a database administrator
- Recognize the different types of Oracle database files and how they are organized within a server file system
- Learn some of the Oracle database administration utilities
- Become familiar with system privileges and user roles
- Understand backup strategies

CHAPTER 11

Introduction to Oracle Database Administration

Introduction The database administrator, or DBA, is the individual (or individuals) responsible for installing, administering, and maintaining a database. In this chapter you will learn about specific Oracle database administration utilities and the tasks performed by DBAs and about the underlying structure of an Oracle database.

The Duties of a DBA

As the complexity of database management systems increases, it becomes more important for there to be a person whose job responsibility is to understand the system's inner workings and oversee database startup activities and its day-to-day operations. The principle duties of an Oracle DBA are:

- Installing and upgrading the Oracle database software on the server
- Installing and upgrading the Oracle utilities (such as SQL*Plus, Oracle Browser, Forms, and Reports) on the client machines
- Performing the physical database design (deciding what data items are stored on specific server drives and directories)
- Starting and shutting down the database
- Creating new user accounts and controlling access to data and resources
- Monitoring data storage space and allocating new storage space as needed
- Assisting in the development of database applications
- Tuning the database for optimum performance
- Performing backup and recovery operations

Installing an Oracle database is much more complex than installing most personal computer software programs. A typical installation often involves many hours of work and might require calls to Oracle technical support personnel before it is completed successfully. However, once the database is installed, the Oracle database administration utilities make configuring the physical database design and performing the other day-to-day administration tasks fairly straightforward. Before you look at specific administrative tools, you will explore the physical structure of an Oracle database.

Physical Structure of an Oracle Database

Oracle is primarily designed to work in multiuser, multitasking computing environments such as UNIX, VMS, and Windows NT. In a **multiuser environment**, many users can run programs on the server at the same time. **Multitasking** means that the server can run several different programs simultaneously. Multiuser, multitasking operating systems are designed specifically to share processing, main memory, and disk storage effectively among multiple users and multiple applications.

In Oracle terminology, a **database** is an organized collection of data stored in datafiles, and an **instance** is the set of processes and memory storage areas that enables users to manipulate this collection of data. An instance has three parts: background processes, shared memory areas, and disk data storage areas.

Background Processes

In a single-user database, the user directly interacts with the datafiles through the DBMS. This interaction is accomplished easily because only one user accesses the files. However, in a multiuser database, interactions are more complicated. What if two users want to update the same record in the same table at the same time? **Background processes** are used to coordinate and accomplish all the tasks needed to maintain the database. For example, when a user updates a database record, one background process writes the update to a main memory buffer, another process makes an entry in the transaction log in case a rollback is issued, and a third process writes the change to the datafile on disk. The system coordinates these processes with one another so they do not contend for the same resource at the same time.

There are four basic kinds of background process tasks in an Oracle database:

- *Servicing user requests*, such as connecting to the database or inserting, updating, viewing, or deleting data. These processes are your link to the Oracle database.
- *Writing data to the datafiles*. When data is inserted or updated, it is saved first in a shared main memory area, and then written to the datafiles on disk.
- *Writing transactions to log files*. Each transaction is read from the main memory area and written to a log file so that in the case of a client or server failure, the system can recover the transactions from the log file.
- *Monitoring database functions*, such as disk space utilization.

Shared Memory Areas

The parts of the server's main memory that are used by Oracle fall into the following four categories:

- The **software code area** is used to store code that is being executed or about to be executed. Oracle's RDBMS code usually is stored in a more protected software code area separated from user programs.
- The **system global area** (**SGA**) is where user transactions are stored until they are written to data or log files. The SGA has four sub-components:
  1. The **database buffer cache**, which contains data records that are waiting to be written to datafiles or that have just been read from datafiles.
  2. The **redo log buffer**, which contains transactions waiting to be written to the online redo log files.
  3. **Shared SQL areas**, which store queries that have been parsed or compiled into executable language, but are waiting to be executed.
  4. The **data dictionary cache**, which stores information about the database, such as information about tables and users.
- The **program** (or **process**) **global area** (**PGA**) separately stores information about each process running on the server. For example, the PGA stores variables that are used by an Oracle Forms application while it is running for each user. Each user running the same Oracle Forms application gets a unique **PGA stack space**, which is memory that is allocated to store variables, arrays, and other specific information for a process.
- **Sort areas** are where records are sorted when an ORDER BY clause is added to a SQL query.

Disk Data Storage Areas

The Oracle DBMS uses seven different types of files to store data: datafiles, online redo log files, archive log files, control files, initialization files, and log and error files. The following sections describe these files, show where they are located, and show what they look like in a standard Windows NT installation.

Datafiles Datafiles contain the database data. Datafiles cannot be read directly using a text editor such as Notepad; they must be accessed using the Oracle DBMS. To store data in a database, the DBA first must create a tablespace. A **tablespace** represents how data is logically stored in the database. A tablespace is associated with one or more datafiles and provides the link to the physical data location. Next you will view your database tablespaces and other tablespaces created by the DBA to store user data.

To view your database tablespaces:

1. Start SQL*Plus and log on to the database.
2. Type the command shown in Figure 11-1. The query output shows tablespaces that are standard for most Oracle systems.

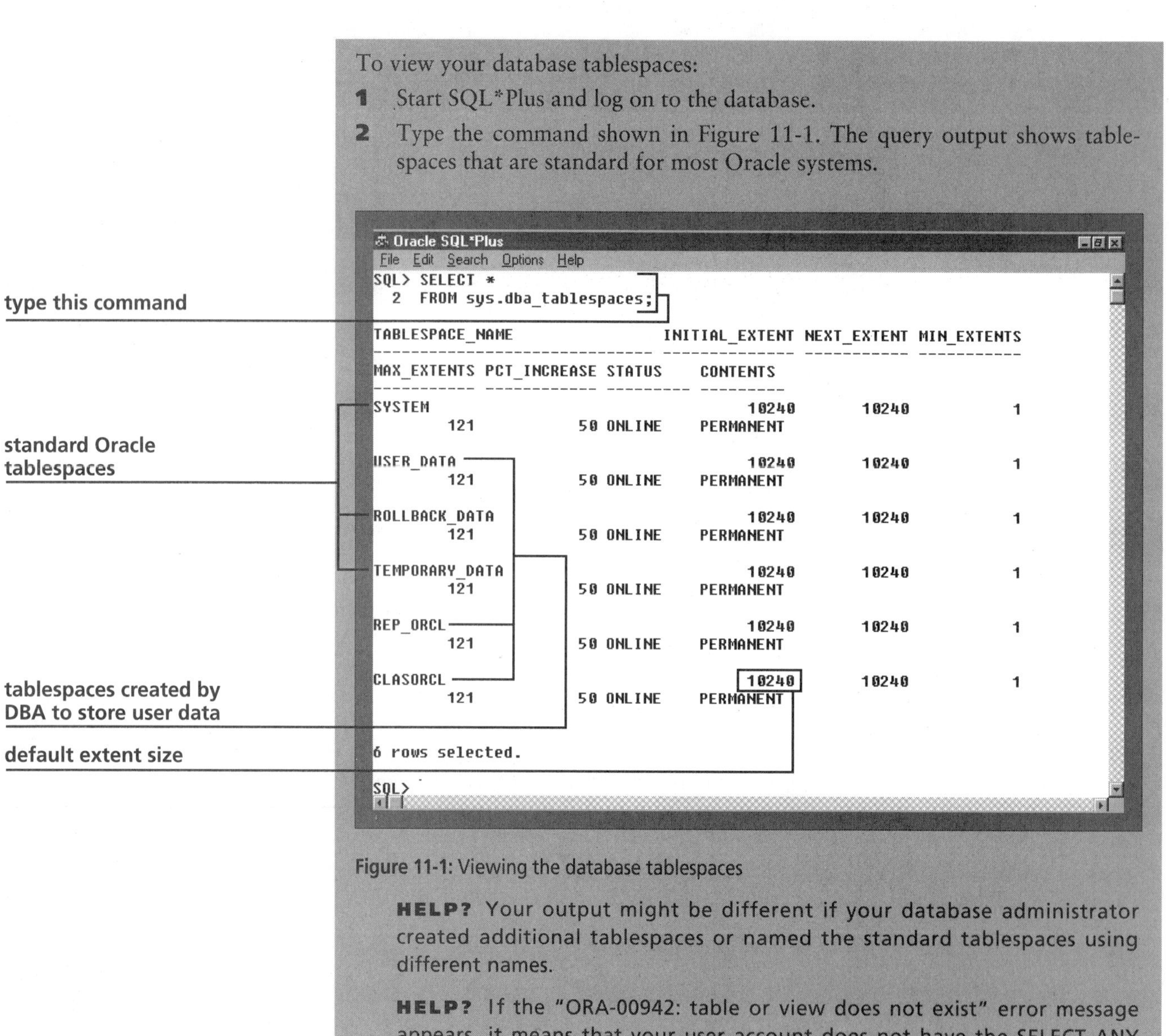

Figure 11-1: Viewing the database tablespaces

HELP? Your output might be different if your database administrator created additional tablespaces or named the standard tablespaces using different names.

HELP? If the "ORA-00942: table or view does not exist" error message appears, it means that your user account does not have the SELECT ANY TABLE privilege. Notify your instructor or technical support person.

The following tablespaces are standard to most Oracle systems:

- The SYSTEM tablespace stores data about the database, such as user accounts and passwords. The SYSTEM tablespace stores data in Oracle tables like the one you just queried (DBA_TABLESPACES).
- The ROLLBACK_DATA tablespace holds the information needed to roll back (undo) the changes made by a transaction. Rollback information is stored in **rollback segments** that include the location of the record that was changed and the data value before the transaction.
- The TEMPORARY_DATA tablespace typically holds data items that are too large to be sorted or processed entirely in main memory. For example, if you execute a SELECT statement with an ORDER BY clause that returns millions of records, the results of the SELECT will be processed in main memory with intermediate results stored in the TEMPORARY_DATA tablespace.

Figure 11-1 also shows that the DBA created the USER_DATA, REP_ORCL, and CLASORCL tablespaces to hold user database tables. Creating multiple user tablespaces enables the DBA to partition the database logically. For example, suppose that the Clearwater Traders and Northwoods University databases were both on the same database server. The tables could be stored in different tablespaces, and then users for one system could not see the other system's tables.

Every time a user creates a table in a tablespace, he or she uses a chunk of memory called an extent. An **extent** is a contiguous amount of storage space on a disk that cannot be used for anything other than its designated table. **INITIAL_EXTENT** is the amount of disk space set aside for the table when it is created. **NEXT_EXTENT** is the amount of disk space that will be acquired by the table when the first extent is filled. **MIN_EXTENTS** is the minimum number of extents that can be allocated for tables in the tablespace, and **MAX_EXTENTS** is the maximum number of extents that can be allocated. Extents allow the table to grow dynamically in size as needed. The default extent size in Oracle is 10,240 bytes, as shown in Figure 11-1.

tip

The Oracle home directory is the main Oracle directory, and all Oracle-related files are stored in its folders. For Windows 95 systems, the home directory usually is named ORAWIN95; for Windows NT systems, the home directory usually is named ORANT.

When the DBA creates a new tablespace, he also must create a datafile that physically holds the tablespace data. Datafiles usually are stored in a folder of the Oracle home directory named \DATABASE\, but datafiles can be stored in any directory. Sometimes they are stored on multiple hard drives so retrievals can occur from several drives simultaneously to speed up data access.

Figure 11-2 shows the file listing for the \ORANT\DATABASE\ folder on a Windows NT database server. The DBA specifies the tablespace data filenames. Usually the DBA will use filenames that are similar to the tablespace names so DBAs easily can identify which file corresponds to which tablespace. The DBA also specifies the datafile size. Note that the datafiles in Figure 11-2 are different sizes. Tablespaces that are expected to contain many tables or tables with large data fields need to have larger datafiles than tablespaces that probably will contain only a few tables with small amounts of data. If the datafile is too large, there will be unused disk space. If the datafile is too small, the DBA must continually create new datafiles when the existing ones are filled. When a tablespace's datafile is filled completely, its users will receive an error message when they try to create a new table. The DBA needs to monitor how full the datafile is and create a new datafile for the tablespace before the current one is completely filled.

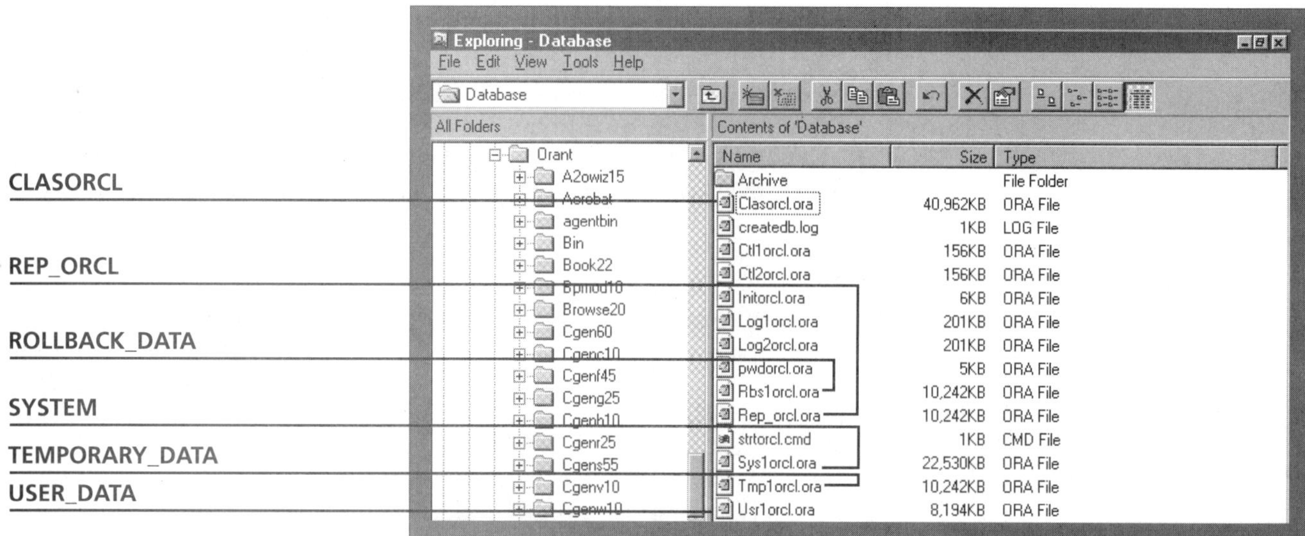

Figure 11-2: Datafiles associated with tablespaces in ORANT\DATABASE folder on server

Online Redo Log Files **Online redo log files** record every database transaction in a different file from the main datafiles so changes can be recovered if a datafile is damaged. There are several online redo log files that work in a circular fashion. At database startup, the first file begins recording transactions and continues recording until it is filled. Then the second file takes over and starts recording. When it is filled, the third file takes over. This sequential process continues until the last redo log file is filled. Then the first file is overwritten with new transactions. All transactions over some time window are thus recorded, with the time window depending on the number of database transactions and the number and size of the redo log files. Next you will view the database redo log files on your system.

To view the database redo log files on your system:

1 Type the command shown in Figure 11-3. The redo log files for your system appear in the output.

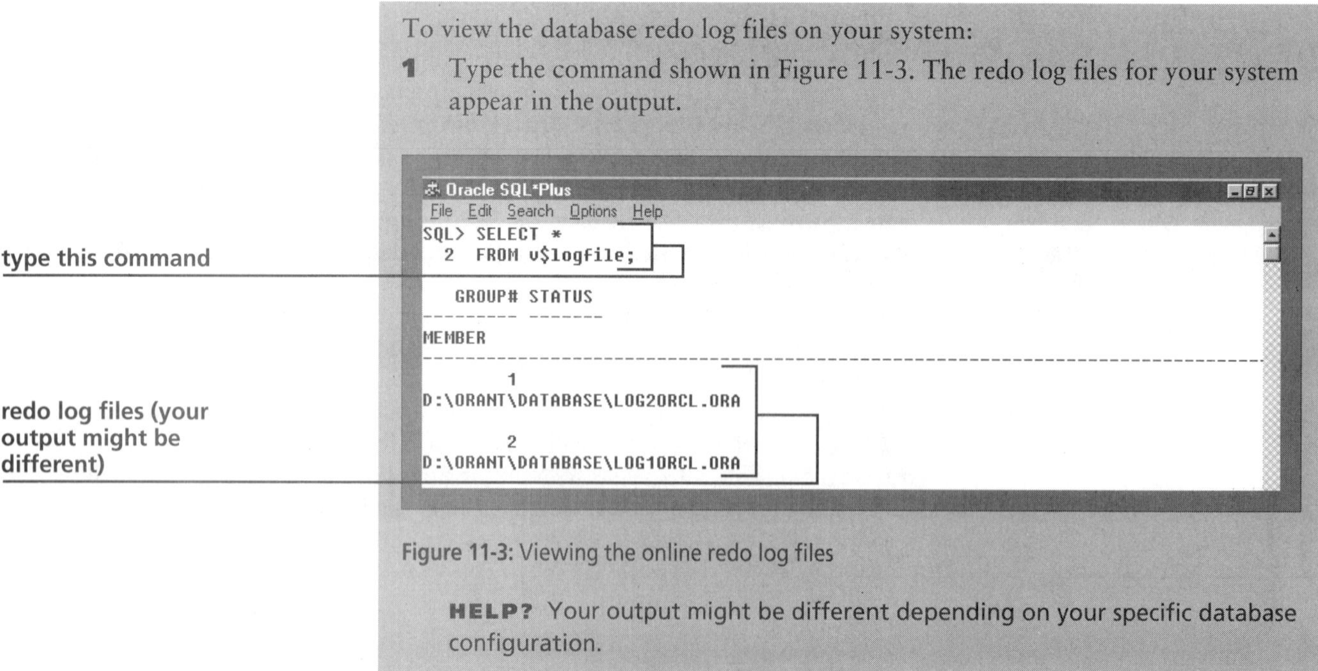

Figure 11-3: Viewing the online redo log files

HELP? Your output might be different depending on your specific database configuration.

The log files also are saved in the \DATABASE folder, as shown in Figure 11-4.

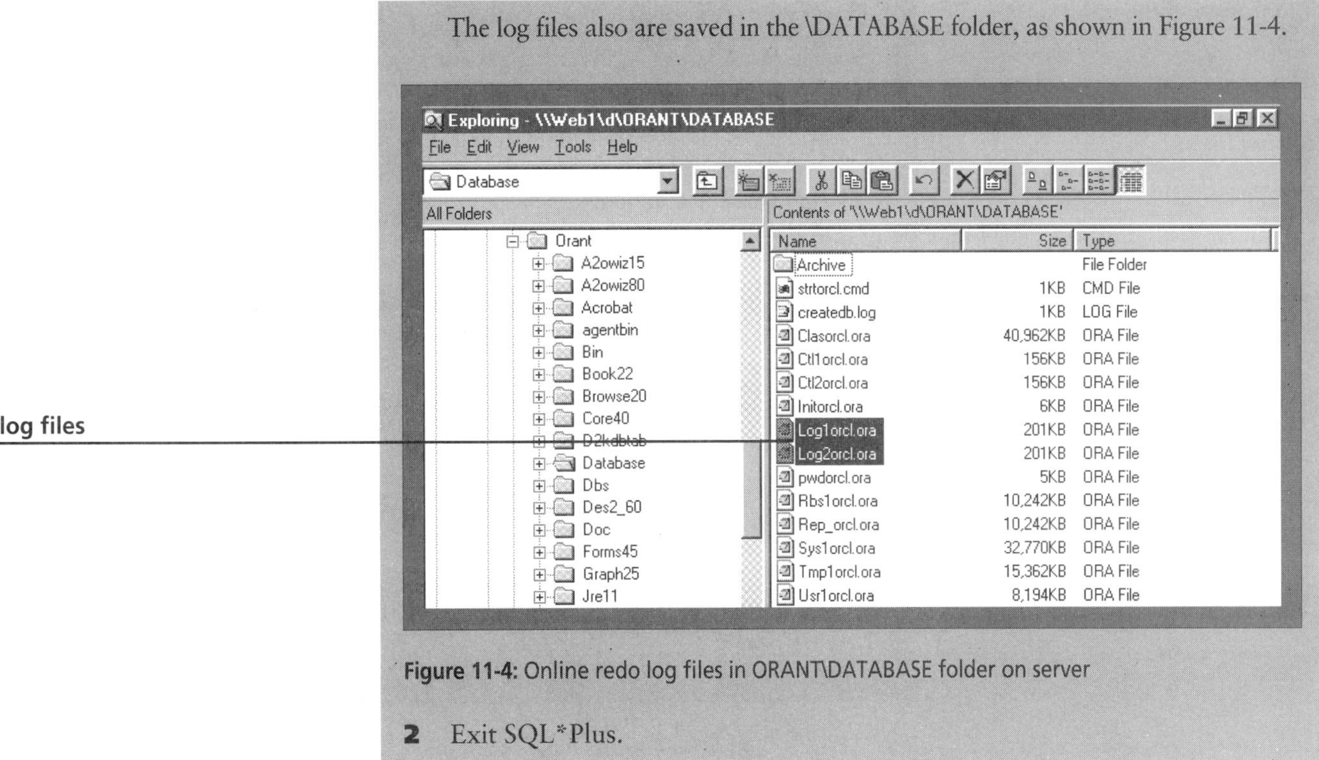

Figure 11-4: Online redo log files in ORANT\DATABASE folder on server

2 Exit SQL*Plus.

Archive Files As noted previously, online redo log files do not exist forever—they eventually fill up and are overwritten. **Archive files** are comprehensive backups of redo log files that usually are kept on magnetic tape. Archive files are not created automatically when a database is installed, so the DBA must issue a specific series of commands to start creating them. If these commands are entered incorrectly, they can stop the entire database. Archive files are an advanced Oracle DBA topic that is beyond the scope of this introductory chapter.

Control Files **Control files** contain a blueprint of the physical layout of the database on the server. Stored information includes the database name and data and redo log filenames. Control files are used internally by the DBMS and are created automatically when the DBA creates a new Oracle instance. The only time that control files cause a problem is when they are missing or damaged. Control files are not editable, but they can be copied, so always try to keep a backup copy on a separate disk drive in case these files are damaged. These files are named ctl1orcl.ora and ctl2orcl.ora and by default are stored in the \DATABASE folder along with the datafiles and the online redo log files.

Initialization Files The main initialization file is named init<SID>.ora, where SID is the system identifier for an Oracle database instance. The SID for the authors' database instance is orcl, so the filename is initorcl.ora. Figure 11-5 shows a portion of this file in Notepad. This is an editable text file that specifies parameters such as the database name, the location of the control files, and a variety of configuration parameters dealing with the SGA, PGA, and other things. Sometimes the DBA needs to edit this file to add a parameter or change an existing parameter's value.

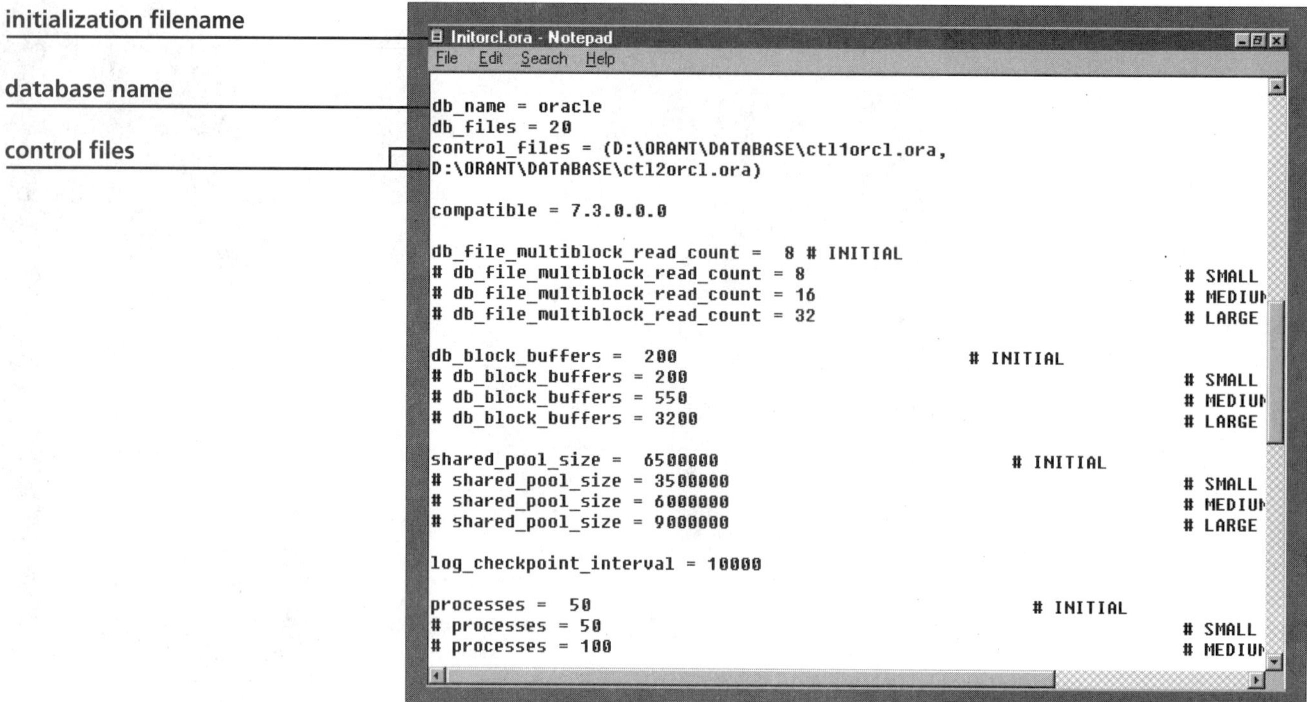

Figure 11-5: Portion of initorcl.ora initialization file

A DBA also might specify additional files that contain further initialization information by using the following line in init<SID>.ora: `ifile = <filename>`. The purpose of using additional initialization files is that the same file can be used by multiple database instances and referred to in each instance's init<SID>.ora file. This might be useful if you are running multiple databases on a single server or on different servers, and each database can access the common initialization files. This way, when you change an initialization property for all database instances, you need to change it only once in a single file.

Log Files **Log files** are written by system processes to record what the processes are doing, which is useful for troubleshooting. For example, if some process is slowing down or crashing the database, the DBA might be able to identify what process is causing the problem by reviewing the log files. Log files always have a .log extension. A search for files with a .log extension in the \ORANT folder on a database server (see Figure 11-6) shows they are stored in many different folders in the Oracle home directory. The log file that records major events of the DBMS itself is called the **alert log file**, which is stored in the file named orclALRT. LOG. (Again, this name is derived from the database SID.)

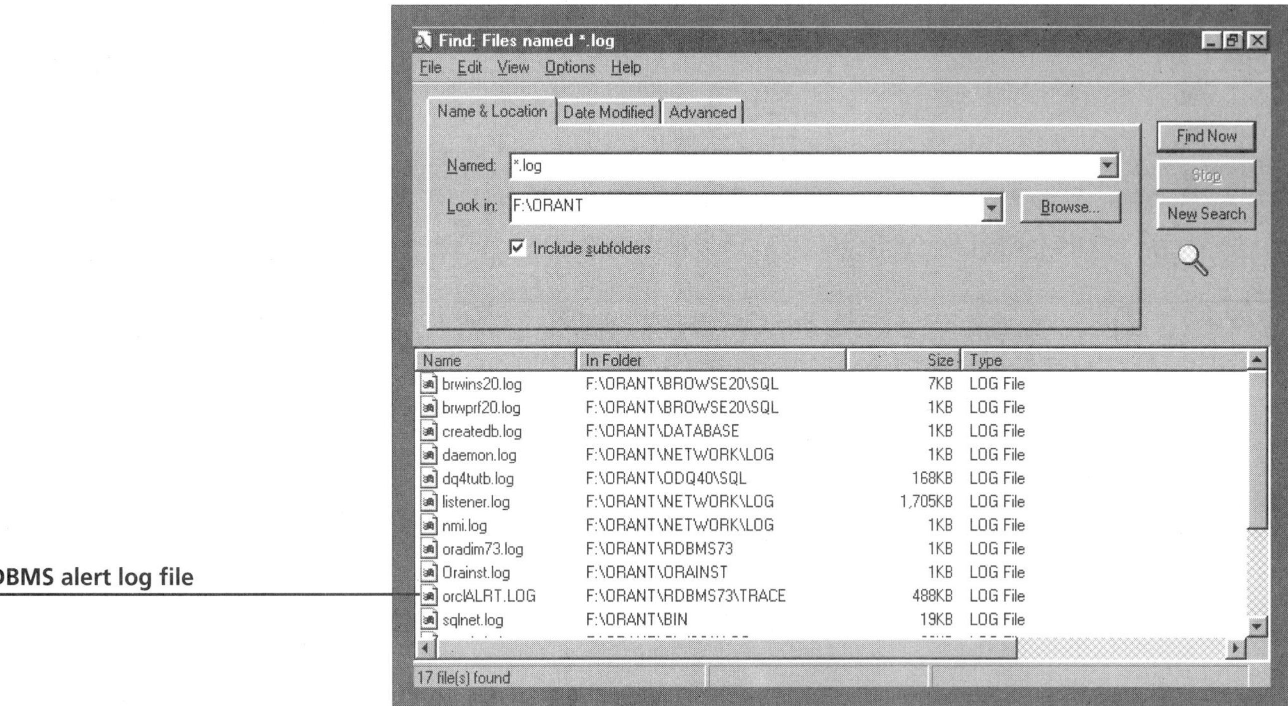

Figure 11-6: Log file listing

Figure 11-7 shows an excerpt (in WordPad) from the orclARLRT.LOG file following the database startup after a server crash and details how a process was recovered and redone.

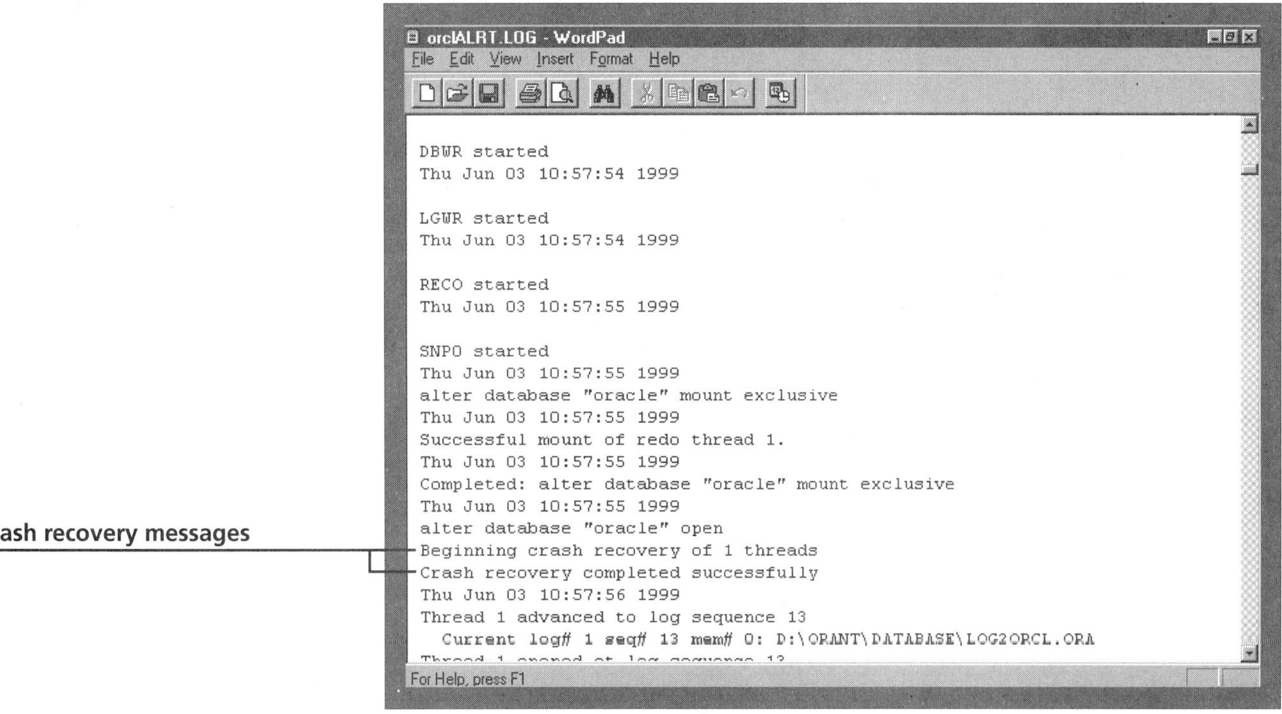

Figure 11-7: Excerpt from orclALRT.LOG file after server crash

Oracle Database Administration Utilities

Although all Oracle database administration tasks can be done using SQL commands, utilities are available to simplify these tasks. In this section, you will view these utilities and see how they are used.

The Instance Manager

Most of the time an Oracle database is left running and is restarted only after power failures or server crashes. (In the case of a power failure, the database will start automatically as soon as the server is rebooted.) The database sometimes is shut down for maintenance activities such as backups or modifying configuration files. Next you will look at the **Instance Manager**, which is used for starting and shutting down the database.

To start the Instance Manager:

1. Click the **Start** button on the taskbar, point to **Programs**, point to **Oracle Enterprise Manager**, and then click **Instance Manager** to start the Instance Manager utility.

   HELP? All of the Oracle database administration utilities are in the Oracle Enterprise Manager program group on the Programs menu. The sequence of steps you use to start these utilities might be slightly different. Ask your instructor or technical support person if you need help.

2. Connect to the database in the usual way. Click the **Normal** option button in the Connect As list.

   HELP? If you are connecting to the database using a student account, you will be able to view this DBA utility, but you will not be able to perform administrative functions unless the DBA has granted you DBA privileges.

tip

You also can start the Instance Manager by opening Windows Explorer and then double-clicking the ORAWIN95\BIN\vai.exe file. Windows NT users will instead double-click the ORANT\BIN\ vai.exe file.

The Database Instance The first selection in the navigation panel on the left side of the screen shows the current database instance, which is the same as your connect string (see Figure 11-8). This name is simply a **database alias** that specifies a network location and a specific database instance running there.

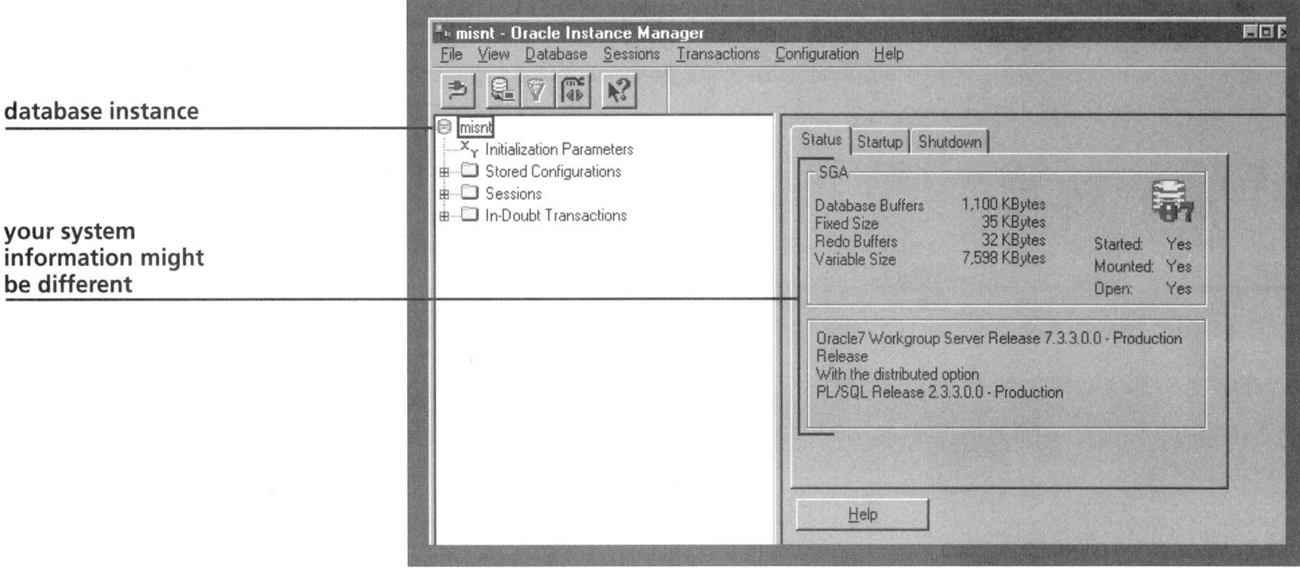

Figure 11-8: Oracle Instance Manager

The right pane currently displays the Status tab, which shows information about the SGA and confirms that the database is currently started, mounted, and open. **Starting** a database means starting the instance, or the underlying processes that run things. **Mounting** a database means associating the specific datafiles with these processes. **Opening** a database means making it available to users. The Startup and Shutdown tables enable the DBA to start and shut down the database. There are three startup options: startup only, mount (which includes startup), and mount and open. The database automatically tries to recover lost transactions and processes at startup. If some required recovery files are damaged or missing, the system might issue an error message informing the DBA of the problem.

If there are several long uncommitted transactions, it might take several minutes to perform an immediate shutdown.

Three different shutdown options exist: normal, immediate, and abort. A **normal shutdown** waits for current users to disconnect and does not allow any new users to connect prior to shutting down. A normal shutdown would be used to perform routine maintenance operations that are not urgent and do not need to interrupt regular work. An **immediate shutdown** does not wait for current users to disconnect, but immediately closes and dismounts the database, and rolls back all uncommitted transactions. An immediate shutdown would be used when it is urgent that the database be shut down immediately or otherwise it might be damaged, such as in the case when a power shutdown is expected or one of the database processes seems to be malfunctioning and possibly harming the database. An **abort shutdown** immediately shuts down the instance without closing or dismounting the database and requires special recovery operations at the next startup. An abort shutdown usually is used only when neither of the other shutdown procedures work, or when an instantaneous power outage is expected and there is not enough time to perform an immediate shutdown.

Next you will examine the Startup and Shutdown tabs to see the available options and parameters for starting and shutting down the database. You are not a DBA, so you do not have the necessary privileges to actually start or shut down your database.

To examine the database instance startup and shutdown options:

1 Click the **Startup** tab (see Figure 11-9). Checking the Force check box means that the DBA wants the database to be started regardless of the state of recovery files. The Force option tells the Instance Manager to ignore errors and start, regardless of what problems might exist. Checking the Restrict check box restricts database access to a limited group of users with special privileges. The DBA might restrict access when he or she needs to make major modifications to the database without interference from other users. The Parameter File text box allows the DBA to specify a specific initialization file other than the default (init<SID>.ora). To start the database, the DBA would select the desired option and then click the Startup button.

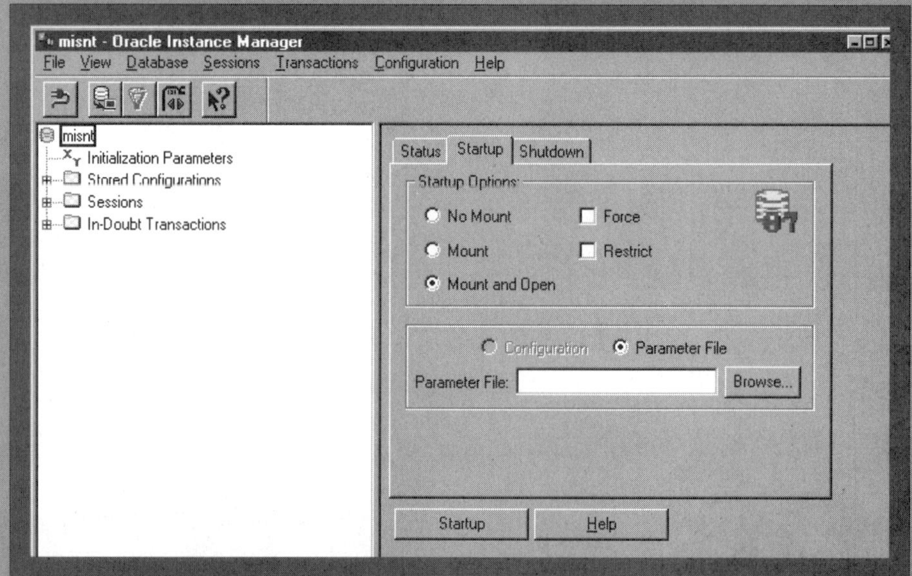

Figure 11-9: Instance Startup tab

2 Click the **Shutdown** tab. Figure 11-10 shows the Shutdown tab, which enables the DBA to shut down the database using one of the three shutdown options.

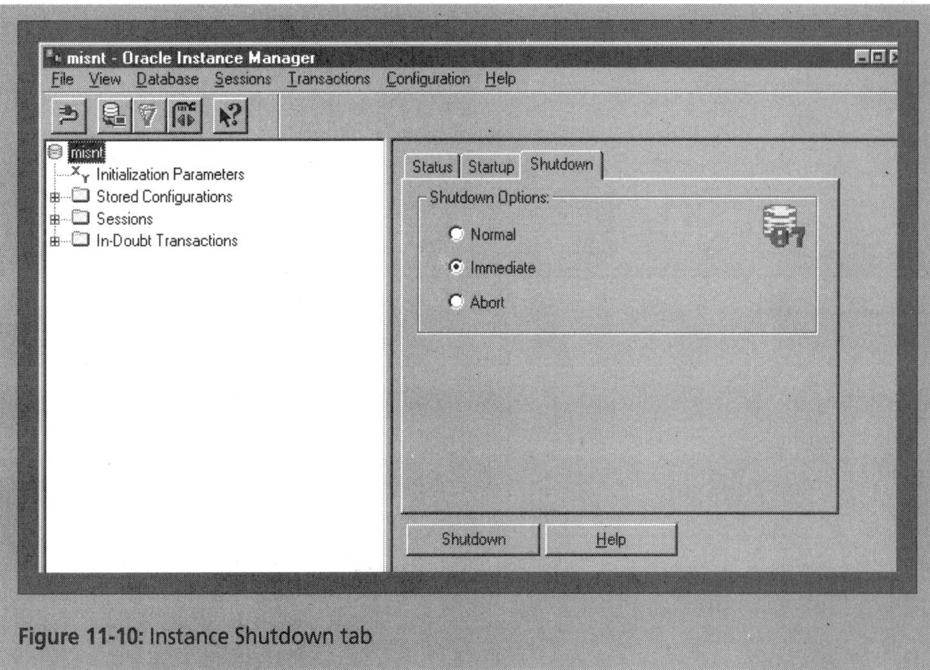

Figure 11-10: Instance Shutdown tab

Other Instance Manager Functions The Instance Manager also enables the DBA to change database initialization parameters, dynamically view what users currently are using the database, and examine in-doubt transactions that were partially recovered by the DBMS.

To examine the other Instance Manager functions:

1 Click **Initialization Parameters** in the left pane of the Instance Manager window. **Initialization parameters** show startup parameter values involving the overall database instance, main memory, file sizes and locations, etc. The DBA can change these parameters if necessary; however, changes are saved and applied only to the current database instance and do not modify the configuration files. If the DBA wants to create a permanent modification, he must modify the configuration file (initorcl.ora) using a text editor.

2 Click **Stored Configurations. Stored configurations** allow the DBA to create instance startup configurations that are stored in the Windows NT registry rather than in the configuration files. If your database has no stored configurations then this folder will be empty.

3 Click **Sessions. Sessions** lists all users currently connected to the database (see Figure 11-11). The only time a user session is ACTIVE is when the user is actively performing an operation that changes the database (such as an INSERT, UPDATE, or DELETE). This screen shows a snapshot of what currently is happening at the instant it is displayed—it is not dynamically updated. Therefore, although several users might be querying the database and actively inserting, updating, and deleting records, they might all be shown as INACTIVE in the snapshot view. Note that six system processes (sessions with Schema name SYS) in Figure 11-11 are listed as ACTIVE. These are the background processes discussed earlier in this chapter.

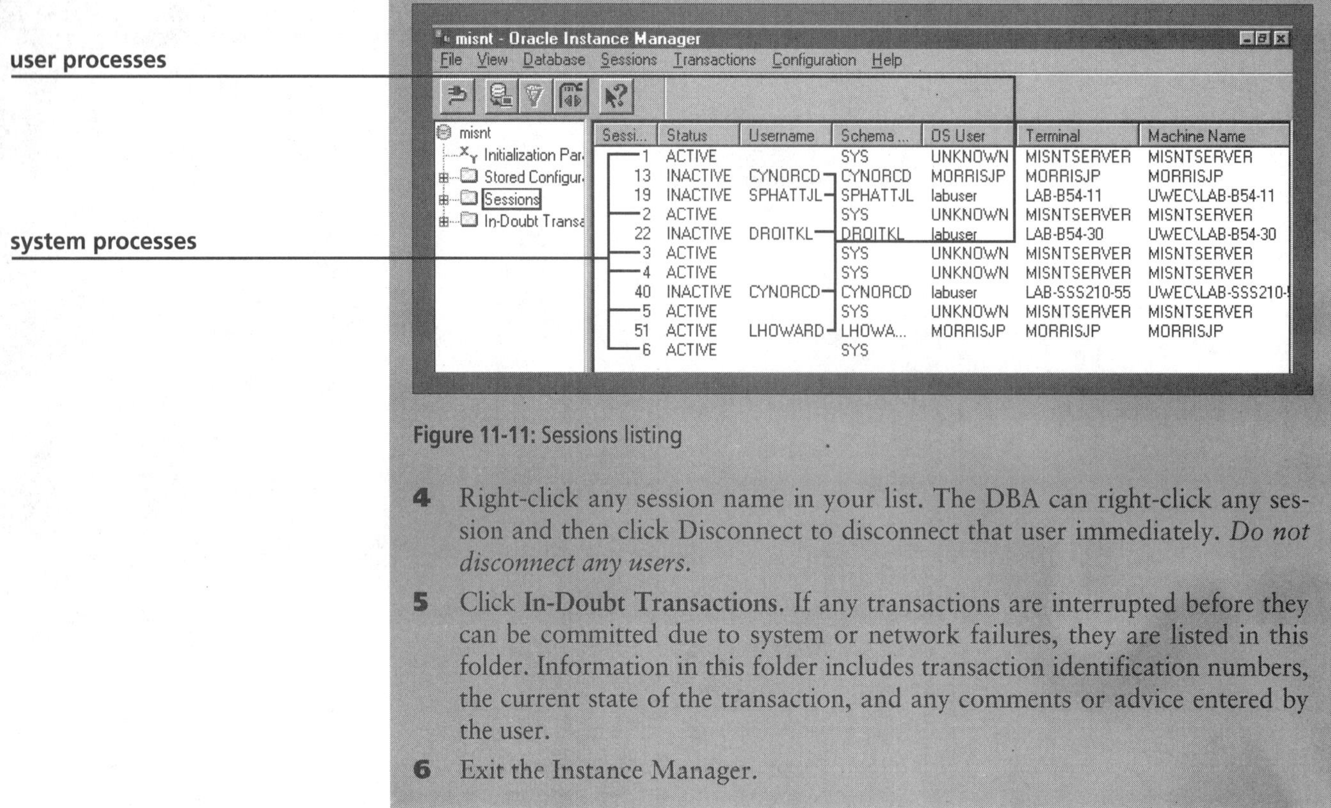

Figure 11-11: Sessions listing

4. Right-click any session name in your list. The DBA can right-click any session and then click Disconnect to disconnect that user immediately. *Do not disconnect any users.*
5. Click **In-Doubt Transactions.** If any transactions are interrupted before they can be committed due to system or network failures, they are listed in this folder. Information in this folder includes transaction identification numbers, the current state of the transaction, and any comments or advice entered by the user.
6. Exit the Instance Manager.

The Storage Manager

The **Storage Manager** enables the DBA to create and maintain tablespaces, datafiles, and rollback segments, as you will see next.

You also can start the Storage Manager from Windows Explorer by double-clicking the ORAWIN95\BIN\vag.exe file. Windows NT users will double-click the file ORANT\ BIN\ vag.exe.

To start the Storage Manager:

1. Click the **Start** button on the taskbar, point to **Programs**, point to **Oracle Enterprise Manager**, and then click **Storage Manager.**
2. Connect to the database in the usual way. Click the **Normal** option button in the Connect As list. The Storage Manager opens, with your database instance name listed as the top entry in the Oracle Navigator window.
3. Click the **Advanced Mode** button on the Storage Manager toolbar.
4. Click the **Tablespaces** folder to see a detailed listing of the tablespace names, and a visual view of how full each tablespace is. See Figure 11-12. As previously mentioned, a default Oracle installation has tablespaces named SYSTEM, ROLLBACK_DATA, and TEMPORARY_DATA.

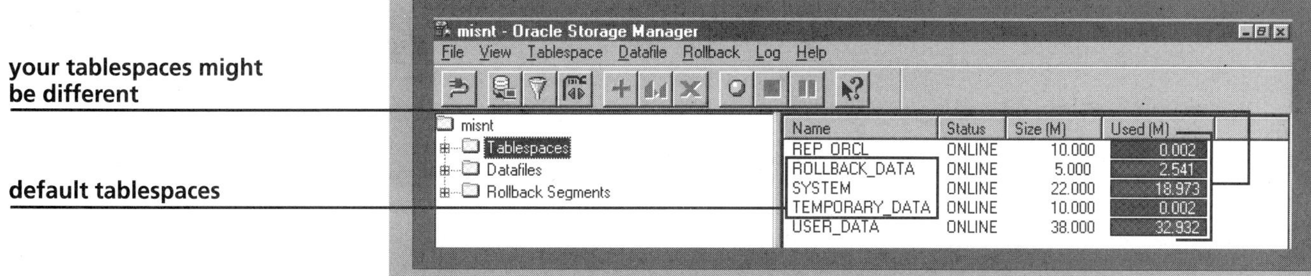

Figure 11-12: Viewing the tablespace details

5. Click the **Tablespaces plus box** ⊞ to view its subfolders.
6. Double-click the **SYSTEM** tablespace icon. You should see two subfolders under SYSTEM named Datafiles and Rollback Segments. The right pane shows the **General** tab, which contains information about the SYSTEM tablespace. See Figure 11-13. You can see that the SYSTEM tablespace currently is online and available to users; this tab also might show that it is offline for maintenance. The General tab also shows the datafiles associated with the tablespace and allows the DBA to create a new datafile. Note that your SYSTEM tablespace datafiles might be different.

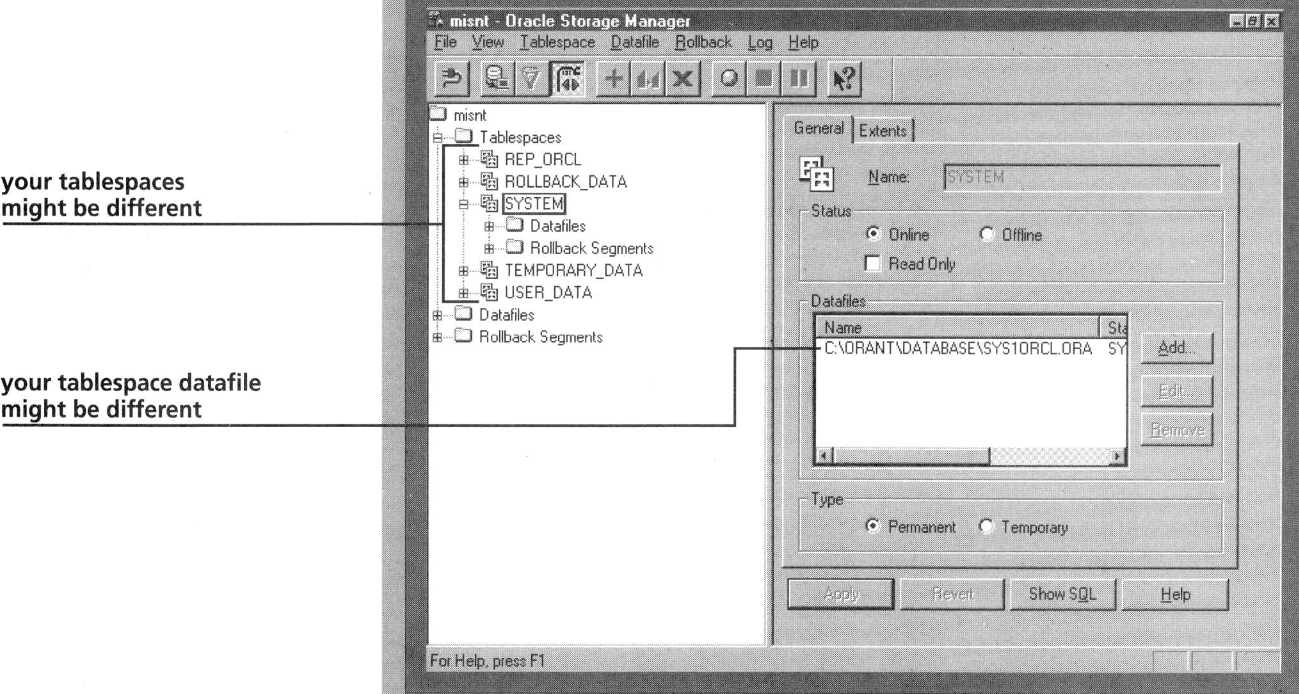

Figure 11-13: SYSTEM tablespace General tab

7. Click the **Extents** tab. An **extent** is a set of contiguous data blocks that is used for storing a specific type of information. Figure 11-14 shows the initial extent size for each table, how large the next extent will be, and the minimum and maximum number of extents. It also allows a DBA to set next extents to increase their size automatically so the DBA won't have to add new extents for a fast-growing table.

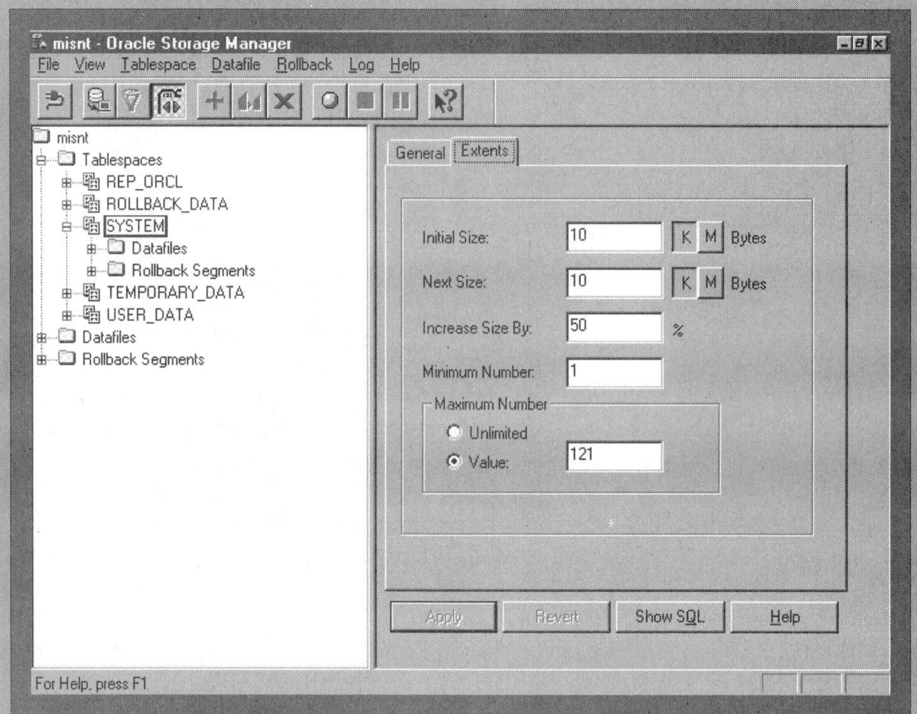

Figure 11-14: Tablespaces Extents tab

HELP? If the Extents tab is not visible, click the Advanced Mode button on the Storage Manager toolbar.

8 Click the **Datafiles plus box** to see a path specification to at least one datafile. Double-click the datafile to view its details. Figure 11-15 shows the General tab for a sample datafile. The filename and size are shown, as well as the status, which determines whether the file is online and usable by the DBMS or offline and not available to users but available to be modified.

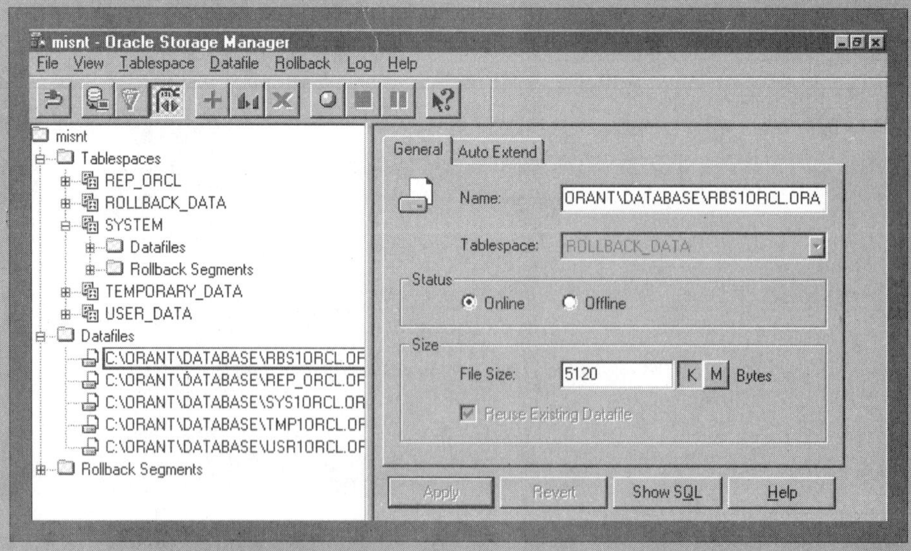

Figure 11-15: Datafile General tab

9 Click the **Auto Extend** tab. The Auto Extend feature is available with Oracle DBMS versions 7.2.0.0.0 and higher, and allows the DBA to specify that the system will increase the datafile's size automatically when the datafile is nearly full. For the datafile shown in Figure 11-16, the DBA has specified that the file automatically will be increased by 5,120 KB each time it comes close to filling up. The advantage of this feature is that the DBA does not have to monitor datafile sizes constantly to ensure that they are not getting too full. The disadvantage is that all of the tablespace data will be placed in one large datafile, and this approach doesn't take advantage of placing datafiles on multiple hard drives to enable faster, parallel data access.

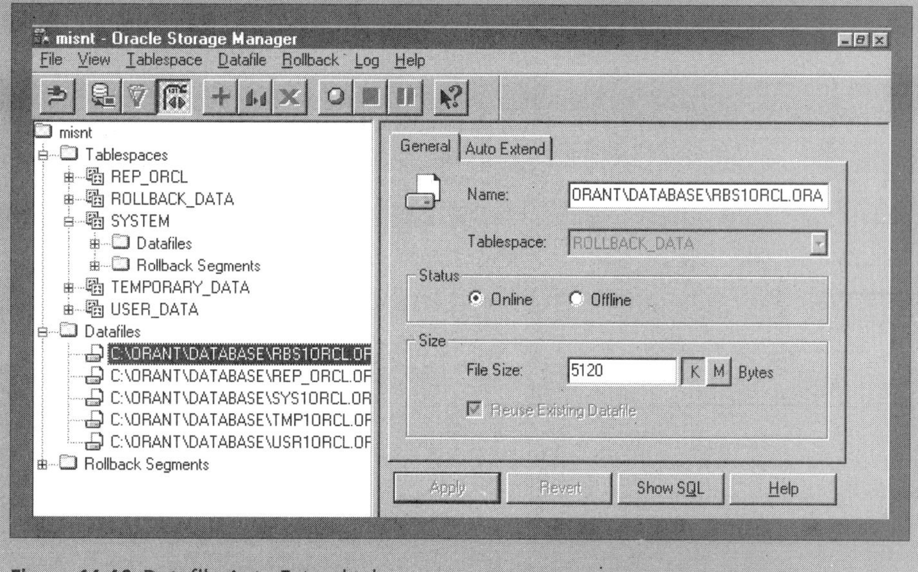

Figure 11-16: Datafile Auto Extend tab

Now that you have examined the existing tablespaces and datafiles, you will learn the process for creating a new tablespace and associated datafiles. You will see the process of creating a tablespace, although you won't actually create one.

To create a new tablespace:

1 Right-click **Tablespaces**. A menu that allows the DBA to create a new tablespace appears. Click **Create** on the menu to open the Create Tablespace dialog box.

2 Enter **SAMPLE** as the name of the tablespace. Whenever a DBA creates a new tablespace, he also must create one or more datafiles to hold the tablespace data.

3 Click the **Add** button for the Datafiles list box, and then enter **SAMPLE_DATA** as the filename. Sizing datafiles is an imprecise process. The DBA doesn't want to make them too large because they consume disk space that can't be used for other things. But if they are too small, the DBA will have to add another datafile shortly. However, trying to accurately estimate how much disk space will be required by a database is difficult to do because many variables are involved. A reasonable approach might be to start with a default value of 10 MB, and monitor the file daily or weekly depending on database activity and add more (and larger) files as needed.

4 Enter **10** as the File Size, and then click M (for megabytes).

5 Click the **Auto Extend** tab.

6 Click the **Enable Auto Extend** check box to select it. Enter **10 MB** as the increment, click the **Maximum Extent Value** option button, and then type 50 MB as the maximum extent limit. Click the **OK** button. Your completed tablespace specification should look like Figure 11-17.

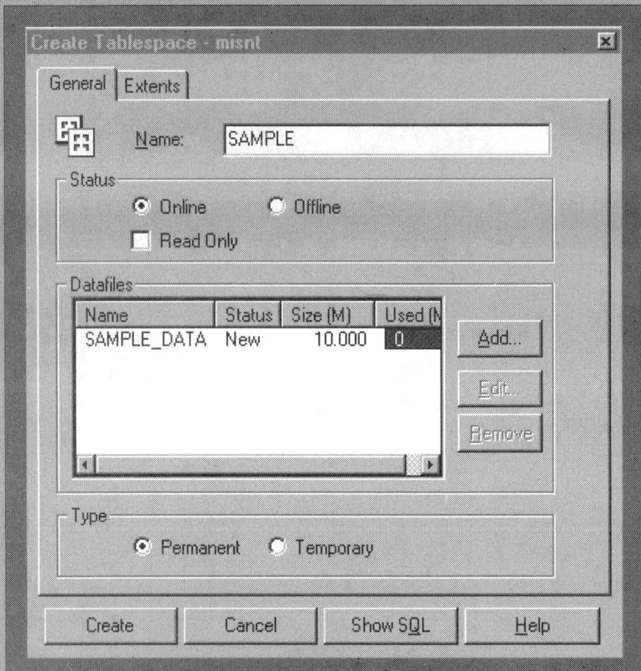

Figure 11-17: New tablespace specification

7 Click the **Show SQL** button. As with many Oracle operations, this utility generates the SQL code that is actually used to perform the operation. Click the **Cancel** button so you won't actually create the tablespace. The Create Tablespace dialog box closes.

HELP? If you click the Create button by mistake, you will receive a message saying you have insufficient system privileges to perform this operation.

8 Click the **Tablespaces minus box** ⊟ to close the Tablespaces node.

9 Click the **Datafiles plus box** ⊞ to open it. This selection provides a way to view datafiles independently of their tablespaces. Close the Datafiles node.

Next you will view information about the rollback segments. Recall that rollback segments are data areas used to record information needed to roll back every uncommitted transaction. By default, transactions are saved to roll back segments in a circular fashion, much like redo logs. When the first rollback segment is filled, then transactions are written to the second log, then to the third log, and so on until all logs are filled. Then the first is overwritten with new transactions.

To view the rollback segment information:

1. Click the **Rollback Segments plus box** ⊞, and then click Rollback Segments. Figure 11-18 shows a list of rollback segments, their sizes, and their **high water mark**, or how much they have been filled at their highest point. The SYSTEM and TEMPORARY_DATA tablespaces have their own private rollback segments named SYSTEM and RB_TEMP. The other tablespaces share the remaining public rollback segments, which are located in the ROLLBACK_DATA tablespace. A database *must* have at least one public rollback segment.

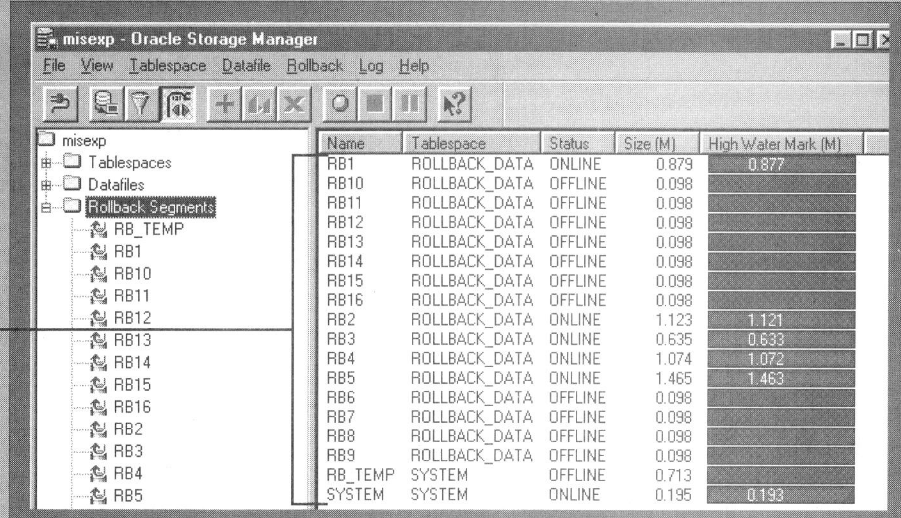

Figure 11-18: Rollback segment listing

2. Click **RB1** in the right pane. The rollback segment detail information shows the selected segment's name and associated tablespace and allows the DBA to take it offline.
3. Click the **Extents** tab. Rollback segments, like tablespaces, can be configured to create new extents automatically as needed. It is best to accept the default parameters for rollback segments unless the system is experiencing performance problems.
4. Exit the Storage Manager.

The Security Manager

The **Security Manager** enables the DBA to create new user accounts and specify the privileges that users have with regards to what they can and cannot do in the database. You will start the Security Manager next and view its contents.

You also can start the Security Manager by opening Windows Explorer and double-clicking the ORAWIN95\BIN\vac.exe file. Windows NT users will use the \ORANT\BIN\vac.exe file.

To start the Security Manager:

1. Click the **Start** button on the taskbar, point to **Programs**, point to **Oracle Enterprise Manager**, and then click **Security Manager**.
2. Connect to the database in the usual way. Click the **Normal** option button in the Connect As list. The Security Manager opens with your database instance name listed as the top entry in the Oracle Navigator window.
3. Click the **Advanced Mode** button on the Security Manager toolbar, and then click the **Users plus box**. You should now see a list of all database users.
4. Scroll down and select your user name. Your screen should look like Figure 11-19.

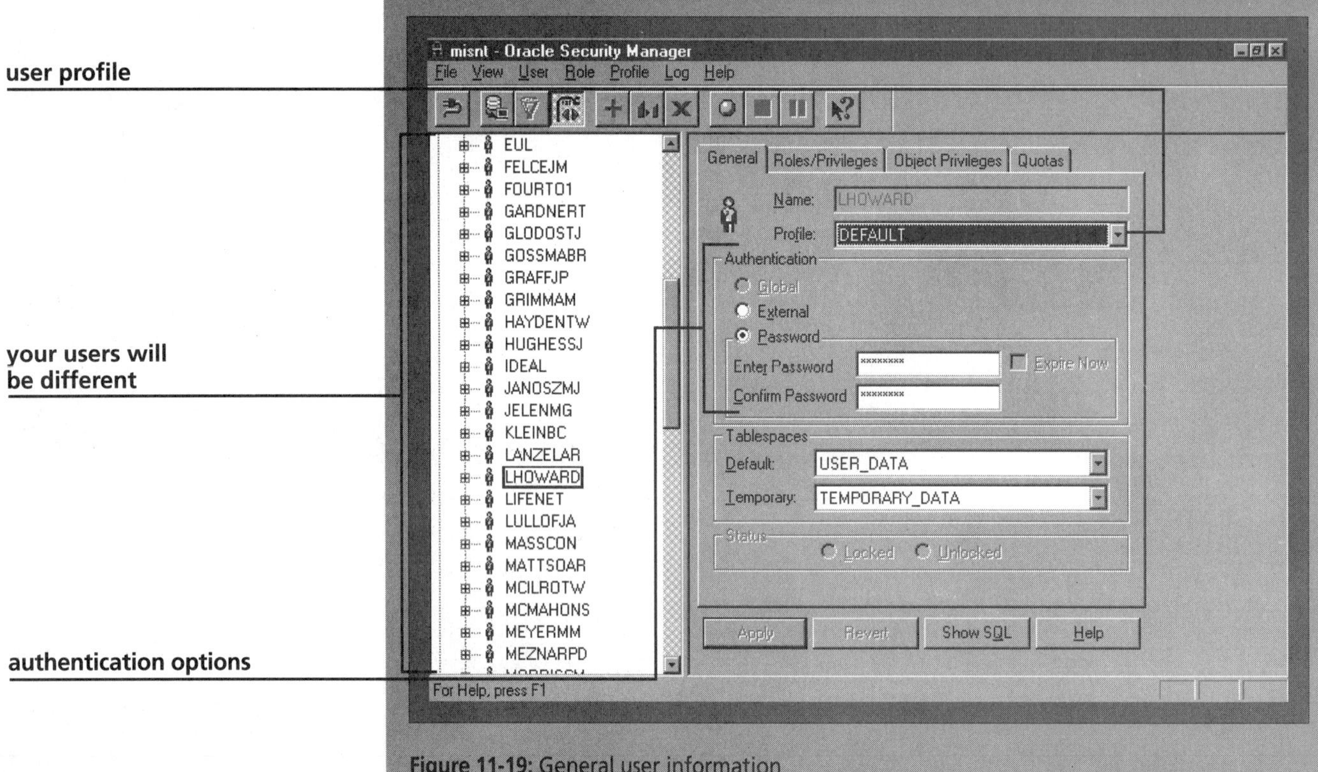

Figure 11-19: General user information

The General tab shows your user name that you selected in the previous set of steps, which cannot be changed, and your user profile. The DBA can specify different **user profiles** to specify certain resource limits for given users. The DBA also can specify the user authentication options. Authentication can be provided using the External option, where the user password is authenticated through the operating system, or the Password option, which provides authentication through the Oracle DBMS. If the Password option is chosen, the password is encrypted and no one, even DBAs, can view passwords. Users can change their password from this screen. This screen also specifies the user's default tablespace where all data tables are stored unless otherwise specified in the CREATE TABLE statement, and the user's temporary tablespace, where temporary query results are stored.

The DBA also can specify each user's roles and privileges. **System privileges** are permissions to perform actions in the database. **Roles** are groups of privileges and other roles that can be created and then assigned to groups of similar users. Next you will view your roles and privileges.

To view your roles and privileges:

1 Click the **Roles/Privileges** tab. The Privilege Type list box lets the DBA specify whether to view roles or privileges. The Available list shows the roles that you can assign to another user, and the Granted list shows the roles currently granted to you. Your roles should look like the ones shown in Figure 11-20.

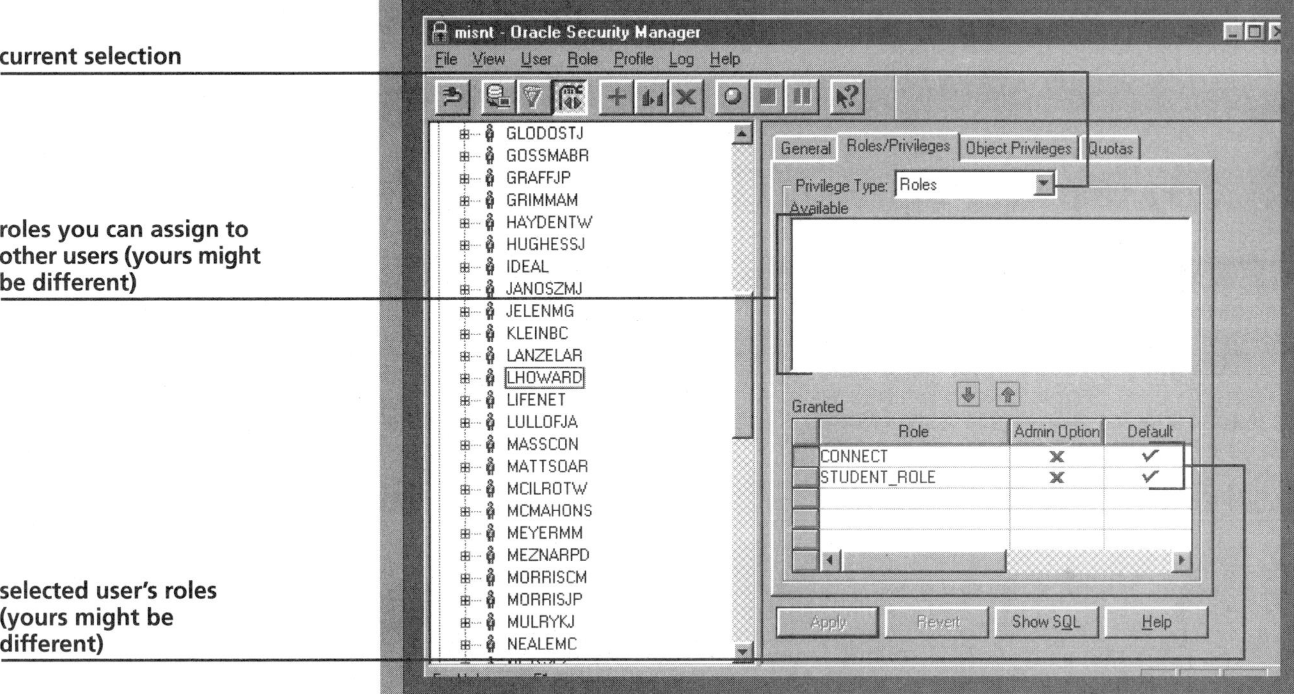

Figure 11-20: User roles

HELP? Your granted roles might display an *x* or a check in the Admin Option or Default columns. Admin Option means that the user has the right to assign this particular role or privilege to other users. A red *x* beside a given role in the Admin Option column means the user *does not have* the Admin Option, whereas a green check means the user *does have* this option. Default means that the user automatically gets the role and its associated privileges at logon, rather than having to issue an explicit SQL command to get the role.

2 Click the **Privilege Type** list arrow, and then click **System Privileges**. There will be no system privileges granted to you. You do have system privileges, however, through the STUDENT_ROLE.

tip

If you do not have the Admin Option for your roles or privileges, then you cannot grant them to other users and your available roles and privileges lists in the upper pane are blank.

3 Click **Roles** in the left pane, and then click **STUDENT_ROLE.**

4 Click the **Roles/Privileges** tab, click the **Privilege Type** list arrow, and then click **System Privileges.** You should see a list of STUDENT_ROLE's granted privileges, which should look similar to Figure 11-21. You have these privileges because the STUDENT_ROLE was granted to you. Next you will look at how roles are created.

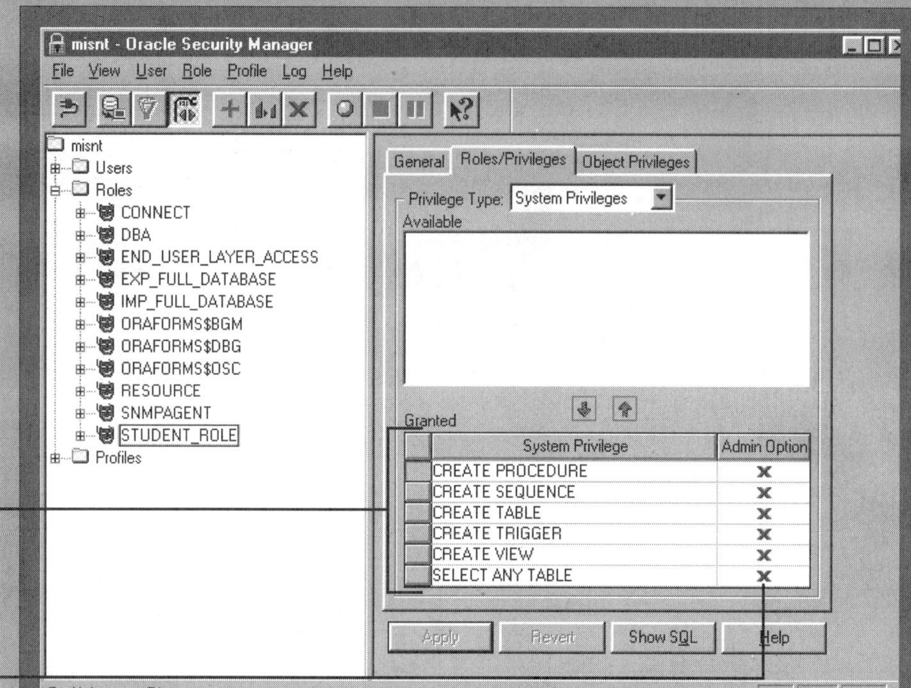

Figure 11-21: User privileges

5 Click **Role** on the menu bar, and then click **Create.** The DBA uses the General tab to specify the new role's name and whether it requires additional authentication beyond the authentication required to connect to the database.

6 Click the **Roles/Privileges** tab. If you were a DBA, your list of available roles would look like Figure 11-22, and your available system privileges would look like Figure 11-23. You are not a DBA so your roles and privileges are limited.

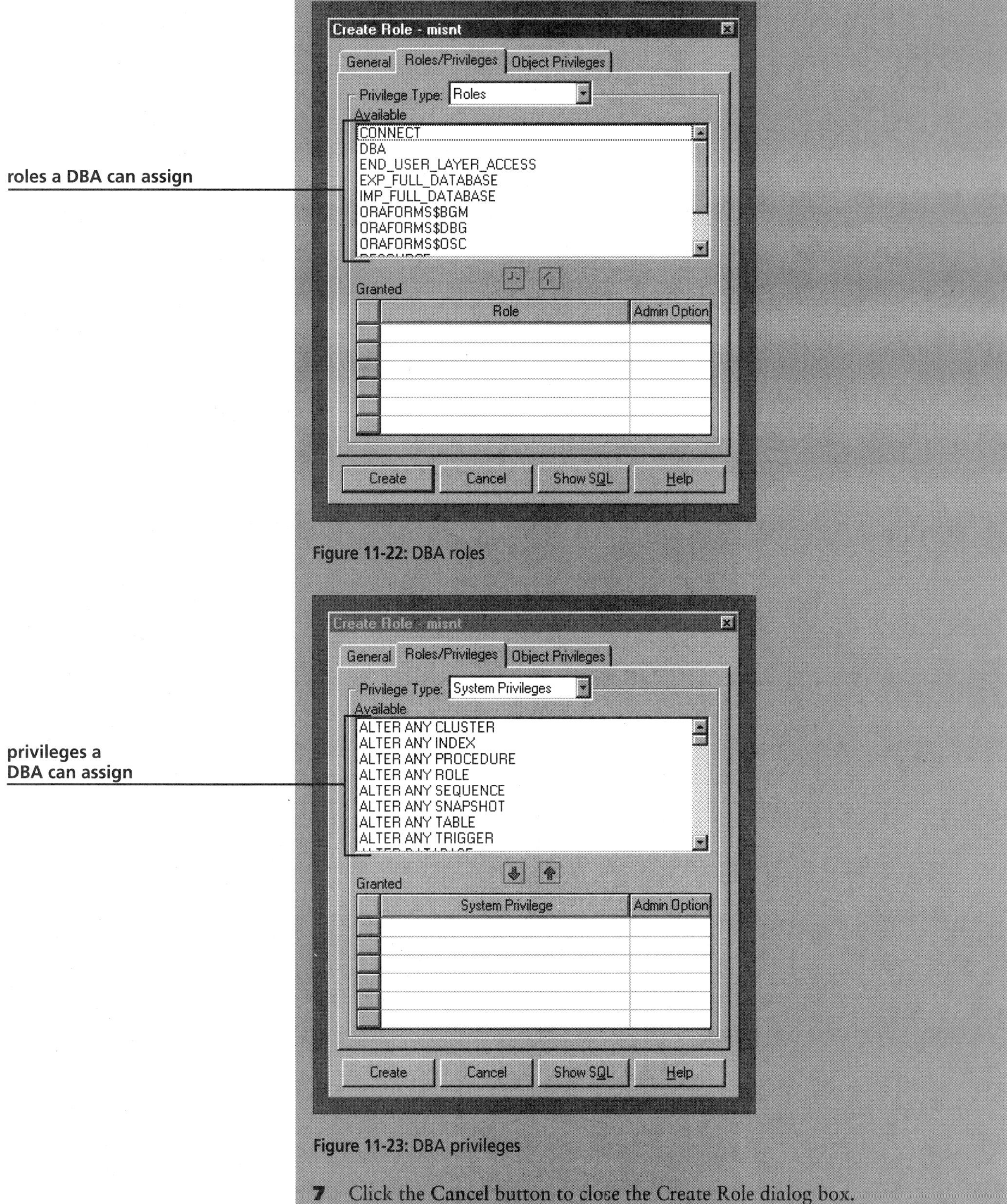

Figure 11-22: DBA roles

Figure 11-23: DBA privileges

7 Click the **Cancel** button to close the Create Role dialog box.

Object privileges enable a user to perform specific actions on objects such as database tables, sequences, or stored procedures. These are the same privileges that you can grant to other users to let them use your tables and sequences. Object privileges have to be granted explicitly by an object's creator. Next you will view your object privileges and give another user some privileges for one of your database tables.

To view your object privileges and grant a privilege to another user:

1. Click the **Object Privileges** tab.
2. Click any user name other than your own in the left panel.
3. Click the **plus box** [+] beside your user name in the Objects list box in the right pane, and then click [+] beside Tables to open your Tables listing.
4. Click any one of your tables. You should now see a list in the Available Privileges box to the right of the objects that shows what privileges are available to be assigned. Available privileges will be different depending on the type of object selected.
5. Select the **ALTER** privilege.
6. Click the **Down Arrow** button [↓] to assign the privilege to another user.
7. Click the **Show SQL** button to view the SQL command that was created to make this change.

   HELP? You might need to scroll down in the window to view the SQL command.

8. Click the **Apply** button to commit the change to the database. Now you will revoke the privilege.
9. Select the privilege you just granted, press the **Up Arrow** button [↑], and then click the **Apply** button.

The Quotas tab allows the DBA to specify and modify the user's disk space quota for each tablespace. The quota determines how much disk space each user can use on the database server for his database objects such as tables, views, and sequences.

To view the quotas for your tablespaces:

1. Click your user name in the left panel.
2. Click the **Quotas** tab. Figure 11-24 shows a typical quota assignment.

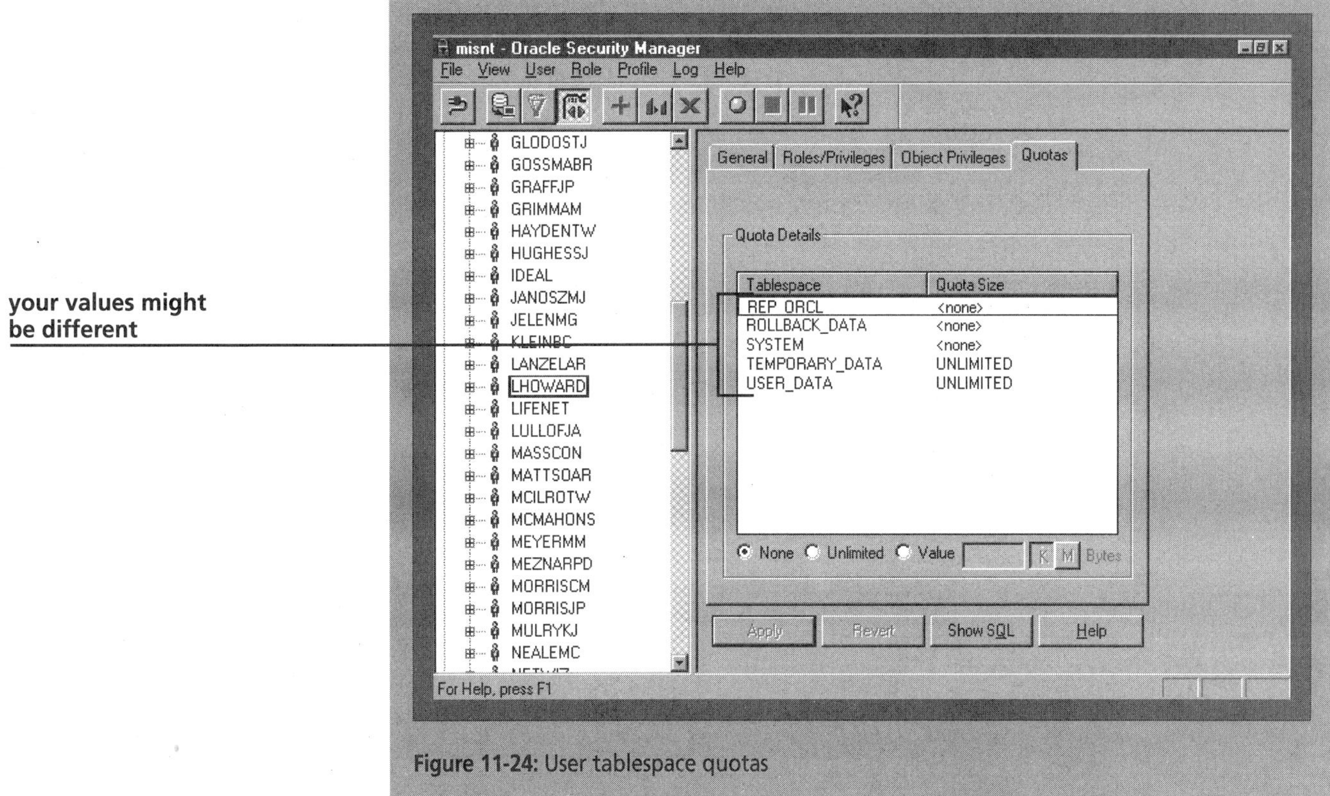

Figure 11-24: User tablespace quotas

Creating a New User Account To create a new user account, the DBA must specify the new user's user name, security authentication scheme, default tablespaces, roles and privileges, and tablespace quotas. Next you will review the steps for creating a new user account, but you will not actually create one.

tip

You also can right-click **Users** in the left panel, and then click **Create** to open the Create User dialog box.

To review the steps for creating a new user account:

1. Click **User** on the menu bar, and then click **Create** to open the Create User dialog box.
2. Enter **NEW_USER** as the user name.
3. Confirm that the **Password** option button is selected, type secret in the Enter Password text box, and then type **secret** again in the Confirm **Password** text box.
4. Select **USER_DATA** for the Default tablespace and **TEMPORARY_DATA** for the Temporary tablespace. Your screen should look like Figure 11-25.

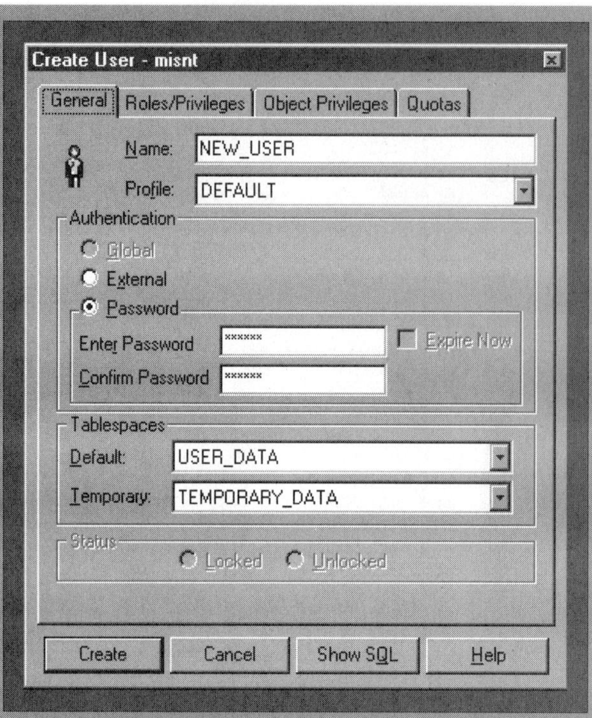

Figure 11-25: Creating a new user

5 Click the **Roles/Privileges** tab. Note that the CONNECT role already is assigned; this is the default role given to all new users.

6 Click the **Quotas** tab, and then give the user **5 MB** on the default tablespace, and **2 MB** on the temporary tablespace. Your screen should look like Figure 11-26.

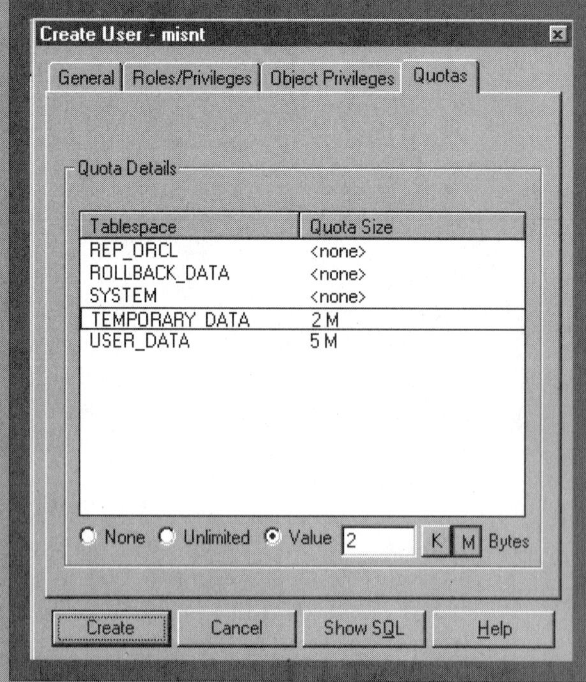

Figure 11-26: New user tablespace quotas

7 Click the **Show SQL** button, and then examine the SQL query used to create the new user. You might need to use the scroll bars to examine all of the query text.
8 Click the **Cancel** button so you won't actually create the new user.
9 Exit the Security Manager.

System Backup

Creating a **backup** simply means making a copy of the database files that can be used in a recovery operation in case of a system failure. Backups can be classified as **cold backups**, where the database is shut down during the backup process, or **hot backups**, where the database remains running.

Cold backups capture a complete snapshot of the database at a single point in time. The cold backup process is as follows:

Note: The following steps can be performed only by a DBA. Students cannot perform system backups.

1. Shut down the database.
2. Make a copy of the following files to a different directory, disk, tape, or machine:
   - All datafiles. These are the files, as shown in Figure 11-2, that correspond to the tablespaces. Your database datafiles might be different.
   - All online redo files. These are the files whose names are listed by the SQL commands shown in Figure 11-3 and Figure 11-4. For your database, there might be a different number of files, and their filenames might be different.
   - All of the initialization files. The main one is named init<SID>.ora, and it usually is stored in the \DATABASE folder inside the Oracle home folder. It might call other initialization files using the ifile = command, and these files also must be backed up.
   - The control files. For the authors' database, these files are named ctl1orcl.ora and ctl2orcl.ora, and are stored in the same folder as the data and online redo files. The names and locations of your control files will be listed in your database initialization file.
3. Restart the database.

Hot backups are necessary for databases that cannot tolerate downtime. Unfortunately, to be able to perform hot backups, your database must create archive files. Setting up a database to create archive files is a tricky task that should not be attempted by a novice database administrator. Unless hot backups are vitally essential, you should use cold backups.

Backup Strategies

The DBA has to reach an agreement with users and managers as to what kind of backup scheme is appropriate for the organization. If the installation is not using archive log files, then in the event of a failure, all transactions are lost since the time of the last cold backup. The DBA and the organization must agree on a backup frequency that matches the potential for data loss—in other words, if the organization can handle a data loss that equals one week's business transactions, then the DBA should back up the database once a week. In some cases, another backup medium, such as paper documents, is kept so it can be used to reconstruct the transactions in the event of a loss. If there is no acceptable amount of data loss, the organization needs to invest in the time and personnel required to set up and maintain log files and create hot backups.

System Recovery

After a backup is created, the recovery process depends on what was lost. If the loss involved data, configuration, initialization, or online redo files, the recovery process involves shutting down the database, copying the files from the last backup into the directory that contains the lost or damaged files, and then restarting the database. If the loss involves part of the Oracle DBMS software, you will need to reinstall the DBMS and then place the backed-up data, configuration, initialization, and online redo files in the appropriate folder.

SUMMARY

- The database administrator (DBA) is the individual (or individuals) responsible for installing, administering, and maintaining a database.
- Oracle is primarily designed to work in multiuser, multitasking computing environments. Multiuser environments allow many users to run programs on the server at the same time. Multitasking means that the same user can run multiple programs simultaneously.
- A database is an organized collection of data stored in datafiles, and an instance is the set of processes and memory storage areas that enable users to manipulate the data. An instance has background processes, shared memory areas, and disk data storage areas. Background processes are used to coordinate and accomplish all the tasks needed to maintain the database.
- The part of the server's main memory that is used by Oracle includes the software code area, where the database programs run, the system global area (SGA), which stores transactions before they are committed to the database, the program global area (PGA), which handles individual user processes, and the sort area, which is used when the ORDER BY clause is added to a SQL query.
- The Oracle DBMS uses datafiles, online redo log files, archive log files, initialization files, control files, and log and error files.
- A tablespace is how data is logically stored in the database. A tablespace is associated with one or more datafiles. Creating multiple user tablespaces enables the DBA to partition the database logically. Every time a user creates a table in a tablespace, he or she uses a chunk of memory called an extent, which is a contiguous amount of storage space on a disk that cannot be used for anything except the designated table. The DBA must monitor how full tablespace datafiles are and create a new datafile before the current one is completely filled.
- Online redo log files record every database transaction in a different file from the main datafiles so changes can be recovered if a datafile is damaged. Archive files are comprehensive backups of redo log files that usually are stored on magnetic tape.
- Control files contain a blueprint of the physical layout of the database on the server, and information such as the database name, datafiles, and redo log files.
- Initialization files are editable text files that specify parameters such as the database name, the location of the control files, and a variety of configuration parameters dealing with SGA, PGA, and other things.

- The database can be started and shut down using the Instance Manager. A normal shutdown waits for current users to disconnect and does not allow any new users to connect prior to shutting down. An immediate shutdown does not wait for current users to disconnect, but immediately closes and dismounts the database. Abort immediately shuts down the instance without closing or dismounting the database, and requires special recovery operations at the next startup.
- The Storage Manager enables the DBA to create and maintain tablespaces, datafiles, and rollback segments. When you create new datafiles, a good rule of thumb is to start with a default value of 10 MB, and monitor the file daily or weekly depending on database activity and add more (and larger) files as needed.
- The Security Manager enables the DBA to create new user accounts and specify the privileges that users have with regards to what they can and cannot do in the database. The DBA can create different user profiles to specify certain resource limits for given users. Privileges are permissions to perform actions in the database. Roles are groups of privileges and other roles that can be created and then assigned to groups of similar users. When a user has a role or privilege with the Admin Option, it means that he has the right to assign this particular role or privilege to other users.
- Creating a backup means making a copy of the database files that can be used in a recovery operation in the case of a system failure. Backups are classified as cold backups, where the database is shut down during the backup process, or hot backups, where the database remains running during the backup process.

REVIEW QUESTIONS

1. List five duties of a DBA.
2. What is the difference between multiuser and multitasking?
3. What is the difference between a database and an instance? What are the three parts of an instance?
4. What are background processes? What are the four basic background process tasks?
5. What are the four main memory areas used by Oracle, and what are they used for?
6. What is the difference between a datafile and a tablespace?
7. What three standard tablespaces exist on most Oracle systems, and what is each used for?
8. What is an extent?
9. What is an online redo log file?
10. Suppose that a database has only three online redo files named redo1, redo2, and redo3. Right now, none are used. How does the DBMS save transactions to these files, assuming it has more transactions to write than there is file space in all three files?
11. What are archive files? What are control files?
12. What are initialization files? What is the default name of the main initialization file?
13. What are log files?
14. What is the Instance Manager used for?
15. What is the difference between a normal, immediate, and an abort shutdown, and when would each be used?
16. What is the Auto Extend feature?
17. When creating a new tablespace, how large should you make the datafile?
18. What is the Security Manager used for?

19. What is the difference between a role and a privilege? What does it mean when a user has the Admin Option for a role or privilege?
20. What is the difference between a system privilege and an object privilege? Who can assign object privileges?
21. List the steps for creating a new user account.
22. What is the difference between a cold backup and a hot backup? How frequently should backups be performed?

EXERCISES

1. List the full pathname(s) to the datafile(s) for each tablespace in your database. (*Hint:* You might need to use the Storage Manager to find this information.)
2. List the full pathnames of your database's online redo log files.
3. Is your database using the Auto Extend feature? If so, name one table with this feature enabled.
4. List the rollback segment names that exist (either online or offline) in your database.
5. List your user roles and privileges.

Appendix A objectives

- Review PL/SQL programming language basics
- Demonstrate methods for concatenating and parsing strings
- Use functions and procedures
- Use the Oracle Procedure Builder to write a procedure
- Learn about packages
- Explain how to create and use database triggers

APPENDIX A

Introduction to PL/SQL, Triggers, and the Procedure Builder

Introduction

PL/SQL is the procedural language used to write procedures and functions for Oracle applications. PL/SQL is the language used within many Oracle development environments, including Forms, Reports, and the PL/SQL Web Agent. PL/SQL also is used to develop **database triggers**, which are custom procedures that execute automatically when INSERT, UPDATE, and DELETE commands are issued to a specified table. The goal of this appendix is to present an overview of the PL/SQL language and provide instructions for creating database triggers. This appendix assumes you have used a procedural programming language, such as Pascal, BASIC, COBOL, FORTRAN, etc. If you need additional information on PL/SQL, your instructor will supplement this appendix with another book or classroom discussion.

PL/SQL Language Basics

PL/SQL was designed to add procedural language programming capabilities to Oracle's SQL language. Valid characters in PL/SQL are:

- Uppercase and lowercase alphabetic letters (PL/SQL is not case sensitive so the characters "A" and "a" are the same to the compiler.)
- Numbers 0 through 9
- Most special characters found on a PC keyboard

Like SQL, variable names must begin with a letter and cannot contain more than 30 characters. Hyphens and spaces are not allowed in variable names. You cannot use reserved words, such as NUMBER, VALUES, BEGIN, or other words used in SQL or PL/SQL commands as variable names. Variable names cannot be the same as table names.

PL/SQL data types are the same types valid for SQL database fields, such as NUMBER, VARCHAR2, and DATE. VARCHAR2 merits additional discussion, however, because its maximum length is 2,000 characters when it is assigned to an Oracle database field and 32,767 characters when it is assigned to a PL/SQL variable. If more than 2,000 characters are required in an Oracle database field, the LONG data type (which stores up to two gigabytes) must be assigned to the column.

Another difference occurs when using the LONG data type. A LONG data type variable in PL/SQL is allowed a maximum length of 32,760 bytes, which is 7 bytes less than a PL/SQL VARCHAR2 variable. Both are much less than the database LONG field's maximum length of two gigabytes. As a result of these size differences, you can insert a PL/SQL VARCHAR2 or LONG variable into a LONG database field. But you cannot insert a value from a LONG type database field that stores more than 32,760 bytes into a LONG PL/SQL variable or a LONG type database field value larger than 32,767 bytes into a PL/SQL VARCHAR2 variable. When LONG database fields hold values larger than a PL/SQL VARCHAR2 variable allows, Oracle provides functions for retrieving the LONG database value in smaller pieces.

Another data type that often is used is the reference data type, which assumes the same data type as a referenced database column or row. Suppose you want to declare a variable named LNAME with the same data type as the FLNAME field in the FACULTY table in the Northwoods University database. The declaration would be written as `LNAME FACULTY.FLNAME%TYPE;`.

Suppose you want to declare a variable to hold an entire row of data. What data type do you use? The following code will declare a variable that holds an entire row of data that was retrieved from the FACULTY table: `FAC_ROW FACULTY%ROWTYPE;`.

PL/SQL program comment statements can be delimited two ways. A **block** of comments that spans several lines can begin with the symbols /* and end with the symbols */. For example, the following code would be read by the compiler as a comment block:

```
/* Script:     orcl_cold_backup
   Purpose:    To perform a complete cold backup on the orcl
               database instance
   Revisions: 9/8/99 JM Script created */
```

If a comment statement appears on a single line, you can delimit it by typing two hyphens at the beginning of the line, as shown in the following example:

```
DECLARE
--variable to hold contents of one row returned by cursor
row_orderline    orderline_cursor%ROWTYPE;
```

The arithmetic and relational operators used in PL/SQL are similar to those used in most programming languages. Figure A-1 describes the arithmetic and relational operators.

Operator	Meaning
+	Addition
-	Subtraction
*	Multiplication
/	Division
**	Exponentiation
<>	Not equal
!=	Not equal
>	Greater than
<	Less than
>=	Greater than or equal to
<=	Less than or equal to
=	Equal (comparison)
:=	Equal (assignment: sets left value equal to right value)

Figure A-1: PL/SQL arithmetic and relational operators

Handling Character Strings

Learning to manipulate character strings is an important topic in any language. For example, you might want to concatenate a last name retrieved from a LNAME field with a first name retrieved from a FNAME field. Or you might need to replace underscores in a string with space characters. Inputs retrieved from users and files might need to be parsed into smaller strings corresponding to the target table's individual fields before inserting them. Suppose you have the following text variables:

Variable Name	Value
LAST_NAME	Sarah
FIRST_NAME	Miller

You would like to combine these two values into one variable named STUDENT_NAME that has the value "Sarah Miller." To join, or concatenate, two character strings, you use the double bar (||) operator in PL/SQL. The command to concatenate these values is `STUDENT_NAME := FIRST_NAME || LAST_NAME;`.

That was pretty simple, but there is a catch. This command puts the two character strings together with no spaces between them, so the value of STUDENT_NAME is now "SarahMiller," which is not what you want—you need to insert a blank space between the first and last name. To do this, use the same command, but concatenate a blank space between the two variable names as an additional character string: `STUDENT_NAME := FIRST_NAME || ' ' || LAST_NAME;`.

You must enclose a string literal within single quotation marks. **Literals** are unchanging data values coded directly into a program. A string literal can enclose any combination of valid PL/SQL characters ('Sarah Miller' for example). If a single quotation mark is used within a string literal, you must type two single quotation marks ('Sarah''s Computer' for example).

Suppose you saved the values for a building code, room, and capacity in three variables as shown next (single quotation marks appear around values to indicate the value is a type string, but remember the CODE_NAME variable shown actually contains CR—not 'CR'):

Variable Name	Value
CODE_NAME	'CR'
ROOM_NUM	'101'
ROOM_CAPACITY	150

You need to display a message that reads "CR Room 101 has 150 seats." The only difficulty is that the ROOM_CAPACITY value is a NUMBER data type and not a CHARACTER data type. You must use the TO_CHAR function to convert the number to a character. The required code to create this text string (which is saved in a variable named TXT_STRG) is:

```
TXT_STRG := CODE_NAME || ' Room '|| ROOM_NUM
            || ' has ' || TO_CHAR(ROOM_CAPACITY) ||
            ' seats.';
```

The only tricky part of this operation is remembering to add spaces before and after the variable values so the strings don't run together. This is also the first time a line of code has spilled into two lines in the code editor. PL/SQL lines of code can span many lines in an editor. When code is compiled, the compiler considers everything up to an ending semicolon to be part of the same line of code. Forgetting to include a semicolon at the end of each line of code will cause errors when you try to compile it.

Now suppose you are formatting several room records and you want each new room location to print on a new line. The ASCII characters for carriage return (ASCII 13) and line feed (ASCII 10) signal the beginning of a new line. The CHR function allows these and other special ASCII characters to be inserted into text strings. The previous room capacity example, modified to start each room on a new line, would be written as:

```
TXT_STRG := CODE_NAME || ' Room '|| ROOM_NUM
            || ' has ' || TO_CHAR(ROOM_CAPACITY) ||
            ' seats.'
            ||CHR(13)||CHR(10);
```

Notice that 13 and 10 in the CHR functions are examples of numeric literals. (Remember literals are unchanging data values coded directly into a program.)

Sometimes when you store retrieved data values in variables, the data values contain blank spaces that pad out the value to its maximum column width. For example, if the string '2103 First St' is stored in a database CHAR field of size 20, the retrieved data value will be '2103 First St   ' (13 characters followed by

7 spaces). The VARCHAR2 database field type doesn't pad stored values, so you mainly deal with this when processing CHAR database field types.

To remove all spaces from the right side of the variable named ADDRESS, use the RTRIM function as follows:

```
TXT_STRG := RTRIM(ADDRESS);
```

The LENGTH function returns the length of a character string. For example, the following program line seeks to determine the length of the current value of CODE_NAME: `BLDG_CODE_LENGTH := LENGTH(CODE_NAME);`. If the value of CODE_NAME is 'CR', then the LENGTH function would return the number 2. If the variable contains additional padded spaces to the right these also will be counted in the length. For example, if CODE_NAME is retrieved from a CHAR type database field of size six, the value of CODE_NAME will be 'CR   ' (CR followed by four spaces) and LENGTH will return the number 6.

The UPPER function converts lowercase letters to uppercase letters. For example, if a variable named FULLNAME stores the value "Mary Smith," the following code will then convert the FULLNAME value to all uppercase letters: `FULLNAME := UPPER(FULLNAME);` and change the value to "MARY SMITH."

The INSTR and SUBSTR functions often are used together to process and modify strings. The INSTR function searches one string and looks for a matching substring. If it finds a matching substring, the starting position of the substring within the original string is returned. If a matching substring is not found, the value 0 is returned. For example, the following code returns the starting position of ' ' or a single space: `SPACE_POSITION := INSTR(FULLNAME, ' ');`.

If the FULLNAME string variable contains the value "Mary Smith," SPACE_POSITION will be set to 5. The parameters used with the INSTR function are:

```
INSTR(string,
      substring,
      [,starting search position in string]
      [,nth appearance in string])
```

The parameters enclosed in square brackets ([and]) are optional. If they are omitted, the starting search position will be one, and the nth appearance will be ignored.

The SUBSTR function allows you to extract a subset of a certain number of characters from a string. To extract the string "Mary" from the string "Mary Smith," use one of the following lines of code:

```
FIRST_NAME := SUBSTR(FULLNAME, 1, 4);
```

or

```
FIRST_NAME := SUBSTR(FULLNAME, 1, INSTR(FULLNAME, ' ')
- 1);
```

The parameters used with SUBSTR are:

```
SUBSTR(string,
       starting position in string,
       length of substring to be returned)
```

A much more complicated use of these two functions allows converting user entered text into Web-compliant HyperText Markup Language (HTML) text. In HTML, the less than (<) and greater than (>) characters delimit HTML tags, so a user innocently entering an equation can wreak havoc with a program designed to display the user's entries in a Web page. The following code scans a string variable that stores the user's comments and replaces every < symbol with the HTML symbols < which will display properly as < in a Web page and will not be interpreted by a Web browser as an HTML tag delimiter:

```
FUNCTION ConvertToHTML (commenttext VARCHAR2) RETURN
VARCHAR2 IS
   pos1     INTEGER   := 1;
   pos2     INTEGER   := 1;
   tmptext VARCHAR2(32767) := '';
BEGIN
   --replace < with &lt;
   pos1 := INSTR(commenttext, '<');
   WHILE pos1 > 0 LOOP
      tmptext := tmptext || SUBSTR(commenttext, pos2,
pos1 - pos2) || '&lt;';
      pos2 := pos1 + 1;
      pos1 := INSTR(comtext, '<', pos2);
   END LOOP;
   --add any text following the last <
   tmptext := tmptext || SUBSTR(comtext, pos2);

RETURN tmptxt;
END;
```

To complete the above process, you need to include a similar loop to replace the > symbols with > (or write a second function to do this).

PL/SQL Program Blocks

PL/SQL procedures and functions are structured in **blocks** with the following format:

```
DECLARE
<variable declarations>
BEGIN
<body containing procedure or function steps>
EXCEPTION
<error handling statements>
END;
```

PL/SQL is a **strongly typed language** in which all variables must be declared prior to use. Strong-typing also means assignments and comparisons can be performed only between variables with the same type. The general format for declaring a variable is `<variable name> <data type>;`. For example, suppose you want to create a variable named COUNT of data type NUMBER. The declaration would be written as `COUNT NUMBER;`.

The variable declaration also can be used to set the initial value of the variable. To assign the initial value zero to COUNT would be written as `COUNT NUMBER := 0;`.

The **body** of a PL/SQL block consists of program statements (which can be assignments, conditional statements, looping statements, calls to procedures, etc.) that lie between the BEGIN and END statements that define the block.

IF/THEN Statements

If a condition evaluates to true, one or more program statements are executed. The IF/THEN structure has the following format:

```
IF <condition> THEN
    <program statements>;
END IF;
```

Here is an example using variable values:

```
IF COUNT = 0 THEN
     DISPLAYED_VALUE := '0';
END IF;
```

Every IF must have a corresponding END IF. Note the difference between the equal comparison operator (=) and the equal assignment operator (:=). An equal sign by itself (=) is used when you are comparing two values in an IF/THEN structure, whereas a colon plus equal sign (:=) is used when you are assigning a new value to a variable.

The IF/THEN/ELSE structure is similar to the IF/THEN structure, except that when the condition evaluates to false, one or more alternative program statements execute. The IF/THEN/ELSE structure has the following general format:

```
IF <condition> THEN
    <program statements>;
ELSE
   <alternative program statements>;
END IF;
```

Here is another example using variable values:

```
IF COUNT = 0 THEN
    DISPLAYED_VALUE := '0';
ELSE
    DISPLAYED_VALUE := 'Not 0';
END IF;
```

IF/THEN/ELSE statements can be nested, as shown in the following example.

```
IF COUNT = 0 THEN
    DISPLAYED_VALUE := '0';
ELSE
    IF COUNT = 1 THEN
      DISPLAYED_VALUE := '1';
    ELSE
      DISPLAYED_VALUE := 'Not 0 or 1';
    END IF;
END IF;
```

An alternative to using a nested IF/THEN/ELSE statement is the IF/THEN/ELSIF structure, which allows you to test for many different conditions. If the first condition is true, then its program statement(s) are executed, and the IF/THEN structure is exited. If an ELSIF condition is true, then its program statement(s) are executed, and the IF/THEN structure is exited. If all conditions are false, then the ELSE program statement(s) are executed. The following code illustrates this structure. The result is equivalent to the previous nested statement.

```
IF COUNT = 0 THEN
    DISPLAYED_VALUE := '0';
ELSIF COUNT = 1 THEN
    DISPLAYED_VALUE := '1';
ELSIF COUNT = 2 THEN
    DISPLAYED_VALUE := '2';
ELSE
    DISPLAYED_VALUE := 'Not 0, 1, or 2';
END IF;
```

Loops

A **loop** repeats an action until some ending condition is reached. Four different looping approaches are available. Each loop usually gets the same result, but one style of loop might be more appropriate to use, depending on what you are doing. To illustrate each loop construct, suppose you want to insert the numbers 1, 2, 3, 4, and 5 into the COUNTER field in COUNT_TABLE as shown in Figure A-2.

COUNTER
1
2
3
4
5

Figure A-2: COUNT_TABLE

The following loop construct to add the column uses an IF/THEN statement. When the IF/THEN condition is true, the program statement EXIT directs program execution to exit the loop.

```
--initialize COUNT to zero
COUNT := 0;

LOOP
  COUNT := COUNT + 1;
  IF COUNT = 6 THEN
    EXIT;
  END IF;
  INSERT INTO COUNT_TABLE VALUES (COUNT);
END LOOP;
```

The following loop structure does the same task as the previous loop, except it detects the ending condition differently:

```
--initialize COUNT to zero
COUNT := 0;

LOOP
  COUNT := COUNT + 1;
  INSERT INTO COUNT_TABLE VALUES (COUNT);
  EXIT WHEN COUNT = 5;
END LOOP;
```

The following loop structure tests the ending condition at the beginning of the loop, so COUNT is incremented one extra time before the loop exits:

```
--initialize COUNT to zero
COUNT := 0;

WHILE COUNT < 5
LOOP
  COUNT := COUNT + 1;
  INSERT INTO COUNT_TABLE VALUES (COUNT);
END LOOP;
```

The following loop construct repeats the loop as many times as the incrementing variable is in a defined series of numbers:

```
--initialize COUNT to zero

FOR COUNT IN 1..5
LOOP
  INSERT INTO COUNT_TABLE VALUES (COUNT);
END LOOP;
```

PL/SQL Cursors

PL/SQL cursors are used to retrieve database data into PL/SQL variables. Cursors can be implicit or explicit. Implicit cursors are used with SELECT statements that return a single record. If more than one record is returned, an error occurs. Implicit cursors have the following format:

```
SELECT <data field(s)>
INTO <declared variable name(s)>
WHERE <search condition that will return a single record>);
```

The variables receiving the data from the query in the INTO clause must be of the same data types as the returned fields.

Here is an implicit cursor that retrieves a specific faculty member's last and first names into the declared variables LNAME and FNAME from the FACULTY table in the Northwoods University database:

```
DECLARE
LNAME          VARCHAR2(30);
FNAME          VARCHAR2(30);

BEGIN
  SELECT FLNAME, FFNAME
  INTO LNAME, FNAME
  FROM FACULTY
  WHERE FID = 1;
  --more program steps that manipulate the retrieved
  --data values
  .
  .
  .
END;
```

Explicit cursors must be used with SELECT statements that might retrieve a variable number of records or that might return no records. Explicit cursors are written in the DECLARE section and processed in the procedure body. Here is an example of an explicit cursor for calculating the total capacity of all rooms in the CR building using the LOCATION table of the Northwoods University database:

```
DECLARE

CURSOR CAPACITY_CURSOR IS
  SELECT CAPACITY
  FROM LOCATION
  WHERE BLDG_CODE = 'CR';

--declare variables using referential data typing
ROOM_CAPACITY      LOCATION.CAPACITY%TYPE;
--declare and initialize variable to hold calculated
total capacity

TOTAL_CAPACITY     LOCATION.CAPACITY%TYPE := 0;

BEGIN
  OPEN CAPACITY_CURSOR;
  LOOP
    FETCH CAPACITY_CURSOR
    INTO ROOM_CAPACITY;
    TOTAL_CAPACITY := TOTAL_CAPACITY + ROOM_CAPACITY;
  EXIT WHEN CAPACITY_CURSOR%NOTFOUND;
  CLOSE CAPACITY_CURSOR;
END;
```

Note the use of the reference data type %TYPE in the declarations of the variables to hold the retrieved room capacities and calculated total capacity. Also note the use of the %NOTFOUND system variable. If the cursor does not fetch a new record successfully, then this variable is true and the loop exits.

A good approach for processing a cursor that retrieves multiple data fields in the SELECT statement uses the reference data type %ROWTYPE. Here is an example of a cursor that retrieves all of the rooms and capacities where BLDG_CODE is 'CR' and displays them as a series of messages to the user:

```
DECLARE
  CURSOR ROOM_DATA_CURSOR IS
    SELECT ROOM, CAPACITY
    FROM LOCATION
    WHERE BLDG_CODE = 'CR';

  --variable to hold contents of one returned row
  ROOM_ROW          ROOM_DATA_CURSOR%ROWTYPE;

BEGIN
  --putting cursor in FOR loop implicitly opens it
  FOR ROOM_ROW IN ROOM_DATA_CURSOR LOOP
      MESSAGE('Room CR '|| ROOM_ROW.ROOM || ' has '
              || TO_CHAR(ROOM_ROW.CAPACITY) || ' seats.');
  END LOOP;
END;
```

When you use the FOR loop, you don't need to explicitly open, fetch, or close the cursor. Also note how the individual field values are accessed in the ROOM_ROW variable by following it with a period and then the field name.

The EXCEPTION Section

Programmers prefer to concentrate on the positive aspects of their programs. Creating programs that generate invoices, process checks, track time usage, and so forth is difficult and time consuming. As a result, programmers tend to breathe a sigh of relief once the program works and overlook or ignore the consequences of a user pressing the wrong key or a critical network link going down. The reality, however, it that users enter incorrect data and press wrong keys, networks fail, computers crash, and anything else that can go wrong will (eventually) go wrong. Programmers can't do much for the user if the user's computer fails, but programmers can and should do everything possible to prevent wrong data from being entered and wrong keystrokes from damaging the system, and to inform the user of errors and how to correct them when they occur. PL/SQL offers exception handling as its primary method for processing errors and informing users of corrective actions. The exception handling section in a PL/SQL block is optional, and if it is present, it is placed as the last code in the block. The exception handling section has the following parameters:

```
DECLARE
      Declarations…
BEGIN
      Lines of code…
EXCEPTION
      WHEN exception_name OR exception_name…
      THEN
            Lines of code to process the exception
END;
```

One common exception is NO_DATA_FOUND. An implicit cursor will generate a NO_DATA_FOUND error if nothing is returned in its query. OTHERS is a catch-all exception handler that allows you to present a message to a user that describes any system error that occurs.

Once an exception occurs, processing in the current PL/SQL execution section is transferred to the EXCEPTION section. In the EXCEPTION section you might choose to correct the error without notifying the user of the problem, you might inform the user of the error without taking corrective action, you might correct the error and inform the user of the error, or you might inform the user of the error and allow the user to decide what action to take. Here is an example of exception handling where ITEMDESC is selected from the ITEM table using an implicit cursor. The example demonstrates exception handling when no data are found using the given item ID:

```
PROCEDURE LOOKUP_ITEM (ITEM_NUM IN NUMBER) IS
      IDESC ITEM.ITEM_DESC%TYPE;
BEGIN
      SELECT ITEMDESC INTO IDESC
      FROM ITEM WHERE ITEMID = ITEM_NUM;
      --more lines of code…
EXCEPTION
      WHEN NO_DATA_FOUND THEN
      --lines of code informing the user no data were
found
WHEN OTHERS THEN
      --put a generic message here that includes
      --the system error code and message
      --(the MESSAGE procedure might be used in Forms
      --Designer)
      MESSAGE('Error Message: ' || SQLERRM);
END;
```

After an EXCEPTION section finishes processing the exception, processing returns to the calling procedure if the block with the exception is in a procedure called from another procedure. Blocks also can be nested within other blocks in the same procedure. Each block can have its own EXCEPTION section. When an exception occurs in a nested block, processing moves to the block's exception section and when finished returns to the enclosing block. Here is an example of nested blocks with exception handling:

```
PROCEDURE DELETE_CUSTOMER (CUST_NUM IN NUMBER) IS
BEGIN
      BEGIN
            DELETE FROM ORDERS WHERE CUSTID = CUST_NUM;
      EXCEPTION
            WHEN OTHERS THEN NULL;
      END;

      BEGIN
            DELETE FROM CUSTOMER WHERE CUSTID = CUST_NUM;
      EXCEPTION
            WHEN OTHERS THEN NULL;
      END;
      --more lines of code
            EXCEPTION
      WHEN OTHERS THEN
            MESSAGE('Error Message: ' || SQLERRM);
END;
```

In the preceding example, a customer might have entries in an ORDERS table. If the ORDERS table has a constraint specifying that CUSTID is a foreign key linked to the CUSTOMER table, attempting to delete the customer's record before deleting the customer's order entries will fail if orders have been entered for the customer. If an attempt is made to delete the customer's order entries, an exception will be generated if there are no orders entered for the customer. By creating a nested block for DELETE FROM ORDERS… and giving it its own EXCEPTION section, control will always return to the next line of code in the enclosing block—regardless of whether the customer has previously made orders. After deleting any orders the customer might have in the ORDER table, a user can safely delete the customer from the CUSTOMER table.

You must be careful with exception handlers when calling one procedure from another. If the called procedure does not have an exception handler, exceptions raised in the called procedure will be processed by the calling procedure's exception handler. When using functions and procedures provided by Oracle, you can't control how exceptions are handled within them. You *can* include an exception handler in every procedure you write. It usually makes more sense to handle an exception in the procedure in which it occurs rather than in a calling procedure. For example, if a procedure fails to retrieve a record, it usually makes more sense to handle the exception in that procedure rather than to force a calling procedure to anticipate what might be happening within the called procedure. Here is an example of what you might want to *avoid* when writing a called function:

```
PROCEDURE CALLING_PROCEDURE () IS
      CUSTOMER_NAME VARCHAR2(50);
BEGIN
      CUSTOMER_NAME := LOOKUP_CUST(12);
      --more lines of code
EXCEPTION
      WHEN OTHERS THEN
            MESSAGE('Error Code: ' || SQLERRM);
END;

FUNCTION LOOKUP_CUST (CUST_NUM IN NUMBER) RETURN
VARCHAR2 IS
      LASTNAME CUSTOMER.LAST%TYPE;
BEGIN
      SELECT LAST INTO LASTNAME
      FROM CUSTOMER WHERE CUSTID = CUST_NUM;
      --more lines of code (notice no EXCEPTION section)
      RETURN LASTNAME;
END;
```

In this example, the EXECUTION section lines of code after `CUSTOMER_NAME := LOOKUP_CUST(12);` will be skipped if no data are found (or if any other exception is raised) in LOOKUP_CUST; and the value of CUSTOMER_NAME will be NULL in the CALLING_PROCEDURE's EXCEPTION section.

Here is a better way to write and call LOOKUP_CUST:

```
PROCEDURE CALLING_PROCEDURE () IS
      CUSTOMER_NAME VARCHAR2(50);
BEGIN
      CUSTOMER_NAME := LOOKUP_CUST(12);
      IF CUSTOMER_NAME IS NULL THEN
            --didn't find the customer, write code to
            --handle this
      END IF
      --more lines of code (not skipped if a LOOKUP_CUST
      --exception occurs)
EXCEPTION
      WHEN OTHERS THEN
            MESSAGE('Error Code: ' || SQLERRM);
END;

FUNCTION LOOKUP_CUST (CUST_NUM IN NUMBER) RETURN
VARCHAR2 IS
      LASTNAME CUSTOMER.LAST%TYPE;
BEGIN
      SELECT LAST INTO LASTNAME
      FROM CUSTOMER WHERE CUSTID = CUST_NUM;
      --more lines of code
      RETURN LASTNAME;
EXCEPTION
      WHEN OTHERS THEN    --you could do something
                          --specific to NO_DATA_FOUND
             RETURN NULL; --or just treat any
                           --exception the same way
END;
```

Functions and Procedures

PL/SQL procedures are code modules that perform tasks. PL/SQL procedures have the following structure:

```
PROCEDURE PROCEDURE_NAME (parameter1 IN OUT datatype,
                          parameter2 IN OUT datatype,
                          etc.) IS
      declarations…
BEGIN
      lines of code…
EXCEPTION
      exception handlers…
END;
```

The IN OUT keywords are optional. By default, parameters are passed as "IN" parameters—even if IN is omitted. An IN only parameter can be read but not modified. IN parameters can be constants, variables, literals, or expressions. For example, all of the following calls to a procedure named SHOW_MESSAGE display "hello world":

```
DECLARE
      CONSTANT_MSG CONSTANT VARCHAR2(50) := 'hello world';
      VARIABLE_MSG VARCHAR2(50);
BEGIN
      SHOW_MESSAGE (CONSTANT_MSG); --passing a constant
      VARIABLE_MSG := 'hello world';
      SHOW_MESSAGE (VARIABLE_MSG); --passing a variable
      SHOW_MESSAGE ('hello world'); --passing a literal
      SHOW_MESSAGE ('hello' || ' ' || 'world'); --passing
      --an expression
END;
```

A parameter passed with the OUT keyword only can be written to but cannot be read within the procedure. When execution returns from the procedure to the calling block, the passed parameter will store the value assigned to it in the procedure. A parameter passed as both IN and OUT can be read and modified. Changes made to the parameter will be seen by the calling block when execution returns to it. Any parameters passed as OUT or IN and OUT must be variables. Constants, literals, and expressions are not allowed.

IN parameters are the most common. IN OUT parameters can be useful, however, if the calling block requires information to be returned to it in modified parameters. There is another way to send information back to a calling block—PL/SQL functions are designed specifically for this purpose. In most cases, functions should be used to send information back to a calling block. If you think you need an OUT parameter, reconsider. Most of the time you will find you are trying to do too much in a single procedure or function. Break your procedure or function down into smaller functions returning the information you need.

Functions are structured as follows:

```
FUNCTION FUNCTION_NAME (parameter1 IN OUT datatype,
                        parameter2 IN OUT datatype, etc.)
                        RETURN VARCHAR2 IS
      declarations...
BEGIN
      lines of code...
      RETURN RETURN_VALUE;
EXCEPTION
      exception handlers...
      RETURN EXCEPTION_NOTICE;
END;
```

Calling a function requires assigning its return value to a variable. For example, a function looking up a customer's name might be called as follows: `CUST_NAME := LOOKUP_CUSTOMER(CUSTID);`.

The Oracle Procedure Builder

The Oracle Procedure Builder can be used to develop, test, and debug PL/SQL programs. The Procedure Builder was introduced in Chapter 10; however, Web PL/SQL requirements prevented using its integrated debugger. This section presents an exercise illustrating how you can use the Procedure Builder to write a procedure to add one hundred records to a table automatically.

tip

Another way to start the Procedure Builder is to start Windows Explorer, and then double-click the file ORAWIN95\BIN\Pb15d32.EXE.

To start the Oracle Procedure Builder and create the table EX1:

1 Click the **Start** button on the taskbar, point to **Programs**, point to **Developer 2000 for Win95** (or NT), and then click **Procedure Builder.**

2 Connect to the database in your usual way.

3 Create a table named EX1 by typing the SQL statement shown in Figure A-3, and then pressing the Enter key.

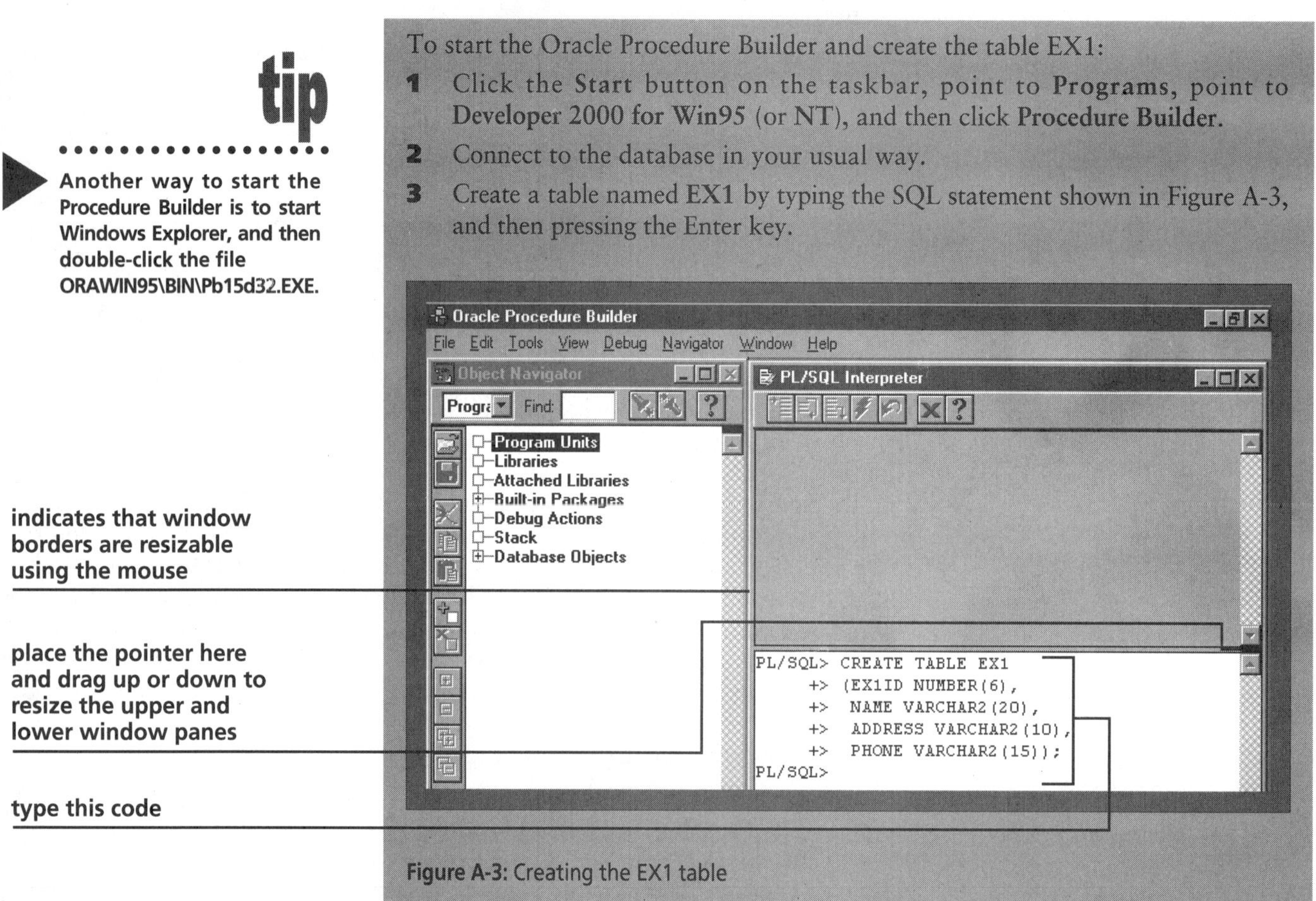

Figure A-3: Creating the EX1 table

Next you will create the program unit that inserts the records.

To create the program unit:

1 Select **Program Units** (Figure A-3) and then click the **Create** button on the Object Navigator toolbar.

2 Make sure that the **Procedure** option button is selected, and then type **Exercise1** for the procedure name, as shown in Figure A-4.

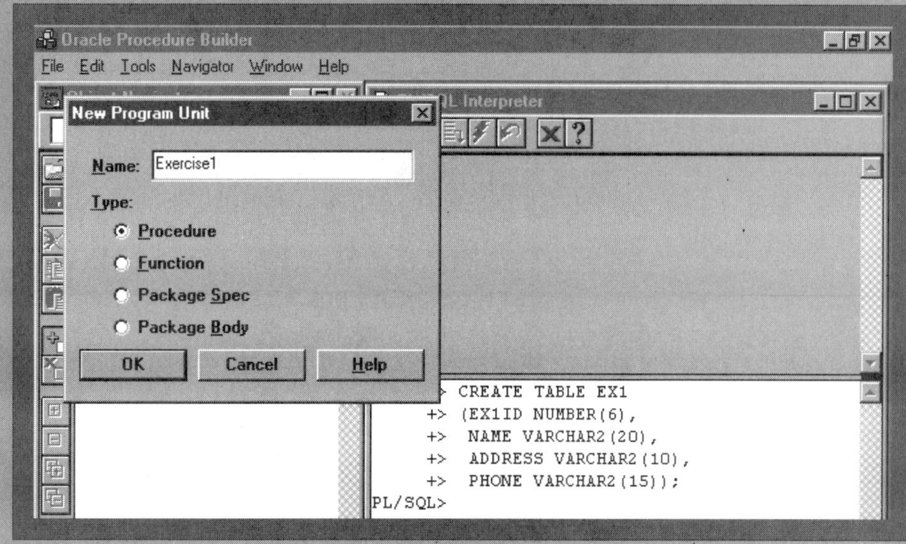

Figure A-4: Creating the EXERCISE1 procedure

3 Click the **OK** button, and then maximize the Program Unit Editor. Enter the code shown in Figure A-5 into the Program Unit Editor, and then compile it.

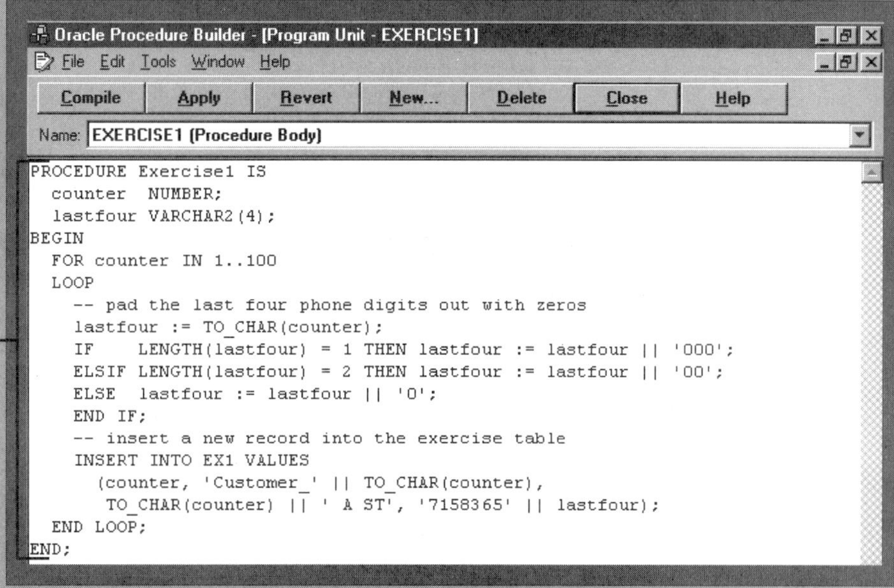


```
PROCEDURE Exercise1 IS
  counter  NUMBER;
  lastfour VARCHAR2(4);
BEGIN
  FOR counter IN 1..100
  LOOP
    -- pad the last four phone digits out with zeros
    lastfour := TO_CHAR(counter);
    IF    LENGTH(lastfour) = 1 THEN lastfour := lastfour || '000';
    ELSIF LENGTH(lastfour) = 2 THEN lastfour := lastfour || '00';
    ELSE  lastfour := lastfour || '0';
    END IF;
    -- insert a new record into the exercise table
    INSERT INTO EX1 VALUES
      (counter, 'Customer_' || TO_CHAR(counter),
       TO_CHAR(counter) || ' A ST', '7158365' || lastfour);
  END LOOP;
END;
```

Figure A-5: Entering 100 records into EX1

4 After successfully compiling the program, close the Program Unit Editor, and then select **EXERCISE1 (Procedure Body)** in the Object Navigator window. You will see the code for EXERCISE1 displayed in the upper pane of the PL/SQL Interpreter window, as shown in Figure A-6.

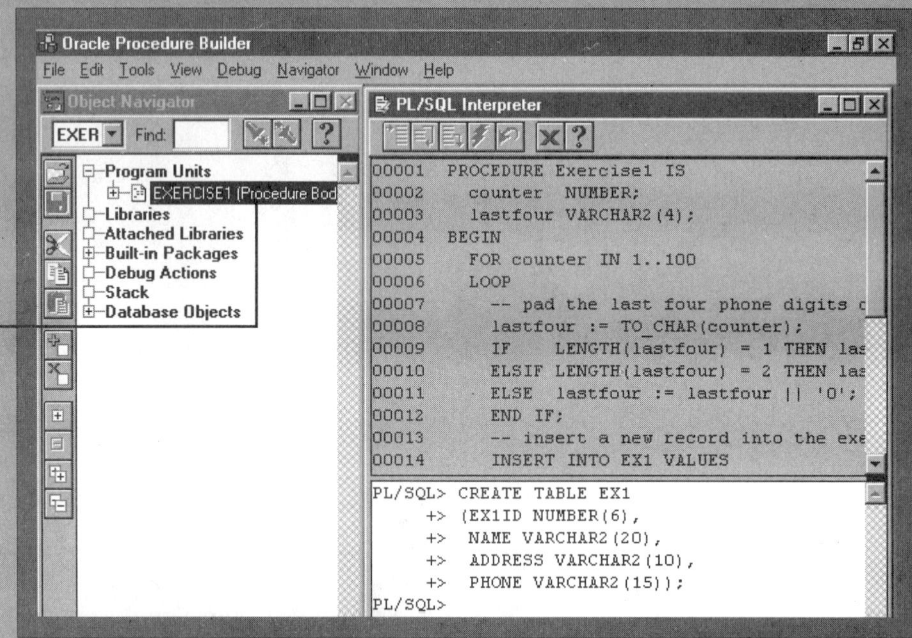

Figure A-6: Loading EXERCISE1 into the PL/SQL Interpreter

HELP? You might need to click Tools on the menu bar, and then click PL/SQL Interpreter to open that window. You also might need to click Window on the menu bar, click Tile, and then rearrange your windows so your screen looks like Figure A-6.

Now you will learn how to use the PL/SQL debugger to set a breakpoint and then single-step through the program unit to observe execution and examine variable values.

To use the PL/SQL debugger:

1 Double-click line 00009 in the PL/SQL Interpreter window to set a breakpoint, as shown in Figure A-7. Type **exercise1;** in the lower pane, and then press the **Enter** key. Program execution will stop at the breakpoint that you just set.

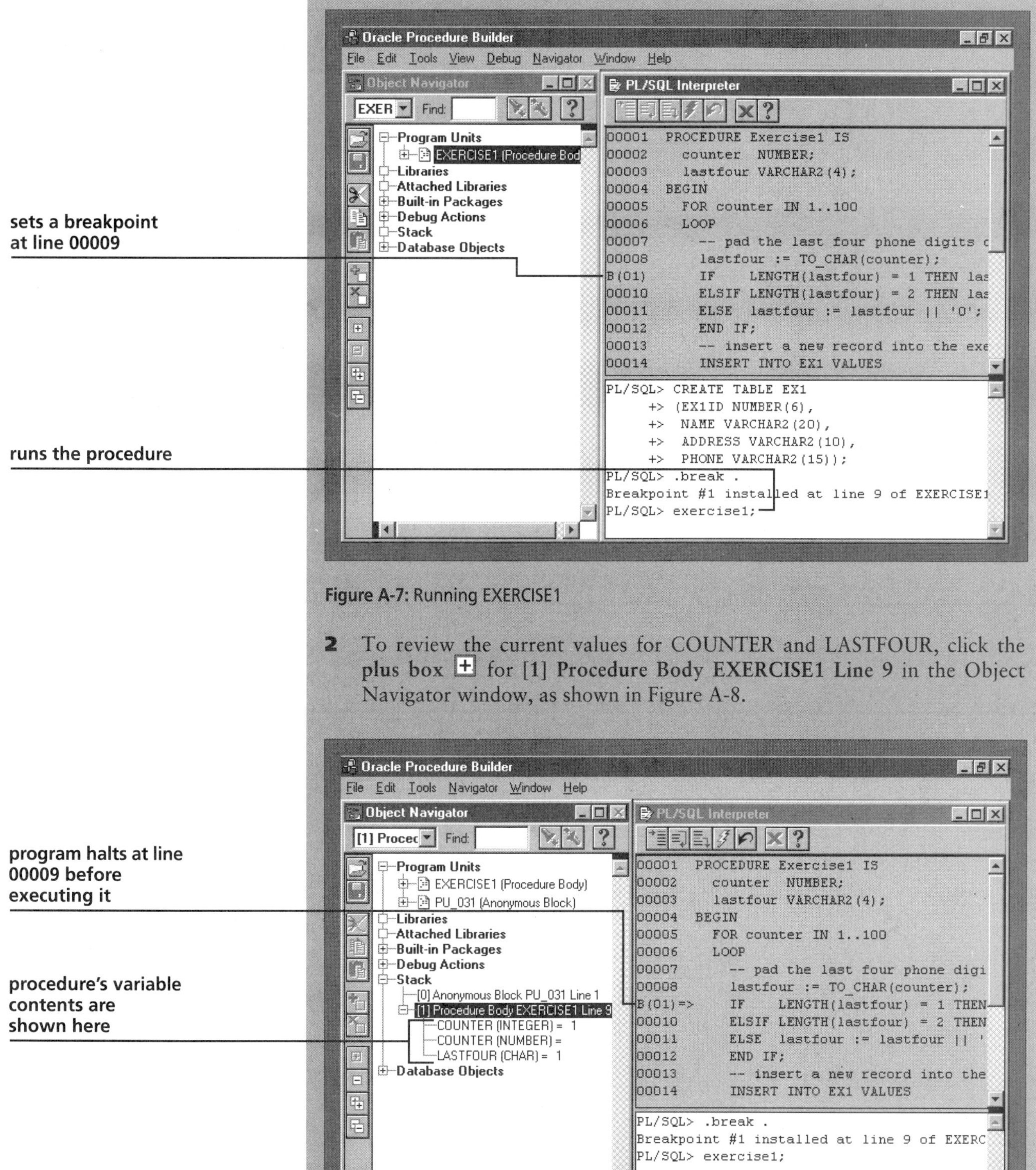

Figure A-7: Running EXERCISE1

2 To review the current values for COUNTER and LASTFOUR, click the **plus box** ⊞ for **[1] Procedure Body EXERCISE1 Line 9** in the Object Navigator window, as shown in Figure A-8.

Figure A-8: Viewing EXERCISE1 variables while running

3 Single step through the procedure by clicking the **Step Into** button on the PL/SQL Interpreter toolbar and observe how the values of COUNTER and LASTFOUR change. Notice the debugger doesn't allow single stepping through some of the procedure lines of code. The Step Into button on the toolbar allows you to step through the lines in called procedures as well as the Exercise1 procedure. The Step Over button will run a line of code calling another procedure, but won't step through the lines of code in the called procedure. The Step Out button finishes running lines of code in the current procedure. The Go button resumes execution (but will still stop on any breakpoints you have set). The Reset button cancels execution and allows you to start over.

4 When you are satisfied that you understand how this works, double-click line 9 again in the upper pane of the PL/SQL Interpreter to remove the breakpoint. Then click the **Go** button on the PL/SQL Interpreter toolbar to finish running the procedure.

Finally, you will confirm that the procedure worked correctly by querying the contents of the EX1 table from the PL/SQL Interpreter.

To confirm that your procedure works correctly:

1 View the contents of the EX1 table by typing **SELECT * FROM EX1;** at the PL/SQL prompt. Figure A 9 shows the query output.

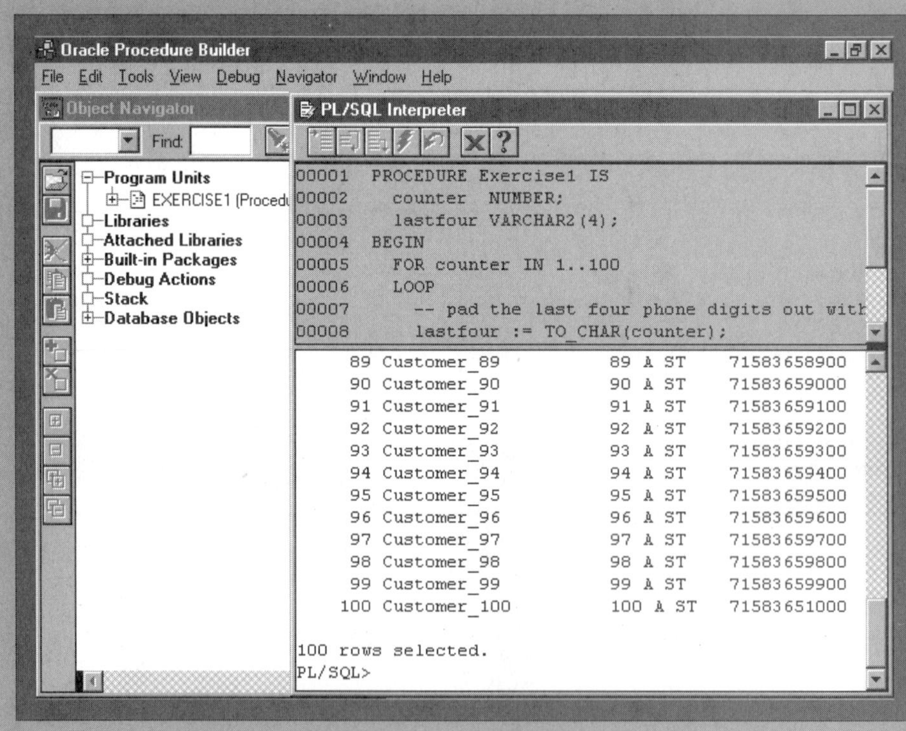

Figure A-9: Result of SELECT * FROM EX1; command

HELP? The EXERCISE1 procedure did not include a COMMIT; command as the last line. The records inserted by your procedure can be selected in the PL/SQL Interpreter, but if you start SQL*Plus and try to select these records, they won't be there. To make these record additions permanent, you must execute a COMMIT command at the PL/SQL Interpreter's PL/SQL prompt.

Next you will save your program unit to your Student Disk, and then open it to confirm that it saved correctly.

To save and reopen your program unit:

1. Double-click **EXERCISE1** in the Object Navigator window to display your code in the Program Unit Editor. Select all of the program unit text, click **Edit** on the menu bar, click **Export**, and then save the selected text to a file named **EX1.pls** in the AppendA folder on your Student Disk.
2. To test opening your saved program unit, delete your EXERCISE1 program unit by selecting it in the Object Navigator window, clicking the **Delete** button on the Object Navigator toolbar, and then clicking the **Yes** button.
3. Click **File** on the menu bar, click **Load**, click the **Find** button, select your saved file from the AppendA folder on your Student Disk, click the **Open** button, and then click the **Load** button.

Another method for saving and restoring a program unit is to create a **library**, which is a file that contains one or more procedures or functions.

To create a library:

1. Select **Libraries** in the Object Navigator window, and then click the **Create** button on the Object Navigator toolbar. A new library appears.
2. Click **EXERCISE1 (Procedure Body)** in the Program Units object, and then drag it to the new library's Program Units, as shown in Figure A-10.

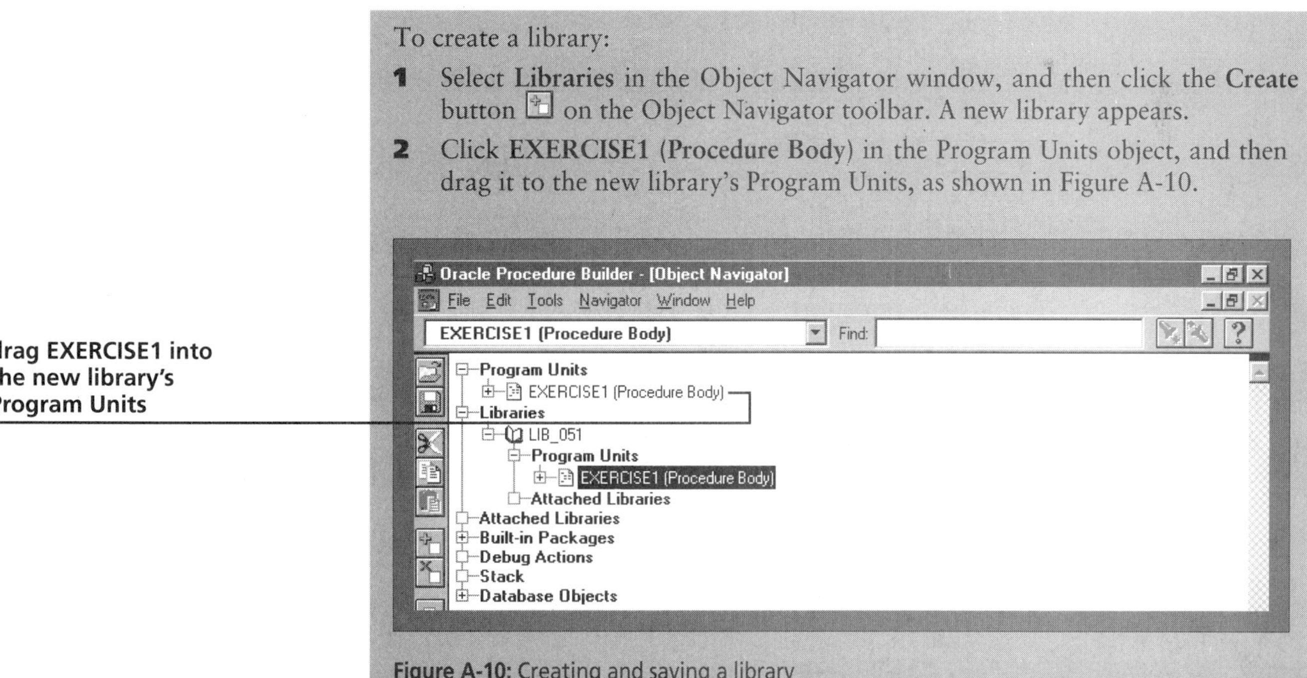

Figure A-10: Creating and saving a library

3 Click the Save button on the Object Navigator toolbar, click the **File System** option button, and then click the **Find** button to browse for the folder you want to save the file in, which is the AppendA folder on your Student Disk.

Debugging a library file requires opening the library file and dragging the procedures and functions contained in it to the top-level Object Navigator Program Units. From this point, debugging procedures are identical to those described in the first exercise. Procedures and functions also can be stored in an Oracle database as stored program units. You can create them there (as you did in the Web assignments for Chapter 10) or create them as file-based program units and drag them to Database Objects/<your user name>/Stored Program Units. Stored program units run on the database server—not on the client. The Web programs in Chapter 10 relied on stored program units. Client applications can be made smaller by offloading some of their processing to the server (using stored program units), but it is easy to overload a database server with this type of processing.

Packages

A **package** is a code library that provides a way to manage large numbers of related programs and variables. A package specification declares the public interface to the package. The **public interface** (package specification) declares programs and variables that can be called by other program units. The **package body** contains the actual implementation of the programs declared in the specification. A specification doesn't have to have a package body, however, except when the specification is used only to declare public variables and data types. Calling a program stored in a package requires prefacing the program with the package name, a period, and the program name. For example, calling the function LOOKUP_CUSTOMER stored in the package named BILLING and passing it a parameter named CUSTID would be written as `CUST_NAME := BILLING.LOOKUP_CUSTOMER(CUSTID);`.

Accessing a variable named CURRENT_NUM declared in the BILLING package specification would be written as `BILLING.CURRENT_NUM`. Variables declared in a package specification are, in effect, global variables to any programs using them. The last example in the next section "Database Triggers" illustrates how a public package variable can be used. Chapter 10 includes a more extensive example for the package SRECORDS.

In addition to creating your own packages, Oracle provides many built-in packages that are accessible to both client (Developer/2000 applications for example) and server programs (Web PL/SQL Agent programs, triggers, etc.). The core functions of the PL/SQL language are contained in the STANDARD and DBMS_STANDARD built-in packages. Other built-in packages extend the core functions to allow submitting and managing regularly scheduled database jobs, and much more. Unlike the core functions, however, calling functions in these packages requires prefacing the function with the name of the package and a period. For example, the built-in TEST_IO package provides functions for opening, reading, writing to, and closing files. The following procedure TESTIO creates and opens a file named test.txt in the C:\TEMP folder, and then writes to it and closes the file.

```
PROCEDURE TESTIO IS
  OUT_FILE TEXT_IO.FILE_TYPE;
  ERR_MSG  VARCHAR(2000);
BEGIN
  OUT_FILE := TEXT_IO.FOPEN('c:\temp\test.txt', 'w');
  TEXT_IO.PUTF (OUT_FILE, 'hello world');
  TEXT_IO.FCLOSE(OUT_FILE);
END;
```

You can search for TEXT_IO in the Procedure Builder's Help system for a complete explanation of the options available with this package.

Debugging a package is almost identical to debugging a procedure or function. Figure A-11 demonstrates running and debugging the EXERCISE1 procedure after it has been declared in a package specification named PACK1 and written in a package body named PACK1.

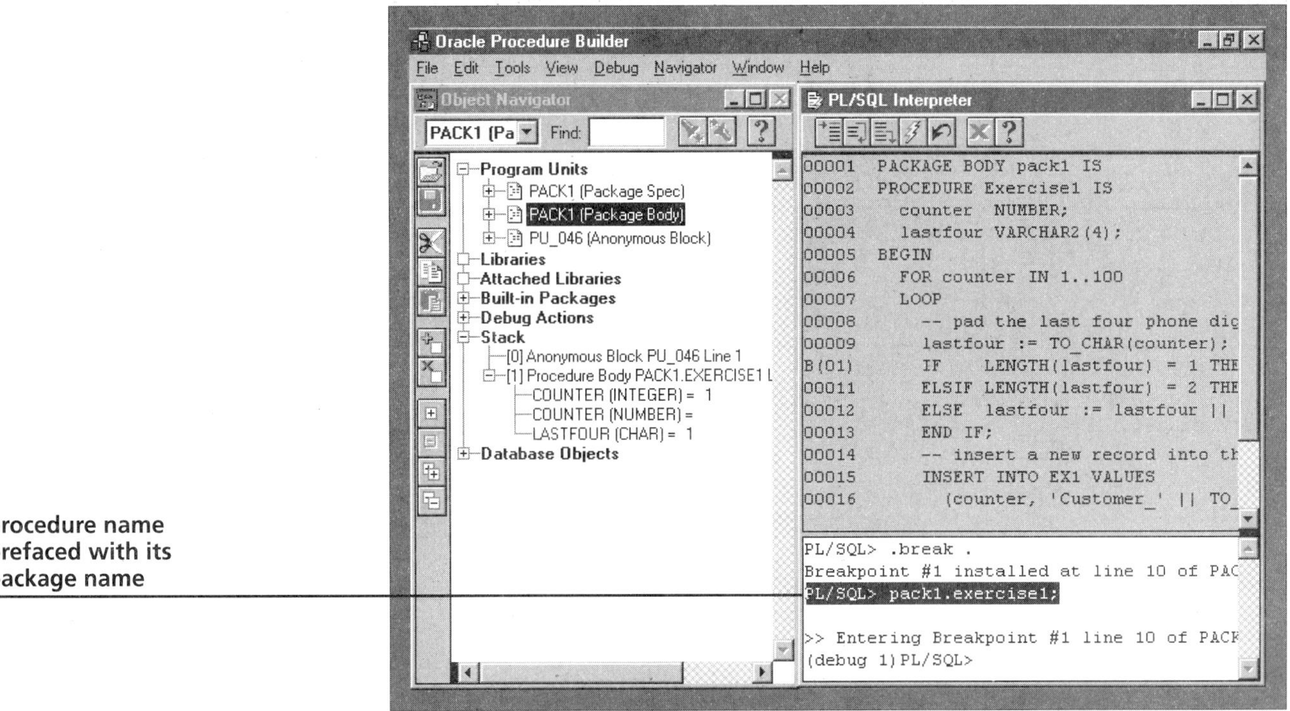

Figure A-11: Debugging a procedure in a package

Database Triggers

Database triggers are procedures that execute in response to the database events of inserting, updating, or deleting a record. Database triggers are similar to procedures, except that a trigger executes whenever the triggering event occurs and a trigger does not accept parameters. When a trigger executes, it is said to be *fired*. Triggers can be used to maintain complex integrity constraints or audit changes made in a table, or to signal other programs that changes were made to a table. If you have been wondering why Oracle does not supply an AUTONUMBER data type for creating surrogate key numbers automatically (like in Microsoft Access), you no longer need to feel deprived. You can use a trigger to duplicate the AUTONUMBER data type, which is a field that automatically increments itself by one each time a new record is added.

At least four Oracle development tools are capable of creating database triggers: the Procedure Builder, Schema Manager, Oracle Navigator, and SQL*Plus. These tools are listed in the order that the authors recommend using them. The Procedure Builder presents the easiest screen to work with. The Schema Manager displays SQL syntax resulting from creating a trigger (which can be copied and pasted into SQL scripts). Oracle Navigator is much like the Schema Manager, but it doesn't display the resulting SQL syntax, which makes it less useful when working with scripts. SQL*Plus is listed last because it offers no check boxes, option buttons, or other helpful messages for creating triggers. The first example will demonstate creating a trigger in all four environments, and then the remaining examples will use the Procedure Builder exclusively.

Types of Triggers

Triggers can fire on INSERTs, DELETEs, and/or UPDATEs. Statement-level triggers can fire before or after the statement executes. Row-level triggers fire once for each row affected by the triggering statement. A table can have many triggers attached to it. In this case, the order of trigger firing will be:

1. If present, fire the *before* statement-level trigger
2. With each row affected by the INSERT, DELETE, or UPDATE:
   - If present, fire the *before* row-level trigger
   - Execute the DELETE or UPDATE on the row
   - If present, fire the *after* row-level trigger
3. If present, fire the *after* statement-level trigger

If the For Each Row check box is checked, you can access the values being inserted into a row and modify them. Even though an INSERT will affect a single row, you might want to make sure the For Each Row check box is selected.

Audit Example

The first example tracks all changes (INSERT, UPDATE, DELETE) made to a table named EMPLOYEE, including who made the change when it was done, and what the old and new values were. This example uses tables named EMPLOYEE and EMP_AUDIT. EMPLOYEE has been simplified for this example to contain just three fields: EMPID, EMPNAME, and PAYSCALE. (A realistic table would break EMPNAME into LAST_NAME, FIRST_NAME, and MIDDLE_INITIAL to facilitate searching and would include many more fields.)

EMP_AUDIT contains the auditing information. Its fields are TYPEACTION (INSERT, UPDATE, DELETE), MADEBY (who made the change), WHENDONE, OLD_EMPID, OLD_EMPNAME, OLD_PAYSCALE, NEW_EMPID, NEW_EMPNAME, and NEW_PAYSCALE. First, you will create the EMPLOYEE and EMP_AUDIT tables.

To create the EMPLOYEE and EMP_AUDIT tables:

1 Start SQL*Plus, and then create the **EMPLOYEE** table with fields **EMPID** (NUMBER, size 6), **EMPNAME** (VARCHAR2, size 30), and **PAYSCALE** (NUMBER, size 1).

2 Create the **EMP_AUDIT** table with fields **TYPEACTION** (CHAR, size 1), **MADEBY** (VARCHAR2, size 30), **WHENDONE** (DATE), **OLD_EMPID** (NUMBER, size 6), **OLD_EMPNAME** (VARCHAR2, size 30), **OLD_PAYSCALE** (NUMBER, size 6), **NEW_EMPID** (NUMBER, size 6), **NEW_EMPNAME** (VARCHAR2, size 30), and **NEW_PAYSCALE** (NUMBER, size 6).

Next you will start the Oracle Procedure Builder and create the trigger to track the changes to the EMPLOYEE table.

To create the trigger:

1 If necessary, start the Procedure Builder and then connect to your user account. Open the following objects: **Database Objects**, **<your account>**, **Tables**, **EMPLOYEE**, and **Triggers**, as shown in Figure A-12.

data types and sizes must match data types and sizes in the EMP_AUDIT table

select Triggers before clicking the Create button

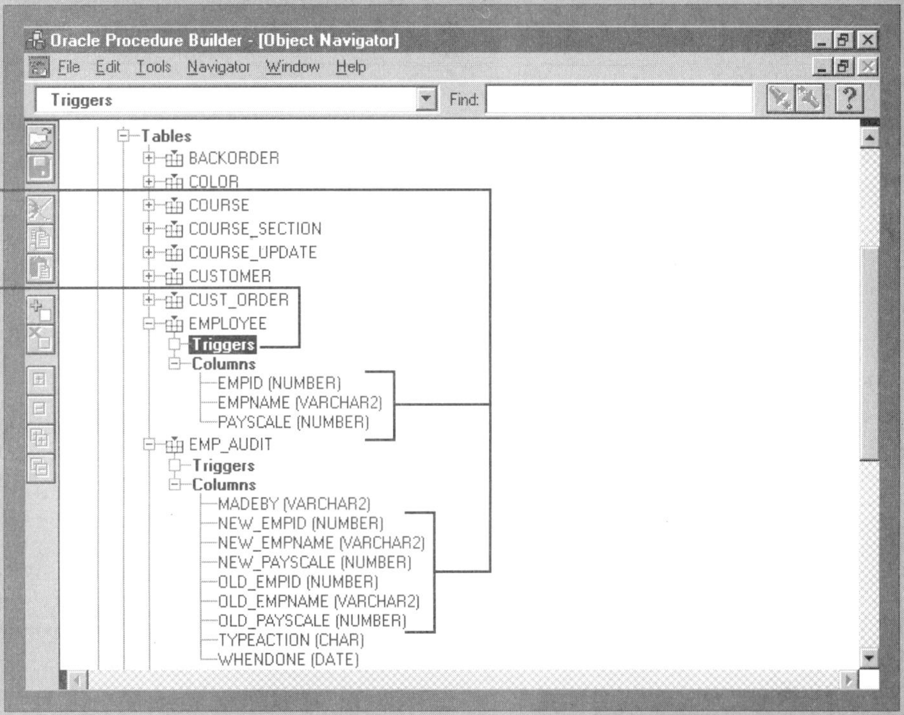

Figure A-12: Creating a trigger in the Procedure Builder

2 Create a new trigger by clicking the Create button on the Object Navigator toolbar. Click the **New** button. Figure A-13 shows the Procedure Builder window and all of the entries required for making the EMPLOYEE_AUDIT trigger.

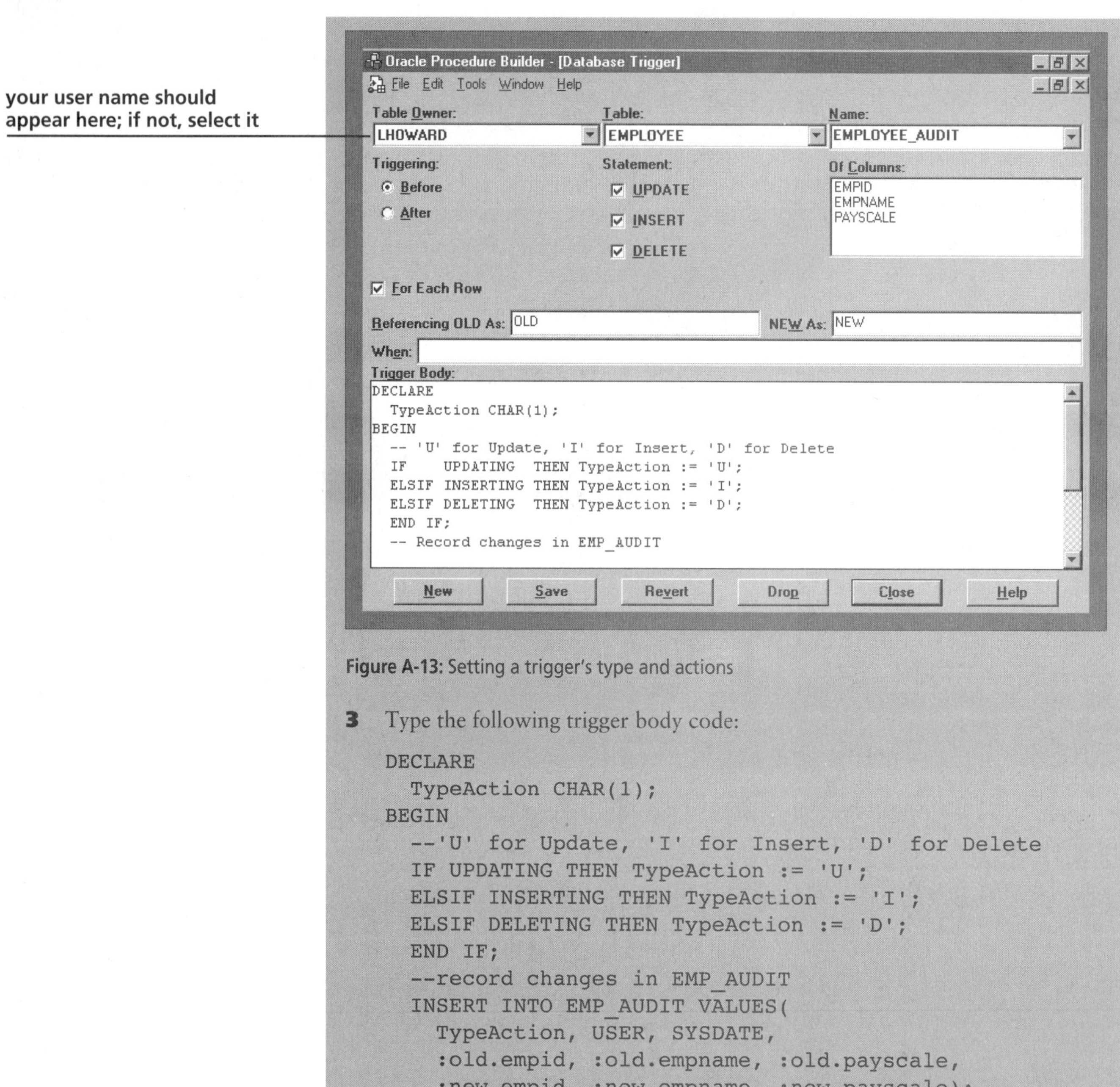

Figure A-13: Setting a trigger's type and actions

3 Type the following trigger body code:

```
DECLARE
  TypeAction CHAR(1);
BEGIN
  --'U' for Update, 'I' for Insert, 'D' for Delete
  IF UPDATING THEN TypeAction := 'U';
  ELSIF INSERTING THEN TypeAction := 'I';
  ELSIF DELETING THEN TypeAction := 'D';
  END IF;
  --record changes in EMP_AUDIT
  INSERT INTO EMP_AUDIT VALUES(
    TypeAction, USER, SYSDATE,
    :old.empid, :old.empname, :old.payscale,
    :new.empid, :new.empname, :new.payscale);
END;
```

4 Click the **Save** button to create the trigger.

Another way to create a trigger is to use the Schema Manager. You must have DBA privileges to use the Schema Manager. There is no *safe* way to allow students to learn to use this utility. Still, if you are a DBA, this utility can be a lifesaver if you aren't sure of the correct SQL syntax for creating different types of triggers.

The Schema Manager will display SQL code generated by your selections and allow you to copy the code to SQL*Plus or scripts. In most cases, the authors recommend using the Procedure Builder for creating your triggers, however. Notice in Figure A-14 the window for writing your PL/SQL code is smaller than the one that opens in the Procedure Builder. In addition, you must press the Tab key to move between two windows to set the trigger properties.

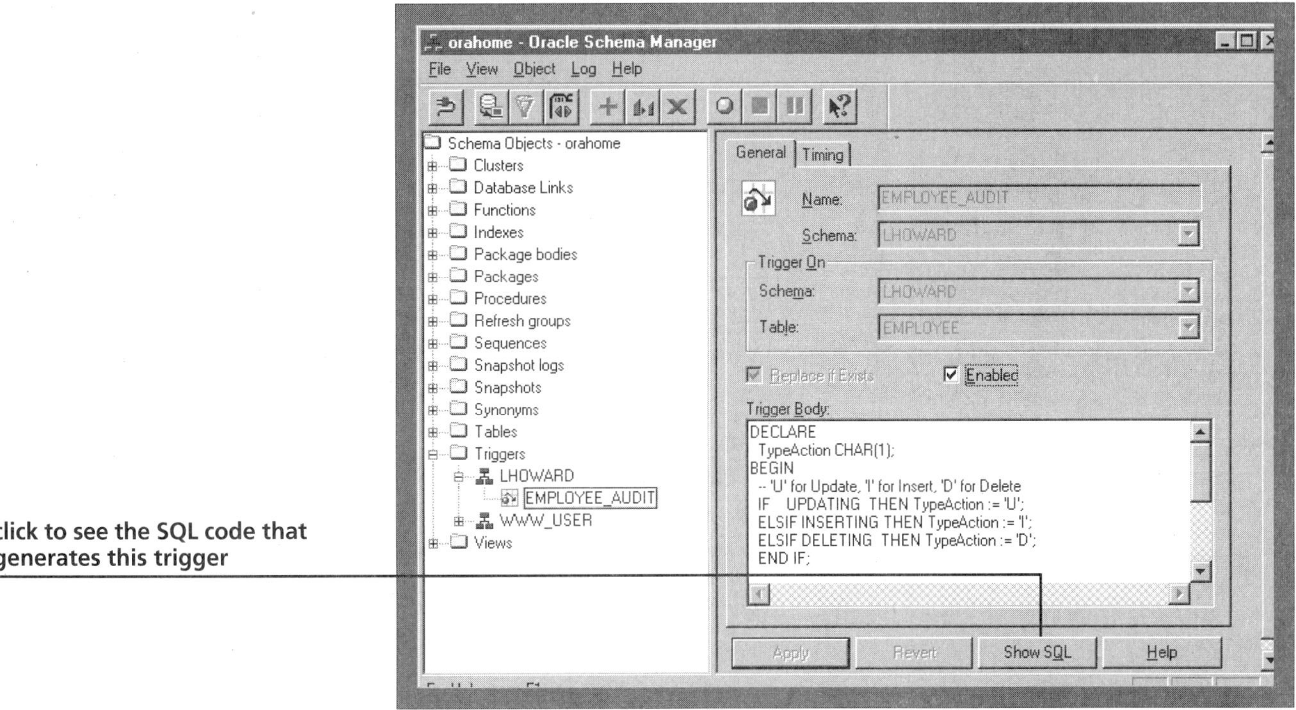

Figure A-14: Creating or viewing triggers in the Schema Manager

A third way to create a trigger is by using the Oracle Navigator. In Figure A-15, the Oracle Navigator displays the EMPLOYEE table and the dialog box for displaying and creating new triggers. Creating a trigger in the Object Navigator starts with selecting a table, right-clicking Trigger, and then clicking New on the menu. (If Oracle Navigator's Connection/Property/Settings are set to Display objects by Object Owner, your sequence will be to right-click your user name, click New on the menu, and then click Trigger.)

As shown in Figure A-15, the method for creating a trigger in the Object Navigator is very similar to the Schema Builder, but unfortunately, the Oracle Navigator won't display the resulting SQL code generated when creating a trigger. If the Body tab is selected, you are presented with a window for entering the trigger code (which is done on the General tab in the Schema Builder).

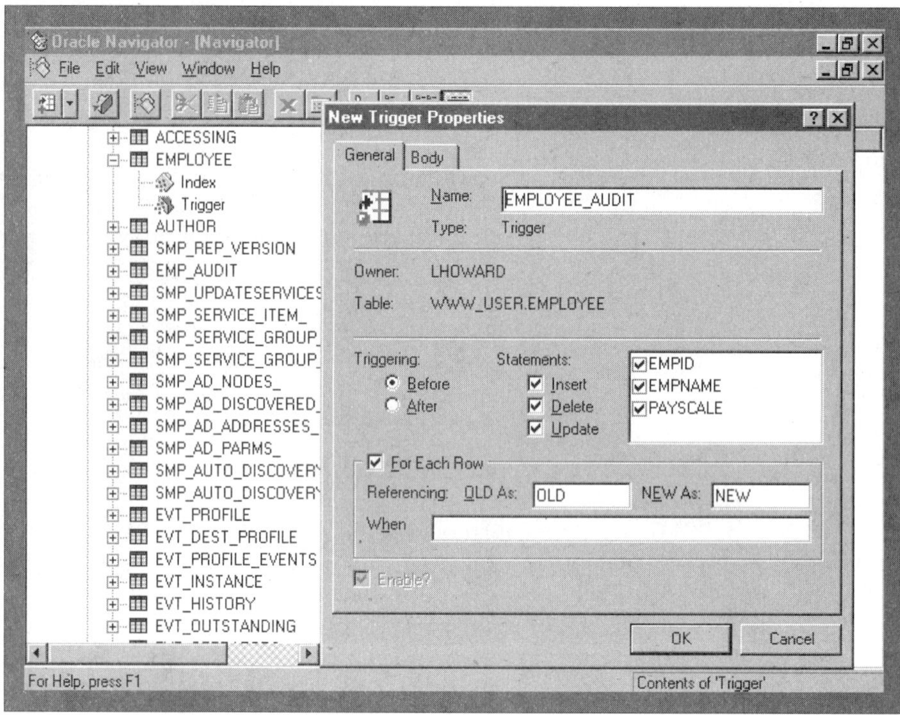

Figure A-15: Creating a trigger in the Oracle Navigator

Finally, Figure A-16 shows how the EMPLOYEE_AUDIT trigger is created in SQL*Plus.

```
Oracle SQL*Plus
File Edit Search Options Help
SQL>
Wrote file afiedt.buf
CREATE OR REPLACE TRIGGER EMPLOYEE_AUDIT
  BEFORE DELETE OR INSERT OR UPDATE
  OF EMPID, EMPNAME, PAYSCALE ON EMPLOYEE
  REFERENCING OLD AS OLD NEW AS NEW
  FOR EACH ROW
DECLARE
  TypeAction CHAR(1);
BEGIN
  -- 'U' for Update, 'I' for Insert, 'D' for Delete
  IF    UPDATING  THEN TypeAction := 'U';
  ELSIF INSERTING THEN TypeAction := 'I';
  ELSIF DELETING  THEN TypeAction := 'D';
  END IF;
  -- Record changes in EMP_AUDIT
  INSERT INTO EMP_AUDIT VALUES(
    TypeAction, USER, SYSDATE,
    :old.empid, :old.empname, :old.payscale,
    :new.empid, :new.empname, :new.payscale);
END;
SQL> /

Trigger created.
```

Figure A-16: Creating a trigger from SQL*Plus

A test of the EMPLOYEE_AUDIT trigger is shown in Figure A-17. If this command is added to a script, the slash shown at the SQL prompt shown in Figure A-16 must be included after the trigger body in the script.

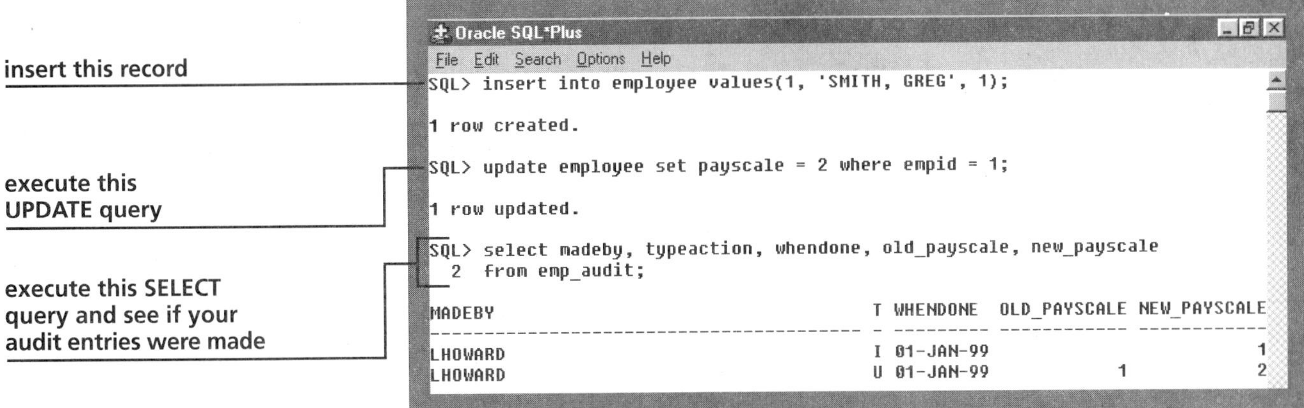

Figure A-17: Verifying the EMPLOYEE_AUDIT trigger

Primary Key/Sequence Example

EMPID is the primary key of the EMPLOYEE table in the previous example. Sequences generally are used to ensure unique primary key values. When a user inserts new records into the EMPLOYEE table, a sequence named EMP_SEQUENCE might be used as follows: `INSERT INTO EMPLOYEE VALUES(EMP_SEQUENCE.NEXTVAL, 'Smith, Greg', 3);`.

If you can complete these examples at the computer, create the sequence named EMP_SEQUENCE in SQL*Plus before continuing by typing the following command: `create sequence EMP_SEQUENCE;`.

Every time you do an INSERT into the EMPLOYEE table you must remember to set EMPID to EMP_SEQUENCE.NEXTVAL or risk a system error from a duplicate primary key. A trigger provides a way to automate this process and ensure that EMPID is always unique. Figure A-18 shows how this is done from the Procedure Builder.

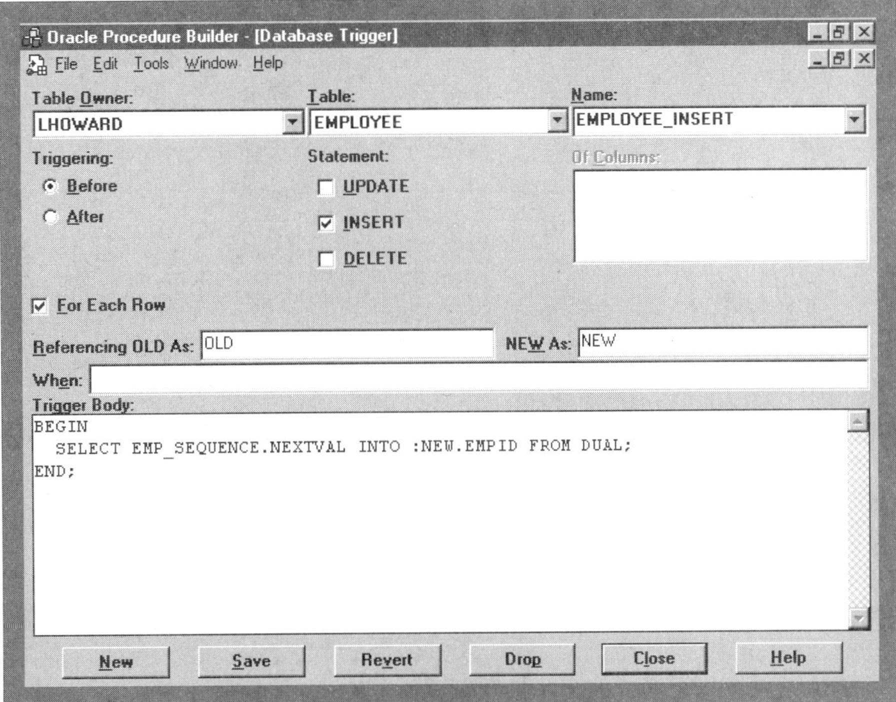

Figure A-18: Automating primary key inserts

Figure A-19 illustrates three ways of inserting records into the EMPLOYEE table after implementing the EMPLOYEE_INSERT trigger. (The initial DELETE FROM EMPLOYEE ensures these examples won't try to assign an EMPID from EMP_SEQUENCE that already is in the table from earlier examples.) The first INSERT uses all the fields and adds a NULL value as a placeholder for EMPID. The second INSERT uses all the fields and adds a numeric placeholder for EMPID (notice the 0 value is ignored here and the EMP_SEQUENCE.NEXTVAL is used). The third INSERT omits EMPID in the specified fields yet still has the value 3 automatically placed in EMPID.

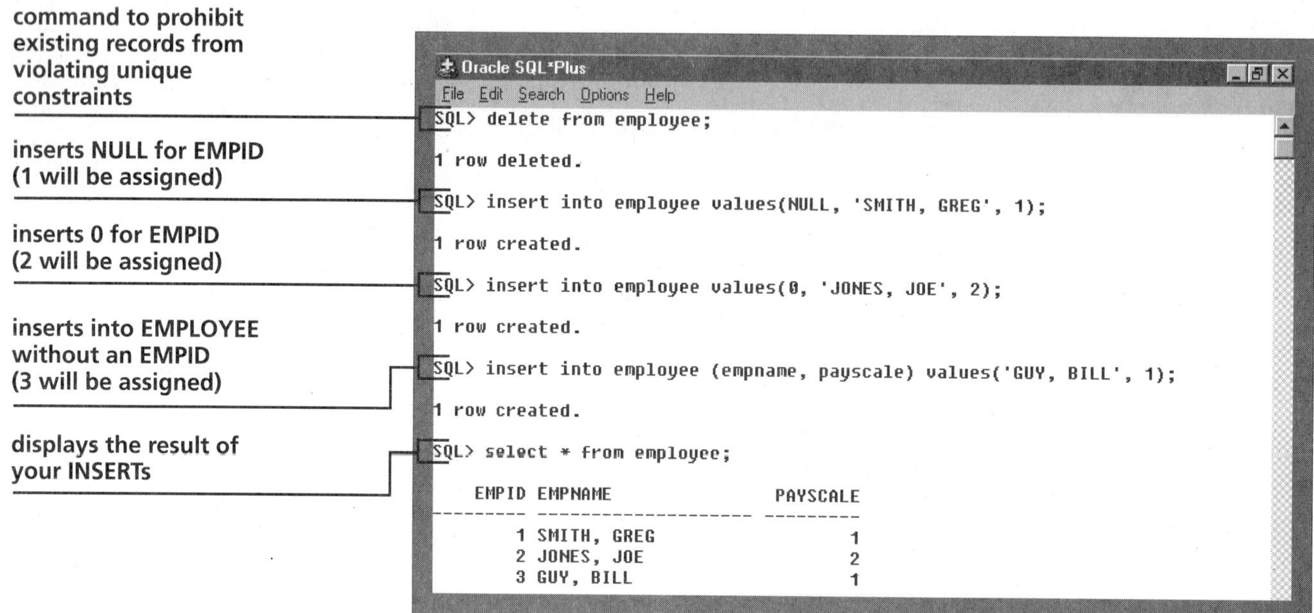

Figure A-19: Observing the actions of the EMPLOYEE_INSERT trigger

Storing the Current Sequence Value

Sometimes you might need to insert an EMPLOYEE record and immediately use the new EMPID assigned to this employee to insert into or update another table. If you use a trigger to assign EMPID, as demonstrated previously, you cannot easily determine the EMPID just assigned to the new employee. You could try a query returning EMPID with the name you just entered in the WHERE clause, but two employees might have the same name—that's one of the reasons for EMPID in the first place. Here is a way around this dilemma.

To store the current sequence value:

1 Create a table named EMPID with a single EMPID field (used only for verifying this example—make sure to use the NUMBER data type and size 6, which is the same as EMPID in EMPLOYEE).

2 Using the Procedure Builder, access your account, then open Database Objects/<your user name>/Stored Program Units, and create a new Package Specification named EMPSEQUENCE.

3 Type the code shown in Figure A-20 into your EMPSEQUENCE package specification.

type this code

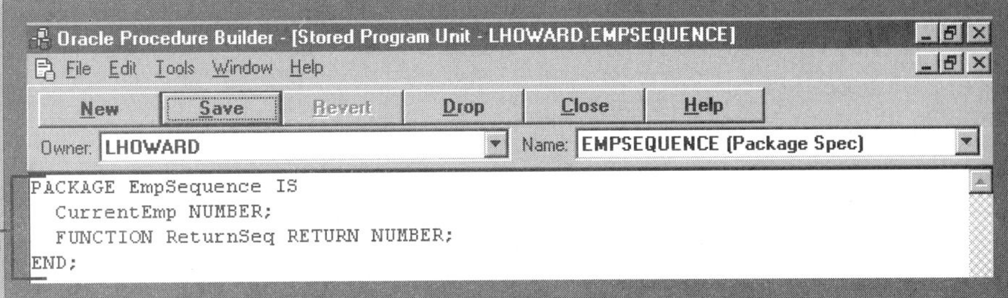

Figure A-20: Creating the EMPSEQUENCE package specification

4 Now create a new package body named EMPSEQUENCE and type the code shown in Figure A-21 into EMPSEQUENCE.

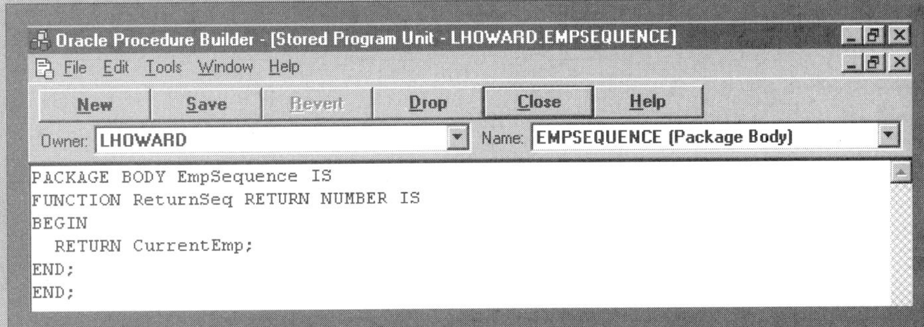

Figure A-21: Writing the EMPSEQUENCE package body

5 Still using the Procedure Builder, select **Tables**, **EMPLOYEE**, **Triggers**, **EMPLOYEE_INSERT**, and then modify the trigger as shown in Figure A-22.

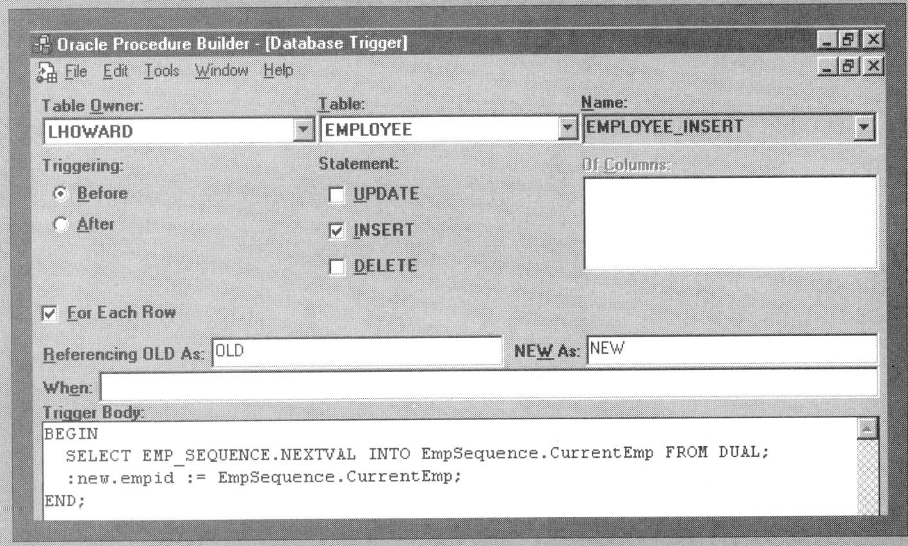

Figure A-22: Modifying the EMPLOYEE_INSERT trigger

6 Next create the procedure shown in Figure A-23. Refer to Figure A-24 to see where the new program unit is created in the Object Navigator.

EMPID is entered automatically by the EMPLOYEE.INSERT trigger and stored in a variable in the EMPSEQUENCE package

EMPSEQUENCE.RETURNSEQ returns the new EMPID that is assigned to CURRENTVAL and inserted into the EMPID table

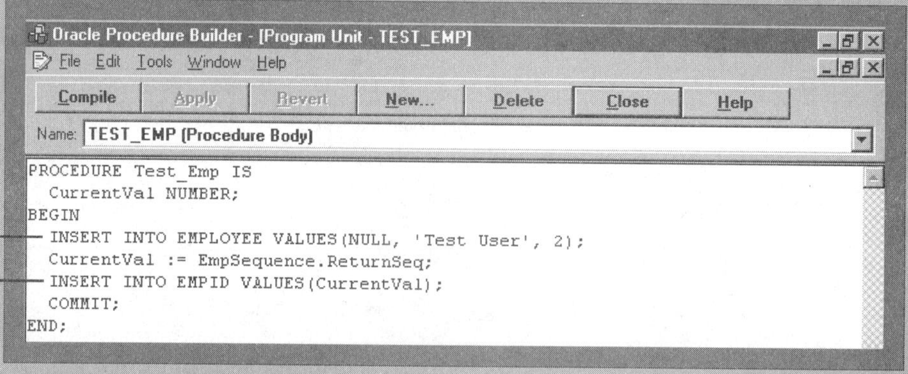

```
PROCEDURE Test_Emp IS
  CurrentVal NUMBER;
BEGIN
  INSERT INTO EMPLOYEE VALUES(NULL, 'Test User', 2);
  CurrentVal := EmpSequence.ReturnSeq;
  INSERT INTO EMPID VALUES(CurrentVal);
  COMMIT;
END;
```

Figure A-23: Testing the EMPLOYEE_INSERT trigger with the EMPSEQUENCE package

runs TEST-EMP

shows the value entered in the EMPID table

compare with the EMPID entered in EMPLOYEE (the values should be the same)

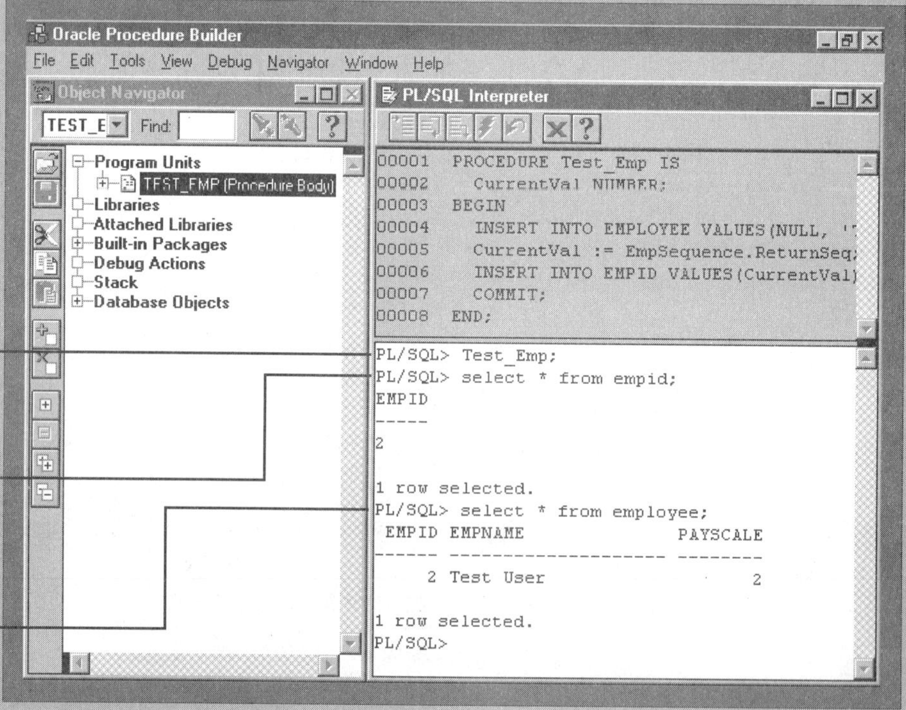

```
00001  PROCEDURE Test_Emp IS
00002    CurrentVal NUMBER;
00003  BEGIN
00004    INSERT INTO EMPLOYEE VALUES(NULL, '
00005    CurrentVal := EmpSequence.ReturnSeq;
00006    INSERT INTO EMPID VALUES(CurrentVal)
00007    COMMIT;
00008  END;
```

```
PL/SQL> Test_Emp;
PL/SQL> select * from empid;
EMPID
-----
2

1 row selected.
PL/SQL> select * from employee;
 EMPID EMPNAME                 PAYSCALE
------ -------------------- --------
     2 Test User                   2

1 row selected.
PL/SQL>
```

Figure A-24: Results from running TEST_EMP

7 Run TESTEMP by first tiling your windows and then arranging your windows to view the Navigator pane and PL/SQL Interpreter side by side, as shown in Figure A-24. Then you can enter `Test_Emp;` and the SELECT statements shown in Figure A-24 to confirm this procedure is working and that the same value for EMPID is inserted in both the EMPID and EMPLOYEE tables.

SUMMARY

- PL/SQL is the procedural language used to write procedures and functions for Oracle applications. Valid PL/SQL characters are uppercase and lowercase letters, numbers, and the special characters found on computer keyboards. PL/SQL variable names must begin with a letter, cannot be longer than 30 characters, and cannot contain blank spaces or hyphens.
- The main PL/SQL data types are NUMBER, VARCHAR2, DATE, and LONG. The VARCHAR2 data type has a maximum length of 32,767 characters when it is assigned to a PL/SQL variable. A LONG data type variable in PL/SQL is allowed a maximum length of 32,760 bytes.
- Reference data types assume the same data type as a referenced database column or row.
- In PL/SQL, a block of comment statements can be delimited by beginning the block with the characters /* and ending the block with the characters */. A single comment line is delimited by beginning it with two hyphens (--).
- To concatenate two character strings, you use the double bar (||) operator in PL/SQL.
- Literals are unchanging values data values coded directly into a program.
- PL/SQL procedures and functions are structured in blocks with a DECLARE, BEGIN, and EXCEPTION sections.
- In PL/SQL, all variables must be declared prior to use, and assignment and comparisons can be performed only between variables with the same type.
- IF/THEN structures evaluate a given condition. Every IF statement must have a corresponding END IF. An equal sign by itself (=) is used when you are comparing two values in an IF/THEN structure. The IF/THEN/ELSE structure is similar, except that when the condition evaluates to false, one or more alternative program statements execute. The IF/THEN/ELSIF structure allows you to test for many different conditions.
- PL/SQL cursors are used to retrieve database data into PL/SQL variables. Implicit cursors are used with SELECT statements that return a single record. Explicit cursors must be used with SELECT statements that might retrieve a variable number of records, or that might return no records.
- Once an exception occurs, processing in the current PL/SQL execution section is transferred to the EXCEPTION section, where you might correct the error without notifying the user of the problem, inform the user of the error without taking corrective action, correct the error and inform the user of the error, or inform the user of the error and allow the user to decide what action to take.
- Blocks can also be nested within other blocks in the same procedure, and each block can have its own exception section. When an exception occurs in a nested block, processing moves to the blocks exception section and when finished returns to the enclosing block.
- PL/SQL procedures are code modules that perform tasks. By default, parameters are passed as "IN" parameters even if IN is omitted, and an IN only parameter can be read but not modified. A parameter passed with the OUT keyword only can be written to, but cannot be read within the procedure. A parameter passed as both IN and OUT can be read and modified.
- Libraries are files that contain one or more procedures or functions.
- A package is a code library that provides a way to manage large numbers of related programs and variables. Oracle provides many built-in packages that are accessible to both client and server programs.
- Database triggers are procedures that execute in response to the database events of inserting, updating, or deleting a record. Database triggers can be created using the Procedure Builder, Schema Manager, Oracle Navigator, and SQL*Plus.

REVIEW QUESTIONS

1. Write on paper a command to concatenate the contents of the variable LNAME and FNAME, with LNAME first, followed by a comma and a space, and then FNAME.
2. Write on paper the PL/SQL declaration for a text variable named MYSTERYTEXT, which is capable of holding up to 2,000 characters.
3. What is the difference between a LONG data type in PL/SQL and in an Oracle database?
4. What are the three sections of a PL/SQL block, and what is the purpose of each section?
5. What are the two approaches for delimiting comment blocks in a PL/SQL program?
6. When should you use a function instead of a procedure?
7. What is a package?
8. What is a library?
9. What is a database trigger? What are the four Oracle utilities you can use to create database triggers?

PROBLEM-SOLVING CASES

1. Write a PL/SQL program block that declares a numeric variable named COUNTER and a string variable named STRINGVAR. Assign the value 100 to COUNTER and the text 'hello world' to STRINGVAR.
2. Write a loop that inserts a number variable named COUNTER into a table named COUNT_TABLE thirteen times. COUNT_TABLE has a single numeric field named COUNTID.
3. Create a PL/SQL block that selects LNAME from CUSTOMER into an implicit cursor where CUSTID = 100. The CUSTOMER table has CUSTID, LNAME, FNAME, and other fields.
4. Write a PL/SQL block with an explicit cursor named CUST_NAMES that retrieves all last and first names from the CUSTOMER table described in Question 3. Concatenate the strings as in Question 1, and then insert the records into a temporary table named CUSTLIST that contains a single field named CNAME.

Index

E

F

G

H

I

J

L

M

N

O

P

S